PERTHES
World Atlas

First Edition

Editor-in-Chief
Guntram H. Herb, Middlebury College

Editors
David H. Kaplan, Kent State University
Mark Monmonier, Syracuse University

Klett-Perthes Verlag
Gotha, Germany

PERTHES
World Atlas

Cartographical and Editorial Office
Klett-Perthes Verlag GmbH, Gotha, Germany
Bernd Creutzburg
Silvia Einsporn
Stephan Frisch
Dr.-Ing. Ulrich Hengelhaupt
Franziska Hohm
Thomas Hönicke
Anja Krüger
Dr.-Ing. Manfred Reckziegel
Katrin Schöbel
Nicole Schramm
Wilfried Schüller
Gerhard Treger

with Assistance of
Ingenieurbüro für Kartographie, Rolf Böhm, Bad Schandau
Ingenieurbüro für Kartographie, Müller und Richert GbR, Gotha
KartoGraFix Hengelhaupt, Suhl

Authors
Prof. Dr. Detlef Busche (World Landforms Map)
Dr. Jürgen Kempf (Africa Ecoregions Map)
Willi Stegner (Economic Maps, Ethnic Maps)

Graphics
Otto Götzl (Geotectonic Processes)
Horst Peuckert † (Ocean Floor)

Flags
Jiří Tenora †, Das Flaggenkabinett, Berlin

Printed and Bound in Germany by
Aprinta, Wemding

ISBN McGraw-Hill: 978-0-07-329073-7
ISBN Klett-Perthes: 978-3-623-00100-5

Preface

The fruit we had for breakfast this morning came from Mexico, Chile, and New Zealand, the coffee from the highlands of Ethiopia, and the tea from Assam. We warmed our rolls in a toaster oven that was designed in Italy and manufactured in China. We sent a text message to our publisher in Germany on a Finnish cell phone with electronic parts from Malaysia and Japan.

Our connections to the rest of the world are multifarious and omnipresent. What is the role of agriculture in Mexico, Chile, and New Zealand? What is the volume of trade between the United States and other parts of the world? Where are the global exchange points for internet data transmissions? Where are the highlands in Ethiopia or the electronic manufacturing centers in Malaysia? Where is Assam? The *Perthes World Atlas* offers answers to these questions and many others.

The idea for this atlas was conceived five years ago, at the Annual Meeting of the Association of American Geographers in New York City during a conversation between Guntram, Lisa Gottschalk of McGraw-Hill and Dietmar Häsler of Klett-Perthes. Astounded by the shortcomings of existing atlases for undergraduate education, which were either out-of-date, heavily biased toward US coverage or contained only simple choropleth maps, the plan was hatched to develop a new, richly informative atlas offering instructive insights to the complex issues and processes of the modern world.

Mark and Dave were immediately taken by the idea and after many discussions with Dietmar and Stephan Frisch of Klett-Perthes, we outlined the major goals for this atlas:

- rich thematic coverage, which includes novel topics, such as maps comparing the numbers and status of women and men throughout the world;
- a comprehensive reference work, with statistical information on all countries and an index listing over 20,000 place and feature names;
- maps compiled from current data, for example, climate maps based on the same classification system used by leading scientific institutes conducting research on global climate change;
- a logical, concise cartographic design that makes it possible to read many different dimensions of a given topic from each map;
- the use of graduated symbols to avoid the misinterpretation likely when the map includes large countries with small populations;
- a highly accessible introduction with little text, lots of graphics, and concrete examples of how to read and interpret maps.

Klett-Perthes was the ideal choice to bring this project to fruition. Staffed with experienced and highly trained cartographic experts, the firm has a long tradition of innovation: Perthes produced one of the first thematic school atlases in the world – Heinrich Berghaus's *Physikalischer Schulatlas* in 1850 – and is renowned for its wall maps and sophisticated atlases and cartographic products. We are proud to present the first edition of our atlas, which reflects a long and intensive collaboration between the editors and the cartographic team of Klett-Perthes in Gotha, Germany.

Guntram H. Herb
David H. Kaplan
Mark Monmonier

Contents

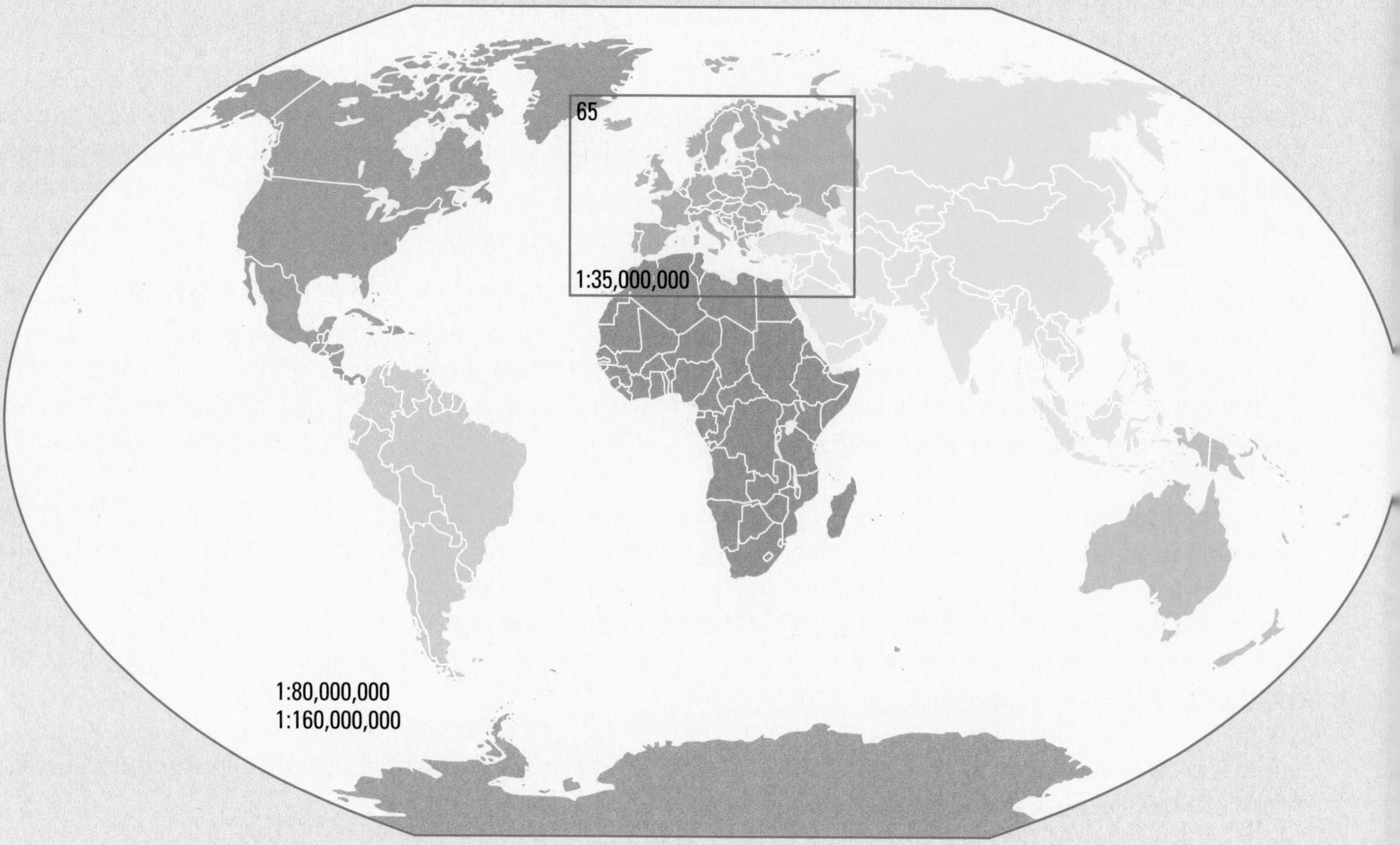
65
1:35,000,000
1:80,000,000
1:160,000,000

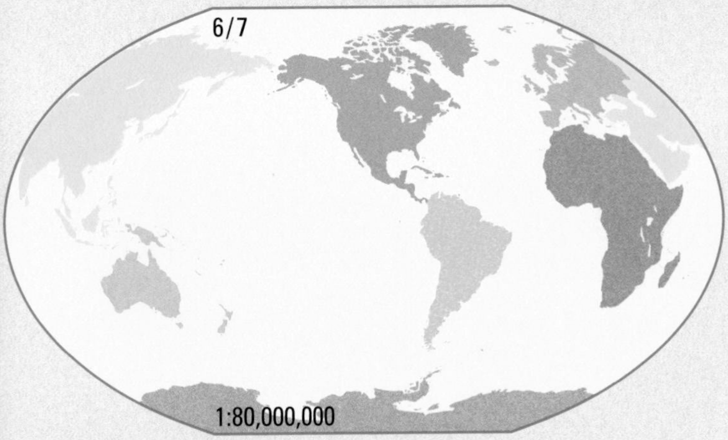
6/7
1:80,000,000

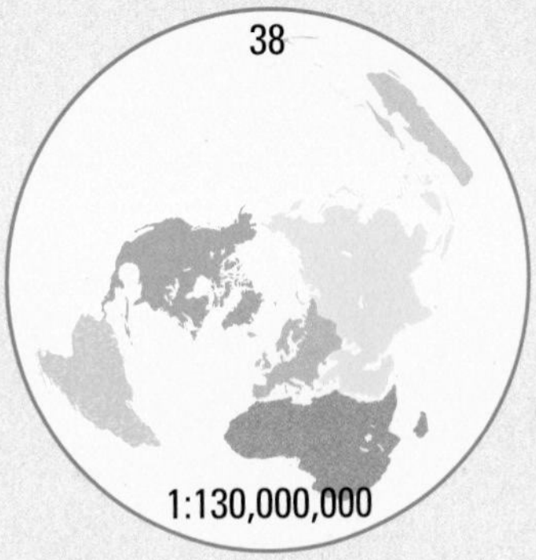
38
1:130,000,000

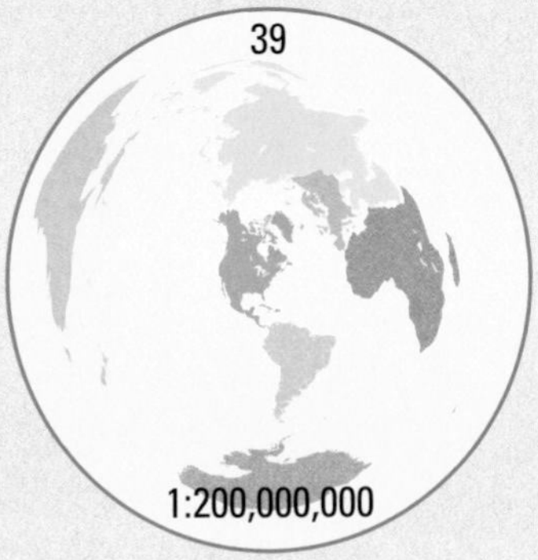
39
1:200,000,000

10/11, 14/15
1:100,000,000
1:160,000,000

12
1:25,000,000

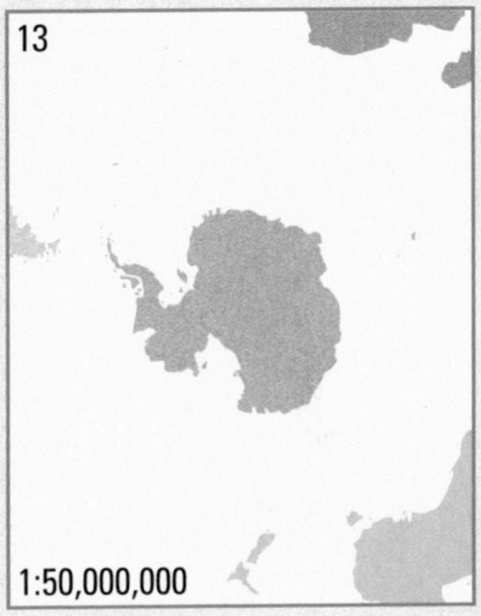
13
1:50,000,000

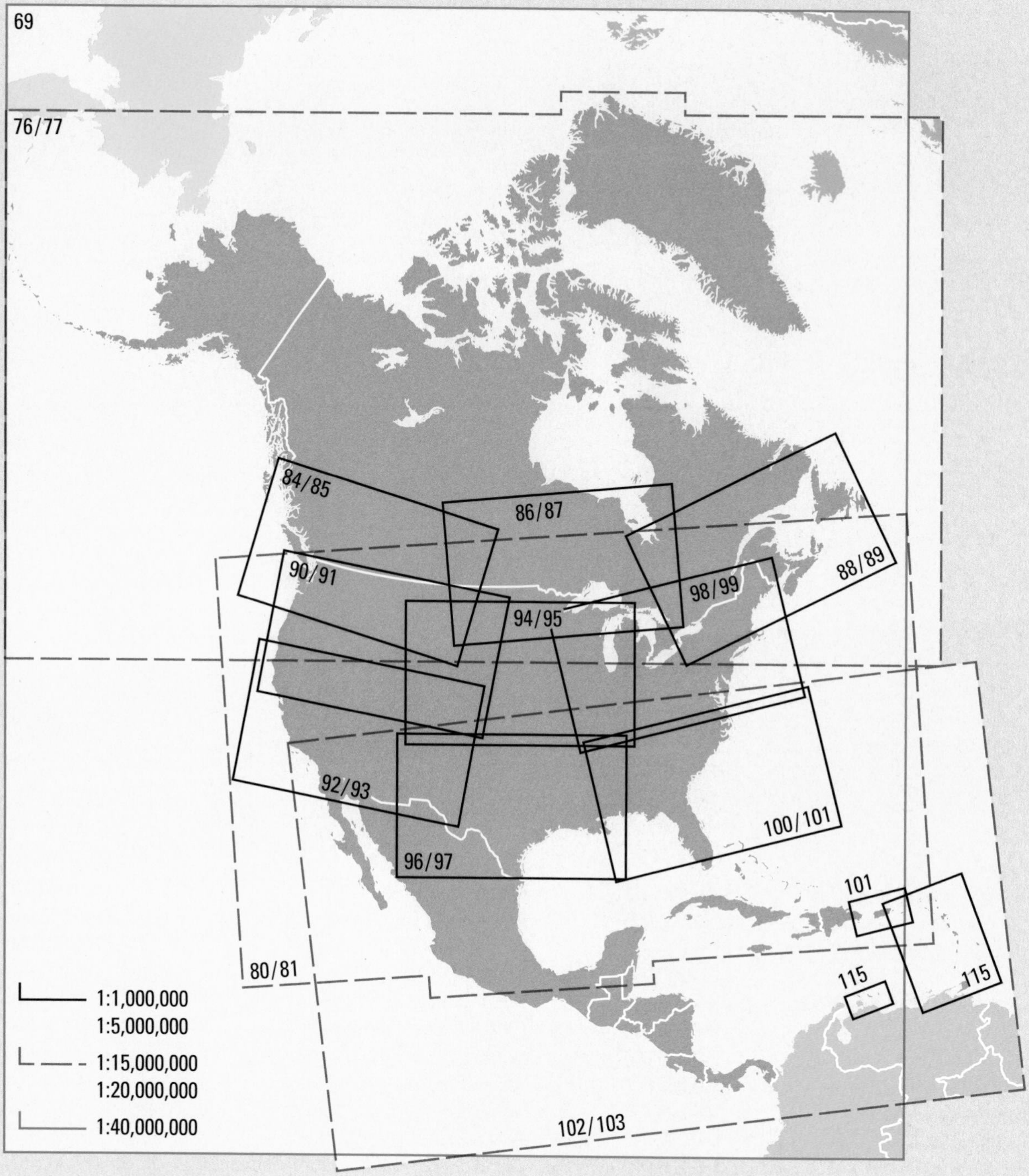

66 The Continents

105
1:5,000,000
1:15,000,000
1:40,000,000
115
115
112/113
114/115

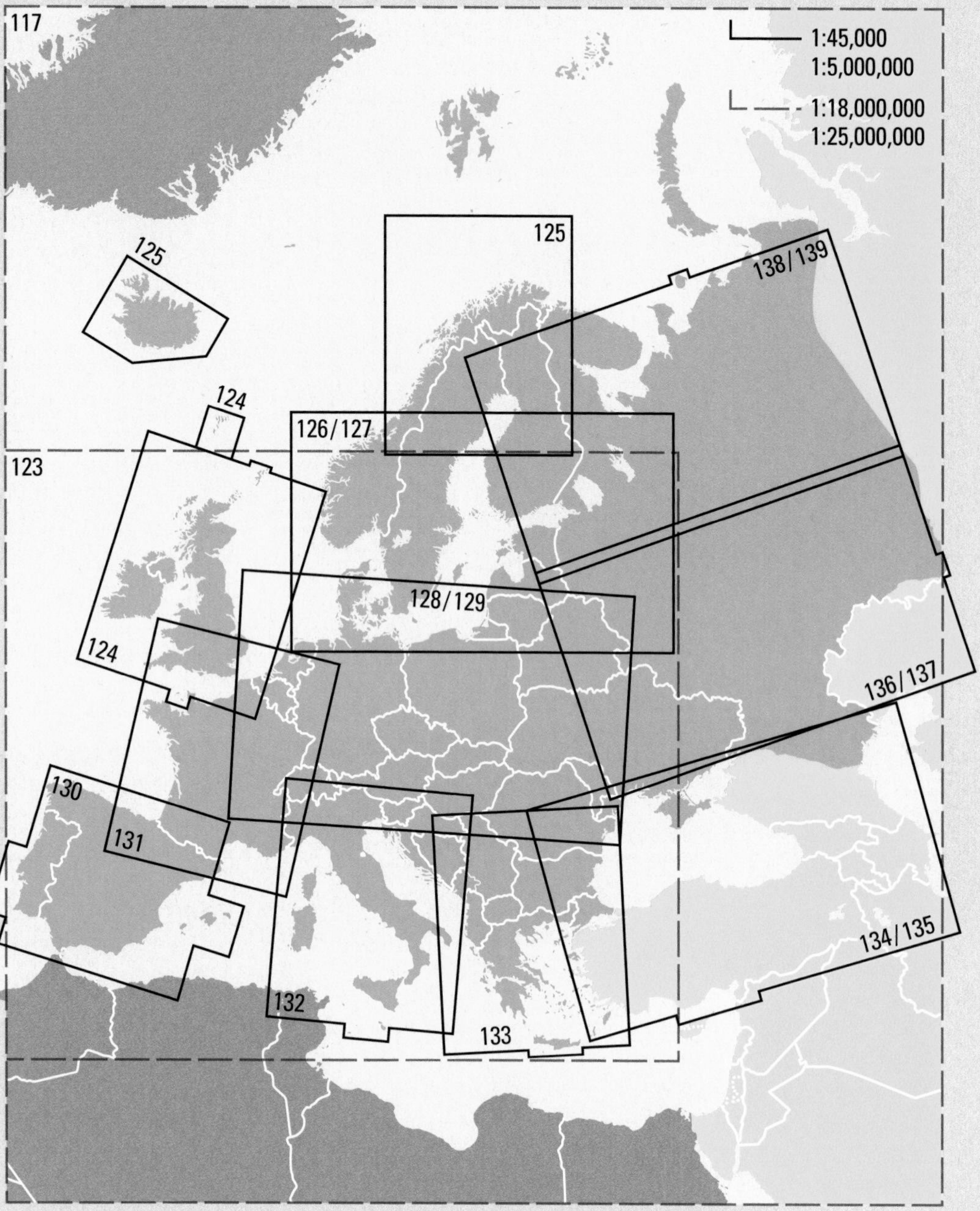
117
1:45,000
1:5,000,000
1:18,000,000
1:25,000,000
125
125
138/139
124
126/127
123
128/129
124
136/137
130
131
132
133
134/135

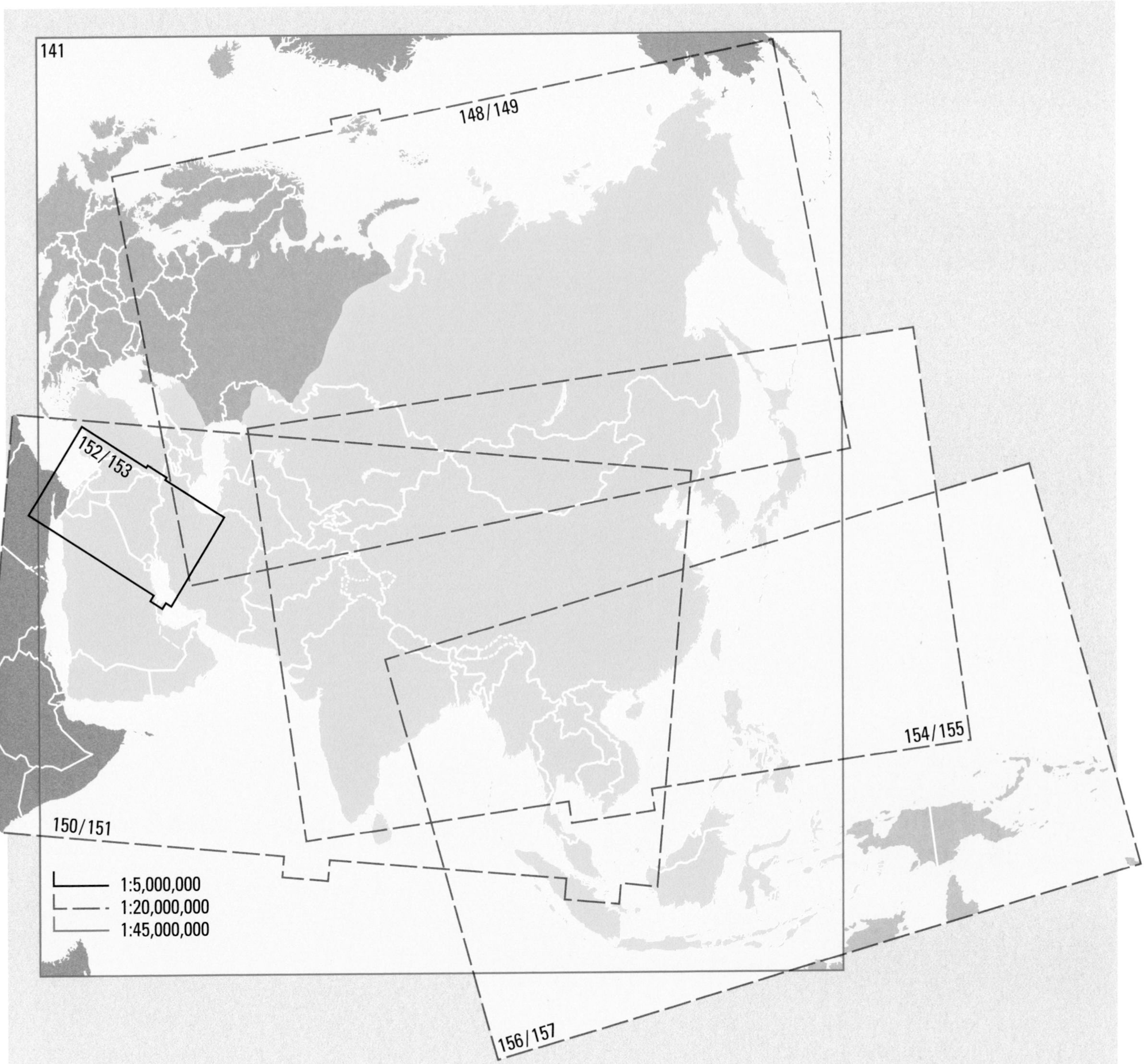
141
148/149
152/153
150/151
154/155
156/157
1:5,000,000
1:20,000,000
1:45,000,000

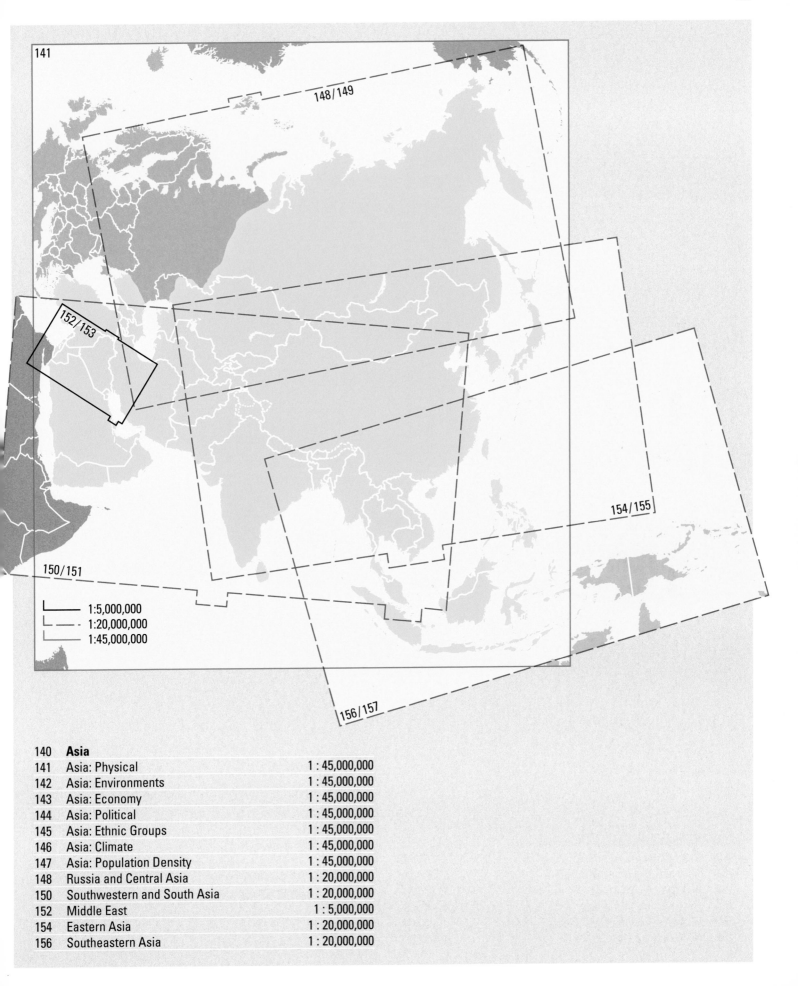

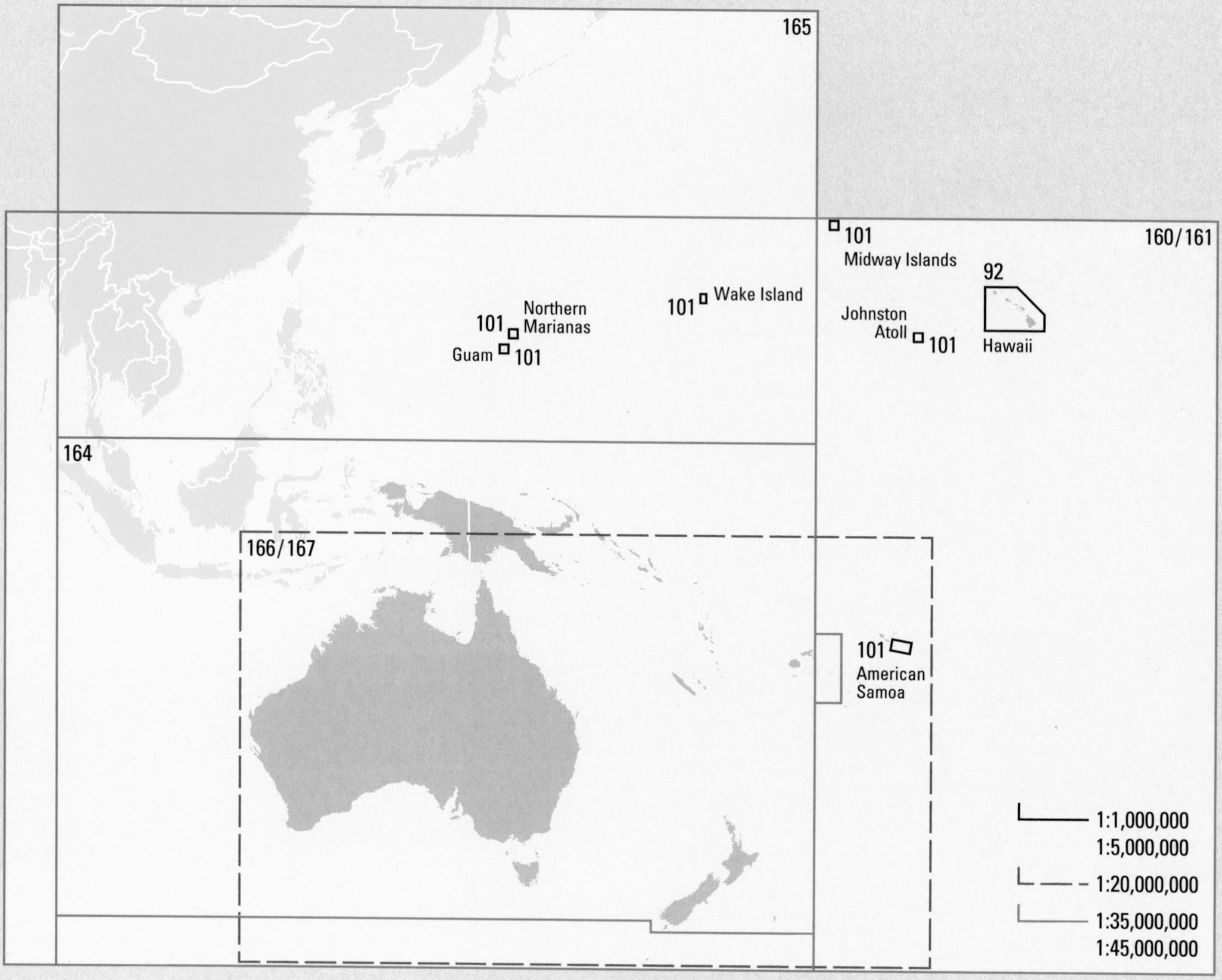
165
160/161
164
166/167
101
Midway Islands
92
Hawaii
Johnston
Atoll
101
101
Wake Island
101
Northern
Marianas
Guam
101
101
American
Samoa
1:1,000,000
1:5,000,000
1:20,000,000
1:35,000,000
1:45,000,000

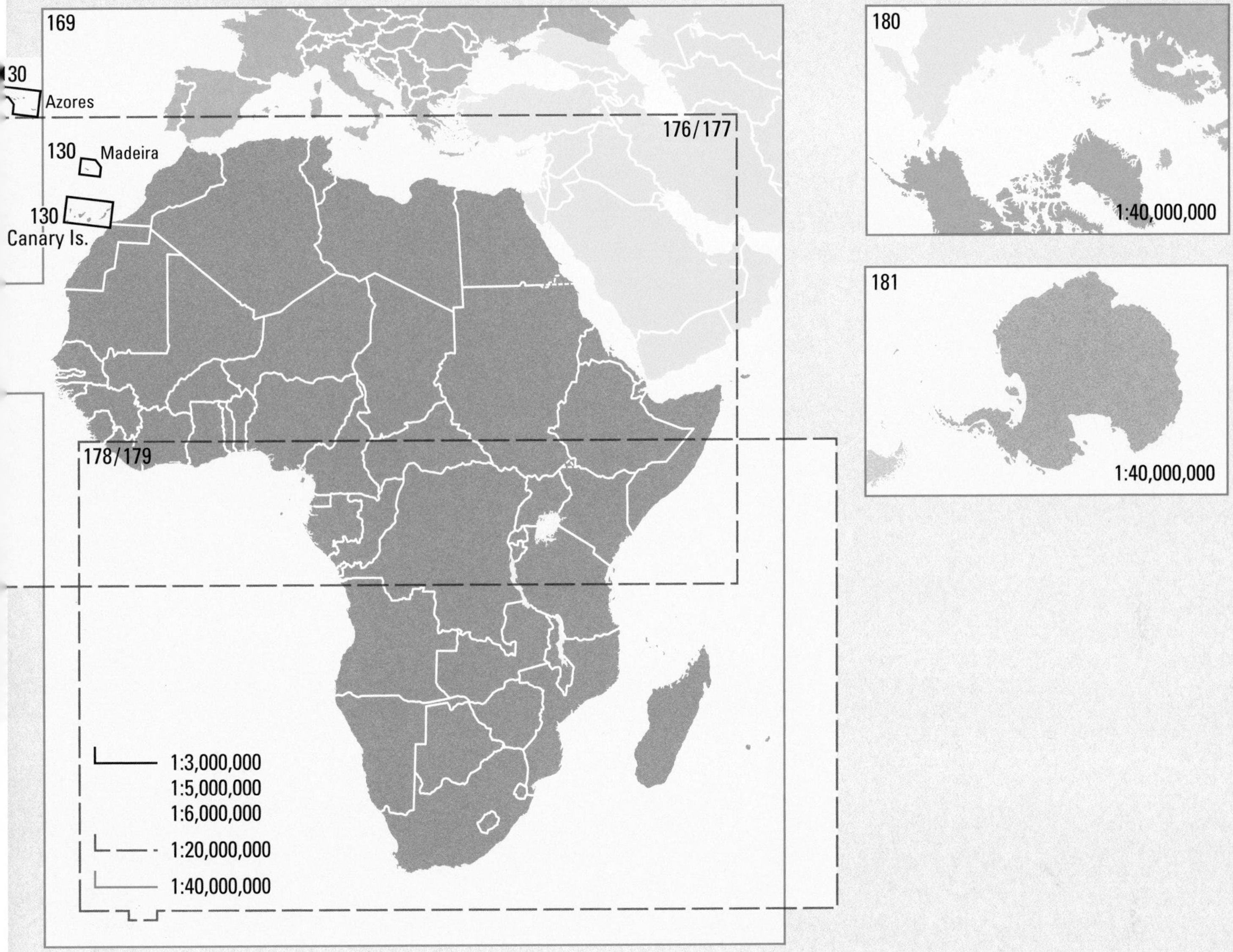
169
130
Azores
130 Madeira
130
Canary Is.
176/177
178/179
1:3,000,000
1:5,000,000
1:6,000,000
1:20,000,000
1:40,000,000
180
1:40,000,000
181
1:40,000,000

Index of Countries

Asia	Statistical Gazetteer	Map
Afghanistan	185	150
Armenia	185	134
Azerbaijan	186	134
Bahrain	186	152
Bangladesh	186	150
Bhutan	187	150
Brunei	187	156
Cambodia	188	156
China	189	154
Christmas Island	*189*	*156*
Cocos (Keeling) Islands	*189*	*156*
Cyprus	190	152
Georgia	192	134
India	194	150
Indonesia	194	156
Iran	194	150
Iraq	194	152
Israel	194	152
Japan	195	154
Jordan	195	152
Kazakhstan	195	148
Korea, North	195	154
Korea, South	195	154
Kuwait	195	152
Kyrgyzstan	195	148
Laos	196	156
Lebanon	196	152
Malaysia	197	156
Maldives	197	150
Mongolia	198	154
Myanmar	198	150
Nepal	198	150
Oman	200	150
Pakistan	200	150
Philippines	200	156
Qatar	201	150
Saudi Arabia	202	150
Singapore	203	156
Sri Lanka	203	150
Syria	204	152
Taiwan	204	154
Tajikistan	204	150
Thailand	204	156
Timor-Leste	204	156
Turkey	205	134
Turkmenistan	205	148
United Arab Emirates	205	150
Uzbekistan	207	148
Vietnam	207	156
Yemen	208	150

Australia and Oceania	Statistical Gazetteer	Map
American Samoa	*185*	*100*
Australia	186	166
Cook Islands	189	160
Fiji	191	166
French Polynesia	*192*	*160*
Guam	*193*	*100*
Johnston Atoll	*195*	*100*
Kiribati	195	160
Marshall Islands	197	160
Micronesia	197	156
Midway Islands	*198*	*100*
Nauru	198	160
New Caledonia	*199*	*166*
New Zealand	199	166
Niue	*199*	*166*
Norfolk Island	*199*	*166*
Northern Mariana Islands	*199*	*100*
Palau	200	156
Papua New Guinea	200	156
Pitcairn Islands	*200*	*160*
Samoa	202	166
Solomon Islands	203	166
Tokelau	*204*	*166*
Tonga	204	166
Tuvalu	205	166
Vanuatu	207	166
Wake Island	*207*	*100*
Wallis and Futuna	*207*	*166*

Africa	Statistical Gazetteer	Map
Algeria	185	176
Angola	185	178
Benin	187	176
Botswana	187	178
Burkina Faso	188	176
Burundi	188	178
Cameroon	188	176
Cape Verde	188	176
Central African Republic	188	176
Chad	188	176
Comoros	189	178
Congo, Dem. Rep. of the	189	178
Congo, Republic of the	189	178
Côte d'Ivoire	190	176
Djibouti	190	176
Egypt	190	176
Equatorial Guinea	191	176
Eritrea	191	176
Ethiopia	191	176
Gabon	192	178
Gambia, The	192	176
Ghana	192	176
Guinea	193	176
Guinea-Bissau	193	176
Kenya	195	178
Lesotho	196	178
Liberia	196	176
Lybia	196	176
Madagascar	196	178
Malawi	196	178
Mali	197	*176*
Mauritania	197	176
Mauritius	197	178
Mayotte	*197*	*178*
Morocco	198	176
Mozambique	198	178
Namibia	198	178
Niger	199	176
Nigeria	199	176
Réunion	*201*	*178*
Rwanda	201	178
Saint Helena	*201*	*178*
Sao Tome and Principe	202	176
Senegal	202	176
Seychelles	202	178
Sierra Leone	202	176
Somalia	203	176
South Africa	203	178
Sudan, The	203	176
Swaziland	204	178
Tanzania	204	178
Togo	204	176
Tunisia	205	176
Uganda	205	178
Western Sahara	207	176
Zambia	208	178
Zimbabwe	208	178

How to Read and Interpret Maps

Centering Maps

In addition to the choice of projection, where a map is centered (and where Earth's skin is torn) affects how the world looks. A comparison of the Winkel Tripel projection world map on the facing page with the Winkel Tripel projection centered on the Pacific Ocean illustrates the importance of centering.

In general, the place at the center will have less distortion than most other places on the map, especially those near the edge.

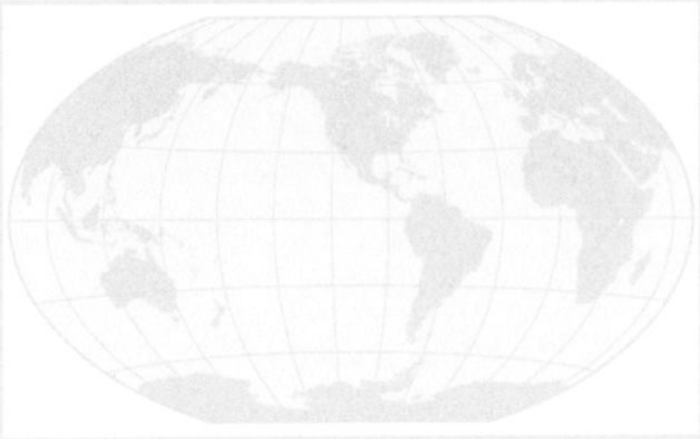

Generalization

Like the written w[illegible] a map is a language – a form of communication. Look closely at a common map, like a road map, and you will be amazed at the amount of information represented. Think about the difficulty of expressing some of the things easily represented on a map in words alone. Road maps stress transportation and how to get between different places. Other maps express or emphasize other geographic concepts.

Maps cannot possibly convey every aspect of the place they cover. As abstractions that condense Earth's complexity into a small space, they must leave many things out. This process is called *generalization*. All maps have to choose the features they represent and those they omit. Without generalization, maps would be hopelessly cluttered.

Scale

[illegible] phers must specify its *scale*, a term that refers to the ratio between length on the map and the corresp[illegible] distance.

A scale of 1:100 means that each inch of map represents 100 inches on the ground. This is called a *representative fraction* because it can be written as 1/100. A scale of 1:100 is useful only for floor plans, gardens, and other small areas. A scale of 1:40,000,000 depicts a large area, like a continent.

Whether a map scale is considered large or small depends on its representative fraction: 1:100 is a huge scale, while 1:100,000,000 is very small. In general, large-scale maps show relatively small areas like a part of a city, while small-scale maps show big areas like the world or the United States.

Examples of Generalization and Scale in the *Perthes World Atlas*

This map of the Eastern Mediterranean, focused on Cyprus, demonstrates how **generalization** works

Some topographic information is represented by shading, but not to the extent of a topographic map. Water depth is not shown.

Only cities of a particular size or importance are represented.

Formation of the coast is smoothed out.

For the most part, only international boundaries are represented. In the case of Cyprus, the internal boundary between Greek and Turkish-dominated regions is considered important enough for inclusion.

This same portion of the world is depicted at three different scales. Note the different levels of generalization in these three maps.

Representative fractions (also called ratio scales)

Scale bars

Origin and Meaning of Atlas

Dictionaries define *atlas* as a book of maps, and some attribute the term to Dutch mapmaker Gerard Mercator, who named his monumental 1595 world atlas after the ancient ruler of Mauritania, chronicled in classical mythology as carrying the world on his shoulders as punishment for leading an unsuccessful revolt against the gods. Mercator's *Atlas sive Cosmographiæ Meditationes de Fabrica Mundi et Fabricati Figura* (Atlas, or Cosmographic Meditations on the Fabric of the World and the Figure of the Fabrick'd) had an enormous impact on cartography – translated from Latin into Dutch, French, German, and English, it was reprinted in various versions over the next century and a half. Even so, the title Father of the Modern Atlas more appropriately belongs to Abraham Ortelius, who published his epic atlas *Theatrum Orbis Terrarum* (Theatre of the Whole World) in 1570. Although *Theatrum* was not the first book of maps – bound collections of sailing charts had been around for a century – Ortelius pioneered the coherent structure of standardized content and quality control.

Gerard Mercator (1574)

Ortelius Map of Ireland (1573)

Atlases Today

Modern atlases address diverse themes. Road atlases help us plan cross-country trips, and street atlases locate addresses, landmarks, parks, and other urban sites. Historical atlases narrate the progression of exploration and settlement, wars and diplomacy, development and trade, while school atlases introduce elementary pupils to world and regional geography. Thematic atlases reflect the enormous diversity of map content. As examples, congressional atlases describe the intricacies of election district boundaries, atlases of the Internet portray the locations, linkages, and impacts of cyberspace, and climate atlases depict the spatial patterns of dozens of averaged weather measurements. By contrast, reference atlases like the *Perthes World Atlas* integrate the geographic details of natural regions, political regions, or the entire world. Some atlases have a narrower geographic focus: national atlases offer an integrated overview of a country's evolution and the spatial diversity of its environment, people, and economy, while state atlases offer a similar treatment for a single state.

Like other reference atlases of the world, the *Perthes World Atlas* includes general reference maps, thematic maps, a geographical index, and a statistical gazetteer.

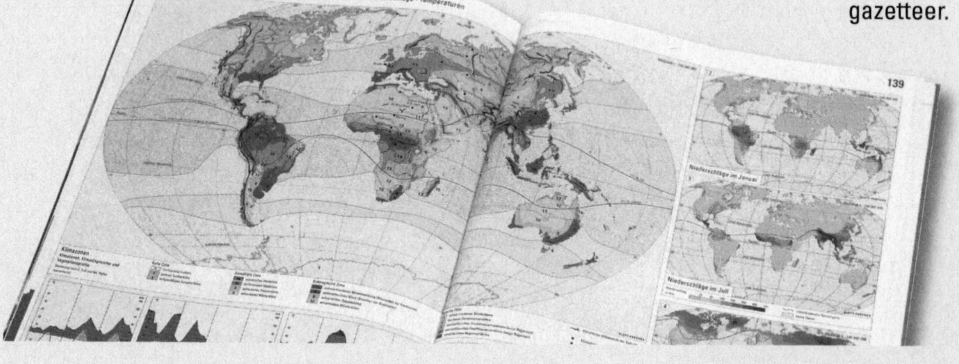

Elements of the *Perthes World Atlas*

Reference maps depict terrain, cities, political boundaries, and rivers at appropriate levels of detail for the whole world or coherent regions of various sizes. Crisscrossed by meridians and parallels to help users find places listed in the index, these maps show a city's larger neighbors, approximate elevation, and relative proximity to the closest ocean, river, or lake.

In this excerpt from the reference map "Asia: Middle East" (p. 152–153) a dotted boundary surrounds the West Bank, a disputed territory controlled by Israel and thus shown in a slightly lighter color.

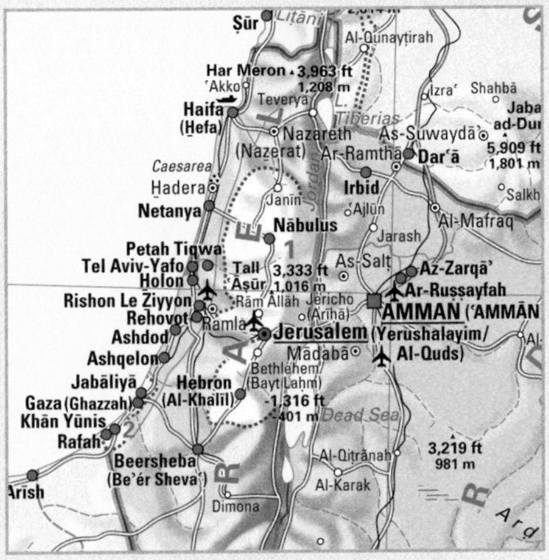

Thematic maps provide geographic overviews for specific themes like precipitation, birth rate, agricultural production, or dominant religion. This excerpt from the thematic map "World: Life Expectancy" (p. 44) shows huge differences between western Europe and southwest Asia in health care and standard of living. The squares represent a country's population, the colors inside the squares show average life expectancy, and abbreviations identify the larger countries by name.

Iceland (toward the northwest) has a comparatively small population with a relatively long average life span. Germany (GER.) has the largest population in the region but lower longevity than Italy (ITA.). Turkey (TUR.) and Ukraine (UKR.) are populous countries whose residents generally die at an earlier age than residents of Sweden (SWE.).

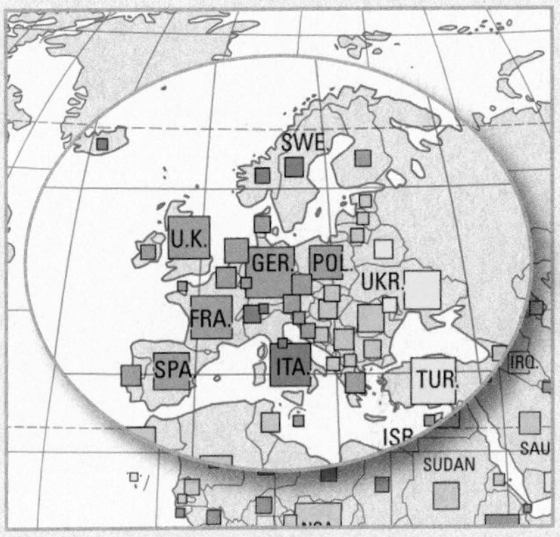

The **geographical index** is an alphabetical inventory of the places and geographic features that are depicted in the maps of the atlas. You can use it to quickly find a place or feature. For example, if you look for "Casablanca" in the index, you will see the entry:

Casablanca
(Ad-Dār al-Bayḍā') **176** F 2

The numbers and letters on the right refer to the page number and points on the reference grid. If you go to the map on page 176 and look for the red letter "F" in the top margin of the map and the red number "2" in the left margin, you will find Casablanca by following a straight line down from "F" and a straight line to the right of "2". Casablanca is a well-known place, but this is not the official name of the city since Moroccans speak Arabic. Therefore, you will find the Arabic transcription next to Casablanca in the index and on the map. The transcription of place names in countries that use different languages and alphabets is rather complicated and even contentious.

Many Arabic places in North Africa are still referred to by their transcriptions into French during the colonial period, even on English language maps. The *Perthes World Atlas* follows the international place name standards set by the United Nations and includes only English transcriptions of Arabic places on its maps. Even so, if you only know a place by its colonial French transcription, you can still find it through the index.

The **statistical gazetteer** lists important information for different countries of the world, such as the size of the territory and population, capital city, administrative organization, languages, religions, currency, and major cities.

As these excerpts from the entry on the United States show, the gazetteer also includes the flag and official name and lists major administrative sub-divisions of countries, such as the 50 American states, and external territories, such as American Samoa or Puerto Rico. All countries are listed by their names in alphabetical order. Inhabited external territories are included under their mother country as well as under their own name, which makes them easier to find.

United States / U.S.A.
United States of America

Area:	9,631,418 km²
Population:	297,043,000 (2004)
Capital:	Washington D.C. (571,000; A: 4,700,000)
Administration:	50 states and the District of Columbia
Languages:	English/regionally Spanish
Religions:	Protestant 58%, Roman Catholic 21%, other Christian 6%, Jewish 2%, Muslim 2%
Currency:	1 dollar = 100 cents

Major cities:
New York (8,084,000; MA: 20,124,000), Los Angeles (3,798,000; MA: 15,781,000), Chicago (2,886,000; A: 7,939,000), Houston (2,010,000; A:

Wisconsin	169,643	5,250,000	Madison
Wyoming	253,349	480,000	Cheyenne

* including inland water

Outlying Territories in the Caribbean:

Navassa
Navassa Island

Area:	5 km²/uninhabited
Population:	75,000 (2004)
Major cities:	Douglas (23,500)

Puerto Rico
Estado Libre Asociado de Puerto Rico/
Commonwealth of Puerto Rico

Area:	9,084 km²
Population:	3,898,000 (2004)
Capital:	San Juan (422,000)
Languages:	Spanish/English
Religions:	Roman Catholic 72%, Protestant 5%

Flat Maps and Coordinates for a Spherical Earth

To understand how map projection works, think of Earth as an orange. Peel off a part of the skin, flatten it out, and the distortion is apparent but minor – much less than for a large section, which cannot be flattened without tearing the skin. Fortunately for geographers and map users, mathematics allows the seamless stretching of the whole globe, or just a portion, into a flat map. To convert the three-dimensional earth into a two-dimensional map, cartographers define locations on the globe with a system of coordinates composed of lines of latitude called *parallels* and lines of longitude called *meridians*. Each intersection of latitude and longitude defines a unique location on the globe.

This is a **parallel**, or line of constant **latitude**, which indicates how far north or south a place on that line is from the equator.

This is the **equator**, along which latitude is 0°.

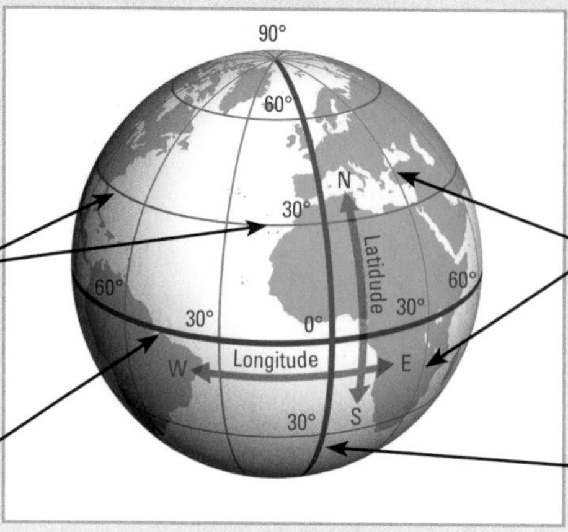

This is a **meridian**, or line of constant **longitude**, which how tells us how far a place is east or west from Greenwich. The greatest longitude from Greenwich in either direction is 180°.

The **prime meridian**, at 0° longitude, passes through Greenwich, England.

Types of Projections

Map projections are created by projecting geographic features from a spherical globe onto one of three simple mathematical surfaces: the **plane**, **cylinder**, and **cone**, which yield projections labeled azimuthal, cylindrical and conic.

The **plane** (azimuthal projection) is generally used for polar maps. Projections for tropical areas are often based on a **cylinder** centered on the equator. Maps for mid-latitude regions like Europe and North American are usually projected onto a **cone** anchored to one or two *standard parallels*, which have the same scale on both map and globe. Conic projections in the *Perthes World Atlas* use two standard parallels because this ensures that the average place can be closer to at least one of the parallels.

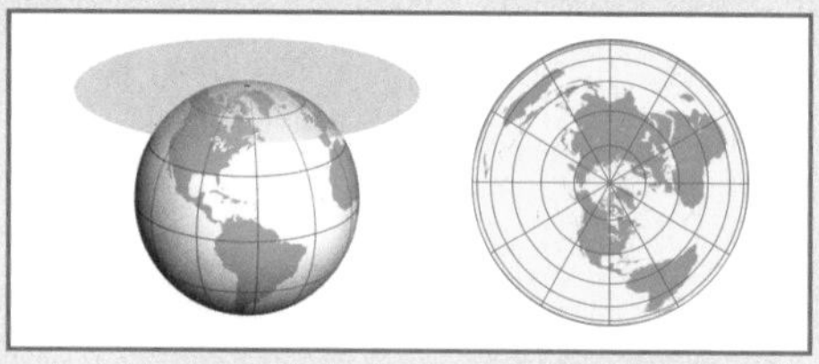

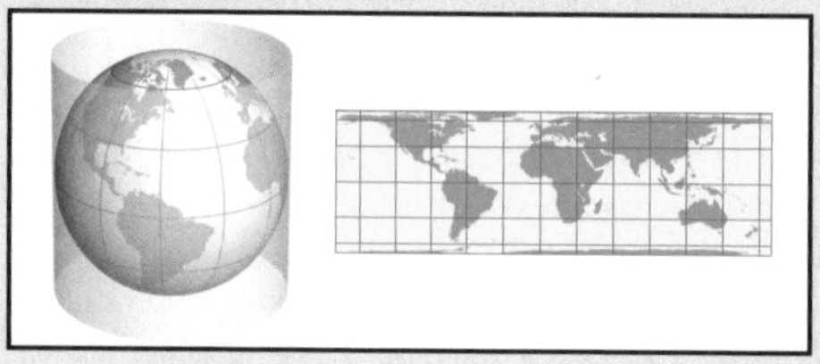

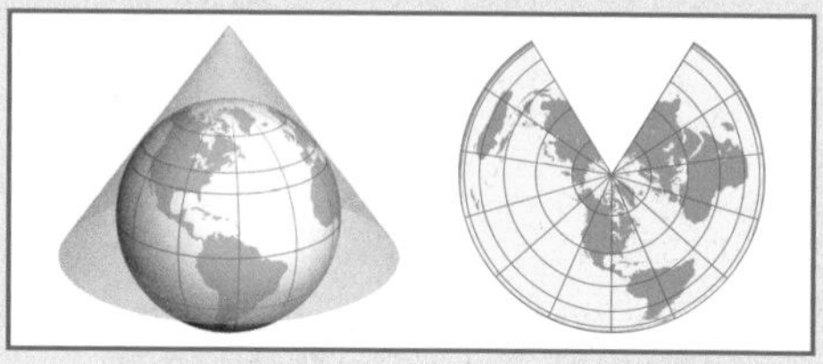

Problems of Distortion

Map projections can distort five geographic properties: area, angles, distance, direction, and gross shapes like the outlines of continents. Although some distortion is unavoidable, angles and relative area can be preserved – but not, unfortunately, in the same projection. Relative area is generally more important than exact angles. Therefore, continental and regional maps in the *Perthes World Atlas* are cast on equal-area projections.

Fitting the whole world onto a single map projection is far trickier than projecting a region or country because of the enormous stretching required. Indeed, distortions of some distances are so extreme that no world map should include a scale bar. Although world projections can preserve relative area exactly, they often incur outrageous distortions of shape, as on the **Peters projection**, which severely stretches continents.

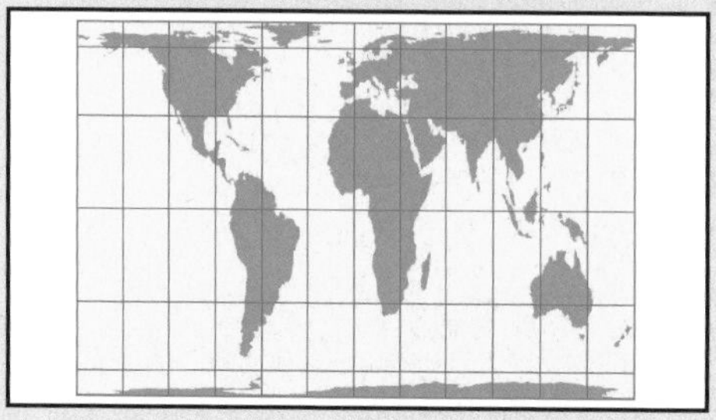

World maps in the *Perthes World Atlas* are cast on the **Winkel Tripel projection**, which offers a balanced treatment of areas and shapes and confines its more severe distortions to the northern and southern polar regions.

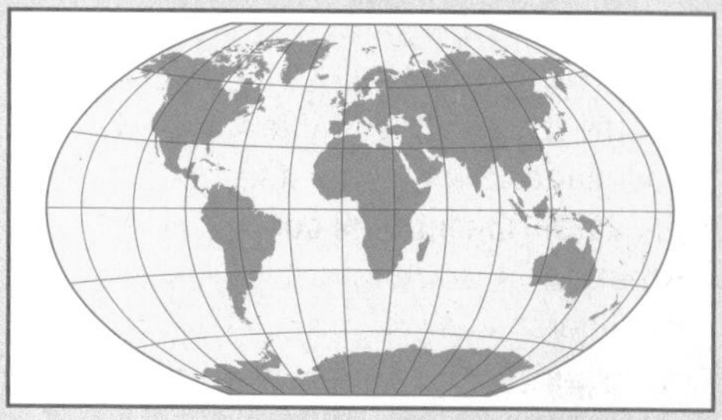

Centering Maps

In addition to the choice of projection, where a map is centered (and where Earth's skin is torn) affects how the world looks. A comparison of the Winkel Tripel projection world map on the facing page with the Winkel Tripel projection centered on the Pacific Ocean illustrates the importance of centering.

In general, the place at the center will have less distortion than most other places on the map, especially those near the edge.

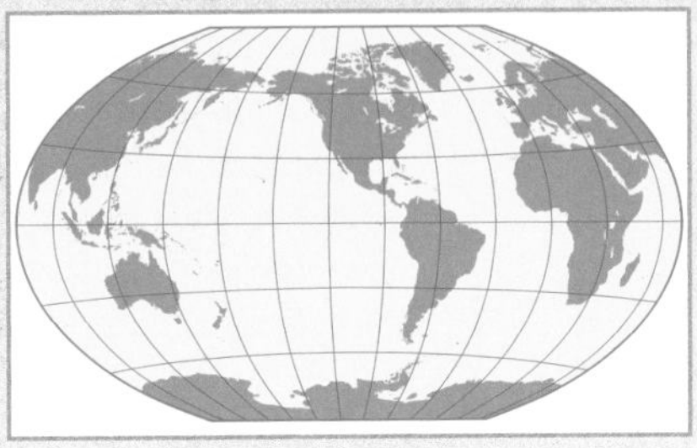

Generalization

Like the written word or mathematics, a map is a language – a form of communication. Look closely at a common map, like a road map, and you will be amazed at the amount of information represented. Think about the difficulty of expressing some of the things easily represented on a map in words alone. Road maps stress transportation and how to get between different places. Other maps express or emphasize other geographic concepts.

Maps cannot possibly convey every aspect of the place they cover. As abstractions that condense Earth's complexity into a small space, they must leave many things out. This process is called *generalization*. All maps have to choose the features they represent and those they omit. Without generalization, maps would be hopelessly cluttered.

Scale

Whenever they make a map, cartographers must specify its *scale*, a term that refers to the ratio between length on the map and the corresponding real-world distance.

A scale of 1:100 means that each inch of map represents 100 inches on the ground. This is called a *representative fraction* because it can be written as 1/100. A scale of 1:100 is useful only for floor plans, gardens, and other small areas. A scale of 1:40,000,000 depicts a large area, like a continent.

Whether a map scale is considered large or small depends on its representative fraction: 1:100 is a huge scale, while 1:100,000,000 is very small. In general, large-scale maps show relatively small areas like a part of a city, while small-scale maps show big areas like the world or the United States.

Examples of Generalization and Scale in the *Perthes World Atlas*

This map of the Eastern Mediterranean, focused on Cyprus, demonstrates how **generalization** works

This same portion of the world is depicted at three different scales. Note the different levels of generalization in these three maps.

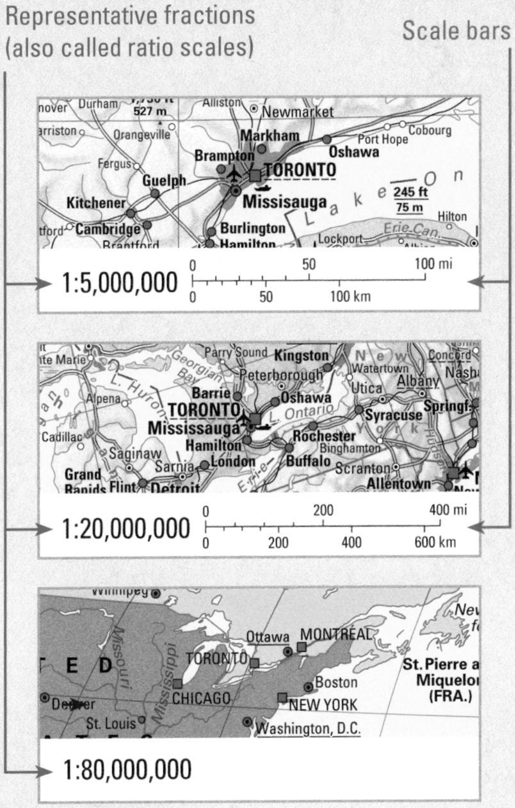

Nuts and Bolts of Maps

Each map is composed of a wide variety of different elements. Knowing what each of these elements means makes it easier for you to find and interpret information on a map. The elements that are depicted depend on the type of map and the scale of the map.

This map of the North Polar Atlantic is a small-scale map in which each unit on the map represents 40,000,000 units on the earth. It is also primarily a physical map that emphasizes physical features like lakes, rivers, coasts, ice, currents, and terrain.

Maps in the atlas include a web of **latitude** and **longitude** lines (**parallels** and **meridians**).

The **scale bar** represents the scale of the map, which indicates how distance on the map corresponds to distance on the earth. The separation of the tics at 0 and 500 represent 500 miles on Earth's surface.

This map uses **color** and **lines** to depict a variety of landforms. Smaller **rivers** are depicted with blue lines, larger **lakes** and seas appear as blue areas bounded by blue lines, and **landforms** are in shades of green and brown.

Maps use boundary lines to represent the **boundaries** between different spatial units. Boundaries between countries are most often depicted, but sometimes internal boundaries are represented as well. On this map, boundaries are shown as red lines. Some boundaries across open water are shown by dashed red lines, like this one, indicating that Spitsbergen belongs to Norway.

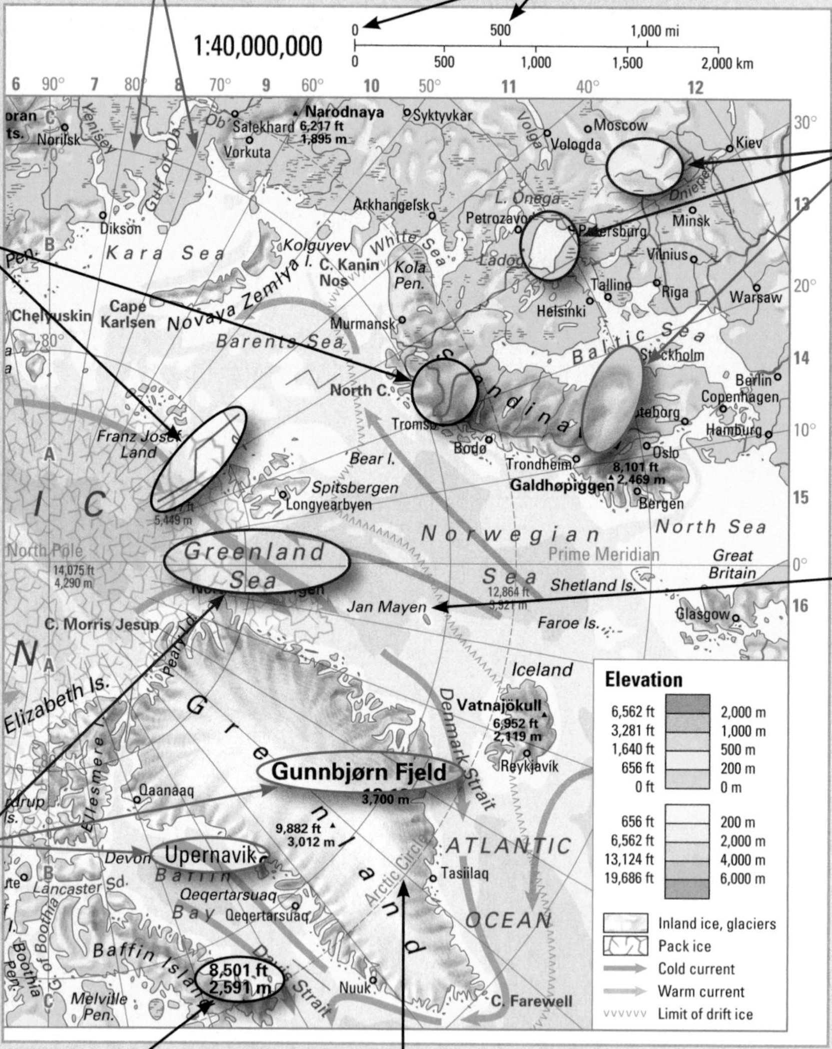

Place names in this atlas are found in the **index**. The index allows you to locate a place by page number and by its position on the map grid. In this case, the index would list "Jan Mayen 180 B 16". The letter indicates a section between two lines of latitude and the number indicates a section between two lines of longitude. Since this is a special projection, the latitude sections are circles and the longitude sections are pie shaped. You can find the island if you follow the red letter "B" along the curve of the latitude lines until you reach the sector with the red number "16".

Names and other **text** are presented using a hierarchical system of fonts, styles, sizes, and colors that provide visual clues to categories of features. For example, **water** features are depicted in blue lettering, while **mountains** and **settlements** are distinguished by different font styles in black lettering.

This map notes significant **elevations**, often high points, in both feet and meters.

Places north of the **Arctic Circle** have at least one period when the sun is above the horizon for more than 24 hours. Everywhere north of the Arctic Circle is in the Polar latitudes.

The **legend** is the part of the map that shows the reader how to interpret various symbols and colors.

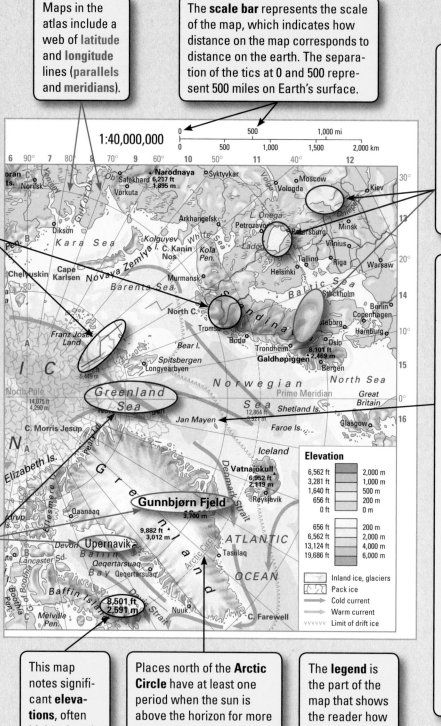

Signs and Symbols

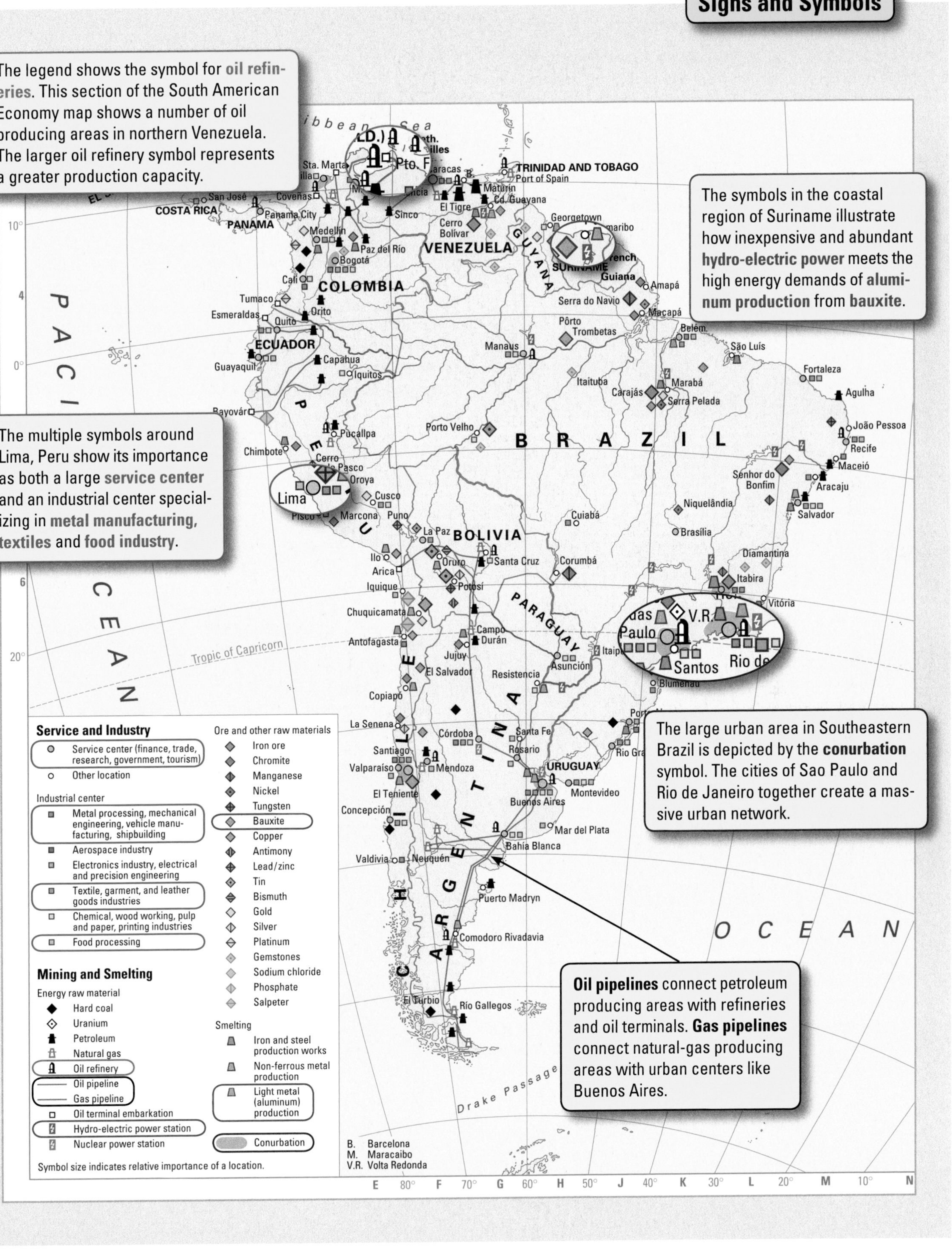

The legend shows the symbol for **oil refineries**. This section of the South American Economy map shows a number of oil producing areas in northern Venezuela. The larger oil refinery symbol represents a greater production capacity.

The symbols in the coastal region of Suriname illustrate how inexpensive and abundant **hydro-electric power** meets the high energy demands of **aluminum production** from **bauxite**.

The multiple symbols around Lima, Peru show its importance as both a large **service center** and an industrial center specializing in **metal manufacturing, textiles** and **food industry**.

The large urban area in Southeastern Brazil is depicted by the **conurbation** symbol. The cities of Sao Paulo and Rio de Janeiro together create a massive urban network.

Oil pipelines connect petroleum producing areas with refineries and oil terminals. **Gas pipelines** connect natural-gas producing areas with urban centers like Buenos Aires.

Choropleths and Arrows

Looks complicated? Sure, but a little effort will yield a lot of insight. The maps in this atlas are designed to be easy-to-read as well as informative. As its title and legend indicate, this map shows several things:

(1) the **direction and size of migration flows**;
(2) **average annual rates of net migration**; and
(3) the **percentage of the world's population** living in an area **with a particular migration pattern**.

Countries are shaded in different colors to indicate **average yearly rates of migration**. Countries with yellow or green shades have experienced net in-migration, with more people moving in than moving out, while in countries with an orange or red color, more migrants have moved out than moved in. If you compare the green shades of Canada and the US, you can see that Canada has a higher average annual rate of in-migration than the United States. Maps that show rates or other values by shading areas of varying sizes – in this case countries – are called **choropleth maps**. The term comes from the Greek *choro*, which means place, and *plethos*, which means magnitude.

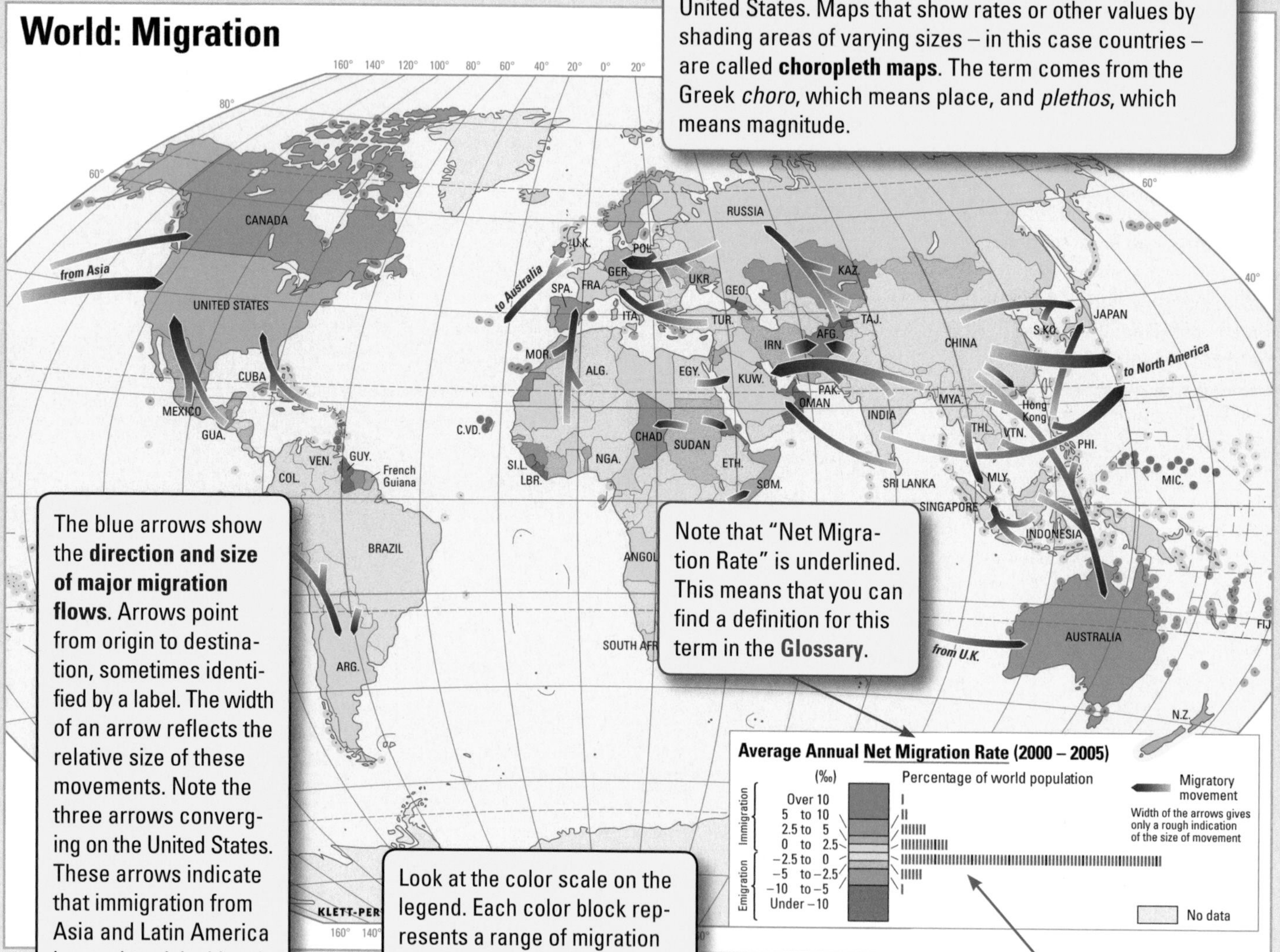

The blue arrows show the **direction and size of major migration flows**. Arrows point from origin to destination, sometimes identified by a label. The width of an arrow reflects the relative size of these movements. Note the three arrows converging on the United States. These arrows indicate that immigration from Asia and Latin America has replaced the historic migrations from Europe.

Note that "Net Migration Rate" is underlined. This means that you can find a definition for this term in the **Glossary**.

Look at the color scale on the legend. Each color block represents a range of migration rates, and its height indicates relative size of the range. For example, the color block for the second darkest shade of green (annual migration rates between 5 % and 10 %) is double the height of the next interval (2.5 % to 5 %). The taller the block, the larger the range of values.

The bars on the right side of the color scale show the **percentage of global population with a given migration rate**. You can see that only about 1 % the world's population lives in countries with the highest rates of net immigration.

Graduated Circles

The map on this page uses graduated circles (circles of different sizes) and a sophisticated legend to present a wealth of information about urban populations in the world. A closer look at the legend indicates that we can read four things from this map:

(1) the change in the size of country's **urban population predicted for 2005 to 2030**;
(2) the **percentage (or share) of a country's population that is urban**;
(3) the **size of a country's population in 2005**; and
(4) **percentage of global population with a given rate of change and a given share of urban population.**

Look at the **different colors of circles** on the map. Note the red circles for the United States and much of Europe and South America and the dark green circles for Niger (NGR.) and Uganda (UGA.). In the United States and other countries with red circles, which are already highly urban, the urban population will grow by no more than 50 %. By contrast, the urban population in Nigeria and other countries with dark green circles will increase between 250 % and 350 %. Note too the purple circles of Russia and much of Eastern Europe, where the share of the urban population is expected to decline over the next 25 years.

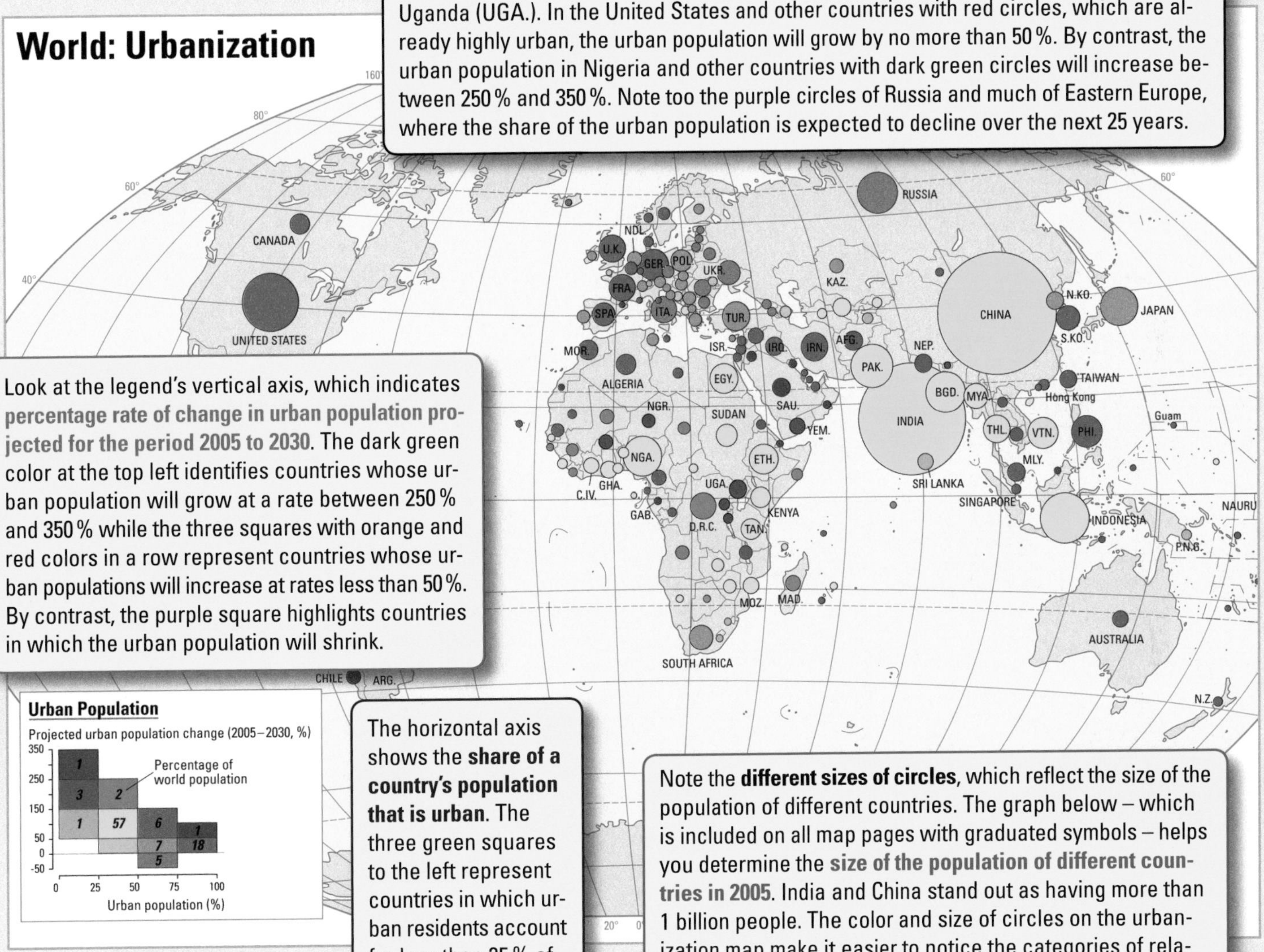

Look at the legend's vertical axis, which indicates **percentage rate of change in urban population projected for the period 2005 to 2030**. The dark green color at the top left identifies countries whose urban population will grow at a rate between 250 % and 350 % while the three squares with orange and red colors in a row represent countries whose urban populations will increase at rates less than 50 %. By contrast, the purple square highlights countries in which the urban population will shrink.

The horizontal axis shows the **share of a country's population that is urban**. The three green squares to the left represent countries in which urban residents account for less than 25 % of the total population. By contrast, the two reddish squares depict highly urbanized countries that are over 75 % urban.

Note the numbers inside the squares, which indicate the **percentage of global population** with a given rate of change and a given share of urban population. More than half (57 %) of the world's population lives in countries with a largely rural population (urban share between 25 % and 50 %) and a projected change between 50 % and 150 %.

Note the **different sizes of circles**, which reflect the size of the population of different countries. The graph below – which is included on all map pages with graduated symbols – helps you determine the **size of the population of different countries in 2005**. India and China stand out as having more than 1 billion people. The color and size of circles on the urbanization map make it easier to notice the categories of relatively small, densely populated countries like Indonesia and Japan, which have significantly larger populations than huge, more sparsely populated nations like Australia and Canada. By contrast, if you look at the choropleth migration map on the facing page, countries with a large land area appear very prominent even if they have small populations.

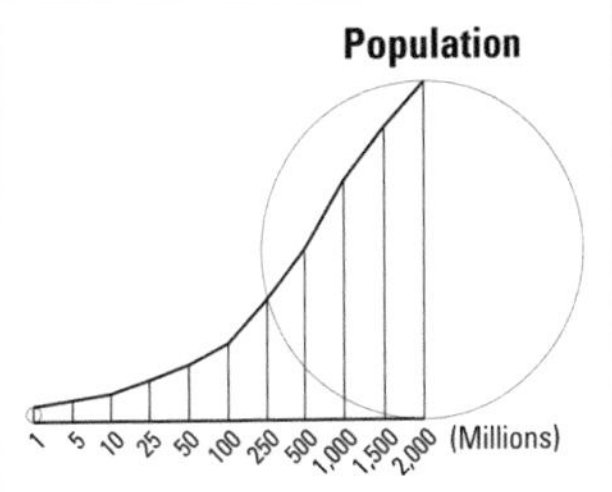

Physical Geographic Issues

An atlas is organized to help you learn more about the world by looking at a variety of maps of the same place or region. When you compare maps of different physical phenomena, such as rainfall and vegetation, with maps of social and economic factors, such as population growth and wealth, you can see new connections and ask new questions. Let's look at some examples in Africa.

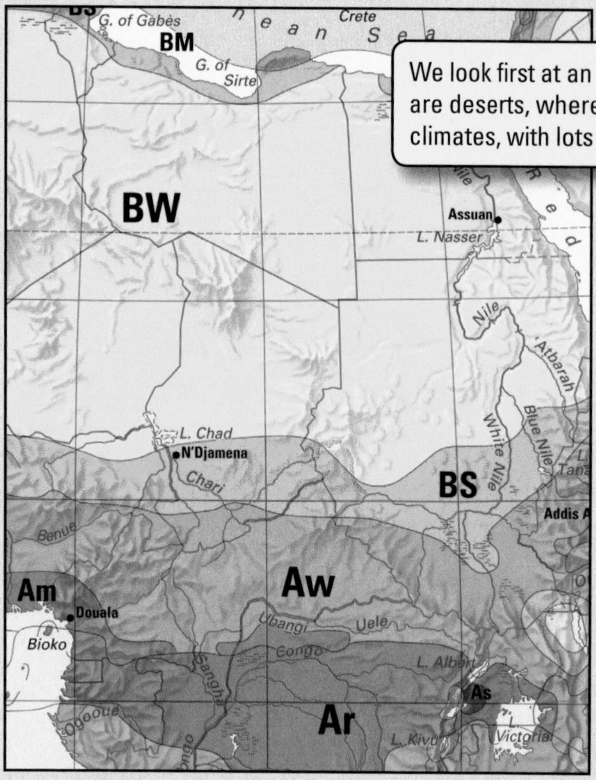

We look first at an excerpt from the "Africa: **Climate**" map (p. 174). The tan areas labeled "BW" are deserts, whereas the "BS" areas are semiarid steppes. Farther south are the tropical "A" climates, with lots of rain, and the "Ar" climates – the wettest and hottest places on Earth.

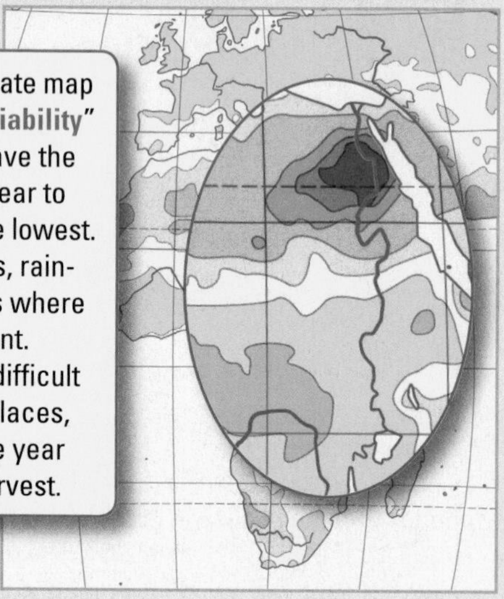

Compare the excerpts for the climate map and the "World: **Precipitation Variability**" map (p. 21). The dark red areas have the highest variation in rainfall from year to year while those in green have the lowest. You can see that in the drier areas, rainfall varies a lot more than in areas where total precipitation is more abundant. Think about agriculture and how difficult it might be to farm in those drier places, where even a little less rain in one year might cost farmers their entire harvest.

Compare the climate map excerpt to the excerpt of the "Africa: **Environments**" map (p. 170). The pink areas on the environment map are "grasslands," and the dark green areas are "evergreen broadleaf forests," which means tropical rainforests. You can see that tropical rainforests generally coincide with an "Ar" climate and grasslands with a "BS" climate.

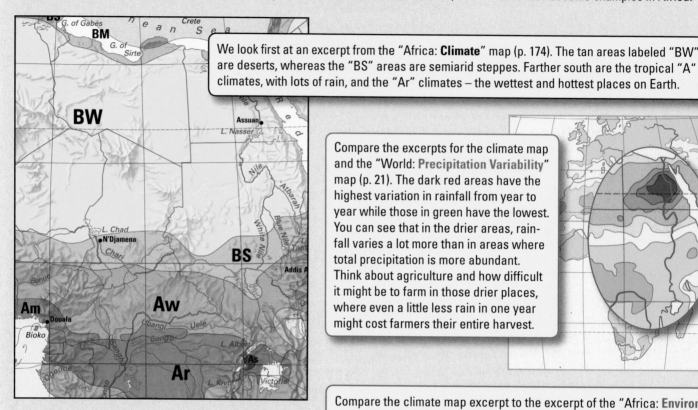

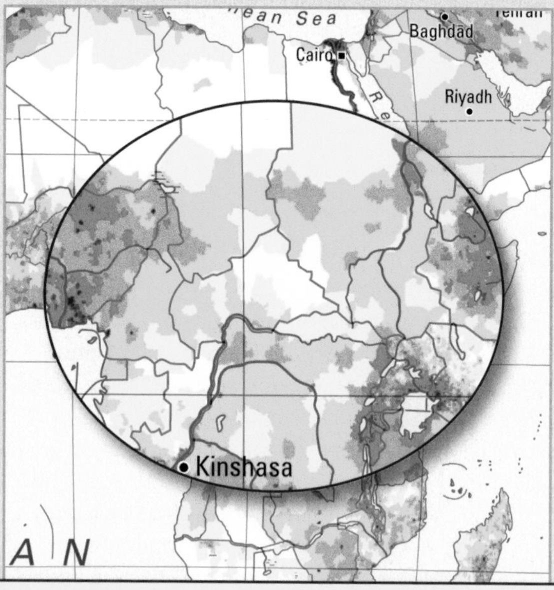

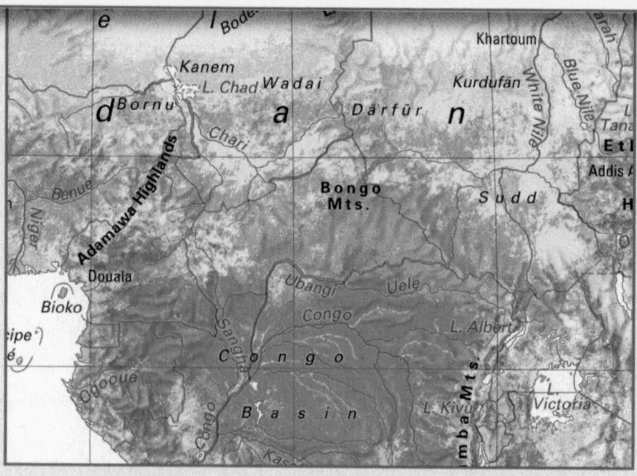

Look at the excerpt from the "World: **Population Density**" map (p. 40–41), on which population density is higher where the shading is darker. Now look at the same area on the **climate** map and note the influence climate on population density, which declines drastically the closer you get to the driest areas, where rainfall becomes so sparse that farming is impossible without irrigation. Now look at the **precipitation variability** map and consider that yearly rainfall becomes less reliable in drier climates. Even so, there is no direct correlation between climate and population density. Look at population densities in the "Aw" climate belt, which includes dense population clusters in the center left part of the map and sparse populations in the center. The **environments** map offers a possible explanation: near its center are the Bongo Mountains, which probably make this area less suitable for agriculture.

Social and Economic Issues

The map comparisons on this page deal with social and economic issues in Africa and Europe.

Let's start with an excerpt from the "World: **Natural Population Development**" map (p. 43). Look at the circles: dark green represents the highest population growth, lighter shades of green show growth rates ranging from high to low, yellow reflects stagnation, and orange indicates decline. You can see that Africa has very high population growth, while most of Europe has stagnation and decline.

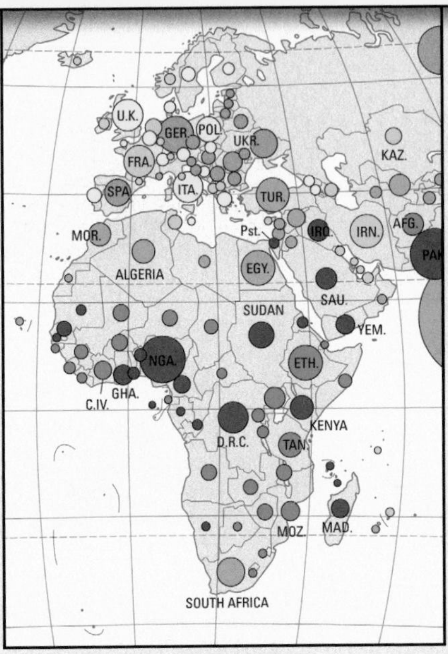

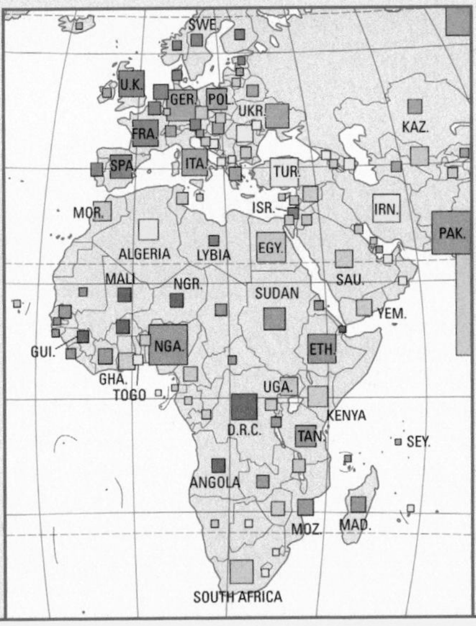

Compare the population growth map excerpt with the "World: **Gross Domestic Product**" map (p. 45) excerpt. Orange and red represents very low yearly per capita GDP (US$ 2,500 or less) while green signifies high yearly per capita GDP's (US$ 20,000 or more). Countries with high population growth have also very low GDP while those with stagnating or declining populations have high GDP. There is clearly a relationship here, but we don't know if one causes the other. Does high population growth put a great strain on the economy, or do poor people have more children to help make ends meet and provide for the parents in their old age? In what kind of economies are children an important source of labor? Map comparison helps you formulate new questions for further inquiry.

The excerpt from the map "World: **Health**"(p. 47) shows infant mortality rates – the orange and red shades indicate that at least 1 in 10 babies die in their first year of life – and the availability of physicians – the circles with a white background mean there are less than 2 physicians for every 10,000 people. Note how countries with high infant mortality rates and few physicians are also those with low **education**, low **Gross Domestic Product**, and high **population growth**.

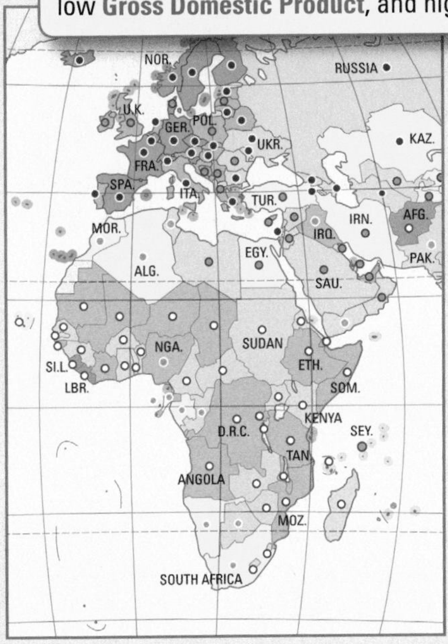

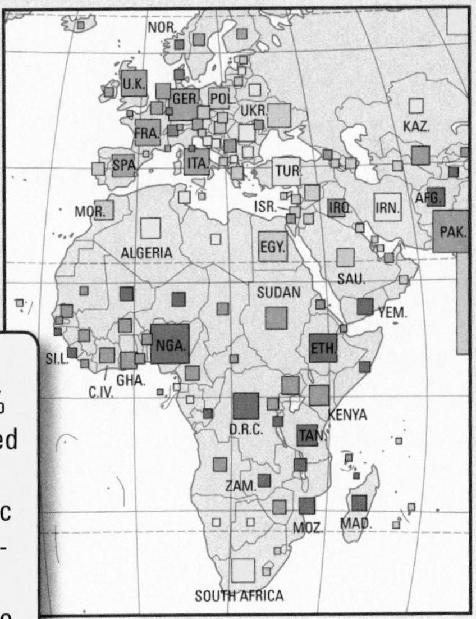

Look at the excerpt from the map "World: **Education**"(p. 44). Green indicates that at least 80 % of the population is enrolled in schools, while red indicates that less than 30 % of the population attends school. Look at the Democratic Republic of the Congo (D.R.C.), which has a very low educational level. The maps of population development and Gross Domestic Product show that the D.R.C. has not only the lowest education level on the continent but also the highest population growth and the lowest GDP. Many countries in Africa have similar socio-economic conditions. Think about the challenges for development. Do low levels of education also mean that people have little knowledge about family planning? What is the link between **education**, **health**, and **population growth**?

We hope that our remarks on the preceding pages have made you eager to explore the wealth of information in the *Perthes World Atlas*.

Guntram H. Herb, David H. Kaplan & Mark Monmonier

Countries

A. & B. Antigua and Barbuda
AFG. Afghanistan
AGO. Angola
ALB. Albania
ALG. Algeria
AND. Andorra
ARG. Argentina
ARM. Armenia
AUS. Australia
AUT. Austria
AZE. Azerbaijan

BBD. Barbados
BDI. Burundi
BEN. Benin
B.FS. Burkina Faso
BGD. Bangladesh
BGM. Belgium
B. & H. Bosnia and Herzegovina
BHM. Bahamas
BHR. Bahrain
BHU. Bhutan
BLR. Belarus
BLZ. Belize
BOL. Bolivia
BOT. Botswana
BRA. Brazil
BRU. Brunei
BUL. Bulgaria

CAN. Canada
C.A.R. Central African Republic
CBD. Cambodia
CHD. Chad
CHL. Chile
CHN. China
C.IV. Côte d'Ivoire
CMN. Cameroon
COL. Colombia
COM. Comoros
CON. Congo
C.RC. Costa Rica
CRO. Croatia
CUB. Cuba
C.VD. Cape Verde
CYP. Cyprus
CZ.R. Czech Republic

DCA. Dominica
DEN. Denmark
DJI. Djibouti
DO.R. Dominican Republic
D.R.C. Congo, Democratic Republic of the

ECU. Ecuador
EGY. Egypt
EQ.G. Equatorial Guinea
ERI. Eritrea
EST. Estonia
ETH. Ethiopia

FIN. Finland
FJI. Fiji
FRA. France

GAB. Gabon
GAM. Gambia
GCE. Greece
GEO. Georgia
GER. Germany
GHA. Ghana
GRA. Grenada
GUA. Guatemala
GU.B. Guinea-Bissau
GUI. Guinea
GUY. Guyana

HON. Honduras
HTI. Haiti
HUN. Hungary

ICE. Iceland
IDN. Indonesia
IND. India
IRE. Ireland
IRN. Iran
IRQ. Iraq
ISR. Israel
ITA. Italy

JAM. Jamaica
JAP. Japan
JOR. Jordan

KAZ. Kazakhstan
KEN. Kenya
KIR. Kiribati
KUW. Kuwait
KYR. Kyrgyzstan

LAO. Laos
LAT. Latvia
LBR. Liberia
LBY. Libya
LEB. Lebanon
LES. Lesotho
LIE. Liechtenstein
LIT. Lithuania
LUX. Luxembourg

MAC. Macedonia, The Former Yugoslav Republic of
MAD. Madagascar
MA.I. Marshall Islands
MCO. Monaco
MDV. Maldives
MEX. Mexico
MIC. Micronesia
MLI. Mali
MLT. Malta
MLY. Malaysia
MNG. Mongolia
MOL. Moldova
MOR. Morocco
MOZ. Mozambique
MRS. Mauritius
MRT. Mauritania
MWI. Malawi
MYA. Myanmar

NAM. Namibia
NAU. Nauru
NEP. Nepal
NGA. Nigeria
NGR. Niger
NIC. Nicaragua
N.KO. Korea, North
NLD. Netherlands
NOR. Norway
N.Z. New Zealand

OMN. Oman

PAK. Pakistan
PAL. Palau
PAN. Panama
PAR. Paraguay
PER. Peru
PHI. Philippines
P.N.G. Papua New Guinea
POL. Poland
POR. Portugal
Pst. Palestine

QAT. Qatar

ROM. Romania
RUS. Russia
RWA. Rwanda

S.AF. South Africa
SAL. El Salvador
SAM. Samoa
SAU. Saudi Arabia
SEN. Senegal
SEY. Seychelles
SGP. Singapore
SI.L. Sierra Leone
S.KO. Korea, South
S. & M. Serbia and Montenegro
S.MA. San Marino
SO.I. Solomon Islands
SOM. Somalia
SPA. Spain
SR.L. Sri Lanka
ST.K. Saint Kitts and Nevis
ST.L. Saint Lucia
S.TO. Sao Tome and Principe
ST.V. Saint Vincent and the Grenadines
SUD. Sudan
SUR. Suriname
SVK. Slovakia
SVN. Slovenia
SWA. Swaziland
SWE. Sweden
SWI. Switzerland
SYR. Syria

TAI. Taiwan
TAJ. Tajikistan
TAN. Tanzania
TGO. Togo
THL. Thailand
TI.L. Timor-Leste
TKM. Turkmenistan
TON. Tonga
T. & T. Trinidad and Tobago
TUN. Tunisia
TUR. Turkey
TUV. Tuvalu

U.A.E. United Arab Emirates
UGA. Uganda
U.K. United Kingdom
UKR. Ukraine
URU. Uruguay
U.S. United States
UZB. Uzbekistan

VAN. Vanuatu
VAT. Vatican City
VEN. Venezuela
VTN. Vietnam

W.SA. Western Sahara

YEM. Yemen

ZAM. Zambia
ZIM. Zimbabwe

Organizations, Institutions, Technical Terms

AETFAT — Association pour l'Etude Taxonomique de la Flore De l'Afrique Tropicale
AIDS — Acquired Immunodeficiency Syndrome
ANZUS — Australia-New Zealand-United States Security Treaty
ASEAN — Association of Southeast Asian Nations
AU — African Union

BGR — Bundesanstalt für Geowissenschaften und Rohstoffe

CIA — Central Intelligence Agency
CIAT — Centro Internacional de Agricultura Tropical
CIESIN — Center for International Earth Science Information Network
CIS — Commonwealth of Independent States
CRED — Center for Research on the Epidemiology of Disasters

DAC — Development Assistance Committee
DAI — Digital Access Index
DWD — Deutscher Wetterdienst

ECOWAS — Economic Community of West African States
EROS — Earth Resources Observation and Science
EU — European Union

FAO — Food and Agriculture Organization of the United Nations
FSC — Forest Stewardship Council

GDP — Gross Domestic Product
GHG — Green House Gasses
GMT — Greenwich Mean Time
GNI — Gross National Income
GWP — Gridded Population of the World
G8 — Group of Eight

HDI — Human Development Index
HIIK — Heidelberger Institut für Internationale Konfliktforschung
HIPC — Heavily Indebted Poor Countries
HIV — Human Immunodeficiency Virus

IGBP — International Geosphere-Biosphere Programme
ILO — International Labour Organization
IMF — International Monetary Fund
IPCC — Intergovernmental Panel on Climate Change
ISIC — International Standard Industrial Classification
ITC — Information and Communications Technology
ITU — International Telecommunication Union
IUCN — International Union for Conservation of Nature and Natural Resources

LAS — League of Arab States

MERCOSUR — Mercado Común del Cono Sur
MET — Middle European Standard Time
MEWT — Middle European Winter Time
MHT — Major Habitat Type
MPI — Migration Policy Institute

NAFTA — North American Free Trade Agreement
NATO — North Atlantic Treaty Organization
NRCS — Natural Resources Conservation Service
NZST — New Zealand Standard Time

OA — Official Aid
OAS — Organization of American States
OCHA — United Nations Office for the Coordination of Humanitarian Affairs
ODA — Official Development Assistance
OECD — Organisation for Economic Co-operation and Development
OPEC — Organization of Petroleum Exporting Countries

PIK — Potsdam-Institut für Klimafolgenforschung
PPP — Purchasing Power Parity
PRB — Population Reference Bureau
PRIO — [International] Peace Research Institute, Oslo

SADC — Southern African Development Community

UN — United Nations
UNAIDS — Joint United Nations Programme on HIV/AIDS
UNCTAD — United Nations Conference on Trade and Development
UNDP — United Nations Development Programme
UNEP — United Nations Environment Programme
UNESCO — United Nations Educational, Scientific and Cultural Organization
UNFCCC — United Nations Framework Convention on Climate Change
UNHCR — United Nations High Commissioner for Refugees
UNPD — United Nations Population Division
UNSO — United Nations Sahelian Office
UNWTO — United Nations World Tourism Organization
USDA — United States Department of Agriculture
USGS — United States Geological Survey
UTC — Coordinated Universal Time

WCMC — World Conservation Monitoring Centre
WEC — World Energy Council
WET — Western European Time
WHO — World Health Organization
WMO — World Meteorological Organization
WTO — World Trade Organization
WWF — World Wildlife Fund

Geographical Terms

A.R. — Autonomous Region
Arch. — Archipelago

C. — Cape
C. — City
Cd. — Ciudad
Co. — Cerro
Cr. — Creek

Depr. — Depression

-fj. — -fjorden

G. — Gulf

I. — Island
Is. — Islands
Ind. Res. — Indian Reservation (in U.S.) Indian Reserve (in CAN.)

J. — Jabal

L. — Lake
La. — Laguna

M. — Monte
Mt. — Mont
Mt. — Mount
Mte. — Monte
Mtn. — Mountain
Mts. — Monts
Mts. — Mountains

N. — North
N. P. — National Park
Nat. Mon. — National Monument
Nat. P. — National Park, National Parc

P. — Pico
P. N. — Parque Nacional
Pen. — Peninsula
Pen. — Península
Pk. — Peak
Pt. — Point
Pta. — Punta

R. — Ra's
R. — Rio
R. — Río
R. — River
Ra. — Range
Rep. — Republic
Res. — Reservoir
Rés. — Réservoir

S. — San, Santa, Santo
S. — São
S. — South
Sa. — Serra
Sa. — Sierra
Sd. — Sound
St. — Saint
St — Saint
Sta. — Santa
Str. — Strait

Foreign Geographical Terms

Adrar (Arabic)	Mountain, Mountains
-älv, -en (Swedish)	River
Bahía (Spanish)	Bay
Baía (Portuguese)	Bay
Baie (French)	Bay
Ben (Scottish)	Mountain
Bereg (Russian)	Coast
Bumu (Turkish)	Cape
Cabo (Portuguese, Spanish)	Cape
Cap (French)	Cape
Cerro (Spanish)	Mountain
Ciudad (Spanish)	Town
Cordillera (Spanish)	Cordillera
Costa (Spanish)	Coast
Côte (French)	Coast
Dag (Turkic languages)	Mountain, Mountains
Dağ, -ı (Turkish)	Mountain, Mountains
Dāgh (Turkic languages)	Mountains
Dağlar, -ı (Turkish)	Mountain, Mountains
Dasht (Farsi)	Desert
Détroit (French)	Strait
Erg [ʿIrq] (Arabic)	Desert
Firth (Scottish)	Bay
-fjörður (Icelandic)	Fjord
Gol (Mongolian)	River
Golfo (Spanish, Italian)	Gulf
Guba (Russian)	Bay
Hamadah (Arabic)	Stony desert
He (Chinese)	River
Hu (Chinese)	Lake
Île, -s (French)	Island, -s
Isla, -s (Spanish)	Island, -s
Jabal (Arabic)	Mountain, Mountains
-järv (Estonian)	Lake
-järvi (Finnish)	Lake
Jiang (Chinese)	River
-joki (Finnish)	River
-jökull (Icelandic)	Glacier
Kamen' (Russian)	Mountain
Kūh (Farsi)	Mountain, Mountains
Lac (French)	Lake
Lagoa (Portuguese)	Lagoon
Laguna (Spanish)	Lagoon
Loch (Scottish)	Lake
Lough (Irish)	Lake
-maa (Estonian, Finnish)	Land
Mar (Italian, Portuguese, Spanish)	Sea
-meer (Dutch)	Lake
Mont (French)	Mountain
Monte (Italian, Portuguese, Spanish)	Mountain
Monts (French)	Mountains
Munţii (Romanian)	Mountains
Nahr (Arabic, Urdu)	River, Canal
-nes (Icelandic)	Cape
Nos (Bulgarian, Russian)	Cape
Nosy (Madagascan)	Island
Nur, Nuur (Mongolian)	Lake
Nuruu (Mongolian)	Mountains
-ö (Swedish)	Island
Ostrow, -a (Russian)	Island, -s
-oy, -a (Norwegian)	Island
Ozero (Russian)	Lake
-pan (African)	Salt pan
Parque Nacional (Spanish)	National Park
Pendi (Chinese)	Plain
Pico (Spanish, Portuguese)	Mountain
Pik (Russian)	Mountain
Playa (Spanish)	Beach
Pointe (French)	Cape
Ponta (Portuguese)	Cape
Porto (Italian, Portuguese)	Harbor, Port
Presa (Spanish)	Reservoir
Puerto (Spanish)	Harbor, Port
Punta (Spanish, Italian)	Cape
Puntan (Chamorro)	Cape
Ra's (Arabic)	Cape
Recife (Portuguese, Spanish)	Reef
Réservoire (French)	Reservoir
Rio (Portuguese)	River
Río (Spanish)	River
Rivière (French)	River
Rt (Croatian)	Cape
Sabkhat (Arabic)	Salt flat
Salar (Spanish)	Salt flat
Salina (Spanish)	Salt flat
San (Japanese, Korean)	Mountain
Serra (Portuguese)	Mountain range
Shan (Chinese)	Mountain, Mountains
Sierra (Spanish)	Mountain range
-sjøn (Norwegian)	Lake
-sjön (Swedish)	Lake
Sopka (Russian)	Volcano
Shuṭṭ (Arabic)	Salt flat
Serranía (Spanish)	Mountain range
Tall (Arabic)	Hill
-tind (Norwegian)	Peak
-van (Swedish)	Lake
-vatn (Icelandic, Norwegian)	Lake
-vesi (Finnish)	Lake
Víla (Portuguese)	Settlement
Villa (Spanish)	Settlement

Hydrographic Features

 Shoreline

Undefined or fluctuating shorline

River, stream

 Seasonal river, intermittent river, wadi

Wadi

Canal

Lake, reservoir

Intermittent lake, reservoir

 Dry lake bed

Swamp, marsh

Salt flat

Physical Features

Elevation

13,124 ft	4,000 m
6,562 ft	2,000 m
3,281 ft	1,000 m
1,640 ft	500 m
656 ft	200 m
328 ft	100 m
0 ft	0 m

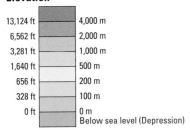

Below sea level (Depression)

Water Depth

656 ft	200 m
6,562 ft	2,000 m
13,124 ft	4,000 m
19,686 ft	6,000 m
26,248 ft	8,000 m

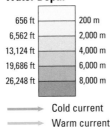

Cold current

Warm current

Inland ice, glaciers

Ice shelf

Pack ice

vvvvvvvvvv Limit of drift ice

Reef

. Elevation above sea level

' Elevation below sea level

Political and other Boundaries

Reference Maps

International boundary

Disputed / undefined boundary

Demarcation line

Territorial limit of a country on water

Internal boundary

Physical and Thematic Maps

International boundary

Disputed / undefined boundary

Demarcation line

Territorial limit of a country on water

Internal boundary

Boundary of national park

Boundary of indian reservation, indian reserve

Settlements

Political Maps ≥ 1:20,000,000

NEW YORK	■	more than 1,000,000 inhabitants
Boston	◉	500,000 – 1,000,000 inhabitants
Regina	●	100,000 – 500,000 inhabitants
Portland	◉	50,000 – 100,000 inhabitants
Key West	○	10,000 – 50,000 inhabitants
Belmopan	○	fewer than 10,000 inhabitants

 Urban agglomeration
(only in maps 1:5,000,000 and 1:15,000,000)

Political Maps ≤ 1:25,000,000

	■	more than 1,000,000 inhabitants
	◉	500,000 – 1,000,000 inhabitants
	●	100,000 – 500,000 inhabitants
	○	fewer than 100,000 inhabitants

∴ Archaelogical/historical site

Physical Maps and Thematic Maps

○ Without classification

Transportation

Expressway, superhighway

Major road

Major railway

Minor railway

Railway tunnel

Ferry

✈ International airport

⚓ Major port

Place Names

Regions

MEXICO	Country
Réunion (FRA.)	Dependent territory and mother country
Nevada	Federal state, province
Cocos I. (C.RC.)	Territory and mainland

Settlements

| Ottawa | National capital |
| Cayenne | Capital city of dependent territory or secondary capital |

NEW YORK	Other Settlements
Boston	
Regina	
Portland	
Key West	
Belmopan	

Physical Features

Andes	Moutains, range
Llano Estacado	Landscape
Sicily	Island
Cape Sable	Cape, headland
Mt. Rainier	Mountain peak, volcano, pass
14,410 ft / 4,392 m	Elevation above sea level, mountain height (in feet and meters)
579 ft / 176 m	Lake surface elevation (in feet and meters)
14,357 ft / 4,376 m	Water depht (in feet and meters)

ATLANTIC OCEAN
Caribbean Sea
Gulf of Maine
Lake Michigan / Seminole Res. } Water bodies

Colorado — River

Lake Eyre — Salt flat

Other Features

Gulf Stream	Current
Yellowstone Nat. Park	National park
North. Cheyenne Ind. Res.	Indian reservation, Indian reserve
Pergamon	Archaeological / histor. site

Measures

Linear, Square, and Cubic Measures

1 inch (in.)	= 25.4 mm	1 mm	= 0.03937 inch
1 foot (ft)	= 0.30479 m	1 m	= 3.28095 feet
1 cubic foot	≈ 0.0283 m³	1 m³	≈ 35.3182 cubic feet
1 mile (mi)	= 1.6093 km	1 km	≈ 0.6214 mile
1 square mile	≈ 2.5898 km²	1 km²	≈ 0.3861 square mile
1 cubic mile	≈ 4.1678 km³	1 km³	≈ 0.2399 cubic mile

1,000 m	3,000 feet
900 m	
800 m	2,500 feet
700 m	
600 m	2,000 feet
500 m	1,500 feet
400 m	
300 m	1,000 feet
200 m	
100 m	500 feet
0 m	0 foot

Other Measures

Temperature (T):

$$T_{Celsius} = (T_{Fahrenheit} - 32) / 1.8$$
$$T_{Fahrenheit} = (T_{Celsius} \cdot 1.8) + 32$$

Speed:

1 km/h ≈ 0.6214 miles per hour/mph

1 mph ≈ 1.6093 km/h

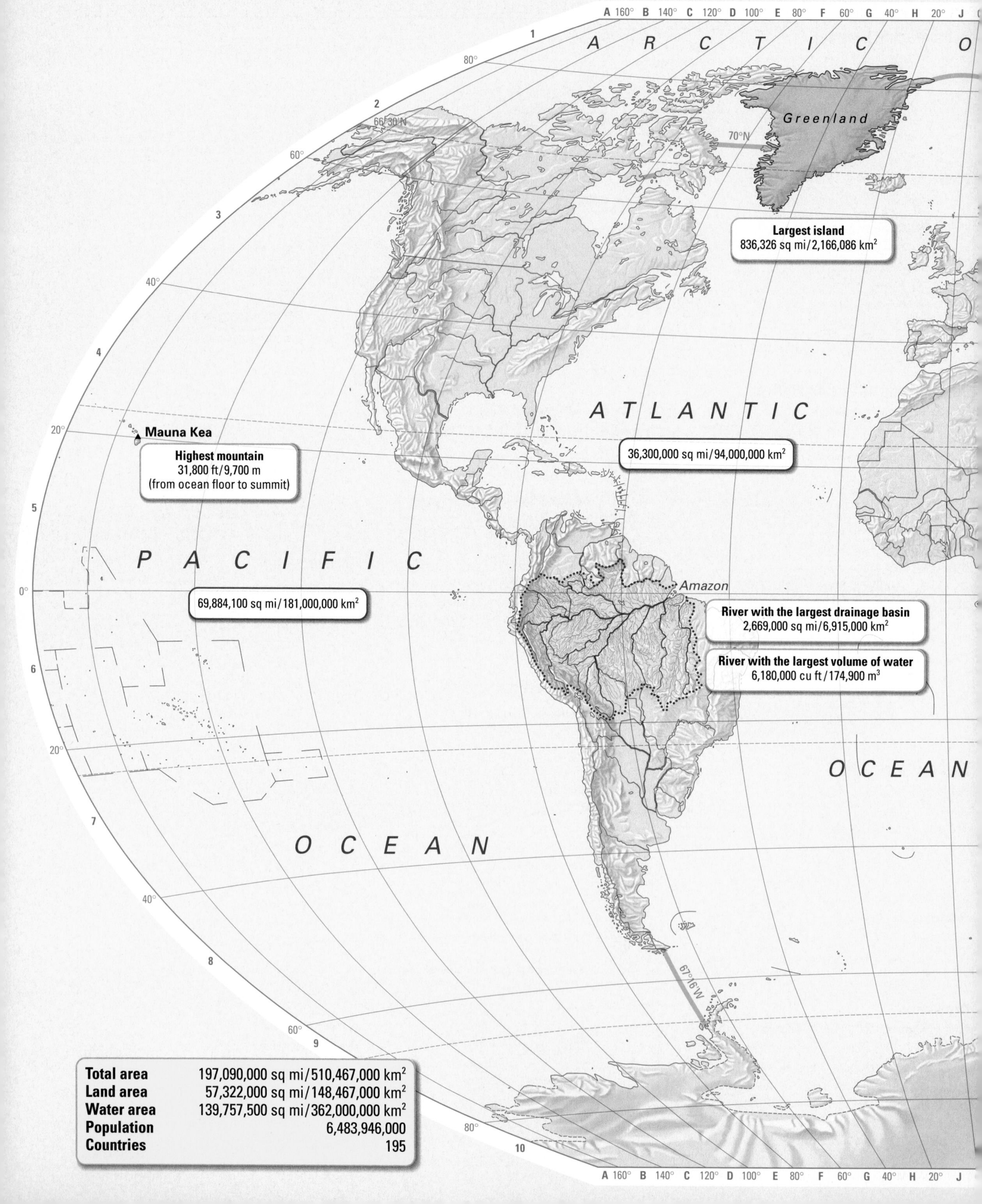

Total area	197,090,000 sq mi/510,467,000 km²
Land area	57,322,000 sq mi/148,467,000 km²
Water area	139,757,500 sq mi/362,000,000 km²
Population	6,483,946,000
Countries	195

The World

5,002,000 sq mi/13,000,000 km²
Largest country
6,592,812 sq mi/17,075,400 km²
R U S S I A
Deepest lake
5,315 ft/1,620 m
Lake Baykal
Caspian Sea
Largest lake
142,000 sq mi/367,000 km²
C H I N A
Most populous country
1,323,805,000
TŌKYŌ
Largest urban agglomeration
30,724,000
Al-ʿAzīzīyah
Dead Sea
Lowest elevation
–1,316 ft/–401 m
(surface)
Mount Everest
Highest elevation
29,035 ft/8,850 m
P A C I F I C
O C E A N
Mariana Trench
Greatest ocean depth
–36,204 ft/–11,035 m
Nile
Longest river
I N D I A N
28,571,400 sq mi/74,000,000 km²
O C E A N
146°55'W
Vostok Station
Lowest recorded temperature
–128,6°F/–89,2°C
KLETT-PERTHES

World: Physical

O C E A N
Franz Josef Land
Severnaya Zemlya
C. Chelyuskin
New Siberian Is.
Laptev Sea
East Siberian Sea
Kara Sea
Novaya Zemlya
Barents Sea
North Cape
Taymyr Pen.
5,581 ft 1,701 m
Central Siberian Plateau
Noril'sk
Cherskiy Ra.
Yakutia
Yakutsk
6,217 ft 1,895 m
Narodnaya
West Siberian Plain
Ural Mts.
Bering Sea
Kamchatka
Klyuchevskaya Sopka
15,584 ft 4,750 m
Sea of Okhotsk
Stanovoy Ra.
Petropavlovsk-Kamchatskiy
Aleutian Is.
Stockholm
St. Petersburg
Nizhniy Novgorod
Yekaterinburg
Omsk
Novosibirsk
Moscow
Sayan
Baykal
Irkutsk
Sakhalin
Kurile Is.
Kurile Trench
Amur
Khabarovsk
35,761 ft 10,900 m
Warsaw
Kiev
Samara
Volga
Carp. Mts.
8,711 ft 2,655 m
14,783 ft 4,506 m
Altay Mts.
Ulan Bator
Manchuria
Vladivostok
Hokkaido
North Pacific Current
18,511 ft 5,642 m
Caucasus
Elbrus
-92 ft -28 m
Caspian Sea
Aral Sea
Ürümqi
Almaty
Gobi
Shenyang
Sea of Japan
Honshu
Black Sea
Rome
Tashkent
Tien Shan
Altun Shan
Beijing
Korea
12,388 ft 3,776 m
Tōkyō
Mt. Fuji
Ōsaka
Ankara
Anatolia
Athens
Elburz Mts.
Tehran
18,605 ft 5,671 m
24,591 ft 7,495 m
Hindu Kush
Kabul
25,338 ft 7,723 m
Kunlun Shan
Xi'an
Yellow R.
Seoul
Kyushu
Shanghai
Japan Current (Kuro Shio)
33,011 ft 10,062 m
Midway Is.
Mediterranean Sea
Baghdad
Iranian Plateau
Tibet
Lahore
24,790 ft 7,556 m
Wuhan
Bonin Is.
Cairo
-1,316 ft -401 m
-436 ft -133 m
Libyan Desert
Nile
Arabian Pen.
Red Sea
Riyadh
Himalayas
Mt. Everest
29,035 ft 8,850 m
Delhi
Chongqing
Yangtze
Ryukyu Is.
P A C I F I C
Guangzhou
12,966 ft 3,952 m
Taiwan
Volcano Is.
30,039 ft 9,156 m
Karachi
Kolkata
Hanoi
Hong Kong
Hainan
Wake I.
Tibesti
11,204 ft 3,415 m
Jeddah
9,777 ft 2,980 m
Ra's al-Hadd
India
Mumbai
Rangoon
Luzon
Mariana Is.
Chad
Khartoum
10,076 ft 3,071 m
N'Djamena
15,158 ft 4,620 m
Sanaa
12,336 ft 3,760 m
Arabian Sea
Bay of Bengal
Chennai
Bangkok
Manila
Philippines
South China Sea
Vityaz Depth
36,204 ft 11,035 m
Marshall Islands
North Equatorial Current
Ethiopian Highlands
Socotra
C. Guardafui
8,842 ft 2,695 m
8,281 ft 2,524 m
Caroline Is.
Equatorial Counter Current
34,439 ft 10,497 m
Addis Ababa
Somali Pen.
Cape Comorin
Colombo
Ceylon
13,455 ft 4,101 m
Kinabalu
Mindanao
Micronesia
Bangui
19,107 ft 5,824 m
North Equatorial Current
Maldives
Kuala Lumpur
Singapore
Melanesia
Congo
Mogadishu
Sumatra
OCEAN
Equator
Congo Basin
L. Victoria
Nairobi
Kilimanjaro
19,331 ft 5,892 m
12,467 ft 3,800 m
Borneo (Kalimantan)
Celebes (Sulawesi)
South Equatorial Current
Gilbert Is.
Kinshasa
Indian Counter Current
16,024 ft 4,884 m
New Guinea
Bismarck Arch.
Phoenix Is.
Dar es Salaam
Seychelles
Chagos Is.
Greater Sunda Is.
Jakarta
Surabaya
Carstensz Pyramid
Luanda
Cabo Delgado
Comoro Is.
INDIAN
Java
12,060 ft 3,676 m
Lesser Sunda Is.
Ellice Is.
Tokelau Is.
Solomon Is.
C. York
Port Moresby
9,849 ft 3,002 m
9,436 ft 2,876 m
Cocos Is.
Lusaka
Mozambique Ch.
Wallis Is.
Coral Sea
Futuna
Antananarivo
Harare
Madagascar
Mascarene Is.
South Equatorial Current
Great Dividing Range
New Hebrides
Tonga Is.
North West Cape
Fiji Is.
Johannesburg
Maputo
Drakensberg
5,023 ft 1,531 m
AUSTRALIA
11,424 ft 3,482 m
20,997 ft 6,400 m
Great Victoria Desert
-39 ft -12 m
New Caledonia
Cape Town
Agulhas Current
3,319 ft 1,011 m
Brisbane
Norfolk I.
Cape of Good Hope
OCEAN
Perth
Kermadec Is.
Cape Leeuwin
Adelaide
7,310 ft 2,228 m
Austr. Alps
Sydney
Amsterdam
Saint-Paul
Mt. Kosciusko
18,605 ft 5,671 m
Melbourne
Tasman Sea
North Island
Polar Current
Crozet Is.
Prince Edward I.
(West Wind Drift)
Tasmania
South East C.
17,280 ft 5,267 m
New Zealand
9,177 ft 2,797 m
Wellington
Kerguelen Is.
South Island
12,349 ft 3,764 m
Mt. Cook
Heard
South West C.
Bounty Is.
Auckland Is.
Antipodes Is.
Macquarie
Campbell Is.
20,505 ft 6,250 m
Wilkes Land
Maud Land
Balleny Is.
13,658 ft 4,163 m
Scott I.
12,447 ft 3,794 m
Ross I.
Ross Sea
Mt. Erebus
A N T A R C T I C A
KLETT-PERTHES
20° L 40° M 60° N 80° O 100° P 120° Q 140° R 160° S 180° T
80° 60° 40° 20° 0° 20° 40° 60° 80°
1 2 3 4 5 6 7 8 9 10

A 80° B 100° C 120° D 140° E 160° F 180° G 160° H 140° J
ARCTIC
Severnaya Zemlya
Kara Sea
C. Chelyuskin
Taymyr Pen.
Laptev Sea
New Siberian Is.
East Siberian Sea
Beaufort Sea
Point Barrow
5,581 ft 1,701 m
Norilsk
Central Siberian Plateau
West Siberian Plain
Yenisey
Lena
Yakutia
Yakutsk
Cherskiy Ra.
Omsk
Ob
Novosibirsk
Baykal
Stanovoy Ra.
Sayan
Irkutsk
Altay Mts.
14,783 ft 4,506 m
ASIA
Ulan Bator
Amur
Khabarovsk
Sea of Okhotsk
Kamchatka
Klyuchevskaya Sopka
15,584 ft 4,750 m
Petropavlovsk-Kamchatskiy
Bering Sea
Aleutian Islands
Alaska
Mt. McKinley
20,321 ft 6,194 m
Alaska Range
Anchorage
G. of Alaska
Kodiak I.
Coast Mts.
Rocky
Yukon
Mackenzie
Yellowknife
Vancouver
Seattle
Almaty
Tien Shan
Ürümqi
Gobi
Manchuria
Sakhalin
Kurile Is.
Oya Shio
35,761 ft 10,900 m
24,591 ft 7,495 m
Altun Shan
Kunlun Shan
25,338 ft 7,723 m
Tibet
Himalayas
29,035 ft 8,850 m
Mt. Everest
24,790 ft 7,556 m
Shenyang
Vladivostok
Beijing
Yellow R.
Sea of Japan
Hokkaido
Honshu
Korea
Söul
12,388 ft 3,776 m
Tokyo
Mt. Fuji
Osaka
Kyushu
Xi'an
Lahore
Delhi
Wuhan
Yangtze
Shanghai
Chongqing
Japan Current (Kuro Shio)
33,011 ft 10,062 m
North Pacific Current
PACIFIC
20,879 ft 6,364 m
California Current
San Francisco
Sa. Nevada
Los Angeles
Ryukyu Is.
Bonin Is.
Midway Is.
Hawaiian Is.
Kolkata
India
Mumbai
Guangzhou
Hong Kong
Hanoi
12,966 ft 3,952 m
Taiwan
Volcano Is.
30,039 ft 9,156 m
Tropic of Cancer
C. San Lucas
Hainan
Bay of Bengal
Rangoon
Bangkok
Chennai
Luzon
Philippines
South China Sea
Manila
Mariana Is.
Wake I.
Honolulu
13,796 ft 4,205 m
Hawaii
19,373 ft 5,905 m
8,842 ft 2,695 m
8,281 ft 2,524 m
Cape Comorin
Colombo
Ceylon
Marshall Islands
Vityaz Depth
36,204 ft 11,035 m
North Equatorial Current
34,439 ft 10,497 m
Caroline Is.
Equatorial Counter Current
13,455 ft 4,101 m
Kinabalu
Mindanao
Micronesia
Kuala Lumpur
Singapore
Sumatra
Maldives
Equator
Melanesia
Polynesia
Kiritimati
17,549 ft 5,349 m
Borneo (Kalimantan)
Celebes (Sulawesi)
12,467 ft 3,800 m
South Equatorial Current
Bismarck Arch.
16,024 ft 4,884 m
New Guinea
Carstensz Pyramid
Gilbert Is.
Phoenix Is.
Jarvis I.
Line Islands
Indian Counter Current
Greater Sunda Is.
Chagos Is.
Jakarta
Java
Surabaya
12,060 ft 3,676 m
Lesser Sunda Is.
Port Moresby
C. York
Solomon Is.
Ellice Is.
Tokelau Is.
Marquesas Is.
Cocos Is.
Wallis Is.
Futuna
Cook Islands
Society Is.
Tuamotu Is.
Coral Sea
New Hebrides
Fiji Is.
Tonga Is.
INDIAN
Gt. Dividing Ra.
5,023 ft 1,531 m
New Caledonia
Tubuai Is.
8,399 ft 2,560 m
South Equatorial Current
North West Cape
Pitcairn Is.
Tropic of Capricorn
AUSTRALIA
Brisbane
-39 ft -12 m
Great Victoria Desert
Norfolk I.
Kermadec Is.
OCEAN
3,319 ft 1,011 m
Perth
Cape Leeuwin
Adelaide
Sydney
Austr. Alps
Mt. Kosciusko
7,310 ft 2,228 m
Melbourne
North Island
Tasman Sea
New Zealand
9,177 ft 2,797 m
Wellington
Mt. Cook
12,349 ft 3,764 m
South Island
OCEAN
18,605 ft 5,671 m
17,280 ft 5,267 m
Amsterdam
Saint-Paul
Tasmania
South East C.
South West C.
Bounty Is.
Antipodes Is.
Westwind
Antarctic Circumpolar Current
Auckland Is.
Campbell Is.
Macquarie
Kerguelen Is.
20,505 ft 6,250 m
Heard
Antarctic Circle
Balleny Is.
Scott I.
Wilkes Land
13,658 ft 4,163 m
Ross Sea
12,447 ft 3,794 m
Ross I.
Mt. Erebus
Amundsen
ANTARCTICA
Elevation
13,124 ft 4,000 m
6,562 ft 2,000 m
3,281 ft 1,000 m
1,640 ft 500 m
656 ft 200 m
0 ft 0 m
Depression
656 ft 200 m
6,562 ft 2,000 m
13,124 ft 4,000 m
19,686 ft 6,000 m
26,248 ft 8,000 m
Inland ice, glaciers
Ice shelf
Pack ice
Cold current
Warm current
Limit of drift ice

O C E A N
Franz Josef Land
Spitsbergen
5,617 ft 1,712 m
Elizabeth Is.
Sverdrup Is.
Ellesmere I.
Devon I.
Greenland
Baffin Bay
Baffin I.
6,660 ft 2,030 m
Gunnbjørn Fjeld
12,139 ft 3,700 m
Novaya Zemlya
Kara Sea
Barents Sea
North Cape
Norwegian Sea
Arctic Circle
Denmark Str.
Greenland Current
6,952 ft 2,119 m
Iceland
Reykjavik
10,111 ft 3,082 m
Nuuk
Davis Str.
Hudson Bay
Labrador
Labrador Sea
Labrador Current
Cape Farewell
Canadian Shield
Winnipeg
AMERICA
Newfoundland
Cape Race
15,420 ft 4,700 m
North Atlantic Drift
British Is.
Scandinavia
8,101 ft 2,469 m
Oslo
Stockholm
Baltic Sea
St. Petersburg
Moscow
Nizhniy Novgorod
Yekaterinburg
Samara
Ural Mts.
6,217 ft 1,895 m
Narodnaya
Ob
North Sea
London
Land's End
Berlin
Warsaw
Kiev
EUROPE
Carp. Mts.
8,711 ft 2,655 m
Paris
Alps
15,772 ft 4,807 m
Rome
Volga
-92 ft -28 m
Caspian Sea
Aral Sea
18,511 ft 5,642 m
Caucasus
Elbrus
Black Sea
Tashkent
Montréal
Toronto
Boston
New York
Washington
Chicago
Denver
St. Louis
Mississippi
Missouri
Plains
Appalachian Mts.
Mt. Mitchell
6,684 ft 2,037 m
Atlanta
Cape Hatteras
Gulf Stream
Dallas
New Orleans
Florida
Gulf of Mexico
Monterrey
Havana
Cuba
Bahama Is.
Bermuda Is.
Sargasso Sea
C. Finisterre
20,751 ft 6,325 m
Azores
Madrid
Lisbon
Mediterranean Sea
Algiers
Tunis
Athens
Ankara
Anatolia
Elburz Mts.
Tehran
18,605 ft 5,671 m
Kabul
Iranian Plateau
Baghdad
Casablanca
Atlas
13,665 ft 4,165 m
Tubqal
Madeira
Canary Is.
Canary Current
3,632 ft 1,107 m
Tripoli
Cairo
-436 ft -133 m
-1,316 ft -401 m
Libyan Desert
Nile
Red Sea
Arabian Pen.
Riyadh
Karachi
9,777 ft 2,980 m
Ra's al-Hadd
Jeddah
ATLANTIC
22,949 ft 6,995 m
Ahaggar
9,574 ft 2,918 m
Sahara
Tibesti
11,204 ft 3,415 m
Arabian Sea
Sierra Madre Occ.
Mexico City
Pico de Orizaba
18,405 ft 5,610 m
Hispaniola
Greater Antilles
Lesser Antilles
North Equatorial Current
C. Nouâdhibou
Cape Verde Is.
Dakar
C. Verde
Niger
Niamey
L. Chad
N'Djamena
Khartoum
10,076 ft 3,071 m
15,158 ft 4,620 m
Sanaa
12,336 ft 3,760 m
Socotra
C. Guardafui
Guatemala City
Caribbean Sea
Punta Gallinas
18,947 ft 5,775 m
Caracas
Llanos
9,219 ft 2,810 m
Guiana Highlands
23,924 ft 7,292 m
Bamako
Conakry
AFRICA
Ethiopian Highlands
Addis Ababa
Somali Pen.
Lagos
13,435 ft 4,095 m
Abidjan
Accra
Guinea Current
G. of Guinea
Bangui
Yaoundé
19,107 ft 5,824 m
Mogadishu
Bogotá
9,889 ft 3,014 m
Galápagos Is.
Quito
Chimborazo
20,703 ft 6,310 m
Amazon
Manaus
Belém
South Equatorial Current
C. Lopez
Congo
Congo Basin
L. Victoria
Nairobi
Kilimanjaro
19,331 ft 5,892 m
Equator
INDIAN
Kinshasa
Punta Negra
Selvas
C. Fernando de Noronha
de São Roque
Recife
Huascarán
22,205 ft 6,768 m
Campos
Ascension
Benguela Current
Luanda
Dar es Salaam
Seychelles
Lima
Andes
SOUTH AMERICA
Salvador
Cabo Delgado
Comoro Is.
Humboldt Current
La Paz
21,464 ft 6,542 m
Brasília
Brazilian Highlands
Brazil Current
St. Helena
Lusaka
9,849 ft 3,002 m
Mozambique Ch.
9,436 ft 2,876 m
9,482 ft 2,890 m
Pico da Bandeira
Rio de Janeiro
20,075 ft 6,119 m
Harare
Antananarivo
Madagascar
Mascarene Is.
Desventurados Is.
Sala-y-Gómez
Asunción
São Paulo
Namib
Windhoek
Aconcagua
22,842 ft 6,963 m
Porto Alegre
Johannesburg
Maputo
Drakensberg
Juan Fernández Is.
Santiago
Pampas
Montevideo
11,424 ft 3,482 m
20,997 ft 6,400 m
OCEAN
Buenos Aires
Río de la Plata
Cape Town
Cape of Good Hope
Agulhas Current
Tristan da Cunha
Gough I.
Patagonia
13,314 ft 4,058 m
Falkland Current
20,380 ft 6,212 m
Antarctic Circumpolar Current
(West Wind Drift)
Prince Edward I.
Falkland Is. (Is. Malvinas)
Tierra del Fuego
South Georgia
Crozet Is.
Str. of Magellan
Cape Horn
Scotia Sea
27,113 ft 8,264 m
Bouvet I.
Kerguelen Is.
17,355 ft 5,290 m
Drake Passage
South Sandwich Is.
South Shetland Is.
South Orkney Is.
18,812 ft 5,734 m
Bellingshausen Sea
Peter I I.
Antarctic Pen.
Mt. Jackson
Alexander I.
10,446 ft 3,184 m
Weddell Sea
Ellsworth Land
Berkner I.
Queen Maud Land
ANTARCTICA
KLETT-PERTHES

A 160° B 140° C 120° D 100° E 80° F 60° G 40° H 20° J
A R C T I C
Queen Elizabeth Is.
Sverdrup Is.
Ellesmere I.
Parry Is.
Beaufort Sea
Devon I.
Baffin Bay
Greenland
Victoria I.
Alaska
Alaska Range
G. of Alaska
Kodiak I.
Aleutian Is.
Coast Mts.
Rocky Mountains
Canadian Shield
Hudson Bay
Labrador
Labrador Sea
Davis Str.
Denmark Str.
Iceland
Arctic Circ
British Is.
North Sea
Newfoundland
NORTH AMERICA
Sa. Nevada
Great Plains
Appalachian Mts.
Mississippi
Azores
Bermuda Is.
Sargasso Sea
Madeira
Atlas
Canary Is.
Florida
Bahama Is.
ATLANTIC
Gulf of Mexico
Cuba
Hispaniola
Greater Antilles
Lesser Antilles
Caribbean Sea
Sa. Madre Occ.
Cape Verde Is.
Sahara
Hawaiian Is.
Hawaii
Tropic of Cancer
PACIFIC
Polynesia
Line Islands
Kiritimati
Jarvis I.
Equator
Galápagos Is.
Llanos
Guiana Highlands
Amazon
Selvas
Campos
SOUTH AMERICA
Andes
Brazilian Highlands
Fernando de Noronha
Ascension
St. Helena
OCEAN
Marquesas Is.
Cook Islands
Society Is.
Tuamotu Is.
Tubuai Is.
Pitcairn Is.
Tropic of Capricorn
Easter I.
Sala-y-Gómez
Desventurados Is.
Juan Fernández Is.
Pampas
Rio de la Plata
Tristan da Cunha
Gough I.
OCEAN
Patagonia
Falkland Is. (Is. Malvinas)
South Georgia
Tierra del Fuego
Str. of Magellan
Scotia Sea
Drake Passage
South Sandwich Is.
South Shetland Is.
South Orkney Is.
Antarctic Circle
Antarctic Pen.
Bellingshausen Sea
Peter I I.
Alexander I.
Weddell Sea
Ellsworth Land
Berkner I.
ANTARC
Landforms
Tertiary planation surfaces and mountains and their Quaternary glacial modification
Dissected Tertiary planation surfaces of mostly medium height and relief cutting across Precambrian metamorphic shield regions
modified by multiple Pleistocene glaciations
Medium-height mountains and uplands of truncated, uplifted and dissected Paleozoic collision zones (Caledonian and Hercynian/Appalachian orogenies) and Mesozoic granitic rocks [G]
modified by multiple Pleistocene glaciations
Dissected plains, plateaus and scarplands of Tertiary planation cutting across gently tilted to horizontal sedimentary rocks of Late Precambrian, Paleozoic and Mesozoic to Tertiary age
blanketed by glacial and fluvioglacial Pleistocene deposits
Planated and dissected plateaus of Mesozoic and Tertiary volcanic rocks, mostly flood basalt, partly modified by Pleistocene glaciations
High-mountain chains of Mesozoic to present collision zones (Alpine orogeny)
modified by multiple Pleistocene valley glaciations
Dissected intermontane plateaus and basins
partly modified by Pleistocene glaciations
with Quaternary, mostly dissected, alluvial fans of arid regions
Extent of last glaciation
Major regions of present glaciation
Southern limit of present continuous permafrost (northern hemisphere)
KLETT-PERTHES

L 40° M 60° N 80° O 100° P 120° Q 140° R 160° S 180° T
O C E A N
Franz Josef Land
Severnaya Zemlya
New Siberian Is.
Laptev Sea
East Siberian Sea
Kara Sea
Novaya Zemlya
Taymyr Pen.
Barents Sea
Central Siberian Plateau
Cherskiy Ra.
Yakutia
West Siberian Plain
Ural Mts
Yenisey
Ob
Lena
Bering Sea
Kamchatka
Sea of Okhotsk
Baykal
Stanovoy Ra.
Aleutian Is.
Sakhalin
Kurile Is.
Sayan
Altay Mts
Amur
Manchuria
Hokkaido
Volga
E U R O P E
Carp. Mts
Caucasus
Caspian Sea
Aral Sea
A S I A
Gobi
Tien Shan
Altun Shan
Sea of Japan
Korea
Honshu
Black Sea
Anatolia
Elburz Mts.
Hindu Kush
Kunlun Shan
Tibet
Himalayas
Yellow R.
Kyushu
Midway Is.
Iranian Plateau
Yangtze
Ryukyu Is.
Bonin Is.
PACIFIC
Volcano Is.
Mediterranean Sea
Libyan Desert
Nile
Red Sea
Arabian Pen.
Taiwan
Mariana Is.
Wake I.
Tibesti
India
Hainan
Luzon
Philippines
Arabian Sea
Bay of Bengal
South China Sea
Marshall Islands
Socotra
Chad
AFRICA
Ethiopian Highlands
Somali Pen.
Caroline Is.
Micronesia
Ceylon
Mindanao
Maldives
Sumatra
Borneo (Kalimantan)
Celebes (Sulawesi)
Melanesia
OCEAN
Equator
Congo Basin
Congo
L. Victoria
Gilbert Is.
Bismarck Arch.
Phoenix Is.
Seychelles
Chagos Is.
Greater Sunda Is.
New Guinea
Ellice Is.
Java
Lesser Sunda Is.
Tokleau Is.
Comoro Is.
INDIAN
Solomon Is.
Cocos Is.
Wallis Is.
Coral Sea
Futuna
Mozambique Ch.
Madagascar
Mascarene Is.
New Hebrides
Tonga Is.
Fiji Is.
Drakensberg
AUSTRALIA
Great Victoria Desert
Gt. Dividing Range
New Caledonia
OCEAN
Norfolk I.
Kermadec Is.
Amsterdam
Saint-Paul
Austr. Alps
Tasman Sea
North Island
Crozet Is.
Tasmania
Prince Edward I.
Kerguelen Is.
New Zealand
South Island
Heard
Bounty Is.
Auckland Is.
Antipodes Is.
Macquarie
Campbell Is.
Queen Maud Land
ANTARCTICA
80° 60° 40° 20° 0° 20° 40°
1 2 3 4 5 6 7 8
Pleistocene and Holocene fluvial, lacustrine, coastal and eolian landforms
Pleistocene and Holocene lowlands with alluvial and lake-alluvial deposits; Pleistocene river terraces, Holocene floodplains, coastal marshes and deltas
Floors of Late Pleistocene ice-dammed glacial meltwater lakes, partly surrounding present lakes
Deposits and shorelines of Mid-Pleistocene to early Holocene pluvial lakes and swamps of arid regions
Quaternary marine terraces [T], near-coastal seafloor raised by glacioisostatic rebound [R] and seafloor of the northern Caspian sea region uplifted by Holocene tectonism [C]
Continental shelf and edge of shelf
Quaternary dune fields (ergs, sand seas)
of hyperarid desert regions, presently active
of semi-arid regions, vegetation-bound
Major Pleistocene loess sheets
Landforms of recent to present volcanism and tectonic deformation, selected mainland and island volcanoes
Eroded and submerged volcanoes topped with coral reefs
Boundary of zone of present-day arid geomorphic processes and resulting surficial features (intermittent runoff, temporary lakes and playas, mostly dissected alluvial fans, desert pavement, eolian sand sheets and sand seas)
L 40° M 60° N 80° O 100° P

World: Ocean Floor

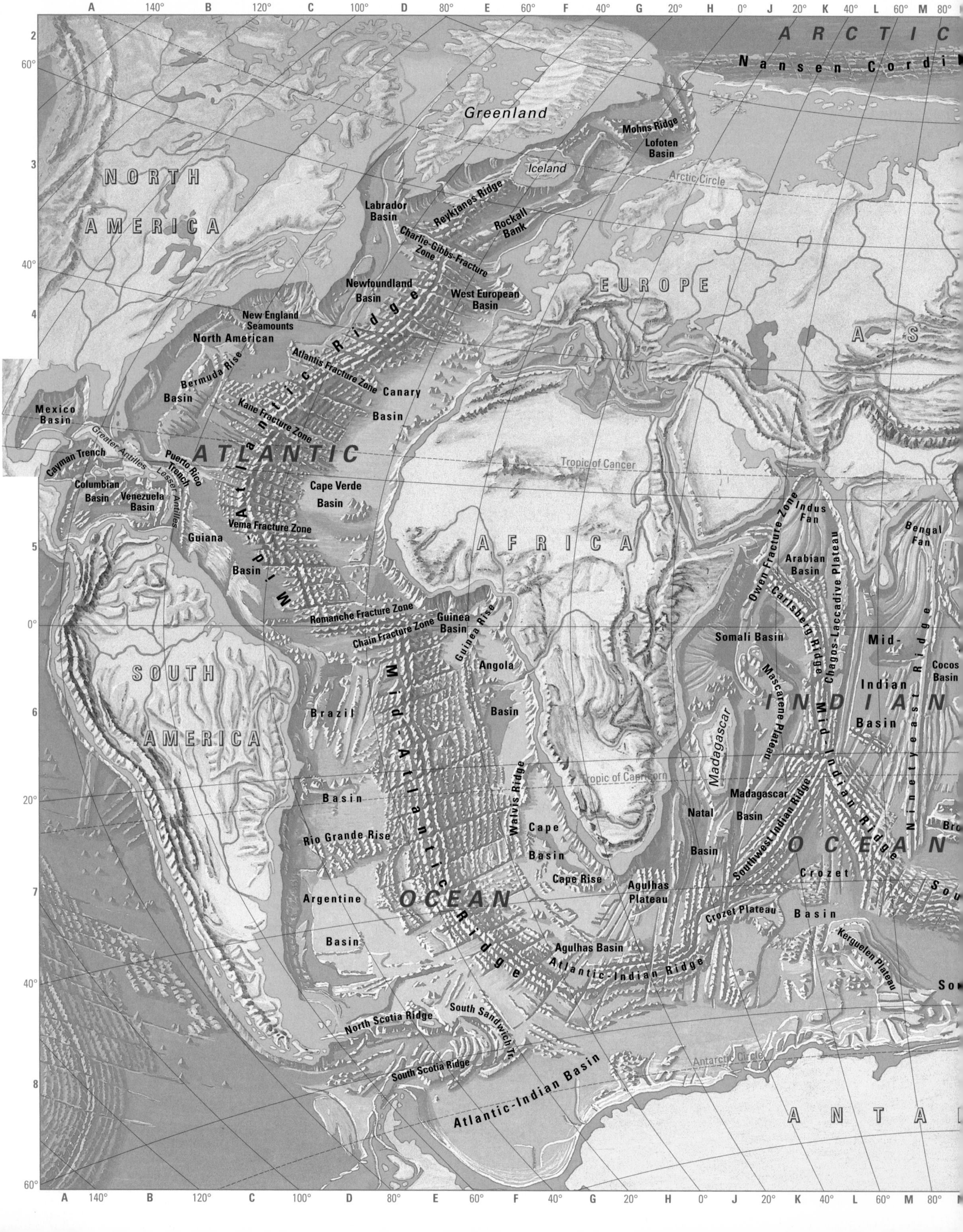
A
140°
B
120°
C
100°
D
80°
E
60°
F
40°
G
20°
H
0°
J
20°
K
40°
L
60°
M
80°
2
3
4
5
6
7
8
60°
40°
20°
0°
ARCTIC
Nansen Cordi
Greenland
Mohns Ridge
Lofoten Basin
Iceland
Arctic Circle
NORTH
AMERICA
Labrador Basin
Reykjanes Ridge
Rockall Bank
Charlie-Gibbs-Fracture Zone
Newfoundland Basin
West European Basin
EUROPE
New England Seamounts
North American
Bermuda Rise
Basin
Atlantis Fracture Zone
Canary
Basin
Mexico Basin
Greater Antilles
Cayman Trench
Puerto Rico Trench
Lesser Antilles
Kane Fracture Zone
ATLANTIC
Tropic of Cancer
AS
Columbian Basin
Venezuela Basin
Cape Verde Basin
Guiana
Basin
Vema Fracture Zone
Mid-Atlantic Ridge
AFRICA
Indus Fan
Owen Fracture Zone
Arabian Basin
Chagos-Laccadive Plateau
Bengal Fan
Carlsberg Ridge
Romanche Fracture Zone
Chain Fracture Zone
Guinea Basin
Guinea Rise
Somali Basin
Mid-
Indian
Basin
Ninetyeast Ridge
Cocos Basin
SOUTH
AMERICA
Angola
Basin
Brazil
Basin
Mascarene Plateau
Mid-Indian Ridge
INDIAN
OCEAN
Madagascar
Tropic of Capricorn
Walvis Ridge
Madagascar Basin
Natal Basin
Rio Grande Rise
Cape Basin
Southwest Indian Ridge
Cape Rise
Agulhas Plateau
Crozet
Basin
Crozet Plateau
Argentine
Basin
OCEAN
Kerguelen Plateau
Agulhas Basin
Atlantic-Indian Ridge
North Scotia Ridge
South Sandwich Tr.
South Scotia Ridge
Antarctic Circle
Atlantic-Indian Basin
ANTA

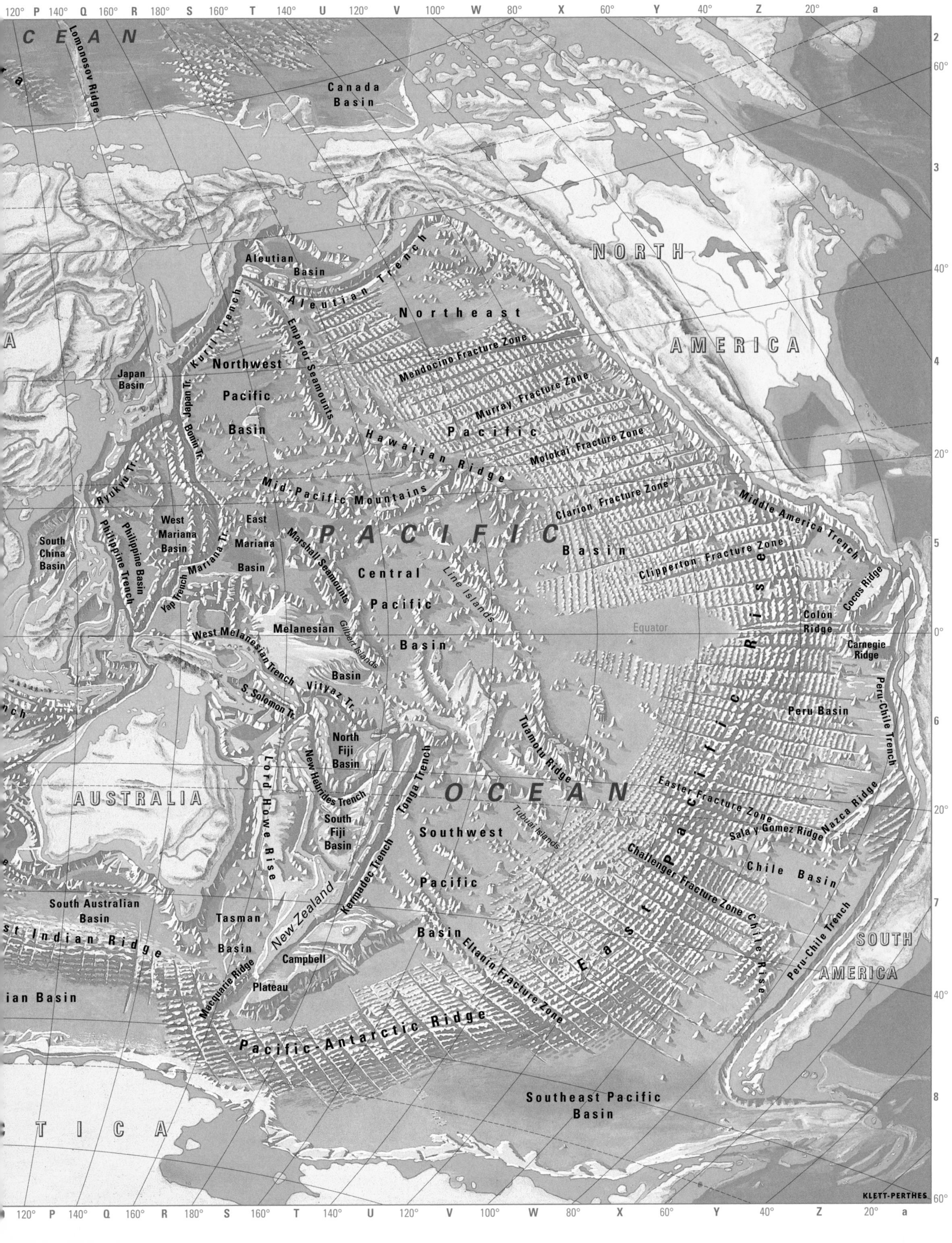

OCEAN
Lomonosov Ridge
Canada Basin
NORTH AMERICA
Aleutian Basin
Aleutian Trench
Kuril Trench
Emperor Seamounts
Northeast
Mendocino Fracture Zone
Northwest Pacific Basin
Japan Basin
Japan Tr.
Bonin Tr.
Murray Fracture Zone
Pacific
Molokai Fracture Zone
Hawaiian Ridge
Mid-Pacific Mountains
Ryukyu Tr.
Clarion Fracture Zone
Middle America Trench
West Mariana Basin
East Mariana Basin
Mariana Tr.
Philippine Basin
Philippine Trench
South China Basin
PACIFIC
Basin
Marshall Seamounts
Central Pacific Basin
Line Islands
Clipperton Fracture Zone
Cocos Ridge
Yap Trench
Colon Ridge
Equator
Carnegie Ridge
West Melanesian Trench
Melanesian Basin
Gilbert Islands
Vityaz Tr.
S. Solomon Tr.
North Fiji Basin
New Hebrides Trench
Tonga Trench
Lord Howe Rise
Tuamotu Ridge
East Pacific Rise
Peru Basin
Peru-Chile Trench
AUSTRALIA
OCEAN
Easter Fracture Zone
South Fiji Basin
Southwest Pacific Basin
Tubuai Islands
Sala y Gomez Ridge
Nazca Ridge
Challenger Fracture Zone
Chile Basin
Kermadec Trench
South Australian Basin
Tasman Basin
New Zealand
Chile Rise
Peru-Chile Trench
SOUTH AMERICA
Indian Ridge
Campbell Plateau
Macquarie Ridge
Eltanin Fracture Zone
ian Basin
Pacific-Antarctic Ridge
Southeast Pacific Basin
TICA
KLETT-PERTHES

1:25,000,000

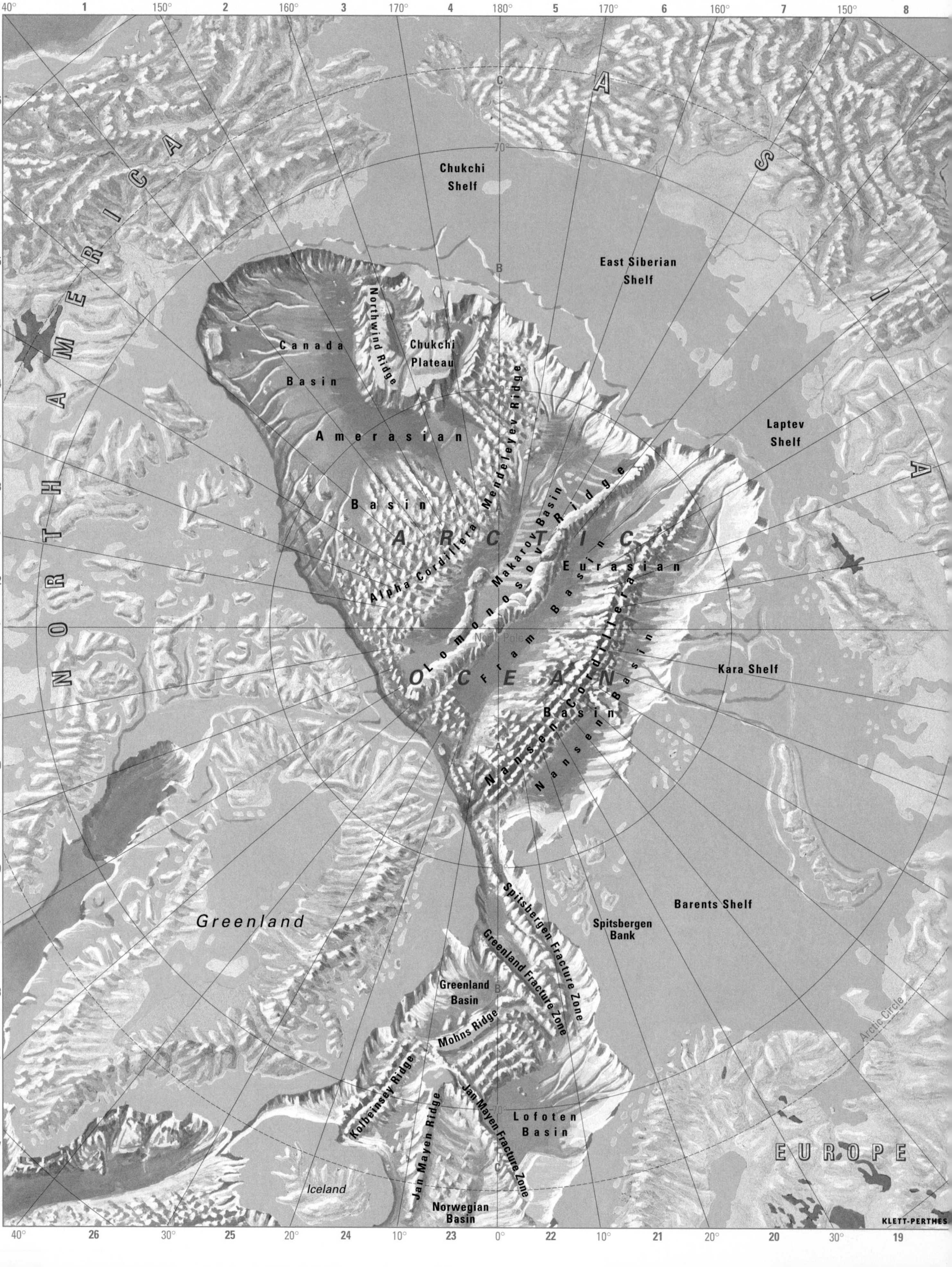
NORTH AMERICA
ASIA
EUROPE
ARCTIC OCEAN
Chukchi Shelf
East Siberian Shelf
Canada Basin
Northwind Ridge
Chukchi Plateau
Amerasian Basin
Mendeleyev Ridge
Makarov Basin
Alpha Cordillera
Lomonosov Ridge
Eurasian Basin
Fram Basin
Nansen Cordillera
Nansen Basin
North Pole
Laptev Shelf
Kara Shelf
Barents Shelf
Spitsbergen Bank
Spitsbergen Fracture Zone
Greenland Fracture Zone
Greenland Basin
Greenland
Mohns Ridge
Kolbeinsey Ridge
Jan Mayen Ridge
Jan Mayen Fracture Zone
Lofoten Basin
Norwegian Basin
Iceland
Arctic Circle
KLETT-PERTHES

South Polar Region: Ocean Floor

c. 1:50,000,000

World: Continental Drift · Plate Tectonics

I The Earth 225 Million Years Ago at the End of the Permian Period

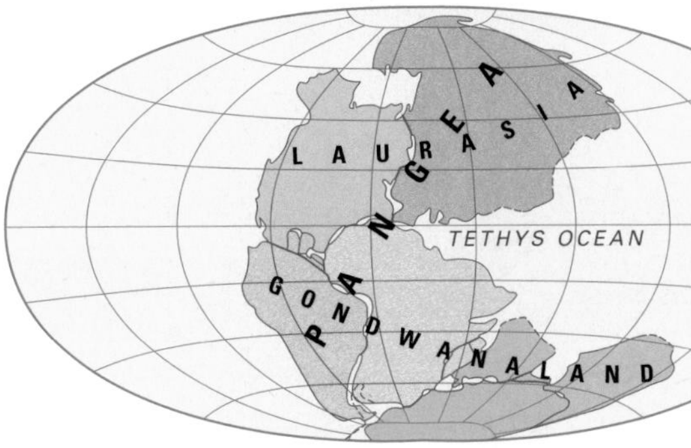

III The Earth at the Present

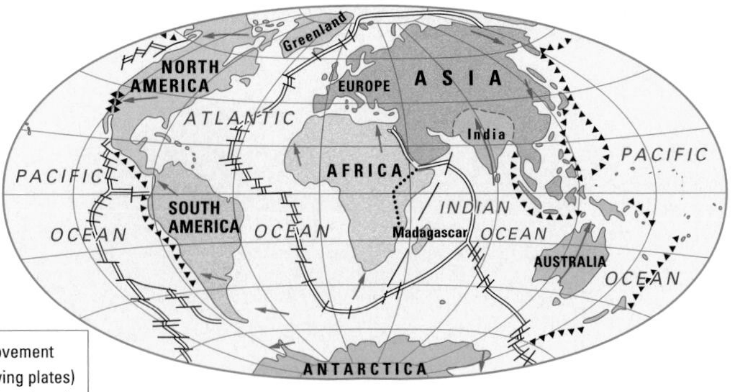

- Direction of plate movement
- Subduction zone (diving plates)
- Transform fault (sliding plates)
- Oceanic Rift zone
- Continental Rift zone
- Transcurrent fault or inactive transform fault

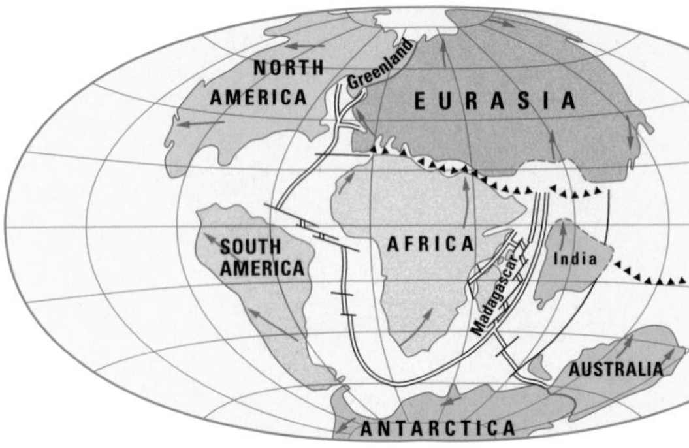

II The Earth 65 Million Years Ago at the End of Cretaceous Period

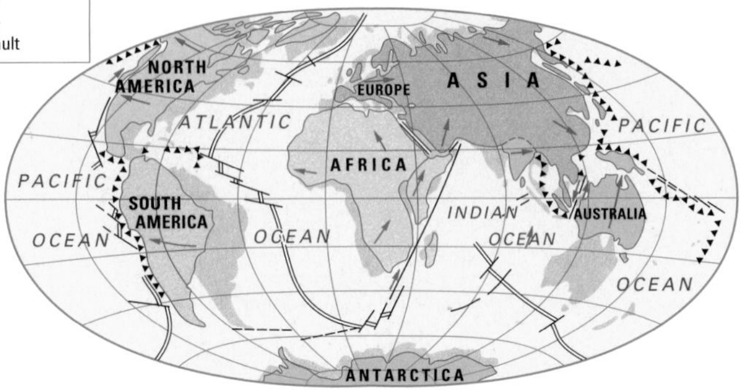

IV The Earth in 50 Million Years

KLETT-PERTHES

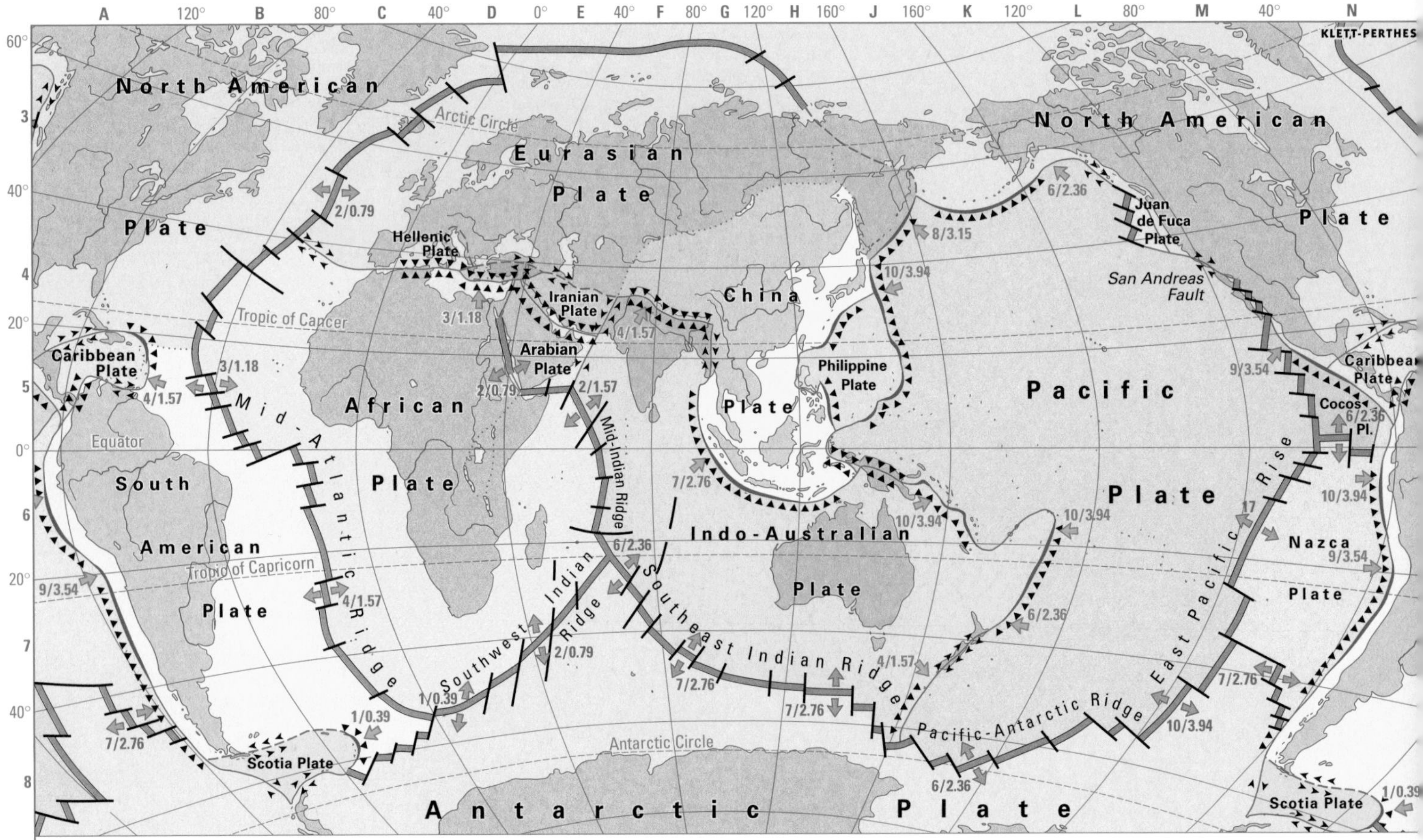

Lithospheric Plates

- Plate boundary
- Uncertain plate boundary
- Supposed plate boundary

Divergent Plate boundary
- Oceanic rift zone
- Direction of plate movement
- 6/2.36 Speed of movement (cm/in. per year)

Convergent Plate boundary (Subduction and Collision Zone)
- Subduction zone (diving plates)
- Collision zone (plates colliding to form a mountain range)
- Direction of plate subduction
- 10/3.94 Speed of subduction (cm/in. per year)
- Ocean trench

Conservative Plate boundary
- Transform fault (sliding plates)
- Transcurrent fault or inactive transform fault

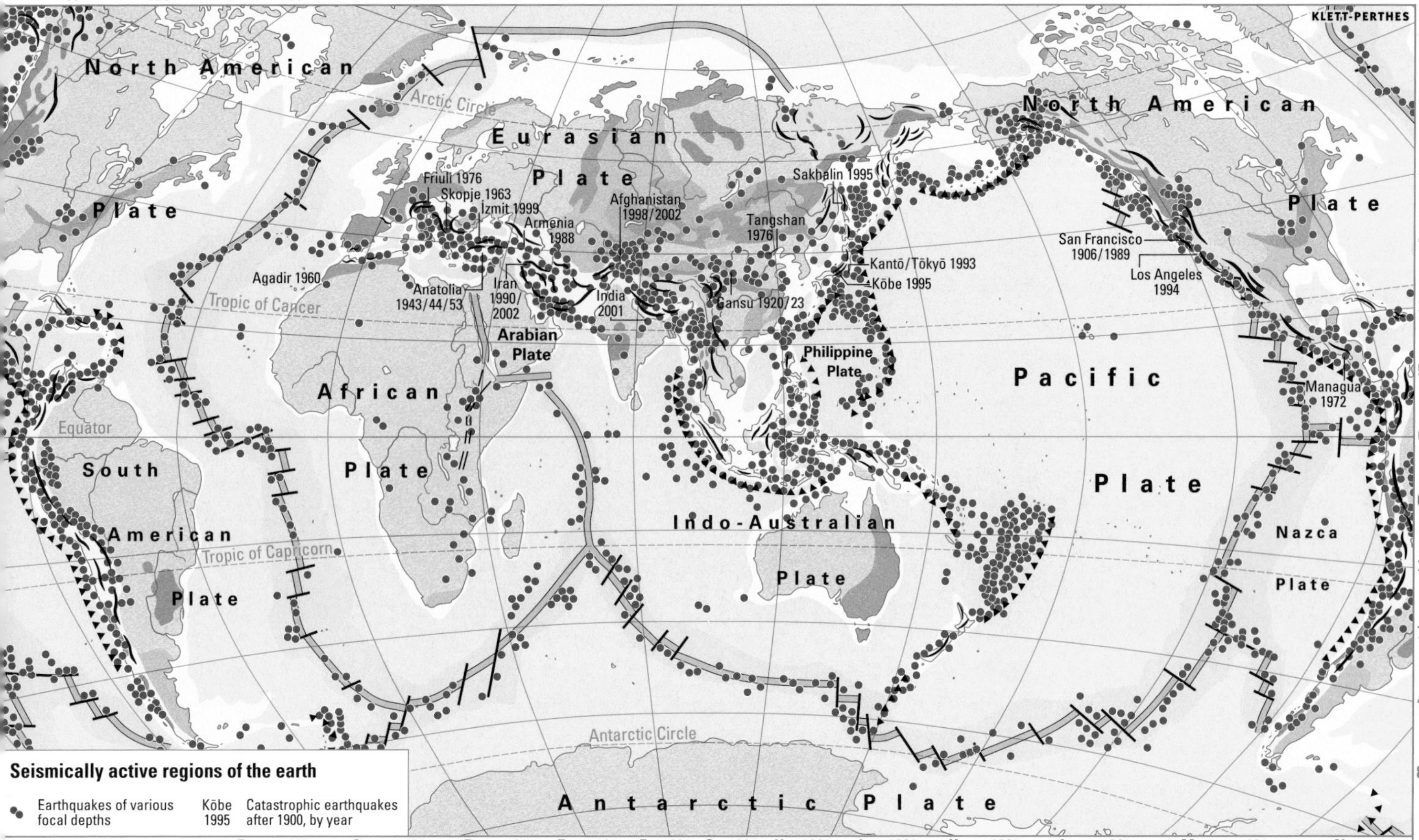

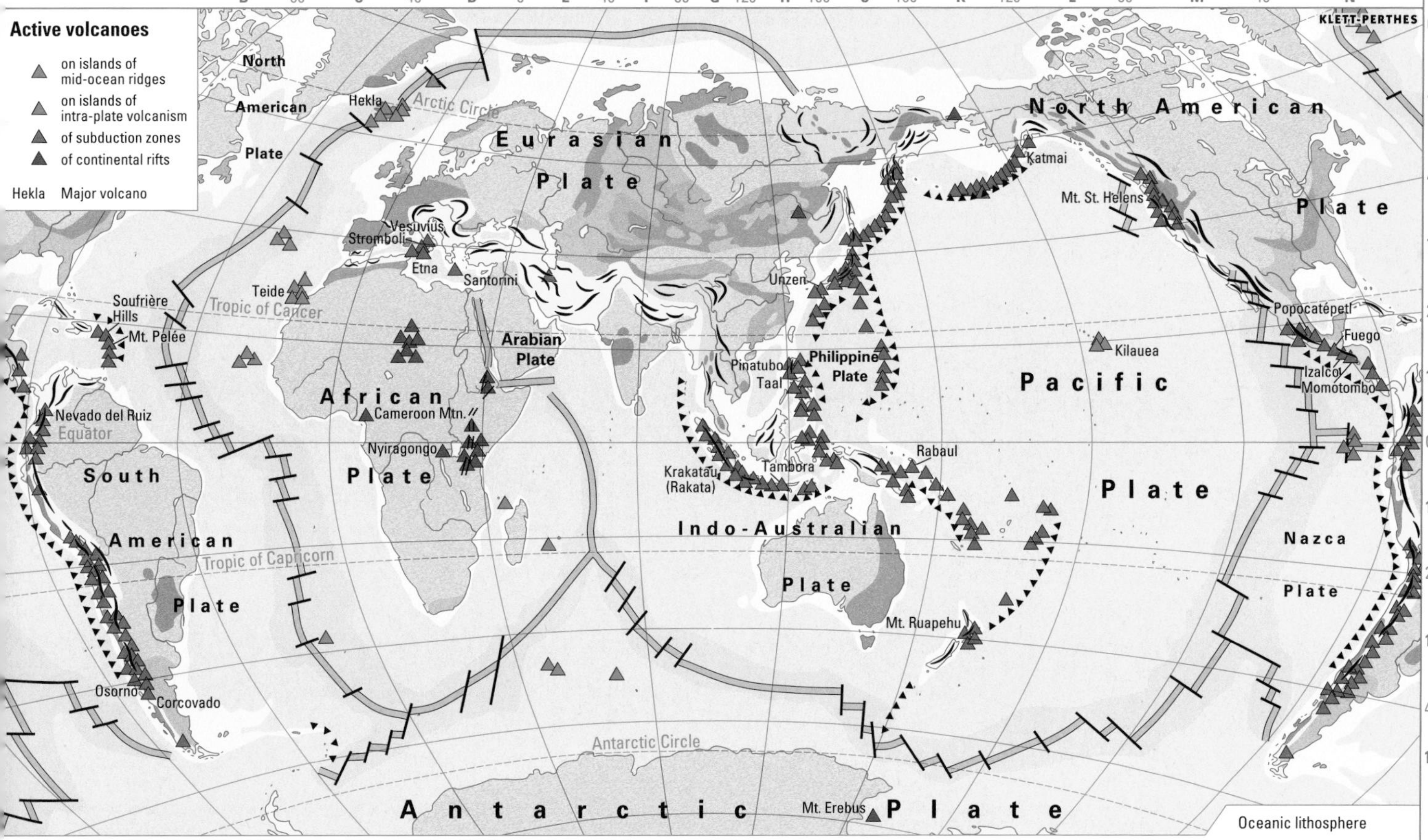

Tectonics

Continents
- Fracture zone, graben

Regions of Alpidic folding
- Alpidic fold mountains
- Orientation of fold trains

Regions of Mesozoic folding
- Mesozoic fold structures
- Orientation of fold trains

Regions of Paleozoic folding
- Caledonian and Hercynian fold structures covered by sedimentary rocks
- Hercynian fold structures
- Caledonian fold structures

- Plateau basalts
- Granitic plutons

Regions of Precambrian folding
- Precambrian shields and platforms

Oceanic realm

Continental lithosphere
- Shelf region with continued continental structures

Oceanic lithosphere
- Mid-oceanic ridge
- Abyssal plain
- Mid-ocean rift zone
- Subduction zone
- Transform fault

Layers of the Earth

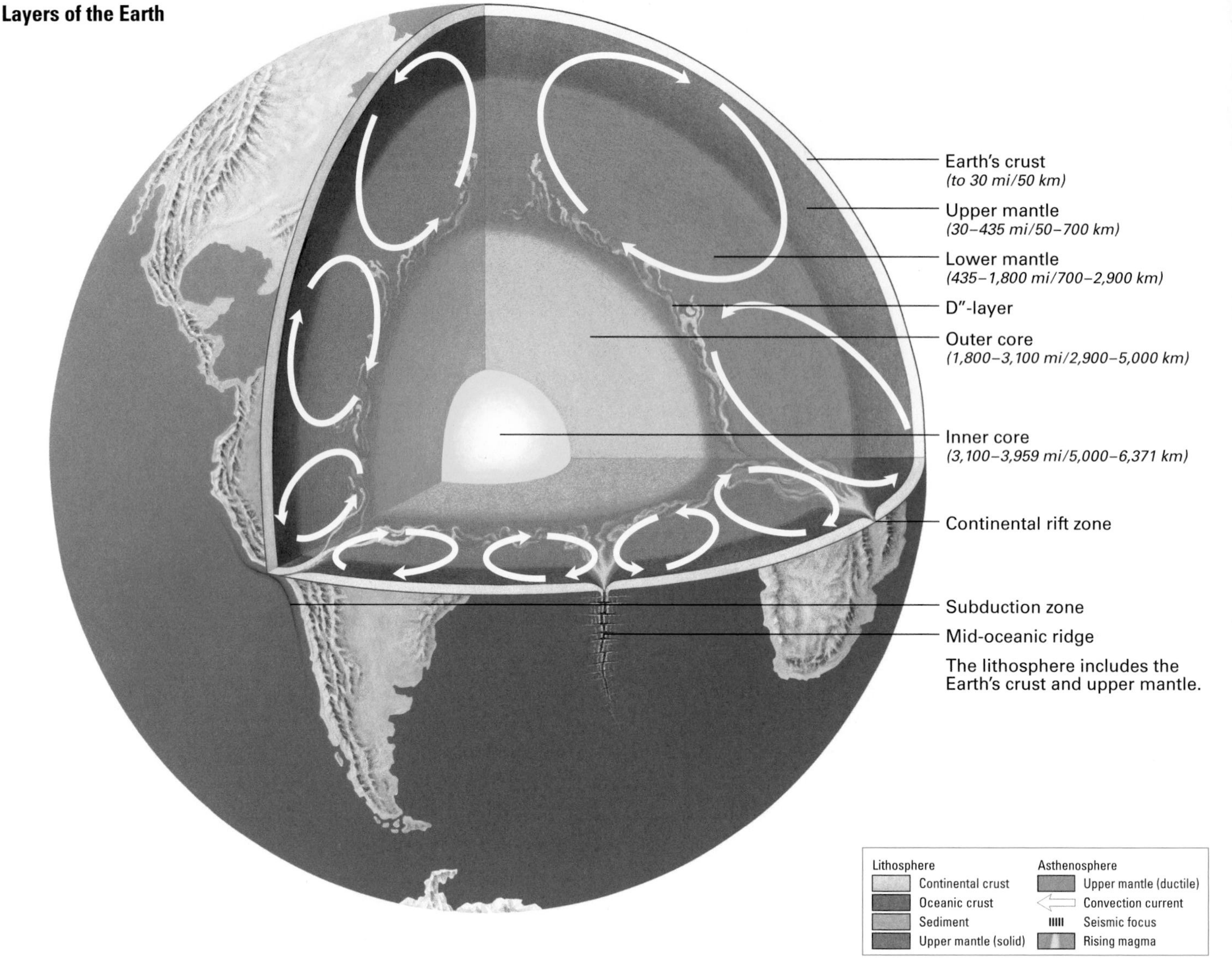
Earth's crust
(to 30 mi/50 km)
Upper mantle
(30–435 mi/50–700 km)
Lower mantle
(435–1,800 mi/700–2,900 km)
D″-layer
Outer core
(1,800–3,100 mi/2,900–5,000 km)
Inner core
(3,100–3,959 mi/5,000–6,371 km)
Continental rift zone
Subduction zone
Mid-oceanic ridge
The lithosphere includes the Earth's crust and upper mantle.
Lithosphere
Continental crust
Oceanic crust
Sediment
Upper mantle (solid)
Asthenosphere
Upper mantle (ductile)
Convection current
Seismic focus
Rising magma

Plate Tectonic Processes

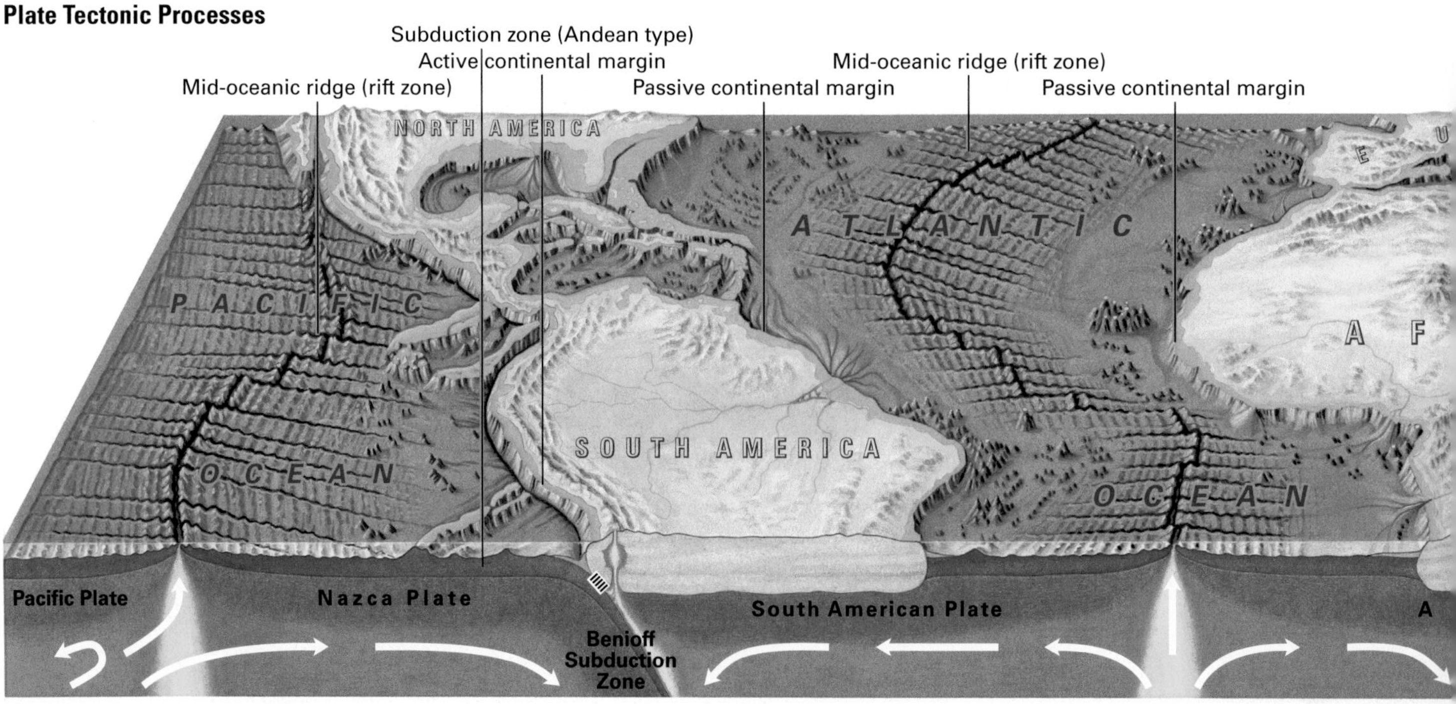
Subduction zone (Andean type)
Active continental margin
Mid-oceanic ridge (rift zone)
Passive continental margin
Mid-oceanic ridge (rift zone)
Passive continental margin
NORTH AMERICA
ATLANTIC
PACIFIC
OCEAN
SOUTH AMERICA
OCEAN
Pacific Plate
Nazca Plate
South American Plate
Benioff Subduction Zone

Subduction

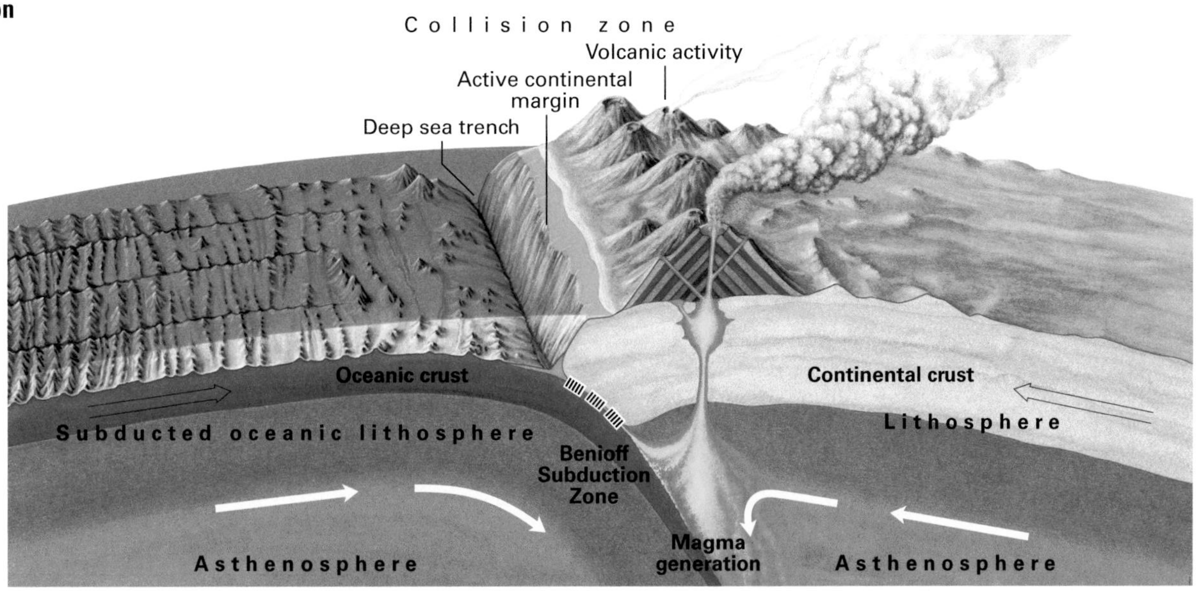
Collision zone
Volcanic activity
Active continental margin
Deep sea trench
Oceanic crust
Continental crust
Subducted oceanic lithosphere
Lithosphere
Benioff Subduction Zone
Asthenosphere
Magma generation
Asthenosphere

Seafloor spreading

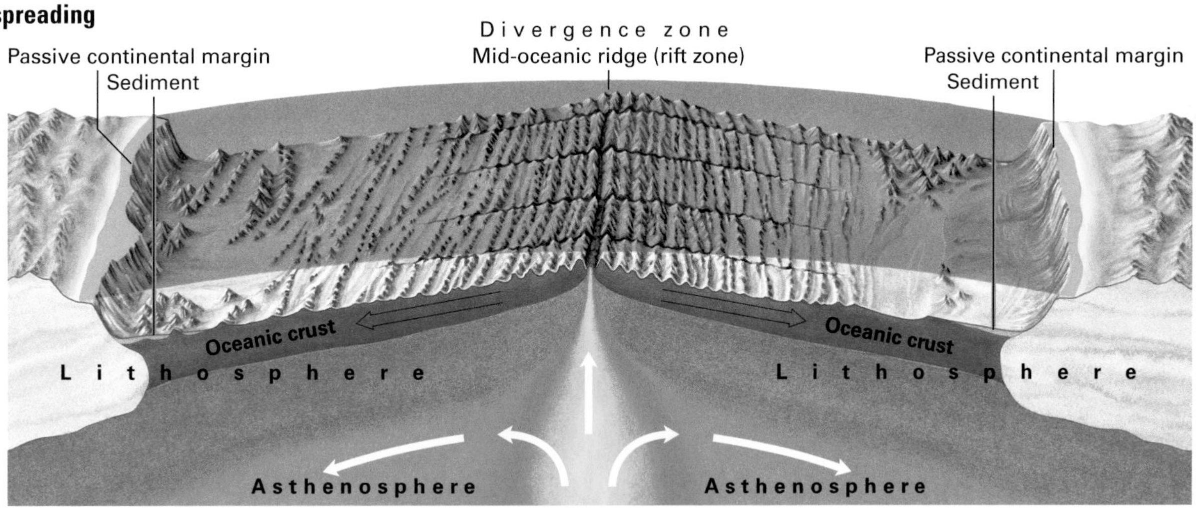
Divergence zone
Mid-oceanic ridge (rift zone)
Passive continental margin
Sediment
Passive continental margin
Sediment
Oceanic crust
Oceanic crust
Lithosphere
Lithosphere
Asthenosphere
Asthenosphere

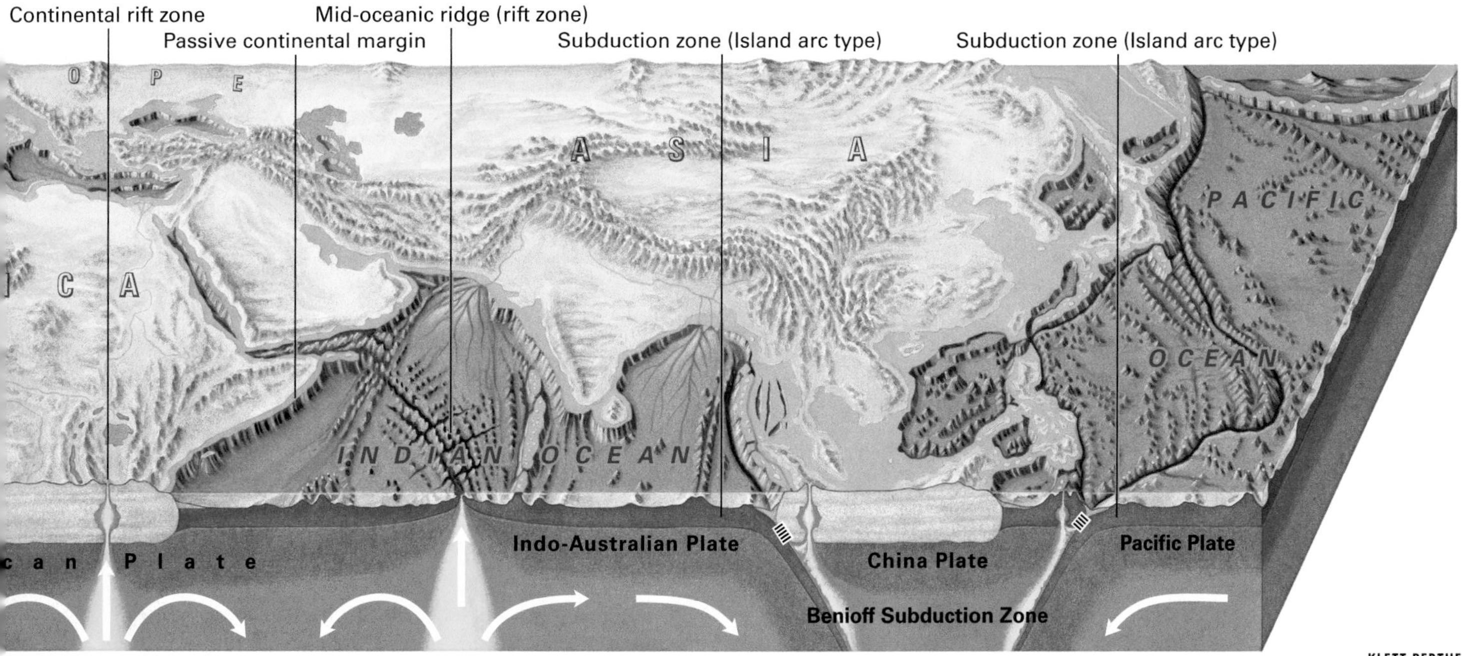
Continental rift zone
Mid-oceanic ridge (rift zone)
Passive continental margin
Subduction zone (Island arc type)
Subduction zone (Island arc type)
O P E
ASIA
C A
PACIFIC
OCEAN
INDIAN OCEAN
can Plate
Indo-Australian Plate
China Plate
Pacific Plate
Benioff Subduction Zone

Climatic Regions (Modified Koeppen System based on Trewartha)

A Tropical Rainy Climates
Absolutely no frost in the region, average temperature of the coldest month at least 18 °C (64.4 °F) over ocean waters

- **Ar** Tropical (permanently) rainy climate
  No more than two months with less than 60 mm (2.4 in.) of monthly rainfall
- **Am** Tropical monsoon rain climate (wet and dry with an extremely wet season)
  More than two months with less than 60 mm (2.4 in.) of monthly rainfall, dry season compensated for by high rainfall during the rainy season, if r ≥ 25 (100 – r*)
- **Aw** Tropical summer rain climate (winter-dry)
  More than 2 winter months with less than 60 mm (2.4 in.) of monthly rainfall
- **As** Tropical winter rain climate (summer-dry)
  More than 2 summer months with less than 60 mm (2.4 in.) of monthly rainfall

B Dry Climates
Boundary condition: r < 20 (t – 10 + 0.3 PS)

- **BS** Steppe climate (semiarid climate)
  Boundary condition: r ≥ 10 (t – 10 + 0.3 PS)
- **BW** Desert climate (arid climate)
  Boundary condition: r < 10 (t – 10 + 0.3 PS)
- **BM** Marine dry climate
  Humid-air dry climate above ocean surfaces with the universally valid boundary condition of r < 20 (t – 10 + 0.3 PS)

C Subtropical Climates
Average temperature of the coldest month less than 18 °C (64.4 °F), 8 to 12 months with an average temperature of at least 10 °C (50.0 °F)

- **Cr** Subtropical (permanently) rainy climate
  Lesser precipitation differences between the extreme months than for Cw or Cs climates
- **Cw** Subtropical summer rain climate (winter-dry)
  Precipitation sum of the wettest summer month at least 10 times that of the driest winter month
- **Cs** Subtropical winter rain climate (summer-dry)
  Precipitation sum of the wettest winter month at least 3 times that of the driest summer month

D Temperate Climates
4 to 7 months with an average temperature of at least 10 °C (50.0 °F)

- **Do** Oceanic temperate climate
  Average temperature of the coldest month 0 °C (32.0 °F) or above
- **Dc** Continental temperate climate
  Average temperature of the coldest month below 10 °C (50.0 °F)

- Meteorological station with climate diagram in the continental maps

Limits of the Regions of Dry Climates

—— r = 20 (t – 10 + 0.3 PS)

– – – r = 10 (t – 10 + 0.3 PS)

r	total annual precipitation [mm]
r*	total precipitation of the driest month [mm]
t	average annual temperature [°C]
PS	percentage of summer precipitation April – September [%]:
	PS = 30 with rainfall concentration in winter
	PS = 50 with rainfall evenly distributed
	PS = 67 with rainfall concentration in summer

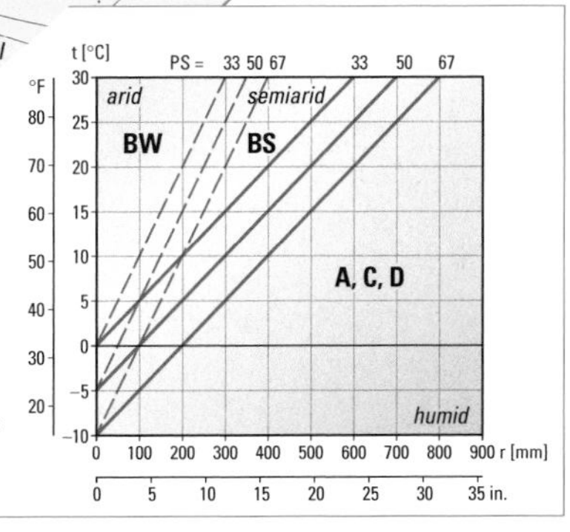

E Boreal Climates
1 to 3 months with an average temperature of at least 10 °C (50.0 °F)

Eo Oceanic boreal climate
Average temperature of the coldest month –10 °C (14.0 °F) or above

Ec Continental boreal climate
Average temperature of the coldest month below –10 °C (14.0 °F)

F Polar Climates
Average temperature of the warmest month below 10 °C (50.0 °F)

FT Tundra climate
Average temperature of the warmest month above 0 °C (32.0 °F)

FI Perpetual frost climate
Average temperature of the warmest month no more than 0 °C (32.0 °F)

World: Precipitation in January and July

1:160,000,000

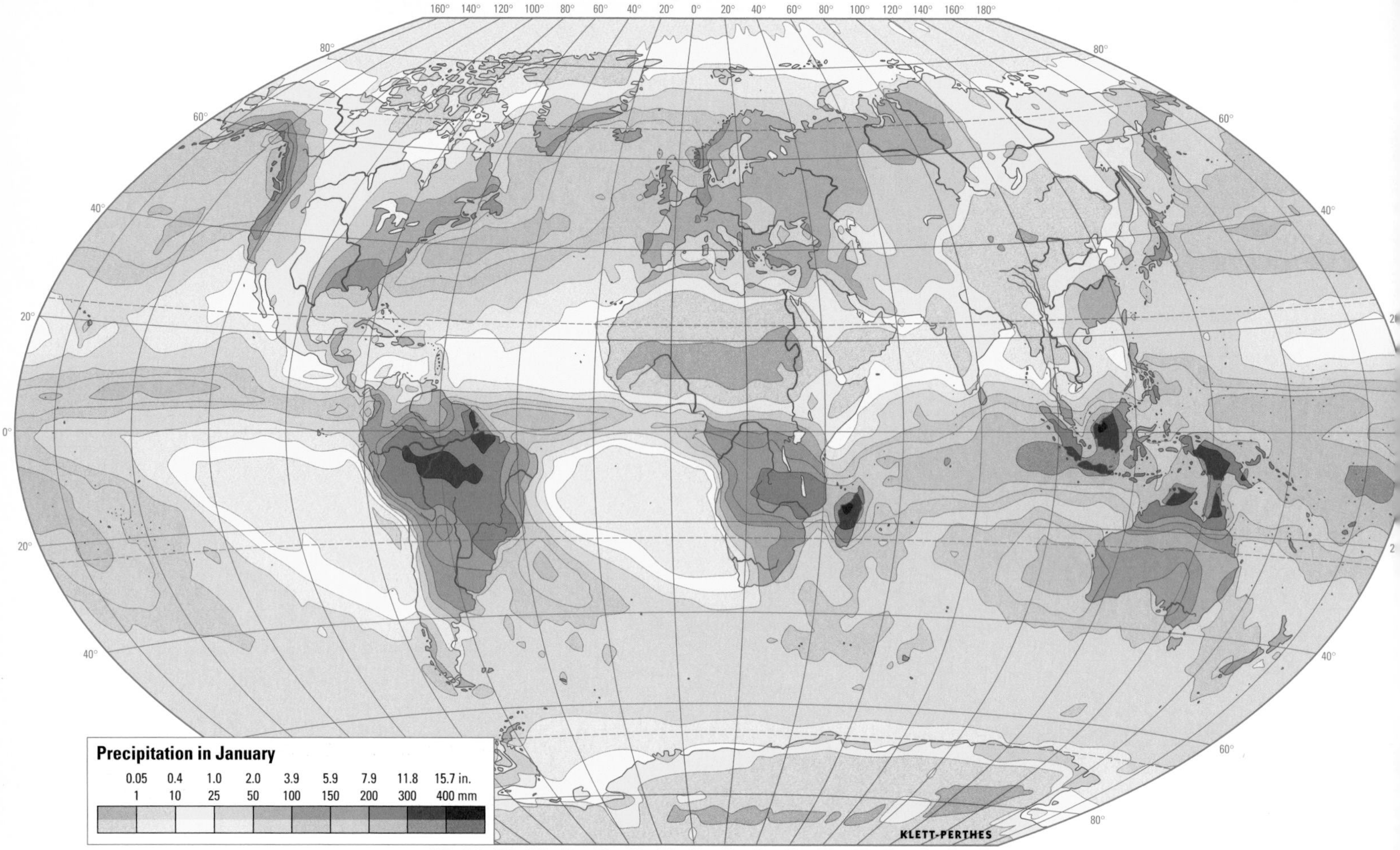

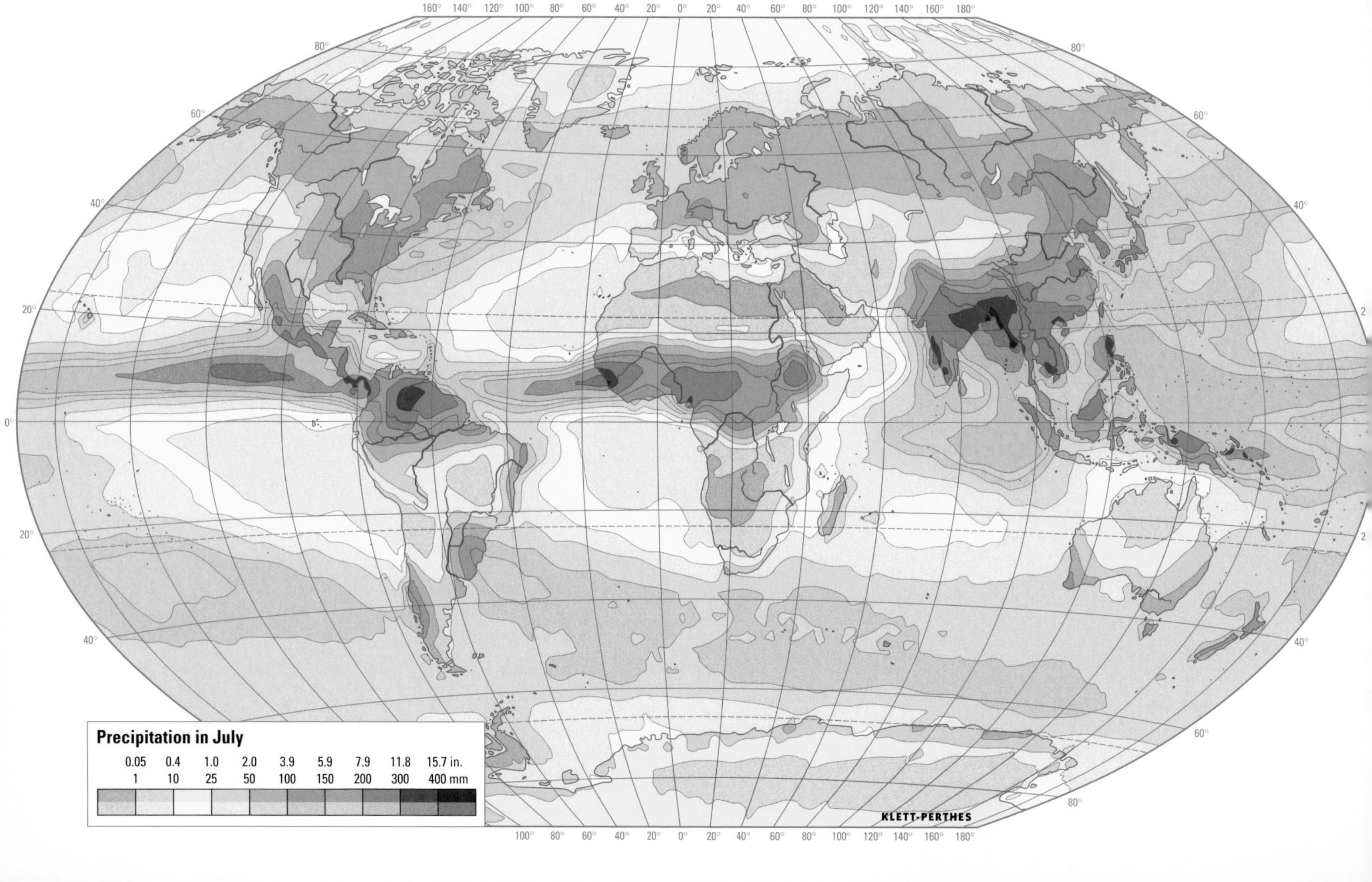

World: Average Annual Precipitation · Precipitation Variability

1:160,000,000

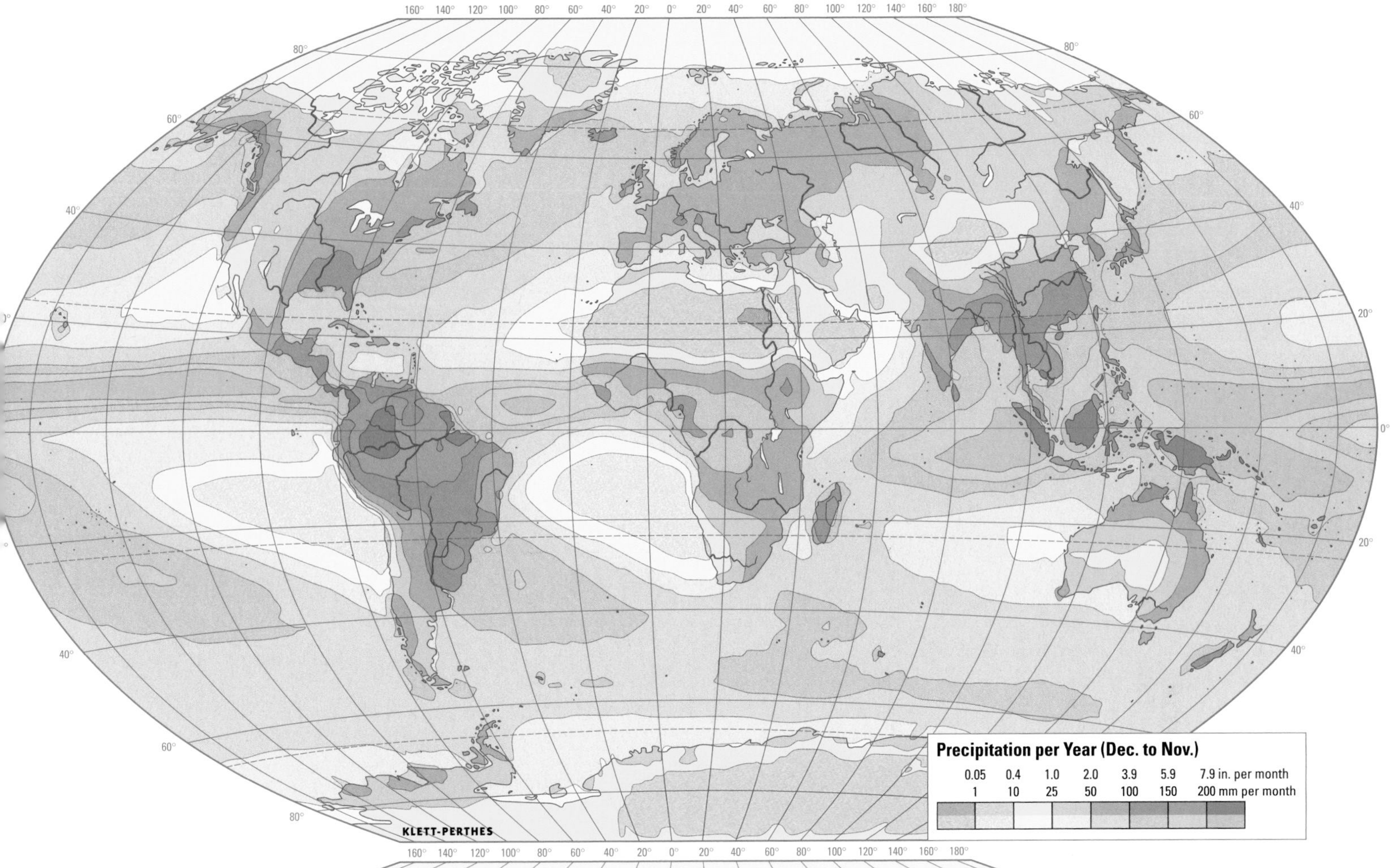

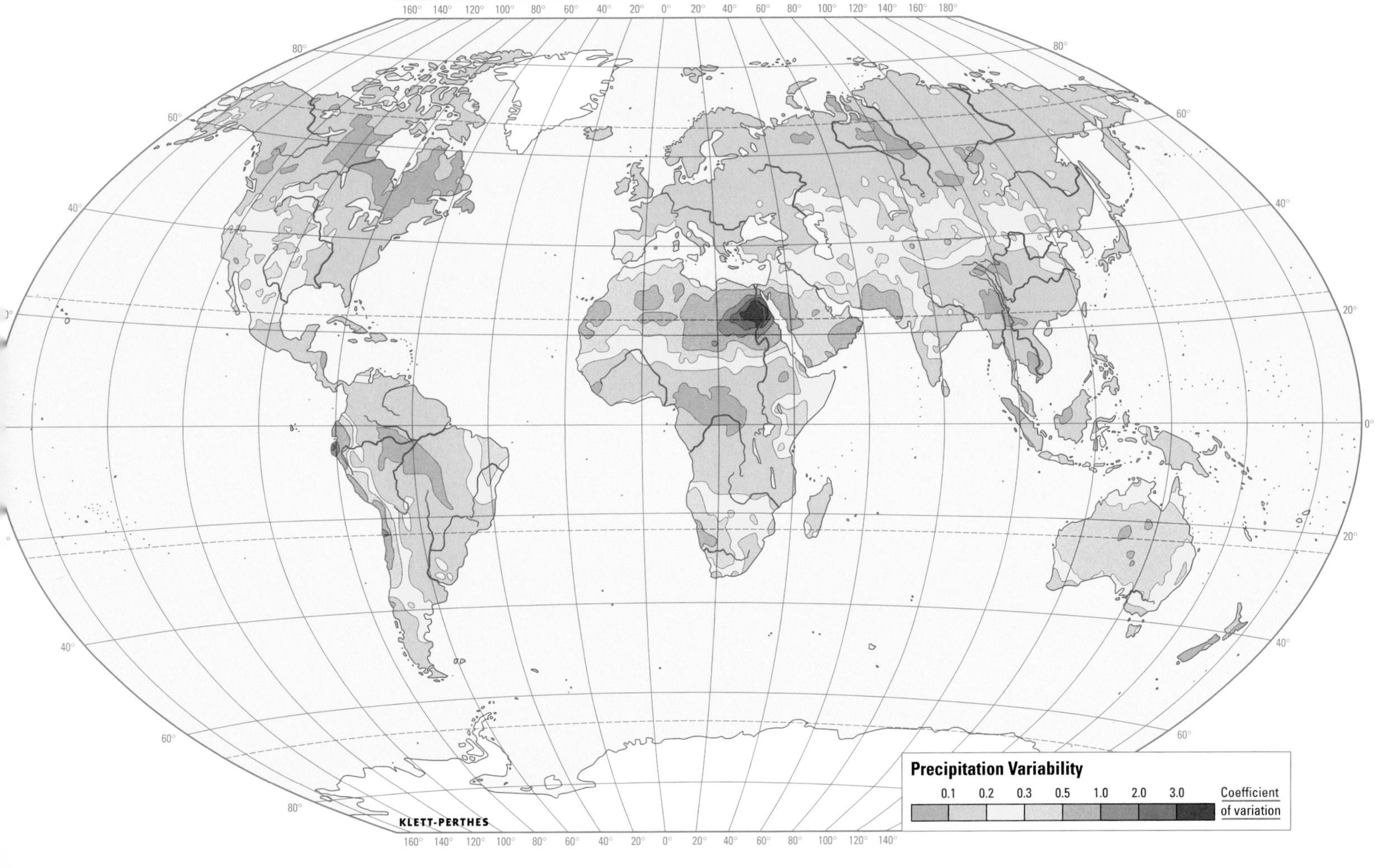

World: Water Resources 2000 · Water Resources 2025

1:160,000,000

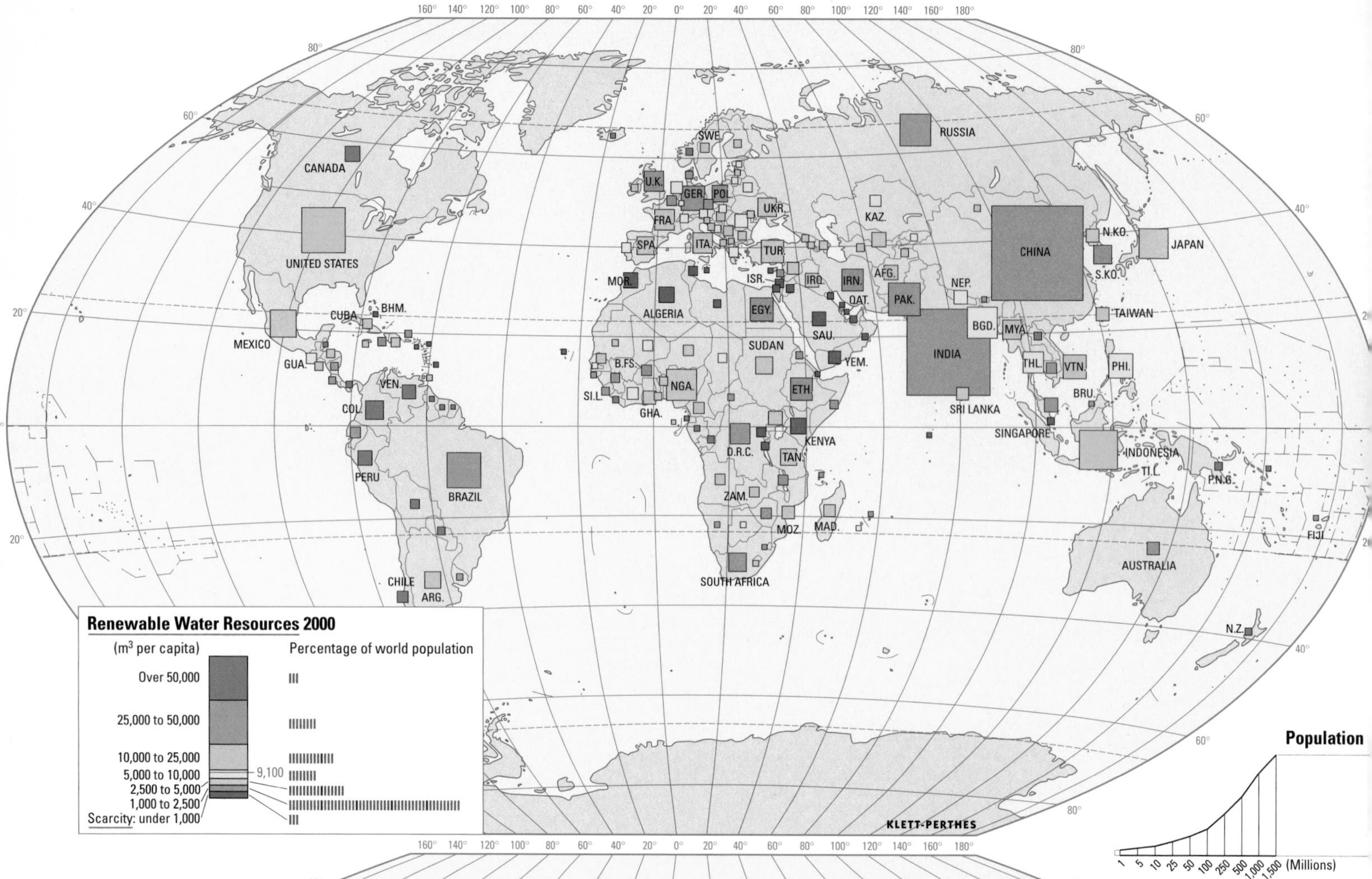

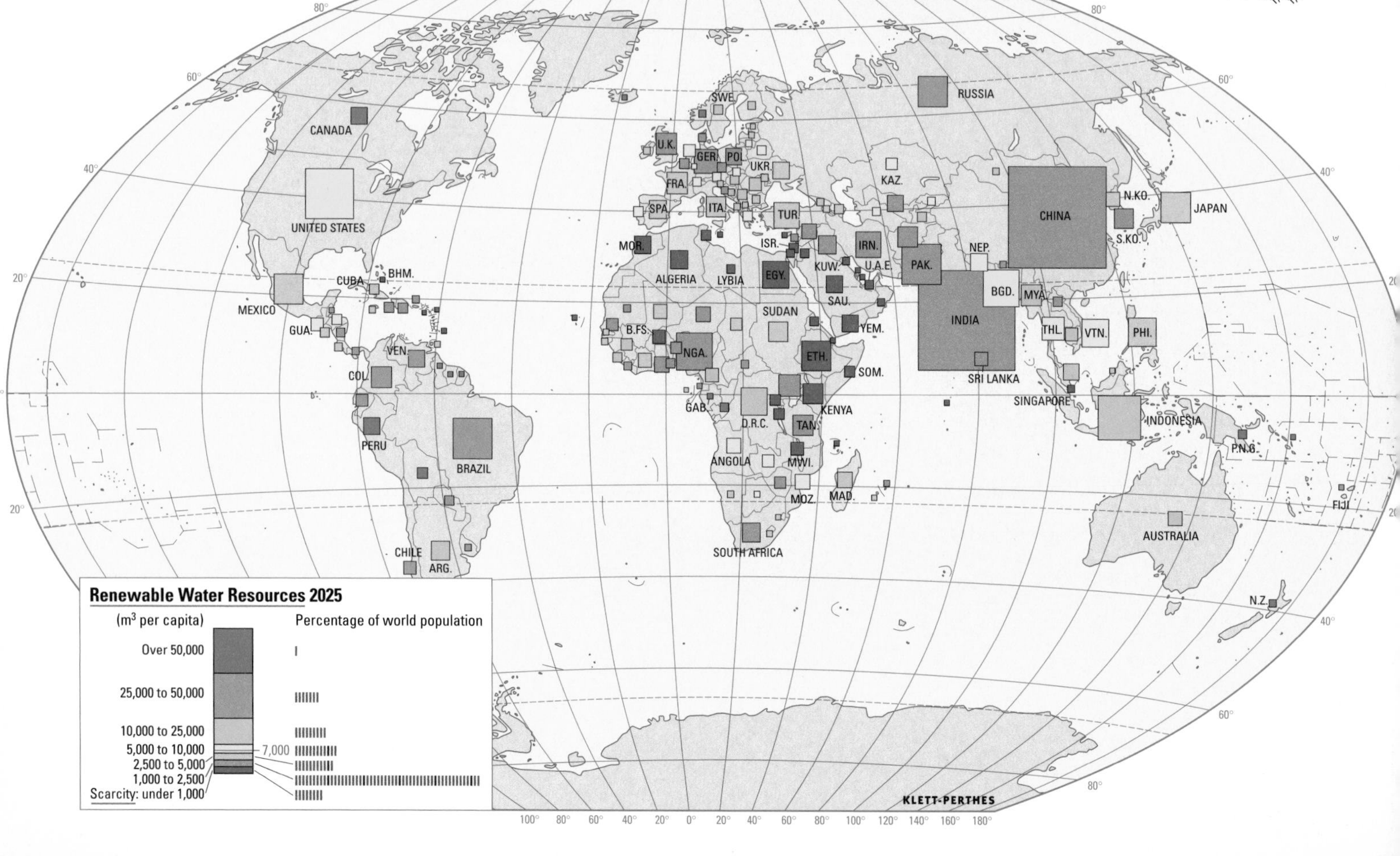

World: Water Use by Sectors · Water Stress

1:160,000,000

Water Use by Sectors

		Percentage of world water use
Dominant domestic use, secondary agricultural		
Absolute dominant domestic use (more than 70%)		
Dominant domestic use, secondary industrial		
Dominant industrial use, secondary domestic		IIII
Absolute dominant industrial use (more than 70%)		II
Dominant industrial use, secondary agricultural		IIIIIIIIIIIII
Dominant agricultural use, secondary industrial		IIIIIIIIIIIIIIIIIIIIIII
Absolute dominant agricultural use (more than 70%)		IIIIIIIIIIIIIIIIIIIIIIIIIIIIIIIIIIIIIIIIIIIIIIIIIIIIIIII
Dominant agricultural use, secondary domestic		IIIIII

Used Water

(km³) 1,000 500 200 100 50 20 10 5 1 0.2

Water Stress

(used water resources per year)

		Percentage of world water resources
Very low (less than 1%)		IIIIIIIIIIIIIIIIIIIIII
Low (1 to 10%)		IIIIIIIIIIIIIIIIIIIIIIIIIIIIIIIIIIIII
Moderate (10 to 20%)		IIIIIIII
Medium to high (20 to 40%)		IIIIIIIIIII
High (40 to 100%)		II
Very high (more than 100%)		
No data		IIII

Water Resources

(km³) 10,000 5,000 2,000 1,000 500 200 100 50 20 10 5

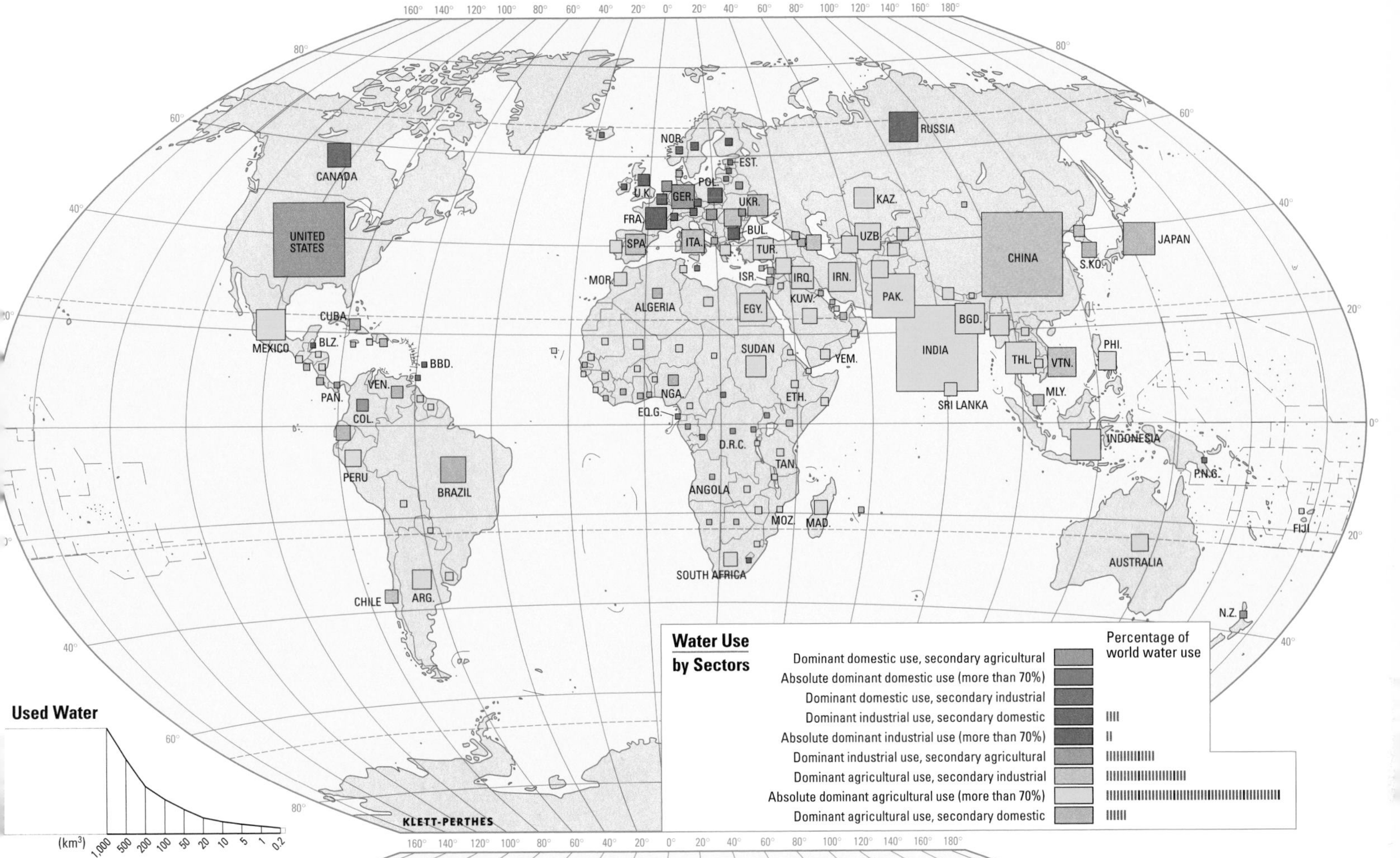

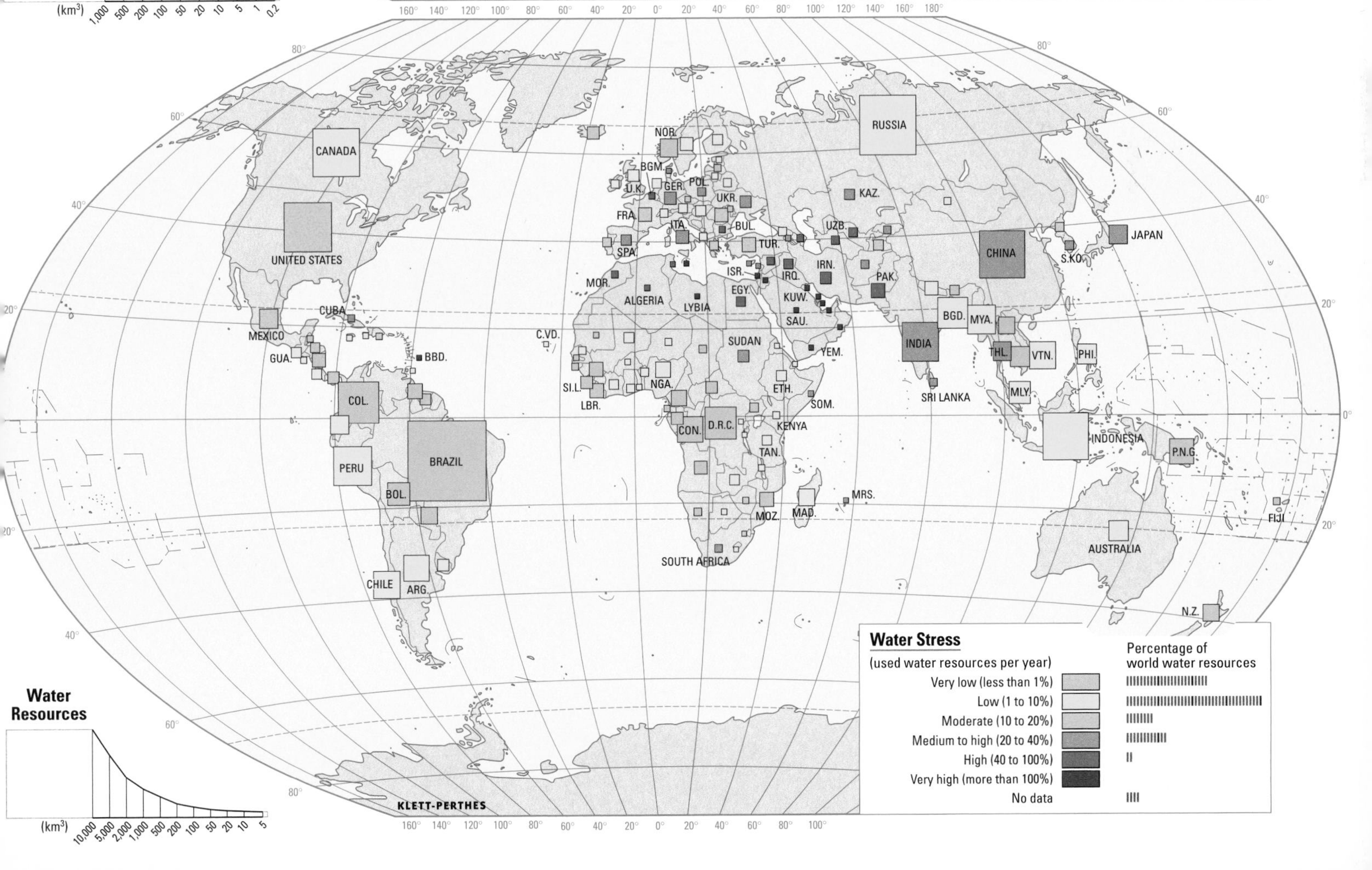

World: Temperatures in January and July

1:160,000,000

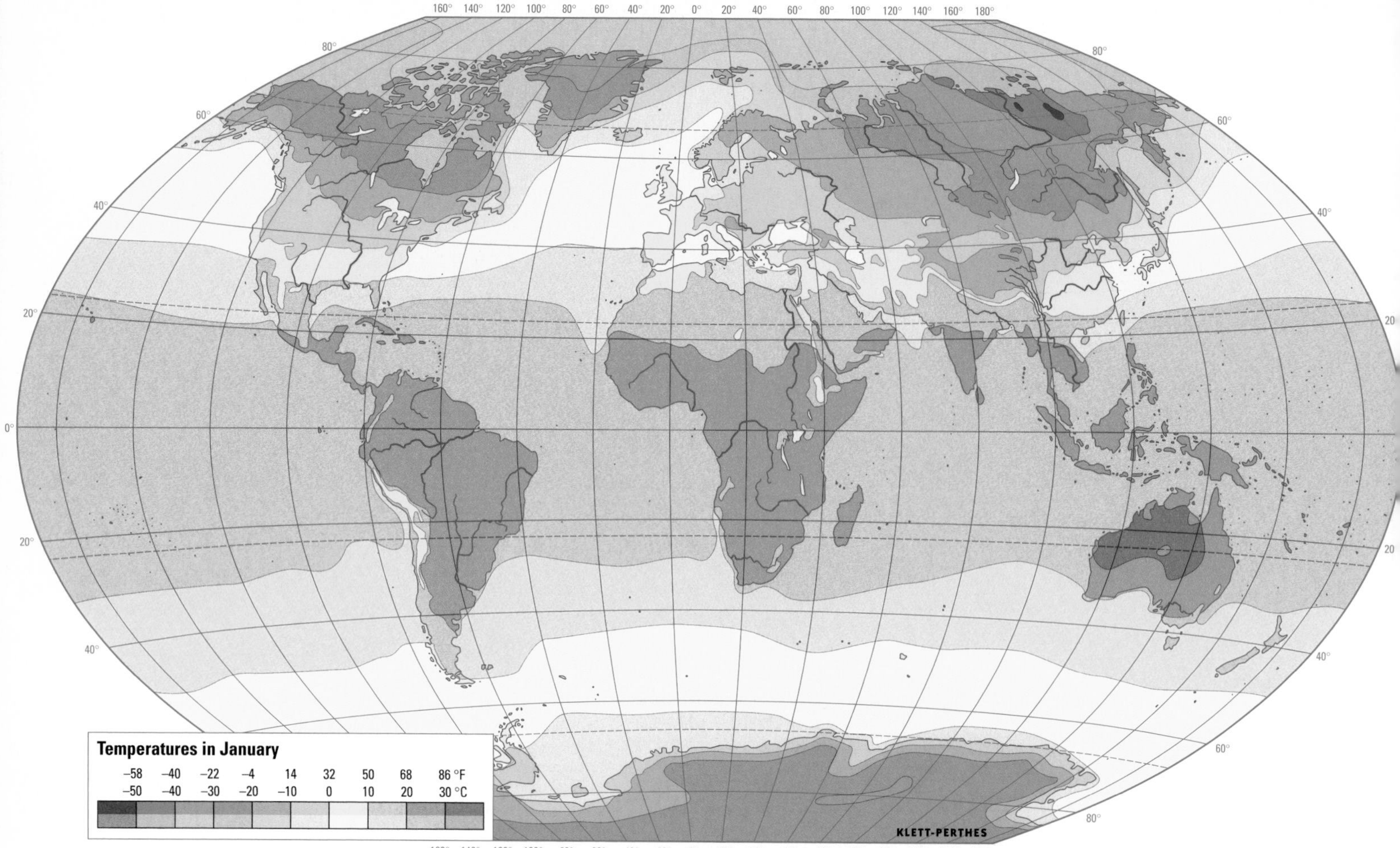

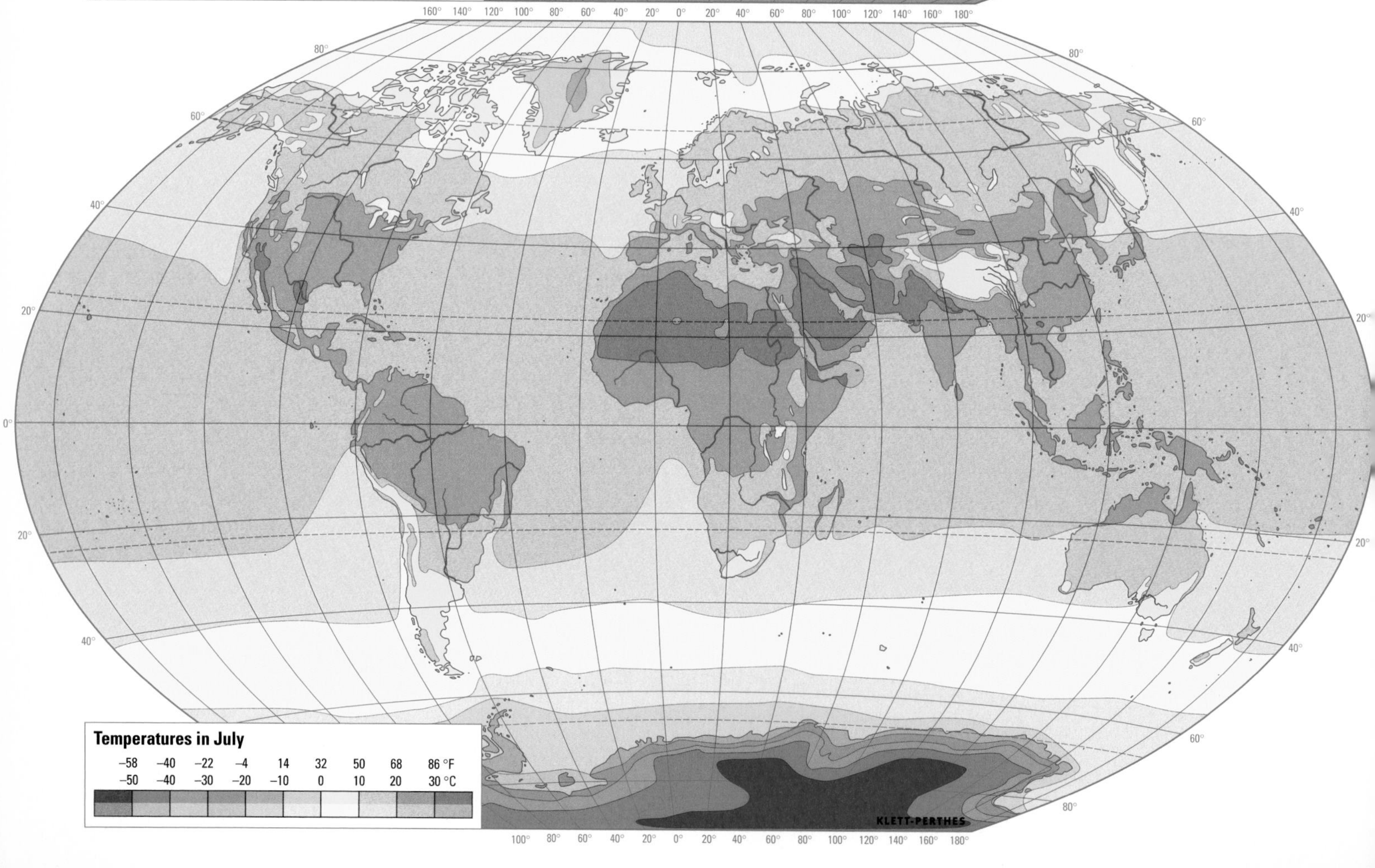

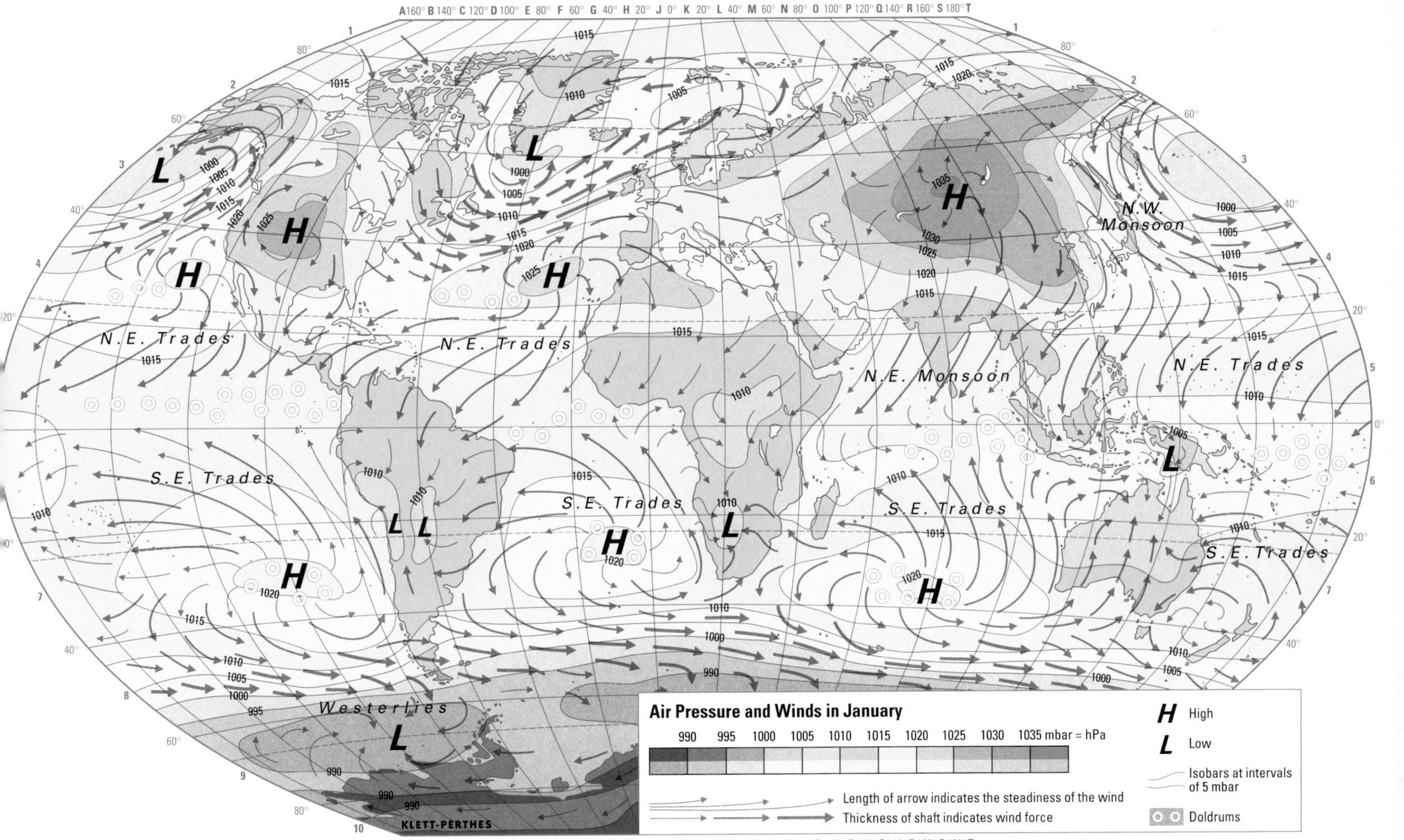

N.E. Trades
N.E. Trades
N.E. Monsoon
N.E. Trades
N.W. Monsoon
S.E. Trades
S.E. Trades
S.E. Trades
S.E. Trades
Westerlies
KLETT-PERTHES
Air Pressure and Winds in January
990 995 1000 1005 1010 1015 1020 1025 1030 1035 mbar = hPa
H High
L Low
Isobars at intervals of 5 mbar
Length of arrow indicates the steadiness of the wind
Thickness of shaft indicates wind force
Doldrums

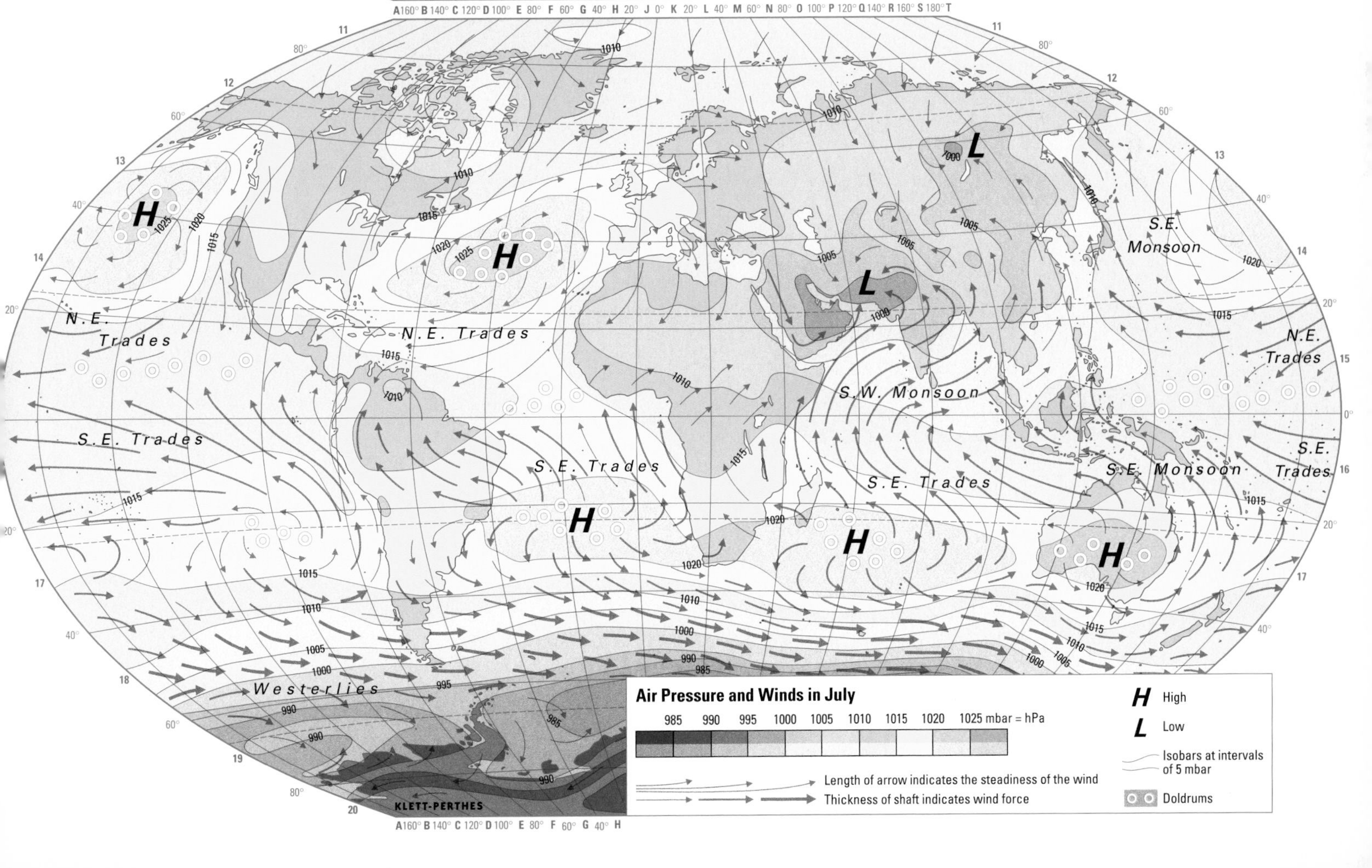

N.E. Trades
N.E. Trades
N.E. Trades
S.E. Monsoon
S.W. Monsoon
S.E. Trades
S.E. Trades
S.E. Trades
S.E. Monsoon
S.E. Trades
Westerlies
KLETT-PERTHES
Air Pressure and Winds in July
985 990 995 1000 1005 1010 1015 1020 1025 mbar = hPa
H High
L Low
Isobars at intervals of 5 mbar
Length of arrow indicates the steadiness of the wind
Thickness of shaft indicates wind force
Doldrums

A 160° B 140° C 120° D 100° E 80° F 60° G 40° H 20° J
1
2
3
4
5
6
80°
60°
40°
20°
0°
20°
A R C T I C
Queen Elizabeth Is.
Sverdrup Is.
Ellesmere I.
Beaufort Sea
Parry Is.
Devon I.
Victoria I.
Baffin Bay
Baffin I.
Greenland
Norw
Arctic Cir
Denmark Str.
Davis Str.
Yukon
Mackenzie
G. of Alaska
Kodiak I.
Aleutian Is.
Hudson Bay
Iceland
British Is.
N E A R C T I C
Labrador Sea
Newfoundland
Missouri
Mississippi
Azores
Bermuda Is.
Madeira
Hawaiian Is.
Hawaii
Tropic of Cancer
A T L A N T I C
Canary Is.
Gulf of Mexico
Bahama Is.
Cuba
Hispaniola
Greater Antilles
Lesser Antilles
Caribbean Sea
Cape Verde Is.
Niger
P A C I F I C
Line Islands
Equator
Kiritimati
Jarvis I.
Galápagos Is.
Amazon
Fernando de Noronha
N E O T R O P I C
Ascension
A F
Marquesas Is.
O C E A N I A
Cook Islands
Society Is.
Tuamotu Is.
St. Helena
O C E A N
O C E A N
Tropic of Capricorn
Tubuai Is.
Pitcairn Is.
Desventurados Is.
Juan Fernández Is.
Río de la Plata
Tristan da Cunha
Gough I.
Falkland Is. (Is. Malvinas)
Tierra del Fuego
South Georgia
Bouvet I.
Str. of Magellan
Scotia Sea
South Sandwich Is.
Drake Passage
South Shetland Is.
South Orkney Is.
Antarctic Circle
A N T
1
3
5
8
10
13

1

2

3

4

5

6

7

8

9

Biomes

1. Tundra
2. Boreal forests/Taiga
3. Temperate conifer forests
4. Temperate broadleaf and mixed forests
5. Temperate grasslands, savannas and shrublands
6. Mediterranean forests, woodlands and shrub
7. Deserts and xeric shrublands
8. Tropical and subtropical coniferous forests
9. Tropical and subtropical moist broadleaf forests
10. Tropical and subtropical dry broadleaf forests
11. Tropical and subtropical grasslands, savannas and shrublands
12. Flooded grasslands and savannas
13. Mangroves
14. Montane grasslands and shrublands

Rock and ice

Biogeographic Realms

N E A R C T I C

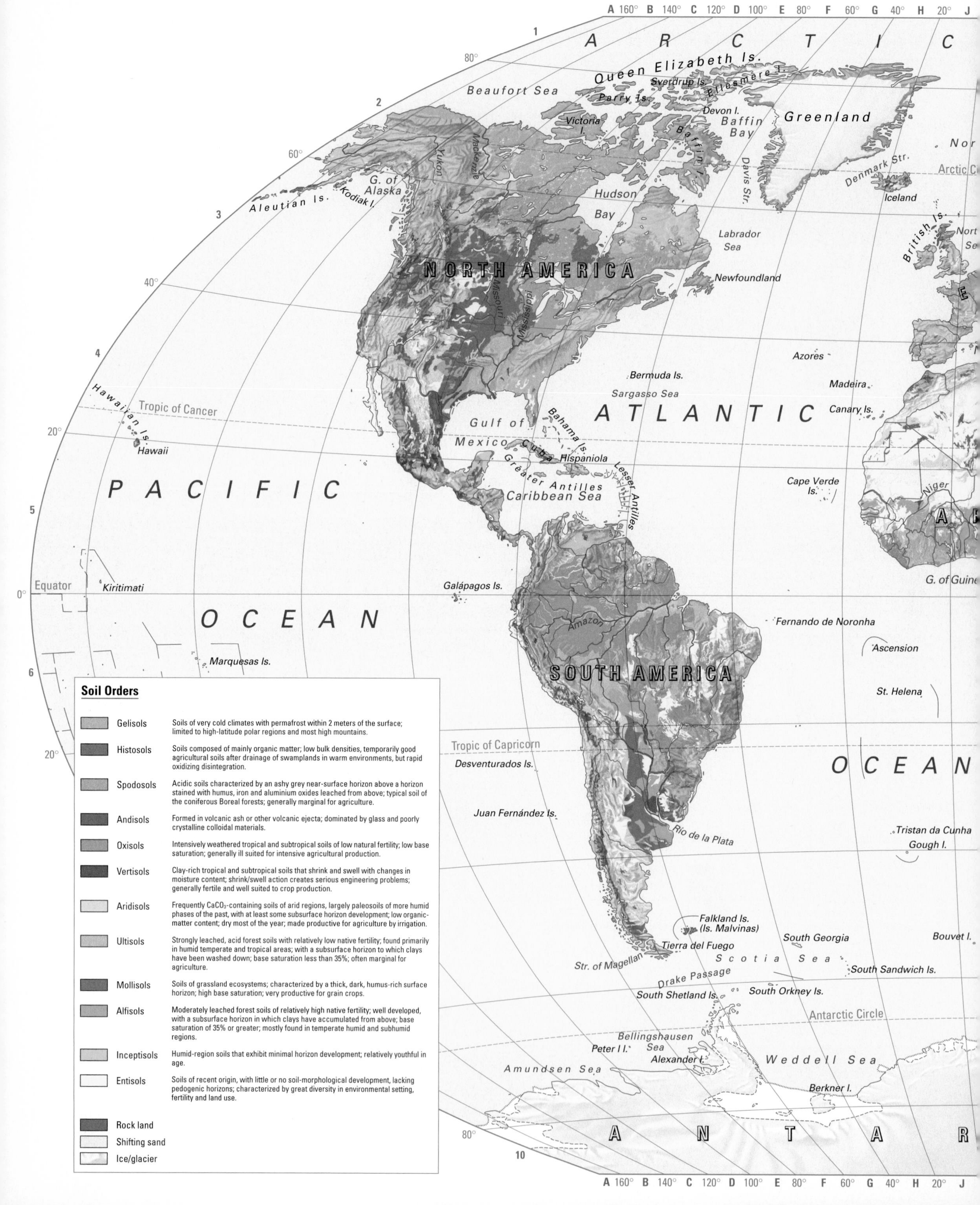

Soil Orders

Gelisols	Soils of very cold climates with permafrost within 2 meters of the surface; limited to high-latitude polar regions and most high mountains.
Histosols	Soils composed of mainly organic matter; low bulk densities, temporarily good agricultural soils after drainage of swamplands in warm environments, but rapid oxidizing disintegration.
Spodosols	Acidic soils characterized by an ashy grey near-surface horizon above a horizon stained with humus, iron and aluminium oxides leached from above; typical soil of the coniferous Boreal forests; generally marginal for agriculture.
Andisols	Formed in volcanic ash or other volcanic ejecta; dominated by glass and poorly crystalline colloidal materials.
Oxisols	Intensively weathered tropical and subtropical soils of low natural fertility; low base saturation; generally ill suited for intensive agricultural production.
Vertisols	Clay-rich tropical and subtropical soils that shrink and swell with changes in moisture content; shrink/swell action creates serious engineering problems; generally fertile and well suited to crop production.
Aridisols	Frequently $CaCO_3$-containing soils of arid regions, largely paleosoils of more humid phases of the past, with at least some subsurface horizon development; low organic-matter content; dry most of the year; made productive for agriculture by irrigation.
Ultisols	Strongly leached, acid forest soils with relatively low native fertility; found primarily in humid temperate and tropical areas; with a subsurface horizon to which clays have been washed down; base saturation less than 35%; often marginal for agriculture.
Mollisols	Soils of grassland ecosystems; characterized by a thick, dark, humus-rich surface horizon; high base saturation; very productive for grain crops.
Alfisols	Moderately leached forest soils of relatively high native fertility; well developed, with a subsurface horizon in which clays have accumulated from above; base saturation of 35% or greater; mostly found in temperate humid and subhumid regions.
Inceptisols	Humid-region soils that exhibit minimal horizon development; relatively youthful in age.
Entisols	Soils of recent origin, with little or no soil-morphological development, lacking pedogenic horizons; characterized by great diversity in environmental setting, fertility and land use.

- Rock land
- Shifting sand
- Ice/glacier

L 40° M 60° N 80° O 100° P 120° Q 140° R 160° S 180° T
O C E A N
Franz Josef Land
Severnaya Zemlya
New Siberian Is.
Laptev Sea
East Siberian Sea
Novaya Zemlya
Kara Sea
Barents Sea
Lena
Yenisey
Ob'
Bering Sea
Sea of Okhotsk
Aleutian Is.
Sakhalin
Kurile Is.
Baykal
Amur
Volga
R O P E
Aral Sea
Caspian Sea
Black Sea
A S I A
Hokkaido
Sea of Japan
Honshu
Kyushu
Yellow R.
Yangtze
Midway Is.
Bonin Is.
Ryukyu Is.
P A C I F I C
Volcano Is.
Taiwan
Wake I.
Mariana Is.
Nile
Red Sea
Hainan
Luzon
Philippines
Arabian Sea
Bay of Bengal
Socotra
South China Sea
Marshall Islands
Caroline Is.
Micronesia
Ceylon
Mindanao
M e l a n e s i a
O C E A N
Maldives
Congo
L. Victoria
Sumatra
Borneo (Kalimantan)
Celebes (Sulawesi)
Bismarck Arch.
Gilbert Is.
Equator
Phoenix Is.
Greater Sunda Is.
New Guinea
Seychelles
Chagos Is.
Java
Lesser Sunda Is.
Solomon Is.
Ellice Is.
Tokleau Is.
Comoro Is.
I N D I A N
Cocos Is.
Wallis Is.
Futuna
Coral Sea
New Hebrides
Madagascar
Mozambique Ch.
Mascarene Is.
Tonga Is.
Fiji Is.
New Caledonia
AUSTRALIA
Norfolk I.
Kermadec Is.
O C E A N
Amsterdam
Saint-Paul
Tasman Sea
North Island
Crozet Is.
Tasmania
New Zealand
Prince Edward I.
Kerguelen Is.
South Island
Bounty Is.
Heard
Auckland Is.
Antipodes Is.
Macquarie
Campbell Is.
Balleny Is.
Scott I.
Ross I.
Ross Sea
C T I C A
KLETT-PERTHES
1 2 3 4 5 6 7 8 9 10
80° 60° 40° 20° 0° 20° 40° 60° 80°

World: Biodiversity · Agriculture

1:160,000,000

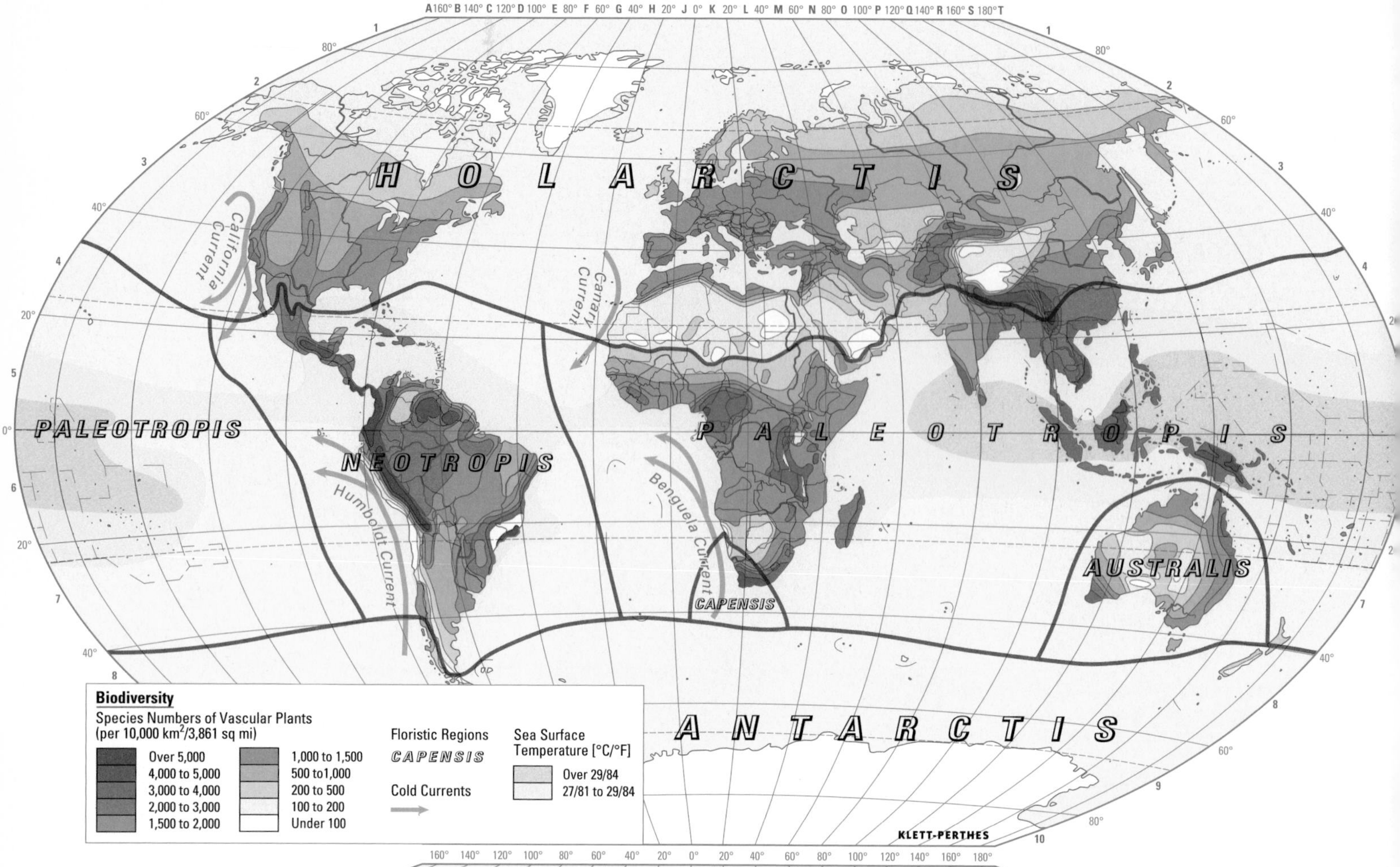

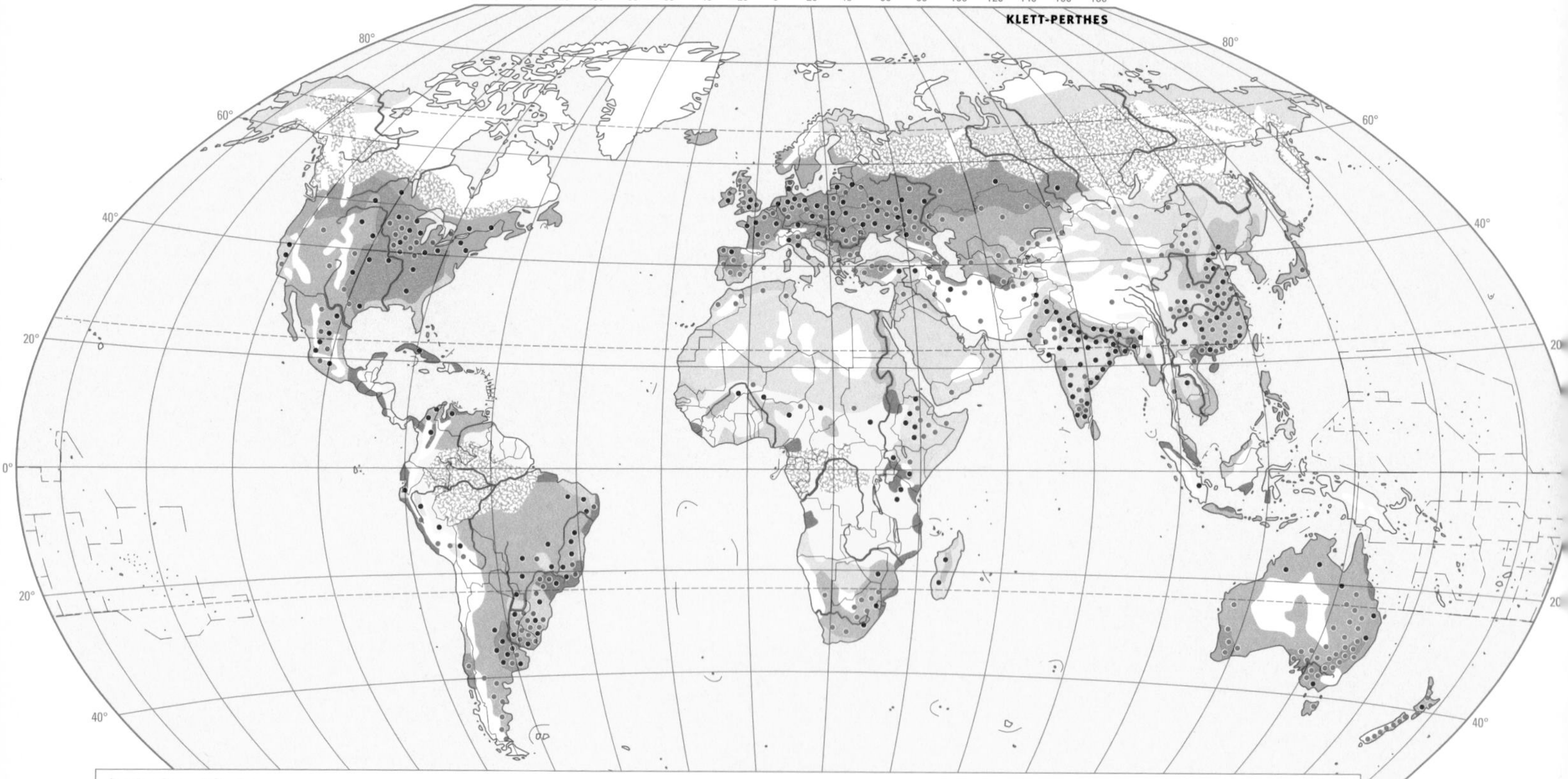

Agricultural Systems

Grassland Systems
- Nomadism
- Ranching (extensive)
- Grazing (intensive, incl. alternate husbandry/ley farming)

Cropping Systems
- Shifting cultivation
- Oasis agriculture with crop rotation
- Traditional smallholders
- Mechanized medium-size and large farms

Permanent Crop Systems
- Plantations and mixed farming
- Plantations with on-site processing

Animal Husbandry
(1 symbol = 5 million animals)
- Cattle
- Sheep
- Pigs

Forests with marginal economic activity (agriculture, animal husbandry, logging, hunting etc.)

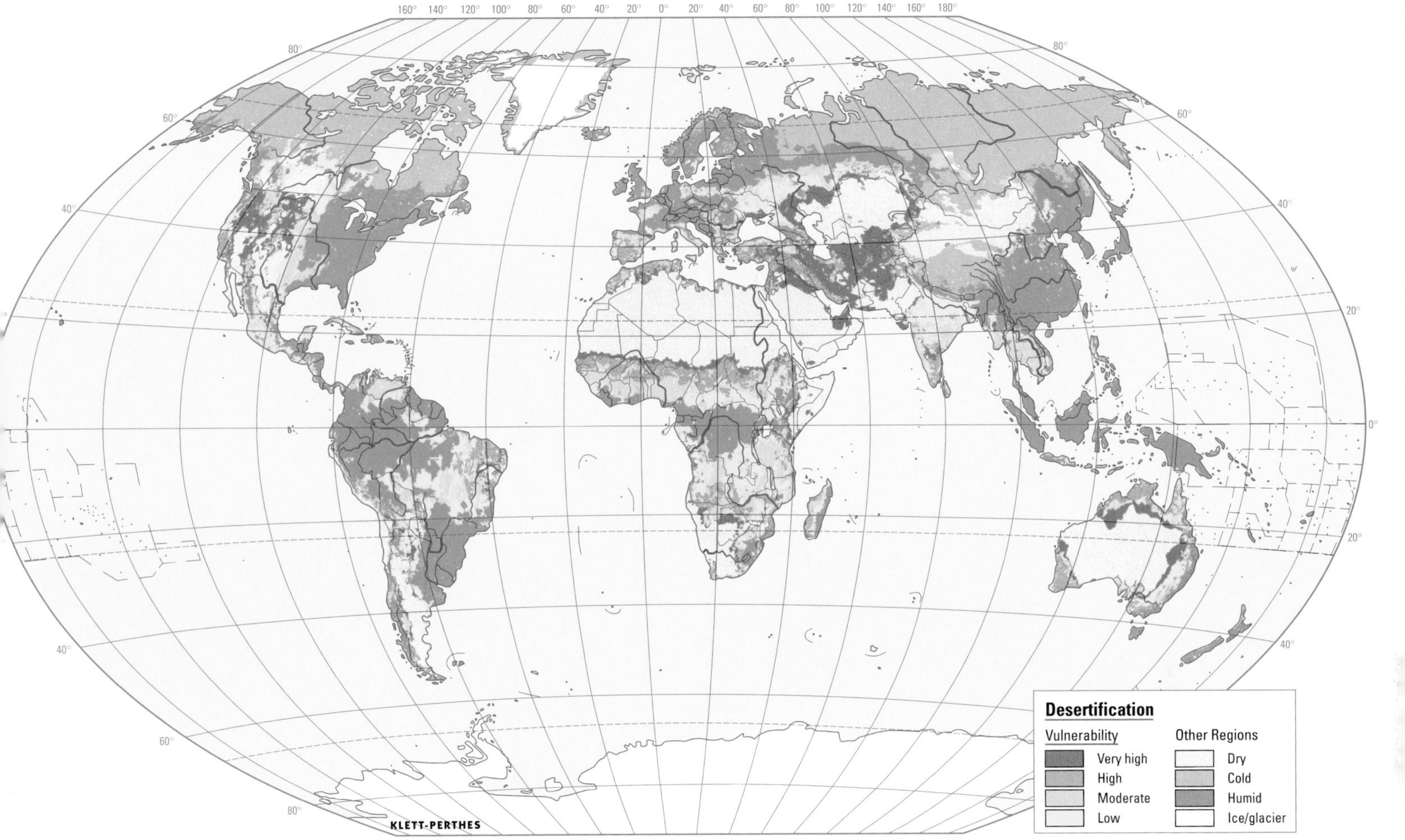
Desertification
Vulnerability
Very high
High
Moderate
Low
Other Regions
Dry
Cold
Humid
Ice/glacier
KLETT-PERTHES

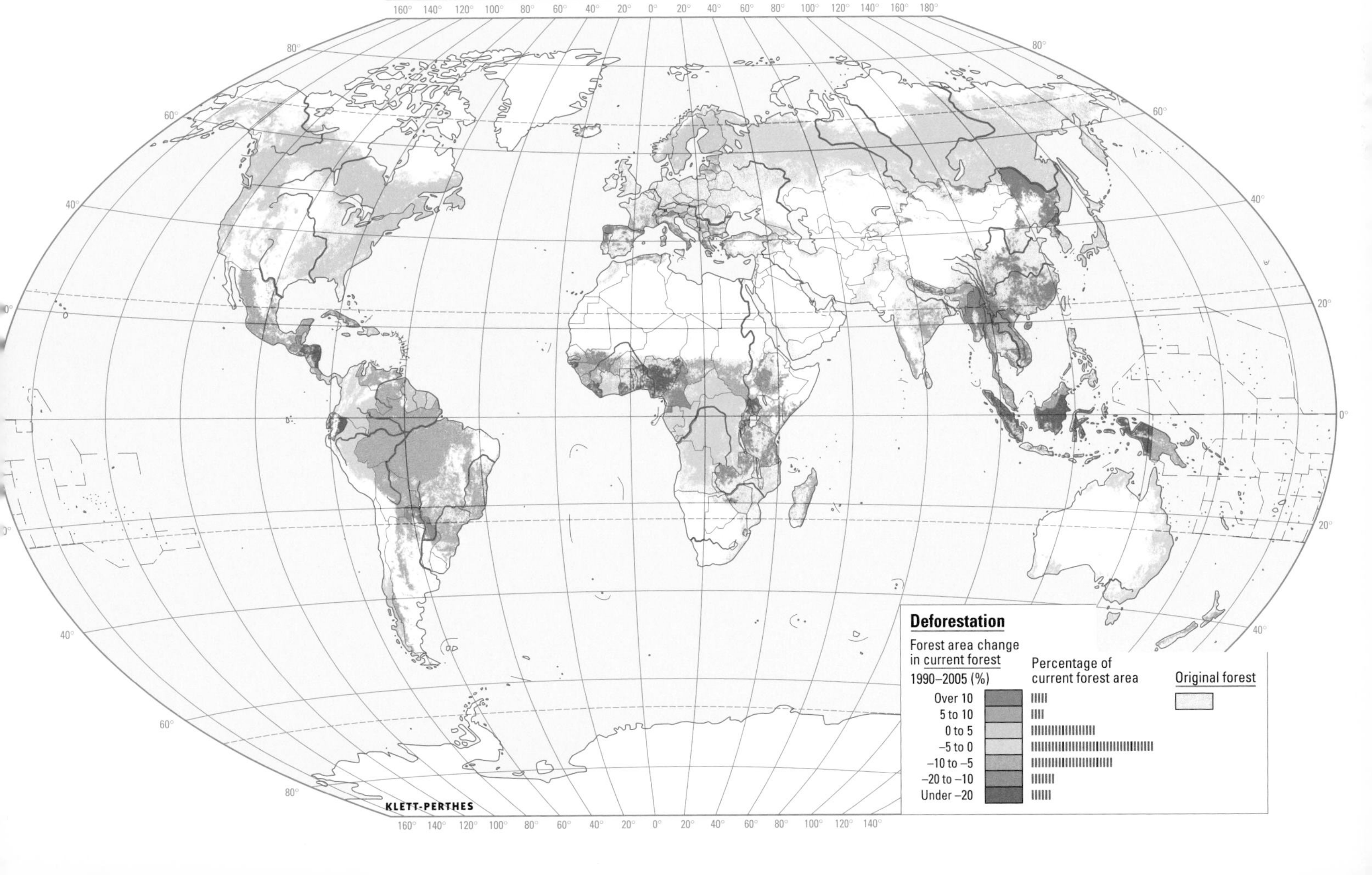
Deforestation
Forest area change in current forest 1990–2005 (%)
Over 10
5 to 10
0 to 5
–5 to 0
–10 to –5
–20 to –10
Under –20
Percentage of current forest area
Original forest
KLETT-PERTHES

Land Cover

Natural Vegetation		
	Evergreen needleleaf forests	Lands dominated by woody vegetation with a percent cover >60% and height exceeding 2 meters. Almost all trees remain green all year. Canopy is never without green foliage.
	Evergreen broadleaf forests	Lands dominated by woody vegetation with a percent cover >60% and height exceeding 2 meters. Almost all trees and shrubs remain green year round. Canopy is never without green foliage.
	Deciduous needleleaf forests	Lands dominated by woody vegetation with a percent cover >60% and height exceeding 2 meters. Consists of seasonal needleleaf tree communities with an annual cycle of leaf-on and leaf-off periods.
	Deciduous broadleaf forests	Lands dominated by woody vegetation with a percent cover >60% and height exceeding 2 meters. Consists of broadleaf tree communities with an annual cycle of leaf-on and leaf-off periods.
	Mixed forests	Lands dominated by trees with a percent cover >60% and height exceeding 2 meters. Consists of tree communities with interspersed mixtures or mosaics of the other four forest types. None of the forest types exceeds 60% of landscape.
	Closed shrublands	Lands with woody vegetation less than 2 meters tall and with shrub canopy cover >60%. The shrub foliage can be either evergreen or deciduous.
	Open shrublands	Lands with woody vegetation less than 2 meters tall and with shrub canopy cover between 10-60%. The shrub foliage can be either evergreen or deciduous.
	Woody savannas	Lands with herbaceous and other understory systems, and with forest canopy cover between 30-60%. The forest cover height exceeds 2 meters.
	Savannas	Lands with herbaceous and other understory systems, and with forest canopy cover between 10-30%. The forest cover height exceeds 2 meters.
	Grasslands	Lands with herbaceous types of cover. Tree and shrub cover is less than 10%.
	Permanent wetlands	Lands with a permanent mixture of water and herbaceous or woody vegetation. The vegetation can be present in either salt, brackish, or fresh water.
Developed and Mosaic Lands		
	Croplands	Lands covered with temporary crops followed by harvest and a bare soil period (e.g., single and multiple cropping systems). Note that perennial woody crops will be classified as the appropriate forest or shrub land cover type.
	Cropland/natural vegetation mosaic	Lands with a mosaic of croplands, forests, shrubland, and grasslands in which no one component comprises more than 60% of the landscape.
	Urban and built-up lands	Land covered by buildings and other man-made structures.
Non-Vegetated Lands		
	Snow and ice	Lands under snow/ice cover throughout the year.
	Barren or sparsely vegetated	Lands with exposed soil, sand, rocks, or snow and never has more than 10% vegetated cover during any time of the year.
	Water bodies	Oceans, seas, lakes, reservoirs, and rivers. Can be either fresh or salt-water bodies.
	No data	

L 40° M 60° N 80° O 100° P 120° Q 140° R 160° S 180° T
O C E A N
Franz Josef Land
Severnaya Zemlya
New Siberian Is.
Laptev Sea
East Siberian Sea
Kara Sea
Novaya Zemlya
Taymyr Pen.
Barents Sea
Central Siberian Plateau
Lena
Yenisey
West Siberian Plain
Ob
Ural Mts.
Yakutia
Bering Sea
Kamchatka
Sea of Okhotsk
Aleutian Is.
Moscow
Volga
L. Baykal
Amur
Sakhalin
Kurile Is.
Altay Mts.
Aral Sea
Manchuria
Hokkaido
Gobi
Sea of Japan
Honshu
Black Sea
Caspian Sea
Tashkent
Tien Shan
Beijing
Korea
Tōkyō
Anatolia
Kunlun Shan
Tibet
Yellow R.
Kyushu
Shanghai
Tehrān
Baghdad
Iranian Plateau
Himalayas
Yangtze
Ryukyu Is.
Midway Is.
Bonin Is.
Cairo
Libyan Desert
Nile
Red Sea
Arabian Pen.
Delhi
PACIFIC
Volcano Is.
Kolkata
India
Taiwan
Mariana Is.
Wake I.
Hainan
Luzon
Arabian Sea
Bay of Bengal
Bangkok
South China Sea
Philippines
Marshall Islands
Socotra
Ethiopian Highlands
Somali Pen.
Ceylon
Caroline Is.
Micronesia
Mindanao
Maldives
OCEAN
Melanesia
Congo
Congo Basin
L. Victoria
Sumatra
Borneo (Kalimantan)
Celebes (Sulawesi)
Equator
Bismarck Arch.
Gilbert Is.
Phoenix Is.
New Guinea
Seychelles
Chagos Is.
Greater Sunda Is.
Jakarta
Java
Lesser Sunda Is.
Ellice Is.
Tokleau Is.
Solomon Is.
Comoro Is.
INDIAN
Cocos Is.
Wallis Is.
Futuna
Coral Sea
New Hebrides
Mozambique Ch.
Madagascar
Mascarene Is.
Tonga Is.
Fiji Is.
AUSTRALIA
Great Dividing Range
New Caledonia
Johannesburg
Great Victoria Desert
Perth
Norfolk I.
Kermadec Is.
OCEAN
Amsterdam
Saint-Paul
Austr. Alps
Sydney
Melbourne
Tasman Sea
North Island
Crozet Is.
Tasmania
New Zealand
Prince Edward I.
Kerguelen Is.
South Island
Heard
Bounty Is.
Auckland Is.
Antipodes Is.
Macquarie
Campbell Is.
Wilkes Land
Balleny Is.
Scott I.
Ross I.
Ross Sea
CTICA
80° 60° 40° 20° 0° 20° 40° 60° 80°
1 2 3 4 5 6 7 8 9 10
KLETT-PERTHES
L 40° M 60° N 80° O 100° P 120° Q 140° R 160° S 180° T

A 160° B 140° C 120° D 100° E 80° F 60° G 40° H 20° J
A R C T I C
Queen Elizabeth Is.
Sverdrup Is.
Ellesmere I.
Parry Is.
Beaufort Sea
Victoria I.
Devon I.
Baffin Bay
Greenland (DEN.)
Jan Mayen (NOR.)
UNITED STATES
Alaska
Anchorage
Yukon
Mackenzie
Arctic Circle
Nuuk
Reykjavik
ICELAND
Faroe Is. (DEN.)
G. of Alaska
Kodiak I.
Aleutian Is.
Hudson Bay
Labrador Sea
Edmonton
C A N A D A
Vancouver
Winnipeg
Seattle
British Is.
UNITED KINGDOM
Dublin
IRELAND
LONDON
Newfoundland
Ottawa
MONTRÉAL
TORONTO
Boston
NEW YORK
CHICAGO
St. Pierre and Miquelon (FRA.)
Missouri
Mississippi
San Francisco
U N I T E D S T A T E S
Washington, D.C.
LOS ANGELES
MADRID
SPAIN
Lisbon
Azores (POR.)
DALLAS
New Orleans
Bermuda (U.K.)
CASABLANCA
MOROCCO
Madeira (POR.)
UNITED STATES
Hawaiian Is.
Honolulu
Hawaii
Tropic of Cancer
M E X I C O
MONTERREY
Gulf of Mexico
A T L A N T I C
Canary Is. (SPA.)
ALGERIA
HAVANA
Nassau
BAHAMAS
CUBA
Western Sahara
MEXICO CITY
Cayman Is.
JAM.
HTI.
DO.R.
MAURITANIA
MALI
Niger
BLZ.
HON.
GUA.
SAL.
NIC.
MANAGUA
C.RC.
PAN.
Caribbean Sea
Aruba
Neth. Antilles
Martinique
ST. LUCIA
ST. V.
BARBADOS
GRENADA
TRINIDAD AND TOBAGO
CAPE VERDE
SEN.
DAKAR
Bamako
B.FS.
GU.B.
GUINEA
CONAKRY
SI.L.
GHA.
C.IV.
ABIDJAN
ACCRA
BEN.
G. of Guinea
CARACAS
VENEZUELA
GUYANA
French Guiana
BOGOTÁ
COLOMBIA
P A C I F I C
Line Islands
Kiritimati
Equator
Jarvis I. (U.S.)
KIRIBATI
Galápagos Is. (ECU.)
ECUADOR
MANAUS
Amazon
BELÉM
(BRA.) Fernando de Noronha
B R A Z I L
RECIFE
Ascension
Tokelau (N.Z.)
Marquesas Is.
PERU
LIMA
SALVADOR
St. Helena (U.K.)
American Samoa (U.S.)
COOK ISLANDS
Society Is.
French Polynesia
Tuamotu Is.
La Paz
BOLIVIA
BRASÍLIA
O C E A N
PARAGUAY
RIO DE JANEIRO
SÃO PAULO
Tropic of Capricorn
Tubuai Is.
Pitcairn (U.K.)
Desventurados Is.
Easter I.
Sala-y-Gómez
(CHL.)
Asunción
PORTO ALEGRE
CHILE
ARGENTINA
SANTIAGO
Juan Fernández Is.
URUGUAY
MONTEVIDEO
BUENOS AIRES
Tristan da Cunha
Gough I.
O C E A N
Falkland Is. (Is. Malvinas) (U.K.)
South Georgia and the South Sandwich Is. (U.K.)
Tierra del Fuego
South Shetland Is.
South Orkney Is.
Antarctic Circle
Bellingshausen Sea
Weddell Sea
Berkner I.
A N T A R
1
2
3
4
5
6
7
9
10
80°
60°
40°
20°
0°
20°
40°
60°
80°
Natural Hazards
Earthquakes
Violent and very violent earthquakes possible (heavy and extreme damage)
Very strong earthquakes possible (moderate damage)
Light to strong earthquakes possible (pictures move, objects fall, nonstructural damage)
Volcanoes
Particularly hazardous volcano
Tsunamis and Storm Surges
Tsunami hazard
Storm surge hazard
Tsunami and storm surge hazard
Tropical Storms and Cyclones
Winds greater than 131 mph (210 km/h)
Winds 111–130 mph (178–209 km/h)
Winds 96–110 mph (154–177 km/h)
Winds 74–95 mph (118–153 km/h)
Principal tracks of tropical storms
A 160° B 140° C 120° D 100° E 80° F 60° G 40° H 20° J

L 40° M 60° N 80° O 100° P 120° Q 140° R 160° S 180° T
O C E A N
Franz Josef Land
Severnaya Zemlya
New Siberian Is.
Laptev Sea
East Siberian Sea
Kara Sea
Novaya Zemlya
Barents Sea
Noril'sk
Yenisey
Lena
Ob'
Yakutsk
Bering Sea
Sea of Okhotsk
Aleutian Is.
Petropavlovsk-Kamchatskiy
Sakhalin
Kurile Is.
FINLAND
R U S S I A
ST. PETERSBURG
NIZHNIY NOVGOROD
YEKATERINBURG
OMSK
NOVOSIBIRSK
Irkutsk
Baykal
Amur
Khabarovsk
LIT.
MOSCOW
WARSAW
SAMARA
Volga
KIEV
UKRAINE
KAZAKHSTAN
Ulan Bator
MONGOLIA
Vladivostok
Hokkaido
ROM.
BUL.
Black Sea
GEO.
Caspian Sea
UZB.
Bishkek
ALMATY
KYR.
TASHKENT
ÜRÜMQI
SHENYANG
BEIJING
NORTH KOREA
SOUTH
SOUL
Sea of Japan
Honshu
TOKYO
OSAKA
JAPAN
GCE.
ANKARA
TURKEY
BAKU
TAJ.
CHINA
XI'AN
Yellow
SHANGHAI
Kyushu
Athens
Mediterranean Sea
IRAQ
TEHRAN
IRAN
KABUL
AFG.
Islamabad
LAHORE
BAGHDAD
CAIRO
EGYPT
Kuwait
PAKISTAN
NEPAL
Kathmandu
DELHI
CHONGQING
Yangtze
WUHAN
Ryukyu Is.
Bonin Is.
PACIFIC
Midway Is. (U.S.)
LIBYA
Nile
Red Sea
SAUDI ARABIA
RIYADH
Abu Dhabi
JEDDAH
KARACHI
BGD.
MYANMAR
KOLKATA
INDIA
GUANGZHOU
HANOI
HONG KONG
TAIWAN
Luzon
Volcano Is.
Wake I. (U.S.)
Northern Mariana Is. (U.S.)
CHAD
KHARTOUM
SUDAN
N'Djamena
ERI.
SANAA
YEMEN
DJI.
ADDIS ABABA
ETHIOPIA
Socotra (YEM.)
Arabian Sea
MUMBAI
RANGOON
Hainan
THAILAND
BANGKOK
VIETNAM
South China Sea
MANILA
PHILIPPINES
Guam (U.S.)
Marshall Islands
Bay of Bengal
CHENNAI
Colombo
SRI LANKA
SOMALIA
C.A.R.
Congo
KUALA LUMPUR
MALAYSIA
SINGAPORE
Mindanao
Caroline Is.
Palikir
Uliga
MICRONESIA
MOGADISHU
Malé
MALDIVES
UGA.
KENYA
NAIROBI
DEM. REP. OF THE CONGO
KINSHASA
BDI.
Victoria
TANZANIA
Sumatra
Borneo (Kalimantan)
Celebes (Sulawesi)
Melanesia
OCEAN
Bairiki
Equator
KIRIBATI
INDIAN
Brit. Indian Ocean Terr. (U.K.)
DAR ES SALAAM
SEYCHELLES
JAKARTA
Java
SURABAYA
INDONESIA
Bismarck Arch.
New Guinea
PAPUA NEW GUINEA
Port Moresby
Solomon Is.
Ellice Is.
Tokleau (N.Z.)
ANDA
ANGOLA
COMOROS
ZAMBIA
LUSAKA
HARARE
ZIM.
MOZAMBIQUE
Christmas I. (AUS.)
Cocos Is. (AUS.)
Wallis and Futuna (FRA.)
SAMOA
Apia
ANTANANARIVO
MADAGASCAR
Réunion (FRA.)
Coral Sea
Coral Sea Is. (AUS.)
VANUATU
Port-Vila
Suva
FIJI
TONGA
NAMIBIA
JOHANNESBURG
MAPUTO
SOUTH AFRICA
AUSTRALIA
New Caledonia (FRA.)
BRISBANE
PERTH
OCEAN
Norfolk I. (AUS.)
Kermadec Is. (N.Z.)
ADELAIDE
SYDNEY
Canberra
Amsterdam
Saint-Paul
MELBOURNE
Tasman Sea
North Island
Prince Edward and Marion Is. (S.AF.)
French Southern Terr.
Crozet Is.
Tasmania
NEW ZEALAND
Wellington
Chatham Is.
Kerguelen Is.
South Island
Bounty Is. (N.Z.)
Heard and the McDonald Is. (AUS.)
Auckland Is. (N.Z.)
Antipodes Is.
Macquarie (AUS.)
Campbell Is. (N.Z.)
Balleny Is.
Scott I.
ANTARCTICA
80°
60°
40°
20°
0°
1 2 3 4 5 6 7 8 9
Natural Disaster (2004, 2005)
Type of Disaster
Slide
Wind storm
Drought
Earthquake
Extreme temperature
Flood
Wave, surge
Epidemic
Disaster Victims
50 to 100 killed
100 to 1,000 killed
1,000 to 10,000 killed
10,000 to 100,000 killed
More than 100,000 killed
Extratropical Storms, Winter Storms
High extratropical storm hazard, mainly in winter
Principal tracks of extratropical storms
Other Natural Hazards
Limit of drift ice
Pack ice (winter maximum)
High seas with wave heights over 5 metres
KLETT-PERTHES

AFG.	AFGHANISTAN	B.FS.	BURKINA FASO	BLR.	BELARUS	C.IV.	CÔTE D'IVOIRE	DJI.	DJIBOUTI	GAB.	GABO
ALB.	ALBANIA	BDI.	BURUNDI	BLZ.	BELIZE	C.RC.	COSTA RICA	DEN.	DENMARK	GAM.	GAMB
ARM.	ARMENIA	BEN.	BENIN	BOT.	BOTSWANA	CBD.	CAMBODIA	DO.R.	DOMINICAN REP.	GCE.	GREEC
AUT.	AUSTRIA	BGD.	BANGLADESH	BRU.	BRUNEI	CMN.	CAMEROON	ERI.	ERITREA	GEO.	GEOR
AZE.	AZERBAIJAN	BGM.	BELGIUM	BUL.	BULGARIA	CRO.	CROATIA	EST.	ESTONIA	GHA.	GHAN
B. & H.	BOSNIA AND HERZEGOVINA	BHR.	BAHRAIN	C.A.R.	CENTRAL AFRICAN REPUBLIC	CYP.	CYPRUS	EQ.G.	EQUATORIAL GUINEA	GUA.	GUATE
		BHU.	BHUTAN			CZ.R.	CZECH REPUBLIC				

GUINEA-BISSAU	KUW.	KUWAIT	MAC.	MACEDONIA	ROM.	ROMANIA	SUR.	SURINAME	TKM.	TURKMENISTAN
HONDURAS	KYR.	KYRGYZSTAN	MOL.	MOLDOVA	RWA.	RWANDA	SVK.	SLOVAKIA	TUN.	TUNISIA
HUNGARY	LAT.	LATVIA	MWI.	MALAWI	S. & M.	SERBIA AND	SVN.	SLOVENIA	U.A.E.	UNITED ARAB
HAITI	LEB.	LEBANON	NLD.	NETHERLANDS		MONTENEGRO	SWA.	SWAZILAND		EMIRATES
ISRAEL	LES.	LESOTHO	NIC.	NICARAGUA	SAL.	EL SALVADOR	SWI.	SWITZERLAND	UGA.	UGANDA
JAMAICA	LIT.	LITHUANIA	PAN.	PANAMA	SEN.	SENEGAL	TAJ.	TAJIKISTAN	UZB.	UZBEKISTAN
JORDAN	LUX.	LUXEMBOURG	QAT.	QATAR	SGP.	SINGAPORE	TGO.	TOGO	ZIM.	ZIMBABWE

World: Time Zones

1:130,000,000

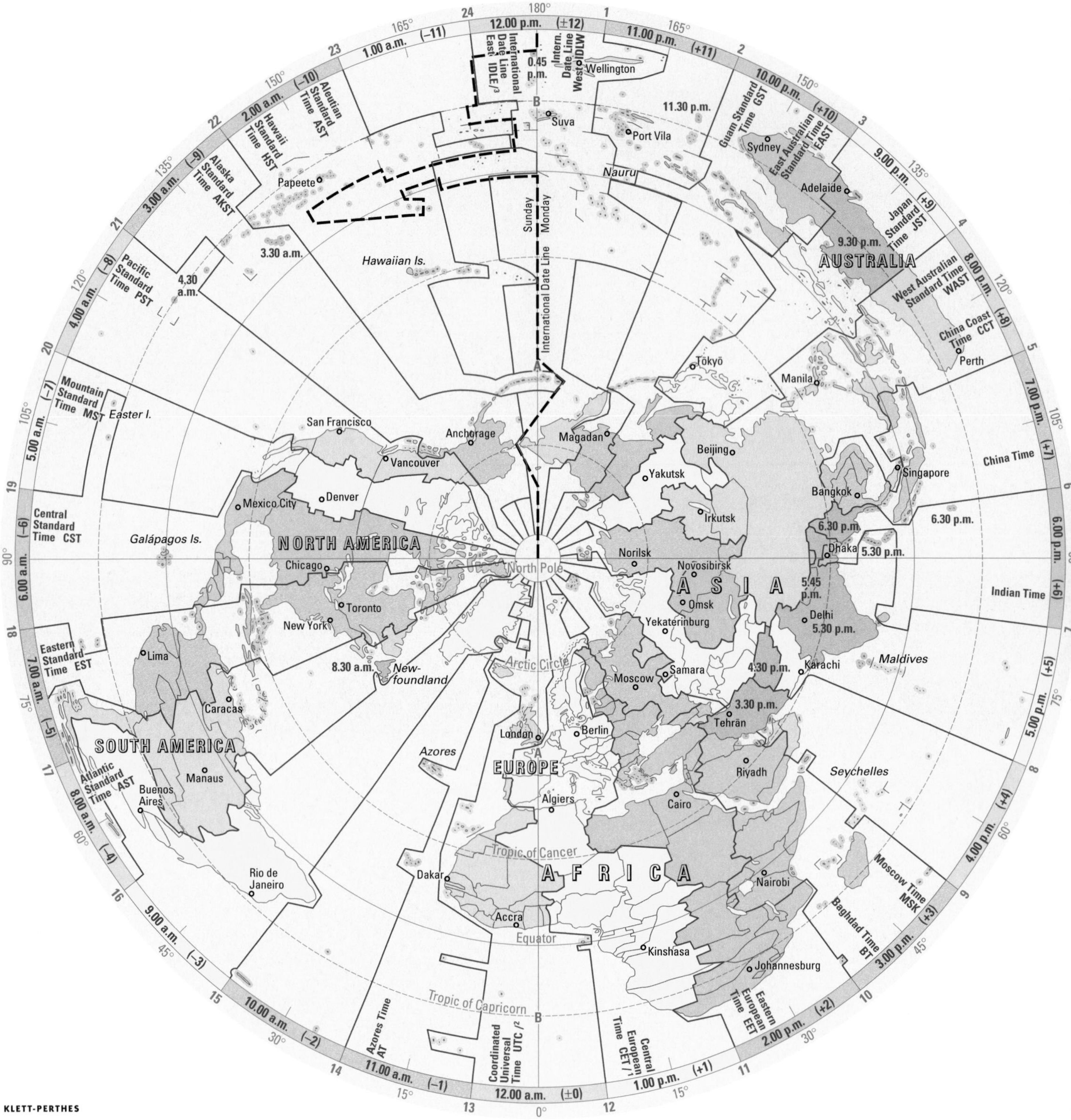

KLETT-PERTHES

Zonal time (disregarding daylight (saving) time/ summer time)

National time

1 Middle European Time MET
Middle European Winter Time MEWT

2 Western European Time WET
Greenwich Mean Time GMT

3 New Zealand Standard Time NZST

Countries with their own time (at 12 a.m. UTC/GMT):

Afghanistan 4.30 p.m.
Australia:
Northern Territory 9.30 p.m.
South Australia 9.30 p.m.
India 5.30 p.m.
Iran 3.30 p.m.
Canada:
Newfoundland 8.30 a.m.
Cocos Islands 6.30 p.m.
Marquesas Islands 3.30 a.m.
Myanmar (Burma) 6.30 p.m.
Nepal 5.45 p.m.
New Zealand:
Chatham Islands 0.45 a.m.
Norfolk Island 11.30 p.m.
Pitcairn Island 4.30 a.m.

Numbers in the outer circle of the map indicate the difference in hours between each zone and Coordinated Universal Time (UTC), also known as Greenwich Mean Time. New York ("−5") is five hours behind London ("0") but three hours ahead of San Francisco ("−8") and five hours ahead of Hawaii ("−10"). Coordinated Universal Time (UTC), which is observed in London and Accra, is also used throughout Antarctica. Since Earth turns around its axis once in 24 hours, you would expect to have 24 different time zones that follow the meridians. However the real delimitation of time zones on the land surface of the earth often follows political boundaries. Some countries and islands use a special national time. For example, the national time of India at 12 a.m. UTC is 4:30 p.m., while the time in Nepal to the north of India is 5:45 p.m. The International Date Line, which largely follows the 180th meridian, marks the line along which a calendar day has to be repeated if you cross it from west to east and skipped if you cross it from east to west.

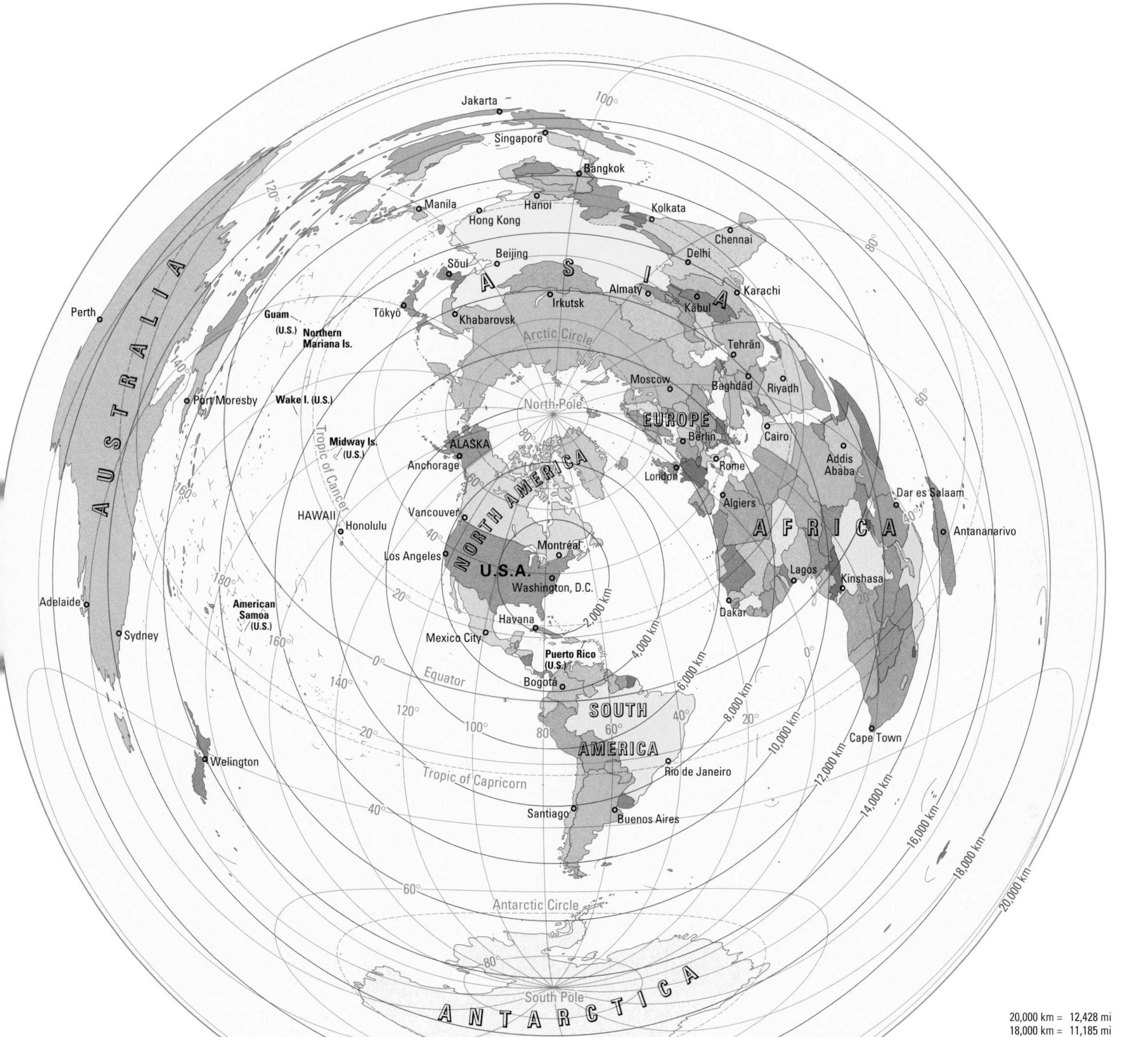

20,000 km =	12,428 mi
18,000 km =	11,185 mi
16,000 km =	9,942 mi
14,000 km =	8,699 mi
12,000 km =	7,456 mi
10,000 km =	6,214 mi
8,000 km =	4,971 mi
6,000 km =	3,728 mi
4,000 km =	2,485 mi
2,000 km =	1,243 mi

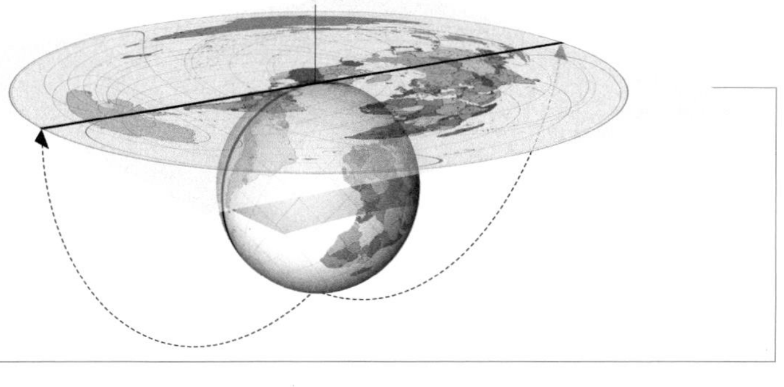

n this azimuthal equidistant projection, scale is constant along all straight lines through the map center or angent point (where the projection plane touches the globe). Because this projection is tangent at Washington, .C., where the latitude and longitude are 38.9° N and 77.0° W, you can easily compare distances from the ational capital to any other place on Earth. To help you estimate the distance, the map includes concentric ircles representing distances between 2,000 and 20,000 km, in 2,000 km increments (2,000 km is approximately ,240 miles.) The outer circle represents Washington's antipode, that is, the point farthest away, on the other ide of the world; in Washington's case, the antipode lies in the Indian Ocean, southwest of Australia. As with ther azimuthal projections, straight lines through the tangent point (map center) also represent great circles, which divide Earth into two equal-size parts. Put differently, each diameter through the center of the map equals he circumference of the globe (see figure on the right).

A 160° B 140° C 120° D 100° E 80° F 60° G 40° H 20° J
A R C T I C
Beaufort Sea
Baffin Bay
G. of Alaska
Hudson Bay
Labrador Sea
Arctic C
London
Toronto
Chicago
New York-Newark
Philadelphia
Madrid
Los Angeles-Long Beach-Santa Ana
Sargasso Sea
Tropic of Cancer
Gulf of Mexico
Miami
A T L A N T I C
Mexico City
Caribbean Sea
P A C I F I C
Bogotá
Equator
G. of Guine
Lima
Belo Horizonte
Rio de Janeiro
São Paulo
O C E A N
Tropic of Capricorn
Santiago
Buenos Aires
O C E A N
Scotia Sea
Antarctic Circle
Bellingshausen Sea
Weddell Sea
Amundsen Sea
80°
60°
40°
20°
0°
1
2
3
4
5
6
7
8
9
10

L 40° M 60° N 80° O 100° P 120° Q 140° R 160° S 180° T
O C E A N
Barents Sea
Kara Sea
Laptev Sea
East Siberian Sea
Bering Sea
Sea of Okhotsk
Sea of Japan
St. Petersburg
Moscow
İstanbul
Tehrān
Baghdād
Cairo
Riyadh
Red Sea
Karachi
Ahmadabad
Mumbai
Lahore
Delhi
Dhaka
Kolkata
Hyderabad
Bangalore
Chennai
Arabian Sea
Bay of Bengal
Beijing
Tianjin
Sŏul
Tōkyō
Ōsaka-Kobe
Wuhan
Shanghai
Hong Kong
Bangkok
South China Sea
Metro Manila
Hô Chi Minh City
Jakarta
Kinshasa
P A C I F I C
O C E A N
Equator
I N D I A N
O C E A N
Coral Sea
Tasman Sea
Ross Sea
80°
60°
40°
20°
0°
1
2
3
4
5
6
7
8
9
10
KLETT-PERTHES
Number of Persons
(per sq mile) (per km²)
Over 2,500 Over 1,000
1,250 to 2,500 500 to 1,000
250 to 1,250 100 to 500
62.5 to 250 25 to 100
12.5 to 62.5 5 to 25
2.5 to 12.5 1 to 5
Under 2.5 Under 1
Urban agglomerations
Over 10 millions inhabitants
5 to 10 millions inhabitants
L 40° M 60° N 80° O 100° P 120° Q 140° R 160° S 180° T

World: Population 2050 · Urbanization

1:160,000,000

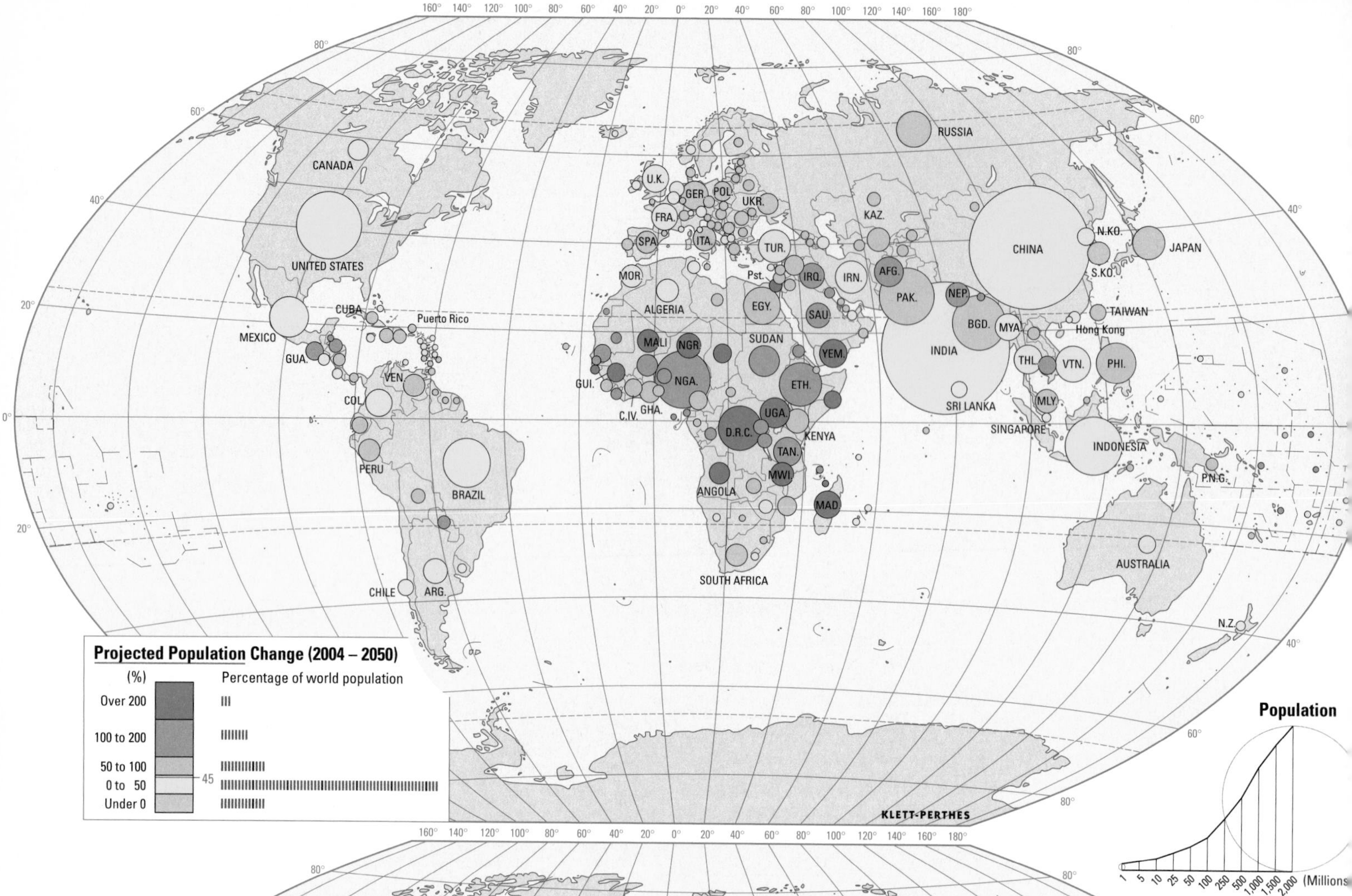

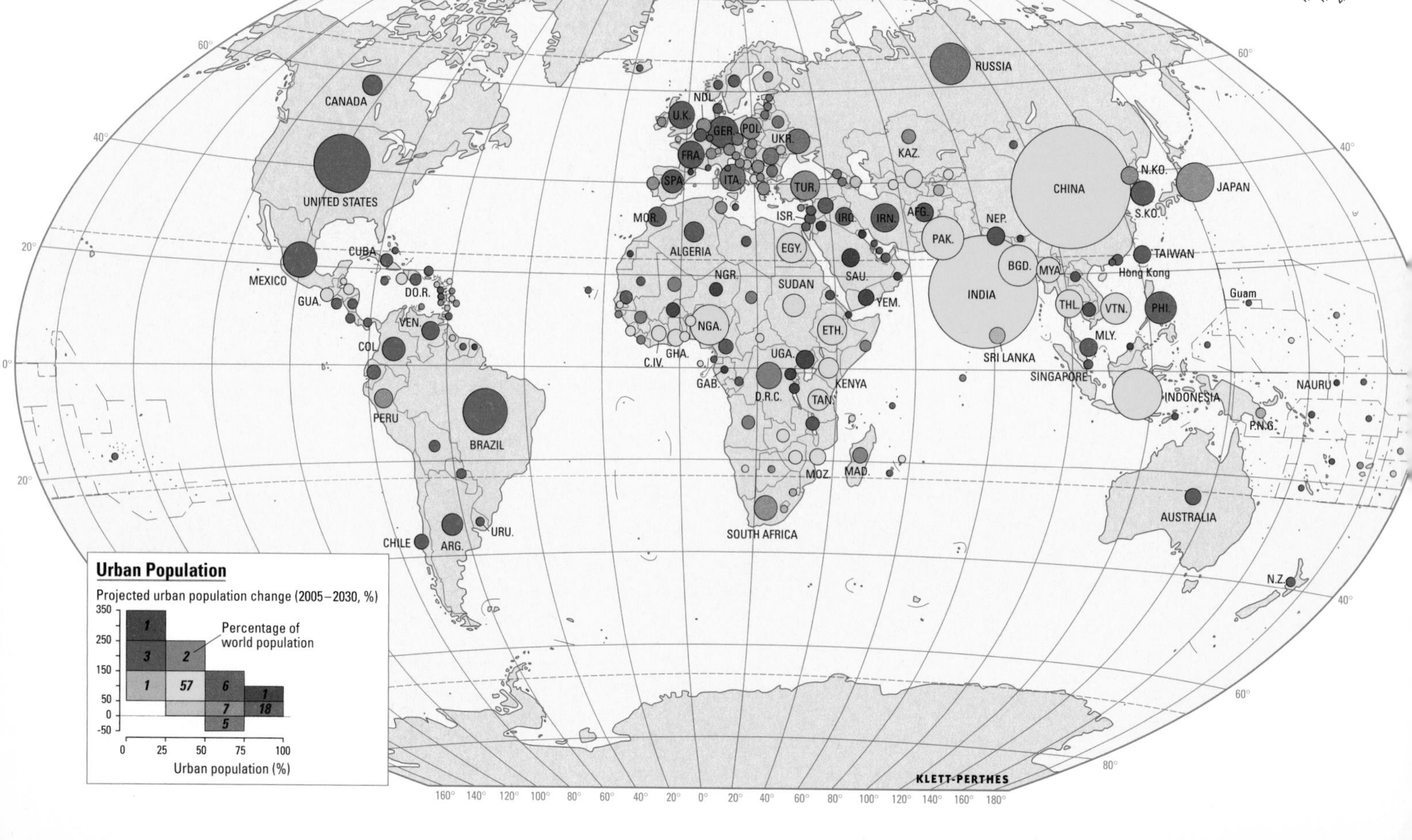

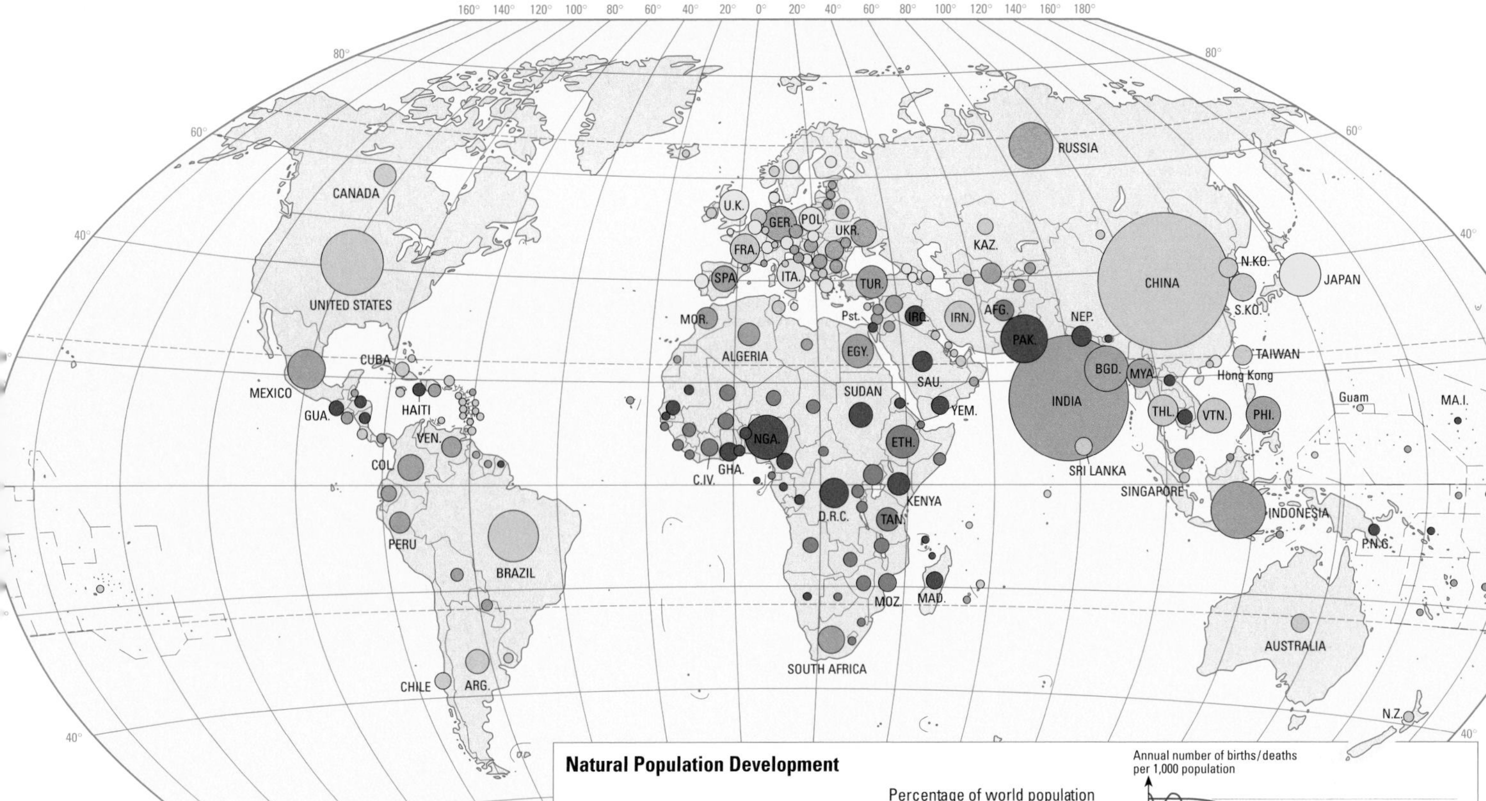
RUSSIA
CANADA
UNITED STATES
MEXICO
CUBA
HAITI
GUA.
VEN.
COL.
PERU
BRAZIL
CHILE
ARG.
U.K.
GER.
POL.
UKR.
FRA.
SPA.
ITA.
TUR.
KAZ.
MOR.
ALGERIA
EGY.
Pst.
IRQ.
IRN.
AFG.
PAK.
NEP.
SAU.
YEM.
SUDAN
ETH.
NGA.
GHA.
C.IV.
D.R.C.
KENYA
TAN.
MOZ.
MAD.
SOUTH AFRICA
CHINA
N.KO.
S.KO.
JAPAN
TAIWAN
Hong Kong
INDIA
BGD.
MYA.
SRI LANKA
THL.
VTN.
PHI.
SINGAPORE
INDONESIA
P.N.G.
Guam
MA.I.
AUSTRALIA
N.Z.
KLETT-PERTHES
Natural Population Development
Percentage of world population
High increase (BR > 30, DR > 15)
Highest increase (BR > 30, DR < 15)
Medium increase (BR = 20 to 30, DR < 15)
Low increase (BR < 20, DR < 15)
Stagnation (BR = DR)
Low decrease (BR < DR)
Annual number of births/deaths per 1,000 population
50
40
30
20
15
10
Birth Rate (BR)
Death Rate (DR)
Time

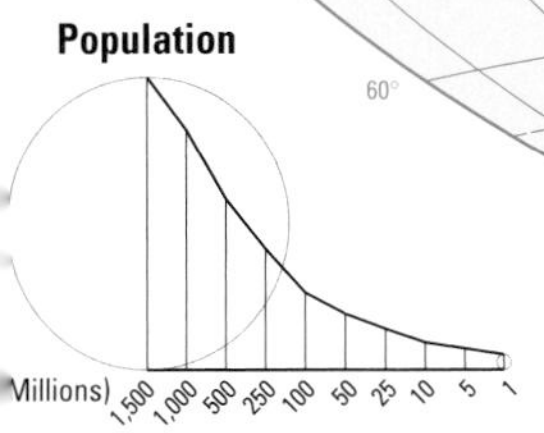
Population
(Millions)
1,500
1,000
500
250
100
50
25
10
5
1

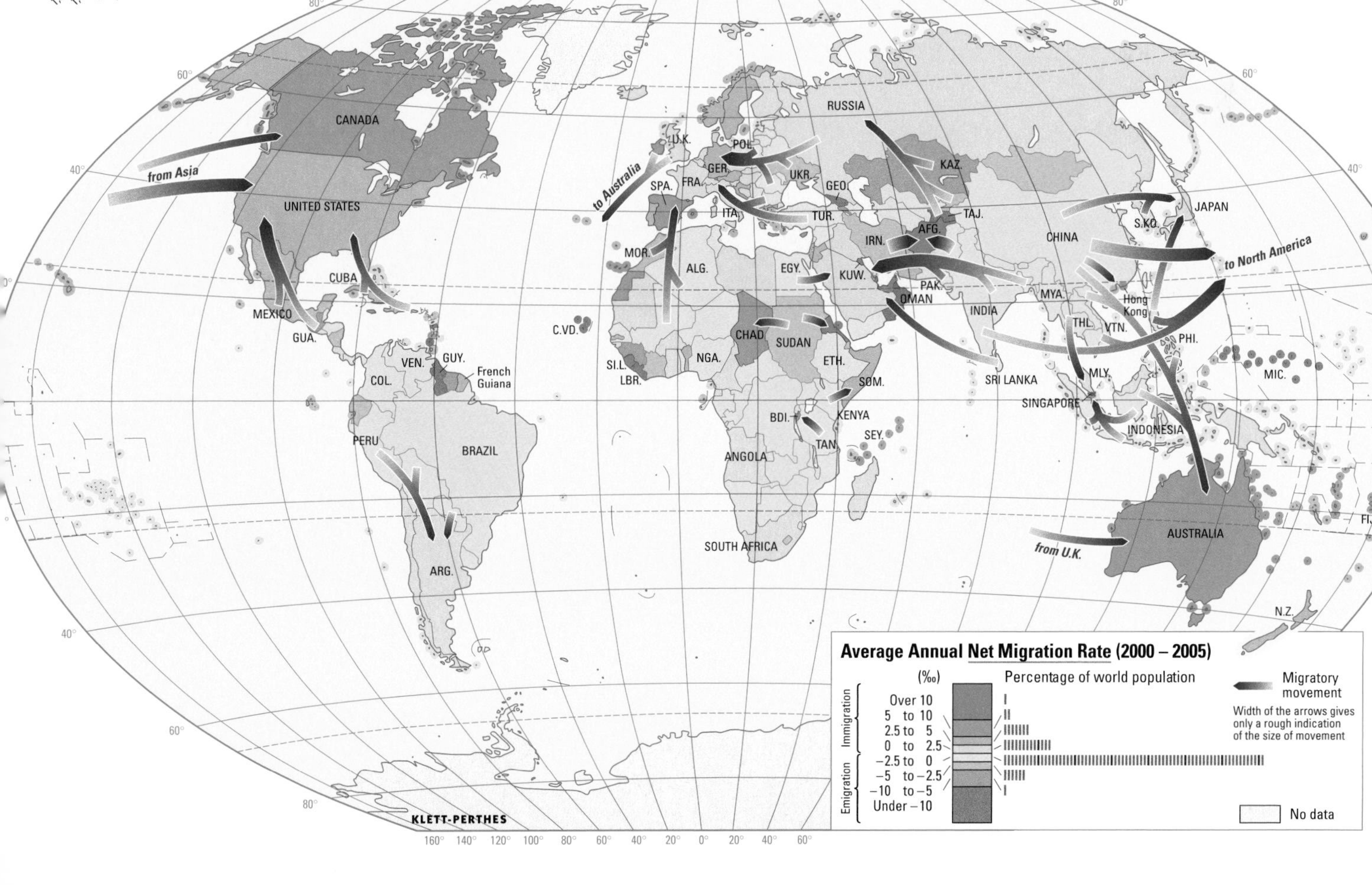
RUSSIA
CANADA
from Asia
UNITED STATES
MEXICO
CUBA
GUA.
VEN.
GUY.
French Guiana
COL.
PERU
BRAZIL
ARG.
to Australia
U.K.
POL.
GER.
SPA.
FRA.
UKR.
GEO.
ITA.
TUR.
KAZ.
TAJ.
MOR.
ALG.
EGY.
IRN.
AFG.
KUW.
PAK.
OMAN
C.V.D.
SI.L.
LBR.
NGA.
CHAD
SUDAN
ETH.
SOM.
KENYA
BDI.
TAN.
SEY.
ANGOLA
SOUTH AFRICA
CHINA
S.KO.
JAPAN
to North America
INDIA
MYA.
Hong Kong
THL.
VTN.
PHI.
SRI LANKA
MLY.
SINGAPORE
INDONESIA
MIC.
FIJI
AUSTRALIA
from U.K.
N.Z.
KLETT-PERTHES
Average Annual Net Migration Rate (2000 – 2005)
(‰)
Percentage of world population
Immigration
Over 10
5 to 10
2.5 to 5
0 to 2.5
Emigration
–2.5 to 0
–5 to –2.5
–10 to –5
Under –10
Migratory movement
Width of the arrows gives only a rough indication of the size of movement
No data

1:160,000,000

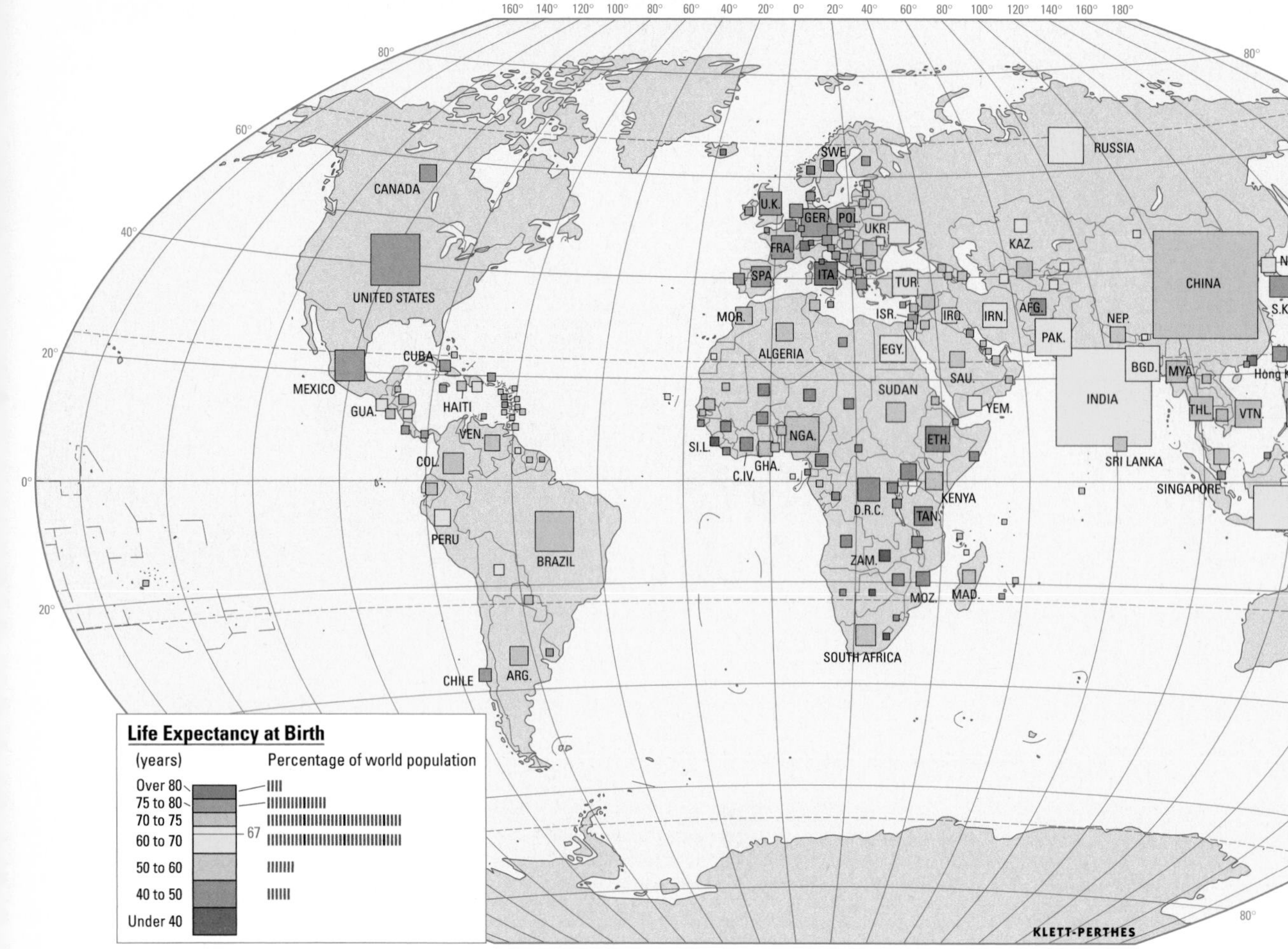
RUSSIA
CANADA
SWE.
U.K.
GER.
POL.
UKR.
FRA.
SPA.
ITA.
TUR.
KAZ.
N.KO.
JAPAN
CHINA
S.KO.
TAIWAN
Hong Kong
UNITED STATES
MEXICO
CUBA
HAITI
GUA.
VEN.
COL.
PERU
BRAZIL
CHILE
ARG.
MOR.
ALGERIA
ISR.
IRQ.
IRN.
AFG.
PAK.
NEP.
EGY.
SAU.
SUDAN
YEM.
INDIA
BGD.
MYA.
THL.
VTN.
PHI.
Guam
SRI LANKA
SINGAPORE
INDONESIA
T.L.
P.N.G.
S.L.
C.IV.
GHA.
NGA.
ETH.
KENYA
D.R.C.
TAN.
ZAM.
MOZ.
MAD.
SOUTH AFRICA
AUSTRALIA
N.Z.
KLETT-PERTHES
Life Expectancy at Birth
(years)
Percentage of world population
Over 80
75 to 80
70 to 75
67
60 to 70
50 to 60
40 to 50
Under 40

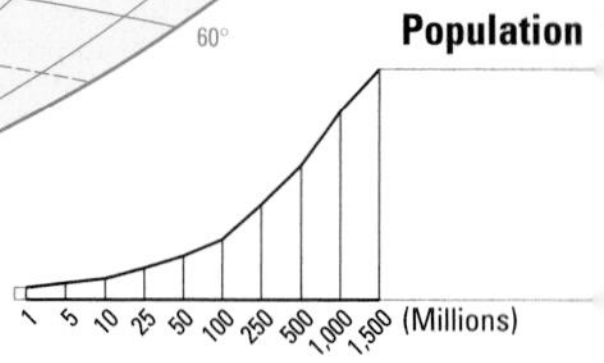
Population
1
5
10
25
50
100
250
500
1,000
1,500
(Millions)

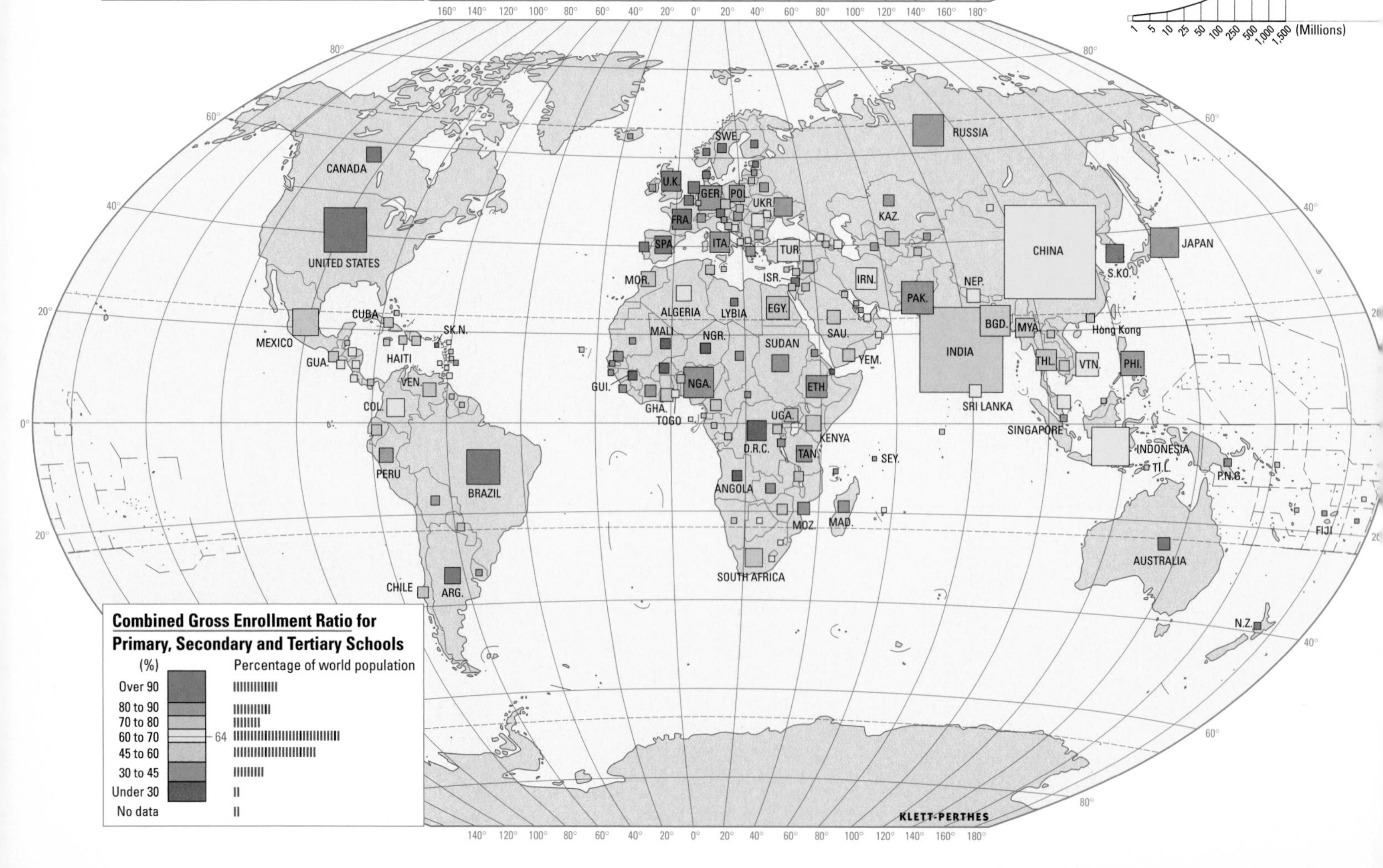
RUSSIA
CANADA
SWE.
U.K.
GER.
POL.
UKR.
FRA.
SPA.
ITA.
TUR.
KAZ.
CHINA
JAPAN
S.KO.
Hong Kong
UNITED STATES
MEXICO
CUBA
SK.N.
HAITI
GUA.
VEN.
COL.
PERU
BRAZIL
CHILE
ARG.
MOR.
ALGERIA
LYBIA
ISR.
IRN.
PAK.
NEP.
EGY.
SAU.
MALI
NGR.
SUDAN
YEM.
INDIA
BGD.
MYA.
THL.
VTN.
PHI.
SRI LANKA
SINGAPORE
INDONESIA
T.L.
P.N.G.
FIJI
GUI.
GHA.
TOGO
NGA.
ETH.
UGA.
KENYA
SEY.
D.R.C.
TAN.
ANGOLA
MOZ.
MAD.
SOUTH AFRICA
AUSTRALIA
N.Z.
KLETT-PERTHES
Combined Gross Enrollment Ratio for Primary, Secondary and Tertiary Schools
(%)
Percentage of world population
Over 90
80 to 90
70 to 80
60 to 70
64
45 to 60
30 to 45
Under 30
No data

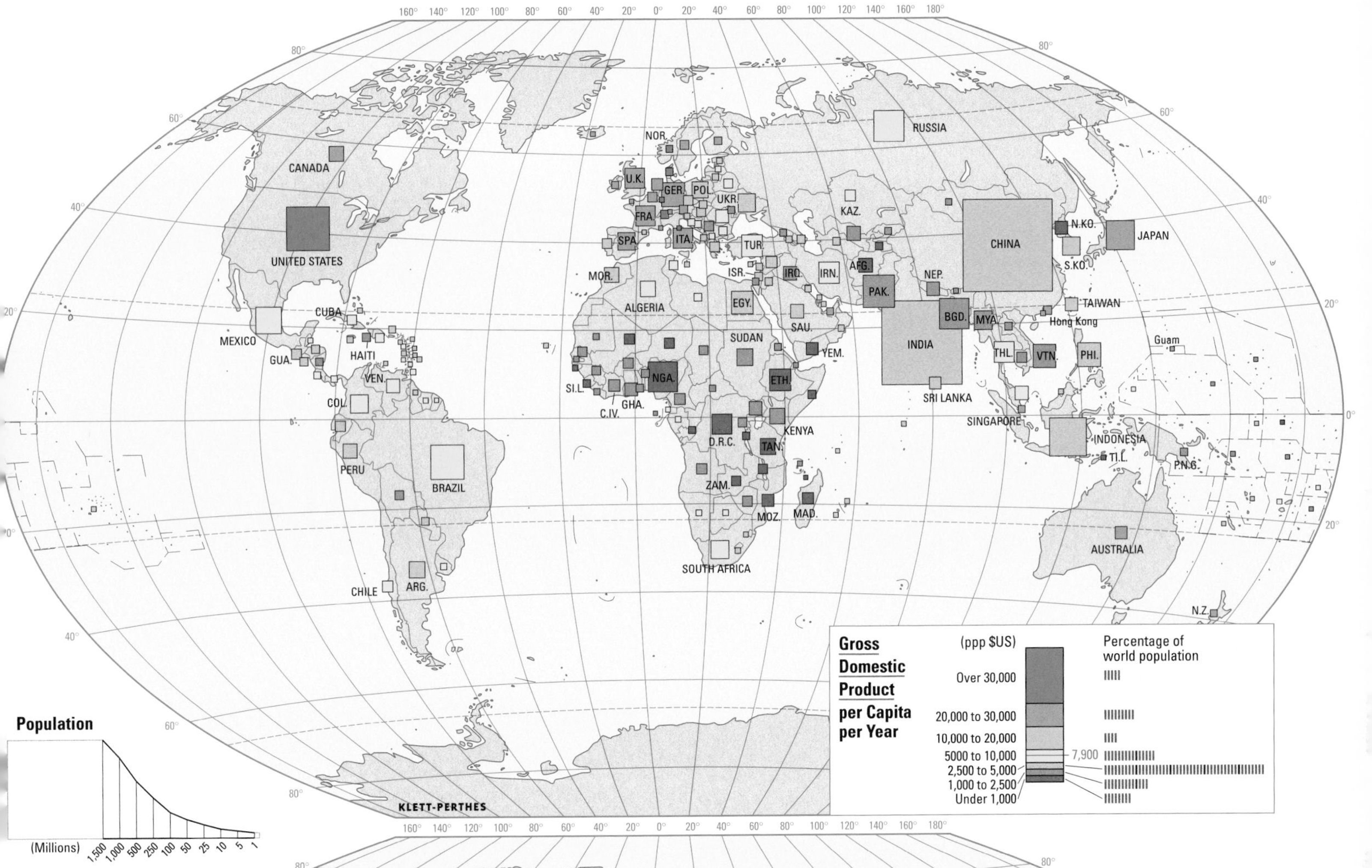
RUSSIA
CANADA
NOR.
U.K.
GER.
POL.
UKR.
FRA.
KAZ.
SPA.
ITA.
TUR.
N.KO.
JAPAN
CHINA
UNITED STATES
MOR.
ISR.
IRQ.
IRN.
AFG.
S.KO.
NEP.
PAK.
ALGERIA
EGY.
TAIWAN
CUBA
SAU.
BGD.
MYA.
Hong Kong
MEXICO
HAITI
SUDAN
YEM.
INDIA
GUA.
VEN.
NGA.
ETH.
THL.
VTN.
PHI.
Guam
SI.L.
COL.
GHA.
C.IV.
SRI LANKA
SINGAPORE
KENYA
D.R.C.
INDONESIA
TAN.
T.L.
PERU
P.N.G.
BRAZIL
ZAM.
MOZ.
MAD.
AUSTRALIA
SOUTH AFRICA
CHILE
ARG.
N.Z.
KLETT-PERTHES
Gross Domestic Product per Capita per Year
(ppp $US)
Over 30,000
20,000 to 30,000
10,000 to 20,000
5000 to 10,000
7,900
2,500 to 5,000
1,000 to 2,500
Under 1,000
Percentage of world population
Population
(Millions)
1,500
1,000
500
250
100
50
25
10
5
1

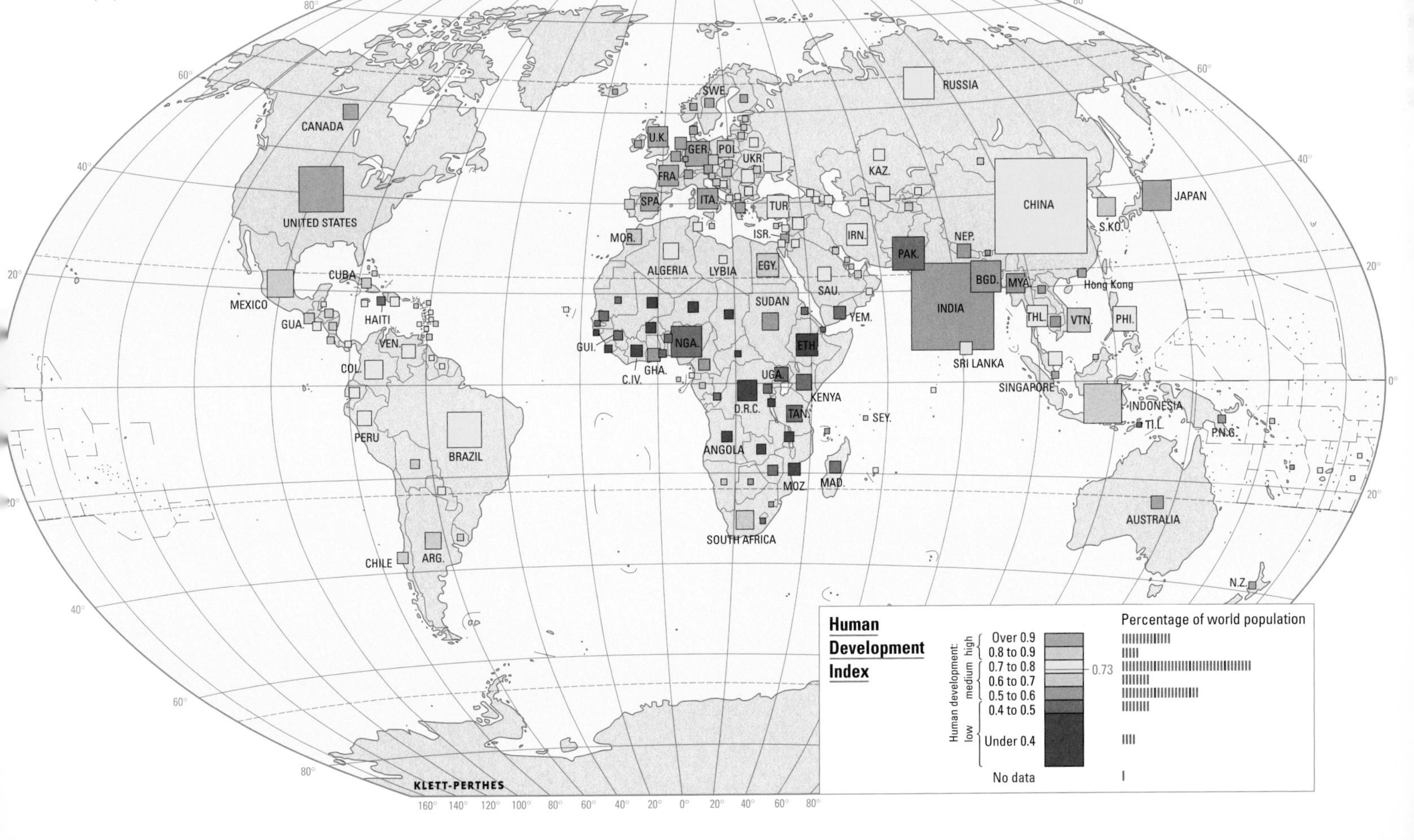
RUSSIA
CANADA
SWE.
U.K.
GER.
POL.
UKR.
FRA.
KAZ.
SPA.
ITA.
TUR.
CHINA
JAPAN
UNITED STATES
MOR.
ISR.
IRN.
S.KO.
NEP.
PAK.
ALGERIA
LYBIA
EGY.
CUBA
SAU.
BGD.
MYA.
Hong Kong
MEXICO
HAITI
SUDAN
YEM.
INDIA
GUA.
VEN.
GUI.
NGA.
ETH.
THL.
VTN.
PHI.
COL.
GHA.
C.IV.
SRI LANKA
UGA.
SINGAPORE
KENYA
D.R.C.
INDONESIA
TAN.
SEY.
T.L.
P.N.G.
PERU
ANGOLA
BRAZIL
MOZ.
MAD.
AUSTRALIA
SOUTH AFRICA
CHILE
ARG.
N.Z.
KLETT-PERTHES
Human Development Index
Human development:
high
medium
low
Over 0.9
0.8 to 0.9
0.7 to 0.8
0.73
0.6 to 0.7
0.5 to 0.6
0.4 to 0.5
Under 0.4
No data
Percentage of world population

1:160,000,000

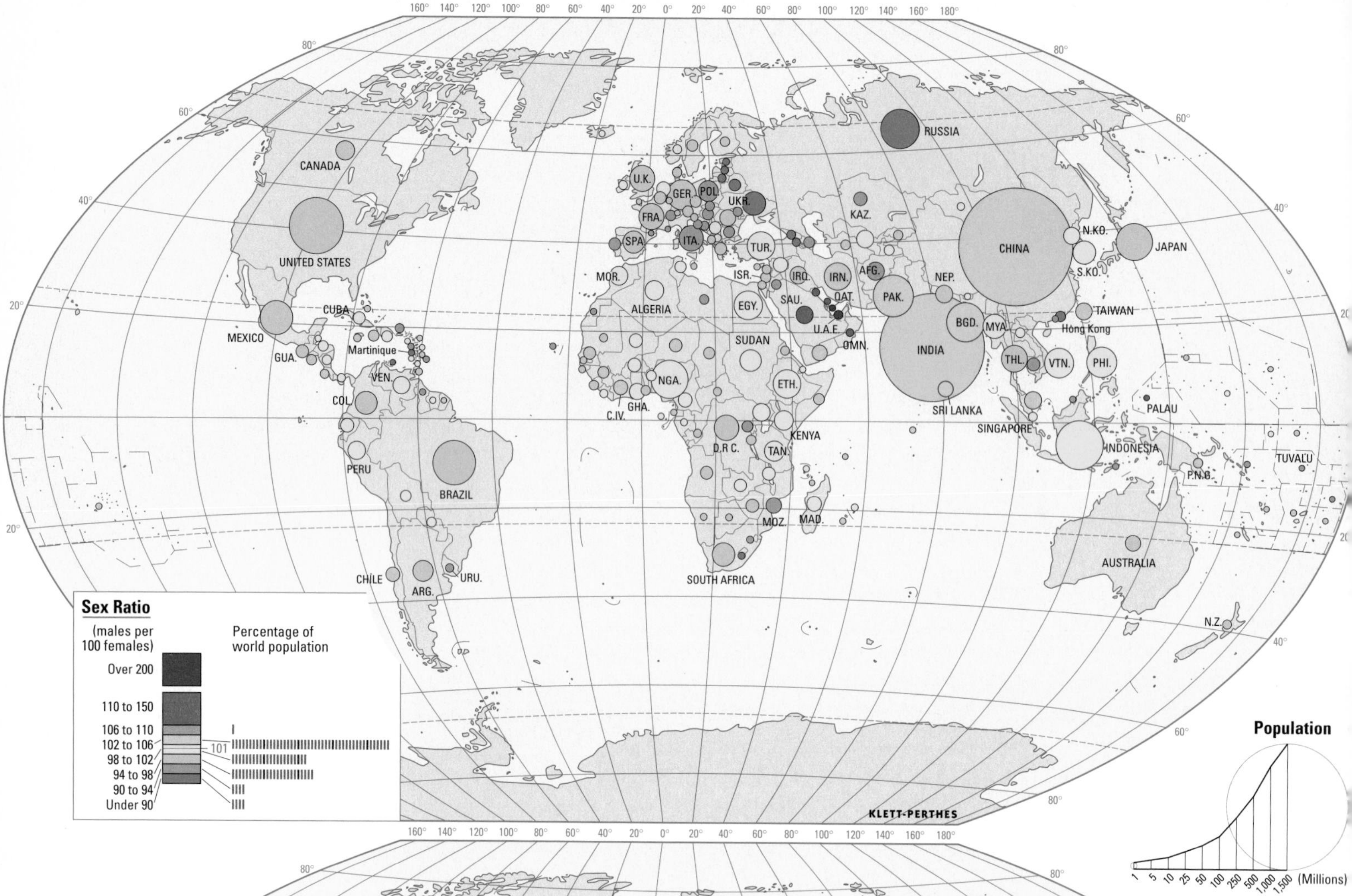

RUSSIA
CANADA
U.K.
GER.
POL.
UKR.
FRA.
KAZ.
N.KO.
JAPAN
SPA.
ITA.
TUR.
CHINA
UNITED STATES
S.KO.
MOR.
ISR.
IRQ.
IRN.
AFG.
NEP.
SAU.
QAT.
PAK.
EGY.
ALGERIA
TAIWAN
CUBA
U.A.E.
BGD.
MYA.
Hong Kong
MEXICO
OMN.
Martinique
SUDAN
INDIA
GUA.
THL.
VTN.
PHI.
VEN.
NGA.
ETH.
COL.
GHA.
C.I.V.
SRI LANKA
PALAU
SINGAPORE
KENYA
D.R.C.
TAN.
INDONESIA
TUVALU
PERU
P.N.G.
BRAZIL
MOZ.
MAD.
AUSTRALIA
CHILE
URU.
ARG.
SOUTH AFRICA
N.Z.
Sex Ratio
(males per 100 females)
Percentage of world population
Over 200
110 to 150
106 to 110
102 to 106
101
98 to 102
94 to 98
90 to 94
Under 90
KLETT-PERTHES
Population
1
5
10
25
50
100
250
500
1,000
1,500
(Millions)

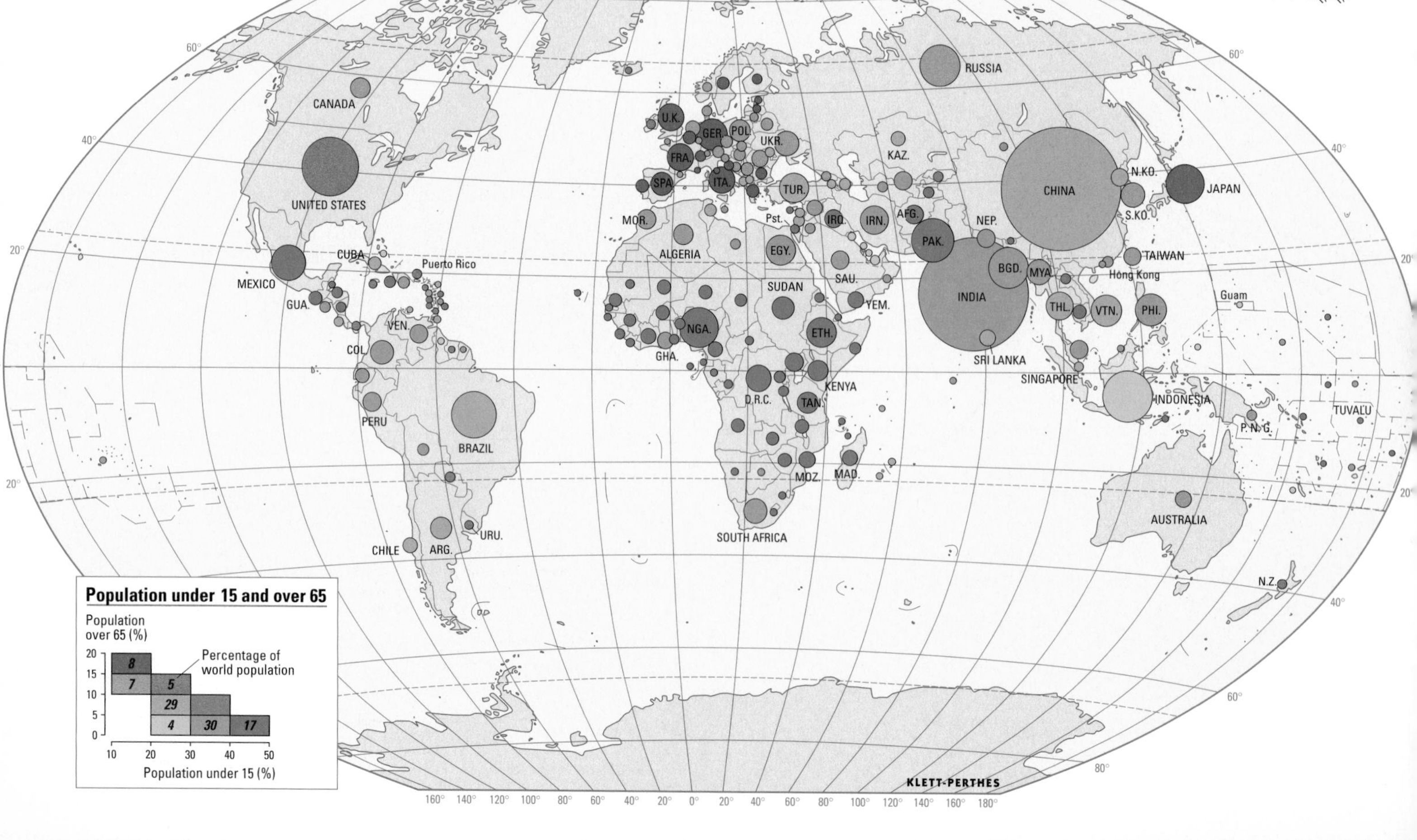

RUSSIA
CANADA
U.K.
GER.
POL.
UKR.
FRA.
KAZ.
N.KO.
JAPAN
SPA.
ITA.
TUR.
CHINA
UNITED STATES
S.KO.
MOR.
Pst.
IRQ.
IRN.
AFG.
NEP.
PAK.
EGY.
ALGERIA
TAIWAN
CUBA
SAU.
BGD.
MYA.
Puerto Rico
Hong Kong
MEXICO
SUDAN
INDIA
GUA.
YEM.
Guam
THL.
VTN.
PHI.
VEN.
NGA.
ETH.
COL.
GHA.
SRI LANKA
SINGAPORE
KENYA
D.R.C.
TAN.
INDONESIA
TUVALU
PERU
P.N.G.
BRAZIL
MOZ.
MAD.
AUSTRALIA
URU.
CHILE
ARG.
SOUTH AFRICA
N.Z.
Population under 15 and over 65
Population over 65 (%)
Percentage of world population
8
7
5
29
4
30
17
Population under 15 (%)
KLETT-PERTHES

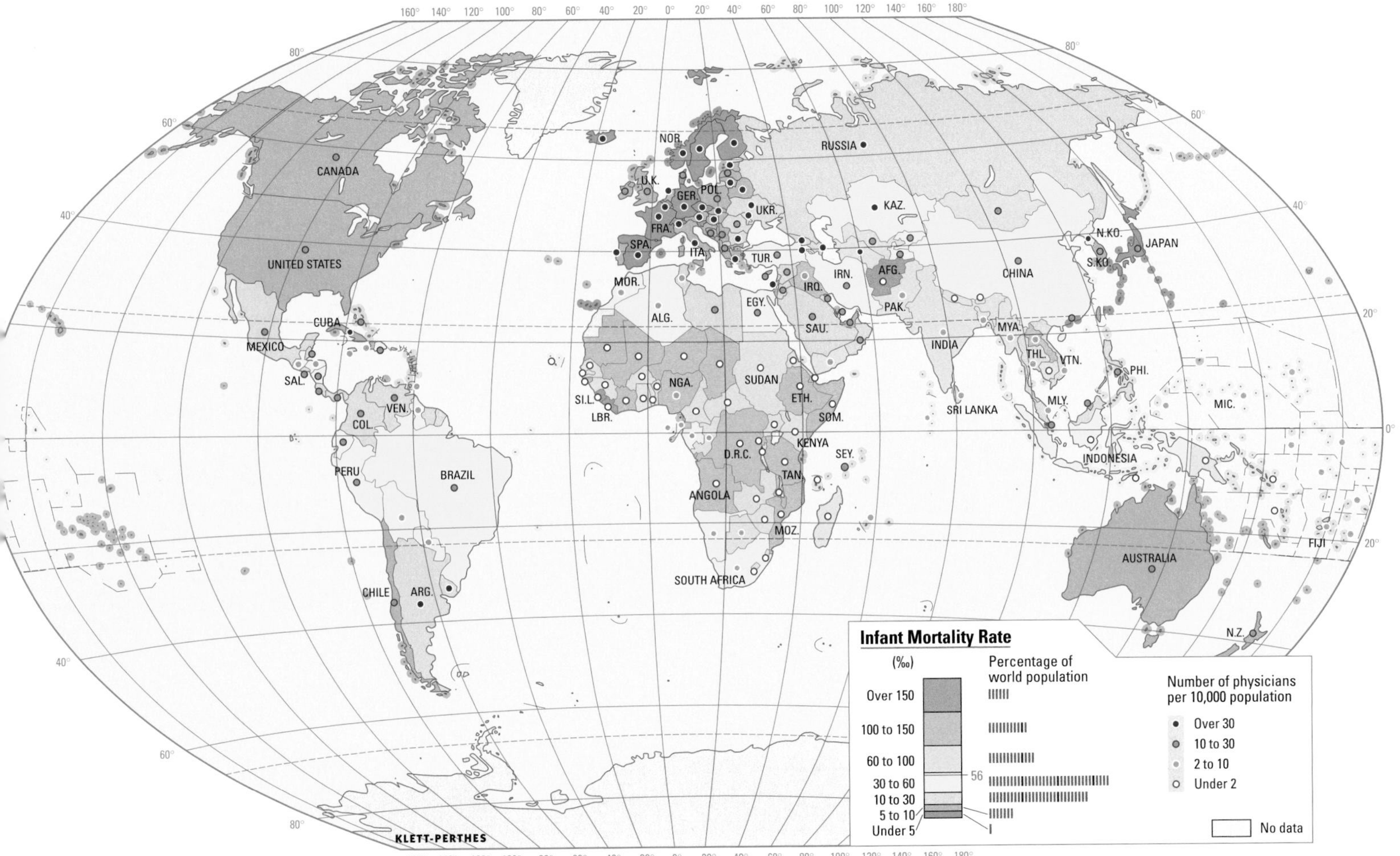

CANADA
UNITED STATES
MEXICO
CUBA
SAL.
VEN.
COL.
PERU
BRAZIL
CHILE
ARG.
NOR.
U.K.
GER.
POL.
FRA.
SPA.
ITA.
UKR.
RUSSIA
KAZ.
TUR.
IRN.
IRQ.
AFG.
PAK.
EGY.
SAU.
MOR.
ALG.
NGA.
SUDAN
ETH.
SOM.
S.L.
LBR.
KENYA
D.R.C.
TAN.
SEY.
ANGOLA
MOZ.
SOUTH AFRICA
INDIA
SRI LANKA
CHINA
MYA.
THL.
VTN.
MLY.
INDONESIA
PHI.
N.KO.
S.KO.
JAPAN
MIC.
AUSTRALIA
FIJI
N.Z.
KLETT-PERTHES
Infant Mortality Rate
(‰)
Over 150
100 to 150
60 to 100
30 to 60
10 to 30
5 to 10
Under 5
56
Percentage of world population
Number of physicians per 10,000 population
Over 30
10 to 30
2 to 10
Under 2
No data

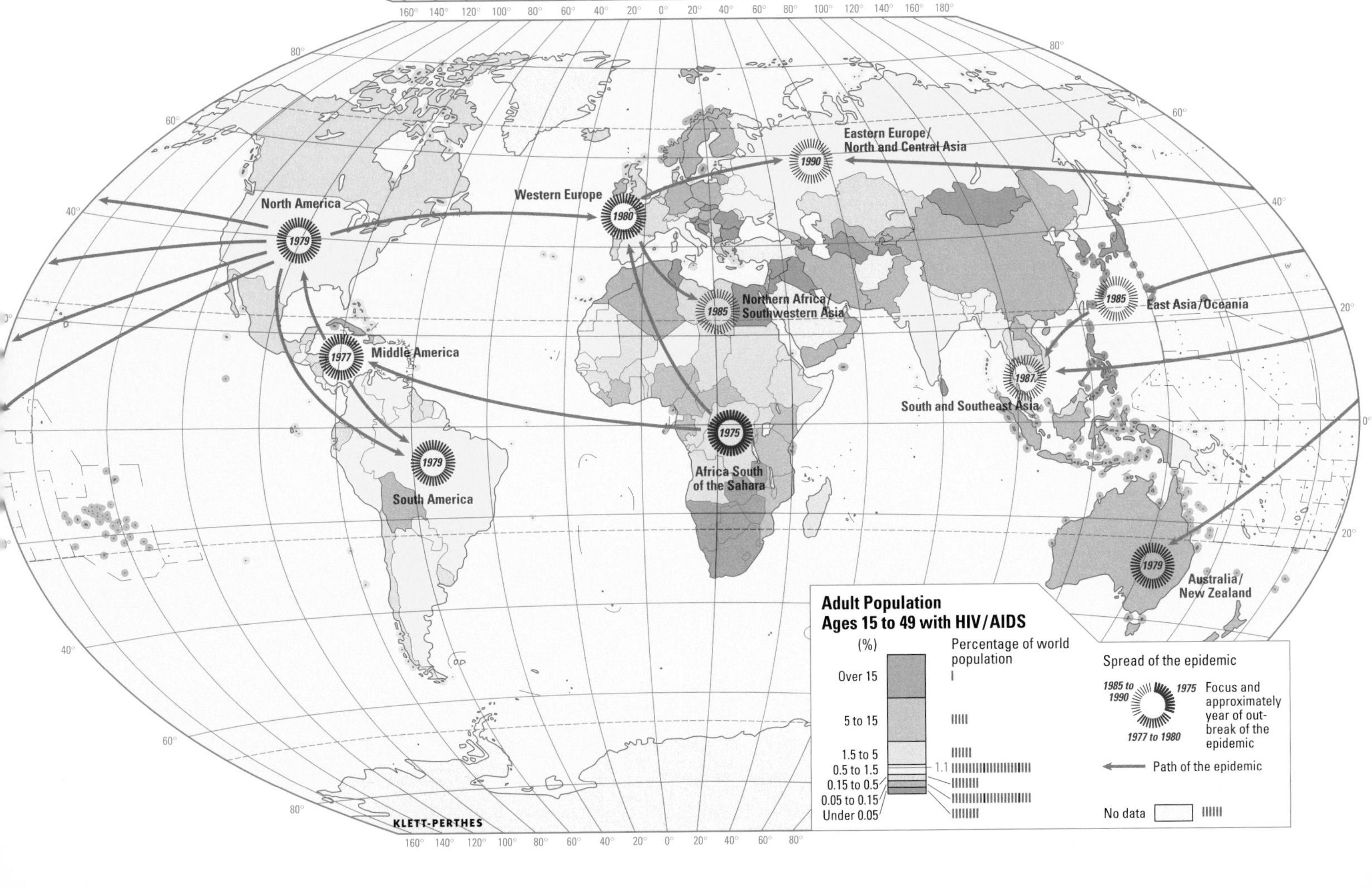

North America
1979
Middle America
1977
South America
1979
Western Europe
1980
Eastern Europe/ North and Central Asia
1990
Northern Africa/ Southwestern Asia
1985
Africa South of the Sahara
1975
East Asia/Oceania
1985
South and Southeast Asia
1987
Australia/ New Zealand
1979
KLETT-PERTHES
Adult Population Ages 15 to 49 with HIV/AIDS
(%)
Over 15
5 to 15
1.5 to 5
0.5 to 1.5
0.15 to 0.5
0.05 to 0.15
Under 0.05
1.1
Percentage of world population
Spread of the epidemic
1985 to 1990
1975
1977 to 1980
Focus and approximately year of outbreak of the epidemic
Path of the epidemic
No data

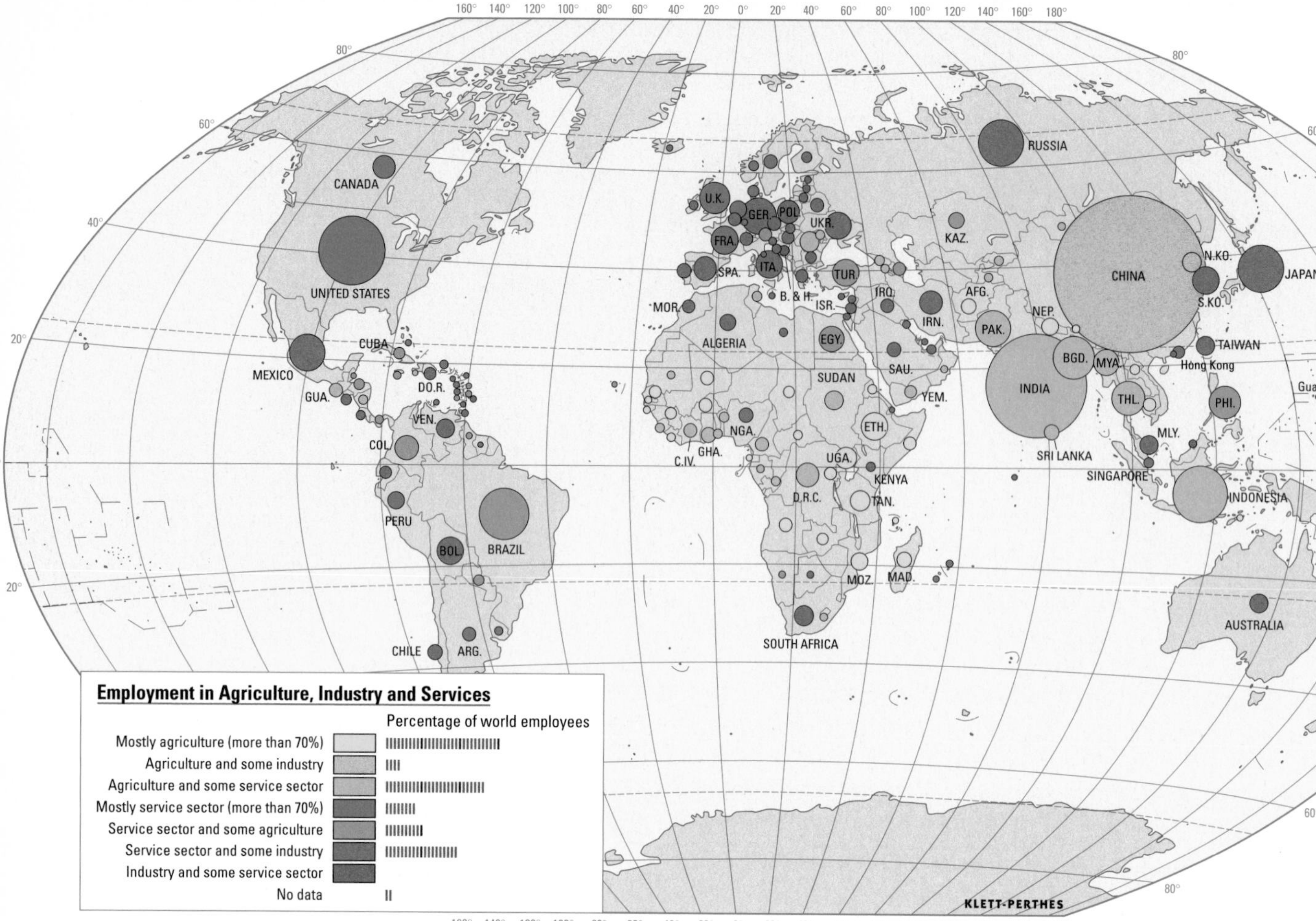
Employment in Agriculture, Industry and Services
Percentage of world employees
Mostly agriculture (more than 70%)
Agriculture and some industry
Agriculture and some service sector
Mostly service sector (more than 70%)
Service sector and some agriculture
Service sector and some industry
Industry and some service sector
No data
RUSSIA
CANADA
UNITED STATES
MEXICO
CUBA
GUA.
DO.R.
VEN.
COL.
PERU
BRAZIL
BOL.
CHILE
ARG.
U.K.
GER.
POL.
UKR.
FRA.
SPA.
ITA.
B. & H.
TUR.
MOR.
ALGERIA
EGY.
ISR.
IRQ.
IRN.
SAU.
YEM.
SUDAN
ETH.
NGA.
GHA.
C.IV.
UGA.
KENYA
TAN.
D.R.C.
MOZ.
MAD.
SOUTH AFRICA
KAZ.
AFG.
PAK.
NEP.
INDIA
BGD.
MYA.
SRI LANKA
CHINA
N.KO.
S.KO.
JAPAN
TAIWAN
Hong Kong
THL.
PHI.
MLY.
SINGAPORE
INDONESIA
Guam
P.N.G.
AUSTRALIA
N.Z.
KLETT-PERTHES

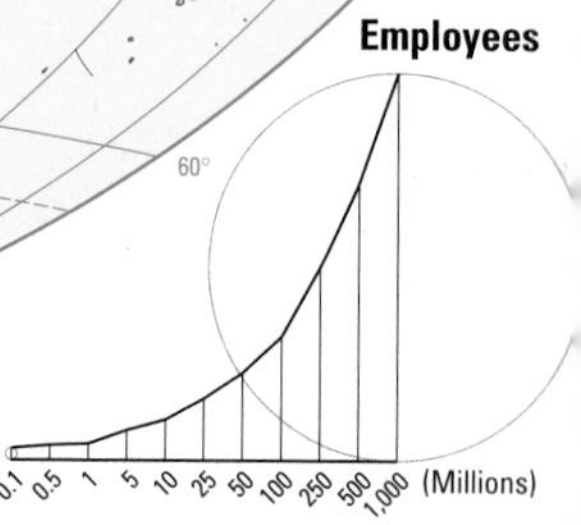
Employees
0.1 0.5 1 5 10 25 50 100 250 500 1,000 (Millions)

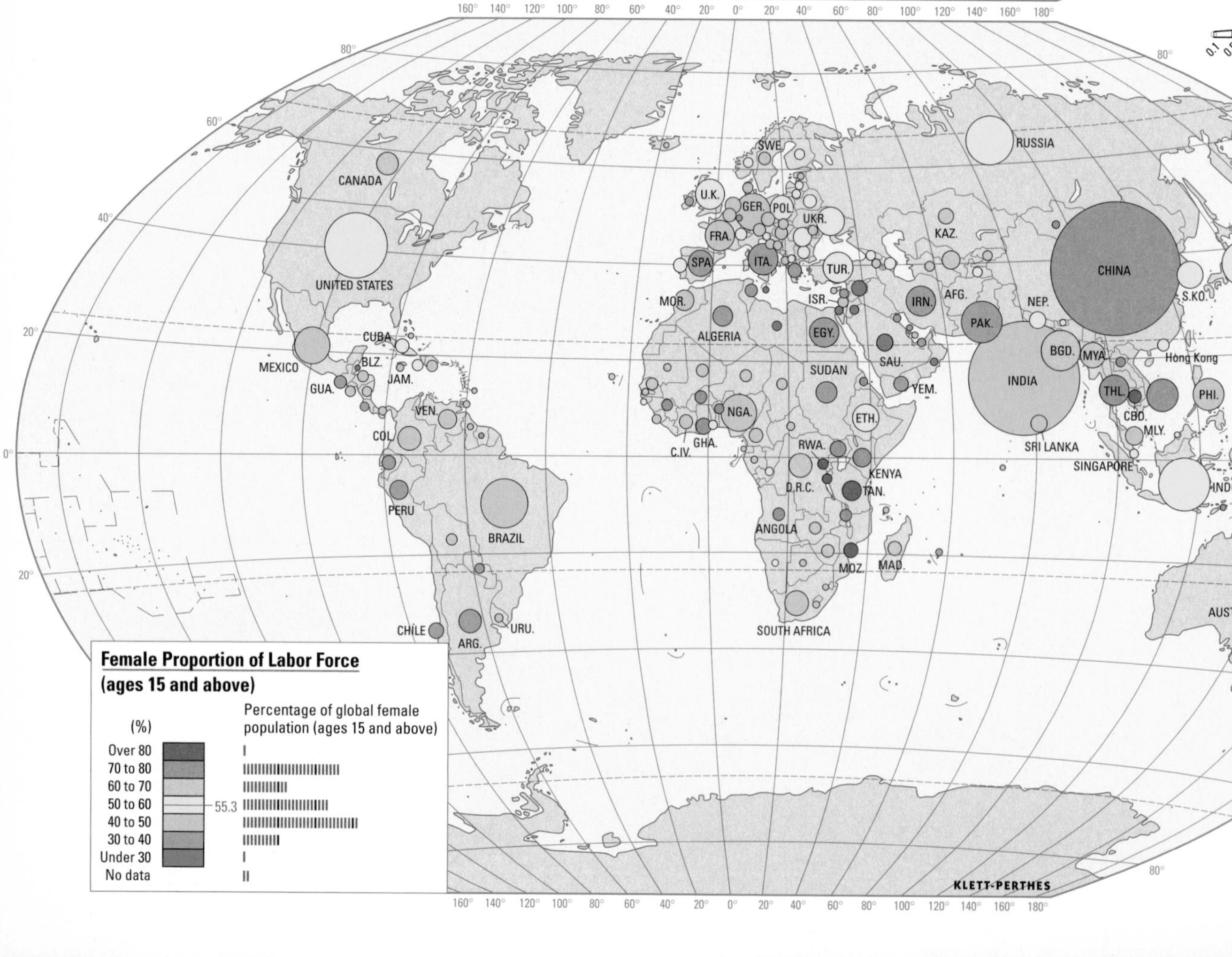
Female Proportion of Labor Force (ages 15 and above)
(%)
Percentage of global female population (ages 15 and above)
Over 80
70 to 80
60 to 70
50 to 60
55.3
40 to 50
30 to 40
Under 30
No data
RUSSIA
SWE.
CANADA
UNITED STATES
MEXICO
CUBA
BLZ.
JAM.
GUA.
VEN.
COL.
PERU
BRAZIL
CHILE
ARG.
URU.
U.K.
GER.
POL.
UKR.
FRA.
SPA.
ITA.
TUR.
MOR.
ALGERIA
EGY.
ISR.
IRN.
SAU.
YEM.
SUDAN
ETH.
NGA.
GHA.
C.IV.
RWA.
KENYA
TAN.
D.R.C.
ANGOLA
MOZ.
MAD.
SOUTH AFRICA
KAZ.
AFG.
PAK.
NEP.
INDIA
BGD.
MYA.
SRI LANKA
CHINA
S.KO.
JAPAN
Hong Kong
THL.
CBO.
PHI.
MLY.
SINGAPORE
INDONESIA
SO.I.
P.N.G.
AUSTRALIA
N.Z.
KLETT-PERTHES

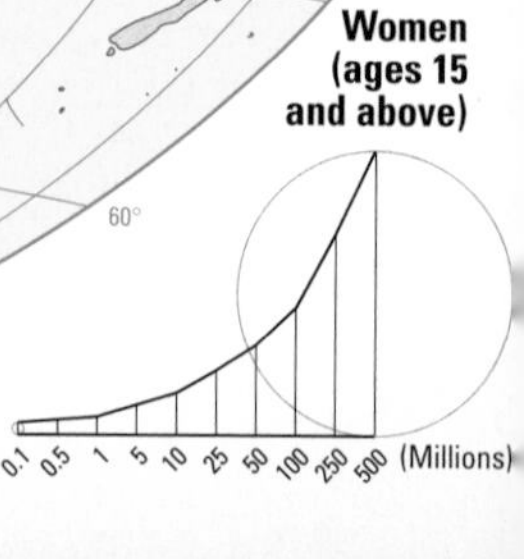
Women (ages 15 and above)
0.1 0.5 1 5 10 25 50 100 250 500 (Millions)

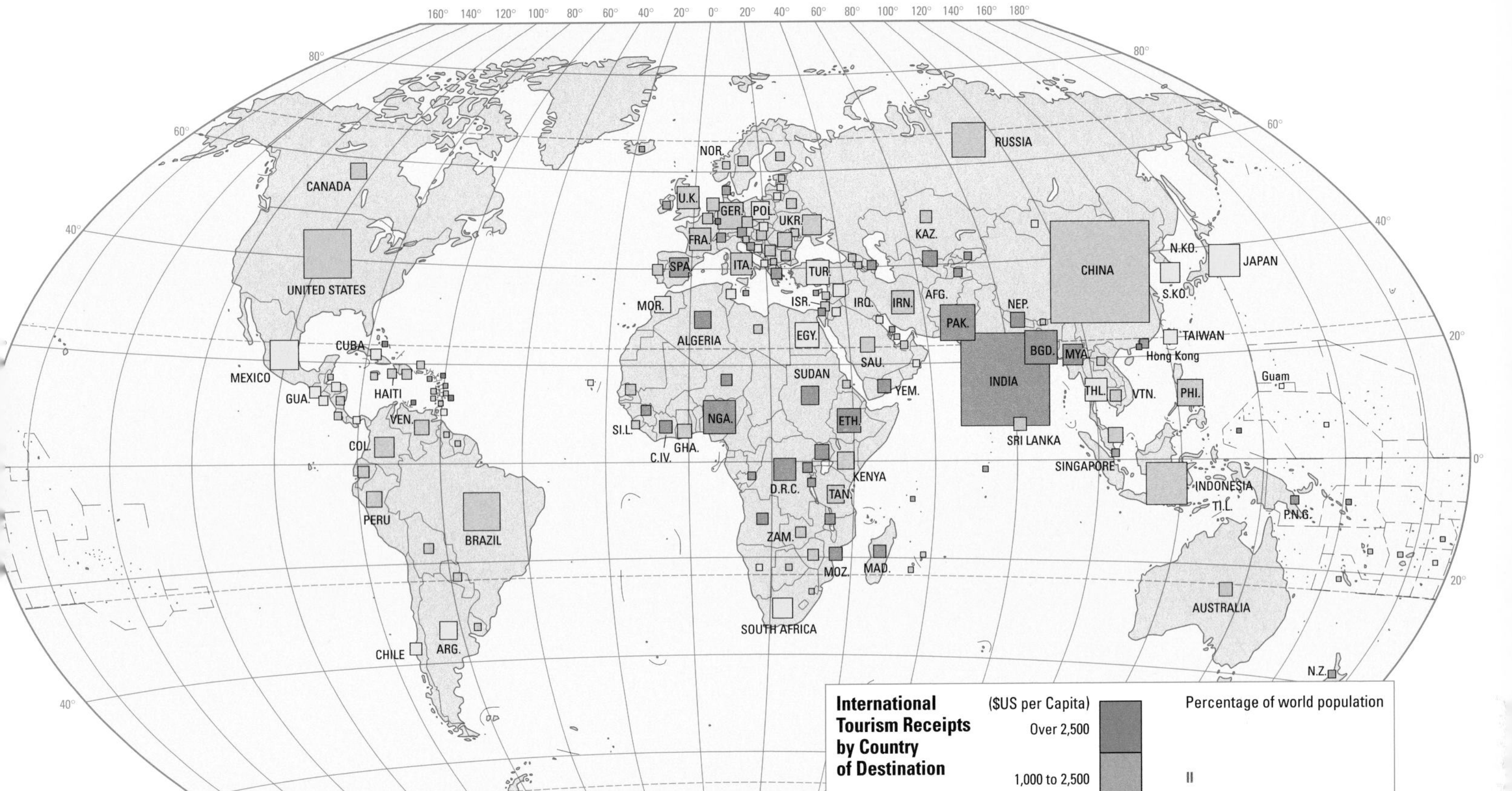
RUSSIA
NOR.
CANADA
U.K.
GER.
POL.
UKR.
KAZ.
FRA.
SPA.
ITA.
TUR.
CHINA
N.KO.
JAPAN
S.KO.
UNITED STATES
MOR.
ISR.
IRQ.
IRN.
AFG.
NEP.
PAK.
ALGERIA
EGY.
TAIWAN
Hong Kong
CUBA
SAU.
BGD.
MYA.
MEXICO
INDIA
SUDAN
YEM.
Guam
GUA.
HAITI
THL.
VTN.
PHI.
VEN.
SI.L.
NGA.
ETH.
C.IV.
GHA.
SRI LANKA
COL.
SINGAPORE
KENYA
D.R.C.
INDONESIA
TAN.
T.L.
PERU
P.N.G.
BRAZIL
ZAM.
MOZ.
MAD.
AUSTRALIA
SOUTH AFRICA
CHILE
ARG.
N.Z.
KLETT-PERTHES
International Tourism Receipts by Country of Destination
($US per Capita)
Over 2,500
1,000 to 2,500
250 to 1,000
50 to 250
10 to 50
Under 10
No data
95,7
Percentage of world population

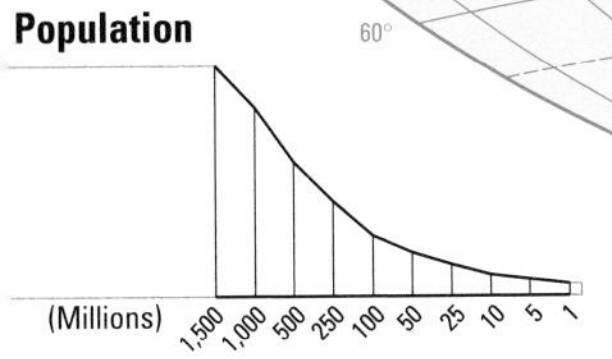
Population
(Millions)
1,500
1,000
500
250
100
50
25
10
5
1

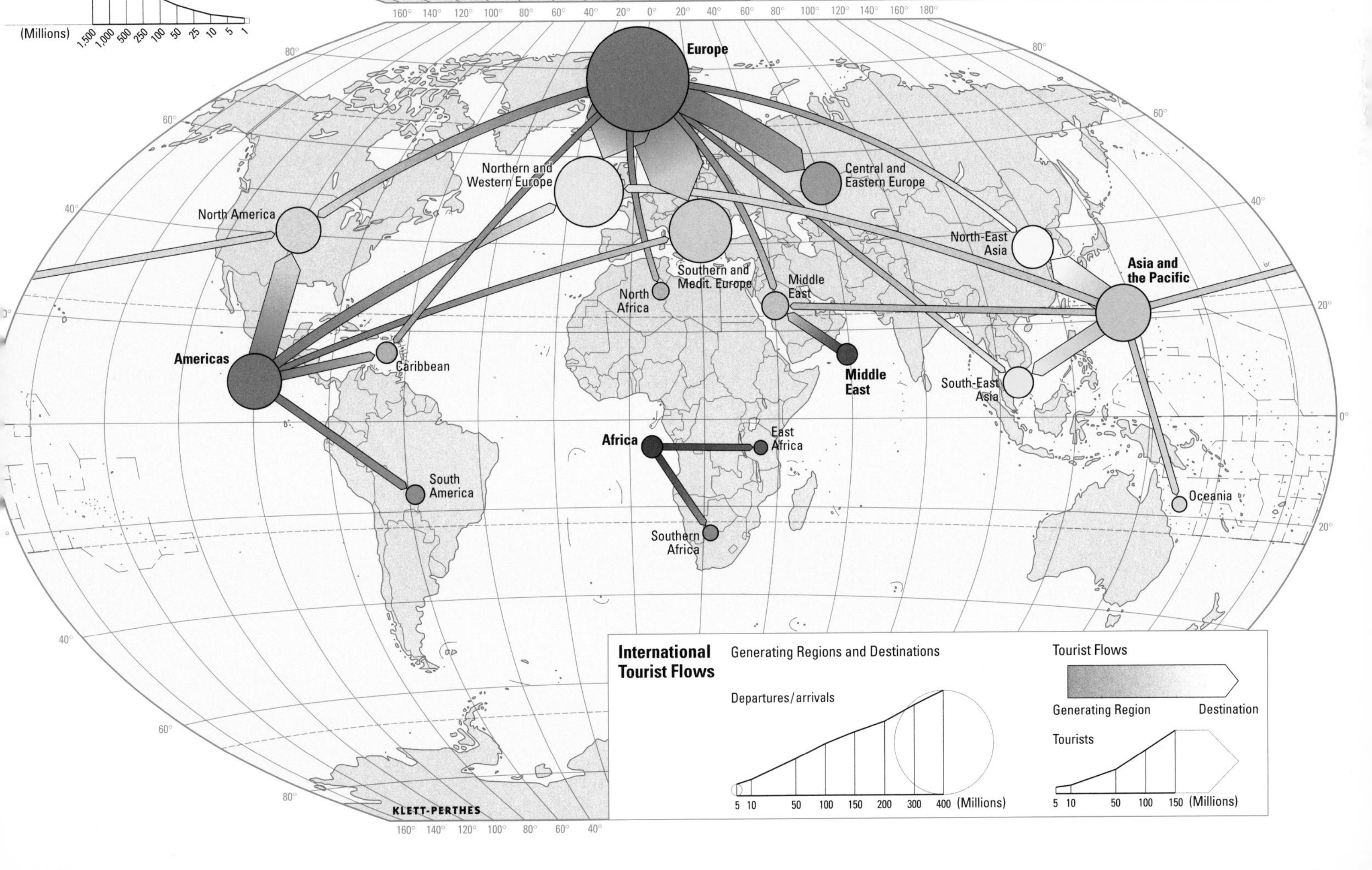
Europe
Northern and Western Europe
Central and Eastern Europe
North America
North-East Asia
Asia and the Pacific
Southern and Medit. Europe
Middle East
North Africa
Americas
Caribbean
Middle East
South-East Asia
Africa
East Africa
South America
Oceania
Southern Africa
KLETT-PERTHES
International Tourist Flows
Generating Regions and Destinations
Departures/arrivals
5 10 50 100 150 200 300 400 (Millions)
Tourist Flows
Generating Region
Destination
Tourists
5 10 50 100 150 (Millions)

1:160,000,000

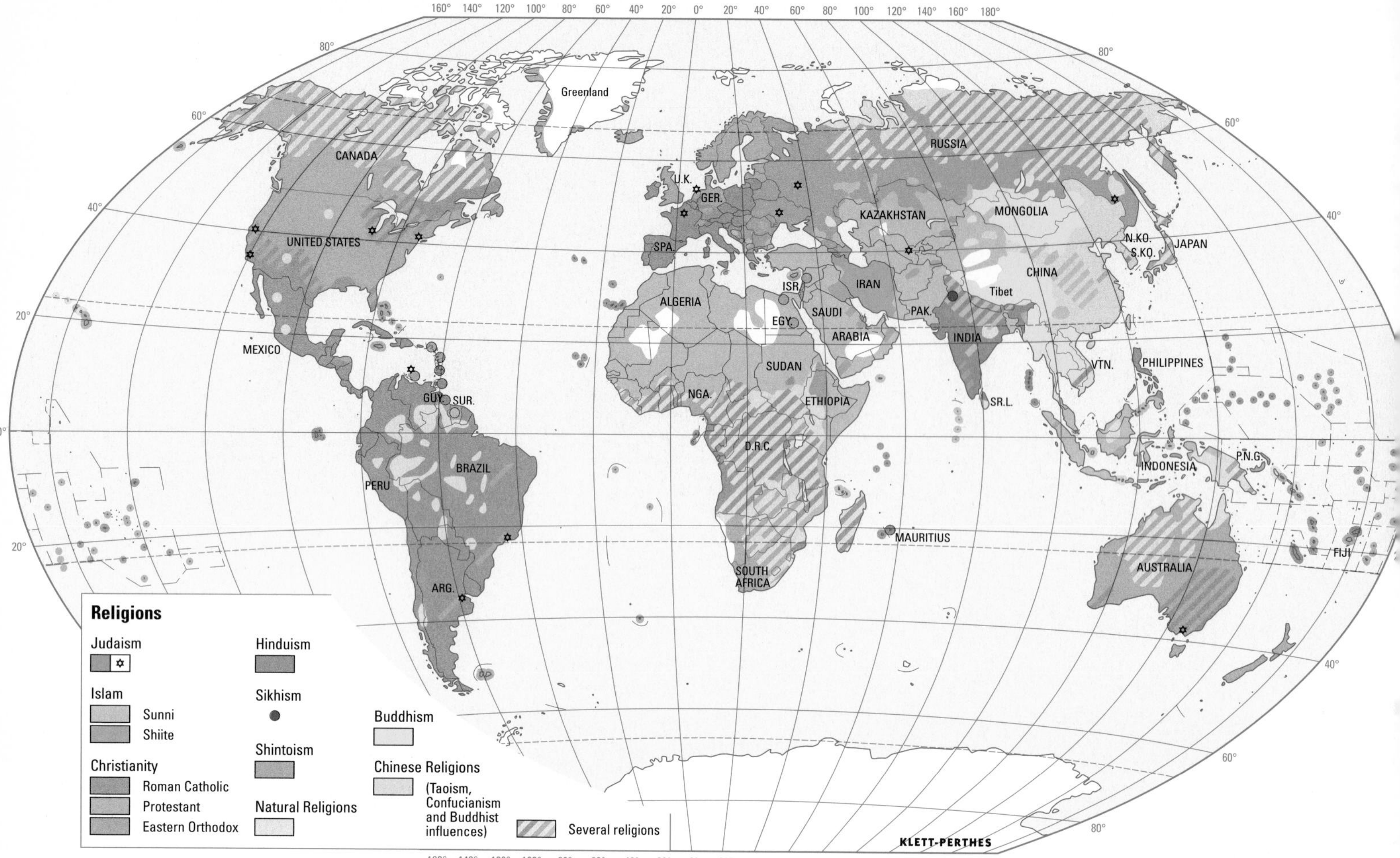
Religions
Judaism
Hinduism
Islam
Sunni
Shiite
Sikhism
Buddhism
Christianity
Roman Catholic
Protestant
Eastern Orthodox
Shintoism
Natural Religions
Chinese Religions
(Taoism, Confucianism and Buddhist influences)
Several religions
Greenland
CANADA
UNITED STATES
MEXICO
GUY.
SUR.
PERU
BRAZIL
ARG.
U.K.
GER.
SPA.
ALGERIA
NGA.
D.R.C.
SOUTH AFRICA
SUDAN
ETHIOPIA
EGY.
ISR.
SAUDI ARABIA
IRAN
PAK.
INDIA
SR.L.
KAZAKHSTAN
RUSSIA
MONGOLIA
CHINA
Tibet
N.KO.
S.KO.
JAPAN
VTN.
PHILIPPINES
INDONESIA
P.N.G.
AUSTRALIA
FIJI
MAURITIUS
KLETT-PERTHES

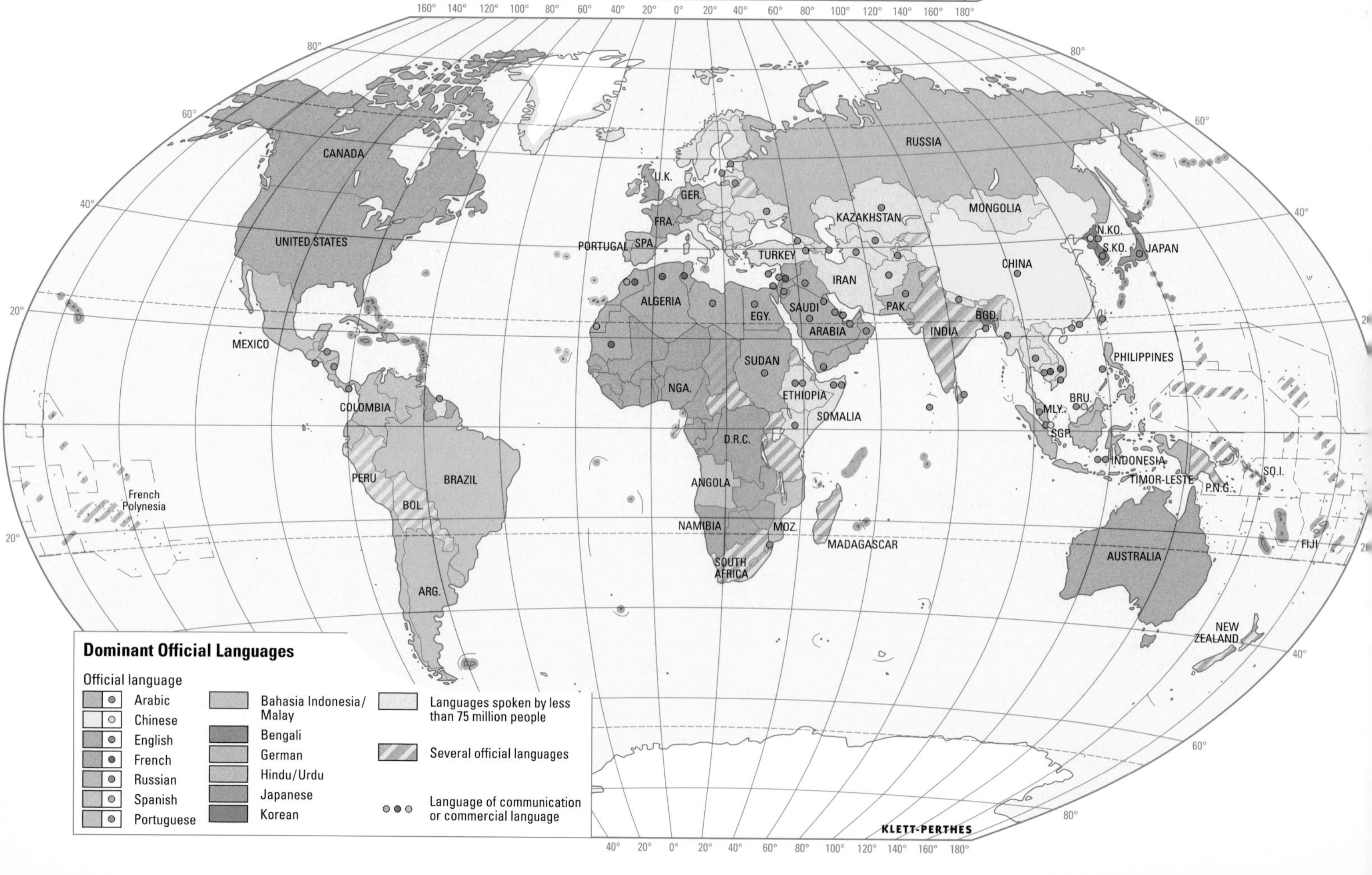
Dominant Official Languages
Official language
Arabic
Chinese
English
French
Russian
Spanish
Portuguese
Bahasia Indonesia/ Malay
Bengali
German
Hindu/Urdu
Japanese
Korean
Languages spoken by less than 75 million people
Several official languages
Language of communication or commercial language
CANADA
UNITED STATES
MEXICO
COLOMBIA
PERU
BOL.
BRAZIL
ARG.
French Polynesia
U.K.
GER.
FRA.
PORTUGAL
SPA.
ALGERIA
NGA.
D.R.C.
ANGOLA
NAMIBIA
MOZ.
SOUTH AFRICA
MADAGASCAR
SUDAN
ETHIOPIA
SOMALIA
EGY.
TURKEY
SAUDI ARABIA
IRAN
PAK.
INDIA
BGD.
KAZAKHSTAN
RUSSIA
MONGOLIA
CHINA
N.KO.
S.KO.
JAPAN
PHILIPPINES
BRU.
MLY.
SGP.
INDONESIA
TIMOR-LESTE
P.N.G.
SO.I.
FIJI
AUSTRALIA
NEW ZEALAND
KLETT-PERTHES

World: Ethnic Diversity · Cultural Regions

1:160,000,000

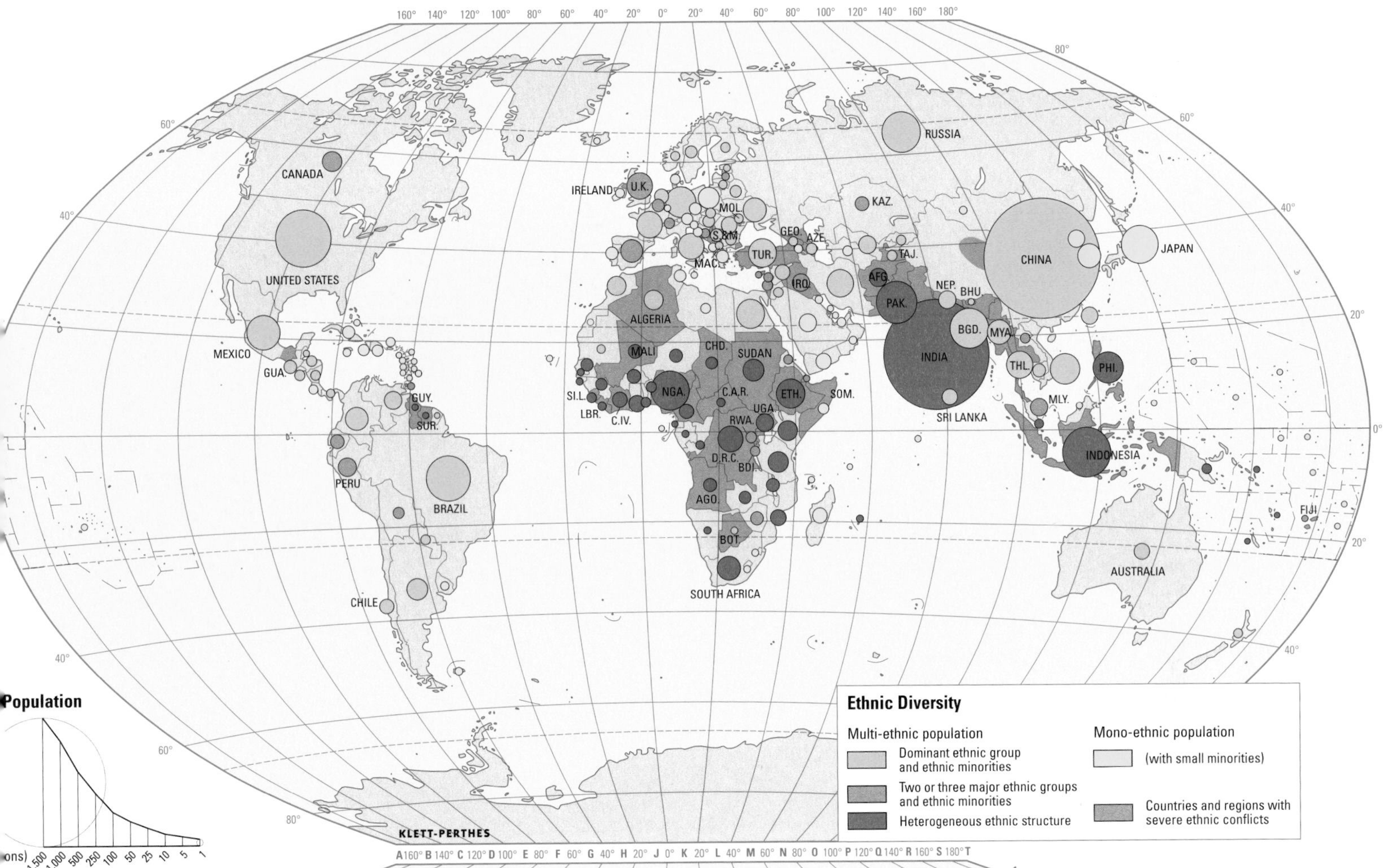
RUSSIA
CANADA
IRELAND
U.K.
KAZ.
MOL.
S.&M.
GEO.
AZE.
TAJ.
MAC.
TUR.
IRQ.
AFG.
JAPAN
CHINA
UNITED STATES
NEP.
BHU.
PAK.
BGD.
MYA.
ALGERIA
MEXICO
INDIA
THL.
PHI.
MALI
CHD.
SUDAN
GUA.
GUY.
SUR.
S.L.
NGA.
C.A.R.
ETH.
SOM.
LBR.
C.IV.
UGA
SRI LANKA
MLY.
RWA.
INDONESIA
D.R.C.
BDI.
PERU
BRAZIL
AGO.
FIJI
BOT.
AUSTRALIA
CHILE
SOUTH AFRICA
Population
(in millions) 1,500 1,000 500 250 100 50 25 10 5 1
KLETT-PERTHES
Ethnic Diversity
Multi-ethnic population
Dominant ethnic group and ethnic minorities
Two or three major ethnic groups and ethnic minorities
Heterogeneous ethnic structure
Mono-ethnic population
(with small minorities)
Countries and regions with severe ethnic conflicts

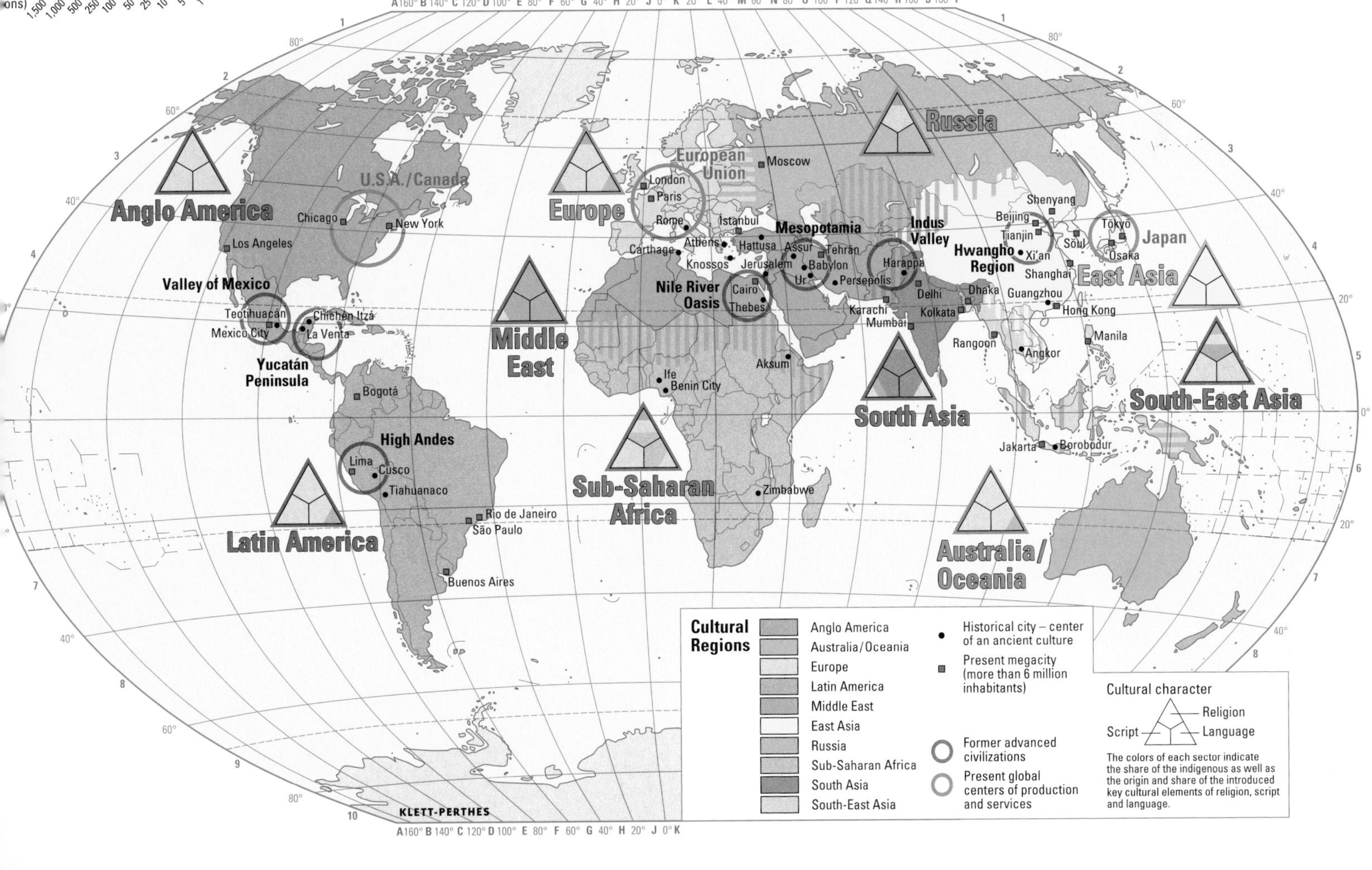
Russia
Moscow
European Union
London
Paris
Rome
U.S.A./Canada
Anglo America
Chicago
New York
Los Angeles
Europe
Istanbul
Athens
Carthage
Knossos
Hattusa
Assur
Mesopotamia
Tehran
Jerusalem
Babylon
Ur
Persepolis
Indus Valley
Harappa
Hwangho Region
Shenyang
Beijing
Tianjin
Xi'an
Soul
Tokyo
Osaka
Japan
Shanghai
East Asia
Valley of Mexico
Teotihuacán
Mexico City
Chichén Itzá
La Venta
Yucatán Peninsula
Middle East
Nile River Oasis
Cairo
Thebes
Karachi
Mumbai
Delhi
Kolkata
Dhaka
Guangzhou
Hong Kong
Manila
Rangoon
Angkor
Ife
Benin City
Aksum
South Asia
South-East Asia
Bogotá
High Andes
Lima
Cusco
Tiahuanaco
Sub-Saharan Africa
Zimbabwe
Jakarta
Borobodur
Rio de Janeiro
São Paulo
Latin America
Australia/Oceania
Buenos Aires
Cultural Regions
Anglo America
Australia/Oceania
Europe
Latin America
Middle East
East Asia
Russia
Sub-Saharan Africa
South Asia
South-East Asia
Historical city – center of an ancient culture
Present megacity (more than 6 million inhabitants)
Former advanced civilizations
Present global centers of production and services
Cultural character
Religion
Script
Language
The colors of each sector indicate the share of the indigenous as well as the origin and share of the introduced key cultural elements of religion, script and language.
KLETT-PERTHES

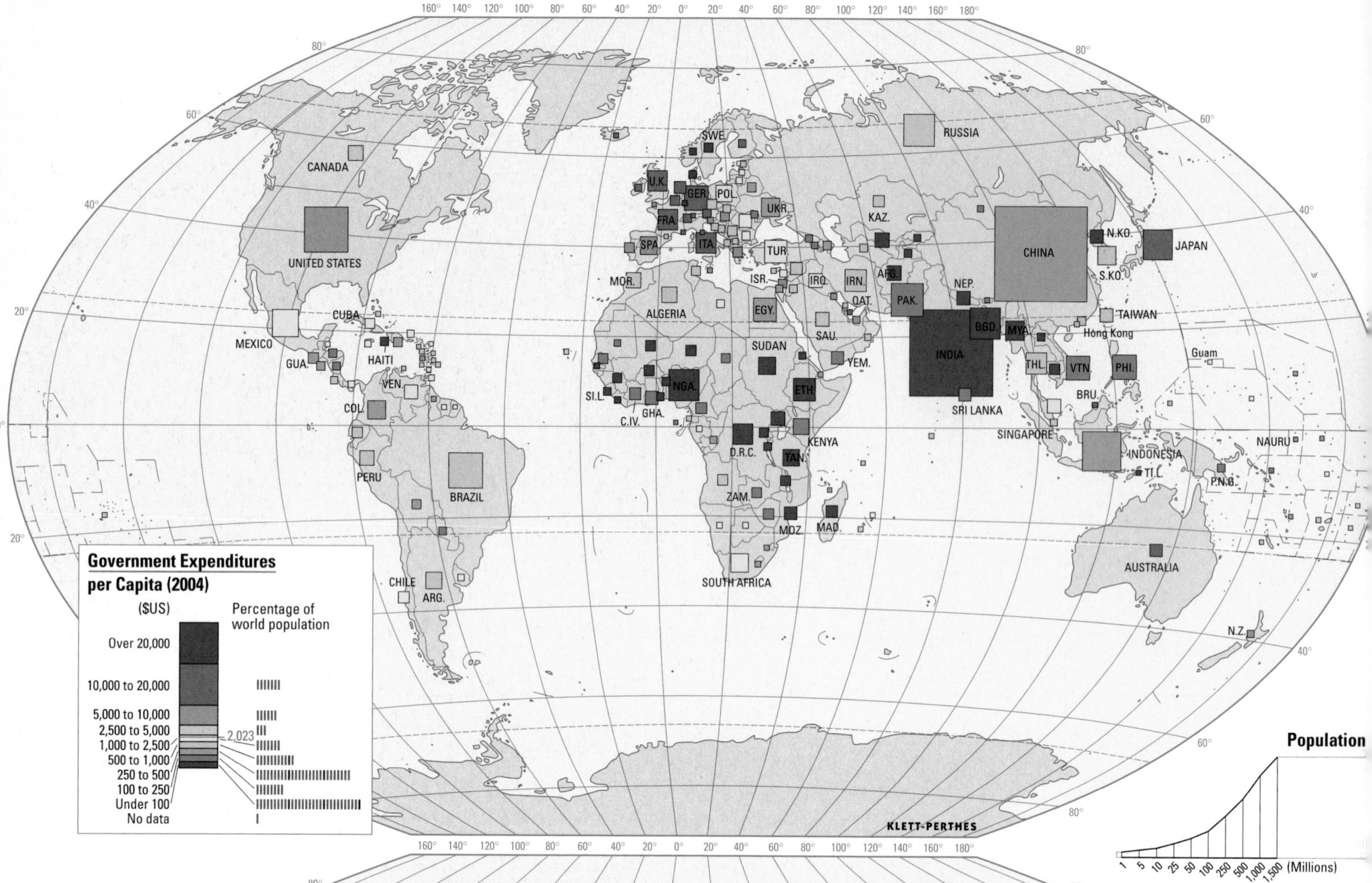
Government Expenditures per Capita (2004)
($US)
Percentage of world population
Over 20,000
10,000 to 20,000
5,000 to 10,000
2,500 to 5,000
2,023
1,000 to 2,500
500 to 1,000
250 to 500
100 to 250
Under 100
No data
CANADA
UNITED STATES
MEXICO
CUBA
GUA.
HAITI
VEN.
COL.
PERU
BRAZIL
CHILE
ARG.
RUSSIA
SWE.
U.K.
GER.
POL.
FRA.
UKR.
SPA.
ITA.
TUR.
MOR.
ISR.
IRQ.
IRN.
AFG.
KAZ.
ALGERIA
EGY.
QAT.
SAU.
YEM.
PAK.
NEP.
BGD.
MYA.
INDIA
SRI LANKA
CHINA
N.KO.
JAPAN
S.KO.
TAIWAN
Hong Kong
THL.
VTN.
PHI.
Guam
BRU.
SINGAPORE
INDONESIA
T.L.
NAURU
P.N.G.
AUSTRALIA
N.Z.
SUDAN
ETH.
NGA.
SI.L.
C.IV.
GHA.
KENYA
D.R.C.
TAN.
ZAM.
MOZ.
MAD.
SOUTH AFRICA
KLETT-PERTHES
Population
1
5
10
25
50
100
250
500
1,000
1,500
(Millions)

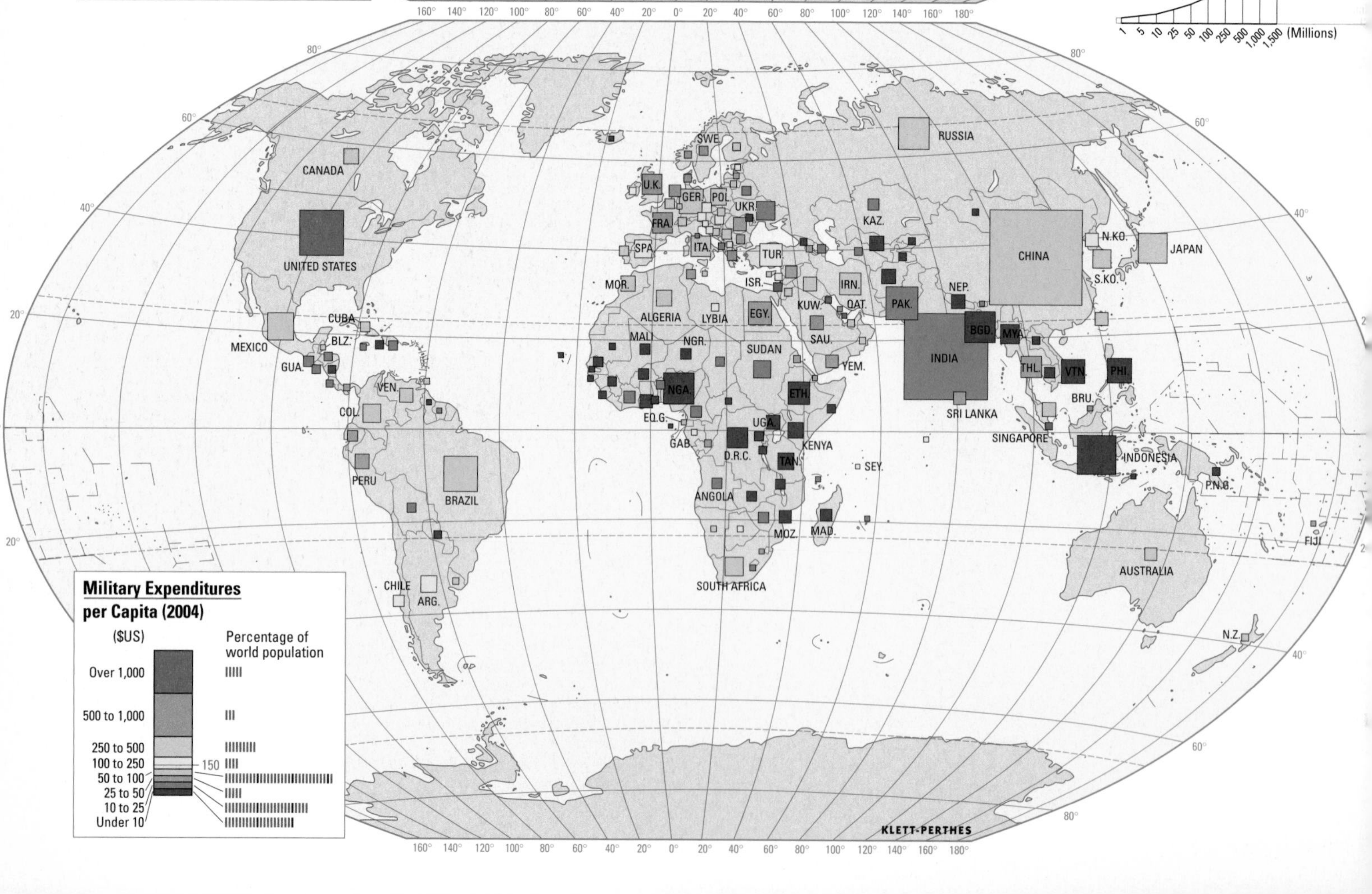
Military Expenditures per Capita (2004)
($US)
Percentage of world population
Over 1,000
500 to 1,000
250 to 500
100 to 250
150
50 to 100
25 to 50
10 to 25
Under 10
CANADA
UNITED STATES
MEXICO
CUBA
BLZ.
GUA.
VEN.
COL.
PERU
BRAZIL
CHILE
ARG.
RUSSIA
SWE.
U.K.
GER.
POL.
UKR.
FRA.
SPA.
ITA.
TUR.
MOR.
ISR.
IRN.
KAZ.
ALGERIA
LYBIA
EGY.
KUW.
QAT.
SAU.
YEM.
MALI
NGR.
SUDAN
NGA.
ETH.
EQ.G.
GAB.
UGA.
KENYA
D.R.C.
TAN.
SEY.
ANGOLA
MOZ.
MAD.
SOUTH AFRICA
PAK.
NEP.
BGD.
MYA.
INDIA
SRI LANKA
CHINA
N.KO.
JAPAN
S.KO.
THL.
VTN.
PHI.
BRU.
SINGAPORE
INDONESIA
P.N.G.
FIJI
AUSTRALIA
N.Z.
KLETT-PERTHES

World: Foreign Direct Investment · Foreign Aid

1:160,000,000

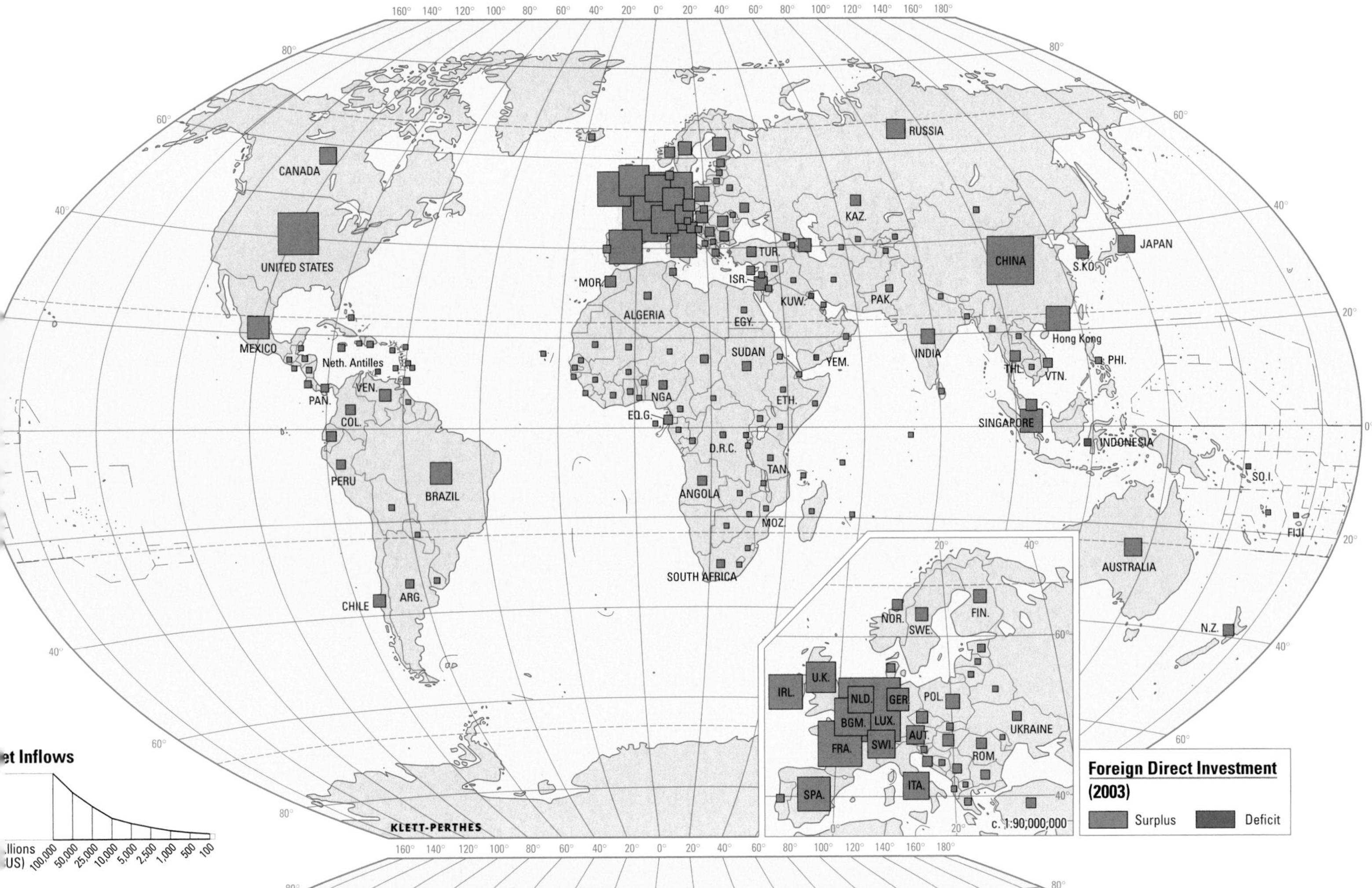
CANADA
UNITED STATES
MEXICO
Neth. Antilles
VEN.
PAN.
COL.
PERU
BRAZIL
ARG.
CHILE
RUSSIA
KAZ.
TUR.
ISR.
KUW.
PAK.
CHINA
JAPAN
S.KO.
Hong Kong
PHI.
INDIA
THL.
VTN.
SINGAPORE
INDONESIA
SO.I.
FIJI
AUSTRALIA
N.Z.
MOR.
ALGERIA
EGY.
SUDAN
YEM.
NGA.
EQ.G.
ETH.
D.R.C.
TAN.
ANGOLA
MOZ.
SOUTH AFRICA
NOR.
SWE.
FIN.
U.K.
IRL.
NLD.
GER.
POL.
BGM.
LUX.
UKRAINE
FRA.
SWI.
AUT.
ROM.
SPA.
ITA.
c. 1:90,000,000
Foreign Direct Investment (2003)
Surplus
Deficit
Net Inflows
(Millions US)
100,000
50,000
25,000
10,000
5,000
2,500
1,000
500
100
KLETT-PERTHES

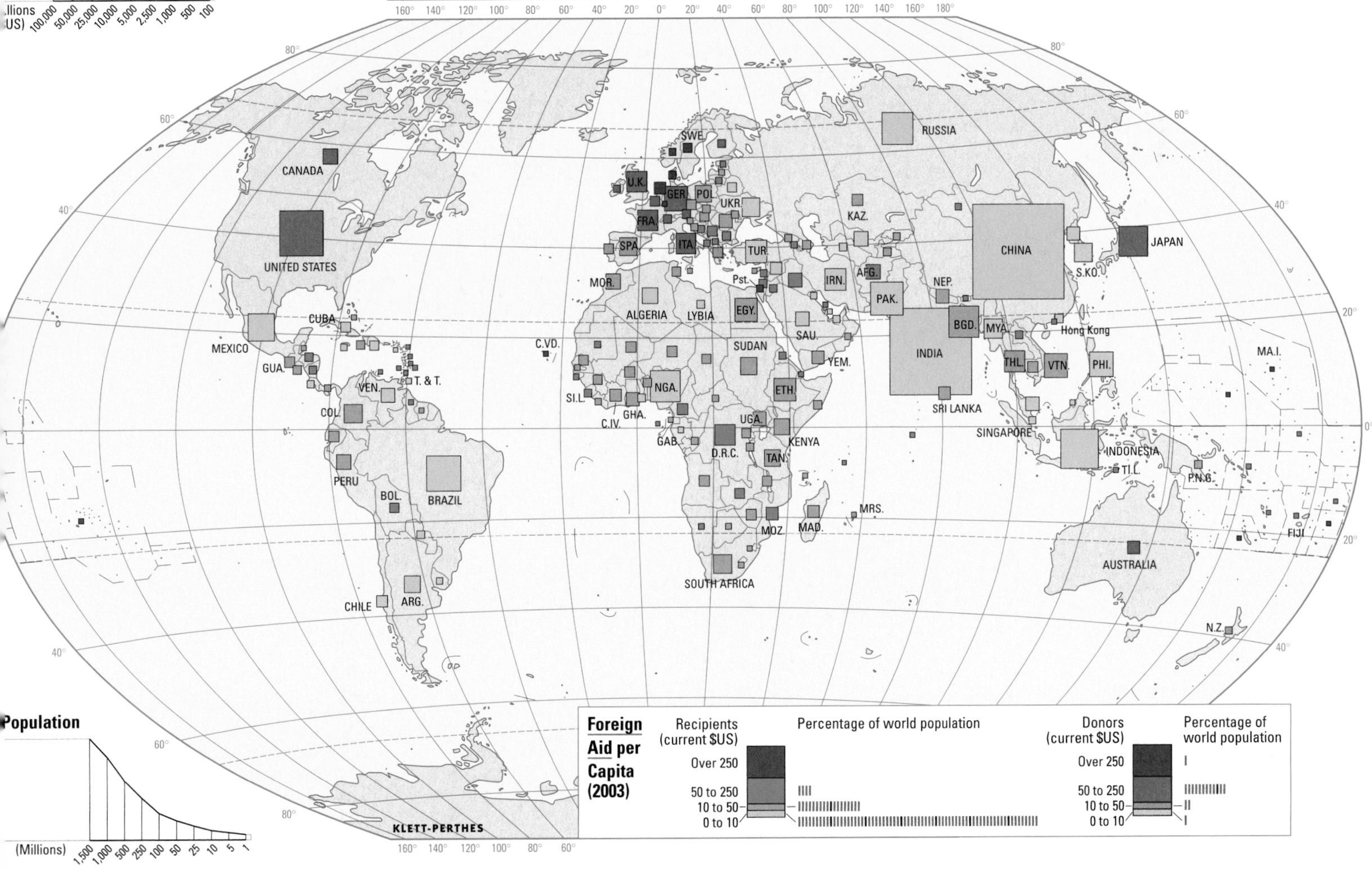
CANADA
UNITED STATES
MEXICO
CUBA
GUA.
VEN.
T. & T.
COL.
PERU
BOL.
BRAZIL
ARG.
CHILE
RUSSIA
SWE.
U.K.
GER.
POL.
UKR.
FRA.
SPA.
ITA.
TUR.
KAZ.
MOR.
ALGERIA
LYBIA
EGY.
Pst.
IRN.
AFG.
PAK.
NEP.
CHINA
JAPAN
S.KO.
BGD.
MYA.
Hong Kong
INDIA
SAU.
YEM.
SUDAN
ETH.
C.VD.
SI.L.
C.IV.
GHA.
NGA.
GAB.
D.R.C.
UGA.
KENYA
TAN.
MRS.
MOZ.
MAD.
SOUTH AFRICA
SRI LANKA
THL.
VTN.
PHI.
SINGAPORE
INDONESIA
TI.L.
P.N.G.
MA.I.
FIJI
AUSTRALIA
N.Z.
Population
(Millions)
1,500
1,000
500
250
100
50
25
10
5
1
Foreign Aid per Capita (2003)
Recipients (current $US)
Percentage of world population
Over 250
50 to 250
10 to 50
0 to 10
Donors (current $US)
Percentage of world population
Over 250
50 to 250
10 to 50
0 to 10
KLETT-PERTHES

1:160,000,000

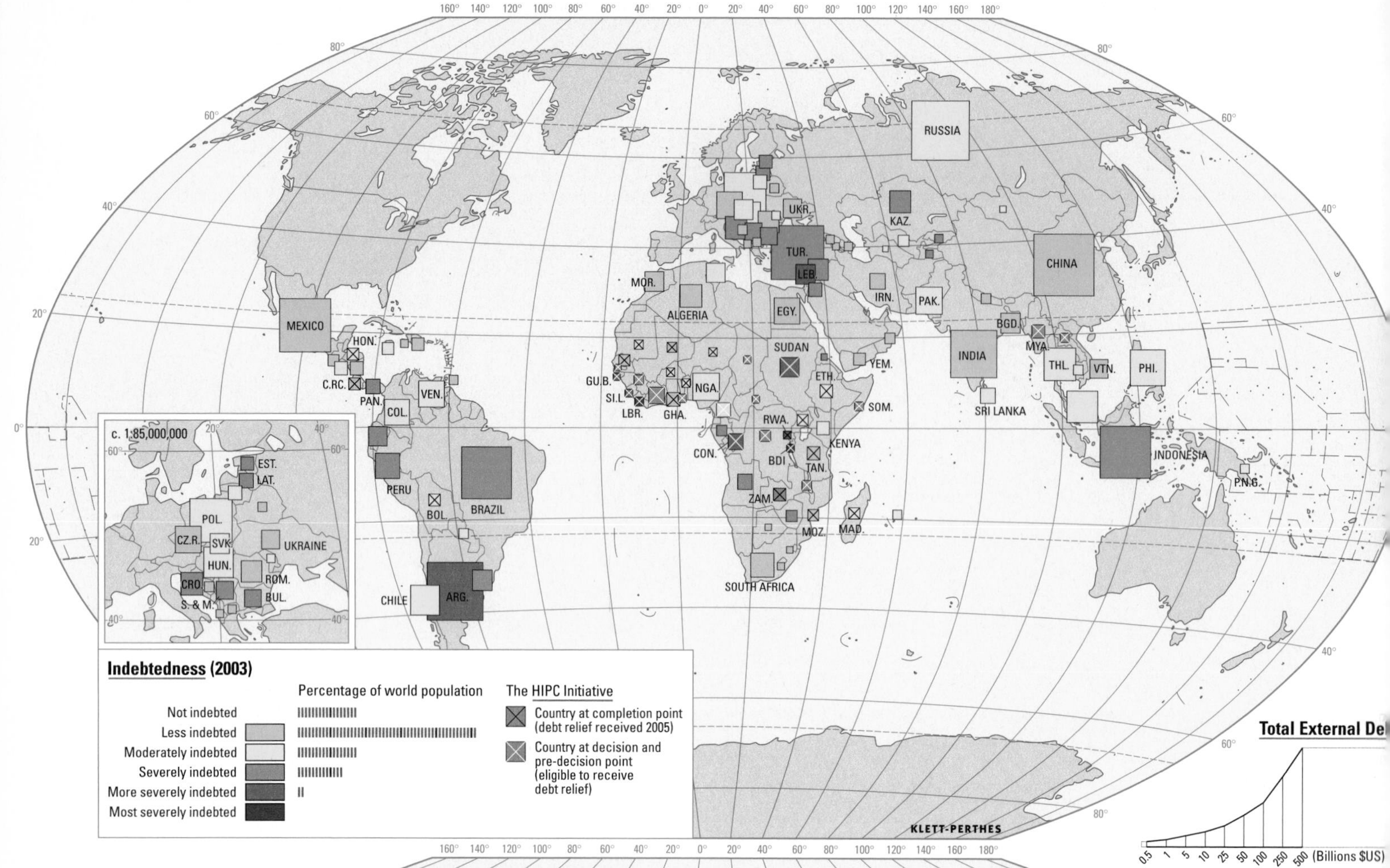

RUSSIA
KAZ.
UKR.
TUR.
LEB.
CHINA
MOR.
ALGERIA
EGY.
IRN.
PAK.
MEXICO
HON.
C.RC.
PAN.
COL.
VEN.
SUDAN
ETH.
YEM.
INDIA
BGD.
MYA.
THL.
VTN.
PHI.
SRI LANKA
GU.B.
SI.L.
LBR.
GHA.
NGA.
SOM.
RWA.
KENYA
CON.
BDI
TAN.
INDONESIA
P.N.G.
PERU
BRAZIL
BOL.
ZAM.
MOZ.
MAD.
SOUTH AFRICA
CHILE
ARG.
c. 1:85,000,000
EST.
LAT.
POL.
CZ.R.
SVK.
HUN.
UKRAINE
CRO.
ROM.
S. & M.
BUL.
Indebtedness (2003)
Percentage of world population
Not indebted
Less indebted
Moderately indebted
Severely indebted
More severely indebted
Most severely indebted
The HIPC Initiative
Country at completion point (debt relief received 2005)
Country at decision and pre-decision point (eligible to receive debt relief)
KLETT-PERTHES
Total External De
0.5 1 5 10 25 50 100 250 500 (Billions $US)

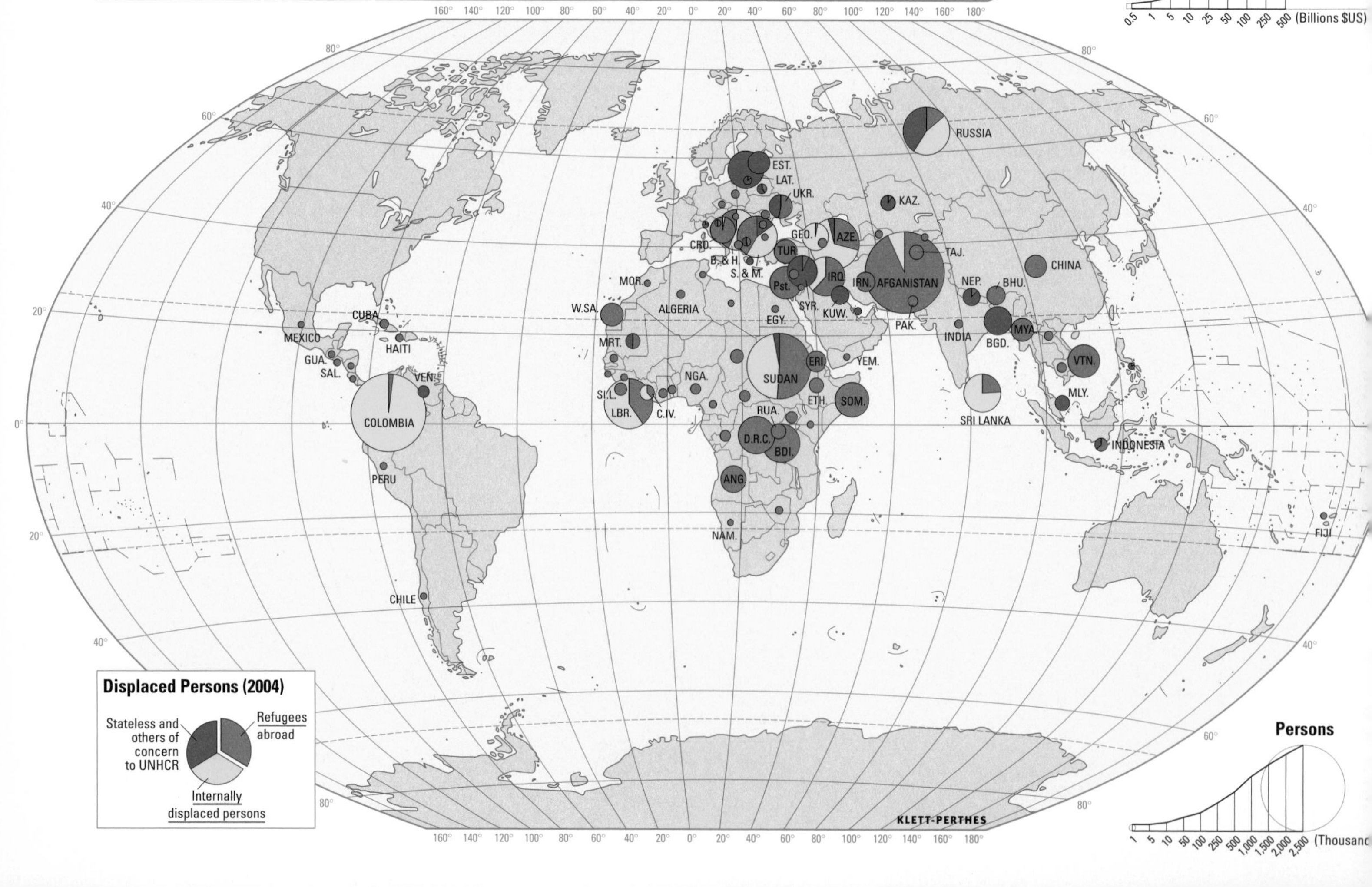

RUSSIA
EST.
LAT.
UKR.
KAZ.
CRO.
GEO.
AZE.
TAJ.
B. & H.
S. & M.
TUR.
CHINA
MOR.
Pst.
IRQ.
IRN.
AFGANISTAN
NEP.
BHU.
SYR.
KUW.
PAK.
W.S.A.
ALGERIA
EGY.
INDIA
BGD.
MYA.
CUBA
MEXICO
HAITI
MRT.
ERI.
YEM.
GUA.
SAL.
VEN.
NGA.
SUDAN
VTN.
SI.L.
ETH.
SOM.
MLY.
LBR.
C.I.V.
SRI LANKA
COLOMBIA
RUA.
D.R.C.
INDONESIA
BDI.
PERU
ANG.
FIJI
NAM.
CHILE
Displaced Persons (2004)
Stateless and others of concern to UNHCR
Refugees abroad
Internally displaced persons
KLETT-PERTHES
Persons
1 5 10 50 100 250 500 1,000 1,500 2,000 2,500 (Thousand

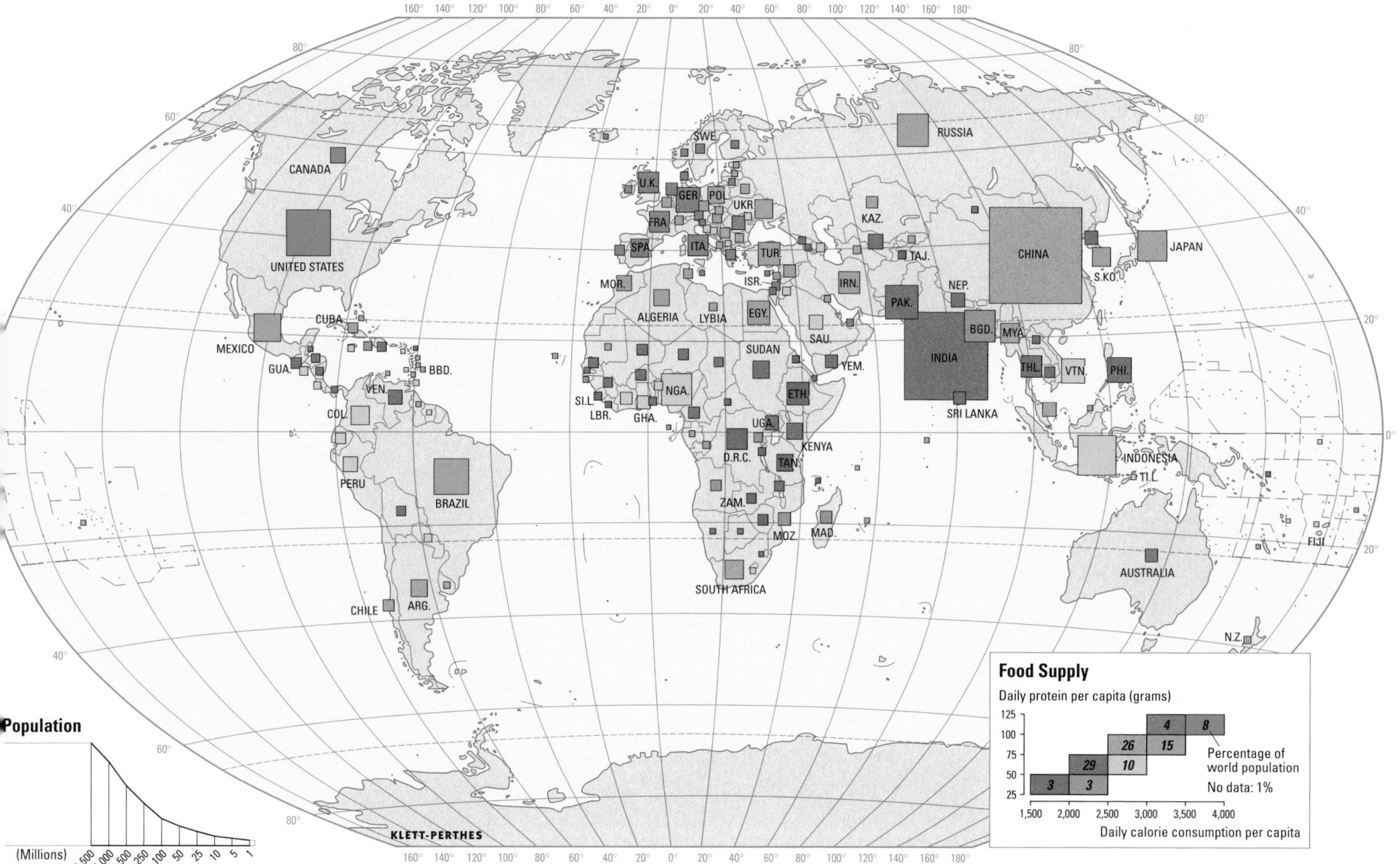

CANADA
UNITED STATES
MEXICO
CUBA
GUA.
BBD.
VEN.
COL.
PERU
BRAZIL
CHILE
ARG.
SWE.
U.K.
GER.
POL.
UKR.
FRA.
SPA.
ITA.
TUR.
MOR.
ALGERIA
LYBIA
EGY.
ISR.
SAU.
YEM.
SUDAN
ETH.
NGA.
SI.L.
LBR.
GHA.
UGA.
KENYA
D.R.C.
TAN.
ZAM.
MOZ.
MAD.
SOUTH AFRICA
RUSSIA
KAZ.
TAJ.
IRN.
PAK.
NEP.
INDIA
SRI LANKA
BGD.
MYA.
THL.
VTN.
PHI.
CHINA
S.KO.
JAPAN
INDONESIA
T.L.
AUSTRALIA
FIJI
N.Z.
KLETT-PERTHES
Population
(Millions)
1,500
1,000
500
250
100
50
25
10
5
1
Food Supply
Daily protein per capita (grams)
125
100
75
50
25
3
3
29
3
26
10
4
15
8
1,500
2,000
2,500
3,000
3,500
4,000
Percentage of world population
No data: 1%
Daily calorie consumption per capita

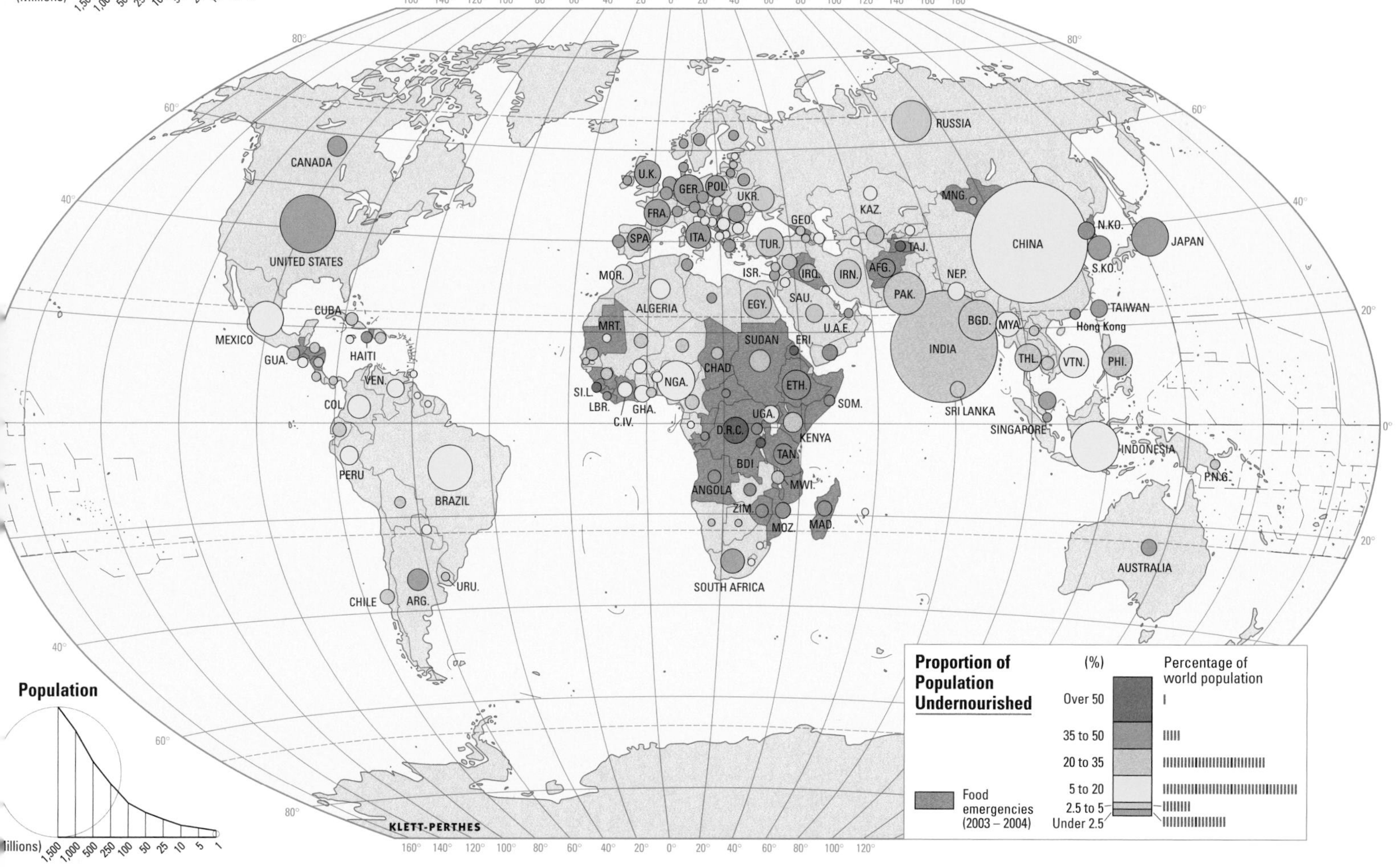

CANADA
UNITED STATES
MEXICO
CUBA
HAITI
GUA.
VEN.
COL.
PERU
BRAZIL
CHILE
ARG.
URU.
U.K.
GER.
POL.
UKR.
FRA.
SPA.
ITA.
TUR.
GEO.
MOR.
ALGERIA
MRT.
EGY.
ISR.
IRQ.
SAU.
U.A.E.
ERI.
SUDAN
CHAD
ETH.
SOM.
NGA.
SI.L.
LBR.
GHA.
C.IV.
UGA.
KENYA
D.R.C.
BDI
TAN.
MWI.
ANGOLA
ZIM.
MOZ.
MAD.
SOUTH AFRICA
RUSSIA
KAZ.
MNG.
TAJ.
AFG.
IRN.
PAK.
NEP.
INDIA
SRI LANKA
BGD.
MYA.
THL.
VTN.
PHI.
SINGAPORE
CHINA
N.KO.
S.KO.
JAPAN
TAIWAN
Hong Kong
INDONESIA
P.N.G.
AUSTRALIA
KLETT-PERTHES
Population
(Millions)
1,500
1,000
500
250
100
50
25
10
5
1
Proportion of Population Undernourished
(%)
Percentage of world population
Over 50
35 to 50
20 to 35
5 to 20
2.5 to 5
Under 2.5
Food emergencies (2003 – 2004)

World: Natural Resources · Agricultural Resources

1:160,000,000

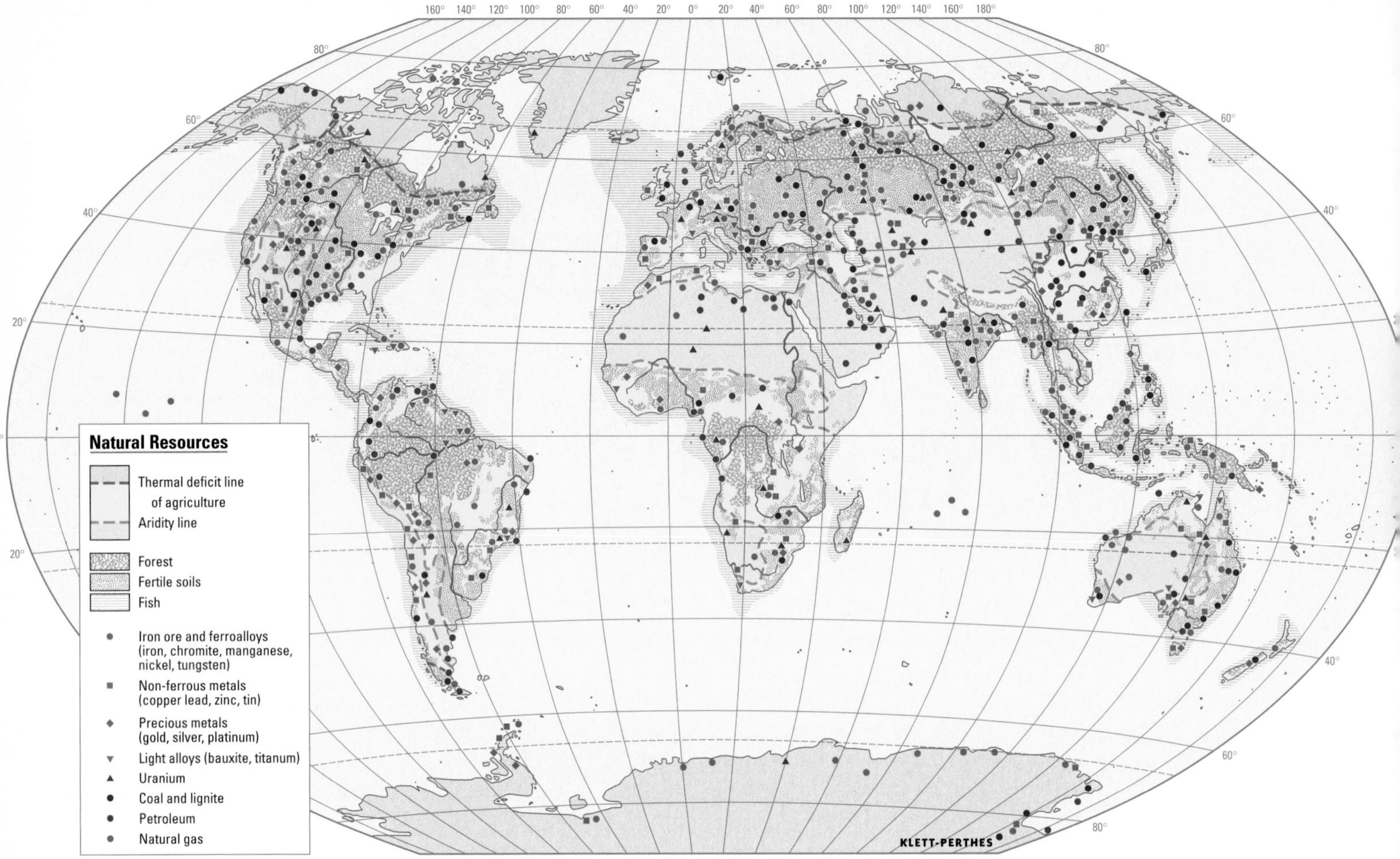
Natural Resources
Thermal deficit line
of agriculture
Aridity line
Forest
Fertile soils
Fish
Iron ore and ferroalloys (iron, chromite, manganese, nickel, tungsten)
Non-ferrous metals (copper lead, zinc, tin)
Precious metals (gold, silver, platinum)
Light alloys (bauxite, titanum)
Uranium
Coal and lignite
Petroleum
Natural gas
KLETT-PERTHES

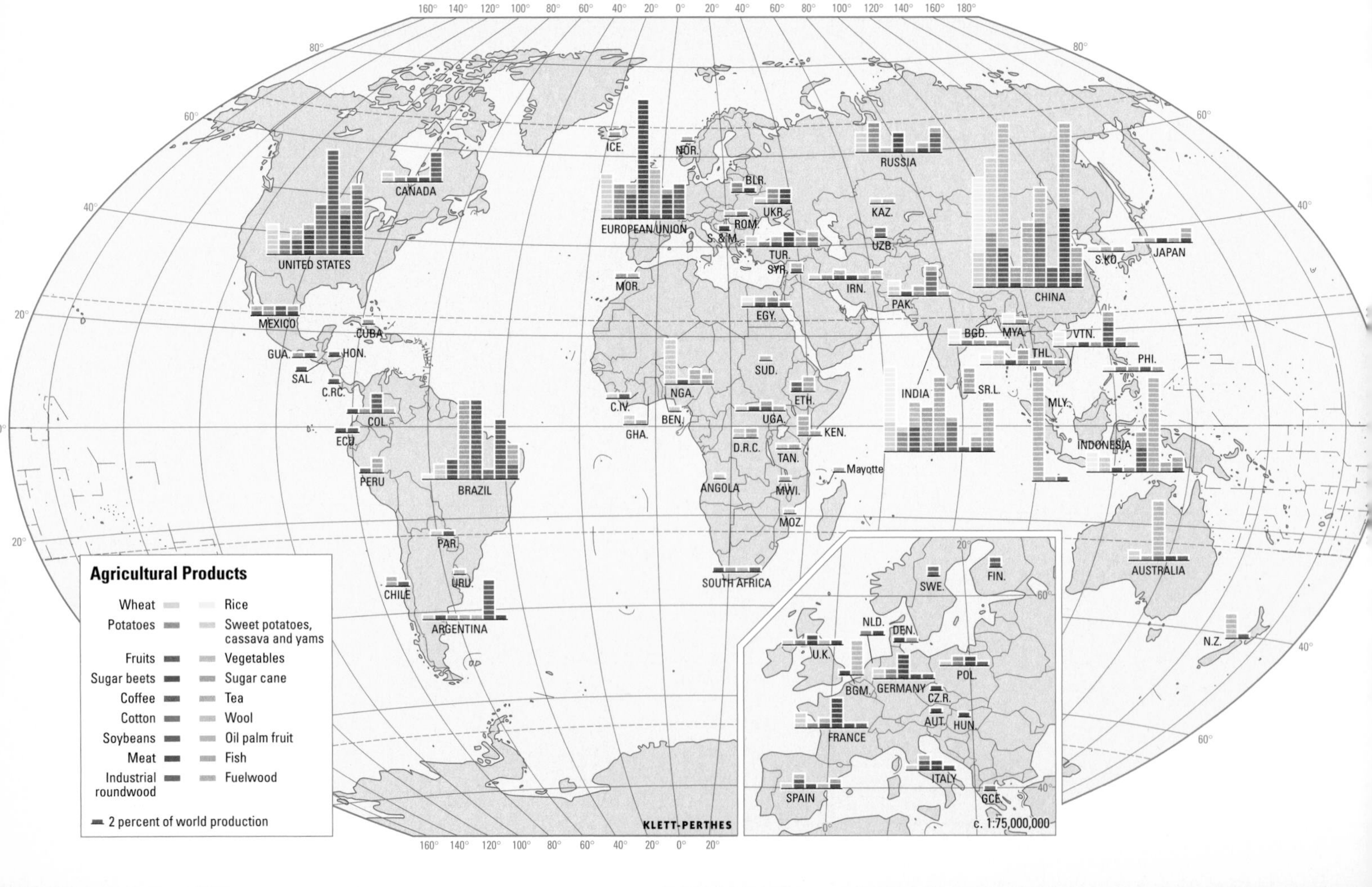
Agricultural Products
Wheat
Potatoes
Fruits
Sugar beets
Coffee
Cotton
Soybeans
Meat
Industrial roundwood
Rice
Sweet potatoes, cassava and yams
Vegetables
Sugar cane
Tea
Wool
Oil palm fruit
Fish
Fuelwood
2 percent of world production
CANADA
UNITED STATES
MEXICO
CUBA
GUA.
HON.
SAL.
C.R.
COL.
ECU.
PERU
BRAZIL
PAR.
CHILE
URU.
ARGENTINA
ICE.
NOR.
EUROPEAN UNION
BLR.
UKR.
ROM.
S.&M.
TUR.
SYR.
MOR.
EGY.
RUSSIA
KAZ.
UZB.
IRN.
PAK.
CHINA
S.KO.
JAPAN
BGD.
MYA.
VTN.
THL.
PHI.
INDIA
SR.L.
MLY.
INDONESIA
C.IV.
GHA.
BEN.
NGA.
SUD.
ETH.
UGA.
KEN.
D.R.C.
TAN.
Mayotte
ANGOLA
MWI.
MOZ.
SOUTH AFRICA
AUSTRALIA
N.Z.
SWE.
FIN.
NLD.
DEN.
U.K.
BGM.
GERMANY
POL.
CZ.R.
AUT.
HUN.
FRANCE
ITALY
SPAIN
GCE.
c. 1:75,000,000
KLETT-PERTHES

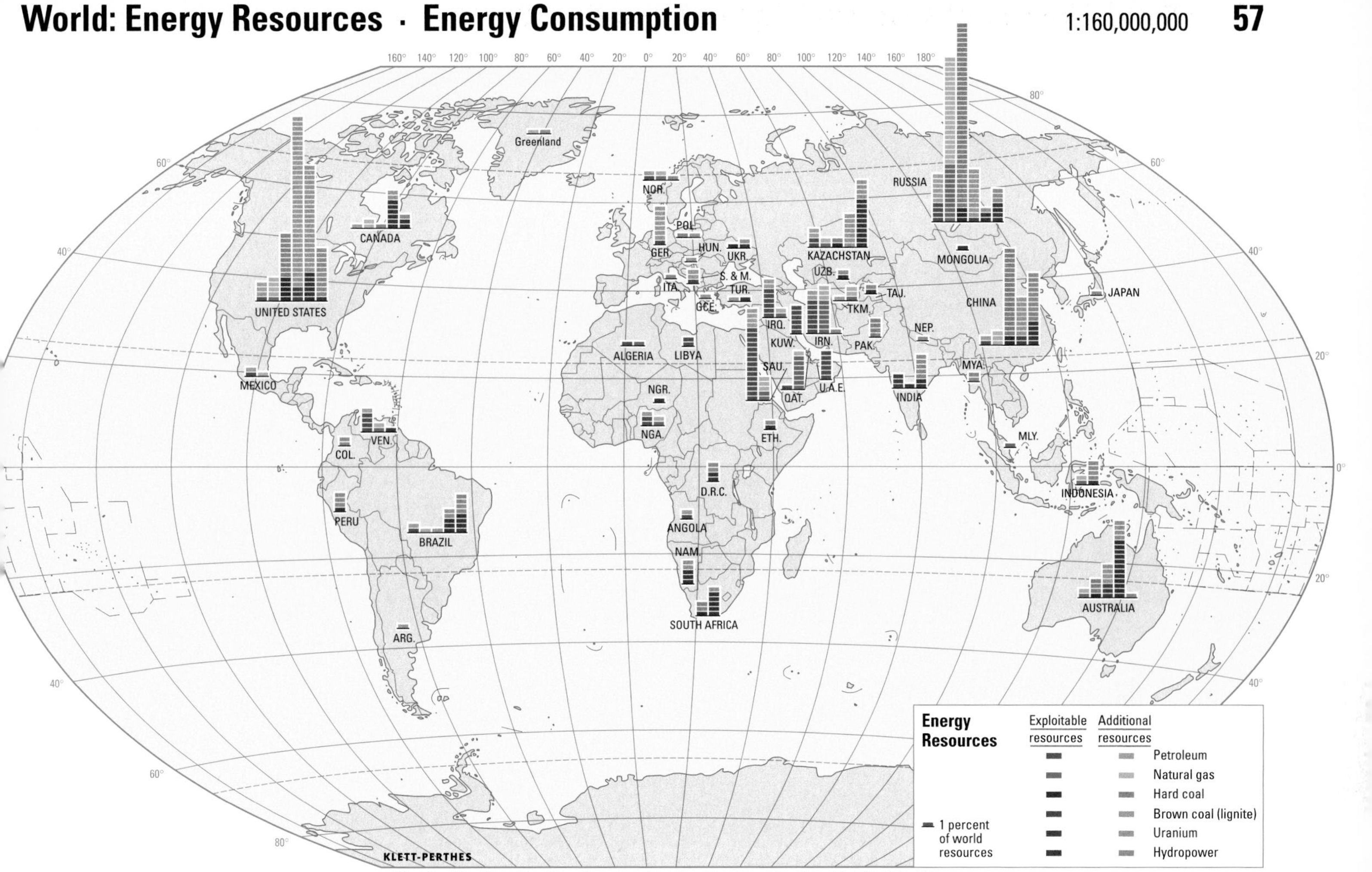
Greenland
NOR.
POL.
GER.
HUN.
UKR.
ITA.
S. & M.
TUR.
GCE.
CANADA
UNITED STATES
RUSSIA
KAZACHSTAN
UZB.
MONGOLIA
TKM.
TAJ.
JAPAN
CHINA
IRQ.
KUW.
IRN.
PAK.
NEP.
SAU.
QAT.
U.A.E.
INDIA
MYA.
ALGERIA
LIBYA
MEXICO
NGR.
NGA.
ETH.
MLY.
VEN.
COL.
PERU
BRAZIL
D.R.C.
ANGOLA
NAM.
INDONESIA
AUSTRALIA
SOUTH AFRICA
ARG.
KLETT-PERTHES
Energy Resources
Exploitable resources
Additional resources
Petroleum
Natural gas
Hard coal
Brown coal (lignite)
Uranium
Hydropower
1 percent of world resources

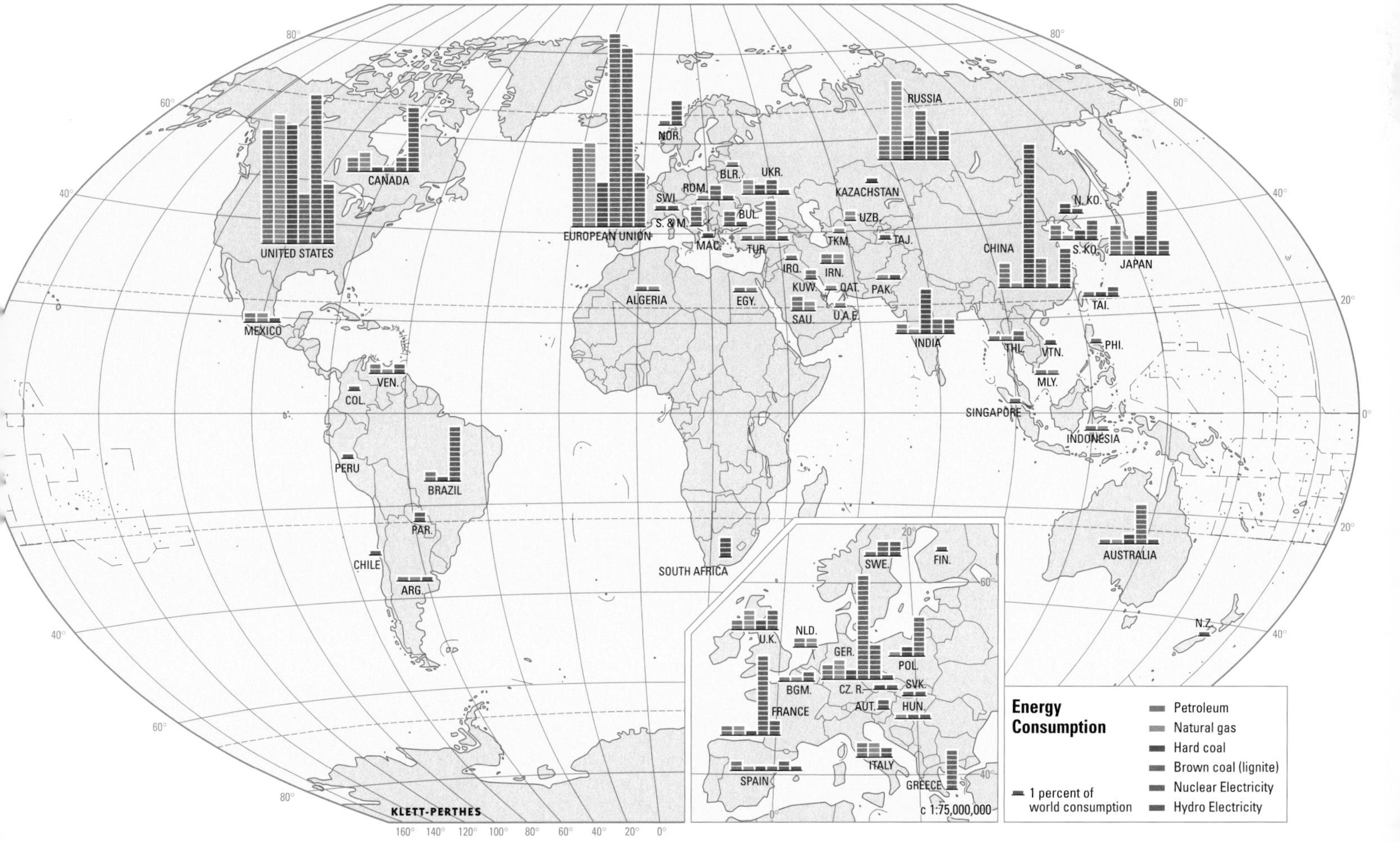
NOR.
RUSSIA
CANADA
BLR.
UKR.
ROM.
SWI.
S. & M.
BUL.
MAC.
TUR.
KAZACHSTAN
UZB.
TKM.
TAJ.
N. KO.
S. KO.
JAPAN
UNITED STATES
EUROPEAN UNION
CHINA
IRQ.
IRN.
KUW.
QAT.
PAK.
SAU.
U.A.E.
ALGERIA
EGY.
INDIA
TAI.
MEXICO
THI.
VTN.
PHI.
MLY.
VEN.
COL.
SINGAPORE
INDONESIA
PERU
BRAZIL
PAR.
CHILE
ARG.
SOUTH AFRICA
AUSTRALIA
N.Z.
KLETT-PERTHES
SWE.
FIN.
U.K.
NLD.
GER.
POL.
BGM.
CZ. R.
SVK.
FRANCE
AUT.
HUN.
ITALY
SPAIN
GREECE
c 1:75,000,000
Energy Consumption
Petroleum
Natural gas
Hard coal
Brown coal (lignite)
Nuclear Electricity
Hydro Electricity
1 percent of world consumption

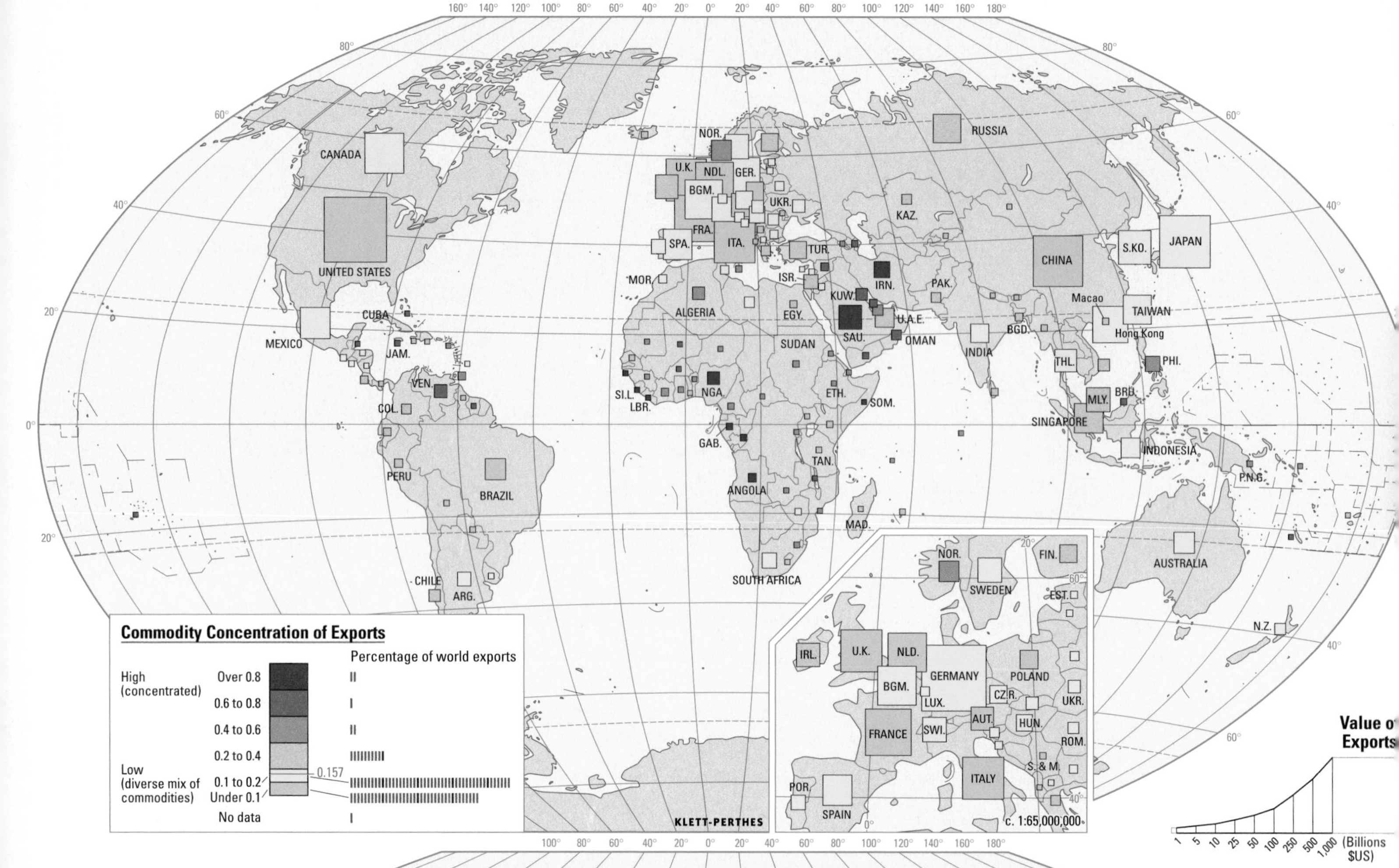

CANADA
UNITED STATES
MEXICO
CUBA
JAM.
VEN.
COL.
PERU
BRAZIL
CHILE
ARG.
NOR.
U.K.
NDL.
GER.
BGM.
UKR.
FRA.
SPA.
ITA.
TUR.
MOR.
ALGERIA
ISR.
EGY.
SUDAN
KUW.
SAU.
IRN.
U.A.E.
OMAN
KAZ.
PAK.
INDIA
BGD.
RUSSIA
CHINA
S.KO.
JAPAN
Macao
TAIWAN
Hong Kong
THL.
PHI.
MLY.
BRU.
SINGAPORE
INDONESIA
P.N.G.
AUSTRALIA
N.Z.
SI.L.
LBR.
NGA
GAB.
ETH.
SOM.
TAN.
ANGOLA
MAD.
SOUTH AFRICA
Commodity Concentration of Exports
Percentage of world exports
High (concentrated)
Over 0.8
0.6 to 0.8
0.4 to 0.6
0.2 to 0.4
Low (diverse mix of commodities)
0.1 to 0.2
0.157
Under 0.1
No data
KLETT-PERTHES
NOR.
FIN.
SWEDEN
EST.
IRL.
U.K.
NLD.
GERMANY
POLAND
BGM.
LUX.
CZ.R.
UKR.
FRANCE
SWI.
AUT.
HUN.
ROM.
S. & M.
ITALY
POR.
SPAIN
c. 1:65,000,000
Value of Exports
1
5
10
25
50
100
250
500
1,000 (Billions $US)

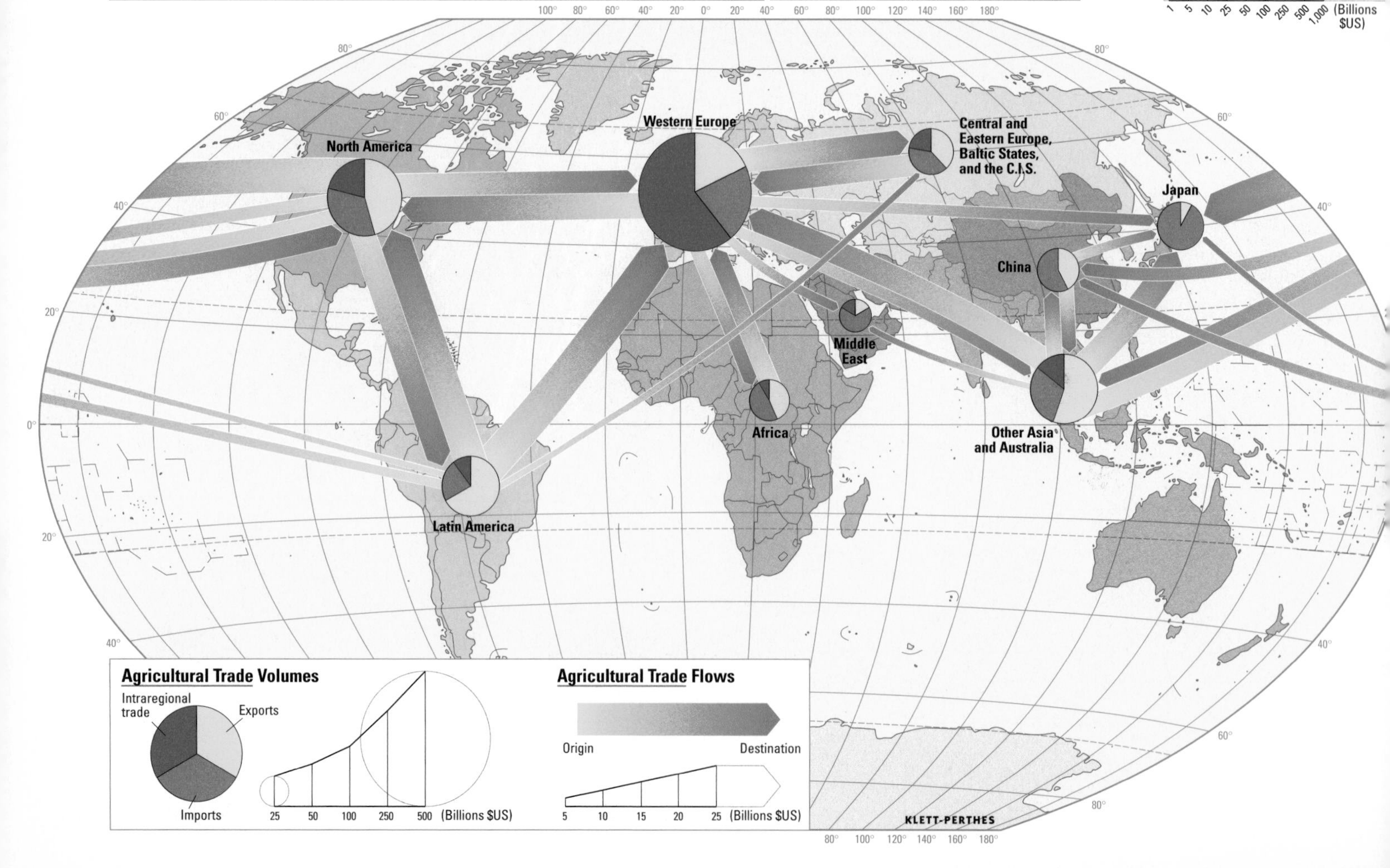

North America
Western Europe
Central and Eastern Europe, Baltic States, and the C.I.S.
Japan
China
Middle East
Africa
Other Asia and Australia
Latin America
Agricultural Trade Volumes
Intraregional trade
Exports
Imports
25
50
100
250
500 (Billions $US)
Agricultural Trade Flows
Origin
Destination
5
10
15
20
25 (Billions $US)
KLETT-PERTHES

World: Trade in Mining Products · Trade in Manufactured Goods

1:160,000,000

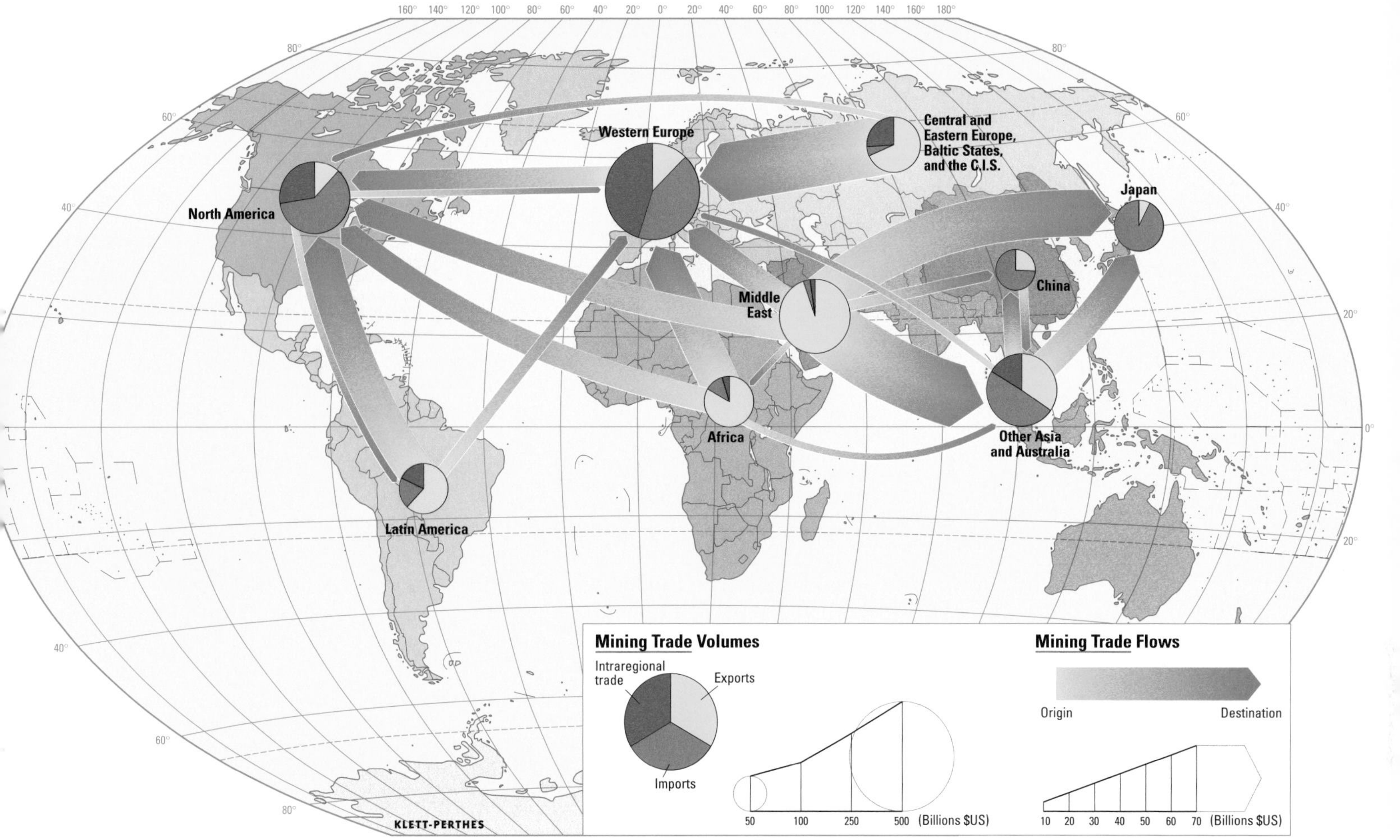

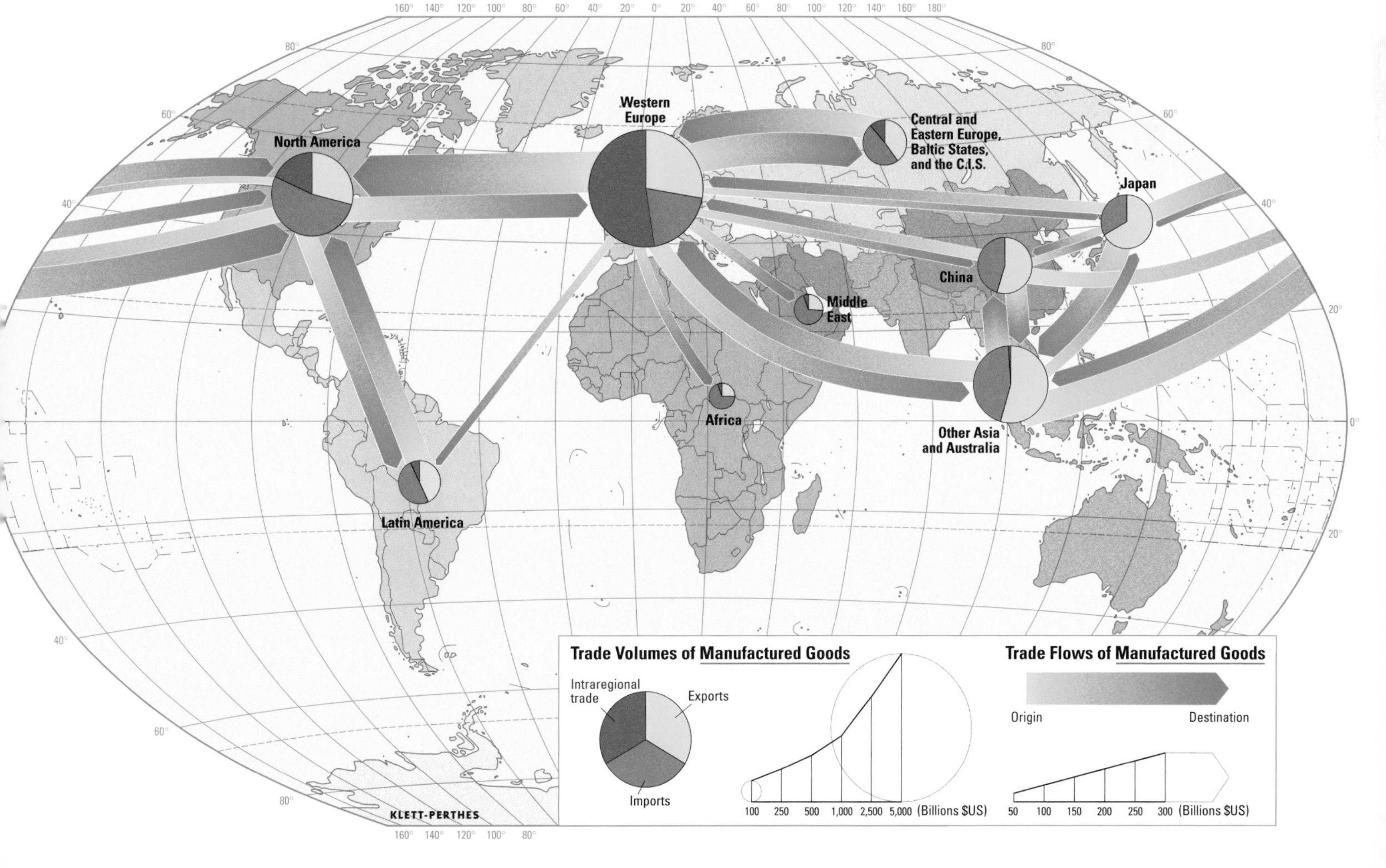

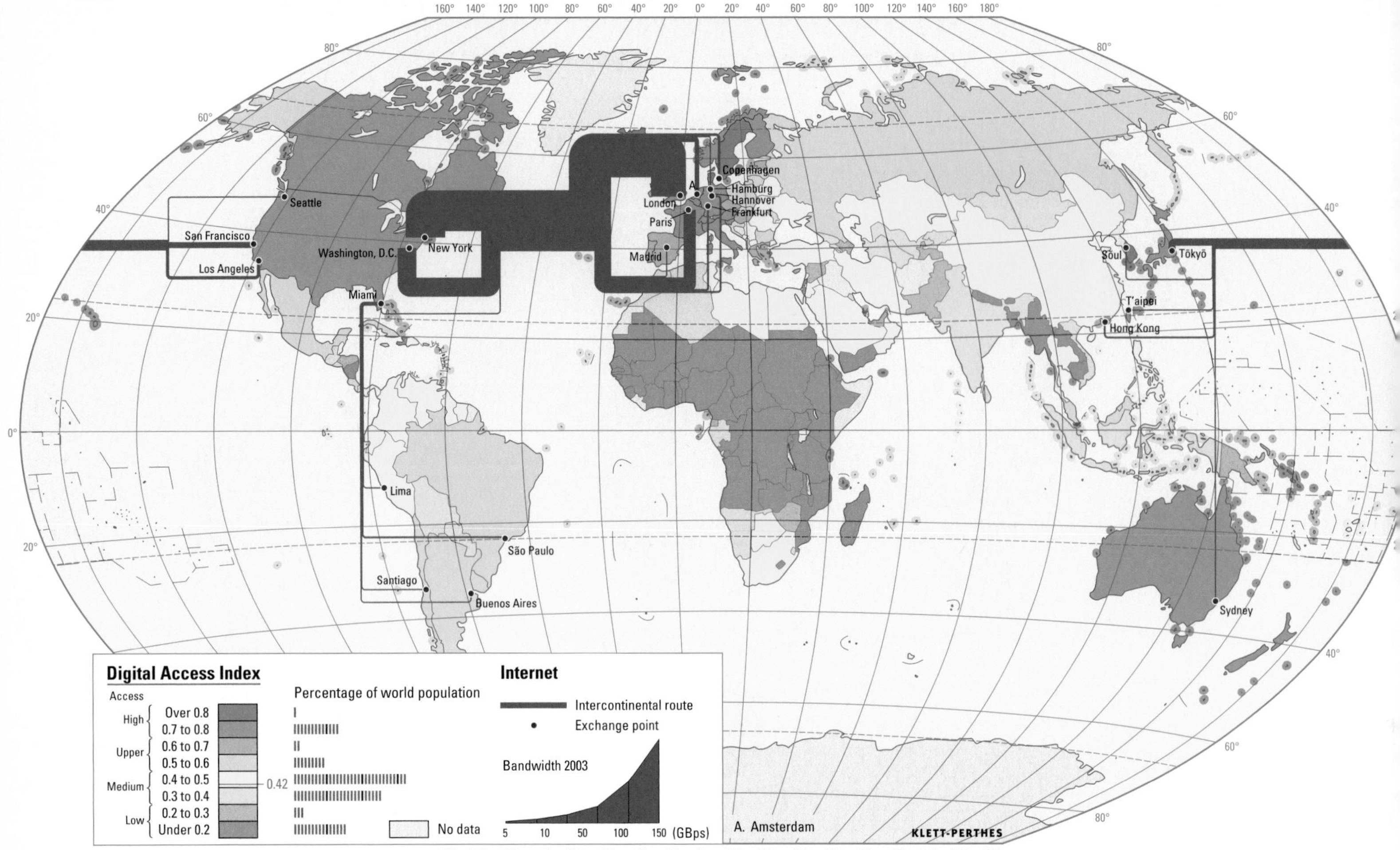

Seattle
San Francisco
Los Angeles
Washington, D.C.
New York
Miami
Lima
São Paulo
Santiago
Buenos Aires
London
Paris
Madrid
Copenhagen
A.
Hamburg
Hannover
Frankfurt
Soul
Tōkyō
T'aipei
Hong Kong
Sydney
Digital Access Index
Access
High
Upper
Medium
Low
Over 0.8
0.7 to 0.8
0.6 to 0.7
0.5 to 0.6
0.4 to 0.5
0.3 to 0.4
0.2 to 0.3
Under 0.2
0.42
Percentage of world population
No data
Internet
Intercontinental route
Exchange point
Bandwidth 2003
5
10
50
100
150 (GBps)
A. Amsterdam
KLETT-PERTHES

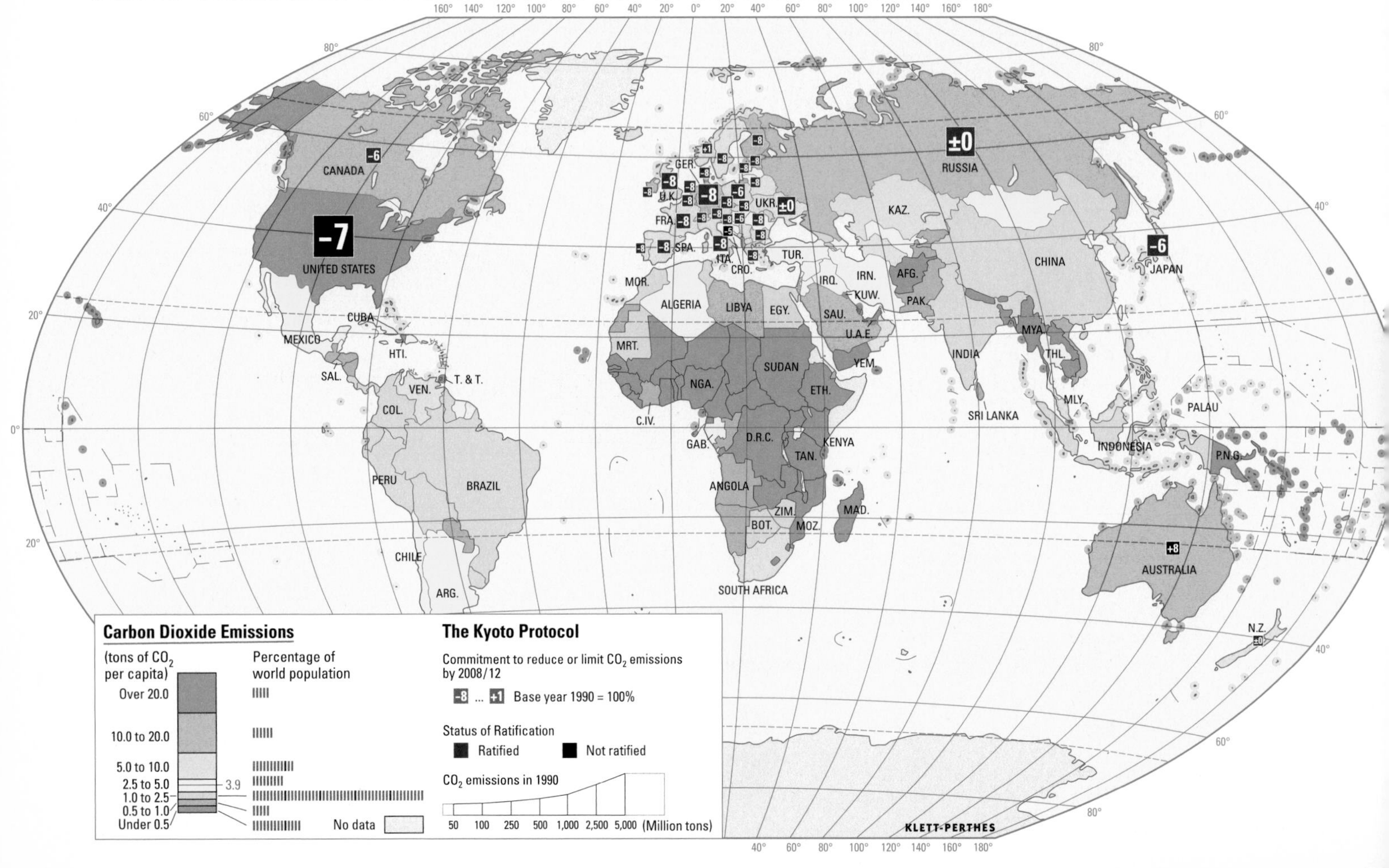

CANADA
-6
UNITED STATES
-7
MEXICO
CUBA
HTI.
SAL.
VEN.
T. & T.
COL.
PERU
BRAZIL
CHILE
ARG.
GER.
U.K.
FRA.
SPA.
ITA.
CRO.
UKR.
±0
TUR.
RUSSIA
KAZ.
CHINA
JAPAN
MOR.
ALGERIA
LIBYA
EGY.
IRQ.
IRN.
KUW.
AFG.
PAK.
SAU.
U.A.E.
YEM.
INDIA
SRI LANKA
MYA.
THL.
MLY.
PALAU
INDONESIA
P.N.G.
MRT.
NGA.
SUDAN
ETH.
C.IV.
GAB.
D.R.C.
KENYA
TAN.
ANGOLA
ZIM.
BOT.
MOZ.
MAD.
SOUTH AFRICA
AUSTRALIA
+8
N.Z.
Carbon Dioxide Emissions
(tons of CO_2 per capita)
Percentage of world population
Over 20.0
10.0 to 20.0
5.0 to 10.0
2.5 to 5.0
1.0 to 2.5
0.5 to 1.0
Under 0.5
3.9
No data
The Kyoto Protocol
Commitment to reduce or limit CO_2 emissions by 2008/12
-8 ... +1 Base year 1990 = 100%
Status of Ratification
Ratified
Not ratified
CO_2 emissions in 1990
50
100
250
500
1,000
2,500
5,000 (Million tons)
KLETT-PERTHES

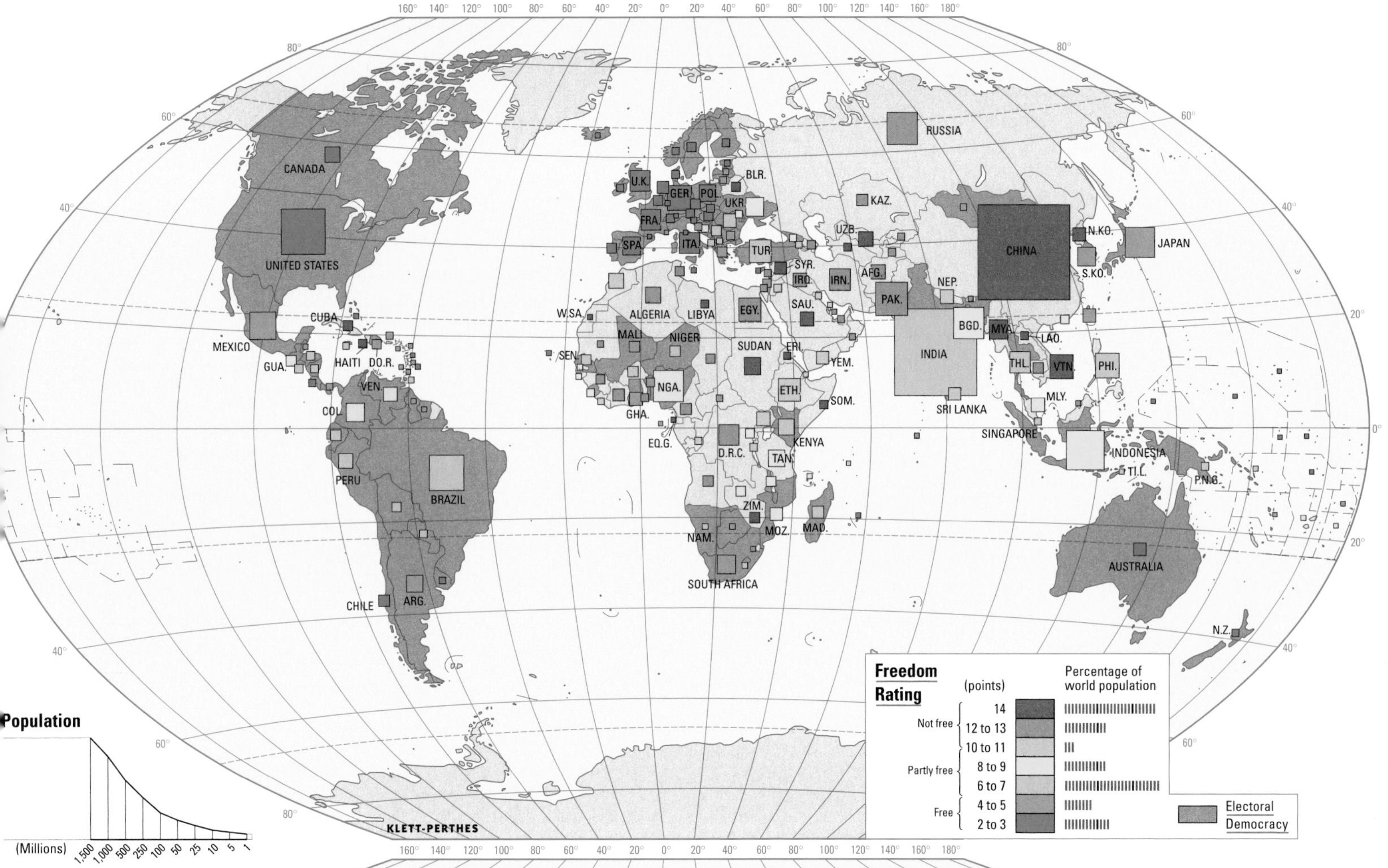
RUSSIA
CANADA
UNITED STATES
MEXICO
CUBA
HAITI
DO.R.
GUA.
VEN.
COL.
PERU
BRAZIL
CHILE
ARG.
U.K.
GER.
POL.
BLR.
UKR.
FRA.
SPA.
ITA.
TUR.
SYR.
IRQ.
IRN.
AFG.
PAK.
KAZ.
UZB.
CHINA
N.KO.
S.KO.
JAPAN
NEP.
BGD.
INDIA
SRI LANKA
MYA.
LAO.
THL.
VTN.
PHI.
MLY.
SINGAPORE
INDONESIA
T.L.
P.N.G.
AUSTRALIA
N.Z.
W.SA.
ALGERIA
LIBYA
EGY.
SAU.
MALI
NIGER
SEN.
SUDAN
ERI.
YEM.
NGA.
ETH.
SOM.
GHA.
EQ.G.
D.R.C.
KENYA
TAN.
ZIM.
NAM.
MOZ.
MAD.
SOUTH AFRICA
KLETT-PERTHES
Freedom Rating
(points)
Percentage of world population
Not free
14
12 to 13
10 to 11
Partly free
8 to 9
6 to 7
Free
4 to 5
2 to 3
Electoral Democracy
Population
(Millions)
1,500
1,000
500
250
100
50
25
10
5
1

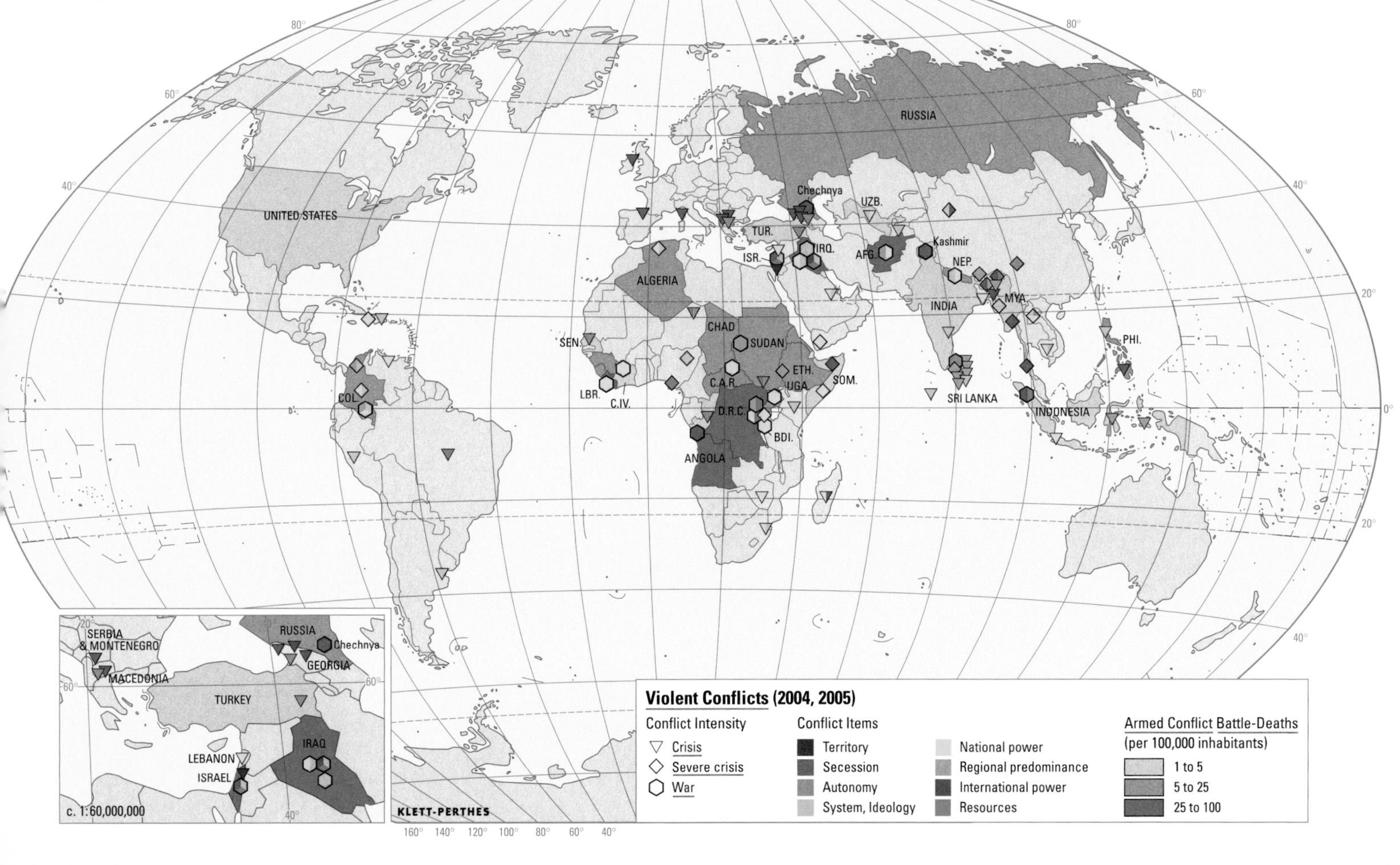
RUSSIA
UNITED STATES
Chechnya
UZB.
Kashmir
TUR.
ISR.
IRQ.
AFG.
NEP.
ALGERIA
INDIA
MYA.
CHAD
SUDAN
SEN.
ETH.
SOM.
PHI.
C.A.R.
UGA.
LBR.
C.IV.
COL.
SRI LANKA
D.R.C.
INDONESIA
BDI.
ANGOLA
SERBIA & MONTENEGRO
MACEDONIA
GEORGIA
TURKEY
IRAQ
LEBANON
ISRAEL
c. 1:60,000,000
KLETT-PERTHES
Violent Conflicts (2004, 2005)
Conflict Intensity
Crisis
Severe crisis
War
Conflict Items
Territory
Secession
Autonomy
System, Ideology
National power
Regional predominance
International power
Resources
Armed Conflict Battle-Deaths (per 100,000 inhabitants)
1 to 5
5 to 25
25 to 100

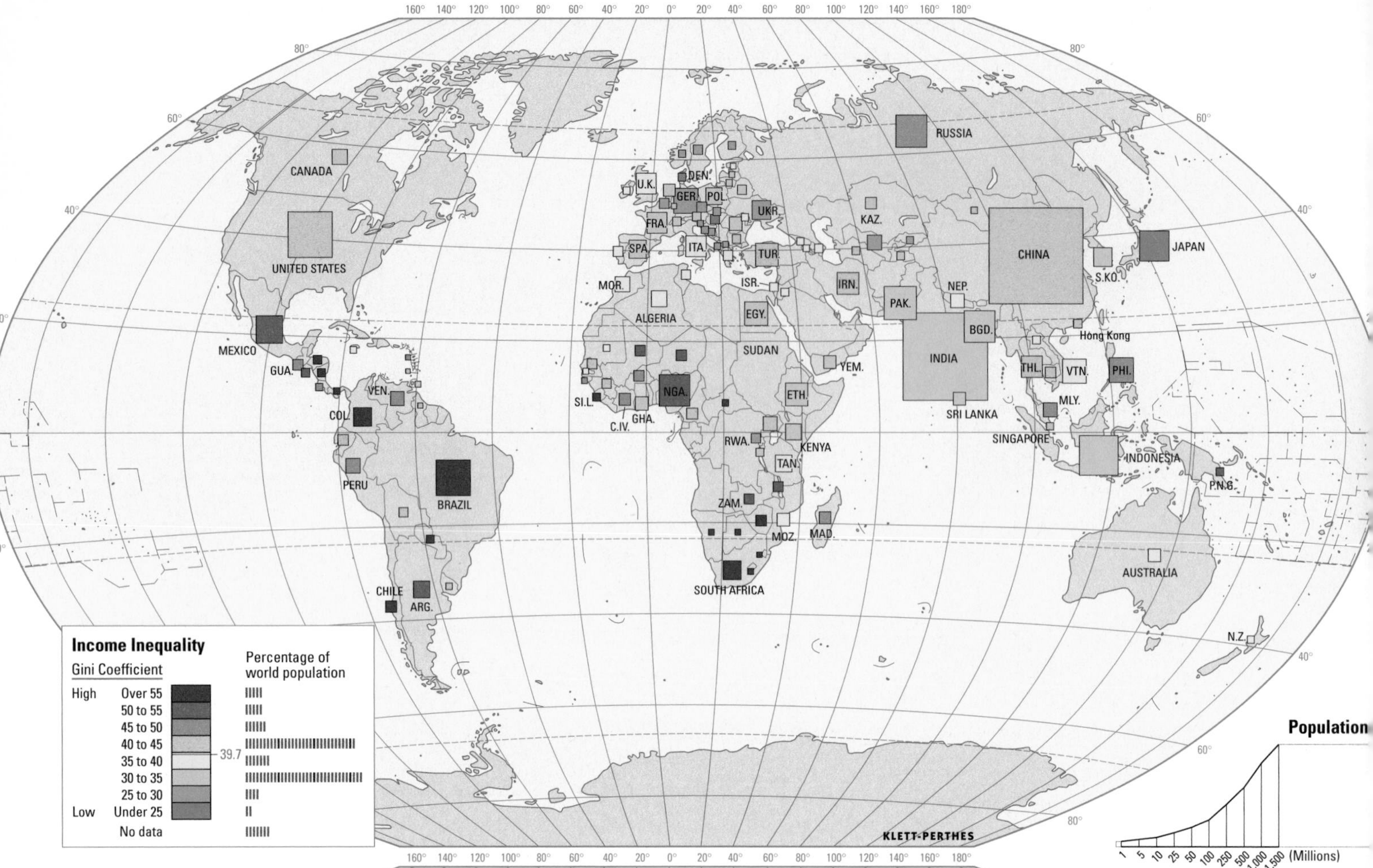
RUSSIA
CANADA
DEN.
U.K.
GER.
POL.
UKR.
FRA.
KAZ.
UNITED STATES
SPA.
ITA.
TUR.
CHINA
JAPAN
S.KO.
MOR.
ISR.
IRN.
NEP.
PAK.
ALGERIA
EGY.
BGD.
Hong Kong
MEXICO
SUDAN
YEM.
INDIA
GUA.
VEN.
SI.L.
NGA.
THL.
VTN.
PHI.
COL.
C.IV.
GHA.
ETH.
MLY.
SRI LANKA
RWA.
KENYA
SINGAPORE
INDONESIA
PERU
TAN.
P.N.G.
BRAZIL
ZAM.
MOZ.
MAD.
AUSTRALIA
SOUTH AFRICA
CHILE
ARG.
N.Z.
KLETT-PERTHES
Income Inequality
Gini Coefficient
Percentage of world population
High Over 55
50 to 55
45 to 50
40 to 45
39.7
35 to 40
30 to 35
25 to 30
Low Under 25
No data
Population
1 5 10 25 50 100 250 500 1,000 1,500 (Millions)

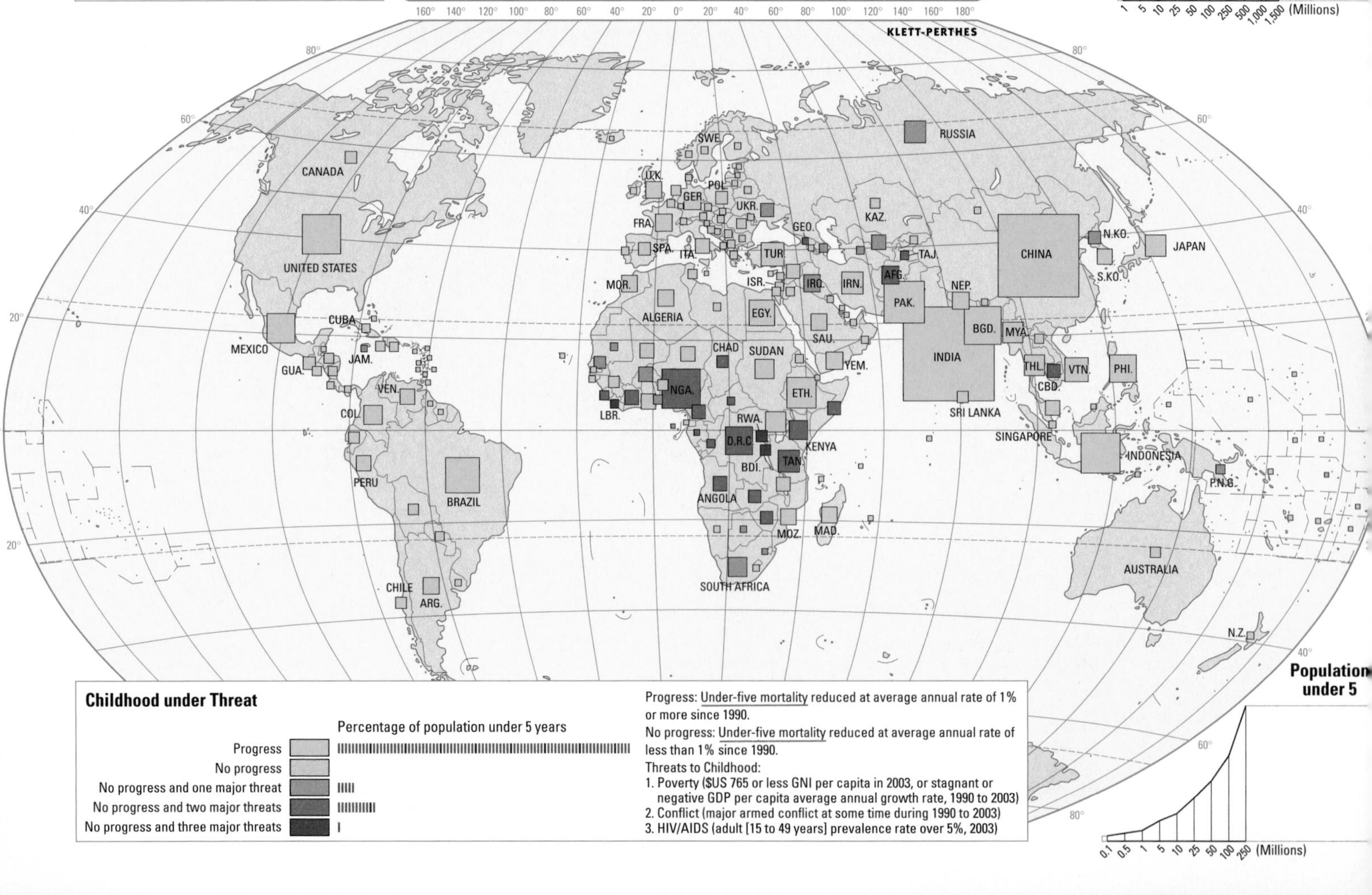
KLETT-PERTHES
RUSSIA
SWE.
CANADA
U.K.
GER.
POL.
UKR.
FRA.
KAZ.
GEO.
UNITED STATES
SPA.
ITA.
TUR.
TAJ.
CHINA
N.KO.
JAPAN
S.KO.
MOR.
ISR.
IRQ.
IRN.
AFG.
NEP.
PAK.
ALGERIA
EGY.
CUBA
BGD.
MYA.
SAU.
MEXICO
JAM.
CHAD
SUDAN
YEM.
INDIA
GUA.
VEN.
NGA.
THL.
VTN.
PHI.
CBD.
ETH.
LBR.
COL.
SRI LANKA
RWA.
KENYA
SINGAPORE
D.R.C.
INDONESIA
BDI.
TAN.
PERU
P.N.G.
ANGOLA
BRAZIL
MOZ.
MAD.
AUSTRALIA
SOUTH AFRICA
CHILE
ARG.
N.Z.
Childhood under Threat
Percentage of population under 5 years
Progress
No progress
No progress and one major threat
No progress and two major threats
No progress and three major threats
Progress: Under-five mortality reduced at average annual rate of 1% or more since 1990.
No progress: Under-five mortality reduced at average annual rate of less than 1% since 1990.
Threats to Childhood:
1. Poverty ($US 765 or less GNI per capita in 2003, or stagnant or negative GDP per capita average annual growth rate, 1990 to 2003)
2. Conflict (major armed conflict at some time during 1990 to 2003)
3. HIV/AIDS (adult [15 to 49 years] prevalence rate over 5%, 2003)
Population under 5
0.1 0.5 1 5 10 25 50 100 250 (Millions)

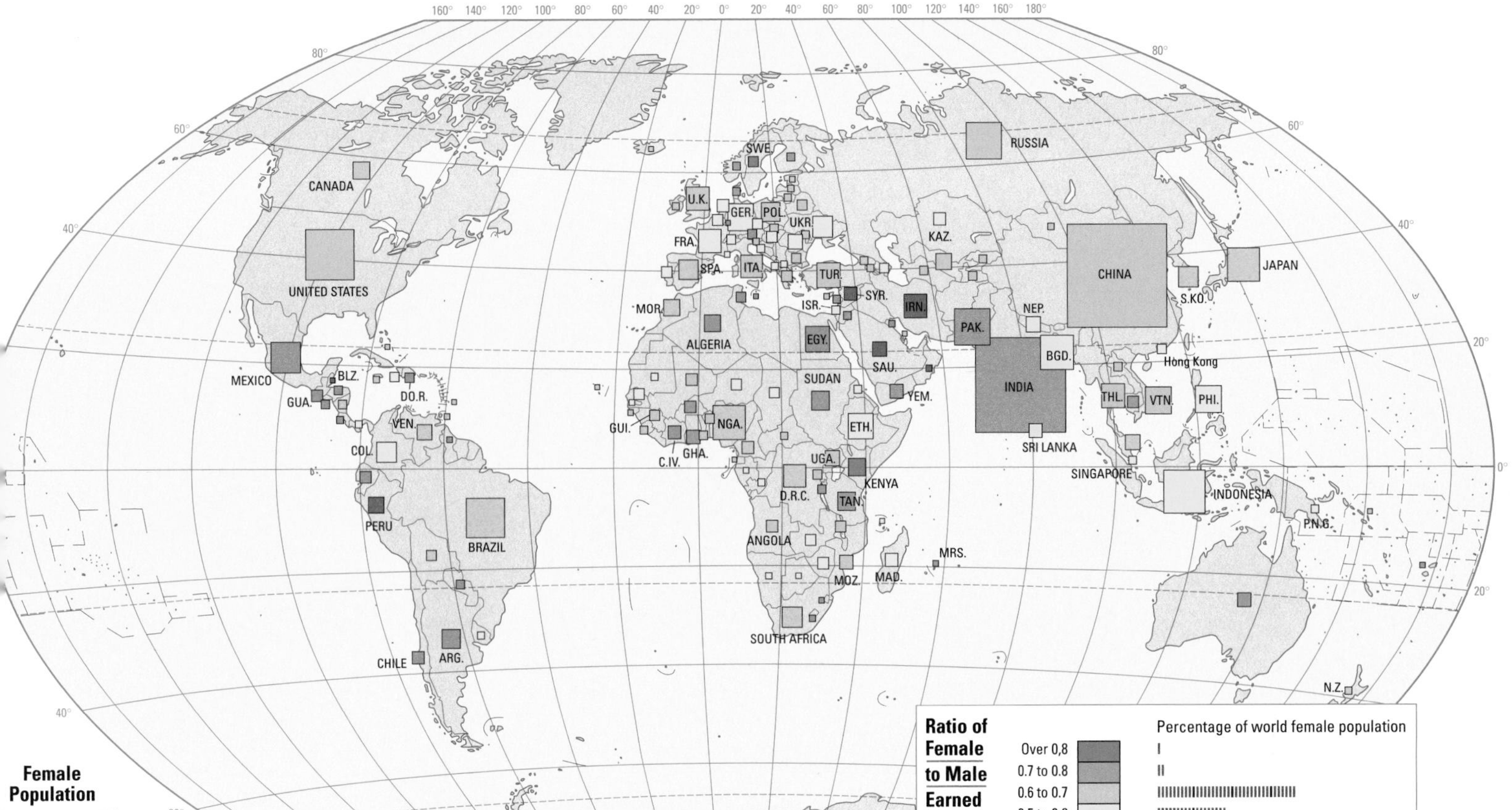

Female Population

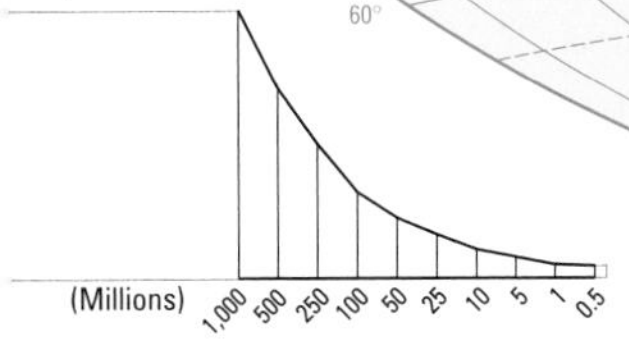

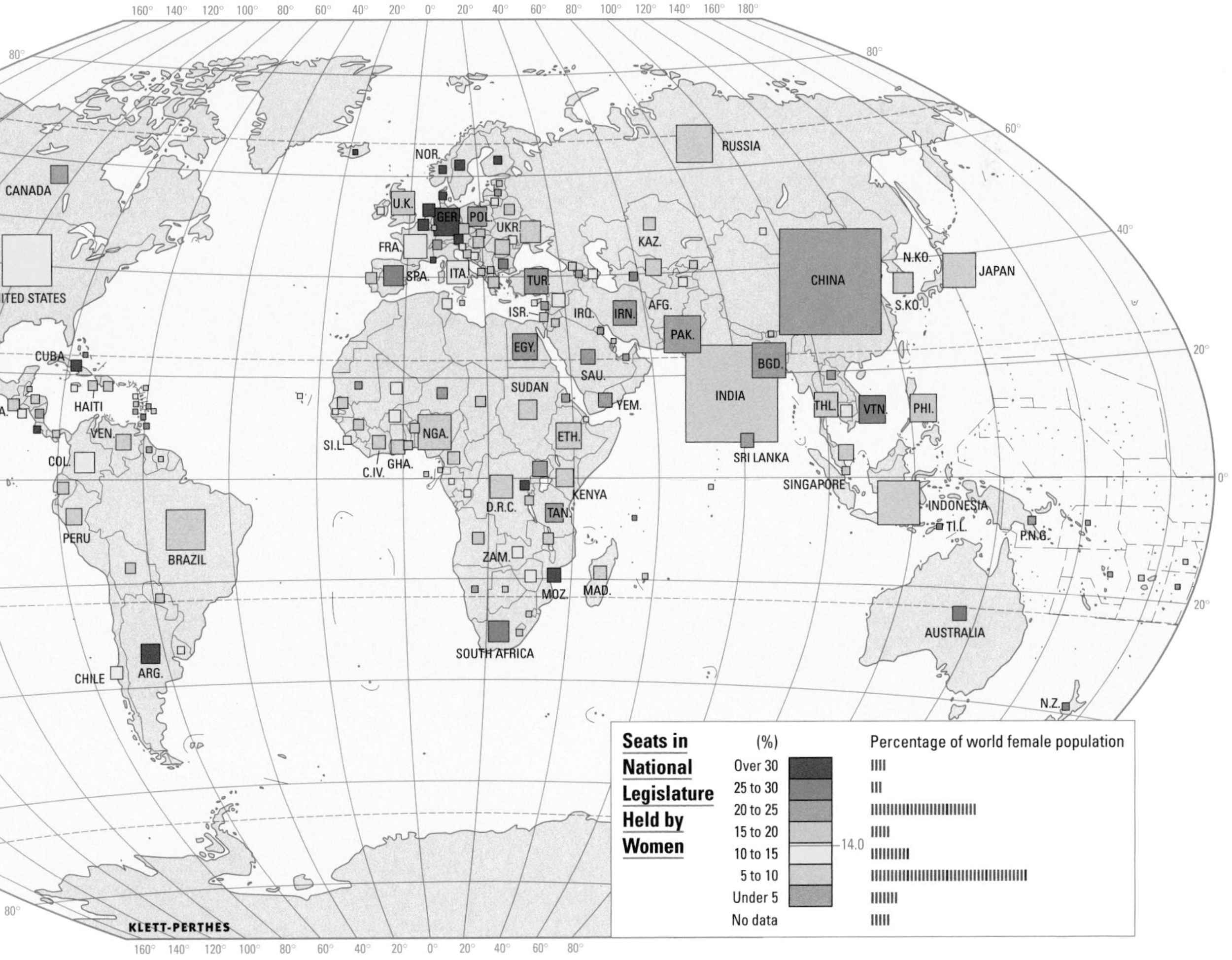

1:160,000,000

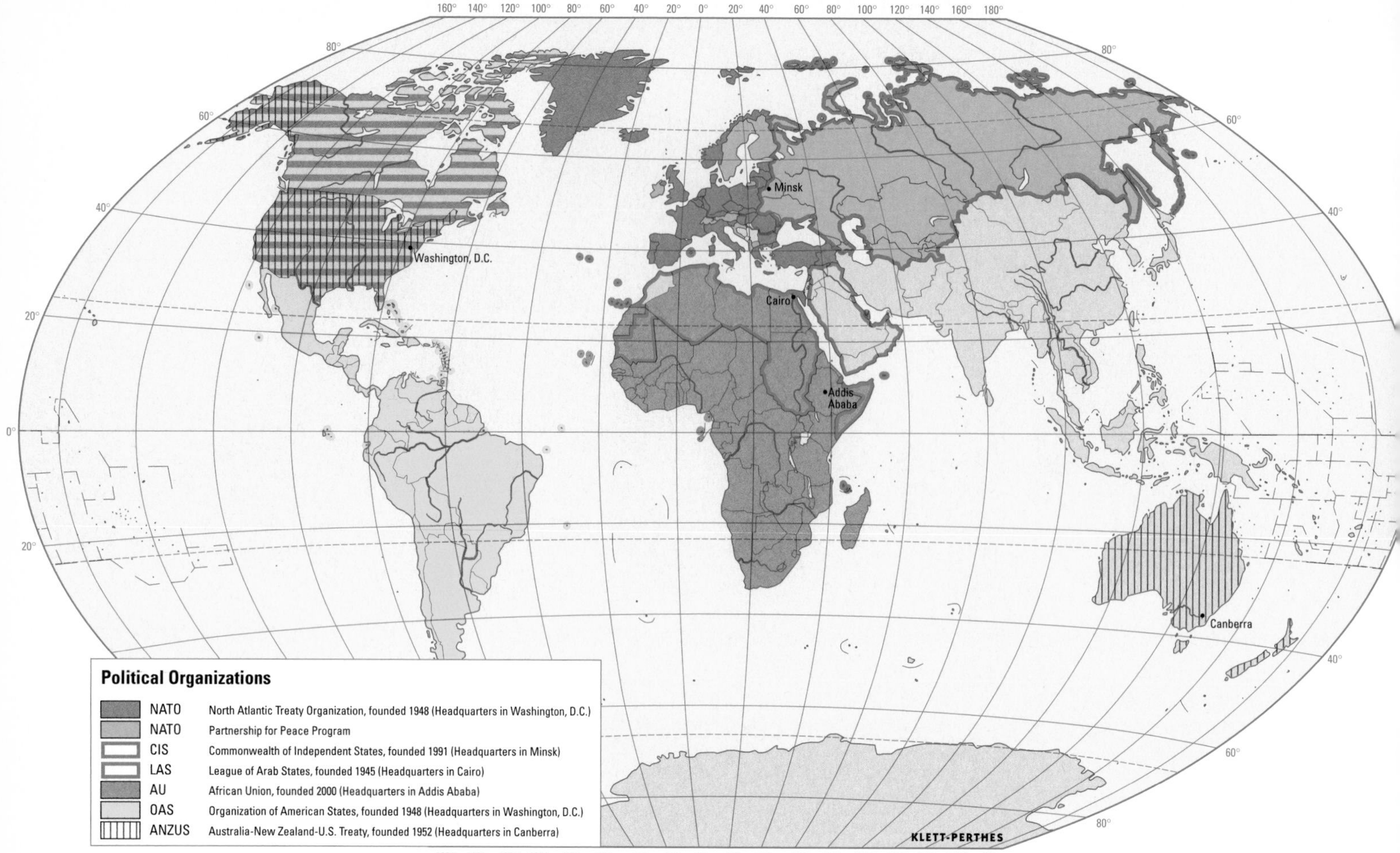

Political Organizations

	NATO	North Atlantic Treaty Organization, founded 1948 (Headquarters in Washington, D.C.)
	NATO	Partnership for Peace Program
	CIS	Commonwealth of Independent States, founded 1991 (Headquarters in Minsk)
	LAS	League of Arab States, founded 1945 (Headquarters in Cairo)
	AU	African Union, founded 2000 (Headquarters in Addis Ababa)
	OAS	Organization of American States, founded 1948 (Headquarters in Washington, D.C.)
	ANZUS	Australia-New Zealand-U.S. Treaty, founded 1952 (Headquarters in Canberra)

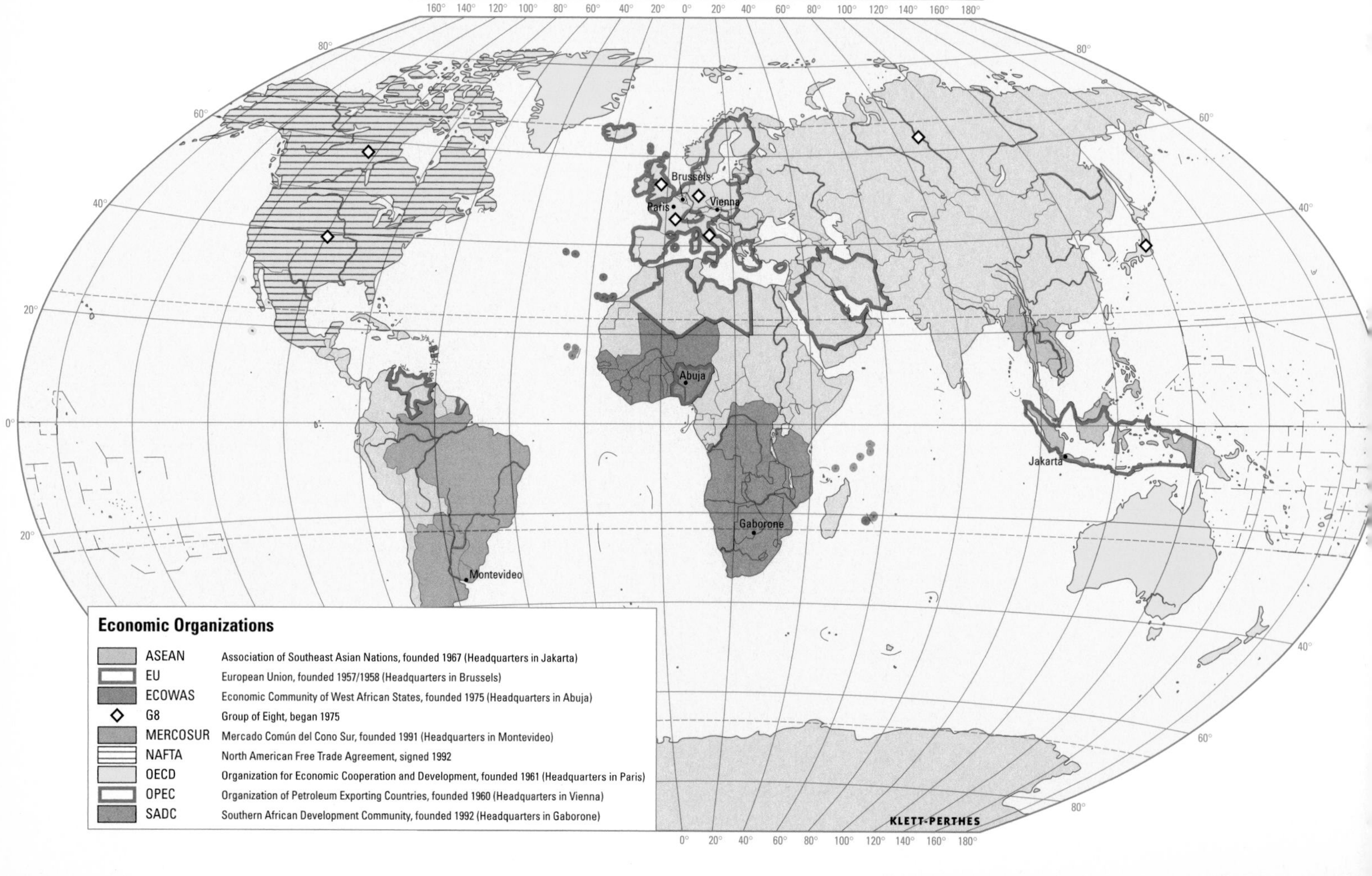

Economic Organizations

	ASEAN	Association of Southeast Asian Nations, founded 1967 (Headquarters in Jakarta)
	EU	European Union, founded 1957/1958 (Headquarters in Brussels)
	ECOWAS	Economic Community of West African States, founded 1975 (Headquarters in Abuja)
◇	G8	Group of Eight, began 1975
	MERCOSUR	Mercado Común del Cono Sur, founded 1991 (Headquarters in Montevideo)
	NAFTA	North American Free Trade Agreement, signed 1992
	OECD	Organization for Economic Cooperation and Development, founded 1961 (Headquarters in Paris)
	OPEC	Organization of Petroleum Exporting Countries, founded 1960 (Headquarters in Vienna)
	SADC	Southern African Development Community, founded 1992 (Headquarters in Gaborone)

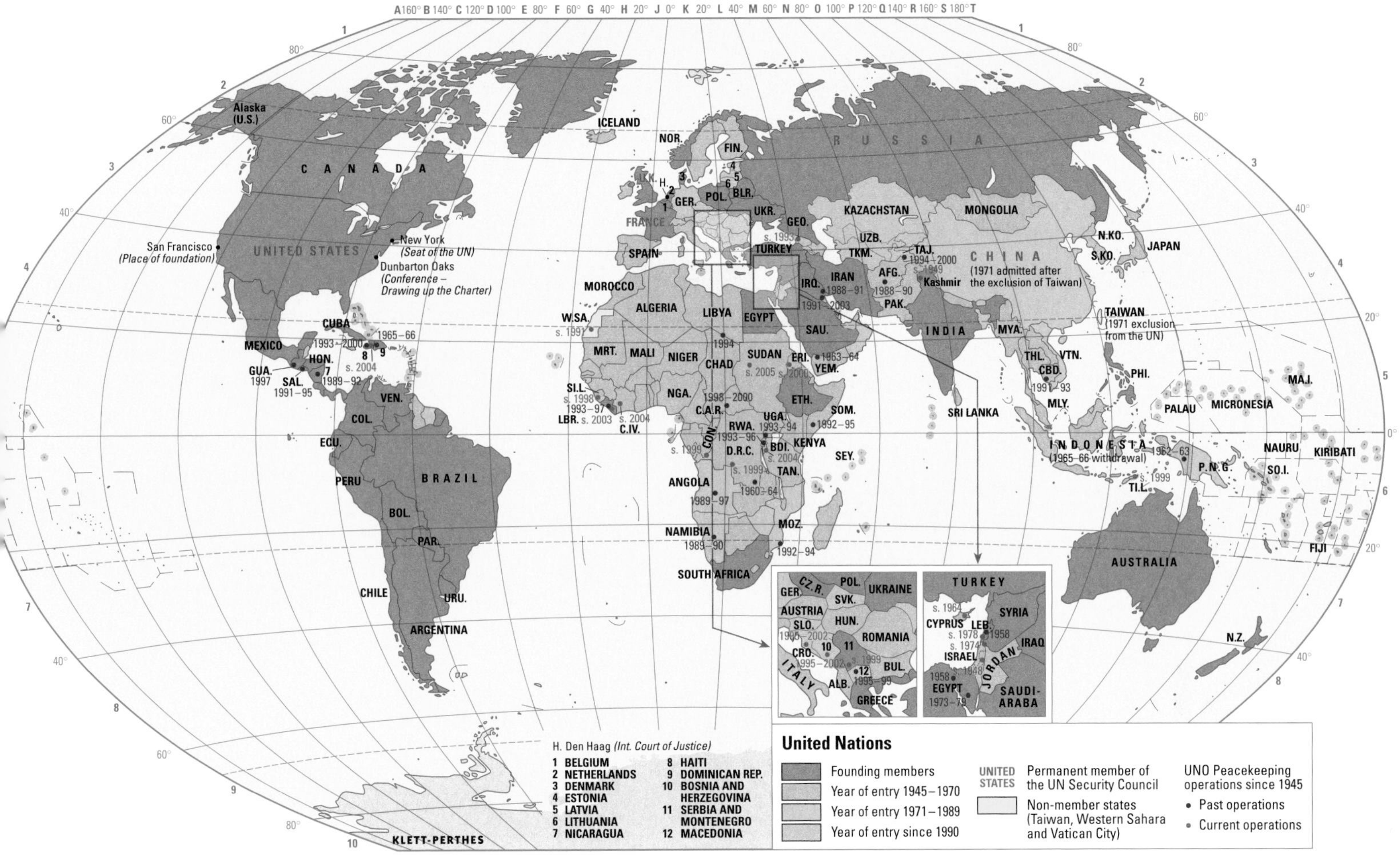
United Nations
Founding members
Year of entry 1945–1970
Year of entry 1971–1989
Year of entry since 1990
UNITED STATES Permanent member of the UN Security Council
Non-member states (Taiwan, Western Sahara and Vatican City)
UNO Peacekeeping operations since 1945
• Past operations
• Current operations
H. Den Haag (Int. Court of Justice)
1 BELGIUM
2 NETHERLANDS
3 DENMARK
4 ESTONIA
5 LATVIA
6 LITHUANIA
7 NICARAGUA
8 HAITI
9 DOMINICAN REP.
10 BOSNIA AND HERZEGOVINA
11 SERBIA AND MONTENEGRO
12 MACEDONIA
KLETT-PERTHES
San Francisco (Place of foundation)
New York (Seat of the UN)
Dunbarton Oaks (Conference – Drawing up the Charter)
CANADA
UNITED STATES
Alaska (U.S.)
ICELAND
RUSSIA
KAZACHSTAN
MONGOLIA
CHINA (1971 admitted after the exclusion of Taiwan)
JAPAN
TAIWAN (1971 exclusion from the UN)
INDIA
INDONESIA (1965–66 withdrawal)
AUSTRALIA
N.Z.
BRAZIL
ARGENTINA
CHILE
PERU
MEXICO
CUBA
ALGERIA
LIBYA
EGYPT
SUDAN
CHAD
NIGER
MALI
ANGOLA
NAMIBIA
SOUTH AFRICA
TURKEY
SYRIA
CYPRUS
ISRAEL
JORDAN
SAUDI-ARABIA
IRAQ
UKRAINE
ROMANIA
GREECE
ITALY

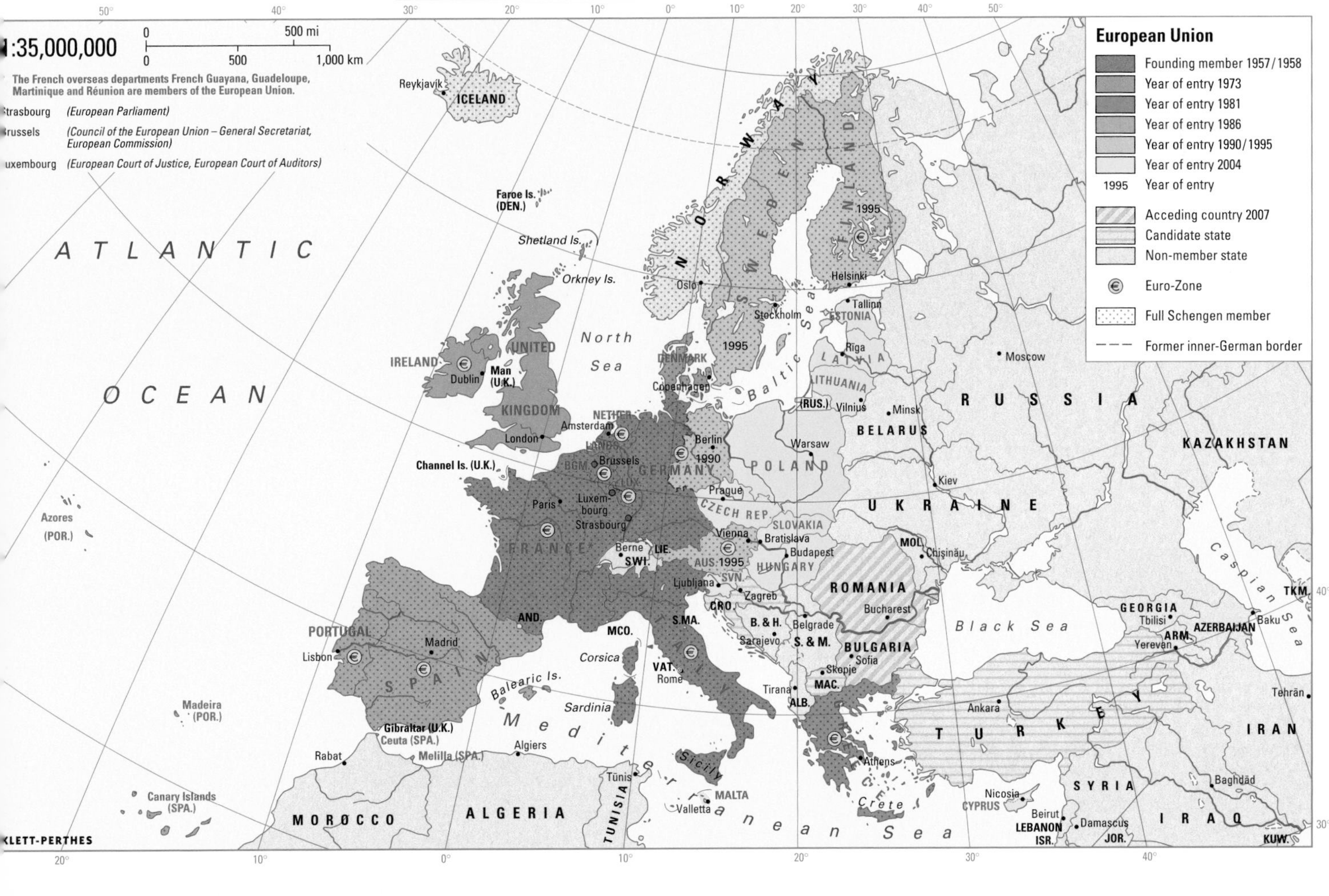
1:35,000,000
0 500 mi
0 500 1,000 km
The French overseas departments French Guayana, Guadeloupe, Martinique and Réunion are members of the European Union.
Strasbourg (European Parliament)
Brussels (Council of the European Union – General Secretariat, European Commission)
Luxembourg (European Court of Justice, European Court of Auditors)
European Union
Founding member 1957/1958
Year of entry 1973
Year of entry 1981
Year of entry 1986
Year of entry 1990/1995
Year of entry 2004
1995 Year of entry
Acceding country 2007
Candidate state
Non-member state
Euro-Zone
Full Schengen member
Former inner-German border
ATLANTIC OCEAN
North Sea
Baltic Sea
Black Sea
Mediterranean Sea
Caspian Sea
ICELAND
NORWAY
SWEDEN
FINLAND
RUSSIA
UNITED KINGDOM
IRELAND
FRANCE
SPAIN
PORTUGAL
GERMANY
POLAND
BELARUS
UKRAINE
ROMANIA
BULGARIA
TURKEY
KAZAKHSTAN
MOROCCO
ALGERIA
TUNISIA
SYRIA
IRAQ
IRAN
KLETT-PERTHES

Grid references (top): A 160° B 140° C 120° D 100° E 80° F 60° G 40° H 20° J

1
80°
60°
2
Greenland
Northice
U.S.
▲ Mt. McKinley
3
C A N A D A
40°
Missouri
L. Superior
Mississippi

EUROPE

Total area:	3,916,000 sq mi / 10,142,000 km²
Population:	692,591,000
Countries:	43
■ Russia (European part)	About 25 % of 6,592,812 sq mi / 17,075,400 km²
👥 Russia (European part)	About 75% of 143,202,000
● Moscow	12,410,000
🏝 Great Britain	84,587 sq mi / 219,081 km²
〰 Lake Ladoga	7,002 sq mi / 18,135 km²
⌇ Volga	2,194 mi / 3,531 km
▲ Mont Blanc	15,771 ft / 4,807 m
▼ Caspian Sea (surface)	−92 ft / −28 m
🌡 Sevilla	122 °F / 50 °C
🌡 Ust'-Shchugër	−67 °F / −55 °C

NORTH AMERICA

Total area:	9,530,000 sq mi / 24,683,000 km²
Population:	516,213,000
Countries:	23
■ Canada	3,855,081 sq mi / 9,984,670 km²
👥 United States	298,213,000
● Mexico City	17,309,000
🏝 Greenland	836,326 sq mi / 2,166,086 km²
〰 Lake Superior	31,700 sq mi / 82,103 km²
⌇ Mississippi-Missouri	3,989 mi / 6,420 km
▲ Mount McKinley	20,320 ft / 6,194 m
▼ Death Valley	−282 ft / −86 m
🌡 Death Valley	134 °F / 57 °C
🌡 Northice	−87 °F / −66 °C

U N I T E D
Death Valley ▼
S T A T E S
20°
MEXICO CITY ●

Great Britain
60°
Mont Blanc
↓ Sevilla
↓ Ifrān

0°
Maracaibo
Amazon
Ucayali
B R A Z I L
SÃO PAULO ●

AFRICA

Total area:	11,683,000 sq mi / 30,260,000 k
Population:	906,068,000
Countries:	54
■ Sudan	967,493 sq mi / 2,505,810 km²
👥 Nigeria	131,530,000
● Cairo	10,834,000
🏝 Madagascar	226,657 sq mi / 587,041 km²
〰 Lake Victoria	26,828 sq mi / 69,484 km²
⌇ Nile	4,145 mi / 6,671 km
▲ Kilimanjaro	19,331 ft / 5,892 m
▼ Lake Asäle (surface)	−515 ft / −157 m
🌡 Al-'Azīzīyah	136 °F / 57,8 °C
🌡 Ifrān	−11 °F / −24 °C

SOUTH AMERICA

Total area:	6,815,000 sq mi / 17,650,000 km²
Population:	375,739,000
Countries:	12
■ Brazil	3,300,153 sq mi / 8,547,404 km²
👥 Brazil	186,405,000
● São Paulo	19,037,000
🏝 Tierra del Fuego	18,148 sq mi / 47,000 km²
〰 Lake Maracaibo	5,217 sq mi / 13,512 km²
⌇ Amazon	4,000 mi / 6,437 km
▲ Aconcagua	22,841 ft / 6,962 m
▼ Salinas Chicas	−138 ft / −42 m
🌡 Rivadavia	120 °F / 49 °C
🌡 Sarmiento	−27 °F / −33 °C

↓ Rivadavia
▲ Aconcagua
Salinas Chicas ▼
↓ Sarmiento
Tierra del Fuego
Alexander I.
Vinson Massif ▲

5
6
20°
7
40°
8
60°
9
80°
10

Legend

■	Largest country
👥	Most populous country
●	Largest urban agglomeration
🏝	Largest island
〰	Largest lake
⌇	Longest river
▲	Highest elevation
▼	Lowest elevation
🌡	Place with the highest recorded temperature
🌡	Place with the lowest recorded temperature

Grid references (bottom): A 160° B 140° C 120° D 100° E 80° F 60° G 40° H 20° J

The Continents

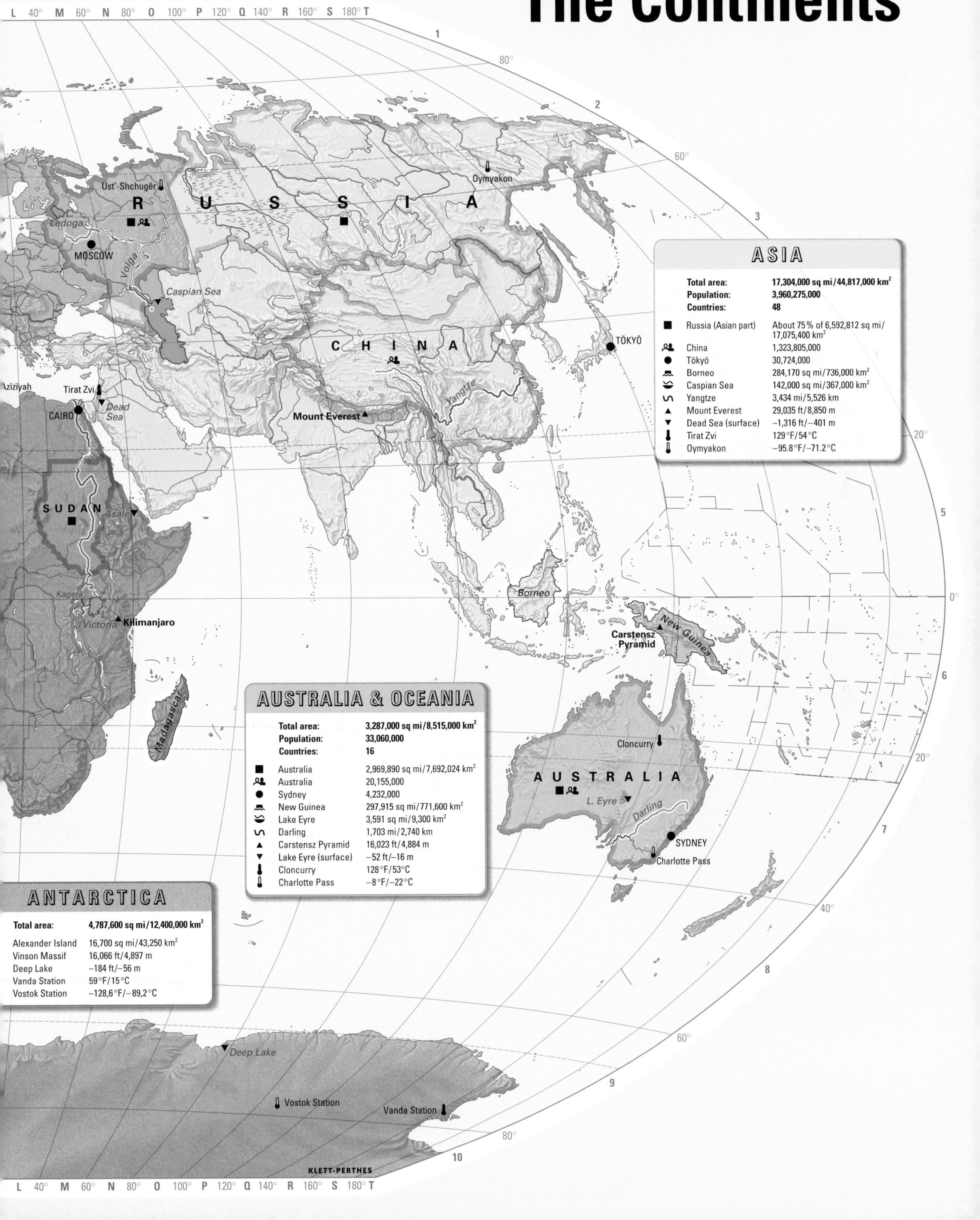

ASIA

	Total area:	**17,304,000 sq mi/44,817,000 km²**
	Population:	**3,960,275,000**
	Countries:	**48**
■	Russia (Asian part)	About 75 % of 6,592,812 sq mi/ 17,075,400 km²
(population)	China	1,323,805,000
●	Tōkyō	30,724,000
(island)	Borneo	284,170 sq mi/736,000 km²
(lake)	Caspian Sea	142,000 sq mi/367,000 km²
(river)	Yangtze	3,434 mi/5,526 km
▲	Mount Everest	29,035 ft/8,850 m
▼	Dead Sea (surface)	–1,316 ft/–401 m
(max. temperature)	Tirat Zvi	129 °F/54 °C
(min. temperature)	Oymyakon	–95.8 °F/–71.2 °C

AUSTRALIA & OCEANIA

	Total area:	**3,287,000 sq mi/8,515,000 km²**
	Population:	**33,060,000**
	Countries:	**16**
■	Australia	2,969,890 sq mi/7,692,024 km²
(population)	Australia	20,155,000
●	Sydney	4,232,000
(island)	New Guinea	297,915 sq mi/771,600 km²
(lake)	Lake Eyre	3,591 sq mi/9,300 km²
(river)	Darling	1,703 mi/2,740 km
▲	Carstensz Pyramid	16,023 ft/4,884 m
▼	Lake Eyre (surface)	–52 ft/–16 m
(max. temperature)	Cloncurry	128 °F/53 °C
(min. temperature)	Charlotte Pass	–8 °F/–22 °C

ANTARCTICA

Total area:	**4,787,600 sq mi/12,400,000 km²**
Alexander Island	16,700 sq mi/43,250 km²
Vinson Massif	16,066 ft/4,897 m
Deep Lake	–184 ft/–56 m
Vanda Station	59 °F/15 °C
Vostok Station	–128,6 °F/–89,2 °C

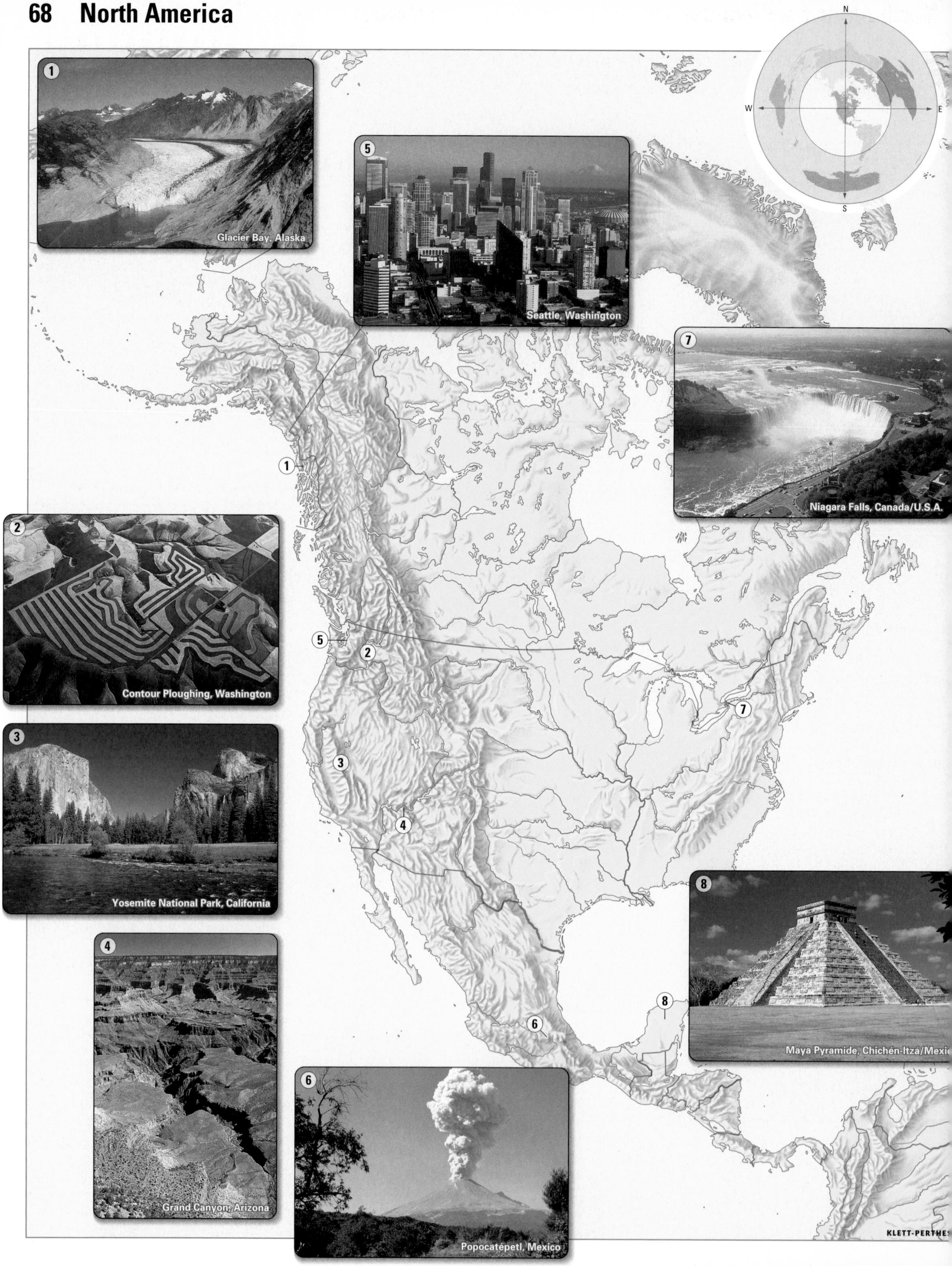

Glacier Bay, Alaska

Contour Ploughing, Washington

Yosemite National Park, California

Grand Canyon, Arizona

Seattle, Washington

Popocatépetl, Mexico

Niagara Falls, Canada/U.S.A.

Maya Pyramide, Chichén-Itzá/Mexic

North America: Physical

1:40,000,000

0 500 1,000 mi
0 500 1,000 1,500 2,000 km

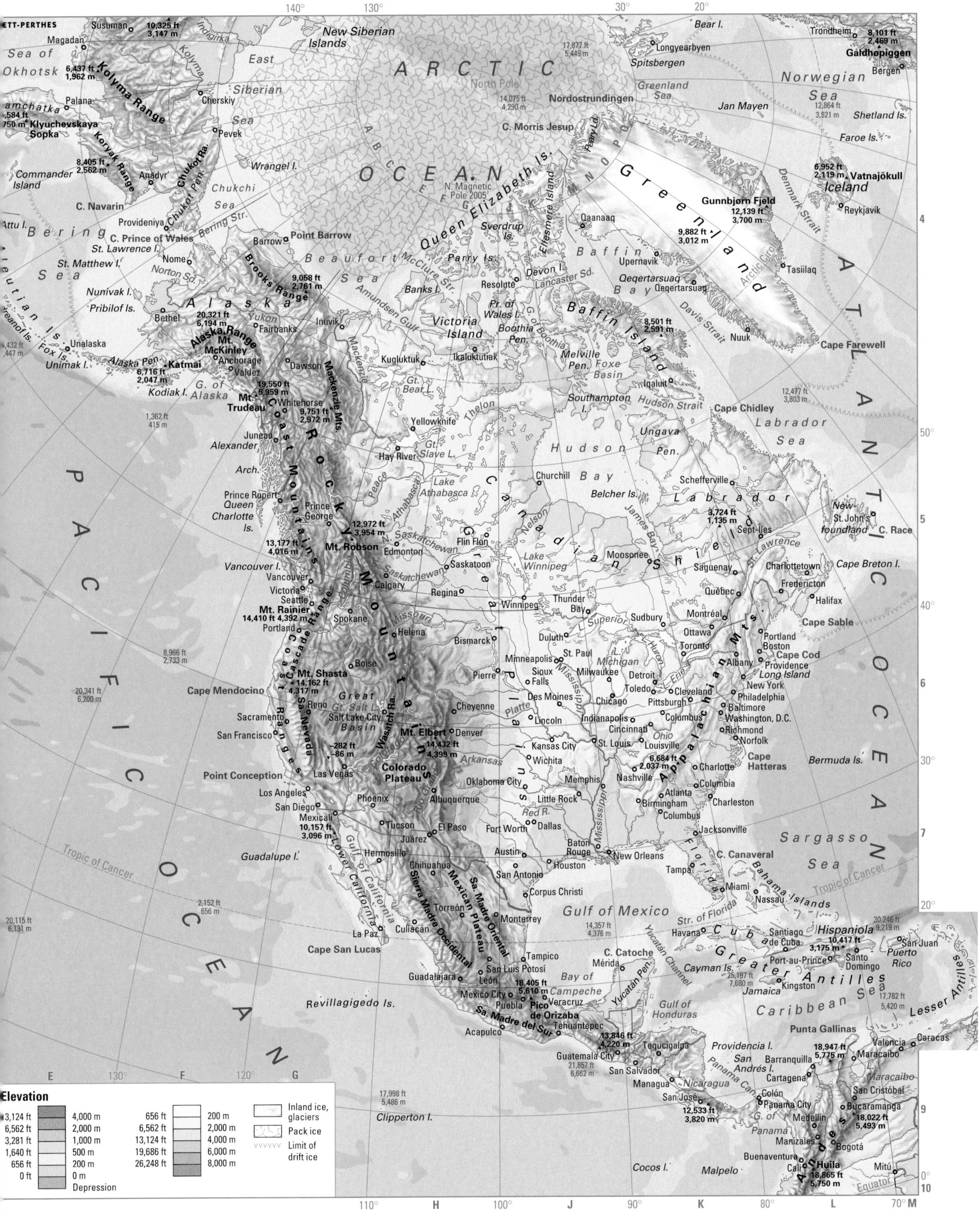

140° 130° 30° 20°
ETT-PERTHES
Susuman 10,325 ft 3,147 m
Magadan
Sea of Okhotsk
6,437 ft 1,962 m
Kolyma Range
Indigirka
Kolyma
New Siberian Islands
East Siberian Sea
ARCTIC OCEAN
North Pole
17,877 ft 5,449 m
14,075 ft 4,290 m
Bear I.
Longyearbyen
Spitsbergen
Greenland Sea
Nordostrundingen
C. Morris Jesup
Peary Ld.
Trondheim
8,101 ft 2,469 m
Galdhøpiggen
Bergen
Norwegian Sea
12,864 ft 3,921 m
Jan Mayen
Shetland Is.
Faroe Is.
Kamchatka
Palana
Cherskiy
Pevek
Klyuchevskaya Sopka
Koryak Range
Chukot Ra.
Chukot Pen.
8,405 ft 2,562 m
Anadyr'
Wrangel I.
Commander Island
Chukchi Sea
N. Magnetic Pole 2005
Queen Elizabeth Is.
Ellesmere Island
Greenland
Gunnbjørn Fjeld 12,139 ft 3,700 m
9,882 ft 3,012 m
6,952 ft 2,119 m
Vatnajökull
Iceland
Reykjavík
Denmark Strait
C. Navarin
Provideniya
Bering Str.
C. Prince of Wales
St. Lawrence I.
Bering Sea
Barrow
Point Barrow
Sverdrup Is.
Qaanaaq
Attu I.
St. Matthew I.
Nome
Norton Sd.
Brooks Range
9,058 ft 2,761 m
Beaufort Sea
McClure Str.
Parry Is.
Devon I.
Lancaster Sd.
Resolute
Baffin Bay
Upernavik
Qeqertarsuaq
Arctic Circle
Tasiilaq
ATLANTIC OCEAN
Nunivak I.
Pribilof Is.
Bethel
Alaska
20,321 ft 6,194 m
Fairbanks
Yukon
Amundsen Gulf
Banks I.
Victoria Island
Pr. of Wales I.
Boothia Pen.
G. of Boothia
Baffin Island
8,501 ft 2,591 m
Davis Strait
Nuuk
Cape Farewell
Aleutian Is.
Andreanof Is.
Fox Is.
Unalaska
Unimak I.
Alaska Range
Mt. McKinley
Inuvik
Mackenzie
Kugluktuk
Ikaluktutiak
Melville Pen.
Foxe Basin
Alaska Pen.
Katmai
Anchorage
Valdez
6,716 ft 2,047 m
Dawson
Mackenzie Mts.
Gt. Bear L.
Iqaluit
12,477 ft 3,803 m
Kodiak I.
G. of Alaska
19,550 ft 5,959 m
Mt. Trudeau
Whitehorse
9,751 ft 2,972 m
Thelon
Southampton I.
Hudson Strait
Cape Chidley
Labrador Sea
1,362 ft 415 m
Yellowknife
Ungava Pen.
Juneau
Alexander Arch.
Coast Mountains
Rocky Mountains
Gt. Slave L.
Hay River
Hudson Bay
PACIFIC OCEAN
Peace
Athabasca
Lake Athabasca
Canadian Shield
Churchill
Belcher Is.
Schefferville
Labrador
Prince Rupert
Queen Charlotte Is.
Prince George
12,972 ft 3,954 m
13,177 ft 4,016 m
Mt. Robson
Edmonton
N. Saskatchewan
Flin Flon
Nelson
James Bay
3,724 ft 1,135 m
Sept-Îles
Newfoundland
St. John's
C. Race
St. Lawrence
Great Plains
Vancouver I.
Vancouver
Victoria
Columbia
S. Saskatchewan
Saskatoon
Calgary
Regina
Lake Winnipeg
Moosonee
Saguenay
Charlottetown
Cape Breton I.
Québec
Fredericton
Halifax
Seattle
Mt. Rainier 14,410 ft 4,392 m
Cascade Range
Spokane
Winnipeg
Thunder Bay
L. Superior
Sudbury
Montréal
Cape Sable
Portland
Missouri
Helena
Bismarck
Duluth
Ottawa
Toronto
Portland
Boston
Cape Cod
8,966 ft 2,733 m
Coast Ranges
Boise
St. Paul
L. Michigan
L. Huron
Appalachian Mts.
Albany
Providence
Long Island
Mt. Shasta 14,162 ft 4,317 m
Minneapolis
Sioux Falls
Mississippi
Milwaukee
Detroit
L. Erie
New York
Philadelphia
20,341 ft 6,200 m
Cape Mendocino
Pierre
Great Basin
Gt. Salt L.
Reno
Sierra Nevada
Salt Lake City
Wasatch Ra.
Cheyenne
Platte
Des Moines
Chicago
Toledo
Cleveland
Pittsburgh
Baltimore
Washington, D.C.
Sacramento
San Francisco
Lincoln
Indianapolis
Columbus
Cincinnati
Ohio
Richmond
Norfolk
Mt. Elbert 14,432 ft 4,399 m
Denver
Kansas City
St. Louis
Louisville
-282 ft -86 m
Wichita
Arkansas
6,684 ft 2,037 m
Nashville
Charlotte
Cape Hatteras
Bermuda Is.
Point Conception
Las Vegas
Colorado Plateau
Colorado
Oklahoma City
Memphis
Atlanta
Columbia
Los Angeles
San Diego
Phoenix
Albuquerque
Rio Grande
Little Rock
Birmingham
Charleston
Mexicali
10,157 ft 3,096 m
Tucson
El Paso
Fort Worth
Dallas
Red R.
Columbus
Jacksonville
Sargasso Sea
Juárez
Baton Rouge
New Orleans
Guadalupe I.
Tropic of Cancer
Hermosillo
Lower California
Gulf of California
Austin
Houston
C. Canaveral
Florida
Tampa
Chihuahua
Sierra Madre Occidental
Mexican Plateau
Sa. Madre Oriental
San Antonio
Corpus Christi
Miami
Bahama Islands
Nassau
2,152 ft 656 m
Torreón
Monterrey
Gulf of Mexico
Str. of Florida
20,115 ft 6,131 m
La Paz
Culiacán
14,357 ft 4,376 m
Havana
Cuba
Santiago de Cuba
Hispaniola
30,246 ft 9,219 m
10,417 ft 3,175 m
San Juan
Puerto Rico
Cape San Lucas
Tampico
C. Catoche
Yucatán Channel
Port-au-Prince
Santo Domingo
Mérida
Cayman Is.
Greater Antilles
Lesser Antilles
San Luis Potosí
Guadalajara
León
Bay of Campeche
Yucatán Pen.
25,197 ft 7,680 m
Kingston
Jamaica
Mexico City
18,405 ft 5,610 m
Pico de Orizaba
Puebla
Veracruz
17,782 ft 5,420 m
Revillagigedo Is.
Gulf of Honduras
Caribbean Sea
Sa. Madre del Sur
Tehuantepec
Punta Gallinas
Acapulco
13,846 ft 4,220 m
Tegucigalpa
Providencia I.
18,947 ft 5,775 m
Valencia
Caracas
Maracaibo
Guatemala City
21,857 ft 6,662 m
San Salvador
San Andrés I.
Barranquilla
Cartagena
Maracaibo
Managua
Nicaragua
Panama Canal
Colón
San Cristóbal
17,998 ft 5,486 m
San José
12,533 ft 3,820 m
Panama City
G. of Panamá
Bucaramanga
Clipperton I.
Medellín
18,022 ft 5,493 m
Manizales
Bogotá
Buenaventura
Cali
Huila 18,865 ft 5,750 m
Andes
Cocos I.
Malpelo
Mitú
Equator
4 50° 5 40° 6 30° 7 20° 9 0° 10
E 130° F 120° G 110° H 100° J 90° K 80° L 70° M
Elevation
ft	m
13,124 ft	4,000 m
6,562 ft	2,000 m
3,281 ft	1,000 m
1,640 ft	500 m
656 ft	200 m
0 ft	0 m
	Depression
ft	m
656 ft	200 m
6,562 ft	2,000 m
13,124 ft	4,000 m
19,686 ft	6,000 m
26,248 ft	8,000 m
Inland ice, glaciers
Pack ice
Limit of drift ice

1:40,000,000

0 500 1,000 mi
0 500 1,000 1,500 2,000 km

North America: Economy

1:40,000,000

0 500 1,000 mi
0 500 1,000 1,500 2,000 km

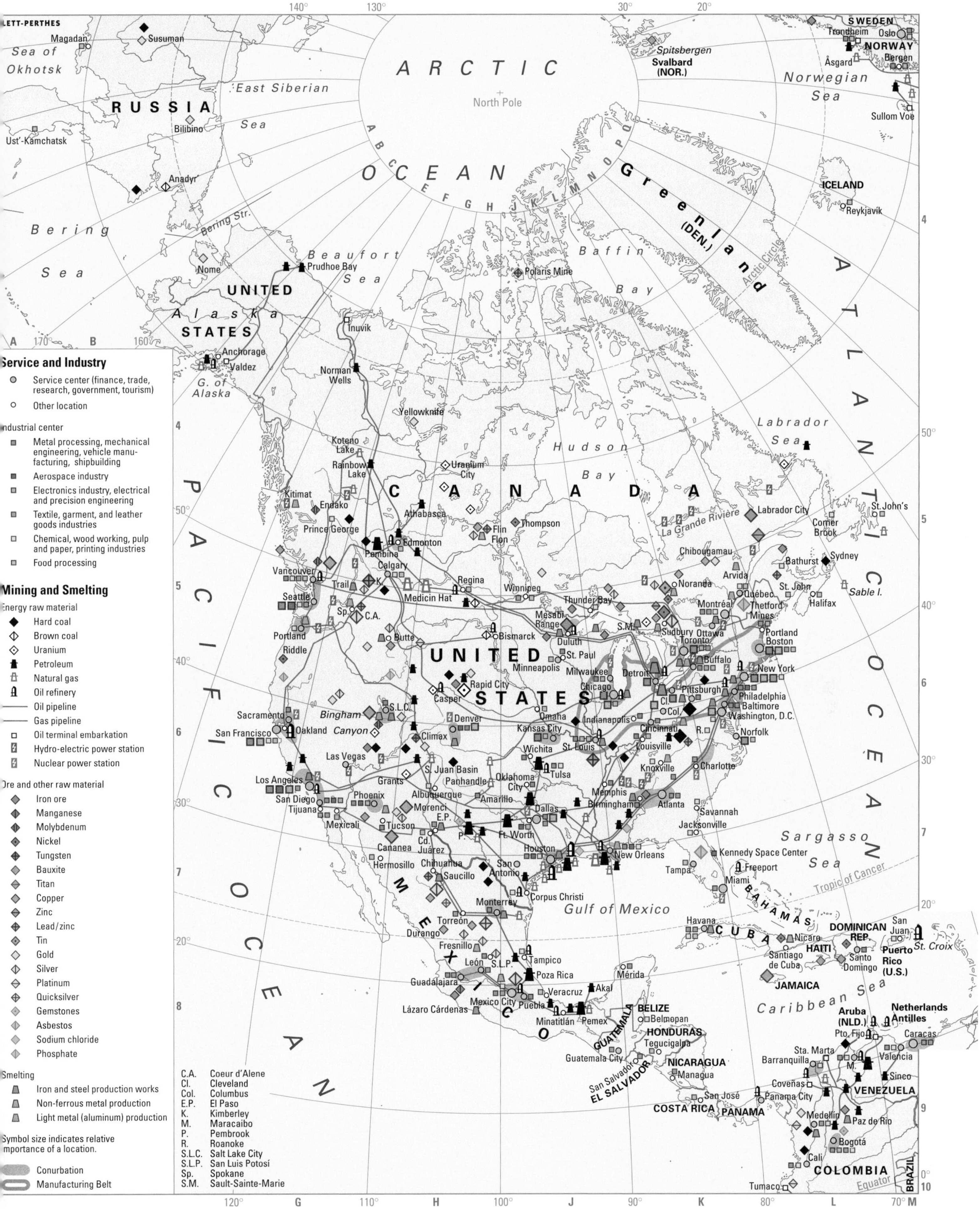

1:40,000,000
0 500 1,000 mi
0 500 1,000 1,500 2,000 km
KLETT-PERTHES
ARCTIC OCEAN
North Pole
PACIFIC OCEAN
ATLANTIC OCEAN
RUSSIA
UNITED STATES
Alaska
CANADA
Greenland (DEN.)
MEXICO
ICELAND
SWEDEN
NORWAY
Hudson Bay
Baffin Bay
Beaufort Sea
Bering Sea
Labrador Sea
Sargasso Sea
Gulf of Mexico
Caribbean Sea
Gulf of California
Tropic of Cancer
Arctic Circle
Equator
CUBA
BAHAMAS
HAITI
DOMINICAN REP.
JAMAICA
BELIZE
GUATEMALA
HONDURAS
EL SALVADOR
NICARAGUA
COSTA RICA
PANAMA
COLOMBIA
VENEZUELA
Bermuda (U.K.)
Washington, D.C.
Ottawa
MEXICO CITY
NEW YORK
LOS ANGELES
CHICAGO
HOUSTON
PHILADELPHIA
TORONTO
MONTRÉAL
HAVANA

North America: Ethnic Groups

1:40,000,000

0 500 1,000 mi
0 500 1,000 1,500 2,000 km

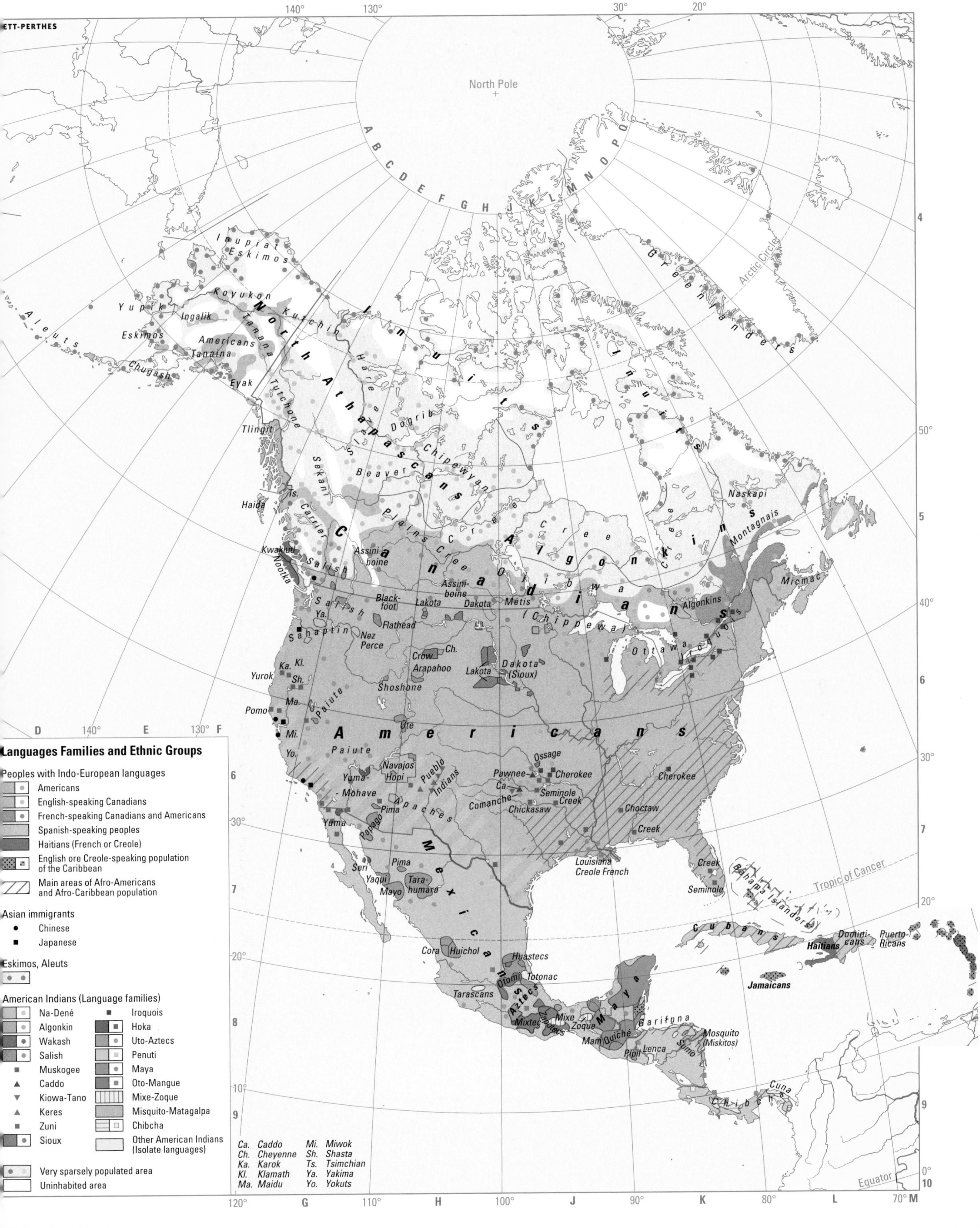

North Pole
Arctic Circle
Tropic of Cancer
Equator
Inupiat Eskimos
Yupik Eskimos
Aleuts
Koyukon
Ingalik
Kutchin
Tanana
Tanaina
Chugash
Eyak
North Americans
North Athapascans
Tutchone
Hare
Dogrib
Slave
Chipewyan
Beaver
Sekani
Tlingit
Haida
Ts.
Carrier
Kwakiutl
Nootka
Salish
Inuits
Greenlanders
Naskapi
Montagnais
Cree
Plains Cree
Assini-boine
Canadians
Algonkins
Ojibwa
Métis
(Chippewa)
Micmac
Algonkins
Iroquois
Ottawa
Blackfoot
Lakota
Dakota
Flathead
Ya.
Sahaptin
Nez Perce
Crow
Ch.
Arapahoo
Dakota (Sioux)
Shoshone
Yurok
Ka.
Kl.
Sh.
Ma.
Pomo
Mi.
Yo.
Paiute
Ute
Americans
Navajos
Hopi
Pueblo Indians
Yuma-Mohave
Apaches
Pima
Yuma
Papago
Ossage
Pawnee
Cherokee
Ca.
Seminole
Creek
Comanche
Chickasaw
Choctaw
Louisiana Creole French
Seminole
Bahama Islanders
Seri
Yaqui
Mayo
Tara-humara
Mexicans
Cora
Huichol
Huastecs
Otomi
Totonac
Tarascans
Aztecs
Mixtec
Zapotecs
Mixe
Zoque
Maya
Mam
Quiché
Garifuna
Pipil
Lenca
Sumo
Mosquito (Miskitos)
Cuna
Chibcha
Cubans
Haitians
Dominicans
Puerto-Ricans
Jamaicans
Languages Families and Ethnic Groups
Peoples with Indo-European languages
Americans
English-speaking Canadians
French-speaking Canadians and Americans
Spanish-speaking peoples
Haitians (French or Creole)
English ore Creole-speaking population of the Caribbean
Main areas of Afro-Americans and Afro-Caribbean population
Asian immigrants
Chinese
Japanese
Eskimos, Aleuts
American Indians (Language families)
Na-Dené
Algonkin
Wakash
Salish
Muskogee
Caddo
Kiowa-Tano
Keres
Zuni
Sioux
Iroquois
Hoka
Uto-Aztecs
Penuti
Maya
Oto-Mangue
Mixe-Zoque
Misquito-Matagalpa
Chibcha
Other American Indians (Isolate languages)
Very sparsely populated area
Uninhabited area
Ca. Caddo
Ch. Cheyenne
Ka. Karok
Kl. Klamath
Ma. Maidu
Mi. Miwok
Sh. Shasta
Ts. Tsimchian
Ya. Yakima
Yo. Yokuts

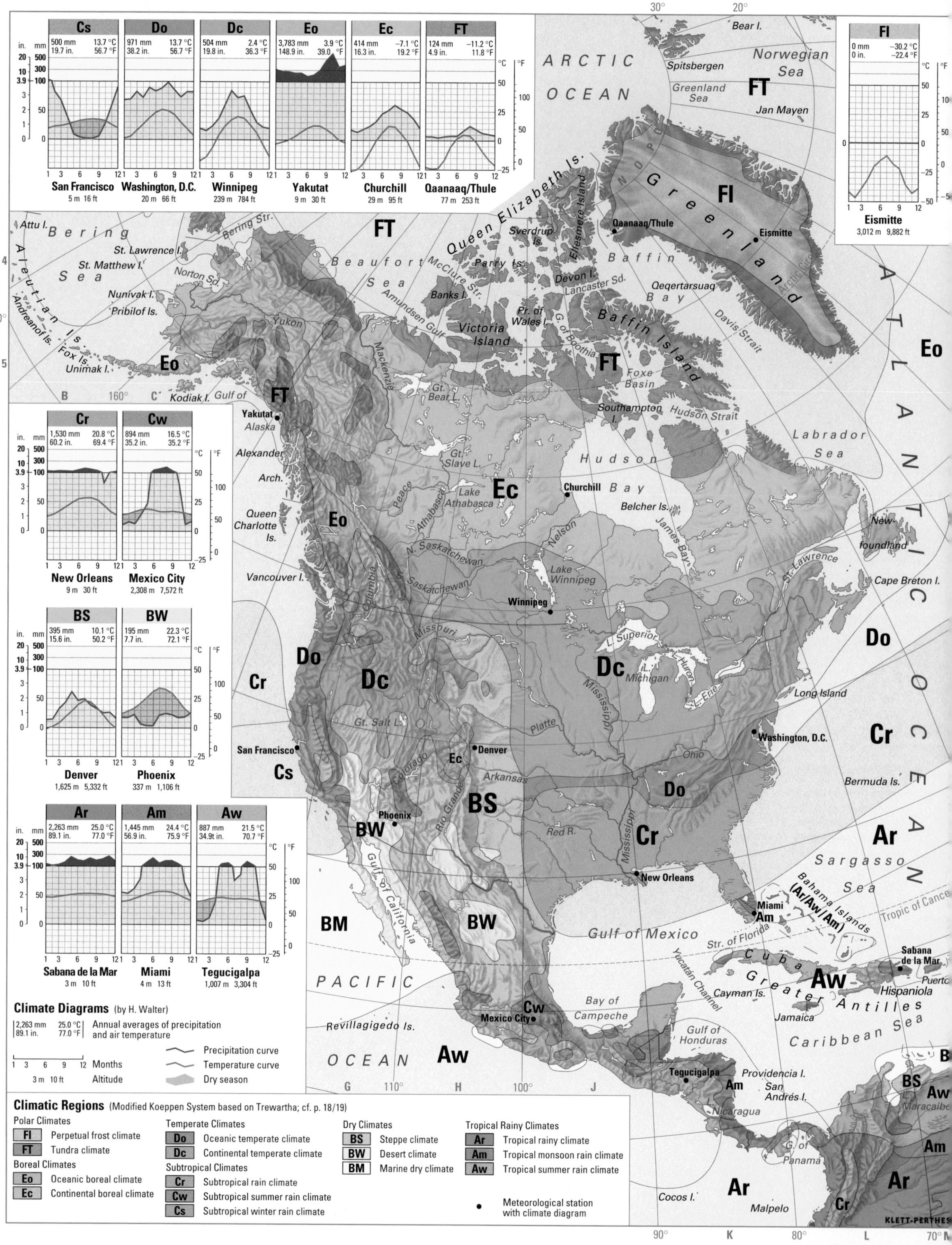

Climatic Regions (Modified Koeppen System based on Trewartha; cf. p. 18/19)

Polar Climates
- **Fl** Perpetual frost climate
- **FT** Tundra climate

Boreal Climates
- **Eo** Oceanic boreal climate
- **Ec** Continental boreal climate

Temperate Climates
- **Do** Oceanic temperate climate
- **Dc** Continental temperate climate

Subtropical Climates
- **Cr** Subtropical rain climate
- **Cw** Subtropical summer rain climate
- **Cs** Subtropical winter rain climate

Dry Climates
- **BS** Steppe climate
- **BW** Desert climate
- **BM** Marine dry climate

Tropical Rainy Climates
- **Ar** Tropical rainy climate
- **Am** Tropical monsoon rain climate
- **Aw** Tropical summer rain climate

• Meteorological station with climate diagram

North America: Natural Hazards

1:40,000,000

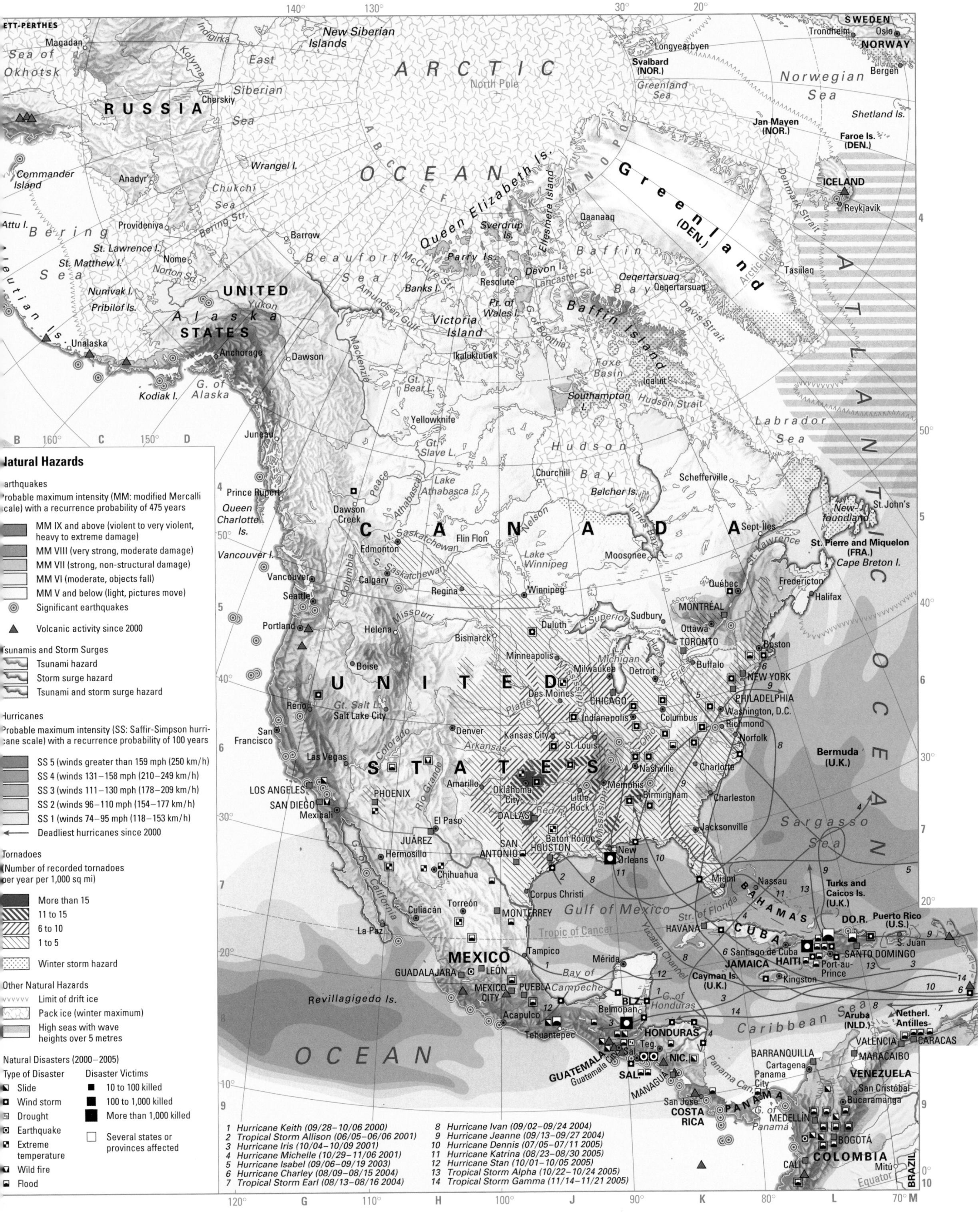
0 500 1,000 mi
0 500 1,000 1,500 2,000 km
ARCTIC OCEAN
North Pole
RUSSIA
UNITED STATES
CANADA
MEXICO
Greenland (DEN.)
ICELAND
ATLANTIC OCEAN
PACIFIC OCEAN
Gulf of Mexico
Caribbean Sea
Sargasso Sea
Hudson Bay
Baffin Bay
Labrador Sea
Bering Sea
Gulf of Alaska
Natural Hazards
Earthquakes
Probable maximum intensity (MM: modified Mercalli scale) with a recurrence probability of 475 years
MM IX and above (violent to very violent, heavy to extreme damage)
MM VIII (very strong, moderate damage)
MM VII (strong, non-structural damage)
MM VI (moderate, objects fall)
MM V and below (light, pictures move)
Significant earthquakes
Volcanic activity since 2000
Tsunamis and Storm Surges
Tsunami hazard
Storm surge hazard
Tsunami and storm surge hazard
Hurricanes
Probable maximum intensity (SS: Saffir-Simpson hurricane scale) with a recurrence probability of 100 years
SS 5 (winds greater than 159 mph (250 km/h)
SS 4 (winds 131–158 mph (210–249 km/h)
SS 3 (winds 111–130 mph (178–209 km/h)
SS 2 (winds 96–110 mph (154–177 km/h)
SS 1 (winds 74–95 mph (118–153 km/h)
Deadliest hurricanes since 2000
Tornadoes
(Number of recorded tornadoes per year per 1,000 sq mi)
More than 15
11 to 15
6 to 10
1 to 5
Winter storm hazard
Other Natural Hazards
Limit of drift ice
Pack ice (winter maximum)
High seas with wave heights over 5 metres
Natural Disasters (2000–2005)
Type of Disaster
Slide
Wind storm
Drought
Earthquake
Extreme temperature
Wild fire
Flood
Disaster Victims
10 to 100 killed
100 to 1,000 killed
More than 1,000 killed
Several states or provinces affected
1 Hurricane Keith (09/28–10/06 2000)
2 Tropical Storm Allison (06/05–06/06 2001)
3 Hurricane Iris (10/04–10/09 2001)
4 Hurricane Michelle (10/29–11/06 2001)
5 Hurricane Isabel (09/06–09/19 2003)
6 Hurricane Charley (08/09–08/15 2004)
7 Tropical Storm Earl (08/13–08/16 2004)
8 Hurricane Ivan (09/02–09/24 2004)
9 Hurricane Jeanne (09/13–09/27 2004)
10 Hurricane Dennis (07/05–07/11 2005)
11 Hurricane Katrina (08/23–08/30 2005)
12 Hurricane Stan (10/01–10/05 2005)
13 Tropical Storm Alpha (10/22–10/24 2005)
14 Tropical Storm Gamma (11/14–11/21 2005)

A
165°
B
170°
C
175°
D
180°
E
175°
F
170°
G
165°
H
160°
J K L M N O P
145°
8
9
10
11
12
50°
45°
40°
35°
N 135°
O
130°
P
125°
Q
120°
90
R
115°
S
110°
91
T
105°
ARCTIC OCEAN
PACIFIC OCEAN
Bering Sea
Beaufort Sea
Chukchi Sea
Gulf of Anadyr'
Gulf of Alaska
Koryak Range
Chukot Range
Chukot Pen.
Karaginskiy I.
Korf
Bering I.
Komandor Is.
Copper I.
C. Olyutorskiy
Ledyanaya
8,405 ft
2,562 m
Anadyr
Cape Navarin
6,079 ft
1,853 m
Ayon I.
C. Shelagskiy
Pevek
6,047 ft
1,843 m
Wrangel I.
3,596 ft
1,096 m
Attu I.
Near Is.
Aleutian Is.
Rat Is.
Andreanof Is.
5,925 ft
1,806 m
Provideniya
C. Chukotskiy
C. Dezhnëv
Bering St.
Saint Lawrence Island
Saint Matthew I.
C. Prince of Wales
4,715 ft
1,437 m
Nome
Seward Pen.
Kotzebue Sd.
Point Barrow
Brooks Range
Prudhoe Bay
C. Romanzof
Norton Sound
Pribilof Is.
Nunivak I.
Yukon
Mt. Isto
9,058 ft
2,761 m
Alaska
Bethel
Kuskokwim Bay
Kuskokwim Mts.
4,508 ft
1,374 m
Kuskokwim
24,432 ft
7,447 m
Umnak I.
Unalaska I.
Fox Islands
Unimak I.
Alaska Pen.
Bristol Bay
Dillingham
Mt. McKinley
20,321 ft
6,194 m
Alaska Range
Fort Yukon
Fairbanks
Porcupine
10,016 ft
3,053 m
Mt. Veniaminof
8,225 ft
2,507 m
Aleutian Ra.
Shumagin Islands
Cook Inlet
Anchorage
Kenai Pen.
Seward
Valdez
Shelikof Str.
Afognak I.
4,439 ft
1,353 m
Kodiak
Kodiak I.
Trinity Islands
Eagle
Dawson
Mt. Trudeau
19,550 ft
5,959 m
Mt. Saint Elias
18,008 ft
5,489 m
1,362 ft
415 m
Whitehorse
Mackenzie Mts.
Keele Peak
9,751 ft
2,972 m
Mackenzie Bay
Inuvik
Mackenzie
Queen Elizabeth Is.
Prince Patrick I.
McClure Strait
Eglinton I.
Melville
C. Prince Alfred
Banks Island
Viscount
Cape Bathurst
Amundsen Gulf
2,149 ft
655 m
Victoria Island
Kugluktuk
Coronation G.
Ikaluktutiak
Cambridge
Gt. Bear L.
Fort Simpson
Yellowknife
Gt. Slave L.
Hay River
Fort Resolution
Liard
Juneau
Chichagof I.
Alexander Arch.
Baranof I.
Mt. Ratz
10,289 ft
3,136 m
Kupreanof I.
Coast Mountains
Rocky Mountains
Fort Nelson
9,652 ft
2,942 m
Mt. Sylvia
Prince of Wales I.
Ketchikan
Dixon Entrance
Prince Rupert
4,101 ft
1,250 m
Queen Charlotte Is.
Hecate Str.
Cape St. James
Peace
Dawson Creek
Grande Prairie
Slave
Athabasca
Uranium City
Fort McMurray
Prince George
Queen Charlotte Sound
Mt. Waddington
13,177 ft
4,016 m
12,972 ft
3,954 m
Mt. Robson
Jasper
Edmonton
N. Saskatchewan
Port Hardy
Vancouver Island
Fraser
Columbia
7,201 ft
2,195 m
Golden Hinde
Courtenay
Kamloops
Vancouver
Victoria
Kelowna
11,870 ft
3,618 m
Mt. Assiniboine
Calgary
Red Deer
Prince Albert
Saskatoon
S. Saskatchewan
Lethbridge
Olympia
Seattle
Mt. St Helens
8,364 ft
2,550 m
Mt. Rainier
14,410 ft
4,392 m
Cascade Range
Spokane
Portland
Salem
Great Falls
Missouri
Helena
Bitterroot Ra.
Billings
Yellowstone
Coast Ra.
8,966 ft
2,733 m
12,662 ft
3,859 m
Borah Peak
Boise
Snake
Idaho Falls
Grand Teton
13,770 ft
4,197 m
13,175 ft
4,016 m
Black Hills
7,242 ft
2,207 m
9,002 ft
2,744 m
14,162 ft
4,317 m
Mt. Shasta
Elevation
13,124 ft
6,562 ft
3,281 ft
1,640 ft
656 ft
0 ft
4,000 m
2,000 m
1,000 m
500 m
200 m
0 m
Depression
656 ft
6,562 ft
13,124 ft
19,686 ft
26,248 ft
200 m
2,000 m
4,000 m
6,000 m
8,000 m
Inland ice, glaciers

Nordostrundingen
C. Morris Jesup
Peary Land
Greenland Sea
Jan Mayen
Faroe Is.
Great Britain
Hebrides
King Frederik VIII Land
Danmarkshavn
Arctic Circle
Lincoln Sea
Cape Columbia
Knud Rasmussen Land
Greenland
King Christian X Land
Ittoqqortoormiit
Akureyri
Vatna-jökull
6,952 ft
2,119 m
Iceland
Reykjavík
Denmark Strait
Gunnbjørn Fjeld
12,139 ft
3,700 m
Ellesmere Island
Axel Heiberg Island
Sverdrup Islands
Amund Ringnes I.
Qaanaaq/ Thule
Dundas
Melville Bay
Norwegian Bay
9,882 ft
3,012 m
King Christian IX Land
Grise Fiord
Jones Sound
Upernavik
Tasiilaq
6,299 ft
1,920 m
Baffin Bay
Corn-wallis I.
Devon I.
Nuugssuaq
Ilulissat
Qeqertarsuaq
Cape Liverpool
Resolute
Lancaster Sound
Bylot I.
6,401 ft
1,951 m
King Frederik VI Coast
Kangerlussuaq
Somerset I.
Brodeur Pen.
Arctic Bay
Prince of Wales Island
Clyde River
Sisimiut
Davis Strait
Baffin Island
Gulf of Boothia
Home Bay
7,546 ft
2,300 m
Nuuk (Godthåb)
Boothia Pen.
8,501 ft
2,591 m
Cape Dyer
Penny Highland
Cumberland Pen.
Qaqortoq
Ivittuut
Cape Farewell
Melville Pen.
King William I.
Prince Charles I.
Cumberland Sd.
Foxe Basin
3,750 ft
1,143 m
Hall Pen.
Labrador Sea
Repulse Bay
Foxe Pen.
Iqaluit/ Frobisher Bay
Meta Incognita Pen.
Frobisher Bay
12,477 ft
3,803 m
Resolution I.
Foxe Channel
Southampton I.
Roes Welcome Sd.
Hudson Strait
ATLANTIC
Cape Chidley
C. Wolsten-holme
Akpatok I.
5,233 ft
1,595 m
Ungava Peninsula
Ungava Bay
Coats Island
Rankin Inlet
Mansel I.
Nain
Kuujjuaq/ Fort Chimo
3,773 ft
1,150 m
Arviat
Ottawa Is.
Port Hope Simpson
Hudson Bay
Inukjuak/ Port Harrison
L. Melville
Happy Valley-Goose Bay
Cape Churchill
Churchill
Schefferville
Smallwood Res.
Grand Falls-Windsor
Gander
St. John's
Labrador (Nunatsiavut)
Belcher Is.
Newfoundland
Avalon Pen.
Cape Race
Labrador City
Corner Brook
2,671 ft
814 m
167 ft
51 m
Nelson
Lynn Lake
Canadian Shield
Mt. Otish
3,724 ft
1,135 m
Île d'Anticosti
St-Pierre
Thompson
Winisk
Chisasibi
Laurentian Highlands
Sept-Îles
Gulf of St. Lawrence
Cabot Str.
James Bay
Lake Mistassini
4,160 ft
1,268 m
C. Gaspé
Îles de la Madeleine
Akimiski I.
Severn
Sydney
St. Lawrence
Mts. Notre-Dame
Charlottetown
Cape Breton I.
Lake Winnipeg
Moosonee
Chibougamau
Saguenay
Sable I.
3,875 ft
1,181 m
Fredericton
Halifax
Albany
Québec
St. John
Manitoba
Appalachian Mts.
Winnipeg
Timmins
Trois-Rivières
Cape Sable
Nipigon
Gulf of Maine
Assiniboine
L. of the Woods
Thunder Bay
Montréal
Augusta
Montpelier
Sudbury
Ottawa
Portland
2,301 ft
701 m
Lake Superior
Sault Sainte Marie
Adirondack Mts.
5,344 ft
1,629 m
OCEAN
Grand Forks
Red R.
Kingston
Concord
Georgian Bay
Duluth
Lake Huron
Albany
Boston
Cape Cod
Bismarck
Fargo
Toronto
L. Ontario
Providence
Hartford
St. Paul
Hamilton
Buffalo
Minneapolis
Green Bay
Lake Michigan
Long Island
Hudson
New York
Missouri
Mississippi
Lansing
Detroit
L. Erie
Erie
Sioux Falls
Milwaukee
Madison
Grand Rapids
Philadelphia
Trenton
KLETT-PERTHES
95
98
99

149
90
91
RUSSIA
ARCTIC OCEAN
Bering Sea
Aleutian Is.
Near Is.
Rat Is.
Andreanof Is.
Fox Islands
Komandor Is.
Bering I.
Copper I.
Attu I.
Attu
Atka
Umnak I.
Unalaska I.
Unalaska
Unimak I.
Cold Bay
Shumagin Islands
Chignik
Pribilof Is.
Nunivak I.
Saint Matthew I.
Saint Lawrence Island
Gambell
C. Chukotskiy
Provideniya
C. Dezhnëv
Uelen
Bering Str.
C. Prince of Wales
Point Hope
Kotzebue
Kotzebue Sd.
Kobuk Valley Nat. Park
Selawik
Gates of the Arctic Nat. Park
Nome
Norton Sound
C. Romanzof
Hooper Bay
Unalakleet
Yukon
Bethel
Kuskokwim Bay
Kuskokwim
Ruby
UNITED STATES
Alaska
Bristol Bay
Dillingham
Newhalen
Lake Clark Nat. Park
Katmai Nat. Park
Kantishna
Denali Nat. Park
College
Fairbanks
Fort Yukon
Circle
Eagle
Wasilla
Palmer
Anchorage
Kenai
Cook Inlet
Homer
Seward
Kenai Fjords Nat. Park
Valdez
Cordova
Wrangell
St. Elias Nat. Park
Tanacross
Shelikof Str.
Afognak I.
Kodiak
Kodiak I.
Trinity Islands
Gulf of Alaska
Yakutat
Il'pyrskiy
Karaginskiy I.
Korf
Kamenskoye
Pakhachi
C. Olyutorskiy
Markovo
Anadyr
Anadyr'
Egvekinot
Gulf of Anadyr'
Beringovskiy
Cape Navarin
Ayon I.
C. Shelagskiy
Pevek
Wrangel I.
Mys Shmidta
Chukchi Sea
Barrow
Point Barrow
Prudhoe Bay
Beaufort Sea
Ivvavik Nat. Park
Vuntut Nat. Park
Mackenzie Bay
Old Crow
Porcupine
Aklavik
Inuvik
Tuktoyaktuk
Dawson
Mayo
Yukon Territory
Carmacks
Faro
Kluane Nat. Park
Whitehorse
Skagway
Glacier Bay Nat. Park
Juneau
Chichagof I.
Sitka
Baranof I.
Alexander Arch.
Kupreanof I.
Wrangell
Prince of Wales I.
Ketchikan
Stewart
Dixon Entrance
Prince Rupert
Hecate Str.
Kitimat
Queen Charlotte Is.
Gwaii Haanas Nat. Park
Cape St. James
Ocean Falls
Queen Charlotte Sound
Port Hardy
Vancouver Island
Courtenay
Port Alberni
Nanaimo
Victoria
Vancouver
Surrey
Abbotsford
British Columbia
Watson Lake
Cassiar
Liard
Fort Nelson
Ware
Fort St. John
Dawson Creek
Prince George
Quesnel
Fraser
Kamloops
Revelstoke
Vernon
Kelowna
Kimberley
Columbia
Peace
Grande Prairie
Jasper
Jasper Nat. Park
Banff Nat. Park
Banff
Alberta
Edson
Edmonton
St. Albert
Sherwood Park
Wetaskiwin
Camrose
Red Deer
Drumheller
Calgary
Lethbridge
Medicine Hat
Swift Current
Moose Jaw
Saskatoon
Prince Albert
Saskatchewan
S. Saskatchewan
Lac la Biche
La Ronge
St. Paul
La Loche
Fort McMurray
Athabasca
Peace River
Fort Vermilion
High Level
Uranium City
Wood Buffalo Nat. Park
Fort Smith
Slave
Hay River
Fort Resolution
Great Slave L.
Fort Providence
Yellowknife
Reliance
Fort Simpson
Nahanni Nat. Park
Mackenzie
Northwest Territories
Tulit'a/Fort Norman
Great Bear L.
Port Radium
Kugluktuk
Coronation G.
Tuktut Nogait Nat. Park
Amundsen Gulf
Uluqsaqtuuq/Holman
Victoria Island
Cape Bathurst
Ikahuuk/Sachs Harbour
Banks Island
Aulavik Nat. Park
C. Prince Alfred
McClure Strait
Eglinton I.
Prince Patrick I.
Queen
Melville
Viscount
Everett
Seattle
Tacoma
Olympia
Aberdeen
Washington
Spokane
Yakima
Vancouver
Portland
Gresham
Salem
Eugene
The Dalles
Kennewick
Oregon
Roseburg
Bend
Crescent City
California
Nampa
Boise
Snake
Idaho
Idaho Falls
Missoula
Helena
Great Falls
Havre
Missouri
Montana
Billings
Yellowstone
Yellowstone Nat. Park
Wyoming
Rapid City
UNITED

1:20,000,000

0 200 400 mi
0 200 400 600 km

95 98 99

A
130°
B
125°
C
84
120°
D
115°
E
85
110°
F
105°
G
100°
86
H
95°
J
2
45°
3
40°
4
35°
5
30°
6
25°
7
20°
8
E
110°
F
102
Golden Hinde
7,201 ft
2,195 m
Courtenay
Vancouver I.
Vancouver
Victoria
Kamloops
Kelowna
Banff
Mt. Assiniboine
11,870 ft
3,618 m
Calgary
Saskatoon
Lethbridge
Medicine Hat
South Saskatchewan
Regina
Qu'Appelle
Lake Winnipeg
L. Winnipegosis
Lake Manitoba
Brandon
Assiniboine
Winnipeg
Kenora
L. of the Woods
Seattle
Olympia
14,410 ft
4,392 m
Mt. Rainier
Astoria
Mt. St. Helens
8,364 ft
2,550 m
Portland
Columbia
Salem
Eugene
Bend
Medford
Klamath Falls
Spokane
Columbia Basin
Kennewick
Kalispell
Missoula
Helena
Butte
Great Falls
Missouri
Billings
Yellowstone
Minot
Souris
Grand Forks
Red R.
Bismarck
Fargo
Duluth
Lake Oahe
Saint Cloud
Mississippi
Minneapolis
Pierre
Black Hills
7,242 ft
2,207 m
Rapid City
Custer
Boise
Snake
Bitterroot Range
12,662 ft
3,859 m
Borah Peak
Idaho Falls
Grand Teton
13,770 ft
4,197 m
13,175 ft
4,016 m
Pocatello
Casper
Sioux Falls
Sioux City
9,002 ft
2,744 m
Mt. Shasta
14,162 ft
4,317 m
Cape Mendocino
Redding
Sacramento
Black Rock Desert
Great Salt Lake
Ogden
Salt Lake City
Uinta Mts.
13,528 ft
4,123 m
Provo
Front Ra.
Cheyenne
Fort Collins
North Platte
Platte
Omaha
Lincoln
Des Moines
Reno
Carson City
San Francisco
San Jose
Stockton
S. Joaquin
Fresno
Great Basin
Wheeler Peak
13,061 ft
3,982 m
Longs Peak
14,255 ft
4,345 m
Denver
Mt. Elbert
14,432 ft
4,399 m
Colorado Springs
Pueblo
Kansas City
Kansas
Missouri
Topeka
Jefferson City
Mt. Whitney
14,495 ft
4,418 m
Death Valley
−282 ft
−86 m
Las Vegas
Cedar City
Lake Powell
L. Mead
Grand Canyon
Durango
Blanca Peak
14,360 ft
4,377 m
Sangre de Cristo Mts.
Dodge City
Arkansas
2,340 ft
713 m
Wichita
Springfield
Bakersfield
Point Conception
Santa Barbara
Mojave Desert
Channel Islands
Los Angeles
Riverside
Colorado Plateau
12,663 ft
3,860 m
Flagstaff
Santa Fe
Albuquerque
Sacramento Mts.
Amarillo
Tulsa
Fayetteville
Oklahoma City
Boston Mts.
Fort Smith
2,900 ft
884 m
Ouachita Mts.
San Diego
Tijuana
Mexicali
Yuma
Gila
Colorado
Phoenix
Lawton
Wichita Falls
Sierra Blanca Peak
12,003 ft
3,659 m
Llano Estacado
Lubbock
Tucson
Plano
Greenville
Dallas
Fort Worth
Longview
Shreveport
10,157 ft
3,096 m
Cerro de la Encantada
Nogales
El Paso
Rio Grande
Odessa
Pecos
Waco
Trinity
Isla Ángel de la Guarda
Guadalupe I.
7,743 ft
2,360 m
Rio Bravo del Norte
Edwards Plateau
Austin
Brazos
Beaumont
Lake Charles
Tiburón I.
Cedros I.
Hermosillo
Yaqui
Houston
Colorado
San Antonio
Galveston
Pta. Sta. Eugenia
Acuña
Chihuahua
Piedras Negras
Eagle Pass
Ciudad Obregón
Creel
Laredo
Corpus Christi
Monclova
Los Mochis
Co. Mohinora
10,830 ft
3,300 m
Cd. Constitución
Brownsville
Reynosa
Matamoros
Torreón
Monterrey
Saltillo
Culiacán
La Paz
7,894 ft
2,406 m
Durango
Cerro Peña Nevada
12,021 ft
3,664 m
Ciudad Victoria
Cape San Lucas
San José del Cabo
Mazatlán
Tropic of Cancer
Islas Tres Marías
San Luis Potosí
Aguascalientes
Tampico
Tepic
9,800 ft
2,987 m
León
Rio Grande de Santiago
Puerto Vallarta
Cape Corrientes
Guadalajara
Revillagigedo Islands
Bay of Campeche
Nevado de Colima
14,600 ft
4,450 m
Uruapan
Morelia
Mexico City
(Cd. de México)
Popocatépetl
17,887 ft
5,452 m
Puebla
Pico de Orizaba
18,405 ft
5,610 m
Veracruz
Manzanillo
Lázaro Cárdenas
Oaxaca
Coatzacoalcos
Villahermosa
Rocky Mountains
Great Plains
Cascade Range
Coast Ranges
Sierra Nevada
Wasatch Ra.
Lower California
Gulf of California
Sierra Madre Occidental
Sierra Madre Oriental
Mexican Plateau
Sierra Madre
Mexican Plateau
PACIFIC OCEAN
Elevation
13,124 ft
4,000 m
6,562 ft
2,000 m
3,281 ft
1,000 m
1,640 ft
500 m
656 ft
200 m
0 ft
0 m
Depression
656 ft
200 m
6,562 ft
2,000 m
13,124 ft
4,000 m
19,686 ft
6,000 m
26,248 ft
8,000 m

1:15,000,000

0 200 400 mi
0 200 400 600 km
87
88
89
103
Canadian Shield
James Bay
Moosonee
Albany
Lake Mistassini
Chibougamau
Laurentian Highlands
Sept-Îles
Anticosti I.
Newfoundland
Avalon Pen.
Cape Race
Gulf of St. Lawrence
C. Gaspé
4,160 ft
1,268 m
Mts. Notre-Dame
St. Lawrence
Magdalene Is.
Cabot Strait
St-Pierre
Rimouski
Saguenay
3,875 ft
1,181 m
Charlottetown
Sydney
Cape Breton Island
Senneterre
Timmins
Québec
Moncton
Fredericton
St. John
Halifax
Sable I.
Bay of Fundy
Lake Superior
Trois-Rivières
Sault Sainte Marie
Sudbury
North Bay
Marquette
Montréal
Sherbrooke
Ottawa
Augusta
Gulf of Maine
Cape Sable
Georgian Bay
Lake Huron
Montpelier
Adirondack Mts.
5,344 ft
1,629 m
White Mts.
Portland
Kingston
Concord
Green Bay
Barrie
Toronto
Lake Ontario
Albany
Boston
Cape Cod
Lake Michigan
Hamilton
Rochester
Saginaw
London
Buffalo
Providence
Nantucket I.
Milwaukee
Lansing
Grand Rapids
Detroit
Hudson
Hartford
New Haven
Madison
Lake Erie
Erie
Scranton
New York
Long Island
Chicago
Toledo
Cleveland
South Bend
Fort Wayne
Pittsburgh
Harrisburg
Trenton
Philadelphia
Peoria
Columbus
Baltimore
Dover
Indianapolis
Washington, D.C.
Annapolis
Spruce Knob
4,861 ft
1,482 m
Cincinnati
Ohio
Charleston
Chesapeake Bay
Evansville
Frankfort
Louisville
Richmond
Newport News
Norfolk
Chesapeake
Allegheny Mts.
Appalachian Mts.
Greensboro
Raleigh
Nashville
Knoxville
Mt. Mitchell
6,684 ft
2,037 m
C. Hatteras
Charlotte
Fayetteville
Memphis
Chattanooga
Greenville
Wilmington
Tennessee
Columbia
Piedmont
Atlanta
Birmingham
Macon
Charleston
Columbus
Savannah
Montgomery
Jackson
Jacksonville
Mobile
Pensacola
Tallahassee
Florida
New Orleans
Cape San Blas
Apalachee Bay
Orlando
Cape Canaveral
Tampa
Saint Petersburg
West Palm Beach
Cape Coral
Fort Lauderdale
Miami
Cape Sable
Florida Keys
Straits of Florida
Gd. Bahama I.
Great Abaco
Eleuthera I.
Nassau
Andros I.
Cat I.
207 ft
63 m
Mt. Alvernia
San Salvador
Bahamas
Long Island
Acklins I.
Caicos Is.
Grand Turk (Cockburn Town)
Turks Is.
Great Inagua
Hamilton
Bermuda Is.
Sargasso Sea
ATLANTIC OCEAN
Gulf of Mexico
Havana (La Habana)
Santa Clara
Cuba
Pinar del Río
Camagüey
Holguín
Cape Maisí
Windward Passage
Cape San Antonio
C. Catoche
Isla de la Juventud
Santiago de Cuba
Manzanillo
Sa. Maestra
Pico Turquino
6,476 ft
1,974 m
Cap-Haïtien
10,417 ft
3,175 m
P. Duarte
Santiago
Santo Domingo
Mona Passage
30,246 ft
9,219 m
San Juan
Co. de Punta
4,390 ft
1,338 m
Ponce
Puerto Rico
Charlotte Amalie
St. Croix
Anegada Passage
St-Martin
St-Barthélemy
Basseterre
Lesser Antilles
Mérida
Cancún
Chichén-Itzá
Cozumel I.
Yucatán Pen.
Yucatán Channel
Greater Antilles
The Bluff
141 ft
43 m
Grand Cayman
Cayman Is.
Georgetown
25,197 ft
7,680 m
Jamaica
Blue Mtn. Peak
7,401 ft
2,256 m
Kingston
Port-au-Prince
8,793 ft
2,680 m
La Selle
Hispaniola
Caribbean Sea
Chetumal
KLETT-PERTHES

84
85
86
102
P A C I F I C O C E A N
U N I T E D S T A T E S
M E X I C O
Washington
Oregon
Idaho
Montana
Wyoming
Nevada
Utah
Colorado
Arizona
New Mexico
North Dakota
South Dakota
Nebraska
Kansas
Oklahoma
Texas
Minnesota
California
Alberta
Saskatchewan
Manitoba
British Columbia
Lower California
Gulf of California
Bay of Campeche
Tropic of Cancer
Vancouver I.
Vancouver
Victoria
Seattle
Tacoma
Spokane
Portland
Salem
Eugene
Boise
Salt Lake City
West Valley City
Provo
Reno
Carson City
Sacramento
San Francisco
Oakland
San Jose
Fresno
Bakersfield
LOS ANGELES
SAN DIEGO
Las Vegas
Henderson
PHOENIX
Tucson
Albuquerque
Santa Fe
Denver
Aurora
Colorado Springs
El Paso
JUÁREZ
TIJUANA
Mexicali
Hermosillo
Chihuahua
Calgary
Regina
Saskatoon
Winnipeg
Billings
Great Falls
Helena
Cheyenne
Bismarck
Omaha
Lincoln
Des Moines
Kansas City
Topeka
Wichita
Oklahoma City
Tulsa
Amarillo
Lubbock
Fort Worth
DALLAS
Austin
HOUSTON
SAN ANTONIO
Corpus Christi
Laredo
MONTERREY
Saltillo
Torreón
Durango
Culiacán
Mazatlán
La Paz
Cape San Lucas
GUADALAJARA
Zapopan
LEÓN
Aguascalientes
San Luis Potosí
Zacatecas
Querétaro
MEXICO CITY (CD. DE MÉXICO)
ECATEPEC
NEZAHUALC.
PUEBLA
Veracruz
Tampico
Morelia
Guadalupe I. (MEX.)
Revillagigedo Islands (MEX.)
Islas Tres Marías
Cape Mendocino
Point Conception
Channel Islands
MA Massachusetts

1:15,000,000

0 200 400 mi
0 200 400 600 km

87 88 89 103

A
B
C
D
128°
124°
120°
2
3
4
52°
48°
44°
U.S.
Alaska
Portland Canal
Behm Canal
4,595 ft
1,400 m
Nass
Lachkaltsap Ind. Res.
Gitanmaa Ind. Res.
Gitsegukla Ind. Res.
Skeena
Skeena Mts.
Shedin Pk.
8,750 ft
2,667 m
Hazelton Mts.
New Hazelton
Babine
Babine Range
Omineca
Omineca Mts.
Takla Lake
Williston Lake
Peace
Fort St. John
Hudson Hope
Mt. Crysdale
7,950 ft
2,423 m
Chetwynd
Dawson Creek
Fairview
Spirit River
Smoky
Mackenzie
Pine Pass
2,851 ft
869 m
Murray
Tumbler Ridge
Beaverlodge
Sexsmith
Grande-Prairie
Sturgeon Lake Ind. Res.
Wapiti
Dundas Island
Tsimpsean Ind. Res.
Mt. McNeil
4,550 ft
1,387 m
Seven Sisters Peaks
9,040 ft
2,755 m
Mt. Cronin
7,822 ft
2,384 m
6,792 ft
2,070 m
Nation
Nechako
Terrace
Smithers
Prince Rupert
Bulkley
Houston
Babine Lake
Stuart Lake
Plateau
Fort St. James
Salmon
Crooked
Sentinel Peak
8,200 ft
2,499 m
Parsnip
Kakwa
Simonette
Little Smoky
Porcher Island
Dolphin Island Ind. Res.
Kitimat
Pitt Island
Greenville Ch.
Douglas Ch.
Atna Peak
9,050 ft
2,758 m
Burns Lake
Francois
British
Columbia
Willow River
McGregor
Mount Sir Alexander
10,740 ft
3,274 m
Grande Cach
Berland
Hawkesbury I.
Banks Island
Gribbell I.
Ootsa Lake
Fraser Lake
Vanderhoof
Nechako
Stony Creek Ind. Res.
Prince George
Willow
Bowron
11,140 ft
3,395 m
Cariboo Mts.
Wildhay
Athabasca
Micheal Peak
7,451 ft
2,271 m
5,500 ft
1,676 m
Princess Royal Island
Caamaño Sound
Aristazabal Island
Eutsuk Lake
Natalkuz Lake
West Road
Fraser Plateau
Nazko
5,758 ft
1,755 m
Quesnel
Wells
Fraser
McBride
12,972 ft
3,954 m
Mount Robson
Jasper
Hinton
Jasper National
Coast Mountains
Kalone Peak
8,390 ft
2,545 m
Dean
Laredo Sound
Ocean Falls
Bella Coola
Milbanke Sound
Bella Bella Ind. Res.
Hunter Island
Quesnel Lake
Mount Sir Wilfrid Laurier
Valemount
11,500 ft
3,505 m
Canoe
Clearwater
Williams Lake
Blue River
Mt. Columbia
12,294 ft
3,747 m
Kinbasket Lake
Calvert Island
Mt. Buxton
3,250 ft
991 m
Owenkeno Lake
Smith Sound
Chilko
Stone Ind. Res.
Chilcotin
Alkali Lake Ind. Res.
Mount Waddington
13,177 ft
4,016 m
Homathko
Chilko Lake
Klinaklini
Clearwater
100 Mile House
Monashee Mountains
N. Thompson
Mt. Sir Sandford
11,556 ft
3,522 m
Queen Charlotte Str.
Good Hope Mtn.
10,630 ft
3,240 m
7,625 ft
2,324 m
Mt. Bowman
Baldy Mtn.
7,500 ft
2,286 m
Barrière
Revelstoke
Mt. Revelstoke Nat. Park
Glacier Nat. P.
Port Hardy
Port McNeill
6,100 ft
1,859 m
Knight Inlet
Bute Inlet
Bridge
Bralorne
Clinton
Adams Lake
Kamloops Ind. Res.
Shuswap
Revelstoke
Quatsino Sound
Port Alice
4,600 ft
1,402 m
Lillooet
Lillooet
Ashcroft
Thompson
Kamloops
Salmon Arm
Mt. Odin
9,750 ft
2,972 m
Upper Arrow Lake
Checleset Bay
Tahsis
Campbell River
Whistler
Gott Peak
9,700 ft
2,956 m
Wedge Mtn.
9,527 ft
2,904 m
Lytton
Okanagan Ind. Res.
6,880 ft
2,097 m
Vernon
Nakusp
Lower Arrow Lake
Nootka Island
Vancouver Island
Golden Hinde
7,201 ft
2,195 m
Courtenay
Cumberland
Nootka Sound
Jervis Inlet
Powell River
Squamish
Squamish
Harrison Lake
Merritt
Douglas Lake Ind. Res.
Okanagan Lake
Kelowna
Strait of Georgia
Sechelt
Vancouver
Burnaby
Surrey
Princeton
Penticton Ind. Res.
Summerland
Penticton
Kettle
Midway Ra.
7,930 ft
2,417 m
Port Alberni
Parksville
Tofino
Nanaimo
Chilliwack
Hope
7,201 ft
2,195 m
Oliver
Osoyoos Ind. Res.
Castlegar
Pacific Rim Nat. Park
Ucluelet
Barkley Sound
Abbotsford
White Rock
Keremeos
Osoyoos
Grand Forks
Trail
Ladysmith
Duncan
Lynden
Lummi Ind. Res.
Bellingham
Mt. Baker
10,777 ft
3,285 m
North Cascades Nat. P.
Okanogan Ra.
Mt. Bonaparte
7,257 ft
2,212 m
Colville
Sidney
Port Renfrew
Victoria
Anacortes
Methow
Omak
Okanogan
Kettle River Ra.
F. D. Roosevelt Lake
6,83
2,084
Makah Ind. Res.
Strait of Juan de Fuca
Sekiu
Mt. Vernon
Oak Harbor
Port Townsend
Tulalip Ind. Res.
Colville Ind. Res.
Spokane Ind. Res.
Newp
Port Angeles
Olympic Nat. P.
Port Gamble Ind. Res.
Marysville
Glacier Peak
10,541 ft
3,213 m
Lake Chelan
Columbia
Mt. Olympus
7,966 ft
2,428 m
Port Madison Ind. Res.
Everett
Coulee Dam
Bellevue
Chelan
Banks Lake
Wilbur
Davenport
Spokane
PACIFIC
OCEAN
Quinault Ind. Res.
Bremerton
Seattle
Kent
Federal Way
Leavenworth
Mt. Stuart
9,415 ft
2,870 m
Wenatchee
Ephrata
Medical Lake
Cheney
Odessa
Coeur d'A
Shelton
Tacoma
Puyallup
Washington
Hoquiam
Elma
Olympia
Lakewood
Mount Rainier Nat. P.
Cle Elum
Yakima
Potholes Res.
Moses Lake
Aberdeen
Ellensburg
Ritzville
Grays Harbor
Mt. Rainier
14,410 ft
4,392 m
Othello
Willapa Bay
South Bend
Centralia
Chehalis
Selah
Pullm
Morton
Cowlitz
Yakima
Snake
Long Beach
3,110 ft
948 m
Toppenish
Richland
Pomeroy
Astoria
Seaside
Mt. St. Helens
8,364 ft
2,550 m
Mt. Adams
12,277 ft
3,742 m
Yakima Ind. Res.
Sunnyside
Pasco
Dayton
Lewi
Longview
Prosser
Kennewick
Walla Walla
6,387 ft
1,947 m
Cascade Range
3,283 ft
1001 m
St. Helens
Lewis
Goldendale
UNITED
White Salmon
Columbia
Milton-Freewater
Hillsboro
Vancouver
Camas
Hood River
Arlington
Hermiston
Pendleton
Umatilla Ind. Res.
Tillamook
Portland
Gresham
The Dalles
Mt. Hood
11,240 ft
3,428 m
Pilot Rock
La Grande
McMinnville
Woodburn
Silverton
Heppner
Blue Mountains
Wall
Eagle Cap
Mt
Lincoln C.
Dallas
Salem
Willamette
Deschutes
Warm Springs Ind. Res.
5,112 ft
1,558 m
N. F. John Day
Oregon
Powder
Newport
Toledo
Mt. Jefferson
10,497 ft
3,199 m
John Day
Baker C.
Corvallis
Albany
Mill City
Madras
Lebanon
4,097 ft
1,249 m
Sweet Home
KLETT-PERTHES

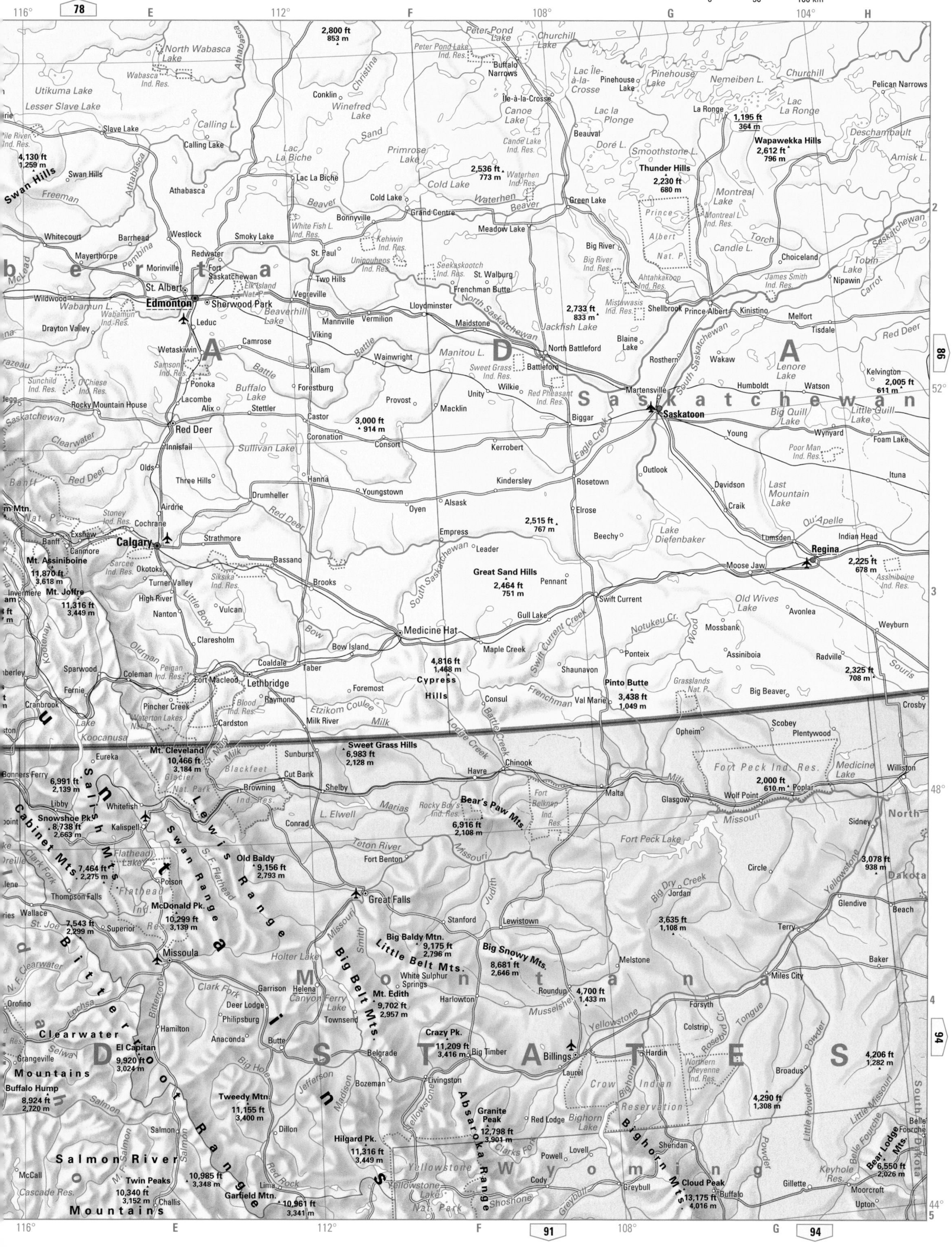
116°
78
E
112°
F
108°
G
104°
H
North Wabasca Lake
Wabasca Ind. Res.
Athabasca
2,800 ft 853 m
Christina
Peter Pond Lake
Peter Pond Lake Ind. Res.
Churchill Lake
Buffalo Narrows
Lac Île-à-la-Crosse
Pinehouse Lake
Nemeiben L.
Churchill
Pelican Narrows
Utikuma Lake
Lesser Slave Lake
Conklin
Winefred Lake
Île-à-la-Crosse
Canoe Lake
Lac la Plonge
La Ronge
Lac La Ronge
1,195 ft 364 m
Slave Lake
Calling L.
Calling Lake
Sand
Primrose Lake
Beauval
Canoe Lake Ind. Res.
Doré L.
Smoothstone L.
Wapawekka Hills 2,612 ft 796 m
Deschambault L.
Amisk L.
4,130 ft 1,259 m
Swan Hills
Lac La Biche
2,536 ft 773 m
Waterhen Ind. Res.
Thunder Hills 2,230 ft 680 m
Freeman
Athabasca
Cold Lake
Cold Lake
Waterhen
Beaver
Green Lake
Montreal Lake
Prince Albert Nat. P.
Montreal L. Ind. Res.
Bonnyville
Grand Centre
White Fish L. Ind. Res.
Meadow Lake
Big River
Whitecourt
Barrhead
Westlock
Smoky Lake
Kehiwin Ind. Res.
Big River Ind. Res.
Candle L.
Torch
Saskatchewan
Mayerthorpe
Pembina
Redwater
St. Paul
Unipouheos Ind. Res.
Seekaskootch Ind. Res.
Choiceland
Tobin Lake
Morinville
Fort Saskatchewan
Elk Island Nat. P.
Two Hills
St. Walburg
Ahtahkakoop Ind. Res.
James Smith Ind. Res.
Nipawin
Carrot
St. Albert
Edmonton
Sherwood Park
Vegreville
Frenchman Butte
Wildwood
Wabamun L.
Wabamun Ind. Res.
Beaverhill Lake
Lloydminster
2,733 ft 833 m
Mistawasis Ind. Res.
Shellbrook
Prince Albert
Kinistino
Melfort
Leduc
Mannville
Vermilion
North Saskatchewan
Maidstone
Jackfish Lake
Tisdale
Red Deer
Drayton Valley
Viking
Blaine Lake
Camrose
Wetaskiwin
Battle
Wainwright
Manitou L.
North Battleford
Wakaw
Samson Ind. Res.
Killam
Sweet Grass Ind. Res.
Battleford
Rosthern
Lenore Lake
Kelvington 2,005 ft 611 m
Sunchild Ind. Res.
O'Chiese Ind. Res.
Ponoka
Forestburg
Wilkie
Martensville
Humboldt
Watson
52°
Lacombe
Buffalo Lake
Provost
Unity
Red Pheasant Ind. Res.
Rocky Mountain House
Alix
Stettler
Castor
Macklin
Saskatoon
Big Quill Lake
Little Quill Lake
Saskatchewan
Red Deer
3,000 ft 914 m
Biggar
Wynyard
Clearwater
Coronation
Young
Innisfail
Sullivan Lake
Consort
Kerrobert
Eagle Creek
Poor Man Ind. Res.
Foam Lake
Olds
Outlook
Banff
Red Deer
Three Hills
Hanna
Kindersley
Rosetown
Davidson
Last Mountain Lake
Ituna
Drumheller
Youngstown
Alsask
Craik
Airdrie
Stoney Ind. Res.
Red Deer
Oyen
2,515 ft 767 m
Elrose
Nat. P.
Cochrane
Exshaw
Empress
Beechy
Lake Diefenbaker
Qu'Appelle
Banff
Canmore
Calgary
Strathmore
Lumsden
Indian Head
Regina
Mt. Assiniboine 11,870 ft 3,618 m
Sarcee Ind. Res.
Okotoks
Bassano
Leader
Great Sand Hills 2,464 ft 751 m
Moose Jaw
2,225 ft 678 m
Assiniboine Ind. Res.
Invermere
Mt. Joffre 11,316 ft 3,449 m
Turner Valley
Siksika Ind. Res.
Brooks
South Saskatchewan
Pennant
High River
Swift Current
Old Wives Lake
3
Nanton
Little Bow
Vulcan
Gull Lake
Avonlea
Kootenay
Bow
Medicine Hat
Notukeu Cr.
Mossbank
Weyburn
Claresholm
Bow Island
Maple Creek
Swift Current Creek
Wood
Ponteix
Assiniboia
Oldman
Coaldale
Taber
4,816 ft 1,468 m
Radville
Souris
Sparwood
Coleman
Peigan Ind. Res.
Cypress Hills
Shaunavon
2,325 ft 708 m
Fernie
Fort Macleod
Lethbridge
Foremost
Pinto Butte 3,438 ft 1,049 m
Grasslands Nat. P.
Big Beaver
Cranbrook
Pincher Creek
Raymond
Consul
Frenchman
Val Marie
Crosby
Blood Ind. Res.
Etzikom Coulee
Waterton Lakes Nat. P.
Cardston
Milk River
Milk
Lodge Creek
Battle Creek
Scobey
Koocanusa
Lake
Opheim
Plentywood
Eureka
Mt. Cleveland 10,466 ft 3,184 m
Sweet Grass Hills 6,983 ft 2,128 m
Sunburst
Chinook
Fort Peck Ind. Res.
Medicine Lake
Williston
Bonners Ferry
6,991 ft 2,139 m
Blackfeet
Glacier Nat. Park
Cut Bank
Havre
Milk
2,000 ft 610 m
Poplar
48°
Libby
Whitefish
Browning
Ind. Res.
Shelby
Fort Belknap Ind. Res.
Malta
Glasgow
Wolf Point
Snowshoe Pk. 8,738 ft 2,663 m
Kalispell
Lewis Range
Marias
Rocky Boy's Ind. Res.
Bear's Paw Mts.
6,916 ft 2,108 m
Missouri
North
Sidney
Cabinet Mts.
Salish Mts.
Swan Range
Conrad
L. Elwell
Fort Peck Lake
Clark Fork
Flathead Lake
Teton River
Missouri
7,464 ft 2,275 m
Old Baldy 9,156 ft 2,793 m
S.F. Flathead
Fort Benton
3,078 ft 938 m
Circle
Dakota
Polson
Flathead Ind. Res.
Great Falls
Judith
Big Dry Creek
Jordan
Yellowstone
Thompson Falls
McDonald Pk. 10,299 ft 3,139 m
Glendive
Wallace
St. Joe
7,543 ft 2,299 m
Superior
Stanford
Lewistown
3,635 ft 1,108 m
Beach
Bitterroot
Missouri
Smith
Big Baldy Mtn. 9,175 ft 2,796 m
Little Belt Mts.
Big Snowy Mts. 8,681 ft 2,646 m
Terry
Missoula
Holter Lake
Melstone
Baker
N.F. Clearwater
White Sulphur Springs
Miles City
Montana
Orofino
Clark Fork
Garrison
Helena
Canyon Ferry Lake
Big Belt Mts.
Mt. Edith 9,702 ft 2,957 m
Roundup
4,700 ft 1,433 m
Lochsa
Deer Lodge
Harlowton
Musselshell
Forsyth
4
Philipsburg
Hamilton
Townsend
Yellowstone
Tongue
Clearwater
Anaconda
Crazy Pk. 11,209 ft 3,416 m
Colstrip
Powder
94
Selway
Butte
Belgrade
Big Timber
Billings
Hardin
Rosebud Cr.
Grangeville
El Capitan 9,920 ft 3,024 m
Big Hole
Laurel
Broadus
4,206 ft 1,282 m
Mountains
Jefferson
Bozeman
Livingston
Northern Cheyenne Ind. Res.
Crow Indian Reservation
Buffalo Hump 8,924 ft 2,720 m
Salmon
Madison
Tweedy Mtn. 11,155 ft 3,400 m
Absaroka Range
Granite Peak 12,798 ft 3,901 m
Red Lodge
Bighorn Lake
Bighorn Mts.
4,290 ft 1,308 m
Little Powder
Little Missouri
South Dakota
Salmon
Dillon
Hilgard Pk. 11,316 ft 3,449 m
Clarks Fork
Sheridan
Belle Fourche
Salmon River
Yellowstone
Powell
Lovell
Wyoming
Keyhole Res.
Bear Lodge Mts. 6,550 ft 2,026 m
McCall
10,985 ft 3,348 m
Red Rock
Yellowstone Lake
Cody
Greybull
Cloud Peak 13,175 ft 4,016 m
Buffalo
Gillette
Moorcroft
Cascade Res.
Twin Peaks 10,340 ft 3,152 m
Challis
Garfield Mtn.
Lima
10,961 ft 3,341 m
Yellowstone Nat. Park
Shoshone
Greybull
Upton
44°
Mountains
Alberta
CANADA
Saskatchewan
United States
Idaho
Bitterroot Range
Lemhi Range
Lewis
5
116°
E
112°
F
91
108°
G
94

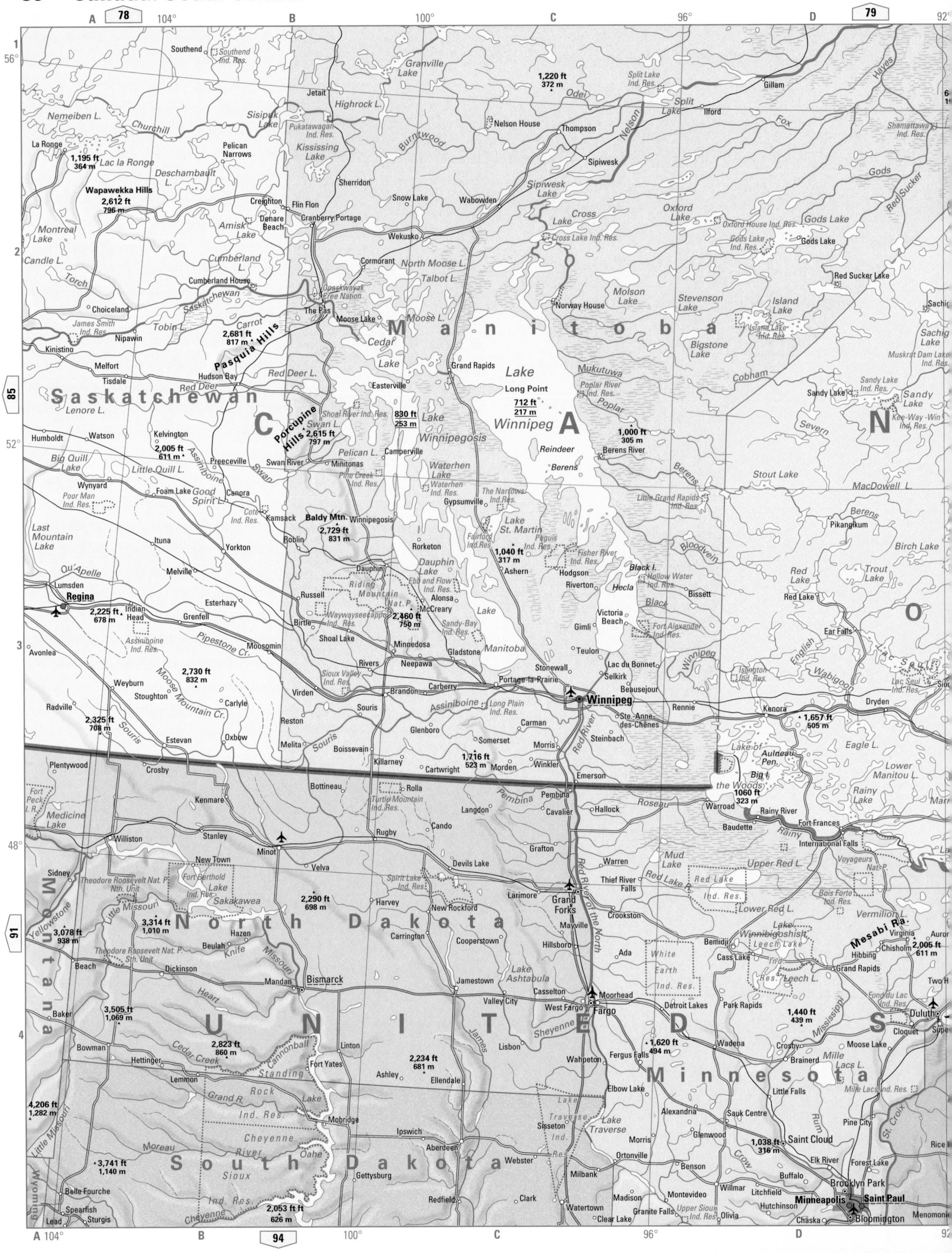

A
78
104°
B
100°
C
96°
D
79
92°
1
56°
2
52°
3
48°
4
85
91
94
Southend
Southend Ind. Res.
Granville Lake
1,220 ft 372 m
Split Lake Ind. Res.
Gillam
Hayes
Jetait
Highrock L.
Odei
Split Lake
Ilford
Nemeiben L.
Sisipuk Lake
Churchill
Pukatawagan Ind. Res.
Nelson House
Thompson
Nelson
Fox
Shamattawa Ind. Res.
La Ronge
Pelican Narrows
Kississing Lake
Burntwood
Sipiwesk
1,195 ft 364 m
Lac la Ronge
Deschambault L.
Sherridon
Gods
Wapawekka Hills
2,612 ft 796 m
Sipiwesk Lake
Red Sucker
Creighton
Flin Flon
Snow Lake
Wabowden
Denare Beach
Cranberry Portage
Oxford Lake
Cross Lake
Montreal Lake
Amisk Lake
Oxford House Ind. Res.
Gods Lake
Gods Lake Ind. Res.
Gods Lake
Candle L.
Wekusko
Cross Lake Ind. Res.
Cumberland L.
Torch
Cormorant
North Moose L.
Talbot L.
Red Sucker Lake
Cumberland House
Opaskwayak Cree Nation
Saskatchewan
Choiceland
The Pas
Norway House
Molson Lake
Stevenson Lake
Island Lake
Sachigo
James Smith Ind. Res.
Tobin L.
Carrot
Moose Lake
Moose L.
Island Lake Ind. Res.
Nipawin
2,681 ft 817 m
Pasquia Hills
Manitoba
Sachigo Lake
Kinistino
Cedar Lake
Bigstone Lake
Muskrat Dam Lake Ind. Res.
Melfort
Grand Rapids
Lake
Mukutuwa
Hudson Bay
Red Deer L.
Cobham
Tisdale
Red Deer
Easterville
Long Point
Poplar River Ind. Res.
Sandy Lake Ind. Res.
Saskatchewan
712 ft 217 m
Sandy Lake
Sandy Lake
Lenore L.
Shoal River Ind. Res.
830 ft 253 m
Poplar
Kee-Way-Win Ind. Res.
Porcupine Hills
Swan L.
Lake
Winnipeg
CANADA
N
Humboldt
Watson
2,615 ft 797 m
Winnipegosis
1,000 ft 305 m
Severn
Kelvington
Reindeer
Berens River
2,005 ft 611 m
Pelican L.
Camperville
Berens
Big Quill Lake
Preeceville
Swan River
Minitonas
Waterhen Lake
Stout Lake
Little Quill L.
Assiniboine
Swan
Pine Creek Ind. Res.
Berens
Waterhen Ind. Res.
MacDowell L.
Wynyard
Foam Lake
Good Spirit L.
Canora
The Narrows Ind. Res.
Poor Man Ind. Res.
Gypsumville
Little Grand Rapids Ind. Res.
Cote Ind. Res.
Kamsack
Baldy Mtn.
Winnipegosis
Lake St. Martin
Berens
Pikangikum
Last Mountain Lake
2,729 ft 831 m
Fairford Ind. Res.
Peguis Ind. Res.
Bloodvein
Birch Lake
Ituna
Roblin
Rorketon
1,040 ft 317 m
Fisher River Ind. Res.
Yorkton
Dauphin Lake
Ashern
Hodgson
Black I.
Trout Lake
Qu'Appelle
Melville
Dauphin
Red Lake
Lumsden
Riding Mountain Nat. P.
Ebb and Flow Ind. Res.
Riverton
Hecla
Hollow Water Ind. Res.
Bissett
Regina
Esterhazy
Russell
Alonsa
Red Lake
2,225 ft 678 m
Indian Head
Grenfell
Waywayseecappo Ind. Res.
2,460 ft 750 m
McCreary
Victoria Beach
Black
O
Assiniboine Ind. Res.
Birtle
Sandy Bay Ind. Res.
Lake
Gimli
Fort Alexander Ind. Res.
Ear Falls
Pipestone Cr.
Shoal Lake
Manitoba
Avonlea
Moosomin
Minnedosa
Gladstone
Teulon
Winnipeg
English
2,730 ft 832 m
Neepawa
Lac du Bonnet
Lac Seul
Rivers
Stonewall
Islington Ind. Res.
Wabigoon
Moose Mountain Cr.
Sioux Valley Ind. Res.
Selkirk
Weyburn
Virden
Brandon
Carberry
Portage-la-Prairie
Beausejour
Lac Seul Ind. Res.
Stoughton
Carlyle
Winnipeg
Rennie
Dryden
Radville
Souris
Assiniboine
Long Plain Ind. Res.
Ste.-Anne-des-Chênes
Kenora
1,657 ft 505 m
2,325 ft 708 m
Reston
Carman
Souris
Estevan
Oxbow
Glenboro
Steinbach
Eagle L.
Melita
Souris
Boissevain
Somerset
Red River
Lake of the Woods
Aulneau Pen.
Plentywood
Killarney
1,716 ft 523 m
Morris
Crosby
Cartwright
Morden
Winkler
Emerson
Big I.
Lower Manitou L.
Bottineau
Rolla
Pembina
1060 ft 323 m
Rainy Lake
Fort Peck I. R.
Kenmare
Turtle Mountain Ind. Res.
Langdon
Pembina
Cavalier
Roseau
Hallock
Warroad
Rainy River
Medicine Lake
Cando
Fort Frances
Williston
Stanley
Minot
Rugby
Baudette
Rainy
International Falls
Grafton
New Town
Velva
Devils Lake
Mud Lake
Voyageurs Nat. P.
Sidney
Theodore Roosevelt Nat. P. Nth. Unit
Fort Berthold Ind. Res.
Lake Sakakawea
Spirit Lake Ind. Res.
Warren
Upper Red L.
Thief River Falls
Red Lake R.
Red Lake Ind. Res.
Bois Forte Ind. Res.
Montana
Yellowstone
Little Missouri
2,290 ft 698 m
Harvey
Larimore
Grand Forks
Red River of the North
3,314 ft 1,010 m
North Dakota
New Rockford
Crookston
Lower Red L.
Vermilion L.
3,078 ft 938 m
Hazen
Carrington
Cooperstown
Mayville
Lake Winnibigoshish
Mesabi Ra.
Virginia
Beulah
Knife
Missouri
Hillsboro
Bemidji
Leech Lake
Chisholm
2,005 ft 611 m
Theodore Roosevelt Nat. P. Sth. Unit
White Earth Ind. Res.
Cass Lake
Hibbing
Beach
Dickinson
Ada
Leech Lake Ind. Res.
Grand Rapids
Mandan
Bismarck
Jamestown
Lake Ashtabula
Heart
Casselton
Moorhead
Fond du Lac Ind. Res.
Baker
3,505 ft 1,069 m
Valley City
West Fargo
Fargo
Detroit Lakes
Park Rapids
1,440 ft 439 m
Duluth
UNITED STATES
Sheyenne
Mississippi
Bowman
2,823 ft 860 m
Cannonball
Linton
James
Lisbon
1,620 ft 494 m
Wadena
Moose Lake
Cloquet
Hettinger
Cedar Creek
Fort Yates
2,234 ft 681 m
Wahpeton
Fergus Falls
Crosby
Brainerd
Mille Lacs L.
Lemmon
Standing Rock Ind. Res.
Ashley
Ellendale
Minnesota
Grand R.
Lake
Elbow Lake
Little Falls
Mille Lacs Ind. Res.
4,206 ft 1,282 m
Mobridge
Lake Traverse Ind. Res.
Alexandria
Sauk Centre
Rum
Little Missouri
Cheyenne River Ind. Res.
Ipswich
Aberdeen
Sisseton
Lake Traverse
Glenwood
Pine City
St. Croix
Moreau
Oahe
Morris
1,038 ft 316 m
Saint Cloud
3,741 ft 1,140 m
South Dakota
Webster
Ortonville
Crow
Elk River
Forest Lake
Wyoming
Sioux
Gettysburg
Milbank
Benson
Buffalo
Brooklyn Park
Belle Fourche
Redfield
Clark
Madison
Montevideo
Willmar
Litchfield
Saint Paul
Spearfish
Ind. Res.
2,053 ft 626 m
Watertown
Granite Falls
Upper Sioux Ind. Res.
Olivia
Hutchinson
Minneapolis
Menomonie
Lead
Sturgis
Cheyenne
Clear Lake
Chaska
Bloomington

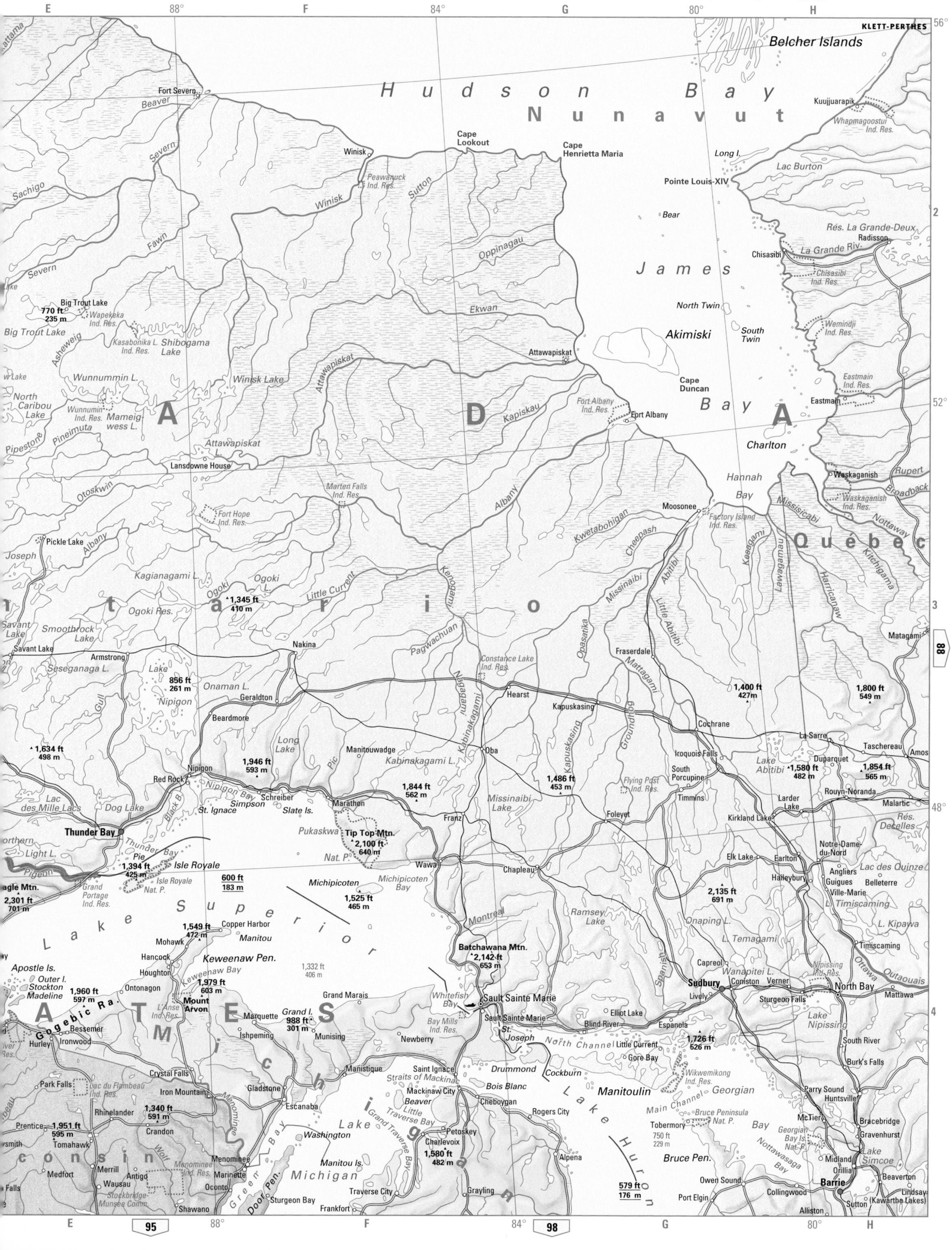
E
F
G
H
88°
84°
80°
56°
52°
48°
2
3
4
KLETT-PERTHES
Belcher Islands
Hudson Bay
Nunavut
Fort Severn
Beaver
Severn
Sachigo
Winisk
Peawanuck Ind. Res.
Sutton
Cape Lookout
Cape Henrietta Maria
Kuujjuarapik
Whapmagoostui Ind. Res.
Long I.
Lac Burton
Pointe Louis-XIV
Bear
Rés. La Grande-Deux
Radisson
Chisasibi
La Grande Riv.
Chisasibi Ind. Res.
James
Fawn
Oppinagau
Ekwan
North Twin
Akimiski
South Twin
Wemindji Ind. Res.
Big Trout Lake
770 ft
235 m
Wapekeka Ind. Res.
Big Trout Lake
Kasabonika L. Ind. Res.
Shibogama Lake
Asheweig
Attawapiskat
Wunnummin L.
Winisk Lake
Cape Duncan
Eastmain Ind. Res.
Eastmain
North Caribou Lake
Wunnumin Ind. Res.
Mameigwess L.
Pineimuta
Pipestone
A
D
A
Kapiskau
Fort Albany Ind. Res.
Fort Albany
Bay
Charlton
Attawapiskat L.
Lansdowne House
Otoskwin
Marten Falls Ind. Res.
Albany
Hannah Bay
Waskaganish
Rupert
Broadback
Waskaganish Ind. Res.
Fort Hope Ind. Res.
Moosonee
Factory Island Ind. Res.
Kwetabohigan
Cheepash
Missisicabi
Nottaway
Pickle Lake
Albany
Joseph
Kesagami
Lawagamau
Québec
Kitchigama
Kagianagami L.
Ogoki
Ogoki L.
1,345 ft
410 m
Little Current
Kenogami
Missinaibi
Abitibi
Little Abitibi
Harricanaw
Ogoki Res.
t a r i o
Savant Lake
Smoothrock Lake
Savant Lake
Pagwachuan
Opasatika
Fraserdale
Mattagami
Matagami
Armstrong
Seseganaga L.
Nakina
Constance Lake Ind. Res.
Lake Nipigon
856 ft
261 m
Onaman L.
Geraldton
Nagagami
Hearst
1,400 ft
427m
1,800 ft
549 m
Gull
Kapuskasing
Groundhog
Beardmore
Cochrane
Long Lake
Manitouwadge
Kabinakagami
Kapuskasing
La Sarre
Taschereau
Amos
1,634 ft
498 m
Pic
Kabinakagami L.
Oba
Iroquois Falls
Lake Abitibi
1,580 ft
482 m
Duparquet
1,854 ft
565 m
Nipigon
1,946 ft
593 m
1,486 ft
453 m
South Porcupine
Red Rock
Nipigon Bay
Schreiber
Marathon
1,844 ft
562 m
Flying Post Ind. Res.
Timmins
Rouyn-Noranda
Lac des Mille Lacs
Dog Lake
Simpson
Slate Is.
Missinaibi Lake
Larder Lake
Malartic
St. Ignace
Black B.
Franz
Foleyet
Kirkland Lake
Rés. Decelles
Thunder Bay
Pukaskwa
Tip Top Mtn.
2,100 ft
640 m
Thunder Bay
Nat. P.
Notre-Dame-du-Nord
Light L.
Pie
1,394 ft
425 m
Isle Royale
Wawa
Chapleau
Elk Lake
Earlton
Angliers
Lac des Quinze
Pigeon
Grand Portage Ind. Res.
Isle Royale Nat. P.
600 ft
183 m
Michipicoten
Michipicoten Bay
Haileybury
Guigues
Belleterre
Eagle Mtn.
2,301 ft
701 m
1,525 ft
465 m
2,135 ft
691 m
Ville-Marie
L. Timiskaming
Lake Superior
Montreal
Ramsey Lake
Onaping L.
L. Kipawa
1,549 ft
472 m
Copper Harbor
Manitou
L. Temagami
Mohawk
Batchawana Mtn.
2,142 ft
653 m
Timiscaming
Hancock
Keweenaw Pen.
Houghton
Keweenaw Bay
1,332 ft
406 m
Spanish
Capreol
Wanapitei L.
Nipissing Ind. Res.
Ottawa
Outaouais
Apostle Is.
Outer I.
Stockton
Madeline
1,979 ft
603 m
Ontonagon
1,960 ft
597 m
Grand Marais
Whitefish Bay
Sudbury
Coniston
Verner
North Bay
Mattawa
Mount Arvon
Sault Sainte Marie
Lively
Sturgeon Falls
Gogebic Ra.
L'Anse Ind. Res.
Marquette
Grand I.
988 ft
301 m
Bay Mills Ind. Res.
Sault Sainte Marie
Elliot Lake
Lake Nipissing
A T E S
Bessemer
Ishpeming
Munising
Blind River
Espanola
1,726 ft
526 m
Hurley
Ironwood
Newberry
St. Joseph
North Channel
Little Current
Gore Bay
South River
Crystal Falls
Manistique
Saint Ignace
Drummond
Cockburn
Burk's Falls
Park Falls
Lac du Flambeau Ind. Res.
Straits of Mackinac
Mackinaw City
Bois Blanc
Wikwemikong Ind. Res.
Manitoulin
Georgian
Parry Sound
Huntsville
Iron Mountain
Gladstone
Beaver
Cheboygan
Lake
Main Channel
Bruce Peninsula Nat. P.
Rhinelander
1,340 ft
591 m
Escanaba
Little Traverse Bay
Rogers City
McTier
Bracebridge
Prentice
1,951 ft
595 m
Crandon
Menominee
Grand Traverse Bay
Washington
Petoskey
Tobermory
750 ft
229 m
Bay
Georgian Bay Is. Nat. P.
Gravenhurst
Tomahawk
Wolf
Charlevoix
1,580 ft
482 m
Lake Huron
Nottawasaga Bay
Lake Simcoe
Midland
Orillia
Wisconsin
Menominee Ind. Res.
Green Bay
Manitou Is.
Alpena
Bruce Pen.
Merrill
Antigo
Marinette
Michigan
Medford
Wausau
Oconto
Door Pen.
Traverse City
Grayling
579 ft
176 m
Owen Sound
Barrie
Beaverton
Stockbridge-Munsee Ind. Res.
Shawano
Sturgeon Bay
Frankfort
Port Elgin
Collingwood
Alliston
Sutton
Lindsay (Kawartha Lakes)
Falls

88
95
98

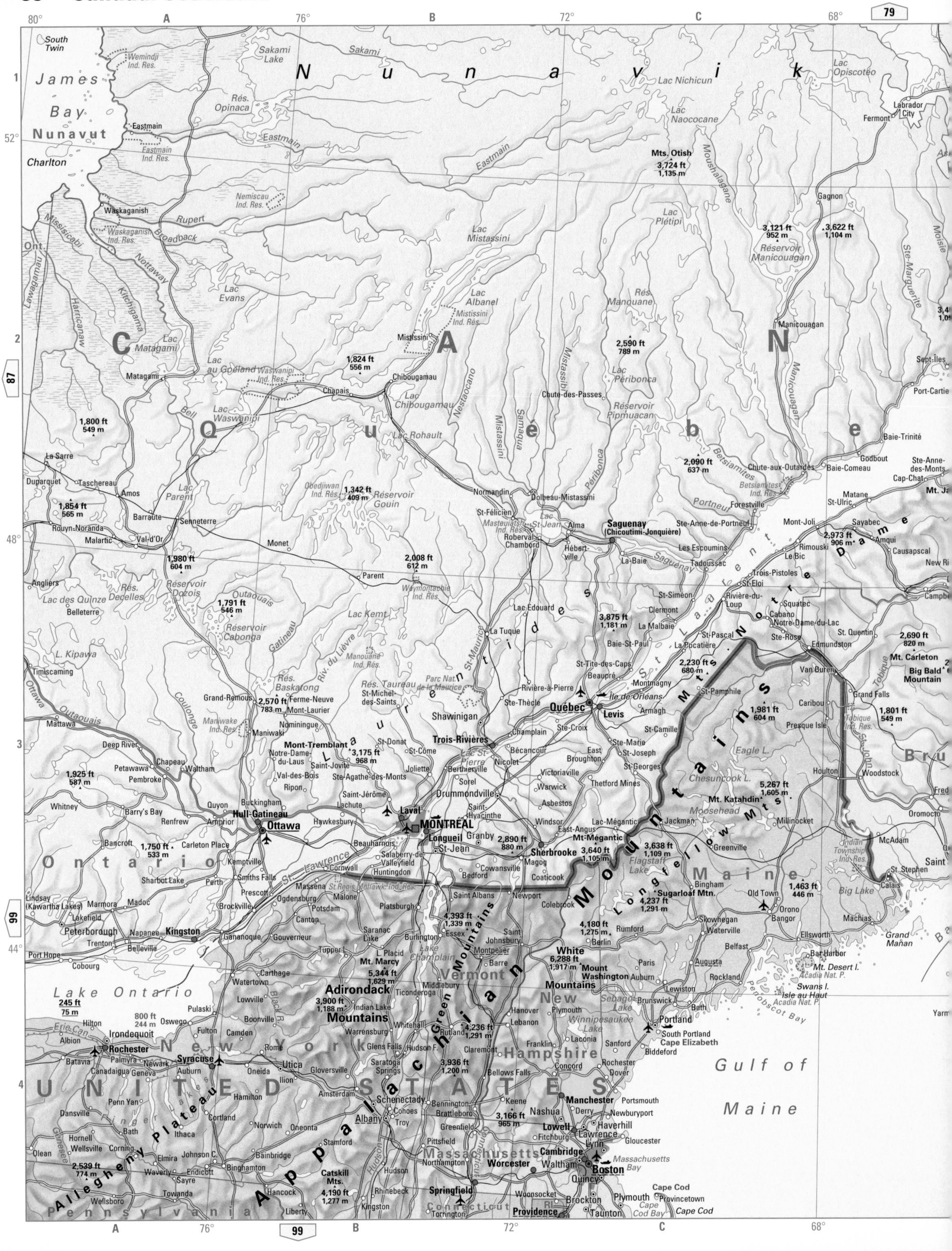

79
87
99
James Bay
Nunavut
Nunavik
Québec
Ontario
Ontario
UNITED STATES
New York
Vermont
New Hampshire
Maine
Massachusetts
Connecticut
Pennsylvania
CANADA
Lake Ontario
Gulf of Maine
Laurentides
Notre Dame
Appalachian Mountains
Adirondack Mountains
Green Mountains
White Mountains
Longfellow Mts.
Allegheny Plateau
Catskill Mts.
Mts. Otish
Mt. Marcy
Mt. Katahdin
Mount Washington
Sugarloaf Mtn.
Mt. Carleton
Mont-Tremblant
Lac Mistassini
Lac Albanel
Lac Evans
Lac Matagami
Lac Nichicun
Lac Naococane
Lac Opiscotéo
Lac Plétipi
Lac Chibougamau
Lac Waswanipi
Lac au Goéland
Lac Parent
Lac Kempt
Lac Édouard
Lac des Quinze
L. Kipawa
Lac Manouane
Lac Péribonca
Rés. Opinaca
Rés. Manouane
Réservoir Manicouagan
Réservoir Pipmuacan
Réservoir Gouin
Réservoir Cabonga
Réservoir Dozois
Rés. Decelles
Rés. Baskatong
Rés. Taureau
Lake Champlain
Moosehead Lake
Chesuncook L.
Eagle L.
Flagstaff Lake
Sebago Lake
Winnipesaukee Lake
Big Lake
Sakami Lake
St. Lawrence
St. Laurent
Saguenay
Eastmain
Rupert
Broadback
Nottaway
Harricanaw
Missisicabi
Kitchigama
Lawagamau
Bell
Outaouais
Gatineau
Coulonge
Ottawa
Riv. du Lièvre
St-Maurice
Mistassini
Mistassibi
Samaqua
Nestaocano
Péribonca
Betsiamites
Portneuf
Manicouagan
Moisie
Ste-Marguerite
Moushalagane
Sakami
Tobique
St. John
Black R.
Hudson
Connecticut
Genesee
Erie Can.
Penobscot Bay
Massachusetts Bay
Cape Cod Bay
Cape Cod
Grand Manan
Mt. Desert I.
Swans I.
Isle au Haut
Acadia Nat. P.
South Twin
Charlton
Eastmain
Waskaganish
Wemindji Ind. Res.
Eastmain Ind. Res.
Nemiscau Ind. Res.
Waskaganish Ind. Res.
Mistissini Ind. Res.
Waswanipi Ind. Res.
Obedjiwan Ind. Rés.
Weymontachie Ind. Rés.
Manouane Ind. Rés.
Maniwake Ind. Res.
Mashteuiatsh Ind. Rés.
Betsiamites Ind. Rés.
Tobique Ind. Res.
Indian Township Ind. Res.
St. Regis Mohawk Ind. Res.
Parc Nat. de la Mauricie
Ont.
Labrador City
Fermont
Gagnon
Manicouagan
Sept-Îles
Port-Cartier
Baie-Trinité
Godbout
Baie-Comeau
Ste-Anne-des-Monts
Cap-Chat
Mt. Ja
Matane
Ste-Ulric
Chute-aux-Outardes
Forestville
Ste-Anne-de-Portneuf
Mont-Joli
Sayabec
Amqui
Causapscal
Rimouski
Le Bic
New Ri
Les Escoumins
Tadoussac
Trois-Pistoles
St-Eloi
Rivière-du-Loup
St-Siméon
Clermont
Squatec
Cabano
Notre-Dame-du-Lac
La Malbaie
Baie-St-Paul
St-Pascal
La Pocatière
Ste-Rose
Edmundston
St. Quentin
Campbe
Chute-des-Passes
Normandin
Dolbeau-Mistassini
St-Félicien
Roberval
Chambord
Alma
Saguenay (Chicoutimi-Jonquière)
Hébertville
La-Baie
Matagami
Chibougamau
Chapais
Mistissini
La Sarre
Duparquet
Taschereau
Amos
Barraute
Senneterre
Rouyn-Noranda
Malartic
Val-d'Or
Monet
Parent
Angliers
Belleterre
Timiscaming
Mattawa
La Tuque
Lac-Édouard
St-Tite-des-Caps
Beaupré
Montmagny
Île de Orléans
Rivière-à-Pierre
Ste-Thècle
Québec
Levis
St-Pamphile
Armagh
Ste-Croix
St-Camille
Caribou
Presque Isle
Van Buren
Grand Falls
Woodstock
Houlton
Fred
Oromocto
McAdam
Saint
St. Stephen
Calais
Grand-Remous
Ferme-Neuve
Mont-Laurier
Nominingue
Maniwaki
St-Michel-des-Saints
Shawinigan
Trois-Rivières
Champlain
St-Donat
St-Côme
Notre-Dame-du-Laus
Saint-Jovite
Val-des-Bois
Ste-Agathe-des-Monts
Ripon
Saint-Jérôme
Lachute
Joliette
Berthierville
Lac-St-Pierre
Sorel
Bécancour
Nicolet
Drummondville
Victoriaville
Warwick
Asbestos
East Broughton
Ste-Marie
St-Joseph
St-Georges
Thetford Mines
Saint-Hyacinthe
Laval
MONTRÉAL
Longueuil
St-Jean
Granby
Windsor
Sherbrooke
Magog
Coaticook
Cowansville
Bedford
East-Angus
Lac-Mégantic
Mt-Mégantic
Jackman
Greenville
Millinocket
Bingham
Old Town
Orono
Bangor
Machias
Ellsworth
Bar Harbor
Skowhegan
Waterville
Augusta
Belfast
Rockland
Rumford
Berlin
Paris
Auburn
Lewiston
Brunswick
Bath
Portland
South Portland
Cape Elizabeth
Biddeford
Sanford
Rochester
Dover
Portsmouth
Newburyport
Haverhill
Gloucester
Lawrence
Lowell
Lynn
Cambridge
Boston
Quincy
Waltham
Fitchburg
Worcester
Brockton
Plymouth
Taunton
Provincetown
Woonsocket
Providence
Torrington
Springfield
Northampton
Greenfield
Brattleboro
Bennington
Keene
Manchester
Nashua
Derry
Concord
Laconia
Franklin
Plymouth
Lebanon
Hanover
Claremont
Bellows Falls
Rutland
Montpelier
Barre
Saint Johnsbury
Newport
Colebrook
Saint Albans
Burlington
Essex
Middlebury
Ticonderoga
Plattsburgh
Malone
Massena
Potsdam
Canton
Ogdensburg
Gouverneur
Tupper L.
Saranac Lake
L. Placid
Carthage
Watertown
Lowville
Boonville
Indian Lake
Whitehall
Warrensburg
Glens Falls
Hudson F.
Saratoga Springs
Schenectady
Albany
Cohoes
Troy
Pittsfield
Hudson
Rhinebeck
Kingston
Liberty
Hancock
Stamford
Oneonta
Norwich
Gloversville
Amsterdam
Utica
Ilion
Rome
Oneida
Syracuse
Auburn
Cortland
Ithaca
Binghamton
Endicott
Johnson C.
Elmira
Corning
Bath
Hornell
Wellsville
Olean
Dansville
Penn Yan
Geneva
Newark
Canandaigua
Palmyra
Batavia
Rochester
Irondequoit
Albion
Hilton
Oswego
Fulton
Camden
Pulaski
Sayre
Waverly
Towanda
Wellsboro
Hull-Gatineau
Ottawa
Buckingham
Quyon
Hawkesbury
Beauharnois
Salaberry-de-Valleyfield
Huntingdon
Cornwall
Kemptville
Smiths Falls
Prescott
Brockville
Perth
Carleton Place
Arnprior
Renfrew
Barry's Bay
Whitney
Pembroke
Petawawa
Chapeau
Waltham
Deep River
Bancroft
Madoc
Marmora
Sharbot Lake
Lindsay (Kawartha Lakes)
Lakefield
Peterborough
Napanee
Kingston
Gananoque
Trenton
Belleville
Port Hope
Cobourg
3,724 ft 1,135 m
3,121 ft 952 m
3,622 ft 1,104 m
2,590 ft 789 m
1,824 ft 556 m
1,800 ft 549 m
2,090 ft 637 m
1,342 ft 409 m
1,854 ft 565 m
1,980 ft 604 m
2,008 ft 612 m
2,973 ft 906 m
1,791 ft 546 m
3,875 ft 1,181 m
2,690 ft 820 m
2,230 ft 680 m
2,570 ft 783 m
1,981 ft 604 m
1,801 ft 549 m
3,175 ft 968 m
1,925 ft 587 m
5,267 ft 1,605 m
2,890 ft 880 m
3,638 ft 1,109 m
3,640 ft 1,105 m
1,750 ft 533 m
1,463 ft 446 m
4,237 ft 1,291 m
4,393 ft 1,339 m
4,180 ft 1,275 m
6,288 ft 1,917 m
5,344 ft 1,629 m
3,900 ft 1,188 m
245 ft 75 m
800 ft 244 m
4,236 ft 1,291 m
3,936 ft 1,200 m
3,166 ft 965 m
2,539 ft 774 m
4,190 ft 1,277 m
80°
76°
72°
68°
52°
48°
44°
A
B
C
1
2
3
4

Labrador
(Nunatsiavut)
Newfoundland and Labrador
Churchill Falls
Ossokmanuan Lake
Goose
Happy Valley-Goose Bay
Mealy Mountains
Churchill
Eagle
2,080 ft 634 m
1,857 ft 566 m
1,893 ft 577 m
1,919 ft 585 m
Atikonak Lake
Alexis
Port Hope Simpson
St Lewis
Natashquan
Little Mecatina
Belle Isle
1,850 ft 564 m
Red Bay
Cape Bauld
2,083 ft 635 m
Petit Mécatina
Strait of Belle Isle
Forteau
Blanc-Sablon
St. Anthony
3,230 ft 984 m
St-Jean
St-Augustin
Grey Islands
1,024 ft 747 m
1,195 ft 364 m
Lac Magpie
Romaine
Aguanish
Olomane
Englee
Harrington Harbour
2,152 ft 656 m
Long Range Mountains
Horse Is.
A
D
A
Natashquan
La Romaine
White Bay
Rivière-au-Tonnerre
Havre-St-Pierre
Baie Verte
New World I.
Fogo
Funk I.
Détroit de Jacques-Cartier
Notre Dame Bay
Port-Menier
2,644 ft 806 m
Gros Morne
Springdale
Nat. P.
Lewisporte
Île d'Anticosti
1,024 ft 312 m
Deer Lake
1,867 ft 569 m
Gander
Baie-du-Renard
1,916 ft 584 m
Badger
Bishop's Falls
Grand Falls-Windsor
Gambo
Bonavista Bay
Détroit d'Honguedo
Louis
Cloridorme
Corner Brook
Bonavista
Grand Lake
Exploits
Terra Nova Nat. P.
Lewis Hills 2,671 ft 814 m
Gaspé
Parc National du Canada Forillon
Stephenville
Newfoundland
Clarenville-Shoal Harbour
Gulf of Saint Lawrence
1,234 ft 376 m
Trinity Bay
St. George's Bay
Chandler
Maelpaeg Res.
Carbonear
Blue Hills of Couteau 1,903 ft 580 m
Grey
St. Alban's
Bay Roberts
St. John's
Mt. Pearl
Conception Bay South
Miscou
Brion
Merasheen I.
Île Lamèque
Shippagan
Îles de la Madeleine
C. Ray
Burgeo
Harbour Breton
Fortune Bay
1,326 ft 404 m
1,066 ft 335 m
Dunville
Avalon Pen.
Channel-Port aux Basques
Placentia Bay
Île du Havre Aubert
Cap-aux-Meules
532 ft 162 m
Cabot Strait
Grand Bank
Marystown
Tracadie-Sheila
St. Paul
Miquelon
St. Pierre and Miquelon (FRA.)
St-Pierre
St. Mary's Bay
Cape Race
Burnt Church Ind. Res.
C. North
Tignish
White Hill 1,747 ft 532 m
Cape Breton Highlands Nat. P.
Prince Edward Island
Prince Edward Island Nat. P.
Summerside
466 ft 142 m
Charlottetown
Souris
Georgetown
Inverness
Sydney Mines
Sydney
Glace Bay
Shediac
Moncton
Northumberland Strait
Whycocomagh Ind. Res.
Baddeck
Riverview
Port Elgin
Sackville
Bras d'Or Lake
Eskasoni Ind. Res.
Cape Breton
Cape Breton Island
Amherst
Pictou
Antigonish
Port Hawkesbury
1,204 ft 367 m
New Glasgow
I. Madame
Truro
Str. of Canso
Nova Scotia
Kentville
Indian Brook Ind. Res.
Sheet Harbour
Windsor
Dartmouth
Halifax
Bridgewater
Liverpool
Sable I.
ATLANTIC
OCEAN
64°
60°
56°
52°
48°
44°
E
F
G
H
1
2
3
4

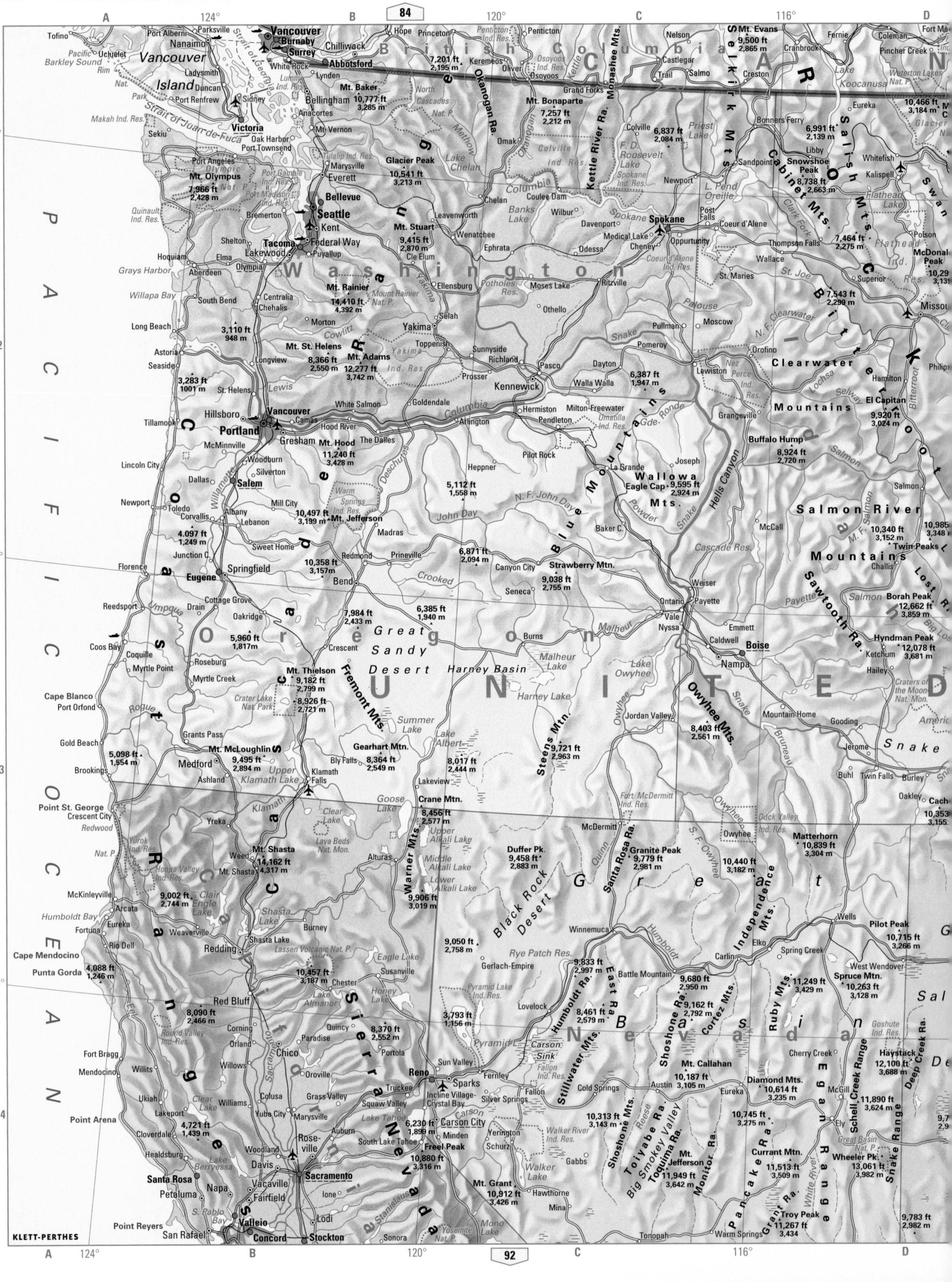

84
92
A
B
C
D
124°
120°
116°
48°
44°
40°
1
2
3
4
British Columbia
CANADA
Washington
Oregon
Idaho
UNITED
Nevada
California
Great Basin
PACIFIC OCEAN
Coast Ranges
Cascade Range
Sierra Nevada
Vancouver Island
Strait of Georgia
Strait of Juan de Fuca
Tofino
Ucluelet
Pacific Rim Nat. P.
Barkley Sound
Port Alberni
Parksville
Nanaimo
Ladysmith
Duncan
Port Renfrew
Sidney
Victoria
Vancouver
Burnaby
Surrey
White Rock
Chilliwack
Abbotsford
Hope
Princeton
Penticton
Keremeos
Oliver
Osoyoos
Grand Forks
Nelson
Castlegar
Trail
Salmo
Creston
Cranbrook
Fernie
Coleman
Pincher Creek
Fort Macleod
Lynden
Bellingham
Anacortes
Mt. Vernon
Oak Harbor
Port Townsend
Port Angeles
Sekiu
Makah Ind. Res.
Everett
Marysville
Bellevue
Seattle
Bremerton
Kent
Federal Way
Tacoma
Lakewood
Puyallup
Olympia
Shelton
Hoquiam
Elma
Aberdeen
Grays Harbor
Willapa Bay
South Bend
Centralia
Chehalis
Long Beach
Astoria
Seaside
Longview
St. Helens
Hillsboro
Vancouver
Portland
Camas
Gresham
Tillamook
McMinnville
Lincoln City
Dallas
Salem
Woodburn
Silverton
Newport
Toledo
Corvallis
Albany
Lebanon
Sweet Home
Junction C.
Florence
Eugene
Springfield
Cottage Grove
Drain
Reedsport
Oakridge
Coos Bay
Coquille
Myrtle Point
Roseburg
Myrtle Creek
Cape Blanco
Port Orford
Gold Beach
Grants Pass
Brookings
Medford
Ashland
Klamath Falls
Point St. George
Crescent City
Redwood Nat. P.
Yreka
Weed
Mt. Shasta
McKinleyville
Arcata
Eureka
Humboldt Bay
Fortuna
Rio Dell
Cape Mendocino
Punta Gorda
Weaverville
Redding
Shasta Lake
Burney
Red Bluff
Corning
Orland
Chico
Paradise
Oroville
Willows
Quincy
Chester
Susanville
Fort Bragg
Mendocino
Willits
Ukiah
Lakeport
Clear Lake
Williams
Colusa
Yuba City
Marysville
Grass Valley
Truckee
Point Arena
Cloverdale
Healdsburg
Santa Rosa
Petaluma
Napa
Vacaville
Fairfield
Davis
Woodland
Sacramento
Roseville
Auburn
South Lake Tahoe
Ione
Lodi
Stockton
Sonora
Vallejo
Concord
San Rafael
Point Reyes
Mt. Baker 10,777 ft 3,285 m
Mt. Olympus 7,966 ft 2,428 m
Glacier Peak 10,541 ft 3,213 m
Mt. Stuart 9,415 ft 2,870 m
Mt. Rainier 14,410 ft 4,392 m
Mt. St. Helens 8,366 ft 2,550 m
Mt. Adams 12,277 ft 3,742 m
Mt. Hood 11,240 ft 3,428 m
Mt. Jefferson 10,497 ft 3,199 m
Mt. Thielson 9,182 ft 2,799 m
Mt. McLoughlin 9,495 ft 2,894 m
Mt. Shasta 14,162 ft 4,317 m
Mt. Bonaparte 7,257 ft 2,212 m
Mt. Evans 9,500 ft 2,865 m
Snowshoe Peak 8,738 ft 2,663 m
Okanogan Ra.
Kettle River Ra.
Monashee Mts.
Selkirk Mts.
Cabinet Mts.
Salish Mts.
Bitterroot Range
Clearwater Mountains
Salmon River Mountains
Sawtooth Ra.
Lost River Ra.
Blue Mountains
Wallowa Mts.
Eagle Cap 9,595 ft 2,924 m
Strawberry Mtn. 9,038 ft 2,755 m
Fremont Mts.
Gearhart Mtn. 8,364 ft 2,549 m
Steens Mtn. 9,721 ft 2,963 m
Crane Mtn. 8,456 ft 2,577 m
Warner Mts.
Owyhee Mts.
Great Sandy Desert
Harney Basin
Crater Lake Nat. Park
Upper Klamath Lake
Lava Beds Nat. Mon.
Black Rock Desert
Santa Rosa Ra.
Granite Peak 9,779 ft 2,981 m
Duffer Pk. 9,458 ft 2,883 m
Independence Mts.
Humboldt Ra.
East Ra.
Stillwater Mts.
Shoshone Ra.
Cortez Mts.
Ruby Mts.
Toiyabe Ra.
Toquima Ra.
Shoshone Mts.
Big Smokey Valley
Monitor Ra.
Pancake Ra.
Grant Ra.
Egan Range
Schell Creek Range
Snake Range
Deep Creek Ra.
Mt. Callahan 10,187 ft 3,105 m
Mt. Jefferson 11,949 ft 3,642 m
Currant Mtn. 11,513 ft 3,509 m
Troy Peak 11,267 ft 3,434
Wheeler Pk. 13,061 ft 3,982 m
Diamond Mts. 10,614 ft 3,235 m
Haystack 12,100 ft 3,688 m
Pilot Peak 10,715 ft 3,266 m
Spruce Mtn. 10,263 ft 3,128 m
Matterhorn 10,839 ft 3,304 m
Mt. Grant 10,912 ft 3,426 m
Freel Peak 10,880 ft 3,316 m
Omak
Chelan
Lake Chelan
Leavenworth
Wenatchee
Cle Elum
Ellensburg
Ephrata
Coulee Dam
Wilbur
Davenport
Spokane
Medical Lake
Cheney
Odessa
Ritzville
Moses Lake
Othello
Yakima
Selah
Toppenish
Sunnyside
Richland
Pasco
Kennewick
Prosser
Walla Walla
Dayton
Pomeroy
Pullman
Moscow
Colville
Newport
Sandpoint
Bonners Ferry
Coeur d'Alene
Post Falls
Wallace
Kellogg
St. Maries
Lewiston
Orofino
Grangeville
Goldendale
White Salmon
Hood River
The Dalles
Arlington
Hermiston
Pendleton
Milton-Freewater
Heppner
Pilot Rock
La Grande
Joseph
Baker C.
Madras
Redmond
Prineville
Bend
Canyon City
Seneca
Burns
Crescent
Lakeview
Ontario
Payette
Weiser
Vale
Nyssa
Caldwell
Boise
Nampa
Emmett
Mountain Home
Jordan Valley
McDermitt
Winnemucca
Lovelock
Gerlach-Empire
Battle Mountain
Carlin
Elko
Wells
Eureka
Austin
Ely
Fallon
Fernley
Sparks
Reno
Sun Valley
Carson City
Yerington
Hawthorne
Gabbs
Tonopah
Mina
Walker Lake
Lake Tahoe
Pyramid Lake
Honey Lake
Eagle Lake
Goose Lake
Harney Lake
Malheur Lake
Lake Owyhee
Alturas
Twin Falls
Jerome
Gooding
Burley
Buhl
Hailey
Ketchum
Challis
Salmon
McCall
Hamilton
Missoula
Polson
Kalispell
Whitefish
Libby
Eureka
Superior
Thompson Falls
Columbia
Snake
Salmon
Clearwater
Yakima
Willamette
Deschutes
John Day
Crooked
Malheur
Owyhee
Humboldt
Klamath
Rogue
Umpqua
Sacramento
KLETT-PERTHES

1:5,000,000

0
50
100 mi
0
50
100 km
112°
E
85
108°
F
104°
G
100°
H
Saskatchewan
Manitoba
Alberta
CANADA
Lethbridge
Foremost
Etzikom Coulee
Cypress Hills
4,816 ft
1,468 m
Shaunavon
Consul
Frenchman
Val Marie
Pinto Butte
3,438 ft
1,049 m
Grasslands Nat. P.
Big Beaver
Radville
2,325 ft
708 m
Souris
Estevan
Oxbow
Melita
Boissevain
Killarney
Rolla
Bottineau
Turtle Mountain Ind. Res.
Milk River
Milk
Sweet Grass Hills
6,983 ft
2,128 m
Sunburst
Cut Bank
Shelby
Lodge Creek
Battle Creek
Chinook
Havre
Opheim
Scobey
Plentywood
Crosby
Kenmare
Rugby
Fort Peck Ind. Res.
Medicine Lake
Stanley
Minot
Velva
Malta
2,000 ft
610 m
Poplar
Williston
New Town
Harvey
Conrad
L. Elwell
Marias
Rocky Boy's Ind. Res.
Bear's Paw Mts.
6,916 ft
2,108 m
Fort Belknap Ind. Res.
Glasgow
Wolf Point
Missouri
Fort Berthold Ind. Res.
Lake Sakakawea
2,290 ft
698 m
Teton River
Fort Benton
Sidney
Theodore Roosevelt Nat. P. N. Unit
Little Missouri
North Dakota
3,314 ft
1,010 m
Beulah
Hazen
Knife
Fort Peck Lake
Great Falls
Judith
Big Dry Creek
Jordan
Circle
3,078 ft
938 m
Theodore Roosevelt Nat. P. S. Unit
Mandan
Bismarck
Stanford
Lewistown
Glendive
Beach
Dickinson
Big Baldy Mtn.
9,175 ft
2,796 m
Little Belt Mts.
Big Belt Mts.
Smith
Holter Lake
Big Snowy Mts.
8,681 ft
2,646 m
3,635 ft
1,108 m
Terry
3,505 ft
1,069 m
Heart
Linton
Montana
Helena
Canyon Ferry L.
Deer Lodge
White Sulphur Springs
Melstone
Roundup
Baker
2,823 ft
860 m
Cannonball
Fort Yates
Mt. Edith
9,702 ft
2,957 m
Harlowton
4,700 ft
1,433 m
Miles City
Bowman
Hettinger
Cedar Creek
Standing
Townsend
Musselshell
Yellowstone
Forsyth
Lemmon
Rock
Grand R.
Ind. Res.
Lake
Mobridge
Butte
Crazy Pk.
11,209 ft
3,416 m
Big Timber
Tongue
Colstrip
Rosebud Cr.
Belgrade
Billings
Hardin
Jefferson
Madison
Bozeman
Livingston
Laurel
Crow
Indian
Reservation
Northern Cheyenne Ind. Res.
Cheyenne
Oahe
River
Broadus
Powder
Moreau
Sioux
Absaroka Range
4,206 ft
1,282 m
Red Lodge
Bighorn
4,290 ft
1,308 m
3,741 ft
1,140 m
Ind. Res.
Dillon
Granite Pk.
12,798 ft
3,901 m
Bighorn Lake
Little Powder
Little Missouri
Hilgard Pk.
11,316 ft
3,449 m
Bighorn Mts.
2,053 ft
626 m
Sheridan
Belle Fourche
South Dakota
Pierre
Clarks F.
Powell
Lovell
13,175 ft
4,016 m
Bear Lodge Mts.
Spearfish
Sturgis
1,570 ft
479 m
Yellowstone
Greybull
Buffalo
Keyhole Res.
6,550 ft
2,026 m
Lead
Rapid City
Bad R.
Shoshone
Cody
Cloud Peak
Gillette
Moorcroft
Philip
Yellowstone Lake
Nat. Park
Greybull
Upton
Black Hills
Mt. Rushmore Nat. Memorial
White R.
Ashton
Worland
Newcastle
7,242 ft
2,207 m
Grand Teton Nat. Park
Francs Pk.
13,153 ft
4,009 m
Badlands Nat. P.
Wind Cave Nat. P.
Pine Ridge
Rexburg
Gd. Teton
13,770 ft
4,197 m
9,872 ft
3,009 m
Owl Creek Mts.
Thermopolis
Hot Springs
3,410 ft
1,039 m
Rosebud
Idaho Falls
Jackson
Wind River
Midwest
Cheyenne
Edgemont
Ind. Res.
Martin
Doubletop Peak
11,740 ft
3,578 m
Boysen Res.
Pine Ridge
UNITED STATES
Wind River Range
Gannett Peak
13,804 ft
4,207 m
Wind
Ind. Res.
Riverton
Casper
Lusk
Chadron
Gordon
Valentine
Blackfoot
Fort Hall
Blackfoot Res.
Douglas
6,135 ft
1,870 m
Pocatello
Pinedale
Lander
Mills
8,244 ft
2,513 m
Wyoming
Glendo Res.
Niobrara
3,400 ft
1,036 m
Soda Springs
9,554 ft
3,034 m
11,378 ft
3,480 m
Wyoming Peak
Wyoming Ra.
Laramie Mts.
McCammon
Meade Peak
Montpelier
Sweetwater
Green Mts.
9,215 ft
2,812 m
Pathfinder Res.
Laramie Peak
10,297 ft
3,131 m
Torrington
Alliance
4,203 ft
1,281 m
Thedford
Shirley Mts.
9,151 ft
2,789 m
Wheatland
Scottsbluff
Nebraska
Preston
Seminoe Res.
8,685 ft
2,647 m
Bear Lake
Basin
Hanna
Hogback Mtn.
5,063 ft
1,543 m
Gering
Bridgeport
Richmond
Kemmerer
Green River
Rawlins
Logan
Wellsville
Rock Springs
Green River
North Platte
Medicine Bow Mts.
Horse Creek
North Platte
Lake McConaughy
Brigham City
Lyman
Saratoga
Medicine Bow Pk.
12,013 ft
3,661 m
Laramie
Kimball
Sidney
Ogallala
North Platte
9,764 ft
2,976 m
Great Salt Lake
Evanston
11,007 ft
3,354 m
Park Range
Cheyenne
Julesburg
Grant
Flaming Gorge Res.
Ogden
Layton
Bountiful
Mt. Zirkel
12,180 ft
3,712 m
Sterling
3,025 ft
922 m
Imperial
13,528 ft
4,123 m
Salt Lake City
Kings Peak
Uinta Mountains
Rocky Mountain Nat. Park
Fort Collins
Windsor
Valley City
West Jordan
Sandy
American Fork
Dinosaur Nat. Mon.
Craig
Yampa
Estes Park
Loveland
Greeley
South Platte
Orem
Provo
Vernal
Steamboat Springs
14,255 ft
4,345 m
Longmont
Brush
Yuma
Wray
40°
Lehi
Utah Lake
Uintah
Roosevelt
Fort Lupton
Fort Morgan
Springville
Duchesne
White River
Granby
Boulder
Brighton
Beaver Creek
Spanish Fork
Santaquin
Meeker
Sheep Mtn.
12,248 ft
3,733 m
Gore Ra.
13,534 ft
4,351 m
Denver
Aurora
Lakewood
Mt. Nebo
11,928 ft
3,636 m
Nephi
West Tavaputs Plateau
Helper
Price
10,450 ft
3,185 m
Ind. Res.
Roan Plateau
Rifle
White River Plateau
Avon
Parker
6,005 ft
1,830 m
Goodland
Colby
Burlington
Wasatch Range
East Tavaputs Plateau
Glenwood Springs
Mt. Lincoln
14,286 ft
4,354 m
Castle Rock
Limon
Oakley
Ephraim
Roan Cliffs
Colorado
Leadville
Mt. Elbert
14,433 ft
4,399 m
Sawatch Ra.
4,039 ft
1,231 m
Delta
Manti
Fruita
Grand Junction
Aspen
Woodland Park
Calhan
Kansas
S. Platte
San Rafael
Green River
Colorado Nat. Mon.
11,234 ft
3,424 m
Pikes Peak
14,108 ft
4,300 m
Colorado Springs
Big Sandy Creek
Cheyenne Wells
Salina
Gunnison
Scott City
Richfield
Mt. Marvine
11,610 ft
3,536 m
Arches Nat. P.
Delta
Black Canyon of the Gunnison Nat. Mon.
Gunnison
Salida
Cañon City
Florence
Fountain
Eads
Sevier
Moab
Mt. Peale
12,721 ft
3,875 m
9,731 ft
2,966 m
Uncompahgre Plateau
Montrose
Pueblo
Ordway
Delano Peak
12,173 ft
3,710 m
Dirty Devil
Capitol Reef Nat. P.
Canyonlands Nat. P.
Naturita
14,309 ft
4,361 m
Uncompahgre Peak
14,294 ft
4,356 m
Arkansas
Rocky Ford
La Junta
Las Animas
Lamar
Arkansas
93
1
2
3
4
48°
44°
86
94

90
KLETT-PERTHES
Brookings
Ashland
Klamath Falls
Lakeview
Crane Mtn.
8,456 ft
2,577 m
Point St. George
Crescent City
Yreka
Mt. Shasta
14,162 ft
4,317 m
Weed
Alturas
Upper Alkali Lake
Middle Alkali Lake
Lower Alkali Lake
Warner Mts.
Duffer Pk.
9,458 ft
2,883 m
Granite Peak
9,779 ft
2,981 m
McDermitt
Santa Rosa Ra.
Owyhee
Matterhorn
10,839 ft
3,304 m
10,440 ft
3,182 m
Independence Mts.
Black Rock Desert
Winnemucca
Humboldt
Elko
Spring Creek
Carlin
McKinleyville
Arcata
Eureka
Weaverville
9,002 ft
2,744 m
Humboldt Bay
Fortuna
Rio Dell
Cape Mendocino
Punta Gorda
4,088 ft
1,246 m
Redding
Shasta Lake
Burney
Lassen Volcanic Nat. P.
10,457 ft
3,187 m
Susanville
Chester
Eagle Lake
Honey Lake
Lake Almanor
Red Bluff
8,090 ft
2,466 m
9,050 ft
2,758 m
Rye Patch Res.
Gerlach-Empire
Pyramid Lake Ind. Res.
Lovelock
9,833 ft
2,997 m
8,461 ft
2,579 m
Humboldt Ra.
East Ra.
Battle Mountain
9,680 ft
2,950 m
9,162 ft
2,792 m
Cortez Mts.
Shoshone Ra.
Ruby Mts.
11,249 ft
3,429 m
Corning
Orland
Willows
Chico
Paradise
Quincy
8,370 ft
2,552 m
Portola
3,793 ft
1,156 m
Pyramid Lake
Sun Valley
Reno
Sparks
Fernley
Carson Sink
Stillwater Mts.
Fallon
Mt. Callahan
10,187 ft
3,105 m
Diamond Mts.
10,614 ft
3,235 m
Eureka
McGill
Fort Bragg
Willits
Mendocino
Ukiah
Lakeport
Oroville
Truckee
Incline Village-Crystal Bay
Grass Valley
Squaw Valley
Williams
Colusa
Yuba City
Marysville
L. Tahoe
6,230 ft
1,899 m
Carson City
Minden
S. Lake Tahoe
Silver Springs
Yerington
Schurz
Walker River Ind. Res.
Cold Springs
Austin
10,313 ft
3,143 m
10,745 ft
3,275 m
Point Arena
4,721 ft
1,439 m
Clear Lake
Cloverdale
Healdsburg
Lake Berryessa
Woodland
Davis
Roseville
Auburn
Sacramento
Freel Peak
10,880 ft
3,316 m
Walker Lake
Gabbs
Shoshone Mts.
Toiyabe Ra.
Big Smokey Valley
Toquima Ra.
Mt. Jefferson
11,949 ft
3,642 m
Monitor Ra.
Pancake Ra.
Currant Mtn.
11,513 ft
3,509 m
White River
Grant Ra.
Santa Rosa
Vacaville
Mt. Grant
10,912 ft
3,426 m
Hawthorne
Petaluma
Napa
Fairfield
Ione
Mina
Troy Pk.
11,267 ft
3,434 m
Warm Springs
Point Reyers
San Rafael
Farallon Is.
Vallejo
Concord
Oakland
Lodi
Stockton
San Francisco
Tracy
Manteca
Sonora
Yosemite Nat. P.
Mono Lake
Tonopah
Fremont
Oakdale
Modesto
Turlock
Yosemite Village
11,726 ft
3,574 m
Mammoth Lakes
White Mts.
14,242 ft
4,341 m
9,404 ft
2,866 m
9,348 ft
2,859 m
San Jose
Merced
Bishop
Diablo Range
3,790 ft
1,155 m
Los Banos
Chowchilla
Big Pine
11,122 ft
3,390 m
Inyo Mts.
Nellis
PACIFIC
Santa Cruz
Gilroy
Watsonville
Monterey Bay
Seaside
Monterey
Hollister
Salinas
Madera
Fresno
Clovis
Kings Canyon Nat. P.
Sanger
Reedley
Death Valley Nat. P.
8,737 ft
2,663 m
Beatty
Mt. Whitney
14,495 ft
4,418 m
Lone Pine
Indian Springs
9,750 ft
2,972 m
Sheep Ra.
Soledad
S. Benito Mtn.
5,248 ft
1,600 m
Selma
Hanford
Visalia
Owens Lake
Panamint Range
Amargosa Ra.
Point Sur
King City
Junipero Serra Peak
5,862 ft
1,787 m
Lemoore
Sequoia N. P.
-282 ft
-86 m
Charleston Pk.
11,919 ft
3,633 m
Spring Mts.
Las Vegas
Coalinga
Corcoran
Tulare
Telescope Peak
11,049 ft
3,368 m
6,384 ft
1,946 m
Pahrump
Spring Valley
OCEAN
Santa Lucia Range
Porterville
Tule River Ind. Res.
8,475 ft
2,583 m
Delano
Wasco
El Paso de Robles
Atascadero
Lake Isabella
Ridgecrest
Searles L.
7,929 ft
2,417 m
Morro Bay
Estelo Bay
San Luis Obispo
Pismo Beach
Arroyo Grande
Bakersfield
Taft
Tehachapi
California C.
Mojave Desert
Soda Lake
San Luis Obispo Bay
Guadalupe
Santa Maria
Mojave
Mt. Pinos
8,831 ft
2,692 m
Rosamond
Barstow
Lompoc
Lancaster
Palmdale
Point Arguelle
Point Conception
Santa Barbara
Santa Clarita
Victorville
Apple Valley
Goleta
San Buenaventura
10,064 ft
3,068 m
Hesperia
Santa Barbara Channel
Thousand Oaks
San Gabriel Mts.
Glendale
Pasadena
San Bernardino
Yucca Valley
Twentynine Palms
S. Miguel
Sta. Cruz
Oxnard
2,471 ft
753 m
Anacapa Is.
LOS ANGELES
Ontario
11,502 ft
3,506 m
San Bernardino Mts.
Banning
Sta. Rosa
Channel Islands Nat. P.
Anaheim
Riverside
Palm Springs
4,353 ft
1,327 m
Long Beach
Moreno Valley
Indio
Hemet
Santa Ana
Temecula
Palm Desert
Sta. Barbara
Mission Viejo
Sta. Catalina
2,126 ft
648 m
Avalon
San Clemente
Salton Sea
S. Nicolas
Palomar Mtn.
6,140 ft
1,872 m
Borrego Sprs.
-235 ft
-72 m
Vista
Oceanside
Escondido
Salton C.
Calipatria
Gulf of Sta. Catalina
Westmorland
Brawley
S. Clemente
China Point
El Centro
Holtville
SAN DIEGO
El Cajon
Chula Vista
Santa Isabel
Calexico
Cuervos
TIJUANA
Tecate
La Rumorosa
Mexicali
Islas de Coronados
Rosarito
La Salada
Baja
Guadalupe Victoria
Punta Salsipuedes
El Sauzal
Ensenada
Bahía de Todos Santos
Isla de Todos Santos
Maneadero
6,675 ft
2,035 m
Golfo de Santa
Ejido Héroes
Santo Tomás
California
San Vicente
Colonia Lázaro Cardenas
Hawaiian Islands
Kilauea
Lehua
5,170 ft
1,578 m
Niihau
Kekaha
Lihue
Kapaa
Hanapepe
Kauai
Kawaihoa Point
Kauai Channel
Kahuku Point
Oahu
Kaena Point
4,040 ft
1,233 m
Hauula
Wahiawa
Waianae
Kaneohe
Pearl City
Kailua
Ewa Beach
Honolulu
Pearl Harbor
Kaiwi Channel
Molokai
Laau Point
Kaunakakai
Pailolo Channel
Lanai City
Wailuku
Lahaina
Kahului
Maui
Kihei
Lanai
10,023 ft
3,055 m
Haleakala Nat. P.
UNITED STATES
Hawaii
Kahoolawe
Alenuihaha Channel
Upolu Point
Hawi
Honokaa
Waimea
PACIFIC
OCEAN
Mauna Kea
13,796 ft
4,205 m
Papaikou
Hilo
Keaau
Kailua
Mountain View
Cape Kumukahi
Mauna Loa
13,678 ft
4,169 m
Kilauea Crater
4,090 ft
1,247 m
Pahoa
Captain Cook
Hawaii Volcanoes Nat. P.
Hawaii (Big Island)
Pahala
Naalehu
Ka Lae
1:5,000,000
Hawaii: East

91

94
96
102
96

A
108°
B
91
104°
C
100°
86
D
85
91
93
96
1
2
3
4
44°
40°
36°
Stanford
Lewistown
Big Dry Creek
Jordan
Circle
Big Snowy Mts.
8,681 ft
2,646 m
3,635 ft
1,108 m
Yellowstone
Glendive
3,078 ft
938 m
3,314 ft
1,010 m
Fort Berthold Ind. Res.
Hazen
Beulah
Knife
Little Missouri
Theodore Roosevelt Nat. P. S. Unit
Carrington
Cooperstown
Jamestown
Harlowton
Roundup
Melstone
Terry
Beach
Dickinson
Mandan
Bismarck
Heart
North Dakota
Musselshell
4,700 ft
1,433 m
Crazy Pk.
11,209 ft
3,416 m
Big Timber
Montana
Miles City
Forsyth
Baker
3,505 ft
1,069 m
2,823 ft
860 m
Cannonball
Linton
James
2,234 ft
681 m
Billings
Yellowstone
Laurel
Colstrip
Rosebud Cr.
Tongue
Powder
Bowman
Hettinger
Cedar Creek
Fort Yates
Ellendale
Ashley
Hardin
Crow
Indian
Reservation
Northern Cheyenne Ind. Res.
Lemmon
Standing
Rock
Grand R.
Ind. Res.
Lake
Mobridge
Absaroka Range
Granite Pk.
12,798 ft
3,901 m
Red Lodge
Bighorn
Bighorn Lake
Broadus
4,206 ft
1,282 m
4,290 ft
1,308 m
Cheyenne
River
Sioux
Ind. Res.
Oahe
Moreau
Ipswich
Aberdeen
Clarks Fork
Yellowstone
Nat. Park
Shoshone
Powell
Lovell
Bighorn Mts.
Sheridan
Little Powder
Little Missouri
3,741 ft
1,140 m
Gettysburg
Redfield
Cody
Greybull
Cloud Peak
13,175 ft
4,016 m
Buffalo
Belle Fourche
Bear Lodge Mts.
6,550 ft
2,026 m
Belle Fourche
Spearfish
Sturgis
Lead
South Dakota
2,053 ft
626 m
Highmore
Miller
Huron
Keyhole Res.
Gillette
Moorcroft
Upton
Francs Pk.
13,153 ft
4,009 m
Worland
Powder
Black Hills
Rapid City
Mt. Rushmore Nat. Memorial
7,242 ft
2,207 m
Cheyenne
1,570 ft
479 m
Pierre
Crow Creek Ind. Res.
Lower Brule Ind. Res.
Bad R.
Fort Thompson
Philip
Rocky
Wind
Owl Creek Mts.
9,872 ft
3,009 m
Thermopolis
Newcastle
Wind Cave Nat. P.
White R.
Chamberlain
Wind River Range
Wind River Ind. Res.
Boysen Res.
Midwest
Cheyenne
Edgemont
Hot Springs
Badlands Nat. P.
Pine Ridge
Ind. Res.
Lake Francis Case
Mitchell
Gannett Peak
13,804 ft
4,207 m
Riverton
2,355 ft
718 m
Pinedale
Lander
Wyoming
Casper
Mills
3,410 ft
1,039 m
Rosebud Ind. Res.
Winner
Platte
Yankton Ind. Res.
Gregory
Pine Ridge
Martin
Rosebud
Wagner
Douglas
Lusk
Chadron
Gordon
Valentine
8,244 ft
2,513 m
6,135 ft
1,870 m
Glendo Res.
Niobrara
Ainsworth
O'Neill
Sweetwater
Green Mts.
9,215 ft
2,812 m
Pathfinder Res.
Laramie Mts.
Laramie Peak
10,297 ft
3,131 m
Niobrara
Elkhorn
8,685 ft
2,647 m
Shirley Mts.
9,151 ft
2,789 m
Seminoe Res.
Wyoming Basin
Hanna
Wheatland
Torrington
Alliance
3,400 ft
1,036 m
4,203 ft
1,281 m
Thedford
Green R.
Rock Springs
Green River
Rawlins
North Platte
Scottsbluff
Gering
Hogback Mtn.
5,063 ft
1,543 m
Bridgeport
Middle Loup
North Loup
Nebraska
Albion
Flaming Gorge Res.
Saratoga
North Platte
Medicine Bow Mts.
Medicine Bow Pk.
12,013 ft
3,661 m
Laramie
Horse Creek
UNITED
Broken Bow
11,007 ft
3,354 m
Park Range
Cheyenne
Kimball
Sidney
L. McConaughy
Ogallala
North Platte
South Loup
Saint Paul
Loup
Mt. Zirkel
12,180 ft
3,712 m
Julesburg
2,820 ft
860 m
Gothenburg
Cozad
Grand Island
Vernal
Dinosaur Nat. Mon.
Yampa
Craig
Grant
Lexington
Kearney
Steamboat Springs
Fort Collins
Windsor
Greeley
Sterling
Estes Park
Loveland
Imperial
3,025 ft
922 m
Platte
White River
Rocky Mountain Nat. Park
14,255 ft
4,345 m
South Platte
Brush
Holdrege
Minden
Hastings
Little Blue
Uintah and Ouray Ind. Res.
Meeker
Sheep Mtn.
12,248 ft
3,733 m
Gore Ra.
Granby
Longmont
Fort Lupton
Fort Morgan
Yuma
McCook
Wray
Republican
Alma
Red Cloud
Superior
Roan Plateau
Rifle
White River Plateau
13,534 ft
4,351 m
Boulder
Brighton
Denver
Lakewood
Aurora
Colorado
Glenwood Springs
Avon
Oberlin
Norton
Phillipsburg
Beaver Creek
6,005 ft
1,830 m
Parker
Castle Rock
Fruita
Grand Junction
Mt. Lincoln
14,286 ft
4,354 m
Leadville
Aspen
Sawatch Ra
Mt. Elbert
14,433 ft
4,399 m
Burlington
Goodland
Colby
Stockton
Beloit
Solomon
Colorado Nat. Mon.
11,234 ft
3,424 m
Gunnison
S. Platte
Woodland Park
Calhan
Limon
Big Sandy Creek
4,039 ft
1,231 m
Oakley
Smoky Hills
Wakeeney
Delta
Colorado
Pikes Pk.
14,108 ft
4,300 m
Colorado Springs
2,120 ft
646 m
Hays
Russell
Mt. Peale
12,721 ft
3,875 m
9,731 ft
2,966 m
Uncompahgre Plateau
Black Canyon of the Gunnison Nat. Park
Gunnison
Montrose
Salida
Fountain
Cheyenne Wells
Smoky Hill R.
Cañon City
Florence
Naturita
Arkansas
Pueblo
Eads
Scott City
Kansas
McPherson
Uncompahgre Peak
14,309 ft
4,361 m
Ouray
Ordway
Great Bend
Monticello
14,294 ft
4,356 m
Sangre de Cristo Range
Larned
Mt. Wilson
14,246 ft
4,342 m
Dolores
Silverton
Great Sand Dunes Nat. Mon.
Center
12,349 ft
3,764 m
Rocky Ford
Las Animas
La Junta
Lamar
Garden City
Kinsley
Hutchinson
9,970 ft
3,041 m
Cortez
Mesa Verde Nat. P.
Monte Vista
San Luis
Blanca Peak
14,360 ft
4,377 m
Walsenburg
4,052 ft
1,235 m
Purgatoire
Arkansas
Dodge City
Pratt
Kingman
San Juan Mts.
13,300 ft
4,054 m
Alamosa
Durango
Ute Mountain
Southern Ute Ind. Res.
Aguilar
Springfield
Ulysses
Antonito
Rio Grande
San Luis Valley
Trinidad
Hugoton
Meade
Red Hills
2,340 ft
713 m
Medicine Lodge
Shiprock
Kirtland
Aztec
Navajo Lake
Chama
11,403 ft
3,476 m
Raton
Liberal
San Juan
Farmington
9,833 ft
2,861 m
Bloomfield
Cimarron
Beaver
Buffalo
Alva
Chaco
Navajo
Jicarilla Apache Ind. Res.
Rio Chama
13,160 ft
4,011 m
Wheeler Peak
Laughlin Peak
8,820 ft
2,688 m
6,062 ft
1,848 m
Boise City
High
Guymon
North Canadian
Cherokee
Cimarron
Newcomb
Taos
Springer
Canadian
Ute Creek
Carrizo Creek
Clayton
Stratford
Perryton
Arizona
Chuska Mts.
New Mexico
Chicoma Mtn.
11,562 ft
3,524 m
San Juan Pueblo
Española
Chimayo
Texas
Plains
Dalhart
Woodward
Seiling
Fairview
Oklahoma

87

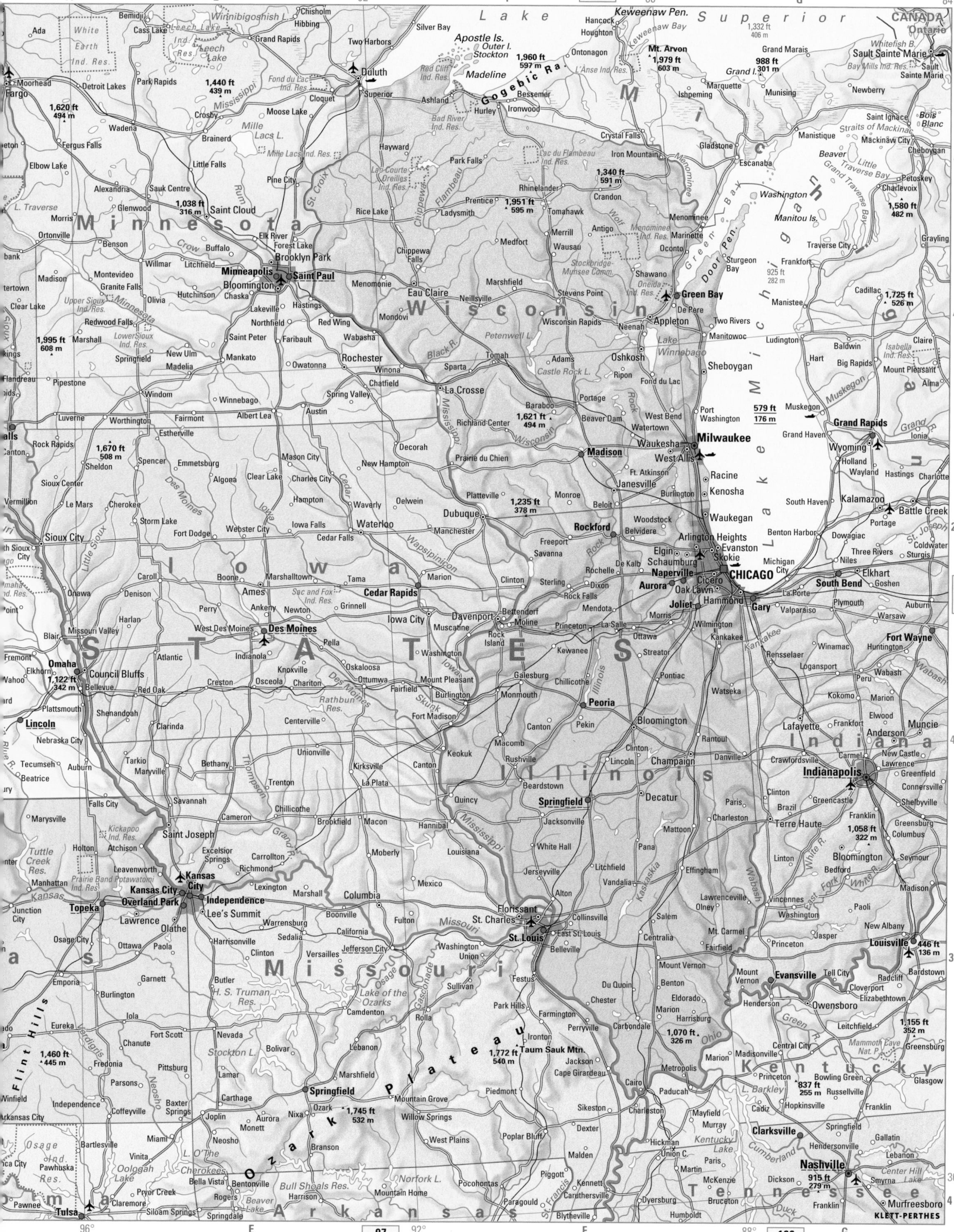
Lake Superior
CANADA
Ontario
Minnesota
Wisconsin
Michigan
Lake Michigan
Iowa
Illinois
Indiana
Missouri
Kentucky
Tennessee
Arkansas
UNITED STATES
Ozark Plateau
Flint Hills
Mississippi
Missouri
Ohio
Wabash
Des Moines
Keweenaw Pen.
Apostle Is.
Gogebic Ra.
Door Pen.
Green Bay
Duluth
Superior
Fargo
Moorhead
Saint Cloud
Minneapolis
Saint Paul
Bloomington
Rochester
La Crosse
Eau Claire
Wausau
Green Bay
Appleton
Oshkosh
Sheboygan
Madison
Milwaukee
Racine
Kenosha
Rockford
CHICAGO
Naperville
Aurora
Joliet
Gary
South Bend
Fort Wayne
Grand Rapids
Kalamazoo
Sioux City
Des Moines
Cedar Rapids
Davenport
Iowa City
Omaha
Council Bluffs
Lincoln
Peoria
Bloomington
Champaign
Springfield
Decatur
Indianapolis
Terre Haute
Evansville
Louisville
Kansas City
Overland Park
Independence
Topeka
St. Louis
Columbia
Jefferson City
Springfield
Tulsa
Clarksville
Nashville
Mt. Arvon 1,979 ft 603 m
Taum Sauk Mtn. 1,772 ft 540 m
KLETT-PERTHES
96°
92°
88°
84°
44°
40°
36°
E
F
G
1
2
3
4

96

97 100

A
B
C
108°
104°
100°
94
93
102
36°
32°
28°
Colorado
Arizona
New Mexico
Rocky Mountains
Sangre de Cristo Ra.
Llano Estacado
High Plains
Caprock Escarpment
UNITED
STATES
Edwards Plateau
Stockton Plateau
Sonora
Chihuahua
Coahuila
Durango
Sinaloa
Nuevo León
MEXICO
Sierra Madre Occidental
Sierra Tarahumara
Bolsón de Mapimí
Serranías del Burro
Sa. del Carmen
Sa. de Tepehuanes
Sa. de los Alamitos
Sa. del Pino
Sa. el Nido
Sa. San Diego
Shiprock
Kirtland
Farmington
Aztec
Bloomfield
Navajo Lake
Chama
11,403 ft
3,476 m
Wheeler Peak
13,160 ft
4,011 m
Taos
Raton
Laughlin Peak
8,820 ft
2,688 m
6,062 ft
1,848 m
Clayton
Liberal
Boise City
Guymon
Buffalo
Beaver
Perryton
Woodward
Stratford
Dalhart
Dumas
Borger
Canadian
Pampa
Lake Meredith
Chuska Mts.
9,833 ft
2,861 m
8,075 ft
2,466 m
Navajo Indian Res.
Newcomb
Chinle
Canyon de Chelly Nat. Mon.
Jicarilla Apache Ind. Res.
Chicoma Mtn.
11,562 ft
3,524 m
Chimayo
Espanola
Los Alamos
Santa Fe
13,101 ft
3,993 m
Springer
Roy
Ganado
Fort Defiance
Window Rock
Jemez Pueblo
Gallup
Thoreau
Chambers
Zuni Mts.
9,255 ft
2,821 m
Mt. Taylor
11,303 ft
3,445 m
Grants
Zuni Pueblo
Petrified Forest Nat. Park
Laguna
Albuquerque
Rio Rancho
Bernalillo
Santo Domingo Pueblo
San Felipe Pueblo
10,679 ft
3,255 m
Las Vegas
Moriarty
Isleta Pueblo
Los Lunas
Belen
Acoma Pueblo
El Malpais Nat. Mon.
Saint Johns
Santa Rosa
Tucumcari
5,150 ft
1,570 ft
Vega
Amarillo
3,676 ft
1,120 m
Canyon
Hereford
Clarendon
Shamrock
Sayre
Elk City
Clinton
Weatherford
Mangum
Hobart
Altus
Memphis
Willard
Vaughn
Fort Sumner
Springerville
Eagar
Baldy Peak
11,590 ft
3,533 m
Alegros Mtn.
10,244 ft
3,122 m
Magdalena
Socorro
South Baldy
10,783 ft
3,287 m
Clovis
Portales
Farwell
Tulia
Childress
Plainview
Floydada
Paducah
Vernon
Burkburnett
Iowa Park
Littlefield
Levelland
Lubbock
Crosbyton
Seymour
Salton
Knox City
Munday
Brownfield
Post
Whitewater Baldy
10,695 ft
3,320 m
Mogollon Mts.
Black Ra.
10,011 ft
3,051 m
Morenci
Clifton
Safford
Carrizozo
12,003 ft
3,659 m
8,958 ft
2730 m
Ruidoso
Mescalero Ind. Res.
Rio Hondo
Roswell
Tularosa
Tularosa Valley
Truth or Consequences
Alamogordo
Hagerman
Artesia
San Andres Mts.
Sacramento Mts.
White Sands Nat. Mon.
Lovington
Silver City
Bayard
Santa Clara Pueblo
Gila
Duncan
Seminole
Lamesa
Snyder
Hamlin
Stamford
Albany
Breckenridge
Bowie
Lordsburg
Las Cruces
8,920 ft
2,719 m
Guadalupe Mts.
Carlsbad
Carlsbad Caverns Nat. Park
Hobbs
Eunice
Loving
Andrews
Big Spring
Colorado City
Sweetwater
Abilene
Cisco
2,621 ft
799 m
Deming
7,402 ft
2,256 m
Anthony
Chaparral
Chiricahua Mts.
9,795 ft
2,986 m
Animas Pk.
8,532 ft
2,600 m
Douglas
El Paso
Juárez
Puerto Palomas
Sunland Park
Socorro
San Elizario
Fabens
Guadalupe Peak
8,749 ft
2,667 m
Guadalupe Mts. Nat. Park
Kermit
West Odessa
Midland
Odessa
Monahans
Pecos
Coleman
Ballinger
Brownwood
La. de Guzmán
Samalayuca
Ascensión
Fort Hancock
Porvenir
El Barreal
Van Horn
Crane
Castle Mtn.
3,153 ft
961 m
Big Lake
McCamey
San Angelo
Eden
Brady
Eagle Mts.
7,497 ft
2,285 m
Rio Grande
Rio Bravo del Norte
Bacerac
7,743 ft
2,360 m
Casas Grandes
Nuevo Casas Grandes
Ahumada
5,390 ft
1,643 m
Davis Mts.
8,378 ft
2,555 m
Fort Stockton
Ozona
Sonora
Mason
Juan Mata Ortiz
Hermenegildo Galeana
Santa María
Moctezuma
Ojos de San Antonio
Alpine
Marfa
6,860 ft
2,091 m
Sanderson
Junction
Fredericksburg
Kerrville
Ricardo Flores Magón
El Carrizo
8,400 ft
2,560 m
Chinati Mts.
7,730 ft
2,353 m
2,800 ft
853 m
El Largo
San Buenaventura
Ignacio Zaragoza
Las Varas
Valentín Gómez Farías
9,515 ft
2,900 m
La. Bavícora
Madera
Presidio
Santiago Mts.
Big Bend Nat. P.
Amistad Res.
Sahuaripa
Temosachic
Benito Juárez
Coyame
Manuel Ojinaga
Hormigas
Conchos
Chisos Mts.
7,825 ft
2,385 m
8,918 ft
2,718 m
Acuña
Del Rio
Jiménez
San Carlos
Uvalde
San Antonio
Hondo
P. Nac. Cumbres de Majalca
Juan Aldama
Manuel Benavides
Yécora
Vicente Guerrero
Adolfo López Mateos
Anáhuac
Chihuahua
Los Alamos
Piedras Negras
Eagle Pass
Crystal City
Pearsall
Moris
P. Nac. Cascada de Basaseachic
Cuauhtémoc
Lázaro Cárdenas
Julimes
Cusihuiriáchi
Meoqui
La Bahia
Zaragoza
Allende
Nava
Carrizo Springs
Dilley
Cotulla
Uruachi
San Juanito
Delicias
La Perla
8,727 ft
2,660 m
Villa Unión
Creel
San Francisco de Borja
Saucillo
Naica
Sabinas
Encinal
8,500 ft
2,591 m
Presa de la Boquilla
Camargo
Santa Elena
Múzquiz
Nueva Rosita
Palau
Témoris
Nonoava
Valle de Zaragoza
Maravillas
Minas de Barroterán
Rio Salado
Hidalgo
Nuevo Laredo
Laredo
990 ft
302 m
Alamos
5,850 ft
1,783 m
Ocampo
Juárez
Progreso
Jiménez
Hebbronville
Baca
Choix
Guachochi
Mariano Balleza
San Francisco del Oro
Hidalgo
Valle de Allende
Laguna del Rey
San Buenaventura
Anáhuac
Lampazos de Naranjo
Zapata
Presa Hidalgo
Morelos
San Miguel
Santa Bárbara
9,908 ft
3,020 m
Villa Coronado
Escalón
Cuatro Ciénegas
Frontera
Monclova
Candela
Falcon Res.
El Fuerte
El Verde
Orestes Pereyra
Ceballos
Castaños
Vallecillo
Sabinas Hidalgo
San Blas
Guadalupe y Calvo
Cerro Mohinora
10,830 ft
3,300 m
Las Nieves
Villa Hidalgo
Conejos
8,400 ft
2,560 m
Villaldama
Guerrero
Mier
Roma
Chorreras
10,335 ft
3,150 m
Santa María del Oro
Sinaloa
Gabriel Leyva Solanos
San Bernardo
El Jaralito
Tlahualilo
Espinazo
Agualeguas
Cerralvo
P. Nac. El Sabinal
Guasave
Palmar de los Sepúlveda
Atascaderos
Bermejillo
Salinas Victoria
Ciénaga de Flores
Paredón
Hidalgo
San Nicolás de los Garza
Apodaca
Monterrey
Guadalupe
P. N. Cumbres de Monterrey
Presa M. R. Gómez

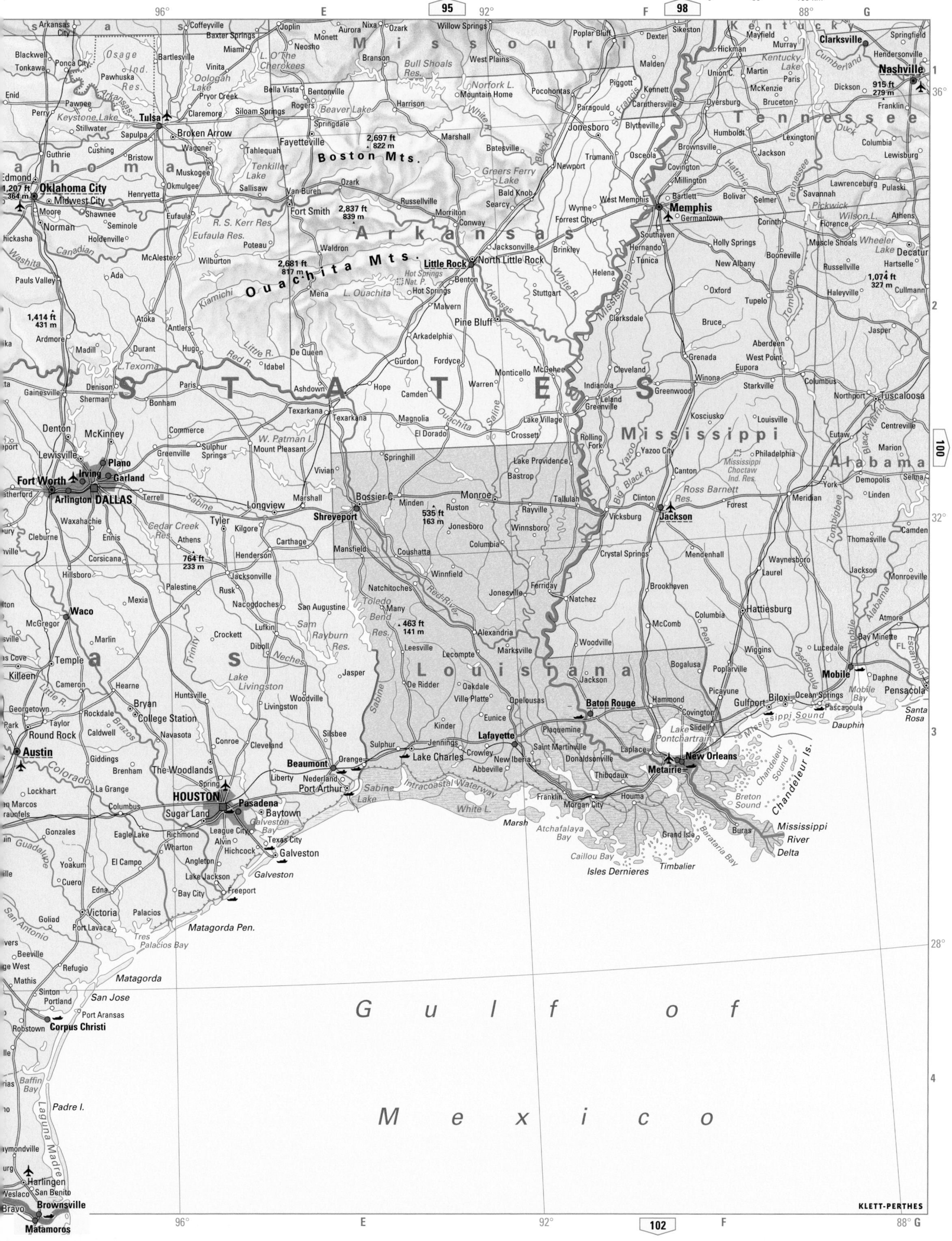
96°
E
95
92°
F
98
88°
G
1
2
3
4
36°
32°
28°
100
102
Missouri
Kentucky
Tennessee
Arkansas
Oklahoma
Mississippi
Alabama
Louisiana
Texas
STATES
Gulf of Mexico
Arkansas City
Coffeyville
Baxter Springs
Joplin
Monett
Aurora
Nixa
Ozark
Willow Springs
Poplar Bluff
Dexter
Sikeston
Mayfield
Murray
Clarksville
Springfield
Hendersonville
Nashville
915 ft
279 m
Franklin
Blackwell
Ponca City
Tonkawa
Osage Ind. Res.
Bartlesville
Miami
Neosho
Branson
Bull Shoals Res.
West Plains
Malden
Hickman
Union C.
Martin
Kentucky Lake
Paris
Dickson
Enid
Pawhuska
Vinita
L. O' The Cherokees
Oologah Lake
Norfork L.
Mountain Home
Pocahontas
Piggott
Kennett
Caruthersville
Dyersburg
McKenzie
Bruceton
Pawnee
Perry
Keystone Lake
Stillwater
Tulsa
Claremore
Pryor Creek
Bella Vista
Bentonville
Rogers
Beaver Lake
Harrison
Paragould
Jonesboro
Blytheville
Humboldt
Lexington
Duck
Cumberland
Cushing
Sapulpa
Broken Arrow
Siloam Springs
Springdale
White R.
Black R.
St. Francis
Guthrie
Bristow
Wagoner
Tahlequah
Fayetteville
2,697 ft
822 m
Boston Mts.
Marshall
Batesville
Trumann
Osceola
Brownsville
Jackson
Columbia
Lewisburg
Edmond
Oklahoma City
1,207 ft
364 m
Midwest City
Muskogee
Okmulgee
Tenkiller Lake
Sallisaw
Van Buren
Ozark
Greers Ferry Lake
Newport
Covington
Millington
Hatchie
Lawrenceburg
Pulaski
Henryetta
Fort Smith
2,837 ft
839 m
Russellville
Bald Knob
Searcy
Morrilton
West Memphis
Wynne
Memphis
Bartlett
Germantown
Bolivar
Selmer
Savannah
Pickwick L.
Wilson L.
Athens
Moore
Norman
Shawnee
Seminole
Eufaula
R. S. Kerr Res.
Eufaula Res.
Conway
Forrest City
Corinth
Florence
Holdenville
Poteau
Waldron
Jacksonville
North Little Rock
Little Rock
Brinkley
Southaven
Hernando
Holly Springs
Muscle Shoals
Wheeler Lake
Decatur
Chickasha
Canadian
McAlester
Wilburton
2,681 ft
817 m
Ouachita Mts.
Hot Springs Nat. P.
Benton
Tunica
New Albany
Booneville
Hartselle
Washita
Pauls Valley
Ada
Kiamichi
Mena
L. Ouachita
Hot Springs
Stuttgart
Helena
Oxford
Russellville
1,074 ft
327 m
Cullmann
Haleyville
Tupelo
Tombigbee
1,414 ft
431 m
Atoka
Malvern
Pine Bluff
Clarksdale
Bruce
Jasper
Ardmore
Antlers
Arkadelphia
Aberdeen
Madill
Durant
Hugo
Little R.
De Queen
Gurdon
Fordyce
Grenada
West Point
L. Texoma
Red R.
Idabel
Monticello
McGehee
Cleveland
Eupora
Winona
Columbus
Northport
Tuscaloosa
Gainesville
Denison
Sherman
Bonham
Paris
Ashdown
Hope
Camden
Warren
Indianola
Greenwood
Starkville
Leland
Greenville
Kosciusko
Louisville
Centreville
Denton
McKinney
Texarkana
Magnolia
El Dorado
Ouachita
Saline
Lake Village
Crossett
Commerce
Eutaw
Marion
Lewisville
Sulphur Springs
W. Patman L.
Mount Pleasant
Greenville
Rolling Fork
Yazoo City
Yazoo
Philadelphia
Mississippi Choctaw Ind. Res.
Plano
Irving
Garland
Springhill
Lake Providence
Bastrop
Vivian
Canton
Demopolis
Selma
York
Fort Worth
Arlington
DALLAS
Terrell
Sabine
Longview
Marshall
Bossier C.
Minden
Monroe
Tallulah
Big Black R.
Clinton
Ross Barnett Res.
Forest
Meridian
Linden
Ruston
535 ft
163 m
Rayville
Vicksburg
Jackson
Camden
Waxahachie
Tyler
Kilgore
Shreveport
Jonesboro
Winnsboro
Thomasville
Cleburne
Ennis
Cedar Creek Res.
Athens
Carthage
Columbia
Corsicana
764 ft
233 m
Henderson
Mansfield
Coushatta
Crystal Springs
Mendenhall
Waynesboro
Laurel
Hillsboro
Jacksonville
Winnfield
Jackson
Monroeville
Palestine
Rusk
Natchitoches
Red River
Jonesville
Ferriday
Natchez
Brookhaven
Mexia
Nacogdoches
San Augustine
Toledo Bend Res.
Many
463 ft
141 m
Alexandria
Columbia
Hattiesburg
Alabama
Waco
Lufkin
Sam Rayburn Res.
McComb
Pearl
Atmore
McGregor
Crockett
Diboll
Marlin
Leesville
Lecompte
Marksville
Woodville
Wiggins
Lucedale
Bay Minette
Mobile
FL
Escambia
Pascagoula
Trinity
Neches
Temple
Killeen
Cameron
Hearne
Jasper
De Ridder
Oakdale
Jackson
Bogalusa
Poplarville
Daphne
Little R.
Bryan
College Station
Lake Livingston
Huntsville
Woodville
Ville Platte
Opelousas
Baton Rouge
Hammond
Picayune
Gulfport
Biloxi
Ocean Springs
Pascagoula
Mobile Bay
Pensacola
Georgetown
Rockdale
Brazos
Livingston
Eunice
Covington
Slidell
Mississippi Sound
Santa Rosa
Dauphin
Taylor
Round Rock
Caldwell
Navasota
Kinder
Silsbee
Lafayette
Plaquemine
Lake Pontchartrain
Austin
Conroe
Cleveland
Sulphur
Jennings
Crowley
Saint Martinville
Laplace
Giddings
Brenham
The Woodlands
Beaumont
Orange
Lake Charles
New Iberia
Donaldsonville
New Orleans
Metairie
Chandeleur Sound
Chandeleur Is.
Colorado
Spring
Liberty
Nederland
Abbeville
Thibodaux
Lockhart
La Grange
Port Arthur
Sabine Lake
Intracoastal Waterway
Franklin
Houma
Breton Sound
San Marcos
New Braunfels
Columbus
HOUSTON
Pasadena
Baytown
Sugar Land
White L.
Morgan City
Gonzales
Eagle Lake
Richmond
League City
Galveston Bay
Marsh
Atchafalaya Bay
Grand Isle
Buras
Mississippi River Delta
Guadalupe
Wharton
Alvin
Texas City
Hitchcock
Barataria Bay
Yoakum
El Campo
Angleton
Galveston
Caillou Bay
Isles Dernieres
Timbalier
Cuero
Lake Jackson
Galveston
Edna
Bay City
Freeport
San Antonio
Goliad
Victoria
Palacios
Port Lavaca
Matagorda Pen.
Tres Palacios Bay
Beeville
George West
Refugio
Mathis
Matagorda
Sinton
Portland
San Jose
Port Aransas
Robstown
Corpus Christi
Baffin Bay
Padre I.
Laguna Madre
Raymondville
Harlingen
San Benito
Weslaco
Brownsville
Bravo
Matamoros
KLETT-PERTHES

87

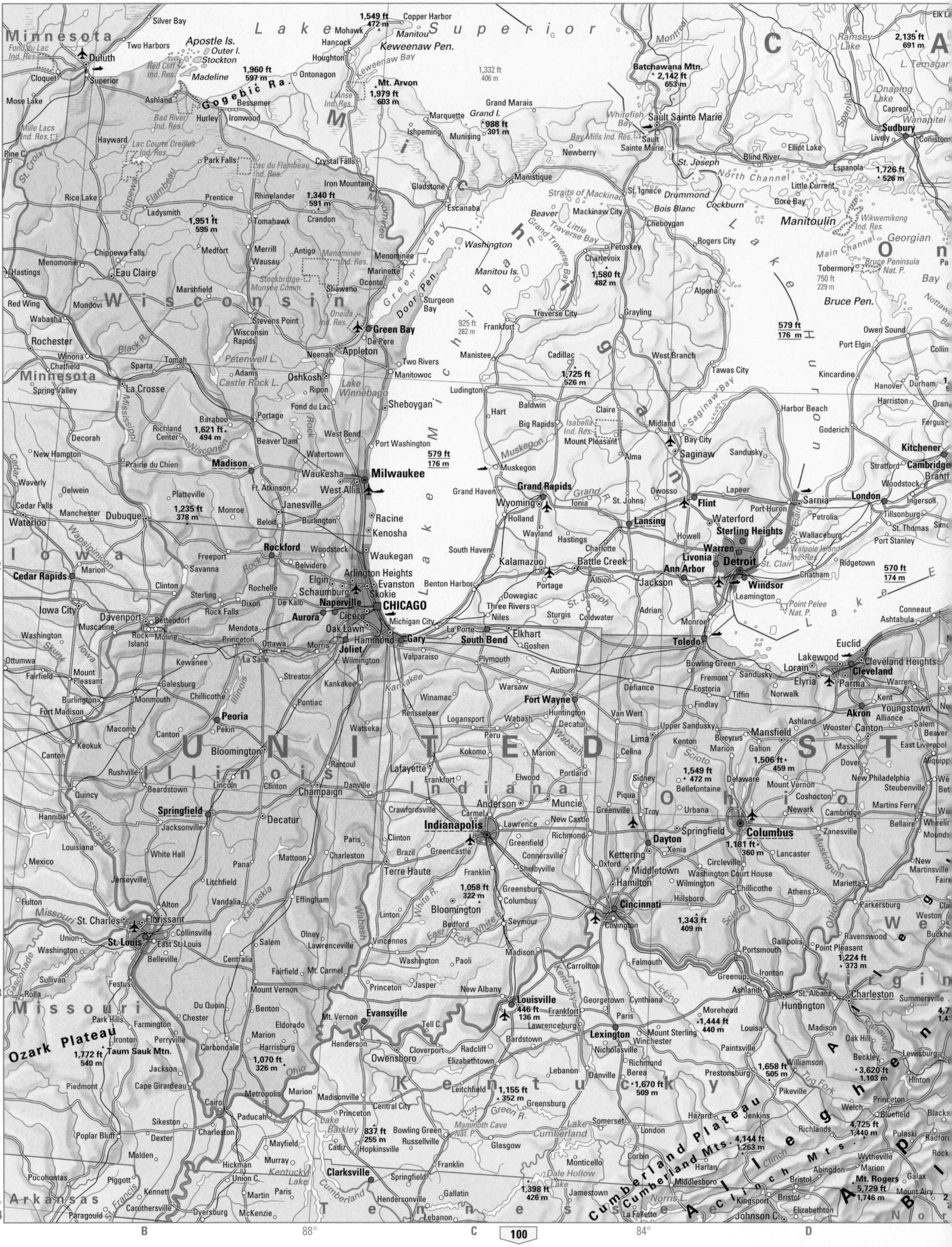

Lake Superior
Minnesota
Duluth
Superior
Two Harbors
Silver Bay
Apostle Is.
Outer I.
Stockton
Madeline
Ashland
Gogebic Ra.
Bessemer
Ironwood
Hurley
Ontonagon
Houghton
Hancock
Mohawk
Copper Harbor
Manitou
Keweenaw Pen.
Keweenaw Bay
Mt. Arvon
1,979 ft
603 m
1,549 ft
472 m
1,960 ft
597 m
Marquette
Grand I.
Grand Marais
Munising
Ishpeming
988 ft
301 m
Newberry
Whitefish Bay
Sault Sainte Marie
Batchawana Mtn.
2,142 ft
653 m
Montreal
Ramsey Lake
Sudbury
Lively
Coniston
Elliot Lake
Blind River
Espanola
St. Joseph
North Channel
Drummond
Cockburn
Manitoulin
Little Current
Gore Bay
Bois Blanc
Cheboygan
Mackinaw City
St. Ignace
Straits of Mackinac
Manistique
Gladstone
Escanaba
Iron Mountain
Crystal Falls
Rhinelander
Crandon
Tomahawk
Prentice
Park Falls
Hayward
Rice Lake
Ladysmith
Medford
Chippewa Falls
Eau Claire
Menomonie
Hastings
Red Wing
Wabasha
Mondovi
Wisconsin
Merrill
Wausau
Antigo
Shawano
Oconto
Marinette
Menominee
Green Bay
Door Pen.
Sturgeon Bay
Stevens Point
Wisconsin Rapids
Appleton
De Pere
Neenah
Oshkosh
Ripon
Lake Winnebago
Fond du Lac
Sheboygan
Two Rivers
Manitowoc
Rochester
Winona
Chatfield
Spring Valley
La Crosse
Sparta
Tomah
Adams
Petenwell L.
Castle Rock L.
Baraboo
1,621 ft
494 m
Portage
Beaver Dam
West Bend
Port Washington
Richland Center
Decorah
New Hampton
Madison
Watertown
Waukesha
Milwaukee
West Allis
Ft. Atkinson
Janesville
Prairie du Chien
Waverly
Oelwein
Platteville
1,235 ft
378 m
Cedar Falls
Manchester
Dubuque
Monroe
Beloit
Burlington
Racine
Kenosha
Waterloo
Iowa
Rockford
Woodstock
Waukegan
Freeport
Belvidere
Cedar Rapids
Marion
Savanna
Clinton
Elgin
Arlington Heights
Evanston
Skokie
Schaumburg
Sterling
Rochelle
Naperville
Aurora
CHICAGO
Cicero
Oak Lawn
Iowa City
Davenport
Bettendorf
Muscatine
Rock Island
Moline
Rock Falls
Dixon
De Kalb
Mendota
Princeton
Ottawa
Morris
Joliet
Hammond
Gary
Michigan City
Washington
Ottumwa
Fairfield
Mount Pleasant
Kewanee
La Salle
Streator
Wilmington
Kankakee
Valparaiso
Galesburg
Burlington
Fort Madison
Monmouth
Chillicothe
Peoria
Pekin
Pontiac
Macomb
Canton
Keokuk
Bloomington
Watseka
Rushville
Quincy
Hannibal
Beardstown
Lincoln
Clinton
Champaign
Rantoul
Danville
Illinois
Springfield
Jacksonville
Decatur
Louisiana
White Hall
Mexico
Pana
Mattoon
Paris
Charleston
Jerseyville
Litchfield
Fulton
Alton
Vandalia
Effingham
St. Charles
Florissant
St. Louis
Collinsville
East St. Louis
Belleville
Union
Washington
Salem
Olney
Lawrenceville
Centralia
Sullivan
Fairfield
Mt. Carmel
Festus
Rolla
Mount Vernon
Missouri
Du Quoin
Benton
Chester
Park Hills
Farmington
Eldorado
Ironton
Perryville
Marion
Harrisburg
Carbondale
1,070 ft
326 m
Ozark Plateau
1,772 ft
Taum Sauk Mtn.
540 m
Jackson
Cape Girardeau
Piedmont
Metropolis
Cairo
Sikeston
Paducah
Charleston
Poplar Bluff
Dexter
Malden
Hickman
Union C.
Martin
Paris
Pocahontas
Piggott
Kennett
Arkansas
Caruthersville
Dyersburg
McKenzie
Paragould
Lake Michigan
Manitou Is.
Washington
Frankfort
Traverse City
Grand Traverse Bay
Beaver
Petoskey
Charlevoix
1,580 ft
482 m
Rogers City
Alpena
Grayling
Manistee
Cadillac
1,725 ft
526 m
West Branch
Tawas City
Ludington
Hart
Baldwin
Big Rapids
Clare
Midland
Bay City
Saginaw
Saginaw Bay
Harbor Beach
Isabella Ind. Res.
Mount Pleasant
Alma
Muskegon
Grand Haven
Grand Rapids
Wyoming
Holland
Ionia
St. Johns
Owosso
Flint
Lapeer
Port Huron
Sarnia
Lansing
Wayland
Hastings
Charlotte
Howell
Waterford
Sterling Heights
Warren
Livonia
Detroit
Windsor
Ann Arbor
Jackson
Battle Creek
Kalamazoo
South Haven
Benton Harbor
Albion
Portage
Dowagiac
Three Rivers
Niles
Sturgis
Coldwater
Adrian
Monroe
Toledo
La Porte
South Bend
Elkhart
Goshen
Plymouth
Auburn
Warsaw
Fort Wayne
Huntington
Winamac
Rensselaer
Logansport
Wabash
Peru
Kokomo
Marion
Lafayette
Frankfort
Elwood
Anderson
Muncie
Portland
Indiana
Crawfordsville
Carmel
Indianapolis
Lawrence
New Castle
Richmond
Greenfield
Connersville
Shelbyville
Clinton
Brazil
Greencastle
Terre Haute
Franklin
1,058 ft
322 m
Greensburg
Columbus
Bloomington
Bedford
Seymour
Linton
Vincennes
Washington
Paoli
Madison
Jasper
Princeton
Evansville
Mt. Vernon
Tell C.
New Albany
Louisville
446 ft
136 m
Henderson
Owensboro
Elizabethtown
Radcliff
Bardstown
Lawrenceburg
Frankfort
Georgetown
Cynthiana
Lexington
Paris
Winchester
Mount Sterling
Nicholasville
Richmond
Berea
Danville
Lebanon
1,670 ft
509 m
Kentucky
Leitchfield
1,155 ft
352 m
Greensburg
Madisonville
Princeton
Central City
Hopkinsville
837 ft
255 m
Cadiz
Lake Barkley
Mayfield
Murray
Bowling Green
Russellville
Mammoth Cave Nat. P.
Glasgow
Franklin
Somerset
Lake Cumberland
London
Corbin
Monticello
Dale Hollow Lake
Clarksville
Springfield
Hendersonville
Gallatin
1,398 ft
426 m
Jamestown
Lebanon
Tennessee
Cumberland Plateau
Cumberland Mts.
4,144 ft
1,263 m
Middlesboro
Harlan
La Follette
Kingsport
Bristol
Johnson C.
Elizabethton
Mt. Rogers
5,729 ft
1,746 m
Lake Huron
Bruce Pen.
Tobermory
Bruce Peninsula Nat. P.
Georgian Bay
Owen Sound
Port Elgin
Kincardine
Hanover
Durham
Harriston
Goderich
Kitchener
Cambridge
Stratford
Brantford
Woodstock
London
Ingersoll
Tillsonburg
St. Thomas
Port Stanley
Petrolia
Wallaceburg
Chatham
Ridgetown
Leamington
Point Pelee Nat. P.
Lake Erie
570 ft
174 m
579 ft
176 m
Conneaut
Ashtabula
Euclid
Lakewood
Cleveland Heights
Cleveland
Lorain
Elyria
Parma
Sandusky
Bowling Green
Fremont
Fostoria
Tiffin
Norwalk
Defiance
Findlay
Kent
Akron
Youngstown
Alliance
Van Wert
Lima
Upper Sandusky
Bucyrus
Mansfield
Ashland
Wooster
Canton
Salem
Kenton
Marion
Galion
Massillon
Celina
1,549 ft
472 m
1,506 ft
459 m
Dover
New Philadelphia
Sidney
Bellefontaine
Delaware
Mount Vernon
Coshocton
Steubenville
Piqua
Troy
Urbana
Newark
Cambridge
Greenville
Springfield
Columbus
Zanesville
Dayton
Xenia
Kettering
1,181 ft
360 m
Lancaster
Oxford
Middletown
Circleville
Washington Court House
Marietta
Hamilton
Wilmington
Chillicothe
Athens
Cincinnati
Covington
Hillsboro
Parkersburg
1,343 ft
409 m
Ohio
Gallipolis
Point Pleasant
Ravenswood
Portsmouth
1,224 ft
373 m
Carrollton
Falmouth
Greenup
Ironton
Ashland
Huntington
St. Albans
Charleston
Morehead
1,444 ft
440 m
Louisa
Madison
Oak Hill
Paintsville
1,658 ft
505 m
Williamson
Prestonsburg
Beckley
3,620 ft
1,103 m
Lewisburg
Pikeville
Hazard
Jenkins
Welch
Bluefield
Richlands
4,725 ft
1,440 m
Wytheville
Marion
Abingdon
Pulaski
Allegheny Mts.
Clinch Mts.
UNITED STATES
CANADA
Ontario
Michigan
Wisconsin
Illinois
Indiana
Ohio
West Virginia
Kentucky
Missouri
Iowa
Minnesota

95

100

1:5,000,000

0 50 100 mi
0 50 100 km
88
101
KLETT-PERTHES
CANADA
Québec
Ontario
New Brunswick
UNITED STATES
New York
Pennsylvania
Maine
Vermont
New Hampshire
Massachusetts
Connecticut
Rhode Island
New Jersey
Delaware
Maryland
Virginia
Carolina
ATLANTIC OCEAN
Gulf of Maine
Long Island
Long Island Sound
Cape Cod
Cape Cod Bay
Delmarva Peninsula
Delaware Bay
Chesapeake Bay
Lake Ontario
Lake Champlain
Appalachian Mountains
Laurentides
Adirondack Mountains
Green Mountains
White Mountains
Longfellow Mts.
Catskill Mts.
Blue Ridge
Shenandoah Mts.
Mt. Marcy 5,344 ft 1,629 m
Mt. Washington 6,288 ft 1,917 m
Mt. Katahdin 5,267 ft 1,605 m
Sugarloaf Mtn. 4,237 ft 1,291 m
Mt. Mégantic 3,640 ft 1,105 m
Mont-Tremblant 3,175 ft 968 m
Blue Knob 3,136 ft 956 m
Catskill Mts. 4,190 ft 1,277 m
MONTRÉAL
Québec
Ottawa
TORONTO
NEW YORK
PHILADELPHIA
Washington, D.C.
Baltimore
Boston
Providence
Hartford
Albany
Augusta
Concord
Montpelier
Trenton
Annapolis
Richmond
Dover
Harrisburg
Portland
Buffalo
Rochester
Syracuse
Springfield
Worcester
New Haven
Bridgeport
Newark
Jersey City
Norfolk
Virginia Beach
Chesapeake
Newport News
Hampton
Portsmouth
Sherbrooke
Trois-Rivières
Kingston
Laval
Longueuil
Lévis
Bangor
Burlington
Scranton
Allentown
Wilmington
Atlantic City
Cape May
Cape May Point
Cape Charles
Cape Henry
Montauk Point
Block Island
Martha's Vineyard
Nantucket
Mt. Desert I.
Bar Harbor
Currituck Sound
Assateague

95
98
97
103
A
B
C
88°
84°
80°
36°
32°
28°
1
2
3
4
Kentucky
Tennessee
Cumberland Plateau
Cumberland Mts.
Clinch Mts.
Appalachian Mountains
Blue Ridge
Piedmont
North Carolina
South Carolina
Georgia
Alabama
Mississippi
Arkansas
Missouri
Louisiana
Florida
Virginia
UNITED STATES
Gulf of Mexico
ATLANTIC OCEAN
Clarksville
Nashville
Memphis
Knoxville
Chattanooga
Huntsville
Birmingham
Montgomery
Atlanta
Athens-Clarke
Augusta-Richmond
Columbia
Charlotte
Winston-Salem
Greensboro
High Point
Asheville
Greenville
Spartanburg
Charleston
North Charleston
Savannah
Macon
Columbus
Albany
Jackson
Mobile
Pensacola
Tallahassee
Jacksonville
Gainesville
Orlando
Tampa
St. Petersburg
Clearwater
Daytona Beach
Deltona
Melbourne
Palm Bay
Port St. Lucie
West Palm Beach
Boynton Beach
Delray Beach
Boca Raton
Coral Springs
Pompano Beach
Ft. Lauderdale
Hollywood
Pembroke Pines
Hialeah
Miami
Miami Beach
Kendall
Homestead
Cape Coral
Fort Myers
New Orleans
Biloxi
Gulfport
Hattiesburg
Tuscaloosa
Hoover
Decatur
Dothan
Mt. Rogers
5,729 ft
1,746 m
Mt. Mitchell
6,684 ft
2,037 m
Brasstown Bald
4,784 ft
1,458 m
Sassafras Mtn.
3,560 ft
1,085 m
Great Smoky Mountains Nat. P.
Eastern Cherokee Ind. Res.
Mississippi Choctaw Ind. Res.
Lake Okeechobee
Lake Seminole
Lake Marion
Lake Moultrie
Lake Murray
Lake Sinclair
Clark Hill Lake
Hartwell Lake
L. Sidney Lanier
Allatoona L.
Weiss L.
Guntersville Lake
Wheeler Lake
Wilson L.
Pickwick L.
Kentucky Lake
Cumberland
Dale Hollow L.
Center Hill Lake
Cherokee L.
Norris Lake
Douglas Lake
Ross Barnett Res.
William Dannelly Res.
Lake Martin
West Point Lake
Okefenokee Swamp
Lake George
L. Apopka
L. Kissimmee
L. Istokpoga
Big Cypress Ind. Res.
Big Cypress Swamp
Brighton Ind. Res.
The Everglades
Everglades Nat. Park
Biscayne Nat. P.
Biscayne Bay
Tampa Bay
Apalachee Bay
Waccasassa Bay
Mobile Bay
Mississippi Sound
Chandeleur Sound
Breton Sound
Chandeleur Is.
Barataria Bay
Mississippi River Delta
St. Helena Sound
Port Royal Sound
Ossabaw Sound
St. Andrew Sound
Cape Canaveral
Cape San Blas
Mississippi
Tennessee
Tombigbee
Alabama
Chattahoochee
Flint
Ocmulgee
Oconee
Altamaha
Savannah
Suwannee
St. Johns
Caloosahatchee
Yazoo
Pearl
Pascagoula
Conecuh
Coosa
Tallapoosa
Black Warrior
Apalachicola
Escambia
Choctawhatchee
Satilla
Ogeechee
I
Gulf of Mexico
Florida
Straits of Florida
Florida Keys
Florida Bay
Key Largo
Marathon
Key West
Marquesas Keys
Dry Tortugas Nat. P.
Pine Is.
Cape Sable
Whitewater Bay
Ten Thousand Is.
Everglades C.
Marco Island
Naples
Bonita Springs
Estero Bay
Sanibel
Pine
North Fort Myers
Charlotte Harb.
Punta Gorda
Clewiston
Belle Glade
Immokalee
Wellington
Jupiter
BAHAMAS
Grand Bahama
Freeport
Northwest Providence Channel
Great Isaac
North Bimini
South Bimini
Andros
KLETT-PERTHES

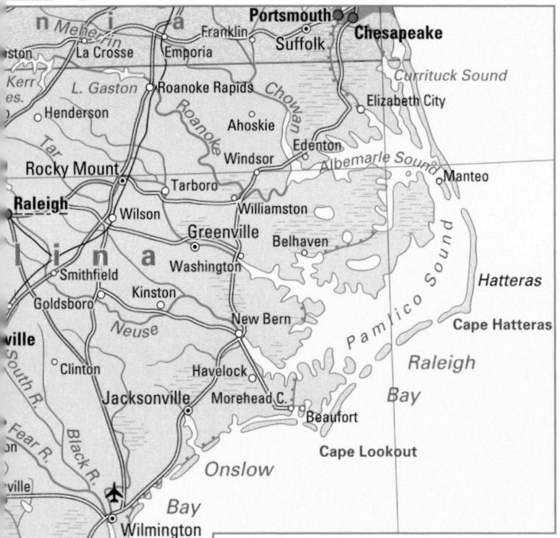
99
D
76°
E
Portsmouth
Chesapeake
Suffolk
Franklin
La Crosse
Emporia
Currituck Sound
L. Gaston
Roanoke Rapids
Elizabeth City
Henderson
Ahoskie
Edenton
Windsor
Albemarle Sound
Rocky Mount
Tarboro
Manteo
Raleigh
Williamston
Wilson
Greenville
Belhaven
Washington
Smithfield
Kinston
Hatteras
Goldsboro
Pamlico Sound
Neuse
New Bern
Cape Hatteras
Clinton
Raleigh
Havelock
Bay
Jacksonville
Morehead C.
Beaufort
Cape Lookout
Onslow
Bay
Wilmington
Southport
Cape Fear
North Myrtle Beach
Long
NTIC

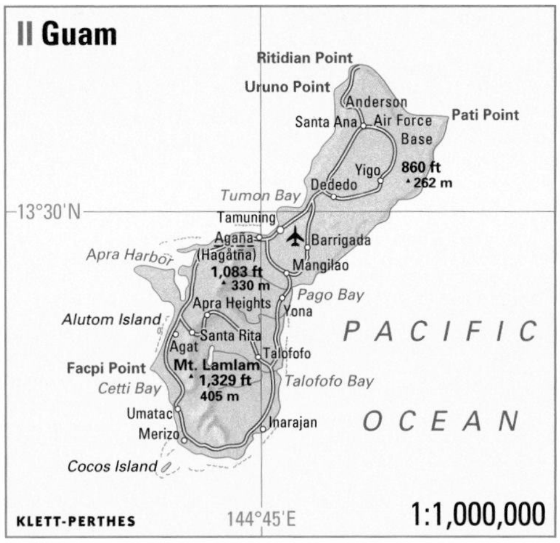
II Guam
Ritidian Point
Uruno Point
Anderson
Santa Ana
Air Force Base
Pati Point
Yigo
860 ft
262 m
Dededo
Tumon Bay
13°30'N
Tamuning
Agaña (Hagåtña)
Barrigada
Apra Harbor
1,083 ft
330 m
Mangilao
Pago Bay
Apra Heights
Yona
Alutom Island
Santa Rita
PACIFIC
Agat
Talofofo
Facpi Point
Mt. Lamlam
1,329 ft
405 m
Talofofo Bay
Cetti Bay
Umatac
Merizo
Inarajan
OCEAN
Cocos Island
KLETT-PERTHES
144°45'E
1:1,000,000

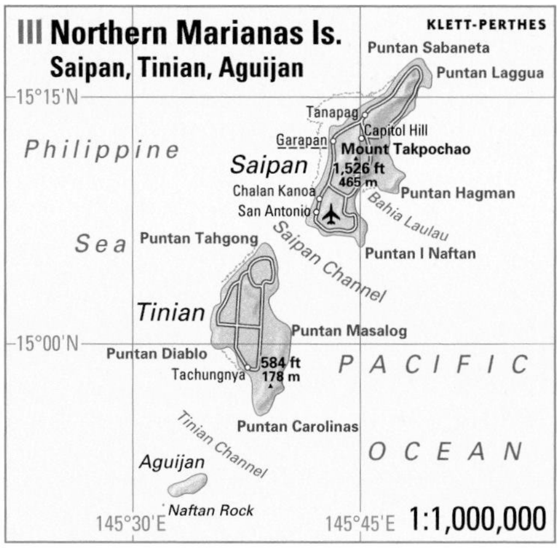
III Northern Marianas Is.
Saipan, Tinian, Aguijan
KLETT-PERTHES
Puntan Sabaneta
Puntan Laggua
15°15'N
Tanapag
Capitol Hill
Garapan
Mount Takpochao
Philippine
Saipan
1,526 ft
465 m
Chalan Kanoa
Puntan Hagman
San Antonio
Bahia Laulau
Sea
Puntan Tahgong
Saipan Channel
Puntan I Naftan
Tinian
Puntan Masalog
15°00'N
Puntan Diablo
584 ft
178 m
PACIFIC
Tachungnya
Tinian Channel
Puntan Carolinas
Aguijan
OCEAN
Naftan Rock
145°30'E
145°45'E
1:1,000,000

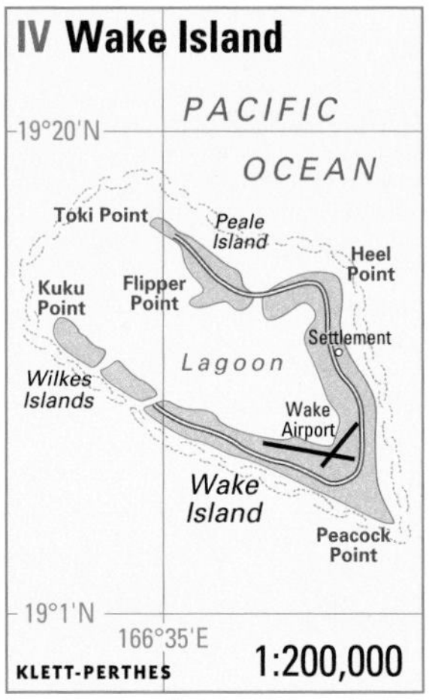
IV Wake Island
PACIFIC
19°20'N
OCEAN
Toki Point
Peale Island
Heel Point
Kuku Point
Flipper Point
Settlement
Lagoon
Wilkes Islands
Wake Airport
Wake Island
Peacock Point
19°1'N
166°35'E
KLETT-PERTHES
1:200,000

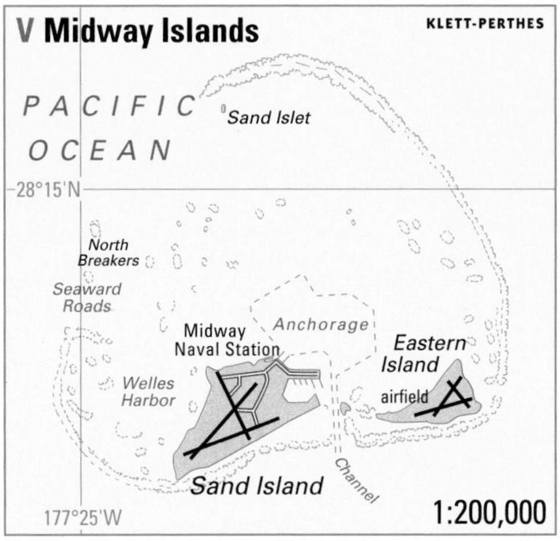
V Midway Islands
KLETT-PERTHES
PACIFIC
OCEAN
Sand Islet
28°15'N
North Breakers
Seaward Roads
Midway Naval Station
Anchorage
Eastern Island
Welles Harbor
airfield
Sand Island
Channel
177°25'W
1:200,000

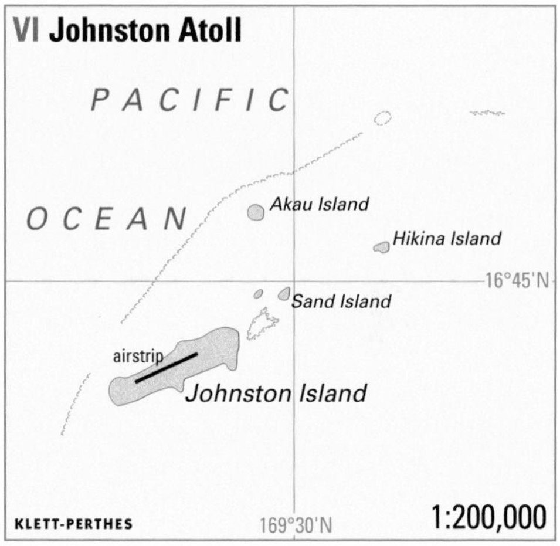
VI Johnston Atoll
PACIFIC
OCEAN
Akau Island
Hikina Island
16°45'N
Sand Island
airstrip
Johnston Island
KLETT-PERTHES
169°30'N
1:200,000

VII American Samoa
14°S
SAMOA
PACIFIC OCEAN
American Samoa
(U. S.)
1,621 ft
494 m
Ofu
Olosega
Nat. Park of Amer. Samoa
2,097 ft
639 m
Tau
3,169 ft
966 m
Maia
Manua Islands
Luma
Nat. Park of Amer. Samoa
Nat. Park of Amer. Samoa
Cape Matatula
Pago Pago
Tula
2,142 ft
653 m
Fagatogo
'Aunu'u
Cape Taputapu
Nu'uuli
Tutuila
Leone
Tafuna
Vaitogi
Steps Point
KLETT-PERTHES
171°W
170°W
1:1,000,000

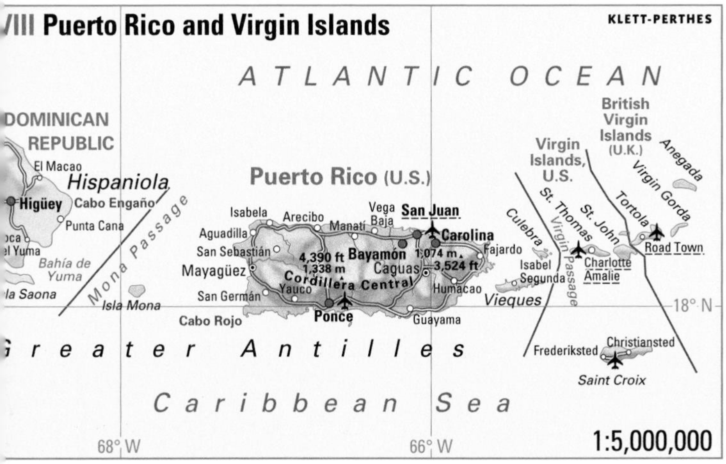
VIII Puerto Rico and Virgin Islands
KLETT-PERTHES
ATLANTIC OCEAN
British Virgin Islands (U.K.)
Anegada
Virgin Islands, U.S.
Virgin Gorda
Tortola
DOMINICAN REPUBLIC
El Macao
Hispaniola
Puerto Rico (U.S.)
St. Thomas
St. John
Higüey
Cabo Engaño
Culebra
Road Town
Punta Cana
Isabela
Arecibo
Vega Baja
San Juan
Carolina
Aguadilla
Manatí
Mona Passage
San Sebastián
4,390 ft
1,338 m
Bayamón
1,074 m
3,524 ft
Fajardo
Charlotte Amalie
Bahía de Yuma
Mayagüez
Cordillera Central
Caguas
Isabel Segunda
Virgin Passage
Yauco
Humacao
Isla Saona
Isla Mona
San Germán
Vieques
18° N
Cabo Rojo
Ponce
Guayama
Frederiksted
Christiansted
Greater Antilles
Saint Croix
Caribbean Sea
68° W
66° W
1:5,000,000

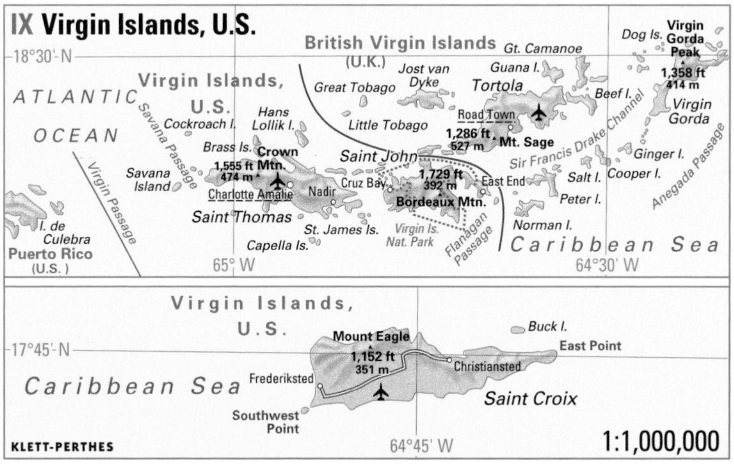
IX Virgin Islands, U.S.
British Virgin Islands (U.K.)
Gt. Camanoe
Dog Is.
Virgin Gorda Peak
18°30' N
1,358 ft
414 m
Virgin Islands, U.S.
Jost van Dyke
Guana I.
ATLANTIC
Great Tobago
Tortola
Beef I.
Savana Passage
Cockroach I.
Hans Lollik I.
Little Tobago
Road Town
Virgin Gorda
OCEAN
1,286 ft
527 m
Mt. Sage
Brass Is.
Crown Mtn.
Saint John
Sir Francis Drake Channel
Ginger I.
Anegada Passage
Savana Island
1,555 ft
474 m
1,729 ft
392 m
East End
Salt I.
Cooper I.
Charlotte Amalie
Nadir
Cruz Bay
Bordeaux Mtn.
Virgin Passage
Peter I.
I. de Culebra
Saint Thomas
St. James Is.
Virgin Is. Nat. Park
Flanagan Passage
Norman I.
Puerto Rico (U.S.)
Capella Is.
Caribbean Sea
65° W
64°30' W
Virgin Islands, U.S.
Buck I.
Mount Eagle
East Point
17°45' N
1,152 ft
351 m
Christiansted
Caribbean Sea
Frederiksted
Saint Croix
Southwest Point
KLETT-PERTHES
64°45' W
1:1,000,000

92
93
94
95
98
120°
115°
110°
105°
100°
95°
90°
30°
25°
20°
15°
10°
5°
LOS ANGELES
Pasadena
Long Beach
Anaheim
Riverside
California
Santa Ana
Oceanside
SAN DIEGO
TIJUANA
Ensenada
Mexicali
Yuma
San Luis Río Colorado
Palm Springs
Brawley
Barstow
Kingman
Grand Canyon Village
12,663 ft
3,860 m
Flagstaff
Prescott
Arizona
Glendale
PHOENIX
Mesa
Chandler
Globe
Tucson
Nogales
Douglas
Cananea
Farmington
Gallup
Santa Fe
Rio Rancho
Holbrook
Zuni Pueblo
Albuquerque
New Mexico
Santa Rosa
Sierra Blanca Peak
12,003 ft
3,659 m
Roswell
Clovis
Las Cruces
El Paso
JUÁREZ
Carlsbad
Hobbs
Trinidad
CO
Dodge City
2,339 ft
713 m
Kansas
Wichita
Independence
Arkansas City
Ponca City
Beaver
Enid
Tulsa
Broken Arrow
Oklahoma
Oklahoma City
Norman
Lawton
Amarillo
Clinton
UNITED STATES
Lubbock
Wichita Falls
Muskogee
Fort Smith
McAlester
2,900 ft
884 m
Joplin
Springfield
Missouri
Fayetteville
Jonesboro
Searcy
Arkansas
Little Rock
Hot Springs
Memphis
Nashville
Pine Bluff
Texarkana
El Dorado
Durant
Sherman
Denton
Plano
Greenville
Garland
Fort Worth
Arlington
DALLAS
Mineral Wells
Sweetwater
Abilene
Odessa
Midland
Pecos
Van Horn
McCamey
San Angelo
Brownwood
Waco
Tyler
Longview
Shreveport
Bossier City
Monroe
Edwards Plateau
Killeen
Palestine
Bryan
Huntsville
Austin
2,800 ft
853 m
Del Rio
Acuña
SAN ANTONIO
Uvalde
Eagle Pass
Piedras Negras
HOUSTON
Pasadena
Galveston
Beaumont
Port Arthur
Lake Charles
Lafayette
Baton Rouge
Metairie
New Orleans
Morgan City
Freeport
Victoria
Louisiana
Alexandria
Natchez
McComb
Hattiesburg
Jackson
Mississippi
Vicksburg
Meridian
Gulfport
Biloxi
Mobile
Tupelo
Corinth
Decatur
Birmingham
Greenville
Winona
Helena
Illinois
Carbondale
Cape Girardeau
Paducah
Poplar Bluff
Bowling Green
Tennessee
Sabinas
Nuevo Laredo
Laredo
Corpus Christi
Monclova
San Nicolás de los Garza
MONTERREY
Guadalupe
Saltillo
Reynosa
McAllen
Harlingen
Brownsville
Matamoros
Linares
Cerro Peña Nevada
12,021 ft
3,664 m
Matehuala
Concepción del Oro
Ciudad Victoria
Sierra Madre Oriental
Gulf of Mexico
Tropic of Cancer
14,357 ft
4,376 m
Cd. Madero
Tampico
Cd. Valles
S. Luis Potosí
9,800 ft
2,987 m
Guanajuato
LEÓN
Irapuato
Querétaro
Tuxpán
Pachuca
Bay of Campeche
ECATEPEC
NEZAHUALCÓYOTEL
MEXICO CITY
(CD. DE MÉXICO)
Toluca
Popocatépetl
17,888 ft
5,452 m
PUEBLA
Pico de Orizaba
18,406 ft
5,610 m
Xalapa Enríquez
Veracruz
Cuernavaca
Tehuacán
Coatzacoalcos
Chilpancingo
12,149 ft
3,703 m
Acapulco
Sierra Madre del Sur
Oaxaca
Tehuantepec
Salina Cruz
Juchitán
Gulf of Tehuantepec
Lázaro Cárdenas
Morelia
Uruapan
Apatzingán
Zamora de Hidalgo
Nevado de Colima
14,600 ft
4,450 m
Colima
Manzanillo
GUADALAJARA
Zapopan
Puerto Vallarta
Cape Corrientes
Tepic
Aguascalientes
Zacatecas
Fresnillo
Río Grande de Santiago
Islas Tres Marías
Revillagigedo Islands
(MEX.)
Mazatlán
Durango
El Salto
Juan Aldama
Sierra Madre Occidental
MEXICO
Torreón
Gómez Palacio
Culiacán
Abasolo
San Bernardo
Co. Mohinora
10,827 ft
3,300 m
Hidalgo
Santa Bárbara
Jiménez
Camargo
Delicias
Chihuahua
Cuauhtémoc
Creel
Manuel Ojinaga
Río Bravo del Norte
Rio Grande
Nuevo Casas Grandes
7,743 ft
2,360 m
Ures
Hermosillo
Guaymas
Ciudad Obregón
Navojoa
Huatabampo
Los Mochis
Santa Rosalía
Loreto
Santo Domingo
Cd. Constitución
La Paz
7,894 ft
2,406 m
San José del Cabo
Cape San Lucas
Gulf of California
Baja California
Lower California
Cedros I.
Tiburón I.
Isla Ángel de la Guarda
Pta. Sta. Eugenia
Guadalupe I.
San Quintín
Cerro de la Encantada
10,157 ft
3,096 m
Sonoita
Channel Islands
Oxnard
Yucatán Pen.
Progreso
Mérida
Tizimín
Valladolid
Chichén-Itzá
C. Catoche
Cozumel
Campeche
Cd. del Carmen
Villahermosa
Francisco Escárcega
Chetumal
Orange Walk
Belize City
BELIZE
Belmopan
Tikal
Flores
San Ignacio
Victoria Peak
3,675 ft
1,120 m
Puerto Barrios
Cobán
Tuxtla Gutiérrez
San Cristóbal de las Casas
Tonalá
Tapachula
13,846 ft
4,220 m
Tajumulco
Quezaltenango
Mixco
Guatemala C.
(Cd. de Guatemala)
Villa Nueva
GUATEMALA
Sierra Madre
Co. Las Minas
9,275 ft
2,827 m
Santa Ana
Nueva San Salvador
Soyapango
San Salvador
EL SALVADOR
San Miguel
La Unión
Chinandega
León
MANAGUA
San Pedro Sula
Choloma
El Progreso
HONDURAS
Comayagua
Tegucigalpa
Usumacinta
Clipperton I.
(French Polynesia)
PACIFIC OCEAN
Cocos I.
(C.RC.)
KLETT-PERTHES

1:15,000,000

0 200 400 mi
0 200 400 600 km

1 Lake Maracaibo, Venezuela

2 Putre, Chile

3 Machupicchu, Peru

4 Osorno, Chile

5 Perito Moreno Glacier, Argentina

6 Amazon near Manaus, Brazil

7 Rio de Janeiro, Brazil

8 Iguaçu Falls, Argentina/Brazil

9 Patagonia, Argentina

Sargasso Sea
Gulf of Mexico
Baton Rouge
Jacksonville
Houston
New Orleans
San Antonio
Tampa
C. Canaveral
Florida
Miami
Bahama Islands
Nassau
Corpus Christi
Str. of Florida
Havana
Cuba
Tropic of Cancer
A T L A N T I C
Tampico
C. Catoche
Mérida
Yucatán Channel
Santiago de Cuba
Greater Antilles
Hispaniola
Bay of Campeche
Yucatán Pen.
Cayman Is.
Port-au-Prince
Santo Domingo
San Juan
Puerto Rico
Veracruz
Jamaica
Kingston
Gulf of Honduras
Guadeloupe
Martinique
Barbados
Caribbean Sea
Lesser Antilles
Tehuantepec
Tegucigalpa
Guatemala City
San Salvador
Managua
L. Nicaragua
Providencia I.
San Andrés I.
Punta Gallinas
Barranquilla
Maracaibo
Caracas
Valencia
Cartagena
Trinidad
Panama Can.
San José
Panama City
G. of Panama
San Cristóbal
Llanos
Orinoco
Ciudad Guayana
Georgetown
Paramaribo
Cayenne
O C E A N
Bucaramanga
Medellín
Manizales
Bogotá
Magdalena
Guiana Highlands
Meta
Boa Vista
Cocos I.
Buenaventura
Cali
Malpelo
Huila
Pasto
Mitú
Pico da Neblina
R. Branco
Macapá
Quito
I. de Marajó
Belém
São Luís
Galápagos Is.
Chimborazo
Caquetá
Japurá
Rio Negro
Amazon
Putumayo
Guayaquil
Manaus
Santarém
Equator
Saint Peter and Paul Rocks
Iquitos
Selvas
Tapajós
Xingu
Madeira
Marañón
Juruá
Purús
Ucayali
Fortaleza
Fernando de Noronha
Rocas
Imperatriz
Teresina
Cabo de São Roque
Natal
João Pessoa
Recife
Punta Negra
Piura
Chiclayo
Trujillo
Chimbote
Pucallpa
Huascarán
Rio Branco
Porto Velho
Tocantins
Parnaíba
Palmas
Juazeiro
Sobradinho Res.
Maceió
Aracaju
Callao
Lima
Huancayo
Cusco
Beni
Mamoré
Guaporé
Campos
Brazilian Highlands
São Francisco
Salvador
Coropuna
Arequipa
La Paz
Titicaca
Cochabamba
Altiplano
Santa Cruz
Cuiabá
Pantanal
Ilhéus
Montes Claros
Goiânia
Uberlândia
Belo Horizonte
Vitória
Pico da Bandeira
Arica
Sucre
Iquique
Campo Grande
Paraná
Paraguay
Ribeirão Prêto
Campinas
Cabo Frio
Rio de Janeiro
Trindade
Martin Vaz
Londrina
São Paulo
Santos
Gran Chaco
Pilcomayo
Antofagasta
Salta
Asunción
Itaipú Res.
Curitiba
Tropic of Capricorn
Atacama
San Miguel de Tucumán
Ciudad del Este
Iguaçu Falls
Resistencia
Florianópolis
Desventurados Is.
Uruguay
Porto Alegre
P A C I F I C O C E A N
Andes
Aconcagua
San Juan
Sa. de Córdoba
Santa Fe
Córdoba
Rosario
Pelotas
Valparaíso
Santiago
Mendoza
Juan Fernández Is.
Buenos Aires
Montevideo
La Plata
Río de la Plata
Pampas
A T L A N T I C
Concepción
Neuquén
Bahía Blanca
Mar del Plata
Temuco
Río Negro
San Carlos de Bariloche
Puerto Montt
Viedma
Chiloé I.
Rawson
Tristan da Cunha
Chonos Arch.
San Valentín
Comodoro Rivadavia
O C E A N
Gough I.
Patagonia
Falkland Is. (Is. Malvinas)
Río Gallegos
Stanley
Str. of Magellan
Punta Arenas
Tierra del Fuego
Staten I.
South Georgia
Ushuaia
Cape Horn
Drake Passage
Scotia Sea
South Sandwich Is.
South Orkney Is.
South Shetland Is.
Antarctic Pen.
Moody Point
Elevation
13,124 ft 4,000 m
6,562 ft 2,000 m
3,281 ft 1,000 m
1,640 ft 500 m
656 ft 200 m
0 ft 0 m
Depression
656 ft 200 m
6,562 ft 2,000 m
13,124 ft 4,000 m
19,686 ft 6,000 m
26,248 ft 8,000 m
Inland ice, glaciers
Ice shelf
Pack ice
Limit of drift ice
KLETT-PERTHES

1:40,000,000

0 500 1,000 mi
0 500 1,000 1,500 2,000 km
Sargasso Sea
Gulf of Mexico
Jacksonville
New Orleans
Houston
San Antonio
Tampa
Florida
Miami
Str. of Florida
Bahama Islands
Havana
Cuba
Yucatán Channel
Tropic of Cancer
ATLANTIC OCEAN
Greater Antilles
Hispaniola
Bay of Campeche
Yucatán
Cayman Is.
Jamaica
Puerto Rico
Gulf of Honduras
Caribbean Sea
Guadeloupe
Martinique
Barbados
Lesser Antilles
Providencia I.
San Andrés I.
Guatemala City
Panama Can.
Cape Verde Islands
Maracaibo
Caracas
Trinidad
L. Nicaragua
Llanos
Orinoco
G. of Panamá
Magdalena
Bogotá
Meta
Guiana Highlands
Cocos I.
Malpelo
PACIFIC OCEAN
Quito
Caquetá
Japurá
Río Negro
R. Branco
Amazon
I. de Marajó
Saint Peter and Paul Rocks
Galápagos Is.
Putumayo
Equator
Andes
Marañón
Ucayali
Selvas
Juruá
Purus
Madeira
Tapajós
Xingu
Rocas
Fernando de Noronha
Tocantins
Parnaíba
Sobradinho Res.
Lima
Guaporé
Mamoré
Beni
Titicaca
Campos
Brazilian Highlands
São Francisco
Brasília
Goiânia
Altiplano
Pantanal
Belo Horizonte
Paraguay
Gran Chaco
Paraná
Vitória
Trindade
Martin Vaz
Atacama
Pilcomayo
São Paulo
Rio de Janeiro
Tropic of Capricorn
Itaipú Res.
Curitiba
Desventurados Is.
Uruguay
Porto Alegre
Sa. de Córdoba
Córdoba
Juan Fernández Is.
Santiago
Buenos Aires
Montevideo
Pampas
Río de la Plata
Río Negro
Chiloé I.
Chonos Arch.
Patagonia
Tristan da Cunha
Gough I.
Falkland Is. (Is. Malvinas)
Str. of Magellan
Tierra del Fuego
Staten I.
South Georgia
Drake Passage
Scotia Sea
South Sandwich Is.
South Orkney Is.
South Shetland Is.
Antarctic Pen.
KLETT-PERTHES
Land Cover
(Explanations on page 32)
Natural Vegetation
Evergreen needleleaf forests
Evergreen broadleaf forests
Deciduous needleleaf forests
Deciduous broadleaf forests
Mixed forests
Closed shrublands
Open shrublands
Woody savannas
Savannas
Grasslands
Permanent wetlands
Developed and Mosaic Lands
Croplands
Cropland/natural vegetation mosaic
Urban and built-up lands
Non-Vegetated Lands
Snow and ice
Barren or sparsely vegetated
Water bodies
No data

0 500 1,000 mi
0 500 1,000 1,500 2,000 km

1:40,000,000

0 500 1,000 mi
0 500 1,000 1,500 2,000 km
UNITED STATES
Jacksonville
Austin
HOUSTON
Baton Rouge
New Orleans
Tampa
C. Canaveral
SAN ANTONIO
Sargasso Sea
Corpus Christi
Miami
Nassau
Gulf of Mexico
Str. of Florida
BAHAMAS
Tropic of Cancer
MEXICO
HAVANA
CUBA
Turks and Caicos Is. (U.K.)
Virgin Islands, U.S.
British Virgin Is. (U.K.)
Yucatán Channel
Tampico
C. Catoche
Cayman Is. (U.K.)
Santiago de Cuba
Hispaniola
ATLANTIC
Mérida
HAITI
DOMINICAN REP.
San Juan
Bay of Campeche
Port-au-Prince
Anguilla (U.K.)
Kingston
SANTO DOMINGO
Puerto Rico (U.S.)
ANTIGUA AND BARBUDA
Veracruz
JAMAICA
Navassa (U.S.)
SAINT KITTS AND NEVIS
Montserrat (U.K.)
Guadeloupe (FRA.)
BELIZE
G. of Honduras
Belmopan
DOMINICA
Caribbean Sea
Martinique (FRA.)
Tehuantepec
GUATEMALA
HONDURAS
Tegucigalpa
Aruba (NLD.)
Neth. Antilles
ST. LUCIA
ST. VINCENT AND THE GRENADINES
BARBADOS
CAPE VERDE
Guatemala City
Providencia I. (COL.)
Punta Gallinas
GRENADA
San Salvador
EL SALVADOR
NICARAGUA
MANAGUA
San Andrés I.
BARRANQUILLA
MARACAIBO
CARACAS
Port of Spain
Nicaragua L.
Panama Canal
Cartagena
Maracaibo L.
VALENCIA
TRINIDAD AND TOBAGO
San José
COSTA RICA
Panama City
PANAMA
San Cristóbal
Orinoco
Ciudad Guayana
G. of Panama
VENEZUELA
GUYANA
Georgetown
OCEAN
MEDELLÍN
Bucaramanga
Magdalena
Paramaribo
Manizales
BOGOTÁ
Meta
Cayenne
Cocos I. (C.RC.)
Buenaventura
SURINAME
French Guiana
Malpelo (COL.)
CALI
COLOMBIA
Boa Vista
Rio Branco
Mitú
Macapá
Saint Peter and Paul Rocks (BRA.)
Pasto
QUITO
Caquetá
Rio Negro
Japurá
Amazon
Galápagos Is. (ECU.)
ECUADOR
Putumayo
MANAUS
BELÉM
São Luís
Equator
GUAYAQUIL
Santarém
Marañón
Iquitos
FORTALEZA
Juruá
Purús
Madeira
Tapajós
Xingu
Imperatriz
Teresina
Rocas
Fernando de Noronha
Piura
Ucayali
Cabo de São Roque
Punta Negra
Chiclayo
Natal
PERU
Tocantins
Parnaíba
João Pessoa
Trujillo
Pucallpa
Rio Branco
Porto Velho
BRAZIL
RECIFE
Chimbote
Palmas
Juazeiro
Maceió
Sobradinho Res.
Aracaju
Callao
LIMA
Huancayo
Cusco
Beni
Mamoré
Guaporé
São Francisco
SALVADOR
Titicaca L.
La Paz
Cuiabá
BRASÍLIA
Montes Claros
Arequipa
Cochabamba
SANTA CRUZ
GOIÂNIA
Ilhéus
BOLIVIA
Sucre
Arica
Uberlândia
BELO HORIZONTE
Iquique
Campo Grande
Paraguay
Ribeirão Prêto
PARAGUAY
Paraná
Vitória
Campinas
CHILE
Londrina
Trindade
Martin Vaz (BRA.)
Pilcomayo
SÃO PAULO
Cabo Frio
Antofagasta
Itaipú Res.
RIO DE JANEIRO
Salta
Santos
Tropic of Capricorn
Asunción
Ciudad del Este
CURITIBA
PACIFIC OCEAN
Desventurados Is. (CHL.)
San Miguel de Tucumán
Resistencia
Florianópolis
Uruguay
PORTO ALEGRE
San Juan
ARGENTINA
Santa Fe
CÓRDOBA
Pelotas
Valparaíso
Mendoza
Rosario
URUGUAY
Juan Fernández Is. (CHL.)
SANTIAGO
BUENOS AIRES
MONTEVIDEO
La Plata
Río de la Plata
Concepción
Bahía Blanca
Mar del Plata
Temuco
Neuquén
Rio Negro
Puerto Montt
San Carlos de Bariloche
Viedma
Chiloé I.
Rawson
Tristan da Cunha (U.K.)
Chonos Arch.
Comodoro Rivadavia
Gough I.
Falkland Is. (Is. Malvinas) (U.K.)
Río Gallegos
Stanley
Str. of Magellan
Punta Arenas
Tierra del Fuego
Staten I.
Ushuaia
Cape Horn
South Georgia and the South Sandwich Is. (U.K.)
Drake Passage
Scotia Sea
South Shetland Is.
South Orkney Is.
Moody Point
KLETT-PERTHES

South America: Ethnic Groups

1:40,000,000

Languages Families and Ethnic Groups

Peoples with Indo-European languages

- Spanish speaking peoples
- Paraguayans (Guaraní and Spanish)
- Brazilians (Portuguese)
- Creole population of the Caribbean and Guiana (English/Dutch/French or mixed languages: Pidgins, Papiamento, Patoá)
- Maroons (Bush Negro/Bosnegers)
- Areas of Afro-Brazilians, Afro-Caribbeans and other Afro-Americans
- Falkland Islanders (English)
- Germans

Asian minorities

- East Indians
- Javanese
- Japanese

American Indians (Language families)

- Chibcha
- Quechua
- Aymara
- Araucanians
- Arawaks
- Caribs
- Tupí-Guaraní
- Pano
- Tukano
- Macro-Gê
- Matacó-Guaicurú
- Mascoi
- Zamuco
- Uru-Chipaya
- Other American Indians (Isolate languages)

- Very sparsely populated area formerly inhabited by indigenous peoples
- Uninhabited area

Am. *Amahuaca*
Ch. *Chipaya*
Gu. *Guayaki (Aché)*
Ma. *Makú*
Mo. *Motitlon*
Si. *Siriono*

1:40,000,000

KLETT-PERTHES
Climate Diagrams (by H. Walter)
2,263 mm 25.0 °C 89.1 in. 77.0 °F Annual averages of precipitation and air temperature
Months
3 m 10 ft Altitude
Precipitation curve
Temperature curve
Dry season
Ar 2,853 mm 26.2 °C 112.3 in. 79.2 °F Iquitos 126 m 413 ft
Am 2,573 mm 26.6 °C 101.3 in. 80.0 °F Macapá 15 m 49 ft
Aw 1,555 mm 20.7 °C 61.2 in. 69.3 °F Brasília 1,158 m 3,799 ft
Aw 912 mm 27.4 °C 35.9 in. 81.3 °F Barranquilla 21 m 69 ft
As 1,595 mm 26.0 °C 62.8 in. 78.8 °F Aracaju 5 m 16 ft
BS 564 mm 27.6 °C 22.2 in. 81.7 °F Maracaibo 65 m 213 ft
BS 235 mm 12.8 °C 9.3 in. 55.0 °F Com. Rivadavia 46 m 151 ft
BW 1 mm 18.7 °C 0.04 in. 65.7 °F Arica 58 m 190 ft
Cs 301 mm 14.3 °C 11.9 in. 57.7 °F Santiago 520 m 1,706 ft
Cw 757 mm 16.4 °C 29.8 in. 61.5 °F Salta 1,221 m 4,006 ft
Cr 1,173 mm 17.5 °C 46.2 in. 63.5 °F Buenos Aires 25 m 82 ft
Do 1,705 mm 10.1 °C 67.1 in. 50.2 °F Puerto Montt 85 m 279 ft
Eo 723 mm 6.3 °C 28.5 in. 43.3 °F Balmaceda 520 m 1,706 ft
FT 524 mm 5.7 °C 20.6 in. 42.3 °F Ushuaia 14 m 46 ft
Climatic Regions
(Modified Koeppen System based on Trewartha; cf. p. 18/19)
Tropical Rainy Climates
Ar Tropical rainy climate
Am Tropical monsoon rain climate
Aw Tropical summer rain climate
As Tropical winter rain climate
Dry Climates
BS Steppe climate
BW Desert climate
BM Marine dry climate
Subtropical Climates
Cr Subtropical rain climate
Cw Subtropical summer rain climate
Cs Subtropical winter rain climate
Temperate Climates
Do Oceanic temperate climate
Dc Continental temperate climate
Boreal Climates
Eo Oceanic boreal climate
Polar Climates
FT Tundra climate
FI Perpetual frost climate
Meteorological station with climate diagram
Sargasso Sea
Gulf of Mexico
Tropic of Cancer
Bahama Islands (Ar/Aw/Am)
Str. of Florida
Cuba
Greater Antilles
Hispaniola
Puerto Rico
Bay of Campeche
Cayman Is.
Gulf of Honduras
Jamaica
Caribbean Sea
Guadeloupe
Martinique
Barbados
Lesser Antilles
Providencia I.
San Andrés I.
Barranquilla
Maracaibo
Trinidad
L. Nicaragua
G. of Panama
Orinoco
Cocos I.
Malpelo
PACIFIC
ATLANTIC
Galápagos Is. (BS/Aw)
Macapá
Saint Peter and Paul Rocks
Equator
Iquitos
Amazon
Rocas
Fernando de Noronha
Sobradinho Res.
Aracaju
Brasília
OCEAN
Arica
Salta
Trindade
Martin Vaz
Tropic of Capricorn
Itaipú Res.
Santiago
Buenos Aires
Río de la Plata
Puerto Montt
Chiloé I.
Chonos Arch.
Balmaceda
Comodoro Rivadavia
Falkland Is. (Is. Malvinas)
Str. of Magellan
Tierra del Fuego
Staten I.
Ushuaia
South Georgia
Drake Passage
Scotia Sea
South Orkney Is.
South Sandwich Is.
South Shetland Is.

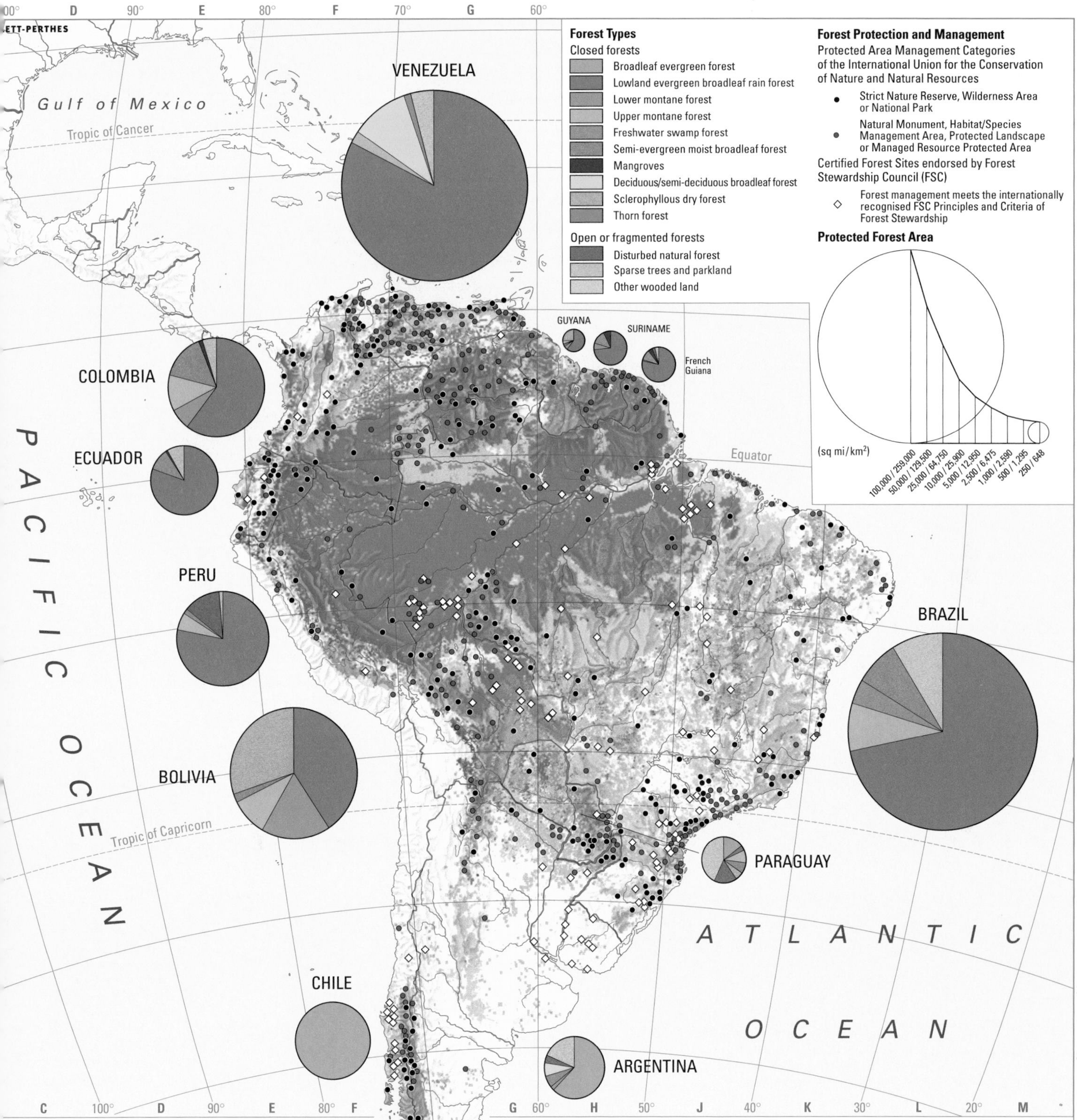
0 500 1,000 mi
0 500 1,000 1,500 2,000 km
Forest Types
Closed forests
Broadleaf evergreen forest
Lowland evergreen broadleaf rain forest
Lower montane forest
Upper montane forest
Freshwater swamp forest
Semi-evergreen moist broadleaf forest
Mangroves
Deciduous/semi-deciduous broadleaf forest
Sclerophyllous dry forest
Thorn forest
Open or fragmented forests
Disturbed natural forest
Sparse trees and parkland
Other wooded land
Forest Protection and Management
Protected Area Management Categories of the International Union for the Conservation of Nature and Natural Resources
Strict Nature Reserve, Wilderness Area or National Park
Natural Monument, Habitat/Species Management Area, Protected Landscape or Managed Resource Protected Area
Certified Forest Sites endorsed by Forest Stewardship Council (FSC)
Forest management meets the internationally recognised FSC Principles and Criteria of Forest Stewardship
Protected Forest Area
(sq mi/km²)
100,000 / 259,000
50,000 / 129,500
25,000 / 64,750
10,000 / 25,900
5,000 / 12,950
2,500 / 6,475
1,000 / 2,590
500 / 1,295
250 / 648
Gulf of Mexico
Tropic of Cancer
Equator
Tropic of Capricorn
PACIFIC OCEAN
ATLANTIC OCEAN
VENEZUELA
COLOMBIA
ECUADOR
PERU
BOLIVIA
CHILE
ARGENTINA
PARAGUAY
BRAZIL
GUYANA
SURINAME
French Guiana
C D E F G H J K L M
100° 90° 80° 70° 60° 50° 40° 30° 20°
5 6 7 8
10° 20° 30°

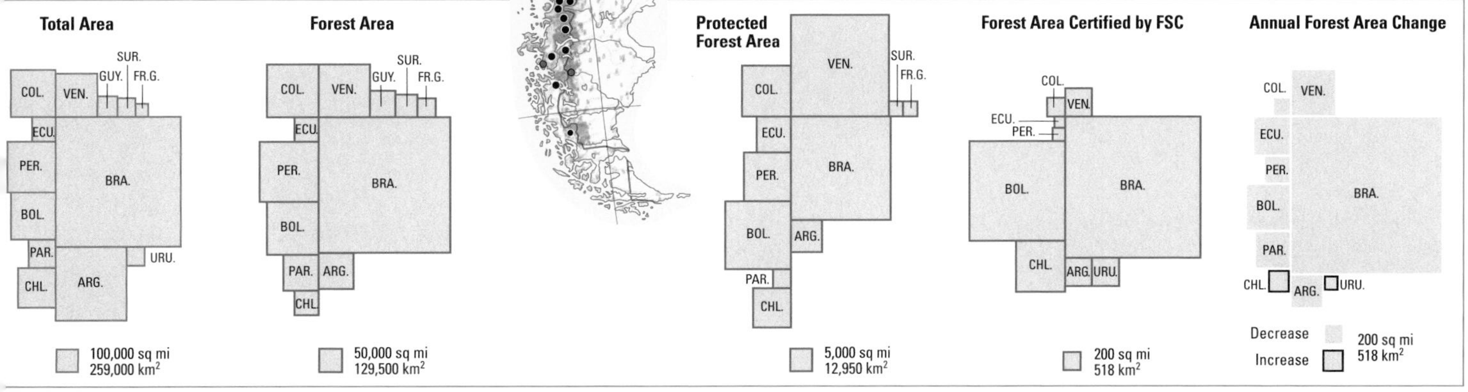
Total Area
COL. VEN. GUY. SUR. FR.G. ECU. PER. BRA. BOL. PAR. URU. CHL. ARG.
100,000 sq mi 259,000 km²
Forest Area
COL. VEN. GUY. SUR. FR.G. ECU. PER. BRA. BOL. PAR. ARG. CHL.
50,000 sq mi 129,500 km²
Protected Forest Area
COL. VEN. SUR. FR.G. ECU. PER. BRA. BOL. ARG. PAR. CHL.
5,000 sq mi 12,950 km²
Forest Area Certified by FSC
COL. VEN. ECU. PER. BOL. BRA. CHL. ARG. URU.
200 sq mi 518 km²
Annual Forest Area Change
COL. VEN. ECU. PER. BOL. BRA. PAR. CHL. ARG. URU.
Decrease
Increase
200 sq mi 518 km²

Caribbean Sea
PACIFIC
OCEAN
Galápagos Is.
(ECU.)
Equator
COLOMBIA
VENEZUELA
ECUADOR
PANAMA
COSTA RICA
NICARAGUA
EL SALVADOR
PERU
BOLIVIA
CHILE
Andes
Cordillera Occidental
Cordillera Central
Cordillera Oriental
Amazon
Managua
Masaya
Granada
León
Chinandega
Matagalpa
Boaco
Rama
Bluefields
L. Nicaragua
San Carlos
Liberia
Puntarenas
Alajuela
San José
Cartago
Limón
Cabo Blanco
Pen. de Nicoya
Cerro Cirripó
12,533 ft
3,820 m
Volcán Barú
11,401 ft
3,475 m
Puerto Armuelles
David
Santiago
Chitré
Azuero Pen.
Coiba
Bocas del Toro
Colón
Arraiján
Panama City
(Panamá)
San Miguelito
Gulf of Panama
Punta Mala
La Palma
Gulf of Darién
El Porvenír
Punta Manzanilla
Panama Canal
San Andrés
San Andrés I.
Providencia I.
(COL.)
Soyapango
San Miguel
San S.
N. S. S.
HON.
Estelí
La Unión
Choluteca
6,529 ft
1,990 m
Cocos I.
(C.RC.)
Malpelo
(COL.)
Marchena
5,601 ft
1,707 m
Volcano Wolf
San Salvador
Santa Cruz
Fernandina
Pto. Ayora
Pto. Baquarizo Moreno
Isabela
Cristóbal
Puerto Villamil
Santa Maria
Española
Punta Gallinas
Guajira Pen.
Aruba
(NLD.)
Oranj.
Netherlands Antilles
Willemstad
Bonaire
Curaçao
Gulf of Venezuela
Blanquilla
Margarita
Ríohacha
Santa Marta
Ciénaga
Barranquilla
Cartagena
Soledad
Valledupar
18,947 ft
5,775 m
Pico Cristóbal Colón
Maicao
Maracaibo
Lake Maracaibo
Cabimas
Punto Fijo
Coro
San Felipe
Puerto Cabello
Catia la Mar
Caracas
Petare
Maracay
Valencia
Cumaná
Barcelona
Barquisimeto
San Juan de los Morros
6,336 ft
1,931 m
Trujillo
San Carlos del Zulia
Valera
Acarigua
S. Carlos
Mérida
Pico Bolívar
16,428 ft
5,007 m
Guanare
Barinas
Calabozo
El Tigre
Ciudad Bolívar
Apure
San Fernando de Apure
Orinoco
San Cristóbal
Cúcuta
Ocaña
El Carmen de Bolívar
Sincelejo
Montería
Turbo
Magdalena
Cauca
Bucaramanga
Floridablanca
Cocuy
18,022 ft
5,493 m
Barrancabermeja
Bello
Medellín
Envigado
Itagüí
Puerto Berrío
Arauca
Puerto Carreño
Puerto Ayacucho
7,497 ft
2,285 m
Co. Yaví
Meta
La Dorada
Tunja
Yopal
Quibdó
Manizales
Pereira
Armenia
Ibagué
Bogotá
Orocué
Puerto Nariño
San Fernando de Atabapo
Girardot
Villavicencio
Tuluá
Buga
Palmira
Cali
Buenaventura
13,944 ft
4,250 m
14,961 ft
4,560 m
Guaviare
Puerto Inírida
Jamundí
Huila
18,865 ft
5,750 m
Neiva
San José del Guaviare
Popayán
Río Negro
Casiquiare
San Carlos de Río Negro
9,889 ft
3,014 m
Pico da Neblina
Vaupés
Mitú
Tumaco
Pasto
Florencia
Mocoa
San Lorenzo
Ipiales
Tulcán
Puerto Asis
Punta Galera
Esmeraldas
Ibarra
Santo Domingo de los Colorados
Quito
Cotopaxi
19,348 ft
5,897 m
Puerto Francisco de Orellana
Caquetá
Araracuara
S. Gabriel da Cachoeira
Santa Isabel do Rio Negro
Tena
Portoviejo
Manta
Quevedo
Chimborazo
6,310 m
20,703 ft
Ambato
Puyo
Babahoyo
Riobamba
Guayaquil
Milagro
Macas
Pta. Sta. Elena
Salinas
Eloy Alfaro
Azogues
Gulf of Guayaquil
Puná I.
Cuenca
Machala
Tumbes
Loja
Zamora
Putumayo
Japurá
Napo
Fonte Boa
Tefé
Iquitos
Leticia
Tabatinga
Benjamin Constant
São Paulo de Olivença
Carauari
Juruá
Marañón
12,907 ft
3,934 m
Talara
Sullana
Paita
Cerro Viejo
Chulucanas
Piura
Jaén
Requena
Yurimaguas
Moyobamba
Chachapoyas
Tarapoto
Juanjuí
Punta Negra
Lambayeque
Chiclayo
Cajamarca
Pacasmayo
Orellana
Ucayali
Eirunepé
Lábrea
Cruzeiro do Sul
Tarauacá
Purús
Boca do Acre
Porto Velho
Trujillo
Uchiza
Pucallpa
Huallaga
Sena Madureira
Rio Branco
Huallanca
22,205 ft
6,768 m
Huascarán
Chimbote
Huaraz
Tingo María
Huánuco
Cerro de Pasco
Barranca
Huacho
Guayaramerín
Guajará-Mirim
Riberalta
Cobija
La Oroya
Chosica
Lima
Callao
Huancayo
Puerto Maldonado
Huancavelica
Quillabamba
Machupicchu
20,575 ft
6,271 m
Salcantay
Ayacucho
Chincha Alta
Pisco
Abancay
Cusco
Sicuani
Sandia
Beni
Mamoré
Santa Ana
Trinidad
Rurrenabaque
Ica
Punta Carreta
Apolo
San Borja
San Ignacio
Puquio
Nazca
21,080 ft
6,425 m
Coropuna
Chala
Juliaca
Puerto Acosta
L. Titicaca
Ancohuma
21,087 ft
6,427 m
19,932 ft
6,075 m
Chachani
Puno
El Alto
La Paz
Illimani
21,201 ft
6,462 m
Arequipa
Guaqui
Viacha
Mollendo
Moquegua
Ilo
Quillacollo
Sacaba
Cochabamba
Santa Cruz
21,464 ft
6,542 m
Sajama
Oruro
Aiquile
Llallagua
Tacna
Putre
Arica
L. Poopó
Challapata
Sucre
Potosí
Iquique
Salar de Uyuni
Uyuni
20,263 ft
6,176 m
Aucanquilcha
Tupiza
Tarija
Villazón
Tocopilla
Chuquicamata
19,751 ft
6,020 m
Calama
La Quiaca
Bermejo
A
B
C
D
E
F
90°
85°
80°
75°
70°
65°
10°
5°
15°
1
2
3
4
5
6
7
102
103
KLETT-PERTHES

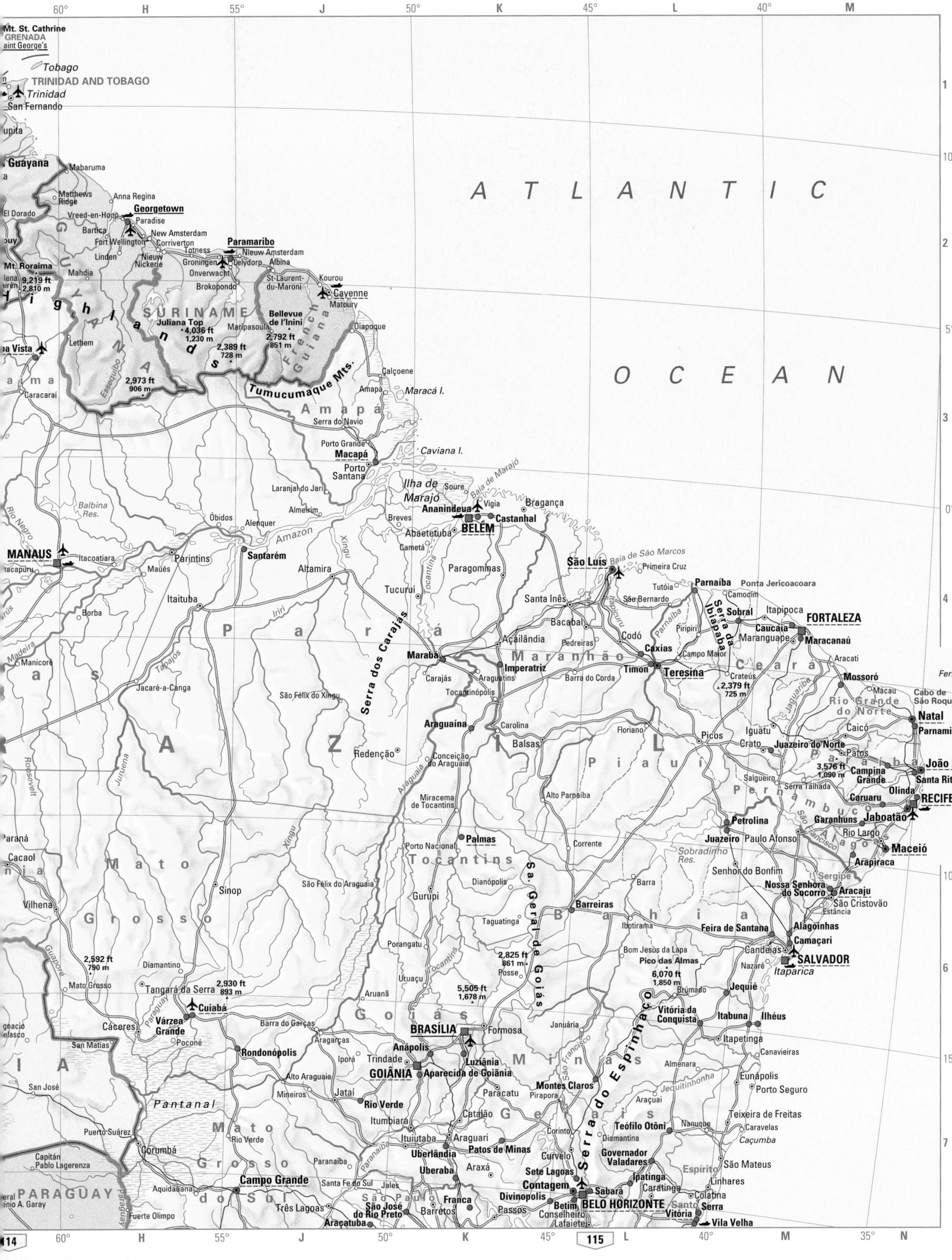
A T L A N T I C
O C E A N
Mt. St. Cathrine
GRENADA
Tobago
TRINIDAD AND TOBAGO
Trinidad
San Fernando
Guayana
Mabaruma
Matthews Ridge
Anna Regina
El Dorado
Vreed-en-Hoop
Georgetown
Paradise
Bartica
New Amsterdam
Fort Wellington
Corriverton
Linden
Nieuw Nickerie
Totness
Paramaribo
Groningen
Nieuw Amsterdam
Lelydorp
Albina
Mt. Roraima
9,219 ft
2,810 m
Mahdia
Onverwacht
Brokopondo
St-Laurent-du-Maroni
Kourou
Cayenne
Matoury
SURINAME
Juliana Top
4,036 ft
1,230 m
Maripasoula
Bellevue de l'Inini
2,792 ft
851 m
French Guiana
Oiapoque
Lethem
2,389 ft
728 m
2,973 ft
906 m
Essequibo
Caracaraí
Tumucumaque Mts.
Calçoene
Amapá
Maracá I.
Amapá
Serra do Navio
Porto Grande
Macapá
Caviana I.
Porto Santana
Ilha de Marajó
Soure
Baía de Marajó
Laranjal do Jari
Vigia
Bragança
Balbina Res.
Rio Negro
Almeirim
Óbidos
Alenquer
Breves
Ananindeua
Castanhal
Abaetetuba
BELÉM
Cametá
Amazon
MANAUS
Itacoatiara
Parintins
Santarém
Maués
Altamira
Xingu
Paragominas
São Luís
Baía de São Marcos
Primeira Cruz
Tucuruí
Tocantins
Tutóia
Parnaíba
Ponta Jericoacoara
Camocim
Santa Inês
São Bernardo
Itapipoca
Itaituba
Borba
Iriri
Serra da Ibiapaba
Sobral
FORTALEZA
Bacabal
Piripiri
Caucaia
Maranguape
Maracanaú
Açailândia
Pedreiras
Codó
Madeira
P a r á
Serra dos Carajás
Marabá
Caxias
Campo Maior
Aracati
Maranhão
Imperatriz
Timon
Teresina
Ceará
Mossoró
Manicoré
Tapajós
Carajás
Araguatins
Barra do Corda
Crateús
2,379 ft
725 m
Macau
Cabo de São Roque
Rocas
Fernando de Noronha (BRA.)
Jacaré-a-Canga
São Félix do Xingu
Tocantinópolis
Rio Grande do Norte
Natal
Parnamirim
Araguaína
Carolina
Floriano
Caicó
Balsas
Picos
Iguatu
Crato
Juazeiro do Norte
Patos
A Z I L
Redenção
Conceição do Araguaia
Piauí
3,576 ft
1,090 m
Campina Grande
João Pessoa
Santa Rita
Roosevelt
Juruena
Araguaia
Salgueiro
Serra Talhada
Olinda
Alto Parnaíba
Miracema de Tocantins
Pernambuco
Caruaru
RECIFE
Jaboatão
Petrolina
Garanhuns
Paraná
Porto Nacional
Palmas
Juazeiro
Paulo Afonso
Rio Largo
Corrente
Alagoas
Maceió
Cacaol
Mato
Tocantins
Sobradinho Res.
Arapiraca
Senhor do Bonfim
Sergipe
Sinop
São Félix do Araguaia
Dianópolis
Barra
Nossa Senhora do Socorro
Aracaju
São Cristovão
Estância
Vilhena
Gurupi
Serra Geral de Goiás
Barreiras
Grosso
Taguatinga
Bahia
Ibotirama
Feira de Santana
Alagoinhas
Camaçari
Guaporé
Porangatu
Bom Jesus da Lapa
Candeias
SALVADOR
2,592 ft
790 m
Diamantino
2,825 ft
861 m
Posse
Pico das Almas
6,070 ft
1,850 m
Itaparica
Nazaré
Mato Grosso
2,930 ft
893 m
Uruaçu
Tangará da Serra
Aruanã
5,505 ft
1,678 m
Brumado
Jequié
Cuiabá
Várzea Grande
Vitória da Conquista
Itabuna
Ilhéus
Cáceres
Barra do Garças
Goiás
BRASÍLIA
Formosa
Januária
Poconé
San Matías
Aragarças
Anápolis
Itapetinga
Canavieiras
Rondonópolis
Iporá
Trindade
Luziânia
Minas
Serra do Espinhaço
Almenara
São Francisco
San José
GOIÂNIA
Aparecida de Goiânia
Alto Araguaia
Montes Claros
Eunápolis
Jequitinhonha
Mineiros
Jataí
Paracatu
Pirapora
Porto Seguro
Pantanal
Rio Verde
Araçuaí
Gerais
Catalão
Itumbiara
Teixeira de Freitas
Puerto Suárez
Mato
Corinto
Teófilo Otôni
Nanuque
Caravelas
Rio Verde
Ituiutaba
Araguari
Diamantina
Caçumba
Corumbá
Patos de Minas
Capitán Pablo Lagerenza
Grosso
Paranaíba
Uberlândia
Curvelo
Governador Valadares
São Mateus
Araxá
Espírito
Uberaba
Sete Lagoas
Ipatinga
Linhares
PARAGUAY
Campo Grande
Santa Fé do Sul
Jales
Contagem
Aquidauana
Caratinga
Colatina
do Sul
São Paulo
Franca
Divinópolis
Sabará
BELO HORIZONTE
Santo
Serra
Betim
Três Lagoas
São José do Rio Preto
Barretos
Passos
Conselheiro Lafaiete
Vitória
Fuerte Olimpo
Araçatuba
Vila Velha
Paraguay
60° 55° 50° 45° 40° 35°
10° 5° 0° 10° 15°
H J K L M N
1 2 3 4 5 6 7

112
PACIFIC
OCEAN
Tropic of Capricorn
Desventurados Is. (CHL.)
Juan Fernández Is. (CHL.)
Robinson Crusoe
Alejandro Selkirk
B O L I V I A
P A R A G U A Y
U R U G U A Y
Gran Chaco
Atacama Desert
Costa
Cordillera de la Costa
Cordillera Patagonica
Pampa
Patagonia
Mesopotamia
Aucanquilcha
Tocopilla
Chuquicamata
Calama
Punta Angamos
Antofagasta
Salar de Atacama
Llullaillaco
Salar de Arizaro
Taltal
Chañaral
Caldera
Ojos del Salado
Copiapó
Pissis
Huasco
Vallenar
Cerro del Toro
La Serena
Coquimbo
Ovalle
Illapel
Aconcagua
Viña del Mar
Valparaiso
Quilpué
San Antonio
SANTIAGO
Puente Alto
San Bernardo
Rancagua
San Fernando
Curicó
Constitución
Talca
Cauquenes
Linares
Talcahuano
Chillán
Concepción
Pta. Lavapié
Coronel
Lebu
Los Angeles
Angol
Temuco
Valdivia
Osorno
Puerto Montt
Ancud
Castro
Chiloé I.
Quellón
Pta. Pabellón
Golfo Corcovado
Chonos Arch.
Puerto Aisén
Coihaique
Taitao Pen.
San Valentín
Chile Chico
Gulf of Peñas
Campana I.
Wellington I.
Murallon
Madre de Dios I.
Queen Adelaide Arch.
Strait of Magellan
Cabo Deseado
Punta Arenas
Riesko
Brunswick Pen.
Dawson I.
Santa Inés I.
Porvenir
Tierra del Fuego
Río Grande
Ushuaia
Yogan
Navarino I.
Hoste I.
Wollaston Is.
Cape Horn
C. San Diego
Staten I.
Tarija
Tupiza
Villazon
La Quiaca
Yacuiba
Villamontes
Tartagal
Bermejo
San Ramón de la Nueva Orán
Embarcación
Jujuy
San Salvador de Jujuy
Salta
San Pedro
San Antonio de los Cobres
Metán
Monte Quemado
San Miguel de Tucumán
Concepción
Catamarca
Tinogasta
Santiago del Estero
Añatuya
San Fernando del Valle de Catamarca
Chilecito
La Rioja
San José de Jáchal
Dean Funes
San Juan
CÓRDOBA
Sierra de Córdoba
Villa Dolores
Villa Krause
Villa María
Mendoza
Villa Nueva
San Martín
San Luis
Río Cuarto
Mercedes
San Rafael
Malargüe
General Pico
Rufino
Junín
Telén
Santa Rosa
General Acha
Domuyo
Chos Malal
Neuquén
Zapala
General Roca
Lanín
Río Negro
Colorado
Sierra Colorada
Carmen de Patagones
Viedma
Punta Rasa
Gulf of San Matías
San Carlos de Bariloche
Valdés Pen.
Puerto Madryn
Trelew
Rawson
Tres Picos
Esquel
Las Plumas
Chubut
C. Dos Bahías
Sarmiento
Comodoro Rivadavia
Gulf of San Jorge
Caleta Olivia
L. Buenos Aires
Las Heras
C. Tres Puntas
Puerto Deseado
Santa Cruz
Gobernador Gregores
Puerto San Julián
San Martin
L. Viedma
L. Argentino
El Calafate
Puerto Santa Cruz
Bahía Grande
Puerto Natales
Río Gallegos
C. Vírgenes
Falkland Islands (Is. Malvinas) (U. K.)
West Falkland
East Falkland
Stanley
Presidencia Roque Sáenz Peña
Resistencia
Corrientes
Formosa
Reconquista
Goya
Santa Fe
Paraná
Rafaela
San Justo
Mar Chiquita
Rosario
San Nicolás de los Arroyos
Zárate
BUENOS AIRES
S. JUSTO
Lomas de Zamora
La Plata
Río de la Plata
Pehuajó
San Carlos de Bolívar
Azul
Olavarría
Tandil
Mar del Plata
Bahía Blanca
Tres Arroyos
Punta Alta
Necochea
Dolores
Punta Norte
Punta Sur
Concordia
Salto
Paysandú
Fray Bentos
Mercedes
Durazno
Trinidad
Colonia del Sacramento
Minas
Cerro Catedral
Las Piedras
Maldonado
Punta del Este
MONTEVIDEO
Rivera
Tacuarembó
Melo
Treinta y Tres
Artigas
Uruguaiana
Santana do Livramento
Bagé
Pelotas
Jaguarão
Mirim
Asunción
Luque
Lambaré
Caacupé
Villarrica
Caazapá
Ciudad del Este
Foz do Iguaçu
Encarnación
Posadas
Oberá
Misiones
Pilar
Concepción
Pozo Colorado
Filadelfia
Doctor Pedro P. Peña
General Eugenio A. Garay
Capitán Pablo Lagerenza
Puerto Suárez
Corumbá
Fuerte Olimpo
Porto Murtinho
Pedro Juan Caballero
Ponta Porã
Dourados
Itaipú Res.
Santo Ângelo
Santo Tomé
São Borja
Cruz Alta
Passo Fundo
Caxias
Chapecó
Santa Maria
Cachoeira do Sul
Novo Hamburgo
Pilcomayo
Bermejo
Paraná
Uruguay
Paraguay
Salado
O
KLETT-PERTHES

1:15,000,000 0 200 400 mi 0 200 400 600 km
1:5,000,000 0 50 100 mi 0 50 100 km

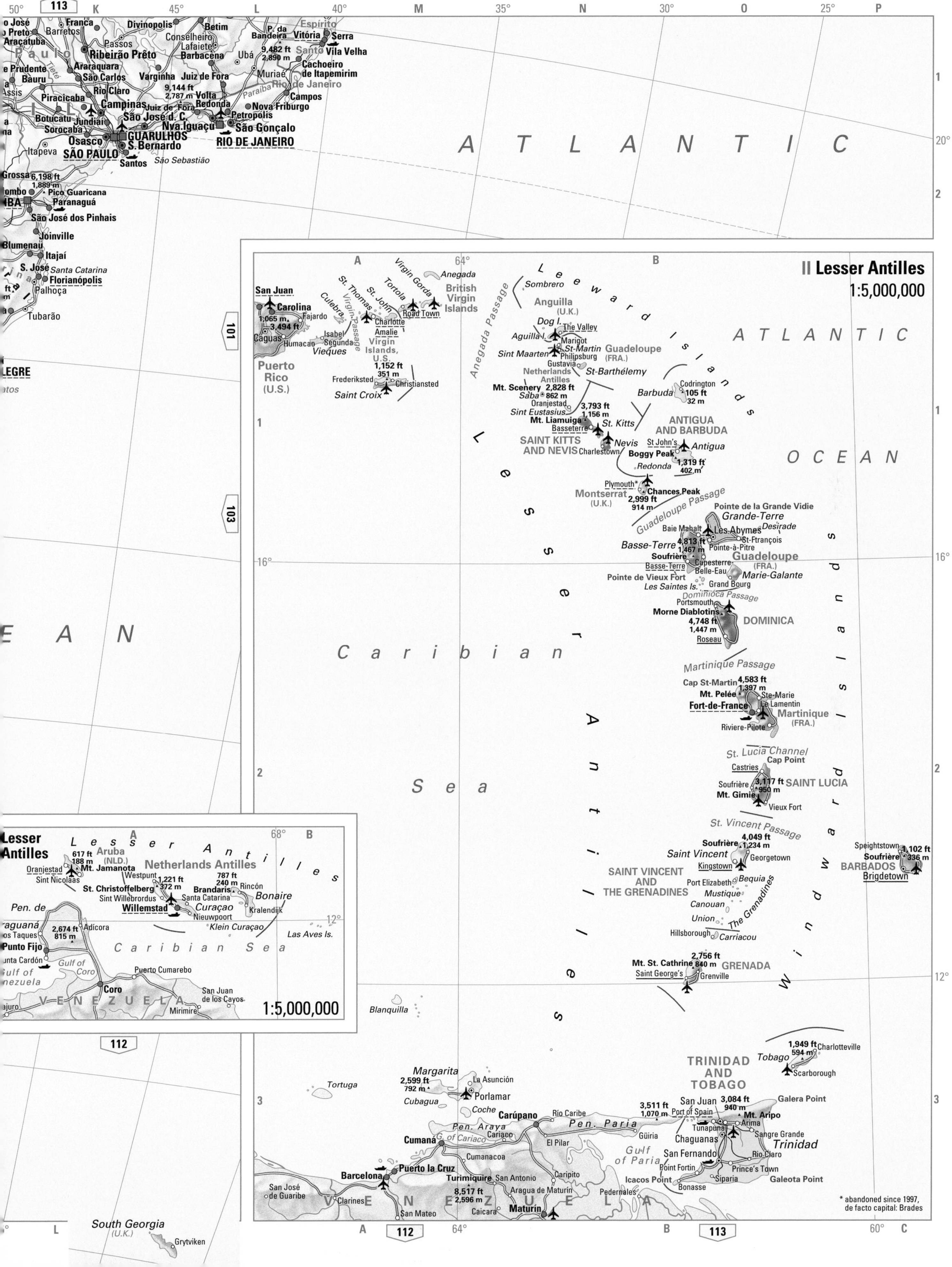

Almannagjá Canyon near Þingvellir, Iceland
Ural Mountains, Russia
Spitsbergen, Svalbard
Lake District, United Kingdom
Lac de Tignes, France
Vineyards, Moldova
Olive Grove near Córdoba, Spain
Florence, Italy
Hagia Sophia, İstanbul/Turkey
N
E
S
W
KLETT-PERTHE

0 200 400 600 mi
0 200 400 600 800 km
ARCTIC OCEAN
Nordostrundingen
Greenland
9,882 ft 3,012 m
King Frederik VIII Land
King Christian X Land
King Christian IX Land
Gunnbjørn Fjeld
12,139 ft 3,700 m
Tasiilaq
Ittoqqortoormiit
Qeqertarsuaq
Baffin
Franz Josef Land
C. Karlsen
Dikson
Taymyr Pen.
Putoran Mts.
5,581 ft 1,701 m
Noril'sk
Kara Sea
Gyda Pen.
Yamal Pen.
Gulf of Ob'
Yenisey
Novaya Zemlya
Kara Str.
Greenland Sea
Spitsbergen
Longyearbyen
5,617 ft 1,712 m
Barents Sea
Bear I.
Jan Mayen
7,470 ft 2,277 m
Denmark Strait
North Cape
Vadsø
Kolguyev I.
C. Kanin Nos
Kanin Pen.
Vorkuta
Salekhard
West Siberian Plain
Khanty-Mansiysk
Nar'yan-Mar
Narodnaya
6,217 ft 1,895 m
Pechora
Ural Mountains
Timan Ridge
Ukhta
Mezen'
Iceland
Reykjavík
Hekla
Vatnajökull
4,892 ft 1,491 m
6,952 ft 2,119 m
Norwegian Sea
12,864 ft 3,921 m
Arctic Circle
Tromsø
Lofoten
Bodø
Kebnekaise
6,926 ft 2,111 m
Lapland
Inari L.
Murmansk
Kola Pen.
3,908 ft 1,191 m
Kirovsk
Rovaniemi
White Sea
Arkhangel'sk
Severodvinsk
Luleå
Oulu
Onega
Vychegda
North. Dvina
Syktyvkar
Kotlas
Serov
Bereznik
Nizhniy Tagil
Yekaterinburg
Perm'
Chelyabinsk
Kama
Sukhona
North Russian Ridge
9,869 ft 3,008 m
Faroe Is.
Trondheim
Ålesund
7,500 ft 2,286 m
Jostedalsbreen
Norrland
Umeå
Gulf of Bothnia
Vaasa
Scandinavia
Karelia
L. Onega
Petrozavodsk
Kirov
Izhevsk
Vyatka
Shetland Is.
Orkney Is.
Rockall
Sognefjorden
Sundsvall
8,101 ft 2,469 m
Bergen
Tampere
Turku
Gävle
Helsinki
L. Ladoga
Vologda
Rybinsk Res.
Yoshkar-Ola
Kazan'
Naberezhnyye Chelny
Ufa
5,190 ft 1,582 m
Oslo
Svealand
Åland Is.
G. of Finland
St. Petersburg
Tallinn
Vel. Novgorod
Yaroslavl'
Ivanovo
Stavanger
Stockholm
Saaremaa
Peipus
Valday Hills
1,125 ft 343 m
Tver'
Volga
Nizhniy Novgorod
Ulyanovsk
Samara
Orenburg
British Isles
Hebrides
Ben Nevis
4,406 ft 1,343 m
Scotland
Aberdeen
Glasgow
Edinburgh
Kristiansand
Skagerrak
Göteborg
Norrköping
Götaland
North Sea
Kattegat
Jylland
Gotland
Riga
Western Dvina
Moscow
Vitsyebsk
Central Russian Upland
Volga Heights
1,152 ft 351 m
Oral
Ireland
Belfast
Newcastle
Dublin
Irish Sea
Great Britain
England
Manchester
Cork
Wales
3,415 ft 1,041 m
3,560 ft 1,085 m
Birmingham
Copenhagen
Malmö
Baltic Sea
Bornholm
Kaliningrad
Kaunas
Vilnius
Smolensk
Tula
Ryazan'
Penza
Tambov
Saratov
Orël
Ural
Land's End
Bristol
London
Greenw.
Amsterdam
Rotterdam
Bremen
Hamburg
Elbe
Gdańsk
Szczecin
Minsk
Bryansk
Voronezh
Kursk
Dnieper
Oka
English Channel
Channel Is.
Le Havre
Lille
Brussels
Düsseldorf
Cologne
Hannover
Poznań
Berlin
Leipzig
Dresden
Oder
Wrocław
Warsaw
Vistula
Łódź
Lublin
Brest
Pripyat Marshes
Homyel'
Kiev
Kharkiv
Zhytomyr
Volgograd
Don
Caspian Depression
Atyrau
-92 ft -28 m
Normandy
Brittany
Rennes
Paris
Seine
Meuse
Frankfurt
Ore Mts.
Sudetes
Prague
Bohemian Forest
Kraków
Volynia
Vinnytsya
Luhans'k
1,204 ft 367 m
Donets Plateau
Dnipropetrovs'k
Donets'k
Astrakhan'
Strasbourg
Stuttgart
Brno
Carpathian Mts.
8,711 ft 2,655 m
L'viv
Podilia
Dniester
Nantes
Loire
Burgundy
Dijon
Rhine
Danube
Vienna
Bratislava
Kryvyy Rih
Mariupol'
Rostov
Aqtau
Bay of Biscay
Munich
Jura Mts.
Berne
Mt. Blanc
Grossglockner
12,461 ft 3,798 m
Graz
Budapest
Gt. Hungarian Plain
Tisza
Iaşi
Chişinău
Mykolayiv
Sea of Azov
Kuban
Stavropol'
Caspian Sea
Makhachkala
C. Finisterre
Gijón
Bordeaux
6,185 ft 1,885 m
Lyon
15,772 ft 4,807 m
Alps
Massif Central
Milan
Ljubljana
Drava
Transylvania
Prut
Odesa
Crimea
Novorossiysk
Krasnodar
Groznyy
Vladikavkaz
Vigo
Cantabrian Mts.
Galicia
Bilbao
Toulouse
Turin
Venice
Zagreb
Timişoara
8,347 ft 2,544 m
Transylvanian A.
Galaţi
Sevastopol'
5,069 ft 1,545 m
Elbrus
Caucasus
18,511 ft 5,642 m
16,556 ft 5,047 m
Sochi
Baku
Kura
Porto
Valladolid
Old Castile
Ebro
Pyrenees
Montpellier
Provence
Genoa
Bologna
Sava
Dinaric Alps
Wallachia
Constanţa
Black Sea
Tbilisi
Gäncä
Zaragoza
Aragon
11,168 ft 3,404 m
Marseille
Nice
Ligurian Sea
Tuscany
Apennines
Adriatic Sea
Sarajevo
Belgrade
Bucharest
Serbia
Niš
Danube
Balkan Mts.
Varna
7,254 ft 2,211 m
Trabzon
Samsun
Yerevan
Ararat
16,946 ft 5,165 m
Tejo
Iberian Peninsula
8,504 ft 2,592 m
Madrid
Catalonia
Barcelona
8,878 ft 2,706 m
Corsica
Florence
9,554 ft 2,912 m
Montenegro
Musala
Sofia
9,597 ft 2,925 m
Bosporus
Pontine Mountains
Erzurum
Tabriz
New Castile
Valencia
Balearic Is.
Menorca
Rome
Tirana
Skopje
Thrace
İstanbul
Van
Seville
Córdoba
Andalusia
Murcia
Palma de M.
Mallorca
Ibiza
6,017 ft 1,834 m
Sardinia
Tyrrhenian Sea
Naples
Vesuvius
4,203 ft 1,281 m
Bari
Apulia
Balkan Pen.
Thessaloniki
Bursa
Ankara
Sivas
Kızılırmak
Orūmīyeh
Urmia
Málaga
Sa. Nevada
Mulhacén
11,424 ft 3,482 m
Strait of Gibraltar
Tanger
Ólympos
Áthos
6,670 ft 2,033 m
Pindus Mts.
9,571 ft 2,917 m
Eskişehir
Kayseri
Erciyes
Malatya
Diyarbakır
Kurdistan
Zagros Mts.
Tigris
Mediterranean Sea
9,472 ft 2,887 m
Cagliari
Calabria
Ionian Is.
Ionian Sea
8,061 ft 2,457 m
İzmir
Aegean Sea
Anatolia
Konya
12,851 ft 3,917 m
Şanlıurfa
Mosul
Kirkūk
Mesopotamia
Rabat
8,088 ft 2,465 m
Ar Rif
Algiers
Oran
Tell Atlas
'Annābah
Palermo
Str. of Sicily
Sicily
Etna
10,903 ft 3,323 m
Catania
Patras
Athens
Taurus Mts.
Gaziantep
Adana
Mersin
Euphrates
Kermānshāh
Fez
Oujda
Constantine
Tūnis
Peloponnese
7,897 ft 2,407 m
Antalya
Aleppo
Baghdād
Saharan Atlas
7,638 ft 2,328 m
High Atlas
Sousse
Malta
Lampedusa
Rhodes
Nicosia
6,408 ft 1,953 m
Cyprus
Ḥims
10,115 ft 3,083 m
Sfax
16,453 ft 5,015 m
Idi
8,058 ft 2,456 m
Crete
Beirut
Damascus
Syrian Desert
Al-Aghwāt
-98 ft -30 m
G. of Gabès
Jarbah
Béchar
9,233 ft 2,814 m
Amman
Jerusalem
-1,316 ft -401 m
Dead Sea
Tripoli
Mişrātah
2,874 ft 876 m
Benghazi
J. al-Akhdar
Gulf of Sirte
Surt
Tripolitania
Cyrenaica
10,981 ft 3,347 m
Port Said
Alexandria
An-Nafūd
Suez
Sinai Pen.
Elat
Ḥā'il
Buraydah
Giza
Cairo
8,652 ft 2,637 m
Tabūk
Sīwah
-436 ft -133 m
Al-Fayyūm
Al-Minyā
Red Sea
Elevation
2,000 m
1,000 m
500 m
200 m
100 m
0 m
Depression
656 ft
6,562 ft
13,124 ft
200 m
2,000 m
4,000 m
Inland ice, glaciers
Pack ice
Limit of drift ice
KLETT-PERTHES
60° A 50° B 40° C 30° D 20° E 10° F 0° G 10° H 20° J 30° K 40° L 50° M 60° N 70° O 80° P 90° Q 100°
H 20° J 30° K 40° L
3 4 5 6 7
60° 50° 40° 30°

1:25,000,000

0 500 1000 mi
0 500 1000 1500 km

ervice and Industry
Service center (finance, trade, research, government, tourism)
Other location
dustrial center
Metal processing, mechanical engineering, vehicle manufacturing, shipbuilding
Electronics industry, electrical and precision engineering
Textile, garment, and leather goods industries
Chemical, wood working, pulp and paper, printing industries
Food processing
Mining and Smelting
Energy raw material
Hard coal
Brown coal
Uranium
Petroleum
Natural gas
Oil refinery
Oil pipeline
Gas pipeline
Oil terminal embarkation
Hydro-electric power station
Nuclear power station (selection)
Ore and other raw materials
Iron ore
Chromite
Cobalt
Manganese
Nickel
Tungsten
Bauxite
Titanium
Copper
Lead/zinc
Tin
Gold
Silver
Platinum
Mercury
Gemstones
Graphite
Sulfur
Sodium chloride
Potassium
Phosphate
Smelting
Iron and steel production works
Non-ferrous metal production
Light metal (aluminum) production
Conurbation
Symbol size indicates relative importance of a location.
m. Amsterdam
nt. Antwerp
r. Bussels
ol. Cologne
n. Dnipropetrovs'k
r. Dresden
Florence
r. Frankfurt/Main
an. Hannover
u. Hunedoara
Ingolstadt
Krasnodar
Leeds
Ljubljana
lan. Manchester
.Ch. Naberezhnyye Chelny
lu. Nuremberg
i. Rijeka
o. Rotterdam
r. Trieste
ek. Yekaterinburg
Zaporizhzhya
ARCTIC OCEAN
Kara Sea
Barents Sea
Norwegian Sea
North Sea
ATLANTIC OCEAN
Mediterranean Sea
Black Sea
Caspian Sea
Red Sea
Arctic Circle
Spitsbergen
Longyearbyen
Svalbard (NOR.)
Faroe Is. (DEN.)
ICELAND
Reykjavík
UNITED KINGDOM
IRELAND
NORWAY
SWEDEN
FINLAND
RUSSIA
ESTONIA
LATVIA
LITHUANIA
BELARUS
UKRAINE
POL.
GER.
CZ.R.
SVK.
AUSTRIA
SWI.
HUNGARY
ROM.
MOL.
BUL.
FRANCE
SPAIN
ORTUGAL
ITALY
GREECE
TURKEY
KAZAKHSTAN
GEO.
ARM.
AZERBAIJAN
IRAN
IRAQ
SYR.
LEBANON
ISRAEL
JORDAN
CYPRUS
SAUDI ARABIA
EGYPT
LIBYA
TUNISIA
ALGERIA
MOROCCO
MALTA
DENMARK
NDL.
BGM.
LUX.
SVN.
CRO.
B. & H.
S. & M.
MAC.
ALB.
Moscow
St. Petersburg
London
Paris
Berlin
Warsaw
Kiev
Vienna
Prague
Budapest
Bucharest
Rome
Madrid
Lisbon
Istanbul
Ankara
Cairo
KLETT-PERTHES

1:25,000,000

0 200 400 600 mi
0 200 400 600 800 km

Europe: Ethnic Groups

1:25,000,000

0 200 400 600 mi
0 200 400 600 800 km

Languages Families and Ethnic Groups

Indo-European family
- Celtic group
- Romance group
- Germanic group
- Slavic group
- Balts
- Albanians
- Greeks
- Armenians
- Iranic group
- Gypsies
- Jews

Afro-Asiatic (Hamito-Semitic) family
- Semitic group

Uralic family
- Finno-Ugric group
- Samoyedes

Altaic family
- Turkic group
- Mongols

Caucasian family

Basques

- Very sparsely populated area
- Uninhabited area

Foreigners, refugees and job-migrants are not shown.

Ar.	*Aromani*
Arm.	*Armenians*
Ba.	*Balkars*
B.M.	*Bosnian Muslims*
Cat.	*Catalans*
Ga.	*Gagauz*
Ge.	*Germans*
Ing.	*Ingushes*
Kab.	*Kabardinians*
Kar.	*Karachays*
Mo.	*Montenegrins*
Ro.	*Rhaeto-Romanch*

KLETT-PERTHES

Europe: Climate

1:25,000,000

0 200 400 600 mi
0 200 400 600 800 km

Climate	Station	Altitude	Precipitation	Temperature
BS	Astrakhan'	−23 m −75 ft	216 mm 8.5 in.	10.0 °C 50.0 °F
Cr	A Coruña	67 m 220 ft	988 mm 38.9 in.	14.1 °C 57.4 °F
Cs	Rome	3 m 10 ft	758 mm 29.8 in.	15.4 °C 59.7 °F
Do	Paris	65 m 213 ft	639 mm 25.2 in.	10.6 °C 51.1 °F
Dc	Moscow	156 m 512 ft	688 mm 27.1 in.	5.0 °C 41.0 °F
Eo	Tromsø	10 m 33 ft	973 mm 38.3 in.	2.8 °C 37.0 °F
Ec	Arkhangel'sk	13 m 43 ft	545 mm 21.5 in.	0.8 °C 33.4 °F
FT	Longyearbyen	29 m 95 ft	183 mm 7.2 in.	−6.5 °C 20.3 °F

Climate Diagrams (by H. Walter)

- Precipitation curve
- Temperature curve
- Dry season

2,263 mm 25.0 °C / 89.1 in. 77.0 °F — Annual averages of precipitation and air temperature
1 3 6 9 12 — Months
3 m 10 ft — Altitude

Arctic Ocean, FI, Franz Josef Land, Longyearbyen, Spitsbergen, FT, Barents Sea, Novaya Zemlya, Bear I., Kara Str., Kolguyev I., Iceland, Norwegian Sea, Tromsø, Inari, Lofoten, Arctic Circle, Ec, Pechora, Ob', White Sea, Arkhangel'sk, Atlantic Ocean, Eo, Faroe Is., North. Dvina, Vychegda, Gulf of Bothnia, Sognefj., Shetland Is., Orkney Is., Rockall, British Isles, Hebrides, Do, L. Onega, Sukhona, Kama, Klarälven, L. Ladoga, Rybinsk Res., Vyatka, Åland Is., G. of Finland, Saaremaa, L. Peipus, Volga, North Sea, Skagerrak, Kattegat, Gotland, Baltic Sea, Moscow, Western Dvina, Irish Sea, Bornholm, Oka, Dc, Dnieper, Elbe, Ural, English Channel, Channel Is., Oder, Vistula, Don, BS, Paris, Seine, Meuse, Rhine, Astrakhan', Loire, Danube, Dniester, Cr, Bay of Biscay, A Coruña, Tisza, Sea of Azov, Kuban, Caspian Sea, FT, Prut, Drava, Sava, Ebro, Po, Ligurian Sea, Adriatic Sea, Black Sea, Kura, Aras, Tejo, Cs, Corsica, Rome, Bosporus, Kızılırmak, L. Van, L. Urmia, Balearic Is., Menorca, Ibiza, Mallorca, Sardinia, Tyrrhenian Sea, Strait of Gibraltar, Mediterranean Sea, Str. of Sicily, Sicily, Ionian Sea, Ionian Is., Aegean Sea, Euphrates, Tigris, Muluya, Malta, Lampedusa, Rhodes, Crete, Cyprus, G. of Gabès, Jarbah, BM, Gulf of Sirte, Dead Sea, BW, Red Sea

Climatic Regions (Modified Koeppen System based on Trewartha; cf. p. 18/19)

Polar Climates
- FI Perpetual frost climate
- FT Tundra climate

Boreal Climates
- Eo Oceanic boreal climate
- Ec Continental boreal climate

Temperate Climates
- Do Oceanic temperate climate
- Dc Continental temperate climate

Subtropical Climates
- Cr Subtropical rain climate
- Cs Subtropical winter rain climate

Dry Climates
- BS Steppe climate
- BW Desert climate
- BM Marine dry climate

• Meteorological station with climate diagram

KLETT-PERTHES

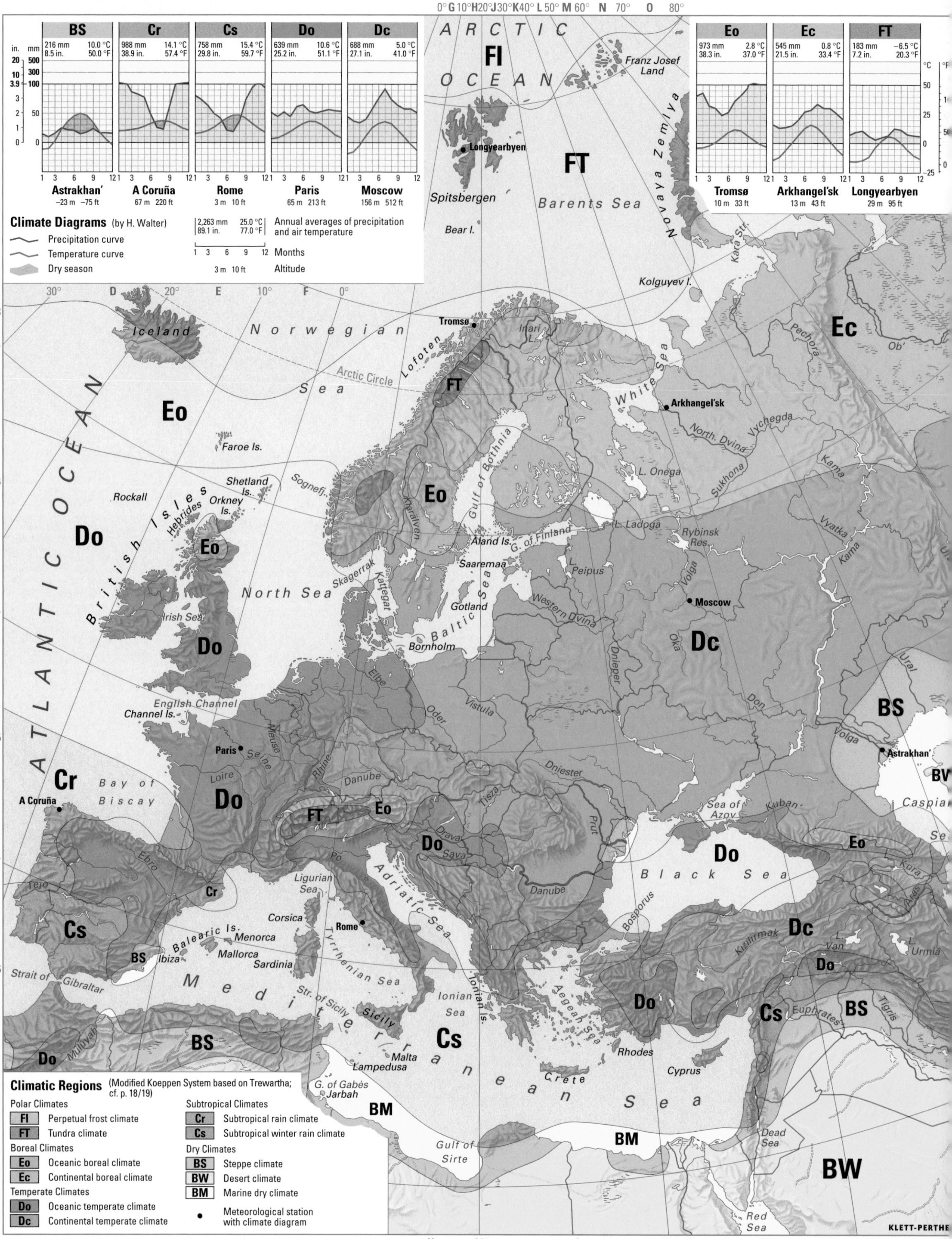

Europe: Tourism

1:18,000,000 — 0 200 400 mi / 0 200 400 600 km

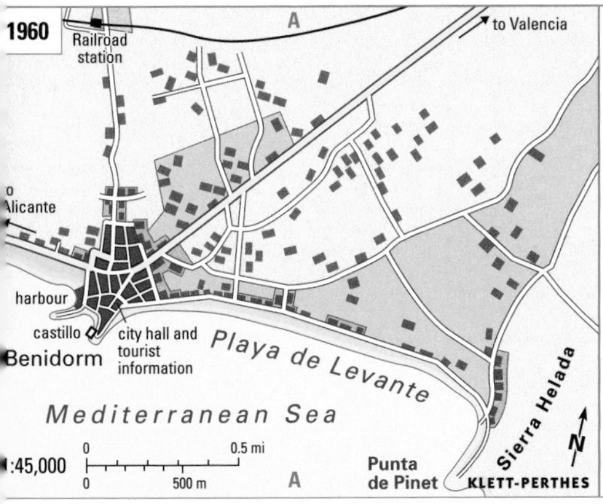

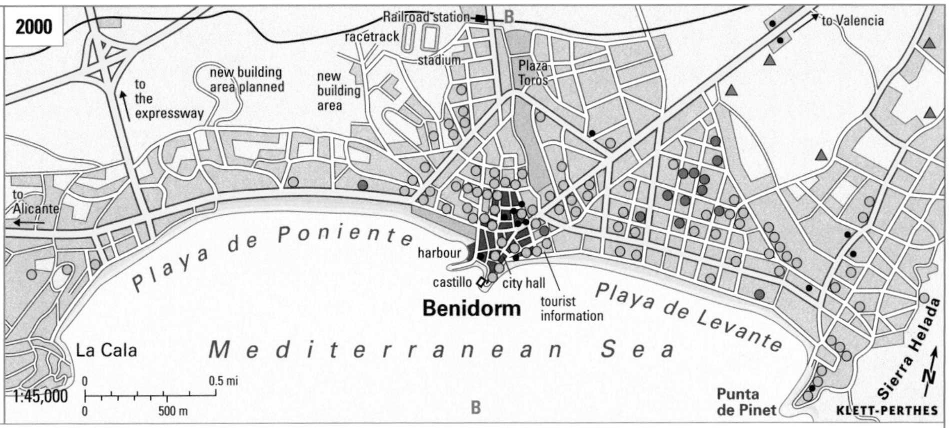

Benidorm 1960 and 2000

From a fishing village to a tourist city on the Costa Blanca

- Old village centre until 1952
- First hotels and guesthouses
- Houses outside the village centre (farmhouses, holiday villas)
- Sandy beach
- Built-up area (mainly hotels, guesthouses, restaurants, shops)
- Gardens
- Park
- Roads
- Hotel with grounds
- Apartment house
- Campsite
- Restaurant, nightclub, discotheque (selection)
- Railroad

1:5,000,000

0 50 100 mi
0 50 100 km
126
131
A B C D E F
9° 6° 3° 0° 3°
63° 57° 54° 51°
Faroe Islands
(DEN.)
2,894 ft
882 m
Slættaratindur
Fuglafjørður
Eysturoy
Klaksvík
Vágar
Miovágur
Streymoy
Tórshavn
Sandoy
Sandur
Skopunarfjørður
2,001 ft
610 m
Gluggarnir
Tvøroyri
Vagur
Suðuroy
ATLANTIC OCEAN
KLETT-PERTHES
ATLANTIC OCEAN
North Sea
UNITED KINGDOM
IRELAND
Northern Ireland
Scotland
Shetland Is.
Unst
Yell
1,476 ft
450 m
Mainland
Lerwick
Sumburgh
Sumburgh Head
Fair Isle
NORWAY
Bergen
Sotra
Osøyri
Bømlo
Haugesund
Karmøy
Skudeneshavn
Orkney Is.
Westray
Sanday
Stronsay
Mainland
Kirkwall
1,565 ft
477 m
Hoy
South Ronaldsay
Pentland Firth
Thurso
Wick
C. Wrath
Butt of Lewis
Outer Hebrides
Lewis
Stornoway
The Minch
2,621 ft
799 m
Rodel
St. Kilda
North Uist
Loch-maddy
Little Minch
Benbecula
South Uist
Lochboisdale
Castlebay
Barra
Sea of the Hebrides
Inner Hebrides
Skye
Portree
Kyle of Lochalsh
Mallaig
Rhum
Coll
Tiree
Mull
3,169 ft
966 m
Tobermory
Oban
Firth of Lorne
Lochgilphead
Jura
Islay
Port Ellen
Kintyre
Arran
Campbeltown
North West Highlands
Tongue
3,153 ft
961 m
Helmsdale
Golspie
Ullapool
Tain
Dingwall
Moray Firth
Inverness
Nairn
Elgin
Banff
Fraserburgh
Keith
Peterhead
Huntly
Spey
3,878 ft
1,182 m
Loch Ness
Fort Augustus
Grantown
Inverurie
Aberdeen
Kingussie
Ben Macdhui
4,298 ft
1,310 m
Dee
Ballater
Stonehaven
Spean Bridge
Ben Nevis
4,406 ft
1343 m
Fort William
Grampian Mountains
Pitlochry
Forfar
Montrose
Arbroath
Tay
Perth
Dundee
Crieff
Cupar
Stirling
Alloa
Kirkcaldy
Firth of Forth
Dunfermline
Falkirk
Dumbarton
Greenock
Rothesay
Paisley
Glasgow
Livingston
Edinburgh
Haddington
Berwick
East Kilbride
Hamilton
Duns
Peebles
Galashiels
Tweed
Kilmarnock
Selkirk
Newtown St. Boswells
Prestwick
Ayr
2,756 ft
840 m
2,677 ft
816 m
Alnwick
Firth of Clyde
Southern Uplands
Hawick
Morpeth
Blyth
Dumfries
Newcastle-upon-Tyne
South Shields
Sunderland
Tyne
Kirkcudbright
Stranraer
North Channel
Carlisle
2,930 ft
893 m
Durham
Hartlepool
Pennines
Penrith
Workington
Darlington
Middlesbrough
Whitehaven
Appleby
Stockton-on-Tees
Whitby
3,212 ft
979 m
Windermere
Tees
Ramsey
Snaefell
2,037 ft
621 m
Douglas
Isle of Man
(U.K.)
Kendal
Northallerton
1,490 ft
454 m
Scarborough
Barrow-in-Furness
Ripon
Bridlington
Flamborough Head
Lancaster
Driffield
Harrogate
York
Skipton
Beverley
Fleetwood
Blackburn
Bradford
Leeds
Kingston-upon-Hull
Blackpool
Preston
Wakefield
Scunthorpe
Southport
Bolton
Bury
Barnsley
Humber
Grimsby
St. Helens
Huddersfield
Doncaster
Liverpool
Rotherham
Louth
Birkenhead
Manchester
Sheffield
Lincoln
Chester
Stoke-on-Trent
Chesterfield
Skegness
Crewe
The Wash
Nottingham
Boston
Hunstanton
Cromer
Derby
Trent
Grantham
King's Lynn
Stafford
Oswestry
Shrewsbury
Walsall
Leicester
Norwich
Great Yarmouth
Welshpool
Wolverhampton
Sutton Coldfield
March
Lowestoft
Dudley
Peterborough
Thetford
Birmingham
Coventry
Diss
Rugby
Wellingborough
Ouse
Worcester
Northampton
Bedford
Cambridge
Ipswich
Hereford
Banbury
Milton Keynes
Harwich
Luton
Colchester
Cheltenham
Severn
Aylesbury
Harlow
Gloucester
Oxford
Watford
Chelmsford
Thames
Southend-on-Sea
Swindon
Slough
LONDON
Gillingham
Margate
Bristol
Reading
Canterbury
Bath
Trowbridge
Basingstoke
Woking
Dover
Crawley
Maidstone
Downs
Folkestone
Salisbury
Hastings
Southampton
Portsmouth
Brighton
Eastbourne
Poole
Bournemouth
Newport
Ventnor
Isle of Wight
Weymouth
Anglesey
Holyhead
Llangefni
Bangor
Caernarfon
Colwyn B.
Snowdon
3,560 ft
1,085 m
Mold
Pwllheli
Ffestiniog
Cambrian Mts
Wales
Cardigan Bay
Aberystwyth
Llandrindod Wells
Cardigan
Fishguard
Brecon
Carmarthen
Merthyr Tydfil
Milford Haven
Llanelli
Neath
Rhondda
Pembroke
Swansea
Newport
Port Talbot
Cardiff
Barry
Bristol Channel
Weston-super-Mare
Barnstaple
Taunton
Bideford
Tiverton
Cornwall
2,037 ft
621 m
Exeter
Yeovil
Newton Abbot
Plymouth
Torquay
Dartmouth
Truro
St. Austell
Penzance
Land's End
Falmouth
Lizard Pt.
Isles of Scilly
English Channel
Alderney
Cap de la Hague
Channel Is.
Cherbourg
St. Peter Port
Guernsey
(U.K.)
Sark
Barneville
St Hélier
Jersey
Baie de la Seine
FRANCE
Le Havre
Honfleur
Rouen
Seine
Fécamp
Bolbec
St-Valéry-en-Caux
Dieppe
Neufchâtel
Barentin
Le Tréport
St-Valéry
Abbeville
Somme
Amiens
705 ft
215 m
Albert
Poix
Montdidier
Beauvais
Compiègne
Soissons
Péronne
St-Quentin
Chauny
Laon
Berck
Arras
Boulogne
Calais
Dunkerque
St-Omer
Hazebrouck
Béthune
Lens
Douai
Lille
Roubaix
Tournai
Valenciennes
Cambrai
Strait of Dover
Flanders
BELGIUM
Kortrijk
Ghent
(Gent)
Bruges
(Brugge)
Ostend
(Oostende)
Terneuzen
Middelburg
NETHERLANDS
Irish Sea
St. George's Channel
Malin Head
Moville
Coleraine
2,467 ft
752 m
Errigal
Ballymoney
1,818 ft
554 m
Letterkenny
Londonderry
Ballymena
Lifford
Larne
Donegal
Lough Neagh
Newtonabbey
Cookstown
Bangor
Donegal Bay
Omagh
Dungannon
Belfast
Lisburn
Erris Head
Mullet Pen.
Sligo
Enniskillen
Lurgan
Downpatrick
Armagh
2,795 ft
852 m
Ballina
Ulster
Newry
Achill I.
Castlebar
Carrick
Cavan
Westport
Ballaghaderreen
Dundalk
2,687 ft
819 m
Longford
Connaught
Roscommon
Navan
Drogheda
Clifden
Tuam
Mullingar
Slyne Head
Lough Corrib
Athlone
Swords
Galway
Athenry
Blanchardstown
Dublin
Galway Bay
Tullamore
Tallaght
Dún Laoghaire
Leinster
Naas
Bray
Aran Is.
Portlaoise
3,038 ft
926 m
Wicklow
Wicklow Mts
Shannon
Ennis
Nenagh
Carlow
Kilkee
Kilrush
Kilkenny
Arklow
Limerick
Thurles
Barrow
Listowel
Munster
Tralee
Abbeyfeale
Tipperary
Enniscorthy
Clonmel
New Ross
Wexford
Cahir
Slea Head
Dingle
Kanturk
2,599 ft
792 m
Carrantuohill
Killarney
Mallow
Suir
Waterford
Rosslare Harbour
Tramore
3,415 ft
1,041 m
Dungarvan
Cork
Youghal
Clonakilty
Bantry
Mizen Head
KLETT-PERTHES

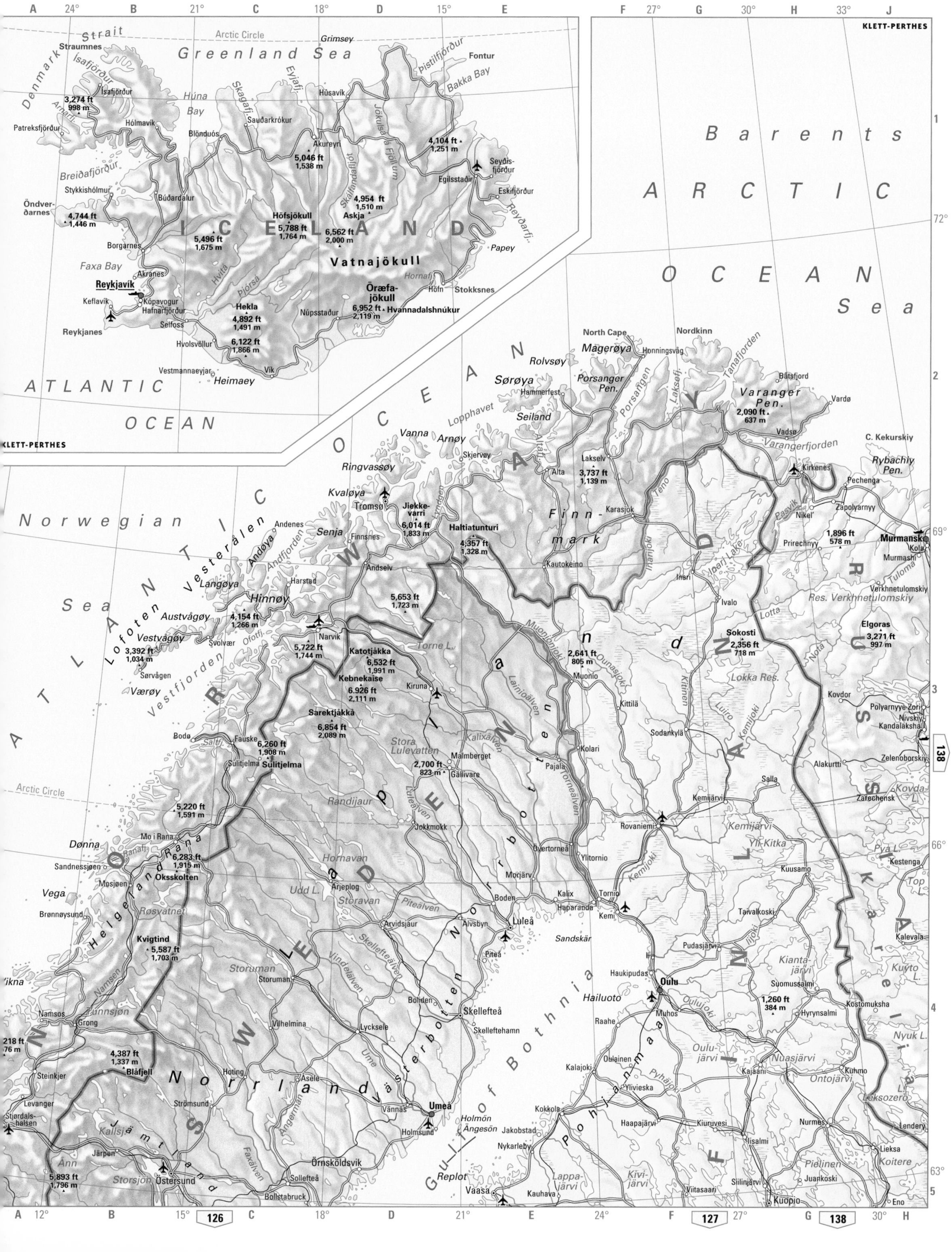
KLETT-PERTHES
Greenland Sea
Denmark Strait
Arctic Circle
Straumnes
Ísafjörður
Grimsey
Fontur
Bakka Bay
Þistilfjörður
Húsavík
Húna Bay
Skagafj.
Eyjafj.
Hólmavík
Sauðarkrókur
Patreksfjörður
Blönduós
Akureyri
4,104 ft 1,251 m
5,046 ft 1,538 m
Seyðisfjörður
Egilsstaðir
Eskifjörður
Breiðafjörður
Stykkishólmur
Búðardalur
Öndverðarnes
4,744 ft 1,446 m
Höfsjökull
5,788 ft 1,764 m
4,954 ft 1,510 m
Askja
6,562 ft 2,000 m
ICELAND
5,496 ft 1,675 m
Borgarnes
Papey
Vatnajökull
Faxa Bay
Akranes
Reykjavík
Keflavík
Kópavogur
Hafnarfjörður
Öræfajökull
Höfn
Stokksnes
Hekla 4,892 ft 1,491 m
Núpsstaður
6,952 ft 2,119 m
Hvannadalshnúkur
Reykjanes
Selfoss
Hvolsvöllur
6,122 ft 1,866 m
Vestmannaeyjar
Heimaey
Vík
ATLANTIC OCEAN
Barents Sea
ARCTIC OCEAN
North Cape
Nordkinn
Magerøya
Honningsvåg
Rolvsøy
Sørøya
Hammerfest
Porsanger Pen.
Båtsfjord
Varanger Pen.
2,090 ft 637 m
Vardø
Seiland
Loppavet
Vanna
Arnøy
Vadsø
Varangerfjorden
C. Kekurskiy
Skjervøy
Ringvassøy
Lakselv
Alta
3,737 ft 1,139 m
Kirkenes
Rybachiy Pen.
Pechenga
Kvaløya
Tromsø
Jiekkevarri
6,014 ft 1,833 m
Karasjok
Finnmark
Zapolyarnyy
Nikel'
Norwegian Sea
Andenes
Vesterålen
Andøya
Senja
Finnsnes
Haltiatunturi
4,357 ft 1,328 m
Prirechnyy
1,896 ft 578 m
Murmansk
Kola
Murmashi
Kautokeino
Andselv
Harstad
Langøya
Hinnøy
Inari
Inarijärvi
Verkhnetulomskiy
Res. Verkhnetulomskiy
Tuloma
Austvågøy
4,154 ft 1,266 m
5,653 ft 1,723 m
Ivalo
Lofoten
Vestvågøy
Svolvær
Narvik
5,722 ft 1,744 m
Torne L.
Lotta
Sokosti 2,356 ft 718 m
Elgoras 3,271 ft 997 m
3,392 ft 1,034 m
Katotjåkka 6,532 ft 1,991 m
Kebnekaise 6,926 ft 2,111 m
2,641 ft 805 m
Muonio
Lokka Res.
Sørvågen
Værøy
Vestfjorden
Kiruna
Kittilä
Kovdor
Polyarnyye Zori
Nivskiy
Kandalaksha
Sarektjåkkå 6,854 ft 2,089 m
Sodankylä
Bodø
Saltfj.
Fauske
6,260 ft 1,908 m
Sulitjelma
Stora Lulevatten
Malmberget
Kolari
Pajala
2,700 ft 823 m
Gällivare
Alakurtti
Zelenoborskiy
Salla
Arctic Circle
5,220 ft 1,591 m
Randijaur
Kemijärvi
Zarechensk
Kovda
Rovaniemi
Mo i Rana
Dønna
Jokkmokk
Övertorneå
Ylitornio
Yli-Kitka
Pya L.
Kestenga
Sandnessjøen
6,283 ft 1,915 m
Oksskolten
Hornavan
Kuusamo
Mosjøen
Vega
Morjärv
Top
Udd L.
Arjeplog
Storavan
Boden
Kalix
Tornio
Haparanda
Kemi
Brønnøysund
Røsvatnet
Piteälven
Taivalkoski
Arvidsjaur
Älvsbyn
Luleå
Sandskär
Kvigtind 5,587 ft 1,703 m
Helgeland
Piteå
Pudasjärvi
Kalevala
Kiantajärvi
Storuman
Haukipudas
Oulu
Kuyto L.
Vikna
Suomussalmi
Hailuoto
Namsen
Boliden
Skellefteå
Muhos
1,260 ft 384 m
Kostomuksha
Hyrynsalmi
Namsos
Tunnsjøen
Grong
Vilhelmina
Lycksele
Skelleftehamn
Raahe
Oulujoki
Oulujärvi
Nyuk L.
4,387 ft 1,337 m
Bläfjell
Hoting
Norrland
Gulf of Bothnia
Kalajoki
Oulainen
Pyhäjoki
Nuasjärvi
Kajaani
Kuhmo
Ontojärvi
Steinkjer
Asele
Västerbotten
Ylivieska
Leksozero
Levanger
Strömsund
Vännäs
Umeå
Kokkola
Kiuruvesi
Nurmes
Lendery
Stjørdalshalsen
Jämtland
Holmön
Ängesön
Jakobstad
Haapajärvi
Iisalmi
Lieksa
Koitere
Kallsjä
Järpen
Nykarleby
Pohjanmaa
Ånn
Faxälven
Örnsköldsvik
Pielinen
5,893 ft 1,796 m
Storsjön
Östersund
Sollefteå
Replot
Lappajärvi
Kivijärvi
Siilinjärvi
Juankoski
Bollstabruck
Vaasa
Kauhava
Viitasaari
Kuopio
Eno
NORWAY
SWEDEN
FINLAND
RUSSIA
Karelia
Lapland
Barents
A B C D E F G H J
24° 21° 18° 15° 27° 30° 33°
72° 69° 66° 63°
12° 15° 18° 21° 24° 27° 30°
1 2 3 4 5
126 127 138

KLETT-PERTHES
125
124
128
ATLANTIC
OCEAN
North
Sea
German
Bight
Skagerrak
Kattegat
Baltic
Gulf of Bothnia
NORWAY
SWEDEN
DENMARK
GERMANY
POLAND
NETHERLANDS
Norrland
Jämtland
Härjedalen
Hälsingland
Svealand
Götaland
Småland
Skåne
Ångermanland
Västerbotten
Telemark
Jylland
Fyn
Sjælland
Hardanger-vidda
Jotunheimen
Jostedalsbreen
Oslo
Stockholm
COPENHAGEN (KØBENHAVN)
Bergen
Trondheim
Stavanger
Kristiansand
Göteborg
Malmö
Helsingborg
Norrköping
Linköping
Jönköping
Örebro
Västerås
Uppsala
Gävle
Falun
Karlstad
Östersund
Sundsvall
Ålborg
Århus
Odense
Esbjerg
Kiel
Lübeck
HAMBURG
Bremerhaven
Rostock
Schwerin
Stralsund
Greifswald
Gdańsk
Gdynia
Elbląg
Koszalin
Kaliningrad
Groningen
Oldenburg
Bornholm
Gotland
Öland
Åland Is.
Rügen
Fehmarn
Lolland
Falster
Møn
Samsø
Læsø
Anholt
Orust
Tjörn
Frøya
Hitra
Smøla
Sotra
Bømlo
Karmøy
Radøy
Indre Solund
Bremanger-landet
Gurskøy
North Frisian Is.
East Frisian Is.
West Frisian Is.
Heligoland
Sylt
Rømø
Vänern
Vättern
Mälaren
Hjälmaren
Siljan
Storsjön
Mjøsa
Femunden
Tyrifjorden
Sognefjorden
Hardangerfjorden
Nordfjord
Trondheimsfj.
Oslofjorden
Pomeranian Bay
Gdańsk Bay
Galdhøpiggen 8,101 ft 2,469 m
Glittertind 8,088 ft 2,465 m
Jostedalsbreen 6,834 ft 2,083 m
Snøhetta 7,500 ft 2,286 m
Gausta 6,178 ft 1,883 m
Blåfjell 4,387 ft 1,337 m
5,893 ft 1,796 m
6,106 ft 1,861 m
4,771 ft 1,454 m
3,100 ft 945 m
2,218 ft 676 m
915 ft 279 m
741 ft 226 m
568 ft 173 m Yding Skovhøj
469 ft 143 m
532 ft 162 m
528 ft 161 m C. Arkona
1,079 ft 329 m
Lindesnes
Skagen
Gotska Sandön
Fårö

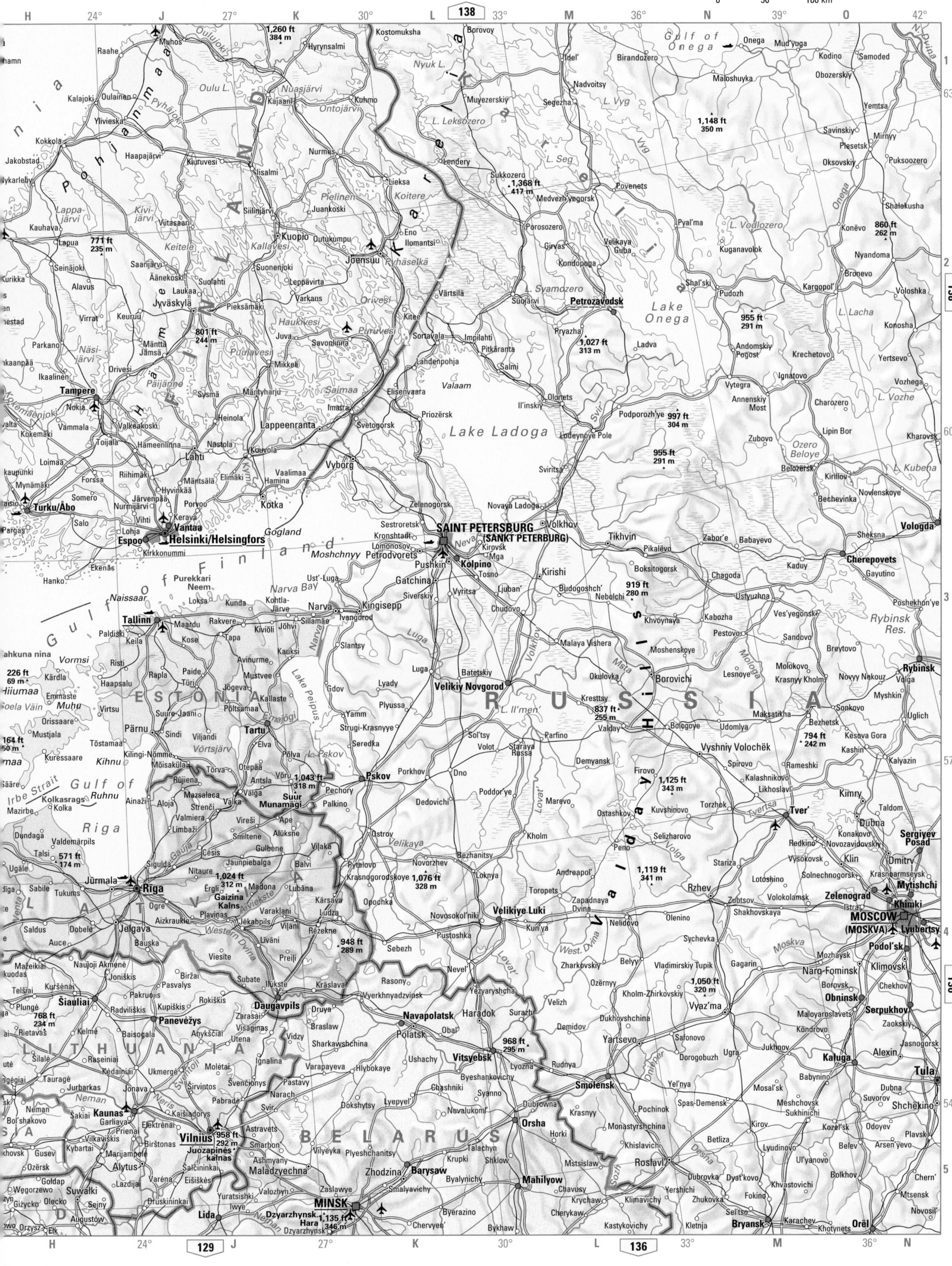
138
136
129
Gulf of Onega
Lake Onega
Lake Ladoga
Gulf of Finland
Gulf of Riga
FINLAND
ESTONIA
LATVIA
LITHUANIA
BELARUS
RUSSIA
Karelia
Valday Hills
Saint Petersburg (Sankt Peterburg)
Helsinki/Helsingfors
Vantaa
Espoo
Turku/Åbo
Tampere
Lahti
Kouvola
Kotka
Hamina
Lappeenranta
Imatra
Vyborg
Mikkeli
Savonlinna
Joensuu
Kuopio
Jyväskylä
Iisalmi
Kajaani
Kuhmo
Nurmes
Lieksa
Kostomuksha
Petrozavodsk
Segezha
Medvezh'yegorsk
Kondopoga
Sortavala
Priozërsk
Tallinn
Narva
Tartu
Pärnu
Rakvere
Paide
Viljandi
Võru
Valga
Pskov
Velikiy Novgorod
Luga
Gatchina
Kolpino
Pushkin
Kirishi
Tikhvin
Volkhov
Cherepovets
Vologda
Rybinsk
Tver'
Torzhok
Rzhev
Vyshniy Volochëk
Borovichi
Velikiye Luki
Nevel'
Riga
Jūrmala
Jelgava
Daugavpils
Rēzekne
Šiauliai
Panevėžys
Kaunas
Vilnius
Alytus
Navapolatsk
Polatsk
Vitsyebsk
Orsha
Barysaw
Minsk
Mahilyow
Smolensk
Roslavl'
Bryansk
Kaluga
Obninsk
Serpukhov
Tula
Moscow (Moskva)
Zelenograd
Khimki
Mytishchi
Lyubertsy
Podol'sk
Sergiyev Posad
Onega
Kargopol'
Lake Peipus
Western Dvina
Neman
Dnieper
Volga
Svir'
Neva
Moskva
Suur Munamägi 1,043 ft 318 m
Gaizina Kalns 1,024 ft 312 m
Juozapinės kalnas 958 ft 292 m
Dzyarzhynsk. Hara 1,135 ft 346 m

KLETT-PERTHES
0°
A
3°
B
6°
C
9°
D
12°
126
E
15°
124
131
132
North Sea
German Bight
Heligoland
Kattegat
Jylland
DENMARK
SWEDEN
Århus
Yding Skovhøj
Samsø
Fyn
Sjælland
COPENHAGEN (KØBENHAVN)
Helsingborg
Malmö
Lund
Kristianstad
Karlskrona
Bornholm
Rønne
Nexø
Lolland
Falster
Møn
Fehmarn
Rügen
C. Arkona
Pomeranian Bay
Esbjerg
Odense
Kolding
Vejle
Horsens
Billund
Skjern
Herning
Silkeborg
Randers
Viborg
Holstebro
Ringkøbing
Skive
Grenå
Halmstad
Nybro
Kalmar
Emmaboda
Karlshamn
Ronneby
Simrishamn
Ystad
Trelleborg
Helsingør
Hillerød
Roskilde
Køge
Næstved
Slagelse
Korsør
Nyborg
Svendborg
Langeland
Nakskov
Nykøbing
Rødby
Gedser
Sassnitz
Haderslev
Åbenrå
Sønderborg
Tønder
Ribe
Westerland
Sylt
Rømø
North Frisian Is.
Schleswig
Flensburg
Husum
Rendsburg
Eckernförde
Kiel
Holstein
Neumünster
Plön
Heide
Itzehoe
Bad Segeberg
Lübeck
Wismar
Rostock
Stralsund
Greifswald
Barth
Bergen
Bad Doberan
Neustadt
Usedom
Wolin
Świnoujście
Kołobrzeg
Darłowo
Kamień Pomorski
Gryfice
Płoty
Świdwin
Goleniów
Szczecin
Stargard Szczeciński
Pomerania
West Frisian Is.
East Frisian Is.
Texel
Borkum
Norderney
Emden
Wilhelmshaven
Cuxhaven
Bremerhaven
Elmshorn
Norderstedt
HAMBURG
Stade
Bremervörde
Schwerin
Mecklenburg-Westpomerania
Parchim
Waren
Neubrandenburg
Güstrow
Demmin
Anklam
Malchin
Pasewalk
Neustrelitz
Prenzlau
Templin
Schwedt
Wittstock
Neuruppin
Angermünde
Eberswalde
Groningen
Leeuwarden
Heerenveen
Assen
Den Helder
Alkmaar
Hoorn
NETHERLANDS
Emmen
Meppel
Zwolle
Amsterdam
Haarlem
Lelystad
Almere
Leiden
The Hague ('s-Gravenhage)
Delft
Utrecht
Amersfoort
Ede
Deventer
Almelo
Enschede
Apeldoorn
Rotterdam
Dordrecht
Nijmegen
Arnhem
Middelburg
Bergen
Breda
's-Hertogenbosch
Tilburg
Eindhoven
Venlo
Papenburg
Oldenburg
Delmenhorst
Bremen
Cloppenburg
Meppen
Lingen
Nordhorn
Rheine
Vechta
Diepholz
Nienburg
Verden
Walsrode
Soltau
Lüneburg
Lüneburger Heide
Uelzen
Dannenberg
Wittenberge
Celle
Salzwedel
Stendal
Gardelegen
Rathenow
Nauen
Brandenburg
Potsdam
BERLIN
Frankfurt
Słubice
Lower Saxony
Hannover
Wolfsburg
Braunschweig
Salzgitter
Hildesheim
Hameln
Minden
Osnabrück
Bielefeld
Gütersloh
Detmold
Münster
Coesfeld
Bocholt
Wesel
Recklinghausen
Lünen
Hamm
Lippstadt
Soest
Paderborn
Gelsenkirchen
Bochum
Dortmund
Moers
Duisburg
Krefeld
Essen
Hagen
Wuppertal
Neuss
Düsseldorf
Mönchengladbach
Ruhr
North Rhine-Westphalia
Cologne (Köln)
Leverkusen
Gummersbach
Aachen
Düren
Bonn
Siegen
Euskirchen
Arnsberg
Marburg
Magdeburg
Wolfenbüttel
Oschersleben
Schönebeck
Halberstadt
Wernigerode
Goslar
Brocken
Harz
Quedlinburg
Köthen
Dessau
Wittenberg
Jüterbog
Luckenwalde
Lübbenau
Cottbus
Guben
Eisenhüttenstadt
Finsterwalde
Göttingen
Nordhausen
Sangerhausen
Sondershausen
Eisleben
Aschersleben
Halle
Bitterfeld
Torgau
Leipzig
Hoyerswerda
Riesa
Großenhain
Weißwasser
Kassel
Hann. Münden
Korbach
Eschwege
Mühlhausen
Merseburg
Weißenfels
Sömmerda
Fritzlar
Eisenach
Gotha
Erfurt
Weimar
Jena
Gera
Altenburg
Meißen
Radebeul
Dresden
Pirna
Bautzen
Görlitz
Zittau
Bad Hersfeld
Alsfeld
Waltershausen
Arnstadt
Thuringia
Thüringer Wald
Glauchau
Chemnitz
Freiberg
Zwickau
Saxony
Saalfeld
Schleiz
Suhl
Meiningen
Ore Mts.
Aue
Plauen
Děčín
Ústí n. L.
Teplice
Most
Chomutov
Klínovec
Liberec
Jablonec
Jelenia Góra
Wałbrzych
Sněžka
Trutnov
Sudety
Gießen
Wetzlar
Fulda
Hesse
Friedberg
Schlüchtern
Bad Neustadt
Coburg
Kronach
Kulmbach
Hof
Selb
Bayreuth
Bamberg
Schweinfurt
Aschaffenburg
Gemünden
Würzburg
Erlangen
Fürth
Nuremberg (Nürnberg)
Ansbach
Weiden
Schwandorf
Amberg
Cheb
Karlovy Vary
Mariánské Lázně
Tachov
Rakovník
Kladno
PRAGUE (PRAHA)
Beroun
Kolín
Pardubice
Čáslav
Havlíčkův Brod
Jihlava
Plzeň
Rokycany
Příbram
Domažlice
Klatovy
Písek
Tábor
Pelhřimov
Strakonice
Vimperk
České Budějovice
Jindřichův Hradec
CZECH REPUBLIC
Bohemian Forest
Gr. Arber
Moravian Hts.
Regensburg
Kelheim
Deggendorf
Straubing
Landshut
Dingolfing
Passau
Ingolstadt
Neuburg
Pfaffenhofen
Neumarkt
Koblenz
Neuwied
Limburg
Bad Homburg
Frankfurt
Hanau
Offenbach
Wiesbaden
Mainz
Rüsselsheim
Darmstadt
Worms
Mannheim
Ludwigshafen
Heidelberg
Speyer
Neustadt
Heilbronn
Karlsruhe
Pforzheim
Stuttgart
Esslingen
Göppingen
Schwäbisch Hall
Baden-Baden
Strasbourg
Kehl
Offenburg
Freiburg
Tübingen
Reutlingen
Sindelfingen
Heidenheim
Aalen
Nördlingen
Donauwörth
Dillingen
Augsburg
Ulm
Neu-Ulm
Biberach
Memmingen
Kaufbeuren
Kempten
Landsberg
Starnberg
MUNICH (MÜNCHEN)
Dachau
Freising
Mühldorf
Rosenheim
Bad Tölz
Chiemsee
Traunstein
Salzburg
Baden-Württemberg
Black Forest
Feldberg
Villingen-Schwenningen
Ravensburg
Friedrichshafen
Konstanz
Lindau
Bregenz
Lake Constance
Bavaria
Bavarian Alps
Zugspitze
Garmisch-Partenkirchen
Watzmann
Berchtesgaden
Hoher Dachstein
Linz
Wels
Steyr
Upper Austria
Braunau
Vöcklabruck
Gmunden
Bad Ischl
Amstetten
St. Pölten
VIENNA (WIEN)
Wiener Neustadt
Lower Austria
Mürzzuschlag
Leoben
Kapfenberg
Graz
Fürstenfeld
Knittelfeld
Bischofshofen
Eisenerz
Liezen
Zell am See
Innsbruck
Schwaz
Kufstein
Imst
Lienz
Grossglockner
Badgastein
Spittal
Villach
Klagenfurt
St. Veit
Wolfsberg
Carinthia
Karawanken
Maribor
Triglav
Julian Alps
Jesenice
Kranj
Ljubljana
Celje
Novo Mesto
Zagreb
Samobor
Trieste
Gorizia
Nova Gorica
Postojna
Karst
Snežnik
Pivka
Bruxelles
Brussels (Brussel / Bruxelles)
Antwerp (Antwerpen)
Ghent (Gent)
Bruges (Brugge)
Ostend (Oostende)
St.-Niklaas
Mechelen
Leuven
Wavre
Hasselt
Genk
Maastricht
Heerlen
Liège (Luik)
Namur
Charleroi
Mons
Tournai
Kortrijk
Flanders
Flemish Region
BELGIUM
Walloon Region
Ardennes
Vaalserberg
Signal de Botrange
Dinant
Bastogne
Arlon
LUXEMBOURG
Luxembourg
Diekirch
Esch-sur-Alzette
Differdange
Trier
Wittlich
Cochem
Prüm
Bad Kreuznach
Idar-Oberstein
Kaiserslautern
Homburg
Pirmasens
Zweibrücken
Saarbrücken
Saarland
Saarlouis
Palatinate
Rhineland-Palatinate
Calais
Dunkerque
Dover
Strait of Dover
Margate
Harwich
Ipswich
Norwich
Great Yarmouth
Lowestoft
Cromer
Diss
UNITED KINGDOM
St-Omer
Boulogne
Hazebrouck
Lille
Roubaix
Lens
Béthune
Douai
Arras
Valenciennes
Cambrai
Abbeville
St-Valéry
Berck
Amiens
Albert
Péronne
St-Quentin
Guise
Hirson
Fourmies
Chauny
Laon
Soissons
Compiègne
Creil
Beauvais
Montdidier
Noyon
Charleville-Mézières
Sedan
Rethel
Reims
Épernay
Châlons-en-Champagne
Verdun
Metz
Thionville
Forbach
St-Avold
Sarreguemines
Nancy
Pont-à-Mousson
Commercy
St-Mihiel
Bar-le-Duc
Vitry-le-François
Lorraine
Champagne
Haguenau
Sarrebourg
Sélestat
Colmar
Mulhouse
St-Dié
Épinal
Remiremont
Luxeuil-les-Bains
Vosges
Grand Ballon
Belfort
Montbéliard
Lure
Vesoul
Besançon
Dole
Dijon
Beaune
Chalon
Autun
Le Creusot
Mâcon
Bourg-en-Bresse
Lons-le-Saunier
Pontarlier
Jura Mts.
PARIS
Nanterre
Versailles
Créteil
Meaux
Fontainebleau
Provins
Étampes
Nemours
Pithiviers
Sens
Troyes
Romilly
Bar-s.-Aube
Bar-s.-S.
Chaumont
Langres
Joinville
Neufchâteau
St-Dizier
Auxerre
Tonnerre
Châtillon
Les Riceys
Montbard
Clamecy
Cosne
La Charité
Nevers
Gien
Briare
Saulieu
Moulins
Commentry
Digoin
Tournus
Roanne
Vichy
Riom
Clermont-Ferrand
Thiers
Ambert
Issoire
Neussargues Moissac
St-Flour
Le Puy
Montbrison
St-Étienne
St-Chamond
Firminy
Annonay
Feurs
Tarare
Villefranche
Lyon
Villeurbanne
Vienne
Romans
Grenoble
Voiron
Chambéry
Aix-les-Bains
Annecy
Annemasse
Thonon-les-Bains
Geneva (Genève)
Lake Geneva
Lausanne
Montreux
Yverdon
Neuchâtel
La Chaux-de-Fonds
Solothurn
Biel
Bern
Fribourg
Thun
Interlaken
Sarnen
Luzern
Zug
Schwyz
Altdorf
Glarus
Olten
Aarau
Basel
Liestal
Lörrach
Zürich
Winterthur
Frauenfeld
Schaffhausen
Herisau
Appenzell
St. Gallen
Vaduz
Feldkirch
Vorarlberg
Chur
Davos
St. Moritz
Bernina
Chiavenna
Sion
Brig
Zermatt
Matterhorn
Dufourspitze
Mt. Blanc
Chamonix
Martigny
Albertville
Aosta
Gran Paradiso
Bourg-St-Maurice
Val-d'Isère
Modane
Ceres
Ivrea
Biella
Borgosesia
Vercelli
Novara
Varese
Como
Lecco
Bergamo
Brescia
Monza
MILAN (MILANO)
Lugano
Locarno
Bellinzona
Domodossola
Verbania
L. Maggiore
L. Como
Sondrio
Bormio
Ortles
Male
Merano
Bozen / Bolzano
Brixen
Bruneck
Mals
Sterzing
Brenner
Similaun
Cortina d'Ampezzo
Pieve di Cadore
Dolomites
Marmolada
Mezzolombardo
Trient / Trento
Rovereto
Feltre
Belluno
Vittorio
Pordenone
Spilimbergo
Gemona
Udine
Tolmin
Conegliano
Bassano
Castelfranco
Treviso
Portogruaro
Verona
Vicenza
Garda
Desenzano
Treviglio
Schio
Riva
S. Dona
Bergamo Alps
Bernese Alps
Rhaetian Alps
Jungfrau
Rhine
Danube
Elbe
Main
Moselle
Meuse
Marne
Seine
Aube
Oise
Somme
Aisne
Saône
Loire
Rhône
Doubs
Isère
Ain
Allier
Inn
Isar
Lech
Enns
Mur
Drau
Sava
Adige
Piave
Oder
Spree
Havel
Saale
Fulda
Weser
Ems
Aller
Vltava
Ohře
SWITZERLAND
AUSTRIA
ITALY
FRANCE
GERMANY
POLAND
SLOVENIA
Zielona Góra
Nowa Sól
Żary
Żagań
Lubsko
Krosno Odrz.
Gubin
Świebodzin
Sulechów
Międzyrzecz
Gorzów Wielkopolski
Kostrzyn
Seelow
Skwierzyna
Dębno
Barlinek
Choszczno
Pyrzyce
Myślibórz
Chojna
Lubin
Legnica
Bolesławiec
Zgorzelec
Jawor
Głogów
Lower Austria
Krems
Styria
Salzburg
Tyrol
Tauern
Windisch

127

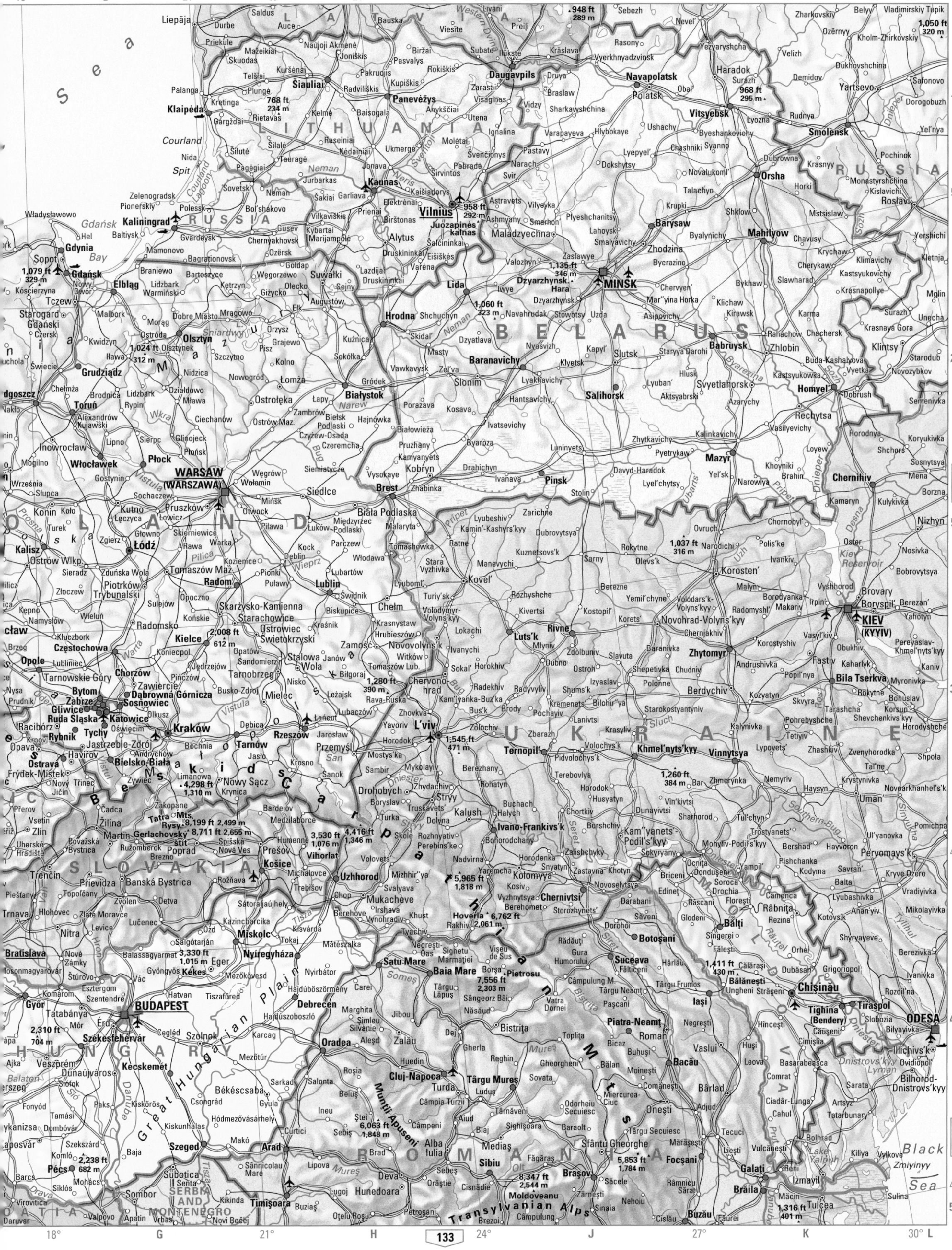

136
134
133

130 Spain and Portugal

0 50 100 mi
0 50 100 km

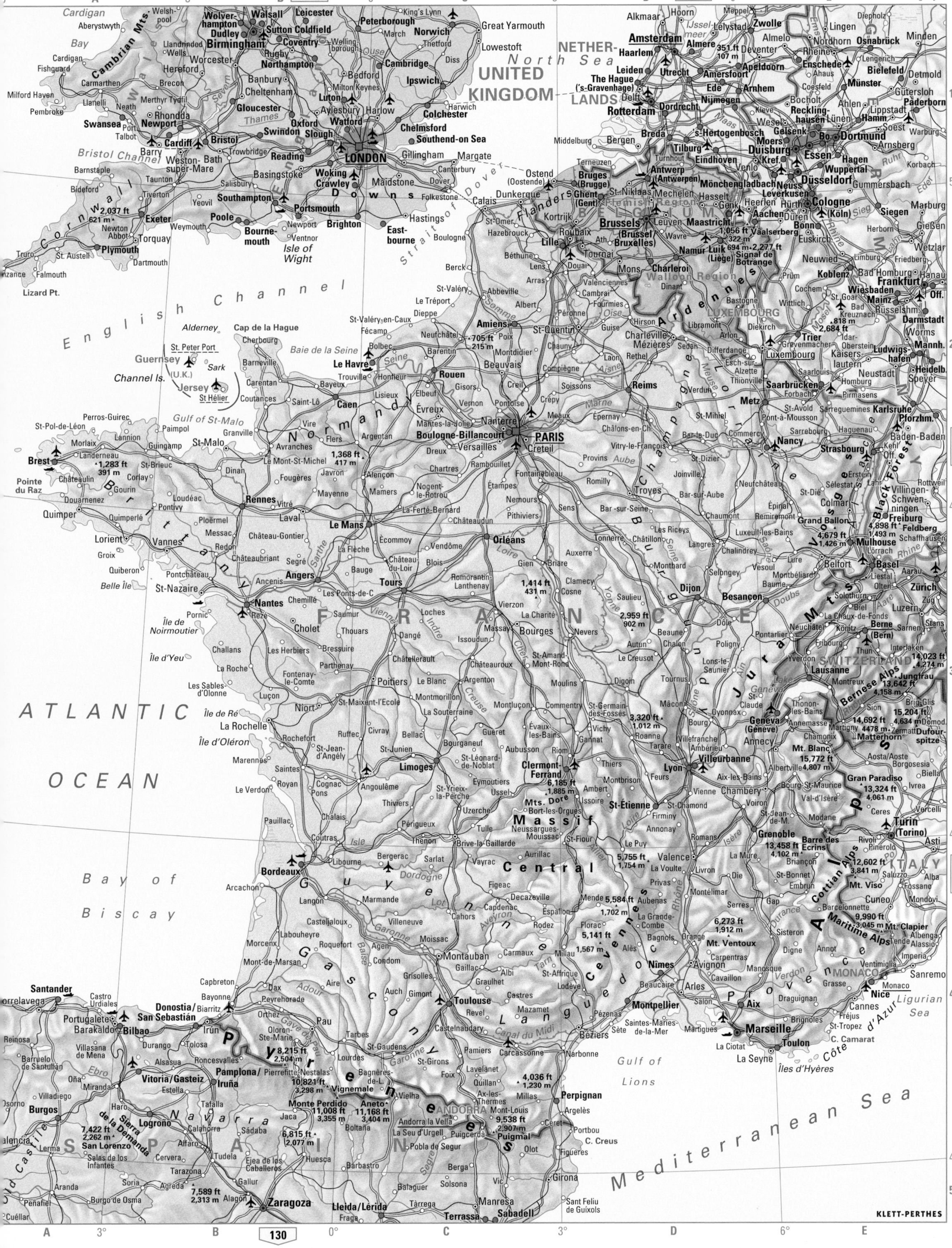

KLETT-PERTHES

124 128 130 132

1:5,000,000

0 50 100 mi
0 50 100 km
128
129
131
176
177
A
B
C
D
E
9°
12°
15°
18°
45°
42°
39°
36°
1
2
3
4
5
SWITZERLAND
AUSTRIA
HUNGARY
SLOVENIA
CROATIA
BOSNIA AND HERZEGOVINA
MONTENEGRO
FRANCE
MONACO
SAN MARINO
VATICAN CITY
MALTA
ALGERIA
TUNISIA
Alps
Bernese Alps
Rhaetian Alps
Bergamo Alps
Dolomites
Julian Alps
Karawanken
Dinaric Alps
Maritime Alps
Cottian Alps
Apennines
Berne (Bern)
Lausanne
Graz
Zagreb
Ljubljana
Trieste
Rijeka
Split
Sarajevo
Banja Luka
Zenica
Tuzla
Mostar
Podgorica
Nikšić
Dubrovnik
Nice
Cannes
Genoa (Genova)
Turin (Torino)
MILAN (MILANO)
Bergamo
Brescia
Verona
Vicenza
Padua (Padova)
Venice (Venezia)
Trento
Bolzano
Modena
Bologna
Ferrara
Ravenna
Rimini
Florence (Firenze)
Prato
Pisa
Livorno
Perugia
Ancona
Pescara
Terni
ROME (ROMA)
Latina
NAPLES (NAPOLI)
Salerno
Foggia
Bari
Taranto
Brindisi
Lecce
Potenza
Catanzaro
Messina
Reggio di Cal.
Palermo
Catania
Syracuse (Siracusa)
Sassari
Cagliari
Ajaccio
Bastia
Bizerte (Binzart)
Tūnis
Ariana (Aryānah)
'Annābah
Valletta
Corsica
Sardinia
Sicily
Elba
Capri
Ischia
Lipari Is.
Egadi Is.
Pontine Is.
Pantelleria
Lampedusa
Linosa
Gozo
Malta
Ligurian Sea
Gulf of Genoa
Tyrrhenian Sea
Adriatic Sea
Ionian Sea
Mediterranean Sea
Gulf of Venice
Gulf of Taranto
Gulf of Manfredonia
Strait of Otranto
Str. of Sicily
Str. of Messina
Str. of Bonifacio
Gulf of Cagliari
G. of Tunis
Vesuvius
Etna
Mt. Blanc
Gran Paradiso
Gran Sasso d'Italia
KLETT-PERTHES

A 18° B 21° C 129 24° D 27° E 30° F
1
2
3
4
5
45°
42°
39°
36°
HUNGARY
CROATIA
BOSNIA AND HERZEGOVINA
SERBIA AND MONTENEGRO
MONTENEGRO
MACEDONIA
ALBANIA
ROMANIA
BULGARIA
GREECE
TURKEY
MOLDOVA
UKRAINE
ITALY
Pécs
Arad
Subotica
Sombor
Timişoara
Osijek
Novi Sad
BELGRADE (BEOGRAD)
Zrenjanin
Banja Luka
Tuzla
Zenica
Sarajevo
Mostar
Dubrovnik
Podgorica
Nikšić
Kragujevac
Niš
Priština
Prizren
Skopje
Kumanovo
Tirana (Tiranë)
Durrës
Elbasan
Vlorë
Korçë
Ohrid
Bitola
Prilep
Sibiu
Braşov
Galaţi
Brăila
Constanţa
Ploieşti
BUCHAREST (BUCUREŞTI)
Craiova
Piteşti
Drobeta-Turnu Severin
Ruse
Varna
Burgas
Sliven
Stara Zagora
Plovdiv
Pleven
SOFIA (SOFIYA)
Shumen
Dobrich
Edirne
Tekirdağ
İSTANBUL
Bursa
Balıkesir
Manisa
İZMİR
Aydın
Denizli
Uşak
Thessaloníki
Kavála
Lárisa
Vólos
Ioánnina
Pátras (Pátra)
Athens (Athína)
Piraeus (Peiraiás)
Peristério
Kallithéa
Kalamáta
Iraklion (Irákleio)
Chaniá
Rhodes
Transylvanian Alps
Carpathian Mts.
Balkan Mountains
Rila
Pirin
Rhodope Mts.
Dinaric Alps
Pindus Mts.
Anatolia
Peloponnese
Chalkidikí
Sporades
Cyclades
Dodecanese
Crete
Ionian Islands
Black Sea
Sea of Marmara
Aegean Sea
Thracian Sea
Mirtoan Sea
Sea of Crete
Ionian Sea
Mediterranean Sea
Adriatic Sea
Strait of Otranto
Danube
Musala 9,597 ft 2,925 m
Olympos 9,571 ft 2,917 m
Moldoveanu 8,347 ft 2,544 m
Botev 7,796 ft 2,376 m
177

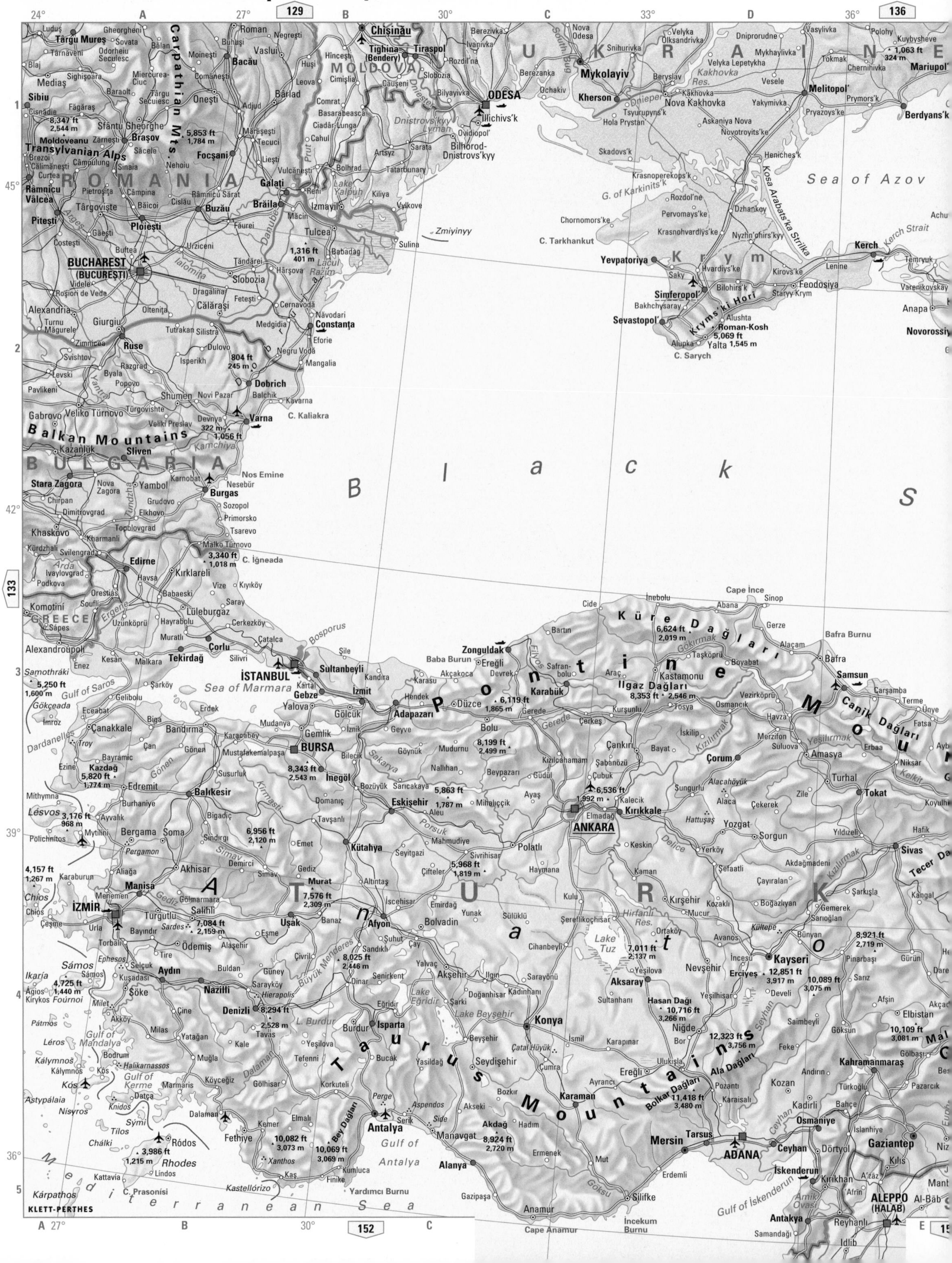
129
136
133
152
UKRAINE
MOLDOVA
ROMANIA
BULGARIA
GREECE
TURKEY
Black Sea
Sea of Azov
Sea of Marmara
Mediterranean Sea
Chişinău
Odesa
Mykolayiv
Kherson
Melitopol'
Mariupol'
Berdyans'k
Tiraspol
Tighina (Bendery)
Bacău
Braşov
Carpathian Mts.
Transylvanian Alps
Ploieşti
Buzău
Galaţi
Brăila
Tulcea
Constanţa
BUCHAREST (BUCUREŞTI)
Ruse
Dobrich
Varna
Shumen
Balkan Mountains
Sliven
Stara Zagora
Burgas
Yambol
Edirne
Kırklareli
Tekirdağ
Çorlu
İSTANBUL
Bosporus
İzmit
Bursa
Gebze
Adapazarı
Zonguldak
Karabük
Kastamonu
Samsun
Küre Dağları
Pontine Mountains
ANKARA
Kırıkkale
Eskişehir
Kütahya
Afyon
Uşak
Balıkesir
Manisa
İZMİR
Aydın
Denizli
Isparta
Antalya
Konya
Karaman
Taurus Mountains
Kayseri
Sivas
Tokat
Amasya
Çorum
Yozgat
Mersin
Tarsus
ADANA
Osmaniye
Kahramanmaraş
Gaziantep
İskenderun
Antakya
ALEPPO (HALAB)
Simferopol'
Sevastopol'
Yevpatoriya
Kerch
Feodosiya
Krym
Lake Tuz
Gulf of Antalya
Rhodes
KLETT-PERTHES

1:5,000,000

0 50 100 mi
0 50 100 km
137
148
153
RUSSIA
GEORGIA
ARMENIA
AZERBAIJAN
IRAN
IRAQ
KAZAKHSTAN
Caspian Sea
Caspian Depression
Kalmykia/Khalmg-Tangch
Yergeni Heights
Chërnyye Zemli
Nogayskaya Step'
Caucasus
Lesser Caucasus
Doğu Toroslar
Karachay-Cherkessia
Kabardino-Balkaria
North Ossetia-Alania
Ingushetia
Chechnya
Dagestan
Abkhazia
Acharia
Adygea
Volgodonsk
Novocherkassk
ROSTOV-NA-DONU
Taganrog
Bataysk
Azov
Astrakhan'
Elista
Stavropol'
Krasnodar
Armavir
Maykop
Nevinnomyssk
Cherkessk
Pyatigorsk
Kislovodsk
Mineral'nyye Vody
Budënnovsk
Nal'chik
Nazran'
Vladikavkaz
Groznyy
Khasavyurt
Makhachkala
Kaspiysk
Derbent
Sochi
Aqua/Sokhumi
Tuapse
Kutaisi
Batumi
Poti
TBILISI
Rustavi
Gyumri
Vanadzor
YEREVAN
Lake Sevan
Gəncə
Mingəçevir
Sumqayıt
BAKU (BAKI)
Xankəndi (Step'anakert)
Naxçıvan
Trabzon
Rize
Erzurum
Erzincan
Kars
Ağri
Van
Lake Van
Tatvan
Muş
Bingöl
Elâzığ
Diyarbakır
Batman
Siverek
Şanlıurfa
Viranşehir
Kızıltepe
Mardin
Al-Qāmishlī
Al-Ḥasakah
MOSUL (AL-MAWṢIL)
Tall 'Afar
Arbīl (Irbīl)
Orūmīyeh
Lake Urmia
Khvoy
TABRĪZ
Marāgheh
Mīāndōwab
Mahābād
Saqqez
Zanjān
Ardabīl
Rasht
Qazvīn
Aqtau
Elbrus 18,511 ft 5,642 m
Kazbek 16,559 ft 5,047 m
Dykhtau 17,074 ft 5,204 m
Bazardüzü Dağı 14,653 ft 4,466 m
Aragats Lerr 13,419 ft 4,090 m
Ararat 16,946 ft 5,165 m
Süphan Dağı 13,314 ft 4,058 m
Kaçkar Dağı 12,901 ft 3,932 m
Qareh Dāgh
Kūh-e Hājī Ebrāhīm 11,811 ft 3,600 m
Tigris
Great Zab
Kura
Aras
Terek
Kuma
Volga
Don

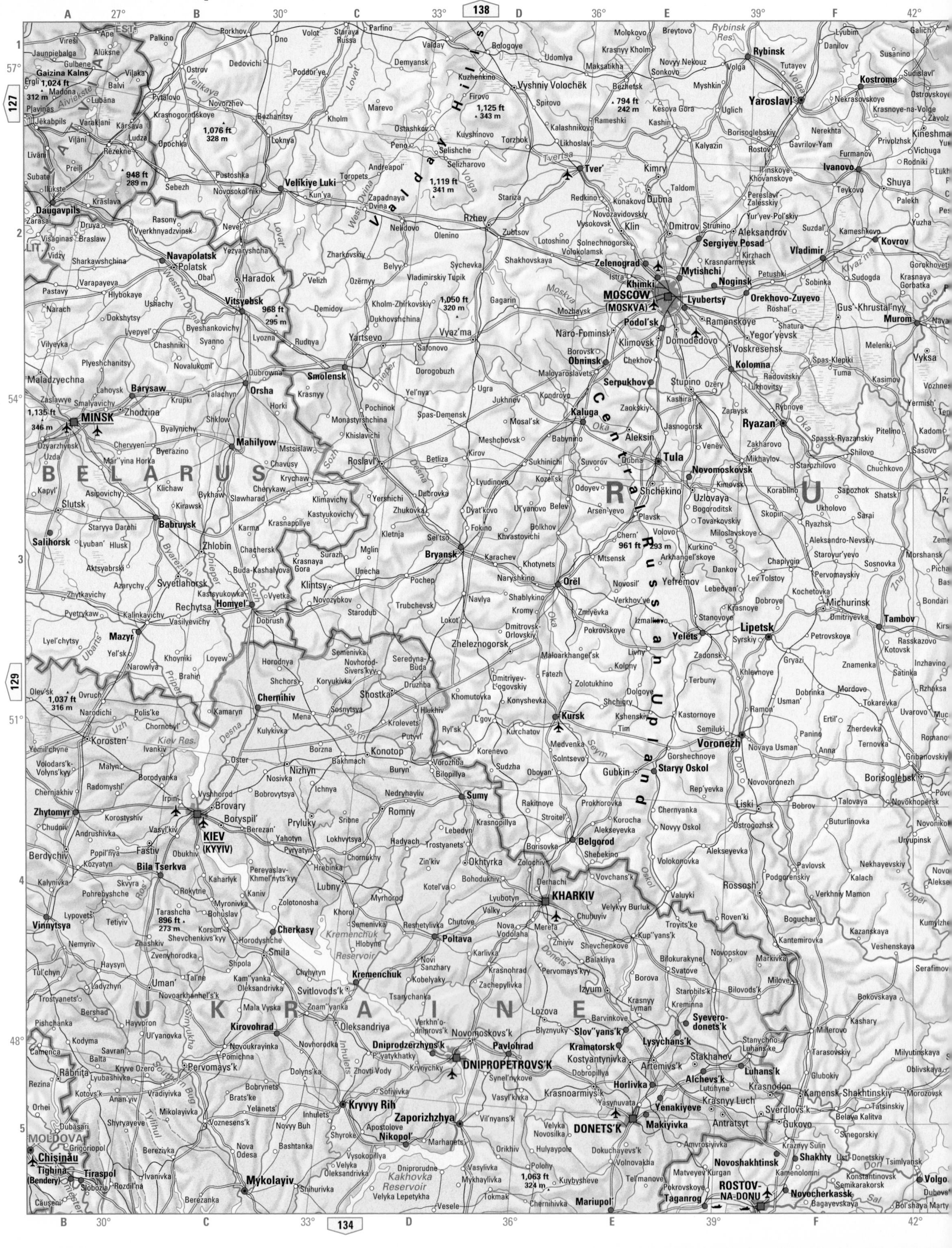
138
134
127
129
A
B
C
D
E
F
27°
30°
33°
36°
39°
42°
57°
54°
51°
48°
1
2
3
4
5
BELARUS
UKRAINE
RU
MOLDOVA
LATVIA
EST.
LIT.
MOSCOW
(MOSKVA)
MINSK
KIEV
(KYYIV)
KHARKIV
DNIPROPETROVS'K
DONETS'K
ROSTOV-NA-DONU
Chişinău
Valday Hills
Central Russian Upland
Volga
Oka
Don
Dnieper
Desna
Western Dvina
Kremenchuk Reservoir
Kakhovka Reservoir
Kiev Res.
Rybinsk Res.
Smolensk
Bryansk
Kaluga
Tula
Orël
Kursk
Voronezh
Lipetsk
Ryazan'
Tver'
Yaroslavl'
Vladimir
Ivanovo
Kostroma
Rybinsk
Tambov
Belgorod
Poltava
Sumy
Chernihiv
Zhytomyr
Vinnytsya
Cherkasy
Kremenchuk
Kirovohrad
Kryvyy Rih
Zaporizhzhya
Mykolayiv
Mariupol'
Taganrog
Luhans'k
Horlivka
Makiyivka
Homyel'
Mahilyow
Vitsyebsk
Babruysk
Orsha
Barysaw
Velikiye Luki
Daugavpils

139

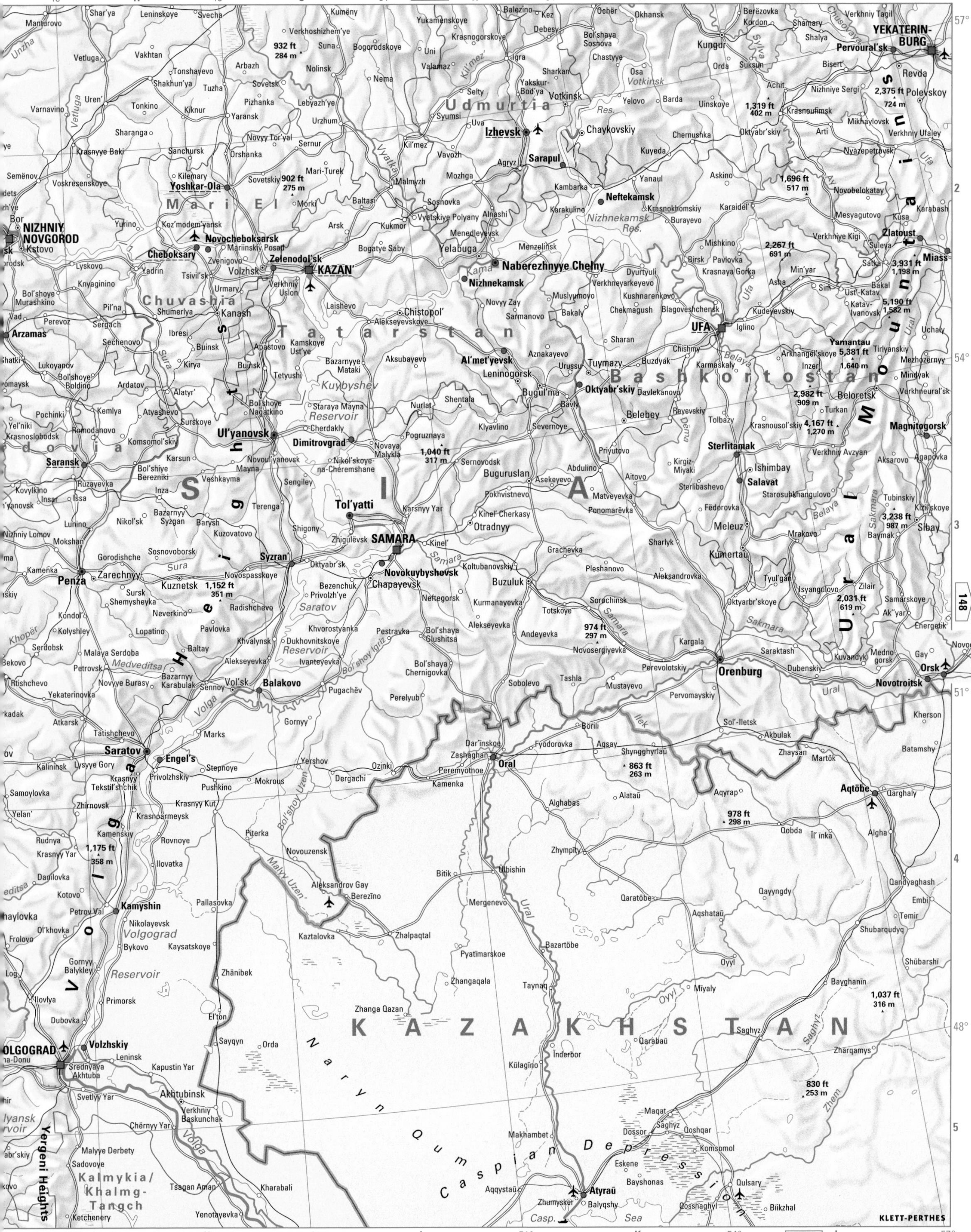
45° H 48° J 51° K 54° L 57° M 60° N
57° 2 54° 3 51° 4 48° 5
Shar'ya
Leninskoye
Svecha
Kumëny
Balezino
Kez
Ochër
Okhansk
Berëzovka
Kordon
Shamary
Verkhniy Tagil
YEKATERIN-BURG
Pervoural'sk
Manturovo
Unzha
Vetluga
Vakhtan
Verkhoshizhem'ye
932 ft 284 m
Suna
Bogorodskoye
Yukamenskoye
Krasnogorskoye
Debesy
Bol'shaya Sosnova
Chastyye
Kungur
Sylva
Chusovaya
Shalya
Tonshayevo
Arbazh
Nolinsk
Uni
Valamaz
Kil'mez'
Igra
Sharkan
Osa
Votkinsk Res.
Orda
Suksun
Bisert'
Revda
Shakhun'ya
Tuzha
Sovetsk
Nema
Yakskur-Bod'ya
Votkinsk
Achit
Nizhniye Sergi
2,375 ft 724 m
Polevskoy
Uren'
Pizhanka
Lebyazh'ye
Selty
Yelovo
Barda
Uinskoye
1,319 ft 402 m
Krasnoufimsk
Varnavino
Tonkino
Kiknur
Yaransk
Urzhum
Udmurtia
Syumsi
Uva
Mikhaylovsk
Sharanga
Novyy Tor'yal
Izhevsk
Chaykovskiy
Chernushka
Oktyabr'skiy
Arti
Verkhniy Ufaley
Krasnyye Baki
Sanchursk
Orshanka
Sernur
Kil'mez'
Vavozh
Agryz
Sarapul
Kuyeda
Nyazepetrovsk
Semënov
Voskresenskoye
Kilemary
Yoshkar-Ola
Sovetskiy
902 ft 275 m
Mari-Turek
Malmyzh
Mozhga
Kambarka
Yanaul
Askino
1,696 ft 517 m
Novobelokatay
Mari El
Morki
Baltasi
Sosnovka
Neftekamsk
Krasnokholmskiy
Karaidel'
Mesyagutovo
Kusa
Karabash
Bor
NIZHNIY NOVGOROD
Kstovo
Yurino
Koz'modem'yansk
Novocheboksarsk
Arsk
Kukmor
Vyatskiye Polyany
Alnashi
Karakulino
Nizhnekamsk Res.
Burayevo
Verkhniye Kigi
Zlatoust
Mariinskiy Posad
Menedleyevsk
Mishkino
2,267 ft 691 m
Suleya
Miass
Cheboksary
Zvenigovo
Zelenodol'sk
KAZAN'
Bogatye Saby
Yelabuga
Menzelinsk
Birsk
Pavlovka
Satka
3,931 ft 1,198 m
Lyskovo
Yadrin
Volzhsk
Kama
Naberezhnyye Chelny
Dyurtyuli
Krasnaya Gorka
Min'yar
Knyaginino
Tsivil'sk
Verkhniy Uslon
Nizhnekamsk
Verkhneyarkeyevo
Asha
Sim
Ust'-Katav
Bol'shoye Murashkino
Urmary
Chuvashia
Laishevo
Novyy Zay
Muslyumovo
Kushnarenkovo
Bakal
Katav-Ivanovsk
5,190 ft 1,582 m
Pil'na
Shumerlya
Kanash
Chistopol'
Sarmanovo
Bakaly
Chekmagush
Blagoveshchensk
Kudeyevskiy
Uchaly
Vad
Perevoz
Sergach
Alekseyevskoye
Tatarstan
UFA
Iglino
Arzamas
Ibresi
Sharan
Yamantau 5,381 ft 1,640 m
Tirlyanskiy
Sechenovo
Kamskoye Ust'ye
Aznakayevo
Chishmy
Arkhangel'skoye
Mezhozërnyy
Buinsk
Apastovo
Al'met'yevsk
Tuymazy
Buzdyak
Karmaskaly
Belaya
Inzer
Lukoyanov
Kirya
Bazarnyye Mataki
Aksubayevo
Urussu
Bashkortostan
Mindyak
Bol'shoye Boldino
Ardatov
Buinsk
Tetyushi
Leninogorsk
Bugul'ma
Oktyabr'skiy
Davlekanovo
2,982 ft 909 m
Beloretsk
Verkhneural'sk
Alatyr'
Kuybyshev Reservoir
Bavly
Pochinki
Bol'shoye Nagatkino
Staraya Mayna
Nurlat
Shentala
Belebey
Rayevskiy
Tolbazy
Krasnousol'skiy
4,167 ft 1,270 m
Turkan
Magnitogorsk
Yel'niki
Krasnoslobodsk
Kemlya
Atyashevo
Surskoye
Cherdakly
Klyavlino
Severnoye
Dëma
Ural Mountains
Romodanovo
Komsomol'skiy
Ul'yanovsk
Dimitrovgrad
Pogruznaya
Novaya Malykla
1,040 ft 317 m
Priyutovo
Sterlitamak
Verkhniy Avzyan
Aksarovo
Agapovka
Mordovia
Saransk
Karsun
Novoul'yanovsk
Nikol'skoye-na-Cheremshane
Sernovodsk
Buguruslan
Abdulino
Kirgiz-Miyaki
Ishimbay
Bol'shiye Berezniki
Mayna
Veshkayma
Sengiley
Asekeyevo
Aitovo
Salavat
Ruzayevka
Inza
RUSSIA
Pokhvistnevo
Matveyevka
Sterlibashevo
Starosubkhangulovo
Tubinskiy
Kovylkino
Insar
Issa
Bazarnyy Syzgan
Terenga
Tol'yatti
Karsnyy Yar
Kinel'-Cherkasy
Ponomarëvka
Fëdorovka
3,238 ft 987 m
Kizil'skoye
Lunino
Nikol'sk
Barysh
Shigony
Otradnyy
Meleuz
Sibay
Nizhniy Lomov
Mokshan
Sosnovoborsk
Kuzovatovo
Zhigulëvsk
SAMARA
Kinel'
Sharlyk
Mrakovo
Baymak
Gorodishche
Syzran'
Oktyabr'sk
Samara
Grachevka
Kumertau
Kamenka
Penza
Zarechnyy
Sura
Novospasskoye
Novokuybyshevsk
Koltubanovskiy
Pleshanovo
Aleksandrovka
Tyul'gan
Zilair
Kuznetsk
1,152 ft 351 m
Bezenchuk
Chapayevsk
Buzuluk
Isyangulovo
2,031 ft 619 m
Samarskoye
Sursk
Shemysheyka
Radishchevo
Privolzh'ye
Neftegorsk
Kurmanayevka
Sorochinsk
Oktyarbr'skoye
Ak"yar
Kondol'
Neverkino
Saratov Reservoir
Totskoye
Energetik
Khopër
Kolyshley
Lopatino
Pavlovka
Khvorostyanka
Pestravka
Alekseyevka
Andeyevka
974 ft 297 m
Sakmara
Serdobsk
Malaya Serdoba
Baltay
Khvalynsk
Dukhovnitskoye
Bol'shaya Glushitsa
Bol'shoy Irgiz
Novosergiyevka
Kargala
Saraktash
Mednogorsk
Novoorsk
Bekovo
Petrovsk
Medveditsa
Alekseyevka
Ivanteyevka
Bol'shaya Chernigovka
Perevolotskiy
Kuvandyk
Gay
Orsk
Rtishchevo
Novyye Burasy
Bazarnyy Karabulak
Sennoy
Vol'sk
Balakovo
Pugachëv
Sobolevo
Tashla
Orenburg
Dubenskiy
Novotroitsk
Yekaterinovka
Perelyub
Mustayevo
Pervomayskiy
Ural
Kadak
Gornyy
Ilek
Sol'-Iletsk
Kherson
Atkarsk
Tatishchevo
Marks
Borili
Akbulak
Batamshy
Saratov
Engel's
Dar'inskoe
Fyodorovka
Aqsay
Shyngghyrlau
Kalininsk
Lysyye Gory
Stepnoye
Yershov
Ozinki
Zashaghan
Oral
863 ft 263 m
Zhaysan
Martök
Krasnyy Tekstil'shchik
Privolzhskiy
Pushkino
Mokrous
Dergachi
Peremyotnoe
Kamenka
Aqtöbe
Qarghaly
Samoylovka
Krasnyy Kut
Alghabas
Alataü
Aqyrap
Zhirnovsk
Krasnoarmeysk
Bol'shoy Uzen'
978 ft 298 m
Yelan'
Volga
Piterka
Qobda
Il'inka
Rudnya
Kamenskiy
Rovnoye
Alfgha
Krasnyy Yar
1,175 ft 358 m
Novouzensk
Zhympity
Ilovatka
Malyy Uzen'
Bitik
Ulbishin
Danilovka
Aleksandrov Gay
Berezino
Qayyngdy
Qandyaghash
Kotovo
Pallasovka
Mergenevo
Qaratöbe
Embi
Petrov Val
Kamyshin
Aqshataü
Temir
Mikhaylovka
Nikolayevsk
Volgograd Reservoir
Zhalpaqtal
Ol'khovka
Kaztalovka
Bazartöbe
Shubarqudyq
Frolovo
Bykovo
Kaysatskoye
Pyatimarskoe
Oyyl
Gornyy Balykley
Zhänibek
Shübarshï
Zhangaqala
Taynaq
Bayghanin
Ilovlya
Primorsk
Miyaly
1,037 ft 316 m
Zhanga Qazan
Dubovka
El'ton
KAZAKHSTAN
Saghyz
VOLGOGRAD
Volzhskiy
Sayqyn
Orda
Qarabaü
Zharqamys
Leninsk
Kapustin Yar
Inderbor
Srednyaya Akhtuba
Kulagino
Akhtubinsk
830 ft 253 m
Zhem
Svetlyy Yar
Naryn Qum
Verkhniy Baskunchak
Maqat
Chërnyy Yar
Makhambet
Dossor
Qoshqar
Yergeni Heights
Malyye Derbety
Komsomol
Sadovoye
Caspian Depression
Eskene
Kalmykia/ Khalmg-Tangch
Bayshonas
Tsagan Aman
Kharabali
Aqqystaü
Atyraü
Qulsary
Zhumysker
Balyqshy
Yenotayevka
Ketchenery
Qosshaghyl
Biikzhal
Casp. Sea
KLETT-PERTHES

148

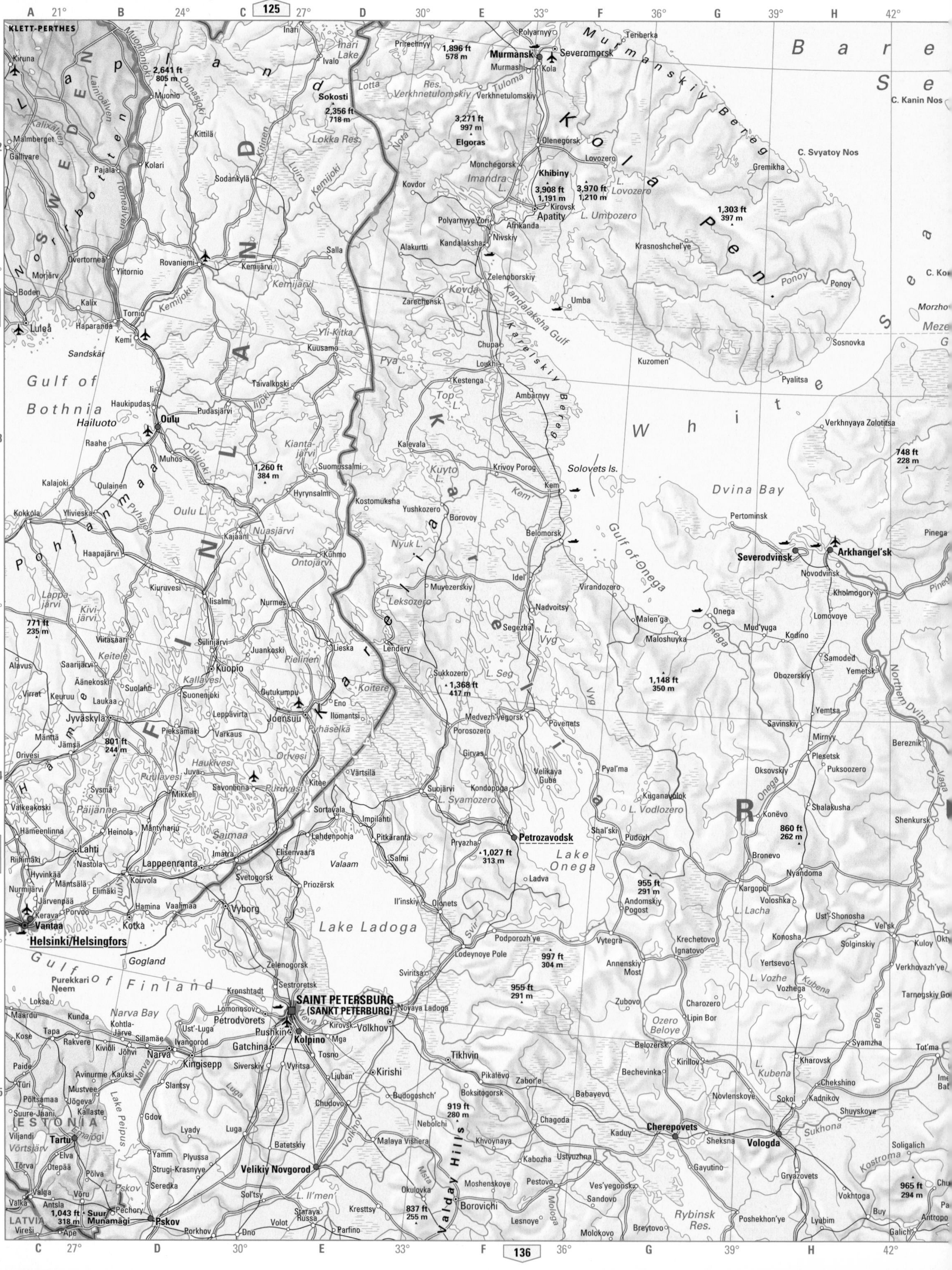

KLETT-PERTHES
125
127
136
Barents Sea
White Sea
Dvina Bay
Gulf of Onega
Kandalaksha Gulf
Karel'skiy Bereg
Murmanskiy Bereg
Kola Pen.
Gulf of Bothnia
Gulf of Finland
Narva Bay
Lake Ladoga
Lake Onega
Lake Peipus
L. Pskov
L. Il'men
Valday Hills
Rybinsk Res.
Ozero Beloye
SWEDEN
Norrbotten
Lappland
FINLAND
Pohjanmaa
Häme
Karelia
ESTONIA
LATVIA
R
Murmansk
Severomorsk
Kola
Polyarnyy
Teriberka
Murmashi
Olenegorsk
Monchegorsk
Apatity
Kirovsk
Khibiny
Kandalaksha
Lovozero
Kovdor
Alakurtti
Umba
Ponoy
Sosnovka
Kuzomen'
Pyalitsa
Kem'
Belomorsk
Solovets Is.
Segezha
Nadvoitsy
Kostomuksha
Kalevala
Petrozavodsk
Kondopoga
Medvezh'yegorsk
Povenets
Pudozh
Vytegra
Kargopol'
Nyandoma
Onega
Severodvinsk
Arkhangel'sk
Novodvinsk
Kholmogory
Pinega
Plesetsk
Mirnyy
Konosha
Vel'sk
Shenkursk
Bereznik
Kharovsk
Sokol
Vologda
Cherepovets
Sheksna
Belozërsk
Kirillov
Babayevo
Tikhvin
Pikalëvo
Boksitogorsk
Kirishi
Volkhov
Novaya Ladoga
Lodeynoye Pole
Podporozh'ye
Olonets
Sortavala
Pitkäranta
Priozërsk
Vyborg
Zelenogorsk
Sestroretsk
Kronshtadt
SAINT PETERSBURG (SANKT PETERBURG)
Kolpino
Pushkin
Gatchina
Tosno
Lomonosov
Petrodvorets
Kingisepp
Ivangorod
Narva
Slantsy
Gdov
Luga
Chudovo
Velikiy Novgorod
Staraya Russa
Borovichi
Okulovka
Malaya Vishera
Pskov
Porkhov
Dno
Tartu
Valga
Võru
Viljandi
Jõhvi
Kohtla-Järve
Sillamäe
Rakvere
Paide
Helsinki/Helsingfors
Vantaa
Kotka
Hamina
Porvoo
Kerava
Lahti
Heinola
Kouvola
Lappeenranta
Imatra
Savonlinna
Mikkeli
Joensuu
Kuopio
Jyväskylä
Iisalmi
Kajaani
Nurmes
Lieksa
Kuhmo
Suomussalmi
Oulu
Raahe
Kokkola
Kemi
Tornio
Haparanda
Luleå
Boden
Kalix
Rovaniemi
Kemijärvi
Salla
Kuusamo
Sodankylä
Kittilä
Muonio
Kiruna
Gällivare
Malmberget
Pajala
Ivalo
Inari
Inari Lake
Sokosti
Kolari
Övertorneå
Saimaa
Päijänne
Oulu L.
Imandra L.
L. Lovozero
L. Umbozero
Kovda L.
Top L.
Kuyto L.
Nyuk L.
L. Vyg
L. Seg
L. Vodlozero
L. Lacha
L. Vozhe
L. Kubena
Svir'
Neva
Volkhov
Msta
Mologa
Sukhona
Kostroma
Vaga
Onega
Northern Dvina
Kemijoki
Tornionjoki
Muonionjoki
Elgoras
Gogland
Hailuoto
Sandskär
Valaam
2,641 ft 805 m
2,356 ft 718 m
3,271 ft 997 m
1,896 ft 578 m
3,908 ft 1,191 m
3,970 ft 1,210 m
1,303 ft 397 m
748 ft 228 m
1,260 ft 384 m
1,148 ft 350 m
1,368 ft 417 m
771 ft 235 m
801 ft 244 m
860 ft 262 m
1,027 ft 313 m
955 ft 291 m
997 ft 304 m
919 ft 280 m
837 ft 255 m
965 ft 294 m
1,043 ft 318 m
Suur Munamägi
C. Kanin Nos
C. Svyatoy Nos
A B C D E F G H
21° 24° 27° 30° 33° 36° 39° 42°
66° 63° 60°

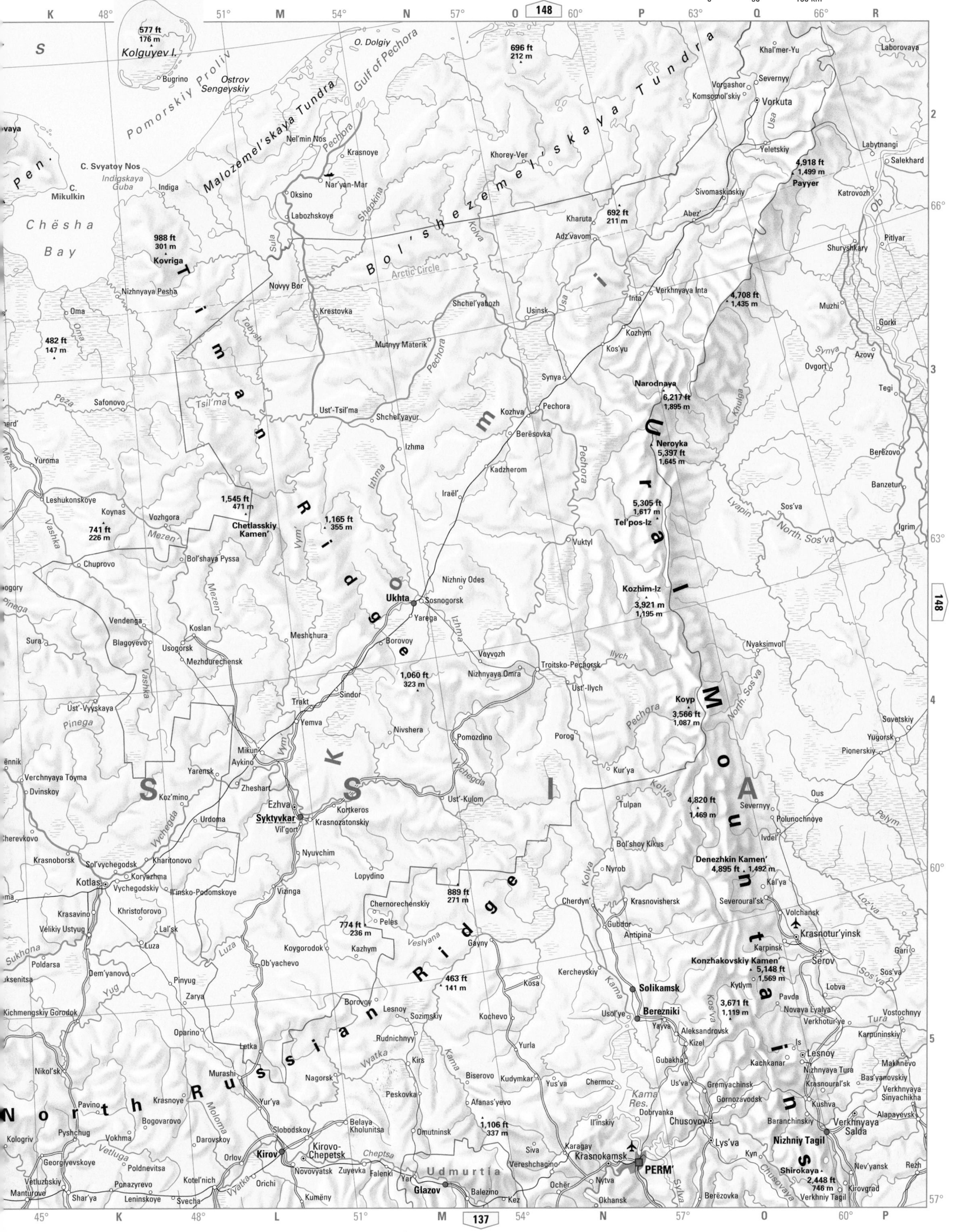
148
137
Kolguyev I.
577 ft
176 m
Bugrino
O. Dolgiy
Gulf of Pechora
Pomorskiy Proliv
Ostrov Sengeyskiy
Malozemel'skaya Tundra
Bol'shezemel'skaya Tundra
Nel'min Nos
Krasnoye
Nar'yan-Mar
Oksino
Labozhskoye
C. Svyatoy Nos
Indigskaya Guba
Indiga
C. Mikulkin
Chësha Bay
988 ft
301 m
Kovriga
Nizhnyaya Pesha
Novyy Bor
Krestovka
Arctic Circle
Oma
482 ft
147 m
Timan Ridge
Safonovo
Peza
Tsil'ma
Ust'-Tsil'ma
Shchel'yayur
Mutnyy Materik
Shchel'yabozh
Usinsk
Khorey-Ver
696 ft
212 m
Kharuta
692 ft
211 m
Adz'vavom
Abez'
Sivomaskinskiy
Vorgashor
Severnyy
Komsomol'skiy
Vorkuta
Khal'mer-Yu
Yeletskiy
Labytnangi
Salekhard
4,918 ft
1,499 m
Payyer
Katrovozh
Ob'
Pitlyar
Shuryshkary
Inta
Verkhnyaya Inta
4,708 ft
1,435 m
Muzhi
Gorki
Kozhym
Kos'yu
Synya
Azovy
Ovgort
Tegi
Narodnaya
6,217 ft
1,895 m
Pechora
Kozhva
Berësovka
Izhma
Neroyka
5,397 ft
1,645 m
Berëzovo
Kadzherom
Banzetur
Iraël'
Yuroma
Leshukonskoye
Koynas
741 ft
226 m
Vozhgora
1,545 ft
471 m
Chetlasskiy Kamen'
1,165 ft
355 m
5,305 ft
1,617 m
Tel'pos-Iz
Lyapin
Sos'va
North. Sos'va
Igrim
Mezen'
Vashka
Chuprovo
Bol'shaya Pyssa
Vuktyl
Nizhniy Odes
Ukhta
Sosnogorsk
Yarega
Kozhim-Iz
3,921 m
1,195 m
Pinega
Vendenga
Koslan
Meshchura
Sura
Blagoyevo
Usogorsk
Mezhdurechensk
Borovoy
Voyvozh
Nyaksimvol'
Troitsko-Pechorsk
Ilych
Nizhnyaya Omra
1,060 ft
323 m
Ust'-Ilych
Sindor
Trakt
Ust'-Vyyskaya
Yemva
Koyp
3,566 ft
1,087 m
Sovetskiy
Nivshera
Pomozdino
Porog
Yugorsk
Pionerskiy
Mikun'
Aykino
Verchnyaya Toyma
Dvinskoy
Yarensk
Kur'ya
Zheshart
Koz'mino
Ezhva
Syktyvkar
Vil'gort
Kortkeros
Krasnozatonskiy
Ust'-Kulom
Vychegda
Kolva
Tulpan
4,820 ft
1,469 m
Severnyy
Polunochnoye
Ous
Pelym
Urdoma
Ivdel'
Nyuvchim
Bol'shoy Kikus
Kotlas
Krasnoborsk
Sol'vychegodsk
Kharitonovo
Koryazhma
Vychegodskiy
Il'insko-Podomskoye
Lopydino
Nyrob
Denezhkin Kamen'
4,895 ft
1,492 m
Kal'ya
Vizinga
889 ft
271 m
Cherdyn'
Krasnovishersk
Severoural'sk
Volchansk
Krasnotur'yinsk
Krasavino
Velikiy Ustyug
Khristoforovo
Chernorechenskiy
Peles
774 ft
236 m
Gubdor
Antipina
Lal'sk
Luza
Sukhona
Koygorodok
Kazhym
Veslyana
Gayny
Karpinsk
Konzhakovskiy Kamen'
5,148 ft
1,569 m
Serov
Gari
Sos'va
Poldarsa
Ob'yachevo
Dem'yanovo
Yug
Pinyug
463 ft
141 m
Kerchevskiy
Kosa
Kama
Solikamsk
Kytlym
3,671 ft
1,119 m
Lobva
Pavda
Zarya
Kichmengskiy Gorodok
Borovoy
Lesnoy
Sozimskiy
Kochevo
Usol'ye
Berezniki
Yayva
Novaya Lyalya
Verkhotur'ye
Tura
Vostochnyy
Karpuninskiy
Oparino
Letka
Rudnichnyy
Yurla
Aleksandrovsk
Kizel
Lesnoy
Makhnëvo
Nikol'sk
Murashi
Vyatka
Kirs
Nagorsk
Biserovo
Kudymkar
Yus'va
Chermoz
Gubakha
Kachkanar
Nizhnyaya Tura
Krasnoural'sk
Bas'yanovskiy
Verkhnyaya Sinyachikha
Gremyachinsk
Gornozavodsk
Us'va
Kushva
Pavino
Krasnoye
Molome
Yur'ya
Peskovka
Afanas'yevo
Kama Res.
Dobryanka
Chusovoy
Baranchinskiy
Alapayevsk
North Russian Ridge
Bogovarovo
Pyshchug
Vokhma
Darovskoy
Slobodskoy
Belaya Kholunitsa
Omutninsk
1,106 ft
337 m
Il'inskiy
Lys'va
Nizhniy Tagil
Verkhnyaya Salda
Kologriv
Vetluga
Orlov
Kirov
Kirovo-Chepetsk
Cheptsa
Siva
Karagay
Krasnokamsk
Perm'
Kyn
Chusovaya
Shirokaya
2,448 ft
746 m
Nev'yansk
Rezh
Georgiyevskoye
Poldnevitsa
Kotel'nich
Novovyatsk
Zuyevka
Falenki
Udmurtia
Vereshchagino
Vetluzhskiy
Manturovo
Ponazyrevo
Shar'ya
Leninskoye
Svecha
Orichi
Kumëny
Yar
Glazov
Balezino
Kez
Ochër
Nytva
Okhansk
Sylva
Berëzovka
Verkhniy Tagil
Kirovgrad
Ural Mountains
Russia
Pen.
K
M
N
O
P
Q
R
L
45°
48°
51°
54°
57°
60°
63°
66°
57°
60°
63°
66°
2
3
4
5

North Passage, Arctic Ocean

Türgen and Kharkhiraa Mountains, Mongolia

Mount Fuji, Japan

Sher-Dor Madrassah, Samarqand/Uzbekistan

Negev Desert, Israel

Plateau of Tibet, China

Rice Field, Sri Lanka

Karst Mountains near Guilin, China

0 500 1,000 mi
0 500 1,000 1,500 2,000 km

1:45,000,000

0 500 1,000 mi
0 500 1,000 1,500 2,000 km
KLETT-PERTHES
ATLANTIC OCEAN
ARCTIC OCEAN
North Pole
PACIFIC OCEAN
INDIAN OCEAN
Greenland Sea
Norwegian Sea
North Sea
Barents Sea
Kara Sea
Laptev Sea
East Siberian Sea
Chukchi Sea
Bering Sea
Bering Str.
Sea of Okhotsk
Sea of Japan
Yellow Sea
East China Sea
South China Sea
Arabian Sea
Bay of Bengal
Andaman Sea
Java Sea
Sulu Sea
Celebes Sea
Banda Sea
Molucca Sea
Baltic Sea
White Sea
Black Sea
Caspian Sea
Aral Sea
Mediterr. Sea
Red Sea
Persian Gulf
G. of Oman
Gulf of Aden
Gulf of Thailand
Alaska
Alaska Pen.
Fox Is.
Aleutian Is.
Commander I.
St. Lawrence I.
Wrangel I.
Chukot Pen.
Chukot Ra.
Koryak Ra.
Kolyma Ra.
Kamchatka
Cherskiy Range
Verkhoyansk Range
Yakutia
Dzhugdzhur Ra.
Stanovoy Ra.
Sikhote-Alin Ra.
Sakhalin
Kurile Is.
Hokkaido
Honshu
Shikoku
Kyushu
Tōkyō
Ōsaka
Ryukyu Is.
Taiwan
Luzon
Manila
Mindoro
Panay
Negros
Palawan
Mindanao
Moluccas
Makassar Str.
Celebes (Sulawesi)
Borneo (Kalimantan)
Greater Sunda Is.
Lesser Sunda Is.
Sumatra
Mentawai Is.
Java
Jakarta
Bali
Flores
Sumba
Equator
Spitsbergen
Bear I.
Franz Josef Land
Severnaya Zemlya
New Siberian Islands
Novaya Zemlya
Kolguyev I.
Kola Pen.
Karelia
Scandinavia
British Isles
Shetland Is.
London
Paris
Berlin
Loire
Rhine
Alps
Carpathian Mts.
Danube
Dniepr
Kiev
Moscow
St. Petersburg
Volga
Donets'k
Crimea
Taymyr Pen.
Putoran Mts.
Central Siberian Plateau
Siberia
West Siberian Plain
Ural Mts.
Yekaterinburg
Ob
Irtysh
Yenisei
Lower Tunguska
Angara
Lena
Kolyma
Indigirka
Lake Baykal
Eastern Sayan
Western Sayan
Yablonovyy Ra.
Amur
Songhua
Manchuria
Gt. Khingan Ra.
Novokuznetsk
Altay Mts.
Khangay
Gobi
Inner Mongolia
Qaraghandy
L. Balqash
Dzungaria
Almaty
Tashkent
Tien Shan
Sinkiang
Tarim
Lop Nur
Takla Makan Desert
Altun Shan
Qaidam Pendi
Kunlun Shan
Tibet
Nyainqêntanglha Shan
Himalayas
Hindu Kush
Karakoram Ra.
Kashmir
Kābul
Punjab
Balūchistān
Indus
Delhi
Hindustan
Ganges
Brahmaputra
Karachi
Tropic of Cancer
India
Deccan
Mumbai
Western Ghats
Eastern Ghats
Chennai
Kolkata
Ceylon
Laccadive Is.
Andaman Is.
Nicobar Is.
Arakan Yoma
Salween
Mekong
Rangoon
Bangkok
Hô Chi Minh City
Malay Pen.
Hainan
Guangzhou
Yangtze
Red Basin
Chengdu
Xi'an
Yellow R.
Great Plain of China
Jinan
Beijing
Shanghai
Korea
Sŏul
Caspian Depr.
Ural
Ustyurt Plateau
Turan Lowland
Syr Darya
Amu Darya
Caucasus
Pontine Mts.
Anatolia
Taurus Mts.
Elburz Mts.
Tehrān
Iranian Plateau
Zagros Mts.
Mesopotamia
Tigris
Euphrates
Baghdād
Cairo
Sinai Pen.
Al-Hijāz
Arabian Peninsula
Riyadh
Najd
Ar-Rub' al-Khālī
Hadramawt
Socotra
Somali Pen.
Shebele
Arctic Circle
30° 40° 140° 150° 50° 60° 70° 80° 90° 100° 110° 120°
A B C D E F G H J K L M N O P Q R S T U V W X Y
Land Cover (Explanations on p. 32)
Natural Vegetation
Evergreen needleleaf forests
Evergreen broadleaf forests
Deciduous needleleaf forests
Deciduous broadleaf forests
Mixed forests
Closed shrublands
Open shrublands
Woody savannas
Savannas
Grasslands
Permanent wetlands
Developed and Mosaic Lands
Croplands
Cropland/natural vegetation mosaic
Urban and built-up lands
Non-Vegetated Lands
Snow and ice
Barren or sparsely vegetated
Water bodies
No data

ATLANTIC OCEAN
ARCTIC OCEAN
North Pole
Greenland (DEN.)
Greenland Sea
Norwegian Sea
Barents Sea
Kara Sea
Laptev Sea
East Siberian Sea
Bering Sea
Sea of Okhotsk
PACIFIC OCEAN
Sea of Japan
Yellow Sea
East China Sea
South China Sea
Sulu Sea
Celebes Sea
Java Sea
Bay of Bengal
Arabian Sea
Caspian Sea
Black Sea
Red Sea
Mediterr. Sea
Tropic of Cancer
Equator
Arctic Circle
RUSSIA
KAZAKHSTAN
MONGOLIA
CHINA
INDIA
PAKISTAN
AFGHANISTAN
IRAN
IRAQ
SAUDI ARABIA
TURKEY
JAPAN
INDONESIA
MALAYSIA
PHILIPPINES
THAILAND
VIETNAM
CAMBODIA
NEPAL
OMAN
YEMEN
Service and Industry
Service center (finance, trade, research, government, tourism)
Other location
Industrial center
Metal processing, mechanical engineering, vehicle manufacturing, shipbuilding
Electronics industry, electrical and precision engineering
Textile, garment, and leather goods industries
Chemical, wood working, pulp and paper, printing industries
Food processing
Natural gas
Oil refinery
Oil pipeline
Gas pipeline
Oil terminal embarkation
Hydro-electric power station
Nuclear power station
Mining and Smelting
Energy raw material
Hard coal
Brown coal
Uranium
Petroleum
Ore and other raw materials
Iron ore
Chromite
Cobalt
Manganese
Molybdenum
Nickel
Tungsten
Bauxite
Copper
Antimony
Lead/zinc
Tin
Gold
Silver
Platinum
Mercury
Gemstones
Asbestos
Graphite
Sodium chloride
Potassium
Phosphate
Smelting
Iron and steel production works
Non-ferrous metal production
Light metal (aluminum) production
Conurbation
Symbol size indicates relative importance of a location.
A. Alexandria
Am. Amsterdam
Ba. Barauni
Be. Belgrade
Bh. Bhilainagar
Br. Brussels
Bu. Bucharest
Bud. Budapest
Bü. Bandar-e Büshehr
Dn. Dnipropetrovs'k
Ed. Edinburgh
Fr. Frankfurt
Gö. Göteborg
H. Hamburg
Ka. Kaliningrad
Kr. Kryvyy Rih
L. London
M. Munich
Nk. Novokuznetsk
P. Prague
Pe. Peshawar
Ra. Raurkela
Ri. Rijeka
S. Samarqand
T.A. Tel Aviv-Yafo
Tb. Tbilisi
Th. Thessaloníki
Tr. Trieste
Tü. Türkmenabat
W. Warsaw
Yek. Yekaterinburg
Zü. Zürich
KLETT-PERTHES

1:45,000,000

0 500 1,000 mi
0 500 1,000 1,500 2,000 km
KLETT-PERTHES
ATLANTIC OCEAN
ARCTIC OCEAN
North Pole
Greenland (DEN.)
CANADA
UNITED STATES
Alaska
Reykjavík
ICELAND
Jan Mayen (NOR.)
Svalbard (NOR.)
Longyearbyen
Faroe Is. (DEN.)
Greenland Sea
Norwegian Sea
Bear I. (NOR.)
Franz Josef Land
Severnaya Zemlya
New Siberian Islands
East Siberian Sea
Laptev Sea
Kara Sea
Barents Sea
Wrangel I.
Point Barrow
Barrow
Nome
C. Pr. of Wales
St. Lawrence I.
C. Dezhnev
Chukchi Sea
Bering Str.
Bering Sea
Unalaska
Fox Is.
Aleutian Is.
Commander I.
Pevek
Anadyr
Cherskiy
British Isles
IRELAND
Dublin
Glasgow
UNITED KINGDOM
LONDON
Shetland Is.
North Sea
NORWAY
Oslo
Trondheim
SWEDEN
Stockholm
FINLAND
Helsinki
DENMARK
COPENHAGEN
Baltic Sea
Tallinn
EST.
LATVIA
Riga
LIT.
Vilnius
(Russia)
North C.
Murmansk
White Sea
Kolguyev I.
Novaya Zemlya
Arkhangelsk
Petrozavodsk
ST. PETERSBURG
Vorkuta
Dikson
Khatanga
C. Chelyuskin
Tiksi
Verkhoyansk
Susuman
Magadan
Palana
Petropavlovsk-Kamchatskiy
Okhotsk
Sea of Okhotsk
Norilsk
Yakutsk
Yakutia
Lena
Aldan
Indigirka
Kolyma
Ob
G. of Ob
Yenisey
Lower Tunguska
RUSSIA
FRANCE
PARIS
Lyon
Loire
Rhine
LUX.
BGM.
NLD.
HAMBURG
GERMANY
BERLIN
MUNICH
SWI.
LIE.
PRAGUE
CZ.R.
POLAND
WARSAW
Kraków
VIENNA
AUT.
SVK.
SVN.
Zagreb
CRO.
BUDAPEST
HUN.
BELARUS
MINSK
UKRAINE
KIEV
ROME
B. & H.
BELGRADE
S. & M.
ROMANIA
BUCHAREST
MOL.
ALBANIA
MAC.
SOFIA
BUL.
Thessaloniki
Danube
Dnieper
ODESA
KHARKIV
DONETS'K
GREECE
Athens
Yaroslavl
Syktyvkar
MOSCOW
NIZHNIY NOVGOROD
PERM'
KAZAN'
Khanty-Mansiysk
YEKATERINBURG
UFA
SAMARA
Voronezh
Volga
VOLGOGRAD
ROSTOV-NA-DONU
Orenburg
CHELYABINSK
OMSK
NOVOSIBIRSK
Krasnoyarsk
Novokuznetsk
Bratsk
Angara
Lake Baykal
Irkutsk
Chita
Amur
Khabarovsk
Sakhalin
Yuzhno-Sakhalinsk
Kurile Is.
Vladivostok
Astrakhan'
Ural
Black Sea
ISTANBUL
İZMIR
ANKARA
TURKEY
Anatolia
Mediterr. Sea
CYPRUS
Nicosia
GEO.
TBILISI
ARM.
YEREVAN
AZE.
BAKU
Caspian Sea
LEBANON
BEIRUT
SYRIA
DAMASCUS
ISRAEL
Jerusalem
AMMAN
JORDAN
EGYPT
MOSUL
TABRIZ
IRAQ
BAGHDAD
Tigris
Euphrates
TEHRAN
IRAN
ISFAHAN
SHIRAZ
MASHHAD
Ashgabat
KUWAIT
Kuwait
Persian Gulf
Gulf of Oman
BAHRAIN
Manama
QAT.
Doha
U.A.E.
Abu Dhabi
OMN.
Muscat
OMAN
Ra's al-Hadd
SAUDI ARABIA
RIYADH
JEDDAH
MECCA
Najd
Al-Hijaz
Red Sea
YEMEN
SANAA
Aden
Şalālah
Gulf of Aden
Socotra (YEM.)
C. Guardafui
DJI.
Djibouti
ERITREA
ETHIOPIA
Hargeysa
SOMALIA
MOGADISHU
Shebele
Aldabra
Mayotte (FRA.)
MADAGASCAR
KAZAKHSTAN
Astana
Irtysh
Qaraghandy
Aral Sea
Syr Darya
Qyzylorda
L. Balqash
UZBEKISTAN
TURKMENISTAN
Amu Darya
TASHKENT
Bishkek
KYRGYZSTAN
ALMATY
Dushanbe
TAJIKISTAN
AFGHANISTAN
Herat
KABUL
Islamabad
Kashmir
PAKISTAN
Balūchistān
Indus
LAHORE
KARACHI
Tropic of Cancer
DELHI
New Delhi
AGRA
KANPUR
VĀRĀNASI
Ganges
AHMADABAD
BHOPAL
NAGPUR
INDIA
MUMBAI
PUNE
HYDERABAD
Arabian Sea
BANGALORE
CHENNAI
Laccadive Is.
Madurai
C. Comorin
SRI LANKA
Colombo
Ceylon
Malé
MALDIVES
INDIAN OCEAN
NEPAL
Kathmandu
Thimphu
BHU.
Brahmaputra
BANGLADESH
DHAKA
KOLKATA
Bay of Bengal
Andaman Is. (IND.)
Nicobar Is.
Andaman Sea
MYANMAR
Mandalay
RANGOON
Salween
MONGOLIA
Ulan Bator
Dzungaria
ÜRÜMQI
Kashi
Tarim
Sinkiang
Lop Nur
Yumen
Inner Mongolia
Hohhot
CHINA
Tibet
Lhasa
LANZHOU
XI'AN
CHENGDU
CHONGQING
GUIYANG
KUNMING
Nanning
Yellow R.
Yangtze
Manchuria
Qiqihar
HARBIN
Songhua
CHANGCHUN
SHENYANG
BEIJING
TIANJIN
DALIAN
TAIYUAN
JINAN
QINGDAO
ZHENGZHOU
NANJING
SHANGHAI
WUHAN
HANGZHOU
NANCHANG
CHANGSHA
FUZHOU
GUANGZHOU
HONG KONG
Macau
TAIPEI
TAIWAN
Ryukyu Is.
Naha
Yellow Sea
East China Sea
NORTH KOREA
PYŎNGYANG
SŎUL
SOUTH KOREA
PUSAN
Sea of Japan
JAPAN
Hokkaido
SAPPORO
SENDAI
Honshu
TŌKYŌ
KYŌTO
ŌSAKA
Shikoku
FUKUOKA
Kyushu
PACIFIC OCEAN
LAOS
Vientiane
VIETNAM
HANOI
Hainan
Da Nang
THAILAND
BANGKOK
CAMBODIA
PHNUM PENH
Mekong
HÔ CHI MINH CITY
Gulf of Thailand
C. Ca Mau
South China Sea
PHILIPPINES
Luzon
MANILA
Mindoro
Panay
Cebu
Negros
Palawan
Sulu Sea
DAVAO
Mindanao
Celebes Sea
Bandar Seri Begawan
BRUNEI
MALAYSIA
KUALA LUMPUR
MEDAN
Kuching
Borneo (Kalimantan)
SINGAPORE
Sumatra
Mentawai Is.
INDONESIA
PALEMBANG
Banjarmasin
UJUNG PANDANG
Makassar Str.
Celebes (Sulawesi)
Molucca Sea
Moluccas
Ambon
Banda Sea
Java Sea
JAKARTA
SURABAYA
Java
Bali
Lesser Sunda Is.
Flores
Sumba
Dili
TIMOR-LESTE
AUSTRALIA
Equator
Arctic Circle
30° 40° 140° 150°
H 50° J 60° K 70° L 80° M 90° N 100° O 110° P 120° Q
ARM. ARMENIA
AUT. AUSTRIA
AZE. AZERBAIJAN
B. & H. BOSNIA AND HERZEGOVINA
BGM. BELGIUM
BHU. BHUTAN
BUL. BULGARIA
CRO. CROATIA
CZ.R. CZECH REPUBLIC
DJI. DJIBOUTI
EST. ESTONIA
GEO. GEORGIA
HUN. HUNGARY
LIE. LIECHTENSTEIN
LIT. LITHUANIA
LUX. LUXEMBOURG
MAC. MACEDONIA
MOL. MOLDOVA
NLD. NETHERLANDS
QAT. QATAR
S. & M. SERBIA AND MONTENEGRO
SVK. SLOVAKIA
SVN. SLOVENIA
SWI. SWITZERLAND
U.A.E. UNITED ARAB EMIRATES

Asia: Ethnic Groups

1:45,000,000

1:45,000,000

0 500 1,000 mi
0 500 1,000 1,500 2,000 km

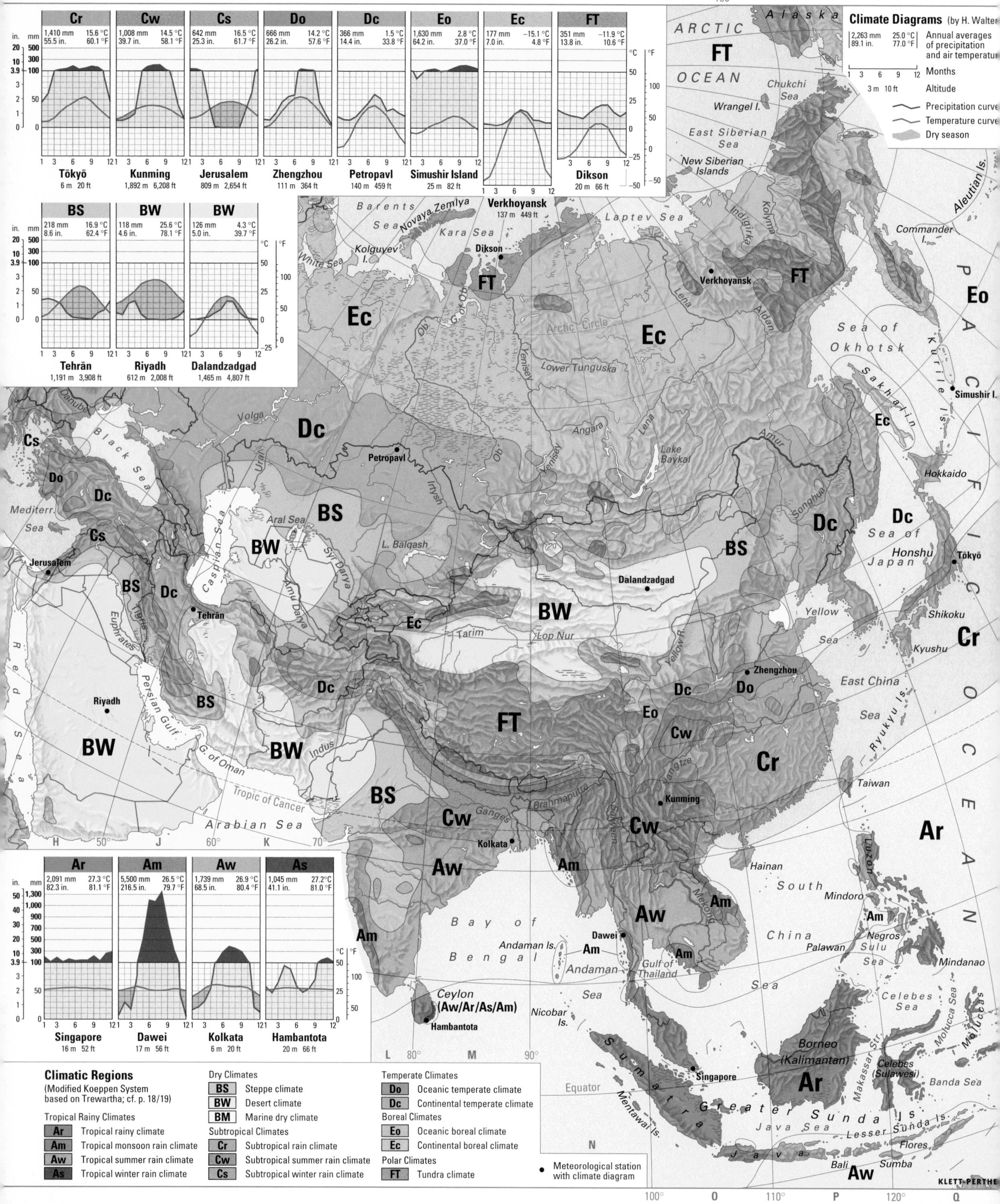
Climate Diagrams (by H. Walter)
2,263 mm 25.0 °C
89.1 in. 77.0 °F
Annual averages of precipitation and air temperature
Months
Altitude
3 m 10 ft
Precipitation curve
Temperature curve
Dry season
Cr
1,410 mm 15.6 °C
55.5 in. 60.1 °F
Tōkyō
6 m 20 ft
Cw
1,008 mm 14.5 °C
39.7 in. 58.1 °F
Kunming
1,892 m 6,208 ft
Cs
642 mm 16.5 °C
25.3 in. 61.7 °F
Jerusalem
809 m 2,654 ft
Do
666 mm 14.2 °C
26.2 in. 57.6 °F
Zhengzhou
111 m 364 ft
Dc
366 mm 1.5 °C
14.4 in. 33.8 °F
Petropavl
140 m 459 ft
Eo
1,630 mm 2.8 °C
64.2 in. 37.0 °F
Simushir Island
25 m 82 ft
Ec
177 mm −15.1 °C
7.0 in. 4.8 °F
Verkhoyansk
137 m 449 ft
FT
351 mm −11.9 °C
13.8 in. 10.6 °F
Dikson
20 m 66 ft
BS
218 mm 16.9 °C
8.6 in. 62.4 °F
Tehrān
1,191 m 3,908 ft
BW
118 mm 25.6 °C
4.6 in. 78.1 °F
Riyadh
612 m 2,008 ft
BW
126 mm 4.3 °C
5.0 in. 39.7 °F
Dalandzadgad
1,465 m 4,807 ft
Ar
2,091 mm 27.3 °C
82.3 in. 81.1 °F
Singapore
16 m 52 ft
Am
5,500 mm 26.5 °C
216.5 in. 79.7 °F
Dawei
17 m 56 ft
Aw
1,739 mm 26.9 °C
68.5 in. 80.4 °F
Kolkata
6 m 20 ft
As
1,045 mm 27.2 °C
41.1 in. 81.0 °F
Hambantota
20 m 66 ft
ARCTIC OCEAN
Alaska
Chukchi Sea
Wrangel I.
East Siberian Sea
New Siberian Islands
Laptev Sea
Kara Sea
Barents Sea
Novaya Zemlya
Kolguyev I.
White Sea
Dikson
Verkhoyansk
Aleutian Is.
Commander I.
PACIFIC OCEAN
Sea of Okhotsk
Kurile Is.
Sakhalin
Simushir I.
Hokkaido
Sea of Japan
Honshu
Tōkyō
Shikoku
Kyushu
Yellow Sea
East China Sea
Ryukyu Is.
Taiwan
Luzon
Mindoro
Negros
Palawan
Sulu Sea
Mindanao
Celebes Sea
Molucca Sea
Moluccas
Celebes (Sulawesi)
Banda Sea
Makassar Str.
Borneo (Kalimantan)
Greater Sunda Is.
Lesser Sunda Is.
Flores
Sumba
Bali
Java Sea
Java
Sumatra
Mentawai Is.
Singapore
Equator
South China Sea
Hainan
Gulf of Thailand
Andaman Sea
Andaman Is.
Nicobar Is.
Bay of Bengal
Ceylon (Aw/Ar/As/Am)
Hambantota
Dawei
Kolkata
Kunming
Zhengzhou
Dalandzadgad
Arabian Sea
Tropic of Cancer
G. of Oman
Persian Gulf
Red Sea
Riyadh
Jerusalem
Tehrān
Mediterr. Sea
Black Sea
Caspian Sea
Aral Sea
L. Balqash
Lake Baykal
Petropavl
Arctic Circle
Danube
Volga
Ural
Euphrates
Tigris
Amu Darya
Syr Darya
Indus
Ganges
Brahmaputra
Salween
Mekong
Yangtze
Yellow R.
Tarim
Lop Nur
Irtysh
Ob'
G. of Ob'
Yenisey
Lower Tunguska
Angara
Lena
Aldan
Indigirka
Kolyma
Amur
Songhua
FT
Ec
Eo
Dc
Do
Cs
Cr
Cw
BS
BW
Ar
Am
Aw
H 50° J 60° K 70°
L 80° M 90°
100° O 110° P 120° Q
150°
N
Climatic Regions
(Modified Koeppen System based on Trewartha; cf. p. 18/19)
Tropical Rainy Climates
Ar Tropical rainy climate
Am Tropical monsoon rain climate
Aw Tropical summer rain climate
As Tropical winter rain climate
Dry Climates
BS Steppe climate
BW Desert climate
BM Marine dry climate
Subtropical Climates
Cr Subtropical rain climate
Cw Subtropical summer rain climate
Cs Subtropical winter rain climate
Temperate Climates
Do Oceanic temperate climate
Dc Continental temperate climate
Boreal Climates
Eo Oceanic boreal climate
Ec Continental boreal climate
Polar Climates
FT Tundra climate
Meteorological station with climate diagram
KLETT-PERTHES

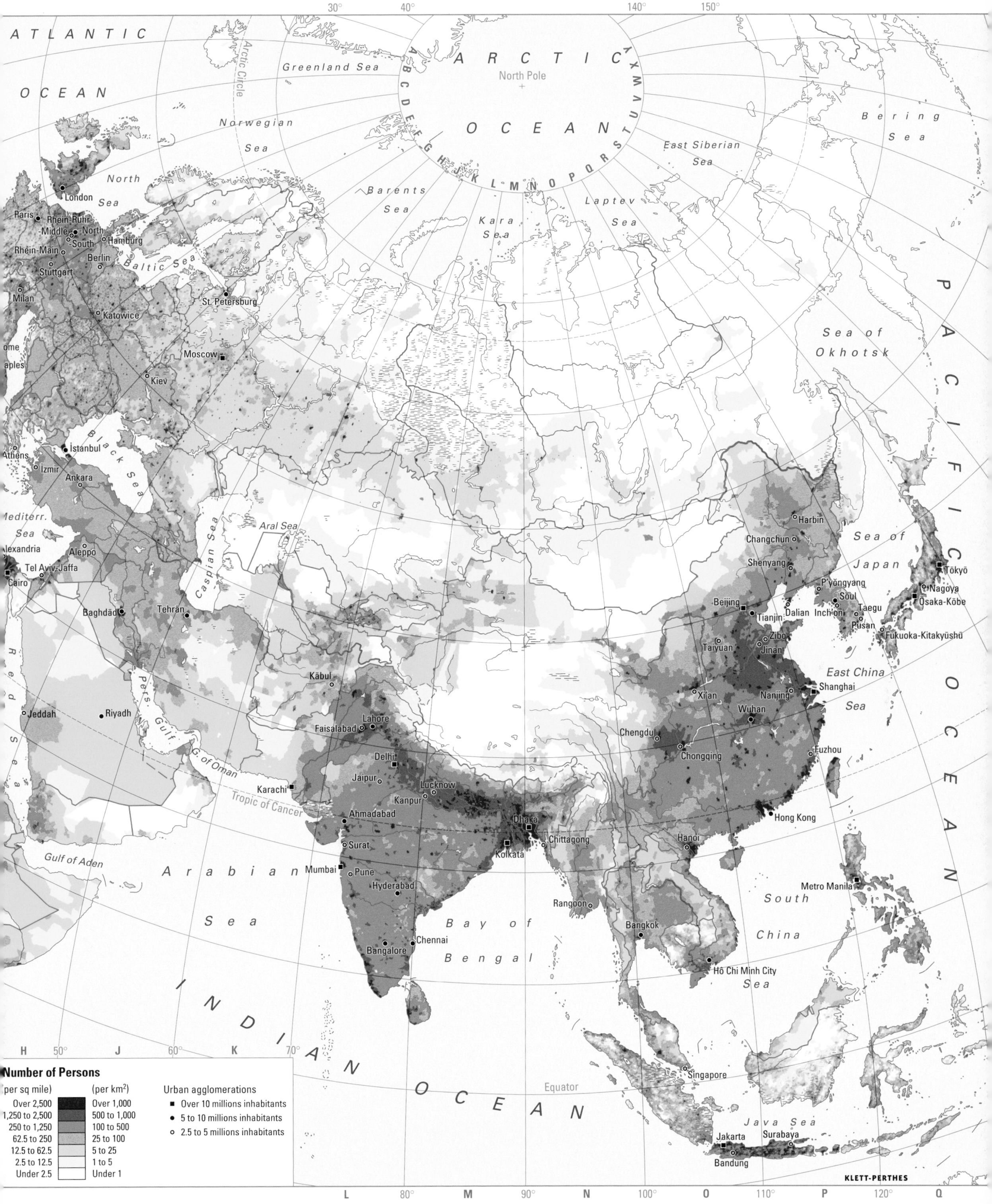

0
500
1,000 mi
0
500
1,000
1,500
2,000 km
30°
40°
140°
150°
ATLANTIC
OCEAN
ARCTIC
OCEAN
North Pole
Arctic Circle
Greenland Sea
Norwegian Sea
North Sea
Barents Sea
Kara Sea
Laptev Sea
East Siberian Sea
Bering Sea
Sea of Okhotsk
PACIFIC OCEAN
Baltic Sea
Black Sea
Caspian Sea
Aral Sea
Mediterr. Sea
Red Sea
Pers. Gulf
G. of Oman
Gulf of Aden
Tropic of Cancer
Arabian Sea
Bay of Bengal
INDIAN OCEAN
Sea of Japan
East China Sea
South China Sea
Java Sea
Equator
London
Paris
Rhein-Ruhr-Middle
North
South
Hamburg
Rhein-Main
Berlin
Stuttgart
Milan
Katowice
St. Petersburg
Moscow
Kiev
Rome
Naples
Athens
İstanbul
İzmir
Ankara
Alexandria
Cairo
Tel Aviv-Jaffa
Aleppo
Baghdād
Tehrān
Jeddah
Riyadh
Kābul
Lahore
Faisalabad
Karachi
Delhi
Jaipur
Lucknow
Kanpur
Ahmadabad
Surat
Mumbai
Pune
Hyderabad
Chennai
Bangalore
Dhaka
Kolkata
Chittagong
Rangoon
Bangkok
Hanoi
Hô Chi Minh City
Singapore
Jakarta
Bandung
Surabaya
Metro Manila
Hong Kong
Fuzhou
Chengdu
Chongqing
Xi'an
Wuhan
Nanjing
Shanghai
Taiyuan
Jinan
Zibo
Beijing
Tianjin
Dalian
Shenyang
Changchun
Harbin
P'yŏngyang
Sŏul
Inch'ŏn
Taegu
Pusan
Tōkyō
Nagoya
Ōsaka-Kōbe
Fukuoka-Kitakyūshū
H
50°
J
60°
K
70°
L
80°
M
90°
N
100°
O
110°
P
120°
Q
Number of Persons
(per sq mile)
(per km²)
Over 2,500
Over 1,000
1,250 to 2,500
500 to 1,000
250 to 1,250
100 to 500
62.5 to 250
25 to 100
12.5 to 62.5
5 to 25
2.5 to 12.5
1 to 5
Under 2.5
Under 1
Urban agglomerations
Over 10 millions inhabitants
5 to 10 millions inhabitants
2.5 to 5 millions inhabitants
KLETT-PERTHES

KLETT-PERTHES
North Sea
Norwegian Sea
Barents Sea
Kara Sea
Baltic Sea
Gulf of Bothnia
White Sea
Black Sea
Caspian Sea
Aral Sea
Sea of Azov
Svalbard (NOR.)
Spitsbergen
Prins Karls Forland
Longyearbyen
Nordaustlandet
Barentsøya
Edgeøya
Bear I.
Franz Josef Land
George Land
Rudolf I.
MacClintock I.
Graham
Vil'tsek I.
Novaya Zemlya
C. Karlsen
Kolguyev I.
Vaygach I.
Kara Strait
White I.
Yamal Pen.
Gyda Pen.
Gulf of Ob
Kola Pen.
C. Kanin Nos
Kanin Pen.
Timan Ridge
Ural Mountains
West Siberian Plain
Ustyurt Plateau
Mughalzhar Hills
Altay Mts
Tarbaghatay Ra.
Dzungaria
Great Salt Desert
Kopet Dagh
Elburz Mts
Karakum
Qizilqum
NORWAY
SWEDEN
FINLAND
ESTONIA
LATVIA
LITHUANIA
POLAND
BELARUS
UKRAINE
MOLDOVA
GEORGIA
ARMENIA
AZERBAIJAN
RUSSIA
KAZAKHSTAN
UZBEKISTAN
TURKMENISTAN
KYRGYZSTAN
TAJIKISTAN
AFGHANISTAN
IRAN
CHINA
DENMARK
GERMANY
NDL.
TURKEY
Oslo
Stockholm
Helsinki/Helsingfors
Tallinn
Riga
Vilnius
WARSAW
BERLIN
COPENHAGEN
HAMBURG
MINSK
KIEV
Chişinău
MOSCOW (MOSKVA)
ST. PETERSBURG
NIZHNIY NOVGOROD
KAZAN'
SAMARA
VOLGOGRAD
ROSTOV-NA-DONU
DONETS'K
KHARKIV
DNIPROPETROVS'K
ODESA
TBILISI
YEREVAN
BAKU
TEHRAN
MASHHAD
Ashgabat (Aşgabat)
TASHKENT (TOSHKENT)
Dushanbe
Bishkek
ALMATY
Astana
OMSK
NOVOSIBIRSK
YEKATERINBURG
CHELYABINSK
PERM'
UFA
ÜRÜMQI
Murmansk
Arkhangel'sk
Petrozavodsk
Syktyvkar
Vorkuta
Salekhard
Surgut
Nizhnevartovsk
Tyumen'
Kurgan
Orenburg
Aqtöbe
Atyraū
Aqtaū
Nukus
Urganch
Bukhara (Buxoro)
Samarqand
Qarshi
Termiz
Herāt
Qaraghandy
Pavlodar
Semey
Öskemen
Barnaul
Novokuznetsk
Kemerovo
Tomsk
Seversk
Abakan
Gorno-Altaysk
Kyzyl
Taraz
Shymkent
Khan-Tengri 22,950 ft 6,995 m
Jengish Chokusu/Shengli Feng 24,407 ft 7,439 m
P. Somoni 24,591 ft 7,495 m
Belukha 14,784 ft 4,506 m
Damāvand 18,606 ft 5,671 m
El'brus 18,511 ft 5,642 m
Galdhøpiggen 8,101 ft 2,469 m
-92 ft -28 m
-433 ft -132 m
Turpan -505 ft -154 m
Hami/Kumul
A. Adygea
Ch. Chechnya
I. Ingushetia
K.-B. Kabardino-Balkaria
K.-C. Karachay-Cherkessia
N.-A. North Ossetia-Alania
128
129
135
150
151
153

ARCTIC OCEAN
Chukchi Sea
East Siberian Sea
Laptev Sea
Bering Sea
Sea of Okhotsk
Sea of Japan
PACIFIC OCEAN
UNITED STATES
JAPAN
NORTH KOREA
SOUTH KOREA
CHINA
MONGOLIA
SAKHA
Central Siberian Plateau
Kamchatka
Sakhalin
Hokkaido
Honshu
Cape Dezhnev
Uelen
Bering Strait
Nunivak
Saint Lawrence I.
Mys Shmidta
Provideniya
Cape Chukotskiy
Chukot Pen.
3,799 ft 1,158 m
St. Matthew I.
Wrangel I.
3,596 ft 1,096 m
De Long Str.
Egvekinot
Gulf of Anadyr'
Chukot Range
6,047 ft 1,843 m
Arctic Circle
Beringovskiy
Anadyr'
Cape Navarin
Cape Shelagskiy
Pevek
Ayon I.
New Siberian Is.
New Siberia
Bear Is.
Bilibino
6,080 ft 1,853 m
Ambarchik
Anyuy Ra.
5,824 ft 1,775 m
Markovo
Ledyanaya
8,406 ft 2,562 m
Koryak Range
Faddeyev I.
Kotel'nyy I.
1,227 ft 374 m
Lyakhov Is.
Little Lyakhov I.
Great Lyakhov I.
Sannikov Str.
Dmitri Laptev Str.
Bel'kovskiy I.
Cherskiy
Gt. Anyuy
Omolon
5,896 ft 1,797 m
Penzhina
4,931 ft 1,503 m
Kamenskoye
Pakhachi
Cape Olyutorskiy
Olyutorskiy Bay
3,429 ft 1,045 m
Korf
Stolbovoy I.
Chokurdakh
Srednekolymsk
Kolyma
Indigirka
Alazeya
3,888 ft 1,185 m
Kolyma Range
Karaginskiy I.
Karaginskiy Bay
Il'pyrskiy
Commander Is.
Copper I.
Bering I.
Shmidt I.
Komsomolets I.
October Revolution I.
Bol'shevik I.
Severnaya Zemlya
965 m
3,166 ft
3,068 ft
935 m
Malyy Taymyr
Vil'kitskiy Str.
C. Chelyuskin
Taymyr Pen.
3,760 ft
1,146 m
Byrranga Mts.
Bol'shoy Begichev I.
L. Taymyr
Kosistyy
Ust'-Olenëk
Tit-Ary
Tiksi
Nizhneyansk
Yana Bay
Severnyy
4,229 ft 1,289 m
Belaya Gora
Druzhina
Deputatskiy
Zyryanka
Evensk
Gizhiga Gulf
Shelikhov Gulf
Penzhina Gulf
Central Mts.
Palana
8,590 ft 2,618 m
Olenëk
1,719 ft 524 m
Lena
Khatanga
Novorybnaya
Anabar
Siktyakh
Verkhoyansk Range
7,169 ft 2,185 m
Selennyakh
Cherskiy Range
8,311 ft 2,533 m
Pobeda
10,325 ft 3,147 m
Seymchan
Merenga
6,437 ft 1,962 m
Tigil'
Klyuchi
Ust'-Kamchatsk
Klyuchevskaya Sopka
15,585 ft 4,750 m
Kheta
Batagay
Adycha
Verkhoyansk
5,801 ft 1,768 m
Susuman
Yagodnoye
Ust'-Nera
8,485 ft 2,586 m
Cape Tolstoy
2,969 ft 905 m
7,838 ft 2,389 m
Sartang
Dulgalakh
Oymyakon
9,708 ft 2,959 m
Magadan
Mil'kovo
Kronotskaya Sopka
11,339 ft 3,456 m
Petropavlovsk-Kamchatskiy
Yelizovo
Vilyuchinsk
Oleněk
Yessey
Kotuy
Zhigansk
7,530 ft 2,295 m
Mотykleу
Kirovskiy
Udachnyy
Aykhal
2,385 ft 727 m
Markha
Vilyuy
Sangar
Khandyga
Aldan
Allakh-Yun'
Okhotsk
Oktyabr'skiy
Ozernovskiy
First Kurile Str.
Ekonda
Vilyuysk
Yakutsk
Nizhniy Bestyakh
Brindakit
Pokrovsk
1,211 ft 369 m
Amga
Ust'-Maya
Nyurba
Tura
2,913 ft 888 m
Chernyshevskiy
Mirnyy
Suntar
Vilyuy Res.
Maya
Dzhugdzhur Ra.
Nel'kan
6,253 ft 1,906 m
Ayan
Cape Yelizaveta
Okha
7,674 ft 2,339 m
Severo-Kuril'sk
Paramushir I.
Onekotan I.
Shiashkotan I.
Kuril Islands
Olëkminsk
Olëkma
Tommot
Chagda
Shantar Is.
Sakhalin Str.
Lensk
Strelka-Chunya
Yerbogachën
Lower Tunguska
Nogliki
Pogibi
Nikolayevsk-na-Amure
5,279 ft 1,609 m
Simushir I.
Taimba
Vanavara
Vitim
5,584 ft 1,702 m
Perevoz
Bol'shoy Nimnyr
Timpton
Gonam
2,412 m 7,914 ft
Chumikan
Lazarev
Aleksandrovsk-Sakhalinskiy
Artëmovskiy
Chul'man
6,585 ft 2,007 m
Neryungri
Stanovoy Range
7,822 ft 2,384 m
Uda
De-Kastri
Tatar Strait
Urup I.
3,104 ft 946 m
Vitimskiy
Bodaybo
Novaya Chara
Nagornyy
Tynda
Ekimchan
Poronaysk
Uglegorsk
Makarov
Ust'-Ilimsk
Kirensk
9,840 ft 2,999 m
Zeya Res.
Sofiysk
Berezovyy
Komsomol'sk-na-Amure
Pivan'
Amursk
Iturup I.
Kuril'sk
Bratsk
Ust'-Kut
8,458 ft 2,578 m
Novyy Uoyan
Upper Angara
Taksimo
Zeya
Fevral'sk
Selemdzha
Chegdomyn
8,662 ft 2,640 m
Sikhote-Alin Range
Sovetskaya Gavan'
Il'inskiy
Kholmsk
Yuzhno-Sakhalinsk
Korsakov
Kunashir I.
Zheleznogorsk-Ilimskiy
Severobaykal'sk
6,424 ft 1,958 m
Yerofey Pavlovich
Magdagachi
Skovorodino
Tygda
Mayskiy
Bureya
6,815 ft 2,077 m
Gornozavodsk
C. Crillon
La Pérouse Strait
Yuzhno-Kuril'sk
Tayshet
Bratsk Reservoir
9,318 ft 2,840 m
6,595 ft 2,010 m
Shimanovsk
Mogocha
Olekma
Shilka
Amur
Svobodnyy
Belogorsk
Khabarovsk
Svetlaya
Wakkanai
Abashiri
Nemuro
8,439 ft 2,572 m
Kurumkan
Lake Baykal
Vitim Ra.
5,584 ft 1,702 m
Bukachacha
Mohe
5,020 ft 1,530 m
Blagoveshchensk
Zavitinsk
Raychikhinsk
Birobidzhan
7,513 ft 2,290 m
Kushiro
Tulun
Romanovka
Zima
Ust'-Barguzin
Nerchinsk
Sretensk
Gornyy Zerentuy
Argun
Jagdaqi
Heihe
Vyazemskiy
Asahikawa
Obihiro
Cheremkhovo
Ust'-Ordynskiy
Yablonovyy Ra.
Chita
Baley
Yitulihe
Great Khingan Range
Wuyiling
Nenjiang
3,435 ft 1,047 m
Fujin
Bikin
Ebetsu
C. Erimo
Otaru
SAPPORO
Usol'ye-Sibirskoye
Angarsk
Ulan-Ude
Irkutsk
Khilok
Olovyannaya
Aginskoye
Borzya
Krasnokamensk
Yichun
Hegang
Shuangyashan
Muroran
Hakodate
Terney
Dal'negorsk
Slyudyanka
Turt
11,454 ft 3,491 m
Munku-Sardyk
Hövsgöl Nuur
Zakamensk
Kyakhta
Khapcheranga
8,278 ft 2,523 m
Onon
Manzhouli
Hulun Nur
Hailar
Yakeshi
Zalantun
Bei'an
Tangyuan
Hailun
Jiamusi
Lesozavodsk
Spassk-Dal'niy
Rudnaya Pristan'
Okushiri
Hachinohe
Tsugaru Str.
Aomori
Sühbaatar
Darhan
9,026 ft 2,751 m
Selenge
Mörön
Bulgan
Erdenet
Choybalsan
Herlen Gol
Qiqihar
DAQING
Suihua
Anda
HARBIN
Jixi
L. Khanka
Ussuriysk
6,086 ft 1,855 m
Vladivostok
Nakhodka
C. Povorotnyy
Morioka
Akita
7,317 ft 2,230 m
Chōkai-san
SENDAI
Ulan Bator (Ulaanbaatar)
Dzuunmod
Öndörhaan
Baruun-Urt
Yirxie
5,738 ft 1,749 m
Ulanhot
Baicheng
Tongyu
Manchuria
Mudanjiang
JILIN
Yanji
Najin
Ch'ŏngjin
Yamagata
Fukushima
Niigata
Aizu-Wakamatsu
Sado
Mito
Utsunomiya
Tsetserleg
Karakorum (Harhorin)
Khangai
Choyr
6,398 ft 1,950 m
CHANGCHUN
Baitou Shan/ Paekdu-san
9,003 ft 2,744 m
Liaoyuan
Hyesan
C.Suzu
Nagano
TOKYO
Funabashi
Mandalgovĭ
Arvayheer
Tongliao
Shuangliao
Kailu
Siping
Baishan
Tonghua
Kimch'aek
Toyama
KAWASAKI
Chiba
YOKOHAMA
Bayanhongor
12,983 ft 3,957 m
Saynshand
Xilinhot
6,657 ft 2,029 m
Linxi
SHENYANG
FUSHUN
Kanggye
Kanazawa
Mt. Fuji
12,389 ft 3,776 m
Govĭ Altayn Nuruu
Gobi
Erenhot
Chifeng
Fuxin
ANSHAN
Benxi
Hüich'ŏn
Hamhŭng
Fukui
Gifu
NAGOYA
Izu Islands
Dalandzadgad
Sonid Youqi
Chaoyang
Jinzhou
Yingkou
Panjin
Dandong
Sinŭiju
P'yŏngsong
Wŏnsan
Ullŭng
Oki Is.
Tottori
KYOTO
OSAKA
KOBE
Sakai
Namp'o
P'YONGYANG
90° 120° 150° 175° 180° 175° 170°
1 2 3 4 5 6 7 8 9 10 11 12
55° 50° 45° 40° 35°
100° 105° 110° 115° 120° 125° 130° 135°
l m n o V W X Y Z a b c
154
155

134
135
148
133
177
Black Sea
Caspian Sea
Mediterranean Sea
Red Sea
Persian Gulf
Gulf of Oman
Gulf of Aden
Arabian Sea
INDIAN
KAZAKHSTAN
RUSSIA
GEORGIA
ARMENIA
AZERBAIJAN
TURKEY
TURKMENISTAN
UZBEKISTAN
SYRIA
LEBANON
ISRAEL
JORDAN
IRAQ
IRAN
KUWAIT
BAHRAIN
QATAR
UNITED ARAB EMIRATES
OMAN
SAUDI ARABIA
YEMEN
EGYPT
SUDAN
ERITREA
DJIBOUTI
ETHIOPIA
SOMALIA
KENYA
AFGHANISTAN
PAKISTAN
CYPRUS
GREECE
BULGARIA
Taurus Mountains
Elburz Mts.
Koppeh Dagh
Garagum
Ustyurt Plateau
Great Salt Desert
Nubian Desert
An-Nafūd
Ad-Dahnā
Ar-Rub' al-Khālī
Ḥadramawt
Balūchestān
Tropic of Cancer
İSTANBUL
ANKARA
İZMİR
BURSA
Athens (Athína)
TBILISI
YEREVAN
BAKU
TASHKENT (TOSHKENT)
Dushanbe
Ashgabat (Aşgabat)
Nicosia (Lefkosía/Lefkoşa)
BEIRUT (BAYRŪT)
DAMASCUS (DIMASHQ)
ALEPPO (ḤALAB)
AMMĀN ('AMMĀN)
Jerusalem (Yerushalayim/Al-Quds)
BAGHDĀD
MOSUL (AL-MAWṢIL)
BASRA (AL-BAṢRAH)
Kuwait (Al-Kuwayt)
TEHRĀN
MASHHAD
ISFAHAN (EṢFAHĀN)
SHĪRĀZ
TABRĪZ
KARAJ
Qom
KABUL
Kandahar (Qandahar)
Quetta
KARACHI
HYDERABAD
ALEXANDRIA (AL-ISKANDARĪYAH)
CAIRO (AL-QĀHIRAH)
GIZA (AL-JĪZAH)
Port Said
Suez (As-Suways)
Luxor (Al-Uqṣur)
Aswān (Assuan)
RIYADH (AR-RIYĀḌ)
JEDDAH (JIDDAH)
MECCA (MAKKAH)
Medina (Al-Madīnah)
Ad-Dammām
Manama (Al-Manāmah)
Doha (Ad-Dawḥah)
Abu Dhabi (Abū Ẓaby)
Dubai (Dubayy)
Muscat (Masqaṭ)
SANAA (SAN'Ā')
Aden ('Adan)
Djibouti/Jībūtī
Asmera
KHARTOUM
OMDURMAN (UMM DURMĀN)
KHARTOUM NORTH (AL-KHARṬŪM BAḤRĪ)
Port Sudan (Būr Sūdān)
ADDIS ABABA (ĀDĪS ĀBEBA)
Hargeysa
Berbera
MOGADISHU (MUQDISHO)
Socotra (YEM.)
KLETT-PERTHES

149
155
156
M O N G O L I A
C H I N A
I N D I A
T i b e t
(A.R. Xizang)
A.R. Xinjiang Uygur
A.R. Inner Mongolia
Q i n g h a i
S i c h u a n
Y u n n a n
G u i z h o u
H u n a n
H u b e i
H e n a n
S h a a n x i
S h a n x i
H e b e i
Shandong
Jiangxi
Fujian
Guangdong
Guangxi
Anhui
Jiangsu
A.R. Ningxia Huizu
K u n l u n S h a n
T i a n S h a n
Qilian Shan
Altun Shan
Nyainqêntanglha Shan
H i m a l a y a s
Karakoram Ra.
Takla Makan Desert
Dzungaria
Badain Jaran Shamo
Qaidam Pendi
Qin Ling
Govĭ Altayn Nuruu
Tarim
Yellow River
Yangtze
Mekong
Salween
Brahmaputra
Ganges
Irrawaddy
BHUTAN
NEPAL
BANGLADESH
MYANMAR
THAILAND
LAOS
CAMBODIA
VIETNAM
MALAYSIA
INDONESIA
SRI LANKA
SINGAPORE
Mt. Everest 29,036 ft 8,850 m
Kangchenjunga
Kula Kangri 24,784 ft 7,554 m
Kathmandu
Thimphu
DELHI
New Delhi
KOLKATA (CALCUTTA)
DHAKA
CHITTAGONG
MUMBAI
CHENNAI (MADRAS)
BANGALORE
HYDERABAD
LUCKNOW
KANPUR
PATNA
AGRA
JAIPUR
BHOPAL
NAGPUR
Visakhapatnam
Colombo (Kolamba)
RANGOON (YANGON)
Mandalay
BANGKOK (KRUNG THEP)
Viangchan
HANOI (HÀ NỘI)
Hai Phong
HÔ CHI MINH CITY (THAN-PHÔ HÔ CHI MINH)
PHNUM PÉNH
KUALA LUMPUR
SINGAPORE
MEDAN
BEIJING
TIANJIN
SHIJIAZHUANG
TAIYUAN
BAOTOU
Hohhot
LANZHOU
XI'AN
ZHENGZHOU
LUOYANG
WUHAN
CHANGSHA
NANCHANG
NANJING
HEFEI
WUXI
CHENGDU
CHONGQING
GUIYANG
KUNMING
Nanning
GUANGZHOU
SHANTOU
Shenzhen
HONG KONG (XIANGGANG)
Macau (Aomen)
ÜRÜMQI
ALMATY
Lhasa
Xining
Golmud
JINAN
QINGDAO
ZIBO
DALIAN
ANSHAN
Hainan
Haikou
B a y o f B e n g a l
Andaman Islands
Nicobar Islands
Andaman and Nicobar Is. (IND.)
A n d a m a n S e a
G. of Thailand
South China Sea
Gulf of Tonking
Paracel Islands (CHN.)
Malay Peninsula
Sumatra
Borneo (Kalimantan)
Ceylon
O C E A N
Arakan Yoma
Tanen Range
Annam Plateau
Eastern Ghats
Western Ghats
An. Anyang
Be. Bengbu
H. Haryana
Hu. Huaibei
Miz. Mizoram
N. Nagaland
Sa. Sanmenxia
Si. Sikkim
Tr. Tripura
Utt. Uttaranchal
Xi. Xianyang
Xu. Xuchang
Ya. Yancheng
Za. Zaozhuang
A.R. Autonomous Region

134
A
32°
B
36°
C
40°
Antalya
Perge
Aspendos
Serik
Side
Elmalı
10,082 ft
3,073 m
10,069 ft
3,069 m
Bey Dağları
Manavgat
Kumluca
Finike
Kaş
Kastellórizo
GREECE
Gulf of Antalya
Yardımcı Burnu
Alanya
8,924 ft
2,720 m
Akdağ
Hadım
Taurus Mts.
Ermenek
Göksu
Mut
Gazipaşa
Anamur
Cape Anamur
TURKEY
Tarsus
Mersin
Erdemli
Silifke
İncekum Burnu
ADANA
Ceyhan
Osmaniye
Karataş
G. of İskenderun
İskenderun
Dörtyol
İslahiye
Kırıkhan
Amik Ovası
Antakya
Reyhanlı
Samandağı
Orontes
Gaziantep
Kilis
A'zāz
'Afrīn
Nizip
Birecik
Şanlıurfa
Suruç
'Ain al-'Arab
Jarābulus
Akçakale
Tall al-Abyaḍ
Manbij
Al-Bāb
ALEPPO
(HALAB)
Idlib
Jabal Ahas
1,903 ft
580 m
Maskanah
Asad Lake
Nahr Balīkh
Al-Mashrafah
Ar-Raqqah
Ath-Thawrah
As-Sabkhah
Euphrates
Tibnī
Marqadā
As-Suwār
Nahr al-Khābūr
Amūdā
Nusaybi
Ra's al-'Ayn
Tall Tamir
Al-Ḥasakah
Ash-Shadādah
Jabal Bishrī
2,845 ft
867 m
Dayr az-Zawr
Al-Buṣayrah
Al-Mayādīn
Subaykhān
Dura-Europos
Abū Kamāl
Wādī al-Miyāh
Jisr ash-Shughūr
Arīḥā
Ma'arrat an-Nu'mān
Suqaylibīyah
Aṣ-Ṣā'rān
Latakia
(Al-Lādhiqīyah)
Jabalah
Jabal as-Sāḥilīyah
4,544 ft
1,385 m
Bāniyās
Maṣyāf
Ḥamāh
Salamīyah
Ar-Rastān
Ṭarṭūs
Ṣāfītā
Ḥimṣ
As-Sukhnah
Tall Kalakh
Al-Quṣayr
Palmyra
(Tudmur)
SYRIA
CYPRUS
Dipkarpaz
C. Andreas
C. Kormakiti
Girne
Güzelyurt
Nicosia
(Lefkosía/Lefkoşa)
Famagusta
(Gazimağusa)
C. Arnauti
Pólis
Troódos
Olympos
6,408 ft
1,953 m
Lárnaka
Dhekelia Sovereign Base Area (U.K.)
C. Greco
Páfos
Limassol
(Lemesós)
Akrotiri Sovereign Base Area (U.K.)
C. Gata
Tripoli
(Ṭarābulus)
Qurnat as-Sawdā'
10,115 ft
3,083 m
Lebanon Mts.
LEBANON
Jūniyah
Baalbek
BEIRUT
(BAYRŪT)
B'abdā
Zaḥlah
Anti Lebanon
An-Nabak
Az-Zabadānī
Al-Quṭayfah
Sab' Ābār
Ṣaydā
DAMASCUS
(DIMASHQ)
Dūmā
Mt. Hermon
9,233 ft
2,814 m
Qaṭanā
An-Nabaṭīyat at-Taḥtā
Līṭānī
Ṣūr
Al-Qunayṭirah
Mukhaywi
Mediterranean Sea
Har Meron
3,963 ft
1,208 m
'Akko
Teverya
L. Tiberias
Haifa
(Ḥefa)
Nazareth
(Nazerat)
Izra'
Shahbā
Jabal ad-Durūz
5,909 ft
1,801 m
As-Suwaydā'
Ar-Ramthā
Dar'ā
Caesarea
Ḥadera
Netanya
Janin
Irbid
'Ajlūn
Salkhad
Syrian Desert
2,684 ft
818 m
Ar-Ruṭbah
2,825 ft
861 m
Nābulus
Jarash
Al-Mafraq
Petah Tiqwa
Tel Aviv-Yafo
Holon
Rishon Le Ziyyon
Rehovot
Ashdod
Ramla
Tall 'Aṣūr
3,333 ft
1,016 m
Rām Allāh
Jericho
(Arīḥā)
As-Salt
Az-Zarqā'
Ar-Ruṣayfah
AMMAN ('AMMĀN)
Jerusalem (Yerushalayim/Al-Quds)
Mādabā
Al-Azraq
JORDAN
ISRAEL
Ashqelon
Jabāliyā
Gaza (Ghazzah)
Khān Yūnis
Rafah
Bethlehem
(Bayt Laḥm)
Hebron
(Al-Khalīl)
-1,316 ft
-401 m
Dead Sea
Beersheba
(Be'ér Sheva)
Dimona
Al-Qiṭrānah
3,219 ft
981 m
Al-Karak
Al-Qurayyāt
Wādī as-Sirḥān
Ard aṣ-Ṣawwān
Ḥamād
Ḥazm al-Jalāmīd
Turayf
3,511 ft
1,070 m
Aṭ-Ṭafīlah
3,550 ft
1,082 m
Negev
3,396 ft
1,035 m
5,696 ft
1,736 m
Petra
Wādī Mūsā
Ma'ān
Al-Jafr
Qa' al-Jafr
Ṭabarjal
Ra's an-Naqb
Elat
Ṭābah
5,755 ft
1,754 m
Jabal Ramm
Aqaba (Al-'Aqabah)
Al-Mudawwarah
4,016 ft
1,224 m
At-Tubayq
Abū Ajram
Sakākah
Qārah
Dawmat al-Jandal
Wādī Fajr
Rashīd
Baltīm
Burullus
Abū Qīr
ALEXANDRIA
(AL-ISKANDARĪYAH)
Dumyāṭ
L. Manzala
Port Said
(Būr Sa'īd)
Kafr ad-Dawwār
Disūq
Kafr ash-Shaikh
Al-Maṭarīyah
Damanhūr
Shirbīn
Al-Manṣūrah
Ḥūsh 'Īsā
Al-Maḥallah al-Kubrā
Al-Qanṭarah
Kafr az-Zayyāt
Mīt Ghamr
As-Sinbillāwayn
Ṭanṭā
Ziftā
Fāqūs
Nasr
Az-Zaqāzīq
Suez Canal
Rummānah
Al-'Arīsh
Shibīn al-Kūm
Al-Ismā'īlīyah
Banhā
Bilbays
Shubrā al-Khaymah
Shibīn al-Qanāṭir
Fā'id
Great Bitter L.
3,589 ft
1,094 m
Wādī al-'Arīsh
GIZA (AL-JĪZAH)
CAIRO
(AL-QĀHIRAH)
Pyramids
Memphis
Saqqārah
Suez
(As-Suways)
An-Nakhl
L. Qārūn
Al-'Ayyāṭ
Aṣ-Ṣaf
As-Sidr
Jabal at-Tīh
Sinai Pen.
Ibshawāy
Sinnūris
Al-Fayyūm
Būsh
Nile
Banī Suwayf
Za'farānah
Abū Zanīmah
5,335 ft
1,626 m
Al-Ḥaql
Ḥālat 'Ammār
Al-Bi'r
Al-Hawjā'
2,979 ft
908 m
SAUDI ARABIA
Al-Fashn
Bibā
EGYPT
Arabian Desert
Abū Rudays
Gulf of Suez
Gulf of Aqaba
8,465 ft
2,580 m
J. al-Lauz
Banī Mazār
Maghāghah
Maṭāy
Dayr Katrīnah
Abū Durbah
Dhahab
J. Katrīnah
8,652 ft
2,637 m
3,392 ft
1,034 m
Al-Qalībah
Jabal ash-Shifā
Samālūṭ
Ra's Ghārib
Maqnā
Tabūk
Al-Minyā
J. Ghārib
5,745 ft
1,751 m
7,435 ft
2,266 m
Aṭ-Ṭūr
J. Sabbāgh
Nabq
Al-'Assāfīyah
Abū Qurqās
Hermopolis
Ar-Rauda
Mallawī
Dayr Mawās
Tall al-'Amarnah
Sharm ash-Shaykh
(Sharm el-Sheikh)
Tīrān
Sanāfīr
Sharmah
J. ad-Dubbāgh
7,710 ft
2,350 m
5,732 ft
1,747 m
Ash-Shawrah
Jamsah
Dalja'
Dayrūṭ
Al-Qūṣīyah
C. Muḥammad
Jūbāl I.
Shadwān I.
Tayma'
Al-Ḥijāz
Abnūb
Manfalūṭ
Ḍubā
Ḥarrat al-'Uwayrid
Asyūṭ
Al-Badārī
Abū Tīj
J. Shā'ib al-Bānāt
7,175 ft
2,187 m
Gifatīn I.
Hurghada
(Al-Ghurdaqah)
Red Sea
4,662 ft
1,421 m
Jaba
Ṭimā
Wādī Qinā
Ṭahṭā
Juhaynah
Akhmīm
Sawhāj
Al-Manshāh
Būr Safājah
Palestine:
1 West Bank
2 Gaza Strip
Al-'Ulā
Ḥafīrat al-'Aydā
Al-Gh
Zargha
1
2
3
4
36°
32°
28°
177

1:5,000,000

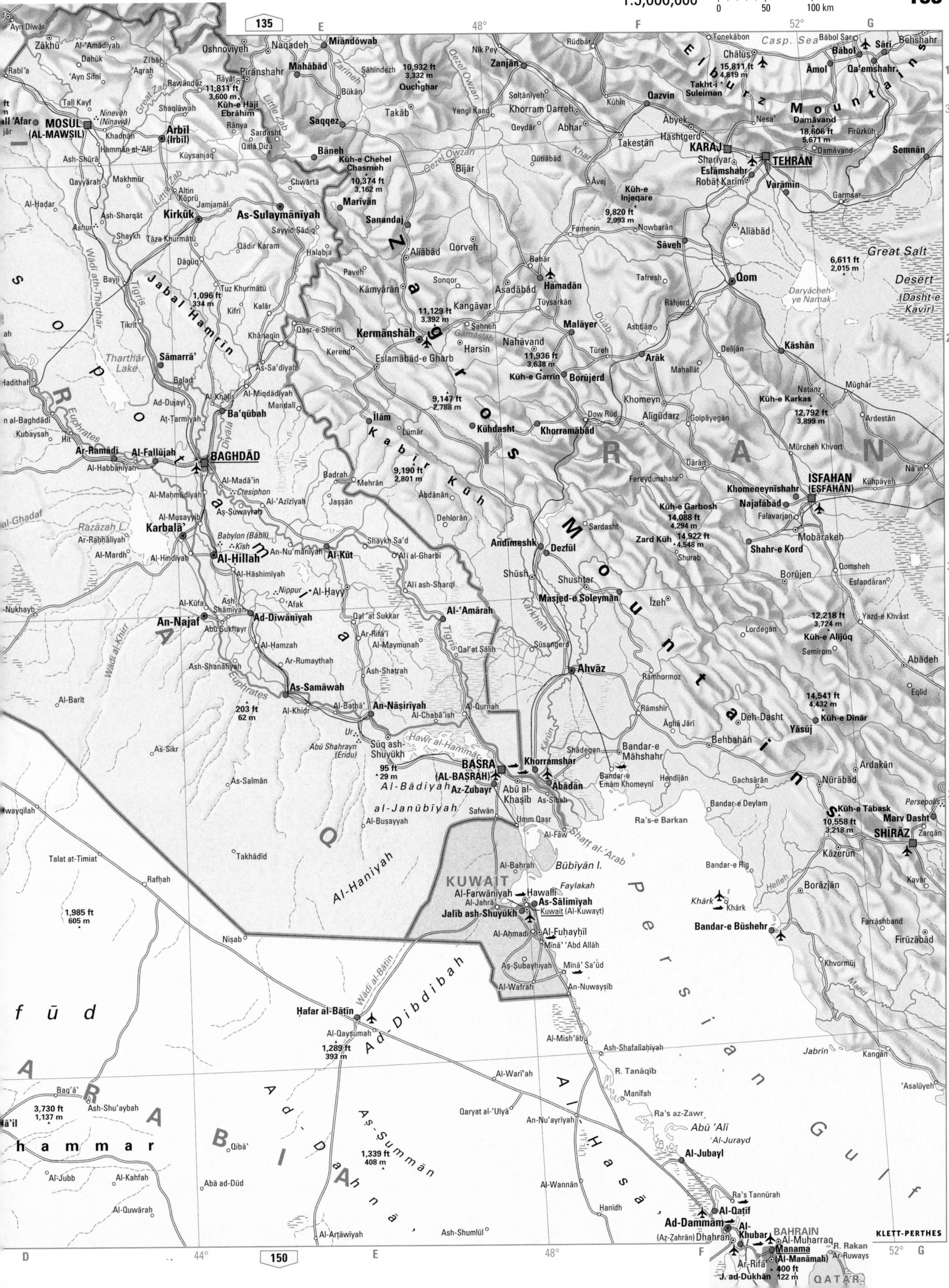
135
150
E
F
G
D
48°
52°
44°
36°
32°
28°
1
2
3
4
Casp. Sea
Elburz Mountains
Zagros Mountains
Kabīr Kūh
Mesopotamia
Jabal Hamrīn
IRAN
IRAQ
ARABIA
KUWAIT
BAHRAIN
QATAR
Persian Gulf
Great Salt Desert (Dasht-e Kavīr)
Daryācheh-ye Namak
An Nafūd
Jabal Shammar
Ad-Dibdibah
Ad-Dahnā
Aş-Şummān
Al-Hasā
Al-Haniyah
Al-Bādiyah al-Janūbīyah
Tigris
Euphrates
Diyālā
Great Zab
Little Zab
Shaţţ al-'Arab
Kārūn
Karkheh
Wādī al-Bāţin
Wādī al-Khirr
Wādī ath-Tharthār
Tharthār Lake
Razāzah L.
Hawr al-Hammār
Būbiyān I.
Faylakah
Khārk
MOSUL (AL-MAWŞIL)
Arbīl (Irbīl)
Kirkūk
As-Sulaymānīyah
BAGHDĀD
Ba'qūbah
Sāmarrā'
Ar-Ramādī
Al-Fallūjah
Karbalā'
Al-Hillah
Al-Kūt
An-Najaf
Ad-Dīwānīyah
Al-'Amārah
As-Samāwah
An-Nāşirīyah
BASRA (AL-BAŞRAH)
Az-Zubayr
Kuwait (Al-Kuwayt)
Al-Jahrā'
Hawallī
As-Sālimīyah
Jalīb ash-Shuyūkh
Al-Aḩmadī
Al-Fuḩayḩīl
Mīnā' 'Abd Allāh
Mīnā' Sa'ūd
Al-Wafrah
Ḩafar al-Bāţin
Al-Qayşūmah
Rafḩah
Nişab
Al-Jubayl
Al-Qaţīf
Ad-Dammām
Dhahran
Al-Khubar
Manama (Al-Manāmah)
Al-Muharraq
TEHRĀN
KARAJ
Qazvīn
Zanjān
Sārī
Bābol
Āmol
Qā'emshahr
Semnān
Qom
Kāshān
Arāk
Hamadān
Kermānshāh
Sanandaj
Saqqez
Mahābād
Bāneh
Marīvān
Ilām
Khorramābād
Borūjerd
Malāyer
Sāveh
Dezfūl
Andīmeshk
Shūsh
Shushtar
Masjed-e Soleymān
Ahvāz
Khorramshahr
Ābādān
Bandar-e Māhshahr
ISFAHAN (ESFAHĀN)
Khomeynīshahr
Najafābād
Shahr-e Kord
Yāsūj
SHĪRĀZ
Marv Dasht
Persepolis
Kāzerūn
Bandar-e Būshehr
Fīrūzābād
Behbahān
Damāvand 18,606 ft 5,671 m
Takht-i Suleiman 15,811 ft 4,819 m
Zard Kūh 14,922 ft 4,548 m
Kūh-e Garbosh 14,088 ft 4,294 m
Kūh-e Dīnār 14,541 ft 4,432 m
Kūh-e Karkas 12,792 ft 3,899 m
Kūh-e Alījūq 12,218 ft 3,724 m
Kūh-e Garrīn 11,936 ft 3,638 m
Kūh-e Hājī Ebrāhīm 11,811 ft 3,600 m
Kūh-e Chehel Chasmeh 10,374 ft 3,162 m
Kūh-e Tābask 10,558 ft 3,218 m
Quchghar 10,932 ft 3,332 m
Kūh-e Injeqare 9,820 ft 2,993 m
Nineveh (Ninawā)
Ashur
Ctesiphon
Babylon (Bābil)
Kish
Nippur
Ur
Abū Shahrayn (Eridu)
KLETT-PERTHES

148
150
151
156
KAZAKHSTAN
UZBEKISTAN
TURKMENISTAN
KYRGYZSTAN
TAJIKISTAN
AFGHANISTAN
PAKISTAN
INDIA
NEPAL
BHUTAN
BANGLADESH
MYANMAR
THAILAND
CAMBODIA
SRI LANKA
MALDIVES
MONGOLIA
CHINA
Aral Sea
Lake Balqash
Tien Shan
Altay Mts.
Western Sayan
Eastern Sayan
Khangai Mts.
Govĭ Altayn Nuruu
Dzungaria
Takla Makan Desert
Kunlun Shan
Altun Shan
Qilian Shan
Tibet
Qinghai
A.R. Xinjiang Uygur
A.R. Xizang
Nyainqêntanglha Shan
Himalaya
Karakoram Ra.
Hindu Kush
Thar Desert
Western Ghats
Eastern Ghats
Arabian Sea
Bay of Bengal
Andaman Sea
Andaman Islands
Andaman and Nicobar Is. (IND.)
Lakshadweep (IND.)
Ceylon
Arakan Yoma
Gulf of Thailand
Tashkent (Toshkent)
Almaty
Bishkek
Dushanbe
Kabul
Islamabad
Peshawar
Rawalpindi
Lahore
Faisalabad
Multan
Karachi
Hyderabad
Quetta
Delhi
New Delhi
Jaipur
Agra
Lucknow
Kanpur
Ahmadabad
Mumbai (Bombay)
Pune
Nagpur
Hyderabad
Bangalore
Chennai (Madras)
Kolkata (Calcutta)
Kathmandu
Mt. Everest 29,036 ft 8,850 m
Thimphu
Dhaka
Chittagong
Mandalay
Rangoon (Yangon)
Bangkok (Krung Thep)
Vientiane (Viangchan)
Hanoi (Ha Nôi)
Phnum Penh
Ho Chi Minh City
Ulan Bator (Ulaanbaatar)
Irkutsk
Ürümqi
Lanzhou
Xining
Chengdu
Chongqing
Kunming
Guiyang
Nanning
Lhasa
Trivandrum (Thiruvananthapuram)
Colombo
Tropic of Cancer

0 200 400 mi
0 200 400 600 km
KLETT-PERTHES
A. R. Autonomous Region
H. Haryana
Hu. Huainan
Ji. Jingdezhen
Ma. Matsuyama
Miz. Mizoram
My. Mymensingh
N. Nagaland
Pa. Panjin
Pi. Pingdingshan
Pu. Punjab
Pu. Puyang
Sa. Sanmenxia
Sh. Shimonoseki
Si. Sikkim
Ta. Takamatsu
To. Tongling
Tr. Tripura
Utt. Uttaranchal
Wa. Wakayama
Xi. Xianyang
Xia. Xiangtan
115° N 120° O 125° 149 P 130° Q 135° R 140° S 145° T 150° U 155° V 160° W 165°
115° N 156 120° O 125° P 130° Q 135° 157 R 140° S 145° T 150°
Sea of Okhotsk
Sakhalin
Tatar Strait
Khabarovsk
Komsomol'sk-na-Amure
Blagoveshchensk
Harbin
Changchun
Jilin
Shenyang
Fushun
Anshan
Dalian
Beijing
Tianjin
Shijiazhuang
Jinan
Qingdao
Zhengzhou
Xuzhou
Nanjing
Hefei
Wuxi
Suzhou
Shanghai
Hangzhou
Ningbo
Nanchang
Changsha
Wenzhou
Fuzhou
Xiamen
Shantou
Guangzhou
Shenzhen
Hong Kong (Xianggang)
Vladivostok
Ch'ŏngjin
Hamhŭng
P'yongyang
North Korea
South Korea
Sŏul
Inch'ŏn
Suwŏn
Taejŏn
Taegu
Kwangju
Pusan
Ulsan
Sea of Japan
Hokkaido
Sapporo
Asahikawa
Hakodate
Honshu
Sendai
Tokyo
Kawasaki
Yokohama
Chiba
Nagoya
Kyoto
Kobe
Ōsaka
Sakai
Hiroshima
Shikoku
Kitakyūshū
Fukuoka
Kyushu
Kumamoto
Kagoshima
Mt. Fuji 12,389 ft 3,776 m
Kuril Islands
Izu Islands
Yellow Sea
Bo Hai
East China Sea
Ryukyu Islands
Okinawa
Naha
Osumi Is.
Amami
Daito Is. (JAP.)
Bonin Is. (JAP.)
Volcano Is. (JAP.)
Marcus I. (JAP.)
Tropic of Cancer
Taiwan
T'aipei
T'aichung
Kaohsiung
Philippine Sea
Okino Tori (JAP.)
Northern Mariana Is. (U.S.)
Mariana Islands
Saipan
Guam (U.S.)
Agana (Hagåtña)
Luzon Strait
Batan Is.
Babuyan Is.
Luzon
Philippines
Manila
Quezon City
Caloocan
Mindoro
Samar
Leyte
Cebu
Palawan
South China Sea
Micronesia
Caroline Is.
Palau
Pacific Ocean

154
A
B
C
D
E
F
G
H
J
85°
90°
95°
100°
105°
110°
115°
120°
25°
20°
15°
10°
5°
0°
Allahabad
Jaunpur
Muzaffarpur
Mirzapur
Satna
VARANASI (BENARES)
PATNA
Gaya
Munger
Bhagalpur
Darbhanga
Ara
Biratnagar
NEPAL
Gangtok
Thimphu
Punakha
BHUTAN
Phuntsholing
Shiliguri
Katihar
Dinajpur
Rangpur
Rajshahi
Guwahati
Shillong
Tezpur
Itanagar
Dibrugarh
Tinsukia
Dispur
Jorhat
Kohima
Imphal
INDIA
Dhanbad
Asansol
Bokaro
Ranchi
Durgapur
Jamshedpur
Korba
Shahdol
Bilaspur
Bhilai
Raipur
Raurkela
Sambalpur
Barddhaman
Kharagpur
Khulna
KOLKATA (CALCUTTA)
Baleshwar
DHAKA
BANGLADESH
Comilla
Agartala
Tongi
Sylhet
Aizawl
Barisal
CHITTAGONG
Cox's Bazar
Bhubaneshwar
Cuttack
Puri
Brahmapur
Devodi Munda
Vizianagaram
Visakhapatnam
5,512 ft 1,680 m
Sittwe (Akyab)
Kyaukpyu
Ramree
Cheduba
Thandwe
Arakan Yoma
Hkakabo Razi 19,295 ft 5,881 m
15,801 ft 4,816 m
Putao
Myitkyina
Bhamo
Kachin
Singkaling Hkamti
Kalemyo
Shwebo
Lashio
Monywa
Myingyan
Mandalay
MYANMAR
Meiktila
Magway
Taunggyi
Shan
Keng Tung
8,544 ft 2,604 m
Pyinmana
Pyay
Toungoo
Henzada
Pegu (Bago)
Pathein
RANGOON (YANGON)
Thaton
Hpa-an
Mawlamyine
G. of Martaban
Mon
Ye
Dawei
Myeik
Mergui Archipelago
C. Negrais
Bay of Bengal
Andaman Sea
2,402 ft 732 m
Andaman Islands (IND.)
Port Blair
Katchall I.
Nicobar Islands (IND.)
Great Nicobar
Baoshan
Dali
Chuxiong
KUNMING
Qujing
Xingyi
Lincang
Yuxi
Simao
Jinghong
Zhaotong
Panzhihua
Xichang
Zigong
Yibin
Luzhou
CHONGQING
Ne.
Fuling
Zunyi
GUIYANG
Anshun
Duyun
Kaili
Dayong
Yuanling
Huaihua
Jinshi
CHINA
Ch.
Yueyang
Yiyang
CHANGSHA
Xia.
Zhuzhou
Loudi
Shaoyang
Hengyang
Leiyang
Hongjiang
Guilin
Liuzhou
Hechi
Bose
Nanning
Wuzhou
Yulin
Qinzhou
Beihai
Zhanjiang
Leizhou Pen.
Haikou
Hainan
Wuzhi Shan 6,126 ft 1,867 m
Sanya
Zhaoqing
Foshan
GUANGZHOU
Shenzhen
HONG KONG (XIANGGANG)
Macau (Aomen)
Jiangmen
Maoming
Shaoguan
Zhangzhou
Xiamen
Shantou
Chaozhou
Meizhou
Longyan
Quanzhou
Putian
FUZHOU
Nanping
Ganzhou
Ji'an
NANCHANG
Jiujiang
Huangshi
Huangshan
HANGZHOU
Ningbo
Shaoxing
Jinhua
Lishui
Wenzhou
Shangrao
Yingtan
Linchuan
6,956 ft 2,120 m
Ji.
Jingdezhen
Chilung
T'AIPEI
T'AICHUNG
Taiwan
Chiai
Yu Shan 12,966 ft 3,952 m
T'ainan
KAOHSIUNG
T'aitung
P'ingtung
Taiwan Str.
C. Garan
Batan Is.
Luzon Strait
Babuyan
Calayan
Mayraira Point
Escarpada Point
Laoag
Vigan
Mt. Pulog 9,610 ft 2,929 m
Tuguegarao
Ilagan
Santiago
San Fernando
Alaminos
Dagupan
Baguio
Luzon
Tarlac
Angeles
Cabanatuan
Olongapo
San Fernando
CALOOCAN
MANILA
QUEZON CITY
Batangas
Lucena
Calapan
Mindoro
Naga
Busuanga
Calamian Group
Culion
Panay
El Nido
Iloilo
Bacolod
Cebu
Negros
Dumaguete
Bayawan
Puerto Princesa
Palawan
Dumaran
Sulu Sea
Balabac
Dipolog
Pagadian
Zamboanga
Sultan Kudarat
Cotabato
Lamitan
Basilan
Jolo
Moro Gulf
Sulu Arch.
Tawitawi
Hanoi (HA NOI)
Viet Tri
Hai Phong
Nam Dinh
Thanh Hoa
Vinh
Dong Hoi
Hue
Da Nang
Quang Ngai
Ngoc Linh 8,524 ft 2,598 m
Quy Nhon
Buon Ma Thuot
Nha Trang
Cam Ranh
Da Lat
Phan Thiet
Bien Hoa
HO CHI MINH CITY (THAN-PHO HO CHI MINH)
Vung Tau
My Tho
Can Tho
Tra Vinh
Rach Gia
Long Xuyen
Bac Lieu
Ca Mau
C. Ca Mau
Con Dao
VIETNAM
Annam Plateau
G. of Tonking
Lao Cai
Phan Si Pan 10,312 ft 3,143 m
Lai Chau
Thai Nguyen
Lang Son
Xam Nua
Louangphrabang
Phou Bia 9,242 ft 2,817 m
8,199 ft 2,499 m
Viangchan
Nong Khai
LAOS
Savannakhet
Pakxe
Saravan
Udon Thani
Nakhon Phanom
Khon Kaen
Ubon Ratchathani
Nakhon Ratchasima
THAILAND
Chiang Rai
Phayao
Chiang Mai
Doi Inthanon 8,452 ft 2,576 m
Lampang
6,601 ft 2,012 m
Tak
Phitsanulok
Nakhon Sawan
Tane Range
Nonthaburi
BANGKOK (KRUNG THEP)
Sara Buri
Samut Prakan
Chon Buri
Phetchaburi
Batdambang
Siemreab
Tonle Sap
CAMBODIA
Kampong Thum
Kampong Cham
Pouthisat
Phnum Aoral 5,948 ft 1,813 m
PHNUM PENH
Prey Veng
Ta Khmau
Chanthaburi
Prachuap Khiri Khan
G. of Thailand
Chumphon
Phangan
Samui
Preah Seihanu
Surat Thani
Nakhon Si Thammarat
Phuket
Trang
Hat Yai
Pattani
Kangar
Perlis
Alor Setar
Kota Baharu
Kedah
George Town (Pinang)
Malay Peninsula
Kuala Terengganu
Taiping
Perak
Ipoh
7,175 ft 2,187 m
Tahan
Kuantan
Pahang
Shah Alam
KUALA LUMPUR
Kelang
Petaling Jaya
Seremban
Melaka
Johor Baharu
SINGAPORE
MALAYSIA
Banda Aceh
Sigli
Lhokseumawe
Meulaboh
Langsa
Leuser 11,231 ft 3,423 m
Binjai
MEDAN
Pematangsiantar
Simeulue
Banyak Is.
Toba L.
Sibolga
Rantauprapat
Nias
Padangsidempuan
Dumai
Bengkalis
Pekanbaru
Riau Arch.
Tanjungpinang
Pini
Tanahmasa
Batu Is.
Tanahbala
Bukittinggi
Padang
Solok
Rengat
Indragiri
Siberut
Muarasiberut
Sipora
Pagai Utara
Pagai Selatan
Mentawai Is.
Kerinci 12,467 ft 3,800 m
Jambi
Lingga Arch.
Bangka
Pangkalpinang
Belitung
Tanjungpandan
Karimata Is.
Karimata Str.
PALEMBANG
Bengkulu
Tebingtinggi
Baturaja
Barisan Ra.
Sumatra
Manna
Kotabumi
Krui
Bandar Lampung
Enggano
C. Rata
Krakatau (Rakata) 2,667 ft 813 m
Merak
JAKARTA
Bekasi
C. Cangkuang
Bogor
Sukabumi
BANDUNG
11,260 ft
Cirebon
Tegal
Pekalongan
3,432 m
Cilacap
M.
SEMARANG
Surakarta
Yogyakarta
Madiun
Kediri
Malang
SURABAYA
Probolinggo
Madura
Sumenep
Java
Java Sea
Karimunjawa Is.
Bawean
Masalembo Besar
Kangean Is.
Sabalana Is.
12,061 ft 3,676 m Semeru
Banyuwangi
Bali
Denpasar
Mataram
Lombok
12,225 ft 3,726 m
Sumbawa
Sumbawabesar
Bima
Labuhanbajo
7,874 ft 2,400 m
Maumere
Flores
Ende
Flores Sea
Savu Sea
Waingapu
Sumba
4,019 ft 1,225 m
Sawu
Roti
Kefamenanu
Ashmore Reef (AUS.)
Cartier I.
Tanahjampea
Kabia
Kabaena
Buton
Bau-Bau
Muna
UJUNG PANDANG
Watampone
Parepare
Rantekombola 11,336 ft 3,455 m
9,183 ft 2,799 m
Malamala
Majene
Mamuju
Palopo
Saroako
Celebes (Sulawesi)
Poso
Luwuk
Palu
Donggala
Gulf of Tomini
Togian Is.
Gorontalo
Tolitoli
9,557 ft 2,913 m
Celebes Sea
Makassar Strait
Samarinda
Balikpapan
Bontang
Tarakan
Tanjungredeb
Sebatik
Tawau
Lahad Datu
Sandakan
Kinabalu 13,455 ft 4,101 m
Kota Kinabalu
Labuan
Bandar Seri Begawan
BRUNEI
Kuala Belait
Miri
Bintulu
Sibu
Sarawak
Sabah
Kuching
Rajang
Iran Ra.
9,702 ft 2,957 m
Borneo (Kalimantan)
Mahakam
Bukit Raya
7,474 ft 2,278 m
Nangapinoh
Sukadana
Ketapang
Pangkalanbuun
Muarateweh
Palangkaraya
Sampit
Barabai
6,208 ft 1,892 m
Kotabaru
Banjarmasin
Martapura
Laut
Cape Selatan
Cape Sambar
Pontianak
Singkawang
Tambelan Is.
Natuna Besar
Natuna Is.
Subi Besar
Anambas Is.
South China Sea
Paracel Islands (CHN.)
C. Sempang Mangayau
Banggi
C. Buliluyan
6,841 ft 2,085 m
INDONESIA
Equator
INDIAN OCEAN
Cocos (Keeling) Islands (AUS.)
Christmas Island (AUS.)
Ch. Changde
Ji. Jingdezhen
M. Magelang
Ma. Mandaue
My. Mymensingh
Ne. Neijiang
N.S. Negeri Sembilan
P. Pinang
Sel. Selangor
Xia. Xiangtan

155
166
161
167
JAPAN
Islands
Naze
Amami
1,634 ft
498 m
Okinawa
Naha
Daito Is.
(JAP.)
Bonin Is.
(JAP.)
Volcano Is.
(JAP.)
Marcus I.
(JAP.)
Tropic of Cancer
Wake Island
(U.S.)
P A C I F I C
O C E A N
Philippine
Sea
Okino Tori
(JAP.)
Asuncion I.
Agrihan
3,166 ft
965 m
Pagan
Northern
Mariana Is.
(U.S.)
Guguan
Sarigan
Anatahan
Mariana Islands
Garapan
Saipan
Tinian
Rota
Agaña
(Hagåtña)
Guam
(U.S.)
Mt. Lamlam 1,332 ft
406 m
MARSHALL
ISLANDS
Bikini Atoll
Enewetak
Atoll
Ujelang
Ulithi
Fais
Colonia
Yap Is.
Ngulu
Sorol
Gaferut
Faraulep
Namonuito
Hall Is.
Ulul
Pikelot
Pulap
Weno
Chuuk Is.
Puluwat
Oroluk
Palikir
Mwokil
Pohnpei
Pingelap
Kosrae
Ngatik
Olimarao
Woleai
Ifalik
Elato
Namoluk
Etal
Satawan
Mortlock Is.
Caroline Islands
MICRONESIA
Nukuoro
Ngcheangel
Babeldaob
Koror
Palau Is.
PALAU
Pulo Anna
Kapingamarangi
Tobi
Helen Reef
Equator
Karakelong
Morotai
5,627 ft
1,715 m
C. Lelai
Halmahera
Ternate
Waigeo
Sorong
Manokwari
Biak
Yapen
Serui
D'Urville C.
Jayapura
Vanimo
Salawati
Doberai Pen.
9,744 ft
2,970 m
Misool
Sarera Bay
Bacan
Obi
Seram Sea
Binaia
9,646 ft
2,940 m
Seram
Fakfak
4,889 ft
1,490 m
Kaimana
Nabire
Enarotali
16,024 ft
4,884 m
Carstensz Pyramid
(Puncak Jayakesuma)
15,519 ft
4,730 m
Oksibil
Amamapare
Ambon
Amahai
Buru
Bandanaira
Adi
Mamberamo
Sepik
Wewak
Maoke Range
New Guinea
Ninigo Is.
Kaniet Is.
Admiralty Is.
Lorengau
Manus I.
Rambutyo
Lou I.
St. Matthias Is.
New Hanover
Kavieng
Tabar Is.
Lihir Is.
New Ireland
Namatanai
Rabaul
Kokopo
7,871 ft
2,399 m
6,769 ft
2,063 m
Feni Is.
Green Is.
Nuguria Is.
Tulun Is.
Takuu Is.
Nukumanu Is.
Ontong Java Atoll
Bismarck Archipelago
Bismarck Sea
Schouten Is.
PAPUA NEW GUINEA
Karkar I.
Madang
Long I.
Umboi I.
New Britain
St. George's Channel
Buka
Mt. Balbi
8,809 ft
2,685 m
Bougainville I.
Arawa
Choiseul
Santa Isabel
Buala
Gizo
New Georgia Is.
Malaita
4,702 ft
1,433 m
Tulaghi
Auki
Honiara
Mt. Makarakomburu
8,028 ft
2,447 m
Kirakira
Guadalcanal
San Cristobal
Solomon Islands
Solomon Sea
Wabag
Mount Hagen
Mendi
14,794 ft 4,509 m
Mt. Wilhelm
4,367 m
14,328 ft
Mt. Giluwe
Goroka
Kundiawa
Lae
Bulolo
Kiunga
Kikori
Kerema
Owen Stanley Ra.
Trobriand Is.
Kiriwina I.
Woodlark I.
Fergusson I.
D'Entrecasteaux Is.
Normanby I.
Misima I.
Popondetta
Gulf of Papua
Mt. Victoria
13,363 ft 4,073 m
Port Moresby
Esa'ala
Alotau
Samarai
Abau
Louisiade Arch.
Rossel I.
Tagula I.
Rennell
SOLOMON ISLANDS
Tual
Kai Is.
Dobo
Wokam
Kobroor
Aru Is.
Trangan
Banda Sea
Moluccas
Damar Is.
Yamdena
Saumlaki
Tanimbar Is.
Selaru
Babar
Leti Is.
Huaki
Bacau
Tutuala
TIMOR-LESTE
Dolak
Digul
Fly
Merauke
Daru
Torres Strait
Badu
Moa
Prince of Wales I.
Cape York
Bamaga
Arafura Sea
Cape Wessel
Melville I.
Croker I.
Wessel Is.
Cape Arnhem
Bathurst I.
Darwin
Jabiru
1,201 ft
366 m
AUSTRALIA
Gulf of Carpentaria
Cape York Pen.
Coen
Coral Sea
Timor Sea
Mindanao
Bislig
DAVAO
Apo
2,954 m
Cape San Agustin
PHILIPPINES
K L M N O P Q R S
130° 135° 140° 145° 150° 155° 160° 165°
25° 20° 15° 10° 5° 0° 5° 10° 15°
3 4 5 6 7 8 9 10 11
KLETT-PERTHES

Himalayas
Brahmaputra
Yangtze
Ganges
Kolkata
Arakan Yoma
Salween
Xi Jiang
Guangzhou
Taiwan Str.
Ryukyu Is.
Taiwan
Daito Is.
Bonin Is.
Volcano Is.
Okino Tori
G. of Tonkin
Hainan
Luzon
Philippine Sea
Mariana Is.
Saipan
Guam
Bay of Bengal
Rangoon
Mekong
Paracel Is.
Manila
Philippines
Mindoro
Bangkok
Tonle Sap
Samar
Panay
Andaman Is.
South China Sea
Negros
Yap Is.
Ho Chi Minh City
Palawan
Sulu Sea
Palau Is.
Chuuk Is.
G. of Thailand
Andaman Sea
Mindanao
Caroline
Nicobar Is.
Malay Pen.
Sulu Arch.
Sangir Is.
Celebes Sea
Micronesia
Halmahera
Str. of Malacca
Singapore
Borneo
(Kalimantan)
Makassar Str.
Molucca Sea
Moluccas
Biak
Admiralty Is.
Bismarck Arch.
Sumatra
Celebes
(Sulawesi)
Seram
Buru
New Guinea
Maoke Range
Sepik
New Britain
Equator
Mentawai Is.
Greater Sunda Is.
Buton
Kai Is.
Aru Is.
Banda Sea
Bougainville
Solomon Sea
Java Sea
Madura
Jakarta
Tanimbar Is.
Dolak
Fly
Sunda Str.
Lesser Sunda Is.
Arafura Sea
Torres Str.
Java
Bali
Flores
Timor
Sumba
Melville I.
Louisiade Arch.
Timor Sea
Arnhem Land
Cape York Pen.
Gulf of Carpentaria
Coral Sea
Christmas I.
Great Barrier Reef
Cocos Is.
Fitzroy
Flinders
Great Dividing Range
Macdonnell Ra.
Australia
L. Eyre
Cooper Cr.
Gt. Victoria Desert
Nullarbor Plain
Darling
Great Australian Bight
Perth
Adelaide
Murray
Sydney
Kangaroo I.
Austral. Alps
Melbourne
King I.
Bass Str.
Tasmania
INDIAN OCEAN
PACIFIC
1
2
3
4
5
9
Land Cover
(Explanations on page 32)
Natural Vegetation
Evergreen needleleaf forests
Evergreen broadleaf forests
Deciduous needleleaf forests
Deciduous broadleaf forests
Mixed forests
Closed shrublands
Open shrublands
Woody savannas
Savannas
Grasslands
Permanent wetlands
Developed and Mosaic Lands
Croplands
Cropland/natural vegetation mosaic
Urban and built-up lands
Non-Vegetated Lands
Snow and ice
Barren or sparsely vegetated
Water bodies
No data
B 90° C 100° D 110° E 120° F 130° G 140° H 150°
90° C 100° D 110° E 120° F 130° G 140° H 150° J
1 20° 2 10° 3 0° 4 10° 5

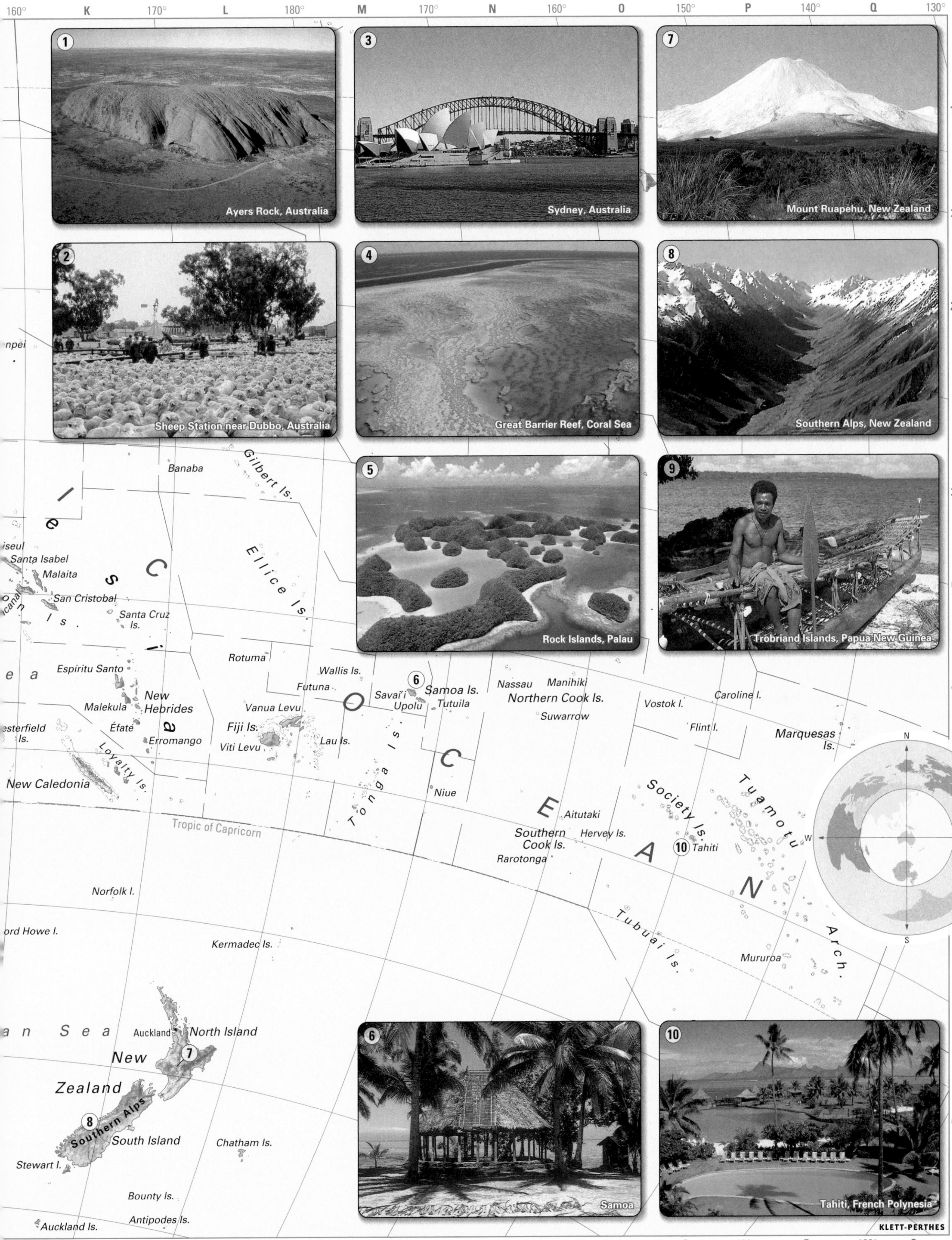

1 Ayers Rock, Australia

3 Sydney, Australia

7 Mount Ruapehu, New Zealand

2 Sheep Station near Dubbo, Australia

4 Great Barrier Reef, Coral Sea

8 Southern Alps, New Zealand

5 Rock Islands, Palau

9 Trobriand Islands, Papua New Guinea

6 Samoa

10 Tahiti, French Polynesia

KLETT-PERTHES

CHINA
JAPAN
INDIA
BANGLADESH
MYANMAR
THAILAND
LAOS
VIETNAM
CAMBODIA
MALAYSIA
BRUNEI
SINGAPORE
PHILIPPINES
INDONESIA
TIMOR-LESTE
PAPUA NEW GUINEA
PALAU
MICRONESIA
AUSTRALIA
TAIWAN
Mt. Everest 29,035 ft 8,850 m
Kathmandu
Thimphu
BHU.
NEP.
DHAKA
KOLKATA
Mandalay
RANGOON
BANGKOK
PHNUM PENH
HO CHI MINH CITY
HANOI
Hai Phong
Vientiane
Huë
Da Nang
Nha Trang
KUNMING
GUIYANG
CHANGSHA
NANCHANG
FUZHOU
Wenzhou
GUANGZHOU
SHANTOU
HONG KONG
Macau
Nanning
T'AIPEI
Naha
MANILA
Cebu
DAVAO
Zamboanga
Mt. Apo 9,692 ft 2,954 m
Kinabalu 13,455 ft 4,101 m
Bandar Seri Begawan
KUALA LUMPUR
MEDAN
Pekanbaru
Padang
PALEMBANG
JAKARTA
BANDUNG
SEMARANG
SURABAYA
Semeru 12,061 ft 3,676 m
Kuching
Pontianak
Samarinda
Banjarmasin
UJUNG PANDANG
Manado
Ambon
Dili
Kupang
Jayapura
Port Moresby
Lae
Rabaul
Koror
Agaña
Garapan
Saipan
Carstensz Pyramid 16,024 ft 4,884 m
Mt. Wilhelm 14,794 ft 4,509 m
Mt. Victoria 13,363 ft 4,073 m
Maoke Range
Darwin
Derby
Port Hedland
North West Cape
Carnarvon
Geraldton
PERTH
Albany
Cape Leeuwin
Alice Springs
Macdonnell Ra.
Ayers Rock 2,844 ft 867 m
Mount Isa
Cairns
Townsville
Mackay
Rockhampton
Broken Hill
Port Augusta
Ceduna
ADELAIDE
Canberra
SYDNEY
Newcastle
Wollongong
Mt. Kosciusko 7,310 ft 2,228 m
Austral. Alps
MELBOURNE
Geelong
Hobart
South East Cape
Tasmania
Great Dividing Range
Great Barrier Reef
Gt. Victoria Desert
Nullarbor Plain
L. Eyre -39 ft -12 m
Cooper Cr.
Darling
Murray
Flinders
Fitzroy
Arnhem Land
Cape York Pen.
C. York
C. Arnhem
Gulf of Carpentaria
Great Australian Bight
Kangaroo I.
King I.
Bass Str.
Torres Str.
Arafura Sea
Timor Sea
Coral Sea
Solomon Sea
Banda Sea
Java Sea
Celebes Sea
Sulu Sea
Molucca Sea
Makassar Str.
South China Sea
Philippine Sea
Bay of Bengal
Andaman Sea
G. of Thailand
G. of Tonking
Str. of Malacca
Sunda Str.
INDIAN OCEAN
Greater Sunda Is.
Lesser Sunda Is.
Moluccas
New Guinea
Borneo (Kalimantan)
Celebes (Sulawesi)
Sumatra
Java
Bali
Flores
Sumba
Madura
Mindanao
Mindoro
Luzon
Samar
Panay
Negros
Palawan
Hainan
Halmahera
Seram
Buru
Buton
Biak
Aru Is.
Kai Is.
Tanimbar Is.
Dolak
Melville I.
Sangir Is.
Sulu Arch.
Mentawai Is.
Malay Pen.
Andaman Is. (IND.)
Nicobar Is. (IND.)
Christmas I. (AUS.)
Cocos Is. (AUS.)
Ashmore (AUS.)
Cartier
Coral Sea Is. (AUS.)
Paracel Is. (CHN.)
Daito Is. (JAP.)
Bonin Is. (JAP.)
Volcano Is. (JAP.)
Marcus I. (JAP.)
Okino Tori (JAP.)
Northern Mariana Is. (U.S.)
Guam (U.S.)
Yap Is.
Palau Is.
Chuuk Is.
Caroline Is.
Admiralty Is.
Bismarck Arch.
New Britain
Bougainville
Louisiade Arch.
Ryukyu Is.
Taiwan Str.
Vityaz Depth 36,204 ft 11,035 m
18,238 ft 5,559 m
34,439 ft 10,497 m
18,605 ft 5,671 m
Elevation
13,124 ft 4,000 m
6,562 ft 2,000 m
3,281 ft 1,000 m
1,640 ft 500 m
656 ft 200 m
0 ft 0 m
Depression
656 ft 200 m
6,562 ft 2,000 m
13,124 ft 4,000 m
19,686 ft 6,000 m
26,248 ft 8,000 m
Inland ice, glaciers
Reef
* free association with New Zealand
BHU. BHUTAN
NEP. NEPAL

1:35,000,000

0 500 1,000 mi
0 500 1,000 1,500 2,000 km
Midway Is. (U.S.)
Hawaiian Islands
UNITED STATES
Tropic of Cancer
Wake I. (U.S.)
Oahu
Honolulu
Maui
Mauna Kea 13,796 ft 4,205 m
Hawaii
Johnston Atoll (U.S.)
25,216 ft 7,686 m
P A C I F I C
Enewetak Atoll
Bikini Atoll
MARSHALL ISLANDS
Ralik Chain
Ratak Chain
Majuro Atoll
Uliga
Palikir
Kosrae
20,751 ft 6,325 m
Kingman Reef
Palmyra Atoll
(U.S.)
Line Islands
Teraina
Tabuaeran
Kiritimati
14,271 ft 4,350 m
Bairiki
Gilbert Is.
Yaren
NAURU
Banaba
Howland I.
Baker I.
(U.S.)
Jarvis I. (U.S.)
KIRIBATI
Kanton
Phoenix Is.
24,002 ft 7,316 m
Equator
SOLOMON ISLANDS
Santa Isabel
Malaita
8,028 ft 2,447 m
San Cristobal
Santa Cruz Is.
TUVALU
Ellice Is.
Funafuti
Malden I.
Atafu
Tokelau (N.Z.)
Starbuck I.
Northern Cook Is.
Penrhyn
Rotuma
Wallis and Futuna (FRA.)
Wallis Is.
Futuna
Matā'utu
SAMOA
6,096 ft 1,858 m
Savai'i
Apia
Upolu
American
Tutuila
Pago Pago
Samoa (U.S.)
Pukapuka
Nassau
Manihiki
Vostok I.
Caroline I.
Flint I.
Suwarrow
Espíritu Santo
6,165 ft 1,879 m
VANUATU
New Hebrides
Malekula
Port Vila
Éfaté
Erromango
Vanua Levu
Viti Levu
Suva
FIJI
Lau Is.
TONGA
COOK ISLANDS*
Marquesas Is.
5,341 ft 1,628 m
New Caledonia (FRA.)
Nouméa
Loyalty Is.
Alofi
NIUE*
Nuku'alofa
Tonga Is.
Southern Cook Is.
Aitutaki
Hervey Is.
Society Is.
Papeete
7,352 ft 2,241 m
Tahiti
Tuamotu Arch.
Tropic of Capricorn
17,398 ft 5,303 m
35,702 ft 10,882 m
Avarua
Rarotonga
French Polynesia
Norfolk (AUS.)
International Date Line
19,819 ft 6,041 m
O C E A N
Lord Howe I. (AUS.)
Kermadec Is. (N.Z.)
Tubuai Is.
Mururoa
North Cape
32,962 ft 10,047 m
Auckland
North Island
Hamilton
East Cape
NEW ZEALAND
Mt. Ruapehu
9,177 ft 2,797 m
Wellington
Monday
Sunday
3,570 ft 1,088 m
Rapa
Oeno I.
Adamstown
Pitcairn I.
Pitcairn (U.K.)
Mt. Cook
12,349 ft 3,764 m
Southern Alps
Christchurch
South Island
Dunedin
Chatham Is. (N.Z.)
Maria Theresa Reef
Stewart I.
Bounty Is. (N.Z.)
Antipodes Is.
Auckland Is. (N.Z.)
KLETT-PERTHES

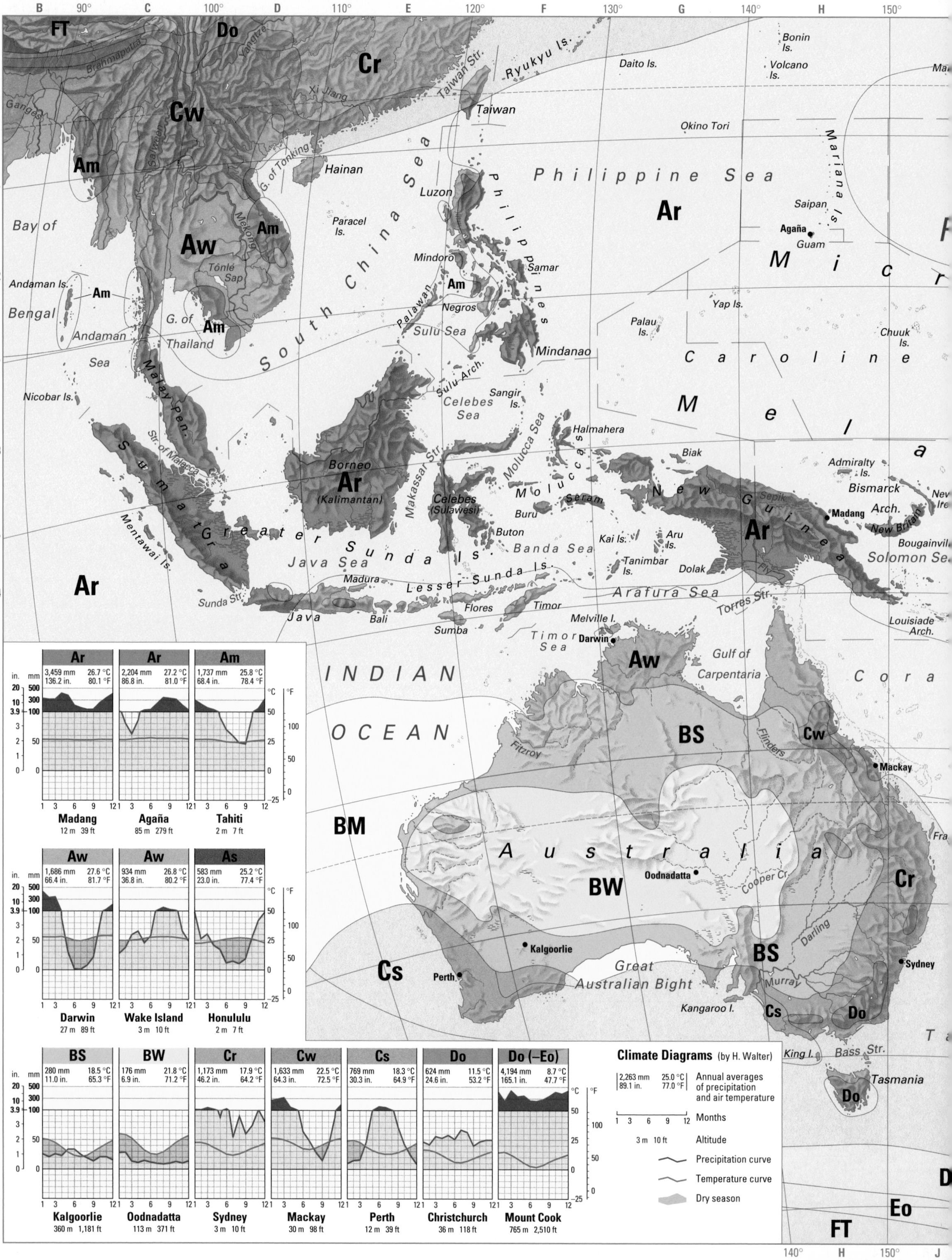
B
90°
C
100°
D
110°
E
120°
F
130°
G
140°
H
150°
1
20°
2
10°
3
0°
4
FT
Do
Cr
Cw
Am
Aw
Ar
BS
BW
BM
Cs
Eo
Brahmaputra
Yangtze
Xi Jiang
Ganges
Salween
Mekong
Bay of Bengal
Andaman Is.
Andaman Sea
Nicobar Is.
G. of Thailand
Tônlé Sap
G. of Tonking
Hainan
Paracel Is.
South China Sea
Taiwan Str.
Taiwan
Ryukyu Is.
Daito Is.
Bonin Is.
Volcano Is.
Okino Tori
Mariana Is.
Saipan
Agaña
Guam
Philippine Sea
Luzon
Philippines
Mindoro
Samar
Palawan
Negros
Sulu Sea
Mindanao
Sulu Arch.
Celebes Sea
Sangir Is.
Malay Pen.
Str. of Malacca
Sumatra
Mentawai Is.
Borneo
(Kalimantan)
Makassar Str.
Celebes
(Sulawesi)
Molucca Sea
Halmahera
Moluccas
Seram
Buru
Buton
Banda Sea
Kai Is.
Aru Is.
Tanimbar Is.
Dolak
Greater Sunda Is.
Java Sea
Madura
Lesser Sunda Is.
Sunda Str.
Java
Bali
Flores
Sumba
Timor
Timor Sea
Melville I.
Darwin
Arafura Sea
Torres Str.
Yap Is.
Palau Is.
Chuuk Is.
Caroline
Micronesia
Melanesia
Biak
New Guinea
Sepik
Fly
Admiralty Is.
Bismarck Arch.
Madang
New Britain
Bougainville
Solomon Sea
Louisiade Arch.
Gulf of Carpentaria
Coral
INDIAN OCEAN
Fitzroy
Flinders
Mackay
Australia
Oodnadatta
Cooper Cr.
Darling
Kalgoorlie
Perth
Great Australian Bight
Kangaroo I.
Murray
Sydney
King I.
Bass Str.
Tasmania
Ar | Ar | Am
3,459 mm 26.7 °C 136.2 in. 80.1 °F
2,204 mm 27.2 °C 86.8 in. 81.0 °F
1,737 mm 25.8 °C 68.4 in. 78.4 °F
Madang 12 m 39 ft
Agaña 85 m 279 ft
Tahiti 2 m 7 ft
Aw | Aw | As
1,686 mm 27.6 °C 66.4 in. 81.7 °F
934 mm 26.8 °C 36.8 in. 80.2 °F
583 mm 25.2 °C 23.0 in. 77.4 °F
Darwin 27 m 89 ft
Wake Island 3 m 10 ft
Honululu 2 m 7 ft
BS | BW | Cr | Cw | Cs | Do | Do (–Eo)
280 mm 18.5 °C 11.0 in. 65.3 °F
176 mm 21.8 °C 6.9 in. 71.2 °F
1,173 mm 17.9 °C 46.2 in. 64.2 °F
1,633 mm 22.5 °C 64.3 in. 72.5 °F
769 mm 18.3 °C 30.3 in. 64.9 °F
624 mm 11.5 °C 24.6 in. 53.2 °F
4,194 mm 8.7 °C 165.1 in. 47.7 °F
Kalgoorlie 360 m 1,181 ft
Oodnadatta 113 m 371 ft
Sydney 3 m 10 ft
Mackay 30 m 98 ft
Perth 12 m 39 ft
Christchurch 36 m 118 ft
Mount Cook 765 m 2,510 ft
in. mm
°C °F
Climate Diagrams (by H. Walter)
2,263 mm 25.0 °C 89.1 in. 77.0 °F
Annual averages of precipitation and air temperature
Months
3 m 10 ft
Altitude
Precipitation curve
Temperature curve
Dry season

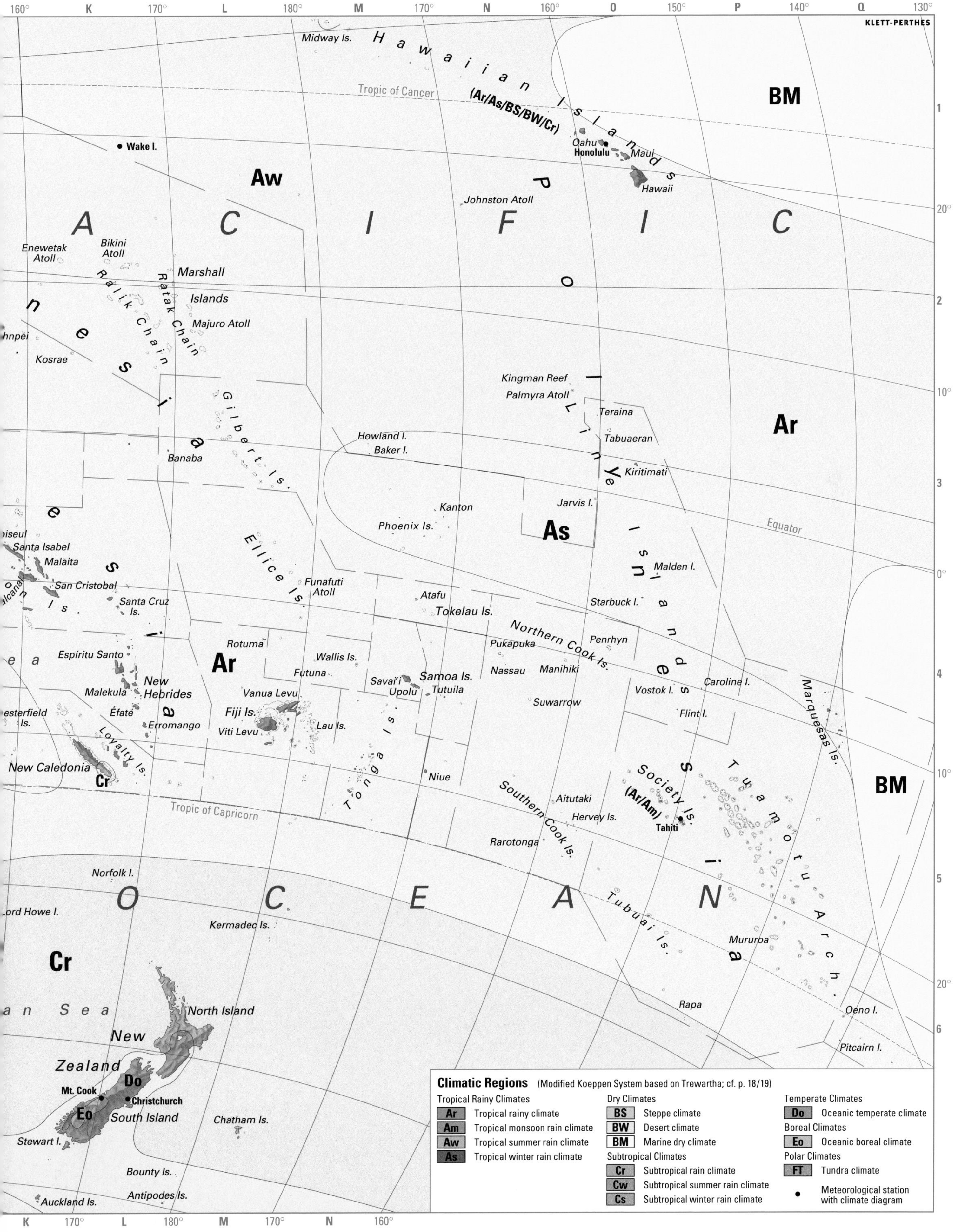
160° K 170° L 180° M 170° N 160° O 150° P 140° Q 130°
KLETT-PERTHES
Midway Is.
Hawaiian Islands
(Ar/As/BS/BW/Cr)
Tropic of Cancer
BM
Oahu
Honolulu
Maui
Hawaii
Wake I.
Aw
Johnston Atoll
PACIFIC
Enewetak Atoll
Bikini Atoll
Marshall Islands
Ralik Chain
Ratak Chain
Majuro Atoll
Kosrae
Polynesia
Kingman Reef
Palmyra Atoll
Teraina
Tabuaeran
Line Islands
Kiritimati
Ar
Gilbert Is.
Banaba
Howland I.
Baker I.
Kanton
Phoenix Is.
Jarvis I.
As
Equator
Micronesia
Santa Isabel
Malaita
San Cristobal
Solomon Is.
Santa Cruz Is.
Ellice Is.
Funafuti Atoll
Malden I.
Atafu
Tokelau Is.
Starbuck I.
Northern Cook Is.
Penrhyn
Pukapuka
Rotuma
Ar
Espíritu Santo
Wallis Is.
Futuna
Samoa Is.
Savai'i
Upolu
Tutuila
Nassau
Manihiki
Vostok I.
Caroline I.
Marquesas Is.
New Hebrides
Malekula
Éfaté
Erromango
Vanua Levu
Fiji Is.
Viti Levu
Lau Is.
Suwarrow
Flint I.
Loyalty Is.
New Caledonia
Cr
Tonga Is.
Niue
Society Is.
(Ar/Am)
Tahiti
Tuamotu Arch.
BM
Southern Cook Is.
Aitutaki
Hervey Is.
Rarotonga
Tropic of Capricorn
Norfolk I.
OCEAN
Lord Howe I.
Kermadec Is.
Tubuai Is.
Mururoa
Cr
Tasman Sea
North Island
New Zealand
Do
Mt. Cook
Christchurch
Eo
South Island
Stewart I.
Chatham Is.
Bounty Is.
Antipodes Is.
Auckland Is.
Rapa
Oeno I.
Pitcairn I.
1 2 3 4 5 6
20° 10° 0° 10° 20°
K 170° L 180° M 170° N 160°
Climatic Regions (Modified Koeppen System based on Trewartha; cf. p. 18/19)
Tropical Rainy Climates
Ar Tropical rainy climate
Am Tropical monsoon rain climate
Aw Tropical summer rain climate
As Tropical winter rain climate
Dry Climates
BS Steppe climate
BW Desert climate
BM Marine dry climate
Subtropical Climates
Cr Subtropical rain climate
Cw Subtropical summer rain climate
Cs Subtropical winter rain climate
Temperate Climates
Do Oceanic temperate climate
Boreal Climates
Eo Oceanic boreal climate
Polar Climates
FT Tundra climate
Meteorological station with climate diagram

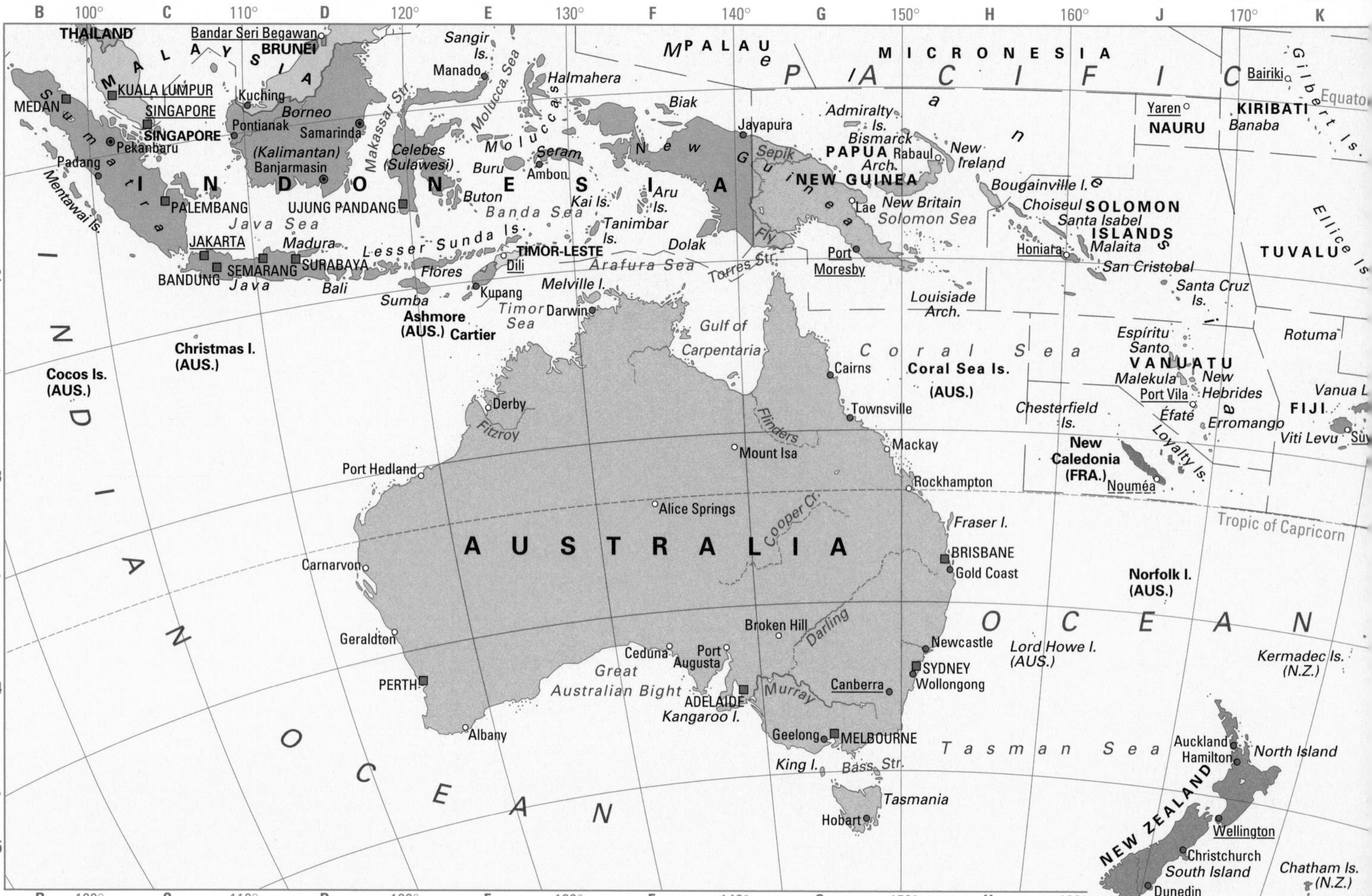
1:45,000,000
0 500 1,000 mi
0 500 1,000 1,500 2,000 km
B C D E F G H J K
100° 110° 120° 130° 140° 150° 160° 170°
0° 10° 20° 30°
1 2 3 4 5
THAILAND
Bandar Seri Begawan
BRUNEI
M A L A Y S I A
KUALA LUMPUR
SINGAPORE
SINGAPORE
MEDAN
Kuching
Pontianak
Borneo
Samarinda
(Kalimantan)
Banjarmasin
Pekanbaru
Padang
Sumatra
Mentawai Is.
I N D O N E S I A
PALEMBANG
UJUNG PANDANG
Java Sea
JAKARTA
Madura
BANDUNG
SEMARANG
SURABAYA
Java
Bali
Lesser Sunda Is.
Sumba
Flores
Kupang
Dili
TIMOR-LESTE
Timor Sea
Ashmore (AUS.)
Cartier
Darwin
Melville I.
Makassar Str.
Celebes (Sulawesi)
Sangir Is.
Manado
Molucca Sea
Halmahera
Moluccas
Seram
Buru
Ambon
Buton
Banda Sea
Kai Is.
Aru Is.
Tanimbar Is.
Arafura Sea
Dolak
Torres Str.
Biak
New Guinea
Jayapura
Sepik
Fly
PALAU
MICRONESIA
P A C I F I C
O C E A N
Admiralty Is.
Bismarck Arch.
Rabaul
New Ireland
PAPUA NEW GUINEA
Lae
New Britain
Solomon Sea
Port Moresby
Bougainville I.
Choiseul
SOLOMON ISLANDS
Santa Isabel
Malaita
Honiara
San Cristobal
Louisiade Arch.
Santa Cruz Is.
Bairiki
Gilbert Is.
Equator
Yaren
NAURU
KIRIBATI
Banaba
Ellice Is.
TUVALU
Rotuma
Espíritu Santo
VANUATU
Malekula
New Hebrides
Port Vila
Éfaté
Erromango
FIJI
Vanua Levu
Viti Levu
Suva
Chesterfield Is.
New Caledonia (FRA.)
Nouméa
Loyalty Is.
Gulf of Carpentaria
Coral Sea
Cairns
Coral Sea Is. (AUS.)
Townsville
Mackay
Flinders
Mount Isa
Derby
Fitzroy
Port Hedland
Rockhampton
Alice Springs
Cooper Cr.
Tropic of Capricorn
Fraser I.
BRISBANE
Gold Coast
A U S T R A L I A
Carnarvon
Norfolk I. (AUS.)
Broken Hill
Darling
Geraldton
Ceduna
Port Augusta
Newcastle
Lord Howe I. (AUS.)
SYDNEY
Wollongong
Kermadec Is. (N.Z.)
PERTH
Great Australian Bight
ADELAIDE
Kangaroo I.
Murray
Canberra
Albany
Geelong
MELBOURNE
King I.
Bass Str.
Tasman Sea
Tasmania
Hobart
Auckland
Hamilton
North Island
NEW ZEALAND
Wellington
Christchurch
South Island
Dunedin
Chatham Is. (N.Z.)
Christmas I. (AUS.)
Cocos Is. (AUS.)
I N D I A N O C E A N
KLETT-PERTHES

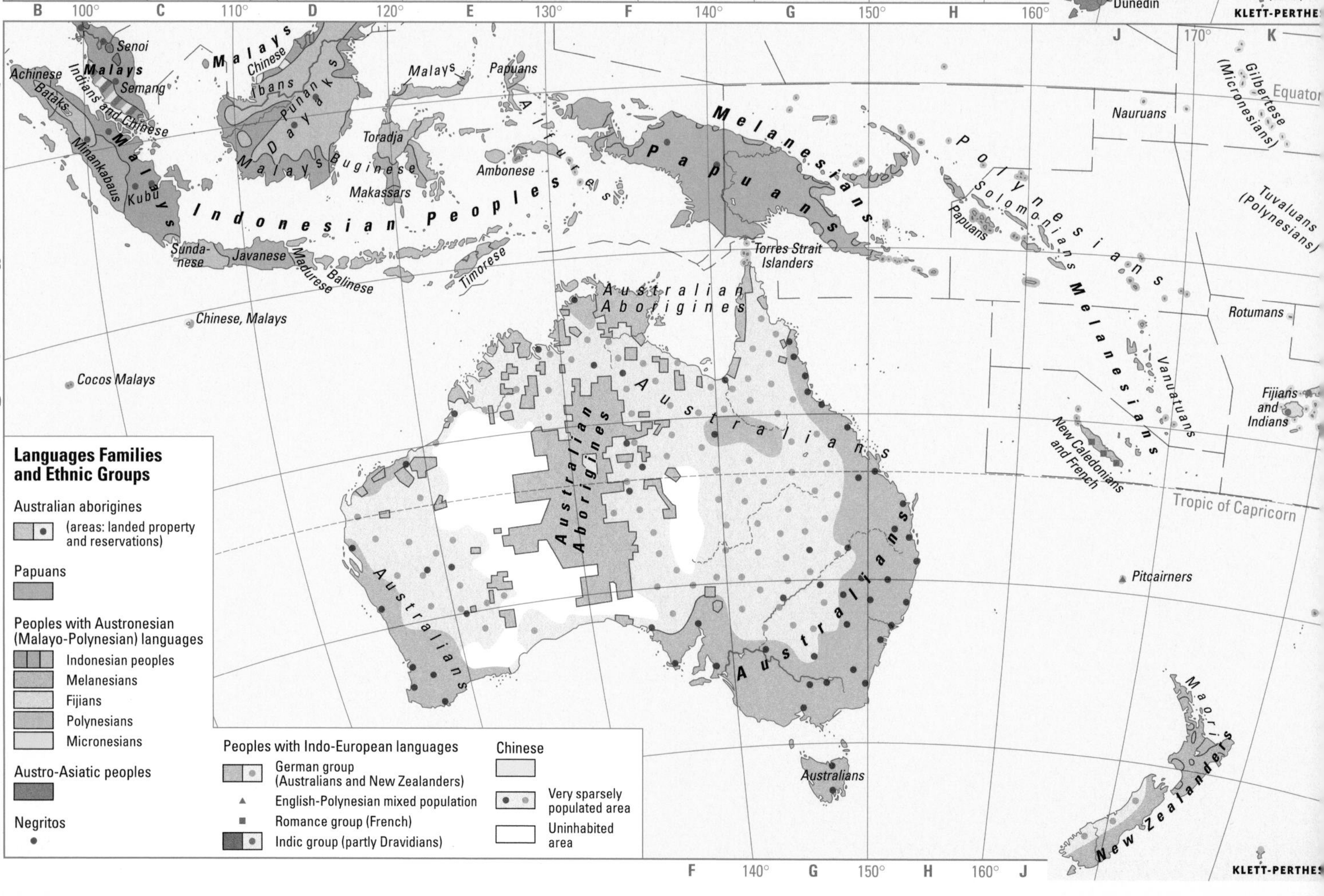
B C D E F G H J K
100° 110° 120° 130° 140° 150° 160° 170°
0° 10°
7 8 9
Senoi
Malays
Semang
Achinese
Bataks
Indians and Chinese
Malays
Minankabaus
Kubu
Malays
Chinese
Ibans
Punans
Dayaks
Malays
Toradja
Buginese
Makassars
Ambonese
Malays
Papuans
Alfures
Indonesian Peoples
Sunda-nese
Javanese
Madurese
Balinese
Timorese
Chinese, Malays
Cocos Malays
Melanesians
Papuans
Torres Strait Islanders
Polynesians
Solomonians
Papuans
Melanesians
Nauruans
Gilbertese (Micronesians)
Equator
Tuvaluans (Polynesians)
Rotumans
Vanuatuans
Fijians and Indians
New Caledonians and French
Tropic of Capricorn
Pitcairners
Australian Aborigines
Australians
Australian Aborigines
Australians
Australians
Australians
Australians
Maoris
New Zealanders
Languages Families and Ethnic Groups
Australian aborigines
(areas: landed property and reservations)
Papuans
Peoples with Austronesian (Malayo-Polynesian) languages
Indonesian peoples
Melanesians
Fijians
Polynesians
Micronesians
Austro-Asiatic peoples
Negritos
Peoples with Indo-European languages
German group (Australians and New Zealanders)
English-Polynesian mixed population
Romance group (French)
Indic group (partly Dravidians)
Chinese
Very sparsely populated area
Uninhabited area
KLETT-PERTHES

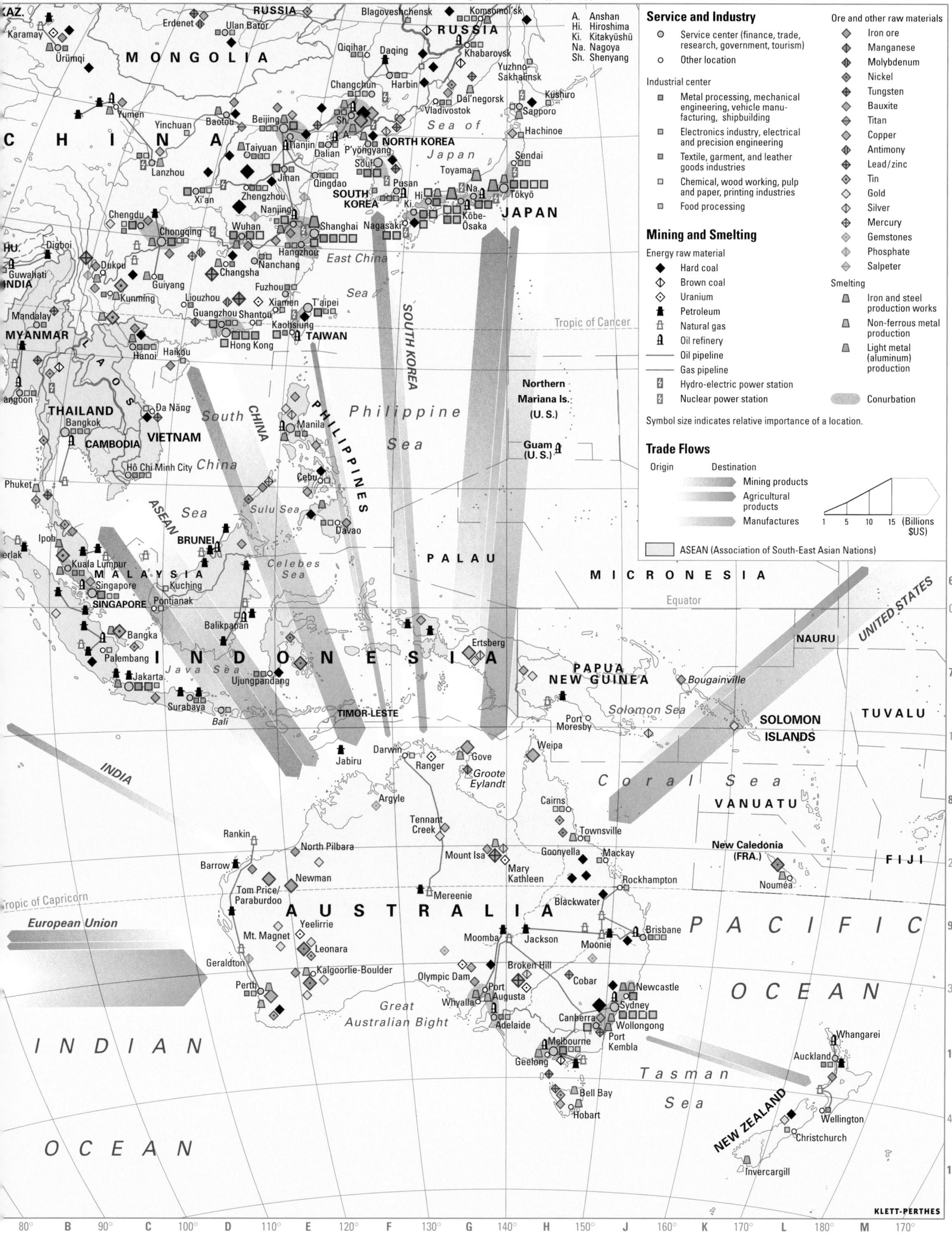

A. Anshan
Hi. Hiroshima
Ki. Kitakyūshū
Na. Nagoya
Sh. Shenyang
Service and Industry
Service center (finance, trade, research, government, tourism)
Other location
Industrial center
Metal processing, mechanical engineering, vehicle manufacturing, shipbuilding
Electronics industry, electrical and precision engineering
Textile, garment, and leather goods industries
Chemical, wood working, pulp and paper, printing industries
Food processing
Mining and Smelting
Energy raw material
Hard coal
Brown coal
Uranium
Petroleum
Natural gas
Oil refinery
Oil pipeline
Gas pipeline
Hydro-electric power station
Nuclear power station
Ore and other raw materials
Iron ore
Manganese
Molybdenum
Nickel
Tungsten
Bauxite
Titan
Copper
Antimony
Lead/zinc
Tin
Gold
Silver
Mercury
Gemstones
Phosphate
Salpeter
Smelting
Iron and steel production works
Non-ferrous metal production
Light metal (aluminum) production
Conurbation
Symbol size indicates relative importance of a location.
Trade Flows
Origin
Destination
Mining products
Agricultural products
Manufactures
1 5 10 15 (Billions $US)
ASEAN (Association of South-East Asian Nations)
RUSSIA
MONGOLIA
CHINA
NORTH KOREA
SOUTH KOREA
JAPAN
TAIWAN
MYANMAR
LAOS
THAILAND
CAMBODIA
VIETNAM
PHILIPPINES
MALAYSIA
SINGAPORE
BRUNEI
INDONESIA
TIMOR-LESTE
PAPUA NEW GUINEA
SOLOMON ISLANDS
VANUATU
NAURU
TUVALU
FIJI
PALAU
MICRONESIA
Northern Mariana Is. (U. S.)
Guam (U. S.)
New Caledonia (FRA.)
AUSTRALIA
NEW ZEALAND
UNITED STATES
INDIA
ASEAN
European Union
Sea of Japan
East China Sea
South China Sea
Philippine Sea
Sulu Sea
Celebes Sea
Java Sea
Solomon Sea
Coral Sea
Tasman Sea
Great Australian Bight
INDIAN OCEAN
PACIFIC OCEAN
Tropic of Cancer
Equator
Tropic of Capricorn
Darwin
Jabiru
Ranger
Gove
Groote Eylandt
Weipa
Cairns
Townsville
Mackay
Goonyella
Rockhampton
Blackwater
Brisbane
Moonie
Jackson
Moomba
Mount Isa
Mary Kathleen
Tennant Creek
Mereenie
Argyle
Rankin
North Pilbara
Barrow
Newman
Tom Price/Paraburdoo
Yeelirrie
Mt. Magnet
Leonara
Geraldton
Kalgoorlie-Boulder
Perth
Olympic Dam
Port Augusta
Whyalla
Adelaide
Broken Hill
Cobar
Newcastle
Sydney
Wollongong
Port Kembla
Canberra
Melbourne
Geelong
Bell Bay
Hobart
Whangarei
Auckland
Wellington
Christchurch
Invercargill
Nouméa
Bougainville
Port Moresby
Ertsberg
KLETT-PERTHES

156
157
Celebes (Sulawesi)
UJUNG PANDANG
Muna
Buton
Kabaena
Baubau
Kabia
Benteng
Sabalana Is.
Tanahjampea
Kangean Is.
Flores Sea
Lomblen
Alor
Wetar
Huaki
Bacau
Dili
Tutuala
TIMOR-LESTE
9,777 ft
2,980 m
Ramelau
Banda Sea
Damar Is.
Babar
Leti Is.
Kai Is.
Trangan
Kobroor
Aru Is.
Yamdena
Tanimbar Is.
Saumlaki
Selaru
Dolak
I N D O N E S I A
Bali
Denpasar
Mataram
Lombok
Sumbawa
Sumbawabesar
12,225 ft
3,726 m
Bima
Labuhanbajo
7,874 ft
2,400 m
Maumere
Endeh
Flores
Savu Sea
Waingapu
4,019 ft
1,225 m
Sumba
Sawu
Kefamenanu
Kupang
Timor
Roti
Timor Sea
Arafura Sea
Melville I.
Croker I.
Bathurst I.
Wessel Islands
Cape Wessel
Cape Arnhem
Darwin
Jabiru
1,201 ft
366 m
Arnhem Land
Pine Creek
Katherine
Ashmore
Ashmore Reef (AUS.)
Cartier
Cape Londonderry
Joseph Bonaparte Gulf
Gulf of Carpentaria
Groote Eylandt
Wellesley Islands
Larrimah
Daly Waters
Victoria
Wyndham
Kimberley
Cape Lévêque
Mount Wells
3,183 ft
970 m
Wave Hill
Derby
Broome
Fitzroy
Halls Creek
Burketown
1,138 ft
347 m
Northern Territory
Tanami Desert
Tanami
Tennant Creek
Camooweal
Mount Isa
Cloncurry
Kajabbi
Great Sandy Desert
Yuendumu
Lake Mackay
Port Hedland
Marble Bar
Dampier
Barrow Is.
Roebourne
North West Cape
Onslow
4,111 ft
1,253 m
Hamersley Range
Ashburton
Newman
Western Australia
5,023 ft
1,531 m
Macdonnell Ranges
Alice Springs
Gibson Desert
Ayers Rock (Uluru)
2,845 ft
867 m
Musgrave Ra.
4,708 ft
1,435 m
Kulgera
Roadhouse
Simpson Desert
A U S T R A L I A
Gascoyne
Carnarvon
Lake Carnegie
Wiluna
Cape Inscription
Denham
Murchison
Meekatharra
2,169 ft
661 m
Great Victoria Desert
South Australia
Oodnadatta
Lake Eyre Basin
Lake Eyre
-39 ft
-12 m
Coober Pedy
Marree
Mount Magnet
Leonora
Laverton
Lake Barlee
Menzies
Mullewa
Geraldton
Dongara
Lake Moore
Nullarbor Plain
Cook
Tarcoola
Kingoonya
Lake Torrens
Lake Gairdner
Ceduna
Kalgoorlie-Boulder
Rawlinna
Coolgardie
Eucla
Fowlers Bay
Streaky Bay
Moora
Meeredin
Norseman
Northam
PERTH
Mandurah
Narrogin
Collie
Bunbury
Katanning
3,642 ft
1,110 m
Cranbrook
Augusta
Cape Leeuwin
Albany
Esperance
Great Australian Bight
Kimba
Whyalla
Port Augusta
Port Pirie
Spencer Gulf
Wallaroo
Mount Hope
Port Lincoln
ADELAIDE
Victor Harbour
Kangaroo Island
Kingscote
Murray Bridge
Leigh Creek
3,901 ft
1,189 m
Lake Frome
112 ft
34 m
Peterborough
Renmark
Wentworth
Mildura
Swan Hill
Murray
Broken Hill
Darling
New South Wales
Cape York Pen.
Coen
Torres Strait
Badu
Moa
Cape York
Bamaga
Prince of Wales I.
Merauke
Digul
Fly
Gulf of Papua
Daru
New Guinea
Kundiawa
Goroka
Lae
Bulolo
Kikori
Kerema
Mt. Victoria
13,363 ft
4,073 m
Port Moresby
Owen Stanley Ra.
Popondetta
Abau
Esa'ala
Alotau
Samarai
Solomon S
Trobriand Is.
Kiriwina
Fergusson I.
D'Entre
Norma
Louisiad Arch.
PAPUA NEW GUINEA
Cooktown
Mossman
Cairns
Mareeba
Bartle Frere
5,322 ft
1,622 m
Innisfail
Coral
Normanton
Croydon
Forsayth
Flinders
Ingham
Townsville
Bowen
Charters Towers
Richmond
Hughenden
4,131 ft
1,259 m
Mackay
Great Dividing Range
Dajarra
Winton
Georgina
Diamantina
Queensland
Clermont
Rockhampt
761 ft
232 m
Great Artesian Basin
Longreach
Barcaldine
Emerald
Blackall
Gladstone
Bund
berg
Yaraka
Tambo
Theodore
Monto
Gayndah
Windorah
Maryborough
Birdsville
Injune
Murgon
Charleville
Miles
Caloundra
3,750
1,143 m
Quilpie
Roma
Dalby
Toowoomba
Warwick
Cooper Creek
Innamincka
Cunnamulla
Dirranbandi
Thargomindah
272 ft
83 m
Goondiwindi
Warrego
Milparinka
Walgett
Moree
Narrabri
Grafto
Lismo
5,276
1,608 m
Armidale
Bourke
Coonamble
Tamworth
Cobar
Nyngan
Dubbo
Ivanhoe
Parkes
Orange
Cessnock
Lithgow
Newc
SYDNE
Wollongo
Griffith
Balranald
4,600 ft
1,402 m
Goulburn
Narrandera
Wagga Wagga
Canberra
Albury
Wodonga
Mt. Kosciusko
7,310 ft
2,228 m
Australian Alps
Nowra
Bega
Bombala
Shepparton
Wangaratta
Bendigo
Horsham
Naracoorte
Victoria
Hamilton
Ballarat
MELBOURNE
Orbost
Cape Howe
Bairnsdale
Mount Gambier
Portland
Warrnambool
Geelong
Wonthaggi
Moe
Sale
Bass Strait
King Island
Currie
Furneaux Is.
Cape Grim
Stanley
Burnie
Devonport
Launceston
Mt. Ossa
5,305 ft
1,617 m
Queenstown
Tasmania
Hobart
South East Cape
INDIAN OCEAN
KLETT-PERTHES

M 160° N 165° O 170° P 175° 161 Q 180° R 175° S 170° T
SOLOMON ISLANDS
Choiseul
Santa Isabel
Buala
New Georgia
Gizo
Rendova
New Georgia Is.
Vangunu
Tulaghi
Auki
Malaita
4,702 ft
1,433 m
Sikaiana
Honiara
8,028 ft
2,447 m
Guadalcanal
Mt. Makarakomburu
Maramasike
Kirakira
San Cristobal
Solomon Islands
Rennell
Nendo
Santa Cruz Islands
Utupua
Vanikolo
Anuta
Tikopia
Torres Is.
Vanua Lava
Banks Islands
VANUATU
Espíritu Santo
Mt. Tabwemasana
6,165 ft
1,879 m
Luganville
Santa Maria
Maewo
Pentecost
Ambrym
Malekula
Épi
Port Vila
Éfaté
Erromango
Tanna
Anatom
New Hebrides
Île Surprise
Chesterfield Is.
Îles Belep
New Caledonia (FRA.)
Poum
Mont Panié
5,341 ft 1,628 m
Koné
New Caledonia
Ouvéa
Lifou
Loyalty Is.
Wé
Maré
Tadine
La Foa
Nouméa
Mont-Dore
Île des Pins
Nanumea
Nanumango
Niutao
Ellice Islands
Nui
Vaitupu
Nukufetau
TUVALU
Funafuti
Nukulaelae
Niulakita
Rotuma
Wallis and Futuna (FRA.)
Matā'utu
Futuna
Taoa
Alofi
Wallis Is.
FIJI
Vanua Levu
3,383 ft
1,031 m
Labasa
Somosomo
Mt. Victoria (Tomanivi)
4,337 ft
1,322 m
Lautoka
Nadi
Levuka
Koro
Taveuni
Viti Levu
Lami
Suva
Gau
Moala
Lakeba
Kadavu
Ono
Matuku
Totoya
Lau Islands
Ono-i-Lau
Tuvana-i-Colo
Ceva-i-Ra
Phoenix Islands
Rawaki
Nikumaroro
Orona
Manra
KIRIBATI
Atafu
Tokelau (N.Z.)
Nukunonu
Fakaofo
SAMOA
Mt. Silisili
6,096 ft
1,858 m
Savai'i
Apia
Upolu
Samoa Islands
Pago Pago
Tutuila
Manua Is.
Lata
3,169 ft
966 m
American Samoa (U.S.)
Niuatoputapu
Tafahi
TONGA
Fonualei
Toku
'Uta Vava'u
Neiafu
Vava'u Is.
3,389 ft
1,033 m
Late
Tofua
Kotu Is.
Pangai
Ha'apai Is.
Nomuka Is.
Nuku'alofa
Tongatapu
Eua
Niue
Alofi
NIUE*
COOK ISLANDS*
Tropic of Capricorn
Norfolk Island (AUS.)
Lord Howe I. (AUS.)
PACIFIC OCEAN
Kermadec Is. (N.Z.)
Tasman Sea
Three Kings
North Cape
Kaitaia
Whangarei
Great Barrier Island
North Shore
Auckland
Manukau
Paeroa
Bay of Plenty
North Island
Hamilton
Tauranga
5,755 ft
1,754 m
Rotorua
East Cape
Waitara
Taumarunui
Whatakane
New Plymouth
Gisborne
Mt. Egmont (Taranaki) 8,261 ft 2,518 m
Mt. Ruapehu
9,177 ft
2,797 m
Napier
Wairoa
Stratford
Hawke Bay
C. Farewell
Wanganui
Hastings
Levin
Nelson
Porirua
Palmerston North
Westport
Lower Hutt
Wellington
Greymouth
Blenheim
Cook Strait
Mount Cook
12,349 ft
3,764 m
Kaikoura
Haast
Southern Alps
Christchurch
Ashburton
L. Te Anau
Timaru
Cromwell
Oamaru
South Island
Dunedin
Invercargill
Milton
Stewart I.
South West Cape
NEW ZEALAND
Chatham Is. (N.Z.)
Bounty Is. (N.Z.)
Auckland Is. (N.Z.)
Antipodes Is. (N.Z.)
* free association with New Zealand
1 2 3 4 5 6 7 8 9
5° 10° 15° 20° 25° 30° 35° 40°
160° N 165° O 170° P 175° Q 180° R 175° S 170° T 165° U 160° V 155° W

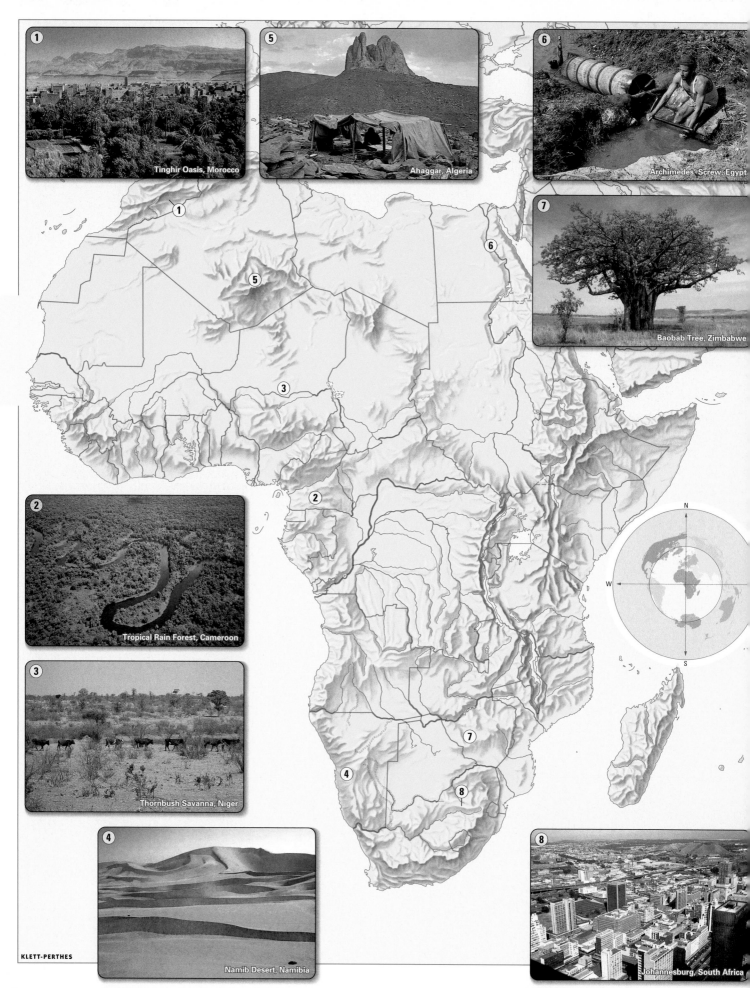

Tinghir Oasis, Morocco

Ahaggar, Algeria

Archimedes' Screw, Egypt

Baobab Tree, Zimbabwe

Tropical Rain Forest, Cameroon

Thornbush Savanna, Niger

Namib Desert, Namibia

Johannesburg, South Africa

A 20° B 10° C 0° D 10° E 20° F 30° G 40° H 50° J 60° K 70° L
ATLANTIC OCEAN
Bay of Biscay
Cape Finisterre
17,976 ft 5,479 m
Paris
Loire
Munich
Danube
Prague
Carpathian Mts.
Dniester
Dnieper
Rostov-na-Donu
Volga
Caspian Depression
-92 ft -28 m
Aral Sea
Qyzylorda
Syr Darya
Turan Lowland
Vienna
Budapest
Alps
15,772 ft 4,807 m
Lyon
Milan
Zagreb
Odesa
Krasnodar
Astrakhan
Ustyurt Plateau
Toulouse
Turin
Belgrade
Bucharest
Crimea
18,511 ft 5,642 m
Caucasus
Elbrus
Caspian Sea
Samarqand
Pyrenees
Apennines
Sofia
Balkan Mts.
9,597 ft 2,925 m
Black Sea
Tbilisi
Amu Darya
Iberian Peninsula
Marseille
Corsica
Adriatic Sea
İstanbul
Pontine Mts.
Yerevan
Kura
Baku
Ashgabat
Madrid
Barcelona
Rome
Ankara
16,945 ft 5,165 m
Lisbon
Valencia
Balearic Is.
Naples
Sardinia
Anatolia
Tabriz
Mashhad
Herāt
Seville
Sa. Nevada
Palermo
Athens
İzmir
Konya
Elburz Mts.
C. Saint Vincent
Algiers
Constantine
Sicily
Aegean Sea
Mosul
Tehrān
Iranian Plateau
8,766 ft 2,672 m
Oran
Tell Atlas
Tūnis
Sfax
Malta
Mediterranean Sea
Cyprus
Aleppo
Euphrates
Tigris
Mesopotamia
Str. of Gibraltar
Rabat
Fez
Saharan Atlas
7,638 ft 2,328 m
G. of Gabès
Crete
Beirut
Damascus
Baghdād
Zagros Mts.
Eşfahān
Madeira
Casablanca
Tughghūrt
Tripoli
Syrian Desert
Marrakech
High Atlas
Béchar
Gt. Western Erg
G. of Sirte
Benghazi
Cyrenaica
Alexandria
Jerusalem
Pt. Said
Ammān
Basra
Kuwait
Shīrāz
Zāhedān
Tubqāl
13,665 ft 4,165 m
Canary Is.
Teide
12,199 ft 3,718 m
Las Palmas
Gt. Eastern Erg
Al-Hamādah al-Hamrā'
Tripolitania
Surt
-436 ft -133 m
Cairo
Sinai Pen.
8,652 ft 2,637 m
An-Nafūd
Persian Gulf
Bandar-e 'Abbās
Tademaït Plateau
Libyan Desert
Sīwah
Arabian Desert
Al-Hijāz
Laâyoune
Erg Ighidi
Erg Chech
Sabhā
Asyūṭ
Nile
Abu Dhabi
Tassili-n-Ajjer
Fazzān
Luxor
Riyadh
Muscat
Tropic of Cancer
Ahaggar
9,574 ft 2,918 m
Tamanrāsat
Assuan
L. Nasser
Medina
Arabian Pen.
Red Sea
Tanezrouft
Tibesti
Emi Koussi
11,204 ft 3,415 m
6,211 ft
J. al-'Uwaynāt
1,893 m
Jeddah
Mecca
Ar-Rub' al-Khālī
Sahara
Adrar des Ifôghas
Aïr
Ténéré
Borkou
Nubian Desert
Port Sudan
'Asīr
Timbuktu
Bodélé
Ennedi
Bayūdah
Atbarah
Şalālah
Senegal
Sahel
Kartoum
Asmera
Sanaa
Hadhramawt
Dakar
Niamey
Kanem
L. Chad
Wadai
J. Marrah
10,076 ft 3,071 m
Dārfūr
Kurdufān
El-Obeid
White Nile
Blue Nile
Ras Dashen
15,158 ft 4,620 m
12,336 ft 3,760 m
Socotra
Gambia
Bamako
Niger
Ouagadougou
Sudan
Kano
Bornu
N'Djamena
Maiduguri
Tana
Aden
Gulf of Aden
Fouta Djallon
Chari
Ethiopian Highlands
Djibouti
C. Guardafui
Conakry
6,391 ft 1,948 m
Adamawa Highlands
4,351 ft 1,326 m
Bongo Mts.
Addis Ababa
Hargeysa
Somali Pen.
Freetown
Komoe
Volta
Kumasi
Ibadan
Benue
Sudd
14,131 ft 4,307 m
Shebele
Monrovia
Grain Coast
Ivory Coast
Gold Coast
Slave Coast
Lagos
Omo
18,684 ft 5,695 m
Abidjan
Accra
Cameroon Mtn.
13,435 ft 4,095 m
Douala
Bangui
Jūbā
C. Palmas
Yaoundé
Ubangi
Uele
L. Turkana
Jubba
G. of Guinea
Bioko
Congo
L. Albert
Mt. Elgon
14,177 ft 4,321 m
Mogadishu
Príncipe
São Tomé
Sangha
Kampala
Equator
Libreville
Congo Basin
Kisangani
16,763 ft 5,110 m
Mitumba Mts.
Kismaayo
C. Lopez
Ogooué
L. Kivu
L. Victoria
Nairobi
Kilimanjaro
19,331 ft 5,892 m
Tana
Brazzaville
Bujumbura
Mombasa
7,461 ft 2,274 m
Kinshasa
Kasai
Kwilu
Kananga
Lualaba
17,306 ft 5,275 m
Seychelle Is.
ATLANTIC
Cuango
L. Tanganyika
Dodoma
Zanzibar
Dar es Salaam
Luanda
Lunda
Shaba
L. Mweru
Luvua
Rungwe
9,715 ft 2,961 m
Aldabra Is.
Ascension
Agalega Is.
Lubumbashi
Luapula
Muchinga Mts.
Ruvuma
Cabo Delgado
Comoro Is.
Cape Bobaomby
Benguela
8,593 ft 2,619 m
Huambo
Ndola
L. Nyasa
Mayotte
18,287 ft 5,574 m
Lilongwe
Maromokotro
9,436 ft 2,876 m
Namibe
Cubango
Cuando
Zambezi
Lusaka
Kafue
Cahora Bassa Res.
Nampula
Mahajanga
L. Kariba
9,849 ft 3,002 m
St. Helena
Harare
Mozambique Channel
8,189 ft 2,496 m
Okavango
Okavango Swamp
Victoria Falls
Madagascar
Toamasina
Kaokoveld
Antananarivo
Beira
Brandberg
8,550 ft 2,606 m
Bulawayo
OCEAN
Limpopo
Save
Port Louis
St-Denis
Mascarene Is.
Windhoek
Kalahari Desert
Pic Boby
8,721 ft 2,658 m
Tropic of Capricorn
16,962 ft 5,170 m
Namib Desert
Gaborone
Transvaal
Pretoria
Maputo
Johannesburg
C. Vohimena
17,257 ft 5,260 m
INDIAN OCEAN
Orange
Vaal
Bloemfontein
11,424 ft 3,482 m
Drakensberg
Durban
8,186 ft 2,495 m
17,873 ft 5,448 m
Cape
Cape Town
Cape of Good Hope
C. Agulhas
Port Elizabeth
Tristan da Cunha
17,611 ft 5,368 m
Gough I.
Elevation
6,562 ft 2,000 m
3,281 ft 1,000 m
1,640 ft 500 m
656 ft 200 m
0 ft 0 m
Depression
656 ft 200 m
6,562 ft 2,000 m
13,124 ft 4,000 m
1 2 3 4 5 6 7 8 9
40° 30° 20° 10° 0° 10° 20° 30°
KLETT-PERTHES

1:40,000,000
0 500 1,000 mi
0 500 1,000 1,500 2,000 km
ATLANTIC OCEAN
Bay of Biscay
Paris
Loire
Danube
Alps
Carpathian Mts.
Dniester
Dnieper
Donets'k
Volga
Caspian Depression
Aral Sea
Syr Darya
Ustyurt Plateau
Turan Lowland
Amu Darya
Caspian Sea
Crimea
Black Sea
Caucasus
Kura
Pyrenees
Iberian Peninsula
Madrid
Sa. Nevada
Barcelona
Corsica
Rome
Apennines
Adriatic Sea
Balkan Mts.
Pontine Mts.
Anatolia
Balearic Is.
Sardinia
Mediterranean Sea
Algiers
Sicily
Tunis
Malta
Aegean Sea
Crete
Cyprus
L. Van
Elburz Mts.
Tehrān
Mesopotamia
Euphrates
Tigris
Baghdād
Zagros Mts.
Iranian Plateau
Str. of Gibraltar
Rabat
Tell Atlas
Saharan Atlas
High Atlas
Madeira
G. of Gabès
Tripoli
Syrian Desert
Canary Is.
Gt. Western Erg
Gt. Eastern Erg
G. of Sirte
Cyrenaica
Cairo
Sinai Pen.
An-Nafūd
Persian Gulf
Tademaït Plateau
Al-Hamadah al-Hamrā'
Tripolitania
Libyan Desert
Arabian Desert
Nile
Red Sea
Al-Hijāz
Arabian Pen.
Riyadh
Najd
Erg Iguidi
Erg Chech
Tassili-n-Ajjer
Fazzān
Tropic of Cancer
Ahaggar
L. Nasser
Ar-Rub' al-Khālī
Tanezrouft
Sahara
Tibesti
Adrar des Ifôghas
Nubian Desert
Cape Verde Is.
Aïr
Ténéré
Borkou
Ennedi
Asir
Senegal
Sahel
Bodélé
Bayuda
'Atbarah
Hadramawt
Khartoum
Gambia
Niger
Kanem
L. Chad
Wadai
Kurdufān
Blue Nile
White Nile
Socotra
Gulf of Aden
Sudan
Bornu
Dārfūr
L. Tana
Fouta Djallon
Chari
Ethiopian Highlands
Addis Ababa
Somali Pen.
Komoe
L. Volta
Ibadan
Benue
Adamawa Highlands
Bongo Mts.
Sudd
Grain Coast
Ivory Coast
Gold Coast
Slave Coast
Lagos
Omo
Shebele
Volta
Douala
Ubangi
Uele
L. Turkana
G. of Guinea
Bioko
Congo
L. Albert
Jubba
Príncipe
São Tomé
Equator
Sangha
Congo Basin
Ogooué
L. Kivu
Mitumba Mts.
L. Victoria
Nairobi
Tana
Kasai
Kinshasa
Seychelle
Lualaba
Zanzibar
Dar es Salaam
Tanganyika
Kwilu
Cuango
Shaba
Luvua
Ascension
Lunda
L. Mweru
Luapula
Aldabra Is.
Agalega
Muchinga Mts.
Ruvuma
L. Nyasa
Comoro Is.
Mayotte
INDIAN OCEAN
Cubango
Cuando
Zambezi
Kafue
Cahora Bassa Res.
St. Helena
L. Kariba
Mozambique Channel
Kaokoveld
Harare
Okavango
Victoria Falls
Okavango Swamp
Madagascar
Namib Desert
Limpopo
Save
Windhoek
Kalahari Desert
Mascarene
Tropic of Capricorn
Transvaal
Johannesburg
Vaal
Orange
Drakensberg
Durban
Cape Town
Cape
Port Elizabeth
Land Cover (Explanations on p. 32)
Natural Vegetation
Evergreen needleleaf forests
Evergreen broadleaf forests
Deciduous needleleaf forests
Deciduous broadleaf forests
Mixed forests
Closed shrublands
Open shrublands
Woody savannas
Savannas
Grasslands
Permanent wetlands
Developed and Mosaic Lands
Croplands
Cropland/natural vegetation mosaic
Urban and built-up lands
Non-Vegetated Lands
Snow and ice
Barren or sparsely vegetated
Water bodies
No data
KLETT-PERTHES

0 500 1,000 mi
0 500 1,000 1,500 2,000 km

1:40,000,000

0 500 1,000 mi
0 500 1,000 1,500 2,000 km

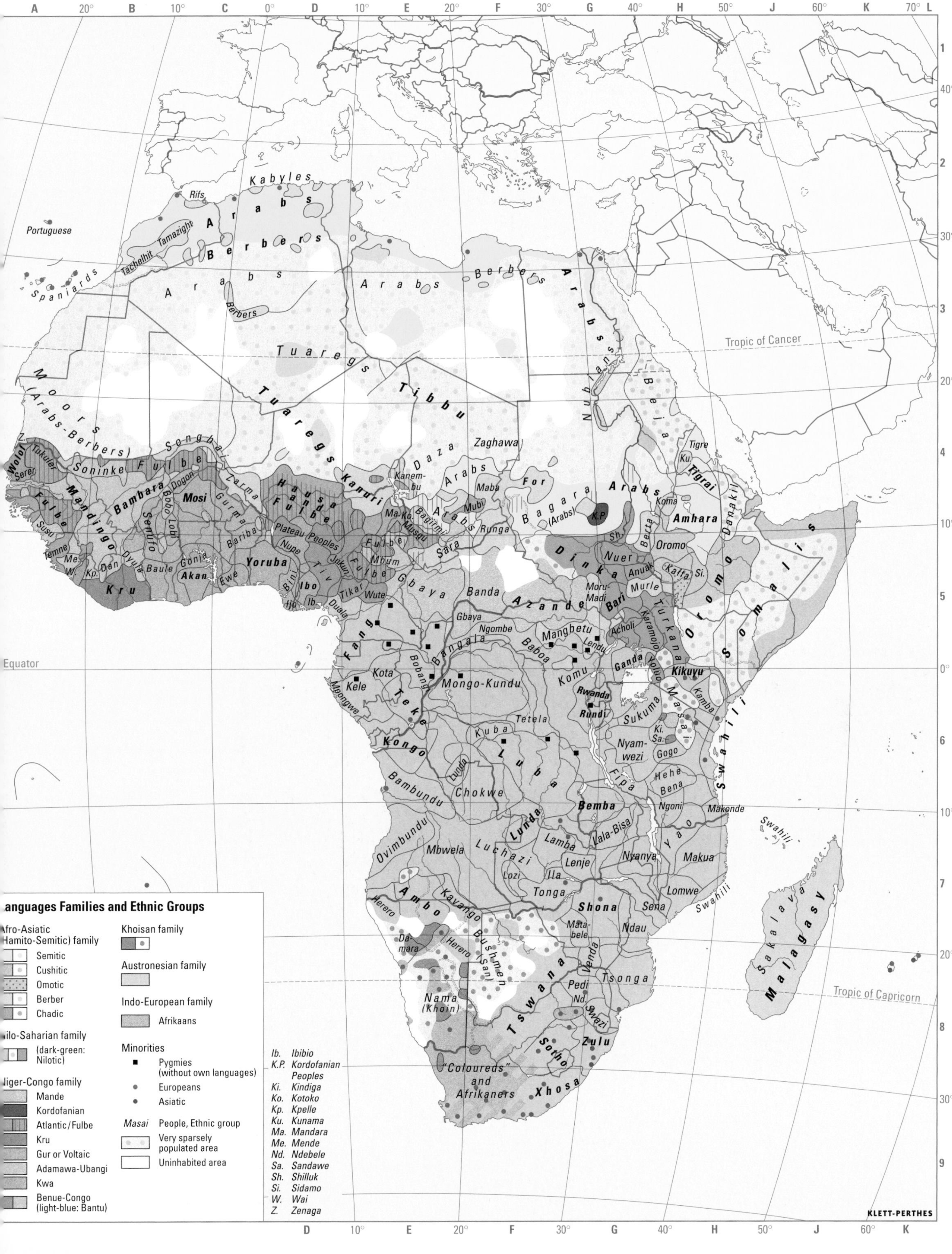
0 500 1,000 mi
0 500 1,000 1,500 2,000 km
A B C D E F G H J K L
20° 10° 0° 10° 20° 30° 40° 50° 60° 70°
1 2 3 4 5 6 7 8 9
40° 30° 20° 10° 0° 10° 20° 30°
Tropic of Cancer
Equator
Tropic of Capricorn
Portuguese
Spaniards
Kabyles
Rifs
Arabs
Tamazight
Tachelhit
Berbers
Tuaregs
Tibbu
Nubians
Beja
Moors (Arabs-Berbers)
Z.
Wolof
Tukuler
Serer
Songhai
Soninke
Fulbe
Mandingo
Bambara
Dogon
Mosi
Gurma
Zarma
Hausa
Kanuri
Daza
Zaghawa
Kanem-bu
Maba
For
Bagara (Arabs)
K.P.
Tigre
Ku.
Tigrai
Koma
Amhara
Danakil
Somalis
Susu
Temne
Me.
W.
Kp.
Dan
Dyula
Senufo
Bobo
Lobi
Bariba
Gonja
Baule
Akan
Ewe
Yoruba
Kru
Plateau Peoples
Nupe
Tiv
Jukun
Bini
Ibo
Ijo
Ib.
Duala
Tikar
Wute
Mbum
Ma.
Ko.
Bagirmi
Musgu
Mubi
Runga
Sara
Gbaya
Banda
Azande
Dinka
Sh.
Nuer
Berta
Oromo
Anuak
Kaffa
Si.
Murle
Moru-Madi
Bari
Turkana
Karamojo
Acholi
Fang
Gbaya
Ngombe
Bangala
Mangbetu
Lendu
Baboa
Bobangi
Kota
Kele
Mpongwe
Mongo-Kundu
Teke
Komu
Ganda
Yoluo
Kikuyu
Kamba
Masai
Rwanda
Rundi
Sukuma
Ki.
Sa.
Swahili
Tetela
Kuba
Kongo
Luba
Nyam-wezi
Gogo
Hehe
Bena
Fipa
Bambundu
Lunda
Chokwe
Bemba
Ngoni
Makonde
Ovimbundu
Mbwela
Luchazi
Lunda
Lamba
Lala-Bisa
Yao
Nyanya
Makua
Lenje
Lozi
Ila
Tonga
Lomwe
Swahili
Herero
Ambo
Kavango
Shona
Sena
Sakalava
Malagasy
Damara
Herero
Bushmen (San)
Mata-bele
Ndau
Venda
Tsonga
Nama (Khoin)
Tswana
Pedi
Nd.
Swazi
Sotho
Zulu
"Coloureds" and Afrikaners
Xhosa
Languages Families and Ethnic Groups
Afro-Asiatic (Hamito-Semitic) family
Semitic
Cushitic
Omotic
Berber
Chadic
Nilo-Saharian family
(dark-green: Nilotic)
Niger-Congo family
Mande
Kordofanian
Atlantic/Fulbe
Kru
Gur or Voltaic
Adamawa-Ubangi
Kwa
Benue-Congo (light-blue: Bantu)
Khoisan family
Austronesian family
Indo-European family
Afrikaans
Minorities
Pygmies (without own languages)
Europeans
Asiatic
Masai People, Ethnic group
Very sparsely populated area
Uninhabited area
Ib. Ibibio
K.P. Kordofanian Peoples
Ki. Kindiga
Ko. Kotoko
Kp. Kpelle
Ku. Kunama
Ma. Mandara
Me. Mende
Nd. Ndebele
Sa. Sandawe
Sh. Shilluk
Si. Sidamo
W. Wai
Z. Zenaga
KLETT-PERTHES

1:40,000,000

0 500 1,000 mi
0 500 1,000 1,500 2,000 km

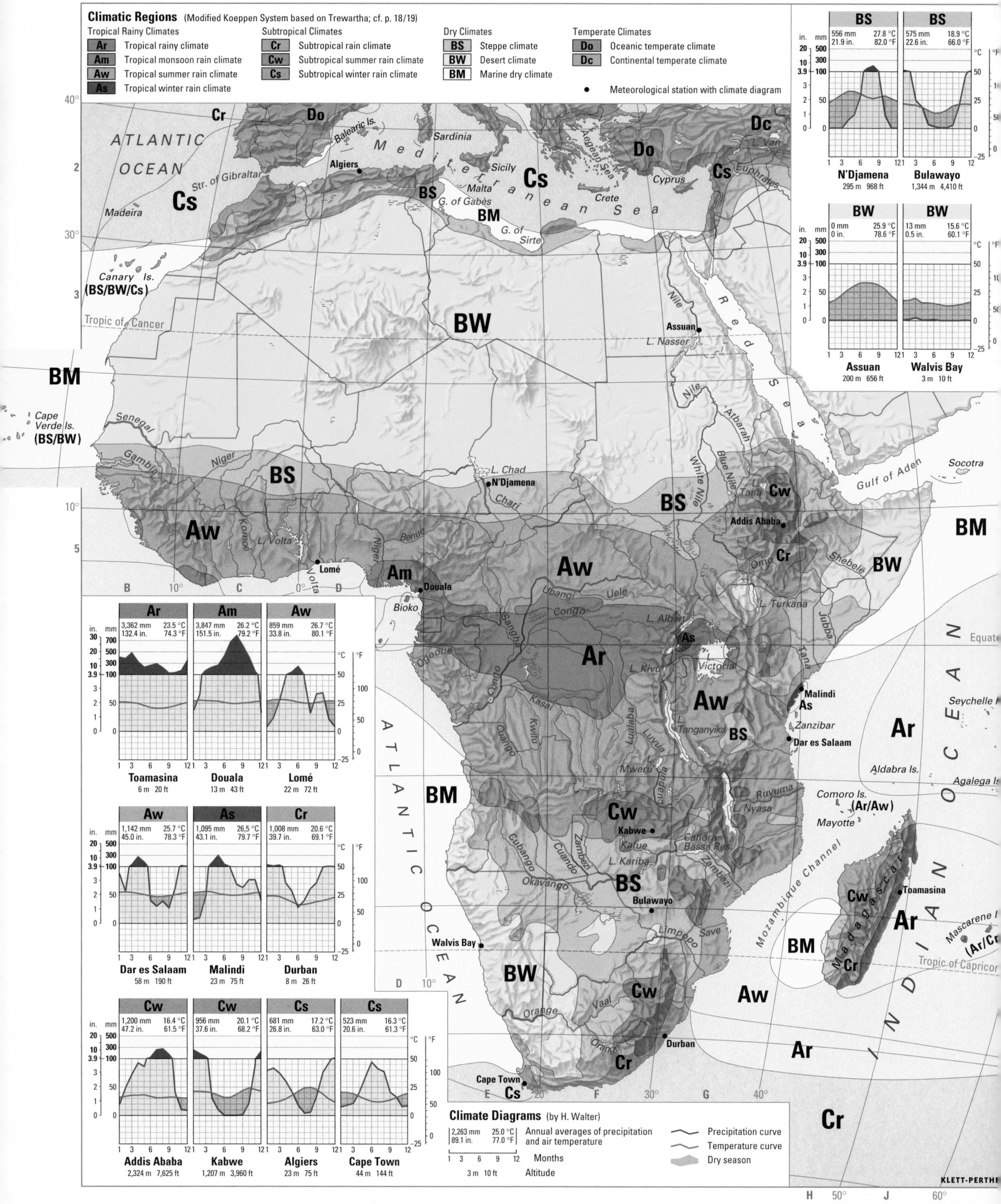

Climatic Regions (Modified Koeppen System based on Trewartha; cf. p. 18/19)
Tropical Rainy Climates
Ar Tropical rainy climate
Am Tropical monsoon rain climate
Aw Tropical summer rain climate
As Tropical winter rain climate
Subtropical Climates
Cr Subtropical rain climate
Cw Subtropical summer rain climate
Cs Subtropical winter rain climate
Dry Climates
BS Steppe climate
BW Desert climate
BM Marine dry climate
Temperate Climates
Do Oceanic temperate climate
Dc Continental temperate climate
Meteorological station with climate diagram
ATLANTIC OCEAN
Madeira
Str. of Gibraltar
Balearic Is.
Sardinia
Mediterranean Sea
Algiers
Sicily
Malta
G. of Gabès
G. of Sirte
Crete
Cyprus
Aegean Sea
L. Van
Euphrates
Canary Is. (BS/BW/Cs)
Tropic of Cancer
Nile
Red Sea
Assuan
L. Nasser
Cape Verde Is. (BS/BW)
Senegal
Gambia
Niger
Atbarah
White Nile
Blue Nile
L. Chad
N'Djamena
Chari
L. Tana
Addis Ababa
Gulf of Aden
Socotra
Komoe
L. Volta
Benue
Volta
Lomé
Douala
Bioko
Omo
Shebele
Ubangi
Uele
Congo
Sangha
Ogooué
L. Albert
L. Turkana
Jubba
Tana
L. Kivu
Victoria
Malindi
Kasai
Kwilu
Cuango
Lualaba
Luvua
L. Tanganyika
Zanzibar
Dar es Salaam
Seychelles
Aldabra Is.
Agalega Is.
Mweru
Luapula
Ruvuma
L. Nyasa
Comoro Is. (Ar/Aw)
Mayotte
Kabwe
Kafue
Cahora Bassa Res.
L. Kariba
Cubango
Cuando
Zambezi
Okavango
Mozambique Channel
Madagascar
Toamasina
Bulawayo
Limpopo
Save
Mascarene Is. (Ar/Cr)
Walvis Bay
Tropic of Capricorn
Orange
Vaal
Durban
Cape Town
ATLANTIC OCEAN
INDIAN OCEAN
Equator
Cr Do Dc Cs BS BM BW Aw Am Ar As Cw
N'Djamena 295 m 968 ft BS 556 mm 21.9 in. 27.8 °C 82.0 °F
Bulawayo 1,344 m 4,410 ft BS 575 mm 22.6 in. 18.9 °C 66.0 °F
Assuan 200 m 656 ft BW 0 mm 0 in. 25.9 °C 78.6 °F
Walvis Bay 3 m 10 ft BW 13 mm 0.5 in. 15.6 °C 60.1 °F
Toamasina 6 m 20 ft Ar 3,362 mm 132.4 in. 23.5 °C 74.3 °F
Douala 13 m 43 ft Am 3,847 mm 151.5 in. 26.2 °C 79.2 °F
Lomé 22 m 72 ft Aw 859 mm 33.8 in. 26.7 °C 80.1 °F
Dar es Salaam 58 m 190 ft Aw 1,142 mm 45.0 in. 25.7 °C 78.3 °F
Malindi 23 m 75 ft As 1,095 mm 43.1 in. 26,5 °C 79.7 °F
Durban 8 m 26 ft Cr 1,008 mm 39.7 in. 20.6 °C 69.1 °F
Addis Ababa 2,324 m 7,625 ft Cw 1,200 mm 47.2 in. 16.4 °C 61.5 °F
Kabwe 1,207 m 3,960 ft Cw 956 mm 37.6 in. 20.1 °C 68.2 °F
Algiers 23 m 75 ft Cs 681 mm 26.8 in. 17.2 °C 63.0 °F
Cape Town 44 m 144 ft Cs 523 mm 20.6 in. 16.3 °C 61.3 °F
Climate Diagrams (by H. Walter)
2,263 mm 89.1 in. 25.0 °C 77.0 °F Annual averages of precipitation and air temperature
Months
3 m 10 ft Altitude
Precipitation curve
Temperature curve
Dry season
KLETT-PERTHES

Africa: Ecoregions

1:40,000,000

0 500 1,000 mi
0 500 1,000 1,500 2,000 km

Vegetation Profiles

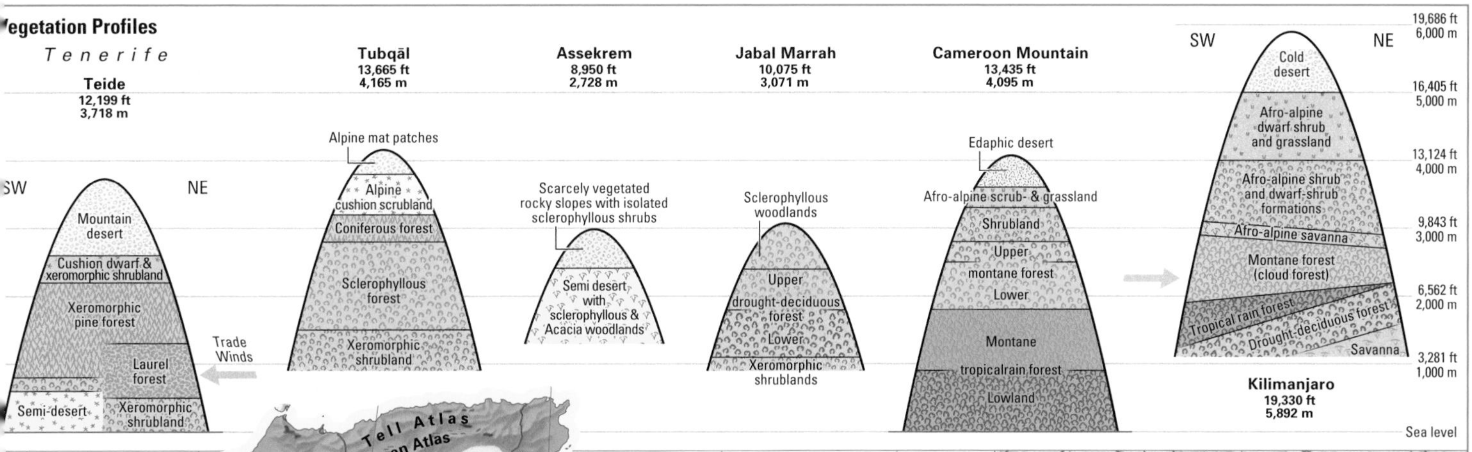

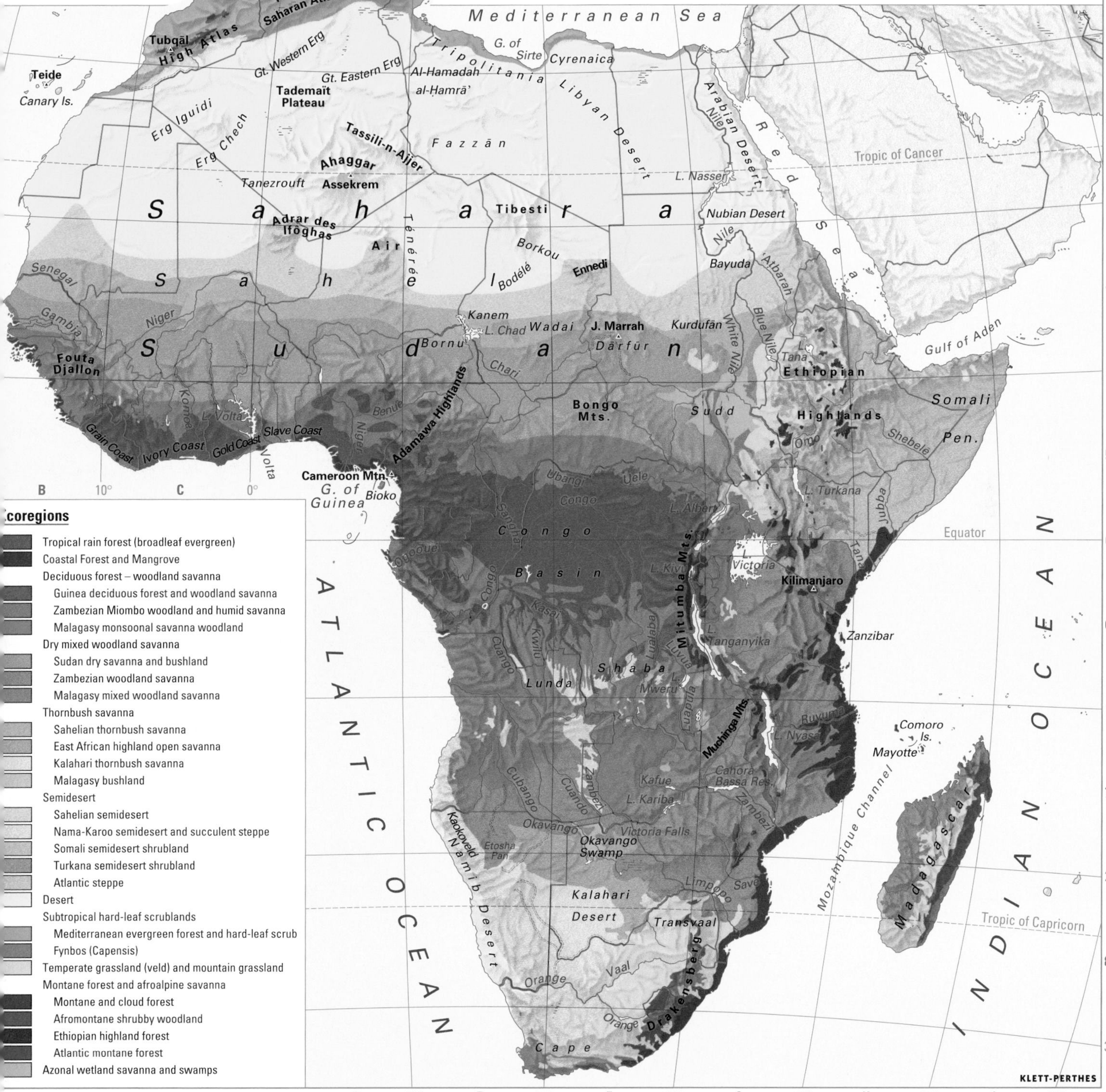

Ecoregions

- Tropical rain forest (broadleaf evergreen)
- Coastal Forest and Mangrove
- Deciduous forest – woodland savanna
  - Guinea deciduous forest and woodland savanna
  - Zambezian Miombo woodland and humid savanna
  - Malagasy monsoonal savanna woodland
- Dry mixed woodland savanna
  - Sudan dry savanna and bushland
  - Zambezian woodland savanna
  - Malagasy mixed woodland savanna
- Thornbush savanna
  - Sahelian thornbush savanna
  - East African highland open savanna
  - Kalahari thornbush savanna
  - Malagasy bushland
- Semidesert
  - Sahelian semidesert
  - Nama-Karoo semidesert and succulent steppe
  - Somali semidesert shrubland
  - Turkana semidesert shrubland
  - Atlantic steppe
- Desert
- Subtropical hard-leaf scrublands
  - Mediterranean evergreen forest and hard-leaf scrub
  - Fynbos (Capensis)
- Temperate grassland (veld) and mountain grassland
- Montane forest and afroalpine savanna
  - Montane and cloud forest
  - Afromontane shrubby woodland
  - Ethiopian highland forest
  - Atlantic montane forest
- Azonal wetland savanna and swamps

130
PORTUGAL
Seville (Sevilla)
Córdoba
Granada
Murcia
Huelva
Málaga
SPAIN
Cádiz
Almería
Strait of Gibraltar
Gibraltar (U.K.)
Ceuta (SPA.)
Tanger (Ţanjah)
Tétouan (Tiţwān)
Al-Husaymah
Al-Qaşr al-Kabīr
Melilla (SPA.)
Oran (Wahrān)
Mustaghānam
ALGIERS (AL-JAZĀ'IR)
Bijāyah
Sakīkdah
Annābah
Bizerte (Binzart)
Carthage
Tunis
Constantine (Qusanţīnah)
Sațīf
Bātnah
Biskrah
Tell Atlas
Sīdī Bal'abbās
Tilimsān
Djelfa (Al-Jilfah)
Kénitra (Al-Qinitrah)
RABAT (AR-RIBĀŢ)
CASABLANCA (AD-DĀR AL-BAYḌĀ')
Meknès (Miknās)
Fez (Fās)
Tāzah
Oujda (Ujdah)
Ar-Rif
Safi (Asfi)
Sattāt
Khurībkah
Banī Mallāl
Aş-Şawīrah
Marrakech (Marrākush)
Tubqal
High Atlas
Agadir (Aghādīr)
Cap Rhir
Warzazāt
Ar-Rashīdiyah
Anti Atlas
Sīdī Ifnī
Kulimīm
Dra'ah
MOROCCO
Béchar (Bashshār)
Abadlah
Banī Abbas
Great Western Erg
Saharan Atlas
Al-Bayadh
Al-Aghwāț
Ghardāyah
Warqlah
Al-Wādī
Tughghūrt
Hāssī Mas'ūd
Great Eastern Erg
Al-Ghulī'ah
Timīmūn
Adrār
Ayn Şalaḥ
Riqqān
Sabkhat Makarrā
Burj Umar Drīs
Al-'Ajilah
Illizi
Ghāt
Janat
Ahaggar
Tahat
Tamanrāsat
Tassili
Ténéré
ALGERIA
Tindūf
Erg Ighidi
Erg Chech
Madeira (POR.)
Porto Santo
Funchal
Selvagens (POR.)
Canary Islands (SPA.)
Santa Cruz de la Palma
La Palma
La Gomera
Hierro
Teide
Tenerife
Santa Cruz de T.
Gran Canaria
Las Palmas
Lanzarote
Arrecife
Fuerteventura
Tarfāyah
Laâyoune (Al-'Ayūn)
Bū Jaydūr
As-Samārah
Western Sahara
Ad-Dākhlah
Tropic of Cancer
Zuwārat
Kaddit al-Jild
Cape Nouâdhibou
Nouâdhibou (Nawadhībū)
Atār
Cape Timirist
Aqjawajat
Tijiqjah
Nouakchott (Nawākshūt)
MAURITANIA
Alāk
Kayhaydi
Kifah
'Ayūn al-'Atrūs
An-Na'mah
Rūṣu
Senegal
Saint-Louis
Louga
Linguère
Matam
Silibābī
Taoudenni
Tanezrouft
Sahara
MALI
Timbuktu (Tombouctou)
Bourem
Niger
Gao
Ménaka
Hombori Tondo
Kidal
Adrar des Ifôghas
Tessalit
Mont Greboun
Iférouane
Aïr
Arlit
Monts Bagzane
Agadèz
NIGER
CAPE VERDE
Santo Antão
Porto Novo
Mindelo
Ribeira Brava
São Nicolau
Sal
Santa Maria
Boa Vista
Cape Verde Is.
Santiago
São Filipe
Fogo
Praia
Cape Verde
DAKAR
Thiès
Diourbel
Fatick
Kaolack
SENEGAL
Nioro
Kayes
Banjul
Serekunda
GAMBIA
Tambacounda
Kolda
Basse Santa Su
Ziguinchor
Bissorã
Gabú
GUINEA-BISSAU
Bissau
Bafatá
Bissagos Is.
Kita
Bamako
Markala
Ségou
Mopti
Bani
San
Koulikoro
Koutiala
Sikasso
Bougouni
Siguiri
Fouta Djallon
Labé
Boké
Kindia
Mamou
CONAKRY
GUINEA
Kankan
Faranah
Kissidougou
Makeni
Koidu
Bintimani
Freetown
SIERRA LEONE
Bo
Kenema
Guéckédou
Mt. Wutéve
Nzérékoré
Sanniquellie
Mts. Nimba
Man
Tubmanburg
Monrovia
LIBERIA
Buchanan
Greenville
Harper
C. Palmas
Zwedru
Guiglo
Daloa
Gagnoa
Odienné
Korhogo
Touba
Katiola
Séguéla
Bouaké
Bondoukou
CÔTE D'IVOIRE
Bouaflé
Yamoussoukro
Abengourou
Divo
Agboville
Anyama
ABIDJAN
Grand-Bassam
San Pedro
Aboisso
Tera
Niamey
Birni N'Konni
Tillabéri
Dosso
Tahoua
Maradi
Zinder
Tessaoua
Diffa
Nguigmi
Ouahigouya
BURKINA FASO
Ouagadougou
Koudougou
Fada N'Gourma
White Volta
Bobo-Dioulasso
Tena Kourou
Banfora
Black Volta
Bolgatanga
Wa
Tamale
L. Volta
GHANA
Kumasi
Sunyani
Obuasi
Koforidua
Cape Coast
Takoradi
Sekondi
C. Three Points
ACCRA
Tema
Teshie
Mt. Afadjato
Kpalimé
Mt. Agou
Lomé
TOGO
Sokodé
Kara
Dapaong
Djougou
Natitingou
BENIN
Kandi
Parakou
Mt. Sokbaro
Atakpamé
Abomey
Porto-Novo
Cotonou
Bight of Benin
Gulf of Guinea
Sokoto
Gusau
Birnin Kebbi
Katsina
Kano
Hadejia
Nguru
Gashua
Bornu
Damaturu
Maiduguri
Funtua
Zaria
Azare
Jos
NIGERIA
KADUNA
Bauchi
Kainji Res.
Minna
Bida
Abuja
Plateau
Lafia
Shere Hill
Gombe
Jimeta
Yola
Jalingo
Benue
Dimlang
Ilorin
Ogbomosho
Oyo
Oshogbo
Iwo
Ado-Ekiti
Ife
Akure
Lokoja
Okene
Makurdi
Gboko
Chappal Waddi
Abeokuta
IBADAN
LAGOS
BENIN CITY
Asaba
Enugu
Abakaliki
Onitsha
Awka
Umuahia
Warri
Aba
Uyo
Calabar
Bamenda
Bafoussam
Nkongsamba
PORT HARCOURT
Cameroon Mtn. (Fako)
Adamawa Highlands
Bight of Biafra
Buea
DOUALA
Edéa
YAOUNDÉ
Pico Basile
Malabo
Bioko
EQUATORIAL GUINEA
Bata
Ebolowa
Ebebiyin
Mongomo
Oyem
Evinayong
Príncipe
Santo António
SAO TOME AND PRINCIPE
São Tomé
Libreville
Equator
C. Lopez
Port Gentil
Lambaréné
GABON
Mt. Iboundji
Mouila
Mt. Berongo
Tchibanga
Mossendjo
Loubomo
Pointe-Noire
Cabinda (ANG.)
Soyo
Nabeul
Sousse (Sūsah)
Al-Qayrawān
Tibissah
J. Shāmbī
Al-Qaşrayn
Qafşah
Sfax
Gabès (Qābis)
Shaţţ al-Jarīd
Madanīn
Tațāwīn
TUNISIA
Ghadāmis
Az-Zāwiyah
Jabal Nafūsah
Ghāt
Gulf of Guinea
ATLANTIC OCEAN
Mediterranean
KLETT-PERTHES

1:20,000,000

0 200 400 mi
0 200 400 600 km

176
Gulf of Guinea
Bight of Benin
Bight of Biafra
Equator
Tropic of Capricorn
A T L A N T I C
O C E A N
Ascension
St. Helena
(U.K.)
Tristan da Cunha
Monrovia
Tubmanburg
Buchanan
Greenville
Harper
C. Palmas
LIBERIA
Guiglo
Daloa
Zwedru
Gagnoa
San Pedro
Yamoussoukro
Divo
Agboville
Abeng
Kumasi
Obuasi
Anyama
ABIDJAN
Aboisso
Grand-Bassam
CÔTE D'IVOIRE
C. Three Points
Takoradi
Sekondi
Cape Coast
Koforidua
GHANA
ACCRA
Tema
Teshie
Kpalimé
Mt. Agou
3,235 ft
986 m
Lomé
Porto-Novo
Coto-nou
BENIN
LAGOS CITY
NIGERIA
Asaba
Enugu
Abakaliki
Onitsha
Awka
Umuahia
Aba
Warri
PORT HARCOURT
Uyo
Calabar
Bamenda
Bafoussam
Nkongsamba
CAMEROON
Cameroon Mtn.(Fako)
13,435 ft
4,095 m
8,990 ft
2,740 m
Buea
DOUALA
Edea
YAOUNDÉ
Bertoua
Pico Basile
9869 ft
3,008 m
Malabo
Bioko
EQUATORIAL GUINEA
Ebolowa
Ebebiyin
Oyem
Mongomo
Evinayong
Bata
Príncipe
Santo António
SAO TOME AND PRINCIPE
São Tomé
Libreville
Makokou
GABON
C. Lopez
Port Gentil
Lambaréné
Mt. Iboundji
5,167 ft
1,575 m
2,963 ft
903 m
Koulamoutou
Moanda
Masuku
Mouila
Mt. Berongou
Mossendjo
Tchibanga
3,412 ft
1,040 m
Sibiti
Loubomo
Brazzaville
Pointe-Noire
Nkayi
Madingou
KINSHASA
4,659 ft
1,420 m
Mont Ngaoui
Bouar
Bozoum
Bossangoa
Kaga Bandoro
Bria
CENTRAL AFRICAN REP.
Sibut
Bambari
Carnot
Berbérati
Boali
Bangui
Mobaye
Nola
Mbaïki
Gemena
Lisala
Ubangi
Sanaga
Sangha
Ouésso
Impfondo
CONGO
Owando
Ewo
Djambala
Mbandaka
Tshuapa
Congo
L. Mai-Ndombe
DEM.
Bandundu
Lukenie
Kasai
Sankuru
Ilebo
Kwilu
Kikwit
OF THE
Kananga
Tshikapa
Mbuji-M
Cabinda
(AGO.)
Boma
Matadi
Mbanza-Ngungu
Soyo
M'Banza Congo
N'Zeto
Uige
Cuango
Lucapa
LUANDA
Caxito
N'Dalatando
Malanje
Lunda
Saurimo
Lulua
Dondo
Cuanza
Porto Amboim
Sumbe
ANGOLA
Lobito
Benguela
Bailundo
Môco
8,593 ft
2,619 m
Huambo
Kuito
Luena
Cunene
Menongue
Namibe
7,563 ft
2,305 m
Lubango
Serra da Chela
Cape Albina
Chiange
Cubango
Cuando
6,805 ft
2,074 m
Baynes Mts.
N'Giva
Cuangar
Rundu
Okavango
Oshikango
Oshakati
Ondangwa
Opuwo
Etosha Pan
Tsumeb
Tsodilo Hills
4,885 ft
1,489 m
Outjo
Otavi
Grootfontein
NAMIBIA
Namib Desert
Brandberg
(Königstein)
8,550 ft
2,606 m
Otjiwarongo
Karibib
Okahandja
Ghanzi
Swakopmund
Windhoek
8,133 ft
2,479 m
Gobabis
Walvis Bay
Rehoboth
Auasberge
Nossob
BOT
Kala
Des
Mariental
Tsabong
Keetmanshoop
Lüderitz
Seeheim
Karasburg
Upington
Alexander Bay
Port Nolloth
Orange
Springbok
Prieska
Upper Karoo
Bitterfontein
AFR
Calvinia
Victoria West
St. Helena Bay
Beaufort West
Saldanha
7,631 ft
2,326 m
Worcester
CAPE TOWN
Table Mtn.
1,087 m 3,566 ft
Bellville
L. Karoo
Cape of Good Hope
Mosselbaai
Cape Agulhas
KLETT-PERTHES

177
SUDAN
ETHIOPIA
SOMALIA
UGANDA
KENYA
TANZANIA
BURUNDI
ZAMBIA
MOZAMBIQUE
ZIMBABWE
MADAGASCAR
SWAZILAND
LESOTHO
COMOROS
SEYCHELLES
MAURITIUS
INDIAN
OCEAN
Mozambique Channel
Madagascar
MOGADISHU
(MUQDISHO)
KAMPALA
NAIROBI
Kigali
Bujumbura
Dodoma
DAR ES SALAAM
LUSAKA
Lilongwe
HARARE
PRETORIA
MAPUTO
ANTANANARIVO
Moroni
Victoria
Port Louis
St-Denis
Mombasa
Zanzibar
Beira
DURBAN
Kisangani
Jūbā
Gulu
Marka
Kismaayo
Jamaame
Baydhabo
Beledweyne
Gaalkacyo
Hobyo
Lake Turkana
Lake Victoria
L. Natron
L. Eyasi
L. Rukwa
L. Mweru
L. Bangweulu
Lake Nyasa
L. Kariba
Cahora Bassa Res.
Kilimanjaro
19,331 ft
5,892 m
Mt. Kenya
17,058 ft
5,199 m
Mt. Elgon
14,177 ft
4,321 m
Margherita Peak
16,766 ft
5,110 m
Arusha
Moshi
Tanga
Malindi
Lamu
Pemba
Mafia
Iringa
Mbeya
Morogoro
Tabora
Mwanza
Kigoma
Musoma
Mtwara
C. Delgado
Nampula
Nacala
Quelimane
Tete
Blantyre
Mutare
Bulawayo
Masvingo
Francistown
Gaborone
Polokwane
Phalaborwa
Matola
Mbabane
Manzini
Pietermaritzburg
Richards Bay
East London
Maseru
Newcastle
Mahajanga
Toamasina
Antsirabe
Fianarantsoa
Toliara
Morondava
Antsirañana
C. Bobaomby
Cape Vohimena
Mayotte
(FRA.)
Aldabra Is.
Cosmoledo Is.
Farquhar Is.
Amirante Is.
Coëtivy
Mahé
Agalega Is.
(MRS.)
Tromelin
(FRA.)
Cargados Carajos Is.
(MRS.)
Réunion
(FRA.)
Rodrigues I.
(MRS.)
Bassas da India
(FRA.)
Europa
(FRA.)
Juan de Nova
(FRA.)
Îles Glorieuses
(FRA.)
Piton des Neiges
10,069 ft
3,069 m
Mt. Piton
2,717 ft
828 m
K L M N O P Q R S
30° 35° 40° 45° 50° 55° 60° 65°
1 2 3 4 5 6 7 8 9
5° 0° 5° 10° 15° 20° 25° 30° 35°

North Polar Region: Physical · Political

1:40,000,000

0 500 1,000 mi
0 500 1,000 1,500 2,000 km

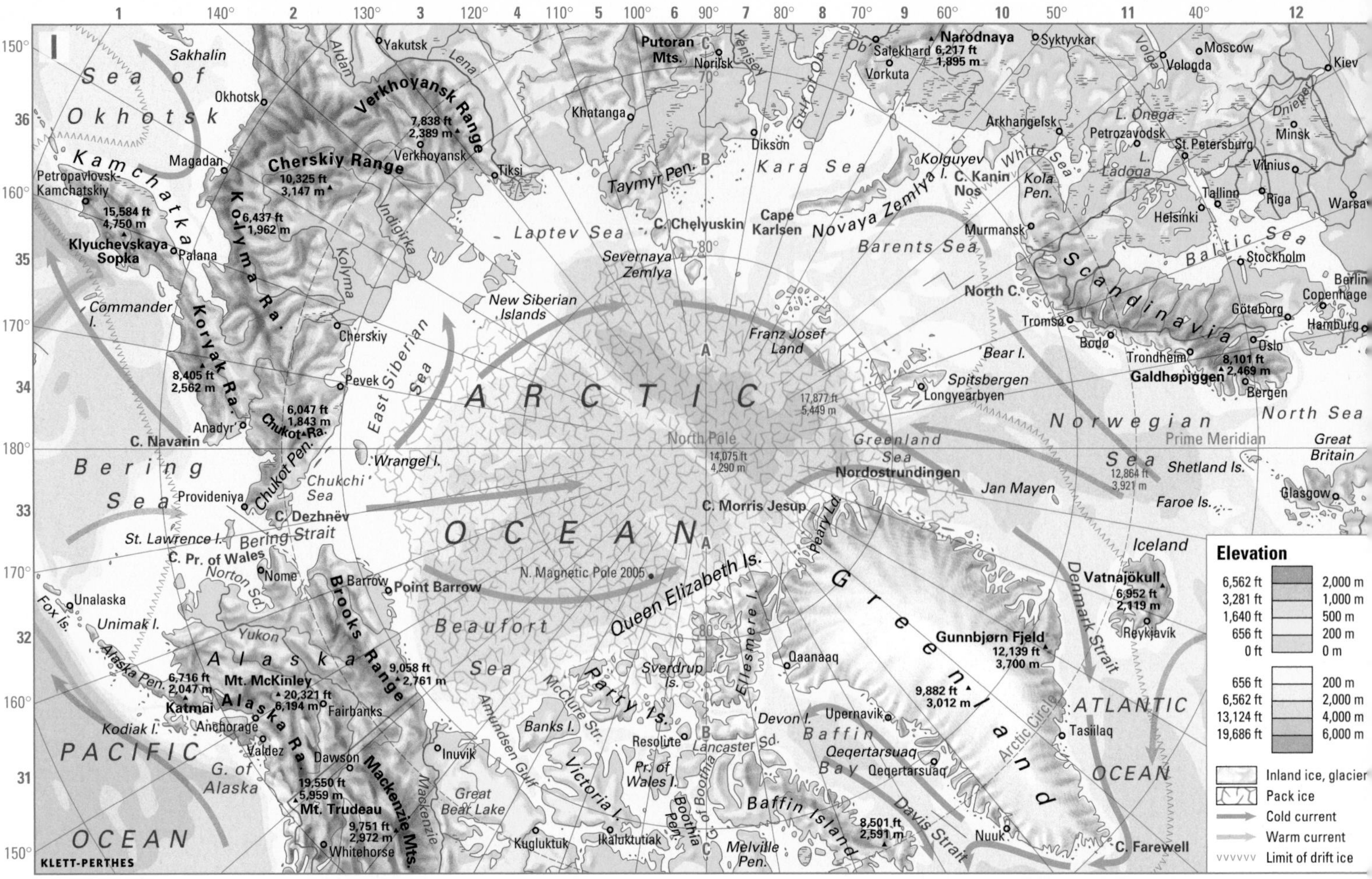

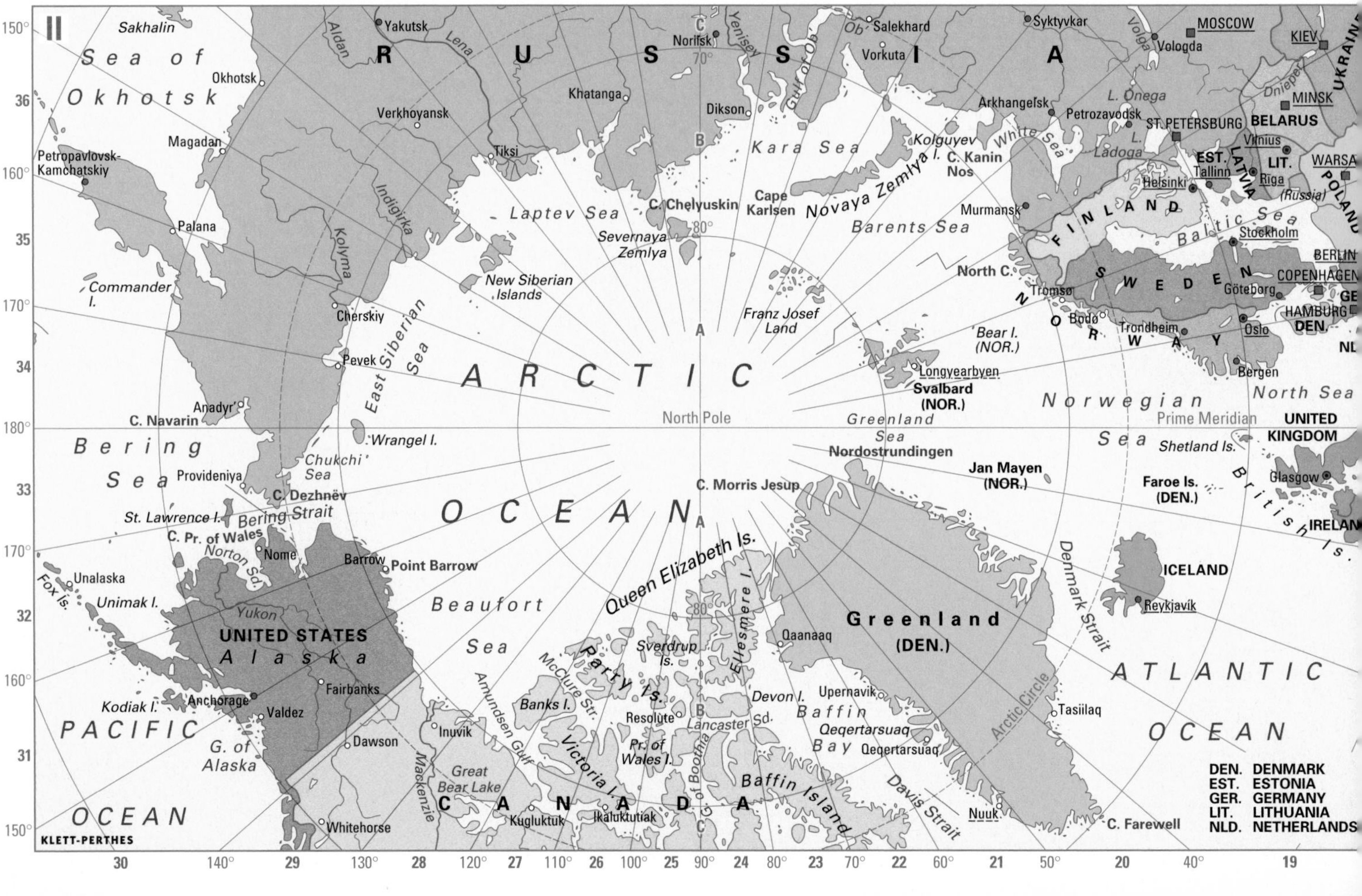

Scale bar: 0 500 1,000 mi; 0 500 1,000 1,500 2,000 km

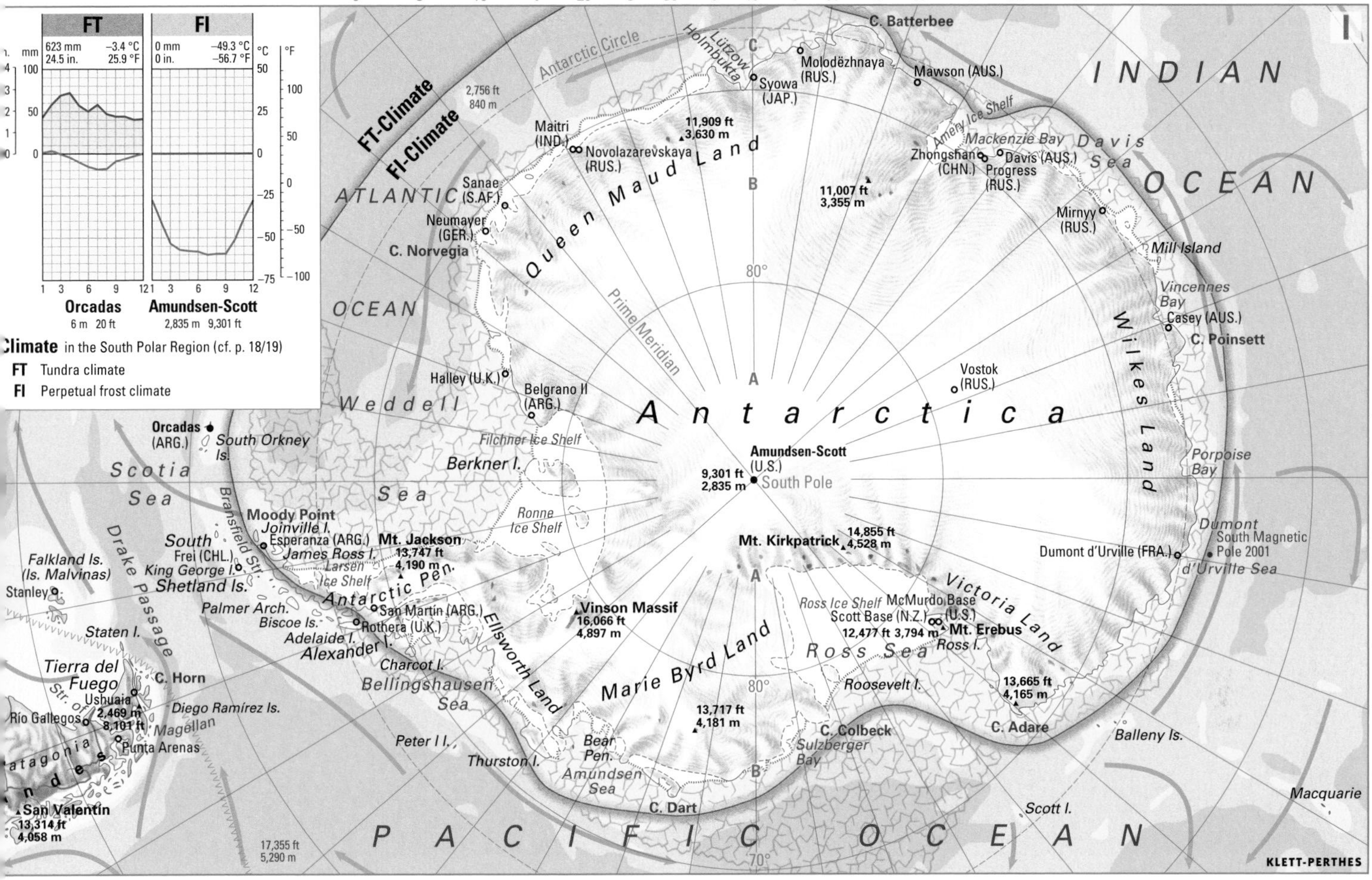
I
FT
FI
623 mm 24.5 in. −3.4 °C 25.9 °F
0 mm 0 in. −49.3 °C −56.7 °F
Orcadas
6 m 20 ft
Amundsen-Scott
2,835 m 9,301 ft
Climate in the South Polar Region (cf. p. 18/19)
FT Tundra climate
FI Perpetual frost climate
FT-Climate
FI-Climate
INDIAN OCEAN
ATLANTIC OCEAN
PACIFIC OCEAN
Antarctica
Antarctic Circle
Prime Meridian
Queen Maud Land
Wilkes Land
Victoria Land
Marie Byrd Land
Ellsworth Land
Antarctic Pen.
Weddell Sea
Scotia Sea
Ross Sea
Davis Sea
Amundsen Sea
Bellingshausen Sea
Dumont d'Urville Sea
Drake Passage
Lützow-Holmbukta
Mackenzie Bay
Amery Ice Shelf
Filchner Ice Shelf
Ronne Ice Shelf
Larsen Ice Shelf
Ross Ice Shelf
C. Batterbee
Molodëzhnaya (RUS.)
Syowa (JAP.)
Mawson (AUS.)
Maitri (IND.)
Novolazarevskaya (RUS.)
11,909 ft 3,630 m
11,007 ft 3,355 m
2,756 ft 840 m
Zhongshan (CHN.)
Davis (AUS.)
Progress (RUS.)
Sanae (S.AF.)
Neumayer (GER.)
C. Norvegia
Mirnyy (RUS.)
Mill Island
Vincennes Bay
Casey (AUS.)
C. Poinsett
Halley (U.K.)
Belgrano II (ARG.)
Vostok (RUS.)
Orcadas (ARG.)
South Orkney Is.
Berkner I.
Amundsen-Scott (U.S.)
9,301 ft 2,835 m
South Pole
Porpoise Bay
Moody Point
Joinville I.
Esperanza (ARG.)
James Ross I.
Mt. Jackson 13,747 ft 4,190 m
Mt. Kirkpatrick 14,855 ft 4,528 m
South Magnetic Pole 2001
Dumont d'Urville (FRA.)
South Shetland Is.
Frei (CHL.)
King George I.
Bransfield Str.
Falkland Is. (Is. Malvinas)
Stanley
Palmer Arch.
San Martín (ARG.)
Vinson Massif 16,066 ft 4,897 m
McMurdo Base (U.S.)
Scott Base (N.Z.)
Mt. Erebus 12,477 ft 3,794 m
Ross I.
Biscoe Is.
Rothera (U.K.)
Adelaide I.
Alexander I.
Charcot I.
Staten I.
Tierra del Fuego
C. Horn
Ushuaia
Str. of Magellan
Río Gallegos
2,469 m 8,101 ft
Diego Ramírez Is.
Punta Arenas
Patagonia
Andes
San Valentín 13,314 ft 4,058 m
Roosevelt I.
13,665 ft 4,165 m
13,717 ft 4,181 m
Peter I I.
Thurston I.
Bear Pen.
C. Colbeck
Sulzberger Bay
C. Adare
Balleny Is.
C. Dart
Scott I.
Macquarie
17,355 ft 5,290 m
KLETT-PERTHES

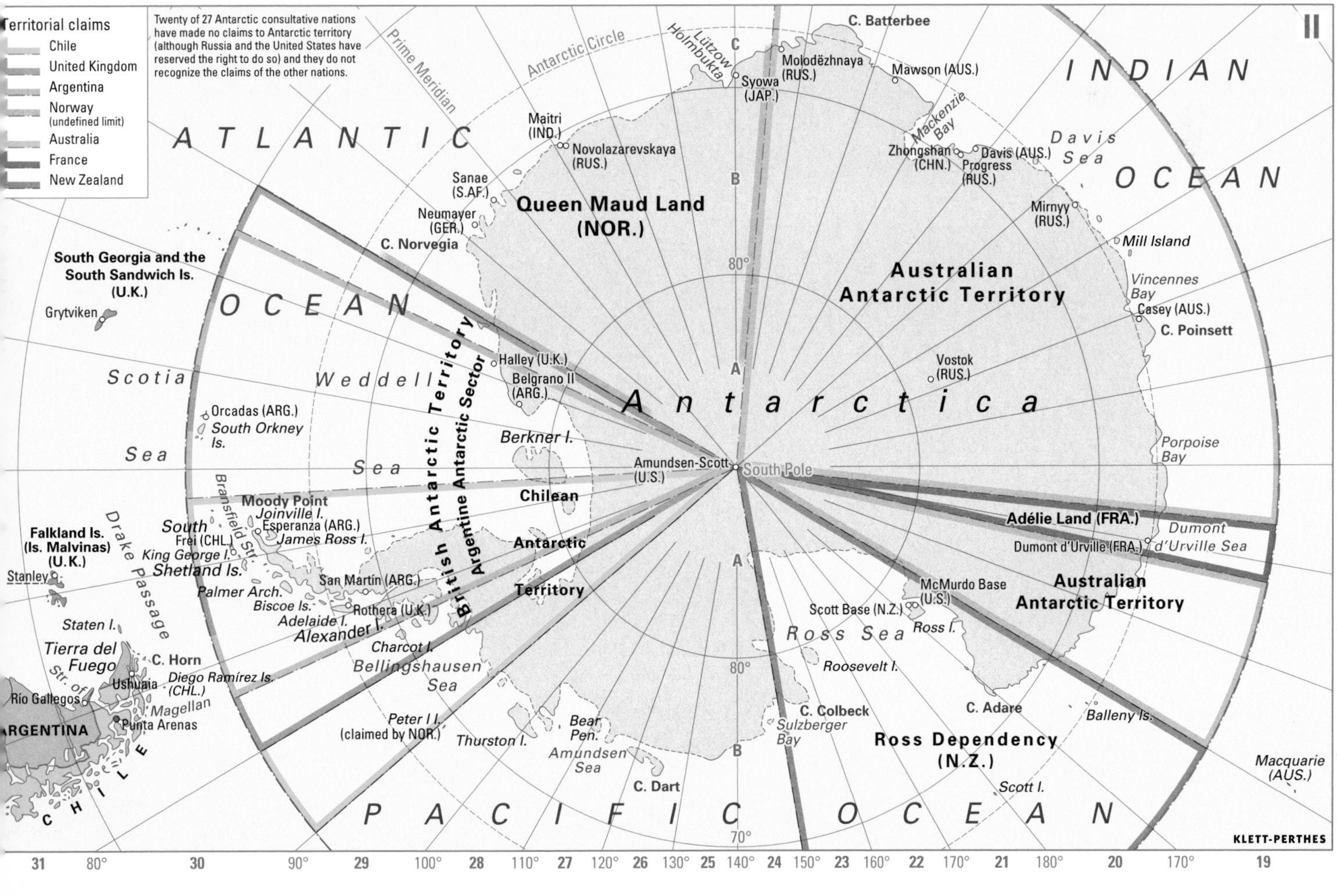
II
Territorial claims
Chile
United Kingdom
Argentina
Norway (undefined limit)
Australia
France
New Zealand
Twenty of 27 Antarctic consultative nations have made no claims to Antarctic territory (although Russia and the United States have reserved the right to do so) and they do not recognize the claims of the other nations.
ATLANTIC OCEAN
INDIAN OCEAN
PACIFIC OCEAN
Antarctica
Queen Maud Land (NOR.)
Australian Antarctic Territory
Adélie Land (FRA.)
Ross Dependency (N.Z.)
British Antarctic Territory
Argentine Antarctic Sector
Chilean Antarctic Territory
South Georgia and the South Sandwich Is. (U.K.)
Grytviken
Falkland Is. (Is. Malvinas) (U.K.)
Stanley
Peter I I. (claimed by NOR.)
Macquarie (AUS.)
Diego Ramírez Is. (CHL.)
ARGENTINA
CHILE
KLETT-PERTHES

Tables and Indexes

Greenland
(part of the Kingdom of Denmark)

rea:	2,166,086 km²
opulation:	57,000 (2005)
apital:	Nuuk (Godthåb) (15,000)
dministration:	3 districts (landsdele)
anguages:	Greenlandic (East Inuit), Danish, English
eligions:	Lutheran 98%
urrency:	Danish krone

ajor cities:
isimiut (6,000), Ilulissat (5,000), Qaqortoq (3,000)

Guatemala
Republic of Guatemala
República de Guatemala

Area:	108,889 km²
Population:	12,599,000 (2005)
Capital:	Guatemala Ciudad/ Cd. de Guatemala (942,000)
Administration:	22 departments
Languages:	Spanish, Mayan languages
Religions:	Roman Catholic 60%, Protestant 30%
Currency:	1 quetzal = 100 centavos

Major cities:
Mixco (384,000), Villa Nueva (302,000), Quezaltenango (120,000), Cobán (52,000)

Guyana
Co-operative Republic of Guyana

Area:	214,969 km²
Population:	751,000 (2005)
Capital:	Georgetown (249,000)
Administration:	10 regions
Languages:	English, Hindi, Urdu, Indian languages
Religions:	Protestant 34%, Hindu 33%, Roman Catholic 20%
Currency:	1 Guyana dollar = 100 cents

Major cities:
Linden (45,000), New Amsterdam (36,000)

Grenada
State of Grenada

rea:	344 km²
opulation:	103,000 (2005)
apital:	Saint George's (4,000)
dministration:	6 councils, 1 dependency
anguages:	English, English Creole, French Creole
eligions:	Roman Catholic 58%, Protestant 38%
urrency:	1 East Caribbean dollar = 100 cents

ajor cities:
ouyave (3,000), Grenville (2,000)

Guernsey
(British crown dependency)
Bailiwick of Guernsey

Area:	78 km²
Population:	65,228 (2005)
Capital:	Saint Peter Port (17,000)
Administration:	none (British crown dependency)
Languages:	English, French
Religions:	Anglican, Roman Catholic, Presbyterian, Baptist
Currency:	British pound and Guernsey pound

Major islands:
Vale (9,600), Castle (9,000), Saint Simpson (8,700)

Haiti
Republic of Haiti
République d'Haïti/
Repiblik Dayti

Area:	27,750 km²
Population:	8,528,000 (2005)
Capital:	Port-au-Prince (991,000)
Administration:	9 departments
Languages:	French/Creole
Religions:	Roman Catholic 70%, Protestant 15%
Currency:	1 gourde = 100 centimes

Major cities:
Carrefour (336,000), Delmas (284,000), Cap-Haïtien (114,000), Gonaïves (64,000)

Guadeloupe
(overseas department of France)
Department of Guadeloupe
Département de la Guadeloupe

rea:	1,703 km²
opulation:	448,000 (2005)
apital:	Basse-Terre (12,000)
dministration:	none (overseas department of France)
anguages:	French, Creole patois
eligions:	Roman Catholic 84%
urrency:	1 euro = 100 cent

ajor cities:
es Abymes (63,000), Baie-Mahault (31,000), e Gosier (29,000), Petit-Bourg (25,000)

Guinea
Republic of Guinea
République de Guinée

Area:	245,857 km²
Population:	9,402,000 (2005)
Capital:	Conakry (1,091,000)
Administration:	33 prefectures and 1 special zone (Conakry)
Languages:	French, Fulani, Malinke
Religions:	Muslim 85%, Christian 8%
Currency:	Guinea franc

Major cities:
Kindia (288,000), Nzérékoré (283,000), Kankan (261,000), Labé (89,000)

Honduras
Republic of Honduras
República de Honduras

Area:	112,492 km²
Population:	7,205,000 (2005)
Capital:	Tegucigalpa (769,000)
Administration:	18 departments
Languages:	Spanish, Indian languages, English
Religions:	Roman Catholic 90%
Currency:	1 lempira = 100 centavos

Major cities:
San Pedro Sula (439,000), La Ceiba (111,000), Choloma (108,000), El Progreso (90,000), Choluteca (76,000), Comayagua (55,000)

Guam
(territory of the U.S.)
Territory of Guam

rea:	549 km²
opulation:	170,000 (2005)
apital:	Agaña/Hagåtña (1,000)
dministration:	none (territory of the U.S.)
anguages:	English, Chamorro, Philippine languages
eligions:	Roman Catholic 90%
urrency:	US dollar

ajor cities:
amuning (11,000), Mangilao (9,000), Yigo (8,000), stumbo (6,000)

Guinea-Bissau
Republic of Guinea-Bissau
República da Guiné-Bissau

Area:	36,125 km²
Population:	1,586,000 (2005)
Capital:	Bissau (292,000)
Administration:	8 regions and the capital
Languages:	Portuguese, Crioulo
Religions:	traditional beliefs 54%, Muslim 38%, Christian 8%
Currency:	1 CFA franc = 100 centimes

Major cities:
Bafatá (18,000), Gabú (9,500)

Hungary
Republic of Hungary
Magyar Köztársaság

Area:	93,029 km²
Population:	10,098,000 (2005)
Capital:	Budapest (1,740,000)
Administration:	19 counties and the capital
Languages:	Hungarian, German, Slovak, Croatian
Religions:	Roman Catholic 63%, Protestant 26%
Currency:	1 forint = 100 fillér

Major cities:
Debrecen (207,000), Miskolc (182,000), Szeged (164,000), Pécs (160,000), Győr (129,000)

This section provides 40 pages of data on 195 countries and their dependent political territories and exclaves. Countries are arranged in alphabetical order by the English short form of their name. Entries also include the English full-length name and the full name in official local languages. For countries with a federal structure, names of administrative units are listed in the customary English form (e.g. North Ossetia-Alania). The same form for these administrative units is used in the maps of the atlas.

Dependent territories and exclaves are listed after their respective nation, and inhabited external territories are listed both after their respective nation and under their own name, to make them easier to find.

Area and population figures for territorial units are based on the statistical yearbook of the Federal Republic of Germany (Statistisches Jahrbuch der Bundesrepublik Deutschland). Figures for federal administrative units are primarily from the Fischer Weltalmanach, an authoritative global statistical survey. Due to differences in the way inland waters are treated in area calculations, some area figures may differ from those of other statistical surveys.

Cities and their associated urban realms are depicted as accurately as possible in reference maps of the atlas. Thus, scale permitting, city symbols have been supplemented by representations of the area of the entire urban agglomeration (cf. Los Angeles). Correspondingly, the statistical gazetteer lists the population of the city proper and the population of a city's agglomeration (A) in relevant cases (cf. Athens). For cities in the U.S.A., the gazetteer lists Metropolitan Statistical Areas (MSAs) as defined by the U.S. Census Bureau.

Population figures are primarily taken from the Fischer Weltalmanach and from publications by national statistical bureaus. These publications also served as the principal source for information on language, religion and currency. Special care has been taken to include the most recer population figures available.

Under languages, the gazetteer mainly lists officia languages, but also includes important non-official lan guages. Official languages are separated by slashes; othe languages are separated by commas.

The gazetteer includes national flags for all countries an inhabited dependent territories. There are three specia cases for flags of inhabited dependencies:

1) The following dependencies do not have a flag of thei own, or have a territorial flag that has not been officiall recognized. In these cases the flag of the mother coun try is depicted as the official flag. These dependencie include: Christmas Island, Cocos Islands, French Guiana Guadeloupe, Johnston Island, Martinique, Mayotte, Mid way Islands, New Caledonia, Réunion, Saint Pierre an Miquelon, Tokelau, Wake Island, Wallis and Futuna.

2) The following dependencies have a flag of their own but it should be noted that the flag may only be hoiste in second position together with the flag of their mothe country. This rule applies to: American Samoa, Anguilla Aruba, Bermuda, British Virgin Islands, Cayman Islands Falkland Islands, Faroe Islands, French Polynesia, Gibral tar, Greenland, Guam, Montserrat, Netherlands Antilles Norfolk Island, Pitcairn Islands, Puerto Rico, Saint Hel ena, Turks and Caicos Islands, Virgin Islands, U.S.

3) The following dependencies have a flag of their own an such a high level of autonomy that they either do no display the flag of their mother country at all or do no have to do so: Guernsey, Jersey, Man, Isle of, Norther Mariana Islands, Niue.

Afghanistan

Islamic Republic of Afghanistan
De Afghānistān Islāmī Dawlat/
Dowlat-e Eslāmī-ye Afghānestān

Area: 652,090 km²
Population: 29,863,000 (2005)
Capital: Kābul (2,956,000)
Administration: 34 provinces
Languages: Pashto/Dari
Religions: Muslim 99%
Currency: 1 afghani = 100 puls
Major cities:
Kandahar/Qandahar (226,000), Herāt (177,000), Jalālābād (168,000), Mazār-e Sharif (128,000), Baghlān (125,000), Kondūz (122,000), Meymaneh (76,000)

Albania

Republic of Albania
Republika e Shqipërisë

Area: 28,748 km²
Population: 3,130,000 (2005)
Capital: Tirana/Tiranë (343,000)
Administration: 12 counties
Languages: Albanian
Religions: Muslim 70%, Albanian Orthodox 20%, Roman Catholic 10%
Currency: 1 lek = 100 qindars
Major cities:
Durrës (100,000), Elbasan (88,000), Shkodër (83,000), Vlorë (78,000), Korçë (55,000)

Algeria

People's Democratic Republic of Algeria
Al-Jumhūrīyah al-Jazā'irīyah ad-Dīmuqrāṭīyah ash-Sha'bīyah

Area: 2,381,741 km²
Population: 32,854,000 (2005)
Capital: Algiers/Al-Jazā'ir (2,956,000)
Administration: 48 provinces (wilayat)
Languages: Arabic, Berber
Religions: Muslim 99,9%
Currency: 1 Alger. dinar = 100 centimes
Major cities:
Oran/Wahrān (656,000), Constantine/Qusantinah (462,000), 'Annābah (349,000), Bātnah (243,000), Saṭīf (212,000), Sīdī Bal'abbās (180,000), Biskrah (171,000), Djelfa/Al-Jilfah (154,000)

American Samoa

(territory of the U.S.)

Territory of American Samoa

Area: 199 km²
Population: 65,000 (2005)
Capital: Pago Pago on Tutuila (4,000)
Administration: none (territory of the U.S.)
Languages: Samoan/English/Tongan
Religions: Christ. Congregationalist 50% Roman Catholic 20%
Currency: 1 dollar = 100 cents
Major cities:
Tafuna (11,000), Nu'uuli (5,000), Leone (4,000)

Andorra

Principality of Andorra
Principat d'Andorra

Area: 468 km²
Population: 67,000 (2005)
Capital: Andorra la Vella (21,000)
Administration: 7 parishes
Languages: Catalan, Spanish, French
Religions: Roman Catholic 92%
Currency: 1 euro = 100 cent
Major cities:
Escaldes-Engordany (15,500), Encamp (10,700), St. Julià de Lòrio (7,800), La Massana (6,600)

Angola

Republic of Angola
República de Angola

Area: 1,246,700 km²
Population: 15,941,000 (2005)
Capital: Luanda (2,623,000)
Administration: 18 provinces
Languages: Portuguese, Bantu languages
Religions: Christian 89%, traditional beliefs
Currency: 1 readjusted kwanza = 100 lwei
Major cities:
Huambo (173,000), Lobito (137,000), Benguela (134,000), Kuito (89,000), Lubango (76,000)

Anguilla

(overseas territory of the U.K.)

Crown Colony of Anguilla

Area: 96 km²
Population: 12,000 (2005)
Capital: The Valley (1,400)
Administration: none (overseas territory of the U.K.)
Languages: English
Religions: Anglican 29%, Methodist 24%, other Protestant 30%
Currency: East Caribbean dollar
Major cities:
South Hill (1,500), North Side (1,200)

Antigua and Barbuda

Area: 457 km²
Population: 81,000 (2005)
Capital: Saint John's (24,000)
Administration: 6 parishes, 2 dependencies
Languages: English, Creole
Religions: Anglican 80%, Roman Catholic 20%
Currency: 1 Eastern Caribbean dollar = 100 cents
Major cities:
Codrington (1,200)

Argentina

Argentine Republic
República Argentina

Area: 2,780,400 km²
Population: 38,747,000 (2005)
Capital: Buenos Aires (2,776,000, A: 12,047,000)
Administration: 23 provinces, 1 federal district
Languages: Spanish, Indian languages
Religions: Roman Catholic 91%, Protestant 2%
Currency: 1 peso = 100 centavos
Major cities:
Córdoba (1,268,000), San Justo (1,254,000), Rosario (906,000), Lomas de Zamora (591,000), La Plata (553,000), Mar del Plata (542,000), San Miguel de Tucumán (526,000), Quilmes (519,000), Almirante Brown (514,000), Merlo (469,000), Salta (463,000), Lanús (453,000), General San Martín (405,000), Moreno (380,000)

External Territory:

Argentine Antarctic Sector

Sector Antártico Argentino
Claimed by Argentina

Area: 1,231,000 km²
Research stations

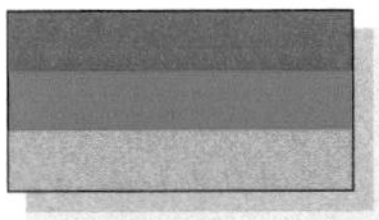

Armenia

Republic of Armenia
Hayastani Hanrapetut'yun

Area: 29,743 km²
Population: 3,016,000 (2005)
Capital: Yerevan (1,246,000)
Administration: 11 provinces
Languages: Armenian, Russian
Religions: Armenian Apostolic Church
Currency: 1 dram = 100 lumas
Major cities:
Gyumri (150,000), Vanadzor (106,000), Vagharshapat (56,000), Hrazdan (53,000), K'ap'an (46,000), Abovyan (45,000)

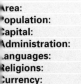

Aruba

(part of the Kingdom of the Netherlands)

Area: 193 km²
Population: 99,000 (2005)
Capital: Oranjestad (30,000)
Administration: none (part of the Kingdom of the Netherlands)
Languages: Dutch, Papiamento
Religions: Roman Catholic 82%, Protestant 8%
Currency: Aruban guilder/florin
Major cities:
Sint Nicolaas (17,000)

Australia
Commonwealth of Australia

Area: 7,692,024 km^2
Population: 20,155,000 (2005)
Capital: Canberra (340,000)
Administration: 6 states, 2 territories
Languages: English, Australian languages
Religions: Roman Catholic 27%, Anglican 21%, other Christian 21%
Currency: 1 Austral. dollar = 100 cents
Major cities:
Sydney (3,602,000; A: 4,232,000), Melbourne (3,489,000), Brisbane (1,653,000), Perth (1,397,000), Adelaide (1,111,000), Newcastle (494,000), Gold Coast (426,000)

	Area km^2	Population 2004	Capital
States			
New South Wales	800,640	6,731,000	Sydney
Queensland	1,730,650	3,882,000	Brisbane
South Australia	983,480	1,534,000	Adelaide
Tasmania	68,400	482,000	Hobart
Victoria	227,420	4,973,000	Melbourne
Western Australia	2,529,880	1,982,000	Perth
Territories			
Australian Capital Territory	2,360	312,000	Canberra
Northern Territory	1,349,130	200,000	Darwin

External Territories:

Ashmore and Cartier Islands
Territory of Ashmore and Cartier Islands

Area: 2 km^2/uninhabited

Australian Antarctic Territory
Claimed by Australia

Area: c. 6,120,000 km^2
Research stations

Christmas Island
Territory of Christmas Island

Area: 135 km^2
Population: 1,500 (2001)

Cocos (Keeling) Islands
Territory of Cocos Islands

Area: 14 km^2
Population: 620 (2001)

Coral Sea Islands
Territory of Coral Sea Islands

Reefs and islands scattered over a sea area of about 1 million km^2 (uninhabited)

Heard and the McDonald Islands
Territory of Heard and the McDonald Islands

Area: 412 km^2/uninhabited

Norfolk Island
Territory of Norfolk Island

Area: 35 km^2
Population: 3,000 (2001)
Capital: Kingston (880)

Austria
Republic of Austria
Republik Österreich

Area: 83,859 km^2
Population: 8,189,000 (2005)
Capital: Vienna/Wien (1,584,000)
Administration: 9 federal states
Languages: German/Slovene/Croatian/Hungarian (regionally)
Religions: Roman Catholic 73%, Protestant 5%
Currency: 1 euro = 100 cent
Major cities:
Graz (226,000), Linz (184,000), Salzburg (143,000), Innsbruck (113,000), Klagenfurt (90,000)

Azerbaijan
Azerbaijani Republic
Azərbaycan Respublikası

Area: 86,600 km^2
Population: 8,411,000 (2005)
Capital: Baku/Bakı (1,840,000)
Administration: 65 districts, 11 city communes, Nakhichevan (Naxçıvan) Aut. Republic, Nagorno-Karabakh Region
Languages: Azerbaijani, Russian
Religions: Muslim 90%
Currency: 1 manat =100 gopik
Major cities:
Gəncə (293,000), Sumqayıt (249,000)

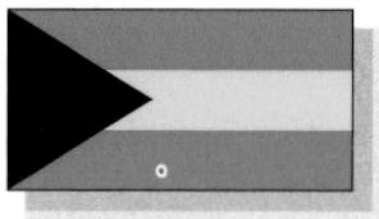

Bahamas, The
Commonwealth of The Bahamas

Area: 13,878 km^2
Population: 323,000 (2005)
Capital: Nassau (211,000)
Administration: 19 districts
Languages: English, Creole
Religions: Baptist 31%, Roman Catholic 16%, Anglican 16%
Currency: 1 Bahamian dollar = 100 cents
Major cities:
Freeport (27,000), Coopers Town (8,000), Marsh Habour (5,000), High Rock (4,000)

Bahrain
Kingdom of Bahrain
Mamlakat al-Baḩrayn

Area: 694 km^2
Population: 727,000 (2005)
Capital: Manama/Al-Manāmah (154,000)
Administration: 12 regions
Languages: Arabic, English
Religions: Muslim 80%
Currency: 1 Bahrain dinar = 1,000 fils
Major cities:
Al-Muḩarraq (92,000), Ar Rifā' (80,000), Hammād (53,000)

Bangladesh
People's Republic of Banglades
Gaṇprajātantrī Bānlādesh

Area: 147,570 km^2
Population: 141,822,000 (2005)
Capital: Dhaka (9,913,000)
Administration: 6 provinces
Languages: Bengali, English
Religions: Muslim 87% (mainly Sunni Hindu 12%
Currency: 1 taka = 100 paisa
Major cities:
Chittagong (3,202,000), Khulna (811,000), Rajshahi (403,000), Sylhet (299,000), Tongi (296,000 Rangpur (264,000), Mymensingh (237,000)

Barbados

Area: 430 km^2
Population: 270,000 (2005)
Capital: Bridgetown (98,000)
Administration: 11 parishes
Languages: English, Bajan
Religions: Anglican 40%, other Protestants 30%, non-denominational 20%
Currency: 1 Barbados dollar = 100 cents
Major cities:
Speightstown (3,500), Bathsheba (1,800)

Belarus
Republic of Belarus
Respublika Belarus'

Area: 207,600 km^2
Population: 9,755,000 (2005)
Capital: Minsk (1,699,000)
Administration: 6 provinces, capital
Languages: Belarusian/Russian
Religions: Russian Orthodox 60%, Roman Catholic 8%
Currency: 1 Belarusian rouble = 100 kopeks
Major cities:
Homyel' (480,000), Mahilyow (361,000), Vitsyebsk (342,000), Hrodna (207,000), Brest (291,000)

Belgium
Kingdom of Belgium
Royaume de Belgique/
Koninkrijk België/
Königreich Belgien

Area: 30,518 km^2
Population: 10,419,000 (2005)
Capital: Brussels/Brussel/Bruxelles (143,000; A: 999,000)
Administration: 3 regions: Flanders, Wallonia, Brussels-Capital
Languages: French/Dutch/German
Religions: Roman Catholic 81%
Currency: 1 euro = 100 cent
Major cities:
Antwerp/Antwerpen (449,000), Ghent/Gent (226,000 Charleroi (200,000), Luik/Liège (185,000)

1 km^2 = 0.3861 square mile

Belize

rea: 22,966 km²
opulation: 270,000 (2005)
apital: Belmopan (8,100)
dministration: 6 districts
anguages: English, English Creole, Spanish
eligions: Roman Catholic 58 %, Protestant 28 %
urrency: 1 Belize dollar = 100 cents
lajor cities:
elize City (49,000), Orange Walk (13,000), an Ignacio (13,000)

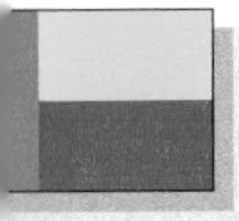

Benin

Republic of Benin
Bénin
République du Bénin

rea: 112,622 km²
opulation: 8,439,000 (2005)
apital: Porto-Novo (210,000) (seat of government: Cotonou)
dministration: 12 regions
anguages: French, 50 tribal languages
eligions: traditional beliefs 60 %, Christian 25 %
urrency: 1 CFA franc = 100 centimes
lajor cities:
otonou (800,000), Parakou (175,000), jougou (132,000), Abomey (82,000)

Bermuda

(overseas territory of the U.K.)

rea: 53 km²
opulation: 64,000 (2005)
apital: Hamilton (890)
dministration: 9 parishes and 2 municipalities
anguages: English, Portuguese
eligions: Anglican 23 %, Roman Catholic 15 %
urrency: Bermudian dollar
lajor cities:
aint George (1,800)

Bhutan

Kingdom of Bhutan
Druk Gyekhab

rea: 46,500 km²
opulation: 2,163,000 (2005)
apital: Thimphu (74,000)
dministration: 20 districts
anguages: Dzongkha, various Tibetan and various Nepalese dialects
eligions: Buddhist 72 %, Hindu 24 %
urrency: 1 ngultrum = 100 chetrum
lajor cities:
huntsholing (60,000)

Bolivia

Republic of Bolivia
República de Bolivia

Area: 1,098,591 km²
Population: 9,182,000 (2005)
Capital: Sucre (judicial, 216,000), La Paz (administrative)
Administration: 9 departments
Languages: Spanish/Quechua/Aymara
Religions: Roman Catholic 85 %
Currency: 1 boliviano = 100 centavos
Major cities:
Santa Cruz (1,136,000), La Paz (793,000), El Alto (650,000), Cochabamba (517,000), Oruro (216,000

Bosnia and Herzegovina

Bosna i Hercegovina/
Bosna i Hercegovina/
Bosna i Hercegovina

Area: 51,197 km²
Population: 4,186,000 (2005)
Capital: Sarajevo (552,000)
Administration: the Bosniak/Croat Federation of B. and H., and Serb Rep.
Languages: Bosnian/Croatian/Serbian
Religions: Muslim 40 %, Orthodox Cath. 31 %, Roman Cath. 15 %
Currency: 1 convertible mark
Major cities:
Tuzla (230,000), Zenica (146,000), Banja Luka (143,000), Mostar (94,000), Bihać (65,000)

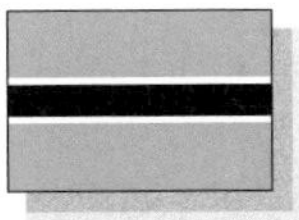

Botswana

Republic of Botswana
Lefatshe la Botswana

Area: 582,000 km²
Population: 1,765,000 (2005)
Capital: Gaborone (186,000)
Administration: 10 districts
Languages: English, Setswana
Religions: predominantly traditional beliefs, Christian 30 %
Currency: 1 pula = 100 thebe
Major cities:
Francistown (82,000), Molepolole (55,000), Selebi-Pikwe (50,000), Maun (44,000), Serowe (42,000), Kanye (41,000)

Brazil

Federative Republic of Brazil
República Federativa do Brasil

Area: 8,547,404 km²
Population: 186,405,000 (2005)
Capital: Brasília (2,231,000)
Administration: 26 states, 1 federal district
Languages: Portuguese
Religions: Roman Catholic 75 %
Currency: 1 real = 100 centavos
Major cities:
São Paulo (10,278,000; A: 19,037,000), Rio de Janeiro (6,094,000; A: 11,570,000), Salvador (2,673,000), Belo Horizonte (2,376,000), Fortaleza (2,375,000), Curitiba (1,758,000)

States	Area km²	Population 2004	Capital
Acre	153,150	621,000	Rio Branco
Alagoas	27,933	2,962,000	Maceió
Amapá	143,454	562,000	Macapá
Amazonas	1,577,820	3,133,000	Manaus
Bahia	567,295	13,613,000	Salvador
Ceará	146,348	7,911,000	Fortaleza
Espírito Santo	46,194	3,321,000	Vitória
Goiás	341,289	5,447,000	Goiânia
Maranhão	333,366	5,977,000	São Luís
Mato Grosso	906,807	2,720,000	Cuiabá
Mato Grosso do Sul	358,159	2,212,000	Campo Grande
Minas Gerais	588,384	18,860,000	Belo Horizonte
Pará	1,253,165	6,753,000	Belém
Paraíba	56,585	3,553,000	João Pessoa
Paraná	199,709	10,066,000	Curitiba
Pernambuco	98,938	8,275,000	Recife
Piauí	252,378	2,961,000	Teresina
Rio de Janeiro	43,910	15,106,000	Rio de Janeiro
Rio Grande do Norte	53,307	2,940,000	Natal
Rio Grande do Sul	282,062	10,661,000	Porto Alegre
Rondônia	238,513	1,491,000	Porto Velho
Roraima	225,116	373,000	Boa Vista
Santa Catarina	95,443	5,724,000	Florianópolis
São Paulo	248,809	36,487,000	São Paulo
Sergipe	22,050	1,916,000	Aracaju
Tocantins	278,421	1,264,000	Palmas
Federal district			
Distrito Federal	5,822	2,254,000	Brasília

British Virgin Islands

(overseas territory of the U.K.)

Area: 153 km²
Population: 22,000 (2005)
Capital: Road Town on Tortola (8,000)
Administration: none (overseas territory of the U.K.)
Languages: English
Religions: Protestant 86 %, Roman Catholic 10 %
Currency: 1 dollar = 100 cents
Major islands:
Tortola (17,000), Virgin Gorda (3,000)

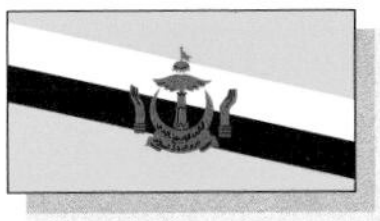

Brunei

State of Brunei Darussalam
Negara Brunei Darussalam

Area: 5,765 km²
Population: 374,000 (2005)
Capital: Bandar Seri Begawan (67,000)
Administration: 4 districts
Languages: Malay, English
Religions: Muslim 67 %, Buddhist 15 %, Christian 10 %
Currency: 1 Brunei dollar = 100 cents
Major cities:
Kuala Belait (21,000), Seria (21,000)

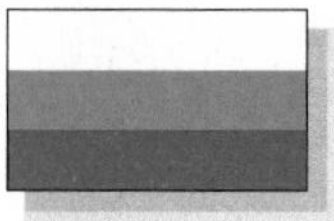

Bulgaria

Republic of Bulgaria
Republika Bŭlgariya

Area: 110,910 km²
Population: 7,726,000 (2005)
Capital: Sofia/Sofiya (1,096,000)
Administration: 8 regions, 1 city commune
Languages: Bulgarian, Turkish
Religions: Bulgarian Orthodox 86%, Muslim 13%
Currency: 1 lev = 100 stotinki
Major cities:
Plovdiv (341,000), Varna (315,000), Burgas (193,000), Ruse (162,000), Stara Zagora (144,000), Pleven (122,000), Sliven (101,000)

Burkina Faso

République Démocratique du Burkina Faso

Area: 274,200 km²
Population: 13,228,000 (2005)
Capital: Ouagadougou (710,000)
Administration: 45 provinces
Languages: French, Arabic
Religions: traditional beliefs 50%, Muslim 40%
Currency: 1 CFA franc = 100 centimes
Major cities:
Bobo-Dioulasso (310,000), Koudougou (72,000), Ouahigouya (52,000), Banfora (50,000)

Burundi

Republic of Burundi
Republika y'Uburundi/
République du Burundi

Area: 27,834 km²
Population: 7,548,000 (2005)
Capital: Bujumbura (319,000)
Administration: 15 provinces
Languages: Kirundi/French
Religions: Christian 68%, traditional beliefs
Currency: 1 Burundi franc = 100 centimes
Major cities:
Gitega (47,000), Muyinga (45,000), Ngozi (40,000), Ruyigi (37,000), Kayanza (26,000), Bururi (23,000)

Cambodia

Kingdom of Cambodia
Preăh Réachéanachâkr Kâmpŭchéa

Area: 181,035 km²
Population: 14,071,000 (2005)
Capital: Phnum Pénh (1,099,000)
Administration: 24 provinces
Languages: Khmer, French, Chinese
Religions: Buddhist 88%, Muslim 2%
Currency: 1 riel = 100 sen
Major cities:
Preah Seihânŭ (156,000), Bâtdâmbâng (140,000), Siĕmréab (120,000)

Cameroon

Republic of Cameroon
République du Cameroun/
Republic of Cameroon

Area: 466,050 km²
Population: 16,322,000 (2005)
Capital: Yaoundé (1,249,000)
Administration: 10 provinces
Languages: French/English
Religions: Christian 53%, traditional beliefs 40%
Currency: 1 CFA franc = 100 centimes
Major cities:
Douala (1,495,000), Garoua (357,000), Bamenda (316,000), Maroua (272,000), Bafoussam (242,000)

Canada

Area: 9,984,670 km² (755,180 km² freshwater)
Population: 32,268,000 (2005)
Capital: Ottawa (828,000; A: 1,146,000)
Administration: 10 provinces, 3 territories
Languages: English/French
Religions: Roman Catholic 45%, Protestant 36%
Currency: 1 Canadian dollar = 100 cents
Major cities:
Toronto (4,367,000), Montréal (3,216,000), Calgary (951,000), Edmonton (938,000), Québec (683,000), Vancouver (546,000)

	Area km²	Population 2004	Capital
Provinces			
Alberta	661,190	3,202,000	Edmonton
British Columbia	947,800	4,196,000	Victoria
Manitoba	649,950	1,170,000	Winnipeg
New Brunswick	73,440	751,000	Fredericton
Newfoundland	405,720	517,000	St. John's
Nova Scotia	55,490	937,000	Halifax
Ontario	1,068,580	12,393,000	Toronto
Prince-Edward-Island	5,660	138,000	Charlottetown
Québec	1,540,680	7,543,000	Québec
Saskatchewan	652,330	995,000	Regina
Territories			
Northwest Territories	1,305,218	43,000	Yellowknife
Nunavut	2,121,102	30,000	Iqaluit
Yukon Territory	483,450	31,000	Whitehorse

Cape Verde

Republic of Cape Verde
República de Cabo Verde

Area: 4,033 km²
Population: 507,000 (2005)
Capital: Praia (95,000)
Administration: 15 counties
Languages: Portuguese
Religions: Roman Catholic 96%
Currency: 1 Cape Verde escudo = 100 centavos
Major cities:
Mindelo (63,000)

Cayman Islands

(overseas territory of the U.K.)

Area: 264 km²
Population: 42,000 (2005)
Capital: George Town on Grand Cayman (21,000)
Administration: 8 districts
Languages: English
Religions: Protestant
Currency: Caymanian dollar
Major islands:
Grand Cayman (40,000), Cayman Brac (1,800), Little Cayman (100)

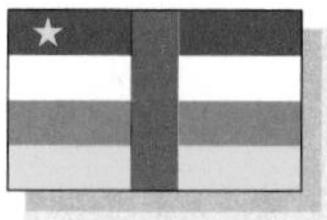

Central African Republic

Ködrö tî Bê-Afrîka/
République centrafricaine

Area: 622,436 km²
Population: 4,038,000 (2005)
Capital: Bangui (636,000)
Administration: 16 prefectures and the capital
Languages: Sango/French
Religions: traditional beliefs 57%, Christian 30%, Muslim 15%
Currency: 1 CFA franc = 100 centimes
Major cities:
Berbérati (61,000), Bouar (58,000), Carnot (58,000), Bambari (52,000), Kaga Bandoro (51,000)

Chad

Republic of Chad
République du Tchad/
Jumhūrīyat Tshād

Area: 1,284,000 km²
Population: 9,749,000 (2005)
Capital: N'Djamena (530,000)
Administration: 18 prefectures
Languages: French/Arabic
Religions: Muslim 50%, Christian 30%
Currency: 1 CFA franc = 100 centimes
Major cities:
Moundou (281,000), Sarh (100,000), Abéché (73,000), Kélo (42,000), Koumra (35,000), Pala (35,000), Am-Timan (28,000), Bongor (27,000)

1 km² = 0.3861 square mile

Chile
Republic of Chile
República de Chile

Area:	756,626 km²
Population:	16,295,000 (2005)
Capital:	Santiago (4,656,000)
Administration:	13 regions
Languages:	Spanish, Indian languages
Religions:	Roman Catholic 77%, Protestant 13%
Currency:	1 Chilean peso = 100 centavos

Major cities:
Puente Alto (493,000), Maipú (464,000),
Viña del Mar (299,000), Antofagasta (298,000),
Valparaíso (270,000), Talcahuano (247,000),
San Bernardo (238,000), Temuco (253,000),
Rancagua (207,000)

External Territories:

Islands in the Pacific Ocean:
Desventurados Islands/Islas Desventurados
Diego Ramírez Island/Islas Diego Ramírez
Easter Island/Isla de Pascua (Rapa Nui)
Juan Fernández Island/Islas Juan Fernández
Sala-y-Gómez

Chilean Antarctic Territory
Territorio Antártico Chileno
Claimed by Chile

Area:	1,250,000 km²

Research stations

China
People's Republic of China
Zhonghua Renmin Gongheguo

Area:	9,596,961 km²
Population:	1,323,805,000 (2005)
Capital:	Beijing (10,839,000)
Administration:	22 provinces, 5 autonomous regions, 4 municipalities, 2 special administrative regions
Languages:	Chinese, minority languages
Religions:	Non-religious 52%, Confucianist 20%, Atheist 12%
Currency:	1 Renminbi (yuan) = 10 jiao

Major cities:
Shanghai (12,887,000), Tianjin (9,156,000),
Hong Kong/Xianggang (6,708,000),
Wuhan (5,169,000), Chongqing (4,900,000),
Harbin (4,266,000), Shenyang (4,828,000),
Guangzhou (3,893,000), Chengdu (3,294,000),
Xi'an (3,123,000), Changchun (3,093,000),
Nanjing (2,740,000), Dalian (2,628,000),
Qingdao (2,543,000), Jinan (2,568,000),
Hangzhou (2,105,000), Zhengzhou (2,035,000),
Shijiazhuang (1,983,000), Taiyuan (1,937,000),
Changsha (1,737,000), Kunming (1,685,000),
Nanjiang (1,650,000), Fuzhou (1,546,000),
Lanzhou (1538000)

Christmas Island
(territory of Australia)
Territory of Christmas Island

Area:	135 km²
Population:	1,500 (2001)
Capital:	The Settlement
Administration:	none (territory of Australia)
Languages:	English, Chinese, Malay
Religions:	Buddhist 36%, Muslim 25%, Christian 18%
Currency:	Australian dollar

Cocos (Keeling) Islands
(territory of Australia)
Territory of Cocos (Keeling) Islands

Area:	14 km²
Population:	630 (2005)
Capital:	West Island
Administration:	none (territory of Australia)
Languages:	Malay (Cocos dialect), English
Religions:	Sunni Muslim 80%, Christian
Currency:	Australian dollar

Colombia
Republic of Colombia
República de Colombia

Area:	1,138,914 km²
Population:	45,600,000 (2005)
Capital:	Bogotá (6,850,000)
Administration:	32 departments, capital
Languages:	Spanish, Indian languages
Religions:	Roman Catholic 95%
Currency:	1 Colombian peso = 100 centavos

Major cities:
Cali (2,288,000), Medellín (1,965,000), Barranquilla
(1,330,000), Cartagena (903,000), Cúcuta (683,000),
Bucaramanga (553,000), Pereira (420,000)

Comoros
Union of the Comoros
Udzima wa Komori
Ittihād al-Qumur
Union des Comores

Area:	1,861 km²
Population:	798,000 (2005)
Capital:	Moroni (60,000)
Administration:	3 districts
Languages:	Comorian, Arabic, French
Religions:	Muslim 99%, Roman Catholic 1%
Currency:	1 Comorian franc = 100 centimes

Major cities:
Mutsamudu (31,000), Mitsamiouli (21,000),
Domoni (19,000), Fomboni (13,000)

Congo, Democratic Republic of the
République démocratique du Congo

Area:	2,344,858 km²
Population:	57,549,000 (2005)
Capital:	Kinshasa (6,789,000)
Administration:	10 regions, capital
Languages:	French
Religions:	Roman Catholic 42%, Protestant 25%
Currency:	1 Congolese franc

Major cities:
Lubumbashi (1,138,000), Mbuji-Mayi (971,000),
Kolwezi (862,000), Kananga (577,000),
Kisangani (536,000), Likasi (397,000)

Congo, Republic of the
République du Congo

Area:	342,000 km²
Population:	3,999,000 (2005)
Capital:	Brazzaville (950,000))
Administration:	10 regions and 1 commune
Languages:	French, Lingala
Religions:	Roman Catholic 54%, traditional beliefs
Currency:	1 CFA franc = 100 centimes

Major cities:
Pointe-Noire (561,000), Loubomo (93,000),
Nkayi (89,000), Mossendjo (28,000)

Cook Islands
(Independant Territory in Free Association with New Zealand)

Area:	237 km²
Population:	18,000 (2005)
Capital:	Avarua (9,000)
Administration:	island councils and district councils
Languages:	English, Cook Islands Maori
Religions:	Protestant 90%, Roman Catholic 10%
Currency:	New Zealand dollar

Major cities:
Mangaia (330), Amuri (280), Omoka (180)

Costa Rica
Republic of Costa Rica
República de Costa Rica

Area:	51,100 km²
Population:	4,327,000 (2005)
Capital:	San José (337,000)
Administration:	7 provinces
Languages:	Spanish, English, Creole
Religions:	Roman Catholic 89%, Protestant 8%
Currency:	1 Costa Rican colon = 100 céntimos

Major cities:
Limón (61,000), Alajuela (48,000),
San Francisco (45,000), Cinco Esquinas (40,000)

Côte d'Ivoire
Republic of Côte d'Ivoire
(Ivory Coast)
République de Côte d'Ivoire

Area: 322,462 km^2
Population: 18,154,000 (2005)
Capital: Yamoussoukro (299,000 (seat of government: Abidjan)
Administration: 18 regions
Languages: French, 60 native dialects
Religions: Muslim 40%, Christian 28%, traditional beliefs
Currency: 1 CFA franc = 100 centimes
Major cities:
Abidjan (3,548,0000), Bouaké (569,000), Daloa (213,000), Korhogo (175,000), Anyama (147,000)

Croatia
Republic of Croatia
Republika Hrvatska

Area: 56,542 km^2
Population: 4,551,000 (2005)
Capital: Zagreb (779,000)
Administration: 20 counties and 1 city
Languages: Croatian, Serbian, Hungarian, Italian
Religions: Roman Catholic 90%, Serbian Orthodox 4%
Currency: 1 kuna = 100 lipa
Major cities:
Split (189,000), Rijeka (144,000), Osijek (90,000), Zadar (73,000), Slavonski Brod (59,000)

Cuba
Republic of Cuba
República de Cuba

Area: 110,860 km^2
Population: 11,269,000 (2005)
Capital: Havana/La Habana (2,185,000)
Administration: 14 provinces, 1 special municipality
Languages: Spanish
Religions: Non-denominational 56%, Roman Catholic 39%
Currency: 1 Cuban peso = 100 centavos
Major cities:
Santiago de Cuba (556,000), Camagüey (348,000), Holguín (319,000), Santa Clara (210,000)

Cyprus
Republic of Cyprus
Kypriakí Dimokratía/
Kıbrıs Cumhuriyeti

Area: 9,251 km^2
Population: 835,000 (2005)
Capital: Nicosia/Lefkosía/Lefkoşa (201,000)
Administration: 6 districts
Languages: Greek/Turkish, English
Religions: Greek Orthodox 80%, Muslim (Sunni) 19%
Currency: 1 Cyprus pound = 100 cents
Major cities:
Limassol/Lemesós (161,000), Lárnaka (71,000), Famagusta (23,000)

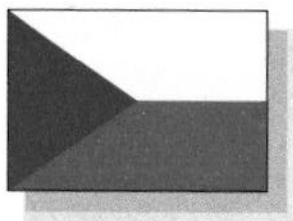

Czech Republic
Česká republika

Area: 78,860 km^2
Population: 10,220,000 (2005)
Capital: Prague/Praha (1,179,000)
Administration: 14 districts
Languages: Czech, Slovak
Religions: Roman Catholic 39%, non-denominational 40%
Currency: 1 koruna = 100 halura
Major cities:
Brno (379,000), Ostrava (319,000), Plzeň (166,000), Olomouc (103,000), Liberec (99,800), České Budějovice (99,000), Hradec Králové (98,000)

Denmark
Kingdom of Denmark
Kongeriget Danmark

Area: 43,094 km^2
Population: 5,431,000 (2005)
Capital: Copenhagen/København (1,086,000)
Administration: 14 counties, 2 municipalities
Languages: Danish, German
Religions: Protestant (Lutheran) 87%
Currency: 1 Danish krone = 100 øre
Major cities:
Århus (223,000), Odense (145,000), Ålborg (121,000), Esbjerg (73,000), Randers (56,000), Kolding (55,000), Vejle (50,000), Horsens (49,000)

Faroe Islands
Føroyar/Færøerne

Area: 1,399 km^2
Population: 47,000 (2005)
Capital: Tórshavn (12,000)
Languages: Faroese/Danish
Religions: Protestant (Lutheran) 95%
Currency: 1 Faroese krona = 100 oyru

Greenland
Kalaallit Nunaat/Grønland

Area: 2,166,086 km^2
Population: 57,000 (2005)
Capital: Nuuk (15,000)
Languages: Inuit/Danish
Religions: Protestant (Lutheran) 98%
Currency: 1 Danish krone = 100 øre

Djibouti
Republic of Djibouti
République de Djibouti/
Jūmhūrīyat Jībūtī

Area: 23,200 km^2
Population: 793,000 (2005)
Capital: Djibouti/Jībūtī (547,000)
Administration: 4 districts
Languages: French/Arabic
Religions: Muslim 97%
Currency: 1 Djibouti franc = 100 centimes
Major cities:
Ali Sabieh (40,000), Tadjoura (22,000), Obock (18,000), Dikhil (12,000)

Dominica
Commonwealth of Dominica

Area: 751 km^2
Population: 79,000 (2005)
Capital: Roseau (19,000)
Administration: 10 parishes
Languages: English, French Creole
Religions: Roman Catholic 80%, Protestant 13%
Currency: 1 East Caribbean dollar = 100 cents
Major cities:
Portsmouth (3,600), Marigot (2,900), Atkinson (2,500)

Dominican Republic
República Dominicana

Area: 48,442 km^2
Population: 8,895,000 (2005)
Capital: Santo Domingo (2,667,000)
Administration: 31 provinces and 1 district
Languages: Spanish
Religions: Roman Catholic 90%
Currency: 1 Dominican peso = 100 centavos
Major cities:
Santiago (581,000), Concepción de la Vega (242,000), San Cristóbal (200,000)

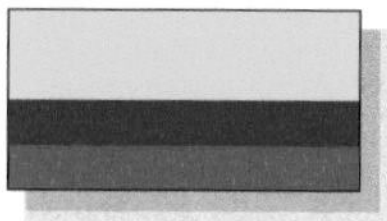

Ecuador
Republic of Ecuador
República del Ecuador

Area: 283,561 km^2
Population: 13,228,000 (2005)
Capital: Quito (1,399,000)
Administration: 22 provinces
Languages: Spanish, Indian languages
Religions: Roman Catholic 93%
Currency: 1 US-$ = 100 cents
Major cities:
Guayaquil (1,952,000), Cuenca (277,000), Santo Domingo de los Colorados (200,000), Machala (198,000), Manta (183,000), Portoviejo (170,000), Eloy Alfaro (168,000), Ambato (154,000)

Egypt
Arab Republic of Egypt
Jumhūrīyat Mişr al-ʿArabīyah

Area: 1,002,000 km^2
Population: 74,033,000 (2005)
Capital: Cairo/Al-Qāhirah (10,834,000)
Administration: 27 governorates
Languages: Arabic, French, English
Religions: Muslim 85%, Christian 10%
Currency: 1 Egypt. pound = 100 piastre
Major cities:
Alexandria/Al-Iskandarīyah (3,380,000), Giza/Al-Jīzah (2,566,000), Shubrā al-Khayma (1,000,000), Port Said/Būr Saʿīd (528,000)

1 km^2 = 0.3861 square mile

El Salvador

Republic of El Salvador
República de El Salvador

Area:	21,041 km²
Population:	6,881,000 (2005)
Capital:	San Salvador (526,000)
Administration:	14 departments
Languages:	Spanish, Indian languages
Religions:	Roman Catholic 80%
Currency:	1 colón = 100 centavos
Major cities:	

Soyapango (330,000), Santa Ana (177,000),
San Miguel (162,000), Mejicanos (160,000),
Nueva San Salvador (125,000), Delgado (72,000)

Equatorial Guinea

Republic of Equatorial Guinea
República de Guinea Ecuatorial

Area:	28,051 km²
Population:	504,000 (2005)
Capital:	Malabo (60,000)
Administration:	7 provinces
Languages:	Spanish, Fang, Bubi, Portuguese patois
Religions:	Roman Catholic 90%
Currency:	1 CFA franc = 100 centimes
Major cities:	

Bata (50,000), Luba (15,000)

Eritrea

State of Eritrea
Hagere Ērtra/Dawlat Iritrīyā

Area:	124,324 km²
Population:	4,401,000 (2005)
Capital:	Āsmera (564,000)
Administration:	10 provinces
Languages:	Tigrinya/Arabic, English
Religions:	Eritrean Orthodox 50%, Muslim 50%
Currency:	1 nakfa = 100 cents
Major cities:	

Aseb (58,000), Keren (38,000), Ādī Ugrī (18,000)

Estonia

Republic of Estonia
Eesti Vabariik

Area:	43,432 km²
Population:	1,330,000 (2005)
Capital:	Tallinn (397,000)
Administration:	15 counties
Languages:	Estonian, Russian
Religions:	Protestant (Lutheran) 13%, Russian Orthodox 11%
Currency:	1 kroon = 100 sents
Major cities:	

Tartu (101,000), Narva (68,000), Pärnu (51,000),
Kohtla-Järve (47,000)

Ethiopia

Federal Democratic Republic of
Ethiopia
Yltyop'iya Federalawi
Demokrasiyawi Ripeblik

Area:	1,112,000 km²
Population:	77,431,000 (2005)
Capital:	Addis Ababa/Ādīs Ābeba (2,753,000)
Administration:	9 regions, 2 self governing-administrations
Languages:	Amharic, English
Religions:	Muslim (Sunni) 45%, Ethiopian Orthodox 40%
Currency:	1 birr = 100 cents
Major cities:	

Dirē Dawa (255,000), Nazrēt (177,000)

Falkland Islands (Islas Malvinas)

*(overseas territory of the U.K.;
also claimed by Argentina)*

Area:	12,173 km²
Population:	3,000 (2005)
Capital:	Stanley on East Falkland (2,000)
Administration:	none (overseas territory of the U.K.)
Languages:	English
Religions:	primarily Anglican, Roman Catholic
Currency:	Falkland Island pound
Major cities:	

East Falkland (2,000), West Falkland (100)

Faroe Islands

(part of the Kingdom of Denmark)
Føroyar/Færøerne

Area:	1,399 km²
Population:	47,000 (2005)
Capital:	Tórshavn (12,000)
Administration:	self-governing overseas administrative division of Denmark
Languages:	Faroese, Danish
Religions:	Evangelical Lutheran 95%
Currency:	1 Faroese krona = 100 oyru
Major cities:	

Klaksvik (5,000), Hoyvik (3,000), Argir (2,000)

Fiji

Republic of the Fiji Islands
MatanituTu-Vaka-i-koya Ko Viti/
Republic of the Fiji Islands

Area:	18,333 km²
Population:	848,000 (2005)
Capital:	Suva (77,000)
Administration:	4 divisions
Languages:	Fijian/English
Religions:	Christian 53%, Hindu 38%, Muslim 8%
Currency:	1 Fiji dollar = 100 cents
Major cities:	

Lautoka (36,000), Nadi (9,200), Labasa (6,500),
Ba (6,300)

Finland

Republic of Finland
Suomen tasavalta/
Republiken Finland

Area:	304,530 km²
Population:	5,249,000 (2005)
Capital:	Helsinki/Helsingfors (559,000)
Administration:	5 provinces, autonomous province Åland
Languages:	Finnish/Swedish
Religions:	Protestant (Lutheran) 85%
Currency:	1 euro = 100 cent
Major cities:	

Espoo (224,000), Tampere (201,000), Vantaa
(184,000), Turku/Åbo (175,000), Oulu (126,000)

France

French Republic
République française

Area:	543,965 km²
Population:	60,496,000 (2005)
Capital:	Paris (2,143,000; A: 9,645,000)
Administration:	22 regions
Languages:	French, regional languages
Religions:	Roman Catholic 81%, Muslim 5%
Currency:	1 euro = 100 cent
Major cities:	

Marseille (798,000; A: 1,350,000), Lyon (416,000;
A: 1,349,000), Toulouse (391,000), Nice (341,000),
Nantes (269,000), Strasbourg (264,000), Mon-
pellier (225,000), Bordeaux (215,000), Rennes
(206,000), Le Havre (191,000), Reims (187,000),
Lille (182,000), Saint-Étienne (180,000), Toulon
(160,000), Grenoble (152,000), Angers (151,000)

Overseas Departments:

French Guiana
Department of Guiana
Département de la Guyane

Area:	83,543 km²
Population:	187,000 (2005)
Capital:	Cayenne (66,000)

Guadeloupe
Department of Guadeloupe
Département de la Guadeloupe

Area:	1,703 km²
Population:	448,000 (2005)
Capital:	Basse-Terre (36,000)

Martinique
Department of Martinique
Département de la Martinique

Area:	1,128 km²
Population:	396,000 (2005)
Capital:	Fort-de-France (131,000)

Réunion
Department of Réunion
Département de la Réunion

Area:	2,504 km²
Population:	785,000 (2005)
Capital:	Saint-Denis (159,000)

Territorial Collectivities:

Mayotte
Territorial Collectivity of Mayotte
Collectivité territoriale de Mayotte

Area:	374 km²
Population:	160,000 (2005)
Capital:	Dzauodi (12,000)

Saint Pierre and Miquelon
Territorial Collectivity of Saint Pierre and Miquelon
Collectivité territoriale de Saint-Pierre-et-Miquelon

Area:	242 km²
Population:	6,000 (2005)
Capital:	Saint-Pierre (5,700)

Overseas Territories:

French Polynesia
Territory of French Polynesia
Territoire de la Polynésie française

Area:	4,000 km²
Population:	257,000 (2005)
Capital:	Papeete (26,000)

French Southern Territories
Territoire des Terres australes et antarctiques françaises

The territories comprise:
Keguelen Islands (7,215 km²)
Crozet Islands (515 km²)
Amsterdam Island (54 km²)
Saint-Paul Island (7 km²)
Adélie Land/Terre Adélie, *claimed by France* (432,000 km²)

New Caledonia
Territory of New Caledonia
Territoire de la Nouvelle-Calédonie

Area:	19,058 km²
Population:	237,000 (2005)
Capital:	Nouméa (83,000)

Wallis and Futuna
Territory of Wallis and Funtuna
Territoire de Wallis-et-Futuna

Area:	255 km² (Wallis 159 km², Futuna 64 km², Alofi 51 km²)
Population:	15,000 (2005)
Capital:	Matâ-Utu (1,300)

French Guiana
(overseas department of France)

Department of Guiana
Département de la Guyane

Area:	83,534 km²
Population:	187,000 (2005)
Capital:	Cayenne (66,000)
Administration:	none (overseas department of France)
Languages:	French, Creole
Religions:	Roman Catholic 75%
Currency:	1 euro = 100 cent

Major cities:
Matoury (26,000), Saint-Laurent-du-Maroni (24,000), Kourou (24,000), Remire-Montjoly (19,000)

French Polynesia
(overseas lands of France)

Territory of French Polynesia
Territoire de la Polynésie française/
Polynesia farani

Area:	4,000 km²
Population:	257,000 (2005)
Capital:	Papeete (26,000)
Administration:	none (overseas lands of France)
Languages:	French/Polynesian
Religions:	Protestant 54%, Roman Catholic 30%
Currency:	Comptoirs Francais du Pacifique franc

Major cities:
Faaa (29,000), Punaauia (26,000), Mahina (14,000)

Gabon
Gabonese Republic
République gabonaise

Area:	267,667 km²
Population:	1,384,000 (2005)
Capital:	Libreville (573,000)
Administration:	9 provinces
Languages:	French, Fang, Bantu languages
Religions:	Roman Catholic 60%, traditional beliefs 30%
Currency:	1 CFA franc = 100 centimes

Major cities:
Port Gentil (109,000), Masuku (43,000), Oyem (31,000), Moanda (30,000), Mouila (22,000)

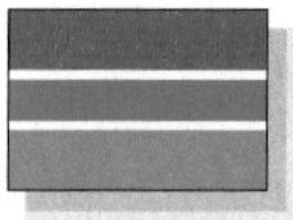

Gambia, The
Republic of The Gambia

Area:	11,295 km²
Population:	1,517,000 (2005)
Capital:	Banjul (34,000, A: 271,000)
Administration:	5 divisions and 1 city
Languages:	English, Mandinka, Fulani, Wolof, Arabic
Religions:	Muslim 85%, Christian 10%
Currency:	1 dalasi = 100 bututs

Major cities:
Serekunda (219,000), Brikama (102,000), Bakau (48,000), Farafenni (37,000), Lamin (17,000), Basse Santa Su (16,000), Sukuta (15,000)

Georgia
Sakartvelo

Area:	69,700 km²
Population:	4,474,000 (2005)
Capital:	Tbilisi (1,082,000)
Administration:	2 autonomous republics, 1 autonomous region, 9 districts
Languages:	Georgian, Russian
Religions:	Georgian Orthodox 84%
Currency:	1 lari = 100 tetri

Major cities:
Kutaisi (186,000), Batumi (122,000), Rustavi (116,000), Zugdidi (69,000), Gori (50,000)

Germany
Federal Republic of Germany
Bundesrepublik Deutschland

Area:	357,027 km²
Population:	82,526,000 (2005)
Capital:	Berlin (3,338,000)
Administration:	16 federal states
Languages:	German
Religions:	Protestant 34%, Roman Catholic 33%
Currency:	1 euro = 100 cent

Major cities:
Hamburg (1,729,000), Munich/München (1,235,00 Cologne/Köln (969,000), Frankfurt a. M. (644,000), Dortmund (591,000), Stuttgart (588,000)

Ghana
Republic of Ghana

Area:	238,539 km²
Population:	22,113,000 (2005)
Capital:	Accra (1,719,000)
Administration:	10 regions
Languages:	English, more than 40 languages
Religions:	Christian 60%, traditional beliefs 35%
Currency:	1 cedi = 100 pesewas

Major cities:
Kumasi (663,000), Tamale (290,000), Tema (263,000), Obuasi (132,000), Teshie (127,000)

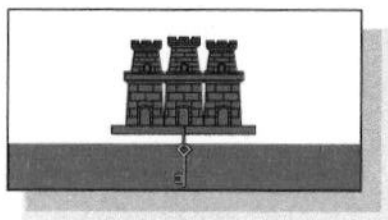

Gibraltar
(overseas territory of the U.K.)

Area:	6 km²
Population:	28,000 (2005)
Capital:	Gibraltar (26,000)
Administration:	none (overseas territory of the U.K.)
Languages:	English, Spanish, Italian, Portuguese
Religions:	Roman Catholic 85%, Churchof England 7%
Currency:	Gibraltar pound

Greece
Hellenic Republic
Elliniki Dimokratía

Area:	131,626 km²
Population:	11,120,000 (2005)
Capital:	Athens/Athína (746,000; A: 3,188,000)
Administration:	13 regions and the Monastic Republic of Mount Athos
Languages:	Greek
Religions:	Greek Orthodox 97%
Currency:	1 lari = 100 tetri

Major cities:
Thessaloníki (364,000), Piraeus/Peiraiás (175,000), Patras/Pátra (161,000), Peristério (140,000)

1 km² = 0.3861 square mile

Greenland
(part of the Kingdom of Denmark)
Kalaallit Nunaat Grønland

rea:	2,166,086 km²
opulation:	57,000 (2005)
apital:	Nuuk (Godthab) (15,000)
dministration:	3 districts (landsdele)
anguages:	Greenlandic (East Inuit), Danish, English
eligions:	Lutheran 98%
urrency:	Danish krone

lajor cities:
isimiut (6,000), Ilulissat (5,000), Qaqortoq (3,000)

Grenada
State of Grenada

rea:	344 km²
opulation:	103,000 (2005)
apital:	Saint George's (4,000)
dministration:	6 councils, 1 dependency
anguages:	English, English Creole, French Creole
eligions:	Roman Catholic 58%, Protestant 38%
urrency:	1 East Caribbean dollar = 100 cents

lajor cities:
ouyave (3,000), Grenville (2,000)

Guadeloupe
(overseas department of France)
Department of Guadeloupe
Département de la Guadeloupe

rea:	1,703 km²
opulation:	448,000 (2005)
apital:	Basse-Terre (12,000)
dministration:	none (overseas department of France)
anguages:	French, Creole patois
eligions:	Roman Catholic 84%,
urrency:	1 euro = 100 cent

lajor cities:
es Abymes (63,000), Baie-Mahalt (31,000), e Gosier (29,000), Petit-Bourg (25,000)

Guam
(territory of the U.S.)
Territory of Guam

rea:	549 km²
opulation:	170,000 (2005)
apital:	Agaña/Hagåtña (1,000)
dministration:	none (territory of the U.S.)
anguages:	English, Chamorro, Philippine languages
eligions:	Roman Catholic 90%
urrency:	US dollar

lajor cities:
amuning (11,000), Mangilao (9,000), Yigo (8,000), stumbo (6,000)

Guatemala
Republic of Guatemala
República de Guatemala

Area:	108,889 km²
Population:	12,559,000 (2005)
Capital:	Guatemala Ciudad/ Cd. de Guatemala (942,000)
Administration:	22 departments
Languages:	Spanish, Mayan languages
Religions:	Roman Catholic 60%, Protestant 30%
Currency:	1 quetzal = 100 centavos

Major cities:
Mixco (384,000), Villa Nueva (302,000), Quezaltenango (120,000), Cobán (52,000)

Guernsey
(British crown dependency)
Bailiwick of Guernsey

Area:	78 km²
Population:	65,228 (2005)
Capital:	Saint Peter Port (17,000)
Administration:	none (British crown dependency)
Languages:	English, French
Religions:	Anglican, Roman Catholic, Presbyterian, Baptist
Currency:	British pound and Guernsey pound

Major islands:
Vale (9,600), Castle (9,000), Saint Simpson (8,700)

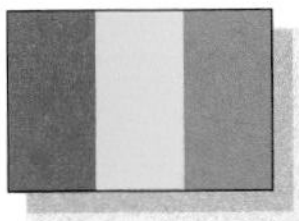

Guinea
Republic of Guinea
République de Guinée

Area:	245,857 km²
Population:	9,402,000 (2005)
Capital:	Conakry (1,091,000)
Administration:	33 prefectures and 1 special zone (Conakry)
Languages:	French, Fulani, Malinke
Religions:	Muslim 85%, Christian 8%
Currency:	Guinea franc

Major cities:
Kindia (288,000), Nzérékoré (283,000), Kankan (261,000), Labé (89,000)

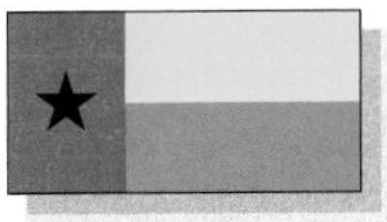

Guinea-Bissau
Republic of Guinea-Bissau
República da Guiné-Bissau

Area:	36,125 km²
Population:	1,586,000 (2005)
Capital:	Bissau (292,000)
Administration:	8 regions and the capital
Languages:	Portuguese, Crioulo
Religions:	raditional beliefs 54%, Muslim 38%, Christian 8%
Currency:	1 CFA franc = 100 centimes

Major cities:
Bafatá (18,000), Gabú (9,500)

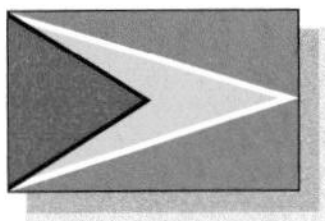

Guyana
Co-operative Republic of Guyana

Area:	214,969 km²
Population:	751,000 (2005)
Capital:	Georgetown (249,000)
Administration:	10 regions
Languages:	English, Hindi, Urdu, Indian languages
Religions:	Protestant 34%, Hindu 33%, Roman Catholic 20%
Currency:	1 Guyana dollar = 100 cents

Major cities:
Linden (45,000), New Amsterdam (36,000)

Haiti
Republic of Haiti
République d'Haïti/
Repiblik Dayti

Area:	27,750 km²
Population:	8,528,000 (2005)
Capital:	Port-au-Prince (991,000)
Administration:	9 departments
Languages:	French/Creole
Religions:	Roman Catholic 70%, Protestant 15%
Currency:	1 gourde = 100 centimes

Major cities:
Carrefour (336,000), Delmas (284,000), Cap-Haïtien (114,000), Gonaïves (64,000)

Honduras
Republic of Honduras
República de Honduras

Area:	112,492 km²
Population:	7,205,000 (2005)
Capital:	Tegucigalpa (769,000)
Administration:	18 departments
Languages:	Spanish, Indian languages, English
Religions:	Roman Catholic 90%
Currency:	1 lempira = 100 centavos

Major cities:
San Pedro Sula (439,000), La Ceiba (111,000), Choloma (108,000), El Progreso (90,000), Choluteca (76,000), Comayagua (55,000)

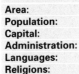

Hungary
Republic of Hungary
Magyar Köztársaság

Area:	93,029 km²
Population:	10,098,000 (2005)
Capital:	Budapest (1,740,000)
Administration:	19 counties and the capital
Languages:	Hungarian, German, Slovak, Croatian
Religions:	Roman Catholic 63%, Protestant 26%
Currency:	1 forint = 100 filler

Major cities:
Debrecen (207,000), Miskolc (182,000), Szeged (164,000), Pécs (160,000), Győr (129,000)

Iceland

Republic of Iceland
Lýðveldið Ísland

Area: 103,000 km²
Population: 295,000 (2005)
Capital: Reykjavík (113,000)
Administration: 8 regions
Languages: Icelandic
Religions: Protestant (Lutheran) 93%, Roman Catholic 1%
Currency: 1 króna = 100 aurar
Major cities:
Kópavogur (25,000), Hafnarfjörður (21,000), Akureyri (16,000)

India

Republic of India
Bhāratīya Gaṇarājya/
Republic of India

Area: 3,287,263 km²*
Population: 1,103,371,000 (2005)*
Capital: New Delhi (295,000)
Administration: 28 states, 7 union territories
Languages: Hindi/English/17 other official languages
Religions: Hindu 80%, Muslim 11%
Currency: 1 rupee = 100 paise

Major cities:
Mumbai/Bombay (11,914,000; A: 16,368,000), Delhi (9,817,000; A: 12,791,000), Kolkata/Calcutta (4,580,000; A: 13,217,000), Bangalore (4,292,000), Chennai/Madras (4,216,000), Ahmadabad (3,515,000), Hyderabad (3,450,000), Pune (2,540,000)

	Area km²	Population 2001	Capital
States			
Andhra Pradesh	275,045	75,728,000	Hyderābād
Arunāchal Pradesh	83,743	1,091,000	Itānagar
Assam	78,438	26,638,000	Dispur
Bihār	99,200	82,879,000	Patna
Chhattisgarh	146,361	20,796,000	Raipur
Goa	3,702	1,344,000	Panaji
Gujarāt	196,024	50,597,000	Gāndhīnagar
Haryāna	44,212	21,083,000	Chandīgarh
Himachal Pradesh	55,673	6,077,000	Shimla
Jammu and Kashmir*	100,569	10,070,000	Srīnagar
Jharkhand	74,677	26,909,000	Rānchi
Karnātaka	191,791	52,734,000	Bangalore
Kerala	38,863	31,839,000	Thiruvananthapuram
Madhya Pradesh	297,085	60,385,000	Bhopāl
Mahārāshtra	307,713	96,752,000	Mumbai
Manipur	22,327	2,389,000	Imphāl
Meghālaya	22,429	2,306,000	Shillong
Mizoram	21,081	891,000	Āīzawl
Nāgāland	16,579	1,989,000	Kohīma
Orissa	155,707	36,707,000	Bhubaneshwar
Punjab	50,362	24,289,000	Chandīgarh
Rājasthān	342,239	56,473,000	Jaipur
Sikkim	7,096	540,000	Gangtok
Tamil Nadu	130,058	62,111,000	Chennai
Tripura	10,486	3,191,000	Agartala
Uttaranchal	63,157	8,480,000	Dehra Dūn
Uttar Pradesh	231,254	166,053,000	Lucknow
West Bengal	88,752	80,221,000	Kolkata (Calcutta)
Union Territories			
Andaman and Nikobar Islands	8,249	356,000	Port Blair
Chandīgarh	114	901,000	Chandīgarh
Dādra and Nagar Haveli	491	220,000	Silvassa
Damān and Diu	112	158,000	Damān
Delhi	1,483	13,783,000	New Delhi
Lakshadweep	32	61,000	Kavaratti
Pondicherry	492	974,000	Pondicherry

* Incl. results for the Indian part of Jammu and Kashmir, the political status of which is still uncertain

Indonesia

Republic of Indonesia
Republik Indonesia

Area: 1,922,570 km²
Population: 222,781,000 (2005)
Capital: Jakarta (9,341,000)
Administration: 33 provinces, incl. 2 special-regions and capital district
Languages: Bahasa Indonesia, 250 (est.) languages or dialects
Religions: Muslim 87%, Christian 10%
Currency: 1 rupiah = 100 sen
Major cities:
Surabaya (2,743,000), Bandung (2,429,000), Medan (1,942,000), Palembang (1,394,000)

Iran

Islamic Republic of Iran
Jomhūrī-ye Eslāmī-ye Īrān

Area: 1,629,807 km²
Population: 69,515,000 (2005)
Capital: Tehrān (6,759,000)
Administration: 28 provinces
Languages: Farsi (Persian), Kurdish, Turkic languages
Religions: Muslim 99%
Currency: 1 rial = 100 dinars
Major cities:
Masshad (1,887,000), Isfahan/Eṣfahān (1,266,000), Tabrīz (1,191,000), Shīrāz (1,053,000), Karaj (1,018,000), Ahvāz (805,000), Qom (778,000)

Iraq

Republic of Iraq
Al-Jumhūrīyah al-ʿIrāqīyah

Area: 438,317 km²
Population: 28,807,000 (2005)
Capital: Baghdād (5,772,000)
Administration: 18 governorates
Languages: Arabic, Kurdish, Turkish
Religions: Muslim 95%
Currency: 1 Iraqi dinar = 1000 fils
Major cities:
Mosul/Al-Mawṣil (1,740,000), Basra/Al-Baṣrah (1,300,000), Arbīl/Irbil (891,000), Kirkūk (784,000), As-Sulaymānīyah (683,000)

Ireland

Éire
Ireland

Area: 70,273 km²
Population: 4,148,000 (2005)
Capital: Dublin (495,000)
Administration: 4 provinces (26 counties, 4 countyboroughs
Languages: Irish/English
Religions: Roman Catholic 88%
Currency: 1 euro = 100 cent
Major cities:
Cork (123,000), Tallaght (63,000), Limerick (54,00
Blanchardstown (50,000), Waterford (45,000)

Israel

State of Israel
Medinat Yisra'el/
Dawlat Isrā'īl

Area: 22,145 km²
Population: 6,725,000 (2005)
Capital: Jerusalem/Yerushalayim/Al-Quds (692,000)
Administration: 6 districts
Languages: Hebrew/Arabic, Yiddish
Religions: Jewish 79%, Muslim 15%
Currency: 1 new sheqel = 100 agorot
Major cities:
Tel Aviv-Yafo (364,000), Haifa/Ḥefa (271,000), Rishon Le Ẓiyyon (215,000), Ashdod (192,000)

Palestinian-administered Territories:

Gaza Strip

Area: 364 km²
Population: 1,299,000 (2002)
Religions: Muslim 99%, Christian 0,7%, Jewish 0,3% (1992)
Major cities:
Gaza/Gazzah (362,000), Khān Yūnis (111,000)

West Bank

Area: 5,633 km²
Population: 2,261,000 (2002)
Religions: Muslim 80%, Jewish 12%, Christian 8% (1992)
Major cities:
Hebron/Al-Khalīl (147,000), Nābulus (121,000), Tulkarm (41,000)

Italy

Italian Republic
Repubblica Italiana/
République italienne/
Italienische Republik

Area: 301,336 km²
Population: 58,093,000 (2005)
Capital: Rome/Roma (2,541,000)
Administration: 20 regions
Languages: Italian/French (regionally)/ German (regionally)
Religions: Roman Catholic over 90%
Currency: 1 euro = 100 cent
Major cities:
Milan/Milano (1,247,000), Naples/Napoli (1,009,00
Turin/Torino (862,000), Palermo (683,000), Genoa/Genova (605,000), Bologna (373,000)

1 km² = 0.3861 square mile

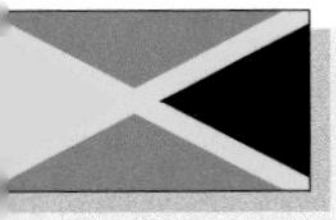

Jamaica

Area:	11,420 km²
Population:	2,651,000 (2005)
Capital:	Kingston (577,000)
Administration:	14 parishes
Languages:	English, Jamaican Creole
Religions:	Protestant 56%, Roman Catholic 5%
Currency:	1 Jamaican dollar = 100 cents

Major cities:
Spanish Town (145,000), Portmore (103,000), Montego Bay (83,000), Mandeville (47,000)

Japan

Nihon-Koku

Area:	377,880 km²
Population:	128,085,000 (2005)
Capital:	Tōkyō (8,483,000) (A: 12,445,000)
Administration:	47 prefectures
Languages:	Japanese, Korean, Chinese
Religions:	Shinto 87%, Buddhist 74%
Currency:	1 yen = 100 sen

Major cities:
Yokohama (3,433,000), Ōsaka (2,484,000), Nagoya (2,109,000), Sapporo (1,823,000), Kōbe (1,478,000), Kyōto (1,387,000), Fukuoka (1,302,000)

Jersey

(British crown dependency)
Bailiwick of Jersey

Area:	116 km²
Population:	90,812 (2005)
Capital:	Saint Helier (29,000)
Administration:	none
Languages:	English, Portuguese
Religions:	Anglican, Roman Catholic, Baptist
Currency:	British pound and Jersey pound

Major cities:
Saint Saviour (12,000), Saint Brelade (11,000), Grouville (4,800)

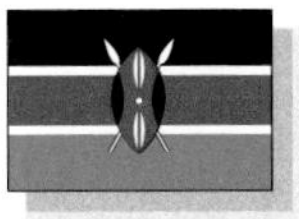

Johnston Atoll

(territory of the U.S.)

Area:	2.6 km²
Population:	No indigenous inhabitants; all US government personnel left the island in May 2005. In previous years, an average of 1,100 military and civilian contractor personnel were present on the island.
note:	closed to the public

Jordan

Hashemite Kingdom of Jordan
Al-Mamlakah al-Urdunīyah al-Hāshimīyah

Area:	89,342 km²
Population:	5,703,000 (2005)
Capital:	Amman/ʿAmmān (1,766,000)
Administration:	12 governorates
Languages:	Arabic
Religions:	Muslim 80%, Christian minority
Currency:	1 Jordan dinar = 1000 fils

Major cities:
Az-Zarqāʾ (477,000), Irbid (258,000), Ar-Ruṣṣayfah (228,000), Aqaba/Al-ʿAqaba (100,000), As-Salṭ (56,000), Mādabā (56,000)

Kazakhstan

Republic of Kazakhstan
Qazaqstan Respublīkasy/ Respublika Kazakhstan

Area:	2,724,900 km²
Population:	14,825,000 (2005)
Capital:	Astana (313,000)
Administration:	14 regions and the capital
Languages:	Kazakh, Russian
Religions:	Muslim 50%, Christian 50%
Currency:	1 tenge = 100 tiyn

Major cities:
Almaty (1,129,000), Qaraghandy (437,000), Shymkent (360,000), Taraz (330,000), Öskemen (311,000), Pavlodar (301,000), Semey (270,000), Aqtöbe (253,000), Qostanay (221,000)

Kenya

Republic of Kenya
Jamhuri ya Kenya

Area:	582,000 km²
Population:	34,256,000 (2005)
Capital:	Nairobi (2,143,000)
Administration:	7 provinces and the capital
Languages:	Kiswahili, English
Religions:	traditional beliefs 60%, Roman Catholic 26%
Currency:	1 Kenya shilling = 100 cents

Major cities:
Mombasa (665,000), Kisumu (323,000), Nakuru (219,000), Eldoret (167,000), Machakos (144,000), Meru (126,000), Nyeri (99,000), Thika (83,000)

Kiribati

Republic of Kiribati
Ribaberikin Kiribati/ Republic of Kiribati

Area:	717 km²
Population:	99,000 (2005)
Capital:	Bairiki (2,200)
Administration:	6 districts
Languages:	Kiribati/English
Religions:	Roman Catholic 53%, Protestant 39%
Currency:	1 Australian dollar = 100 cents

Island Groups:
Gilbert Islands, Phoenix Islands, Line Islands

Korea, North

Democratic People's Republic of Korea
Chosŏn Minjujuŭi In'min Konghwaguk

Area:	120,538 km²
Population:	22,488,000 (2005)
Capital:	P'yŏngyang (2,741,000)
Administration:	9 provinces, 2 special cities
Languages:	Korean, Russian, Chinese
Religions:	Atheist 68%, traditional beliefs
Currency:	1 won = 100 chon

Major cities:
Namp'o (731,000), Hamhŭng (710,000), Ch'ŏngjin (582,000), Kaesŏng (334,000), Sinŭiju (326,000), Wŏnsan (300,000), Kanggye (211,000)

Korea, South

Republic of Korea
Taehan Min'guk

Area:	99,538 km²
Population:	47,817,000 (2005)
Capital:	Sŏul (10,231,000)
Administration:	9 provinces, 7 special cities
Languages:	Korean, English, Japanese
Religions:	Protestant 31%, Confucianist 22%, Buddhist 19%
Currency:	1 won = 100 chon

Major cities:
Pusan (3,655,000), Taegu (2,474,000), Inch'ŏn (2,466,000), Taejŏn (1,366,000), Kwangju (1,351,000), Suwŏn (1,154,000), Ulsan (883,000)

Kuwait

State of Kuwait
Dawlat al-Kuwayt

Area:	17,818 km²
Population:	2,687,000 (2005)
Capital:	Kuwait/Al-Kuwayt (29,000)
Administration:	5 governorates
Languages:	Arabic, English
Religions:	Muslim 95%, Christian 2%
Currency:	1 Kuwait dinar = 1000 fils

Major cities:
As-Sālimīyah (130,000), Jalīb ash-Shuyūkh (102,000), Hawallī (82,000), Al-Fuḥayḥīl (51,000)

Kyrgyzstan

Kyrgyz Republic
Kyrgyz Respublikasy/ Kyrgyzskaya Respublika

Area:	199,900 km²
Population:	5,264,000 (2005)
Capital:	Bishkek (750,000)
Administration:	7 provinces and the capital
Languages:	Kyrgyz/Russian
Religions:	Muslim (Sunni) 75%, Russian Orthodox 20%
Currency:	1 som = 100 tyiyn

Major cities:
Osh (209,000), Džalal-Abad (70,000), Karaköl (64,000), Tokmak (59,000), Kara-Balta (55,000)

Laos

Lao People's Democratic Republic
Sathalanalat Paxathipatai Paxaxôn Lao

Area:	236,800 km²
Population:	5,924,000 (2005)
Capital:	Viangchan (663,000)
Administration:	16 provinces, 1 municipality, 1 special zone
Languages:	Lao, French, English
Religions:	Buddhist 58%, Tribal religionist 34%
Currency:	1 kip = 100 at

Major cities:
Savannakhét (68,000), Louangphrabang (58,000)

Latvia

Republic of Latvia
Latvijas Republika

Area:	64,589 km²
Population:	2,307,000 (2005)
Capital:	Rīga (764,000)
Administration:	26 districts, 7 special cities
Languages:	Latvian, Russian
Religions:	Lutheran 55%, Roman Catholic 24%
Currency:	1 lats = 100 santimi

Major cities:
Daugavpils (115,000), Liepāja (89,000), Jelgava (63,000), Jūrmala (56,000)

Lebanon

Lebanese Republik
Al-Jumhūrīyah al-Lubnānīyah

Area:	10,452 km²
Population:	3,577,000 (2005)
Capital:	Beirut/Bayrūt (2,115,000)
Administration:	5 governorates and the capital
Languages:	Arabic, Armenian, French, English
Religions:	Muslim 60%, Christian 40%
Currency:	1 Leban. pound = 100 piastres

Major cities:
Tripoli/Ṭarābulus (200,000), Ṣaydā (140,000), Ṣūr (110,000), An-Nabatīyat at-Tahtā (98,000)

Lesotho

Kingdom of Lesotho
Mmuso wa Lesotho/
Kingdom of Lesotho

Area:	30,355 km²
Population:	1,795,000 (2005)
Capital:	Maseru (271,000)
Administration:	10 districts
Languages:	Sesotho/English
Religions:	Roman Catholic 44%, Protestant 30%
Currency:	1 loti = 100 lisente

Major cities:
Teyateyaneng (14,000), Mafeteng (13,000), Hlotse (10,000)

Liberia

Republic of Liberia

Area:	111,369 km²
Population:	3,283,000 (2005)
Capital:	Monrovia (550,000)
Administration:	14 counties
Languages:	English, Gola, Kpelle
Religions:	traditional beliefs 70%, Muslim 20%, Christian 10%
Currency:	1 Liberian dollar = 100 cents

Major cities:
Zwedru (37,000), Harper (33,000), Buchanan (28,000)

Libya

Socialist People's Libyan Arab Jamahiriya
Al-Jamāhīrīyah al-'Arabīyah al-Lībīyah ash-Sha'bīyah al-Ishtirākīyah

Area:	1,759,540 km²
Population:	5,853,000 (2005)
Capital:	Tripoli/Ṭarābulus (1,776,000)
Administration:	13 regions (baladiyat)
Languages:	Arabic, Tuareg
Religions:	Muslim 97%
Currency:	1 Libyan dinar = 1000 dirhams

Major cities:
Benghazi/Banghāzī (655,000), Al-Khums (271,000), Miṣrātah (191,000), Az-Zāwiyah (140,000), Ṭubruq (137,000), Al-Baydā' (122,000), Darnah (113,000)

Liechtenstein

Principality of Liechtenstein
Fürstentum Liechtenstein

Area:	160 km²
Population:	35,000 (2005)
Capital:	Vaduz (5,000)
Administration:	11 communes
Languages:	German
Religions:	Roman Catholic 83%, Protestant 7%
Currency:	1 Swiss franc = 100 centimes

Major cities:
Schaan (5,600), Triesen (5,000), Balzers (4,000)

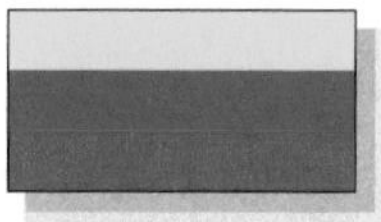

Lithuania

Republic of Lithuania
Lietuvos Respublika

Area:	65,300 km²
Population:	3,431,000 (2005)
Capital:	Vilnius (543,000)
Administration:	10 provinces
Languages:	Lithuanian, Russian
Religions:	Roman Catholic 80%, Russian Orthodox, Protestant
Currency:	1 litas = 100 centas

Major cities:
Kaunas (381,000), Klaipėda (194,000), Šiauliai (136,000), Panevėžys (122,000), Alytus (71,000), Marijampolė (48,000)

Luxembourg

Grand Duchy of Luxembourg
Groussherzogtum Lëtzebuerg/
Großherzogtum Luxemburg/
Grand-Duché de Luxembourg

Area:	2,586 km²
Population:	465,000 (2005)
Capital:	Luxembourg (77,000)
Administration:	3 districts incl. 12 cantons
Languages:	Letzeburgish/German/French
Religions:	Roman Catholic 95%
Currency:	1 euro = 100 cent

Major cities:
Esch-sur-Alzette (27,000), Differdange (18,000), Dudelange (17,000)

Macedonia, The Former Yugoslav Republic

porenešna jugoslovenska Repubika Makedonija

Area:	25,713 km²
Population:	2,034,000 (2005)
Capital:	Skopje (467,000)
Administration:	123 communes
Languages:	Macedonian, Albanian, Turkish
Religions:	Macedonian Orthodox 67% Muslim 30%
Currency:	1 denar = 100 deni

Major cities:
Kumanovo (103,000), Bitola (86,000), Prilep (73,000), Tetovo (71,000)

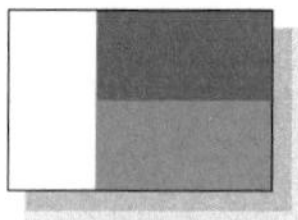

Madagascar

Republic of Madagascar
Repoblikan'i Madagasikara/
République de Madagascar

Area:	587,041 km²
Population:	18,606,000 (2005)
Capital:	Antananarivo (1,111,000)
Administration:	6 provinces
Languages:	Malagasy/French
Religions:	traditional beliefs 52%, Roman Catholic 25%, Protestant 20%
Currency:	1 Malagsy franc = 100 centimes

Major cities:
Fianarantsoa (130,000), Toamasina (127,000)

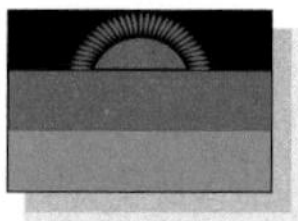

Malawi

Republic of Malawi
Mfuko la Malaŵi/
Republic of Malawi

Area:	118,484 km²
Population:	12,884,000 (2005)
Capital:	Lilongwe (598,000)
Administration:	3 regions
Languages:	Chichewa/English
Religions:	Christian 75%, traditional beliefs 10%
Currency:	1 kwacha = 100 tambala

Major cities:
Blantyre (646,000), Mzuzu (102,000), Zomba (90,000), Nioro (67,000), Karonga (28,000), Kasungu (28,000)

1 km² = 0.3861 square mile

Malaysia

Area: 330,242 km²
Population: 25,347,000 (2005)
Capital: Kuala Lumpur (1,298,000)
Administration: 13 states, 2 federal territories
Languages: Malay, Chinese, Tamil
Religions: Muslim 53%, Buddhist 17%
Currency: 1 ringgit = 100 sen
Major cities:
Ipoh (566,000), Kelang (563,000), Petaling Jaya (438,000), Johor Baharu (385,000), Shah Alam (320,000), Kuantan (238,000)

Maldives

Republic of Maldives
Divehi Raajjeyge Jumhooriyyaa

Area: 298 km²
Population: 329,000 (2005)
Capital: Malé (74,000)
Administration: 20 districts (administrative atolls) and the capital district
Languages: Maldivian (Divehi)
Religions: Sunni Muslim 99%
Currency: 1 rufiyaa = 100 laari

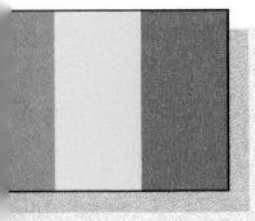

Mali

Republic of Mali
République du Mali

Area: 1,248,574 km²
Population: 13,518,000 (2005)
Capital: Bamako (954,000)
Administration: 8 regions and the capital
Languages: French, Bambara
Religions: Muslim 80%, traditional beliefs 18%
Currency: 1 CFA franc = 100 centimes
Major cities:
Sikasso (128,000), Mopti (116,000), Ségou (102,000), Kayes (83,000), Koutiala (95,000)

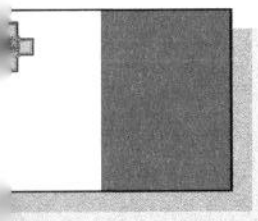

Malta

Republic of Malta
Repubblika ta' Malta/
Republic of Malta

Area: 316 km²
Population: 402,000 (2005)
Capital: Valletta (7,200)
Administration: 6 regions
Languages: Maltese/English
Religions: Roman Catholic 93%, Anglican
Currency: 1 Maltese lira = 100 cents
Major cities:
Birkirkara (22,000), Qormi (19,000), Mosta (18,000), Zabbar (15,000)

Man, Isle of

(British crown dependency)

Area: 572 km²
Population: 77,000 (2005)
Capital: Douglas (25,000)
Administration: 24 local authorities
Languages: English
Religions: Anglican, Roman Catholic
Currency: British pound and Manx pound
Major cities:
Onchan (9,000), Ramsey (8,000), Peel (4,000)

Marshall Islands

Republic of the Marshall Islands

Area: 181 km²
Population: 62,000 (2005)
Capital: Dalap-Uliga-Darrit (16,000)
Administration: 33 districts
Languages: English, Marshallese
Religions: Protestant 63%, Roman Catholic 7%
Currency: 1 U.S. dollar = 100 cents
Major cities:
Ebeye (9,300), Rairok (3,800)

Martinique

(overseas department of France)

Department of Martinique
Département de la Martinique

Area: 1,128 km²
Population: 396,000 (2005)
Capital: Forte de France (89,000)
Administration: none (overseas department of France)
Languages: French, Creole patois
Religions: Roman Catholic 78%
Currency: 1 euro = 100 cent
Major cities:
Le Lamentin (89,000), Le Robert (24,000), Schoelcher (22,000), Sainte-Marie (20,000)

Mauritania

Islamic Republic of Mauritania
Al-Jumhūrīyah al-Islāmīyah al-Mūrītānīyah

Area: 1,025,520 km²
Population: 3,069,000 (2005)
Capital: Nouakchott/Nawākshūṭ (415,000)
Administration: 13 regions
Languages: Arabic, French, Wolof
Religions: Muslim 99,6%
Currency: 1 ouguiya = 5 khoums
Major cities:
Nouâdhibou/Nawadhībū (73,000), Rūsū (49,000), Kayhaydi (34,000), Zuwārat (34,000), Kīfah (33,000)

Mauritius

République of Maurice

Area: 2,040 km²
Population: 1,245,000 (2005)
Capital: Port Louis (144,000)
Administration: 9 districts, 3 dependencies
Languages: English, French
Religions: Hindu 53%, Christian 30%
Currency: 1 Mauritius rupee = 100 cents
Major cities:
Beau Bassin-Rose Hill (104,000), Vacoas-Phoenix (100,000), Curepipe (79,000)

Mayotte

(territorial collectivity of France)

Territorial Collectivity of Mayotte
Collectivité territoriale de Mayotte

Area: 374 km²
Population: 160,000 (2002)
Capital: Dzaoudzi (12,000)
Administration: none
Languages: French
Religions: Muslim 98%, Roman Catholic
Currency: 1 euro = 100 cent
Major cities:
Mamoudzou (55,000), Koungou (18,000), Sada (9,000)

Mexico

United Mexican States
Estados Unidos Mexicanos

Area: 1,964,375 km²
Population: 107,029,000 (2005)
Capital: Mexico City/Cd. de México (8,605,000) (A: 17,309,000)
Administration: 31 states, 1 federal district
Languages: Spanish, Mayan dialects
Religions: Roman Catholic 90%
Currency: 1 Mexican peso = 100 centavos
Major cities:
Guadalajara (1,648,000), Ecatepec (1,619,000), Puebla (1,346,000), Nezahualcóyotel (1,225,000), Juárez (1,218,000), Tijuana (1,212,000)

Micronesia

Federated States of Micronesia

Area: 701 km²
Population: 110,000 (2005)
Capital: Palikir
Administration: 4 states
Languages: English, 9 indigenous languages
Religions: Roman Catholic 59%, Protestant 39%
Currency: 1 U.S. dollar = 100 cents
Major cities:
Weno (16,000), Nett (5,900), Kitti (5,100), Tol (4,800)

Midway Islands
(territory of the U.S.)

Area:	5 km^2
Population:	No indigenous inhabitants; approximately 40 people live on the atoll (staff of US Fish and Wildlife Service and service contractors)

Montserrat
(overseas territory of the U.K.)

Area:	101 km^2
Population:	4,000 (2005)
Capital:	Plymouth (destroyed by the volcano in 1997); interim government: Brades
Administration:	3 parishes
Languages:	English
Religions:	Anglican
Currency:	East Caribbean dollar

Namibia
Republic of Namibia

Area:	824,269 km^2
Population:	2,031,000 (2005)
Capital:	Windhoek (234,000)
Administration:	13 regions
Languages:	English, Afrikaans, German
Religions:	Protestant 62%, Roman Catholic 20%
Currency:	1 Namibia dollar = 100 cents

Major cities:
Walvis Bay (50,000), Oshakati (37,000), Ondangwa (33,000), Rehoboth (21,000), Swakopmund (18,000), Rundu (18,000)

Moldova
Republic of Moldova
Respublica Moldova

Area:	33,800 km^2
Population:	4,206,000 (2005)
Capital:	Chişinău (662,000)
Administration:	32 raions (including Gagauz Autonomous Region and Transdniestrian Republic)
Languages:	Moldovian, Russian
Religions:	predominantly Eastern Orthodox
Currency:	1 leu = 100 bani

Major cities:
Tiraspol (187,000), Bălţi (151,000)

Morocco
Kingdom of Morocco
Al-Mamlakah al-Maghribīyah

Area:	458,730 km^2 (without Western Sahara)
Population:	31,478,000 (2005)
Capital:	Rabat (1,623,000)
Administration:	16 regions
Languages:	Arabic, Berber, French
Religions:	Muslim 89%
Currency:	1 dirham = 100 centimes

Major cities:
Ad-Dār al-Baydā (Casablanca) (2,934,000), Fās (947,000), Marrākuš (823,000), Aġādīr (679,000), Ṭanğah (Tanger) (670,000), Miknās (536,000)

Nauru
Republic of Nauru

Area:	21 km^2
Population:	14,000 (2005)
Capital:	Yaren (4,000)
Administration:	14 districts
Languages:	Nauruan/English
Religions:	Protestant 60%, Roman Catholic 30%
Currency:	1 Australian dollar = 100 cents

Monaco
Principaltiy of Monaco
Principauté de Monaco

Area:	1.95 km^2
Population:	35,000 (2005)
Capital:	Monaco (1,000)
Administration:	4 districts
Languages:	French, Monegasque, Italian and English
Religions:	Roman Catholic 90%, Protestant 6%
Currency:	1 euro = 100 cent

Major cities:
Monte Carlo (16,000), La Condamine (12,000)

Mozambique
Republic of Mozambique
República de Moçambique

Area:	799,380 km^2
Population:	19,792,000 (2005)
Capital:	Maputo (1,114,000)
Administration:	10 provinces and the capital
Languages:	Portuguese, Kiswahili
Religions:	traditional beliefs 47%, Christian 37%, Muslim 18%
Currency:	1 metical = 100 centavos

Major cities:
Matola (521,000), Beira (487,000), Nampula (372,000), Chimoio (210,000), Nacala (194,000)

Nepal
Kingdom of Nepal
Nepāl Adhirājya

Area:	147,181 km^2
Population:	27,133,000 (2005)
Capital:	Kathmandu (672,000)
Administration:	5 regions
Languages:	Nepali, Maithili, Bhojpuri
Religions:	Hindu 80%, Buddhist 10%
Currency:	1 Nepalese rupee = 100 paisa

Major cities:
Biratnagar (167,000), Lalitpur (163,000), Pokhara (156,000), Birganj (112,000)

Mongolia
Mongol Uls

Area:	1,564,100 km^2
Population:	2,646,000 (2005)
Capital:	Ulan Bator/Ulaanbaatar (760,000)
Administration:	21 provinces, 1 municipality
Languages:	Khalkha Mongol, Russian, Kazakh
Religions:	Buddhist 90%, trad. beliefs
Currency:	1 tugrik = 100 möngö

Major cities:
Darhan (73,000), Erdenet (66,000), Choybalsan (42,000), Ölgiy (30000)

Myanmar
Union of Myanmar
Pyidaungzu Myanma Naingngandaw

Area:	676,578 km^2
Population:	50,519,000 (2005)
Capital:	Rangoon/Yangon (4,504,000)
Administration:	7 states, 7 divisions
Languages:	Burmese, English
Religions:	Buddhist 87%, Christian 6%
Currency:	1 kyat = 100 pyas

Major cities:
Mandalay (533,000), Mawlamyine (220,000), Pegu/Bago (151,000), Pathein (144,000), Taunggyi (108,000), Sittwe/Akyab (108,000), Monywa (107,000)

Netherlands, The
Kingdom of The Netherlands
Koninkrijk der Nederlanden

Area:	33,873 km^2
Population:	16,229,000 (2005)
Capital:	Amsterdam (737,000) (seat of government: The Hague/'s-Gravenhage)
Administration:	12 provinces
Languages:	Dutch/Frisian (regionally)
Religions:	Roman Catholic 30%, Protestant 20% Muslim 6%
Currency:	1 euro = 100 cent

1 km^2 = 0.3861 square mile

lajor cities:
otterdam (600,000), The Hague/'s-Gravenhage 458,000), Utrecht (265,000), Eindhoven (206,000), ilburg (198,000), Groningen (177,000), reda (164,000)

)verseas Territories:

ruba

rea: 193 km^2
opulation: 99,000 (2005)
apital: Oranjestad (30,000)
anguages: Dutch, Papiamento
urrency: Aruban guilder/florin
lajor cities:
int Nicolaas (17,000)

letherlands Antilles

ederlandse Antillen

rea: 800 km^2
opulation: 183,000 (2005)
apital: Willemstad (133,000)
anguages: Dutch, Papiamento, English
urrency: Netherlands Antillean guilder
lajor cities:
rincess Quarter (13,000), Cole Bay (7,000)

New Zealand

Area: 270,500 km^2
Population: 4,028,000 (2005)
Capital: Wellington (166,000)
Administration: 16 regions
Languages: English/Maori
Religions: Christian 62%, Maori Churches
Currency: 1 New Zealand dollar = 100 cents
Major cities:
Auckland (337,000), Christchurch (322,000), Manukau (282,000), North Shore (184,000)

Independant Territory in Free Association with New Zealand

Niue

Republic of Niue

Area: 260 km^2
Population: 1,700 (2005)
Capital: Alofi (600)

Overseas Territories:

Ross Dependency

Claimed by New Zealand

Area: 750,310 km^2
Research stations

Tokelau

Area: 12 km^2
Population: 1,000 (2005)

Nigeria

Federal Republic of Nigeria

Area: 923,768 km^2
Population: 131,530,000 (2005)
Capital: Abuja (403,000)
Administration: 36 states and the capital
Languages: English, French, Hausa
Religions: Muslim 45%, Protestant 26%, Roman Catholic 12%
Currency: 1 naira = 100 kobo
Major cities:
Lagos (9,954,000), Kano (3,413,000), Ibadan (3,202,000), Kaduna (1,563,000), Port Harcourt (1,133,000), Benin City (1,113,000)

Niue

(Independant Territory in Free Association with New Zealand)

Republic of Niue

Area: 260 km^2
Population: 1,700 (2005)
Capital: Alofi (600)
Administration: 14 villages
Languages: Niuean, English
Religions: Ekalesia Niue (Niuean Church) 75%, Latter-Day Saints 10%
Currency: New Zealand dollar
Major cities:
Hakupu (220), Tamakautoga (140), Tuapa (130)

Netherlands Antilles

(part of the Kingdom of the Netherlands)

Nederlandse Antillen

rea: 800 km^2
opulation: 183,000 (2005)
apital: Willemstad (133,000)
dministration: none (part of the Kingdom of the Netherlands)
anguages: Dutch, Papiamento, English
eligions: Roman Catholic 80%, Protestant 8%
urrency: Netherlands Antillean guilder
Major cities:
rincess Quarter (13,000), Cole Bay (7,000)

Nicaragua

Republik of Nicaragua
República de Nicaragua

Area: 119,838 km^2
Population: 5,487,000 (2005)
Capital: Managua (1,039,000)
Administration: 15 departments, 2 autonomous regions
Languages: Spanish, Indian languages
Religions: Roman Catholic 89%, Protestant 5%
Currency: 1 córdoba = 100 centavos
Major cities:
León (150,000), Chinandega (129,000), Masaya (123,000), Granada (93,000)

Norfolk Island

(territory of Australia)

Territory of Norfolk Island

Area: 35 km^2
Population: 3,000 (2001)
Capital: Kingston (880)
Administration: none (territory of Australia)
Languages: English, Norfolk
Religions: Church of England 35%, Roman Catholic 12%, Uniting Church 11%
Currency: Australian dollar

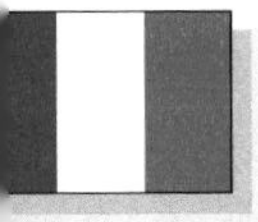

New Caledonia

(overseas territory of France)

Territory of New Caledonia
Territoire de la Nouevelle-Calédonie

Area: 19,058 km^2
Population: 237,000 (2005)
Capital: Nouméa (83,000)
Administration: none (overseas territory of France)
Languages: French, Melanesian and Polynesian dialects
Religions: Roman Catholic 55%
Currency: Comptoirs Francais du Pacifique franc
Major cities:
Mont-Dore (26,000), Dumbéa (14,000)

Niger

Republic of Niger
République du Niger

Area: 1,267,000 km^2
Population: 13,957,000 (2005)
Capital: Niamey (675,000)
Administration: 8 departments
Languages: French, Hausa, Djerma
Religions: Muslim 95%, traditional beliefs
Currency: 1 CFA franc = 100 centimes
Major cities:
Zinder (171,000), Maradi (147,000), Agadèz (77,000), Tahoua (72,000), Arlit (67,000), Dosso (43,000)

Northern Mariana Islands

(commonwealth in political union with the U.S.)

Commonwealth of the Northern Mariana Islands

Area: 464 km^2
Population: 81,000 (2005)
Capital: Garapan on Saipan (4,000)
Administration: none (commonwealth in political union with the U.S.)
Languages: English, Chamorro,
Religions: Roman Catholic
Currency: US dollar
Major cities:
San Antonio (6,000), San Vincente (5,000), Tanapag (4,000)

Norway
Kingdom of Norway
Kongeriket Norge

Area: 385,155 km²
Population: 4,620,000 (2005)
Capital: Oslo (523,000)
Administration: 19 counties
Languages: Norwegian, Sami
Religions: Protestant (Lutheran) 89%
Currency: 1 Norwegian krone = 100 øre
Major cities:
Bergen (237,000), Trondheim (154,000), Stavanger (112,000), Kristiansand (75,000)

Svalbard
Svalbard

Area/Population: 61,020 km²/2,600 inhabitants

Jan Mayen
Area: 377 km²/uninhabited

External Territories:

Bouvet Island
Bouvetøya

Area: 59 km²/uninhabited

Peter I Island
Peter I. Øy, *Claimed by Norway*

Area: c. 180 km²/uninhabited

Queen Maud Land
Dronning Maud Land, *Claimed by Norway*

Area: 2,500,000 km²/uninhabited

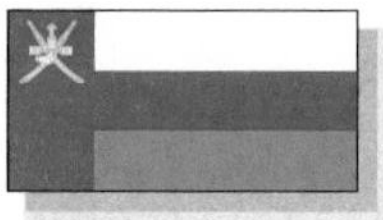

Oman
Sultanate of Oman
Salṭanat ʿUmān

Area: 309,500 km²
Population: 2,567,000 (2005)
Capital: Muscat/Masqaṭ (A: 540,000)
Administration: 59 provinces
Languages: Arabic, Baluchi, English
Religions: Muslim 88%
Currency: 1 Omani rial = 1000 baiza
Major cities:
As-Sīb (248,000), Ṣalālah (186,000), Ṣuḥār (135,000), Ruwī (117,000), Saḥam (103,000), Nazwá (85,000), Ar-Rustāq (81,000), Maṭraḥ (79,000)

Pakistan
Islamic Republic of Pakistan
Jamhūryat Islāmī Pākistān

Area: 796,096 km² (excluding the disputed area of Kashmir)
Population: 157,935,000 (2005)
Capital: Islamabad (799,000)
Administration: 4 provinces, capital, Tribal Areas
Languages: Urdu, Panjabi, Sindhi
Religions: Muslim almost 100%
Currency: 1 Pakistan rupee = 100 paisa
Major cities:
Karachi (9,269,000), Lahore (5,063,000), Faisalabad (1,977,000), Rawalpindi (1,406,000)

Palau
Republic of Palau
Belu'u er a Belau/
Republic of Palau

Area: 490 km²
Population: 20,000 (2005)
Capital: Koror (11,000)
Administration: 16 states
Languages: Palauan/English
Religions: Roman Catholic 41%, Protestant 25%, traditional beliefs 25%
Currency: 1 U.S. dollar = 100 cents
Major cities:
Melekeok, Ngetbong, Airai

Panama
Republic of Panama
República de Panamá

Area: 75,517 km²
Population: 3,232,000 (2005)
Capital: Panama City/Panamá (416,000)
Administration: 9 provinces and 1 territory
Languages: Spanish, Indian languages
Religions: Roman Catholic 86%, Protestant 2%
Currency: 1 balboa = 100 centésimos
Major cities:
San Miguelito (294,000), David (77,000), Colón (71,000), Santiago (41,000)

Papua New Guinea
Independent State of Papua New Guinea
Papua-Niugini/
Gau Hedinarai ai Papua-Matamata Guinea

Area: 462,243 km²
Population: 5,887,000 (2005)
Capital: Port Moresby (254,000)
Administration: 19 provinces, National Capital District
Languages: English/Pidgin/Motu
Religions: Protestant 58%, Roman Catholic 33%
Currency: 1 kina = 100 toea
Major cities:
Lae (78,000), Arawa (36,000), Mount Hagen (28,000), Madang (27,000), Wewak (23,000)

Paraguay
Republic of Paraguay
República del Paraguay/
Tetâ Paraguay

Area: 406,752 km²
Population: 6,158,000 (2005)
Capital: Asunción (561,000)
Administration: 17 departments and the capital
Languages: Spanish/Guaraní
Religions: Roman Catholic 90%
Currency: 1 guaraní = 100 céntimos
Major cities:
Ciudad del Este (223,000), San Lorenzo (203,000), Luque (170,000), Capiatá (154,000), Lambaré (120,000), Fernando de la Mora (114,000)

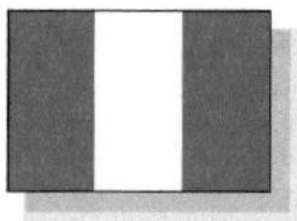

Peru
Republic of Peru
República del Perú

Area: 1,285,216 km²
Population: 27,968,000 (2005)
Capital: Lima (7,912,000)
Administration: 25 departments
Languages: Spanish/Quechua/Aymara
Religions: Roman Catholic 89%, Protestant 3%
Currency: 1 nuevo sol = 100 céntimos
Major cities:
Arequipa (710,000), Trujillo (604,000), Callao (512,000), Chiclayo (583,000), Iquitos (334,000), Piura (308,000), Huancayo (305,000)

Philippines
Republic of the Philippines
Republika ng Pilipinas

Area: 300,000 km²
Population: 83,054,000 (2005)
Capital: Manila (1,581,000)
Administration: 79 provinces and 115 chartered cities
Languages: Pilipino, Tagalog, English
Religions: Roman Catholic 83%, Protestant 5%
Currency: 1 Philipp. peso=100 centavo
Major cities:
Quezon City (2,174,000), Caloocan (1,178,000), Davao (1,147,000), Cebu (777,000)

Pitcairn Islands
(overseas territory of the U.K.)
Pitcairn, Henderson, Ducie, and Oeno Islands

Area: 35.5 km² (Pitcairn 4.6 km², Henderson 31 km², Oeno 5 km², Ducie 4 km²)
Population: 45 (2003)
Capital: Adamstown on Pitcairn (is the only settlement)
Administration: none (overseas territory of the U.K.)
Languages: English, Pitcairnese (a mixture of English and Tahitian)
Religions: Seventh-Day Adventist 100%
Currency: New Zealand dollar

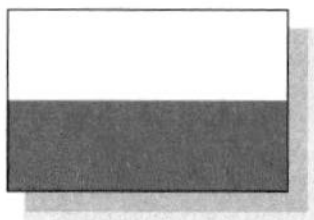

Poland
Republic of Poland
Rzeczpospolita Polska

Area: 312,685 km²
Population: 38,530,000 (2005)
Capital: Warsaw/Warszawa (1,672,000)
Administration: 16 provinces (voivodships)
Languages: Polish, German, Ukrainian
Religions: Roman Catholic 91%
Currency: 1 złoty = 100 groszy
Major cities:
Łódź (789,000), Kraków (759,000), Wrocław (640,000), Poznań (579,000), Gdańsk (461,000), Szczecin (415,000), Bydgoszcz (374,000)

1 km² = 0.3861 square mile

Portugal

Portuguese Republic
República Portuguesa

rea:	91,906 km²
opulation:	10,495,000 (2005)
apital:	Lisbon/Lisboa (557,000; A: 2,050,000)
dministration:	18 districts, 2 autonomous regions
anguages:	Portuguese
eligions:	Roman Catholic 92%, Protestant 2%
urrency:	1 euro = 100 cent

lajor cities:
orto (263,000), Amadora (175,000), Braga 12,000), Coimbra (104,000), Funchal (on Madei-) (104,000), Setúbal (97,000), Agualva-Cacém 2,000), Vila Nova de Gaia (70,000)

utonomous Regions:

zores
utonomous Region of the Azores
çores

rea:	2352 km²
opulation:	242,000 (2001)
apital:	Ponta Delgada (20,000)

ladeira
utonomous Region of Madeira

rea:	795 km²
opulation:	243,000 (2001)
apital:	Funchal (104,000)

Puerto Rico

(commonwealth associated with the U.S.)

Estado Libre Asociado de Puerto Rico/
Commonwealth of Puerto Rico

rea:	9,084 km²
opulation:	3,955,000 (2005)
apital:	San Juan (418,000)
dministration:	none (commonwealth associated with the U.S.)
anguages:	Spanish/English
eligions:	Roman Catholic 72%, Protestant 5%
urrency:	1 dollar = 100 cents

lajor cities:
ayamón (204,000), Ponce (153,000), arolina (170,000), Caguas (87,000)

Qatar

State of Qatar
Dawlat Qaṭar

rea:	11,437 km²
opulation:	813,000 (2005)
apital:	Doha/Ad-Dawḥah (339,000)
dministration:	9 municipalities
anguages:	Arabic, Urdu, Farsi (Persian), English
eligions:	Muslim (Sunni) 92%, Hindu
urrency:	1 Qatari riyal = 100 dirhams

lajor cities:
r-Rayyān (273,000), Al-Wakrah (31,000)

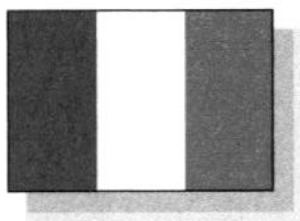

Réunion

(overseas department of France)

Department of Reunion
Département de la Réunion

Area:	2,504 km²
Population:	785,000 (2005)
Capital:	Saint-Denis (158,000)
Administration:	none (overseas department of France)
Languages:	French, Creole
Religions:	Roman Catholic 92%
Currency:	1 euro = 100 cent

Major cities:
Saint-Paul (99,000), Saint-Pierre (77,000), Le Tampon (70,000), Saint-André (49,000)

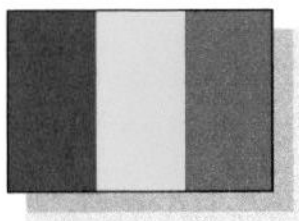

Romania

România

Area:	238,391 km²
Population:	21,711,000 (2005)
Capital:	Bucharest/Bucureşti (1,922,000)
Administration:	41 counties and the capital
Languages:	Romanian, Hungarian, German
Religions:	Romanian Orthodox 87%
Currency:	1 leu = 100 bani

Major cities:
Iaşi (322,000), Timişoara (318,000), Cluj-Napoca (318,000), Constanţa (311,000), Craiova (303,000)

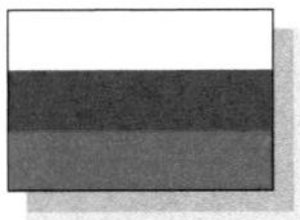

Russia

Russian Federation
Rossiyskaya Federatsiya

Area:	17,075,400 km²
Population:	143,202,000 (2005)
Capital:	Moscow/Moscwa (8,718,000; A: 12,410,000)
Administration:	21 republics, 1 autonomous oblast, 10 autonomous areas (avtonomnyy okrug), 6 territories (kray), 49 provinces (oblast), 2 cities of federal status: Moskva, Sankt Peterburg
Languages:	Russian, languages of the minorities
Religions:	Russian Orthodox 24%, Muslim 10–15%
Currency:	1 rouble = 100 kopeks

Major cities:
Saint Petersburg/Sankt Peterburg (4,628,000), Novosibirsk (1,393,000), Nižnij Novgorod (1,343,000), Ekaterinburg (1,257,000), Samara (1,146,000), Omsk (1,138,000), Kazan´ (1,090,000), Ufa (1,088,000), Čeljabinsk (1,081,000), Perm´ (1,005,000), Volgograd (1,011,000), Rostov-n.-D. (998,000), Voronež (902,000), Saratov (864,000), Krasnojarsk (759,000), Tol´jatti (724,000), Ul´janovsk (662,000), Iževsk (650,000), Krasnodar (635,000), Jaroslavl´ (609,000), Chabarovsk (604,000), Vladivostok (597,000), Irkutsk (587,000), Barnaul (573,000), Novokuzneck (565,000), Penza (525,000), Rjazan´ (524,000), Lipeck (519,000)

Republics	Area km²	Population 2001	Capital
Adygea	7,600	447,000	Maykop
Altay	92,600	206,000	Gorno-Altaysk
Bashkortostan	143,600	4,109,000	Ufa
Buryatia	351,300	1,029,000	Ulan-Ude
Chechnya	15,700	608,000	Groznyy
Khakassia	61,900	580,000	Abakan
Chuvashia	18,300	1,351,000	Cheboksary
Dagestan	50,300	2,166,000	Makhachkala
Ingushetia	3,600	461,000	Nazran'
Kabardino-Balkaria	12,500	790,000	Nal'chik
Kalmykia/Khalmg Tangch	75,900	314,000	Ėlista
Karachay-Cherkessia	14,100	433,000	Cherkessk
Karelia	172,400	762,000	Petro-zavodsk
Komi	415,900	1,124,000	Syktyvkar
Mari El	23,200	755,000	Yoskar-Ola
Mordovia	26,200	920,000	Saransk
Sakha	3,103,200	974,000	Yakutsk
North Ossetia-Alania	8,000	679,000	Vladikavkaz
Tatarstan	67,836	3,773,000	Kazan'
Tuva	170,500	311,000	Kyzyl
Udmurtia	42,100	1,627,000	Izhevsk

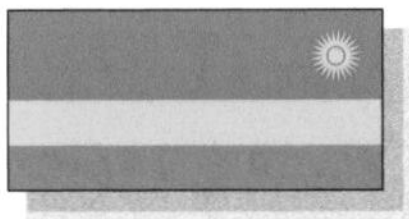

Rwanda

Rwandese Republic
Republika y'u Rwanda/
République rwandaise/
Rwandese Republic

Area:	26,338 km²
Population:	9,038,000 (2005)
Capital:	Kigali (412,000)
Administration:	12 prefectures
Languages:	Kinyarwanda/French/English
Religions:	Christian c. 50%, traditional beliefs c. 50%
Currency:	1 Rwanda franc = 100 centimes

Major cities:
Butare (43,000), Ruhengeri (29,000)

Saint Helena

(overseas territory of the U.K.)

Crown Colony of Saint Helena and Dependencies

Area:	410 km² (St. Helena 122 km²)
Population:	5,000 (2005)
Capital:	Jamestown (640)
Administration:	1 administrative area and 2 dependencies
Languages:	English
Religions:	Anglican (majority)
Currency:	Saint Helenian pound

Dependencies:
Ascension (88 km²/1,100 inh.), Tristan da Cunha (98 km²/300 inh.), Gough (90 km²/uninh.), Inaccessible (10 km²/uninh.), Nightingale (2 km²/uninh.)

Saint Kitts and Nevis
Federation of St. Kitts and Nevis

Area:	261 km²
Population:	43,000 (2005)
Capital:	Basseterre (13,000)
Administration:	14 parishes
Languages:	English, English Creole
Religions:	Anglican 36%, Methodist 32%, Roman Catholic 11%
Currency:	1 Eastern Caribbean dollar = 100 cents

Major cities:
Charlestown (1,700)

Samoa
Independent State of Samoa
Malo Tutoatasi o Samoa/
Independent State of Samoa

Area:	2,935 km²
Population:	185,000 (2005)
Capital:	Apia (34,000)
Administration:	11 districts
Languages:	Samoan/English
Religions:	Protestant 71%, Roman Catholic 22%
Currency:	1 tala = 100 sene

Major cities:
Sataua, Salelologa

Senegal
Republic of Senegal
République du Sénégal

Area:	196,722 km²
Population:	11,658,000 (2005)
Capital:	Dakar (2,079,000)
Administration:	10 regions
Languages:	French/Wolof
Religions:	Muslim 94%, Christian 5%
Currency:	1 CFA franc = 100 centimes

Major cities:
Thiès (256,000), Kaolack (228,000), Ziguinchor (181,000), Saint-Louis (132,000)

Saint Lucia

Area:	616 km²
Population:	161,000 (2005)
Capital:	Castries (A: 64,000)
Administration:	10 districts
Languages:	English, English Creole
Religions:	Roman Catholic 77%, Protestant 19%
Currency:	1 Eastern Caribbean dollar = 100 cents

Major cities:
Vieux Fort (23,000), Micoud (15,000), Soufrière (14,000), Gros Islet (12,000)

San Marino
Republic of San Marino
Repubblica di San Marino

Area:	61 km²
Population:	28,000 (2005)
Capital:	San Marino (4,400)
Administration:	9 districts (castelli)
Languages:	Italian
Religions:	Roman Catholic 93%
Currency:	1 euro = 100 cent

Major cities:
Serravalle (7,300)

Serbia and Montenegro
Srbija i Crna Gora

Area:	102,173 km²
Population:	10,503,000 (2005)
Capital:	Belgrade/Beograd (1,281,00
Administration:	2 republics
Languages:	Serbian, Croatian, Albanian
Religions:	Serbian Orthodox 44%, Roman Catholic 31%
Currency:	1 new dinar = 100 para

Major cities:
Novi Sad (234,000), Niš (178,000), Priština (165,000 Kragujevac (146,000), Podgorica (139,000), Subotica (99,000)

Saint Pierre and Miquelon
(territorial collectivity of France)
Territorial Collectivity of Saint Pierre and Miquelon/Collectivité territoriale de Saint-Pierre-et-Miquelon

Area:	242 km²
Population:	6,000 (2005)
Capital:	Saint-Pierre (5,700)
Administration:	none
Languages:	French
Religions:	Roman Catholic 99%
Currency:	1 euro = 100 cent

Sao Tome and Principe
Democratic Republic of Sao Tome and Principe
República Democrática de São Tomé e Príncipe

Area:	1,001 km²
Population:	157,000 (2005)
Capital:	São Tomé (52,000)
Administration:	6 districts on São Tomé, self-government of Príncipe
Languages:	Portuguese, Portuguese Creole
Religions:	Roman Catholic 80%, Protestant 10%
Currency:	1 dobra = 100 cêntimos

Major cities:
Santo António (1,000)

Seychelles
Republic of Seychelles
Repiblik Sesel/
Republic of Seychelles/
République des Seychelles

Area:	455 km²
Population:	81,000 (2005)
Capital:	Victoria (60,000)
Administration:	23 districts
Languages:	Creole/English/French
Religions:	Roman Catholic 90%, Anglican 8%
Currency:	1 Seychelles rupee = 100 cents

Saint Vincent and the Grenadines

Area:	388 km²
Population:	119,000 (2005)
Capital:	Kingstown (14,000)
Administration:	6 parishes
Languages:	English, English Creole
Religions:	Protestant 75%, Roman Catholic 9%
Currency:	1 Eastern Caribbean dollar = 100 cents

Major cities:
Georgetown (St. Vincent) (14,000)

Saudi Arabia
Kingdom of Saudi Arabia
Al-Mamlakah al-ʻArabīyah as-Saʻūdīyah

Area:	2,250,000 km²
Population:	24,573,000 (2005)
Capital:	Riyād/Ar-Riyād (4,087,000)
Administration:	13 regions
Languages:	Arabic, English
Religions:	Muslim 98%
Currency:	1 riyal = 100 halalas

Major cities:
Jeddah/Jiddah (3,192,000), Mecca/Makkah (1,355,000), Medina/Al-Madīnah (891,000), Ad-Dammām (764,000), Aṭ-Ṭā'if (658,000)

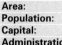

Sierra Leone
Republic of Sierra Leone

Area:	71,740 km²
Population:	5,525,000 (2005)
Capital:	Freetown (837,000)
Administration:	4 provinces
Languages:	traditional beliefs 52%, Muslim 39%
Religions:	1 leone = 100 cents
Currency:	1 Qatari riyal = 100 dirhams

Major cities:
Koidu (116,000), Makeni (116,000), Bo (84,000), Kenema (74,000)

1 km² = 0.3861 square mile

Singapore

Republic of Singapore
Republik Singapura/
Republic of Singapore/
Xinjiapo Gongheguo/
Singapur Kutiyarasu

Area: 682 km²
Population: 4,326,000 (2005)
Capital: Singapura (3,263,000)
Administration: 5 divisions
Languages: Malay/English/Chinese/Tamil
Religions: Buddhist 32%, Taoist 22%, Muslim 15%, Christian 13%
Currency: 1 Singapore dollar = 100 cents

Slovakia

Slovak Republic
Slovenská republika

Area: 49,035 km²
Population: 5,401,000 (2005)
Capital: Bratislava (428,000)
Administration: 8 regions
Languages: Slovak/Hungarian
Religions: Roman Cath. 60%, Protestant 8%
Currency: 1 Slovak koruna = 100 haliers
Major cities:
Košice (236,000), Prešov (93,000), Nitra (87,000), Žilina (85,000), Banská Bystrica (83,000)

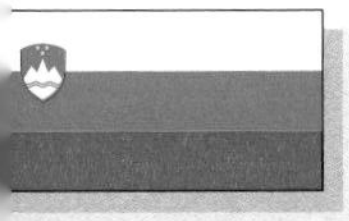

Slovenia

Republic of Slovenia
Republika Slovenija

Area: 20,273 km²
Population: 1,967,000 (2005)
Capital: Ljubljana (264,000)
Administration: 182 municipalities, and 11 urban municipalities
Languages: Slovene, Croatian, Hungarian, Italian
Religions: Christian 74%, Muslim 2%
Currency: 1 tolar = 100 stotins
Major cities:
Maribor (94,000), Celje (38,000), Kranj (36,000), Velenje (27,000), Koper (24,000)

Solomon Islands

Area: 28,446 km²
Population: 478,000 (2005)
Capital: Honiara (50,000)
Administration: 9 provinces, Capital Territory
Languages: English, Melanesian languages
Religions: Christian c. 95%
Currency: 1 Solomon Islands dollar = 100 cents
Major cities:
Gizo (7,000), Auki (5,000), Kirakira (3,000), Buala (2,000)

Somalia

Somali Republic
Jamhuuriyadda Soomaaliya

Area: 637,657 km²
Population: 8,228,000 (2005)
Capital: Mogadishu/Muqdisho (1,212,000)
Administration: 18 regions
Languages: Somali, Arabic, Italian
Religions: Muslim (Sunni) almost 100%
Currency: 1 Somali shilling = 100 cents
Major cities:
Hargeysa (328,000), Berbera (233,000), Marka (230,000), Kismaayo (183,000)

South Africa

Republic of South Africa/
iRiphabliki yaseMtzantsi Afrika/
iRiphabliki yaseNingizimu Afrika/
Rephaboliki ya Afrika-Borwa
Republiek van Suid-Afrika/

Area: 1,219,090 km²
Population: 47,432,000 (2005)
Capital: Pretoria (1,474,000) legislative centre: Cape Town judical centre: Bloemfontein
Administration: 9 provinces
Languages: Zulu/Xhosa/Afrikaans/Pedi/English/Tswana/Sotho/Tsonga/Swazi/Venda/Ndebele
Religions: Christian 78%, traditional beliefs 10%, Hindu 2%
Currency: 1 rand = 100 cents
Major cities:
Cape Town (2,984,000), Durban (2,531,000), Johannesburg (1,976,000), Soweto (1,465,000), Port Elizabeth (776,000), Benoni (488,000), Vereeniging (463,000), Pietermaritzburg (458,000), East London (426,000), Tembisa (377,000), Bloemfontein (349,000), Boksburg (348,000), Vanderbjilpark (338,000), Newcastle (309,000), Krugersdorp (270,000)

External Territory:

Prince Edward and Marion Islands

Prince Edward Island: 41 km²/uninhabited
Marion Island: 388 km²/uninhabited

Spain

Kingdom of Spain
Reino de España/
Regne d'Espanya/
Reino de España/
Espainiako Erresuma

Area: 504,790 km²
Population: 43,064,000 (2005)
Capital: Madrid (3,017,000)
Administration: 17 autonomous communities
Languages: Castilian Spanish/Catalan (reg.)/Galician (reg.)/Basque (reg.)
Religions: Roman Catholic 96%
Currency: 1 euro = 100 cent
Major cities:
Barcelona (1,527,000), Valencia (792,000), Seville/Sevilla (704,000), Zaragoza (620,000), Málaga (536,000), Murcia (378,000), Las Palmas (371,000), Palma de Mallorca (358,000), Bilbao (354,000), Valladolid (319,00), Córdoba (315,000), Alicante (294,000), Vigo (288,000), Gijón (270,000)

Places under Spanish Sovereignty in North Africa:

Ceuta

Place of Ceuta

Area: 19 km²
Population: 72,000 (2001)

Melilla

Place of Mellia

Area: 13 km²
Population: 66,000 (2001)

Sri Lanka

Dem. Socialist. Rep. of Sri Lanka
Shrī Laṅkā Prajātāntrika Samājavādī Janarajaya/
Ilankai Jananāyaka Choṣhalichak Kuṭiyarachu

Area: 65,610 km²
Population: 20,743,000 (2005)
Capital: Colombo (642,000)
Administration: 9 provinces
Languages: Sinhala/Tamil, English
Religions: Buddhist 69%, Hindu 16%, Muslim 8%
Currency: 1 Sri Lankan rupee = 100 cents
Major cities:
Moratuwa (177,000), Yāpanaya (Jaffna) (146,000), Negombo (122,000), Sri Jayawardenepura 116,000)

Sudan, The

Republic of the Sudan
Jumhūrīyat as-Sūdān

Area: 2,505,810 km²
Population: 36,233,000 (2005)
Capital: Khartoum/Al-Kharṭūm (2,731,000)
Administration: 26 states
Languages: Arabic, English
Religions: Muslim 70%, trad. beliefs 20%
Currency: 1 Sudanese dinar = 100 piastres
Major cities:
Omdurman/Umm Durmān (1,271,000), Khartou North/Al-Kharṭūm Baḥrī (1,256,000)

Suriname

Republic of Suriname
Republiek Suriname

Area: 163,820 km²
Population: 449,000 (2005)
Capital: Paramaribo (205,000)
Administration: 9 districts, capital district
Languages: Dutch, English, Hindi
Religions: Hindu 27%, Roman Catholic 23%, Muslim 20%, Protestant 19%
Currency: 1 Suriname guilder = 100 cents
Major cities:
Lelydorp (16,000), Nieuw Nickerie (11,000)

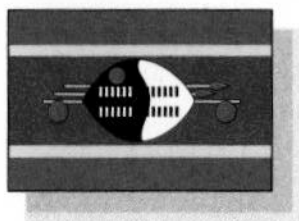

Swaziland

Kingdom of Swaziland
Umbuso waka'Ngwane

Area: 17,364 km^2
Population: 1,032,000 (2005)
Capital: Mbabane (80,000)
Administration: 4 districts
Languages: Swazi, English
Religions: Christian 78%, traditional beliefs 21%
Currency: 1 lilangeni = 100 cents
Major cities:
Manzini (78,000)

Sweden

Kingdom of Sweden
Konungariket Sverige

Area: 410,934 km^2
Population: 9,041,000 (2005)
Capital: Stockholm (762,000)
Administration: 21 counties (län)
Languages: Swedish, Finnish, Sami
Religions: Protestant (Lutheran) 89%, Roman Catholic 2%
Currency: 1 krona = 100 öre
Major cities:
Göteborg (474,000), Malmö (267,000), Uppsala (181,000), Linköping (136,000), Västerås (130,000), Örebro (126,000)

Switzerland

Swiss Confederation
Schweiz. Eidgenossenschaft/
Confédération suisse/
Confederazione Svizzera/
Confederaziun Svizr

Area: 41,285 km^2
Population: 7,252,000 (2005)
Capital: Berne/Bern (123,000)
Administration: 20 cantons, 6 demi-cantons
Languages: German/French/Italian/Romansch
Religions: Roman Catholic 42%, Protestant 35%
Currency: 1 Swiss franc = 100 centimes
Major cities:
Zürich (343,000), Geneva/Genève (178,000), Basel (165,000), Lausanne (116,000)

Syria

Syrian Arab Republic
Al-Jumhūrīyah al-ʿArabīyah as-Sūrīyah

Area: 185,180 km^2, including the Golan Heights (1,154 km^2)
Population: 19,043,000 (2005)
Capital: Damascus/Dimashq (2,195,000)
Administration: 13 provinces, capital district
Languages: Arabic, Kurdish, Armenian
Religions: Muslim 90%, Christian 9%
Currency: 1 Syrian pound = 100 piastres
Major cities:
Aleppo/Halab (2,229,000), Ḥimṣ (811,000), Latakia/Al-Lādhiqīyah (312,000), Hamāh (264,000)

Taiwan

Republic of China
Ta Chung-Hwa Min-Kwo

Area: 36,006 km^2
Population: 22,301,000 (2000)
Capital: T'aipei (2,640,000)
Administration: 5 municipalities, 16 counties, 2 special municipalities
Languages: Mandarin Chinese
Religions: Buddhist 43%, Taoist 34%
Currency: 1 New Taiwan dollar = 100 cents
Major cities:
Kaohsiung (1,494,000), T'aichung (1,006,000), T'ainan (741,000), Panch'iao (533,000)

Tajikistan

Republic of Tajikistan
Jumhurii Tojikiston
Respublika Tadzhikistan

Area: 143,100 km^2
Population: 6,507,000 (2005)
Capital: Dushanbe (576,000)
Administration: 3 provinces, Badakhshan Autonomous Republic and the capital
Languages: Tajik, Russian, Uzbek
Religions: Muslim (mainly Sunni) 80%
Currency: 1 Somoni = 100 Diram
Major cities:
Khujand (147,000), Kŭlob (80,000)

Tanzania

United Republic of Tanzania
Jamhuri ya Muungano wa Tanzania/
United Republic of Tanzania

Area: 883,749 km^2
Population: 38,329,000 (2005)
Capital: Dodoma (204,000) (seat of government: Dar es Salaam)
Administration: 26 regions
Languages: Swahili/English
Religions: Muslim 35%, Roman Catholic 33%, Protestant 13%
Currency: 1 Tanzania shilling = 100 cents
Major cities:
Dar es Salaam (1,436,000), Mwanza (223,000), Tanga (188,000), Zanzibar (158,000)

Thailand

Kingdom of Thailand
Ratcha Anachak Thai

Area: 513,115 km^2
Population: 64,233,000 (2005)
Capital: Bangkok/Krung Thep (6,320,000)
Administration: 5 regions
Languages: Thai, Chinese, Malay, English
Religions: Buddhist 94%, Muslim 4%
Currency: 1 baht = 100 stangs
Major cities:
Nonthaburi (291,000), Udon Thani (220,000), Nakhon Ratchasima (204,000), Hat Yai (186,000)

Timor-Leste

The Democratic Republic of Timor-Leste
Repúblika Democrátika Timor Loro Sa'e/República Democrática de Timor-Leste

Area: 18,889 km^2
Population: 947,000 (2005)
Capital: Dili (56,000)
Administration: 13 administrative districts
Languages: Tetum, Portuguese, Bahasa Indonesia
Religions: Catholic 91%
Currency: 1 U.S. dollar = 100 cent
Major cities:
Dare (19,000), Baucau (14,000), Maliana (12,000), Ermera (12,000)

Togo

Togolese Republic
République togolaise

Area: 56,785 km^2
Population: 6,145,000 (2005)
Capital: Lomé (375,000 A: 1,194,000)
Administration: 5 regions
Languages: French/Ewe/Kabye
Religions: traditional beliefs 50%, Christian 35%, Muslim (Sunni) 15%
Currency: 1 CFA franc = 100 centimes
Major cities:
Sokodé (99,000), Kpalimé (79,000), Atakpamé (67,000), Kara (51,000), Tsévié (38,000)

Tokelau

(overseas territory of New Zealand)

Area: 12 km^2
Population: 1,000 (2005)
Capital: none; each atoll has its own administrative center
Administration: none (overseas territory of New Zealand)
Languages: Tokelauan, English
Religions: Protestant 70%, Roman Catholic 28%
Currency: New Zealand dollar

Tonga

Kingdom of Tonga
Pule'anga Tonga

Area: 649 km^2
Population: 102,000 (2005)
Capital: Nuku'alofa (22,000)
Administration: 5 divisions
Languages: Tongan, English
Religions: Protestant 44%, Roman Catholic 16%
Currency: 1 pa'anga = 100 seniti
Islands (Pop.):
Tongatapu (67,000), Vava'u (16,000), Ha'apai (8,100), Eua (4,900)

1 km^2 = 0.3861 square mile

Trinidad and Tobago

Republic of Trinidad and Tobago

Area: 5,128 km²
Population: 1,305,000 (2005)
Capital: Port of Spain (49,000)
Administration: 10 counties
Languages: English, French, Spanish
Religions: Christian 40%, Hindu 24%
Currency: 1 Trinidad and Tobago dollar = 100 cents

Major cities:
San Fernando (55,000), Arima (30,000)

Tunisia

Republic of Tunisia
Al-Jumhūrīyah at-Tūnisīyah

Area: 162,155 km²
Population: 10,102,000 (2005)
Capital: Tūnis (691,000)
Administration: 24 Governorates
Languages: Arabic, French
Religions: Muslim (mainly Sunni) 99%
Currency: 1 Tunisian dinar = 1000 millimes

Major cities:
Sfax/Ṣafāqis (263,000), Aryānah (206,000), Sousse/Sūsah (149,000), Al-Qayrawān (115,000), Gabes/Qābis (109,000)

Turkey

Republic of Turkey
Türkiye Cumhuriyeti

Area: 779,452 km²
Population: 73,193,000 (2005)
Capital: Ankara (3,203,000)
Administration: 81 provinces
Languages: Turkish, Kurdish, Arabic
Religions: Muslim 99%
Currency: 1 Turkish lira = 100 kurush
Major cities:
İstanbul (8,832,000), İzmir (2,250,000), Bursa (1,184,000), Adana (1,133,000), Gaziantep (862,000), Konya (761,000), Antalya (606,000)

Turkmenistan

Turkmenistan

Area: 488,100 km²
Population: 4,833,000 (2005)
Capital: Ashgabat/Aşgabat (605,000)
Administration: 5 regions
Languages: Turkmen, Russian, Uzbek
Religions: Muslim (mainly Sunni) 90%
Currency: 1 manat = 100 tenesi
Major cities:
Türkmenabat (203,000), Daşhowuz (165,000), Mary (123,000), Balkanabat (119,000), Türkmenbaşi (70,000)

Turks and Caicos Islands

(overseas territory of the U.K.)

Area: 430 km²
Population: 26,000 (2005)
Capital: Cockburn Town on Grand Turk (100)
Administration: none (overseas territory of the U.K.)
Languages: English
Religions: Baptist 40%; Anglican 18%, Methodist 16%
Currency: US dollar
Major islands:
Providenciales (13,000), Grand Turk (4,000)

Tuvalu

Area: 27 km²
Population: 10,000 (2005)
Capital: Vaiaku (4,000, on island)
Administration: 9 atolls
Languages: Tuvaluan/English
Religions: Protestant 98%
Currency: 1 Australian dollar = 100 cents

Uganda

Republic of Uganda
Jamhuri ya Uganda/
Republic of Uganda

Area: 242,554 km²
Population: 28,816,000 (2005)
Capital: Kampala (1,209,000)
Administration: 56 districts
Languages: Kiswahili/English, Bantu languages
Religions: Roman Catholic 40%, Protestant 26%, Muslim 5%
Currency: 1 Uganda shilling = 100 cents

Major cities:
Gulu (113,000), Lira (90,000), Jinja (87,000)

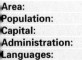

Ukraine

Ukrayina
Ukraina

Area: 603,700 km²
Population: 46,481,000 (2005)
Capital: Kiev/Kyyiv (2,611,000)
Administration: 24 provinces, 2 municipalities, Aut. Republic of Crimea
Languages: Ukrainian, Russian
Religions: Orthodox, Roman Cath. 11%
Currency: 1 hryvna = 100 kopiykas
Major cities:
Karkiv (1,470,000), Dnipropetrovs'k (1,065,000), Odesa (1,029,000), Donets'k (1,016,000), Zaporizhzhya (815,000)

United Arab Emirates

Al-Imārāt al-ʿArabīyah al-Muttaḥidah

Area: 83,600 km²
Population: 4,496,000 (2005)
Capital: Abū Ẓabī (552,000)
Administration: 7 emirates
Languages: Arabic, Hindi, Urdu, Farsi, English
Religions: Muslim 96%
Currency: 1 dirham = 100 fils
Major cities:
Dubayy (941,000), Ash-Shāriqah (450,000), Al-ʿAyn (348,000), ʿAghmān (225,000), Ras al-Khaymah (102,000), Al-Fughayrah (54,000)

United Kingdom

United Kingdom of Great Britain and Northern Ireland

Area: 243,820 km²
Population: 59,668,000 (2005)
Capital: London (7,172,000; A: 7,375,000)
Administration: *England:* Greater London, 6 metropolitan counties, 34 nonmetropolitan counties, 46 unitary authorities
Wales: 22 unitary authorities
Scotland: 32 unitary authorities
Northern Ireland: 26 districts
Languages: English, Welsh, Scottish, Gaelic
Religions: Protestant 43%, Roman Catholic 11%
Currency: 1 pound sterling = 100 pence
Major cities:
Birmingham (971,000; A: 2,284,000), Glasgow (630,000; A: 1,168,000), Liverpool (469,000), Leeds (443,000; A: 1,499,000), Sheffield (440,000), Edinburgh (431,000), Bristol (421,000), Manchester (394,000; A: 2,245,000), Leicester (331,000), Coventry (303,000)

	Area km²	Population 2001	Capital
England	130,439	49,139,000	London
Wales	20,768	2,903,000	Cardiff
Scotland	78,783	5,062,000	Edinburgh
Northern Ireland	14,120	1,685,000	Belfast

Crown Dependencies:

Channel Islands: Guernsey, Jersey

Area: 194 km² (Jersey 116 km²; Guernsey and dependencies 78 km²)
Population: 145,000 (2005)
Major cities: St. Helier (29,000) on Jersey, St. Peter Port (17,000) on Guernsey

Isle of Man

Area: 572 km²
Population: 77,000 (2005)
Major cities: Douglas (25,000)

Dependent Territories:

Anguilla
Crown Colony of Anguilla

Area: 96 km²
Population: 12,000 (2005)
Capital: The Valley (1,400)

Bermuda

Area: 53 km²
Population: 64,000 (2005)
Capital: Hamilton (890)

British Antarctic Territory
Claimed by the United Kingdom, Argentina and partly by Chile

Area: c. 1,710,000 km²
(South Orkney Is., South Shetland Is., Antarctic Pen., Filchner and Ronne Ice Shelves, Coast Land)
Research stations

British Indian Ocean Territory
Claimed by Mauritius

Area: 60 km² (land area)
Population: No permanent population

British Virgin Islands

Area: 153 km²
Population: 22,000 (2005)
Capital: Road Town on Tortola (8,000)

Cayman Islands

Area: 264 km²
Population: 42,000 (2005)
Capital: George Town (21,000)

Falkland Islands (Islas Malvinas)
Claimed by Argentina

Area: 12,173 km²
Population: 3,000 (2005)
Capital: Stanley (2,000)

Gibraltar
Colony of Gibraltar

Area: 6 km²
Population: 28,000 (2005)

Montserrat

Area: 101 km²
Population: 4,000 (2005)
Capital: interim government: Brades

Pitcairn Islands
Pitcairn, Henderson, Ducie, and Oeno Islands

Area: 35.5 km²
Population: 45 inhabitants (2003)
Capital: Adamstown

Saint Helena
Crown Colony of Saint Helena and Dependencies

Area: 410 km² (St. Helena 122 km²)
Population: 5,000 (2005)
Capital: Jamestown (640)

South Georgia and the South Sandwich Islands
Claimed by Argentina

Area: 3,755 km²/337 km²
Population:
South Georgia: no permanent population
South Sandwich Islands: uninhabited

Turks and Caicos Islands

Area: 430 km²
Population: 26,000 (2005)
Capital: Grand Turk (3,800)

United States / U.S.A.
United States of America

Area: 9,631,418 km²
Population: 298,213,000 (2005)
Capital: Washington D.C. (563,000; MSA: 5,090,000)
Administration: 50 states and the District of Columbia
Languages: English/regionally Spanish
Religions: Protestant 58%, Roman Catholic 21%, other Christian 6%, Jewish 2%, Muslim 2%
Currency: 1 dollar = 100 cents
Major cities:
New York (8,086,000; MSA: 18,641,000), Los Angeles (3,820,000; MSA: 12,829,000), Chicago (2,869,000; MSA: 9,334,000), Houston (2,010,000; MSA: 5,076,000), Philadelphia (1,479,000; MSA: 5,773,000), Phoenix (1,388,000; MSA: 3,593,000), San Diego (1,267,000; MSA: 2,931,000), San Antonio (1,215,000; MSA: 1,821,000), Dallas (1,208,000; MSA: 5,590,000), Detroit (911,000; MSA: 4,484,000), San Jose (898,000), Indianapolis (783,000), Jacksonville (774,000), San Francisco (752,000; MSA: 4,157,000), Columbus (728,000), Austin (672,000), Memphis (646,000), Baltimore (629,000; MSA: 2,616,000), Milwaukee (587,000), Forth Worth (585,000), El Paso (584,000), Boston (582,000; MSA: 4,440,000), Seattle (569,000; MSA: 3,142,000), Denver (557,000)

MSA Metropolitan Statistical Area

	Area* km²	Population 2004	Capital
States			
Alabama	135,775	4,530,000	Montgomery
Alaska	1,700,138	655,000	Juneau
Arizona	295,276	5,744,000	Phoenix
Arkansas	137,742	2,753,000	Little Rock
California	424,002	35,894,000	Sacramento
Colorado	269,618	4,601,000	Denver
Connecticut	14,358	3,504,000	Hartford
Delaware	6,448	830,000	Dover
District of Columbia	177	554,000	Washington
Florida	170,314	17,397,000	Tallahassee
Georgia	153,952	8,829,000	Atlanta
Hawaii	28,313	1,262,000	Honolulu
Idaho	216,456	1,393,000	Boise
Illinois	150,007	12,714,000	Springfield
Indiana	94,328	6,238,000	Indianapolis
Iowa	145,754	2,954,000	Des Moines
Kansas	213,111	2,736,000	Topeka
Kentucky	104,665	4,146,000	Frankfort
Louisiana	134,275	4,516,000	Baton Rouge
Maine	91,653	1,317,000	Augusta
Maryland	32,134	5,558,000	Annapolis
Massachusetts	27,337	6,417,000	Boston
Michigan	250,465	10,113,000	Lansing
Minnesota	225,182	5,101,000	Saint Paul
Mississippi	125,443	2,903,000	Jackson
Missouri	180,546	5,755,000	Jefferson City
Montana	380,850	927,000	Helena
Nebraska	200,358	1,747,000	Lincoln
Nevada	286,367	2,335,000	Carson City
New Hampshire	24,219	1,300,000	Concord
New Jersey	22,590	8,699,000	Trento
New Mexico	314,939	1,903,000	Santa F
New York	141,080	19,227,000	Alban
North Carolina	139,397	8,541,000	Raleig
North Dakota	183,123	634,000	Bismarc
Ohio	116,103	11,459,000	Columbu
Oklahoma	181,048	3,524,000	Oklahom City
Oregon	254,819	3,595,000	Salen
Pennsylvania	119,291	12,406,000	Harrisbur
Rhode Island	4,002	1,081,000	Providenc
South Carolina	82,902	4,198,000	Columbi
South Dakota	199,744	771,000	Pierr
Tennessee	109,158	5,901,000	Nashvill
Texas	695,676	22,490,000	Austi
Utah	219,902	2,389,000	Salt Lak City
Vermont	24,903	612,000	Montpelie
Virginia	110,792	7,460,000	Richmon
Washington	184,672	6,204,000	Olympi
West Virginia	62,759	1,815,000	Charlesto
Wisconsin	169,643	5,509,000	Madiso
Wyoming	253,349	507,000	Cheyenn

* including inland water

Outlying Territories in the Caribbean:

Navassa
claimed by Haiti
Navassa Island

Area/Population: 5 km²/uninhabited

Puerto Rico
Estado Libre Asociado de Puerto Rico/ Commonwealth of Puerto Rico

Area: 9,084 km²
Population: 3,955,000 (2005)
Capital: San Juan (418,000)
Languages: Spanish/English
Religions: Roman Catholic 72%, Protestant 5%
Currency: 1 dollar = 100 cents
Major cities:
Bayamón (204,000), Ponce (153,000), Carolina (170,000), Caguas (87,000)

Virgin Islands, U. S.
United States Virgin Islands

Area: 386 km²
Population: 112,000 (2005)
Capital: Charlotte Amalie (11,000)
Languages: English, Spanish, Creole

Outlying Territories in the Pacific Ocean:

American Samoa
Territory of American Samoa

Area: 199 km²
Population: 65,000 (2005)
Capital: Pago Pago on Tutuila (4,000
Languages: Samoan/English/Tongan

Baker Island

Area: 2.3 km²/uninhabited

Guam
Territory of Guam

Area: 549 km²
Population: 170,000 (2005)
Capital: Agaña/Hagåtña (1,000)
Languages: English, Chamorro, Philippine languages

1 km² = 0.3861 square mile

owland Island
rea: 2.3 km^2/uninhabited

arvis Island
rea: 7.7 km^2/uninhabited

ohnston Island
rea: 2.6 km^2
opulation: No indigenous inh.; all US government personnel left the island. In prev. years, an average of 1,100 military and civilian contractor personnel was present on the island.

ingman Reef
rea: 8 km^2/uninhabited

lidway Islands
rea: 5 km^2
opulation: 40 (2005)

Iorthern Mariana Islands
ommonwealth of the Northern Mariana Islands

rea: 464 km^2
opulation: 81,000 (2005)
apital: Garapan on Saipan (4,000)
anguages: English, Chamorro

'almyra Island
rea: 6 km^2/uninhabited

Vake Island
rea: 7.8 km^2
opulation: c. 200 (2005)

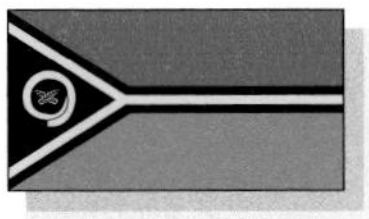

Vanuatu
Republic of Vanuatu
Ripablik blong Vanuatu/
Republic of Vanuatu/
République de Vanuatu

Area: 12,109 km^2
Population: 211,000 (2005)
Capital: Port Vila (34,000)
Administration: 6 provinces
Languages: Bislama/English/French
Religions: Christian 80%, traditional beliefs
Currency: 1 vatu = 100 centimes
Major cities:
Luganville (10,000)

Virgin Islands, U. S.
(territory of the U.S.)

United States Virgin Islands

Area: 386 km^2
Population: 112,000 (2005)
Capital: Charlotte Amalie (11,000)
Administration: none (territory of the U.S.)
Languages: English, Spanish, Creole
Religions: Baptist 42%, Roman Catholic 34%
Currency: US dollar
Major cities:
Anna's Retreat (8,000), Charlotte Amelie West (5,000), Frederiksted Southeast (3,000)

Vatican City
The Vatican City State
Status Civitatis Vaticanae/
Stato della Città del Vaticano

Area: 0,44 km^2
Population: 700 (2005)
Languages: Latin/Italian
Religions: Roman Catholic 100%
Currency: 1 euro = 100 cent

Wake Island
(territory of the U.S.)

Area: 7.8 km^2
Population: no indigenous inhabitants U.S. military personnel have left the islands, but contractor personnel remain, 200 contractor personnel were present (2005)

Uruguay
Oriental Republic of Uruguay
República Oriental del Uruguay

rea: 176,215 km^2
opulation: 3,463,000 (2005)
apital: Montevideo (1,379,000)
dministration: 19 departments
anguages: Spanish
eligions: Roman Catholic 78%, Protestant 2%
urrency: 1 Uruguayan peso = 100 centésimos
lajor cities:
alto (105,000), Paysandú (84,000), Maldonado 57,000), Las Piedras (66,000), Rivera (63,000)

Venezuela
Republic of Venezuela
República Bolivariana de Venezuela

Area: 912,050 km^2
Population: 26,749,000 (2005)
Capital: Caracas (1,976,000)
Administration: 23 states and capital district
Languages: Spanish, Indian languages
Religions: Roman Catholic 93%, Protestant 5%
Currency: 1 bolívar = 100 céntimos
Major cities:
Maracaibo (1,764,000), Valencia (1,339,000), Barquisimeto (876,000), Ciudad Guayana (704,000), Petare (369,000), Maracay (394,000)

Wallis and Futuna
(overseas territory of France)

Territory of the Wallis and Futuna Islands
Territoire des Wallis-et-Futuna

Area: 255 km^2
Population: 15,000 (2005)
Capital: Matâ'utu (1,300)
Administration: none (overseas territory of France)
Languages: French, Polynesian languages
Religions: Roman Catholic 97%
Currency: Comptoirs Francais du Pacifique franc
Major cities:
Alele (900), Utufua (750), Ono (750)

Uzbekistan
Republic of Uzbekistan
O'zbekiston Respublikasi
Respublika Uzbekistan

rea: 447,400 km^2
opulation: 26,593,000 (2005)
apital: Tashkent/Toshkent (2,197,000)
dministration: 12 provinces, Karakalpak Autonomous Republic
anguages: Uzbek, Russian
eligions: Muslim (Sunni) 88%
urrency: 1 sum = 100 teen
lajor cities:
amangan (377,000), Samarqand (362,000), ndijon (324,000), Bukhara/Buxoro (238,000)

Vietnam
Socialist Republic of Vietnam
Công-hòa xã-hôi chu-nghia Viêt-Nam

Area: 331,690 km^2
Population: 84,238,000 (2005)
Capital: Hanoi/Ha Nôi (2,842,000)
Administration: 8 regions
Languages: Vietnamese, Chinese, French
Religions: Buddhist 55%, Roman Catholic 5%
Currency: 1 dong = 100 xu
Major cities:
Chi Minh City/Thanh-Phô Hô Chi Minh (5,378,000), Hai Phong (591,000), Đa Năng (459,000), Buôn Ma Thuôt (384,000), Huê (277,000)

Western Sahara
Al-Jumhūrīyah al-ʻArabīyah aṣ-Ṣaḥrāwīyah ad-Dīmuqrāṭīyah

Area: 252,146 km^2
Population: 316,000 (2005)
Capital: Laâyoune/Al-ʻAyūn (139,000)
Administration: 4 provinces
Languages: Arabic, Spanish
Religions: Muslim almost 100%
Currency: Moroccan dirham
Major cities:
As-Samārah (44,000), Ad-Dākhla (39,000), Bū Jaydūr (23,000)

Yemen

Republic of Yemen
Al-Jumhūrīyah al-Yamanīyah

Area:	527,968 km^2
Population:	20,975,000 (2005)
Capital:	Ṣan'ā' (1,590,000)
Administration:	17 governorates
Languages:	Arabic
Religions:	Muslim 99%
Currency:	1 Yemeni rial = 100 fils

Major cities:
'Adan (Aden) (608,000), Ta'izz (318,000), Al-Ḥudaydah (300,000), Al-Mukallā (122,000), Ibb (103,000)

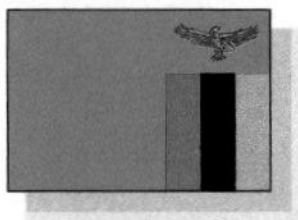

Zambia

Republic of Zambia

Area:	752,614 km^2
Population:	11,668,000 (2005)
Capital:	Lusaka (1,718,000)
Administration:	9 provinces
Languages:	English, Bantu languages
Religions:	Christian 72%, traditional beliefs 27%
Currency:	1 kwacha = 100 ngwee

Major cities:
Ndola (375,000), Kitwe (364,000), Kabwe (177,000), Chingola (147,000), Mufulira (122,000), Luanshya (116,000), Livingstone (109,000)

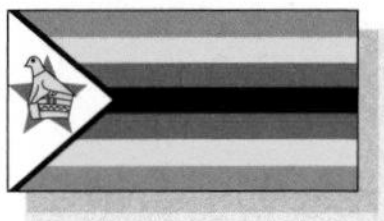

Zimbabwe

Republic of Zimbabwe

Area:	390,757 km^2
Population:	13,010,000 (2005)
Capital:	Harare (1,868,000)
Administration:	10 provinces
Languages:	English, Shona, Sindebele Bantu languages
Religions:	Christian 55%, tradit. beliefs
Currency:	1 Zimbabwe dollar = 100 cents

Major cities:
Bulawayo (1,004,000), Chitungwiza (424,000), Mutare (159,000), Gweru (158,000)

1 km^2 = 0.3861 square mile

Earth Dimensions

Radius at the equator	6378,160 km
Half axis	6356,775 km
Amount of flattening of the geoid at the poles	1/298,254
Circumference at the equator	40075,161 km
Circumference over the poles	40008,006 km
Length of a degree at the equator	111,320 km
Average length of a meridian degree	111,133 km
Total surface	510,068 million km^2
Land surface (c. 29%)	c. 148,1 million km^2
Ocean surface (c. 71%)	c. 362,0 million km^2
Mass	5,976 x 10^{24} kg
Volume	1,083 x 10^{12} km^3
Mean density	5,517 g/cm^3
Sideric time per rotation	23^h 56^m $4{,}09^s$
Mean distance Earth-Sun	149,598 million km
Distance Earth–Sun in aphelion (farthest from sun)	152,099 million km
Distance Earth–Sun in perihelion (nearest to sun)	147,096 million km
Length of the earth's orbit around the sun	939,886 million km
Tilt of the earth's axis in relation to its orbital plane (ecliptic), in 2000	23° 26' 21'', 4
Average orbital speed around the sun	29,783 km/s
Sidereal year	365^d 6^h 9^m 9^s
Tropical year	365^d 5^h 48^m 46^s
Average distance Earth–Moon	384,400 km
Distance Earth–Moon in apogee (farthest from earth)	406,740 km
Distance Earth–Moon in perigee (nearest to earth)	356,410 km
Sidereal month	27^d 7^h 43^m 12^s
Synodic month	29^d 12^h 44^m 3^s

The Continents

	Area in km^2	Population 2005
Europe	10,142,000	692,591,000
Asia	44,817,000	3,960,275,000
Australia and Oceania	8,515,000	33,060,000
Africa	30,260,000	906,068,000
North America	24,683,000	516,213,000
South America	17,650,000	375,739,000
Antarctica	12,400,000	–
World	148,467,000	6,483,946,000

Countries and their Areas

	km²
1. Russia	17,075,400
2. Canada	9,984,670
3. United States	9,631,418
4. China	9,596,961
5. Brazil	8,547,404
6. Australia	7,692,024
7. India	3,287,263
8. Argentina	2,780,400
9. Kazakhstan	2,724,900
10. Sudan, The	2,505,810
11. Algeria	2,381,741
12. Congo, Dem. Rep. of the	2,344,858
13. Saudi Arabia	2,250,000
14. Mexico	1,964,375
15. Indonesia	1,922,570
16. Libya	1,759,540
17. Iran	1,629,807
18. Mongolia	1,564,100
19. Peru	1,285,216
20. Chad	1,284,000
21. Niger	1,267,000
22. Mali	1,248,574
23. Angola	1,246,700
24. South Africa	1,219,090
25. Colombia	1,138,914
26. Ethiopia	1,112,000
27. Bolivia	1,098,591
28. Mauritania	1,025,520
29. Egypt	1,002,000
30. Nigeria	923,768
31. Venezuela	912,050
32. Tanzania	883,749
33. Namibia	824,269
34. Mozambique	799,380
35. Pakistan	796,096
36. Turkey	779,452
37. Chile	756,626
38. Zambia	752,614
39. Myanmar	676,578
40. Afghanistan	652,090
41. Somalia	637,657
42. Central African Republic	622,436
43. Ukraine	603,700
44. Madagascar	587,041
45. Botswana	582,000
46. Kenya	582,000
47. France	543,965
48. Yemen	527,968
49. Thailand	513,115
50. Spain	504,790
51. Turkmenistan	488,100
52. Cameroon	466,050
53. Papua New Guinea	462,243
54. Morocco	458,730
55. Uzbekistan	447,400
56. Iraq	438,317
57. Sweden	410,934
58. Paraguay	406,752
59. Zimbabwe	390,757
60. Norway	385,155
61. Japan	377,880
62. Germany	357,027
63. Congo, Republic of the	342,000
64. Vietnam	331,690
65. Malaysia	330,242

	km²
66. Côte d'Ivoire	322,462
67. Poland	312,685
68. Oman	309,500
69. Finland	304,530
70. Italy	301,336
71. Philippines	300,000
72. Ecuador	283,561
73. Burkina Faso	274,200
74. New Zealand	270,500
75. Gabon	267,667
76. Western Sahara	252,146
77. Guinea	245,857
78. United Kingdom	243,820
79. Uganda	242,554
80. Ghana	238,539
81. Romania	238,391
82. Laos	236,800
83. Guyana	214,969
84. Belarus	207,600
85. Kyrgyzstan	199,900
86. Senegal	196,722
87. Syria	185,180
88. Cambodia	181,035
89. Uruguay	176,215
90. Suriname	163,820
91. Tunisia	162,155
92. Bangladesh	147,570
93. Nepal	147,181
94. Tajikistan	143,100
95. Greece	131,626
96. Eritrea	124,324
97. Korea, North	120,538
98. Nicaragua	119,838
99. Malawi	118,484
100. Benin	112,622
101. Honduras	112,492
102. Liberia	111,369
103. Bulgaria	110,910
104. Cuba	110,860
105. Guatemala	108,889
106. Iceland	103,000
107. Serbia and Montenegro	102,173
108. Korea, South	99,538
109. Hungary	93,029
110. Portugal	91,906
111. Jordan	89,342
112. Azerbaijan	86,600
113. Austria	83,859
114. United Arab Emirates	83,600
115. Czech Republic	78,860
116. Panama	75,517
117. Sierra Leone	71,740
118. Ireland	70,273
119. Georgia	69,700
120. Sri Lanka	65,610
121. Lithuania	65,300
122. Latvia	64,589
123. Togo	56,785
124. Croatia	56,542
125. Bosnia and Herzegovina	51,197
126. Costa Rica	51,100
127. Slovakia	49,035
128. Dominican Republic	48,442
129. Bhutan	46,500
130. Estonia	43,432

	km
131. Denmark	43,09
132. Switzerland	41,28
133. Guinea-Bissau	36,12
134. Taiwan	36,00
135. Netherlands, The	33,87
136. Moldova	33,80
137. Belgium	30,51
138. Lesotho	30,35
139. Armenia	29,74
140. Albania	28,74
141. Solomon Islands	28,44
142. Equatorial Guinea	28,05
143. Burundi	27,83
144. Haiti	27,75
145. Rwanda	26,33
146. Macedonia	25,71
147. Djibouti	23,20
148. Belize	22,96
149. Israel	22,14
150. El Salvador	21,04
151. Slovenia	20,27
152. Timor-Leste	18,88
153. Fiji	18,33
154. Kuwait	17,81
155. Swaziland	17,36
156. Bahamas, The	13,87
157. Vanuatu	12,10
158. Qatar	11,43
159. Jamaica	11,42
160. Gambia, The	11,29
161. Lebanon	10,45
162. Cyprus	9,25
163. Brunei	5,76
164. Trinidad and Tobago	5,12
165. Cape Verde	4,03
166. Samoa	2,93
167. Luxembourg	2,58
168. Mauritius	2,04
169. Comoros	1,86
170. Sao Tome and Principe	1,00
171. Dominica	75
172. Kiribati	71
173. Micronesia	70
174. Bahrain	69
175. Singapore	68
176. Tonga	64
177. Saint Lucia	61
178. Palau	49
179. Andorra	46
180. Antigua and Barbuda	45
181. Seychelles	45
182. Barbados	43
183. St. Vincent and the Grenadines	38
184. Grenada	34
185. Malta	31
186. Maldives	29
187. Saint Kitts and Nevis	26
188. Cook Islands	23
189. Marshall Islands	18
190. Liechtenstein	16
191. San Marino	6
192. Tuvalu	2
193. Nauru	2
194. Monaco	1.9
195. Vatican City	0.4

1 km² = 0.3861 square mile

	Inhabitants 2005
1. China	1,315,844,000
2. India	1,103,371,000
3. United States	298,213,000
4. Indonesia	222,781,000
5. Brazil	186,405,000
6. Pakistan	157,935,000
7. Russia	143,202,000
8. Bangladesh	141,822,000
9. Nigeria	131,530,000
10. Japan	128,085,000
11. Mexico	107,029,000
12. Vietnam	84,238,000
13. Philippines	83,054,000
14. Germany	82,526,000
15. Ethiopia	77,431,000
16. Egypt	74,033,000
17. Turkey	73,193,000
18. Iran	69,515,000
19. Thailand	64,233,000
20. France	60,496,000
21. United Kingdom	59,668,000
22. Italy	58,093,000
23. Congo, Dem. Rep. of the	57,549,000
24. Myanmar	50,519,000
25. Korea, South	47,817,000
26. South Africa	47,432,000
27. Ukraine	46,481,000
28. Colombia	45,600,000
29. Spain	43,064,000
30. Argentina	38,747,000
31. Poland	38,530,000
32. Tanzania	38,329,000
33. Sudan, The	36,233,000
34. Kenya	34,256,000
35. Algeria	32,854,000
36. Canada	32,268,000
37. Morocco	31,478,000
38. Afghanistan	29,863,000
39. Uganda	28,816,000
40. Iraq	28,807,000
41. Peru	27,968,000
42. Nepal	27,133,000
43. Venezuela	26,749,000
44. Uzbekistan	26,593,000
45. Malaysia	25,347,000
46. Saudi Arabia	24,573,000
47. Korea, North	22,488,000
48. Taiwan	22,301,000
49. Ghana	22,113,000
50. Romania	21,711,000
51. Yemen	20,975,000
52. Sri Lanka	20,743,000
53. Australia	20,155,000
54. Mozambique	19,792,000
55. Syria	19,043,000
56. Madagascar	18,606,000
57. Côte d'Ivoire	18,154,000
58. Cameroon	16,322,000
59. Chile	16,295,000
60. Netherlands, The	16,229,000
61. Angola	15,941,000
62. Kazakhstan	14,825,000
63. Cambodia	14,071,000
64. Niger	13,957,000
64. Mali	13,518,000
65. Burkina Faso	13,228,000
Ecuador	13,228,000
67. Zimbabwe	13,010,000
68. Malawi	12,884,000
69. Guatemala	12,559,000
70. Zambia	11,668,000
71. Senegal	11,658,000
72. Cuba	11,269,000
73. Greece	11,120,000
74. Serbia and Montenegro	10,503,000
75. Portugal	10,495,000
76. Belgium	10,419,000
77. Czech Republic	10,220,000
79. Tunisia	10,102,000
80. Hungary	10,098,000
81. Belarus	9,755,000
82. Chad	9,749,000
83. Guinea	9,402,000
84. Bolivia	9,182,000
85. Sweden	9,041,000
86. Rwanda	9,038,000
87. Dominican Republic	8,895,000
88. Haiti	8,528,000
89. Benin	8,439,000
90. Azerbaijan	8,411,000
91. Somalia	8,228,000
92. Austria	8,189,000
93. Bulgaria	7,726,000
94. Switzerland	7,252,000
95. Honduras	7,205,000
96. Burundi	7,548,000
97. El Salvador	6,881,000
98. Israel	6,725,000
99. Tajikistan	6,507,000
100. Paraguay	6,158,000
101. Togo	6,145,000
102. Laos	5,924,000
103. Papua New Guinea	5,887,000
104. Libya	5,853,000
105. Jordan	5,703,000
106. Sierra Leone	5,525,000
107. Nicaragua	5,487,000
108. Denmark	5,431,000
109. Slovakia	5,401,000
110. Kyrgyzstan	5,264,000
111. Finland	5,249,000
112. Turkmenistan	4,833,000
113. Norway	4,620,000
114. Croatia	4,551,000
115. United Arab Emirates	4,496,000
116. Georgia	4,474,000
117. Eritrea	4,401,000
118. Costa Rica	4,327,000
119. Singapore	4,326,000
120. Moldova	4,206,000
121. Bosnia and Herzegovina	4,186,000
122. Ireland	4,148,000
123. Central African Republic	4,038,000
124. New Zealand	4,028,000
125. Congo, Republic of the	3,999,000
126. Lebanon	3,577,000
127. Uruguay	3,463,000
128. Lithuania	3,431,000
129. Liberia	3,283,000
130. Panama	3,232,000
131. Albania	3,130,000
132. Mauritania	3,069,000
133. Armenia	3,016,000
134. Kuwait	2,687,000
135. Jamaica	2,651,000
136. Mongolia	2,646,000
137. Oman	2,567,000
138. Latvia	2,307,000
139. Bhutan	2,163,000
140. Macedonia	2,034,000
141. Namibia	2,031,000
142. Slovenia	1,967,000
143. Lesotho	1,795,000
144. Botswana	1,765,000
145. Guinea-Bissau	1,586,000
146. Gambia, The	1,517,000
147. Gabon	1,384,000
148. Estonia	1,330,000
149. Trinidad and Tobago	1,305,000
150. Mauritius	1,245,000
151. Swaziland	1,032,000
152. Timor-Leste	947,000
153. Fiji	848,000
154. Cyprus	835,000
155. Qatar	813,000
156. Comoros	798,000
157. Djibouti	793,000
158. Guyana	751,000
159. Bahrain	727,000
160. Cape Verde	507,000
161. Equatorial Guinea	504,000
162. Solomon Islands	478,000
163. Luxembourg	465,000
164. Suriname	449,000
165. Malta	402,000
166. Brunei	374,000
167. Maldives	329,000
168. Bahamas	323,000
169. Western Sahara	316,000
170. Iceland	295,000
171. Barbados	270,000
Belize	270,000
173. Vanuatu	211,000
174. Samoa	185,000
175. Saint Lucia	161,000
176. Sao Tome and Principe	157,000
177. St. Vincent and the Grenadines	119,000
178. Micronesia	110,000
179. Grenada	103,000
180. Tonga	102,000
181. Kiribati	99,000
182. Antigua and Barbuda	81,000
Seychelles	81,000
184. Dominica	79,000
185. Andorra	67,000
186. Marshall Islands	62,000
187. Saint Kitts and Nevis	43,000
188. Monaco	35,000
189. Liechtenstein	35,000
190. San Marino	28,000
191. Palau	20,000
192. Cook Islands	18,000
193. Nauru	14,000
194. Tuvalu	10,000
195. Vatican City	700

Major Mountains

North America

Mount McKinley (Alaska Range)	6,194 m
Mount Logan) (Saint Elias Mountains)	5,959 m
Pico de Orizaba (Mexico)	5,610 m
Popocatépetl (Mexico)	5,452 m
Nevado de Colima (Sierra Madre Occidental)	4,450 m
Mount Whitney (Sierra Nevada)	4,418 m
Mount Elbert (Rocky Mountains)	4,399 m
Mount Rainier (Cascade Range)	4,392 m
Tajumulco (Sierra Madre)	4,220 m
Mount Waddington (Coast Mountains)	4,016 m
Cerro Mohinora (Sierra Madre Occidental)	3,992 m
Mount Robson (Rocky Mountains)	3,954 m
Chirripó Grande (Cordillera de Talamanca)	3,820 m
Gunnbjørn Fjeld (Greenland)	3700 m
Cerro Peña Nevada (Sierra Madre Oriental)	3,664 m
Pico Duarte (Hispaniola)	3,175 m
Blue Mountain Peak (Jamaica)	2,256 m
Mount Mitchell (Appalachian Mountains)	2,037 m
Pico Turquino (Sierra Maestra)	1,974 m

South America

Aconcagua (Andes)	6,962 m
Pissis (Andes)	6,882 m
Ojos del Salado (Andes)	6,880 m
Huascarán (Andes)	6,768 m
Llullaillaco (Andes)	6,723 m
Sajama (Andes)	6,542 m
Illimani (Andes)	6,462 m
Chimborazo (Andes)	6,310 m
Cotopaxi (Andes)	5,897 m
Pico Cristóbal Colón (Sierra Nevada de Santa Marta)	5,775 m
Huila (Andes)	5,750 m
Pico Bolívar (Cordillera de Mérida)	5,007 m
San Valentín (Cordillera Patagónica)	4,058 m
Pico da Neblina (Guiana Highlands)	3,014 m
Pico da Bandeira (Brazilian Highlands)	2,890 m
Yogan (Tierra del Fuego)	2,469 m

Europe

Mont Blanc (Western Alps)	4,807 m
Dufourspitze, Monte Rosa (Pennine Alps)	4,634 m
Matterhorn (Pennine Alps)	4,478 m
Finsteraarhorn (Bernese Alps)	4,274 m
Jungfrau (Bernese Alps)	4,158 m
Pelvoux (Western Alps)	4,102 m
Gran Paradiso (Alpi Graie)	4,061 m
Bernina (Rhaetian Alps)	4,049 m
Ortles (Central Alps)	3,905 m
Monte Viso (Cottian Alps)	3,841 m
Grossglockner (Hohe Tauern)	3,798 m
Mulhacén (Sierra Nevada)	3,481 m
Aneto (Pyrenees)	3,404 m
Marmolada (Dolomites)	3,342 m
Etna (Sicily)	3,323 m
Zugspitze (Bavarian Alps)	2,962 m
Musala (Rila)	2,925 m
Ólympos (Piería)	2,917 m
Vihren (Pirin)	2,914 m
Gran Sasso d'Italia (Abruzzi)	2,912 m
Triglav (Julian Alps)	2,864 m
Monte Cinto (Corsica)	2,706 m
Jezerca (North Albanian Alps)	2,694 m
Gerlachovský Štít (High Tatra)	2,655 m
Picos de Europa (Cantabrian Mountains)	2,648 m
Almanzor (Sierra de Gredos)	2,592 m
Grintavec (Karawanken)	2,559 m
Moldoveanu (Transylvanien Alps)	2,544 m
Durmitor (Dinaric Alps)	2,522 m
Galdhøpiggen (Scandinavia)	2,469 m
Ídi (Crete)	2,456 m
Ágios Ilías (Taïgetos)	2,407 m
Botev (Balkan Maountains)	2,376 m
Pietrosu (Carpathian Mountains)	2,303 m
Golyam Pereli (Rhodope Mountains)	2,191 m
Öræfajökull (Iceland)	2,119 m
Kebnekaise (Scandinavia)	2,111 m
Ďumbier (Low Tatra)	2,043 m

Asia

Mt. Everest (Himalayas)	8,850 m
K2 (Karakoram Range)	8,611 m
Dhaulagiri (Himalayas)	8,167 m
Nanga Parbat (Himalayas)	8,125 m
Muztag Feng (Kunlun Shan)	7,723 m
Kongur Shan (Kunlun Shan)	7,719 m
Tirich Mir (Hindu Kush)	7,690 m
Gongga Shan (Daxue Shan)	7,556 m
Peak Somoni (Pamirs)	7,495 m
Jengish Chokusu/ Shengli Feng (Tien Shan)	7,439 m
Lenin Pik (Trans Alai)	7,134 m
Nyainqêntanglha (Nyainqêntanglha Shan)	7,111 m
Damāvand (Elburz Mountains)	5,671 m
El'brus (Caucasus)	5,642 m
Pik Piramidalnyy (Turkestan Range)	5,621 m
Chimtarga (Zeravshan Range)	5,489 m
Ararat (Armenian Highlands)	5,165 m
Klyuchevskaya Sopka (Kamchatka)	4,750 m
Zard Kūh (Zagros Mountains)	4,548 m
Belukha (Altay)	4,506 m
Uludoruk (Eastern Taurus Mount.)	4,135 m
Kinabalu (Borneo)	4,101 m
Ich Bogd (Govi Altayn Nuruu)	3,957 m
Kaçkar (Pontine Mountains)	3,932 m
Erciyeş (Anatolia)	3,917 m
Otgon Tenger (Khangai)	3,905 m
Kerinci (Sumatra)	3,800 m
Mount Fuji (Honshu)	3,776 m
Rinjani (Lombok)	3,726 m
Semeru (Java)	3,676 m
Nabī Shua'yb (Yemen)	3,760 m
Munku-Sardyk (Eastern Sayan)	3,491 m
Rantekombola (Celebes)	3,455 m
Pobeda (Cherskiy Range)	3,147 m
Phan Si Pang (Hoanglien Son)	3,143 m
Kyzyl Taiga (Western Sayan)	3,121 m
Qurnat as Sawdā' (Lebonan Mount.)	3,083 m
J. ash Shām (Oman Mountains)	2,980 m
Mount Apo (Mindanao)	2,954 m
Mount Pulog (Luzon)	2,929 m
Baitou Shan/Paekdu-san (China/North Korea)	2,744 m
Anai Mudi (Western Ghats)	2,695 m
J. Katrīna (Sinai Peninsula)	2,637 m
Pidurutalagala (Ceylon)	2,524 m
Tahan (Malay Peninsula)	2,187 m
Tardoki-Jani (Sikhote Alin Range)	2,077 m
Ólympus (Cyprus)	1,953 m

Australia an Oceania

Carstensz Pyramid/ Puncak Jayakesuma (Maoke Range)	4,884 m
Mount Wilhelm (Bismarck Range)	4,509 m
Mauna Kea (Hawaii)	4,205 m
Mount Victoria (Owen Stanley Range)	4,073 m
Mount Cook (Southern Alps)	3,754 m
Mount Ruapehu (North Island, New Zealand)	2,797 m
Mount Balbi (Bougainville Isl.)	2,685 m
Mount Popomanaseu (Guadalcanal)	2,331 m
Mont Orohena (Tahiti)	2,241 m
Mount Kosciusko (Australian Alps)	2,228 m
Mount Tabwemasana (Espiritu Santo)	1,879 m
Mont Panié (New Caledonia)	1,628 m
Mount Ossa (Tasmania)	1,617 m
Mount Victoria (Viti Levu)	1,322 m

Africa

Kilimanjaro (Tanzania)	5,892 m
Mount Kenya (Kenya)	5,199 m
Margherita Peak (Ruwenzori)	5,110 m
Ras Dashen (Ethiopian Highlands)	4,620 m
Tubqāl (High Atlas)	4,165 m
Cameroon Mountain (Cameroon)	4,095 m
Pico de Teide (Tenerife)	3,718 m
Thabana Ntlenyana (Drakensberg)	3,482 m
Emi Koussi (Tibesti)	3,415 m
Kinyeti (Lolibai)	3,187 m
Jebel Marrah (Darfur)	3,071 m
Piton des Neiges (Réunion)	3,069 m
Pico Basile (Bioko)	3,008 m
Sapitwa (Mlanje)	3,002 m
Tahat (Ahaggar)	2,918 m
Maromokotro (Madagascar)	2,876 m
Môco (Bié Plateau)	2,619 m
Brandberg (Namibia)	2,606 m
Kompasberg (Sneeuberg)	2,504 m
Shimbiris (Somalia)	2,416 m
Kartala (Ngazidja)	2,361 m
Bintimani (Loma Mountains)	1,948 m
Pico Ruivo (Madeira)	1,847 m
Shere Hill (Jos Plateau)	1,780 m
Tamgue (Fouta Djallon)	1,538 m
Table Mountain (South Africa)	1,087 m

Antarctica

Vinson Massif	4,897 m
Mount Kirkpatrick	4,528 m
Mount Jackson	4,190 m
Mount Erebus	3,794 m

1 m = 3,28095 ft

orth America	
ississippi/Missouri	6,420 km
ackenzie/Peace River	4,241 km
ississippi	3,778 km
issouri	3,725 km
ukon	3,185 km
o Grande/ Rîo Bravo del Norte	2,840 km
elson/Saskatchewan	2,575 km
rkansas	2,348 km
olorado	2,333 km
hio/Allegheny	2,101 km
olumbia	2,000 km
nake	1,670 km
hurchill	1,609 km
razos	1,485 km
ennessee/French Broad	1,421 km
aser	1,368 km
aint Lawrence	1,287 km
udson	492 km

outh America	
mazonas	6,437 km
araná/Rîo de la Plata	4,264 km
adeira	3,240 km
urus	3,211 km
ão Francisco	3,199 km
apurá/Caquetá	2,816 km
ocantins	2,699 km
rinoco	2,575 km
araguay	2,549 km
io Negro	2,253 km
apajós/Juruena	2,200 km
ingu	2,100 km
ruguay	1,609 km
agdalena	1,538 km

Europe	
Volga	3,531 km
Danube	2,858 km
Ural	2,428 km
Dniepr	2,201 km
Kama	2,032 km
Don	1,870 km
Pechora	1,809 km
Oka	1,480 km
Belaya	1,430 km
Dniester	1,352 km
Rhine	1,320 km
Vyatka	1,314 km
Northern Dvina/Sukhona	1,302 km
Elbe	1,165 km
Desna	1,130 km
Vychegda	1,130 km
Donets	1,053 km
Vistula	1,047 km
Western Dvina	1,020 km
Loire	1,020 km
Tagus	1,007 km
Tisza	966 km
Prut	950 km
Meuse/Maas	933 km
Oder	912 km
Ebro	910 km
Rhône	812 km
Seine	776 km
Klarälven/Göta Älv	720 km
Po	652 km
Glomma	598 km
Maritsa	533 km
Kemijoki	483 km
Tevere	393 km
Shannon	361 km
Thames	346 km

Asia	
Yangtze	5,526 km
Yellow River	5,464 km
Amur/Shilka/Onon	4,416 km
Ob/Katun	4,345 km
Lena	4,313 km
Irtysh	4,248 km
Mekong	4,184 km
Yenisey	4,102 km
Syr Darya/Naryn	3,012 km
Lower Tunguska	2,989 km
Indus	2,897 km
Brahmaputra	2,896 km
Tarim/Yarkant	2,750 km
Euphrates	2,736 km
Amu Darya/Panj/Vakhan	2,574 km
Kolyma	2,513 km
Ganges	2,511 km
Salween	2,414 km
Aldan	2,242 km
Xi Jiang	2,129 km
Irrawaddy	2,092 km
Sungari	1,927 km
Tigris	1,899 km

Australia and Oceania	
Darling	2,740 km
Murray	2,570 km
Murrumbidgee	2,160 km
Lachlan	1,480 km
Sepik	1,127 km
Fly	1,120 km
Flinders	832 km
Waikato	425 km

Africa	
Nile/Kagera	6,671 km
Congo	4,374 km
Niger	4,184 km
Zambezi	2,736 km
Ubangi/Uele	2,300 km
Kasai	2,153 km
Orange River	2,092 km
Cubango/Okavango	1,800 km
Juba	1,650 km
Limpopo	1,600 km
Volta	1,600 km
Lomami	1,450 km
Senegal	1,430 km
Chari	1,400 km
Vaal	1,251 km
Gambia	1,127 km

Major Islands (In some cases small adjacent islands are included.)

North America	
Greenland	2,166,086 km²
Baffin Island	688,808 km²
Victoria Island	217,291 km²
Ellesmere Island	196,237 km²
Newfoundland	112,300 km²
Cuba	105,007 km²
Hispaniola	75,606 km²
Banks Island	70,028 km²
Devon Island	55,247 km²
Axel Heiberg Island	43,178 km²
Melville Island	42,150 km²
Southampton Island	41,215 km²
Prince of Wales Island	33,338 km²
Vancouver Island	31,285 km²
Somerset Island	24,786 km²
Bathurst Island	16,042 km²
Prince Patrick Island	15,848 km²
King William Island	13,111 km²
Ellef Ringnes Island	11,250 km²
Bylot Island	11,067 km²
Jamaica	10,962 km²
Cape Breton Island	10,311 km²
Puerto Rico	8,644 km²
Andros Island	5,957 km²
Long Island	4,463 km²
Guadeloupe	1,433 km²

South America	
Tierra del Fuego	47,000 km²
Chiloé Island	8,395 km²
East Falkland	6,605 km²
Isabela Island	5,825 km²
Trinidad	4,820 km²
West Falkland	4,532 km²

Europe	
Great Britain	219,081 km²
Iceland	103,000 km²
Ireland	84,420 km²
Novaya Zemlya (North Island)	48,904 km²
Spitsbergen	39,044 km²
Novaya Zemlya (South Island)	33,275 km²
Sicily	25,426 km²
Sardinia	23,813 km²
North East Land	14,530 km²
Corsica	8,682 km²
Crete	8,263 km²
Sjælland	7,016 km²
Kolguyev	5,250 km²
Euboea	3,655 km²
Mallorca	3,505 km²
Vaigach Island	3,383 km²
Gotland	3,001 km²
Fyn	2,977 km²
Saaremaa	2,714 km²
Hinnøy	2,198 km²
Lésvos	1,630 km²
Rhodes	1,398 km²
Öland	1,344 km²
Lolland	1,241 km²
Hiiumaa	965 km²
Rügen	926 km²
Menorca	683 km²
Corfu	592 km²
Bornholm	588 km²
Isle of Man	572 km²
Krk	410 km²
Malta	246 km²
Fehmarn	185 km²
Île d'Oléron	175 km²

Asia	
Borneo (Kalimantan)	736,000 km²
Sumatera	425,000 km²
Honshu	227,414 km²
Celebes (Sulawesi)	180,000 km²
Java	126,650 km²
Luzon	104,700 km²
Mindanao	94,600 km²
Hokkaido	78,073 km²
Sachalin	76,400 km²
Ceylon	65,610 km²
Kyushu	36,554 km²
Taiwan	36,000 km²
Hainan	34,000 km²
Timor	33,850 km²
Shikoku	18,256 km²
Halmahera	17,800 km²
Seram	17,150 km²
Flores	14,250 km²
October Revolution Island	14,200 km²
Sumbawa	13,280 km²
Samar	13,080 km²
Negros	12,700 km²
Bangka	11,930 km²
Palawan	11,785 km²
Kotelnyy Island	11,665 km²
Panay	11,515 km²
Bolshevik Island	11,312 km²
Sumba	11,150 km²
Mindoro	9,735 km²
Buru	9,500 km²
Cyprus	9,251 km²
Komsomolets Island	9,200 km²
Wrangel Island	7,300 km²
New Siberia	6,200 km²

Australia and Oceania	
New Guinea	771,600 km
South Island (New Zealand)	151,971 km
North Island (New Zealand)	114,489 km
Tasmania	64,410 km
New Britain	36,500 km
New Caledonia	16,177 km
Viti Levu	10,429 km
Hawaii (Big Island)	10,414 km
Bougainville Island	10,050 km
New Ireland	8,600 km
Guadalcanal	6,475 km
Melville Island	5,800 km
Vanua Levu	5,556 km
Kangaroo Island	4,350 km
Espíritu Santo	3,677 km
Savai'i	1,715 km
Tahiti	1,042 km

Africa	
Madagaskar	587,041 km
Socotra	3,580 km
Réunion	2,512 km
Tenerife	2,057 km
Bioko	2,017 km
Mauritius	1,865 km
Zanzibar	1,658 km
Ngazidja	1,148 km
Santiago	991 km
Pemba	984 km
Madeira	740 km

Antarctic Region	
Kerguelen Island	5,820 km
South Georgia	3,755 km
Ross Island	2,300 km

1 km² = 0.3861 square mile

Major Lakes (* excluding islands)

orth America

ake Superior	82,103 km²
ake Huron	59,570 km²
ake Michigan	57,757 km²
reat Bear Lake	31,328 km²
reat Slave Lake	28,568 km²
ake Erie	25,667 km²
ake Winnipeg	24,387 km²
ake Ontario	19,011 km²
ake Nicaragua	8,029 km²
ake Athabasca	7,935 km²
eindeer Lake	6,651 km²
reat Salt Lake	5,905 km²
ettilling Lake	5,542 km²
ake Winnipegosis	5,374 km²
ake Manitoba	4,624 km²

Europe

Lake Ladoga	18,135 km²
Lake Onega	9,720 km²
Vänern*	5,584 km²
Lake Peipus	3,550 km²
Vättern*	1,899 km²
Saimaa	1,460 km²
Lake Seg	1,200 km²
Mälaren*	1,140 km²
Beloye Ozero	1,125 km²
Inari Lake	1,085 km²
Päijänne*	1,054 km²
Lake Ilmen	982 km²
Oulu Lake	893 km²
Balaton	592 km²
Lake Geneva	580 km²
Lake Constanze	572 km²
Hjälmaren	484 km²
Lough Neagh	388 km²
Lake Garda	370 km²
Mjøsa	368 km²
Torne Lake	322 km²
Lake Neusiedl	320 km²
Lake Neuchâtel	218 km²
Lago Maggiore	212 km²
Müritz	110 km²
Chiemsee	80 km²
Loch Ness	65 km²

Australia and Oceania

Lake Eyre	c. 9,300 km²
Lake Torrens	c. 5,700 km²
Lake Gairdner	c. 4,700 km²
Lake Taupo	606 km²

outh America

ake de Maracaibo	13,512 km²
ake Titicaca	8,288 km²
ake Poopó	2,530 km²
ago Argentino	1,415 km²
ake Nahuel Huapi	550 km²

Asia

Caspian Sea	367,000 km²
Baykal	31,499 km²
Lake Balkhash	18,428 km²
Aral Sea	c. 17,000 km²
Ysyk-Köl	6,099 km²
Koko Nor	5,000 km²
Lake Urmia	4,686 km²
Lake Tajmyr	4,560 km²
Lake Khanka	4,401 km²
Lake Van	3,713 km²
Lake Sevan	1,360 km²
Dead Sea	910 km²
Lake Biwa	672 km²

Africa

Lake Victoria	69,484 km²
Lake Tanganyika	32,893 km²
Lake Nyassa	28,878 km²
Lake Chad	10,000–25,000 km²
Lake Turkana	6,405 km²
Lake Albert	5,374 km²
Lake Mweru	4,920 km²
Lake Tana	3,630 km²
Lac Kivu	2,650 km²
Lake Edward	2,200 km²

Additional Resources
Estimated resources based on general geologic conditions as well as proven resources that cannot be recovered under current economic conditions or with existing available technology.

Agricultural Trade
Trade in food (food and live animals, beverages and tobacco, animal and vegetable oils, fats and waxes, oilseeds and oleaginous fruit), raw materials (hides, skins and furskins, crude rubber, cork and wood, pulp and waste paper, textile fibres and their wastes, crude animal and vegetable materials).

Armed Conflict
An armed conflict is defined as a contested incompatibility that concerns government and/or territory where the use of armed force between two parties, of which at least one is the government of a state, results in at least 25 battle-related deaths (PRIO 2005).

Battle-Deaths
Deaths resulting directly from violence inflicted through the use of armed force by a party to an armed conflict during contested combat. Contested combat is use of armed force by a party to an armed conflict against any person or target during which the perpetrator faces the immediate threat of lethal force being used by another party to the conflict against him/her and/or allied fighters (Lacina & Gleditsch 2005).

Biodiversity
Number and variety of living organisms; includes genetic diversity, species diversity, and ecological diversity.

Biogeographical Realm
Continental-scale biogeographic regions defined by differences in geologic and climatic history which contain distinct assemblages of plants and animals, particularly at higher taxonomic levels.

Biome (formally known as Major Habitat Types or MHTs)
Broad kinds of ecoregions that:
a) experience comparable climatic regimes;
b) have similar vegetation structure;
c) display similar spatial patterns of biodiversity;
d) contain flora and fauna with similar guild structures and life histories;
e) have similar minimum requirements and thresholds for maintaining certain biodiversity features; and
f) have similar sensitivities to human disturbance.

Birth Rate
The annual number of births per 1,000 total population. This rate is often referred to as "crude birth rate" since it does not take a population's age structure into account.

Carbon Dioxide Emissions
The emissions data are in accordance with the source categories of the IPCC Guidelines for National Greenhouse Gas Inventories. The sources considered are: Fuel combustion, energy industries, transport, industrial processes, solvent and other product use, agriculture and waste. Not included are emissions resulting from fuel sold to ships or aircraft engaged in international transport and emissions from biomass burning or emissions or removals from the land-use change and forestry sector.

Climate Diagram (by H. Walter)
Climate diagrams summarize average climatic variables by month. these diagrams by H. Walter, months are placed along the bottom hor zontal axis. Average precipitation and temperature are indicated alor the left and right axes, respectively. 20 mm of monthly precipitation (le axis) equals 10 °C average temperature (right axis). When the precipit tion curve falls below the temperature curve, the gap between the emphasizes a dry season. When the precipitation curve exceeds th temperature curve, this denotes a moist season.

Coefficient of variation
The coefficient of variation is defined as the ratio of standard deviatio to the average. It is a measure of relative variability. A high coefficie of variation means that the standard deviation is high compared to a erage. This means that precipitation in single years may differ consi erably from the long term average.

Combined Gross Enrollment Ratio [for Primary, Secondary and Tertia Schools]
The number of students enrolled in primary, secondary and tertiary le els of education, regardless of age, as a percentage of the populatio of official school age for the three levels.

Commodity Concentration of Exports
The related measure used by UNCTAD is the Hirschman index, which calculated using the shares of products in a country's exports. The max mum value of the index is 1, and its minimum (theoretical) value is zer for a country with no exports. The lower the index, the less concen trated are a country's exports.

Crisis
A crisis is a tense situation in which at least one of the parties uses vi lent force in sporadic incidents.

Current Forest
Land spanning more than 0.5 hectares with trees higher than 5 mete and a canopy cover of more than 10 percent, or trees able to reac these thresholds in situ. It does not include land that is predominant under agricultural or urban land use.

Death Rate
The annual number of deaths per 1,000 total population. This rate is o ten referred to as "crude death rate" since it does not take a popul tion's age structure into account.

Deforestation
A non-temporary change of land use from forest to other land use depletion of forest crown cover to less than 10 percent. Clear cuts (eve with stump removal) if shortly followed by reforestation for forestry pu poses are not considered deforestation.

Desertification
Land degradation in arid, semi-arid and dry sub-humid areas resultin from various factors, including climate variations and human activitie

Digital Access Index (DAI)
The index combines eight variables, covering five areas, to provide a overall country score. The areas are availability of infrastructure (fixe telephone subscribers per 100 inhabitants, mobile cellular subscribe

r 100 inhabitants), affordability of access (Internet access price as rcentage of GNI per capita), educational level (adult literacy, comned primary, secondary and tertiary school enrolment level), quality ICT services (international Internet bandwidth [bits] per capita, broadnd subscribers per 100 inhabitants), and Internet usage (Internet uss per 100 inhabitants).

oregion

ecoregion is defined as a large area of land or water that contains a ographically distinct assemblage of natural communities that
- share a large majority of their species and ecological dynamics;
- share similar environmental conditions, and;
- interact ecologically in ways that are critical for their long-term persistence.

ectoral Democracy

qualify as an electoral democracy, a state must have satisfied the lowing criteria:
- A competitive, multiparty political system.
- Universal adult suffrage for all citizens (with exceptions for restrictions that states may legitimately place on citizens as sanctions for criminal offenses).
- Regularly contested elections conducted in conditions of ballot secrecy, reasonable ballot security, and in the absence of massive voter fraud that yields results that are unrepresentative of the public will.
- Significant public access of major political parties to the electorate through the media and through generally open political campaigning.

nployment in Agriculture, Industry and Services

e agriculture, industry and services sectors are defined by the International Standard Industrial Classification (ISIC) System:
- The agricultural sector comprises activities in agriculture, hunting, forestry and fishing.
- The industry sector comprises mining and quarrying, manufacturing, construction and public utilities (electricity, gas and water).
- The services sector consists of wholesale and retail trade, restaurants and hotels, transport, storage and communications, finance, insurance, real estate and business services, and community, social and personal services.

rozone

ropean Union member states which have adopted the Euro (€) as their mmon currency.

ploitable Resources

oven resources that are recoverable under present economic conditions with existing available technology.

male and Male Earned Income

male and male earned income are crudely estimated on the basis of ta on the ratio of the female non-agricultural wage to the male nonricultural wage, the female and male shares of the economically ace population, the total female and male population and GDP per capita PP US$).

male Proportion of Labor Force

e share of the female population ages 15 and above who supply, or e available to supply, labour for the production of goods and services.

Foreign Aid

Foreign aid includes both official development assistance (ODA) and official aid (OA).

Foreign Direct Investment

Foreign direct investment is net inflow of investment to acquire a lasting management interest (10 percent or more of voting stock) in an enterprise operating in an economy other than that of the investor. It is the sum of equity capital, reinvestment of earnings, other long-term capital, and short-term capital as shown in the balance of payments.

Freedom Rating

Countries are evaluated based on a checklist of questions on political rights (electoral process, political pluralism and participation, functioning of government, discretionary political rights) and civil liberties (freedom of expression and belief, associational and organizational rights, rule of law, personal autonomy and individual rights) that are derived in large measure from the Universal Declaration of Human Rights (Freedom House 2005).

Full Schengen Member

The EU has set up a Schengen area – consisting of EU member states that have signed the Schengen agreements (1985 and 1990) on the free movement of persons and the harmonization of border controls in Europe. Member states are: Austria, Belgium, Denmark, Finland, France, Germany, Greece, Italy, Luxembourg, Netherlands, Portugal, Spain, and Sweden. In addition, non-EU states Iceland and Norway have been included in the Schengen area since 1996 (full members in 2001).

Gini Coefficient

The Gini Coefficient measures the extent to which the distribution of income (or consumption) among individuals or households within a country deviates from a perfectly equal distribution. A value of 0 represents perfect equality, and a value of 100 perfect inequality.

Government Expenditures

The sum of the final consumption expenditures of the general government, plus property income paid, plus subsidies paid, plus social benefits other than in-kind paid, plus other current transfers paid, plus net capital transfers paid, plus Gross capital formation and net acquisitions of non-produced non-financial assets, minus consumption of fixed capital.

Gross Domestic Product (GDP)

The sum of value added by all resident producers in the economy plus any product taxes (less subsidies) not included in the valuation of output. It is calculated without making deductions for depreciation of fabricated capital assets or for depletion and degradation of natural resources. Value added is the net output of an industry after adding up all outputs and subtracting intermediate inputs.

Gross National Income (GNI)

Gross national income (GNI) is the sum of value added by all resident producers plus any product taxes (less subsidies) not included in the valuation of output plus net receipts of primary income (compensation of employees and property income) from abroad.

HIPC Initiative

The HIPC (Heavily Indebted Poor Countries) Initiative currently identifies 38 countries, 32 of them in Sub-Saharan Africa, as potentially eligible to receive debt relief. Through the HIPC Initiative, nominal debt service relief of more than US$ 56 billion has been approved for 28 countries, reducing their Net Present Value of external debt by approximately two-thirds. Of these countries, 19 have reached the completion point and have been granted unconditional debt service relief of over US$ 37 billion.

Human Development Index (HDI)
A composite index measuring average achievement in the three basic dimensions of human development – a long and healthy life (life expectancy at birth), knowledge (combined gross enrollment ratio for schools) and a decent standard of living (Gross Domestic Product per capita).

Indebtedness
Present value of debt is the sum of short-term external debt plus the discounted sum of total debt service payment due on public, public guaranteed, and private non-guaranteed long-term external debt over the life of existing loans. Countries with a present value of debt service greater than 220 % of exports or 80 % of Gross National Income (GNI) were classified as severely indebted, countries that were not severely indebted but whose present value of debt service exceeded 132 % of exports or 48 % of GNI were classified as moderately indebted, and countries that did not fall into either group were classified as less indebted.

Infant Mortality Rate
The annual number of deaths of infants under age 1 per 1,000 live births.

Internally Displaced Persons
A person who, owing to well-founded fear, or fact, of being persecuted for reasons of race, ethnicity, religion, nationality, membership of a particular social group or political opinion, has moved from her/his habitual place of residence within the country of his/her nationality and is unable or, owing to such fear, is unwilling to return to it.

Life Expectancy at Birth
The average number of years a newborn infant can expect to live under current mortality levels.

Manufactured Goods
Iron and steel, chemicals, other semi-manufactures, machinery and transport equipment (power-generating machinery, other non-electrical machinery, office machines and telecommunications equipment, electrical machinery and apparatus, automotive products, other transport equipment), textiles, clothing, and other consumer goods.

Military Expenditures
The figure is calculated by multiplying the estimated defense spending in percentage terms by the Gross Domestic Product (GDP) calculated on an exchange rate basis, not Purchasing Power Parity (PPP) terms. Dollar figures for military expenditures should be treated with caution because of different price patterns and accounting methods among nations, as well as wide variations in the strength of their currencies.

Mining Trade
Trade in ores and other minerals (crude fertilizers and crude minerals, metalliferous ores and metal scrap), fuels, and non-ferrous metals.

Natural Resources
Materials that occur in nature and are essential or useful to humans, such as water, air, land, forests, fish and wildlife, topsoil, and minerals.

Net Migration Rate
The number of immigrants minus the number of emigrants over a p riod, divided by the person-years lived by the population of the recei ing country over that period. It is expressed as net number of migran per 1,000 population.

Official Aid (OA)
Official aid loans must meet the same criteria as Official Development A sistance (ODA), but are made to countries and territories in transitior

Official Development Assistance (ODA)
Official development assistance comprises grants or loans to develo ing countries and territories on the OECD/DAC list of aid recipients th are undertaken by the official sector with promotion of economic dev opment and welfare as the main objective and at concessional fina cial terms (if a loan, having a grant element of at least 25 %). Technic cooperation is included. Grants, loans and credits for military purpos are excluded.

Original Forest
The world's estimated original forest cover between the end of the la ice age and the expansion of the Europeans – c. 8,000 years ago.

Population under 15 and over 65
The total population in these ages is often considered the "depende ages".

Projected Population
Projected population based upon reasonable assumptions on the f ture course of fertility, mortality and migration. Projections are bas upon official country projections, series issued by the UN or the U Census Bureau, or Population Reference Bureau projections.

Purchasing-power parity (PPP)
The number of currency units required to buy goods equivalent to wh can be bought with one unit of the currency of the base country or wi one unit of the common currency of a group of countries. Also referr to as Purchasing Power Standard. The PPP may be calculated over of GDP, but also at levels of aggregation, like capital formation

Refugee
A person who, owing to well-founded fear, or fact, of being persecut for reasons of race, ethnicity, religion, nationality, membership of a pa ticular social group or political opinion, is outside the country of his/h nationality and is unable or, owing to such fear, is unwilling to avail hir herself of the protection of that country; or who, not having a nation ity and being outside the country of former habitual residence as a r sult of such events, is unable or, owing to such fear, is unwilling to r turn to it.

Renewable Water Resources
Renewable water resources is the sum of internal and external rene able water resources. It corresponds to the maximum theoretical amou of water available for a country on an average year on a long referen period.

Seats in National Legislature Held by Women
Refers to seats in a lower or single house or an upper house or sena where relevant.

evere Crisis
conflict is considered to be a severe crisis if violent force is repeatdly used in an organized way.

ex Ratio
umber of males per 100 females in the population.

oil Orders
oil taxonomy at the highest hierarchical level identifies 12 soil orders. he names for the orders and taxonomic soil properties relate to Greek, atin, or other root words that reveal something about the soil.

otal External Debt
otal external debt is debt owed to non-residents repayable in foreign urrency, goods, or services. It is the sum of public, publicly guaraned, and private non-guaranteed long-term debt, use of IMF credit, and hort-term debt. Short-term debt includes all debt having an original aturity of one year or less and interest in arrears on long-term debt.

nder-Five Mortality
he probability that a newborn baby will die before reaching age five, if ubject to current age-specific mortality rates.

ndernourished
FAO's estimates, food consumption is expressed in terms of dietary nergy, and people in households consuming less than a certain miniium energy requirement are considered to be undernourished. The inimum daily requirement, which takes into account the calories needd to maintain body weight while performing light activity, varies from ountry to country but is approximately 1,900 kcal per capita, dependg on age, sex and average height.

rban Population
opulation living in urban areas as defined according to the national efinition used in the most recent population census. Typically, the popution living in towns of 2,000 or more or in national or provincial capitals classified "urban".

iolent Conflict
conflict is defined as the clashing of interests on national values of ome duration and magnitude between at least two parties (organized roups, states, groups of states, organizations) that are determined to ursue their interests and win their cases. A violent conflict is a type of onflict in which violent force is used at least sporadically by at least ne conflict party (HIIK 2004).

ulnerability
efines the extent to which climate change may damage or harm a sysm. It depends not only on a system's sensitivity but also on its ability adapt to new climatic conditions.

Var
war is a type of violent conflict in which violent force is used with a ertain continuity in an organized and systematic way. The conflict pares exercise extensive measures, depending on the situation. The exnt of destruction is massive and of long duration.

Water Stress
Water stress is defined as a country's estimated volume of water used per annum expressed as a percentage of the estimated available water resource. Four levels of stress are identified:

1. Low water stress (water use of less than 10 % of the available water resource).
2. Moderate water stress (water use in the range 10 to 20 % of the available resource).
3. Medium to high water stress (water use in the range 20 to 40 % of the available resource).
4. High water stress (water use of more than 40 % of the available water resource).

Water Scarcity
When fresh water availability falls below 1,000 cubic meters per person per year, countries experience chronic water scarcity, in which the lack of water begins to hamper economic development and human health and well-being.

Water Use
Annual gross quantity of water produced and used for agricultural, industrial and domestic purposes. It does not include other in-situ uses: energy, mining, recreation, navigation, fisheries and the environment, which are typically non-consumptive uses of water. Water use = a) agricultural water use + b) domestic water use + c) industrial use.

a) Annual quantity of water used for agricultural purposes including irrigation and livestock watering. By default, livestock water use is accounted for in agricultural water use. However, some countries include it in domestic water withdrawal. Methods for computing agricultural water withdrawal vary from country to country.
b) Annual quantity of water use for domestic purposes. It is usually computed as the total amount of water supplied by public distribution networks, and usually includes the withdrawal by those industries connected to public networks.
c) Annual quantity of water use by self-supplied industries not connected to any distribution network.

Finding a name

The index contains all names that appear in the maps of the atlas

Names are arranged alphabetically

Letters with diacritical marks are alphabetized like regular letters. The ligatures æ and œ are treated as "ae" and "oe", respectively. The special letter ð is regarded as dh, þ as th, ə as e, and the German ß as ss.

Names that are abbreviated in the maps of the atlas are always spelled out in the index:

Cheyenne [= Ch.]

Additions (in parentheses) show local names. Local names are also listed separately and include a reference to the primary name.

Venice (Venezia)
Venezia → Venice

Finding the location of a name

The numbers and letters after each place name indicate the page number of the map, the letter of the reference grid column, and the number of the reference grid row. The place is located at the intersection of the row and column on the page listed. However, on two-page map spreads, the index only lists the number of the left page, even if the place is located on the right page. If there is more than one map on a page, the page number is followed by a Roman numeral that refers to the specific map.

Center Hill Lake	**100** B 1/2
Port of Spain	**114** II B 3
Walburg, Saint	**84** F 2

Additional information

- Thematic entries in the index are marked with special symbols. Explanations for these symbols are included at the bottom of the index pages. For example, a mountain peak is listed as follows:

Adelunga ▲	**148** P 10

- Entries with identical names include additional geographic information in brackets:

Aberdeen *[U.K.]*
Aberdeen *[U.S., Maryland]*
Aberdeen *[U.S., Mississippi]*
Aberdeen *[U.S., South Dakota]*
Aberdeen *[U.S., Washington]*

Long Island *[Bahamas]*
Long Island *[Canada]*
Long Island *[Papua New Guinea]*
Long Island *[U.S.]*

A

Aachen 128 C 3
Aalen 128 D 3
Äänekoski 126 J 2
Aarau 128 C 4
Aare ∽ 128 C 4
Aasiaat 78 de 5
Aba 176 J 7
Abā ad-Dūd 152 E 4
Ābādān 152 F 3
Ābādeh 152 G 3
Abadla → ʿAbadlah
ʿAbadlah 176 G 2
Abaetetuba 112 JK 4
Abakaliki 176 J 7
Abakan 148 ST 8
Abana 134 D 2/3
Abancay 112 E 6
Abashiri 154 ST 3
Abasolo 102 DE 3
Abau 156 O 10
Abaza 148 ST 8
Abbeville *[France]* 131 C 2
Abbeville *[U.S., Louisiana]* 96 E 3
Abbeville *[U.S., South Carolina]* 100 C 2
Abbeyfeale 124 AB 4
Abbotsford 84 C 3
Ābdānān 152 E 2
Abdulino 136 K 3
Abéché 176 LM 6
Abengourou 176 FG 7
Åbenrå 126 D 4
Abeokuta 176 H 7
Aberdeen *[U.K.]* 124 D 2
Aberdeen *[U.S., Maryland]* 98 E 3
Aberdeen *[U.S., Mississippi]* 96 F 2
Aberdeen *[U.S., South Dakota]* 94 D 1
Aberdeen *[U.S., Washington]* 90 B 2
Aberystwyth 124 C 4
Abez' 138 P 2
Abhā 150 E 7
Abhar 152 F 1
Abidjan 176 FG 7
Abilene *[U.S., Kansas]* 94 D 3
Abilene *[U.S., Texas]* 96 D 2
Abingdon 98 D 3
Abinsk 134 E 2
Abitibi ∽ 86 G 3
Abitibi, Lake ◡ 86 GH 3
Abitibi, Little ∽ 86 G 3
Abkhaz ⚇ 121 KL 5
Abkhazia ⛉ 134 F 2
Abnūb 152 A 4
Åbo/Turku 126 H 2
Aboisso 176 G 7
Abomey 176 H 7
Abrantes 130 B 2
Abruzzi ⛉ 132 C 2
Absaroka Range ▲▲ 90 E 2/3
Abū Ajram 152 C 3
Abū ʿAlī ⌓ 152 F 4
Abū al-Khaṣīb 152 EF 3
Abu Dhabi (Abū Ẓaby) 150 G 6
Abū Durbah 152 B 3
Abū Ḥamad 176 OP 5
Abu Hamed → Abū Ḥamad
Abuja 176 J 7
Abū Kamāl 152 D 2
Abū Qīr 152 A 3
Abū Qurqās 152 A 4
Abū Rudays 152 B 3
Abū Shahrayn (Eridu) ∴ 152 E 3
Abū Ṣukhayr 152 E 3
Abū Tīj 152 A 4
Abū Ẓaby → Abu Dhabi 150 G 6
Abū Zanīmah 152 B 3
Abyaḍ, Ra's al-)≋ 132 B 4
Ābyek 152 F 1
Abymes, Les 115 II B 1
Acadia National Park ⌂ 98 GH 1/2
Açailândia 112 K 4
Acapulco 102 E 5
Acarigua 112 EF 2
Accra 176 GH 7/8
Acharia ⛉ 134 FG 3
Acharnés 133 C 4
Aché ⚇ → Guayaki [= Gu.] 109 H 7
Achelóos ∽ 133 C 3
Achikulak 134 G 2
Achill Island ⌓ 124 A 4
Achinese ⚇ 145 N 9
Achinsk 148 ST 7
Achisu 134 HJ 2
Achit 136 M 2
Acholi ⚇ 173 G 5
Achuyevo 134 E 1
Acireale 132 D 4
Acklins Island ⌓ 102 KL 4
Acoma Pueblo ⧗ 92 F 3
Aconcagua ▲ 114 E 4
A Coruña 130 B 1
Acqui Terme 132 A 2
Acre ⛉ 112 EF 5/6
Acuña 96 C 3
Ada *[U.S., Minnesota]* 94 D 1
Ada *[U.S., Oklahoma]* 96 D 2
Adair, Bahía de ≋) 92 D 4
Adamawa Highlands ▲▲ 176 K 7
Adams 94 F 2
Adams, Mount ▲ 90 B 2
Adams Lake ◡ 84 D 3
Adamstown 160 QR 6
ʿAdan → Aden 150 EF 8
Adana 134 D 4
Adapazarı 134 C 3
Adare, Cape)≋ 181 I BC 20/19
Ad-Dahmānī 132 AB 5
Ad-Dahnā' ⌳ 150 EF 5
Ad-Dākhla 176 D 4
Ad-Damāzīn 176 OP 6
Ad-Dāmir 176 O 5
Ad-Dammām 152 F 4
Ad-Dār al-Bayḍā' → Casablanca 176 EF 2
Ad-Dawḥah → Doha 150 G 5
ad-Dayr, Jabal ▲ 176 O 6
Ad-Dibdibah ⌳ 152 E 3
Addis Ababa (Ādīs Ābeba) 176 P 6/7
Ad-Dīwānīyah 152 E 2/3
ad-Dubbāgh, Jabal ▲ 152 BC 4
Ad-Dujayl 152 DE 2
ad-Dukhān, Jabal ▲ 152 F 4
ad-Durūz, Jabal ▲ 152 C 2
Ad-Duwaym 176 O 6
Adel 100 C 3
Adelaide 166 HJ 7
Adelaide Island ⌓ 181 I C 32/31
Adélie Land ⛉ 181 II B 17/16
Adelunga ▲ 148 P 10
Aden (ʿAdan) 150 EF 8
Aden, Gulf of ≋) 150 FG 8
Adi ⌓ 156 I 8
Adícora 115 I A 2
Adige ∽ 132 B 1
Adilcevaz 134 G 4
Adīrī 176 K 3
Adirondack Mountains ▲▲ 98 F 1/2
Ādīs Ābeba → Addis Ababa 176 P 6/7
Ādī Ugrī 176 P 6
Adıyaman 134 E 4
Adjud 128 K 4
Admiralty Islands ⌓ 156 O 8
Ado-Ekiti 176 J 7
Adolfo López Mateos 96 B 3
Adour ∽ 131 B 4
Adra 130 C 3
Adrano 132 C 4
Adrār 176 GH 3
Adrar des Ifôghas ▲▲ 176 H 5
Adrian 98 C 2
Adriatic Sea ≋ 132 CD 2/3
Ādwa 176 P 6
Adycha ∽ 148 c 5
Adygea ⛉ 134 F 2
Adz'vavom 138 O 2
Aegean Islands ⌓ 123 F 4
Aegean Sea ≋ 133 D 3/4
A Estrada 130 B 1
Aeta ⚇ 145 Q 8
Afadjato, Mount ▲ 176 GH 7
ʿAfak 152 E 2
Afanas'yevo 138 MN 5
Affrique, Saint- 131 CD 4
Afghanistan ⛊ 150 JK 4/3
Afgooye 176 Q 8
Afognak Island ⌓ 76 KL 7
Africa ⊛ 4 JL 5
Africa, Sub-Saharan ⊛ 51 JK 7
African Plate ⤼ 14 DE 5/6
Afrikanda 138 EF 2
Afrikaners ⚇ 173 EF 9
ʿAfrīn 152 C 1
Afro-Caribbeans ⚇ 109 G 3
Afrotropic ⊛ 26 JM 6
Afşin 134 E 4
Afyon 134 C 4
Agadèz 176 J 5
Agadir (Aghādīr) 176 EF 2
Agalega Islands ⌓ 178 Q 5
Agaña (Hagåtña) 101 II
Agapovka 136 M 3
Agartala 150 P 6
Agat 101 II
Agata di Militello, Sant' 132 C 4
Agathe-des-Monts, Sainte- 88 B 3
Agboville 176 G 7
Ağcabədi 134 H 3
Ağdam 134 H 3
Ağdaş 134 H 3
Agen 131 C 4
Aghādīr → Agadir 176 EF 2
Āghā Jārī 152 F 3
Aghwāt, Al- 176 H 2
Aginskoye 148 X 8
Ágios Efstrátios ⌓ 133 D 3
Ágios Ilías ▲ 133 C 4
Ágios Kírykos 133 D 4
Ágios Nikólaos 133 D 5
Agou, Mont ▲ 176 GH 7
Agra 150 M 5
Agreda 130 D 2
Ağri 134 G 3
Agrigento 132 C 4
Agrihan ⌓ 156 O 4
Agrínio 133 C 4
Agropoli 132 C 3
Agryz 136 K 2
Ağsu 134 J 3
Agua Caliente Indian Reservation ⧗ 92 C 3
Aguadilla 101 VIII
Agualeguas 96 D 4
Agualva-Cacém 130 A 2/3
Aguanish ∽ 88 E 2
Agua Prieta 92 E 4
Aguascalientes 102 E 4
Águeda 130 B 2
Aguiar 130 B 2
Aguijan ⌓ 101 III
Aguilar 94 B 3
Aguilas 130 D 3
Aguilla Island ⌓ 115 II B 1
Agulha 107 K 5
Agulhas, Cape)≋ 178 HJ 9/10
Agulhas Basin ⩫ 13 E 6/7
Agulhas Current ⥲ 4 L 7
Agulhas Plateau ⩫ 13 EF 7
Agustin, Cape San)≋ 156 KL 6
Ahaggar ▲▲ 176 HJ 4
Ahar 134 H 4
Ahas, Jabal ▲ 152 C 2
Ahaus 128 C 2
Ahlat 134 G 4
Ahlbeck 128 E 2
Ahlen 128 C 2
Ahmadabad 150 L 6
Aḥmadī, Al- 152 E 3
Ahmadnagar 150 LM 7
Ahoskie 100 D 1
Ahtahkakoop Indian Reserve ⧗ 84 G 2
Ahumada 96 B 3
Ahvāz 152 F 3
Aḥwār 150 F 8
Aigen 128 E 3
Aígina ⌓ 133 C 4
Aígio 133 C 4
Aiken 100 C 2
Aimaq ⚇ 145 K 6
Ain ∽ 131 D 3
ʿAin al-ʿArab 152 C 1
Ainaži 126 HJ 3

⛊ Independent country
◐ Dependent territory
⛉ Federal state, province, territory
⚇ People, ethnic group, tribe
⧗ Indian reservation/reserve
⌂ National Park
⊓ Industrial region
∴ Historical site
⛺ Research station
⊛ Continent, realm
⌳ Region, peninsula
▲▲ Mountain range, mountains
▲ Peak
)(Pass
* Ice shelf, glacier

River, canal
Waterfall
Lake, lakes, reservoir
Swamp
Salt flat
Sea
Strait
Bay, gulf
Cape
Island, islands
Ocean current
Ocean floor landforms
Tectonic feature
Atmospheric phenomena
Time zone
Geographical grid

Alexandria (Al-Iskandarīyah) *[Egypt]* **152** A 3
Alexandroúpoli **133** D 3
Alexandrów Kujawski **128** G 2
Alexis ∽ **88** F 1
Aleysk **148** R 8
Al-Fahs **132** B 4
Al-Fallūjah **152** DE 2
Alfambra **130** D 2
Alfaro **130** D 1
Al-Farwānīyah **152** E 3
Al-Fāshir **176** N 6
Al-Fashn **152** A 3
Al-Fāw **152** F 3
Al-Fayyūm **152** A 3
Al-Fuḥayḥīl **152** F 3
Al-Fūlah **176** N 6
Alfures ⚇ **164** EF 8
Algarve ⊾ **130** B 3
Algeciras **130** C 3
Algeria ■ **176** FJ 3
Algha **136** LM 4
Alghabas **136** K 4
al-Ghadaf, Wādī ∽ **152** D 2
Al-Ghayḍah **150** G 7
Al-Ghazzālah **152** D 4
Alghero **132** A 3
Al-Ghulīʿah **176** H 2
Al-Ghurdaqah → Hurghada **152** B 4
Algiers (Al-Jazāʾir) **176** H 1
Algona **94** E 2
Algonkins ⚇ **73** JM 4-5
Al-Habbānīyah **152** D 2
Al-Ḥaḍar **152** D 2
al-Ḥadd, Raʾs)≋ **150** J 6
Al-Ḥamād ⊾ **152** CD 2/3
Al-Hamadah al-Ḥamrāʾ ⊾ **169** E 2/3
Al-Ḥammāmāt **132** B 4
Al-Ḥamzah **152** E 3
Al-Haniyah ⊾ **152** E 3
Al-Ḥaql **152** B 3
Al-Ḥasāʾ ⊾ **152** F 4
Al-Ḥasakah **152** D 1
Al-Hāshimīyah **152** E 2
Al-Hawīyah **150** E 6
Al-Hawjāʾ **152** C 3
Al-Ḥayy **152** E 2
Al-Ḥijāz ⊾ **150** D 5/6
Al-Ḥillah **152** E 2
Al-Hindīyah **152** DE 2
Al-Hoceima → Al-Husaymah
Al-Ḥudaydah **150** E 8
Al-Hufūf **150** F 5/6
Al-Husaymah **176** G 1
ʿAlīābād *[Iran, Kordestān]* **152** E 2
ʿAlīābād *[Iran, Qom]* **152** F 2
Aliağa **134** B 4
Aliákmonas ∽ **133** C 3
ʿAlī al-Gharbī **152** E 2
ʿAlī ash-Sharqī **152** E 2
Alicante **130** D 3
Alice **96** D 4
Alice Springs **166** GH 5
Aligarh **150** M 5
Alīgūdarz **152** F 2
Alījūq, Kūh-e ▲ **152** FG 3
Alingsås **126** E 3
Aliquippa **98** DE 2
Ali Sabieh **176** Q 6
Al-Iskandarīyah → Alexandria **152** A 3
Al-Ismāʿīlīyah **152** AB 3
Alix **84** E 2
Al-Jafr **152** C 3
Al-Jaghbūb **176** M 3
Al-Jahrāʾ **152** E 3
Al-Jawf **176** M 4
Al-Jazāʾir → Algiers **176** H 1
Aljezur **130** AB 3
Al-Jilfah → Djelfa **176** H 1/2
Al-Jīzah → Giza **152** A 3
Al-Jubayl **152** F 4
Al-Jubb **152** D 4
Al-Junaynah **176** M 6
Al-Jurayd ⌓ **152** F 4
Aljustrel **130** B 3
Al-Kāf **132** A 4
Al-Kahfah **152** D 4
Alkali Lake, Lower ⌣ **92** BC 1
Alkali Lake, Middle ⌣ **92** BC 1
Alkali Lake, Upper ⌣ **92** BC 1
Alkali Lake Indian Reserve ⧖ **84** C 3
Al-Karak **152** B 3
Al-Khalīl → Hebron **152** B 3
Al-Khāliṣ **152** E 2
Al-Khārijah **176** NO 3
Al-Kharj **150** F 6
Al-Kharṭūm → Khartoum **176** NO 5/6
Al-Kharṭūm Baḥrī → Khartoum North **176** OP 5
Al-Khiḍr **152** E 3
al-Khirr, Wādī ∽ **152** D 3
Al-Khubar **152** F 4
Al-Khums **176** KL 2
Alkmaar **128** B 2
Al-Kūfa **152** DE 2
Al-Kūt **152** E 2
Al-Kuwayt → Kuwait **152** F 3
Al-Lādhiqīyah → Latakia **152** B 2
Allahabad **150** MN 5
Allakh-Yunʾ **148** C 6
Allatoona Lake ⌣ **100** B 2
al-Lauz, Jabal ▲ **152** B 3
Allegany Indian Reservation ⧖ **98** E 2
Allegheny ∽ **98** E 2
Allegheny Mountains ▲▲ **80** KL 4
Allegheny Plateau ▲▲ **98** DF 3/2
Allendale **100** C 2
Allende **96** C 3
Allentown **98** EF 2
Aller ∽ **128** D 2
Alliance *[U.S., Nebraska]* **94** C 2
Alliance *[U.S., Ohio]* **98** D 2
Allier ∽ **131** D 3/4
Allison [= 2] ⊃ **75** J 7
Alliston **98** E 1
Alloa **124** C 3
Alma *[Canada]* **88** C 2
Alma *[U.S., Michigan]* **98** C 2
Alma *[U.S., Nebraska]* **94** D 2
Almada **130** A 3
Al-Madāʾin **152** E 2
Almadén **130** C 3
Al-Madīnah → Medina **150** DE 6
Al-Mafraq **152** C 2
Al-Maḥallah al-Kubrā **152** A 3
Al-Mahdīyah **176** K 1
Al-Maḥmūdīyah **152** DE 2
Al-Manāmah → Manama **152** F 4
Al-Manāqil **176** O 6
Almannagjá Canyon ⊾ **116** ①
Almanor, Lake ⌣ **92** B 1
Almansa **130** D 3
Al-Manshāh **152** AB 4
Al-Manṣūrah **152** AB 3
Almarcha, La **130** D 2
Al-Mardh **152** D 2
Al-Marj **176** M 2
Almas, Pico, das ▲ **112** L 6
Al-Mashrafah **152** C 1
Al-Maṭariyah **152** AB 3
Almaty **148** Q 10
Al-Mawṣil → Mosul **152** D 1
Al-Mayādīn **152** CD 2
Al-Maymunah **152** E 3
Almazán **130** D 2
Almeirim **112** J 4
Almelo **128** C 2
Almenara **112** L 7
Almendra, Lake ⌣ **130** BC 2
Almendralejo **130** BC 3
Almere **128** B 2
Almería **130** D 3
Alʼmetʼyevsk **136** K 2
Älmhult **126** E 4
Al-Mijlad **176** N 6
al-Milk, Wādī ∽ **176** N 5
Al-Minyā **152** A 3
Al-Miqdādīyah **152** E 2
Al-Mishʾāb **152** F 3
al-Miyāh, Wādī ∽ **152** C 2
Almodôvar **130** B 3
Almonte **130** B 3
Al-Mubarraz **150** F 5
Al-Mudawwarah **152** BC 3
Al-Muḥarraq **152** F 4
Al-Mukallā **150** FG 8
Al-Mukhā **150** E 8
Almuñecar **130** C 3
Al-Musayyib **152** DE 2
Almyrós **133** C 3
Alnashi **136** K 2
Alnwick **124** D 3
Alofi **166** T 4
Alofi ⌓ **166** R 3
Aloja **126** J 3
Alonsa **86** C 3
Alor ⌓ **156** JK 9
Álora **130** C 3
Alor Setar **156** E 6
Alotau **156** OP 10
Alpena **98** D 1
Alpha [= 13] ⊃ **75** L-M 7-8
Alpha Cordillera ⏠ **12** A 33/3
Alpine **96** C 3
Alps ▲▲ **117** GH 5
Alps, Australian ▲▲ **166** KL 8
Alps, Bavarian ▲▲ **128** DE 4
Alps, Bergamo ▲▲ **132** B 1
Alps, Bernese ▲▲ **128** C 4
Alps, Cottian ▲▲ **131** E 4
Alps, Dinaric ▲▲ **132** CD 1/2
Alps, Julian ▲▲ **132** C 1
Alps, Maritime ▲▲ **131** E 4
Alps, Rhaetian ▲▲ **128** D 4
Alps, Southern ▲▲ **166** OP 9
Alps, Transylvanian ▲▲ **133** CD 1/2
Al-Qaḍārif **176** OP 6
Al-Qāhirah → Cairo **152** A 3
Al-Qalʿah **132** A 4
Al-Qalībah **152** C 3
Al-Qāmishlī **152** D 1
Al-Qanṭarah **152** AB 3
Al-Qaṣr *[Egypt]* **176** N 3
Al-Qaṣr *[Saudi Arabia]* **152** D 4
Al-Qaṣr al-Kabīr **176** F 2/1
Al-Qaṣrayn **176** JK 1/2
Al-Qaṭīf **152** F 4
Al-Qatrūn **176** KL 4
Al-Qayrawān **176** J 1
Al-Qayṣūmah **152** E 3
Al-Qiniṭrah → Kénitra **176** EF 2
Al-Qiṭrānah **152** BC 3
Al-Quds → Jerusalem **152** BC 3
Al-Qunayṭirah **152** BC 2
Al-Qurayyāt **152** C 3
Al-Qurnah **152** E 3
Al-Quṣayr *[Egypt]* **176** OP 3
Al-Quṣayr *[Syria]* **152** C 2
Al-Qūṣīyah **152** A 4
Al-Quṭayfah **152** C 2
Al-Quwārah **152** D 4
Als ⌓ **126** D 4
Alsace ⊾ **131** E 3/2
Alsask **84** F 3
Alsasua **130** D 1
Alsfeld **128** D 3
Alta **125** E 2
Altafjorden ≋) **125** E 2
Altai □ → Altay
Altai Mountains ▲▲ → Altay Mountains
Altamaha ∽ **100** C 3
Altamira **112** J 4
Altamura **132** D 3
Altavista **98** E 3
Altay *[China]* **154** G 2
Altay *[Mongolia]* **154** J 2
Altay □ **148** S 8
Altayans ⚇ **145** M 4
Altay Mountains ▲▲ **148** RU 8/9
Altdorf **128** C 4
Altenburg **128** E 2/3
Altin Köprü **152** E 2
Altıntaş **134** C 3
Altiplano ⊾ **112** F 7/8
Alto, El **112** F 7
Alto Adige/South Tyrol, Trentino- □ **132** BC 1
Alto Araguaia **112** J 7
Alton **94** F 3
Altoona **98** E 2
Alto Parnaíba **112** KL 5
Altun Shan ▲▲ **154** GH 4
Alturas **92** B 1
Altus **96** D 2

■ Independent country
◧ Dependent territory
□ Federal state, province, territory
⚇ People, ethnic group, tribe
⧖ Indian reservation/reserve
⌂ National Park
⊓ Industrial region
∴ Historical site
⊿ Research station
⊛ Continent, realm
⊾ Region, peninsula
▲▲ Mountain range, mountains
▲ Peak
)(Pass
* Ice shelf, glacier

l-ʿUbaydī 152 D 2
l-Ubayyiḍ → El-Obeid 176 NO 6
lūksne 126 JK 3
l-ʿUlā 152 C 4
lupka 134 D 2
l-Uqṣur → Luxor 176 O 3
lushta 134 D 2
lutom Island 101 II
l-ʿUwaynāt, Jabal 176 N 4
l-ʿUwayqīlah 152 D 3
lva 96 D 1
lvdalen 126 E 2
lvernia, Mount 102 K 4
lvin 96 E 3
lvsbyn 125 DE 4
l-Wādī 176 J 2
l-Wafrah 152 EF 3
l-Wajh 150 D 5
l-Wakrah 150 G 6/5
l-Wannān 152 EF 4
l-Warīʿah 152 E 4
l-Winzah 132 A 5
lytus 126 H 4
lzira 130 D 2
Amādīyah, Al- 152 D 1
madora 130 A 3
mahai 156 K 8
mahuaca [= Am.] 109 F 5/6
mål 126 E 3
maliáda 133 C 4
mamapare 156 M 9
mami 154 PQ 6
mand-Mont-Rond, Saint- 131 CD 3
mantea 132 D 3
mapá 112 J 3
mapá 112 J 3
Amārah, Al- 152 E 3
margosa 92 C 3
margosa Range 92 C 2/3
marillo 96 C 2
masya 134 DE 3
mazon 112 E 4
mazonas 112 EH 5
mbarchik 148 h 5
mbarnyy 138 F 3
mbato 112 D 4
mbatondrazaka 178 OP 6
mbérieu 131 D 3
mbert 131 D 3
mbo 173 E 7
mbon 156 K 8
mbonese 145 Q 10
mbovombe 178 NO 8/7
mbrolauri 134 G 2
mbrym 166 O 4
mderma 148 N 5
merasian Basin 12 BA 35/3
merican Falls 90 D 3
merican Falls Reservoir 90 D 3
merican Fork 92 E 1
mericans 73 GK 6/CD 3
merican Samoa 160 MN 5
merican Samoa *[Detail map]* 101 VII
merican Samoa, National Park of 101 VII
mericus 100 BC 2

Amersfoort 128 B 2
Amery Ice Shelf 181 I BC 9/10
Ames 94 E 2
Amfilochía 133 BC 4
Amfípoli 133 CD 3
Ámfissa 133 C 4
Amga 148 b 6
Amga 148 ab 6
Amhara 173 G 4
Amherst 88 DE 3
Amiens 131 C 2
ʿĀmij, Wādī 152 D 2
Amik Ovasi 134 DE 4
Amindivi Islands 150 L 8
Amirante Islands 178 P 4/3
Amisk Lake 86 B 2
Amistad Reservoir 96 C 3
Amman (ʿAmmān) 152 BC 3
Āmol 152 G 1
Amora 130 B 3
Amorgós 133 D 4
Amos 88 A 2
Amour, Côte d' 123 C 3
Amparafaravola 178 O 6
Amposta 130 E 2
Amqui 88 D 2
Amravati 150 M 6
Amritsar 150 M 4
Amsterdam *[Netherlands]* 128 B 2
Amsterdam *[U.S.]* 98 F 2
Amsterdam 4 N 7
Amstetten 128 EF 3
Am-Timan 176 M 6
Amūdā 152 D 1
Amu Darya 148 N 10/11
Amund Ringnes Island 76 VW 3
Amundsen Gulf 76 PR 4/5
Amundsen-Scott 181 I A 34/33
Amundsen Sea 181 I B 28/27
Amur 148 a 8
Amursk 148 C 8/9
Amvrosiyivka 136 EF 5
Ana, Santa *[Bolivia]* 112 F 6
Ana, Santa *[El Salvador]* 102 H 6
Ana, Santa *[Guam]* 101 II
Ana, Santa *[U.S.]* 92 C 3
Anabar 148 X 4
Anacapa Islands 92 C 3
Anaconda 90 D 2
Anacortes 90 B 1
Anadarko 96 D 2
Anadyr' 148 L 6
Anadyr' 148 kj 5
Anadyr', Gulf of 148 m 6
Anáfi 133 D 4
ʿĀnah 152 D 2
Anaheim 92 C 3
Anáhuac *[Mexico, Chihuahua]* 96 B 3
Anáhuac *[Mexico, Nuevo León]* 96 C 4
Anai Mudi 150 M 8
Anambas Islands 156 F 7
Anamur 134 CD 4
Anamur, Cape 134 CD 5/4
Ananindeua 112 K 4
Anan'yiv 136 BC 5

Anapa 134 E 2
Anápolis 112 JK 7
Anatahan 156 O 4
Anatolia 134 BG 3/4
Anatom 166 OP 5
Añatuya 114 G 3
Ancenis 131 B 3
Anchorage 78 L 6
Anchorage 101 V
Ancohuma 112 F 7
Ancona 132 C 2
Ancud 114 E 7
Anda 154 P 2
Åndalsnes 126 C 2
Andalusia 100 B 3
Andalusia 130 BD 3
Andalusia 117 F 6
Andaman and Nicobar Islands 150 OP 9
Andamanese 145 N 8
Andaman Islands 150 P 8
Andaman Sea 150 Q 8/9
Andenes 125 C 2
Andermatt 128 CD 4
Anderson *[U.S., Indiana]* 98 C 2
Anderson *[U.S., South Carolina]* 100 C 2
Anderson Air Force Base 101 II
Andes 105 FG 5/8
Andes, High 51 FG 6
Andeyevka 136 K 3
Andfjorden 125 C 3/2
Andhra Pradesh 150 MN 8/7
Andijon 148 P 10
Andīmeshk 152 EF 2
Andırın 134 DE 4
Andomskiy Pogost 138 G 4
Andorra 130 D 2
Andorra 130 E 1
Andorra la Vella 130 E 1
Andøya 125 C 3/2
Andreanof Islands 76 EF 8
Andreapol' 136 C 2
Andreas, Cape 152 B 2
Andreas Fault, San 14 K 4
Andrés, San 102 J 6
Andrés Island, San 102 J 6
Andres Mountains, San 92 F 3
Andrews 96 C 2
Andrew Sound, Saint 100 C 3
Andria 132 D 3
Ándros 133 D 4
Ándros 133 D 4
Andros Island 102 K 4
Andrushivka 128 K 3
Andrychów 128 G 3
Andselv 125 D 2/3
Andújar 130 C 3
Anegada 101 VIII
Anegada Passage 115 II B 1
Aneto 130 E 1
Angamos, Punta 114 E 2
Angara 148 U 7
Angara, Upper 148 X 7
Angarsk 148 VW 8
Ånge 126 F 2

Ángel de la Guarda, Isla 102 C 2/3
Angeles 156 HJ 4
Angeles, Los *[Chile]* 114 E 5
Angeles, Los *[U.S.]* 92 C 3
Ängelholm 126 E 4
Angelo, San 96 CD 3
Ângelo, Santo 114 J 3
Angerman 126 F 1
Ångermanland 126 FG 1
Angermünde 128 E 2
Angers 131 B 3
Ängesön 126 H 1
Angkor 156 E 5
Anglesey 124 C 4
Angleton 96 E 3
Angliers 88 A 3
Anglo America 51 BD 4/3
Angoche 178 MN 6
Angol 114 E 5
Angola 178 GJ 5
Angola Basin 10 J 6
Angoulême 131 C 3
Angra do Heroísmo 130 C 5
Angren 148 P 10
Anguilla 115 II B 1
Anhui 154 N 5
Animas, Las 94 C 3
Animas Peak 92 E 4
Anina 133 C 1
Ankang 154 L 5
Ankara 134 CD 3
Ankeny 94 E 2
Anklam 128 E 2
Ånn 126 E 1
Anna 136 F 3
Annaba → ʿAnnābah
ʿAnnābah 132 A 4
An-Nabak 152 C 2
An-Nabatīyat at-Taḥtā 152 B 2
An-Nafūd 152 CD 3
An-Najaf 152 DE 2/3
An-Nakhl 152 B 3
An-Naʿmah 176 F 5
Anna Maria Key 100 C 4
Annam Plateau 156 EF 4/5
Annapolis 98 E 3
Ann Arbor 98 D 2
Anna Regina 112 H 2
An-Nāṣirīyah 152 E 3
Annecy 131 DE 3
Anne-de-Portneuf, Sainte- 88 C 2
Anne-des-Chênes, Sainte- 86 C 3
Anne-des-Monts, Sainte- 88 D 2
Annemasse 131 E 3
Annenskiy Most 138 G 4
Anniston 100 B 2
Annonay 131 D 3
Annot 131 E 4
An-Nuʿayrīyah 152 EF 4
An-Nuhūd 176 N 6
An-Nukhayb 152 D 2
An-Nuʿmānīyah 152 E 2
An-Nuwayṣīb 152 F 3
Anqing 154 N 5
Ansbach 128 D 3

River, canal
Waterfall
Lake, lakes, reservoir
Swamp
Salt flat
Sea
Strait
Bay, gulf
Cape
Island, islands
Ocean current
Ocean floor landforms
Tectonic feature
Atmospheric phenomena
Time zone
Geographical grid

Anse Indian Reservation, L' **98** B 1
Anshan **154** O 3
Anshun **154** L 6
Antakya **134** DE 4
Antalaha **178** P 5
Antalya **134** C 4
Antalya, Gulf of **134** C 4
Antananarivo **178** NO 6
Antanifotsy **178** O 6
Antão, Santo **176** BC 5
Antarctandes **13** CB 34
Antarctic **26** JN 9
Antarctica **181** I AB 36/15
Antarctic Circle **4** H 9
Antarctic Circumpolar Current (West Wind Drift) **6** B-S 8
Antarctic Peninsula **181** I CB 32
Antarctic Plate **14** DK 9/10
Antarctis **30** JR 9/8
Antequera **130** C 3
Anthony **92** F 3
Anthony, Saint **88** G 2
Anti Atlas **176** F 3/2
Anticosti, Île d' **88** E 2
Antigo **94** F 1
Antigonish **88** E 3
Antigua **115** II B 1
Antigua and Barbuda **115** II B 1
Antikýthira **133** C 5
Anti Lebanon **152** C 2
Antilles, Greater **102** JM 4/5
Antilles, Lesser **102** MN 5/6
Antioco, Sant' **132** A 3/4
Antipina **138** NO 4
Antipodes Islands **166** QR 10
Antírrio **133** C 4
Antlers **96** E 2
Antofagasta **114** E 2
Anton, Sankt **128** D 4
Antoni de Portmany, San **130** E 2/3
Antonio, Cape San **102** HJ 4
Antonio, San *[Chile]* **114** E 4
Antonio, San *[Northern Mariana Is.]* **101** III
Antonio, San *[U.S.]* **96** D 3
Antonio, San *[Venezuela]* **115** II B 3
Antonio, San **96** D 3
António, Santo **176** J 8
Antonio de los Cobres, San **114** F 2
Antonito **94** B 3
Antratsyt **136** EF 4/5
Antrodoco **132** C 2
Antropovo **138** J 5
Antsirabe **178** O 6
Antsirañana **178** OP 5
Antsla **126** J 3
Antwerp (Antwerpen) **131** D 1
Anuak **173** G 5
Anuradhapura **150** N 9
Anuta **166** O 3
Anxi **154** J 3
Anyama **176** G 7
Anyang **154** MN 4
Anykščiai **126** J 4
Anyuy, Great **148** h 5
Anyuy, Little **148** hj 5
Anyuy Range **148** hj 5
Anzhero-Sudzhensk **148** ST 7
Anzio **132** C 3
Aomen → Macau **154** M 7
Aomori **154** RS 3
Aosta/Aoste **132** A 1
Apaches **73** GH 6
Apalachee Bay **100** BC 3
Apalachicola **100** B 3
Apalachicola **100** B 3
Aparecida de Goiânia **112** K 7
Apastovo **136** J 2
Apatin **133** B 1
Apatity **138** F 2
Apatzingán **102** E 5
Ape **126** JK 3
Apeldoorn **128** C 2
Apennines **132** BD 2/3
Apia **166** S 3
Apo, Mount ▲ **156** K 6
Apodaca **96** CD 4
Apolo **112** F 6
Apopka, Lake **100** C 3
Apostle Islands **94** F 1
Apostolove **136** D 5
Appalachian Mountains **80** KO 5/2
Appenzell **128** D 4
Appleby **124** D 3
Appleton **94** FG 1
Apple Valley **92** C 3
Appomattox **98** E 3
Apra Harbor **101** II
Apra Heights **101** II
Aprilia **132** C 3
Apsheronsk **134** F 2
Apucarana **114** JK 2
Apulia **132** D 3
Apulia **123** E 3
Apure **112** F 2
Apuriña **109** G 5
Apuseni, Munţii **128** H 4
Aqaba (Al-ʿAqabah) **152** B 3
Aqaba, Gulf of **152** B 3
Aqjawajat **176** E 5
Aqqystaū **136** J 5
ʿAqrah **152** D 1
Aqsay **136** K 3
Aqshataū **136** L 4
Aqsorang bīigi ▲ **148** PQ 9
Aqsū **148** P 8
Aqtaū **134** JK 2
Aqtöbe **136** LM 4
Aqua/Sokhumi **134** F 2
Aquidauana **112** H 8
Aquila, L' **132** C 2
Aqyrap **136** L 4
Ara **150** N 5
ʿAraʿar **152** D 3
ʿAraʿar, Wādī **152** D 3
Arabian Basin **10** M 5
Arabian Desert **169** G 3
Arabian Peninsula **141** GJ 7/8
Arabian Plate **14** F 4/5
Arabian Sea **150** JK 7
Arabs *[Africa]* **173** B-G 2-4
Arabs *[Asia]* **145** G-J 6-8
Araç **134** D 3
Aracaju **112** M 6
Aracati **112** M 4
Araçatuba **114** JK 2
Araçuai **112** L 7
Arad **128** GH 4
ʿArafat, Jabal ▲ **150** DE 6
Arafura Sea **156** LM 9
Aragarças **112** J 7
Aragats Lerr ▲ **134** G 3
Aragón **130** D 2/1
Aragon **117** FG 5
Aragua de Maturín **115** II B 3
Araguaia **112** JK 5
Araguaína **112** K 5
Araguari **112** K 7
Araguatins **112** K 5
Arāk **152** F 2
Arakan Yoma **150** P 6/7
Aral **148** N 9
Aral Sea **148** MN 9/10
Aranda **130** C 2
Aran Islands **124** A 4
Aranjuez **130** C 2
Arapahoo **73** H 5
Arapiraca **112** M 6/5
Arapkir **134** E 3
Arará **109** H 5
Araracuara **112** E 4
Araraquara **114** K 2
Ararat **134** GH 3
Ararat ▲ **134** G 3
Aras **134** FG 3
Arauca **112** EF 2
Araucanians **109** FG 8/9
Arawa **156** Q 9
Arawaks **109** H 4
Araxá **112** K 7
Araya, Península de **115** II AB 3
Ārba Minch **176** P 7
Arbazh **136** J 1
Arber, Großer ▲ **128** E 3
Arbīl (Irbīl) **152** DE 1
Arbroath **124** D 3
Arcachon **131** B 4
Arcadia **100** C 4
Arcangelo, Sant' **132** D 3
Arcata **92** AB 1
Arches National Park **92** E 2
Arco **90** D 3
Arcos de la Frontera **130** C 3
Arctic Bay **78** XY 4
Arctic Circle **4** JK 2
Arctic Institute Islands **148** RS 3
Arctic Ocean **180** I BA
Arda **133** D 3
Ardabīl **134** J 4
Ardahan **134** G 3
Ardakān **152** G 3
Årdal **119** G 3
Ard aṣ-Ṣawwān **152** C 3
Ardatov *[Russia, Mordovia]* **136** H 2
Ardatov *[Russia, Nizhegorod]* **136** G 2
Ardennes **131** DE 2
Ardestān **152** G 2
Ardmore **96** D 2
Arecibo **101** VIII
Arena, Point **92** AB 2
Arendal **126** CD 3
Arequipa **112** E 7
Arévalo **130** C 2
Arezzo **132** BC 2
Argelès **131** D 4
Argent, Côte d' **123** C 3
Argenta **132** B 2
Argentan **131** C 2
Argentina **114** EG 7/3
Argentine Antarctic Sector **181** II B 31/36
Argentine Basin **13** FE 36/1
Argentinians **109** GH 9/7
Argentino, Lake **114** EF 8
Argenton **131** C 3
Argeş **133** D 1/2
Árgos **133** C V
Argostóli **133** B 4
Arguelle, Point **92** B 3
Argun **134** H 2
Argun' **148** YZ 8
Argyle **165** FG 8
Arhavi **134** F 3
Århus **126** D 4
Ariana (Aryānah) **132** B 4
Ariano Irpino **132** D 3
Arica **112** E 7
Arīḥā → Jericho *[Palestina]* **152** B 2/3
Arīḥā *[Syria]* **152** C 2
Arima **115** II B 3
Aripo, Mount ▲ **115** II B 3
Ariquemes **112** G 5
ʿArīsh, Al- **152** B 3
ʿArīsh, Wādī al- **152** B 3
Aristazabal Island **84** A 2
Ariza **130** D 2
Arizaro, Salar de **114** F 2/3
Arizona **92** DE 3
Årjäng **126** E 3
Arjeplog **125** CD 4
Arkadak **136** G 3
Arkadelphia **96** E 2
Arkansas **96** EF 2
Arkansas **96** EF 2
Arkansas City **94** D 3
Arkhangel'sk **138** HJ 3
Arkhangel'skoye *[Russia, Bashkortostan]* **136** LM 2
Arkhangel'skoye *[Russia, Tula]* **136** E 3
Arkhipo-Osipovka **134** EF 2
Arklow **124** BC 4
Arkona, Cape **128** E 1
Arlan ▲ **148** L 10
Arles **131** D 4
Arlington *[U.S., Oregon]* **90** BC 2
Arlington *[U.S., Texas]* **96** D 2
Arlington *[U.S., Virginia]* **98** E 3
Arlington Heights **94** FG 2
Arlit **176** J 5
Arlon **131** D 2
Armagh *[Canada]* **88** C 3
Armagh *[U.K.]* **124** B 3
Armavir *[Armenia]* **134** G 3
Armavir *[Russia]* **134** F 2
Armenia **112** D 3

Independent country
Dependent territory
Federal state, province, territory
People, ethnic group, tribe
Indian reservation/reserve
National Park
Industrial region
Historical site
Research station
Continent, realm
Region, peninsula
Mountain range, mountains
▲ Peak
)(Pass
* Ice shelf, glacier

menia 134 GH 3
menians [= Arm.] 121 L 5/6
midale 166 L 7
mstrong 86 E 3
narfjörður 125 AB 2
nauti, Cape 152 AB 2
nhem 128 C 2
nhem, Cape 166 H 3
nhem Land 166 GH 3
no 132 B 2
nøy 125 DE 2
nprior 88 A 3
nsberg 128 C 2
nstadt 128 D 3
omani [= Ar.] 121 J 5
rona 130 E 5
rpaçay 134 G 3
rqalyq 148 O 9/8
r-Raḥḥālīyah 152 D 2
-Ramādī 152 D 2
r-Ramthā 152 BC 2
rran 124 C 3
-Raqqah 152 C 1/2
rras 131 C 2
r-Rashīdiyah 176 FG 2
r-Rastān 152 C 2
r-Rauḍa 152 A 4
r-Rayyān 150 FG 6/5
rrecife 130 G 5
r-Ribāṭ → Rabat 176 EF 2
r-Rif 176 FG 2
r-Rifā‘ 152 F 4
r-Rifā‘ī 152 E 3
r-Riyāḍ → Riyadh 150 EF 6
rrow Lake, Lower 84 D 3
rrow Lake, Upper 84 D 3
rroyo Grande 92 BC 3
r-Rub‘ al-Khālī 150 FG 7/6
r-Rumaythah 152 E 3
r-Ruṣṣayfah 152 C 2/3
r-Ruṭbah 152 D 2
r-Ruways 152 F 4
rsen'yevo 136 E 3
rsk 136 J 2
rta *[Greece]* 133 C 3
rtà *[Spain]* 130 F 2
rtashat 134 G 3
rṭāwīyah, Al- 152 E 4
rtemisa 102 J 4
rtemivs'k 136 E 4
rtëmovsk 148 T 8
rtëmovskiy 148 XY 7
rtesia 92 F 3
rtesian Basin, Great 166 HJ 5/6
rti 136 M 2
rtigas 114 H 4
rt'ik 134 G 3
rtsyz 134 B 1
rtvin 134 F 3
rtyom 134 J 3
rua 178 L 2
ruanã 112 J 6
ruba 115 I A 1
rucas 130 F 5
ru Islands 156 LM 9
runachal Pradesh 150 PQ 5
rusha 178 M 3
ruwimi 178 K 2
rvayheer 154 K 2

Arviat 78 W 6
Arvida 71 LM 5
Arvidsjaur 125 D 4
Arvika 126 E 3
Arvon, Mount ▲ 98 BC 1
Aryānah → Ariana 132 B 4
Arys 148 O 10
Arzamas 136 G 2
Arzgir 134 G 1
Arzīw 119 G 6
Asaba 176 J 7
Asadābād *[Afghanistan]* 150 L 4
Asadābād *[Iran]* 152 F 2
Asad Lake 152 C 1
Asahikawa 154 RS 3
Asālē, Lake 66 L 5
‘Asalūyeh 152 G 4
Asansol 150 O 6
Āsayita 176 Q 6
Asbestos 88 C 3
Asbury Park 98 F 2
Ascensión *[Bolivia]* 112 G 7
Ascensión *[Mexico]* 96 A 3
Ascension 178 B 4
Aschaffenburg 128 D 3
Aschersleben 128 D 2
Ascoli Piceno 132 C 2
‘Aseb 176 Q 6
Asekeyevo 136 K 3
Āsela 176 PQ 7
Åsele 126 F 1
Asenovgrad 133 D 3
Asfī → Safi 176 EF 2
Aşgabat → Ashgabat 148 MN 11
Asha 136 M 2
Ashburton 166 P 9
Ashburton 166 D 5
Ashcroft 84 C 3
Ashdod 152 B 3
Ashdown 96 E 2
Asheboro 100 D 2
Ashern 86 C 3
Asheville 100 C 2
Asheweig 86 E 2
Ash Fork 92 D 3
Ashgabat (Aşgabat) 148 MN 11
Ashland *[U.S., Kentucky]* 98 D 3
Ashland *[U.S., Ohio]* 98 D 2
Ashland *[U.S., Oregon]* 90 B 3
Ashland *[U.S., Virginia]* 98 E 3
Ashland *[U.S., Wisconsin]* 94 F 1
Ashley 94 D 1
Ashmore 166 E 3
Ashmore Reef 166 E 3
Ashmyany 128 J 1
Ashqelon 152 B 3
Ash-Shadādah 152 D 1
Ash-Shafallaḥīyah 152 F 3/4
ash-Sham, Jabal ▲ 150 H 6
Ash-Shāmīyah 152 E 2/3
Ash-Shanāfīyah 152 E 3
Ash-Shāriqah 150 H 5/6
Ash-Sharqāt 152 D 2
Ash-Shaṭrah 152 E 3
Ash-Shawrah 152 B 4
ash-Shifā’, Jabal 152 BC 3/4
Ash-Shu‘aybah 152 D 4
Ash-Shumlūl 152 E 4

Ash-Shūrā 152 D 1
Ashtabula 98 D 2
Ashtabula, Lake 94 D 1
Ashtarak 134 G 3
Ashtīān 152 F 2
Ashton 90 E 2
Ashuanipi Lake 88 D 1
Ashur ∴ 152 D 2
Asia 4 MP 3
Asinara 132 A 3
Asino 148 RS 7
Asipovichy 128 K 2
‘Asīr 150 E 7
Aşkale 134 F 3
Askaniya Nova 134 D 1
Askim 126 D 3
Askino 136 L 2
Askja ▲ 125 D 2
Aşlanduz 134 H 3
Āsmera 176 PQ 5/6
Åsnen 126 EF 4
Asosa 176 O 6
Aspen 94 B 3
Aspendos ∴ 134 C 4
As-Sabkhah 152 C 2
As-Sa‘dīyah 152 E 2
Aş-Şaf 152 A 3
‘Assāfīyah, Al- 152 C 3
as-Sāḥilīyah, Jabal 152 C 2
Aş-Şalīf 143 H 8
As-Sālimīyah 152 F 3
As-Sallūm 176 N 2
As-Salmān 152 E 3
As-Salṭ 152 B 2
Assam 150 PQ 5
As-Samārah 176 EF 3
As-Samāwah 152 E 3
Assamese 145 N 7
Aş-Şā‘rān 152 C 2
Assateague 98 F 3
aş-Şawāb, Wādī 152 D 2
as-Sawdā’, Jabal 176 KL 3
Aş-Şawīrah 176 EF 2
Assekrem ▲ 175 D 3
Assen 128 C 2
As-Sīb 150 H 6
As-Sībah 152 F 3
As-Sidr 152 B 3
As-Sidrah 176 L 2
As-Sikr 152 D 3
As-Sinballāwayn 152 AB 3
Assiniboia 84 G 3
Assiniboine 73 G-H 4-5
Assiniboine 86 B 2/3
Assiniboine, Mount ▲ 84 E 3
Assiniboine Indian Reserve 86 B 3
as-Sirḥān, Wādī 152 C 3
Assis 114 JK 2
Assisi 132 C 2
Assuan (Aswān) 176 O 4
Aş-Şubayḥiyah 152 EF 3
As-Sukhnah 152 C 2
As-Sulaymānīyah 152 E 2
As-Sulayyil 150 F 6
Aş-Şummān 152 E 4
As-Suwār 152 D 2
As-Suwaydā’ 152 BC 2
Aş-Şuwayrah 152 E 2

As-Suways → Suez 152 B 3
Astana 148 P 8
Astara 134 J 4
Asti 132 A 2
Astorga 130 BC 1
Astoria 90 AB 2
Astrakhan' 134 J 1
Astravets 128 J 1
Asturias 130 BC 1
Astypálaia 133 D 4
Asunción 114 H 3
Asunción, La 115 II B 3
Asuncion Island 156 O 4
Aswān → Assuan 176 O 4
Asyūṭ 152 A 4
Atacama, Salar de 114 F 2
Atacama Desert 114 EF 3/2
Atafu 166 S 2
Atakpamé 176 H 7
Atalánti 133 C 4
‘Atāq 150 F 8
Aṭār 176 E 4
Atascadero 92 B 3
Atascaderos 96 B 4
Atasū 148 P 9
Atatürk Reservoir 134 EF 4
Atbara → ‘Aṭbarah
‘Aṭbarah 176 OP 5
‘Aṭbarah 176 OP 5
Atbasar 148 O 8
Atchafalaya Bay 96 F 3
Atchison 94 E 3
Ath 131 D 2
Athabasca 84 E 2
Athabasca 76 S 7
Athabasca, Lake 76 ST 7
Athapascans, North 73 CH 3/4
Athenry 124 B 4
Athens *[U.S., Alabama]* 100 B 2
Athens *[U.S., Ohio]* 98 D 3
Athens *[U.S., Tennessee]* 100 B 2
Athens *[U.S., Texas]* 96 E 2
Athens (Athína) *[Greece]* 133 CD 4
Athens-Clarke 100 C 2
Athína → Athens 133 CD 4
Athlone 124 B 4
Áthos 133 D 3
ath-Tharthār, Wādī 152 D 2
Ath-Thawrah 152 C 2
Ati 176 L 6
Atikokan 86 E 3
Atikonak Lake 88 D 1
Atka 78 F 8
Atkarsk 136 G 3
Atlanta 100 BC 2
Atlantic 94 E 2
Atlantic City 98 F 3
Atlantic-Indian Basin 13 C 36/3
Atlantic-Indian Ridge 13 DE 5/8
Atlantic Ocean 6 MQ 4/7
Atlantic Standard Time 38 B 17
Atlantis Fracture Zone 10 FG 4
Atlas, High 176 FG 2
Atlas, Saharan 176 GH 2
Atlas, Tell 176 HJ 1

River, canal
Waterfall
Lake, lakes, reservoir
Swamp
Salt flat
Sea
Strait
Bay, gulf
Cape
Island, islands
Ocean current
Ocean floor landforms
Tectonic feature
Atmospheric phenomena
Time zone
Geographical grid

Atmore **100** B 3
Atna Peak ▲ **84** AB 2
Atoka **96** D 2
Ätran ∽ **126** E 3
Atroari 👥 **109** GH 5
Aṭ-Ṭafīlah **152** B 3
Aṭ-Ṭā'if **150** E 6
Aṭ-Ṭarif **132** A 4
Aṭ-Ṭarmīyah **152** DE 2
Attawapiskat **86** G 2
Attawapiskat ∽ **86** F 2
Attawapiskat Lake ◡ **86** F 2
at-Tīh, Jabal ▲▲ **152** B 3
Attu **78** C 8
Aṭ-Ṭubayq ▲▲ **152** C 3
Attu Island ⌓ **76** C 8
At-Tūnj **176** N 7
Aṭ-Ṭūr **152** B 3
Atyashevo **136** H 2
Atyraū **136** K 5
Auasberge ▲▲ **178** H 7
Aube ∽ **131** D 2
Aubenas **131** D 4
Auburn *[U.S., Alabama]* **100** B 2
Auburn *[U.S., California]* **92** B 2
Auburn *[U.S., Indiana]* **98** C 2
Auburn *[U.S., Maine]* **98** G 1
Auburn *[U.S., Nebraska]* **94** DE 2
Auburn *[U.S., New York]* **98** E 2
Aubusson **131** C 3
Aucanquilcha ▲ **112** F 8
Auce **126** H 4
Auch **131** C 4
Auckland **166** P 8
Auckland Islands ⌓ **166** NO 11
Aue **128** E 3
Augsburg **128** D 3
Augusta *[Australia]* **166** C 7
Augusta *[Italy]* **132** D 4
Augusta *[U.S.]* **98** G 1
Augusta-Richmond **100** C 2
Augustin, Saint- **88** F 2
Augustine, Saint **100** C 3
Augustine, San **96** E 3
Augustów **128** H 2
Auki **166** N 2
Aulavik National Park ⌂ **78** PQ 4
Aulneau Peninsula ⛰ **86** D 3
'Aunu'u ⌓ **101** VII
Aurillac **131** C 4
Aurora *[U.S., Colorado]* **94** B 3
Aurora *[U.S., Illinois]* **94** F 2
Aurora *[U.S., Minnesota]* **86** DE 4
Aurora *[U.S., Missouri]* **94** E 3
Aurora *[U.S., Nebraska]* **94** D 2
Austell, Saint **124** C 5
Austin *[U.S., Minnesota]* **94** E 2
Austin *[U.S., Nevada]* **92** C 2
Austin *[U.S., Texas]* **96** D 3
Australasia ⊕ **26** PS 7
Australia ⊕ **6** CE 7
Australia ■ **166** DK 5/6
Australia, South □ **166** FH 6/7
Australia, Western □ **166** DF 5/6
Australian
  Aborigines 👥 **164** E-G 8-9
Australian Alps ▲▲ **166** KL 8
Australian Antarctic
  Territory □ **181** II B-C 10-18
Australian Bight,
  Great ≈) **166** FG 7/8
Australians 👥 **164** D-H 9-12
Australis ⊕ **30** PR 7
Austria ■ **128** DF 4/3
Austria, Lower □ **128** F 3
Austria, Upper □ **128** E 3
Austrians 👥 **121** H 5
Austvågøy ⌓ **125** B 3
Autun **131** D 3
Auvergne ⛰ **123** D 3
Auxerre **131** D 3
Auyán Tepuy ▲ **112** G 2
Auyuittuq National
  Park ⌂ **78** bc 5
Avalon **92** C 3
Avalon Peninsula ⛰ **88** G 3
Avanos **134** D 4
Avarua **160** N 6
Ávdira **133** D 3
Aveiro **130** B 2
Āvej **152** F 2
Avellino **132** CD 3
Aves Islands, Las ⌓ **115** I B 2
Avesta **126** F 2
Aveyron ∽ **131** C 4
Avezzano **132** C 3
Avigliano **132** D 3
Avignon **131** D 4
Ávila **130** C 2
Avilés **130** BC 1
Avinurme **126** J 3
Avola **132** D 4
Avold, Saint- **131** E 2
Avon **94** B 3
Avondale **92** D 3
Avonlea **84** G 3
Avranches **131** B 2
Āwasa **176** P 7
Āwash ∽ **176** Q 6
Awbārī **176** K 3
Aweil → Uwayl
Awjilah **176** M 3
Awka **176** J 7
Axel Heiberg Island ⌓ **76** VX 2/3
Ax-les-Thermes **131** C 4
Ay ∽ **136** M 2
Ayacucho **112** DE 6
Ayagöz **148** QR 9
Ayamonte **130** B 3
Ayan **148** c 7
Ayaş **134** C 3
Aybastı **134** E 3
Aydın **134** B 4
Ayers Rock (Uluru) ▲ **166** G 5/6
Aykhal **148** X 5
Aykino **138** L 4
Aylesbury **124** D 4
Aymara 👥 **109** FG 6/7
'Ayn, Al- **150** H 6
'Ayn al-Bāyḍā' **132** A 5
'Ayn aṣ-Ṣafrā' **176** G 2
'Ayn Dīwār **152** D 1
'Ayn Ṣālaḥ **176** H 3
'Ayn Sifnī **152** D 1
Ayon Island ⌓ **148** j 4/5
Ayoré 👥 **109** GH 6
Ayoûn el-Atroûs
  → 'Ayūn al-'Atrūs
Ayr **124** C 3
Ayrancı **134** D 4
'Ayūn, Al- → Laâyoune **176** DE 3
'Ayūn al-'Atrūs **176** F 5
Ayvalık **134** AB 3
'Ayyāṭ, Al- **152** A 3
Azahar, Costa del ⛰ **123** CD 4/3
Azande 👥 **173** F 5
Azare **176** JK 6
Azarychy **128** K 2
A'zāz **152** C 1
Azerbaijan ■ **134** HJ 3
Azerbaijanis
  (Azeri) 👥 **145** H 5/6
'Azīzīyah, Al- *[Iraq]* **152** E 2
'Azīzīyah, Al- *[Libya]* **66** KL 4
Aznakayevo **136** K 2
Azogues **112** D 4
Azores □ **130** BD 5
Azores ⌓ **4** H 4
Azores Time ◷ **38** B 14
Azov **134** F 1
Azov, Sea of ≋ **134** DE 1
Azovy **138** Q 3
Azraq, Al- **152** C 3
Aztec **92** EF 2
Aztecs 👥 **73** J 8/7
Azuaga **130** C 3
Azuero Peninsula ⛰ **102** J 7
Azul **114** GH 5
Azur, Côte d' ⛰ **131** E 4
Az-Zabadānī **152** C 2
Az-Zaqāzīq **152** AB 3
Az-Zarqā' **152** C 2
Az-Zāwiyah **176** K 2
az-Zawr, Ra's ⟩≋ **152** F 4
Az-Zubayr **152** E 3
Az-Zuwaytīnah **119** J 6

B

Ba'āj, Al- **152** D 1
Baalbek → Ba'labakk
Baardheere **176** Q 8
Bāb, Al- **152** C 1
Baba Burun ⟩≋ **134** C 3
Babadag **133** E 2
Babaeski **134** B 3
Babahoyo **112** CD 4
Bāb al-Mandab ≍ **150** EF 8
Babar ⌓ **156** L 9
Babati **178** M 3
Babayevo **138** G 5
Babayurt **134** H 2
B'abdā **152** B 2
Babeldaob ⌓ **156** L 6
Bābil ∴ → Babylon **152** E 2
Babine ∽ **84** B 2
Babine Lake ◡ **84** B 2
Babine Range ▲▲ **84** B 2
Baboa 👥 **173** F 5
Bābol **152** G 1
Bābol Sar **152** G 1
Babruysk **128** K 2
Babuyan Island ⌓ **156** J 4
Babuyan Islands ⌓ **156** J 4
Babylon (Bābil) ∴ **152** E 2
Babynino **136** DE 2
Baca **96** A 4
Bacabal **112** K 4
Bacan ⌓ **156** K 8
Bacău *[Romania]* **128** JK 4
Bacau *[Timor-Leste]* **156** K 9
Bacerac **96** A 3
Back ∽ **76** TU 5
Bačka Palanka **133** B 1
Bac Liêu **156** F 6
Bacolod **156** J 5
Badain Jaran Shamo ⛰ **154** K 3
Badajoz **130** B 3
Badalona **130** E 2
Badārī, Al- **152** A 4
Baddeck **88** E 3
Bad Doberan **128** D 1
Baden **128** F 4
Baden-Baden **128** C 3
Baden-Württemberg □ **128** CD 3
Badgastein **128** E 4
Badger **88** F 2
Bad Hersfeld **128** D 3
Bad Homburg **128** C 3
Bad Ischl **128** E 4
Bādiyah al-
  Janūbīyah, Al- ⛰ **152** E 3
Bad Kreuznach **128** C 3
Badlands National
  Park ⌂ **94** C 2
Bad Mergentheim **128** D 3
Bad Neustadt an
  der Saale **128** D 3
Badrah **152** E 2
Bad River ∽ **94** C 1
Bad River Indian
  Reservation X **94** F 1
Bad Segeberg **128** D 1/2
Bad Tölz **128** DE 4
Badu ⌓ **166** J 2/3
Baena **130** C 3
Bafatá **176** DE 6
Baffin Bay ≈)
  [Arctic Ocean] **76** ac 4
Baffin Bay ≈)
  [Gulf of Mexico] **96** D 4
Baffin Island ⌓ **76** Yb 4/5
Bafoussam **176** K 7
Bafra **134** E 3
Bafra Burnu ⟩≋ **134** E 3
Bagara 👥 **173** F 4
Bagayevskaya **134** F 1
Bagé **114** J 4
Baghdād **152** E 2
Baghdad Time ◷ **38** B 10
Bagheria **132** C 4
Baghlān **150** K 3
Bagirmi 👥 **173** E 4/5
Bagnères-de-Luchon **131** C 4
Bagnols **131** D 4
Bago → Pegu **150** Q 7
Bagrationovsk **128** GH 1
Baguio **156** J 4
Bagzane, Monts ▲▲ **176** J 5
Bāḥah, Al- **150** E 7
Bahama Island,
  Grand ⌓ **102** K 3
Bahama Islanders 👥 **73** L 7
Bahama Islands ⌓ **80** MN 6/7
Bahamas ■ **102** KL 3/4

■ Independent country
◘ Dependent territory
□ Federal state, province, territory
👥 People, ethnic group, tribe
X Indian reservation/reserve
⌂ National Park
Π Industrial region
∴ Historical site
◺ Research station
⊕ Continent, realm
⛰ Region, peninsula
▲▲ Mountain range, mountains
▲ Peak
)(Pass
* Ice shelf, glacier

River, canal
Waterfall
Lake, lakes, reservoir
Swamp
Salt flat
Sea
Strait
Bay, gulf
Cape
Island, islands
Ocean current
Ocean floor landforms
Tectonic feature
Atmospheric phenomena
Time zone
Geographical grid

Barkley Sound	84 B 3
Bârlad	128 K 4
Bar-le-Duc	131 D 2
Barlee, Lake	166 DE 6
Barletta	132 D 3
Barlinek	128 F 2
Barmer	150 L 5
Barnaul	148 R 8
Barnesville	100 B 2
Barneville	131 B 2
Barnsley	124 D 4
Barnstaple	124 C 4
Barquisimeto	112 EF 1/2
Barra	112 L 6
Barra	124 B 3
Barra, Ponta da	178 M 7
Barraco, El	130 C 2
Barra do Corda	112 KL 5
Barra do Garças	112 J 7
Barranca	112 D 6
Barrancabermeja	112 DE 2
Barranquilla	112 D 1
Barraute	88 A 2
Barre	98 F 1
Barreal, El	96 B 3
Barre des Ecrins	131 E 3/4
Barreiras	112 L 6
Barretos	112 K 8
Barrhead	84 E 2
Barrie	98 E 1
Barrière	84 CD 3
Barrier Reef, Great	160 HJ 5
Barrigada	101 II
Barrow *[U.S.]*	78 J 4
Barrow *[Australia]*	165 E 9
Barrow	124 B 4
Barrow, Point	76 JK 4
Barrow-in-Furness	124 CD 3
Barrow Islands	166 CD 5
Barruelo de Santullán	130 C 1
Barry	124 C 4
Barry's Bay	88 A 3
Barstow	92 C 3
Bar-sur-Aube	131 D 2
Bar-sur-Seine	131 D 2
Barth	128 E 1
Barthélemy, Saint-	115 II B 1
Bartica	112 H 2
Bartın	134 C 3
Bartle Frere	166 JK 4
Bartlesville	96 DE 1
Bartlett	100 A 2
Bartolomeo, San	132 D 3
Bartoszyce	128 GH 1
Bartow	100 C 4
Barú, Volcán	102 J 7
Baruun-Urt	154 M 2
Barvinkove	136 E 4
Barysaw	128 K 1
Barysh	136 H 3
Basarabeasca	128 K 4
Basel	128 C 4
Basento	132 D 3
Bashkirs	121 M-N 4
Bashkortostan	136 LM 2/3
Bashmakovo	136 G 3
Bashshār → Béchar	176 G 2
Bashtanka	136 C 5
Basilan	156 J 6
Basile, Pico	176 J 8
Basilicata	132 D 3
Basingstoke	124 D 4
Başkale	134 G 4
Baskatong, Réservoir	88 B 3
Basque Country	130 CD 1
Basques	121 F 5
Başra (Al-Başrah)	152 E 3
Bassano *[Canada]*	84 EF 3
Bassano *[Italy]*	132 BC 1
Bassas da India	178 MN 7
Basse Santa Su	176 E 6
Basse-Terre *[Guadeloupe]*	115 II B 1/2
Basseterre *[St. Kitts and Nevis]*	115 II B 1
Basse-Terre	115 II B 1
Bass Strait	166 JK 8
Bastānābād	134 H 4
Bastia	132 B 2
Bastogne	131 DE 2
Bastrop	96 F 2
Bas'yanovskiy	138 P 5
Bata	176 J 8
Batagay	148 b 5
Bataks	145 N 9
Batamshy	136 M 4
Batang	154 JK 6
Batangas	156 HJ 5
Batan Islands	156 J 3
Batavia	98 E 2
Bataysk	134 F 1
Batchawana Mountain	86 F 4
Bătdâmbâng	156 E 5
Batesburg-Leesville	100 C 2
Batesville	96 EF 2
Batetskiy	138 E 5
Bath *[U.K.]*	124 D 4
Bath *[U.S., Maine]*	98 G 2
Bath *[U.S., New York]*	98 E 2
Baṭḥā', Al-	152 E 3
Bathurst	88 D 3
Bathurst, Cape	76 PQ 4
Bathurst Island *[Australia]*	166 F 3
Bathurst Island *[Canada]*	76 UV 3
Bāṭīn, Wādī al-	152 E 3
Batken	148 OP 11
Batman	134 F 4
Batna → Bātnah	
Bātnah	176 HJ 1
Baton Rouge	96 F 3
Båtsfjord	125 GH 2
Batterbee, Cape	181 I C 8/9
Batticaloa	150 N 9
Battipaglia	132 CD 3
Battle	84 E 2
Battle Creek	98 C 2
Battle Creek	90 E 1
Battleford	84 F 2
Battle Mountain	92 C 1
Batu	176 P 7
Batu Islands	156 D 8
Batumi	134 F 3
Baturaja	156 EF 8
Baubau	156 J 9
Bauchi	176 J 6
Baudette	86 D 3
Bauge	131 BC 3
Bauld, Cape	88 G 2
Baule	173 C 5
Baume	131 E 3
Baure	109 G 6
Bauru	114 K 2
Bauska	126 J 4
Bautzen	128 E 2
Bavaria	128 DE 3
Bavarian Alps	128 DE 4
Bavispe	96 A 3
Bavly	136 K 2
Bawean	156 G 9
Bawiṭi, Al-	176 N 3
Baxter Springs	94 E 3
Bayadh, Al-	176 GH 2
Bayamo	102 K 4
Bayamon	101 VIII
Bayanhongor	154 JK 2
Bayan Obo	154 LM 3
Bayard	92 E 3
Bayat	134 D 3
Bayawan	156 J 6
Bayburt	134 F 3
Bay City *[U.S., Michigan]*	98 D 2
Bay City *[U.S., Texas]*	96 E 3
Bayḍā', Al- *[Libya]*	176 M 2
Bayḍā', Al- *[Yemen]*	150 F 8
Baydaratskaya Guba	148 NO 4/5
Baydhabo	176 QR 8
Bayeux	131 B 2
Bayghanīn	136 L 4
Bayındır	134 B 4
Bay Islands	102 H 5
Bayjī	152 D 2
Baykal, Lake	148 W 8
Baykit	148 U 6
Baykonur (Bayqongyr)	148 NO 9
Baymak	136 M 3
Bay Mills Indian Reservation	98 C 1
Bay Minette	100 B 3
Baynes Mountains	178 G 6
Bay of ... → ..., Bay of	
Bayonet Point	100 C 3
Bayonne	131 B 4
Bayovár	107 E 5
Bayqongyr → Baykonur	148 NO 9
Baÿramaly	148 N 11
Bayramic	134 AB 3
Bayreuth	128 DE 3
Bay Roberts	88 G 3
Bayrūt → Beirut	152 B 2
Bayshonas	136 K 5
Bayt Laḥm → Bethlehem	152 B 3
Baytown	96 E 3
Bayūdah	169 G 4
Baza	130 D 3
Bazardüzü Dağı	134 HJ 3
Bazarnyye Mataki	136 J 2
Bazarnyy Karabulak	136 H 3
Bazarnyy Syzgan	136 H 3
Bazartöbe	136 K 4
Bazhong	154 L 5
Be, Nosy	178 O 5
Beach	94 BC 1
Beacon	98 F 2
Bear	86 G 2
Beardmore	86 F 3
Beardstown	94 F 3
Bear Island	148 D 4
Bear Islands	148 h 4
Bear Lake	90 E 3
Bear Lodge Mountains	90 F 2
Bear Peninsula	181 I B 28/27
Bearskin Lake Indian Reserve	86 E 2
Bear's Paw Mountains	90 E 1
Beatrice	94 D 2
Beatty	92 C 2
Beaucaire	131 D 4
Beaufort *[U.S., North Carolina]*	100 D 2
Beaufort *[U.S., South Carolina]*	100 C 2
Beaufort Sea	76 LO 4/3
Beaufort West	178 J 9
Beauharnois	88 B 3
Beaumont	96 E 3
Beaune	131 D 3
Beaupré	88 C 3
Beausejour	86 CD 3
Beauvais	131 C 2
Beauval	84 G 2
Beaver *[U.S., Oklahoma]*	96 C 1
Beaver *[U.S., Utah]*	92 D 2
Beaver	73 FG 4
Beaver *[Canada, Alberta/ Saskatchewan]*	84 F 2
Beaver *[Canada, Ontario]*	86 E 2
Beaver	98 C 1
Beaver Creek	94 C 3
Beaver Dam	94 F 2
Beaver Falls	98 D 2
Beaverhill Lake	84 EF 2
Beaver Lake	96 E 1
Beaverlodge	84 D 2
Beaverton	98 E 1
Beawar	150 LM 5
Bécancour	88 BC 3
Béchar (Bashshār)	176 G 2
Bechevinka	138 G 5
Beckley	98 D 3
Bedford *[Canada]*	88 B 3
Bedford *[U.K.]*	124 D 4
Bedford *[U.S., Indiana]*	98 C 3
Bedford *[U.S., Virginia]*	98 E 3
Bedfort	98 E 2/3
Bednodem'yanovsk	136 G 3
Beechy	84 G 3
Beef Island	101 IX
Beersheba (Be'ér Sheva')	152 B 3
Beeville	96 D 3
Bega	166 KL 8
Begna	126 CD 2
Behbahān	152 F 3
Behm Canal	84 A 2
Behshahr	152 G 1
Bei'an	154 OP 2
Beihai	154 L 7
Beijing	154 MN 3/4
Beira	178 M 6

Independent country
Dependent territory
Federal state, province, territory
People, ethnic group, tribe
Indian reservation/reserve
National Park
Industrial region
Historical site
Research station
Continent, realm
Region, peninsula
Mountain range, mountains
Peak
Pass
Ice shelf, glacier

River, canal
Waterfall
Lake, lakes, reservoir
Swamp
Salt flat
Sea
Strait
Bay, gulf
Cape
Island, islands
Ocean current
Ocean floor landforms
Tectonic feature
Atmospheric phenomena
Time zone
Geographical grid

■ Independent country
◨ Dependent territory
□ Federal state, province, territory
⚇ People, ethnic group, tribe
Ⲭ Indian reservation/reserve
⌂ National Park
Π Industrial region
∴ Historical site
⛫ Research station
⊕ Continent, realm
⩘ Region, peninsula
▲▲ Mountain range, mountains
▲ Peak
)(Pass
* Ice shelf, glacier

ue Ridge 98 DE 3
ue River 84 D 2
ue River, Little 94 D 2
uff 92 E 2
uff, The ▲ 102 K 4/5
umenau 114 K 3
y Falls 90 B 3
yth 124 D 3
ythe 92 D 3
ytheville 96 F 2
yznyuky 136 E 4
o 176 E 7
o. = Bochum 128 C 2
oaco 102 H 6
oali 176 L 8
oa Vista 112 G 3
oa Vista 176 C 5
obangi 173 E 5/6
obaomby, Cape 178 OP 5
obbio 132 B 2
obo 173 C 4
obo-Dioulasso 176 G 6
obrov 136 F 3/4
obrovytsya 136 C 4
obrynets' 136 C 5/4
oby, Pic ▲ 178 O 7
oca del Yuma 101 VIII
oca do Acre 112 F 5
oca Raton 100 CD 4
ocas del Toro 102 J 7
ocayna, La 130 FG 5
ochnia 128 G 3
ocholt 128 C 2
ochum [= Bo.] 128 C 2
ocşa 133 C 1
odaybo 148 XY 7
odélé 169 E 4
oden 125 E 4
odø 125 B 3
odrum 134 B 4
ogalusa 96 F 3
ogatye Saby 136 J 2
oğazlıyan 134 D 3
oggy Peak ▲ 115 II B 1
ogomila 133 C 3
ogor 156 F 9
ogoroditsk 136 E 3
ogorodsk 136 G 2
ogorodskoye 136 JK 1
ogotá 112 E 3
ogovarovo 138 K 5
oguchar 136 F 4
o Hai 154 NO 4
ohemian Forest 128 E 3
ohodukhiv 136 D 4
ohol 156 JK 6
ohorodchany 128 J 3
ohuslav 136 C 4
ois Blanc 98 CD 1
oise 90 CD 3
oise City 96 C 1
ois Forte Indian
Reservation 86 D 3
oissevain 86 B 3
okaro 150 O 6
oké 176 E 6
okovskaya 136 F 4
oksitogorsk 138 F 5
ol 176 KL 6

Bolbec 131 C 2
Bolesławiec 128 F 2
Bolgatanga 176 G 6
Bolhrad 134 B 1
Boliden 125 D 4
Bolivar *[U.S., Missouri]* 94 E 3
Bolivar *[U.S., Tennessee]* 100 A 2
Bolívar, Pico ▲ 112 E 2
Bolivia 112 FH 7
Bolivians 109 G 6/7
Bolkar Dağları 134 D 4
Bolkhov 136 D 3
Bollnäs 126 F 2
Bollstabruck 126 FG 1
Bolmen 126 E 4
Bolnisi 134 G 3
Bologna 132 B 2
Bologoye 136 D 1
Bolsena, Lake 132 B 2
Bol'shakovo 128 H 1
Bol'shaya Chernigovka 136 J 3
Bol'shaya Glushitsa 136 JK 3
Bol'shaya Martynovka 134 FG 1
Bol'shaya Pyssa 138 L 3
Bol'shaya Sosnova 136 L 1
Bol'shevik Island 148 WY 3
Bol'shezemel'skaya
Tundra 138 MQ 2
Bol'shiye Berezniki 136 H 2/3
Bol'shoy Begichev
Island 148 XY 4
Bol'shoye Boldino 136 GH 2
Bol'shoye Murashkino 136 G 2
Bol'shoye Nagatkino 136 HJ 2
Bol'shoy Igriz 136 J 3
Bol'shoy Kikus 138 O 4
Bol'shoy Nimnyr 148 Za 7
Bol'shoy Uzen' 136 HJ 4/3
Bolsón de Mapimí 96 BC 3/4
Boltaña 130 DE 1
Bolton 124 D 4
Bolu 134 C 3
Bolvadin 134 C 4
Bolzano/Bozen 132 BC 1
Boma 178 G 4
Bombala 166 KL 8
Bombay → Mumbai 150 L 7
Bom Jesus da Lapa 112 L 6
Bømlo 126 B 3
Bomu 178 J 2
Bon, Cap 132 B 4
Bonāb 134 H 4
Bonaire 115 I AB 1
Bonaparte, Mount ▲ 90 C 1
Bonasse 115 II B 3
Bonavista 88 G 2
Bonavista Bay 88 G 2
Bondari 136 G 3
Bondo 178 J 2
Bondoukou 176 G 7
Bongo Mountains 169 F 5
Bongor 176 L 6
Bonham 96 DE 2
Bonifacio 132 AB 3
Bonifacio, Strait of 132 AB 3
Bonifay 100 B 3
Bonin Islands 154 S 6
Bonin Trench 10 Q 4
Bonita Springs 100 C 4

Bonn 128 C 3
Bonners Ferry 90 CD 1
Bonnet, Saint- 131 E 4
Bonnyville 84 F 2
Bontang 156 H 7
Boone *[U.S., Iowa]* 94 E 2
Boone
[U.S., North Carolina] 100 C 1
Booneville 96 F 2
Boonville
[U.S., Missouri] 94 E 3
Boonville
[U.S., New York] 98 F 2
Boosaaso 176 R 6
Boothia, Gulf of 76 WX 4/5
Boothia Peninsula 76 VW 4
Boquilla, Presa de la 96 B 4
Bor *[Russia]* 136 G 2
Bor *[Serbia]* 133 C 2
Bor → Būr *[Sudan]*
Bor *[Turkey]* 134 D 4
Borah Peak ▲ 90 D 2
Borås 126 E 3
Borāzjān 152 F 3
Borba 112 H 4
Bordeaux 131 B 4
Bordeaux Mountain ▲ 101 IX
Borden Island 76 ST 3
Bordj Omer Driss
→ Burj Umar Drīs
Borgarnes 125 B 2
Borger 96 C 2
Borges Blanques, Les 130 E 2
Borgholm 126 F 4
Borgo 132 B 2
Borgosesia 132 A 1
Börili 136 K 3
Borisoglebsk 136 FG 3
Borisoglebskiy 136 EF 1
Borisovka 136 DE 4
Borja, San 112 F 6/7
Borja, São 114 HJ 3
Borjomi 134 G 3
Borkou 169 EF 4
Borkum 128 C 2
Borlänge 126 EF 2
Bormio 132 B 1
Borneo (Kalimantan) 156 GH 7/8
Bornholm 126 F 4
Bornu 176 K 6
Borobodur ∴ 51 PQ 6
Borodyanka 128 K 3
Bororo 109 H 6
Borova 136 E 4
Borovichi 138 F 5
Borovoy
[Russia, Karelia] 138 E 3
Borovoy *[Russia, Kirov]* 138 M 5
Borovoy *[Russia, Komi]* 138 M 3
Borovsk 136 DE 2
Borrego Springs 92 C 3
Borşa 128 J 4
Borshchiv 128 J 3
Bort-les-Orgues 131 CD 3
Borūjen 152 F 2/3
Borūjerd 152 F 2
Boryslav 128 H 3
Boryspil' 136 C 4
Borzna 136 C 3

Borzya 148 Y 8
Bosa 132 A 3
Bosanska Gradiška 132 D 1
Bosanska Krupa 132 D 2
Bosanski Novi 132 D 1
Bose 154 L 7
Bosilegrad 133 C 2
Bosna 132 DE 2/1
Bosnia and
Herzegovina 132 DE 2
Bosnia and Herzegovina,
Federation of 132 DE 2
Bosnian Muslims
[= B.M.] 121 H 5
Bosporus 134 B 3
Bossangoa 176 L 7
Bossier City 96 E 2
Bosten Hu 154 G 3
Boston *[U.K.]* 124 DE 4
Boston *[U.S.]* 98 G 2
Boston Mountains 96 E 2
Botev ▲ 133 D 2
Botevgrad 133 CD 2
Bothnia, Gulf of 117 HJ 3
Botlikh 134 H 2
Botocudos 109 J-K 6-7
Botoşani 128 JK 4
Botshabelo 178 K 8
Botswana 178 JK 7
Bottineau 90 G 1
Botucatu 114 K 2
Bouaflé 176 F 7
Bouaké 176 G 7
Bouar 176 KL 7
Bouârfa → Būʿarfah
Bougainville Island 156 Q 9
Bougouni 176 F 6
Boujdour → Bū Jaydūr
Boulder 94 B 2/3
Boulder City 92 D 3
Boulogne 131 C 2
Boulogne-Billancourt 131 C 2
Bountiful 92 E 1
Bounty Islands 166 Q 10
Bourem 176 G 5
Bourg 131 D 3
Bourganeuf 131 C 3
Bourges 131 C 3
Bourg-Saint-Maurice 131 E 3
Bourke 166 K 7
Bournemouth 124 D 5
Bousso 176 L 6
Bouvet Island 36 JK 8
Bouvet Island 4 JK 8
Bow 84 F 3
Bow, Little 84 E 3
Bowen 166 K 4/5
Bowie *[U.S., Arizona]* 92 E 3
Bowie *[U.S., Maryland]* 98 E 3
Bowie *[U.S., Texas]* 96 D 2
Bow Island 84 F 3
Bowling Green
[U.S., Kentucky] 98 C 3
Bowling Green
[U.S., Ohio] 98 CD 2
Bowman 94 C 1
Bowman, Mount ▲ 84 C 3
Bowron 84 C 2
Boyabat 134 D 3

River, canal
Waterfall
Lake, lakes, reservoir
Swamp
Salt flat
Sea
Strait
Bay, gulf
Cape
Island, islands
Ocean current
Ocean floor landforms
Tectonic feature
Atmospheric phenomena
Time zone
Geographical grid

■ Independent country
◧ Dependent territory
□ Federal state, province, territory
⚇ People, ethnic group, tribe
Ⲗ Indian reservation/reserve
⌂ National Park
Ⲡ Industrial region
∴ Historical site
⌓ Research station
◉ Continent, realm
⌙ Region, peninsula
▲▲ Mountain range, mountains
▲ Peak
)(Pass
* Ice shelf, glacier

C

River, canal
Waterfall
Lake, lakes, reservoir
Swamp
Salt flat
Sea
Strait
Bay, gulf
Cape
Island, islands
Ocean current
Ocean floor landforms
Tectonic feature
Atmospheric phenomena
Time zone
Geographical grid

Independent country
Dependent territory
Federal state, province, territory
People, ethnic group, tribe
Indian reservation/reserve
National Park
Industrial region
Historical site
Research station
Continent, realm
Region, peninsula
▲▲ Mountain range, mountains
▲ Peak
)(Pass
✱ Ice shelf, glacier

River, canal
Waterfall
Lake, lakes, reservoir
Swamp
Salt flat
Sea
Strait
Bay, gulf
Cape
Island, islands
Ocean current
Ocean floor landforms
Tectonic feature
Atmospheric phenomena
Time zone
Geographical grid

Chaniá **133** CD 5
Channel Islands *[U.K.]* **131** AB 2
Channel Islands *[U.S.]* **92** BC 3
Channel Islands National Park **92** BC 3
Channel-Port aux Basques **88** F 3
Chantada **130** B 1
Chanthaburi **156** E 5
Chanute **94** E 3
Chao Phraya **156** DE 4/5
Chaoyang **154** NO 3
Chaozhou **154** N 7
Chapais **88** B 2
Chaparral **92** F 3
Chapayevsk **136** J 3
Chapeau **88** A 3
Chapecó **114** J 3
Chapel Hill **100** D 2
Chapleau **86** G 4
Chaplygin **136** F 3
Chappal Waddi ▲ **176** JK 7
Charcot Island **181** I CB 31/30
Chari **176** L 6
Chārīkār **150** KL 3
Charité, La **131** C 3
Chariton **94** E 2
Charleroi **131** D 2
Charles, Cape **98** F 3
Charles, Saint *[U.S., Maryland]* **98** E 3
Charles, Saint *[U.S., Missouri]* **94** F 3
Charles City **94** E 2
Charleston *[U.S., Illinois]* **94** FG 3
Charleston *[U.S., Missouri]* **94** F 3
Charleston *[U.S., South Carolina]* **100** D 2
Charleston *[U.S., West Virginia]* **98** D 3
Charlestown **115** II B 1
Charleville **166** JK 6
Charleville-Mézières **131** D 2
Charlevoix **98** C 1
Charley [= 6] **75** L-M 5-8
Charlie-Gibbs-Fracture Zone **10** FH 3
Charlotte *[U.S., Michigan]* **98** C 2
Charlotte *[U.S., North Carolina]* **100** C 2
Charlotte Amalie **101** IX
Charlotte Harbor **100** C 4
Charlotte Pass **66** RS 7
Charlottesville **98** E 3
Charlottetown **88** E 3
Charlotteville **115** II B 3
Charlston Peak ▲ **92** D 2/3
Charlton **86** H 3
Charozero **138** G 4
Charters Towers **166** JK 4/5
Chartres **131** C 2
Chashniki **128** K 1
Chaska **94** E 1
Chastyye **136** L 1
Châteaubriant **131** B 3
Château-du-Loir **131** C 3
Châteaudun **131** C 2/3
Château-Gontier **131** B 3
Châteaulin **131** A 2
Châteauroux **131** C 3
Châtellerault **131** C 3
Chatfield **94** EF 2
Chatham **98** D 2
Chatham Islands **166** RS 9
Chatham Rise **13** E 23/22
Châtillon **131** D 3
Chattahoochee **100** B 3
Chattahoochee **100** B 3
Chattanooga **100** B 2
Chaumont **131** D 2
Chauny **131** CD 2
Chaux-de-Fonds, La **128** C 4
Chaves **130** B 2
Chavusy **128** L 2
Chaykovskiy **136** L 2
Cheb **128** E 3
Cheboksary **136** H 2
Cheboygan **98** CD 1
Chechen' Island **134** HJ 2
Chechens **121** L 5
Chechnya □ **134** H 2
Checleset Bay **84** AB 3
Cheduba **150** P 7
Cheektowaga **98** E 2
Cheepash **86** G 3
Chegdomyn **148** bc 8
Chehalis **90** B 2
Chehel Chasmeh, Kūh-e ▲ **152** E 2
Cheju **154** P 5
Cheju Island **154** OP 5
Chekhov **136** E 2
Chekmagush **136** L 2
Chekshino **138** H 5
Chela, Serra da **178** G 6
Chelan **90** BC 2
Chelan, Lake **90** B 1
Chełm **128** H 2/3
Chelmsford **124** E 4
Chełmża **128** G 2
Cheltenham **124** D 4
Chelyabinsk **148** NO 8/7
Chelyuskin, Cape **148** WX 3
Chemehuevi Indian Reservation **92** D 3
Chemillé **131** B 3
Chemnitz **128** E 3
Cheney **90** C 2
Chengde **154** N 3
Chengdu **154** K 5
Chennai (Madras) **150** N 8
Chenzhou **154** M 6
Cheptsa **138** M 5
Cher **131** C 3
Cherbourg **131** B 2
Cherdakly **136** J 2
Cherdyn' **138** N 4
Cheremkhovo **148** UV 8
Cherepanovo **148** R 8
Cherepovets **138** G 5
Cherevkovo **138** JK 4
Chergui, Chott ech → Shuṭṭ ash-Sharqī
Cherkasy **136** C 4
Cherkess **121** KL 5
Cherkessk **134** F 2
Cherlak **148** PQ 8
Chermoz **138** N 5
Chern' **136** E 3
Chernihiv **136** C 3
Chernihivka **134** E 1
Chernivtsi **128** J 3
Chernjakhiv **128** K 3
Chernogorsk **148** T 8
Chernorechenskiy **138** M 4
Chernushka **136** L 2
Chernyakhovsk **128** H 1
Chernyanka **136** E 4
Chernyshevskiy **148** WX 6
Chërnyye Zemli **134** H 1
Chërnyy Yar **136** H 4/5
Cherokee *[U.S., Iowa]* **94** E 2
Cherokee *[U.S., Oklahoma]* **96** D 1
Cherokee **73** J-K 6
Cherokee Lake **100** C 1
Cherry Creek **92** D 2
Cherskiy **148** gh 5
Cherskiy Range **148** cf 5/6
Cherven Bryag **133** CD 2
Chervonohrad **128** HJ 3
Chervyen' **128** K 2
Cherykaw **128** L 2
Chesapeake **98** EF 3
Chesapeake Bay **98** EF 3
Chësha Bay **138** K 2
Chester *[U.K.]* **124** D 4
Chester *[U.S., California]* **92** B 1
Chester *[U.S., Illinois]* **94** F 3
Chester *[U.S., Pennsylvania]* **98** F 3
Chesterfield **124** D 4
Chesterfield Islands **166** MN 4/5
Chestertown **98** EF 3
Chesuncook Lake **98** G 1
Chetlasskiy Kamen' ▲ **138** L 3
Chetumal **102** H 5
Chetwynd **84** C 2
Cheyenne **90** F 3
Cheyenne **94** BC 2
Cheyenne [= Ch.] **73** H 5
Cheyenne River Sioux Indian Reservation **94** C 1
Cheyenne Wells **94** C 3
Chhattisgarh □ **150** N 7/6
Chiai **154** NO 7
Chiange **178** G 6
Chiang Mai **156** DE 4
Chiang Rai **156** DE 4
Ch'iatura **134** G 2
Chiavari **132** B 2
Chiavenna **132** B 1
Chiba **154** S 4/5
Chibcha **73** KL 9
Chibougamau **88** B 2
Chibougamau, Lac **88** B 2
Chibuto **178** L 7
Chicago **94** G 2
Chichagof Island **76** N 7
Chichén-Itzá ∴ **102** H 4
Chickasaw **73** J 6
Chickasha **96** D 2
Chiclayo **112** CD 5
Chico **92** B 2
Chico **114** F 6
Chicoma Mountain ▲ **92** F 2
Chicoutimi-Jonquière → Saguenay **88** C 2
Chidley, Cape **76** c 6/7
Chiemsee **128** E 4
Chieti **132** C 2
Chifeng **154** N 3
Chignik **78** J 7
Chihuahua **96** B 3
Chihuahua □ **96** B 3
Chilcotin **84** C 3
Childress **96** C 2
Chile ■ **108** FG 9/7
Chilean Antarctic Territory □ **181** II BA 33/3
Chileans **109** FG 8/7
Chile Basin **10** W 7
Chile Chico **114** E 7
Chilecito **114** F 3
Chile Rise **10** W 7/8
Chililabombwe **178** K 5
Chilko **84** BC 3
Chilko Lake **84** BC 3
Chillán **114** E 5
Chillicothe *[U.S., Illinois]* **94** F 2
Chillicothe *[U.S., Missouri]* **94** E 3
Chillicothe *[U.S., Ohio]* **98** D 3
Chilliwack **84** C 3
Chiloé Island **114** DE 6
Chilpancingo **102** F 5
Chilung **154** O 6
Chimayo **92** F 2/3
Chimborazo ▲ **112** CD 4
Chimbote **112** D 5
Chimoio **178** L 6
Chin □ **150** P 6
China ■ **154** GM 5
China Coast Time **38** B 5
Chinandega **102** H 6
China Plate **14** GH 4/5
China Point **92** C 3
China Time **38** B 6
Chinati Mountains **96** B 3
Chincha Alta **112** D 6
Chinchilla de Monte Aragón **130** D 2/3
Chincoteague **98** F 3
Chinde **178** M 6
Chinese **145** N-R 5-9
Chinese *[Christmas I.]* **164** C 9
Chingola **178** K 5
Chinhoyi **178** KL 6
Chinle **92** E 2
Chinook **90** E 1
Chins **145** N 7
Chioggia **132** C 1
Chionótrypa ▲ **133** CD 3
Chíos **133** D 4
Chíos **133** D 4
Chipata **178** L 5
Chipaya [= Ch.] **109** G 6
Chipewyan **73** GH 3/4
Chipman **88** D 3
Chippewa → Ojibwa **73** HK 4/5
Chippewa **94** F 1

■ Independent country
◘ Dependent territory
□ Federal state, province, territory
People, ethnic group, tribe
Indian reservation/reserve
National Park
Industrial region
∴ Historical site
Research station
Continent, realm
Region, peninsula
Mountain range, mountains
▲ Peak
)(Pass
✱ Ice shelf, glacier

hippewa Falls 94 F 1
hiquitanos 109 GH 6
hirchiq 148 OP 10
hiricahua Mountains 92 E 4
hiriguano 109 G 7/6
hirpan 133 D 2
hisasibi 86 H 2
hisasibi Indian Reserve 86 H 2
hishmy 136 L 2
hisholm 94 E 1
hişinău 128 K 4
hisos Mountains 96 C 3
histopol' 136 JK 2
hita 148 X 8
hitrāl 150 L 3
hitré 102 JK 7
hittagong 150 P 6
hitungwiza 178 KL 6
hkalovsk 136 G 2
hochiti Pueblo 92 F 3
hocos 109 F 4
hoctaw 73 K 6
hoctawhatchee 100 B 3
hodzież 128 F 2
hoiceland 84 G 2
hoiseul 166 M 2
hoix 96 A 4
hojna 128 E 2
hojnice 128 F 2
hōkai-san ▲ 154 RS 4
hokurdakh 148 ef 4/5
hokwé 178 L 7
hokwe 173 EF 6
holet 131 B 3
holoma 102 H 5
holuteca 102 H 6
homa 178 K 6
homutov 128 E 3
hon Buri 156 E 5
h'ŏngjin 154 PQ 3
h'ŏngju 154 P 4
hongqing 154 L 6
hŏnju 154 P 4
honos Archipelago 114 DE 6/7
hop 128 H 3
hornobyl' 136 BC 3
hornomors'ke 134 C 1
hornukhy 136 D 4
horreras ▲ 96 B 4
hortkiv 128 J 3
horzów 128 G 3
hosica 112 D 6
hos Malal 114 EF 5
hoszczno 128 F 2
hott ech Chergui → Shuṭṭ ash-Sharqī
hott el Djerid → Shuṭṭ al-Jarīd
hott Melrhir → Shuṭṭ Malghir
howan 100 D 1
howchilla 92 BC 2
hoybalsan 154 M 2
hoyr 154 L 2
hristchurch 166 PQ 9
hristiansted 101 IX
hristina 84 F 2/1
hristmas Island 156 F 10
Christoffelberg, Sint ▲ 115 I A 1
Chuang 145 O 7
Chubut 114 EF 6
Chubut 114 F 6
Chuchkovo 136 F 2
Chudniv 128 K 3
Chudovo 138 E 5
Chugash 73 C 4
Chuhuyiv 136 E 4
Chukchi 145 UV 3
Chukchi Plateau 12 B 3/4
Chukchi Sea 76 FG 5
Chukchi Shelf 12 B 4
Chukhloma 138 J 5
Chukot Peninsula 148 mn 5
Chukot Range 148 km 5
Chukotskiy, Cape 148 n 6
Chula Vista 92 C 3
Chul'man 148 Za 7
Chulucanas 112 D 5
Chulym 148 R 7
Chulym 148 S 7
Chumikan 148 bc 8
Chumphon 156 DE 5
Ch'unch'ŏn 154 PQ 4
Chupa 138 E 2
Chuprovo 138 K 3
Chuquicamata 114 F 2
Chur 128 D 4
Churchill 78 W 7
Churchill [Canada, Manitoba] 76 VW 7
Churchill [Canada, New Foundland and Labrador] 88 E 1
Churchill, Cape 76 W 7
Churchill Falls 88 DE 1
Churchill Lake 84 FG 1/2
Chuska Mountains 92 E 2/3
Chusovaya 138 O 5
Chusovoy 138 O 5
Chute-aux-Outardes 88 C 2
Chute-des-Passes 88 BC 2
Chutove 136 D 4
Chuuk Islands 156 P 6
Chuvashia 136 H 2
Chuwash 121 L 4
Chuxiong 154 K 7
Chwārtā 152 E 2
Chyhyryn 136 C 4
Ciadâr-Lunga 128 K 4
Cibecue 92 E 3
Cicero 94 FG 2
Cide 134 C 3
Ciechanów 128 GH 2
Ciego de Ávila 102 K 4
Ciénaga 112 DE 1
Ciénaga de Flores 96 CD 4
Cienfuegos 102 J 4
Cieza 130 D 3
Çifteler 134 C 3
Cihanbeyli 134 C 4
Cilacap 156 F 9
Cimarron 96 D 1/2
Cimişlia 128 K 4
Cincinnati 98 CD 3
Çine 134 B 4
Cintas Largas 109 H 6
Cinto, Monte ▲ 132 AB 2
Ciotat, La 131 D 4
Circeo, Cape 132 C 3
Circle [U.S., Alaska] 78 M 5
Circle [U.S., Montana] 90 F 2
Circleville 98 D 3
Cirebon 156 F 9
Cirripó, Cerro ▲ 102 J 7
Cirze 134 FG 4
Cisco 96 D 2
Cislău 133 D 1
Cisnădie 128 HJ 4
Cistierna 130 C 1
Città di Castello 132 C 2
Ciudad Bolívar 112 FG 2
Ciudad Constitución 102 C 4/3
Ciudad de Guatemala → Guatemala City 102 G 6
Ciudad del Carmen 102 G 5
Ciudad del Este 114 HJ 2/3
Ciudad de México → Mexico City 102 EF 5
Ciudad Guayana 112 G 2
Ciudad Madero 102 F 4
Ciudad Obregón 102 C 3
Ciudad Piar 112 G 2
Ciudad Real 130 C 3
Ciudad Rodrigo 130 BC 2
Ciudad Valles 102 EF 4
Ciudad Victoria 102 F 4
Ciutadella 130 F 2
Civitanova Marche 132 C 2
Civitavecchia 132 B 2/3
Civray 131 C 3
Çivril 134 B 4
Clair, Lake Saint 98 D 2
Clair, Saint 98 D 2
Claire 98 C 2
Clair Engle Lake 92 B 1
Clair Fork 96 D 2
Clamecy 131 D 3
Clanton 100 B 2
Clapier, Mont(e) ▲ 131 E 4
Clara, Santa 102 K 4
Clara Pueblo, Santa 92 EF 3
Claremont 98 FG 2
Claremore 96 E 1
Clarence Town 102 K 4
Clarendon 96 C 2
Clarenville-Shoal Marbour 88 G 2
Claresholm 84 E 3
Clarinda 94 E 2
Clarines 115 II A 3
Clarion Fracture Zone 10 TU 5
Clarita, Santa 92 C 3
Clark 94 D 1
Clark Fork 90 D 2
Clark Hill Lake 100 C 2
Clarksburg 98 DE 3
Clarksdale 96 F 2
Clarks Fork 90 E 2
Clarksville 100 B 1
Claude, Saint- 131 DE 3
Clay Center 94 D 3
Clayton 92 G 2
Clear Lake [U.S., Iowa] 94 E 2
Clear Lake [U.S., South Dakota] 94 D 1
Clear Lake [U.S., California] 92 B 1
Clear Lake [U.S., California] 92 B 2
Clearwater [Canada] 84 CD 3
Clearwater [U.S.] 100 C 3/4
Clearwater [Canada, Alberta] 84 E 2
Clearwater [Canada, British Columbia] 84 C 2
Clearwater, North Fork 90 CD 2
Clearwater Mountains 90 D 2
Cleburne 96 D 2
Cle Elum 90 B 2
Clemente, San 92 C 3
Clemente, San 92 C 3
Clemson 100 C 2
Clermont [Australia] 166 K 5
Clermont [Canada] 88 C 3
Clermont-Ferrand 131 CD 3
Cleveland [U.S., Mississippi] 96 F 2
Cleveland [U.S., Ohio] 98 D 2
Cleveland [U.S., Tennessee] 100 B 2
Cleveland [U.S., Texas] 96 E 3
Cleveland, Mount ▲ 90 D 1
Cleveland Heights 98 D 2
Clewiston 100 C 4
Clifden 124 A 4
Clifton 92 E 3
Clifton Forge 98 E 3
Climax 71 H 6
Clinch 98 D 3
Clinch Mountains 98 D 3
Clinton [Canada] 84 C 3
Clinton [U.S., Illinois] 94 F 2
Clinton [U.S., Indiana] 98 C 3
Clinton [U.S., Iowa] 94 F 2
Clinton [U.S., Mississippi] 96 F 2
Clinton [U.S., Missouri] 94 E 3
Clinton [U.S., North Carolina] 100 D 2
Clinton [U.S., Oklahoma] 96 D 2
Clinton [U.S., South Carolina] 100 C 2
Clipperton Fracture Zone 10 UV 5
Clipperton Island 102 D 6
Clonakilty 124 B 4
Cloncurry 166 J 5
Clonmel 124 B 4
Cloppenburg 128 C 2
Cloquet 94 E 1
Cloridorme 88 D 2
Cloud, Saint 94 E 1
Cloud Peak ▲ 90 F 2
Cloverdale 92 B 2
Cloverport 98 C 3
Clovis [U.S., California] 92 C 2
Clovis [U.S., New Mexico] 92 G 3
Cluj-Napoca 128 H 4
Clyde, Firth of 124 C 3
Clyde River 78 bc 4/5
Cnl. Oviedo = Coronel Oviedo 114 H 3

River, canal
Waterfall
Lake, lakes, reservoir
Swamp
Salt flat
Sea
Strait
Bay, gulf
Cape
Island, islands
Ocean current
Ocean floor landforms
Tectonic feature
Atmospheric phenomena
Time zone
Geographical grid

Independent country
Dependent territory
Federal state, province, territory
People, ethnic group, tribe
Indian reservation/reserve
National Park
Industrial region
∴ Historical site
Research station
Continent, realm
Region, peninsula
Mountain range, mountains
▲ Peak
)(Pass
∗ Ice shelf, glacier

River, canal
Waterfall
Lake, lakes, reservoir
Swamp
Salt flat
Sea
Strait
Bay, gulf
Cape
Island, islands
Ocean current
Ocean floor landforms
Tectonic feature
Atmospheric phenomena
Time zone
Geographical grid

Independent country
Dependent territory
Federal state, province, territory
People, ethnic group, tribe
Indian reservation/reserve
National Park
Industrial region
Historical site
Research station
Continent, realm
Region, peninsula
Mountain range, mountains
Peak
Pass
Ice shelf, glacier

River, canal
Waterfall
Lake, lakes, reservoir
Swamp
Salt flat
Sea
Strait
Bay, gulf
Cape
Island, islands
Ocean current
Ocean floor landforms
Tectonic feature
Atmospheric phenomena
Time zone
Geographical grid

Independent country
Dependent territory
Federal state, province, territory
People, ethnic group, tribe
Indian reservation/reserve
National Park
Industrial region
∴ Historical site
Research station
Continent, realm
Region, peninsula
Mountain range, mountains
▲ Peak
)(Pass
✱ Ice shelf, glacier

st Liverpool 98 D 2
st London 178 KL 9
stmain 88 A 1
stmain 88 AB 1
stmain Indian
Reserve 88 A 1/2
stman 100 C 2
st Mariana Basin 10 Q 5
ston [U.S., Maryland] 98 F 3
ston
[U.S., Pennsylvania] 98 F 2
st Pacific Rise 10 UV 8/5
st Point 100 B 2
st Point 101 IX
st Range 92 C 1
st Saint Louis 94 F 3
st Siberian Sea 148 el 4
st Siberian Shelf 12 B 6/7
st Tavaputs Plateau 92 E 2
st Timor
→ Timor-Leste
tonton 100 C 2
u Claire 94 F 1
b and Flow Indian
Reserve 86 C 3
ebiyin 176 K 8
erswalde 128 E 2
etsu 154 S 3
inur Hu 154 F 2/3
oli 132 D 3
olowa 176 K 8
ro 130 C 1
catepec 102 EF 5/4
ceabat 134 A 3
ija 130 C 3
kernförde 128 D 1
commoy 131 C 3
uador 112 D 4
uadorians 109 D-F 4-5
d 126 D 3
Dair, Jebel ▲
→ ad-Dayr, Jabal
Damer → Ad-Dāmīr
Dueim
→ Ad-Duwaym
de 128 B 2
déa 176 K 8
en
[U.S., North Carolina] 100 D 1
den [U.S., Texas] 96 D 3
denton 100 D 1
der 128 CD 3/2
dessa 133 C 3
dgefield 100 C 2
dgemont 94 BC 2
dgeøya 148 EF 3
dinburg 96 D 4
dinburgh 124 CD 3
dineţ 128 K 3
dirne 134 A 3
dith, Mount ▲ 90 E 2
djeleh → Al-ʿAjīlah
dmond 96 D 2
dmonton 84 E 2
dmundston 88 CD 3
dna 96 D 3
dremit 134 B 3
dson 84 D 2
dward, Lake 178 K 3

Edwards Plateau 96 CD 3
Eel 92 B 1
Éfaté 166 O 4
Effingham 94 F 3
Eforie 133 E 2
Egadi Islands 132 BC 4
Egan Range 92 D 2
Eger 128 G 4
Egersund 126 BC 3
Egilsstaðir 125 DE 2
Eglinton Island 76 QR 3
Egmont, Mount
(Taranaki) ▲ 166 OP 8/9
Eğridir 134 C 4
Eğridir, Lake 134 C 4
Egvekinot 148 m 5
Egypt 176 NO 3
Eindhoven 128 B 2
Eirunepé 112 EF 5
Eisenach 128 D 3/2
Eisenerz 128 E 4
Eisenhüttenstadt 128 E 2
Eisenstadt 128 F 4
Eišiškės 126 J 4
Eisleben, Lutherstadt 128 D 2
Eismitte 74 OP 2/3
Eivissa → Ibiza 130 E 3
Ejea de los Caballeros 130 D 1
Ejido, El 130 CD 3
Ejido Héroes 92 CD 4
Ejin Qi 154 K 3
Ekenäs 126 H 3
Ekibastuz 148 PQ 8
Ekimchan 148 b 8
Ekofisk 119 G 4
Ekonda 148 VW 5
Ekwan 86 G 2
El Alto 112 F 7
Elassóna 133 C 3
Elat 152 B 3
Elato 156 O 6
Elâzığ 134 F 4
Elba 100 B 3
Elba 132 B 2
El Barraco 130 C 2
El Barreal 96 B 3
Elbasan 133 B 3
El Bayadh → Al-Bayadh
Elbe 128 F 3
Elbert, Mount ▲ 94 B 3
Elberton 100 C 2
Elbeuf 131 C 2
Elbistan 134 E 4
Elbląg 128 G 1
Elbow Lake 94 D 1
El'brus ▲ 134 G 2
Elburz Mountains 150 G 3
El Cajon 92 C 3
El Calafate 114 E 8
El Campo 96 D 3
El Capitan ▲ 90 D 2
El Carmen de Bolívar 112 D 2
El Carrizo 96 B 3
El Centro 92 D 3
Elche 130 D 3
Elche de la Sierra 130 D 3
El Cozón 92 D 4
Elda 130 D 3
Eldorado [Argentina] 114 J 3

El Dorado
[U.S., Arkansas] 96 E 2
Eldorado [U.S., Illinois] 94 F 3
El Dorado [U.S., Kansas] 94 D 3
El Dorado [Venezuela] 112 G 2
Eldoret 178 M 2
El Ejido 130 CD 3
Elektrėnai 126 J 4
Elena, Punta Santa 112 C 4
Elena, Santa 96 C 4
Elena de Uairén, Santa 112 G 2/3
Eleşkirt 134 G 3
Eleuthera Island 102 KL 3
El Faiyûm → Al-Fayyūm
El Fasher → Al-Fāshir
El Fuerte 96 A 4
El Fula → Al-Fūlah
El Geneina
→ Al-Junaynah
Elgin 94 F 2
Elgin 124 C 2
El Goléa → Al-Ghulīʿah
Elgon, Mount ▲ 178 L 2
Elgoras ▲ 138 E 2
Elias, Mount Saint ▲ 76 M 6/7
Elias National Park,
Wrangell-Saint 78 M 6/7
Əli Bayramlı 134 J 3
Elimäki 126 J 2
Elisenvaara 138 DE 4
Elista 134 G 1
Elizabeth 98 F 2
Elizabeth, Cape 98 G 2
Elizabeth City 100 D 1
Elizabethton 100 C 1
Elizabethtown 98 C 3
Elizario, San 96 B 3
El Jaralito 96 B 4
Ełk 128 H 2
El Kala → Al-Qalʿah
Elk City 96 D 2
El Khârga → Al-Khārija
Elkhart 98 C 2
Elkhorn 94 D 2
Elkhorn 94 D 2
Elkhovo 133 D 2
Elkin 100 C 1
Elkins 98 E 3
Elk Island National
Park 84 E 2
Elk Lake 86 G 4
Elko 92 D 1
Elk River 94 E 1
Elkton 98 E 3
El Largo 96 A 3
Ellef Ringnes Island 76 TV 3
Ellen, Mount ▲ 92 E 2
Ellendale 94 D 1
Ellensburg 90 B 2
Ellesmere Island 76 Yb 3/2
Ellice Islands 166 Q 2/3
Elliot Lake 86 G 4
Ellisras → Lephalae
Ellsworth 98 GH 1
Ellsworth Land 181 I B 31/29
Ellsworth Range 13 BA 32/31
Elma 90 B 2
El Macao 101 VIII
Elmadağ 134 D 3

Elmalı 134 B 4
El Malpais National
Monument 92 E 3
Elmira 98 E 2
Elmshorn 128 D 2
El Muglad → Al-Mijlad
El Nido 156 H 5
El-Obeid (Al-Ubayyiḍ) 176 NO 6
Eloi, Saint- 88 C 2/3
El Oued → Al-Wādī
Eloy 92 E 3
Eloy Alfaro 112 D 4
El Paso 96 B 3
El Paso de Robles 92 B 3
El Pilar 115 II B 3
El Porvenír 102 K 7
El Progreso 102 H 5
El Puerto de Santa 130 BC 3
El Reno 96 D 2
Elrose 84 FG 3
El Sabinal, Parque
Nacional 96 CD 4
El Salto 102 D 4
El Salvador 107 G 7
El Salvador 102 GH 6
El Sauzal 92 C 4
El Simbillâwein
→ As-Sinballāwayn
Eltanin Fracture Zone 13 DE 28/25
El Tarf → Aṭ-Ṭarif
El Teniente 107 F 8
El Tigre 112 G 2
El'ton 136 H 4
El Turbio 107 F 10
Elva 126 J 3
Elvas 130 B 3
El Vendrell 130 E 2
El Verde 96 B 4
Elverum 126 DE 2
Elwell, Lake 90 E 1
Elwood 98 C 2
Ely [U.S., Minnesota] 86 E 4
Ely [U.S., Nevada] 92 D 2
Elyria 98 D 2
Emajõgi 126 JK 3
Emāmrūd 150 GH 3
Emån 126 F 3
Embarcación 114 G 2
Embi 136 M 4
Embrun 131 E 4
Embu 178 M 3
Emden 128 C 2
Emerald 166 K 5
Emeraude, Côte 123 C 3
Emerson 86 C 3
Emet 134 B 3
Emi Koussi ▲ 176 L 5
Emilia-Romagna 132 BC 2
Emine, Nos 133 E 2
Emirdağ 134 C 4
Emmaboda 126 F 4
Emmaste 126 H 3
Emmen 128 C 2
Emmetsburg 94 E 2
Emmett 90 C 3
Emperor Seamounts 10 R 3/4
Empoli 132 B 2
Emporia [U.S., Kansas] 94 DE 3
Emporia [U.S., Virginia] 98 E 3

River, canal
Waterfall
Lake, lakes, reservoir
Swamp
Salt flat
Sea
Strait
Bay, gulf
Cape
Island, islands
Ocean current
Ocean floor landforms
Tectonic feature
Atmospheric phenomena
Time zone
Geographical grid

Empress 84 F 3
Ems 128 C 2
Enarotali 156 M 8
Encantada, Cerro de la ▲ 102 B 2
Encarnación 114 H 3
Encinal 96 D 4
Encino 96 D 4
Endako 71 F 4
Endeh 156 J 9
Endicott 98 EF 2
Energetik 136 M 3
Enewetak Atoll 156 R 5
Enez 134 A 3
Engaño, Cabo 101 VIII
Engel's 136 H 3
Enggano 156 E 9
England 124 D 3/4
England 117 FG 4
Englee 88 FG 2
English 121 F 4
English 86 D 3
English Channel 124 CE 5
Enid 96 D 1
Enköping 126 F 3
Enna 132 C 4
En-Nahud → An-Nuhūd 98 F 5
Ennedi ▲▲ 176 M 5
Ennis *[Ireland]* 124 B 4
Ennis *[U.S.]* 96 D 2
Enniscorthy 124 BC 4
Enniskillen 124 B 3
Enns 128 E 4
Eno 126 L 2
Enschede 128 C 2
Ensenada 92 C 4
Enshi 154 L 5
Entebbe 178 L 2/3
Enterprise 100 B 3
Entre Ríos 114 GH 4
Entroncamento 130 B 2
Enugu 176 J 7
Envigado 112 D 2
Épernay 131 D 2
Ephesos ∴ 134 B 4
Ephraim 92 E 2
Ephrata 90 C 2
Épi 166 O 4
Épinal 131 E 2
Epirus 133 BC 3
Eqlīd 152 G 3
Equator 4 B 5
Equatorial Counter Current 6 FK 5
Equatorial Guinea 176 J 8
Erbaa 134 E 3
Erciş 134 G 3/4
Erciyeş ▲ 134 D 4
Érd 128 G 4
Erdek 134 B 3
Erdemli 134 D 4
Erdenet 154 KL 2
Erebus, Mount ▲ 181 I B 19/18
Erechim 114 J 3
Ereğli *[Turkey, Konya]* 134 D 4
Ereğli *[Turkey, Zonguldak]* 134 C 3
Erenhot 154 M 3
Ereymentaū 148 P 8
Erfurt 128 D 2/3
Erg, Great Eastern 176 J 3/2
Erg, Great Western 176 GH 2
Ergani 134 F 4
Erg Chech 176 G 4/3
Ergene 134 A 3
Erg Ighidi 176 FG 3
Ērgli 126 J 4
Eridu ∴ → Abū Shahrayn 152 E 3
Erie 98 DE 2
Erie, Lake 98 DE 2
Erie Canal 98 E 2
Erimo, Cape 154 S 3
Eritrea 176 PQ 5/6
Erlangen 128 D 3
Ermenek 134 CD 4
Ermoúpoli 133 D 4
Er Rachidia → Ar-Rashīdiyah
Er Rif ▲▲ → Ar-Rif
Errigal ▲ 124 B 3
Erris Head 124 A 3
Erromango 166 O 4
Ersekë 133 B 3
Erstein 131 E 2
Ertil' 136 F 3
Ertīs 148 PQ 8
Ertsberg 165 G 7
Eruh 134 G 4
Erwin 100 C 1
Erzincan 134 EF 3
Erzurum 134 F 3
Esa'ala 156 OP 9/10
Esbjerg 126 C 4
Escalón 96 B 4
Escambia 100 B 3
Escanaba 98 C 1
Escarpada Point 156 J 4
Esch-sur-Alzette 131 DE 2
Eschwege 128 D 2
Escondido 92 C 3
Escoumins, Les 88 C 2
Eṣfahān → Isfahan 152 FG 2
Esfandāran 152 G 3
Esil 148 O 8
Eskasoni Indian Reserve 88 E 3
Eskene 136 K 5
Eskifjörður 125 E 2
Eskilstuna 126 F 3
Eskimos 145 W 3
Eskişehir 134 C 3
Esla 130 C 1
Eslamābād-e Gharb 152 E 2
Eslāmshahr 152 F 2
Eslöv 126 E 4
Eşme 134 B 4
Esmeraldas 112 D 3
Espalion 131 CD 4
Espanola *[Canada]* 86 G 4
Espanola *[U.S.]* 92 F 3
Española 112 B 4
Esperance 166 E 7
Esperanza 181 II C 33
Espinazo 96 C 4
Espinhaço, Serra do ▲▲ 112 L 7/6
Espírito Santo 114 L 1/2
Espíritu Santo 166 NO 3/4
Espoo 126 J 2
Esquel 114 E 6
Essaouira → Aṣ-Ṣawīrah
Es Semara → As-Samārah
Essen 128 C 2
Essequibo 112 H 3
Essex 98 F 1
Esslingen am Neckar 128 D 3
Estacado, Llano 96 C 2
Estância 112 M 6
Este, Punta del 114 J 4
Estelí 102 H 6
Estella 130 D 1
Estelo Bay 92 B 3
Estepona 130 C 3
Esterhazy 86 B 3
Estero Bay 100 C 4
Estes Park 94 B 2
Estevan 86 B 3
Estherville 94 E 2
Estonia 126 J 3
Estonians 121 J 4
Estrada, A 130 B 1
Estrela, Serra da ▲▲ 123 C 4/3
Estremadura 130 AB 3/2
Esztergom 128 G 4
Etal 156 P 6
Étampes 131 C 2
Ethiopia 176 OQ 7
Ethiopian Highlands ▲▲ 169 GH 4/5
Étienne, Saint- 131 D 3
Etna, Monte ▲ 132 CD 4
Etne 126 C 3
Etosha Pan 178 H 6
Etsch 132 B 1
Etzikom Coulee 84 F 3
Eua 166 S 5
Euboea 133 CD 4
Eucla 166 F 7
Euclid 98 D 2
Eufaula *[U.S., Alabama]* 100 B 3
Eufaula *[U.S., Oklahoma]* 96 E 2
Eufaula Reservoir 96 E 2
Eugene 90 B 2/3
Eugenia, Punta Santa 102 B 3
Eulalia del Río, Santa 130 E 2/3
Eunápolis 112 M 7
Eunice *[U.S., Louisiana]* 96 E 3
Eunice *[U.S., New Mexico]* 92 G 3
Euphrates 150 DE 3
Eupora 96 F 2
Eurasian Basin 12 A 9/20
Eurasian Plate 14 EG 2/3
Eureka *[U.S., California]* 92 AB 1
Eureka *[U.S., Kansas]* 94 D 3
Eureka *[U.S., Montana]* 90 D 1
Eureka *[U.S., Nevada]* 92 C 2
Europa 178 N 7
Europa, Picos de ▲▲ 130 C 1
Europe 4 JM 3
European Union 51 KL 2/3
Euskirchen 128 C 3
Eustasius, Sint 115 II B 1
Eustis 100 C 3
Eutaw 100 AB 2
Eutsuk Lake 84 B 2
Evans, Lac 88 A 2
Evans, Mount ▲ 84 D 3
Evanston *[U.S., Illinois]* 94 G 2
Evanston *[U.S., Wyoming]* 90 E 3
Evansville 98 C 3
Évaux-les-Bains 131 CD 3
Evenks 145 N-S 3-4
Evens 145 Q-U 2-3
Evensk 148 gh 6
Everest, Mount ▲ 150 O 5
Everett 90 B 2
Everglades, The 100 C 4
Everglades City 100 C 4
Everglades National Park 100 I C 4
Evinayong 176 K 8
Evje 126 C 3
Évora 130 B 3
Évreux 131 C 2
Ewa Beach 92 I BC 2
Ewe 173 D 5
Ewo 178 GH 3
Excelsior Springs 94 E 3
Exeter 124 C 5
Exploits 88 F 2
Exshaw 84 E 3
Extremadura 130 BC 3/2
Eyak 73 D 3
Eyasi, Lake 178 LM 3
Eyjafjörður 125 C 1
Eymoutiers 131 C 3
Eyre, Lake 166 GH 6
Eysturoy 124 A 2
Ezhva 138 L 4
Ezine 134 A 3

F

Fabens 96 B 3
Fabriano 132 C 2
Facpi Point 101 II
Factory Island Indian Reserve 86 GH 3
Fada 176 M 5
Fada N'Gourma 176 GH 6
Faddeyev Island 148 de 3/4
Faenza 132 BC 2
Făgăraş 128 J 4
Fagatogo 101 VII
Fagernes 126 D 2
Fagersta 126 F 2/3
Fahs, Al- 132 B 4
Faial 130 B 5
Fā'id 152 B 3
Fairbanks 78 L 5
Fairbury 94 D 2
Fairfield *[U.S., California]* 92 B 2
Fairfield *[U.S., Illinois]* 94 FG 3
Fairfield *[U.S., Iowa]* 94 EF 2
Fairford Indian Reserve 86 C 3
Fair Isle 124 D 2
Fairmont *[U.S., Minnesota]* 94 E 2
Fairmont *[U.S., West Virginia]* 98 D 3

Independent country
Dependent territory
Federal state, province, territory
People, ethnic group, tribe
Indian reservation/reserve
National Park
Industrial region
∴ Historical site
Research station
Continent, realm
Region, peninsula
▲▲ Mountain range, mountains
▲ Peak
)(Pass
∗ Ice shelf, glacier

rview *[Canada]* 84 D 1
rview *[U.S.]* 96 D 1
s 156 N 6
salabad 150 KL 4
zabad 150 N 5
ardo 101 VIII
r, Wādī 152 C 3
kaofo 166 S 2
kfak 156 L 8
ko ▲ → Cameroon
Mountain 176 J 8
avarjan 152 F 2
con Reservoir 96 D 4
lenki 138 M 5
eşti 128 K 4
furrias 96 D 4
lkenberg 126 DE 4
lkirk 124 C 3
lkland, East 114 H 8
lkland, West 114 G 8
lkland Current 6 MN 8
lkland Islanders 109 H 10
lkland Islands
(Islas Malvinas) 114 GH 8
lköping 126 E 3
llon 92 C 2
llon Indian
Reservation 92 C 2
ll River 98 G 2
lls City 94 E 3
llūjah, Al- 152 DE 2
lmouth *[U.K.]* 124 C 5
lmouth
[U.S., Kentucky] 98 CD 3
lmouth
[U.S., Massachusetts] 98 G 2
lster 126 E 4
lticeni 128 J 4
lun 126 F 2
magusta
(Gazimajusa) 152 B 2
menin 152 F 2
ng 173 E 5
no 132 C 2
qūs 152 AB 3
rafangana 178 O 7
rāh 150 J 4
rallon Islands 92 B 2
ranah 176 EF 6/7
rasān Islands 150 DE 7
raulep 156 N 6
rewell, Cape
[Greenland] 76 g 7
rewell, Cape
[New Zealand] 166 P 9
rgo 94 D 1
rg'ona 148 P 11/10
ribault 94 E 1
rjestaden 126 F 4
rmington
[U.S., Missouri] 94 F 3
rmington
[U.S., New Mexico] 92 E 2
rmville 98 E 3
rnham, Mount ▲ 84 D 3
ro *[Canada]* 78 O 6
ro *[Portugal]* 130 B 3
rö 126 G 3
roe Islands 124 AB 2
Faroe Islands 117 F 3
Faroese 121 F 3
Fårösund 126 G 3
Farquhar Islands 178 OP 5
Farragut 100 B 1/2
Farrāshband 152 FG 3
Fársala 133 C 3
Farsund 126 C 3
Farwānīyah, Al- 152 E 3
Farwell 96 C 2
Fās → Fez 176 G 2
Fasā 150 G 5
Fāshir, Al- 176 N 6
Fashn, Al- 152 A 3
Fastiv 136 BC 4
Fatezh 136 DE 3
Fatick 176 D 6
Fatsa 134 E 3
Făurei 133 E 1/2
Fauske 125 C 3
Fāw, Al- 152 F 3
Fawn 86 E 2
Faxa Bay 125 B 2
Faxälven 126 F 1
Faya (Largeau) 176 LM 5
Fayetteville
[U.S., Arkansas] 96 E 1/2
Fayetteville
[U.S., North Carolina] 100 D 2
Fayetteville
[U.S., Tennessee] 100 B 2
Fâyid → Fā'id
Faylakah 152 F 3
Fayyūm, Al- 152 A 3
Fazzān 176 KL 3
Fdayrik 171 B 3
Fe, Santa *[Argentina]* 114 G 4
Fe, Santa *[U.S.]* 92 F 3
Fe, Santa 114 G 4
Fear, Cape 100 D 2
Fécamp 131 BC 2
Federal Way 90 B 2
Federation of Bosnia
and Herzegovina 132 DE 2
Fëdorovka 136 L 3
Fe do Sul, Santa 112 J 8/7
Fehmarn 128 D 1
Feira de Santana 112 LM 6
Feke 134 D 4
Feldberg ▲ 128 C 4
Feldkirch 128 D 4
Félicien, Saint- 88 B 2
Felipe, San 112 F 1
Felipe Pueblo, San 92 F 3
Feliu de Guíxols, Sant 130 E 2
Félix do Araguaia, São 112 J 6
Félix do Xingu, São 112 J 5
Feltre 132 B 1
Femunden 126 D 2
Feni Islands 156 PQ 8
Feodosiya 134 DE 1/2
Fereydunshahr 152 F 2
Fergus 98 D 2
Fergus Falls 94 DE 1
Fergusson Island 156 P 9
Ferme-Neuve 88 B 3
Fermo 132 C 2
Fermont 88 D 1
Fermoselle 130 BC 2
Fernandina 112 A 4
Fernandina Beach 100 C 3
Fernando, San *[Chile]* 114 EF 4
Fernando, San
*[Philippines,
Central Luzon]* 156 J 4/5
Fernando, San
[Philippines, Ilocos] 156 HJ 4
Fernando, San *[Spain]* 130 B 3
Fernando, San
[Trinidad and Tobago] 115 II B 3
Fernando de Apure,
San 112 F 2
Fernando de Atabapo,
San 112 F 3
Fernando del Valle de
Catamarca, San 114 F 3
Fernando de
Noronha 112 N 4
Fernie 84 E 3
Fernley 92 C 2
Ferrara 132 BC 2
Ferriday 96 F 3
Ferrol 130 B 1
Ferté-Bernard, La- 131 C 2
Fès → Fez (Fās)
Festus 94 F 3
Feteşti 133 E 2
Fethiye 134 B 4
Fetsund 126 C 3
Feurs 131 D 3
Fevral'sk 148 ab 8
Feyzābād 150 KL 3
Fez (Fās) 176 G 2
Fezzan → Fazzān
Ffestiniog 124 C 4
Fianarantsoa 178 O 7
Fidenza 132 B 2
Fier 133 B 3
Figeac 131 C 4
Figueira da Foz 130 AB 2
Figueres 130 EF 1
Figuig → Fikīk
Fiji 166 PQ 4
Fijians 164 K 9
Fiji Basin, North 10 R 6/7
Fikīk 176 G 2
Filadelfia 114 GH 2
Filchner Ice Shelf ✱ 181 I BA 34/35
Filiaşi 133 C 2
Filiatrá 133 C 4
Filipe, São 176 BC 6
Filippiáda 133 B 3
Filipstad 126 E 3
Fillmore 92 D 2
Filyos 134 C 3
Findlay 98 D 2
Finger Lakes 98 E 2
Finike 134 C 4
Finisterre, Cape 130 AB 1
Finland 120 J 3
Finnish Lakes 123 F 1
Finnmark 125 EF 2
Finns 121 J 3
Finnsnes 125 D 2
Finsterwalde 128 E 2
Fiour, Saint- 131 D 3
Fipa 173 G 6
Firminy 131 D 3
Firovo 136 D 1
First Kurile Strait 148 fg 8
Firth of Clyde 124 C 3
Firth of Forth 124 D 3
Firth of Lorne 124 BC 3
Firūzābād 152 G 3
Fīrūzkūh 152 G 2
Fisher River Indian
Reserve 86 C 3
Fishguard 124 C 4
Fitchburg 98 G 2
Fitzgerald 100 C 3
Fitzroy 166 E 4
Fiumicino 132 BC 3
Fjord Coast 123 D 2/1
Flagstaff 92 E 3
Flagstaff Lake 98 G 1
Flambeau 94 F 1
Flamborough Head 124 DE 3/4
Flaming Gorge
Reservoir 90 E 3
Flanagan Passage 101 IX
Flanders 131 CD 2/1
Flandreau 94 D 1/2
Flathead 73 GH 5
Flathead, South Fork 90 D 1/2
Flathead Indian
Reservation 90 D 2
Flathead Lake 90 D 1/2
Flèche, La 131 BC 3
Fleetwood 124 C 4
Flekkefjord 126 C 3
Flemings 121 G 4
Flemish Region 131 D 2/1
Flen 126 F 3
Flensburg 128 D 1
Flers 131 B 2
Flinders 166 J 4
Flin Flon 86 B 2
Flint 98 D 2
Flint 100 B 2
Flint Hills ▲▲ 94 D 3
Flint Island 160 OP 5
Flipper Point 101 IV
Flix 130 E 2
Florac 131 D 4
Florence *[U.S., Alabama]* 100 AB 2
Florence *[U.S., Arizona]* 92 E 3
Florence *[U.S., Colorado]* 94 B 3
Florence *[U.S., Oregon]* 90 A 2/3
Florence
[U.S., South Carolina] 100 CD 2
Florence (Firenze) *[Italy]* 132 B 2
Florencia 112 DE 3
Flores 102 GH 5
Flores *[Indonesia]* 156 J 9
Flores *[Portugal]* 130 A 5
Flores Sea 156 HJ 9
Floreşti 128 K 4
Floresville 96 D 3
Floriano 112 L 5
Florianópolis 114 K 3
Florida 100 BC 3/4
Florida 80 L 5/6
Florida, Straits of 100 I CD 4
Florida Bay 100 I C 4
Floridablanca 112 E 2
Florida Keys 100 I C 4
Flórina 133 C 3

River, canal
Waterfall
Lake, lakes, reservoir
Swamp
Salt flat
Sea
Strait
Bay, gulf
Cape
Island, islands
Ocean current
Ocean floor landforms
Tectonic feature
Atmospheric phenomena
Time zone
Geographical grid

Independent country
Dependent territory
Federal state, province, territory
People, ethnic group, tribe
Indian reservation/reserve
National Park
Industrial region
Historical site
Research station
Continent, realm
Region, peninsula
Mountain range, mountains
▲ Peak
)(Pass
* Ice shelf, glacier

erte Olimpo **114** H 2
erteventura ⌓ **130** F 5
glafjørður **124** A 2
ḩayḩīl, Al- **152** F 3
ji, Mount ▲ **154** R 4/5
jian ▽ **154** N 6
jin **154** Q 2
kui **154** QR 4
kuoka **154** PQ 5
kushima **154** S 4
lah, Al- **176** N 6
lbe ⚇ **173** B-E 4-5
lda **128** D 3
lda ∽ **128** D 2
ling **154** L 6
lnio ⚇ **109** K 5
lton *[U.S., Missouri]* **94** F 3
lton *[U.S., New York]* **98** E 2
nabashi **154** S 4
nafuti **166** QR 2
nafuti ⌓ **166** Q 2
nchal **130** B 6
ndão **130** B 2
ndy, Bay of ≋) **88** D 3
ndy National Park ⌂ **88** D 3
nk Island ⌓ **88** G 2
ntua **176** J 6
rgun, Kūh-e ▲ **150** H 5
rmanov **136** F 1
rneaux Islands ⌓ **166** KL 9
rstenfeld **128** F 4
rstenwalde **128** E 2
rth **128** D 3
scaldo **132** D 3
shun **154** OP 3
tuna ⌓ **166** R 3
xin **154** O 3
yang **154** MN 5
yun **154** G 2
zhou **154** NO 6
zuli **134** H 3
n ⌓ **126** D 4
odorovka **136** K 3

G

aalkacyo **176** R 7
abbs **92** C 2
abès, Gulf of ≋) **176** K 2
abès (Qābis) **176** JK 2
abon ◼ **178** FG 3
aborone **178** K 7/8
abriel da Cachoeira, São **112** F 4
abriel Leyva Solanos **96** A 4
abriel Mountains, San ▲▲ **92** C 3
abrovo **133** D 2
abú **176** E 6
achsārān **152** F 3
adag **150** M 7
adsden **100** B 2
aels ⚇ **121** F 4
ăeşti **133** D 2
aeta **132** C 3
aferut ⌓ **156** O 6
affney **100** C 2
afsa → Qafşah

Gagarin **136** D 2
Gagauz [= Ga.] ⚇ **121** J 5
Gagliano del Capo **132** E 3
Gagnoa **176** F 7
Gagnon **88** CD 2
Gagra **134** F 2
Gaillac **131** C 4
Gainesville *[U.S., Florida]* **100** C 3
Gainesville *[U.S., Georgia]* **100** C 2
Gainesville *[U.S., Texas]* **96** D 2
Gairdner, Lake ⩌ **166** GH 7
Gaithersburg **98** E 3
Gaizina Kalns ▲ **126** J 4
Galápagos Islands ⌓ **112** AB 3
Galashiels **124** CD 3
Galaţi **133** E 1
Galatina **132** E 3
Galax **98** D 3
Gáldar **130** F 5
Galdhøpiggen ▲ **126** C 2
Galeota Point)≋ **115** II B 3
Galera, Punta)≋ **112** C 3
Galera Point)≋ **115** II B 3
Galesburg **94** F 2
Gali **134** F 2
Galibi ⚇ **109** H 4
Galich **138** HJ 5
Galicia ▽ **130** B 1
Galicians ⚇ **121** F 5
Galion **98** D 2
Galite, La ⌓ → Jālīţā
Gallatin **100** B 1
Galle **150** MN 9
Gallen, Sankt **128** D 4
Gallinas, Punta)≋ **112** E 1
Gallipoli **132** E 3
Gallipolis **98** D 3
Gällivare **125** DE 3
Gallup **92** E 3
Gallur **130** D 2
Galveston **96** E 3
Galveston ⌓ **96** E 3
Galveston Bay ≋) **96** E 3
Galway **124** A 4
Galway Bay ≋) **124** A 4
Gāmāsīāb ∽ **152** E 2
Gambēla **176** O 7
Gambell **78** F 6
Gambia ◼ **176** DE 6
Gambia ∽ **176** E 6
Gambo **88** G 2
Gamburtsev Mountains ▲▲ **13** AB 13/14
Gamış Dağı ▲ **134** H 3
Gamma [= 14] ☁ **75** K-M 8
Ganado **92** E 3
Gananoque **88** AB 3
Ganda ⚇ **173** G 6/5
Gandajika **178** J 4
Gander **88** G 2
Gāndhīdhām **150** K 6
Gandhinagar **150** L 6
Gandia **130** DE 2/3
Ganganagar **150** LM 5
Ganges ∽ **150** M 5
Gangi **132** C 4
Gangtok **150** O 5
Gannat **131** D 3

Gannett Peak ▲ **90** E 3
Gansu ▽ **154** JL 3/5
Gantang **154** K 4
Gantiadi **134** F 2
Ganyushkīn **134** J 1
Ganzhou **154** N 6
Gao **176** H 5
Gap **131** DE 4
Gar **154** F 5
Garabogaz aÿlagy ◒ **148** L 10
Garagum ⛬ **148** MN 10/11
Garagum Canal ∽ **148** N 11
Garan, Cape)≋ **154** O 7
Garanhuns **112** M 5
Garapan **101** III
Garapan **156** NO 4
Garbahaarey **176** Q 8
Garbosh, Kūh-e ▲ **152** F 2
Garda, Lake ◒ **132** B 1
Gardelegen **128** D 2
Garden City **94** C 3
Gardēz **150** K 4
Garfield Mountain ▲ **90** D 2
Gargždai **126** H 4
Gari **138** P 5
Garifuna ⚇ **73** K 8
Garissa **178** MN 3
Garland **96** D 2
Garliava **126** H 4
Garmī **134** HJ 3/4
Garmisch-Partenkirchen **128** D 4
Garmsar **152** G 2
Garnett **94** E 3
Garo ⚇ **145** MN 7
Garonne ∽ **131** C 4
Garoowe **176** RS 7
Garoua **176** K 7
Garovillas **130** B 2
Garrīn, Kūh-e ▲ **152** F 2
Garrison **90** D 2
Garue **178** M 6
Gary **98** C 2
Garzê **154** JK 5
Gasconade ∽ **94** F 3
Gascony ⛬ **131** BC 4
Gascoyne ∽ **166** D 5/6
Gashua **176** K 6
Gaspé **88** D 2
Gasteiz/Vitoria **130** D 1
Gaston, Lake ◒ **100** D 1
Gastonia **100** C 2
Gata, Cabo de)≋ **130** D 3
Gata, Cape)≋ **152** B 2
Gata, Sierra de ▲▲ **130** B 2
Gatchina **138** DE 5
Gates of the Arctic National Park ⌂ **78** JK 5
Gatesville **96** D 3
Gatineau ∽ **88** B 3
Gau ⌓ **166** QR 4
Gaudens, Saint- **131** C 4
Gauja ∽ **126** J 3
Gausta ▲ **126** C 3
Gávdos ⌓ **133** D 5
Gave de Pau ∽ **131** B 4
Gävle **126** F 2
Gavrilov-Yam **136** F 1
Gaxun Nur ◒ **154** JK 3
Gay **136** M 3

Gaya **150** NO 6
Gayndah **166** L 6
Gayny **138** MN 4
Gayutino **138** G 5
Gaza (Ghazzah) **152** B 3
Gaza Strip [= 2] ▽ **152** B 3
Gaziantep **134** E 4
Gazimajusa → Famagusta **152** B 2
Gazipaşa **134** C 4
Gazli **143** K 5
Gbaya ⚇ **173** E-F 5
Gboko **176** JK 7
Gdańsk **128** G 1
Gdańsk Bay ≋) **128** G 1
Gdov **138** D 5
Gdynia **128** G 1
Gearhart Mountain ▲ **90** B 3
Gebze **134** B 3
Gedaref → Al-Qadārif
Gediz **134** B 3
Gediz ∽ **134** B 4
Gedser **126** DE 4
Geelong **166** J 8
Geesthacht **128** D 2
Geilo **126** C 2
Geithus **126** D 3
Gejiu **154** K 7
Gela **132** C 4
Gelendzhik **134** E 2
Gelibolu **134** AB 3
Gelsenkirchen **128** D 2
Gemena **178** HJ 2
Gemerek **134** E 3
Gemlik **134** B 4
Gemona **132** C 1
Gemünden **128** D 3
Genalē ∽ **176** PQ 7
Genç **134** F 4
Gəncə **134** H 3
General Acha **114** G 5
General Eugenio A. Garay **114** G 2
General Pico **114** FG 5
General Roca **114** F 5
General Santos **156** K 6
Genesee ∽ **98** E 2
Geneva *[U.S., Alabama]* **100** B 3
Geneva *[U.S., Nebraska]* **94** D 2
Geneva *[U.S., New York]* **98** E 2
Geneva (Genève) *[Switzerland]* **128** BC 4
Geneva, Lake ◒ **128** C 4
Genève → Geneva **128** BC 4
Genil ∽ **130** C 3
Genk **131** D 2
Genoa (Genova) **132** AB 2
Genoa, Gulf of ≋) **132** AB 2
Genova → Genoa **132** AB 2
Gent → Ghent **131** D1/2
George **178** J 9
George, Lake ◒ **100** C 3
George, Point Saint)≋ **92** A 1
George, Saint **92** D 2
George, Saint ⌓ **100** B 3
George Land ⌓ **148** JK 3/4
Georges, Saint- *[Canada]* **88** C 3
George's, Saint *[Grenada]* **115** II B 2
George's Bay, Saint ≋) **88** F 2

∽ River, canal
⟆ Waterfall
◒ Lake, lakes, reservoir
≂ Swamp
⩌ Salt flat
≋ Sea
≍ Strait
≋) Bay, gulf
)≋ Cape
⌓ Island, islands
⇄ Ocean current
≙ Ocean floor landforms
⌁ Tectonic feature
☁ Atmospheric phenomena
◷ Time zone
⊕ Geographical grid

■ Independent country
◗ Dependent territory
▽ Federal state, province, territory
⚇ People, ethnic group, tribe
Ⴟ Indian reservation/reserve
⌂ National Park
Industrial region
∴ Historical site
Research station
⊛ Continent, realm
⊵ Region, peninsula
▲▲ Mountain range, mountains
▲ Peak
)(Pass
✳ Ice shelf, glacier

rgān 150 GH 3
rgona 132 B 2
ri 134 G 2/3
ris 134 H 3
rizia 132 C 1
rki 138 Q 3
r'kiy Reservoir 136 G 1/2
rlitz 128 E 2
rnji Vakuf 132 DE 2
rno-Altaysk 148 RS 8
rno-Badakhshan 150 L 3
rnozavodsk [Russia, Perm'] 138 O 5
rnozavodsk [Russia, Sakhalin] 148 cd 9
rnyy 136 J 3
rnyy Balykley 136 GH 4
rnyy Zerentuy 148 Y 8
rodets 136 G 2
rodishche 136 H 3
rodovikovsk 134 FG 1
roka 156 O 9
rokhovets 136 FG 2
rontalo 156 J 7
rshechnoye 136 E 3
ryachi Klyuch 134 EF 2
rzów Wielkopolski 128 EF 2
shen 98 C 2
shute Indian Reservation 92 D 1
slar 128 D 2
spić 132 D 2
stivar 133 BC 3
stynin 128 G 2
ta Älv 126 DE 3
taland 126 EF 3
teborg 126 D 3
tha 128 D 2/3
thenburg 94 CD 2
tland 126 G 3
to Islands 154 P 5
tse Delchev 133 CD 3
tska Sandön 126 G 3
ttingen 128 D 2
tt Peak 84 C 3
ugh Island 169 B 9
uin, Réservoir 88 B 2
ulburn 166 K 7
uménissa 133 C 3
urin 131 A 2
uveia 130 B 2
uverneur 98 F 1
ve 165 G 8
vernador Valadares 112 L 7
vĭ Altayn Nuruu 154 JK 3
ya 114 H 3
öyçay 134 HJ 3
öynük 134 C 3
zo 132 C 4/5
rachevka 136 K 3
racias á Dios, Cape 102 J 5/6
raciosa [Portugal] 130 B 5
raciosa [Spain] 130 G 5
rado 130 B 1
rafton [Australia] 166 L 6
rafton [U.S., North Dakota] 86 C 3
rafton [U.S., West Virginia] 98 DE 3
Graham 96 D 2
Graham, Mount 92 E 3
Graham Bell Island 148 OQ 2
Grahamstown 178 JK 9
Grain Coast 169 BC 5
Grajewo 128 H 2
Grampian Mountains 124 C 3/2
Gramsh 133 B 3
Granada [Nicaragua] 102 HJ 6
Granada [Spain] 130 C 3
Granbury 96 D 2
Granby [Canada] 88 B 3
Granby [U.S.] 94 B 2/3
Gran Canaria 130 F 6
Gran Chaco 114 GH 3/2
Grand Bahama Island 102 K 3
Grand Ballon 131 E 2/3
Grand Bank 88 FG 3
Grand-Bassam 176 G 7/8
Grand Bourg 115 II B 2
Grand Canyon 92 D 2/3
Grand Canyon National Park 92 D 2
Grand Canyon Village 92 D 2/3
Grand Cayman 102 J 5
Grand Centre 84 F 2
Grande, Bahía 114 F 8
Grande, La 90 C 2
Grande, Rio 80 F 4
Grande Cach 84 D 2
Grande-Combe, La 131 D 4
Grande de Santiago, Río 102 E 4
Grande-Deux, Réservoir La 86 H 2
Grande-Prairie 84 D 2
Grande Rivière, La 71 LM 4
Grande Ronde 90 C 2
Grande-Terre 115 II B 1
Grande Vidie, Pointe de la 115 II B 1
Grand Falls 88 D 3
Grand Falls-Windsor 88 G 2
Grand Forks [Canada] 84 D 3
Grand Forks [U.S.] 86 C 4
Grand Haven 98 C 2
Grandioznyy, Pik 148 UV 8
Grand Island 94 D 2
Grand Island 98 C 1
Grand Isle 96 F 3
Grand Junction 94 AB 3
Grand Lake 88 F 2
Grand Manan 88 D 3
Grand Marais 98 C 1
Grândola 130 AB 3
Grand Portage Indian Reserve 86 E 4
Grand Rapids [Canada] 86 C 2
Grand Rapids [U.S., Michigan] 98 C 2
Grand Rapids [U.S., Minnesota] 94 E 1
Grand-Remous 88 AB 3
Grand River [U.S., Michigan] 98 C 2
Grand River [U.S., Missouri] 94 E 3
Grand River [U.S., South Dakota] 94 C 1
Grand Teton 90 E 3
Grand Teton National Park 90 E 3
Grand Traverse Bay 98 C 1
Grand Turk (Cockburn Town) 102 LM 4
Grange, La [U.S., Geogia] 100 B 2
Grange, La [U.S., Texas] 96 D 3
Grangeville 90 C 2
Granite Falls 94 E 1
Granite Peak [U.S., Montana] 90 E 2
Granite Peak [U.S., Nevada] 92 C 1
Gran Paradiso 132 A 1
Gran Sasso d'Italia 132 C 2
Grant 94 C 2
Grant, Mount 92 C 2
Grantham 124 D 4
Grantown 124 CD 2
Grant Range 92 D 2
Grants 92 EF 3
Grants Pass 90 B 3
Granville 131 B 2
Granville Lake 86 BC 1
Gräsö 126 G 2
Grasse 131 E 4
Grasslands National Park 84 G 3
Grass Valley 92 B 2
Graulhet 131 C 4
Gravataí 114 JK 3/4
Gravenhurst 86 H 4
Grayling 98 C 1
Grays Harbor 90 A 2
Graz 128 F 4
Great Abaco 102 K 3
Great Anyuy 148 h 5
Great Artesian Basin 166 HJ 5/6
Great Australian Bight 166 FG 7/8
Great Barrier Island 166 Q 8
Great Barrier Reef 160 HJ 5
Great Basin 92 CD 1/2
Great Basin National Park 92 D 2
Great Bear Lake 76 QR 5
Great Belt 126 D 4
Great Bend 94 D 3
Great Bitter Lake 152 B 3
Great Britain 117 FG 4
Great Camanoe 101 IX
Great Dividing Range 166 JK 5/7
Great Eastern Erg 176 J 3/2
Greater Antilles 102 JM 4/5
Greater Sunda Islands 160 DF 4
Great Falls 90 E 2
Great Hungarian Plain 128 GH 4
Great Inagua 102 L 4
Great Isaac 100 I D 4
Great Khingan Range 154 O 2/1
Great Lyakhov Island 148 cd 4
Great Nicobar 150 P 9
Great Plain of China 141 P 6
Great Plains 69 HJ 4/6
Great Salt Desert 150 GH 4
Great Salt Lake 92 D 1
Great Salt Lake Desert 92 D 1/2
Great Sand Dunes National Monument 94 B 3
Great Sand Hills 84 F 3
Great Sandy Desert [Ausralia] 166 EF 5
Great Sandy Desert [U.S.] 90 B 3
Great Slave Lake 76 RS 6
Great Smoky Mountains National Park 100 C 2
Great Tobago 101 IX
Great Victoria Desert 166 EG 6
Great Western Erg 176 GH 2
Great Yarmouth 124 E 4
Great Yenisey 148 U 8
Great Zab 152 DE 1
Greboun, Mont 176 J 5
Greco, Cape 152 B 2
Gredos, Sierra de 130 C 2
Greece 133 BD 3/4
Greeks 121 J-K 5-6
Greeley 94 B 2
Green Bay 94 G 1
Green Bay 98 C 1
Greenbrier 98 DE 3
Greencastle 98 C 3
Greeneville 100 C 1
Greenfield [U.S., Indiana] 98 C 3
Greenfield [U.S., Massachusetts] 98 F 2
Green Islands 156 PQ 8/9
Green Lake 84 G 2
Greenland 78 hf 2/6
Greenland 76 gh 3/5
Greenland Basin 12 B 23
Greenland Current 6 NP 2
Greenlanders 73 NO 2/3
Greenland Fracture Zone 12 B 23/22
Greenland Sea 117 EG 2
Green Mountains [U.S., Vermont] 98 F 2/1
Green Mountains [U.S., Wyoming] 90 EF 3
Greenock 124 C 3
Green River [U.S., Utah] 92 E 2
Green River [U.S., Wyoming] 90 E 3
Green River [U.S., Kentucky] 98 C 3
Green River [U.S., Wyoming/Utah] 92 E 1
Greensboro 100 D 1/2
Greensburg [U.S., Indiana] 98 C 3
Greensburg [U.S., Kentucky] 98 C 3
Greensburg [U.S., Pennsylvania] 98 E 2
Greenup 98 D 3
Green Valley 92 E 4
Greenville [Liberia] 176 EF 7/8

River, canal
Waterfall
Lake, lakes, reservoir
Swamp
Salt flat
Sea
Strait
Bay, gulf
Cape
Island, islands
Ocean current
Ocean floor landforms
Tectonic feature
Atmospheric phenomena
Time zone
Geographical grid

H

Independent country
Dependent territory
Federal state, province, territory
People, ethnic group, tribe
Indian reservation/reserve
National Park
Industrial region
Historical site
Research station
Continent, realm
Region, peninsula
Mountain range, mountains
Peak
Pass
Ice shelf, glacier

guenau 131 E 2
ida 73 E 4
ifa (Hefa) 152 B 2
ikou 154 LM 8
'il 152 D 4
ilar 154 NO 2
iley 90 D 3
ileybury 86 GH 4
ilun 154 P 2
iluoto 125 EF 4
inan 154 LM 8
inan 154 LM 8
ines City 100 C 3
i Phong 156 F 3
iti 102 L 5
itians 73 L 8
iyan 154 K 4
jdúböszörmény 128 H 4
jdúszoboszló 128 H 4
ji Ebrāhīm, Kūh-e 152 E 1
jnówka 128 H 2
-kha 150 P 6
kkâri 134 G 4
kodate 154 S 3
lab → Aleppo 152 C 1/2
labja 152 E 2
la'ib 176 P 4
lat 'Ammār 152 BC 3
lden 126 D 3
leakala National Park 92 I CD 2
leyville 100 B 2
lifax 88 E 3
likarnassos 134 B 4
ling 126 D 2
llasan 154 OP 5
lle/Saale 128 D 2
llefors 126 EF 3
lley 181 II B 36
ll Islands 156 P 6
llock 86 C 3
ll Peninsula 76 b 6
llsberg 126 F 3
lls Creek 166 F 4
llstavik 126 FG 2/3
lmahera 156 KL 7
lmstad 126 E 4
lsingland 126 F 2
ltiatunturi 125 DE 2
lych 128 J 3
mād, Al- 152 CD 2/3
madah
al-Ḥamrā', Al 169 E 2/3
madān 152 F 2
māh 152 C 2
mar 126 D 2
mbantota 146 M 9
mburg 128 D 2
me 126 J 2
meenlinna 126 J 2
meln 128 D 2
mersley Range 166 D 5
mhŭng 154 PQ 4
mi/Kumul 154 H 3
milton *[Australia]* 166 J 8
milton *[Bermuda]* 82 O 5
milton *[Canada]* 98 E 2
milton *[New Zealand]* 166 PQ 8
milton *[U.K.]* 124 C 3
Hamilton *[U.S., Montana]* 90 D 2
Hamilton *[U.S., New York]* 98 F 2
Hamilton *[U.S., Ohio]* 98 C 3
Hamilton *[U.S., Texas]* 96 D 3
Hamina 126 JK 2
Hamlin 96 C 2
Hamm 128 C 2
Ḥammāmāt, Al- 132 B 4
Hammamet → Al-Ḥammāmāt
Hammān al-ʿAlīl 152 D 1
Hammerfest 125 E 2
Hammond *[U.S., Indiana]* 98 C 2
Hammond *[U.S., Louisiana]* 96 F 3
Hammonton 98 F 3
Hampton *[U.S., Iowa]* 94 E 2
Hampton *[U.S., Virginia]* 98 EF 3
Hampton Bays 98 FG 2
Hamrīn, Jabal 152 DE 2
Hāmūn-e Sāberī 150 HJ 4
Ḥamzah, Al- 152 E 3
Hanang 178 LM 3
Hanapepe 92 I B 2
Hanau 128 D 3
Hancock *[U.S., Michigan]* 98 B 1
Hancock *[U.S., New York]* 98 F 2
Handan 154 M 4
Hanford 92 C 2
Hangzhou 154 O 5/6
Hani 134 F 4
Hani 145 O 7
Ḥanīdh 152 F 4
Haniyah, Al- 152 E 3
Hanko 126 H 3
Hanna *[Canada]* 84 F 3
Hanna *[U.S.]* 90 F 3
Hannah Bay 86 GH 3
Hannibal 94 F 3
Hannover 128 D 2
Hannoversch Münden 128 D 2
Hanoi (Ha Nôi) 156 EF 3
Hanover *[Canada]* 98 D 1
Hanover *[U.S., New Hampshire]* 98 FG 2
Hanover *[U.S., Pennsylvania]* 98 E 3
Hans Lollik Island 101 IX
Hanstholm 126 C 3
Hantsavichy 128 J 2
Hanzhong 154 L 5
Haparanda 125 EF 4
Happy Valley-Goose Bay 88 E 1
Ḥaql, Al- 152 B 3
Ḥaraḍ 150 FG 6
Haradok 128 L 1
Harappa 51 NO 4
Harare 178 KL 6
Harbin 154 P 2
Harbor Beach 98 D 2
Harbour Breton 88 FG 3
Hardangerfjorden 126 BC 3/2
Hardangervidda 126 C 2/3
Hardin 90 F 2
Hare 73 F 3
Härer 176 Q 7
Hargeysa 176 QR 7
Harhorin → Karakorum 154 K 2
Harīrūd 150 J 4
Harjavalta 126 H 2
Härjedalen 126 E 2
Harlan *[U.S., Iowa]* 94 E 2
Harlan *[U.S., Kentucky]* 98 D 3
Hârlău 128 JK 4
Harlingen 96 D 4
Harlow 124 DE 4
Harlowton 90 E 2
Har Meron 152 B 2
Harney Basin 90 BC 3
Harney Lake 90 C 3
Härnösand 126 FG 2
Haro 130 CD 1
Harper 176 F 8
Ḥarrat al-ʿUwayriḍ 152 C 4
Harricanaw 88 A 2
Harriman 100 B 1/2
Harrington Harbour 88 F 2
Harrisburg *[U.S., Illinois]* 94 F 3
Harrisburg *[U.S., Pennsylvania]* 98 E 2
Harrison 96 E 1
Harrisonburg 98 E 3
Harrison Lake 84 C 3
Harrisonville 94 E 3
Harriston 98 D 2
Harrogate 124 D 3/4
Harry S. Truman Reservoir 94 E 3
Harsīn 152 E 2
Hârşova 133 E 2
Harstad 125 C 3
Hart 98 C 2
Hartford 98 F 2
Hartlepool 124 D 3
Hartselle 100 B 2
Hartsville 100 CD 2
Hartwell Lake 100 C 2
Har Us Nuur 154 H 2
Harvey 86 C 4
Harwich 124 E 4
Haryana [= H.] 150 M 5
Harz 128 D 2
Ḥasā', Al- 152 F 4
Ḥasakah, Al- 152 D 1
Hasan Dağı 134 D 4
Hāshimīyah, Al- 152 E 2
Hashtgerd 152 F 1/2
Hashtpar 134 J 4
Hashtrud 134 H 4
Hasselt 131 D 1/2
Ḥassī al-Raml 119 G 6
Ḥāssī Masʿūd 176 J 2
Hassi Messaoud → Ḥāssī Masʿūd
Hässleholm 126 E 4
Hastings *[New Zealand]* 166 Q 9/8
Hastings *[U.K.]* 124 E 5
Hastings *[U.S., Michigan]* 98 C 2
Hastings *[U.S., Minnesota]* 94 E 1
Hastings *[U.S., Nebraska]* 94 D 2
Hatchie 100 A 2
Hatteras 100 E 2
Hatteras, Cape 100 E 2
Hattiesburg 96 F 3
Hattuşaş 134 D 3
Hatvan 128 G 4
Hat Yai 156 E 6
Haugesund 126 B 3
Haukeligrend 126 C 3
Haukipudas 125 F 4
Haukivesi 126 K 2
Hausa 173 D 4
Haut, Isle au 98 GH 1/2
Hauula 92 I C 2
Havana (La Habana) 102 J 4
Havasu, Lake 92 D 3
Havasupai Indian Reservation 92 D 3
Havel 128 E 2
Havelock 100 D 2
Haverhill 98 G 2
Havířov 128 G 3
Havlíčkův Brod 128 F 3
Havre 90 E 1
Havre, Le 131 BC 2
Havre Aubert, Île du 88 E 3
Havre-Saint-Pierre 88 E 2
Havsa 134 AB 3
Havza 134 D 3
Hawaii 92 I BC 2
Hawaii (Big Island) 92 I CD 3
Hawaiian Islands 160 MO 1/2
Hawaiian Ridge 10 ST 4
Hawaii Standard Time 38 B 22
Hawaii Volcanoes National Park 92 I D 3
Ḥawallī 152 EF 3
Hawi 92 I D 2
Hawick 124 D 3
Hawīyah, Al- 150 E 6
Hawjā', Al- 152 C 3
Hawke Bay 166 Q 8
Hawkesbury 88 B 3
Hawkesbury Island 84 A 2
Hawkinsville 100 C 2
Hawr al-Hammār 152 E 3
Hawrān, Wādī 152 D 2
Hawthorne 92 C 2
Haydarābād 134 GH 4
Hayden 92 E 3
Hayes 86 D 1
Haymana 134 C 3
Hayrabolu 134 B 3
Hay River 78 R 6
Hays 94 D 3
Haystack, Mount 92 D 2
Haysville 94 D 3
Haysyn 128 K 3
Hayvoron 128 KL 3
Hayward 94 F 1
Ḥayy, Al- 152 E 2
Hazaras 145 K 6
Hazard 98 D 3
Hazebrouck 131 C 2
Hazelton Mountains 84 AB 2
Hazen 94 C 1
Hazlehurst 100 C 3
Hazleton 98 F 2
Ḥazm al-Jalāmid 152 D 3
Healdsburg 92 B 2

River, canal
Waterfall
Lake, lakes, reservoir
Swamp
Salt flat
Sea
Strait
Bay, gulf
Cape
Island, islands
Ocean current
Ocean floor landforms
Tectonic feature
Atmospheric phenomena
Time zone
Geographical grid

Independent country
Dependent territory
Federal state, province, territory
People, ethnic group, tribe
Indian reservation/reserve
National Park
Industrial region
∴ Historical site
Research station
Continent, realm
Region, peninsula
▲▲ Mountain range, mountains
▲ Peak
)(Pass
✱ Ice shelf, glacier

River, canal
Waterfall
Lake, lakes, reservoir
Swamp
Salt flat
Sea
Strait
Bay, gulf
Cape
Island, islands
Ocean current
Ocean floor landforms
Tectonic feature
Atmospheric phenomena
Time zone
Geographical grid

Independent country
Dependent territory
Federal state, province, territory
People, ethnic group, tribe
Indian reservation/reserve
National Park
Industrial region
Historical site
Research station
Continent, realm
Region, peninsula
Mountain range, mountains
▲ Peak
)(Pass
∗ Ice shelf, glacier

River, canal
Waterfall
Lake, lakes, reservoir
Swamp
Salt flat
≋ Sea
Strait
≋) Bay, gulf
)≋ Cape
⁂ Island, islands
⇄ Ocean current
⩕ Ocean floor landforms
Tectonic feature
☁ Atmospheric phenomena
◷ Time zone
Geographical grid

Independent country
Dependent territory
Federal state, province, territory
People, ethnic group, tribe
Indian reservation/reserve
National Park
Industrial region
Historical site
Research station
Continent, realm
Region, peninsula
Mountain range, mountains
▲ Peak
)(Pass
* Ice shelf, glacier

River, canal
Waterfall
Lake, lakes, reservoir
Swamp
Salt flat
Sea
Strait
Bay, gulf
Cape
Island, islands
Ocean current
Ocean floor landforms
Tectonic feature
Atmospheric phenomena
Time zone
Geographical grid

⛊ Independent country
◧ Dependent territory
⛉ Federal state, province, territory
⚇ People, ethnic group, tribe
⧖ Indian reservation/reserve
⇧ National Park
⨅ Industrial region
∴ Historical site
⊿ Research station
⊛ Continent, realm
⊵ Region, peninsula
▲▲ Mountain range, mountains
▲ Peak
)(Pass
✱ Ice shelf, glacier

River, canal
Waterfall
Lake, lakes, reservoir
Swamp
Salt flat
Sea
Strait
Bay, gulf
Cape
Island, islands
Ocean current
Ocean floor landforms
Tectonic feature
Atmospheric phenomena
Time zone
Geographical grid

Independent country
Dependent territory
Federal state, province, territory
People, ethnic group, tribe
Indian reservation/reserve
National Park
Industrial region
∴ Historical site
Research station
Continent, realm
Region, peninsula
Mountain range, mountains
▲ Peak
)(Pass
∗ Ice shelf, glacier

River, canal
Waterfall
Lake, lakes, reservoir
Swamp
Salt flat
Sea
Strait
Bay, gulf
Cape
Island, islands
Ocean current
Ocean floor landforms
Tectonic feature
Atmospheric phenomena
Time zone
Geographical grid

Kupang 156 J 10
Kupiškis 126 J 4
Kupreanof Island 76 NO 7
Kup"yans'k 136 E 4
Kuqa 154 F 3
Kura 134 G 3
Kūrchatov [Kazakhstan] 148 Q 9/8
Kurchatov [Russia] 136 D 3
Kürdəmir 134 J 3
Kurdistan 117 L 6
Kurds 145 H-J 6
Kurdufān 169 FG 4
Kŭrdzhali 133 D 3
Küre Dağları 134 D 3
Kuressaare 126 H 3
Kureyka 148 ST 5
Kurgan 148 O 7
Kurganinsk 134 F 2
Kuria Muria Islands 150 H 7
Kurikka 126 H 2
Kurile Islands 148 eg 10/9
Kuril'sk 148 e 9/10
Kuril Trench 10 QR 3
Kurkino 136 E 3
Kurmanayevka 136 K 3
Kurnool 150 M 7
Kuro Shio
→ Japan Current 6 DE 4
Kursavka 134 G 2
Kuršėnai 126 H 4
Kursk 136 E 3
Kurskaya 134 G 2
Kurşunlu 134 D 3
Kurtalan 134 F 4
Kurumkan 148 WX 8
Kur'ya 138 O 4
Kusa 136 M 2
Kuşadası 134 B 4
Kushchevskaya 134 F 1
Kushiro 154 ST 3
Kushnarenkovo 136 L 2
Kushva 138 OP 5
Kuskokwim 76 JK 6
Kuskokwim Bay 76 H 7
Kuskokwim
Mountains 76 JK 6
Kūstī 176 O 6
Kūt, Al- 152 E 2
Kütahya 134 C 3
Kutaisi 134 G 2
Kutch, Gulf of 150 K 6
Kutchin 73 DE 3
Kutina 132 D 1
Kutno 128 G 2
Kuujjuaq/Fort Chimo 78 ab 7
Kuujjuarapik 86 H 2
Kuusamo 125 G 3/4
Kuvandyk 136 LM 3
Kuvshinovo 136 D 1
Kuwait 152 E 3
Kuwait (Al-Kuwayt) 152 F 3
Kuybysheve 136 E 5
Kuybyshev Reservoir 136 J 2
Kuyeda 136 L 2
Kūysanjaq 152 E 1
Kuyto 138 E 3
Kuytun 154 F 3
Kuzhenkino 136 D 1
Kuznetsk 136 H 3
Kuznetsovs'k 128 J 2
Kuźnica 128 H 2
Kuzomen' 138 G 2
Kuzovatovo 136 H3
Kvaløya 125 CD 2
Kvigtind ▲ 125 B 4
Kwakiutl 73 EF 4/5
Kwangju 154 OP 4
Kwekwe 178 K 6
Kwetabohigan 86 G 3
Kwidzyn 128 G 2
Kwilu 178 H 3
Kyakhta 148 W 8
Kyaukpyu 150 P 7
Kybartai 126 H 4
Kyle of Lochalsh 124 BC 2
Kyllíni 133 BC 4
Kyllíni ▲ 133 C 4
Kými 133 D 4
Kymi 126 J 2
Kyn 138 O 5
Kyōto 154 QR 4/5
Kyparissía 133 C 4
Kyrgyzstan 148 PQ 10
Kyritz 128 E 2
Kýthira 133 C 4
Kýthnos 133 CD 4
Kytlym 138 O 5
Kyushu 154 Q 5
Kyustendil 133 C 2
Kyyiv → Kiev 136 C 4
Kyzyl 148 T 8
Kyzyl Taiga ▲ 148 S 8

L

La Almarcha 130 D 2
La Asunción 115 II B 3
Laau Point 92 I C 2
Laâyoune (Al-ʿAyūn) 176 DE 3
Laba 134 F 2
La Bahia 96 C 3
La-Baie 88 C 2
La Bañeza 130 BC 1
Labasa 166 QR 4
Labé 176 E 6
La Biche, Lac 84 EF 2
Labin 132 C 1
Labinsk 134 F 2
La Bocayna 130 FG 5
Laborovaya 138 R 2
Labouheyre 131 B 4
Labozhskoye 138 M 2
Labrador, Newfound-
land and 78 cd 7/9
Labrador
(Nunatsiavut) 76 ac 7/8
Labrador Basin 10 F 3
Labrador City 88 D 1
Labrador Current 6 N 3
Labrador Sea 76 ce 6/7
Lábrea 112 G 5
Labuan 156 GH 6
Labuhanbajo 156 HJ 9
Labytnangi 138 R 2
Laç 133 B 3
Lac ... → ..., Lac ...
La Cala 123 B 5
La Carolina 130 C 3
Laccadive Islands 150 L 8
Lac Courte Oreilles
Indian Reservation 94 F 1
Lac du Bonnet 86 C 3
Lac du Flambeau Indian
Reservation 94 F 1
Lac Édouard 88 BC 3
La Ceiba 102 H 5
Lacha, Lake 138 GH 4
La Charité 131 C 3
La Chaux-de-Fonds 128 C 4
Lachkaltsap Indian
Reserve 84 A 2
Lachute 88 B 3
La Ciotat 131 D 4
Lac La Biche 84 F 2
Lac-Mégantic 88 C 3
Lacombe 84 E 2
Laconia 98 G 2
Lacq 119 FG 5
La Crosse [U.S., Virginia] 98 E 3
La Crosse
[U.S., Wisconsin] 94 F 2
Lac Seul Indian
Reserve 86 D 3
Lacul Razim 133 E 2
Ladhaki 145 L 6
Lādhiqīyah, Al-
→ Latakia 152 B 2
Ladins 121 H 5
Ladoga, Lake 138 E 4
La Dorada 112 DE 2
Ladva 138 F 4
Ladysmith [Canada] 84 BC 3
Ladysmith [South Africa] 178 KL 8
Ladysmith [U.S.] 94 F 1
Ladyzhyn 136 B 4
Lae 156 O 9
Læsø 126 D 3
Lafayette [U.S., Indiana] 98 C 2
Lafayette
[U.S., Louisiana] 96 EF 3
La-Ferté-Bernard 131 C 2
Lafia 176 J 7
La Flèche 131 BC 3
La Foa 166 NO 5
La Follette 100 BC 1
La Fuente de San
Esteban 130 BC 2
La Galite → Jāliṭā
Lagan' 134 H 1
Lagan 126 E 4
Lågen 126 D 2
Lages 114 J 3
Laggua, Puntan 101 III
Laghouat → Al-Aghwāt
Lagkadás 133 C 3
Lagoa dos Patos 114 JK 4
Lago Maggiore 132 A 1
La Gomera 130 E 5/6
Lagos [Nigeria] 176 H 7
Lagos [Portugal] 130 B 3
Lago Trasimeno 132 C 2
La Grande 90 C 2
La Grande-Combe 131 D 4
La Grande-Deux,
Réservoir 86 H 2
La Grande Rivière 71 LM 4
La Grange [U.S., Geogia] 100 B 2
La Grange [U.S., Texas] 96 D 3
Laguna 92 F 3
Laguna ...
→ ..., Laguna ...
Laguna Bavicora 96 B 3
Laguna del Rey 96 C 4
La Habana → Havana 102 J 4
Lahad Datu 156 H 6/7
Lahaina 92 I C 2
Lahdenpohja 138 E 4
Lāhījān 134 J 4
Lahn 128 C 3
Lahndas 145 L 6
Lahore 150 LM 4
Lahoysk 128 K 1
Lahr/Schwarzwald 128 C 3
Lahti 126 J 2
Laï 176 L 7
Lai Châu 156 E 3
Lainioälven 125 E 3
Laishevo 136 J 2
La Junta 94 BC 3
Lake ...
→ ..., Lake
Lakeba 166 R 4
Lake Charles 96 E 3
Lake City [U.S., Florida] 100 C 3
Lake City
[U.S., South Carolina] 100 D 2
Lake Clark National
Park 78 K 6
Lake District 123 C 2
Lake Eyre Basin 166 H 6
Lakefield 88 A 3
Lake Havasu City 92 D 3
Lake Isabella 92 C 3
Lake Jackson 96 E 3
Lakeland 100 C 3
Lake Placid 98 F 1
Lakeport 92 B 2
Lake Providence 96 F 2
Lake Traverse Indian
Reservation 94 D 1
Lakeview 90 BC 3
Lake Village 96 F 2
Lakeville 94 E 1
Lakewood
[U.S., Colorado] 94 B 3
Lakewood
[U.S., New Jersey] 98 F 2
Lakewood [U.S., Ohio] 98 D 2
Lakewood
[U.S., Washington] 90 B 2
Lakonía, Gulf of 133 C 4
Lakota 73 G-H 5
Laksefjorden 125 FG 2
Lakselv 125 F 2
Lakshadweep 150 KL 8
Lala-Bisa 173 FG 7
La Línea 130 C 3
Lalitpur 150 NO 5
La Loche 78 T 7
Lal'sk 138 KL 4
La Maddalena 132 B 3
La Malbaie 88 C 3
Lamar [U.S., Colorado] 94 C 3
Lamar [U.S., Missouri] 94 E 3
Lamba 173 F 7

Independent country
Dependent territory
Federal state, province, territory
People, ethnic group, tribe
Indian reservation/reserve
National Park
Industrial region
Historical site
Research station
Continent, realm
Region, peninsula
Mountain range, mountains
▲ Peak
Pass
Ice shelf, glacier

River, canal
Waterfall
Lake, lakes, reservoir
Swamp
Salt flat
Sea
Strait
Bay, gulf
Cape
Island, islands
Ocean current
Ocean floor landforms
Tectonic feature
Atmospheric phenomena
Time zone
Geographical grid

Independent country
Dependent territory
Federal state, province, territory
People, ethnic group, tribe
Indian reservation/reserve
National Park
Industrial region
Historical site
Research station
Continent, realm
Region, peninsula
Mountain range, mountains
▲ Peak
)(Pass
∗ Ice shelf, glacier

River, canal
Waterfall
Lake, lakes, reservoir
Swamp
Salt flat
Sea
Strait
Bay, gulf
Cape
Island, islands
Ocean current
Ocean floor landforms
Tectonic feature
Atmospheric phenomena
Time zone
Geographical grid

M

Independent country
Dependent territory
Federal state, province, territory
People, ethnic group, tribe
Indian reservation/reserve
National Park
Industrial region
Historical site
Research station
Continent, realm
Region, peninsula
Mountain range, mountains
Peak
Pass
Ice shelf, glacier

Madā'in, Al- **152** E 2
Madama **176** K 4
Madame, Isle **88** E 3
Madang **156** O 9
Madanīyīn **176** K 2
Madawrūsh **132** A 5/4
Maddalena, La **132** B 3
Madeira **130** B 6
Madeira **112** G 5
Madeira **176** D 2
Madeleine, Îles de la **88** E 3
Madelia **94** E 1
Madeline **94** F 1
Maden **134** F 4
Madera *[Mexico]* **96** AB 3
Madera *[U.S.]* **92** B 2
Madhya Pradesh **150** M 6
Madill **96** D 2
Madīnah, Al- → Medina **150** DE 6
Madingou **178** G 3
Madison *[U.S., Indiana]* **98** C 3
Madison *[U.S., Minnesota]* **94** D 1
Madison *[U.S., Nebraska]* **94** D 2
Madison *[U.S., South Dakota]* **94** D 1
Madison *[U.S., West Virginia]* **98** D 3
Madison *[U.S., Wisconsin]* **94** F 2
Madison **90** E 2
Madisonville **98** C 3
Madiun **156** G 9
Madoc **88** A 3
Madoi **154** J 4/5
Madona **126** J 4
Madras → Chennai *[India]* **150** N 8
Madras *[U.S.]* **90** B 2
Madre, Laguna **96** D 4
Madre, Sierra **102** GH 5/6
Madre de Dios Island **114** D 7/8
Madre del Sur, Sierra **102** EF 5
Madre Occidental, Sierra **102** DE 2/4
Madre Oriental, Sierra **102** EF 3/4
Madrid **130** C 2
Madrid **130** C 2
Madridejos **130** C 2
Madura **156** G 9
Madurai **150** M 9
Madurese **145** P 10
Maelpaeg Reservoir **88** F 2/3
Maestra, Sierra **102** K 5/4
Maewo **166** O 3/4
Mafia **178** N 4
Mafraq, Al- **152** C 2
Magadan **148** f 7
Magdagachi **148** Za 8
Magdalena *[Bolivia]* **112** G 6
Magdalena *[U.S.]* **92** F 3
Magdalena **112** E 2
Magdalena **114** E 6
Magdeburg **128** DE 2
Magelang [= M.] **156** FG 9
Magellan, Strait of **114** D-F 8
Magerøya **125** F 2
Maghāghah **152** A 3
Maglobek **134** G 2
Magnetic Pole, North **180** I AB 30/27
Magnetic Pole, South **181** I C 16
Magnitogorsk **136** M 3
Magnolia **96** E 2
Magog **88** BC 3
Magpie, Lac **88** D 2
Magway **150** PQ 6
Mahābād **134** H 4
Mahajanga **178** NO 6
Mahakam **156** H 7/8
Mahalapye **178** JK 7
Maḥallah al-Kubrā, Al- **152** A 3
Maḥallāt **152** F 2
Mahanadi **150** N 6
Maha Nuwara **150** MN 9
Maharashtra **150** LM 7/6
Mahdia *[Guyana]* **112** H 2
Mahdia → Mahdīyah, Al- *[Tunisia]*
Mahdīyah, Al- **176** K 1
Mahe **150** LM 8
Mahé **178** Q 4
Mahilyow **128** L 1/2
Maḥmūdīyah, Al- **152** DE 2
Mahmudiye **134** C 3
Mahón **130** F 2
Maia **101** VII
Maicao **112** E 1
Maidstone *[Canada]* **84** F 2
Maidstone *[U.K.]* **124** E 4
Maidu [= Ma.] **73** F 5/6
Maiduguri **176** K 6
Main **128** D 3
Main Channel **98** D 1
Mai-Ndombe, Lake **178** H 3
Maine **98** G 1
Maine, Gulf of **98** G 2
Mainland *[U.K., Orkney Is.]* **124** C 2
Mainland *[U.K., Shetland Is.]* **124** D 1
Maintirano **178** N 6
Mainz **128** C 3
Maisí, Cape **102** L 4
Maitri **181** II C 3/4
Maixent-l'Ecole, Saint- **131** BC 3
Majāz al-Bāb **132** B 4
Majene **156** H 8
Majī **176** P 7
Majuro Atoll **160** L 3
Makah Indian Reservation **90** A 1
Makarakomburu, Mount **166** MN 3
Makarikari Salt Pan **178** JK 7
Makariv **128** K 3
Makarov **148** d 9
Makarov Basin **12** A 4/7
Makarska **132** D 2
Makar'yev **136** G 1
Makassars **145** PQ 10
Makassar Strait **156** H 8
Makeni **176** E 7
Makhachkala **134** HJ 2
Makhambet **136** JK 5
Makhmūr **152** D 2
Makhnëvo **138** P 5
Makiyivka **136** E 5
Makkah → Mecca **150** DE 6
Makó **128** G 4
Makokou **178** G 2
Makonde **173** GH 6/7
Maksatikha **136** DE 1
Makthar **132** B 5
Mākū **134** G 3
Makú [= Ma.] **109** F 4
Makua **173** G 7
Makurdi **176** J 7
Makushi **109** GH 4
Mala, Punta **102** K 7
Malabo **176** J 8
Malacca, Strait of **156** DE 7
Malacky **128** F 3
Malad City **90** D 3
Maladzyechna **128** J 1
Málaga **130** C 3
Malagasy **173** H 8/7
Malagón **130** C 2
Malaita **166** N 2
Malakāl **176** O 7
Malamala **156** J 8
Malang **156** G 9
Malanje **178** H 4
Mälaren **126** F 3
Malargüe **114** F 5
Malartic **88** A 2
Malaryta **128** HJ 2
Malatya **134** E 4
Malatya Dağları **134** E 4
Mala Vyska **136** C 4
Malawi **178** LM 5/6
Malayalis **145** L 8/9
Malaya Serdoba **136** H 3
Malaya Vishera **138** EF 5
Malāyer **152** F 2
Malay Peninsula **156** EF 6
Malays **145** O-Q 9-10
Malays, Cocos **164** BC 9
Malaysia **156** EG 7/6
Malazgirt **134** G 3
Malbaie, La **88** C 3
Malbork **128** G 2
Malchin **128** E 2
Malden **94** F 3
Malden Island **160** O 4
Maldive Islanders **145** L 9
Maldives **150** L 10
Maldives **141** L 9
Maldonado **114** HJ 4
Malè *[Italy]* **132** B 1
Malé *[Maldives]* **150** L 10
Maléa, Cape **133** C 4
Malegaon **150** M 6
Malek Kandī **134** H 4
Malekula **166** O 4
Malen'ga **138** G 3
Malheur **90** C 3
Malheur Lake **90** C 3
Mali **176** FG 6/4
Mali Lošinj **132** C 2
Malindi **178** N 3
Malin Head **124** B 3
Malīq **132** A 5/4
Malkara **134** AB 3
Malko Tŭrnovo **133** E 2
Mallaig **124** BC 2/3
Mallawī **152** A 4
Mallorca **130** F 2
Mallow **124** B 4
Malmberget **125** DE 3
Malmö **126** E 4
Malmyzh **136** JK 2
Malo, Gulf of Saint- **131** B 2
Malo, Saint- **131** B 2
Maloarkhangel'sk **136** DE 3
Malone **98** F 1
Małopolska **128** GH 3
Maloshuyka **138** G 3
Maloyaroslavets **136** DE 2
Malozemel'skaya Tundra **138** LM 2
Malpaso **130** DE 6
Malpelo **112** C 3
Malpica de Bergantiños **130** AB 1
Mals **132** B 1
Malta **90** EF 1
Malta **132** C 5
Malta **132** C 5
Maltese **121** H 6
Malung **126** E 2
Malvern **96** E 2
Malvinas, Islas → Falkland Islands **114** GH 8
Malyn **128** K 3
Malyye Derbety **136** GH 5
Malyy Taymyr **148** WY 3
Malyy Uzen' **136** HJ 4
Mam **73** J 8
Mamberamo **156** M 8
Mameigwess Lake **86** E 2
Mamers **131** C 2
Mammoth Cave National Park **98** C 3
Mammoth Lakes **92** C 2
Mamonovo **128** G 1
Mamoré **112** F 6
Mamou **176** E 6/7
Mamoudzou **178** O 5
Mamuju **156** H 8
Man **176** F 7
Man, Isle of **124** C 3
Manacapuru **112** G 4
Manacor **130** F 2
Manado **156** K 7
Managua **102** H 6
Manakara **178** O 7
Manama (Al-Manāmah) **152** F 4
Mananara Avaratra **178** OP 6
Mananjary **178** O 7
Manāqil, Al- **176** O 6
Manassas **98** E 3
Manatí **101** VIII
Manaus **112** G 4
Manavgat **134** C 4
Manbij **152** C 1
Mancha **130** CD 3/2
Manchester *[U.K.]* **124** D 4
Manchester *[U.S., Iowa]* **94** F 2
Manchester *[U.S., New Hampshire]* **98** G 2
Manchuria **154** OP 2/3
Manchus **145** Q 6/5
Manciano **132** B 2

River, canal
Waterfall
Lake, lakes, reservoir
Swamp
Salt flat
Sea
Strait
Bay, gulf
Cape
Island, islands
Ocean current
Ocean floor landforms
Tectonic feature
Atmospheric phenomena
Time zone
Geographical grid

Independent country
Dependent territory
Federal state, province, territory
People, ethnic group, tribe
Indian reservation/reserve
National Park
Industrial region
Historical site
Research station
Continent, realm
Region, peninsula
Mountain range, mountains
Peak
Pass
Ice shelf, glacier

Marsá Maṭrūḥ **176** N 2
Marseille **131** DE 4
Marsh **96** EF 3
Marshall
[U.S., Arkansas] **96** E 2
Marshall
[U.S., Minnesota] **94** DE 1
Marshall
[U.S., Missouri] **94** E 3
Marshall [U.S., Texas] **96** E 2
Marshall Islands **160** L 2/3
Marshall
Seamounts **10** R 5
Marshalltown **94** E 2
Marshfield
[U.S., Missouri] **94** E 3
Marshfield
[U.S., Wisconsin] **94** F 1
Marsh Harbour **102** K 3
Marsico Nuovo **132** D 3
Märsta **126** F 3
Marta, Santa **112** DE 1
Martaban, Gulf of **150** Q 7
Martapura **156** H 8
Marten Falls Indian
Reserve **86** F 3
Martensville **84** G 2
Marte R. Gomez,
Presa **96** D 4
Martha's Vineyard **98** G 2
Martigny **128** C 4
Martigues **131** D 4
Martin [Slovakia] **128** G 3
Martin
[U.S., South Dakota] **94** C 2
Martin
[U.S., Tennessee] **100** A 1
Martin, Cap Saint- **115** II B 2
Martin, Lake **100** B 2
Martin, Lake Saint **86** C 3
Martín, Lake San **114** E 7
Martin, Saint- **115** II B 1
Martín, San **114** F 4
Martín, San **181** II C 32
Martina Franca **132** D 3
Martinez **100** C 2
Martinique **115** II B 2
Martinique Passage **115** II B 2
Martinsburg **98** E 3
Martins Ferry **98** D 2
Martinsville **98** E 3
Martin Vaz **105** L 7/6
Martinville, Saint **96** F 3
Martök **136** L 4
Martos **130** C 3
Martuni **134** GH 3
Marv Dasht **152** G 3
Marvine, Mount **92** E 2
Mary **148** N 11
Mary, Saint **84** E 3
Maryborough **166** L 6
Mar"yina Horka **128** K 2
Mary Kathleen **165** H 9
Maryland **98** EF 3
Marys, Saint **98** E 2
Mary's Bay, Saint **88** G 3
Marystown **88** G 3
Marysville
[U.S., California] **92** B 2
Marysville
[U.S., Kansas] **94** D 3
Marysville
[U.S., Washington] **90** B 1
Maryville
[U.S., Missouri] **94** E 2
Maryville
[U.S., Tennessee] **100** C 2
Marzūq **176** K 3
Masai **173** G 6
Masaka **178** L 3
Masalembo Besar **156** GH 9
Masallı **134** J 4
Masalog, Puntan **101** III
Masaya **102** H 6
Masbate **156** J 5
Masbate **156** J 5
Mascarene Islands **169** J 8
Mascarene Plateau **10** LM 6/7
Mascoi **109** GH 7
Maseru **178** K 8
Mashhad **150** HJ 3
Mashrafah, Al- **152** C 1
Maṣīrah **150** HJ 6
Masjed-e Soleymān **152** F 2/3
Maskanah **152** C 1
Mason **96** D 3
Mason City **94** E 2
Maspalomas **130** F 6
Masqaṭ → Muscat **150** HJ 6
Massa **132** B 2
Massachusetts **98** FG 2
Massachusetts Bay **98** G 2
Massay **131** C 3
Massena **98** F 1
Massif Central **131** CD 3/4
Massillon **98** D 2
Masteuiatsh Indian
Reserve **88** B 2
Masty **128** J 2
Masuku **178** G 3
Masunga **178** K 7
Masvingo **178** KL 7
Maṣyāf **152** C 2
Matabele **173** F 7/8
Mataco **109** G 7
Matadi **178** G 4
Matagalpa **102** HJ 6
Matagami **88** A 2
Matagami, Lac **88** A 2
Matagorda **96** D 3
Matagorda
Peninsula **96** E 3
Matam **176** E 5
Matamoros **96** D 4
Matane **88** D 2
Matanzas **102** J 4
Matara **150** N 9
Mataram **156** H 9
Maṭariyah, Al- **152** AB 3
Mataró **130** E 2
Matatula, Cape **101** VII
Matâ'utu **166** R 3
Maṭāy **152** A 3
Matehuala **102** E 4
Mateo, San **115** II A 3
Matera **132** D 3
Mátészalka **128** H 3/4
Mateur → Māṭir
Mateus, São **112** M 7
Mathis **96** D 3
Mathura **150** M 5
Matías, Gulf of San **114** G 6
Matías, San **112** H 7
Māṭir **132** B 4
Mato Grosso **112** H 6
Mato Grosso **112** H 6
Mato Grosso do Sul **112** HJ 7/8
Matola **178** L 8
Matoury **112** J 3
Maṭraḥ **150** H 6
Matsés **109** F 5
Matsue **154** Q 4
Matsuyama [= Ma.] **154** Q 5
Mattagami **86** G 3
Mattawa **88** A 3
Matterhorn
[Switzerland/Italy] **128** C 4
Matterhorn [U.S.] **92** D 1
Matthew Island,
Saint **76** F 6/7
Matthews, Saint **100** C 2
Matthews Ridge **112** GH 2
Matthias Islands,
Saint **156** OP 8
Mattoon **94** F 3
Matuku **166** Q 4
Maturín **112** G 2
Matveyevka **136** KL 3
Matveyev Kurgan **136** EF 5
Maud Subglacial
Basin **13** BA 4/7
Maués **112** H 4
Maui **92** I CD 2
Maumere **156** J 9
Maun **178** J 7
Mauna Kea **92** I D 3
Mauna Loa **92** I D 3
Maurice, Parc
National de la **88** B 3
Maurice, Saint **88** B 3
Mauritania **176** EF 5/3
Mauritius **178** QR 7
Mawé **109** H 5
Mawlamyine **150** Q 7
Mawqaq **152** D 4
Mawṣil, Al- → Mosul **152** D 1
Mawson **181** II C 9
Maxixe **178** LM 7
Maya **73** JK 8/7
Maya **148** bc 7
Mayādīn, Al- **152** CD 2
Mayagüez **101** VIII
Mayari **102** KL 4
Mayenne **131** B 2
Mayerthorpe **84** E 2
Mayfield **98** B 3
Maykop **134** F 2
Maymunah, Al- **152** E 3
Mayn **148** k 6
Mayna **136** HJ 2/3
Mayo **78** NO 6
Mayo **73** GH 7
Mayo **96** A 4
Mayotte **178** O 5
Mayotte **169** H 7
May Point, Cape **98** F 3
Mayraira Point **156** HJ 4
Mayskiy [Russia, Amur] **148** ab 8
Mayskiy [Russia,
Kabardino-Balkaria] **134** G 2
Mayville **94** D 1
Mazabuka **178** K 6
Mazamet **131** C 4
Mazar **154** E 4
Mazara del Vallo **132** BC 4
Mazār-e Sharif **150** JK 3
Mazatlán **102** D 4
Mažeikiai **126** H 4
Mazirbe **126** H 3
Mazsalaca **126** J 3
Mazury **128** GH 2/1
Mazyr **128** K 2
Mbabane **178** L 8
Mbaïki **176** L 8
Mbala **178** L 4
Mbale **178** LM 2
Mbandaka **178** HJ 3
M'Banza Congo **178** GH 4
Mbanza-Ngungu **178** H 4
Mbarara **178** L 3
Mbeya **178** L 4
Mbuji-Mayi **178** J 4
Mbum **173** E 5
Mbwela **173** E 7
Mbya **109** HJ 7
McAdam **88** D 3
McAlester **96** DE 2
McAllen **96** D 4
McBride **84** CD 2
McCall **90** CD 2
McCamey **96** C 3
McCammon **90** D 3
McClintock Channel **76** UV 4
McClure Strait **76** QS 3/4
McComb **96** F 3
McConaughy, Lake **94** C 2
McCook **94** C 2
McCreary **86** C 3
McDermitt **92** C 1
McDonald Islands,
Heard and the **36** NO 8
McDonald Peak **90** D 2
McDonough **100** BC 2
McGehee **96** F 2
McGill **92** D 2
McGregor **96** D 3
McGregor **84** C 2
McKenzie **100** AB 1
McKinley, Mount **76** KL 6
McKinleyville **92** A 1
McKinney **96** D 2
McLead **84** DE 2
McLennan **84** D 2
McLoughlin, Mount **90** B 3
McMinnville
[U.S., Oregon] **90** B 2
McMinnville
[U.S., Tennessee] **100** B 2
McMurdo Base **181** II B 19/18
McNeil, Mount **84** A 2
McPherson **94** D 3
McRae **100** C 2
McTier **86** GH 4
M'Daourouch
→ Madawrūsh
Mead, Lake **92** D 2

River, canal
Waterfall
Lake, lakes, reservoir
Swamp
Salt flat
Sea
Strait
Bay, gulf
Cape
Island, islands
Ocean current
Ocean floor landforms
Tectonic feature
Atmospheric phenomena
Time zone
Geographical grid

■ Independent country
◘ Dependent territory
□ Federal state, province, territory
⚇ People, ethnic group, tribe
⧖ Indian reservation/reserve
⇧ National Park
⩍ Industrial region
∴ Historical site
⌂ Research station
⊛ Continent, realm
⊵ Region, peninsula
▲▲ Mountain range, mountains
▲ Peak
)(Pass
✱ Ice shelf, glacier

ddletown [U.S., Ohio] 98 CD 3
d-Indian Basin ⩠ 10 MN 6
id-Indian Ridge ⩠ 10 MN 6/7
idland [Canada] 98 E 1
idland
[U.S., Michigan] 98 CD 2
idland [U.S., Texas] 96 C 3
d-Pacific
Mountains ⩠ 10 QS 4/5
idway Islands ⛊ 160 M 1
idway Islands ⛊
[Detail map] 101 V
idway Naval Station 101 V
idway Range ⛰ 84 D 3
idwest 90 F 3
idwest City 96 D 2
idyat 134 F 4
iędzychód 128 F 2
iędzyrzec Podlaski 128 H 2
iędzyrzecz 128 F 2
ielec 128 H 3
ier 96 D 4
iercurea-Ciuc 128 J 4
ieres 130 BC 1
iguel, San 102 H 6
iguel, San ∽ 96 B 4
iguel, San ⌓ 92 B 3
iguel, São ⌓ 130 CD 6
iguel de Tucumán,
San 114 FG 3
iguel d'Oeste, São 114 J 3
iguelito, San 102 K 7
ihalıççik 134 C 3
ihiel, Saint- 131 D 2
ijlad, Al- 176 N 6
ikhaylov 136 F 2
ikhaylovka 136 G 4
ikhaylovsk 136 M 2
ikhaylovskiy 148 QR 8
ikkeli 126 K 2
iknās → Meknès 176 FG 2
ikolayivka 136 C 5
ikulkin, Cape)≋ 138 K 2
ikun' 138 L 4
ilagro 112 D 4
ilan (Milano) 132 B 1
ilas 134 B 4
ilazzo 132 CD 4
ilbank 94 D 1
ilbanke Sound ≍ 84 A 2
ildura 166 J 7
iles 166 KL 6
iles City 90 F 2
ilet ∴ 134 B 4
ilford
[U.S., Delaware] 98 F 3
ilford [U.S., Utah] 92 D 2
ilford Haven 124 C 4
ilicz 128 F 2
iliés 133 C 3
ilk ∽ 90 D 1
ilk, Wādī al- ∽ 176 N 5
il'kovo 148 g 7/8
ilk River 84 EF 3
illas 131 C 4
illau 131 CD 4
ill City 90 B 2
illedgeville 100 C 2
ille Lacs, Lac des ◡ 86 E 3
Mille Lacs Indian
Reservation ⧗ 94 E 1
Mille Lacs Lake ◡ 94 E 1
Miller 94 D 1
Millerovo 136 F 4
Millington 100 A 2
Millinocket 98 G 1
Mill Island ⌓ 181 I C 13
Mills 90 F 3
Millville 98 F 3
Mílos 133 D 4
Mílos ⌓ 133 D 4
Miloslavskoye 136 EF 3
Milove 136 F 4
Milparinka 166 J 6
Milton 166 P 10
Milton-Freewater 90 C 2
Milton Keynes 124 DE 4
Milwaukee 94 G 2
Milyutinskaya 136 FG 4
Mina 92 C 2
Mīnā' 'Abd Allāh 152 F 3
Minankabaus ⚇ 145 NO 9/10
Minas 114 H 4
Minas, Cerro Las ▲ 102 GH 6
Mīnā' Sa'ūd 152 F 3
Minas de Barroterán 96 C 4
Minas Gerais ▽ 112 KL 7
Minatitlán 71 J 8
Minch, Little ≍ 124 B 2
Minch, The ≍ 124 BC 2
Mindanao ⌓ 156 K 6
Mindelo 176 C 5
Minden [Germany] 128 C 2
Minden
[U.S., Louisiana] 96 E 2
Minden
[U.S., Nebraska] 94 D 2
Minden [U.S., Nevada] 92 C 2
Mindoro ⌓ 156 HJ 5
Mindyak 136 M 3
Mineiros 112 J 7
Mineral'nyye Vody 134 G 2
Mineral Wells 96 D 2
Mingəçevir 134 H 3
Mingəçevir Reservoir ◡ 134 H 3
Minglanilla 130 D 2
Minho ⩘ 130 B 2
Minicoy Island ⌓ 150 L 9
Minitonas 86 B 2
Min Jiang ∽ 154 K 5
Minna 176 J 7
Minneapolis 94 E 1
Minnedosa 86 C 3
Minnesota ▽ 82 HJ 2
Minnesota ∽ 94 E 1
Miño ∽ 130 B 1
Minot 90 G 1
Minsk [Belarus] 128 K 2
Mińsk [Poland] 128 H 2
Minusinsk 148 T 8
Min Xian 154 K 5
Minyā, Al- 152 A 3
Min'yar 136 M 2
Míovágur 124 A 2
Miqdādīyah, Al- 152 E 2
Miquelon ⌓ 88 F 3
Miquelon,
Saint Pierre and ⛊ 88 F 3
Mira 130 B 2
Miracema de Tocantins 112 K 5
Miramichi 88 D 3
Miranda [Portugal] 130 B 2
Miranda [Spain] 130 D 1
Mirandela 130 B 2
Miri 156 G 7
Mirimire 115 I A 2
Mirim Lagoon ◡ 114 J 4
Mirnyy
[Russia, Arkhangel'sk] 138 H 4
Mirnyy [Russia, Sakha] 148 XY 6
Mirnyy ⊿ 181 II C 11/12
Mirpur Khas 150 KL 5
Mirtoan Sea ≋ 133 CD 4
Mirzapur 150 N 6
Miscou ⌓ 88 D 3
Mish'āb, Al- 152 F 3
Mishkino 136 L 2
Misima Island ⌓ 156 P 10
Misiones ▽ 114 HJ 3
Miskitos ⚇
→ Mosquito 73 K 8
Miskolc 128 GH 3
Misool ⌓ 156 L 8
Miṣrātah 176 L 2
Missinaibi ∽ 86 G 3
Missinaibi Lake ◡ 86 FG 3
Mission 96 D 4
Mission Viejo 92 C 3
Missisauga 98 E 2
Missisicabi ∽ 88 A 2
Mississippi ▽ 96 F 2
Mississippi ∽ 80 J 2
Mississippi Choctaw
Indian Reservation ⧗ 96 F 2
Mississippi River
Delta ⩘ 96 F 3
Mississippi Sound ≍ 96 F 3
Missoula 90 D 2
Missouri ▽ 94 EF 3
Missouri ∽ 80 F 2
Missouri, Little ∽ 90 F 2
Missouri Valley 94 DE 2
Mistassibi ∽ 88 C 2
Mistassini ∽ 88 B 2
Mistassini, Lac ◡ 88 B 2
Mistawasis Indian
Reserve ⧗ 84 G 2
Mistissini 88 D 2
Mistissini Indian
Reserve ⧗ 88 B 2
Mistretta 132 C 4
Mitchell 94 D 2
Mitchell, Mount ▲ 100 C 2
Mīt Ghamr 152 A 3
Míthymna 133 D 3
Mito 154 S 4
Mits'iwwa' 176 PQ 5
Mittersill 128 E 4
Mitú 112 E 3
Mitumba Mountains ⛰ 178 K 4/3
Miwok [= Mi.] ⚇ 73 F 6
Mixco 102 GH 5/6
Mixe ⚇ 73 J 8
Mixtec ⚇ 73 J 8
Miyāh, Wādī al- ∽ 152 C 2
Miyako ⌓ 154 P 7
Mīyaly 136 KL 4
Miyazaki 154 Q 5
Mizen Head)≋ 124 A 4
Mizhhir"ya 128 H 3
Mizoram [= Miz.] ▽ 150 P 6
Mjölby 126 F 3
Mjøsa ◡ 126 D 2
Mladá Boleslav 128 F 3
Mladenovac 133 B 2
Mława 128 G 2
Mljet ⌓ 132 D 2
Mlyniv 128 J 3
Mmabatho 178 K 8
Mo i Rana 125 B 3
Moa 102 KL 4
Moa ⌓ 166 J 3
Moab 92 E 2
Moala ⌓ 166 QR 4
Moanda 178 G 3
Moapa 92 D 2
Mobārakeh 152 FG 2
Mobaye 176 M 8
Moberly 94 E 3
Mobile 100 AB 3
Mobile ∽ 100 AB 3
Mobile Bay ≋) 100 AB 3
Mobridge 94 CD 1
Moçambique 178 N 6
Mochis, Los 102 CD 3
Mochudi 178 K 7
Mocímboa da Praia 178 N 5
Mocksville 100 C 2
Môco ▲ 178 GH 5
Mocoa 112 D 3
Moctezuma 96 B 3
Mocuba 178 M 6
Modane 131 E 3
Modena 132 B 2
Modesto 92 B 2
Modica 132 C 4
Modimolle 178 K 7
Moe 166 K 8
Moers 128 C 2
Mogadishu (Muqdisho) 176 R 8
Mogilno 128 C 2
Mogocha 148 YZ 8
Mogollon Mountains ⛰ 92 E 3
Mogollon Plateau ⛰ 92 E 3
Mogotón ▲ 102 H 6
Mohács 128 G 4
Mohave, Lake ◡ 92 D 3
Mohave, Yuma- ⚇ 73 G 6
Mohawk 98 B 1
Mohe 154 O 1
Mohinora, Cerro ▲ 96 B 4
Mohns Ridge ⩠ 12 B 23/22
Mohyliv-Podil's'kyy 128 K 3
Moiave ∽ 92 C 3
Moineşti 128 J 4
Mo i Rana 125 B 3
Mõisaküla 126 J 3
Moisie ∽ 88 D 2
Moissac 131 C 4
Mojave 92 C 3
Mojave Desert ⩘ 92 C 3
Mojos ⚇ 109 G 6
Mokhovaya ▲ 138 JK 2
Mokolo 176 K 6
Mokp'o 154 OP 4/5
Mokrous 136 HJ 3

∽ River, canal
≷ Waterfall
◡ Lake, lakes, reservoir
⩪ Swamp
⩌ Salt flat
≋ Sea
≍ Strait
≋) Bay, gulf
)≋ Cape
⌓ Island, islands
⇄ Ocean current
⩠ Ocean floor landforms
⌁ Tectonic feature
☁ Atmospheric phenomena
◷ Time zone
⊕ Geographical grid

Moksha 136 G 2
Mokshan 136 GH 3
Mola di Bari 132 D 3
Mold 124 C 4
Moldavians 121 J 5
Molde 126 C 2
Moldova 128 K 3/4
Moldova Nouă 133 C 2
Moldoveanu 133 D 1
Molepolole 178 JK 7
Molėtai 126 J 4
Molfetta 132 D 3
Molina 130 D 2
Molina de Segura 130 D 3
Moline 94 F 2
Molise 132 CD 3
Mollendo 112 E 7
Molodëzhnaya 181 II C 7/8
Mologa 138 F 5
Molokai 92 I C 2
Molokai Fracture Zone 10 TU 4
Molokovo 136 E 1
Moloma 138 L 5
Molson Lake 86 C 2
Moluccas 156 KL 7/9
Molucca Sea 156 JK 8
Mombasa 178 MN 3
Mombuey 130 BC 1
Momotombo 15 L 15
Mon 150 Q 7
Mon 145 N 8
Møn 126 E 4
Mona, Isla 101 VIII
Monaco 131 E 4
Monaco 131 E 4
Monahans 96 C 3
Mona Passage 101 VIII
Monashee Mountains 84 D 3
Monastyrshchina 136 C 2
Monchegorsk 138 E 2
Mönchengladbach 128 BC 2
Monclova 96 C 4
Moncton 88 D 3
Mondovi *[Italy]* 132 A 2
Mondovi *[U.S.]* 94 F 1
Monemvasía 133 C 4
Monet 88 B 2
Monett 94 E 3
Monfalcone 132 C 1
Monforte 130 B 1
Mongo 176 L 6
Mongo-Kundu 173 EF 6
Mongolia 154 HM 2
Mongolia, Inner 141 OQ 5
Mongomo 176 K 8
Mongu 178 J 6
Monitor Range 92 C 2
Monmouth 94 F 2
Mono Lake 92 C 2
Monopoli 132 D 3
Monreal del Campo 130 D 2
Monreale 132 C 4
Monroe *[U.S., Georgia]* 100 C 2
Monroe *[U.S., Louisiana]* 96 EF 2
Monroe *[U.S., Michigan]* 98 D 2
Monroe *[U.S., North Carolina]* 100 C 2
Monroe *[U.S., Wisconsin]* 94 F 2
Monroeville 100 B 3
Monrovia 176 E 7
Mons 131 D 2
Monsoon, North East 25 QR 3/4
Monsoon, North West 25 MO 5
Monsoon, South East 25 Q-S 14-16
Monsoon, South West 25 MO 15
Mönsterås 126 F 3/4
Mont ... → ..., Mont
Montagnais 73 LM 4
Montague 92 D 4
Montalbán 130 D 2
Montalbano Ionico 132 D 3
Montana 133 C 2
Montana 90 DF 2
Montauban 131 C 4
Montauk Point 98 G 2
Montbard 131 D 3
Montbéliard 131 E 3
Montbrison 131 D 3
Mont-de-Marsan 131 B 4
Montdidier 131 C 2
Mont-Dore 166 O 5
Monte ... → ..., Monte ...
Montecristo 132 B 2
Montefiascone 132 C 2
Montego Bay 102 K 5
Montélimar 131 D 4
Montemor-o-Novo 130 B 3
Montenegrins [= Mo.] 121 H 5
Montenegro 117 HJ 5
Montenegro, Serbia and 133 BC 2
Montepuez 178 M 5
Montepulciano 132 B 2
Monte Quemado 114 G 3
Monterey 92 B 2
Monterey Bay 92 B 2
Montería 112 D 2
Montero 112 G 7
Monterrey 96 C 4
Monterrey, Parque Nacional de 96 C 4
Montes Claros 112 KL 7
Montevarchi 132 B 2
Montevideo *[U.S.]* 94 E 1
Montevideo *[Uruguay]* 114 HJ 5/4
Monte Vista 94 B 3
Montgomery 100 B 2
Monticello *[U.S., Arkansas]* 96 F 2
Monticello *[U.S., Kentucky]* 98 C 3
Monticello *[U.S., New York]* 98 F 2
Monticello *[U.S., Utah]* 92 E 2
Monti del Gennargentu 132 AB 3
Montilla 130 C 3
Mont-Joli 88 C 2
Mont-Laurier 88 B 3
Mont-Louis 88 D 2
Mont-Louis 131 C 4
Montluçon 131 C 3
Montmagny 88 C 3
Montmorillon 131 C 3
Monto 166 L 5
Montoro 130 C 3
Montpelier *[U.S., Idaho]* 90 E 3
Montpelier *[U.S., Vermont]* 98 F 1
Montpellier 131 D 4
Montréal 88 B 3
Montreal 86 FG 4
Montreal Lake 84 G 2
Montreal Lake Indian Reserve 84 G 2
Montreux 128 C 4
Montrose *[U.K.]* 124 D 3
Montrose *[U.S.]* 94 B 3
Monts ... → ..., Monts
Mont-Saint-Michel, Le 131 B 2
Montserrat 115 II B 1
Monywa 150 PQ 6
Monza 132 B 1
Moody Point 181 I C 33
Moomba 165 G 9
Moonie 165 HJ 9
Moora 166 D 7
Moorcroft 90 F 2
Moore 96 D 2
Moore, Lake 166 D 6/7
Moorhead 94 D 1
Moors 173 BC 3/4
Moosehead Lake 98 G 1
Moose Jaw 84 G 3
Moose Lake *[Canada]* 86 B 2
Moose Lake *[U.S.]* 94 E 1
Moose Lake 86 C 2
Moose Mountain Creek 86 B 3
Moosomin 86 B 3
Moosonee 86 G 3
Mopti 176 G 6
Moquegua 112 E 7
Mór 128 G 4
Mora *[Spain]* 130 C 2
Morå *[Sweden]* 126 E 2
Mora 96 B 2
Moradabad 150 MN 5
Morąg 128 G 2
Moraleja 130 B 2
Moratuwa 150 N 9
Morava 128 F 3
Moravian Heights 128 EF 3
Moray Firth 124 C 2
Morcenx 131 B 4
Morden 86 C 3
Mordovia 136 GH 2
Mordovo 136 F 3
Mordvinians 121 L-M 4
Moreau 94 C 1
Moree 166 KL 6
Morehead 98 D 3
Morehead City 100 D 2
Morelia 102 E 5/4
Morella 130 D 2
Morelos 96 B 4
Morena, Sierra 130 BD 3
Morenci 92 E 3
Moreno Valley 92 C 3
Morgan City 96 F 3
Morganton 100 C 2
Morgantown 98 E 3
Moriarty 92 F 3
Morinville 84 E 2
Morioka 154 S 4
Moris 96 A 3
Moritz, Sankt 128 D 4
Morjärv 125 E 3
Morki 136 J 2
Morlaix 131 A 2
Morne Diablotins 115 II B 2
Morne Seychellios 178 PQ 3
Morocco 176 EG 3/2
Morogoro 178 M 4
Moro Gulf 156 J 6
Morombe 178 N 7
Mörön 154 K 2
Morondava 178 N 7/6
Morón de la Frontera 130 C 3
Moroni 178 N 5
Moros 145 Q 9
Morotai 156 KL 7
Morozovsk 136 FG 4
Morpeth 124 D 3
Morrasale 148 OP 5/4
Morrilton 96 E 2
Morris *[Canada]* 86 C 3
Morris *[U.S., Illinois]* 94 F 2
Morris *[U.S., Minnesota]* 94 DE 1
Morris Jesup, Cape 76 fj 1/2
Morristown 100 C 1
Morro Bay 92 B 3
Morshansk 136 FG 3
Mortlock Islands 156 PQ 6/7
Morton 90 B 2
Moru-Madi 173 FG 5
Morzhovets Island 138 J 2
Mosal'sk 136 D 2
Moscow *[U.S.]* 90 C 2
Moscow (Moskva) *[Russia]* 136 E 2
Moscow Time 38 B 9
Mosel 128 C 3
Moses Lake 90 C 2
Moshchnyy 126 K 3
Moshenskoye 138 F 5
Moshi 178 M 3
Mosi 173 C 4
Mosjøen 125 B 4
Moskva → Moscow 136 E 2
Moskva 136 DE 2
Mosonmagyaróvár 128 FG 4
Mosquito (Miskitos) 73 K 8
Mosquito Lagoon 100 C 3
Moss 126 D 3
Mossbank 84 G 3
Mosselbaai 178 J 9
Mossendjo 178 G 3
Mossman 166 K 4
Mossoró 112 M 4/5
Most 128 E 3
Mostaganem → Mustaghānam
Mostar 132 DE 2
Móstoles 130 C 2

Independent country
Dependent territory
Federal state, province, territory
People, ethnic group, tribe
Indian reservation/reserve
National Park
Industrial region
Historical site
Research station
Continent, realm
Region, peninsula
Mountain range, mountains
Peak
Pass
Ice shelf, glacier

Mostovskoy 134 F 2
Mostys'ka 128 H 3
Mosul (Al-Mawṣil) 152 D 1
Mota del Cuervo 130 D 2
Motala 126 F 3
Motilla del Palancar 130 D 2
Motitlon [= Mo.] 109 F 4
Motril 130 C 3
Motru 133 C 2
Motykley 148 ef 7
Mouila 178 G 3
Moulins 131 CD 3
Moulouya
→ Mulūyah
Moultrie 100 C 3
Moultrie, Lake 100 C 2
Moundou 176 L 7
Moundsville 98 D 3
Mount ... → ..., Mount
Mountain Grove 94 EF 3
Mountain Home
[U.S., Arkansas] 96 EF 1
Mountain Home
[U.S., Idaho] 90 D 3
Mountain Khmers 145 O 8
Mountain Standard
Time 38 B 20
Mountain View 92 I D 3
Mount Airy 100 C 1
Mount Carmel 94 FG 3
Mount Desert Island 98 GH 1
Mount Gambier 166 HJ 8
Mount Hagen 156 N 9
Mount Hope 166 GH 7
Mount Isa 166 H 5
Mount Magnet 166 DE 6
Mount Pearl 88 G 3
Mount Pleasant
[U.S., Iowa] 94 F 2
Mount Pleasant
[U.S., Michigan] 98 C 2
Mount Pleasant
[U.S., South Carolina] 100 D 2
Mount Pleasant
[U.S., Texas] 96 E 2
Mount Rainier
National Park 90 B 2
Mount Revelstoke
National Park 84 D 3
Mount Rushmore
National Memorial 94 C 2
Mount Shasta 92 B 1
Mount Sterling 98 D 3
Mount Vernon
[U.S., Illinois] 94 F 3
Mount Vernon
[U.S., Indiana] 98 BC 3
Mount Vernon
[U.S., Ohio] 98 D 2
Mount Vernon
[U.S., Washington] 90 B 1
Moura 130 B 3
Moushalagane 88 C 1/2
Moville 124 B 3
Mo'ynoq 148 M 10
Moyobamba 112 D 5
Mozambique 178 LM 7/5
Mozambique
Channel 178 MN 7/5

Mozdok 134 GH 2
Mozhaysk 136 DE 2
Mozhga 136 K 2
Mpanda 178 L 4
Mpika 178 L 5
Mpongwe 173 DE 6
Mrągowo 128 H 2
Mrakovo 136 LM 3
Msta 138 F 5
Mstsislaw 128 L 1
Mtsensk 136 E 3
Mtskheta 134 GH 3
Mtwara 178 N 4/5
Muarasiberut 156 D 8
Muarateweh 156 G 8
Mubarraz, Al- 150 F 5
Mubi 176 K 6
Mubi 173 EF 4
Muchinga
Mountains 178 L 5
Muchkapskiy 136 G 3
Mucur 134 D 3
Mudanjiang 154 PQ 3
Mudanya 134 B 3
Mudawwarah, Al- 152 BC 3
Mud Lake 86 CD 3
Mudurnu 134 C 3
Mud'yuga 138 GH 3
Mufulira 178 K 5
Mughalzhar Hills 148 M 9
Mūghār 152 G 2
Muğla 134 B 4
Mugodzhary
Mountains
→ Mughalzhar Hills
Muḥammad, Cape 152 B 4
Muḥarraq, Al- 152 F 4
Mühldorf 128 E 3
Mühlhausen/Thüringen 128 D 2
Muhos 125 F 4
Muhu 126 H 3
Mujarridah 132 AB 4
Mujarridah-
Mountains 132 AB 4
Mukacheve 128 H 3
Mukallā, Al- 150 FG 8
Mukhā, Al- 150 E 8
Mukhaywīr 152 D 2
Mukutuwa 86 C 2
Mula 130 D 3
Mulhacén 130 C 3
Mulhouse 128 C 4
Mull 124 BC 3
Mullet Peninsula 124 A 3
Mullewa 166 D 6
Mullingar 124 B 4
Multan 150 L 4
Mulūyah 176 G 2
Mumbai (Bombay) 150 L 7
Mumra 134 HJ 1
Mūn, Jabal 176 M 6
Muna 156 J 8/9
München → Munich 128 D 3
Muncie 98 C 2/3
Mundas 145 M 7
Munday 96 D 2
Mundurucus 109 H 5
Mungbere 178 K 2
Munger 150 O 5

Munich (München) 128 D 3
Munising 98 C 1
Munku-Sardyk 154 JK 1
Münster 128 C 2
Munster 124 AB 4
Munţii Apuseni 128 H 4
Munzur Dağları 134 EF 3
Muonio 125 EF 3
Muonionjoki 125 E 3
Muqdisho
→ Mogadishu 176 R 8
Mur 128 E 4
Murá 109 G-H 5
Muradiye 134 G 4
Murallón 114 E 7
Murashi 138 L 5
Murat 134 B 4/3
Murat 134 G 3
Muratlı 134 B 3
Muravera 132 B 3
Muravlenko 148 PQ 6
Mūrcheh Khvort 152 FG 2
Murchison 166 CD 6
Murcia 130 D 3
Murcia 130 D 3
Murcia 130 D 3
Murdochville 88 D 2
Mure, La 131 D 4
Mureş 128 J 4
Murfreesboro 100 B 2
Murgap 148 N 11
Murgon 166 L 6
Muriaé 114 L 2
Müritz 128 E 2
Murle 173 G 5
Murmansk 138 EF 2
Murmanskiy Bereg 138 FG 1/2
Murmashi 138 E 2
Murnau 128 D 4
Murom 136 F 2
Muroran 154 S 3
Muros 130 A 1
Murray 98 B 3
Murray [Australia] 166 J 7/8
Murray [Canada] 84 C 2
Murray, Lake 100 C 2
Murray Bridge 166 HJ 8
Murray Fracture
Zone 10 TU 4
Murska Sobota 132 D 1
Mururoa 160 PQ 6
Murwara 150 MN 6
Mürzzuschlag 128 F 4
Muş 134 F 4
Musa Ālī Terara 176 PQ 6
Musala 133 CD 2
Musayyib, Al- 152 DE 2
Muscat (Masqaṭ) 150 HJ 6
Muscatine 94 F 2
Muscle Shoals 100 B 2
Musgrave Range 166 FG 6
Musgu 173 E 4/5
Musina 178 KL 7
Muskegon 98 C 2
Muskegon 98 C 2
Muskingum 98 D 3
Muskogee 96 E 2
Muskrat Dam Lake
Indian Reserve 86 DE 2

Muslyumovo 136 K 2
Musoma 178 LM 3
Musselshell 90 E 2
Mustafakemalpaşa 134 B 3
Mustaghānam 176 GH 1
Mustang 150 N 5
Mustayevo 136 K 3
Mustique 115 II B 2
Mustjala 126 H 3
Mustvee 126 J 3
Mut 134 D 4
Mutare 178 L 6
Mutnyy Materik 138 MN 2/3
Mutsamudu 178 NO 5
Muyezerskiy 138 E 3
Muzaffarpur 150 NO 5
Muzhi 138 Q 3
Múzquiz 96 C 4
Muztag Feng 154 G 4
Mwali 178 N 5
Mwanza 178 L 3
Mwene-Ditu 178 J 4
Mweru, Lake 178 KL 4
Mwokil 156 QR 6
Myanmar 150 PQ 6
Mycenæ 133 C 4
Myeik 150 Q 8
Myingyan 150 Q 6
Myitkyina 150 Q 5/6
Mykhaylivka 134 D 1
Mykolayiv
[Ukraine, L'viv] 128 HJ 3
Mykolayiv
[Ukraine, Mykolayiv] 134 C 1
Mýkonos 133 D 4
Mýkonos 133 D 4
Mymensingh 150 P 6
Mynämäki 126 H 2
Myrhorod 136 D 4
Mýrina 133 D 3
Myronivka 136 C 4
Myrtle Beach 100 D 2
Myrtle Creek 90 B 3
Myrtle Point 90 AB 3
Myshkin 136 E 1
Mysore 150 M 8
Mys Shmidta 148 m 5
My Tho 156 F 5/6
Mytilíni 133 D 3
Mytishchi 136 E 2
Mzimba 178 L 5
Mzuzu 178 L 5

N

Naalehu 92 I D 3
Naas 124 B 4
Nabak, An- 152 C 2
Nabatīyat at-Tahtā, An- 152 B 2
Nabatiyet et Tahta
→ An-Nabatīyat
at-Tahtā
Naberezhnyye Chelny 136 KL 2
Nabeul → Nābul
Nabire 156 LM 8
Nabī Shu'ayb 150 E 7
Nabq 152 B 3
Nābul 132 B 4

River, canal
Waterfall
Lake, lakes, reservoir
Swamp
Salt flat
Sea
Strait
Bay, gulf
Cape
Island, islands
Ocean current
Ocean floor landforms
Tectonic feature
Atmospheric phenomena
Time zone
Geographical grid

Independent country
Dependent territory
Federal state, province, territory
People, ethnic group, tribe
Indian reservation/reserve
National Park
Industrial region
Historical site
Research station
Continent, realm
Region, peninsula
Mountain range, mountains
▲ Peak
Pass
Ice shelf, glacier

egro, Río [Colombia/ Venezuela/Brazil] 112 F 3
egros 156 J 5/6
egru Vodă 133 E 2
ehoiu 133 D 1
eiafu 166 S 4
eijiang 154 KL 5/6
eillsville 94 F 1
eiva 112 DE 3
ek'emtē 176 OP 7
ekhayevskiy 136 F 4
ekrasovskoye 136 F 1
eksø 126 F 4
elidovo 136 CD 2
eligh 94 D 2
el'kan 148 c 7
ellis 92 C 2
ellore 150 N 8
el'min Nos 138 M 2
elson [Canada] 84 D 3
elson [New Zealand] 166 P 9
elson 76 VW 7
elson House 86 C 2
elspruit 178 L 8
éma → Na'mah, An- [Mauritania]
ema [Russia] 136 JK 1
eman 128 H 1
eman 128 J 2
emeiben Lake 84 G 2
emiscau Indian Reserve 88 A 2
emours 131 C 2
'emuro 154 T 3
emyriv 128 K 3
enagh 124 B 4
endo 166 NO 3
enjiang 154 P 2
entsy [Asia] 145 LM 3
entsy [Europe] 121 LN 3
eosho 94 E 3
eosho 94 E 3
eotropic 26 FH 6
eotropis 30 EH 6
epal 150 NO 5
'ephi 92 DE 2
erchinsk 148 XY 8
erekhta 136 F 1
eresnica 133 C 2
eretva 132 DE 2
eris 126 J 4
eroyka 138 OP 3
erpio 130 D 3
erva 130 B 3
eryungri 148 Za 7
es' 138 JK 2
esa' 152 F 1
esebŭr 133 E 2
eskaupstaður 119 EF 3
esoddtangen 126 D 3
ess, Loch 124 C 2
estaocano 88 B 2
éstos 133 D 3
etanya 152 B 2
etherlands 128 BC 2
etherlands Antilles [Northern island group] 115 II B 1
Netherlands Antilles [Southern island group] 115 I AB 1
Neubrandenburg 128 E 2
Neuchâtel 128 C 4
Neufchâteau 131 DE 2
Neufchâtel 131 C 2
Neumarkt in der Oberpfalz 128 DE 3
Neumayer 181 II CB 1/2
Neumünster 128 D 1
Neuquén 114 F 5
Neuquén 114 EF 5
Neuruppin 128 E 2
Neuse 100 D 2
Neusiedl, Lake 128 F 4
Neuss 128 C 2
Neussargues-Mouissac 131 C 3
Neustadt an der Weinstraße 128 C 3
Neustadt in Holstein 128 D 1/2
Neustrelitz 128 E 2
Neu-Ulm 128 D 3
Neuwied 128 C 3
Neva 138 E 5
Nevada 94 E 3
Nevada 92 CD 2
Nevada, Sierra [Spain] 130 CD 3
Nevada, Sierra [U.S.] 92 BC 1/3
Nevado de Colima 102 DE 5
Nevado del Ruiz 15 C 15
Nevel' 136 B 2
Neverkino 136 H 3
Nevers 131 D 3
Nevesinje 132 E 2
Nevinnomyssk 134 G 2
Nevis 115 II B 1
Nevis, Saint Kitts and 115 II B 1
Nevşehir 134 D 4
Nev'yansk 138 P 5
New Albany [U.S., Indiana] 98 C 3
New Albany [U.S., Mississippi] 96 F 2
New Amsterdam 112 H 2
Newar 145 M 7
Newark [U.S., Delaware] 98 F 3
Newark [U.S., New Jersey] 98 F 2
Newark [U.S., New York] 98 E 2
Newark [U.S., Ohio] 98 D 2
New Bedford 98 G 2
New Bern 100 D 2
Newberry [U.S., Michigan] 98 C 1
Newberry [U.S., South Carolina] 100 C 2
New Braunfels 96 D 3
New Britain 156 OP 9
New Brunswick 98 F 2
New Brunswick 88 D 3
Newburgh 98 F 2
Newburyport 98 G 2
New Caledonia 166 MN 5
New Caledonia 166 NO 5
New Caledonians 164 J 9/10
New Castile 130 CD 2
Newcastle [Australia] 166 L 7
Newcastle [South Africa] 178 K 8
New Castle [U.S., Indiana] 98 C 3
New Castle [U.S., Pennsylvania] 98 DE 2
Newcastle [U.S., Wyoming] 90 F 3
Newcastle-upon-Tyne 124 D 3
Newcomb 92 E 2
New Delhi 150 M 5
New England Seamounts 10 EF 4/3
Newfoundland 88 FG 2
Newfoundland and Labrador 78 cd 7/9
Newfoundland Basin 10 FG 3
New Georgia 166 M 2
New Georgia Islands 166 M 2
New Glasgow 88 E 3
New Guinea 156 LO 8/9
Newhalen 78 J 7/6
New Hampshire 98 G 2
New Hampton 94 EF 2
New Hanover 156 P 8
New Haven 98 F 2
New Hazelton 84 B 2
New Hebrides 166 OP 3/4
New Hebrides Trench 10 R 6/7
New Iberia 96 EF 3
New Ireland 156 P 8
New Jersey 98 F 2/3
New London 98 FG 2
Newman 166 DE 5
Newmarket 98 E 1/2
New Martinsville 98 D 3
New Mexico 92 FG 3
Newnan 100 B 2
New Orleans 96 F 3
New Philadelphia 98 D 2
New Plymouth 166 P 8
Newport [U.K., England] 124 D 5
Newport [U.K., Wales] 124 C 4
Newport [U.S., Arkansas] 96 F 2
Newport [U.S., Oregon] 90 A 2
Newport [U.S., Rhode Island] 98 G 2
Newport [U.S., Vermont] 98 FG 1
Newport [U.S., Washington] 90 C 1
Newport News 98 E 3
New Richmond 88 D 2
New Rockford 86 C 4
New Ross 124 B 4
Newry 124 BC 3
New Siberia 148 fg 3/4
New Siberian Islands 148 bg 3
New Smyrna Beach 100 C 3
New South Wales 166 JL 7
Newton [U.K., Iowa] 94 E 2
Newton [U.S., Kansas] 94 D 3
Newtonabbey 124 C 3
Newton Abbot 124 C 5
New Town 90 G 1/2
Newtown Saint Boswells 124 D 3
New Ulm 94 E 1
New World Island 88 G 2
New York 98 F 2
New York 98 EF 2
New Zealand 166 PR 10/8
New Zealanders 164 JK 12/11
New Zealand Standard Time [= 3] 38 B 24
Neya 136 G 1
Nezahualcóyotl 102 F 5/4
Nez Perce 73 G 5
Nez Perce Indian Reservation 90 C 2
Nganassans 145 MO 2
Nganglong Kangri 154 F 5
Ngaoui, Mont 176 KL 7
Ngaoundéré 176 K 7
Ngatik 156 Q 6
Ngaya, Jebel 176 M 7
Ngazidja 178 N 5
Ngcheangel 156 L 6
N'Giva 178 H 6
Ngoc Linh 156 F 4
Ngombe 173 F 5
Ngoni 173 G 6/7
Ngoring Hu 154 J 5
Nguigmi 176 K 6
Ngulu 156 M 6
Nguru 176 K 6
Nha Trang 156 FG 5
Niagara 98 E 2
Niagara Falls 98 E 2
Niagara Falls 68 ⑦
Niamey 176 H 6
Nias 156 D 7
Nicaragua 102 HJ 6
Nicaragua, Lake 102 J 6
Nicaro 71 L 7/8
Nice 131 E 4
Nichicun, Lac 88 C 1
Nicholasville 98 C 3
Nicobar, Great 150 P 9
Nicobarese 145 N 9
Nicobar Islands 150 P 9
Nicolaas, Sint 115 I A 1
Nicolas, San 92 C 3
Nicolás de los Arroyos, San 114 G 4
Nicolás de los Garza, San 96 C 4
Nicolau, São 176 C 5
Nicolet 88 B 3
Nicosia (Lefkosía/Lefkoşa) 152 B 2
Nicoya, Península de 102 H 6/7
Nida 126 G 4
Nido, Sierra el 96 B 3
Nidzica 128 G 2
Nienburg (Weser) 128 CD 2
Nieuw Amsterdam 112 J 2
Nieuw Nickerie 112 H 2
Nieuwpoort 115 I A 1/2
Nieves, Las 96 B 4
Niğde 134 D 4
Niger 176 JK 5
Niger 176 EF 6

River, canal
Waterfall
Lake, lakes, reservoir
Swamp
Salt flat
Sea
Strait
Bay, gulf
Cape
Island, islands
Ocean current
Ocean floor landforms
Tectonic feature
Atmospheric phenomena
Time zone
Geographical grid

Nigeria 176 JK 6
Nigríta 133 C 3
Niigata 154 R 4
Niihau 92 I A 2
Nijar 130 D 3
Nijmegen 128 B 2
Nikel' 125 GH 2
Niklaas, Sint 131 D 1
Nikolayevsk 136 H 4
Nikolayevsk-na-Amure 148 cd 8
Nikol'sk *[Russia, Penza]* 136 H 3
Nikol'sk *[Russia, Vologda]* 138 K 5
Nikol'skoye-na-Cheremshane 136 J 2/3
Nikopol' 136 D 5
Nīk Pey 134 J 4
Niksar 134 E 3
Nikšič 133 B 2
Nikumaroro 166 RS 2/1
Nile 176 O 3
Nile, Blue 176 O 6
Nile, White 176 O 7
Nile River Oasis 51 KL 4
Niles 98 C 2
Nimba, Monts 176 F 7
Nîmes 131 D 4
Nimule 176 O 8
Nīnawā ∴ → Nineveh 152 D 1
Ninetyeast Ridge 10 N 7/5
Nineveh (Nīnawā) ∴ 152 D 1
Ningbo 154 O 6
Ningde 154 NO 6
Ningdu 154 N 6
Ninghai 154 O 6
Ningxia Huizu, Autonomous Region 154 KL 4
Ninigo Islands 156 N 8
Niobrara 94 C 2
Nioro 176 F 5
Niort 131 B 3
Nipawin 84 H 2
Nipigon 86 EF 3
Nipigon, Lake 86 E 3
Nipigon Bay 86 F 3
Nipissing, Lake 86 H 4
Nipissing Indian Reserve 86 H 4
Nippur ∴ 152 E 2
Niquelândia 107 J 6
Nir 134 H 4
Niš 133 C 2
Nişab 152 E 3
Nišava 133 C 2
Nisko 128 H 3
Nissan 126 E 4/3
Nísyros 133 E 4
Nītaure 126 J 3
Nitra 128 G 3
Niuatoputapu 166 RS 4
Niue 166 T 4
Niue 166 T 4
Niulakita 166 Q 3
Niutao 166 Q 2
Nivshera 138 M 4
Nivskiy 138 EF 2
Nixa 94 E 3
Niyālā 176 N 6
Nizamabad 150 MN 7
Nizhnekamsk 136 K 2
Nizhnekamsk Reservoir 136 L 2
Nizhneudinsk 148 U 8/7
Nizhnevartovsk 148 QR 6
Nizhneyansk 148 bc 4
Nizhniy Bestyakh 148 b 6
Nizhniy Chir 136 G 4
Nizhniye Sergi 136 M 2
Nizhniy Lomov 136 G 3
Nizhniy Novgorod 136 GH 2
Nizhniy Odes 138 N 3
Nizhniy Tagil 138 O 5
Nizhnyaya Omra 138 N 4
Nizhnyaya Pesha 138 KL 2
Nizhnyaya Poyma 148 UV 7
Nizhnyaya Tura 138 OP 5
Nizhyn 136 C 3/4
Nizip 134 E 4
Nkayi 178 G 3
Nkongsamba 176 K 7/8
Nogales 92 E 4
Nogays 121 L 5
Nogayskaya Step' 134 H 2
Nogent-le-Rotrou 131 C 2
Noginsk 136 EF 2
Nogliki 148 d 8
Nogoonnuur 154 GH 2
Noia 130 B 1
Noirmoutier, Île de 131 B 3
Nokia 126 H 2
Nola 176 L 8
Nolinsk 136 J 1
Nome 78 GH 6
Nominingue 88 B 3
Nomuka Islands 166 S 5
Nong Khai 156 E 4
Nonoava 96 B 4
Nonthaburi 156 DE 5
Nootka 73 F 4/5
Nootka Island 84 B 3
Nootka Sound 84 B 3
Noranda 71 L 5
Nordaustlandet 148 EG 2
Nordegg 84 D 2
Norderney 128 C 2
Norderstedt 128 D 2
Nordfjord 126 BC 2
Nordfjordeid 126 C 2
Nordhausen 128 D 2
Nordhorn 128 C 2
Nordkinn 125 G 2
Nördlingen 128 D 3
Nordostrundingen 76 no 2/3
Norfolk *[U.S., Nebraska]* 94 D 2
Norfolk *[U.S., Virginia]* 98 E 3
Norfolk Island 166 O 6
Norfork Lake 96 EF 1
Noril'sk 148 S 5
Norman 96 D 2
Normanby Island 156 P 9/10
Normandin 88 B 2
Normandy 131 BC 2
Norman Island 101 IX
Normanton 166 J 4
Norman Wells 71 EF 3
Norrbotten 125 DE 4/3
Nørresundby 126 D 3
Norris Lake 100 C 1
Norristown 98 F 2
Norrköping 126 F 3
Norrland 125 BD 4
Norrtälje 126 G 3
Norseman 166 E 7
Norte, Punta 114 HJ 5
North, Cape 88 EF 3
Northallerton 124 D 3
Northam 166 D 7
North America 6 JL 3
North American Basin 10 EF 4
North American Plate 14 KM 2/4
Northampton *[U.K.]* 124 D 4
Northampton *[U.S.]* 98 F 2
North and East Greenland, National Park of 78 gj 3/5
North Athapascans 73 CH 3/4
North Atlantic Drift 6 OQ 3/2
North Augusta 100 C 2
North Battleford 84 FG 2
North Bay 86 H 4
North Bimini 100 I D 4
North Breakers 101 V
North Canadian 96 D 1
North Cape *[New Zealand]* 166 PQ 7
North Cape *[Norway]* 125 F 2
North Caribou Lake 86 E 2
North Carolina 100 CD 2
North Cascades National Park 90 B 1
North Channel *[Atlantic Ocean/Irish Sea]* 124 BC 3
North Channel *[Canada, Lake Huron]* 86 G 4
North Charleston 100 CD 2
North Dakota 86 BC 4
North East Monsoon 25 QR 3/4
Northeast Pacific Basin 10 SU 3/5
North East Trades 25 C-T 6-7
North Equatorial Current *[Atlantic Ocean]* 6 NO 4/5
North Equatorial Current *[Indian Ocean]* 4 MO 5
North Equatorial Current *[Pacific Ocean]* 6 FK 5
Northern Cheyenne Indian Reservation 90 F 2
Northern Cook Islands 160 NO 4/5
Northern Dvina 138 HJ 3/4
Northern Ireland 124 BC 3
Northern Light Lake 86 E 3
Northern Mariana Islands 156 N 4
Northern Mariana Islands *[Detail map]* 101 III
Northern Sos'va 138 OP 4
Northern Sporades 133 D 3/4
Northern Territory 166 GH 4/5
Northfield 94 E 1
North Fiji Basin 10 R 6/7
North Fork Clearwater 90 CD 2
North Fork John Day 90 C 2
North Fort Myers 100 C 4
North Frisian Islands 128 C 1
Northice 66 G 2
North Island 166 OP 8
North Korea 154 PQ 3/4
North Little Rock 96 EF 2
North Loup 94 D 2
North Magnetic Pole 180 I AB 30/27
North Moose Lake 86 BC 2
North Myrtle Beach 100 D 2
North Ossetia-Alania 134 G 2
North Pacific Current 6 EH 4/3
North Pilbara 165 F 8/9
North Platte 94 C 2
North Platte 94 B 2
North Pole 180 II A
Northport 100 B 2
North Rhine-Westphalia 128 CD 2/3
North Russian Ridge 138 JN 5/4
North Saskatchewan 84 DE 2
North Scotia Ridge 13 D 35/1
North Sea 117 FG 4
North Shore 166 P 8
North Thompson 84 D 2/3
North Twin 86 G 2
North Uist 124 B 2
Northumberland Strait 88 DE 3
North Wabasca Lake 84 E 1/2
North West Cape 166 C 5
North-West Frontier 150 L 3/4
North West Highlands 124 C 3/2
North West Monsoon 25 MO 5
Northwest Pacific Basin 10 QR 3/4
Northwest Providence Channel 100 I D 4
Northwest Territories 78 PS 6/5
Northwind Ridge 12 B 2
Norton 94 D 3
Norton Sound 76 H 6
Norvegia, Cape 181 I CB 1
Norwalk *[U.S., Connecticut]* 98 F 2
Norwalk *[U.S., Ohio]* 98 D 2
Norway 120 GJ 4/2
Norway House 86 C 2
Norwegian Basin 12 C 23
Norwegian Bay 76 WX 3
Norwegians 121 G-H 2-4
Norwegian Sea 117 FG 3
Norwich *[U.K.]* 124 E 4
Norwich *[U.S., Connecticut]* 98 G 2
Norwich *[U.S., New York]* 98 F 2
Nos Emine 133 E 2
Nosivka 136 C 4
Nossa Senhora do Socorro 112 M 6

Independent country
Dependent territory
Federal state, province, territory
People, ethnic group, tribe
Indian reservation/reserve
National Park
Industrial region
∴ Historical site
Research station
Continent, realm
Region, peninsula
Mountain range, mountains
▲ Peak
)(Pass
∗ Ice shelf, glacier

ossob 178 H 7
osy Be 178 O 5
osy Sainte Marie 178 OP 6
ota 138 DE 2
oteć 128 F 2
oto 132 D 4
otodden 126 CD 3
otre Dame, Monts 88 CD 3/2
otre Dame Bay 88 G 2
otre-Dame-du-Lac 88 CD 3
otre-Dame-du-Laus 88 B 3
otre-Dame-du-Nord 86 H 4
ottawasaga Bay 98 D 1
ottaway 88 A 2
ottingham 124 D 4
otukeu Creek 84 G 3
ouâdhibou, Cape 176 CD 4
ouâdhibou (Nawadhībū) 176 D 4
ouakchott (Nawākshūṭ) 176 D 5
ouméa 166 NO 5
ova Friburgo 114 L 2
ova Gorica 132 C 1
ova Iguaçu 114 L 2
ova Kakhovka 134 D 1
ovalukoml' 128 K 1
ova Mambone 178 M 7
ova Odesa 136 C 5
ovara 132 A 1
ova Scotia 88 DE 3
ova Scotia 88 DE 3
ova Vodolaha 136 DE 4
ovaya Chara 148 YZ 7
ovaya Ladoga 138 EF 4
ovaya Lyalya 138 OP 5
ovaya Malykla 136 J 2/3
ovaya Usman' 136 F 3
ovaya Zemlya 148 LN 4/3
ova Zagora 133 D 2
ové Zámky 128 G 3/4
ovhorodka 136 CD 4
ovhorod-Sivers'kyy 136 CD 3
ovi Bečej 133 B 1
ovi Ligure 132 AB 2
ovi Pazar *[Bulgaria]* 133 E 2
ovi Pazar *[Serbia]* 133 B 2
ovi Sad 133 B 1
ovi Sanzhary 136 D 4
ovlenskoye 138 GH 5
ovoaleksandrovsk 134 FG 1
ovoanninskiy 136 G 4
ovoarkhanhel's'k 136 C 4
ovoazovs'k 134 E 1
ovobelokatay 136 M 2
ovocheboksarsk 136 HJ 2
ovocherkassk 134 F 1
ovodvinsk 138 H 3
ovo Hamburgo 114 J 3
ovohrad-Volyns'kyy 128 K 3
ovokhopërsk 136 FG 3
ovokubansk 134 F 1
ovokuybyshevsk 136 JK 3
ovokuznetsk 148 S 8
ovolazarevskaya 181 II B 4/5
ovo Mesto 132 CD 1
ovomoskovsk *[Russia]* 136 EF 2
ovomoskovs'k *[Ukraine]* 136 D 4
ovonikolayevskiy 136 G 4
ovoorsk 136 M 3
Novopavlovsk 134 G 2
Novopokrovskaya 134 F 1
Novopskov 136 EF 4
Novorossiysk 134 E 2
Novorybnaya 148 WX 4
Novorzhev 136 B 1
Novoselytsya 128 J 3
Novosergiyevka 136 K 3
Novoshakhtinsk 136 F 5
Novosibirsk 148 QR 8/7
Novosil' 136 E 3
Novosokol'niki 136 BC 2
Novospasskoye 136 HJ 3
Novotroitsk 136 M 3
Novotroyits'ke 134 D 1
Novoukrayinka 136 C 4
Novoul'yanovsk 136 HJ 2
Novouzensk 136 J 4
Novovolyns'k 128 HJ 3
Novovoronezh 136 F 3
Novovyatsk 138 L 5
Novozavidovskiy 136 E 2
Novozybkov 136 C 3
Nový Jičín 128 G 3
Novyy Bor 138 M 2
Novyy Buh 136 C 5
Novyye Burasy 136 H 3
Novyy Nekouz 136 E 1
Novyy Oskol 136 E 4
Novyy Port 148 P 5
Novyy Tor'yal 136 J 1/2
Novyy Uoyan 148 X 7
Novyy Urengoy 148 Q 5
Novyy Vasyugan 148 Q 7
Novyy Zay 136 K 2
Nowa Sól 128 F 2
Nowbarān 152 F 2
Nowogród 128 H 2
Nowra 166 L 8
Nowshak 150 L 3
Nowy Dwór 128 G 1
Nowy Sącz 128 GH 3
Noyabr'sk 148 PQ 6
Nuasjärvi 125 G 4
Nu'ayrīyah, An- 152 EF 4
Nubian Desert 176 OP 4
Nubians 173 FG 4/3
Nueces 96 C 3
Nuer 173 G 5
Nueva Gerona 102 J 4
Nueva Rosita 96 C 4
Nueva San Salvador 102 GH 6
Nuevitas 102 K 4
Nuevo Casas Grandes 96 B 3
Nuevo Laredo 96 CD 4
Nuevo León 96 CD 4
Nuguria Islands 156 PQ 8
Nuhūd, An- 176 N 6
Nui 166 Q 2
Nukhayb, An- 152 D 2
Nuku'alofa 166 R 5
Nukufetau 166 Q 2
Nukulaelae 166 Q 2
Nukumanu Islands 156 QR 8
Nukunonu 166 S 2
Nukuoro 156 PQ 7
Nukus 148 MN 10
Nullarbor Plain 166 FG 7
Nu'mānīyah, An- 152 E 2
Numedalslågen 126 CD 2
Nunatsiavut → Labrador 76 ac 7/8
Nunavik 88 BC 1
Nunavut 78 Ub 5
Nunivak Island 76 G 7
Nuoro 132 B 3
Nupe 173 D 5
Núpsstaður 125 CD 2
Nura 148 OP 8
Nūrābād 152 F 3
Nuremberg (Nürnberg) 128 D 3
Nuristanis [= N.] 145 L 6
Nurlat 136 JK 2
Nurmes 126 K 1
Nurmijärvi 126 HJ 2
Nürnberg → Nuremberg 128 D 3
Nusaybin *[Syria]* 152 D 1
Nusaybin *[Turkey]* 134 F 4
Nuugssuaq 76 ef 4
Nuuk/Godthåb 78 de 6
Nu'uuli 101 VII
Nuwayṣīb, An- 152 F 3
Nyagan' 148 NO 6
Nyainqêntanglha Shan 154 GJ 5/6
Nyaksimvol' 138 P 4
Nyala → Niyālā
Nyamwezi 173 G 6
Nyandoma 138 H 4
Nyanya 173 G 7
Nyasa, Lake 178 L 5
Nyasvizh 128 J 2
Nyazepetrovsk 136 M 2
Nyborg 126 D 4
Nybro 126 F 4
Nyda 148 PQ 5
Nyeri 178 M 3
Nyingchi 154 H 6
Nyiragongo 15 E 15/16
Nyírbátor 128 H 4
Nyíregyháza 128 GH 4
Nykarleby 126 H 1
Nykøbing 126 E 4
Nyköping 126 F 3
Nylstroom → Polokwane
Nymburk 128 F 3
Nynäshamn 126 G 3
Nyngan 166 K 7
Nyrob 138 NO 4
Nysa 128 F 3
Nyssa 90 C 3
Nytva 138 N 5
Nyuk Lake 138 E 3
Nyuksenitsa 138 JK 4
Nyurba 148 YZ 6
Nyuvchim 138 LM 4
Nyzhn'ohirs'kyy 134 D 1
Nzérékoré 176 EF 7
N'Zeto 178 G 4
Nzwani 178 NO 5

O

Oahe, Lake 94 C 1
Oahu 92 I C 2
Oakdale *[U.S., California]* 92 B 2
Oakdale *[U.S., Louisiana]* 96 E 3
Oak Harbor 90 B 1
Oak Hill 98 D 3
Oakland 92 B 2
Oak Lawn 94 FG 2
Oakley *[U.S., Idaho]* 90 D 3
Oakley *[U.S., Kansas]* 94 C 3
Oakridge *[U.S., Oregon]* 90 B 3
Oak Ridge *[U.S., Tennessee]* 100 B 1
Oamaru 166 P 10/9
Oaxaca 102 F 5
Ob' 148 R 8
Ob', Gulf of 148 P 5/4
Oba 86 FG 3
Obal' 128 K 1
Oban 124 C 3
O Barco 130 B 1
Obedjiwan Indian Reserve 88 B 2
Oberá 114 HJ 3
Oberlin 94 C 3
Oberstdorf 128 D 4
Obi 156 K 8
Óbidos 112 H 4
Obihiro 154 S 3
Oblivskaya 136 FG 4
Obninsk 136 DE 2
Obo 176 N 7
Obock 176 Q 6
Oboyan' 136 DE 3
Obozerskiy 138 H 3
Obrenovac 133 B 2
Obuasi 176 G 7
Obukhiv 136 C 4
Ob'yachevo 138 L 4
Ocala 100 C 3
Ocampo 96 C 4
Ocaña *[Colombia]* 112 E 2
Ocaña *[Spain]* 130 C 2
Occidental, Cordillera *[Colombia]* 112 D 3/2
Occidental, Cordillera *[Peru]* 112 DE 6/7
Ocean City *[U.S., Maryland]* 98 F 3
Ocean City *[U.S., New Jersey]* 98 F 3
Ocean Falls 84 AB 2
Oceania 26 R-C 5-6
Oceanside 92 C 3
Ocean Springs 96 F 3
Ochakiv 134 C 1
Ochamchire 134 F 2
Ochenyrd 148 OP 5
Ochër 138 N 5
O'Chiese Indian Reserve 84 E 2
Ocmulgee 100 C 2/3
Ocniţa 128 K 3
Oconee 100 C 2
Oconto 94 FG 1
October Revolution Island 148 VX 2/3
Oda → Ūda, Jabal
Odda 126 C 2/3
Odei 86 C 1
Odemira 130 AB 3
Ödemiş 134 B 4

River, canal
Waterfall
Lake, lakes, reservoir
Swamp
Salt flat
Sea
Strait
Bay, gulf
Cape
Island, islands
Ocean current
Ocean floor landforms
Tectonic feature
Atmospheric phenomena
Time zone
Geographical grid

Odense	**126**	D 4
Oder	**128**	FG 3
Odesa	**134**	C 1
Ödeshög	**126**	EF 3
Odessa *[U.S., Texas]*	**96**	C 3
Odessa *[U.S., Washington]*	**90**	C 2
Odienné	**176**	F 7
Odin, Mount ▲	**84**	D 3
Odivelas	**130**	AB 3
Odorheiu Secuiesc	**128**	J 4
Odoyev	**136**	E 3
Oelwein	**94**	F 2
Oeno Island	**160**	QR 6
Of	**134**	F 3
Ofanto	**132**	D 3
Offenbach	**128**	CD 3
Offenburg	**128**	C 3
Ofotfjorden	**125**	C 3
Ofu	**101**	VII
Ogallala	**94**	C 2
Ogbomosho	**176**	H 7
Ogden	**92**	D 1
Ogdensburg	**98**	F 1
Ogeechee	**100**	C 2
Oglio	**132**	B 1
Ogoki	**86**	F 3
Ogoki Lake	**86**	F 3
Ogoki Reservoir	**86**	E 3
Ogooué	**178**	G 3
Ogre	**126**	J 4
Ogulin	**132**	D 1
Ohio	**98**	D 2
Ohio	**98**	D 3
Ohře	**128**	E 3
Ohrid	**133**	BC 3
Ohrid, Lake	**133**	B 3
Oiapoque	**112**	J 3
Oil City	**98**	E 2
Oise	**131**	D 2
Ōita	**154**	Q 5
Ojibwa (Chippewa)	**73**	HK 4/5
Ojos del Salado ▲	**114**	F 3
Ojos de San Antonio	**96**	B 3
Oka	**136**	DE 3
Okahandja	**178**	H 7
Okanagan Indian Reserve	**84**	D 3
Okanagan Lake	**84**	D 3
Okanogan	**90**	C 1
Okanogan Range	**90**	BC 1
Okara	**150**	LM 4
Okavango	**178**	HJ 6
Okavango Swamp	**178**	J 6
Okayama	**154**	Q 4/5
Okeechobee	**100**	C 4
Okeechobee, Lake	**100**	C 4
Okefenokee Swamp	**100**	C 3
Okene	**176**	J 7
Okha	**148**	d 8
Okhansk	**136**	L 1
Okhotsk	**148**	d 7
Okhotsk, Sea of	**148**	ef 7/9
Okhtyrka	**136**	D 4
Okiep	**171**	E 8/9
Oki Islands	**154**	Q 4
Okinawa	**154**	P 6
Okinawa	**154**	P 6
Okino Tori	**154**	R 7
Oklahoma	**96**	DE 2
Oklahoma City	**96**	D 2
Okmulgee	**96**	E 2
Okotoks	**84**	E 3
Oksibil	**156**	N 8/9
Oksino	**138**	M 2
Oksovskiy	**138**	H 4
Oksskolten ▲	**125**	B 4
Oktyabr'sk	**136**	J 3
Oktyabr'skiy *[Russia, Arkhangel'sk]*	**138**	J 4
Oktyabr'skiy *[Russia, Bashkortostan]*	**136**	KL 2
Oktyabr'skiy *[Russia, Kamchatka]*	**148**	fg 8
Oktyabr'skiy *[Russia, Perm']*	**136**	LM 2
Oktyabr'skiy *[Russia, Volgograd]*	**136**	G 5
Oktyarbr'skoye	**136**	L 3
Okulovka	**138**	EF 5
Okushiri	**154**	R 3
Öland	**126**	F 4
Olathe	**94**	E 3
Olavarría	**114**	G 5
Olbia	**132**	B 3
Old Baldy ▲	**90**	D 2
Old Castile	**130**	C 2/1
Old Crow	**78**	N 5
Oldenburg (Oldenburg)	**128**	C 2
Oldman	**84**	E 3
Olds	**84**	E 3
Old Town	**98**	G 1
Old Wives Lake	**84**	G 3
Olean	**98**	E 2
Olecko	**128**	H 1
Olëkma	**148**	Y 8
Olëkminsk	**148**	YZ 6
Oleksandrivka	**136**	C 4
Oleksandriya	**136**	D 4
Olenegorsk	**138**	F 2
Olenëk	**148**	X 5
Olenëk	**148**	WX 5
Olenino	**136**	D 2
Oléron, Île d'	**131**	B 3
Oleśnica	**128**	F 2
Ölets	**145**	O 5/6
Olevs'k	**128**	K 2
Ölgiy	**154**	H 2
Olhão	**130**	B 3
Olimarao	**156**	NO 6
Olinda	**112**	MN 5
Olivenza	**130**	B 3
Oliver	**84**	D 3
Olivia	**94**	E 1
Ol'khovka	**136**	G 4
Olkusz	**128**	G 3
Olmaliq	**148**	OP 10
Olney	**94**	F 3
Olomane	**88**	E 2
Olomouc	**128**	F 3
Olonets	**138**	EF 4
Olongapo	**156**	HJ 5/4
Oloron-Sainte-Marie	**131**	B 4
Olosega	**101**	VII
Olot	**130**	E 1
Olovyannaya	**148**	Y 8
Olsztyn	**128**	GH 2
Olsztynek	**128**	G 2
Olt	**133**	D 1
Olten	**128**	C 4
Olteniţa	**133**	D 2
Oltu	**134**	F 3
Olympia	**90**	B 2
Olympia ∴	**133**	C 4
Olympic Dam	**165**	G 10
Olympic National Park	**90**	B 2
Ólympos ▲ *[Cyprus]*	**152**	B 2
Ólympos ▲ *[Greece]*	**133**	C 3
Olympus, Mount ▲	**90**	AB 2
Ólynthos ∴	**133**	C 3
Olyutorskiy, Cape	**148**	jk 7
Olyutorskiy Bay	**148**	jk 6/7
Oma	**138**	K 2
Oma	**138**	K 2
Omagh	**124**	B 3
Omaha	**94**	D 2
Omaha Indian Reservation	**94**	D 2
Omak	**90**	C 1
Oman	**150**	GH 7/6
Oman, Gulf of	**150**	H 6
Omdurman (Umm Durmān)	**176**	NO 5
Omer, Saint-	**131**	C 2
Omineca	**84**	B 2
Omineca Mountains	**84**	B 1/2
Omo	**176**	P 7
Omolon	**148**	gh 6
Omsk	**148**	PQ 7
Omutninsk	**138**	M 5
Oña	**130**	C 1
Onaman Lake	**86**	F 3
Onancock	**98**	F 3
Onaping Lake	**86**	G 4
Onawa	**94**	DE 2
Onda	**130**	D 2
Ondangwa	**178**	H 6
Öndörhaan	**154**	LM 2
Öndverðarnes	**125**	A 2
Onega	**138**	G 3
Onega	**138**	H 4
Onega, Gulf of	**138**	FG 3
Onega, Lake	**138**	FG 4
One Hundred Mile House	**84**	C 3
Oneida	**98**	F 2
Oneida Indian Reservation	**94**	F 1
O'Neill	**94**	D 2
Onekotan Island	**148**	f 8/9
Oneonta *[U.S., Alabama]*	**100**	B 2
Oneonta *[U.S., New York]*	**98**	F 2
Oneşti	**128**	J 4
Oni	**134**	G 2
Onitsha	**176**	J 7
Ono	**166**	Q 4
Ono-i-Lau	**166**	R 5
Onon	**148**	X 8
Onslow	**166**	CD 5
Onslow Bay	**100**	D 2
Ontario *[U.S., California]*	**92**	C 3
Ontario *[U.S., Oregon]*	**90**	C 2/3
Ontario	**78**	WY 8
Ontario, Lake	**98**	E 2
Ontojärvi	**125**	G 4
Ontonagon	**98**	B 1
Ontong Java Atoll	**156**	QR 9
Onverwacht	**112**	H 2
Oodnadatta	**166**	GH 6
Oologah Lake	**96**	E 1
Oostende → Ostend	**131**	C 1
Ootsa Lake	**84**	B 2
Oparino	**138**	KL 5
Opasatika	**86**	G 3
Opaskwayak Cree Nation	**86**	B 2
Opatija	**132**	C 1
Opatów	**128**	H 3
Opava	**128**	F 3
Opelika	**100**	B 2
Opelousas	**96**	EF 3
Opheim	**90**	F 1
Opinaca, Réservoir	**88**	A 1
Opiscotéo, Lac	**88**	D 1
Opochka	**136**	B 2
Opoczno	**128**	G 2
Opole	**128**	FG 3
Opp	**100**	B 3
Oppdal	**126**	D 2
Oppinagau	**86**	G 2
Oppurtunity	**90**	C 2
Opuwo	**178**	G 6
Oqsuqtooq	**78**	VW 5
Oradea	**128**	H 4
Öræfajökull *	**125**	D 2
Oral	**136**	K 3
Oran (Wahrān)	**176**	G 1
Orange *[Australia]*	**166**	K 7
Orange *[France]*	**131**	D 4
Orange *[U.S., Texas]*	**96**	E 3
Orange *[U.S., Virginia]*	**98**	E 3
Orange	**178**	H 8
Orangeburg	**100**	C 2
Orangeville	**98**	D 1
Orange Walk	**102**	H 5
Oranienburg	**128**	E 2
Oranjestad *[Aruba]*	**115**	I A 1
Oranjestad *[Netherlands Antilles]*	**115**	II B 1
Orantes	**152**	C 2/1
Oraon	**145**	M 7
Orapa	**178**	K 7
Orăştie	**128**	H 4
Orbetello	**132**	B 2
Orbost	**166**	K 8
Orcadas	**181**	I DC 34
Orda *[Kazakhstan]*	**136**	H 4
Orda *[Russia]*	**136**	LM 1
Ordes	**130**	B 1
Ordos	**145**	OP 6
Ordu	**134**	E 3
Ordubad	**134**	H 4
Ordway	**94**	BC 3
Örebro	**126**	EF 3
Oregon	**90**	BC 3
Orekhovo-Zuyevo	**136**	F 2
Orël	**136**	E 3
Orellana	**112**	DE 5
Orem	**92**	E 1
Ore Mountains	**128**	E 3
Orenburg	**136**	L 3
Orestes Pereyra	**96**	B 4

Independent country
Dependent territory
Federal state, province, territory
People, ethnic group, tribe
Indian reservation/reserve
National Park
Industrial region
∴ Historical site
Research station
Continent, realm
Region, peninsula
Mountain range, mountains
▲ Peak
)(Pass
* Ice shelf, glacier

P

River, canal
Waterfall
Lake, lakes, reservoir
Swamp
Salt flat
Sea
Strait
Bay, gulf
Cape
Island, islands
Ocean current
Ocean floor landforms
Tectonic feature
Atmospheric phenomena
Time zone
Geographical grid

Independent country
Dependent territory
Federal state, province, territory
People, ethnic group, tribe
Indian reservation/reserve
National Park
Industrial region
Historical site
Research station
Continent, realm
Region, peninsula
Mountain range, mountains
Peak
Pass
Ice shelf, glacier

Patos, Lagoa dos **114** JK 4
Patos de Minas **112** K 7
Patras (Pátra) **133** C 4
Patreksfjörður **125** A 2
Pattani **156** E 6
Patti **132** C 4
Pau **131** B 4
Pauillac **131** B 3
Paul, Saint *[Canada]* **84** F 2
Paul, Saint *[U.S., Minnesota]* **94** E 1
Paul, Saint *[U.S., Nebraska]* **94** D 2
Paul, Saint *[Canada]* **88** E 3
Paul, Saint- *[French Southern Territories]* **4** NO 7/8
Paulo, São **114** K 2
Paulo, São **114** JK 2
Paulo Afonso **112** M 5
Paulo de Olivença, São **112** F 4
Pauls Valley **96** D 2
Pavda **138** OP 5
Paveh **152** E 2
Pavia **132** B 1
Pavino **138** K 5
Pavlikeni **133** D 2
Pavlodar **148** Q 8
Pavlohrad **136** DE 4
Pavlovka *[Russia, Bashkortostan]* **136** L 2
Pavlovka *[Russia, Ul'yanovsk]* **136** H 3
Pavlovo **136** G 2
Pavlovsk **136** F 4
Pavlovskaya **134** F 1
Pawhuska **96** D 1
Pawnee **96** D 1
Pawnee **73** HJ 6
Paxoí **133** B 3
Payette **90** C 2
Payette **90** D 2
Payne/Kangirsuk **78** a 6
Paysandú **114** H 4
Payson **92** E 3
Payyer **138** Q 2
Paz, La *[Argentina]* **114** H 4
Paz, La *[Bolivia]* **112** F 7
Paz, La *[Mexico]* **102** CD 4
Pazar **134** F 3
Pazarcık **134** E 4
Pazardzhik **133** D 2
Paz del Río **107** FG 4
Pazin **132** C 1
Pea **100** B 3
Peace **76** R 7
Peace River **84** D 1
Peachtree **100** B 2
Peacock Point **101** IV
Peak Samani → Peak Somoni
Peak Somoni **150** L 3
Peale, Mount **92** E 2
Peale Island **101** IV
Pearl **96** F 3
Pearl City **92** I B 2
Pearl Harbor **92** I BC 2
Pearsall **96** D 3
Peary Land **76** hk 2
Peawanuck Indian Reserve **86** F 2
Peć **133** B 2
Pechenga **125** H 2
Pechora **138** O 3
Pechora **138** O 4
Pechora, Gulf of **138** N 2
Pechory **138** D 5
Pecos **96** C 3
Pecos **96** B 2
Pécs **128** FG 4
Pedernales **115** II B 3
Pedi **173** FG 8
Pedreiras **112** KL 4
Pedro, San *[Argentina]* **114** G 2
Pedro, San *[Côte d'Ivoire]* **176** FG 8
Pedro, San *[Paraguay]* **114** H 2
Pedro, San **92** E 3
Pedro Juan Caballero **114** H 2
Pedro Sula, San **102** H 5
Peebles **124** C 3
Pee Dee **100** D 2
Pegu (Bago) **150** Q 7
Peguis Indian Reserve **86** C 3
Pehuajó **114** G 5
Peigan Indian Reserve **84** E 3
Peipus, Lake **126** K 3
Peiraiás → Piraeus **133** C 4
Pekalongan **156** FG 9
Pekanbaru **156** E 7/8
Pekin **94** F 2
Peking → Beijing
Pelée, Mount **115** II B 2
Peleng **156** J 8
Peles **138** M 4
Pelhřimov **128** EF 3
Pelican Lake **86** B 2
Pelican Narrows **86** B 2
Pelješac **132** D 2
Pella **94** E 2
Peloponnese **133** C 4
Pelotas **114** J 4
Pelym **138** P 4
Pematangsiantar **156** D 7
Pemba **178** N 5
Pemba **178** MN 4/3
Pembina *[Canada]* **71** G 4
Pembina *[U.S.]* **86** C 3
Pembina *[Canada]* **84** D 2
Pembina *[Canada/U.S.]* **86** C 3
Pembroke *[Canada]* **88** A 3
Pembroke *[U.K.]* **124** C 4
Pembroke Pines **100** CD 4
Pembrook [= P.] **71** H 6
Pemex **71** J 8
Pemón **109** G 4
Peñafiel **130** C 2
Peña Nevada, Cerro **102** EF 4
Peñaranda de Bracamonte **130** C 2
Peñarroya **130** D 2
Peñarroya-Pueblonuevo **130** C 3
Peñas, Cabo de **130** C 1
Peñas, Gulf of **114** DE 7
Pendleton **90** C 2
Pend Oreille, Lake **90** C 1/2
Peniche **130** A 2
Península ... → ..., Península ...
Pennant **84** F 3
Penne **132** C 2
Penn Hills **98** E 2
Pennines **124** D 3/4
Pennsylvania **98** E 2
Penn Yan **98** E 2
Penny Highland **76** bc 5
Peno **136** C 2
Penobscot Bay **98** G 1/2
Penrhyn **160** O 4
Penrith **124** CD 3
Pensacola **100** B 3
Pensacola Mountains **13** A 36/4
Pentecost **166** O 4
Penticton **84** D 3
Penticton Indian Reserve **84** CD 3
Pentland Firth **124** CD 2
Penza **136** GH 3
Penzance **124** BC 5
Penzhina **148** hj 6
Penzhina Gulf **148** h 6
Peoria *[U.S., Arizona]* **92** D 3
Peoria *[U.S., Illinois]* **94** F 2
Perak **156** DE 7
Perdido, Monte **130** D 1
Perehins'ke **128** HJ 3
Pereira **112** D 2/3
Perelyub **136** J 3
Peremyotnoe **136** JK 3
Pereslavl'-Zalesskiy **136** EF 2
Perevolotskiy **136** KL 3
Perevoz *[Russia, Irkutsk]* **148** XY 7
Perevoz *[Russia, Nizhegorod]* **136** GH 2
Pereyaslav-Khmel'nyts'kyy **136** C 4
Pergamon **134** B 4/3
Perge **134** C 4
Péribonca **88** C 2
Péribonca, Lac **88** C 2
Périgueux **131** C 3
Peristério **133** C 4
Perito Moreno Glacier **104** ⑤
Perla, La **96** B 3
Perlak **143** N 9
Perlis **156** DE 6
Perm' **138** NO 5
Përmet **133** B 3
Permyaks, Komi- **121** M 3/4
Pernambuco **112** LM 5
Pernik **133** C 2
Péronne **131** CD 2
Pérouse Strait, La **148** d 9
Perpignan **131** CD 4
Perros-Guirec **131** A 2
Perry *[U.S., Florida]* **100** C 3
Perry *[U.S., Georgia]* **100** C 2
Perry *[U.S., Iowa]* **94** E 2
Perry *[U.S., Oklahoma]* **96** D 1
Perryton **96** C 1
Perryville **94** F 3
Persepolis **152** G 3
Persian Gulf **150** FG 5
Persians **145** H-J 6-7
Pertek **134** F 4
Perth *[Australia]* **166** CD 7
Perth *[Canada]* **88** A 3
Perth *[U.K.]* **124** C 3
Pertominsk **138** GH 3
Peru **98** C 2
Peru **112** DE 5/6
Peru Basin **10** VW 6
Peru-Chile Trench **10** W-X 6-8
Peru Current → Humboldt Current
Perugia **132** C 2
Peruvians **109** F 5/6
Pervomaysk *[Russia]* **136** G 2
Pervomays'k *[Ukraine]* **136** C 5/4
Pervomays'ke **134** D 1
Pervomayskiy *[Russia, Orenburg]* **136** L 3
Pervomayskiy *[Russia, Tambov]* **136** F 3
Pervomays'kyy **136** E 4
Pervoural'sk **136** M 1/2
Pesaro **132** C 2
Pescara **132** C 2
Pescara **132** C 2
Peschanokopskoye **134** F 1
Peshawar **150** KL 4
Peshkopi **133** B 3
Peski **136** G 3
Peskovka **138** M 5
Pêso da Régua **130** B 2
Pestovo **138** F 5
Pestravka **136** J 3
Pestyaki **136** G 2
Petah Tiqwa **152** B 2
Petaling Jaya **156** E 7
Petaluma **92** B 2
Petare **112** F 1
Petatlan **96** B 4
Petawawa **88** A 3
Petenwell Lake **94** F 1/2
Peter, Saint **94** E 1
Peter and Paul Rocks, Saint **105** L 4
Peterborough *[Australia]* **166** HJ 7
Peterborough *[Canada]* **88** A 3
Peterborough *[U.K.]* **124** DE 4
Peterburg, Sankt → Saint Petersburg **138** E 4/5
Peterhead **124** D 2
Peter I Island **181** I C 30
Peter Island **101** IX
Peter Pond Lake **84** F 1
Peter Pond Lake Indian Reserve **84** F 1/2
Peter Port, Saint **131** B 2
Petersburg *[U.S., Virginia]* **98** E 3
Petersburg *[U.S., West Virginia]* **98** E 3
Petersburg, Saint *[U.S.]* **100** C 4
Petersburg, Saint (Sankt Peterburg) *[Russia]* **138** E 4/5

River, canal
Waterfall
Lake, lakes, reservoir
Swamp
Salt flat
Sea
Strait
Bay, gulf
Cape
Island, islands
Ocean current
Ocean floor landforms
Tectonic feature
Atmospheric phenomena
Time zone
Geographical grid

⛊ Independent country
⛉ Dependent territory
▿ Federal state, province, territory
👥 People, ethnic group, tribe
⧖ Indian reservation/reserve
⌂ National Park
⌶ Industrial region
∴ Historical site
⛫ Research station
◍ Continent, realm
⌳ Region, peninsula
▲▲ Mountain range, mountains
▲ Peak
)(Pass
✱ Ice shelf, glacier

Plön **128** D 1
Plonge, Lac La **84** G 2
Płońsk **128** G 2
Płoty **128** F 2
Plovdiv **133** D 2
Plumas, Las **114** F 6
Plungė **126** H 4
Plyeshchanitsy **128** K 1
Plymouth *[Montserrat]* **115** II B 1
Plymouth *[U.K.]* **124** C 5
Plymouth *[U.S., Indiana]* **98** C 2
Plymouth *[U.S., Massachusetts]* **98** G 2
Plymouth *[U.S., New Hampshire]* **98** G 2
Plyussa **138** D 5
Plzeň **128** E 3
Pniewy **128** F 2
Po **132** A 2
Pobeda ▲ **148** e 5
Pobla de Segur **130** E 1
Pocatello **90** DE 3
Pocatière, La **88** C 3
Pochayiv **128** J 3
Pochep **136** D 3
Pochinki **136** G 2
Pochinok **136** CD 2
Pocohontas **96** F 1
Poconé **112** H 7
Poços de Caldas **107** HJ 7
Poddor'ye **136** C 1
Podgorenskiy **136** F 4
Podgorica **133** B 2
Podilia **117** JK 5
Podkova **133** D 3
Podol'sk **136** E 2
Podporozh'ye **138** F 4
Pogibi **148** d 8
Pogradec **133** B 3
Pogruznaya **136** JK 2
Pohjanmaa **126** HJ 1
Pohnpei **156** Q 6
Pohrebyshche **128** KL 3
Poinsett, Cape **181** I C 14
Point, Cap **115** II B 2
Point(e) ... → ..., Point(e) ...
Pointe-à-Pitre **115** II B 1
Pointe-Noire **178** FG 3
Point Fortin **115** II B 3
Point Hope **78** G 5
Point Imperial ▲ **92** DE 2
Point Pelee National Park **98** D 2
Point Pleasant *[U.S., New Jersey]* **98** F 2/3
Point Pleasant *[U.S., West Virginia]* **98** D 3
Poitiers **131** C 3
Poix **131** C 2
Pokhara **150** NO 5
Pokhvistnevo **136** K 3
Pokrovsk **148** a 6
Pokrovskoye *[Russia, Orël]* **136** E 3
Pokrovskoye *[Russia, Rostov]* **136** E 5
Polacca **92** E 3
Pola de Gordón, La **130** C 1
Poland **128** FH 2
Polaris Mine **71** JL 2
Polar Subglacial Basin **13** A 34/11
Polatlı **134** C 3
Polatsk **128** K 1
Poldarsa **138** K 4
Pol-de-Léon, Saint- **131** A 2
Poldnevitsa **138** K 5
Poles **121** H-J 4-5
Polessk **128** GH 1
Polevskoy **136** N 2
Polichnítos **133** D 3
Poligny **131** D 3
Polillo Islands **156** J 5
Pólis **152** B 2
Polis'ke **128** K 2
Polohy **136** E 5
Polokwane **178** K 7
Polonne **128** K 3
Polson **90** D 2
Poltava **136** D 4
Poltavskaya **134** E 1
Pölten, Sankt **128** F 3
Põltsamaa **126** J 3
Polunochnoye **138** P 4
Põlva **126** JK 3
Polyarnyy **138** EF 1
Polyarnyye Zori **138** E 2
Polýgyros **133** C 3
Polynesia **160** NP 2/6
Polynesians **164** H-K 8-9
Pombal **130** B 2
Pomerania **128** EG 2
Pomeranian Bay **128** E 1
Pomeroy **90** C 2
Pomichna **136** C 4
Pomo **73** F 6
Pomorskiy Proliv **138** LM 2
Pomozdino **138** N 4
Pompano Beach **100** CD 4
Pompei ∴ **132** C 3
Ponazyrevo **138** K 5
Ponca City **96** D 1
Ponce **101** VIII
Pondicherry **150** MN 8
Pondicherry **150** L-N 7-8
Pond Inlet **78** Za 4
Ponferrada **130** BC 1
Poniente, Playa de **123** B 5
Ponoka **84** E 2
Ponomarëvka **136** KL 3
Ponoy **138** H 2
Ponoy **138** H 2
Pons **131** B 3
Ponta ... → ..., Ponta ...
Ponta Delgada **130** CD 6
Ponta Grossa **114** JK 2/3
Pont-à-Mousson **131** E 2
Ponta Porã **114** HJ 2
Pontarlier **131** DE 3
Pontchartrain, Lake **96** F 3
Pontchâteau **131** B 3
Ponte de Sôr **130** B 2
Ponteix **84** G 3
Pontevedra **130** AB 1
Pontiac **94** F 2
Pontianak **156** F 8/7
Pontine Islands **132** C 3
Pontine Mountains **134** CF 3
Pontivy **131** B 2/3
Ponto do Sol **130** A 6
Pontoise **131** C 2
Ponts-de-Cé, Les **131** BC 3
Poole **124** D 5
Poopó, Lake **112** F 7
Poor Man Indian Reserve **84** G 3
Popayán **112** D 3
Popil'nya **128** K 3
Poplar **90** F 1
Poplar **86** C 2
Poplar Bluff **94** F 3
Poplar River Indian Reserve **86** C 2
Poplarville **96** F 3
Popocatépetl ▲ **102** EF 5
Popondetta **156** O 9
Popovo **133** D 2
Poprad **128** G 3
Porangatu **112** JK 6
Porazava **128** J 2
Porbandar **150** K 6
Porcher Island **84** A 2
Porcuna **130** C 3
Porcupine **76** MN 5
Porcupine Hills **86** B 2
Pordenone **132** C 1
Poreč **132** C 1
Pori **126** H 2
Porirua **166** P 9
Porkhov **136** B 1
Porlamar **115** II B 3
Pornic **131** B 3
Porog **138** N 4
Poronaysk **148** d 9
Porosozero **138** EF 4
Porpoise Bay **181** I C 15/16
Porsangen **125** F 2
Porsanger Peninsula **125** F 2
Porsgrunn **126** D 3
Porsuk **134** C 3
Portage *[U.S., Michigan]* **98** C 2
Portage *[U.S., Wisconsin]* **94** F 2
Portage-la-Prairie **86** C 3
Port Alberni **84** B 3
Portalegre **130** B 2
Portales **92** G 3
Port Alfred **178** K 9
Port Alice **84** B 3
Port Angeles **90** AB 1/2
Port Aransas **96** D 4
Port Arthur **96** E 3
Port Augusta **166** H 7
Port-au-Prince **102** L 5
Port Blair **150** P 8
Portbou **130** EF 1
Port-Cartier **88** D 2
Port Charlotte **100** C 4
Port Colborne **98** E 2
Porte, La **98** C 2
Port Elgin *[Canada, New Brunswick]* **88** DE 3
Port Elgin *[Canada, Ontario]* **98** D 1
Port Elizabeth *[South Africa]* **178** K 9
Port Elizabeth *[St. Vincent and the Grenadines]* **115** II B 2
Port Ellen **124** B 3
Porterville **92** C 3
Port Gamble Indian Reservation **90** B 2
Port Gentil **178** F 3
Port Harcourt **176** HJ 7/8
Port Hardy **84** AB 3
Port Harrison/Inukjuak **78** YZ 7
Port Hawkesbury **88** E 3
Port Hedland **166** D 4/5
Port Hope **88** A 3/4
Port Hope Simpson **88** F 1
Port Huron **98** D 2
Portimão **130** B 3
Port Jervis **98** F 2
Port Kembla **165** J 10
Portland *[Australia]* **166** HJ 8
Portland *[U.S., Indiana]* **98** C 2
Portland *[U.S., Maine]* **98** G 2
Portland *[U.S., Oregon]* **90** B 2
Portland *[U.S., Texas]* **96** D 4
Portland Canal **84** A 2
Portlaoise **124** B 4
Port Lavaca **96** D 3
Port Lincoln **166** GH 7
Port Louis **178** Q 6/7
Port Madison Indian Reservation **90** B 2
Port McNeill **84** B 3
Port-Menier **88** D 2
Portmore **102** K 5
Port Moresby **156** NO 9
Portneuf **88** C 2
Port Nolloth **178** H 8
Porto **130** B 2
Porto Alegre **114** JK 4
Porto Amboim **178** G 5
Porto Empedocle **132** C 4
Portoferraio **132** B 2
Port of Spain **115** II B 3
Porto Grande **112** J 3
Portogruaro **132** C 1
Portola **92** B 2
Porto Moniz **130** AB 6
Porto Murtinho **114** H 2
Porto Nacional **112** K 6
Porto-Novo *[Benin]* **176** H 7
Porto Novo *[Cape Verde]* **176** BC 5
Port Orange **100** C 3
Port Orford **90** A 3
Porto Santana **112** J 4
Porto Santo **130** B 5/6
Porto Santo **130** B 5
Porto Seguro **112** M 7
Porto Torres **132** A 3
Pôrto Trombetas **107** H 5
Porto-Vecchio **132** B 3
Porto Velho **112** FG 5
Portoviejo **112** C 4
Port Pirie **166** H 7
Port Radium **78** RS 5
Portree **124** BC 2
Port Renfrew **84** BC 3
Port Royal Sound **100** CD 2

River, canal
Waterfall
Lake, lakes, reservoir
Swamp
Salt flat
Sea
Strait
Bay, gulf
Cape
Island, islands
Ocean current
Ocean floor landforms
Tectonic feature
Atmospheric phenomena
Time zone
Geographical grid

Port Said (Būr Sa'īd) **152** B 3
Port Saint Joe **100** B 3
Port Saint Lucie **100** CD 4
Portsmouth *[Dominica]* **115** II B 2
Portsmouth *[U.K.]* **124** D 5
Portsmouth *[U.S., New Hampshire]* **98** G 2
Portsmouth *[U.S., Ohio]* **98** D 3
Portsmouth *[U.S., Virginia]* **98** E 3
Port Stanley **98** D 2
Port Sudan (Būr Sūdān) **176** P 4/5
Port Talbot **124** C 4
Port Townsend **90** B 1
Portugal **130** B 3/2
Portugalete **130** C 1
Portuguese *[Africa]* **173** B 2
Portuguese *[Europe]* **121** F 6/5
Port Vila **166** O 4
Port Washington **94** G 2
Porvenir *[Chile]* **114** EF 8
Porvenir *[Mexico]* **96** B 3
Porvenír, El **102** K 7
Porvoo **126** J 2
Posadas **114** H 3
Poshekhon'ye **138** H 5
Poso **156** J 8
Posof **134** G 3
Posse **112** K 6
Post **96** C 2
Post Falls **90** C 2
Postmasburg **171** EF 8
Postojna **132** C 1
Poteau **96** E 2
Potenza **132** D 3
Potholes Reservoir **90** C 2
Poti **134** F 2
Potiguara **109** K 5
Potomac **98** E 3
Potosí **112** FG 7
Potsdam *[Germany]* **128** E 2
Potsdam *[U.S.]* **98** F 1
Pottstown **98** EF 2
Pottsville **98** EF 2
Pötürge **134** EF 4
Poughkeepsie **98** F 2
Poum **166** N 5
Poŭthĭsăt **156** E 5
Považská Bystrica **128** G 3
Povenets **138** F 4
Póvoa de Varzim **130** AB 2
Povorino **136** G 3
Povorotnyy, Cape **148** bc 10
Powder *[U.S., Oregon]* **90** C 2
Powder *[U.S., Wyoming/Montana]* **90** F 2
Powder, Little **90** F 2
Powell **90** E 2
Powell, Lake **92** E 2
Powell River **84** BC 3
Poyang Hu **154** N 6
Pozantı **134** D 4
Požarevac **133** C 2
Poza Rica **71** J 7
Požega **132** D 1
Poznań **128** F 2
Pozoblanco **130** C 3
Pozo Colorado **114** H 2
Pozzallo **132** C 4
Pozzuoli **132** C 3
Prachuap Khiri Khan **156** DE 5
Prague (Praha) **128** E 3
Praha → Prague **128** E 3
Praia **176** C 5/6
Prairie Band Potawatomi Indian Reservation **94** DE 3
Prairie du Chien **94** F 2
Prasonísi, Cape **133** E 5
Prata, Costa de **123** BC 4/3
Prato **132** B 2
Pratt **94** D 3
Prattville **100** B 2
Preah Seihânŭ **156** E 6/5
Preeceville **86** B 2/3
Preiļi **126** J 4
Prentice **94** F 1
Prenzlau **128** E 2
Přerov **128** F 3
Presa ... → ..., Presa ...
Prescott *[Canada]* **88** B 3
Prescott *[U.S.]* **92** D 3
Prescott Valley **92** D 3
Preševo **133** C 2
Presidencia Roque Sáenz Peña **114** G 3
Presidente Epitácio **114** J 2
Presidente Prudente **114** JK 2
Presidio **96** B 3
Prešov **128** H 3
Prespa, Lake **133** B 3
Presque Isle **98** GH 1
Preston *[U.K.]* **124** CD 4
Preston *[U.S.]* **90** E 3
Prestonsburg **98** D 3
Prestwick **124** C 3
Pretoria **178** KL 8
Préveza **133** B 3/4
Prey Vêng **156** F 5
Pribilof Islands **76** FG 7
Příbram **128** E 3
Price **92** E 2
Priego **130** C 3
Priekule **126** H 4
Prienai **126** HJ 4
Prieska **178** J 8
Priest Lake **90** C 1
Prievidza **128** G 3
Prijedor **132** D 2
Prilep **133** C 3
Primeira Cruz **112** L 4
Primorsk **136** H 4
Primorsko **133** E 2
Primorsko-Akhtarsk **134** E 1
Primošten **132** D 2
Primrose Lake **84** F 2
Prince Albert **84** G 2
Prince Albert National Park **84** G 2
Prince Alfred, Cape **76** OQ 4
Prince Charles Island **76** Z 5
Prince Charles Mountains **13** B 10/11
Prince Edward and Marion Islands **36** L 8
Prince Edward Island **88** E 3
Prince Edward Island **4** LM 8
Prince Edward Island National Park **88** E 3
Prince George **84** C 2
Prince of Wales, Cape **76** FG 6/5
Prince of Wales Island *[Australia]* **166** J 3
Prince of Wales Island *[Canada]* **76** UV 4
Prince of Wales Island *[U.S.]* **76** O 7/8
Prince Patrick Island **76** PQ 3
Prince Rupert **84** A 2
Princess Royal Island **84** A 2
Prince's Town **115** II B 3
Princeton *[Canada]* **84** C 3
Princeton *[U.S., Illinois]* **94** F 2
Princeton *[U.S., Indiana]* **98** C 3
Princeton *[U.S., Kentucky]* **98** C 3
Princeton *[U.S., West Virginia]* **98** D 3
Príncipe **176** J 8
Prineville **90** B 2
Prins Karls Forland **148** C 3
Priob'ye **148** NO 6
Priozërsk **138** E 4
Pripet **128** J 2
Pripyat Marshes **117** J 4
Prirechnyy **138** DE 2
Priština **133** C 2
Pritzwalk **128** DE 2
Privas **131** D 4
Privolzhsk **136** F 1
Privolzhskiy **136** H 3
Privolzh'ye **136** J 3
Priyutnoye **134** G 1
Priyutovo **136** KL 3
Prizren **133** BC 2
Probolinggo **156** GH 9
Proddatur **150** MN 7/8
Progreso *[Mexico, Coahuila]* **96** C 4
Progreso *[Mexico, Yucatán]* **102** GH 4
Progreso, El **102** H 5
Progress **181** II C 10/11
Prokhladnyy **134** G 2
Prokhorovka **136** E 4
Prokop'yevsk **148** RS 8
Prokuplje **133** C 2
Proletarsk **134** FG 1
Prosna **128** FG 2
Prosser **90** BC 2
Prostějov **128** F 3
Provençals **121** G 5
Provence **131** DE 4
Providence **98** G 2
Providencia Island **102** JK 6
Provideniya **148** n 5/6
Provincetown **98** G 2
Provins **131** D 2
Provo **92** E 1
Provost **84** F 2
Prudhoe Bay **78** L 4
Prudnik **128** F 3
Prüm **128** C 3
Pruszków **128** G 2
Prut **128** K 4
Pruzhany **128** HJ 2
Pryazha **138** F 4
Pryazoys'ke **134** DE 1
Pryluky **136** C 4
Prymors'k **134** E 1
Pryor Creek **96** E 1
Przemyśl **128** H 3
Psará **133** D 4
Psebay **134** F 2
Pskov **138** D 5
Pskov, Lake **138** D 5
Ptolemaïda **133** C 3
Ptuj **132** D 1
Pucallpa **112** DE 5
Puchezh **136** G 2
Pudasjärvi **125** F 4
Pudozh **138** G 4
Puebla **102** F 5
Puebla de Sanabria **130** B 1
Pueblo **94** B 3
Pueblo Colorado Wash **92** E 3
Pueblo Indians **73** H 6
Puente Alto **114** EF 4
Puente-Genil **130** C 3
Puerto Acosta **112** F 7
Puerto Aisén **114** E 6/7
Puerto Armuelles **102** J 7
Puerto Asís **112** D 3
Puerto Ayacucho **112** F 2
Puerto Ayora **112** AB 4
Puerto Baquarizo Moreno **112** B 4
Puerto Barrios **102** H 5
Puerto Berrío **112** E 2
Puerto Cabello **112** F 1
Puerto Cabezas **102** J 6
Puerto Carreño **112** F 2
Puerto Cumarebo **115** I A 2
Puerto de la Cruz *[Spain, Canary Is., Fuerteventura]* **130** FG 5/6
Puerto de la Cruz *[Spain, Canary Is., Tenerife]* **130** E 5
Puerto del Rosario **130** G 5
Puerto de Pozo Negro **130** G 5
Puerto de Santa, El **130** BC 3
Puerto Deseado **114** FG 7
Puerto Francisco de Orellana **112** D 3/4
Puerto Iguazú **114** J 3
Puerto Inírida **112** F 3
Puerto la Cruz **112** G 1/2
Puerto Lempira **102** J 5
Puertollano **130** C 3
Puerto Madryn **114** F 6
Puerto Maldonado **112** EF 6
Puerto Montt **114** DE 6
Puerto Nariño **112** F 3
Puerto Natales **114** E 8
Puerto Padre **102** K 4
Puerto Palomas **96** B 3
Puerto Peñasco **92** D 4
Puerto Plata **102** L 4/5

Independent country
Dependent territory
Federal state, province, territory
People, ethnic group, tribe
Indian reservation/reserve
National Park
Industrial region
Historical site
Research station
Continent, realm
Region, peninsula
Mountain range, mountains
Peak
Pass
Ice shelf, glacier

uerto Princesa **156** H 6/5
uerto Ricans **73** M 8
uerto Rico **101** VIII
uerto Rico **80** O 8
uerto Rico Trench **10** EF 4/5
uerto San Julián **114** F 7
uerto Santa Cruz **114** F 8
uerto Suárez **112** H 7
uerto Vallarta **102** D 4
uerto Villamil **112** A 4
ugachëv **136** J 3
uigcerdà **130** E 1
uigmal **131** C 4
ukapuka **160** N 5/4
ukaskwa National Park **86** F 3
ukatawagan Indian Reserve **86** B 2
ukë **133** B 2/3
uksoozero **138** H 4
ula **132** C 2
ulap **156** OP 6
ulaski *[U.S., New York]* **98** E 2
ulaski *[U.S., Tennessee]* **100** B 2
ulaski *[U.S., Virginia]* **98** D 3
uławy **128** H 2
ullman **90** C 2
ulo Anna **156** L 6
ulog, Mount **156** J 4
ülümür **134** F 3
uluwat **156** OP 6
uná Island **112** C 4
unakha **150** P 5
unan **145** P 10/9
uncak Jayakesuma → Carstensz Pyramid **156** LM 8
une **150** LM 7
unjab *[India]* **150** LM 4/5
unjab *[Pakistan]* **150** KL 5
unjabis **145** L 6
uno **112** EF 7
unta ... → ..., Punta ...
unta Alta **114** G 5
unta Arenas **114** EF 8
unta Cana **101** VIII
unta Cardón **115** I A 2
unta Gorda **100** C 4
untan ... → ..., Puntan ...
untarenas **102** HJ 6
unto Fijo **112** E 1
unxsutawney **98** E 2
uquio **112** E 6
ur **148** Q 5
urekkari Neem **126** J 3
urgatoire **94** BC 3
uri **150** O 7
urús **112** F 5
uruvesi **126** K 2
usan **154** PQ 5
ushkin **138** DE 5
ushkino **136** H 3
ustoshka **136** B 2
utao **150** Q 5
utian **154** N 6
utoran Mountains **148** TU 5
utre **112** F 7

Putumayo **112** E 4
Putyvl' **136** D 3
Puulavesi **126** JK 2
Puy, Le **131** D 3/4
Puyallup **90** B 2
Puyang [= Pu.] **154** N 4
Puyo **112** D 4
Pweto **178** K 4
Pwllheli **124** C 4
Pya Lake **138** E 2/3
Pyalitsa **138** H 2
Pyal'ma **138** G 4
Pyasina **148** ST 4
Pyatigorsk **134** G 2
Pyatīmarskoe **136** JK 4
P"yatykhatky **136** D 4
Pyay **150** Q 7
Pyetrykaw **128** K 2
Pyhäjoki **126** J 1
Pyhäselkä **126** KL 2
Pyinmana **150** PQ 7
Pýlos **133** C 4
P'yŏngsong **154** OP 4
P'yŏngyang **154** P 4
Pyramid Lake **92** C 2
Pyramid Lake Indian Reservation **92** C 1
Pyramids **152** A 3
Pyrenees **130** DE 1
Pýrgos *[Greece, Crete]* **133** D 5
Pýrgos *[Greece, Peloponnese]* **133** C 4
Pyryatyn **136** C 4
Pyrzyce **128** E 2
Pyshchug **138** K 5
Pytalovo **136** B 1/2

Q

Qa' al-Jafr **152** C 3
Qaanaaq/Thule **78** bc 3
Qābis → Gabès **176** JK 2
Qaḍārif, Al- **176** OP 6
Qādir Karam **152** E 2
Qa'emshahr **152** G 1
Qafṣah **176** J 2
Qāhirah, Al- → Cairo **152** A 3
Qaidam Pendi **154** HJ 4
Qalā Diza **152** E 1
Qal'ah, Al- **132** A 4
Qalāt **150** K 4
Qal'at Ṣāliḥ **152** E 3
Qal'at Sukkar **152** E 3
Qal'eh-ye Now **150** JK 3/4
Qalībah, Al- **152** C 3
Qālmah **132** A 4
Qamanittuaq/Baker Lake **78** VW 6
Qamdo **154** J 5
Qāmishlī, Al- **152** D 1
Qanā **152** D 4
Qandahar → Kandahar **150** JK 4
Qandarān-Hūrand **134** H 4
Qandyaghash **136** M 4
Qanṭarah, Al- **152** AB 3
Qapshaghay **148** PQ 10
Qaqortoq **78** f 6
Qarabaū **136** K 4
Qaraghandy **148** PQ 9/8
Qaraghayly **148** PQ 9
Qārah **152** D 3
Qaratöbe **136** K 4
Qarazhal **148** P 9
Qardho **176** R 7
Qar'eh Aqāj **134** H 4
Qareh Dāgh **134** H 4
Qareh Sū **134** H 4/3
Qarghaly **136** M 4
Qarkilik/Ruoqiang **154** GH 4
Qarqan **154** G 4
Qarqan/Qiemo **154** FG 4
Qarsaqbay **148** NO 9
Qarshi **148** NO 11
Qārūn, Lake **152** A 3
Qaryat al-'Ulyā **152** E 4
Qasigiannguit **78** ef 5
Qaṣr, Al- *[Egypt]* **176** N 3
Qaṣr, Al- *[Saudi Arabia]* **152** D 4
Qaṣr al-Kabīr, Al- **176** F 2/1
Qaṣrayn, Al- **176** JK 1/2
Qāṣr-e Shīrīn **152** E 2
Qaṭanā **152** C 2
Qatar **150** G 5
Qaṭīf, Al- **152** F 4
Qatrūn, Al- **176** KL 4
Qaṭṭārah Depression **176** N 2/3
Qax **134** H 3
Qayrawān, Al- **176** J 1
Qayṣūmah, Al- **152** E 3
Qayyārah **152** D 2
Qayyngdy **136** L 4
Qazax **134** H 3
Qazıməmməd **134** J 3
Qazvīn **152** F 1
Qəbələ **134** H 3
Qenâ → Qinā
Qeqertarsuaq **78** de 4/5
Qeqertarsuaq **76** ce 4
Qeydār **152** F 1
Qezel Owzan **134** H 4
Qibā' **152** E 4
Qiemo/Qarqan **154** FG 4
Qilian Shan **154** JK 4
Qinā **176** O 3
Qinā, Wādī **152** B 4
Qingdao **154** O 4
Qinghai **154** HK 4/5
Qinhuangdao **154** NO 4
Qiniṭrah, Al- → Kénitra **176** EF 2
Qin Ling **154** L 5
Qinzhou **154** L 7
Qiqihar **154** O 2
Qiṭrānah, Al- **152** BC 3
Qizilqum **148** NO 10
Qobda **136** L 4
Qom **152** F 2
Qomsheh **152** FG 2
Qo'ng'irot **148** M 10
Qo'qon **148** OP 10
Qornet es Saouda → Qurnat as-Sawdā'
Qorveh **152** E 2
Qoryooley **176** Q 8
Qoshqar **136** K 5
Qosshaghyl **136** K 5
Qostanay **148** NO 8
Qoṭūr **134** G 4
Quang Ngai **156** FG 4/5
Quanzhou *[China, A.R. Guangxi]* **154** LM 6
Quanzhou *[China, Fujian]* **154** N 6
Qu'Apelle **84** G 3
Quartu Sant'Elena **132** B 3
Quartzsite **92** D 3
Quatsino Sound **84** A 3
Quba **134** J 3
Quchghar **134** H 4
Quds, Al- → Jerusalem **152** BC 3
Québec **88** C 3
Québec **78** Zb 8
Quechua **109** F-G 5-7
Quedlinburg **128** DE 2
Queen Adelaide Archipelago **114** DE 8
Queen Charlotte Islands **76** O 8
Queen Charlotte Sound **76** OP 8
Queen Charlotte Strait **84** AB 3
Queen Elizabeth Islands **76** QY 3/2
Queen Maud Gulf **76** UV 5
Queen Maud Land **181** II B 2/6
Queen Maud Land **181** I B 2/7
Queensland **166** HK 5
Queenstown *[Australia]* **166** JK 9
Queenstown *[South Africa]* **178** K 9
Quelimane **178** M 6
Quellón **114** E 6
Quentin, Saint *[Canada]* **88** D 3
Quentin, Saint- *[France]* **131** CD 2
Querétaro **102** EF 4
Queshan **154** MN 5
Quesnel **84** C 2
Quesnel **84** C 2
Quesnel Lake **84** C 2
Quetta **150** K 4/5
Quevedo **112** CD 4
Quezaltenango **102** G 6
Quezon City **156** J 5
Quiaca, La **114** FG 2
Quibdó **112** D 2
Quiberon **131** A 3
Quiché **73** JK 8
Quillabamba **112** E 6
Quillacollo **112** F 7
Quillan **131** C 4
Quill Lake, Little **86** B 3
Quilpie **166** JK 6
Quilpué **114** E 4
Quimper **131** A 3
Quimperlé **131** A 3
Quinault Indian Reservation **90** A 2
Quincy *[U.S., California]* **92** B 2
Quincy *[U.S., Florida]* **100** B 3
Quincy *[U.S., Illinois]* **94** F 3
Quincy *[U.S., Massachusetts]* **98** G 2
Quinn **92** C 1
Quintanar de la Orden **130** CD 2
Quintanar del Rey **130** D 2
Quintín, San **102** B 3/2

River, canal
Waterfall
Lake, lakes, reservoir
Swamp
Salt flat
Sea
Strait
Bay, gulf
Cape
Island, islands
Ocean current
Ocean floor landforms
Tectonic feature
Atmospheric phenomena
Time zone
Geographical grid

Quinto 130 D 2
Quinze, Lac des 88 A 3
Quispamsis 88 D 3
Quitman 100 C 3
Quito 112 D 4
Qujing 154 K 6
Qulaybīyah 132 B 4
Qulsary 136 L 5
Qultay 134 K 1
Qum Muryn 134 JK 2
Qunayṭirah, Al- 152 BC 2
Qurayyāt, Al- 152 C 3
Qŭrghonteppa 150 KL 3
Qurnah, Al- 152 E 3
Qurnat as-Sawdā' ▲ 152 C 2
Qusanṭinah
→ Constantine 176 J 1
Qusar 134 J 3
Quṣayr, Al- *[Egypt]* 176 OP 3
Quṣayr, Al- *[Syria]* 152 C 2
Qūṣīyah, Al- 152 A 4
Qusmuryn 148 NO 8
Quṭayfah, Al- 152 C 2
Qūtīābād 152 F 2
Quwārah, Al- 152 D 4
Quy Nhơn 156 FG 5
Quyon 88 A 3
Q'vareli 134 H 3
Qyzylorda 148 O 9

R

Raahe 125 F 4
Rab 132 C 2
Rab 132 C 2
Rába 128 F 4
Rabat (Ar-Ribāṭ) 176 EF 2
Rabaul 156 P 8
Rabaul ▲ 15 HJ 16
Rabī'a 152 D 1
Râbniţa 128 K 4
Race, Cape 88 G 3
Rach Gia 156 EF 6/5
Racibórz 128 FG 3
Racine 94 G 2
Rădăuţi 128 J 4
Radcliff 98 C 3
Radebeul 128 E 2
Radekhiv 128 J 3
Radford 98 D 3
Radishchevo 136 HJ 3
Radisson 86 H 2
Radom 128 GH 2
Radomsko 128 G 2/3
Radomyshl' 128 K 3
Radoviš 133 C 3
Radovitskiy 136 F 2
Radøy 126 B 2
Raduzhnyy 148 QR 6
Radviliškis 126 HJ 4
Radville 84 G 3
Radyvyliv 128 J 3
Rafael, Cerro San ▲ 114 H 3
Rafael, San *[Argentina]* 114 F 4
Rafael, San *[U.S.]* 92 B 2
Rafael, San 92 E 2
Rafaela 114 G 4
Rafah 152 B 3
Rafḥah 152 D 3
Rafsanjān 150 H 4
Ragusa 132 CD 4
Rahachow 128 L 2
Raḥḥālīyah, Ar- 152 D 2
Rahimyar Khan 150 KL 5
Rāhjerd 152 F 2
Raichur 150 M 7
Rainbow Lake 71 FG 4
Rainier, Mount ▲ 90 B 2
Rainy 86 D 3
Rainy Lake 86 D 3
Rainy River 86 D 3
Raipur 150 N 6
Raisio 126 H 2
Rajahmundry 150 N 7
Rajang 156 G 7
Rajasthan 150 LM 5
Rajasthanis 145 L 7
Rajkot 150 L 6
Rajshahi 150 O 6
Rakan, Ra's 152 F 4
Rakata ▲ → Krakatau 156 E 9
Rakhine 150 P 6/7
Rakhiv 128 HJ 2/3
Rakitnoye 136 DE 4
Rakovník 128 E 3
Rakovski 133 D 2
Rakvere 126 J 3
Raleigh 100 D 2
Raleigh Bay 100 DE 2
Ralik Chain 160 K 2/3
Rama 102 J 6
Ramādī, Ar- 152 D 2
Rām Allāh 152 B 3
Rambouillet 131 C 2
Rambutyo 156 O 8
Ramelau ▲ 156 K 9/10
Ramenskoye 136 EF 2
Rameshki 136 E 1
Rāmhormoz 152 F 3
Ramla 152 B 3
Ramm, Jabal ▲ 152 BC 3
Râmnicu Sărat 133 DE 1
Râmnicu Vâlcea 133 CD 1
Ramon' 136 F 3
Ramón de la Nueva
Orán, San 114 FG 2
Ramotswa 178 K 8
Rampur 150 MN 5
Ramree 150 P 7
Ramsey 124 C 3
Ramsey Lake 86 G 4
Rāmshīr 152 F 3
Ramthā, Ar- 152 BC 2
Rana 125 B 3
Ranafjorden 125 B 3
Rancagua 114 EF 4
Ranchi 150 N 6
Randers 126 D 4
Randijaur 125 CD 3
Ranger 165 G 8
Rangoon (Yangon) 150 PQ 7
Rangpur 150 OP 5/6
Rankin 165 E 8
Rankin Inlet 78 WX 6
Rantauprapat 156 DE 7
Rantekombola ▲ 156 HJ 8
Rantoul 94 FG 2
Rānya 152 E 1
Rapa 160 P 6
Rapallo 132 B 2
Rapid City 94 C 1
Rapla 126 J 3
Rappahannock 98 E 3
Raqqah, Ar- 152 C 1/2
Rarotonga 160 NO 6
Ra's ... → ..., Ra's ...
Rasa, Punta 114 G 6
Ra's al-'Ayn 152 D 1
Ra's al-Jabal 132 B 4
Ra's al-Khaymah 150 H 5
Ra's an-Naqb 152 B 3
Râscani 128 K3/4
Ras Dashen ▲ 176 P 6
Raseiniai 126 H 4
Ra's Ghārib 152 B 3
Rashīd 152 A 3
Rashīdiyah, Ar- 176 FG 2
Rasht 134 J 4
Raška 133 B 2
Ra's Lānūf 119 H 6/7
Rasony 128 K 1
Rass Jebel
→ Ra's al-Jabal
Rasskazovo 136 FG 3
Rastān, Ar- 152 C 2
Ra's Tannūrah 152 F 4
Rata, Cape 156 E 9
Ratak Chain 160 KL 2/3
Rathbun Reservoir 94 E 2
Rathenow 128 E 2
Rat Islands 76 DE 8
Ratlam 150 LM 6
Ratnagiri 150 L 7
Ratne 128 J 2
Raton 92 F 2
Ratz, Mount ▲ 76 O 7
Rauḍa, Ar- 152 A 4
Raufoss 126 D 2
Rauma 126 H 2
Raurkela 150 NO 6
Răuţel 128 K 4
Rava-Ruska 128 H 3
Ravenna 132 C 2
Ravensburg 128 D 4
Ravenswood 98 D 3
Rawa 128 G 2
Rāwah 152 D 2
Rawaki 166 ST 1
Rawalpindi 150 LM 4
Rawāndūz 152 E 1
Rawicz 128 F 2
Rawlinna 166 F 7
Rawlins 90 F 3
Rawson 114 G 6
Ray, Cape 88 F 3
Rāyāt 152 E 1
Raychikhinsk 148 ab 9
Rayevskiy 136 L 2/3
Raymond 84 E 3
Raymondville 96 D 4
Rayville 96 F 2
Rayyān, Ar- 150 FG 6/5
Raz, Pointe du 131 A 2
Razāzah Lake 152 D 2
Razgrad 133 D 2
Razim, Lacul 133 E 2
Ré, Île de 131 B 3
Reading *[U.K.]* 124 D 4
Reading *[U.S.]* 98 F 2
Rechytsa 128 L 2
Recife 112 N 5
Recife, Cape 178 K 9
Recklinghausen 128 C 2
Reconquista 114 GH 3
Red Basin 141 O 6/7
Red Bay 88 F 2
Red Bluff 92 B 1
Red Cliff Indian
Reservation 94 F 1
Red Cloud 94 D 2
Red Deer 84 E 2
Red Deer
[Canada, Alberta/
Saskatchewan] 84 E 3
Red Deer *[Canada,*
Saskatchewan/
Manitoba] 86 B 2
Red Deer Lake 86 B 2
Redding 92 B 1
Redenção 112 J 5
Redfield 94 D 1
Red Hills 94 CD 3
Redkino 136 DE 2
Red Lake 86 D 3
Red Lake 86 D 3
Red Lake, Lower 86 D 4
Red Lake, Upper 86 D 3
Red Lake Indian
Reservation 86 D 3/4
Red Lake River 86 CD 4
Red Lodge 90 E 2
Redmond 90 B 2
Red Oak 94 E 2
Redon 131 B 3
Redonda 115 II B 1
Redondela 130 B 1
Red Pheasant Indian
Reserve 84 FG 2
Red River
[China/Vietnam] 156 E 3
Red River *[U.S.]* 96 D 2
Red River of the
North 86 C 3/4
Red Rock 86 E 3
Red Rock 90 D 2
Red Sea 150 DE 5/7
Red Spruce Knob ▲ 98 DE 3
Red Sucker 86 D 2
Red Sucker Lake 86 D 2
Red Volta 176 G 6
Redwater 84 E 2
Red Wing 94 E 1
Redwood Falls 94 E 1
Redwood National
Park 92 A 1
Reedley 92 C 2
Reedsport 90 A 3
Reedville 98 E 3
Reese 92 C 2
Refahiye 134 EF 3
Refugio 96 D 3
Regensburg 128 E 3
Reggane → Riqqān
Reggio di Calabria 132 D 4
Reggio nell'Emilia 132 B 2

eghin 128 J 4
egina 84 G 3
egis Mohawk Indian Reservation, Saint 98 F 1
ehoboth 178 H 7
ehovot 152 B 3
ei, Costa 123 DE 4
eidsville 100 D 1
eims 131 D 2
eindeer 86 C 2
eindeer Lake 76 UV 7
einosa 130 C 1
eliance 78 T 6
emiremont 131 DE 2/3
emo, San 132 A 2
emontnoye 134 G 1
endova 166 M 2
endsburg 128 CD 1
enfrew 88 A 3
engat 156 E 8
eni 134 B 1
enmark 166 HJ 7
ennell 166 N 3
ennes 131 B 2
ennie 86 D 3
eno 92 BC 2
eno 132 B 2
eno, El 96 D 2
ensselaer 98 C 2
entína 133 C 3
eplot 126 GH 1
epublican 94 C 2
epulse Bay 78 WX 5
ep'yevka 136 E 3
equena *[Peru]* 112 E 5
equena *[Spain]* 130 D 2
eservoir/ Réservoir ... → ..., Reservoir/ Réservoir ...
eshetylivka 136 D 4
esistencia 114 GH 3
eşiţa 133 C 1
esolute 78 V 4
esolution Island 76 c 6
eston 86 B 3
ethel 131 D 2
éthymno 133 D 5
éunion 178 PQ 6/7
eus 130 E 2
eutlingen 128 D 3
evda 136 N 2
evel 131 C 4
evelstoke 84 D 3
evelstoke, Lake 84 D 3
evillagigedo Islands 102 C 5
exburg 90 E 3
eyðarfjörður 125 E 2
eyers, Point 92 B 2
eykjanes 125 B 2
eykjanes Ridge 10 G 3/2
eykjavík 125 B 2
eynosa 96 D 4
ezé 131 B 3
ēzekne 126 K 4
ezh 138 P 5
ezina 128 K 4
haetian Alps 128 D 4
Rhaeto-Romanch [= Ro.] 121 GH 5
Rheine 128 C 2
Rhein-Main 147 D 5
Rhein-Ruhr 118 G 4
Rhein-Ruhr-Middle 147 D 5/4
Rhein-Ruhr-North 147 D 5/4
Rhein-Ruhr-South 147 DE 5/4
Rhine 128 D 4
Rhinebeck 98 F 2
Rhinelander 94 F 1
Rhineland-Palatinate 128 C 3
Rhir, Cap 176 E 2
Rhode Island 98 G 2
Rhodes 133 E 4
Rhodope Mountains 133 CD 3
Rhondda 124 CD 4
Rhône 131 E 3
Rhum 124 B 3
Rias, Las 123 C 3
Riau Archipelago 156 E 7
Ribadeo 130 B 1
Ribāţ, Ar- → Rabat 176 EF 2
Ribe 126 CD 4
Ribeira 130 AB 1
Ribeira Brava 176 BC 5
Ribeira Grande 130 D 5/6
Ribeirão Prêto 114 K 2
Riberalta 112 F 6
Ricardo Flores Magón 96 B 3
Rice Lake 94 EF 1
Riceys, Les 131 D 3
Richards Bay 178 L 8
Richfield 92 D 2
Richibucto Indian Reserve 88 D 3
Richland 90 C 2
Richland Center 94 F 2
Richlands 98 D 3
Richmond *[Australia]* 166 J 5
Richmond *[U.S., Indiana]* 98 C 3
Richmond *[U.S., Kentucky]* 98 CD 3
Richmond *[U.S., Missouri]* 94 E 3
Richmond *[U.S., Texas]* 96 DE 3
Richmond *[U.S., Utah]* 92 DE 1
Richmond *[U.S., Virginia]* 98 E 3
Riddle 71 F 5
Ridgecrest 92 C 3
Ridgetown 98 D 2
Riding Mountain National Park 86 BC 3
Ried 128 E 3
Riesa 128 E 2
Riesi 132 C 4
Riesko 114 E 8
Rietavas 126 H 4
Rieti 132 C 2
Rif, Ar- 176 FG 2
Rifāʿ, Ar- 152 F 4
Rifāʿī, Ar- 152 E 3
Rifle 94 B 3
Rifs 173 C 2
Rīga 126 J 4
Riga, Gulf of 126 HJ 3
Rigolet 78 d 7/8
Riihimäki 126 J 2
Rijeka 132 C 1
Rila 133 C 2
Rimini 132 C 2
Rimouski 88 CD 2
Rincón 115 I A 1
Ringkøbing 126 C 4
Ringsted 126 DE 4
Ringvassøy 125 CD 2
Rio/Río ... → ..., Rio/Río
Riobamba 112 D 4
Rio Branco 112 F 5
Río Bravo 96 D 4
Río Caribe 115 II B 3
Rio Claro *[Brazil]* 114 K 2
Rio Claro *[Trinidad and Tobago]* 115 II B 3
Río Cuarto 114 G 4
Rio de Janeiro 114 L 2
Rio de Janeiro 114 LM 2
Río de la Plata 114 H 4/5
Rio Dell 92 AB 1
Río Gallegos 114 F 8
Río Grande *[Argentina]* 114 F 8
Rio Grande *[Brazil]* 114 J 4
Rio Grande City 96 D 4
Rio Grande do Norte 112 M 5
Rio Grande do Sul 114 HJ 3/4
Rio Grande Rise 13 F 1
Ríohacha 112 E 1
Rioja, La 114 F 3
Rioja, La *[Argentina]* 114 F 3/4
Rioja, La *[Spain]* 130 D 1
Rio Largo 112 M 5
Riom 131 CD 3
Río Negro 114 FG 5/6
Rio Rancho 92 F 3
Rio Verde *[Brazil, Goiás]* 112 JK 7
Rio Verde *[Brazil, Mato Grosso do Sul]* 112 J 7
Ripon *[Canada]* 88 B 3
Ripon *[U.K.]* 124 D 3
Ripon *[U.S.]* 94 F 2
Riqqān 176 GH 3
Rishon Le Ẕiyyon 152 B 3
Risør 126 D 3
Risti 126 HJ 3
Rita, Santa *[Brazil]* 112 N 5
Rita, Santa *[Guam]* 101 II
Ritidian Point 101 II
Ritzville 90 C 2
Riva 132 B 1
Rivadavia 66 FG 7
Rivera 114 H 4
Riverhead 98 F 2
Rivers 86 BC 3
Riverside 92 C 3
Riverton *[Canada]* 86 C 3
Riverton *[U.S.]* 90 E 3
Riverview 88 D 3
Riviera 123 D 3
Riviera del Sole 123 E 3
Rivière-à-Pierre 88 BC 3
Rivière-au-Tonnerre 88 D 2
Rivière du Lièvre 88 B 3
Rivière-du-Loup 88 C 3
Riviere-Pilote 115 II B 2
Rivne 128 J 3
Rivoli 132 A 1/2
Riyadh (Ar-Riyāḍ) 150 EF 6
Rize 134 F 3
Rizzuto, Cape 132 D 4
Rjukan 126 C 3
Road Town 101 IX
Roan Cliffs 92 E 2
Roanne 131 D 3
Roanoke *[U.S., Alabama]* 100 B 2
Roanoke *[U.S., Virginia]* 98 E 3
Roanoke 100 D 1
Roanoke Rapids 100 D 1
Roan Plateau 94 AB 3
Robāţ Karīm 152 F 2
Robert S. Kerr Reservoir 96 E 2
Roberval 88 B 2
Robinson Crusoe 114 D 4
Roblin 86 B 3
Robson, Mount 84 D 2
Robstown 96 D 4
Roca, Cabo da 130 A 3
Rocas 112 N 4
Rocha 114 J 4
Roche, La 131 B 3
Rochefort 131 B 3
Rochegda 138 J 4
Rochelle 94 F 2
Rochelle, La 131 B 3
Rochester *[U.S., Minnesota]* 94 EF 1
Rochester *[U.S., New Hampshire]* 98 G 2
Rochester *[U.S., New York]* 98 E 2
Rock 94 F 2
Rockall 117 E 4
Rockall Bank 10 GH 3/2
Rockdale 96 D 3
Rock Falls 94 F 2
Rockford 94 F 2
Rockhampton 166 L 5
Rock Hill 100 C 2
Rockingham 100 D 2
Rock Island 94 F 2
Rock Islands [= ⑤] 158 G 3
Rockland 98 G 1
Rock Rapids 94 DE 2
Rock Springs 90 E 3
Rockwood 100 B 2
Rocky Boy's Indian Reservation 90 E 1
Rocky Ford 94 BC 3
Rocky Mount *[U.S., North Carolina]* 100 D 1/2
Rocky Mount *[U.S., Virginia]* 98 DE 3
Rocky Mountain House 84 E 2
Rocky Mountain National Park 94 B 2
Rocky Mountains 69 EH 3/6
Roda, La 130 D 2
Rødberg 126 CD 2
Rødby 126 D 4
Rodel 124 B 2
Rodez 131 C 4
Rodniki 136 FG 1
Ródos 133 E 4

River, canal
Waterfall
Lake, lakes, reservoir
Swamp
Salt flat
Sea
Strait
Bay, gulf
Cape
Island, islands
Ocean current
Ocean floor landforms
Tectonic feature
Atmospheric phenomena
Time zone
Geographical grid

S

Independent country
Dependent territory
Federal state, province, territory
People, ethnic group, tribe
Indian reservation/reserve
National Park
Industrial region
Historical site
Research station
Continent, realm
Region, peninsula
Mountain range, mountains
▲ Peak
Pass
* Ice shelf, glacier

abah **156** H 6
abalana Islands **156** H 9
abana de la Mar **74** M 7/8
abaneta, Puntan **101** III
abanözü **134** D 3
abará **112** L 7
abbāgh, Jabal ▲ **152** B 3
abhā **176** KL 3
abile **126** H 3/4
abinal, Parque Nacional El **96** CD 4
abinas **96** C 4
abinas *[Mexico, Coahuila]* **96** C 3/4
abinas *[Mexico, Nuevo León]* **96** C 4
abinas Hidalgo **96** CD 4
abine **96** E 2
abine Lake **96** E 3
abirabad **134** J 3
abkhah, As- **152** C 2
abkhat Makarghan **176** H 3
able, Cape *[Canada]* **88** D 4
able, Cape *[U.S.]* **101** I
able Island **88** F 4
ables-d'Olonne, Les **131** B 3
ablinskoye **134** G 2
abzevār **150** H 3
acaba **112** FG 7
ac and Fox Indian Reservation **94** EF 2
ăcele **128** J 4
achigo **86** DE 2
achigo **86** E 2
achigo Lake **86** DE 2
achkhere **134** G 2
achs Harbour/Ikahuuk **78** OP 4
ackville **88** D 3
acramento **92** B 2
acramento **92** B 2
acramento Mountains **92** F 3
ádaba **130** D 1
a'dah **150** E 7
a'dīyah, As- **152** E 2
ado **154** R 4
adovoye **136** GH 5
adrātah **132** A 4
af, Aṣ- **152** A 3
afāqis → Sfax **176** K 1/2
äffle **126** E 3
afford **92** E 3
afi (Aṣfī) **176** EF 2
āfītā **152** C 2
afonovo *[Russia, Arkhangel'sk]* **138** K 3
afonovo *[Russia, Smolensk]* **136** D 2
afranbolu **134** C 3
afwān **152** E 3
aga *[China]* **154** G 6
aga *[Japan]* **154** P 5
agar **150** M 6
age, Mount ▲ **101** IX
aghand **143** J 6
aghyz *[Kazakhstan, Atyraū]* **136** K 5
Saghyz *[Kazakhstan, Atyraū]* **136** L 4
Saghyz **136** L 4
Saginaw **98** D 2
Saginaw Bay **98** D 2/1
Sagres **130** B 3
Saguaro National Park **92** E 3
Saguenay **88** C 2
Saguenay (Chicoutimi-Jonquière) **88** C 2
Sagunto **130** DE 2
Sahagún **130** C 1
Ṣaḥam **150** H 6
Sahaptin **73** FG 5
Sahara **176** FM 4
Saharan Atlas **176** GH 2
Saharanpur **150** MN 4/5
Sahel **169** CE 4
Sāḥilīyah, Jabal as- **152** C 2
Sāhīndezh **134** H 4
Sahiwal **150** L 4
Ṣaḥneh **152** EF 2
Sahuaripa **96** A 3
Saïda → Ṣaydā
Saigon → Hô Chi Minh City (Than-Phô Hô Chi Minh)
Saimaa **126** K 2
Saimbeyli **134** DE 4
Saint-Affrique **131** CD 4
Saint Alban's *[Canada]* **88** G 3
Saint Albans *[U.S., Vermont]* **98** F 1
Saint Albans *[U.S., West Virginia]* **98** D 3
Saint Albert **84** E 2
Saint-Amand-Mont-Rond **131** CD 3
Saint Andrew Sound **100** C 3
Saint Anthony **88** G 2
Saint-Augustin **88** F 2
Saint Augustine **100** C 3
Saint Austell **124** C 5
Saint-Avold **131** E 2
Saint-Barthélemy **115** II B 1
Saint-Bonnet **131** E 4
Saint-Brieuc **131** AB 2
Saint-Camille **88** C 3
Saint Catharines **98** E 2
Saint Catherines **100** C 3
Saint Cathrine, Mount ▲ **115** II B 2
Saint-Chamond **131** D 3
Saint Charles *[U.S., Maryland]* **98** E 3
Saint Charles *[U.S., Missouri]* **94** F 3
Saint Clair **98** D 2
Saint Clair, Lake **98** D 2
Saint-Claude **131** DE 3
Saint Cloud **94** E 1
Saint-Côme **88** B 3
Saint Croix **94** E 1
Saint Croix **101** IX
Saint-Denis **178** PQ 7
Saint-Dié **131** E 2
Saint-Dizier **131** D 2
Saint-Donat **88** B 3
Sainte-Agathe-des-Monts **88** B 3
Sainte-Anne-de-Portneuf **88** C 2
Sainte-Anne-des-Chênes **86** C 3
Sainte-Anne-des-Monts **88** D 2
Sainte-Croix **88** C 3
Saint Elias, Mount ▲ **76** M 6/7
Saint Elias National Park, Wrangell- **78** M 6/7
Saint-Eloi **88** C 2/3
Sainte-Marguerite **88** D 2
Sainte-Marie *[Canada]* **88** C 3
Sainte-Marie *[Martinique]* **115** II B 2
Sainte Marie, Nosy **178** OP 6
Sainte-Rose **88** C 3
Saintes **131** B 3
Saintes Islands, Les **115** II B 2
Saintes-Maries-de-la-Mer **131** D 4
Sainte-Thècle **88** BC 3
Saint-Étienne **131** D 3
Saint-Félicien **88** B 2
Saint-Flour **131** D 3
Saint Francis **96** F 2/1
Saint-François **115** II B 1
Saint-Gaudens **131** C 4
Saint George **92** D 2
Saint George **100** B 3
Saint George, Point **92** A 1
Saint-Georges *[Canada]* **88** C 3
Saint George's *[Grenada]* **115** II B 2
Saint George's Bay **88** F 2
Saint George's Channel *[Atlantic Ocean/ Irish Sea]* **124** BC 4
Saint George's Channel *[Bismarck Sea/ Solomon Sea]* **156** P 8/9
Saint-Germain-des-Fossés **131** D 3
Saint-Girons **131** C 4
Saint Helena **178** C 6
Saint Helena **169** C 7
Saint Helena Bay **178** H 9
Saint Helena Sound **100** CD 2
Saint Helens *[U.K.]* **124** CD 4
Saint Helens *[U.S.]* **90** B 2
Saint Helens, Mount ▲ **90** B 2
Saint Hélier **131** B 2
Saint-Hyacinthe **88** B 3
Saint Ignace **98** C 1
Saint Ignace **86** EF 3
Saint James, Cape **76** O 8
Saint James Islands **101** IX
Saint-Jean **88** B 3
Saint-Jean **88** D 2
Saint-Jean, Lac **88** BC 2
Saint-Jean-d'Angély **131** B 3
Saint-Jean-de-Maurienne **131** DE 3
Saint-Jérôme **88** B 3
Saint Joe **90** D 2
Saint John **88** D 3
Saint John **88** D 3
Saint John **101** IX
Saint John's *[Antigua and Barbuda]* **115** II B 1
Saint John's *[Canada]* **88** G 3
Saint Johns *[U.S., Arizona]* **92** E 3
Saint Johns *[U.S., Michigan]* **98** C 2
Saint Johns **100** C 3
Saint Johnsbury **98** F 1
Saint-Joseph *[Canada]* **88** C 3
Saint Joseph *[U.S.]* **94** E 3
Saint Joseph **98** C 2
Saint Joseph **86** FG 4
Saint Joseph, Lake **86** F 3
Saint-Jovite **88** B 3
Saint-Junien **131** C 3
Saint Kilda **124** B 2
Saint Kitts **115** II B 1
Saint Kitts and Nevis **115** II B 1
Saint-Laurent **88** C 3/2
Saint-Laurent-du-Maroni **112** J 2/3
Saint Lawrence **88** B 3
Saint Lawrence, Gulf of **88** E 2
Saint Lawrence Island **76** FG 6
Saint-Léonard-de-Noblat **131** C 3
Saint Lewis **88** F 1
Saint-Lô **131** B 2
Saint-Louis *[Senegal]* **176** D 5
Saint Louis *[U.S.]* **94** F 3
Saint Lucia **115** II B 2
Saint Lucia Channel **115** II B 2
Saint-Maixent-l'Ecole **131** BC 3
Saint-Malo **131** B 2
Saint-Malo, Gulf of **131** B 2
Saint-Marc **102** L 5
Saint Maries **90** C 2
Saint-Martin **115** II B 1
Saint-Martin, Cap **115** II B 2
Saint Martin, Lake **86** C 3
Saint Martinville **96** F 3
Saint Mary **84** E 3
Saint Marys **98** E 2
Saint Mary's Bay **88** G 3
Saint Matthew Island **76** F 6/7
Saint Matthews **100** C 2
Saint Matthias Islands **156** OP 8
Saint Maurice **88** B 3
Saint-Michel-des-Saints **88** B 3
Saint-Mihiel **131** D 2
Saint-Nazaire **131** B 3
Saint-Omer **131** C 2
Saint-Pamphile **88** C 3
Saint-Pascal **88** C 3
Saint Paul *[Canada]* **84** F 2
Saint Paul *[U.S., Minnesota]* **94** E 1
Saint Paul *[U.S., Nebraska]* **94** D 2
Saint Paul *[Canada]* **88** E 3

– River, canal
– Waterfall
– Lake, lakes, reservoir
– Swamp
– Salt flat
– Sea
– Strait
– Bay, gulf
– Cape
– Island, islands
– Ocean current
– Ocean floor landforms
– Tectonic feature
– Atmospheric phenomena
– Time zone
– Geographical grid

Saint-Paul ⌓ *[French Southern Territories]* **4** NO 7/8
Saint Peter **94** E 1
Saint Peter and Paul Rocks ⌓ **105** L 4
Saint Peter Port **131** B 2
Saint Petersburg *[U.S.]* **100** C 4
Saint Petersburg (Sankt Peterburg) *[Russia]* **138** E 4/5
Saint-Pierre **88** FG 3
Saint-Pierre, Lac ◡ **88** B 3
Saint Pierre and Miquelon ◐ **88** F 3
Saint-Pol-de-Léon **131** A 2
Saint Quentin *[Canada]* **88** D 3
Saint-Quentin *[France]* **131** CD 2
Saint Regis Mohawk Indian Reservation Ⲭ **98** F 1
Saint-Siméon **88** C 3
Saint Simons ⌓ **100** C 3
Saint Stephen **88** D 3
Saint Thomas **98** D 2
Saint Thomas ⌓ **101** IX
Saint-Tite-des-Caps **88** C 3
Saint-Tropez **131** E 4
Saint-Ulric **88** D 2
Saint-Valéry **131** C 2
Saint-Valéry-en-Caux **131** BC 2
Saint Vincent ⌓ *[St. Vincent and the Grenadines]* **115** II B 2
Saint Vincent ⌓ *[U.S.]* **100** B 3
Saint Vincent, Cape)≋ **130** AB 3
Saint Vincent and the Grenadines ■ **115** II B 2
Saint Vincent Passage ≊ **115** II B 2
Saint Walburg **84** F 2
Saint-Yrieix-la-Perche **131** C 3
Saipan ⌓ **101** III
Saipan Channel ≊ **101** III
Sajama ▲ **112** F 7
Sakai **154** R 5
Sakākah **152** D 3
Sakakawea, Lake ◡ **90** G 2
Sakalava ⚇ **173** H 8/7
Sakami ∽ **88** B 1
Sakami Lake ◡ **88** A 1
Sakarya ∽ **134** C 3
Sakha ▽ **148** Xb 5/6
Sakhalin ⌓ **148** de 8/9
Sakhalin Strait ≊ **148** d 6
Šakiai **126** H 4
Sakīkdah **176** J 1
Sakmara ∽ **136** M 3
Saky **134** D 1/2
Sal ∽ **134** FG 1
Sal ⌓ **176** C 5
Sala **126** F 3
Salaberry-de-Valleyfield **88** B 3
Sala Consilina **132** D 3
Salada, Laguna ◡ **92** CD 3
Salado ∽ **114** G 3
Salado, Río ∽ **96** C 4
Şalālah **150** GH 7
Salamanca *[Spain]* **130** C 2
Salamanca *[U.S.]* **98** E 2
Salamīyah **152** C 2
Salar ... ⋓ → ..., Salar ...
Salars [= S.] ⚇ **145** O 6
Salas de los Infantes **130** CD 1/2
Salavat **136** L 3
Salawati ⌓ **156** KL 8
Sala-y-Gómez ⌓ **6** KL 7
Sala y Gomez Ridge ⏖ **10** VW 7
Salcantay ▲ **112** E 6
Šalčininkai **126** J 4
Saldanha **178** H 9
Saldus **126** H 4
Sale **166** K 8
Salekhard **138** R 2
Salem *[India]* **150** M 8
Salem *[U.S., Illinois]* **94** F 3
Salem *[U.S., Ohio]* **98** D 2
Salem *[U.S., Oregon]* **90** B 2
Salem *[U.S., South Dakota]* **94** D 2
Salerno **132** C 3
Salgótarján **128** G 3
Salgueiro **112** LM 5
Sali **132** D 2
Salida **94** B 3
Şalīf, Aş- **143** H 8
Salihli **134** B 4
Salihorsk **128** JK 2
Salima **178** LM 5
Sālimīyah, As- **152** F 3
Salina *[U.S., Kansas]* **94** D 3
Salina *[U.S., Utah]* **92** E 2
Salina ⌓ **132** CD 4
Salina Cruz **102** F 5
Salinas *[Ecuador]* **112** C 4
Salinas *[U.S.]* **92** B 2
Salinas ∽ **92** B 2
Salinas Chicas ⋓ **66** FG 7
Salinas Grandes ⋓ **114** FG 4/3
Salinas Victoria **96** C 4
Saline ∽ **96** E 2
Salisbury *[U.K.]* **124** D 4
Salisbury *[U.S., Maryland]* **98** F 3
Salisbury *[U.S., North Carolina]* **100** C 2
Salish ⚇ **73** FG 4-5
Salish Mountains ▲▲ **90** D 1/2
Salkhad **152** C 2
Salla **125** G 3
Salle, La **94** F 2
Sallisaw **96** E 2
Sallūm, As- **176** N 2
Salmān, As- **152** E 3
Salmās **134** G 4
Salmi **138** E 4
Salmo **84** D 3
Salmon **90** D 2
Salmon ∽ *[Canada]* **84** C 2
Salmon ∽ *[U.S.]* **90** D 2
Salmon, Middle Fork ∽ **90** D 2
Salmon Arm **84** D 3
Salmon River Mountains ▲▲ **90** D 2
Salo **126** H 2
Salon **131** D 4
Salonta **128** H 4
Salsipuedes, Punta)≋ **92** C 3/4
Salsk **134** F 1
Salt, As- **152** B 2
Salta **114** FG 2
Salta ▽ **114** FG 3
Saltfjorden ≋) **125** BC 3
Salt Fork ∽ **96** C 2
Salt Island ⌓ **101** IX
Salt Lake, Great ◡ **92** D 1
Salt Lake, Little ◡ **92** D 2
Salt Lake City **92** E 1
Salto **114** H 4
Salto, El **102** D 4
Salto del Guairá **114** HJ 2
Salton **96** C 2
Salton City **92** CD 3
Salton Sea ◡ **92** D 3
Salt River ∽ **92** E 3
Salt River Indian Reservation Ⲭ **92** E 3
Saluzzo **132** A 2
Salvador **112** M 6
Salvador, El **107** G 7
Salvador, El ■ **102** GH 6
Salvador, San **102** GH 6
Salvador, San ⌓ *[Bahamas]* **102** L 4
Salvador, San ⌓ *[Ecuador]* **112** AB 3/4
Salvador de Jujuy, San **114** FG 2
Salween ∽ **154** J 5
Salyan **134** J 3
Salzburg **128** E 4
Salzburg ▽ **128** E 4
Salzgitter **128** D 2
Salzwedel **128** D 2
Samagaltay **148** TU 8
Samalayuca **96** B 3
Samālūţ **152** A 3
Samandağı **134** D 4
Samani, Peak ▲ → Somoni, Peak
Samaqua ∽ **88** B 2
Samar ⌓ **156** K 5
Samara **136** J 3
Samara ∽ **136** K 3
Samārah, As- **176** EF 3
Samarai **156** OP 10
Samarinda **156** H 7/8
Samarqand **148** O 11/10
Sāmarrā' **152** DE 2
Samarskoye **136** M 3
Samāwah, As- **152** E 3
Şamaxı **134** J 3
Sambalpur **150** NO 6
Sambar, Cape)≋ **156** FG 8
Sambir **128** H 3
Samit ⚇ → Lapps **121** HK 3
Samoa ■ **166** S 3
Samoa Islands ⌓ **166** ST 3/4
Samobor **132** D 1
Samoded **138** H 3
Samokov **133** C 2
Sámos **133** D 4
Sámos ⌓ **133** D 4
Samothráki ⌓ **133** D 3
Samoylovka **136** G 3
Sampit **156** G 8
Sam Rayburn Reservoir ◡ **96** E 3
Samsø ⌓ **126** D 4
Samson Indian Reserve Ⲭ **84** E 2
Samsun **134** E 3
Samt'redia **134** FG 2/3
Samui ⌓ **156** E 6
Samut Prakan **156** E 5
San **176** F 6
San ⚇ → Bushmen **173** F 7/8
San ∽ **128** H 3
Sanaa (San'ā') **150** EF 7/8
Sanae ◿ **181** II C 2
Sanāfīr ⌓ **152** B 4
Sanaga ∽ **176** K 8
San Agustin, Cape)≋ **156** KL 6
Sanana **156** K 8
Sanana ⌓ **156** K 8
Sanandaj **152** E 2
San Andreas Fault ⌁ **14** K 4
San Andrés **102** J 6
San Andrés Island ⌓ **102** J 6
San Andres Mountains ▲▲ **92** F 3
San Angelo **96** CD 3
San Antoni de Portmany **130** E 2/3
San Antonio *[Chile]* **114** E 4
San Antonio *[Northern Mariana Is.]* **101** III
San Antonio *[U.S.]* **96** D 3
San Antonio *[Venezuela]* **115** II B 3
San Antonio ∽ **96** D 3
San Antonio, Cape)≋ **102** HJ 4
San Antonio de los Cobres **114** F 2
San Augustine **96** E 3
San Bartolomeo **132** D 3
San Benedetto **132** C 2
San Benito **96** D 4
San Benito Mountain ▲ **92** B 2
San Bernadino **92** C 3
San Bernardino Mountains ▲▲ **92** C 3
San Bernardo *[Chile]* **114** EF 4
San Bernardo *[Mexico]* **96** B 4
San Blas **96** A 4
San Blas, Cape)≋ **100** B 3
San Borja **112** F 6/7
San Buenaventura *[Mexico, Chihuahua]* **96** B 3
San Buenaventura *[Mexico, Coahuila]* **96** C 4
San Buenaventura *[U.S.]* **92** C 3
San Carlos *[Mexico]* **96** C 3
San Carlos *[Nicaragua]* **102** J 6
San Carlos *[U.S.]* **92** E 3
San Carlos *[Venezuela]* **112** F 2
San Carlos de Bariloche **114** EF 6
San Carlos de Bolívar **114** G 5
San Carlos del Zulia **112** E 2
San Carlos de Río Negro **112** F 3
San Carlos Indian Reservation Ⲭ **92** E 3
Sanchursk **136** H 1/2
San Clemente **92** C 3
San Clemente ⌓ **92** C 3

■ Independent country
◐ Dependent territory
▽ Federal state, province, territory
⚇ People, ethnic group, tribe
Ⲭ Indian reservation/reserve
⇧ National Park
⊓ Industrial region
∴ Historical site
◿ Research station
⊛ Continent, realm
⊾ Region, peninsula
▲▲ Mountain range, mountains
▲ Peak
)(Pass
∗ Ice shelf, glacier

∽ River, canal
Waterfall
⌣ Lake, lakes, reservoir
Swamp
Salt flat
≋ Sea
≍ Strait
≋) Bay, gulf
)≋ Cape
∩ Island, islands
Ocean current
Ocean floor landforms
Tectonic feature
Atmospheric phenomena
Time zone
Geographical grid

Independent country
Dependent territory
Federal state, province, territory
People, ethnic group, tribe
Indian reservation/reserve
National Park
Industrial region
∴ Historical site
Research station
Continent, realm
Region, peninsula
▲▲ Mountain range, mountains
▲ Peak
)(Pass
∗ Ice shelf, glacier

River, canal
Waterfall
Lake, lakes, reservoir
Swamp
Salt flat
Sea
Strait
Bay, gulf
Cape
Island, islands
Ocean current
Ocean floor landforms
Tectonic feature
Atmospheric phenomena
Time zone
Geographical grid

Seyhan 134 D 4
Seyitgazi 134 C 3
Seym 136 E 3
Seymchan 148 ef 6
Seymour *[U.S., Indiana]* 98 C 3
Seymour *[U.S., Texas]* 96 D 2
Seyne, La 131 D 4
Sfântu Gheorghe 128 J 4
Sfax (Şafāqis) 176 K 1/2
's-Gravenhage
→ The Hague 128 B 2
Shaanxi 154 LM 4
Shaba 178 JK 4/5
Shabestar 134 H 4
Shablykino 136 D 3
Shache/Yarkant 154 E 4
Shackleton Range ▲▲ 13 BA 1/4
Shadādah, Ash- 152 D 1
Shādegan 152 F 3
Shadwān Island 152 B 4
Shafallaḥīyah, Ash- 152 F 3/4
Shah Alam 156 DE 7
Shahbā 152 C 2
Shahdol 150 N 6
Shahjahanpur 150 N 5
Shahr-e Kord 152 F 2
Shahrisabz 148 O 11
Shāhrūd → Emāmrūd
Shā'ib al-Bānat, Jabal ▲ 152 B 4
Shaim 119 N 3/4
Shakhovskaya 136 D 2
Shakhtīnsk 148 P 9
Shakhty 136 F 5
Shakhun'ya 136 H 1
Shalakusha 138 H 4
Shalqar 148 M 9
Shal'ski 138 FG 4
Shalya 136 M 1
Sham, Jabal ash- ▲ 150 H 6
Shamary 136 M 1
Shamattawa Indian
Reserve 86 D 2
Shambajinagar 150 LM 6/7
Shāmbī, Jabal ▲ 176 JK 1
Shāmīyah, Ash- 152 E 2/3
Shammar, Jabal ▲▲ 152 D 4
Shamokin 98 E 2
Shamrock 96 C 2
Shan 150 Q 6
Shan 145 N 7
Shanāfīyah, Ash- 152 E 3
Shandī 176 O 5
Shandong 154 N 4
Shandong Peninsula 154 NO 4
Shanghai 154 O 5
Shangrao 154 N 6
Shangri-La 154 JK 6
Shannon 124 B 4
Shantar Islands 148 c 7/8
Shantou 154 N 7
Shanxi 154 M 4
Shaoguan 154 M 7
Shaoxing 154 NO 6
Shaoyang 154 M 6
Shapkina 138 MN 2
Shaqlāwah 152 DE 1
Shar 148 QR 9
Sharaf-Khāneh 134 H 4
Sharan 136 L 2
Sharanga 136 H 1
Sharbot Lake 88 A 3
Sharhorod 128 K 3
Shāriqah, Ash- 150 H 5/6
Sharīyar 152 F 2
Sharkan 136 KL 1
Sharkawshchina 128 K 1
Sharlyk 136 L 3
Sharmah 152 B 3
Sharm ash-Shaykh
(Sharm el Sheikh) 152 B 4/3
Sharon 98 D 2
Sharqāt, Ash- 152 D 2
Shar'ya 138 K 5
Shashemenē 176 PQ 7
Shashi 154 M 5/6
Shasta, Mount ▲ 92 B 1
Shasta [= Sh.] 73 F 5
Shasta Lake 92 B 1
Shasta Lake 92 B 1
Shatki 136 G 2
Shatoy 134 H 2
Shaṭrah, Ash- 152 E 3
Shatsk 136 F 3
Shaṭṭ al-'Arab 152 F 3
Shatura 136 F 2
Shaunavon 84 FG 3
Shavante 109 H 6
Shawano 94 F 1
Shawinigan 88 B 3
Shawnee 96 D 2
Shawrah, Ash- 152 B 4
Shaykh 152 D 2
Shaykh Sa'd 152 E 2
Shchëkino 136 E 3
Shchel'yabozh 138 N 2
Shchel'yayur 138 MN 3
Shchigry 136 E 3
Shchors 136 C 3
Shchūchīnsk 148 P 8
Shchuchyn 128 J 2
She 145 P 7
Shebekino 136 E 4
Shebelē 176 Q 7
Sheberghān 150 JK 3
Sheboygan 94 G 2
Shediac 88 D 3
Shedin Peak ▲ 84 B 1/2
Shedok 134 F 2
Sheep Mountain ▲ 94 B 3
Sheep Range ▲▲ 92 D 2
Sheet Harbour 88 E 3
Sheffield 124 D 4
Sheksna 138 GH 5
Shelagskiy, Cape 148 jk 4
Shelby *[U.S., Montana]* 90 E 1
Shelby
[U.S., North Carolina] 100 C 2
Shelbyville
[U.S., Indiana] 98 C 3
Shelbyville
[U.S., Tennessee] 100 B 2
Sheldon 94 E 2
Shelikhov Gulf 148 g 6/7
Shelikof Strait 76 JK 7
Shelkovskaya 134 H 2
Shellbrook 84 G 2
Shelton 90 B 2
Shemysheyka 136 H 3
Shenandoah 94 E 2
Shenandoah
Mountains ▲▲ 98 E 3
Shenandoah National
Park 98 E 3
Shendi → Shandī
Shengli Feng/
Jengish Chokusu ▲ 154 F 3
Shenkursk 138 J 4
Shentala 136 K 2
Shenyang 154 O 3
Shenzhen 154 MN 7
Shepetivka 128 K 3
Shepparton 166 JK 8
Sherbrooke 88 C 3
Shere Hill ▲ 176 JK 6/7
Sherente 109 J 5
Sheridan 90 F 2
Sherman 96 D 2
Sherridon 86 B 2
's-Hertogenbosch 128 BC 2
Sherwood Park 84 E 2
Shetland Islands 124 DE 1
Shevchenkove 136 E 4
Shiashkotan Island 148 fg 9
Shibām 150 F 7
Shibīn al-Kūm 152 A 3
Shibīn al-Qanāṭir 152 A 3
Shibîn el Kôm
→ Shibīn al-Kūm
Shibogama Lake 86 EF 2
Shifā', Jabal ash- ▲▲ 152 BC 3/4
Shigony 136 J 3
Shihezi 154 G 3
Shijiazhuang 154 MN 4
Shikoku 154 QR 5
Shiliguri 150 O 5
Shilik 148 Q 10
Shilka 148 Y 8
Shillong 150 P 5
Shilluk [= Sh.] 173 G 5/4
Shilovo 136 F 2
Shimanovsk 148 a 8
Shimbiris ▲ 176 R 6
Shimla 150 M 4
Shimoga 150 LM 8
Shimonoseki [= Sh.] 154 Q 5
Shinyanga 178 L 3
Shiono, Cape 154 R 5
Shipibo 109 F 5
Shiping 154 K 7
Shippagan 88 D 3
Shiprock 92 E 2
Shīrāz 152 G 3
Shirbīn 152 A 3
Shirley Mountains ▲▲ 90 F 3
Shirokaya ▲ 138 O 5
Shiyan 154 LM 5
Shizuishan 154 L 4
Shklow 128 KL 1
Shkodër 133 B 2
Shmidt Island 148 TV 2
Shmidt Subglacial
Basin 13 BC 15/14
Shoal Lake 86 B 3
Shoal River Indian
Reserve 86 B 2
Shona 173 FG 7
Shors [= Sh.] 145 M 4
Shoshone 73 GH 5
Shoshone 90 E 2
Shoshone Mountains ▲▲ 92 C 2
Shoshone Range ▲▲ 92 C 2/1
Shostka 136 CD 3
Show Low 92 E 3
Shoyna 138 J 2
Shpakovskoye 134 G 1
Shpola 136 C 4
Shreveport 96 E 2
Shrewsbury 124 D 4
Shū 148 P 10
Shuangliao 154 O 3
Shuangyashan 154 Q 2
Shu'aybah, Ash- 152 D 4
Shubarqudyq 136 LM 4
Shūbarshī 136 M 4
Shubrā al-Khaymah 152 A 3
Shuiding 154 F 3
Shumagin Islands 76 HJ 8
Shumen 133 D 2
Shumerlya 136 H 2
Shumlūl, Ash- 152 E 4
Shums'k 128 J 3
Shūrā, Ash- 152 D 1
Shurab 152 F 2
Shuryshkary 138 Q 3
Shūsh 152 EF 2
Shushenskoye 148 TU 8
Shushtar 152 F 2
Shuswap Lake 84 D 3
Shuṭṭ al-Jarīd 176 J 2
Shuṭṭ ash-Sharqī 176 GH 2
Shuṭṭ Malghir 176 HJ 2
Shuya 136 F 2
Shuyskoye 138 H 5
Shwebo 150 PQ 6
Shymkent 148 OP 10
Shyngghyrlaū 136 KL 3/4
Shyroke 136 D 5
Shyryayeve 136 BC 5
Sīah Chashmeh 134 G 3/4
Sialkot 150 LM 4
Siamese → Thai 145 N-O 8
Siátista 133 C 3
Šiauliai 126 H 4
Sīb, As- 150 H 6
Sībah, As- 152 F 3
Sibay 136 M 3
Šibenik 132 D 2
Siberia 141 LQ 3/4
Siberut 156 D 8
Sibiti 178 G 3
Sibiu 128 J 4
Sibolga 156 D 7
Sibu 156 G 7
Sibut 176 L 7
Sichuan 154 JK 5
Sicily 132 C 4
Sicily 132 D 4
Sicily, Strait of 132 BC 4
Sicuani 112 E 6
Šid 133 B 1
Sidamo [= Si.] 173 G 5
Side ∴ 134 C 4
Side, Cape 132 B 4
Siderno 132 D 4
Síderos, Cape 133 D 5
Sīdī Bal'abbās 176 GH 1

Independent country
Dependent territory
Federal state, province, territory
People, ethnic group, tribe
Indian reservation/reserve
National Park
Industrial region
∴ Historical site
Research station
Continent, realm
Region, peninsula
▲▲ Mountain range, mountains
▲ Peak
Pass
Ice shelf, glacier

River, canal
Waterfall
Lake, lakes, reservoir
Swamp
Salt flat
Sea
Strait
Bay, gulf
Cape
Island, islands
Ocean current
Ocean floor landforms
Tectonic feature
Atmospheric phenomena
Time zone
Geographical grid

Independent country
Dependent territory
Federal state, province, territory
People, ethnic group, tribe
Indian reservation/reserve
National Park
Industrial region
∴ Historical site
Research station
Continent, realm
Region, peninsula
Mountain range, mountains
▲ Peak
)(Pass
✱ Ice shelf, glacier

Southport [U.S.] 100 D 2
South Portland 98 G 2
South River 86 H 4
South River 100 D 2
South Ronaldsay 124 D 2
South Sandwich Islands, South Georgia and the 181 II D 35/36
South Sandwich Trench 13 DC 2/3
South Saskatchewan 84 F 3
South Scotia Ridge 13 C 35/1
South Shetland Islands 181 I DC 33/32
South Shields 124 D 3
South Sioux City 94 D 2
South Solomon Trench 10 QR 6
South Tasman Rise 13 DE 20/19
South Twin 86 H 2
South Tyrol 132 BC 1
South Uist 124 B 2
South West Cape 166 NO 10
Southwest Indian Ridge 10 LM 7
South West Monsoon 25 MO 15
Southwest Pacific Basin 10 ST 7/8
Southwest Point 101 IX
Sovata 128 J 4
Sovetsk [Russia, Kaliningrad] 128 H 1
Sovetsk [Russia, Kirov] 136 J 1
Sovetskaya Gavan' 148 cd 9
Sovetskiy [Russia, Khanty-Mansiy] 138 Q 4
Sovetskiy [Russia, Mari El] 136 J 2
Sowa 178 K 7
Soweto 178 K 8
Soyapango 102 H 6
Soyo 178 G 4
Soyra 176 PQ 6
Sozh 128 L 2/1
Sozimskiy 138 M 5
Sozopol 133 E 2
Spain 130 BD 2
Spainards [Europe] 121 F 5/6
Spaniards [Africa] 173 B 3
Spanish 86 G 4
Spanish Fork 92 DE 1/2
Spanish Town 102 K 5
Spánta, Cape 133 C 5
Sparks 92 C 2
Sparta 94 F 2
Spartanburg 100 C 2
Spárti 133 C 4
Spartivento, Cape 132 D 4
Sparwood 84 E 3
Spas-Demensk 136 D 2
Spas-Klepiki 136 F 2
Spassk-Dal'niy 148 b 9/10
Spassk-Ryazanskiy 136 F 2
Spean Bridge 124 C 3
Spearfish 94 C 1
Speightstown 115 II BC 2
Spencer 94 E 2
Spencer Gulf 166 H 8/7
Spey 124 C 2
Speyer 128 C 3
Spezia, La 132 B 2
Spilimbergo 132 C 1
Spirit Lake Indian Reservation 86 C 3/4
Spirit River 84 D 2
Spirovo 136 D 1
Spišská Nová Ves 128 GH 3
Spitsbergen 117 GH 2
Spitsbergen Bank 12 B 21/20
Spitsbergen Fracture Zone 12 B 22/21
Spittal 128 E 4
Split 132 D 2
Split Lake 86 CD 1/2
Split Lake Indian Reserve 86 C 1
Spokane 90 C 2
Spokane 90 C 2
Spokane Indian Reservation 90 C 1
Spoleto 132 C 2
Sporades, Northern 133 D 3/4
Sporades, Southern 133 DE 4/5
Spree 128 E 2
Spring 96 E 3
Springbok 178 H 8
Spring Creek 92 D 1
Springdale [Canada] 88 F 2
Springdale [U.S.] 96 E 1
Springe 128 D 2
Springer 92 F 2
Springerville 92 E 3
Springfield [U.S., Colorado] 94 C 3
Springfield [U.S., Illinois] 94 F 3
Springfield [U.S., Massachusetts] 98 F 2
Springfield [U.S., Minnesota] 94 E 1
Springfield [U.S., Missouri] 94 E 3
Springfield [U.S., Ohio] 98 D 3
Springfield [U.S., Oregon] 90 B 2
Springfield [U.S., Tennessee] 100 B 1
Spring Hill [U.S., Florida] 100 C 3
Springhill [U.S., Louisiana] 96 E 2
Spring Mountains 92 D 2/3
Spring Valley [U.S., Minnesota] 94 EF 2
Spring Valley [U.S., Nevada] 92 D 3
Springville 92 E 1
Spruce Knob 98 E 3
Spruce Mountain 92 D 1
Squamish 84 C 3
Squamish 84 C 3
Squatec 88 C 3
Squaw Valley 92 B 2
Srbobran 133 B 1
Srebrenica 132 E 2
Srednekolymsk 148 ef 5
Srednyaya Akhtuba 136 GH 4
Sremska Mitrovica 133 B 1/2
Sretensk 148 Y 8
Sribne 136 CD 4
Sri Jayawardenepura 150 N 9
Sri Lanka 150 N 9
Srinagar 150 M 4
Srnetica 132 D 2
Środa Wielkopolska 128 F 2
Stade 128 D 2
Stafford 124 D 4
Stakhanov 136 EF 4
Stalowa Wola 128 H 3
Stamford [U.S., Connecticut] 98 F 2
Stamford [U.S., New York] 98 F 2
Stamford [U.S., Texas] 96 D 2
Stan [= 12] 75 J-K 7-8
Standing Rock Indian Reservation 94 C 1
Stanford 90 E 2
Stanislaus 92 BC 2
Stanley [Australia] 166 K 9
Stanley [U.K.] 114 H 8
Stanley [U.S.] 90 G 1
Stanovoye 136 EF 3
Stanovoy Range 148 Zb 7
Stans 128 C 4
Stanychno-Luhans'ke 136 F 4
Starachowice 128 H 2/3
Stara Vyzhivka 128 J 2
Staraya Mayna 136 J 2
Staraya Russa 136 C 1
Stara Zagora 133 D 2
Starbuck Island 160 O 4
Stargard Szczecinski 128 F 2
Stariza 136 D 2
Starke 100 C 3
Starkville 96 F 2
Starnberg 128 D 3/4
Starobils'k 136 E 4
Starodub 136 CD 3
Starogard Gdański 128 FG 2
Starokostyantyniv 128 K 3
Starominskaya 134 EF 1
Starosubkhangulovo 136 LM 3
Staroyur'yevo 136 F 3
Starozhilovo 136 F 2
Staryya Darohi 128 K 2
Staryy Krym 134 D 2
Staryy Oskol 136 E 3
State College 98 E 2
Staten Island 114 G 8
Statesboro 100 C 2
Statesville 100 C 2
Staunton 98 E 3
Stavanger 126 B 3
Stavropol' 134 G 1/2
Steamboat Springs 94 B 2
Steens Mountain 90 C 3
Stege 126 E 4
Ştei 128 H 4
Steinbach 86 C 3
Steinkjer 126 D 1
Stendal 128 D 2
Step'anakert → Xankəndı 134 H 3
Step'anavan 134 G 3
Stephen, Saint 88 D 3
Stephenville [Canada] 88 F 2
Stephenville [U.S.] 96 D 2
Stepnogor 148 P 8
Stepnoye 136 H 3
Steps Point 101 VII
Sterlibashevo 136 L 3
Sterling [U.S., Colorado] 94 C 2
Sterling [U.S., Illinois] 94 F 2
Sterling Heights 98 D 2
Sterlitamak 136 L 3
Sterzing 132 B 1
Stettler 84 E 2
Steubenville 98 D 2
Stevenson Lake 86 D 2
Stevens Point 94 F 1
Stewart 78 OP 7
Stewart Island 166 O 10
Steyr 128 E 3/4
Stillwater 96 D 1
Stillwater Mountains 92 C 2
Štip 133 C 3
Stirling 124 C 3
Stjørdalshalsen 126 D 1
Stockbridge-Munsee Community 94 F 1
Stockerau 128 F 3
Stockholm 126 G 3
Stockton [U.S., California] 92 B 2
Stockton [U.S., Kansas] 94 D 3
Stockton 94 F 1
Stockton Lake 94 E 3
Stockton-on-Tees 124 D 3
Stockton Plateau 96 C 3
Stöeng Trĕng 156 F 5
Stoke-on-Trent 124 D 4
Stokksnes 125 E 2
Stolbovoy Island 148 ac 4
Stolin 128 J 2
Stonehaven 124 D 3
Stone Indian Reserve 84 C 2/3
Stonewall 86 C 3
Stoney Indian Reserve 84 E 3
Stony Creek Indian Reserve 84 B 2
Stony Tunguska 148 TU 6
Stora Lulevatten 125 D 3
Storavan 125 D 4
Storm Lake 94 E 2
Stornoway 124 BC 2
Storozhynets' 128 J 3/4
Storsjön 126 E 1
Storuman 125 C 4
Storuman 125 C 4
Stoughton 86 B 3
Stout Lake 86 D 2
Stowbtsy 128 JK 2
Strait(s) of ... → ..., Strait of
Strakonice 128 E 3
Stralsund 128 E 1
Stranraer 124 C 3
Strasbourg 131 E 2
Străşeni 128 K 4
Stratford [Canada] 98 D 2
Stratford [New Zealand] 166 P 8/9
Stratford [U.S.] 96 C 1
Strathmore 84 E 3
Straubing 128 E 3

River, canal
Waterfall
Lake, lakes, reservoir
Swamp
Salt flat
Sea
Strait
Bay, gulf
Cape
Island, islands
Ocean current
Ocean floor landforms
Tectonic feature
Atmospheric phenomena
Time zone
Geographical grid

Straumnes)≋ **125** AB 1
Strawberry Mountain ▲ **90** C 2
Streaky Bay **166** G 7
Streator **94** F 2
Strelka-Chunya **148** VW 6
Strenči **126** J 3
Streymoy ◓ **124** A 2
Strezhevoy **148** PQ 6
Stroitel' **136** E 4
Stromboli ▲ **15** DE 13/14
Stromboli ◓ **132** D 4
Strömstad **126** D 3
Strömsund **126** EF 1
Stronsay ◓ **124** D 2
Struga **133** B 3
Strugi-Krasnyye **138** D 5
Struma ∽ **133** C 2/3
Strumica **133** C 3
Strunino **136** E 2
Stryy **128** HJ 3
Stryy ∽ **128** H 3
Stuart, Mount ▲ **90** B 2
Stuart Lake ◡ **84** B 2
Stupino **136** E 2
Sturgeon Bay **94** G 1
Sturgeon Falls **86** GH 4
Sturgeon Lake ◡ **86** E 3
Sturgeon Lake Indian Reserve ⛺ **84** D 2
Sturgis *[U.S., Michigan]* **98** C 2
Sturgis *[U.S., South Dakota]* **94** C 1
Štúrovo **128** G 4
Stuttgart *[Germany]* **128** D 3
Stuttgart *[U.S.]* **96** F 2
Stykkishólmur **125** B 2
Styria ▽ **128** EF 4
Suakin → Sawākīn
Subate **126** J 4
Şubayḩiyah, Aş- **152** EF 3
Subaykhān **152** D 2
Subi Besar ◓ **156** FG 7
Subotica **133** B 1
Subrâ el Kheima → Subrā al-Khaymah
Sub-Saharan Africa ⊕ **51** JK 7
Suceava **128** J 4
Sucre **112** FG 7
Sudan ⛊ **176** MO 6
Sudan ⌒ **169** CF 4
Sudbury **86** G 4
Sudd ⌒ **169** FG 5
Sudetes ▲▲ **128** F 3
Suðuroy ◓ **124** A 2
Sudislavl' **136** FG 1
Sudogda **136** F 2
Sudr → Sidr, As-
Sudzha **136** D 3
Sue ∽ **176** N 7
Sueca **130** DE 2
Suez (As-Suways) **152** B 3
Suez, Gulf of ≋) **152** B 3
Suez Canal ∽ **152** B 3
Suffolk **98** E 3
Sūfjān **134** H 4
Sugar Land **96** DE 3
Sugarloaf Mountain ▲ **98** G 1
Şuḩār **150** H 6
Sühbaatar **154** KL 1/2
Suhl **128** D 3
Şuhut **134** C 4
Suide **154** LM 4
Suihua **154** P 2
Suining **154** KL 5
Suir ∽ **124** B 4
Suiti, Cape)≋ **134** J 3
Sukabumi **156** F 9
Sukadana **156** G 8
Sukhinichi **136** D 2
Sukhnah, As- **152** C 2
Sukhona ∽ **138** H 5
Sukkozero **138** EF 3
Sukkur **150** K 5
Suksun **136** M 1/2
Sukuma ⚉ **173** G 6
Sula ∽ **138** M 2
Sulak ∽ **134** H 2
Sulawesi ◓ → Celebes **156** HJ 8
Sulaymānīyah, As- **152** E 2
Sulayyil, As- **150** F 6
Sulechów **128** F 2
Sulejów **128** G 2
Suleya **136** M 2
Sulina **133** EF 1/2
Sulitjelma **125** C 3
Sulitjelma ▲ **125** C 3
Sullam Voe **119** F 4/3
Sullana **112** CD 4
Sullivan **94** F 3
Sullivan Lake ◡ **84** E 2/3
Sulmona **132** C 3
Sulphur **96** E 3
Sulphur Springs **96** E 2
Sultanbeyli **134** B 3
Sultanhanı **134** D 4
Sultan Kudarat **156** J 6
Sulu Archipelago ◓ **156** HJ 7/6
Sülüklü **134** C 4
Suluova **134** D 3
Sulūq **176** M 2
Sulu Sea ≋ **156** HJ 6
Sulzberger Bay ≋) **181** I B 24/22
Sumatra ◓ **156** DF 7/8
Sumba ◓ **156** HJ 10
Sumbawa ◓ **156** H 9
Sumbawabesar **156** H 10/9
Sumbawanga **178** KL 4
Sumbe **178** G 5
Sumburgh **124** D 2
Sumburgh Head)≋ **124** D 2
Sumenep **156** GH 9
Şummān, Aş- ⌒ **152** E 4
Summer Lake ◡ **90** B 3
Summerland **84** D 3
Summerside **88** DE 3
Summersville **98** D 3
Summerville *[U.S., Georgia]* **100** B 2
Summerville *[U.S., South Carolina]* **100** C 2
Sumo ⚉ **73** K 8
Šumperk **128** F 3
Sumqayıt **134** J 3
Sumter **100** CD 2
Sumy **136** D 4
Suna **136** J 1
Sunburst **90** DE 1
Sunbury **98** E 2
Sunchild Indian Reserve ⛺ **84** E 2
Sunda Islands, Greater ◓ **160** DF 4
Sunda Islands, Lesser ◓ **160** EF 4
Sundanese ⚉ **145** O 10
Sunda Strait ≋ **160** D 4
Sunderland **124** D 3
Sundsvall **126** FG 2
Sungurlu **134** D 3
Sunland Park **92** F 4
Sunndalsøra **126** CD 2
Sunne **126** E 3
Sunnyside **90** BC 2
Sunrise Manor **92** D 2
Suntar **148** Y 6
Sun Valley **92** C 2
Sunyani **176** G 7
Suojärvi **138** EF 4
Suolahti **126** J 2
Suomussalmi **125** G 4
Suonenjoki **126** K 2
Superior *[U.S., Arizona]* **92** E 3
Superior *[U.S., Montana]* **90** D 2
Superior *[U.S., Nebraska]* **94** D 2
Superior *[U.S., Wisconsin]* **94** EF 1
Superior, Lake ◡ **86** EF 4
Süphan Dağı ▲ **134** G 3
Sūq Ahrās **132** A 4
Sūq ash-Shuyūkh **152** E 3
Suqaylibīyah **152** C 2
Şūr *[Lebanon]* **152** B 2
Şūr *[Oman]* **150** H 6
Sur, Point)≋ **92** B 2
Sur, Punta)≋ **114** H 5
Sura **138** K 3
Sura ∽ **136** H 3
Surabaya **156** GH 9
Surakarta **156** G 9
Surat **150** L 6
Surat Thani **156** DE 6
Surazh *[Belarus]* **128** L 1
Surazh *[Russia]* **136** C 3
Surdulica **133** C 2
Surgut **148** PQ 6
Surigao **156** K 6
Suriname ⛊ **112** HJ 3
Surovikino **136** G 4
Surprise, Île ◓ **166** NO 4
Surrey **84** C 3
Sursk **136** H 3
Surskoye **136** H 2
Surt **176** L 2
Sürüç **134** E 4
Suruí ⚉ **109** G 6
Sūsah → Sousse **176** K 1
Sūsangerd **152** F 3
Susanino **136** F 1
Susanville **92** B 1
Suşehri **134** E 3
Susquehanna ∽ **98** EF 2
Sussex **88** D 3
Susu ⚉ **173** B 4/5
Susuman **148** e 6
Susurluk **134** B 3
Sutlej ∽ **150** L 5
Sutton *[Canada]* **98** E 1
Sutton *[U.S.]* **94** D 2
Sutton ∽ **86** F 2
Sutton Coldfield **124** D 4
Suure-Jaani **126** J 3
Suur Munamägi ▲ **126** JK 3
Suva **166** Q 4
Suvorov **136** E 2
Suwałki **128** H 1
Suwannee ∽ **100** C 3
Suwār, As- **152** D 2
Suwarrow ◓ **160** NO 5
Suwaydā', As- **152** BC 2
Şuwayrah, Aş- **152** E 2
Suways, As- → Suez **152** B 3
Suwŏn **154** OP 4
Suyutkina Kosa, Cape)≋ **134** HJ 2
Suzdal' **136** F 2
Suzhou *[China, Anhui]* **154** N 5
Suzhou *[China, Jiangsu]* **154** O 5
Suzu, Cape)≋ **154** R 4
Svalbard ◗ **120** GH 2
Svalyava **128** H 3
Svanetis Kedi ▲▲ **134** G 2
Svatove **136** E 4
Svealand ⌒ **126** EF 3/2
Svecha **138** KL 5
Sveg **126** E 2
Švenčionys **126** J 4
Svendborg **126** D 4
Šventoji ∽ **126** J 4
Sverdlovs'k **136** F 4
Sverdrup Islands ◓ **76** TX 3
Svetlaya **148** c 9
Svetlograd **134** G 1
Svetlyy **148** N 8
Svetlyy Yar **136** GH 4
Svetogorsk **138** D 4
Svilengrad **133** D 3
Svir **128** J 1
Svir' ∽ **138** F 4
Sviritsa **138** E 4
Svishtov **133** D 2
Svitavy **128** F 3
Svitlovods'k **136** CD 4
Svobodnyy **148** ab 8
Svolvær **125** BC 3
Svyatoy Nos, Cape)≋ *[Russia, Arkhangel'sk]* **138** KL 2
Svyatoy Nos, Cape)≋ *[Russia, Murmansk]* **138** H 2
Svyetlahorsk **128** K 2
Swahili ⚉ **173** G-H 6-7
Swainsboro **100** C 2
Swakopmund **178** G 7
Swan ∽ **86** B 2/3
Swan Hill **166** J 8
Swan Hills **84** E 2
Swan Hills ▲▲ **84** DE 2
Swan Lake ◡ **86** B 2
Swan Range ▲▲ **90** D 1/2
Swan River **86** B 2
Swansea **124** C 4

⛊ Independent country
◗ Dependent territory
▽ Federal state, province, territory
⚉ People, ethnic group, tribe
⛺ Indian reservation/reserve
⌂ National Park
⊓ Industrial region
∴ Historical site
⌓ Research station
⊕ Continent, realm
⌒ Region, peninsula
▲▲ Mountain range, mountains
▲ Peak
)(Pass
* Ice shelf, glacier

Swans Island 98 GH 1
Swazi 173 FG 8
Swaziland 178 L 8
Sweden 120 HJ 4/3
Swedes 121 H-J 3-4
Sweet Grass Hills 90 E 1
Sweet Grass Indian Reserve 84 F 2
Sweet Home 90 B 2
Sweetwater *[U.S., Tennessee]* 100 BC 2
Sweetwater *[U.S., Texas]* 96 CD 2
Sweetwater 90 E 3
Świdnica 128 F 3
Świdnik 128 H 2
Świdwin 128 F 2
Świebodzin 128 F 2
Świecie 128 FG 2
Swift Current 84 G 3
Swift Current Creek 84 FG 3
Swindon 124 D 4
Świnoujście 128 E 2
Swiss 121 G 5
Switzerland 128 CD 4
Swords 124 BC 4
Syamozero, Lake 138 EF 4
Syamzha 138 H 4
Syanno 128 KL 1
Sychevka 136 D 2
Sydney *[Australia]* 166 L 7
Sydney *[Canada]* 88 E 3
Sydney Mines 88 E 3
Syeverodonets'k 136 EF 4
Sykía 133 C 3
Syktyvkar 138 L 4
Sylacauga 100 B 2
Sylhet 150 P 5/6
Sylt 128 C 1
Sylva 136 M 1
Sylvania 100 C 2
Sylvia, Mount 76 PQ 7
Sými 133 E 4
Synel'nykove 136 DE 4
Synya 138 O 3
Synya 138 Q 3
Syowa 181 II CB 7
Syracuse *[U.S.]* 98 EF 2
Syracuse (Siracusa) *[Italy]* 132 D 4
Syr Darya 148 O 10
Syria 152 CD 2/1
Syrian Desert 152 CD 2
Sýros 133 D 4
Syrskiy 136 EF 3
Sysmä 126 J 2
Syumsi 136 K 1/2
Syzran' 136 HJ 3
Szamotuły 128 F 2
Szczecin 128 E 2
Szczecinek 128 F 2
Szczytno 128 H 2
Szeged 128 G 4
Székesfehérvár 128 G 4
Szekszárd 128 G 4
Szentendre 128 G 4
Szolnok 128 G 4
Szombathely 128 F 4

T

Taal 15 G 15
Tābah 152 B 3
Tabar Islands 156 P 8
Tabarjal 152 C 3
Tabarka → Ṭabarqah
Ṭabarqah 132 A 4
Tābask, Kūh-e 152 FG 3
Tabatinga 112 F 4
Taber 84 EF 3
Tablas 156 J 5
Table Mountain 178 H 9
Tábor 128 E 3
Tabora 178 L 3
Tabrīz 134 H 4
Tabuaeran 160 O 3
Tabūk 152 C 3
Tabursuq 132 B 4
Tabwemasana, Mount 166 NO 4
Täby 126 G 3
Tacana 109 G 6
Tachelhit 173 C 3/2
Tacheng 154 F 2
Tachov 128 E 3
Tachungnya 101 III
Tacloban 156 K 5
Tacna 112 E 7
Tacoma 90 B 2
Tacuarembó 114 HJ 4
Tademaït Plateau 169 D 3
Tadine 166 O 5
Tadjoura 176 Q 6
Ta'Dmejrek 132 C 5
Tadoussac 88 C 2
Taegu 154 PQ 4
Taejŏn 154 P 4
Taëzhnyy 148 U 7
Tafahi 166 S 4
Tafalla 130 D 1
Ṭafīlah, Aṭ- 152 B 3
Tafresh 152 F 2
Taft 92 C 3
Taftān, Kūh-e 150 HJ 5
Tafune 101 VII
Tagalog 145 PQ 8
Taganrog 134 EF 1
Taganrog, Gulf of 134 E 1
Tagbilaran 156 JK 6
Taguatinga 112 K 6
Tagula Island 156 P 10
Tagum 156 K 6
Tagus → Tejo 130 B 2
Tahan 156 E 7
Tahat 176 J 4
Tahgong, Puntan 101 III
Tahiti 160 P 5
Tahkuna nina 126 H 3
Tahlequah 96 E 2
Tahoe, Lake 92 B 2
Tahoe, South Lake 92 B 2
Tahoua 176 J 6
Tahsis 84 B 3
Ṭahṭā 152 A 4
Tai'an 154 N 4
T'aichung 154 O 7
Ṭā'if, Aṭ- 150 E 6
Tai Hu 154 NO 5
Taimba 148 U 6
Taimyr, Lake → Taymyr, Lake
Taimyr Peninsula → Taymyr Peninsula
Tain 124 C 2
T'ainan 154 NO 7
Taínaron, Cape 133 C 4
T'aipei 154 O 7
Taiping 156 DE 7
Taitao Peninsula 114 D 7
T'aitung 154 O 7
Taivalkoski 125 G 4
Taiwan 154 O 7
Taiwan 154 O 7
Taiwan Strait 154 NO 7/6
Taiyuan 154 M 4
Taizhou 154 O 5
Ta'izz 150 EF 8
Tajerouine → Tajīrwīn
Tajikistan 150 KL 3
Tajiks 145 K-L 6
Tajīrwīn 132 A 5
Tajumulco 102 G 5/6
Tak 156 D 4
Takāb 134 H 4
Takamatsu [= Ta.] 154 Q 5
Takestān 152 F 2
Takhādīd 152 E 3
Ta Khmau 156 EF 5
Takht-i Suleiman 152 F 1
Takla Lake 84 B 2
Takla Makan Desert 154 EG 4
Takoradi 176 G 8
Takpochao, Mount 101 III
Taksimo 148 XY 7
Takuu Islands 156 Q 8
Talachyn 128 K 1
Talara 112 C 4
Talarrubias 130 C 2/3
Talas 148 P 10
Talat at-Timiat 152 D 3
Talaud Islands 156 JK 7
Talavera de la Reina 130 C 2
Talbot Lake 86 C 2
Talca 114 E 5
Talcahuano 114 E 5
Taldom 136 E 2
Taldyqorghan 148 Q 10/9
Taliabu 156 J 8
Talladega 100 B 2
Tall 'Afar 152 D 1
Tallaght 124 B 4
Tallahassee 100 BC 3
Tall al-Abyaḍ 152 C 1
Tall al-'Amarnah 152 A 4
Tallapoosa 100 B 2
Tall 'Āṣūr 152 B 2/3
Tallinn 126 J 3
Tall Kalakh 152 BC 2
Tall Kayf 152 D 1
Tall Tamir 152 D 1
Tallulah 96 F 2
Tal'menka 148 RS 8
Talnakh 148 ST 5/4
Tal'ne 136 C 4
Talofofo 101 II
Talofofo Bay 101 II
Tāloqān 150 KL 3
Talovaya 136 F 3
Talsi 126 H 3
Taltal 114 E 3
Tama 94 E 2
Tamala 136 G 3
Tamale 176 G 7
Tamanrāsat 176 J 4
Tamanrasset → Tamanrāsat
Tamási 128 FG 4
Tamaulipas 96 D 4
Tamazight 173 C 2
Tambacounda 176 E 6
Tambelan Islands 156 F 7
Tambo 166 K 6
Tambora 15 GH 16
Tambov 136 FG 3
Tamil Nadu 150 M 9/8
Tamils 145 L-M 8-9
Tampa 100 C 4
Tampa Bay 100 C 4
Tampere 126 H 2
Tampico 102 F 4
Tamuning 101 II
Tamworth 166 L 7
Tana 178 N 3
Tana, Lake 176 P 6
Tanacross 78 LM 6
Tanafjorden 125 G 2
Tanahbala 156 D 8
Tanahjampea 156 J 9
Tanahmasa 156 D 8
Tanaina 73 CD 3
Tanami 166 FG 4/5
Tanami Desert 166 G 4/5
Tanana 73 CD 3
Tanapag 101 III
Tanāqīb, Ra's 152 F 4
Tanaro 132 A 2
Ţăndărei 133 E 2
Tandil 114 H 5
Tane Range 156 D 4
Tanezrouft 176 GH 4
Tanga 178 M 3/4
Tanganyika, Lake 178 KL 3/4
Tangará da Serra 112 H 6/7
Tangier (Tanjah) 130 BC 4
Tangshan 154 N 3/4
Tangyuan 154 P 2
Tanimbar Islands 156 L 9
Tanjah → Tangier 130 BC 4
Tanjungpandan 156 F 8
Tanjungpinang 156 EF 7
Tanjungredeb 156 H 7
Tanna 166 O 4
Ţanţā 152 A 3
Tanzania 178 LM 4
Taoa 166 R 3
Taormina 132 D 4
Taos 92 F 2
Taoudenni 176 G 4
Tapa 126 J 3
Tapachula 102 G 5/6
Tapajós 112 H 5
Tapauá 112 G 5
Tappahannock 98 E 3
Taputapu, Cape 101 VII
Taques, Los 115 I A 2
Tar 100 D 1
Tara 148 P 7

River, canal
Waterfall
Lake, lakes, reservoir
Swamp
Salt flat
Sea
Strait
Bay, gulf
Cape
Island, islands
Ocean current
Ocean floor landforms
Tectonic feature
Atmospheric phenomena
Time zone
Geographical grid

Independent country
Dependent territory
Federal state, province, territory
People, ethnic group, tribe
Indian reservation/reserve
National Park
Industrial region
∴ Historical site
Research station
Continent, realm
Region, peninsula
Mountain range, mountains
▲ Peak
)(Pass
* Ice shelf, glacier

Thailand **156** E 4
Thailand, Gulf of **156** E 5
Thai Nguyên **156** F 3
Thames **124** D 4
Thandwe **150** P 7
Thanh Hoa **156** F 4/3
Thanjavur **150** MN 8
Than-Phô Hô Chi Minh → Hô Chi Minh City **156** FG 5
Thar Desert **150** L 5
Thargomindah **166** J 6
Tharsis **130** B 3
Tharthār, Wādī ath- **152** D 2
Tharthār Lake **152** D 2
Thásos **133** D 3
Thásos **133** D 3
Thaton **150** Q 7
Thawrah, Ath- **152** C 2
Thebes **176** O 3
The Bluff **102** K 4/5
Thècle, Sainte- **88** BC 3
The Dalles **90** B 2
Thedford **94** C 2
The Everglades **100** C 4
The Grenadines **115** II B 2
The Hague ('s-Gravenhage) **128** B 2
Thelon **76** U 6
The Minch **124** BC 2
The Narrows Indian Reserve **86** C 3
Thenon **131** C 3/4
Theodore **166** KL 6
Theodore Roosevelt National Park (North Unit) **90** FG 2
Theodore Roosevelt National Park (South Unit) **90** G 2
The Pas **86** B 2
Thermopolis **90** EF 3
Thessaloníki **133** C 3
Thessaloníki, Gulf of **133** C 3
Thessaly **133** C 3
Thetford **124** E 4
Thetford Mines **88** C 3
The Valley **115** II B 1
The Wash **124** E 4
The Woodlands **96** DE 3
Thibodaux **96** F 3
Thief River Falls **86** C 3/4
Thielson, Mount **90** B 3
Thiers **131** D 3
Thiès **176** D 5/6
Thimphu **150** OP 5
Þingvellier **116** ①
Thionville **131** DE 2
Thíra **133** D 4
Thíra (Santorini) **133** D 4
Thiruvananthapuram → Trivandrum **150** LM 9
Thisted **126** C 4/3
Þistilfjörður **125** DE 1
Thíva **133** C 4
Thiviers **131** C 3
Þjórsá **125** C 2
Thomas, Saint **98** D 2
Thomas, Saint **101** IX
Thomaston **100** BC 2
Thomasville *[U.S., Alabama]* **100** B 3
Thomasville *[U.S., Georgia]* **100** C 3
Thompson **86** C 2
Thompson *[Canada]* **84** C 3
Thompson *[U.S.]* **94** E 2/3
Thompson, North **84** D 2/3
Thompson Falls **90** CD 2
Thomson **100** C 2
Thonon-les-Bains **131** E 3
Thoothukkuddi **150** MN 9
Thoreau **92** EF 3
Thouars **131** BC 3
Thousand Oaks **92** C 3
Thrace **117** J 5
Thracian Sea **133** D 3
Three Gorges Reservoir **154** LM 5
Three Hills **84** E 3
Three Kings **166** OP 7
Three Points, Cape **176** G 8
Three Rivers *[U.S., Michigan]* **98** C 2
Three Rivers *[U.S., Texas]* **96** D 3
Thrissur **150** LM 8
Thule/Qaanaaq **78** bc 3
Thun **128** C 4
Thunder Bay **86** E 3
Thunder Bay **86** E 3
Thunder Hills **84** G 2
Thuringia **128** DE 3
Thuringian Forest **128** D 2/3
Thurles **124** B 4
Thurso **124** C 2
Thurston Island **181** I CB 29/28
Thyborøn **126** C 4
Tiahuanaco **51** FG 6
Tianjin **154** NO 4
Tianshui **154** KL 4/5
Tibbu **173** E 3/4
Tiberias, Lake **152** BC 2
Tibesti **176** L 4
Tibet **141** MN 6
Tibet (Autonomous Region Xizang) **154** FH 5
Tibetans **145** MO 6
Tibissah **176** J 1
Tibnī **152** C 2
Tiburón Island **102** C 3
Ticino **123** DE 3
Ticonderoga **98** F 2
Tidjikja → Tijiqjah
Tien Shan **154** DH 3
Tierp **126** F 2
Tierra del Fuego **114** F 8
Tierra del Fuego **114** F 8
Tieté **114** K 2
Tiffin **98** D 2
Tifton **100** C 3
Tighina (Bendery) **128** K 4
Tigil' **148** g 7
Tignes, Lac de **116** ⑦
Tignish **88** E 3
Tigrai **173** G 4
Tigre **173** G 4
Tigre, El **112** G 2
Tigris **150** E 3/4
Tīh, Jabal at- **152** B 3
Tijiqjah **176** E 5
Tijuana **92** C 3
Tikal **102** GH 5
Tikar **173** DE 5
Tikhoretsk **134** F 1
Tikhvin **138** F 5
Tikopia **166** O 3
Tikrīt **152** D 2
Tiksi **148** a 4
Tikuna **109** FG 5
Tilburg **128** B 2
Tilimsān **176** GH 2/1
Tillabéri **176** H 6
Tillamook **90** AB 2
Tillsonburg **98** D 2
Tílos **133** E 4
Tim **136** E 3
Ţimā **152** A 4
Timan Ridge **138** LM 2/3
Timaru **166** P 9
Timashëvsk **134** EF 1
Timbalier **96** F 3
Timbira **109** J 5
Timbuktu (Tombouctou) **176** FG 5
Timimoun → Timimūn
Timīmūn **176** GH 3
Timirist, Cape **176** D 5
Timiscaming **88** A 3
Timiscaming, Lake **86** H 4
Timişoara **128** GH 4
Timmins **86** G 3
Timon **112** L 5
Timor **156** JK 10/9
Timorese **145** Q 11/10
Timor-Leste **156** K 9
Timor Sea **166** F 3
Timpton **148** a 7
Timrå **126** F 2
Tindouf → Tindūf
Tindūf **176** F 3
Tinerhir Oasis → Tinghir Oasis
Tinghir Oasis **168** ⑤
Tingo María **112** DE 5
Tinian **101** III
Tinian Channel **101** III
Tinogasta **114** F 3
Tínos **133** D 4
Tínos **133** D 4
Tinsukia **150** Q 5
Tipperary **124** B 4
Tipton, Mount **92** D 3
Tip Top Mountain **86** F 3
Tirān **152** B 4
Tirana (Tiranë) **133** B 3
Tiraspol **128** KL 4
Tirat Zvi **66** L 4
Tire **134** B 4
Tiree **124** B 3
Tiriyó **109** H 4
Tirlyanskiy **136** M 2
Tírnavos **133** C 3
Tirso **132** AB 3
Tirso, Santo **130** B 2
Tiruchchirappalli **150** MN 8/9
Tisdale **84** G 2
Tisza **117** HJ 5
Tiszafüred **128** G 4
Tit-Ary **148** a 4
Tite-des-Caps, Saint- **88** C 3
Titicaca, Lake **112** F 7
Titov vrh **133** B 2
Titule **178** K 2
Titusville **100** C 3
Tiţwān → Tétouan **176** F 1
Tiv **173** D 5
Tiverton **124** C 5
Tizimín **102** H 4
Tjörn **126** D 3
Tlahualilo **96** C 4
Tlemcen → Tilimsān
Tlingit **73** E 4
Tlyarata **134** H 2
Toamasina **178** OP 6
Toba **109** H 7
Tobago **115** II B 3
Tobago, Great **101** IX
Tobago, Little **101** IX
Tobago, Trinidad and **115** II B 3
Toba Lake **156** D 7
Tobarra **130** D 3
Tobermory *[Canada]* **98** D 1
Tobermory *[U.K.]* **124** BC 3
Tobi **156** L 7
Tobin Lake **86** B 2
Tobique **88** D 3
Tobique Indian Reserve **88** D 3
Tobol **148** O 7
Tobol'sk **148** OP 7
Tobysh **138** LM 2
Tocantinópolis **112** K 5
Tocantins **112** K 6
Tocantins **112** K 6
Toccoa **100** C 2
Tocopilla **114** E 2
Todos Santos **112** FG 7
Todos Santos, Bahía de **92** C 4
Todos Santos, Isla de **92** C 4
Tofino **84** B 3
Tofua **166** R 4/5
Togian Islands **156** J 7/8
Togo **176** H 7
Tohono O'odham Nation **92** DE 3/4
Toijala **126** HJ 2
Toiyabe Range **92** C 2
Tokaj **128** H 3/4
Tokar → Ţawkar
Tokarevka **136** F 3
Tokat **134** E 3
Tokelau **166** S 2
Toki Point **101** IV
Tokmak **134** DE 1
Toku **166** S 4
Tokushima **154** QR 5
Tōkyō **154** R 4
Tôlañaro **178** O 8/7
Tolbazy **136** L 3
Toledo *[Spain]* **130** C 2
Toledo *[U.S., Ohio]* **98** D 2
Toledo *[U.S., Oregon]* **90** B 2
Toledo Bend Reservoir **96** E 3

River, canal
Waterfall
Lake, lakes, reservoir
Swamp
Salt flat
Sea
Strait
Bay, gulf
Cape
Island, islands
Ocean current
Ocean floor landforms
Tectonic feature
Atmospheric phenomena
Time zone
Geographical grid

■ Independent country
◘ Dependent territory
▢ Federal state, province, territory
⚇ People, ethnic group, tribe
Δ Indian reservation/reserve
⌂ National Park
⊓ Industrial region
∴ Historical site
⊿ Research station
⊕ Continent, realm
⊾ Region, peninsula
▲▲ Mountain range, mountains
▲ Peak
)(Pass
* Ice shelf, glacier

River, canal
Waterfall
Lake, lakes, reservoir
Swamp
Salt flat
Sea
Strait
Bay, gulf
Cape
Island, islands
Ocean current
Ocean floor landforms
Tectonic feature
Atmospheric phenomena
Time zone
Geographical grid

V

Independent country
Dependent territory
Federal state, province, territory
People, ethnic group, tribe
Indian reservation/reserve
National Park
Industrial region
Historical site
Research station
Continent, realm
Region, peninsula
Mountain range, mountains
Peak
Pass
Ice shelf, glacier

Vagur 124 A 2
Váh 128 FG 3
Vaitogi 101 VII
Vaitupu 166 Q 2
Vakh 148 R 6
Vakhtan 136 H 1
Valaam 138 E 4
Valamaz 136 K 1
Valday 136 CD 1
Valday Hills 136 CD 2/1
Valdemārpils 126 H 3
Valdemarsvik 126 F 3
Valdepeñas 130 CD 3
Val-des-Bois 88 B 3
Valdés Peninsula 114 G 6
Valdez 78 L 6
Val-d'Isère 131 E 3
Valdivia 114 E 5
Val-d'Or 88 A 2
Valdosta 100 C 3
Vale *[Georgia]* 134 G 3
Vale *[U.S.]* 90 C 2/3
Valemount 84 D 2
Valença 130 B 1/2
Valence 131 D 4
Valencia *[Spain]* 130 DE 2
Valencia *[Venezuela]* 112 F 1/2
Valencia, Gulf of 130 E 2
Valencia de Alcántara 130 B 2
Valencian Community 130 DE 3/2
Valenciennes 131 D 2
Valentín, San 114 E 7
Valentine 94 C 2
Valentín Gómez Farías 96 B 3
Valera 112 E 2
Valéry, Saint- 131 C 2
Valéry-en-Caux, Saint- 131 BC 2
Valga 126 J 3
Valjevo 133 B 2
Valka 126 J 3
Valkeakoski 126 J 2
Valky 136 D 4
Valladolid *[Mexico]* 102 H 4
Valladolid *[Spain]* 130 C 2
Vall d'Uixo, La 130 DE 2
Vallecillo 96 C 4
Valle d'Aosta/ Vallee d'Aoste 132 A 1
Valle de Allende 96 B 4
Valle de Zaragoza 96 B 4
Valledupar 112 E 1
Vallee d'Aoste/ Valle d'Aosta 132 A 1
Vallehermoso 130 E 5
Valleio 92 B 2
Vallenar 114 E 3
Valletta 132 C 5
Valley, The 115 II B 1
Valley City 94 D 1
Valley of Mexico 51 CD 4
Valleyview 84 D 2
Valls 130 E 2
Val Marie 84 G 3
Valmiera 126 J 3
Valozhyn 128 J 1
Valparaíso *[Chile]* 114 E 4
Valparaiso *[U.S.]* 98 C 2
Valpovo 132 E 1
Valuyki 136 E 4
Valverde 130 E 6
Valverde del Camino 130 B 3
Vammala 126 H 2
Van 134 G 4
Van, Lake 134 G 4
Vanadzor 134 G 3
Vanavara 148 V 6
Van Buren *[Canada]* 88 CD 3
Van Buren *[U.S., Arkansas]* 96 E 2
Van Buren *[U.S., Maine]* 98 GH 1
Vancouver *[Canada]* 84 C 3
Vancouver *[U.S.]* 90 B 2
Vancouver Island 84 B 3
Vandalia 94 F 3
Vanda Station 66 RS 9
Vanderhoof 84 C 2
Vänern 126 E 3
Vänersborg 126 E 3
Vangunu 166 M 2
Van Horn 96 B 3
Vanikolo 166 O 3
Vanimo 156 N 8
Vanna 125 D 2
Vännäs 126 G 1
Vannes 131 B 3
Vansbro 126 E 2
Vantaa 126 J 2
Vanua Lava 166 O 3
Vanua Levu 166 Q 4
Vanuatu 166 MO 3
Vanuatuans 164 JK 9/10
Van Wert 98 C 2
Vara, Pico, da 130 D 5/6
Varakļani 126 J 4
Varāmīn 152 F 2
Vārānasi (Benares) 150 N 5/6
Varangerfjorden 125 GH 2
Varanger Peninsula 125 GH 2
Varapayeva 128 JK 1
Varas, Las 96 A 3
Varaždin 132 D 1
Varberg 126 E 3
Vardar 133 C 3
Vardø 125 H 2
Varėna 126 J 4
Varenikovskaya 134 E 1
Vareš 132 E 2
Varese 132 AB 1
Vårgårda 126 E 3
Varginha 114 KL 2
Varkaus 126 K 2
Varna 133 E 2
Värnamo 126 E 3
Varnavino 136 GH 1
Varto 134 F 3
Värtsilä 138 E 4
Varzaqān 134 H 40
Várzea Grande 112 H 7
Vashka 138 K 3/4
Vasilyevichy 128 KL 2
Vaslui 128 K 4
Västerås 126 F 3
Västerbotten 125 DE 4
Västerdalälven 126 E 2
Västervik 126 F 3
Vasto 132 C 2
Vasylivka 136 D 5
Vasyl'kiv 136 BC 4
Vasyl'kivka 136 DE 4
Vasyugan 148 Q 7
Vatican City 132 BC 3
Vatnajökull 125 D 2
Vatra Dornei 128 J 4
Vättern 126 E 3
Vaughn 92 F 3
Vaupés 112 E 3
Vava'u Islands 166 S 4
Vavozh 136 K 2
Vawkavysk 128 HJ 2
Växjö 126 EF 4
Vaygach Island 148 MN 4
Vayrac 131 C 4
Vechta 128 C 2
Vedeno 134 H 2
Vega 96 C 2
Vega 125 A 4
Vega, La 102 LM 5
Vega Baja 101 VIII
Vegas, Las *[U.S., Nevada]* 92 D 2
Vegas, Las *[U.S., New Mexico]* 92 F 3
Vegreville 84 F 2
Veit, Sankt 128 E 4
Vejer de la Frontera 130 B 3
Vejle 126 D 4
Velas 130 BC 5
Velebit 132 D 2
Velenje 132 CD 1
Veles 133 C 3
Vélez Málaga 130 C 3
Vélez Rubio 130 D 3
Velika 132 D 1
Velika Gorica 132 D 1
Velika Plana 133 C 2
Velikaya 136 B 1
Velikaya Guba 138 F 4
Veliki Preslav 133 DE 2
Veliki Risnjak 132 CD 1
Velikiye Luki 136 C 2
Velikiy Novgorod 138 DE 5
Velikiy Ustyug 138 K 4
Veliko Tŭrnovo 133 D 2
Velingrad 133 D 2/3
Velizh 136 C 2
Vella Lavella 166 LM 2
Velletri 132 C 3
Vellore 150 M 8
Vel'sk 138 HJ 4
Velva 90 G 1/2
Velyka Lepetykha 134 D 1
Velyka Novosilka 136 E 5
Velyka Oleksandrivka 136 D 5
Velykyy Burluk 136 E 4
Vema Fracture Zone 10 FG 5
Venda 173 FG 8
Vendenga 138 K 3
Vendôme 131 C 3
Vendrell, El 130 E 2
Veneto 132 BC 1
Venëv 136 E 2
Venezia → Venice 132 C 1
Venezia Giulia, Friuli- 132 C 1
Venezuela 112 FG 2
Venezuela, Gulf of 112 E 1
Venezuela Basin 10 E 5
Venezuelans 109 FG 4
Veniaminof, Mount 76 HJ 7
Venice 100 C 4
Venice, Gulf of 132 C 1
Venice (Venezia) 132 C 1
Venlo 128 BC 2
Vennesla 126 C 3
Venosa 132 D 3
Venta 126 H 4
Venta, La 51 EF 5
Ventimiglia 132 A 2
Ventnor 124 D 5
Ventoux, Mont 131 D 4
Ventspils 126 H 3
Veps 121 K 4
Veracruz 102 F 5
Verbania 132 AB 1
Vercelli 132 A 1
Verchnyaya Toyma 138 K 4
Verde 92 E 3
Verde, Cape 176 D 6/5
Verde, Costa 123 C 3
Verde, El 96 B 4
Verden 128 D 2
Verdigris 94 DE 3
Verdon 131 E 4
Verdon, Le 131 B 3
Verdun 131 D 2
Vereeniging 178 KL 8
Vereshchagino 138 MN 5
Verín 130 B 1/2
Verkhneimbatsk 148 RS 6
Verkhnetulomskiy 138 EF 2
Verkhnetulomskiy, Reservoir 138 DE 2
Verkhneural'sk 136 M 3
Verkhneyarkeyevo 136 KL 2
Verkhniy Avzyan 136 M 3
Verkhniy Baskunchak 136 H 4
Verkhniye Kigi 136 M 2
Verkhniy Mamon 136 F 4
Verkhniy Tagil 138 OP 5
Verkhniy Ufaley 136 MN 2
Verkhniy Uslon 136 J 2
Verkhn'odniprovs'k 136 D 4
Verkhnyaya Inta 138 P 2/3
Verkhnyaya Salda 138 P 5
Verkhnyaya Sinyachikha 138 P 5
Verkhnyaya Zolotitsa 138 HJ 3
Verkhoshizhem'ye 136 J 1
Verkhotur'ye 138 P 5
Verkhovazh'ye 138 J 4
Verkhov'ye 136 E 3
Verkhoyansk 148 ab 5
Verkhoyansk Range 148 ac 4/6
Vermeille, Côte 123 D 3
Vermilion 84 F 2
Vermilion Lake 86 D 4
Vermillion 94 D 2
Vermont 98 F 1
Vernal 92 E 1
Verner 86 G 4
Vernon *[Canada]* 84 D 3
Vernon *[France]* 131 C 2
Vernon *[U.S.]* 96 D 2
Vero Beach 100 CD 4
Véroia 133 C 3
Verona 132 B 1
Versailles *[France]* 131 C 2

River, canal
Waterfall
Lake, lakes, reservoir
Swamp
Salt flat
Sea
Strait
Bay, gulf
Cape
Island, islands
Ocean current
Ocean floor landforms
Tectonic feature
Atmospheric phenomena
Time zone
Geographical grid

Independent country
Dependent territory
Federal state, province, territory
People, ethnic group, tribe
Indian reservation/reserve
National Park
Industrial region
Historical site
Research station
Continent, realm
Region, peninsula
▲▲ Mountain range, mountains
▲ Peak
Pass
Ice shelf, glacier

W

∽ River, canal
≾ Waterfall
◡ Lake, lakes, reservoir
⩰ Swamp
⩊ Salt flat
≋ Sea
≂ Strait
≋) Bay, gulf
)≋ Cape
⌓ Island, islands
⇄ Ocean current
⩠ Ocean floor landforms
⌁ Tectonic feature
☁ Atmospheric phenomena
◷ Time zone
⊕ Geographical grid

[symbol] Independent country
[symbol] Dependent territory
[symbol] Federal state, province, territory
[symbol] People, ethnic group, tribe
[symbol] Indian reservation/reserve
[symbol] National Park
[symbol] Industrial region
[symbol] Historical site
[symbol] Research station
[symbol] Continent, realm
[symbol] Region, peninsula
▲▲ Mountain range, mountains
▲ Peak
)(Pass
* Ice shelf, glacier

Wilbur 90 C 2
Wilburton 96 E 2
Wildhay 84 D 2
Wildwood 84 E 2
Wilhelm, Mount 156 NO 9
Wilhelmshaven 128 D 2
Wilkes-Barre 98 F 2
Wilkesboro 100 C 1
Wilkes Islands 101 IV
Wilkes Land 181 I C 13/16
Wilkes Subglacial Basin 13 AB 16/19
Wilkie 84 F 2
Willamette 90 B 2
Willapa Bay 90 A 2
Willard 92 F 3
Willcox 92 E 3
Willebrordus, Sint 115 I A 1
Willemstad 115 I A 1
William Dannelly Reservoir Lake 100 B 2
Williams *[U.S., Arizona]* 92 D 3
Williams *[U.S., California]* 92 B 2
Williamsburg 98 E 3
Williams Lake 84 C 2
Williamson 98 D 3
Williamsport 98 E 2
Williamston 100 D 2
Willingboro 98 F 2/3
Williston *[U.S., Florida]* 100 C 3
Williston *[U.S., North Dakota]* 90 G 1
Williston Lake 84 C 1
Willits 92 B 2
Willmar 94 E 1
Willow 84 C 2
Willow River 84 C 2
Willows 92 B 2
Willow Springs 94 EF 3
Wilmington *[U.S., Delaware]* 98 EF 3
Wilmington *[U.S., Illinois]* 94 FG 2
Wilmington *[U.S., North Carolina]* 100 D 2
Wilmington *[U.S., Ohio]* 98 D 3
Wilson 100 D 2
Wilson, Mount 94 AB 3
Wilson Lake 100 B 2
Wiluna 166 E 6
Winamac 98 C 2
Winchester *[U.S., Kentucky]* 98 CD 3
Winchester *[U.S., Tennessee]* 100 B 2
Winchester *[U.S., Virginia]* 98 E 3
Wind 90 E 3
Wind Cave National Park 94 BC 2
Windermere 124 CD 3
Windhoek 178 H 7
Windom 94 E 2
Windorah 166 J 5/6
Window Rock 92 E 3
Wind River Indian Reservation 90 E 3
Wind River Range 90 E 3
Windsor *[Canada, Nova Scotia]* 88 D 3
Windsor *[Canada, Québec]* 88 C 3
Windsor *[U.S., Colorado]* 94 B 2
Windsor *[U.S., North Carolina]* 100 D 1
Windward Islands 115 II B 3/1
Windward Passage 102 L 4
Winefred Lake 84 F 2
Winfield 94 D 3
Winisk 86 F 2
Winisk 86 F 2
Winisk Lake 86 F 2
Winkler 86 C 3
Winnebago 94 E 2
Winnebago, Lake 94 FG 1/2
Winnebago Indian Reservation 94 D 2
Winnemuca 92 C 1
Winner 94 CD 2
Winnfield 96 E 3
Winnibigoshish, Lake 94 E 1
Winnipeg 86 C 3
Winnipeg 86 D 3
Winnipeg, Lake 86 C 2
Winnipegosis 86 B 3
Winnipegosis, Lake 86 C 2
Winnipesaukee Lake 98 G 2
Winnsboro 96 F 2
Winona *[U.S., Minnesota]* 94 EF 1/2
Winona *[U.S., Mississippi]* 96 F 2
Winslow 92 E 3
Winston-Salem 100 C 1/2
Winter Haven 100 C 3/4
Winterthur 128 CD 4
Winton 166 J 5
Winzah, Al- 132 A 5
Wisconsin 94 F 1
Wisconsin 94 F 2
Wisconsin Rapids 94 F 1
Wismar 128 D 2
Witków 128 H 3
Wittenberg, Lutherstadt 128 E 2
Wittenberge 128 D 2
Wittlich 128 C 3
Wittstock 128 E 2
Wkra 128 G 2
Władysławowo 128 FG 1
Włocławek 128 G 2
Włodawa 128 H 2
Wokam 156 LM 9
Woking 124 D 4
Woleai 156 N 6
Wolf 94 F 1
Wolf, Volcano 112 A 3/4
Wolfenbüttel 128 D 2
Wolf Point 90 F 1
Wolfsberg 128 EF 4
Wolfsburg 128 D 2
Wolin 128 E 2/1
Wollaston Islands 114 FG 9
Wollaston Lake 78 U 7
Wollaston Lake 76 TU 7
Wollongong 166 L 7
Wolof 173 B 4
Wołomin 128 H 2
Wołów 128 F 2
Wolstenholme, Cape 76 YZ 6
Wolverhampton 124 CD 4
Wŏnsan 154 P 4
Wonthaggi 166 JK 8
Wood 84 G 3
Wood Buffalo National Park 78 S 7
Woodburn 90 B 2
Woodland 92 B 2
Woodland Park 94 B 3
Woodlands, The 96 DE 3
Woodlark Island 156 P 9
Woods, Lake of the 86 D 3
Woodstock *[Canada, New Brunswick]* 88 D 3
Woodstock *[Canada, Ontario]* 98 D 2
Woodstock *[U.S.]* 94 F 2
Woodville *[U.S., Mississippi]* 96 F 3
Woodville *[U.S., Texas]* 96 E 3
Woodward 96 D 1
Woonsocket 98 G 2
Wooster 98 D 2
Worbis, Leinefelde- 128 D 2
Worcester *[South Africa]* 178 HJ 9
Worcester *[U.K.]* 124 D 4
Worcester *[U.S.]* 98 FG 2
Workington 124 C 3
Worland 90 F 2
Worms 128 C 3
Worthington 94 E 2
Wowoni 156 J 8
Wrangel Island 148 I 4
Wrangell 78 O 7
Wrangell-Saint Elias National Park 78 M 6/7
Wrath, Cape 124 C 2
Wray 94 C 2
Wright 100 B 3
Wright Patman Lake 96 E 2
Wrocław 128 F 2/3
Września 128 FG 2
Wudu 154 KL 5
Wuhai 154 L 4
Wuhan 154 M 5
Wuhu 154 N 5
Wunnumin Indian Reserve 86 E 2
Wunnummin Lake 86 E 2
Wupatki National Monument 92 DE 3
Wuppertal 128 C 2
Würzburg 128 D 3
Wute 173 E 5
Wuteve, Mount 176 EF 7
Wuwei 154 K 4
Wuxi 154 NO 5
Wuyiling 154 P 2
Wuzhi Shan 154 L 8
Wuzhou 154 LM 7
Wyndham 166 F 4
Wynne 96 F 2
Wynyard 84 G 3
Wyoming 98 C 2
Wyoming 90 EF 3
Wyoming Basin 90 EF 3
Wyoming Peak 90 E 3
Wyoming Range 90 E 3
Wytheville 98 D 3

X

Xaafuun 176 S 6
Xaçmaz 134 J 3
Xai-Xai 178 LM 8
Xakriaba 109 J 6
Xalapa Enríquez 102 FG 5
Xam Nua 156 E 3
Xankəndı (Step'anakert) 134 H 3
Xanlar 134 H 3
Xánthi 133 D 3
Xanthos 134 B 4
Xátiva 130 D 3
Xenia 98 D 3
Xhosa 173 FG 9
Xiamen 154 N 7
Xi'an 154 LM 5
Xiangfan 154 M 5
Xianggang → Hong Kong 154 MN 7
Xiangtan [= Xia.] 154 M 6
Xianyang [= Xi.] 154 L 5
Xiaogan 154 MN 5
Xichang 154 K 6
Xigazê 154 G 6
Xi Jiang 154 LM 7
Xilinhot 154 N 3
Xingtai 154 M 4
Xingu 112 J 6
Xinguanos 109 H 6/5
Xingyi 154 L 6
Xining 154 K 4
Xinjiang Uygur, Autonomous Region 154 EH 3
Xinxiang 154 MN 4/5
Xinyang 154 MN 5
Xinzhou 154 M 4
Xinzo 130 B 1
Xizang, Autonomous Region → Tibet 154 FH 5
Xorkol 154 H 4
Xuanhua 154 MN 3
Xuchang 154 MN 5
Xuddur 176 Q 8
Xuwen 154 L 7
Xuzhou 154 N 5

Y

Ya'an 154 K 5
Yablonovyy Range 148 XY 8
Yacuíba 112 G 8
Yadkin 100 C 1
Yadrin 136 H 2
Yafran 176 K 2
Yagodnoye 148 ef 6
Yahotyn 136 C 4
Yakeshi 154 NO 2

River, canal
Waterfall
Lake, lakes, reservoir
Swamp
Salt flat
Sea
Strait
Bay, gulf
Cape
Island, islands
Ocean current
Ocean floor landforms
Tectonic feature
Atmospheric phenomena
Time zone
Geographical grid

Independent country
Dependent territory
Federal state, province, territory
People, ethnic group, tribe
Indian reservation/reserve
National Park
Industrial region
Historical site
Research station
Continent, realm
Region, peninsula
Mountain range, mountains
▲ Peak
)(Pass
* Ice shelf, glacier

b, Great 152 DE 1
b, Little 152 E 1
badānī, Az- 152 C 2
bol 150 J 4
bor'e 138 F 5
brze 128 G 3
būrūn'e 134 J 1
catecas 102 E 4
cháro 133 C 4
chepylivka 136 D 4
dar 132 D 2
donsk 136 E 3
'farānah 152 B 3
fra 130 B 3
gań 128 F 2
gazig → Zaqāzīq, Az-
ghawa 173 F 4
ghouan → Zaghwān
ghwān 132 B 4
greb 132 D 1
gros Mountains 141 HJ 6/7
āhedān 150 HJ 5
aḥlah 152 BC 2
ahlé → Zaylah
aječar 133 C 2
akamensk 148 VW 8
akharovo 136 F 2
ākhū 152 D 1
akopane 128 G 3
ákynthos 133 BC 4
ákynthos 133 B 4
alaegerszeg 128 F 4
alantun 154 O 2
alău 128 H 4
alishchyky 128 J 3
alṭan 176 L 3
ambezi 178 J 5
ambia 178 JL 6/5
amboanga 156 HJ 6
ambra 132 B 4
ambrów 128 H 2
amora *[Ecuador]* 112 D 4
amora *[Spain]* 130 C 2
amora de Hidalgo 102 DE 5/4
amość 128 H 3
áncara 130 D 2
anesville 98 D 3
anjān 134 J 4
anzibar 178 M 4
anzibar 178 MN 4
aokskiy 136 E 2
aozhuang 154 NO 4/5
apadnaya Dvina 136 C 2
apala 114 F 5
'aparo 109 F 5
apata 96 D 4
apolyarnyy 125 H 2
'apopan 102 E 4
aporizhzhya 136 D 5
apotecs 73 J 8
'aqatala 134 H 3
aqāzīq, Az- 152 AB 3
ara 134 E 3
'arafshon 148 NO 10
'aragoza *[Mexico]* 96 C 3
'aragoza *[Spain]* 130 D 2
'aranj 150 J 4

Zarasai 126 J 4
Zárate 114 GH 4
Zaraysk 136 EF 2
Zard Kūh 152 F 2
Zarechensk 138 E 2
Zarechnyy 136 H 3
Zarghaṭ 152 D 4
Zaria 176 J 6
Zarichne 128 J 2
Zarīneh 134 H 4
Zarma 173 D 4
Zărneşti 128 J 4
Zarqā', Az- 152 C 2
Zarqān 152 G 3
Żary 128 F 2
Zarya 138 L 4
Zashaghan 136 JK 3
Zaslawye 128 JK 1
Zastavna 128 J 3
Zavetnoye 134 G 1
Zavidovici 132 E 2
Zavitinsk 148 ab 8/9
Zavolzhsk 136 G 1
Zavolzh'ye 136 G 2
Zawiercie 128 G 3
Zāwiyah, Az- 176 K 2
Zawr, Ra's az- 152 F 4
Zaysan 148 RS 9
Zaysan, Lake 148 RS 9
Zbarazh 128 J 3
Zbąszyń 128 F 2
Žďár 128 F 3
Zdolbuniv 128 J 3
Zduńska Wola 128 G 2
Zeitz 128 DE 2
Zelenchukskaya 134 F 2
Zelënnik 138 JK 4
Zelenoborskiy 138 EF 2
Zelenodol'sk 136 J 2
Zelenogorsk
[Russia, Krasnoyarsk] 148 TU 7
Zelenogorsk
[Russia, Leningrad] 138 DE 4
Zelenograd 136 E 2
Zelenogradsk 128 G 1
Zelenokumsk 134 G 2
Zel'va 128 J 2
Zembra → Zambra
Zemetchino 136 G 3
Zenaga [= Z.] 173 B 4
Zenica 132 DE 2
Zermatt 128 C 4
Zernograd 134 F 1
Zeya 148 a 8
Zeya 148 a 8
Zeya Reservoir 148 ab 8
Zgierz 128 G 2
Zgorzelec 128 F 2
Zhabinka 128 J 2
Zhalpaqtal 136 J 4
Zhangaqala 136 J 4
Zhangaqazaly 148 N 9
Zhanga Qazan 136 J 4
Zhangatas 148 OP 10
Zhangjiakou 154 MN 3
Zhangye 154 K 4
Zhangzhou 154 N 7
Zhänibek 136 H 4
Zhanjiang 154 LM 7

Zhaoqing 154 M 7
Zhaotong 154 KL 6
Zharkent 148 QR 10
Zharkovskiy 136 C 2
Zharqamys 136 L 4/5
Zhashkiv 136 BC 4
Zhaysan 136 L 4
Zhejiang 154 NO 6
Zheleznogorsk
[Russia, Krasnoyarsk] 148 T 7
Zheleznogorsk
[Russia, Kursk] 136 D 3
Zheleznogorsk-Ilimskiy 148 VW 7
Zhem 148 M 9
Zhengzhou 154 MN 5
Zhenyuan 154 L 6
Zherd' 138 JK 3
Zherdevka 136 F 3
Zheshart 138 L 4
Zhezqazghan 148 OP 9
Zhigansk 148 Z 5
Zhigulëvsk 136 J 3
Zhirnovsk 136 GH 3/4
Zhitiqara 148 N 8
Zhlobin 128 L 2
Zhmerynka 128 K 3
Zhob 150 K 4
Zhodzina 128 K 1/2
Zhongning 154 L 4
Zhongshan 181 II BC 9/10
Zhosaly 148 NO 9
Zhovkva 128 H 3
Zhovti Vody 136 D 4
Zhukovka 136 D 3
Zhumysker 136 K 5
Zhuzhou 154 M 6
Zhydachiv 128 HJ 3
Zhympīty 136 K 4
Zhytkavichy 128 K 2
Zhytomyr 128 K 3
Zia Pueblo 92 F 3
Zībār 152 D 1
Zibo 154 N 4
Ziębice 128 F 3
Zielona Góra 128 F 2
Ziftā 152 A 3
Zigong 154 K 6
Ziguinchor 176 D 6
Zilair 136 M 3
Zile 134 D 3
Žilina 128 G 3
Zillah 176 L 3
Zima 148 V 8
Zimbabwe 178 KL 6
Zimbabwe 178 L 7
Zimnicea 133 D 2
Zimovniki 134 G 1
Zinder 176 JK 6
Zinjibār 150 F 8
Zin'kiv 136 D 4
Zion National Park 92 D 2
Zirkel, Mount 94 B 2
Zittau 128 E 2/3
Zlaté Moravce 128 G 3
Zlatoust 136 M 2
Zlín 128 FG 3
Zlītan 176 KL 2
Złocieniec 128 F 2
Złoczew 128 G 2

Złotów 128 F 2
Zmeinogorsk 148 R 8
Zmiyëvka 136 E 3
Zmiyinyy 134 C 1
Zmiyiv 136 E 4
Zna 136 F 3
Znamenka 136 F 3
Znam"yanka 136 CD 4
Żnin 128 F 2
Znojmo 128 F 3
Zoigê 154 K 5
Zolochiv
[Ukraine, Kharkiv] 136 DE 4
Zolochiv
[Ukraine, L'viv] 128 J 3
Zolotonosha 136 C 4
Zolotukhino 136 E 3
Zomba 178 M 6/5
Zonguldak 134 C 3
Zoque 73 J 8
Zorita 130 C 2
Zouar 176 L 4
Zouérat → Zuwārat
Zrenjanin 133 B 1
Zubayr, Az- 152 E 3
Zubova Polyana 136 G 2/3
Zubovo 138 G 4
Zubtsov 136 D 2
Ẓūfār 150 GH 7
Zug 128 C 4
Zugdidi 134 FG 2
Zugspitze 128 D 4
Zújar 130 C 3
Zulu 173 FG 8
Zuni Indian
Reservation 92 E 3
Zuni Mountains 92 E 3
Zuni Pueblo 92 E 3
Zunyi 154 L 6
Zürich 128 C 4
Zuwārah 176 K 2
Zuwārat 176 E 4
Zuwaytīnah, Az- 119 J 6
Zuyevka 138 LM 5
Zvenigovo 136 HJ 2
Zvenyhorodka 136 C 4
Zvolen 128 G 3
Zvornik 133 B 2
Zwedru 176 F 7
Zwettl 128 EF 3
Zwickau 128 E 3
Zwolle 128 C 2
Zyryan 148 R 9
Zyryanka 148 ef 5
Zyudev Island 134 J 1
Żywiec 128 G 3

River, canal
Waterfall
Lake, lakes, reservoir
Swamp
Salt flat
Sea
Strait
Bay, gulf
Cape
Island, islands
Ocean current
Ocean floor landforms
Tectonic feature
Atmospheric phenomena
Time zone
Geographical grid

Alexander GlobalAtlas für Baden-Württemberg. Gotha, 2004.
Alexander KombiAtlas Erdkunde, Geschichte, Sozialkunde, Wirtschaft. Gotha 2003.
Auswärtiges Amt der Bundesrepublik Deutschland: Länder- und Reiseinformationen [auswaertiges-amt.de/www/de/laenderinfos/index_html].

Barthlott, W., Biedinger, N., Braun, G., Feig, F., Kier, G., & J. Mutke (1999): Global Biodiversity: Species numbers of vascular plants. Bonn [botanik.uni-bonn.de/system/phytodiv.htm].
BGR (2005): Reserven, Ressourcen und Verfügbarkeit von Energierohstoffen 2004 – Kurzstudie. Hannover.
Bundeszentrale für politische Bildung: Wissen, Lexika, Begriffe nachschlagen [bpb.de/wissen/H75VXG,0,0,Begriffe_nachschlagen.html].
Castles, St., & M. J. Miller (2003): The Age of Migration. Basingstoke.
CIA: The World Factbook 2005 [cia.gov/cia/publications/factbook/].
CIESIN, Columbia University, CIAT: Gridded Population of the World (GWP), Version 3 [sedac.ciesin.columbia.edu/gpw].
CRED: EM-DAT – The International Disaster Database [em-dat.net/].

Der Fischer Weltalmanach 2006. Frankfurt a.M., 2005.
Diercke Länderlexikon. Braunschweig, 2005.
Diercke Weltatlas. Braunschweig, 2005.
DWD: Global Precipitation Climatology Centre [orias.dwd.de/GPCC/GPCC_Visualizer].

Engelman, R., & P. LeRoy (1993): Sustaining Water – Population and the Future of Renewable Water Supplies [cnie.org/pop/pai/water-12.html].

FAO (2000): Definitions and Basic Principles of Sustainable Forest Managements in Relation to Criteria and Indictors [fao.org/docu ments/show_cdr.asp?url_file=/docrep/003/x6896e/x6896e0e.htm].
FAO (2002): Monitoring Food Deprivation and Related Indicators. Rome [adb.org/documents/events/2002/reta5917/monitoring.pdf].
FAO (2003): Review of World Water Resources by Country. Rome [fao.org/documents/show_cdr.asp?url_file=/DOCREP/005/Y4473E/Y4473E00.HTM].
FAO (2004): The State of Food Insecurity in the World 2004. Rome [fao.org/documents/show_cdr.asp?url_file=/docrep/007/y5650e/y5650e00.htm].
FAO (2004): Global Forest Resources. Assessment Update 2005. Terms and Definitions [fao.org/forestry/site/fra2005-terms/en].
FAO: FAOSTAT Data – Food Balance Sheets [faostat.fao.org/faostat/collections?version=ext&hasbulk=0&subset=nutrition].
FAO: FAOSTAT Data – Agricultural Production [faostat.fao.org/faostat/collections?version=ext&hasbulk=0&subset=agriculture].
FAO: Global Forest Resources Assessment [fao.org/forestry/site/32033/en].
Fitchard, K. (2003): Mapping the Global Internet [telephonyonline.com/mag/telecom_intelligence_broadband_economy_41/index.html].
Fiziko-geograficheskiy Atlas Mira. Moscow, 1964.
Freedom House: Freedom in the World 2005 [freedomhouse.org/template.cfm?page=35&year=2005].
Freedom House: Map of Freedom 2005 [freedomhouse.org/template.cfm?page=20&year=2005].

HIIK (2004): Conflict Barometer 2004. Heidelberg [hiik.de/en/index_e.htm].

ILO (2001): Key Indicators of the Labour Market. Geneva.
IPCC (1995): Scientific-Technical Analyses of Impacts, Adaptations and Mitigation of Climate Change. Cambridge [ipcc.ch/pub/sarsum2.htm].
ITU [2003]: ITU Digital Access Index: World's First Global ICT Ranking [itu.int/newsarchive/press_releases/2003/30.html].

Kyoto Protocol to the UNFCC [unfccc.int/resource/docs/convkp/kpeng.pdf].
Kyoto Protocol – Status of Ratification [unfccc.int/files/essential_background/kyoto_protocol/application/pdf/kpstats.pdf].

Lacina, B., & N. P. Gleditsch (2005). Monitoring Trends in Global Combat: A New Dataset of Battle Deaths. European Journal of Population, 21 (2/3): 145 – 166.

Meller, E., Middelschulte, A., Milojcic, G., Reichel, W., & G. Schöning (2004): Jahrbuch der europäischen Energie- und Rohstoffwirtschaft 2005. Essen.
Metcalf, Th. R. (2005): Tropical Storms, Worldwide [solar.ifa.hawaii.edu/Tropical/tropical.html].
MPI: Migration Information Source [migrationinformation.org/GlobalData/].
Münchener Rückversicherungs-Gesellschaft (1998): World Map of Natural Hazards. München.

OCHA: OCHA Natural and Environmental Disaster Reporting and Involvement in 2005 [reliefweb.int/rw/RWB.NSF/db900SID/AHAA-6LDW2W?OpenDocument].
OECD (2002): New Definition of General Government Total Expenditures. Paris [oecd.org/dataoecd/9/17/1949944.doc].
OECD: International Migration Data [oecd.org/document/36/0,2340,en_2825_494553_2515108_1_1_1_1,00.html].
OECD: Aid Statistics, Donor Aid Charts [oecd.org/countrylist/0,2578,en_2649_34447_1783495_1_1_1_1,00.html].
Olson, D. M., Dinerstein, E., et al. (2001): Terrestrial Ecoregions of the World: A New Map of Life on Earth. BioScience, 51 (11): 933 – 938 [worldwildlife.org/science/pubs/bioscience.pdf].

PRB (2004): 2004 World Population Data Sheet. Washington, D.C. [prb.org/pdf04/04WorldDataSheet_Eng.pdf].
PIK, Department of Climate System (2005): PIK data bank [Observation period: 1974 – 2003].
PriMetrica, Inc. (2003): Major Interregional Internet Routes [thispointer.com/images/gig2004fig15zoom.gif].
PRIO (2005): Armed Conflict Dataset Codebook. Oslo [prio.no/cscw/armedconflict].

Schroeder, F.-G. (1998): Lehrbuch der Pflanzengeographie. Wiesbaden.
Smithsonian Institution: Global Volcanism Program [volcano.si.edu/world/].
Snead, R. E. (1972): Atlas of World Physical Features. New York, London, Sydney, Toronto.
Stalker, P.: Stalker's Guide to International Migration [pstalker.com/migration/index.htm].
Statistisches Bundesamt Deutschland: Länderprofile [destatis.de/allg/d/veroe/l_profile/lprofil_ueb.htm].
Statistisches Jahrbuch 2005 für das Ausland. Wiesbaden, 2005.

he Statesman's Yearbook: The Politics, Cultures and Economies of the World. Basingstoke, 2004.

he Weather Underground: Hurricane Archive [wunderground.com/hurricane/at2005.asp].

he World Bank Group: World Development Indicators – Data Query [devdata.worldbank.org/data-query/].

he World Bank Group: World Development Indicators [devdata.worldbank.org/wdi2005/Section4.htm].

he World Bank Group: Development Education Program. Glossary [unesco.org/education/tlsf/theme_c/mod13/www.worldbank.org/depweb/english/modules/glossary.htm].

he World Bank Group: Millennium Development Goals [ddp-ext.world bank.org/ext/GMIS/gdmis.do?siteId=2&menuId=LNAV01HOME1]

dvardy, M. D. F. (1975). A classification of the biogeographical provinces of the world. Morges. = IUCN Occasional Paper, 18.

N: Peacekeeping operations [un.org/Depts/dpko/dpko/index.asp].

NAIDS (2004): Report on the global AIDS epidemic 2004. Geneva [unaids.org/bangkok2004/report_pdf.html].

NCTAD (2004): UNCTAD Handbook of Statistics 2004. New York, Geneva. [unctad.org/en/docs/tdstat29_enfr.pdf].

NDP [2004]: Human Development Report 2004. New York [hdr.undp.org/reports/global/2004/pdf/hdr04_complete.pdf].

NEP: The GEO Data Portal [geodata.grid.unep.ch].

NEP, WCMC: Global Distribution of Original and Remaining Forests [unep-wcmc.org/index.html?].

NESCO, AETFAT, UNSO: White's Vegetation Map of Africa [geodata.grid.unep.ch].

NFCCC [2005]: GHG – Definitions [ghg.unfccc.int/definitions.html].

NHCR (2005): Refugee Status Determination – Identifying who is a refugee. Geneva [unhcr.ch/cgi-bin/texis/vtx/home/opendoc.pdf?tbl=RSDLEGAL&id=43141f5d4].

NHCR (2005): 2004 Global Refugee Trends. Geneva [unhcr.org/cgi-bin/texis/vtx/events/opendoc.pdf?tbl=STATISTICS&id=42b283744].

NICEF (2004): The State of the World's Children 2005. New York [unicef.org/sowc05/english/sowc05.pdf].

nited Nations Statistical Yearbook 2002–2004. New York, 2005.

UNPD (2004): World Urbanisation Prospects. The 2003 Revison. New York [un.org/esa/population/publications/wup2003/WUP2003Report.pdf].

UNPD (2005): World Population Prospects: The 2004 Revision. New York [un.org/esa/population/publications/WPP2004/2004Highlights_finalrevised.pdf].

UNWTO: Facts and Figures, Tourism Indicators [world-tourism.org/facts/menu.html].

UNWTO (2004): Tourism Market Trends 2004 – World Overview & Tourism Topics. Madrid.

USDA, NRCS: Global Soil Regions Map [soils.usda.gov/use/worldsoils/mapindex/order.html].

USDA, NRCS: Global Desertification Vulnerability Map [soils.usda.gov/use/worldsoils/mapindex/desert.html].

USGS: World Petroleum Assessment 2000 – Description and Results [pubs.usgs.gov/dds/dds-060/].

USGS: Glossary [biology.usgs.gov/s+t/noframe/z999.htm].

USGS, EROS Data Center (2000): Global 1 km Land Cover – IGBP Legend (1993) [geodata.grid.unep.ch].

Weber, L., & G. Zsak (2003): World Mining Data. Vienna [wmc.org.pl/wmd2003.pdf]

WEC: Survey of Energy Resources [worldenergy.org/wec-geis/publications/reports/ser/overview.asp].

White, F. (1983): Vegetation of Africa – a descriptive memoir to accompany the Unesco / AETFAT / UNSO vegetation map of Africa. Paris. = Natural Resources Research Report, XX.

WHO (2005): World Health Statistics 2005. Geneva [who.int/healthinfo/statistics/whostat2005en1.pdf].

WMO, UNESCO (1997): The World Water – is there enough? [unesco.org/science/waterday2000/Brochure.htm].

WTO: International Trade Statistics 2004. [wto.org/english/res_e/statis_e/its2004_e/its2004_e.pdf].

WWF [2002]: WWF Ecoregions – Terrestrial Ecoregions Legend [geodata.grid.unep.ch].

WWF [2002]: WWF Ecoregions – Major Habitat Types (Biomes) Legend [geodata.grid.unep.ch].

WWF: Conservation Science – Terrestrial Ecoregions of the World [worldwildlife.org/science/data/attributes.cfm].

icture Credits

rco Digital Images, Lünen 26.3 (D. Meissner); Australische Botschaft, erlin 159.2; Avenue Images, Hamburg Titelbild (imagesbroker/Arco/aTerraMagica); Bähr, Kiel 104.1; Blickwinkel, Witten 27.12; Bricks, Erurt 68.8; Corbis, Düsseldorf 159.5 (Amos Nachoum); Eckenfelder, Weigenlupnitz 116.3; Ehlers, Bonn 168.6; Enkelmann, Filderstadt 68.4, 140.6; erster, Zumikon 68.2; getty images, Munich 68.6; Hahn, Stuttgart 68.7; ess, Buckow 116.1; Hokenmaier, Wäschenbeuren 168.1; Itar Tass, oscow 116.8, 140.1; Jürgens Ost + Europa Photo, Berlin 26.2; Kastner, ürnberg 140.5; Klett Archiv 116.7; Kraus, Wäschenbeuren 68.5; Leicht, Mutlangen 68.3; Maresch, Rutesheim 159.3, 159.7; MEV, Augsburg 168.2; Mitsubishi, Rüsselsheim 140.7; Mühr, Karlsruhe 104.2; Müller, Würzburg 140.8; Newig, Flintbek 116.5, 116.9, 168.8; Pasca, Tübingen 104.7; Reckziegel, Schnepfenthal 26.4, 140.2; Ria „Nowosti", Berlin 116.6; Richter, Röttenbach 26.5, 26.8, 26.9, 27.10, 27.13, 116.4; Rother, Schwäbisch Gmünd 27.14, 68.1, 104.4, 104.5, 104.6, 104.8, 104.9, 116.2, 140.3, 140.4, 159.6, 159.8, 159.9, 159.10, 168.4, 168.5; Schmidtke, Melsdorf 168.7; Schulz, Schwäbisch Gmünd 168.3; Still Pictures, London 26.1 (Patrick Frischknecht), 26.7 (Ted Mead); Stock4B, Munich 26.6 (Peter von Felbert); Tierbildarchiv Angermayer, Holzkirchen 27.11; von der Ruhren, Aachen 104.3; Zauner, Ludwigsburg 159.1, 159.4.